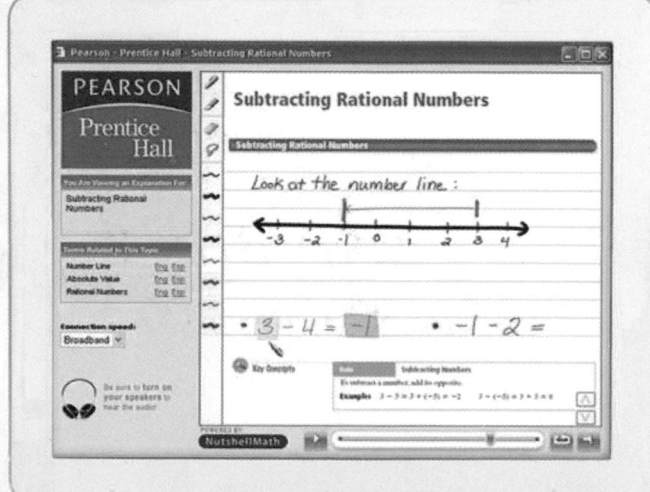
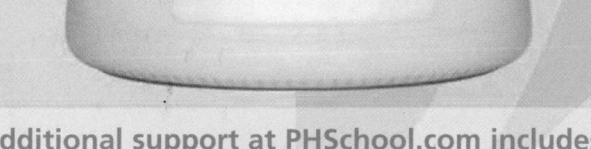

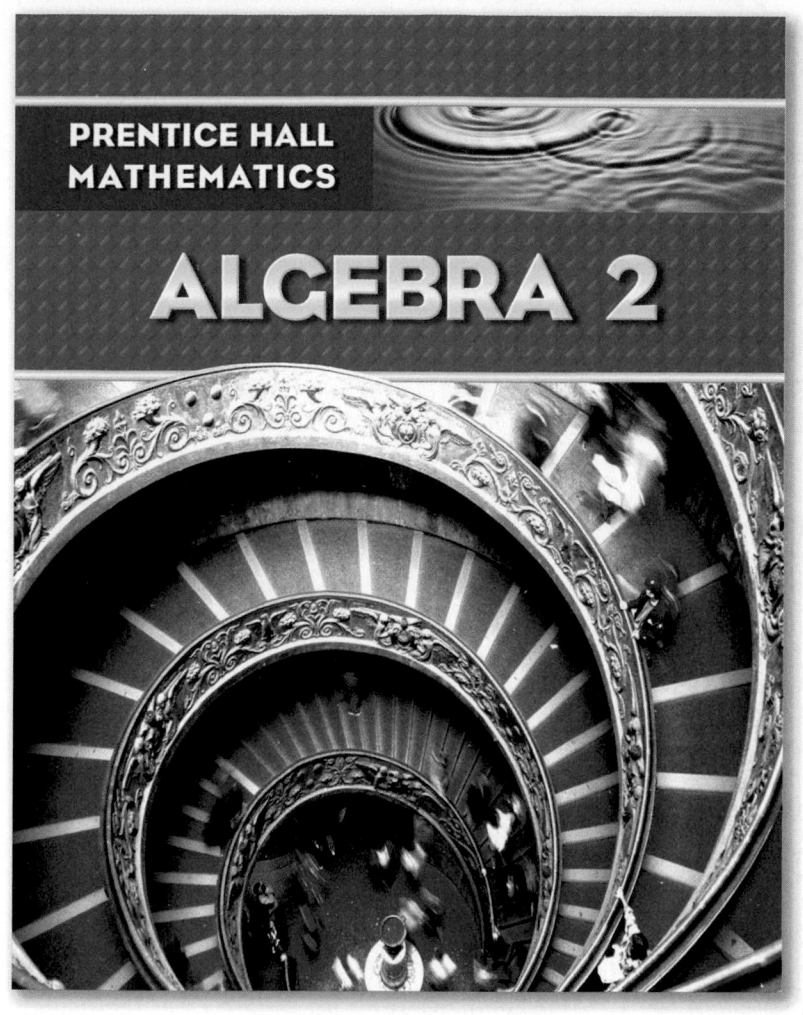

PRENTICE HALL MATHEMATICS

ALGEBRA 2

Allan E. Bellman

Sadie Chavis Bragg

Randall I. Charles

Basia Hall

William G. Handlin, Sr.

Dan Kennedy

PEARSON

Prentice Hall

Boston, Massachusetts
Upper Saddle River, New Jersey

Authors

Series Authors

Dan Kennedy, Ph.D., is a classroom teacher and the Lupton Distinguished Professor of Mathematics at the Baylor School in Chattanooga, Tennessee. A frequent speaker at professional meetings on the subject of mathematics education reform, Dr. Kennedy has conducted more than 50 workshops and institutes for high school teachers. He is coauthor of textbooks in calculus and precalculus, and from 1990 to 1994 he chaired the College Board's AP Calculus Development Committee. He is a 1992 Tandy Technology Scholar and a 1995 Presidential Award winner.

Randall I. Charles, Ph.D., is Professor Emeritus in the Department of Mathematics and Computer Science at San Jose State University, San Jose, California. He began his career as a high school mathematics teacher, and he was a mathematics supervisor for five years. Dr. Charles has been a member of several NCTM committees and is the former Vice President of the National Council of Supervisors of Mathematics. Much of his writing and research has been in the area of problem solving. He has authored more than 75 mathematics textbooks for kindergarten through college.

Basia Hall currently serves as Manager of Instructional Programs for the Houston Independent School District. With 30 years teaching experience, Ms. Hall has served as a department chair, instructional specialist, instructional supervisor, a school improvement facilitator, and a professional development (TEXTEAMS) trainer. Ms. Hall has developed curriculum for Algebra 1, Geometry, and Algebra 2 and contributed to the development of the Texas Essential Knowledge and Skills. A recipient of the 1992 Presidential Award for Excellence in Mathematics Teaching, Ms. Hall is also a past president of the Texas Association of Supervisors of Mathematics, and she is a state representative for the National Council of Supervisors of Mathematics (NCSM).

Acknowledgments appear on pages 1023–1025, which constitute an extension of this copyright page.

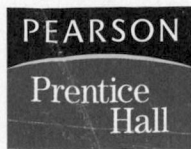

PEARSON
Prentice
Hall

ISBN 0-13-133998-2
4 5 6 7 8 9 10   10 09 08 07 06

Algebra 1 and Algebra 2 Authors

Allan E. Bellman is a Lecturer/Supervisor in the School of Education at the University of California, Davis. Before coming to Davis, he was a mathematics teacher for 31 years in Montgomery County, Maryland. He has been an instructor for both the Woodrow Wilson National Fellowship Foundation and the T^3 program. Mr. Bellman has a particular expertise in the use of technology in education and speaks frequently on this topic. He was a 1992 Tandy Technology Scholar.

Sadie Chavis Bragg, Ed.D., is Senior Vice President of Academic Affairs at the Borough of Manhattan Community College of the City University of New York. A former professor of mathematics, she is a past president of the American Mathematical Association of Two-Year Colleges (AMATYC), co-director of the AMATYC project to revise the standards for introductory college mathematics before calculus, and an active member of the Benjamin Banneker Association. Dr. Bragg has coauthored more than 50 mathematics textbooks for kindergarten through college.

William G. Handlin, Sr., is a classroom teacher and Department Chairman of Technology Applications at Spring Woods High School in Houston, Texas. Awarded Life Membership in the Texas Congress of Parents and Teachers for his contributions to the well-being of children, Mr. Handlin is also a frequent workshop and seminar leader in professional meetings throughout the world.

Geometry Authors

Laurie E. Bass is a classroom teacher at the 9–12 division of the Ethical Culture Fieldston School in Riverdale, New York. Ms. Bass has a wide base of teaching experience, ranging from grade 6 through Advanced Placement Calculus. She was the recipient of a 2000 Honorable Mention for the RadioShack National Teacher Awards. She has been a contributing writer of a number of publications, including software-based activities for the Algebra 1 classroom. Among her areas of special interest are cooperative learning for high school students and geometry exploration on the computer. Ms. Bass has been a presenter at a number of local, regional, and national conferences.

Art Johnson, Ed.D., is a professor of mathematics education at Boston University. He is a mathematics educator with 32 years of public school teaching experience, a frequent speaker and workshop leader, and the recipient of a number of awards. Dr. Johnson received the Tandy Prize for Teaching Excellence in 1995, a Presidential Award for Excellence in Mathematics Teaching in 1992, and New Hampshire Teacher of the Year, also in 1992. He was profiled by the Disney Corporation in the American Teacher of the Year Program.

Reviewers

Algebra 1 Reviewers

Mary Lou Beasley
Southside Fundamental
Middle School
St. Petersburg, Florida

Blanche Smith Brownley
Washington, D.C., Public
Schools
Washington, D.C.

Joseph Caruso
Somerville High School
Somerville, Massachusetts

Belinda Craig
Highland West Junior High
School
Moore, Oklahoma

Jane E. Damaske
Lakeshore Public Schools
Stevensville, Michigan

Stacey A. Ego
Warren Central High School
Indianapolis, Indiana

Earl R. Jones
Formerly, Kansas City
Public Schools
Kansas City, Missouri

Jeanne Lorenson
James H. Blake High School
Silver Spring, Maryland

John T. Mace
Hibbett Middle School
Florence, Alabama

**Ann Marie Palmieri-
Monahan**
Director of Mathematics
Bayonne Board of Education
Bayonne, New Jersey

Marie Schalke
Woodlawn Middle School
Long Grove, Illinois

Julie Welling
LaPorte High School
LaPorte, Indiana

Sharon Zguzenski
Naugatuck High School
Naugatuck, Connecticut

Geometry Reviewers

Marian Avery
Great Valley High School
Malvern, Pennsylvania

Mary Emma Bunch
Farragut High School
Knoxville, Tennessee

Karen A. Cannon
K–12 Mathematics
Coordinator
Rockwood School District
Eureka, Missouri

Johnnie Ebbert
Department Chairman
DeLand High School
DeLand, Florida

Russ Forrer
Math Department Chairman
East Aurora High School
Aurora, Illinois

Andrea Kopco
Midpark High School
Middleburg Heights, Ohio

Gordon E. Maroney III
Camden Fairview High
School
Camden, Arkansas

Charlotte Phillips
Math Coordinator
Wichita USD 259
Wichita, Kansas

Richard P. Strausz
Farmington Public Schools
Farmington, Michigan

Jane Tanner
Jefferson County
International
Baccalaureate School
Birmingham, Alabama

Karen D. Vaughan
Pitt County Schools
Greenville, North Carolina

Robin Washam
Math Specialist
Puget Sound Educational
Service District
Burien, Washington

Algebra 2 Reviewers

Josiane Fouarge
Landry High School
New Orleans, Louisiana

Susan Hvizdos
Math Department Chair
Wheeling Park High School
Wheeling, West Virginia

Kathleen Kohler
Kearny High School
Kearny, New Jersey

Julia Kolb
Leesville Road High School
Raleigh, North Carolina

Deborah R. Kula
Sacred Hearts Academy
Honolulu, Hawaii

Betty Mayberry
Gallatin High School
Gallatin, Tennessee

John L. Pitt
Formerly, Prince William
  County Schools
Manassas, Virginia

Margaret Plouvier
Billings West High School
Billings, Montana

Sandra Sikorski
Berea High School
Berea, Ohio

Tim Visser
Grandview High School
Cherry Creek School District
Aurora, Colorado

Content Consultants

Ann Bell
Mathematics
Prentice Hall Consultant
Franklin, Tennessee

Blanche Brownley
Mathematics
Prentice Hall Consultant
Olney, Maryland

Joe Brumfield
Mathematics
Prentice Hall Consultant
Altadena, California

Linda Buckhalt
Mathematics
Prentice Hall Consultant
Derwood, Maryland

Andrea Gordon
Mathematics
Prentice Hall Consultant
Atlanta, Georgia

Eleanor Lopes
Mathematics
Prentice Hall Consultant
New Castle, Delaware

Sally Marsh
Mathematics
Prentice Hall Consultant
Baltimore, Maryland

Bob Pacyga
Mathematics
Prentice Hall Consultant
Darien, Illinois

Judy Porter
Mathematics
Prentice Hall Consultant
Fuquay-Varena, North Carolina

Rose Primiani
Mathematics
Prentice Hall Consultant
Harbor City, New Jersey

Jayne Radu
Mathematics
Prentice Hall Consultant
Scottsdale, Arizona

Pam Revels
Mathematics
Prentice Hall Consultant
Sarasota, Florida

Barbara Rogers
Mathematics
Prentice Hall Consultant
Raleigh, North Carolina

Michael Seals
Mathematics
Prentice Hall Consultant
Edmond, Oklahoma

Margaret Thomas
Mathematics
Prentice Hall Consultant
Indianapolis, Indiana

From the Authors

Dear Student,

Welcome! Mathematics is a powerful tool with far-reaching applications in daily life. We have designed a unique and engaging program that will enable you to tap into the power of mathematics and develop lifelong skills. As you will discover, mathematics is all around us!

Building mathematical skills and an understanding of concepts is an ongoing process—a journey taken both inside and outside of the classroom. This text is designed to help make sense of the mathematics you encounter in and out of class each day.

Your skills and confidence will increase through practice and review. The concepts presented in this text will become an integral part of your thinking as you put them to use. Work the examples so that you understand the concepts and the processes presented. Then do your homework. Ask yourself how new concepts relate to old ones. Make the connections!

This text will also help you be successful on the tests you take in class as well as on high-stakes tests like the SAT, ACT, or state exams. The practice problems in each lesson will prepare you for the format and content of these tests. No surprises!

Be sure to use your teacher as a resource. Ask questions! Someone else in your class most likely has the same question in mind and will be grateful that you decided to ask it.

We wish you all the best this year as you work through this text. The mathematical skills you build and refine will prepare you not only for future success as a student, but also as a member of a vibrant technological society.

Sincerely,

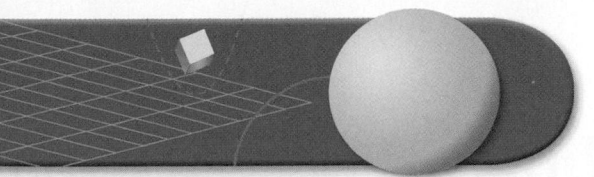

Contents in Brief

Connect Your Learning xxii

Using Your Book for Success xxvi

Beginning-of-Course Diagnostic Test xxxii

Chapter 1   Tools of Algebra 2

Chapter 2   Functions, Equations, and Graphs 52

Chapter 3   Linear Systems 116

Chapter 4   Matrices 166

Chapter 5   Quadratic Equations and Functions 236

Chapter 6   Polynomials and Polynomial Functions 304

Chapter 7   Radical Functions and Rational Exponents 366

Chapter 8   Exponential and Logarithmic Functions 428

Chapter 9   Rational Functions 486

Chapter 10   Quadratic Relations and Conic Sections 544

Chapter 11   Sequences and Series 598

Chapter 12   Probability and Statistics 646

Chapter 13   Periodic Functions and Trigonometry 708

Chapter 14   Trigonometric Identities and Equations 776

Extra Practice: Skills and
Word Problems 836

Skills Handbook

Draw a Diagram 864

Try, Check, Revise 865

Look for a Pattern and Make a Table 866

Solve a Simpler Problem 867

Use Logical Reasoning 868

Work Backward 869

Percents and Percent Applications 870

Operations With Fractions 871

Ratios and Proportions 872

Simplifying Expressions With Integers 873

Evaluating Formulas and Solving
Literal Equations 874

Area and Volume 875

The Coordinate Plane, Midpoint,
and Slope 876

Solving Linear Equations and Inequalities . . 877

Absolute Value Equations and Inequalities . . 878

Graphing Two-Variable Equations
and Inequalities 879

Operations With Exponents 880

Factoring and Operations With Polynomials . 881

Scientific Notation and Significant Digits . . . 882

Operations With Radicals 883

The Pythagorean Theorem and
the Distance Formula 884

Bar Graphs and Circle Graphs 885

Descriptive Statistics and Histograms 886

Operations With Rational Expressions 887

Tables

Measures 888

Symbols 889

Squares and Square Roots 890

Trigonometric Ratios 891

Random Numbers 892

Properties and Formulas 893

English/Spanish Illustrated
Glossary 899

Answers to Instant Check System™ . . 945

Selected Answers 974

Index 1007

Acknowledgments 1023

Chapter

1

Tools of Algebra

Student Support

✓ Instant Check System

Check Your Readiness 2

Check Skills You'll Need 4, 12, 18, 26, 33, 39

Quick Check 6, 7, 8, 12, 13, 14, 19, 20, 21, 27, 28, 33, 34, 35, 36, 40, 41, 42

Checkpoint Quiz 24, 38

Vocabulary 🔊

New Vocabulary 4, 12, 18, 26, 33, 39

Vocabulary Tip 5, 7, 8, 19, 34, 40

Vocabulary Review 47

GO Online

Video Tutor Help 18, 27

Active Math 6, 28, 42

Homework Video Tutor 9, 16, 22, 30, 37, 44

Lesson Quizzes 9, 17, 23, 31, 37, 45

Vocabulary Quiz 47

Chapter Test 50

Algebra at Work 24

✓ **Check Your Readiness** 2

1-1 **Properties of Real Numbers** 4

1-2 **Algebraic Expressions** 12
   • **Activity Lab** Writing Expressions From Tables, 11

1-3 **Solving Equations** 18
   • **Activity Lab** Technology: Spreadsheets, 25

   ✓ **Checkpoint Quiz 1** 24

1-4 **Solving Inequalities** 26
   • **Guided Problem Solving** Understanding Math
                   Problems, 32

1-5 **Absolute Value Equations and Inequalities** 33

   ✓ **Checkpoint Quiz 2** 38

1-6 **Probability** 39

Assessment and Test Prep
   • **Test-Taking Strategies:** Writing Gridded Responses, 46
   • Chapter Review, 47
   • Chapter Test, 50
   • **Standardized Test Prep:** Reading Comprehension, 51

Chapter 2

Functions, Equations, and Graphs

Student Support

 Instant Check System

Check Your Readiness 52

Check Skills You'll Need 55, 62, 72, 78, 88, 93, 101

Quick Check 55, 56, 57, 58, 63, 64, 65, 66, 67, 72, 73, 74, 78, 79, 80, 89, 90, 94, 95, 96, 102, 103, 104

Checkpoint Quiz 77, 100

Vocabulary ◀))

New Vocabulary 55, 62, 72, 78, 88, 93, 101

Vocabulary Tip 57, 64, 72, 83, 88, 93, 101

Vocabulary Builder 85

Vocabulary Review 109

GO Online

Video Tutor Help 58, 67, 73, 103

Active Math 57, 89, 95, 102

Homework Video Tutor 60, 68, 75, 82, 91, 98, 105

Lesson Quizzes 61, 69, 75, 83, 91, 99, 105

Vocabulary Quiz 109

Chapter Test 112

Algebra at Work 77

 Check Your Readiness 52

2-1 Relations and Functions 55
• Algebra 1 Review: The Coordinate Plane, 54

2-2 Linear Equations 62
• Extension: Piecewise Functions, 71

2-3 Direct Variation 72

Checkpoint Quiz 1 77

2-4 Using Linear Models 78
• **Vocabulary Builder** High-Use Academic Words, 85
• **Activity Lab** Technology: Finding a Line of Best Fit, 86

2-5 Absolute Value Functions and Graphs 88

2-6 Families of Functions 93

Checkpoint Quiz 2 100

2-7 Two-Variable Inequalities 101
• **Guided Problem Solving** Understanding Math Problems, 107

DK • **Activity Lab** Applying Functions, 114

Assessment and Test Prep
• **Test-Taking Strategies:** Writing Short Responses, 108
• Chapter Review, 109
• Chapter Test, 112
• **Standardized Test Prep:** Cumulative Review, 113

Chapter 3

Linear Systems

Student Support

 **Instant Check System**

Check Your Readiness 116

Check Skills You'll Need 118, 125, 133, 139, 146, 152

Quick Check 119, 120, 125, 126, 127, 134, 135, 140, 141, 147, 148, 153, 154, 155, 156

Checkpoint Quiz 138, 151

Vocabulary ◀))

New Vocabulary 118, 125, 139, 146

Vocabulary Tip 120, 123, 139, 140, 141, 148

Vocabulary Review 161

GO Online

Video Tutor Help 120, 127

Active Math 118, 127, 135, 141

Homework Video Tutor 122, 129, 136, 143, 149, 158

Lesson Quizzes 123, 129, 137, 143, 149, 159

Vocabulary Quiz 161

Chapter Test 164

Algebra at Work 151

☑ **Check Your Readiness** 116

3-1 **Graphing Systems of Equations** 118

3-2 **Solving Systems Algebraically** 125
- **Activity Lab** Technology: Parametric Equations, 124
- **Guided Problem Solving** Understanding Word Problems, 131
- **Activity Lab** Solving Systems Using Tables, 132

3-3 **Systems of Inequalities** 133

☑ **Checkpoint Quiz 1** 138

3-4 **Linear Programming** 139
- **Activity Lab** Technology: Linear Programming, 145

3-5 **Graphs in Three Dimensions** 146

☑ **Checkpoint Quiz 2** 151

3-6 **Systems With Three Variables** 152

Assessment and Test Prep
- **Test-Taking Strategies:** Writing Extended Responses, 160
- Chapter Review, 161
- Chapter Test, 164
- **Standardized Test Prep:** Reading Comprehension, 165

Chapter 4

Matrices

Student Support

 **Instant Check System**

Check Your Readiness 166

Check Skills You'll Need 168, 174, 182, 191, 199, 206, 214, 221

Quick Check 168, 169, 170, 175, 176, 177, 182, 183, 184, 185, 186, 192, 193, 194, 195, 200, 201, 202, 203, 207, 208, 214, 215, 216, 217, 221, 222, 223, 224

Checkpoint Quiz 189, 211

Vocabulary 🔊

New Vocabulary 168, 174, 182, 191, 199, 214, 221

Vocabulary Tip 168, 176, 183, 191, 192, 196, 207, 222

Vocabulary Review 229

GO Online

Video Tutor Help 174, 200

Active Math 175, 193

Homework Video Tutor 171, 179, 187, 197, 204, 210, 215, 225

Lesson Quizzes 173, 179, 189, 197, 205, 209, 219, 227

Vocabulary Quiz 229

Chapter Test 232

A Point in Time 211

☑ **Check Your Readiness** **166**

4-1 **Organizing Data Into Matrices** **168**

4-2 **Adding and Subtracting Matrices** **174**
  • **Activity Lab** Technology: Working With Matrices, 181

4-3 **Matrix Multiplication** **182**

  ☑ **Checkpoint Quiz 1** **189**

4-4 **Geometric Transformations With Matrices** **191**
  • **Geometry Review:** Geometric Transformations, 190

4-5 **2 × 2 Matrices, Determinants, and Inverses** **199**

4-6 **3 × 3 Matrices, Determinants, and Inverses** **206**
  • **Extension:** Networks, 212

  ☑ **Checkpoint Quiz 2** **211**

4-7 **Inverse Matrices and Systems** **214**
  • **Guided Problem Solving** Understanding Math
                        Problems, 220

4-8 **Augmented Matrices and Systems** **221**

  • **Activity Lab** Applying Inequalities, 234

Assessment and Test Prep
  • **Test-Taking Strategies:** Interpreting Data, 228
  • Chapter Review, 229
  • Chapter Test, 232
  • **Standardized Test Prep:** Cumulative Review, 233

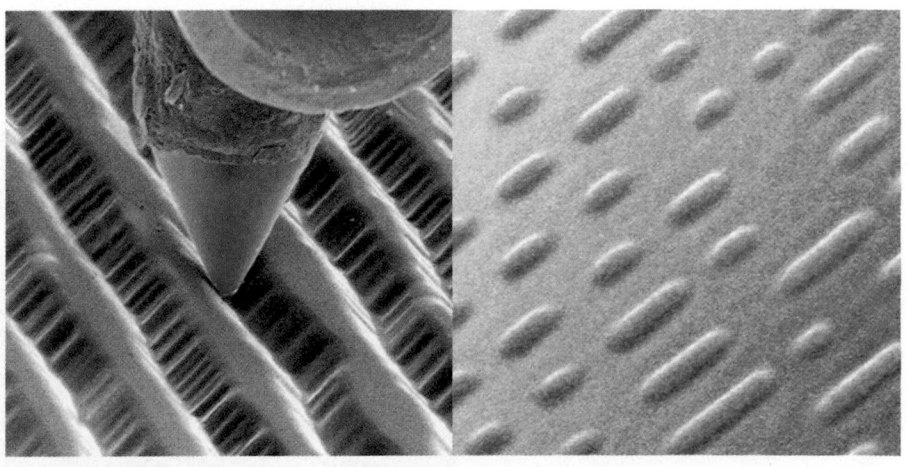

Chapter 5

Quadratic Equations and Functions

☑ **Check Your Readiness** 236

5-1 Modeling Data With Quadratic Functions 238
  • **Activity Lab** Technology: Modeling Using Residuals, 244

5-2 Properties of Parabolas 245

5-3 Transforming Parabolas 252

  ☑ **Checkpoint Quiz 1** 258

5-4 Factoring Quadratic Expressions 259

5-5 Quadratic Equations 267
  • Algebra 1 Review: Square Roots and Radicals, 266
  • **Activity Lab** Writing Equations From Roots, 273

5-6 Complex Numbers 274

  ☑ **Checkpoint Quiz 2** 280

5-7 Completing the Square 282
  • **Activity Lab** Hands-On: Completing the Square, 281
  • **Guided Problem Solving** Understanding Word
                              Problems, 288

5-8 The Quadratic Formula 289
  • **Activity Lab** Technology: Quadratic Inequalities, 296

Assessment and Test Prep
  • **Test-Taking Strategies:** Using a Variable, 298
  • Chapter Review, 299
  • Chapter Test, 302
  • **Standardized Test Prep:** Reading Comprehension, 303

Student Support

☑ Instant Check System

Check Your Readiness 236

Check Skills You'll Need 238, 245, 252, 259, 267, 274, 282, 289

Quick Check 239, 240, 245, 246, 247, 253, 254, 255, 259, 260, 261, 262, 263, 267, 268, 269, 274, 275, 276, 277, 282, 283, 284, 285, 290, 291, 292

Checkpoint Quiz 258, 280

Vocabulary

New Vocabulary 238, 252, 259, 267, 274, 282, 289

Vocabulary Tip 238, 245, 246, 253, 259, 260, 269, 275, 282, 284

Vocabulary Review 299

GO Online

Video Tutor Help 274, 282, 290

Active Math 247, 253, 269, 292

Homework Video Tutor 242, 249, 257, 265, 270, 279, 286, 294

Lesson Quizzes 243, 249, 257, 265, 271, 279, 287, 295

Vocabulary Quiz 299

Chapter Test 302

Algebra at Work 251

Chapter 6

Polynomials and Polynomial Functions

Student Support

 **Instant Check System**

Check Your Readiness 304

Check Skills You'll Need 306, 313, 320, 327, 335, 341, 345, 353

Quick Check 307, 308, 309, 313, 314, 315, 316, 321, 322, 323, 327, 328, 329, 330, 336, 337, 338, 342, 343, 345, 346, 347, 354, 355

Checkpoint Quiz 326, 351

Vocabulary

New Vocabulary 306, 313, 320, 327, 335, 341, 345, 353

Vocabulary Tip 307, 310, 314, 315, 316, 320, 322, 329, 335, 342

Vocabulary Builder 334

Vocabulary Review 359

GO Online

Video Tutor Help 321, 347

Active Math 316, 323

Homework Video Tutor 310, 318, 325, 332, 339, 343, 349, 356

Lesson Quizzes 311, 319, 325, 331, 339, 343, 351, 357

Vocabulary Quiz 359

Chapter Test 362

Algebra at Work 326

✓ **Check Your Readiness** 304

6-1 Polynomial Functions 306
  • Extension: End Behavior, 312

6-2 Polynomials and Linear Factors 313

6-3 Dividing Polynomials 320

  ✓ **Checkpoint Quiz 1** 326

6-4 Solving Polynomial Equations 327
  • **Guided Problem Solving** Understanding Word
                              Problems, 333
  • **Vocabulary Builder** Continuous and Discrete, 334

6-5 Theorems About Roots of Polynomial Equations 335

6-6 The Fundamental Theorem of Algebra 341

6-7 Permutations and Combinations 345

  ✓ **Checkpoint Quiz 2** 351

6-8 The Binomial Theorem 353
  • **Activity Lab** Pascal's Triangle, 352

  • **Activity Lab** Applying Quadratic Functions, 364

Assessment and Test Prep
  • **Test-Taking Strategies:** Drawing a Diagram, 358
  • Chapter Review, 359
  • Chapter Test, 362
  • **Standardized Test Prep:** Cumulative Review, 363

Chapter 7

Radical Functions and Rational Exponents

Student Support

✓ **Instant Check System**

Check Your Readiness 366

Check Skills You'll Need 369, 374, 380, 385, 391, 398, 406, 414

Quick Check 370, 371, 374, 375, 376, 377, 380, 381, 382, 385, 386, 387, 388, 391, 392, 393, 398, 399, 400, 407, 408, 409, 415, 416, 417

Checkpoint Quiz 384, 404

Vocabulary

New Vocabulary 369, 374, 380, 385, 391, 398, 406, 414

Vocabulary Tip 369, 370, 385, 398, 399, 408

Vocabulary Review 423

GO Online

Video Tutor Help 381, 387

Active Math 371, 417

Homework Video Tutor 373, 378, 383, 389, 395, 402, 411, 418

Lesson Quizzes 373, 379, 383, 389, 395, 403, 411, 419

Vocabulary Quiz 423

Chapter Test 426

Algebra at Work 412

✓ **Check Your Readiness** 366

7-1 Roots and Radical Expressions 369
  • Algebra 1 Review: Properties of Exponents, 368

7-2 Multiplying and Dividing Radical Expressions 374

7-3 Binomial Radical Expressions 380

✓ **Checkpoint Quiz 1** 384

7-4 Rational Exponents 385

7-5 Solving Square Root and Other Radical Equations 391
  • Geometry Review: Radical Expressions in
    Formulas, 397

7-6 Function Operations 398
  • **Guided Problem Solving** Understanding Word
    Problems, 405

✓ **Checkpoint Quiz 2** 404

7-7 Inverse Relations and Functions 406
  • **Activity Lab** Technology: Graphing Inverses, 413

7-8 Graphing Square Root and Other Radical Functions 414
  • **Activity Lab** Technology: Radical Inequalities, 420

Assessment and Test Prep
  • **Test-Taking Strategies:** Finding Multiple Correct
    Answers, 422
  • Chapter Review, 423
  • Chapter Test, 426
  • **Standardized Test Prep:** Reading Comprehension, 427

Chapter 8

Exponential and Logarithmic Functions

Student Support

 **Instant Check System**

Check Your Readiness 428

Check Skills You'll Need 430, 439, 446, 454, 461, 470

Quick Check 430, 431, 432, 433, 434, 439, 440, 441, 442, 446, 447, 448, 449, 455, 456, 461, 462, 463, 464, 470, 471, 472

Checkpoint Quiz 445, 468

Vocabulary

New Vocabulary 430, 439, 446, 461, 470

Vocabulary Tip 433, 434, 443, 447, 449, 455, 470

Vocabulary Builder 460

Vocabulary Review 479

GO Online

Video Tutor Help 447, 455

Active Math 434, 440, 448

Homework Video Tutor 436, 443, 450, 458, 466, 474

Lesson Quizzes 437, 445, 451, 459, 467, 473

Vocabulary Quiz 479

Chapter Test 482

A Point in Time 475

⟨✓⟩ **Check Your Readiness** **428**

8-1 Exploring Exponential Models **430**
  • **Activity Lab** Technology: Fitting Exponential
    Curves to Data, 438

8-2 Properties of Exponential Functions **439**

  ⟨✓⟩ **Checkpoint Quiz 1** **445**

8-3 Logarithmic Functions as Inverses **446**
  • **Guided Problem Solving** Understanding Word
    Problems, 453

8-4 Properties of Logarithms **454**
  • **Vocabulary Builder** Reasonable Context, 460

8-5 Exponential and Logarithmic Equations **461**
  • **Activity Lab** Technology: Linear and
    Exponential Models, 469

  ⟨✓⟩ **Checkpoint Quiz 2** **468**

8-6 Natural Logarithms **470**
  • **Activity Lab** Technology: Exponential and
    Logarithmic Inequalities, 476

  • **Activity Lab** Applying Exponential Functions, 484

Assessment and Test Prep
  • **Test-Taking Strategies:** Testing Multiple Choices, 478
  • Chapter Review, 479
  • Chapter Test, 482
  • **Standardized Test Prep:** Cumulative Review, 483

Chapter 9

Rational Functions

Student Support

✓ **Instant Check System**

Check Your Readiness 486

Check Skills You'll Need 488, 495, 501, 509, 514, 522, 531

Quick Check 489, 490, 495, 496, 497, 498, 502, 503, 504, 505, 509, 510, 511, 515, 516, 517, 522, 523, 524, 532, 533, 534

Checkpoint Quiz 508, 520

Vocabulary

New Vocabulary 488, 495, 501, 509, 514, 531

Vocabulary Tip 488, 490, 495, 496, 501, 533

Vocabulary Review 539

GO Online

Video Tutor Help 511, 516, 523

Active Math 489, 497, 504

Homework Video Tutor 492, 499, 506, 512, 518, 525, 535

Lesson Quizzes 493, 499, 507, 513, 519, 527, 535

Vocabulary Quiz 539

Chapter Test 542

Algebra at Work 537

✓ **Check Your Readiness** 486

9-1 Inverse Variation 488

9-2 The Reciprocal Function Family 495
  • **Activity Lab** Technology: Graphing Rational
            Functions, 494

9-3 Rational Functions and Their Graphs 501

    ✓ **Checkpoint Quiz 1** 508

9-4 Rational Expressions 509

9-5 Adding and Subtracting Rational Expressions 514

    ✓ **Checkpoint Quiz 2** 520

9-6 Solving Rational Equations 522
  • **Activity Lab** Extraneous Solutions, 521
  • **Activity Lab** Technology: Rational Inequalities, 528
  • **Guided Problem Solving** Understanding Word
            Problems, 530

9-7 Probability of Multiple Events 531

Assessment and Test Prep
  • **Test-Taking Strategies:** Eliminating Answers, 538
  • Chapter Review, 539
  • Chapter Test, 542
  • **Standardized Test Prep:** Reading Comprehension, 543

Chapter 10

Quadratic Relations and Conic Sections

 Check Your Readiness **544**

10-1 Exploring Conic Sections **547**
   • **Activity Lab** Hands-On: Conic Sections, 546
   • **Activity Lab** Technology: Graphing Conic Sections, 554

10-2 Parabolas **555**

10-3 Circles **561**
   • **Activity Lab** Technology: Using Parametric
                    Equations, 567

 Checkpoint Quiz 1 . . . . **566**

10-4 Ellipses **568**

10-5 Hyperbolas **574**
   • **Guided Problem Solving** Understanding Math
                    Problems, 581

 Checkpoint Quiz 2 . . . . **580**

10-6 Translating Conic Sections **582**
   • **Activity Lab** Technology: Solving Quadratic
                    Systems, 589

   • **Activity Lab** Applying Conic Sections, 596

Assessment and Test Prep
   • **Test-Taking Strategies:** Choosing *Cannot Be Determined*, 590
   • Chapter Review, 591
   • Chapter Test, 594
   • **Standardized Test Prep:** Cumulative Review, 595

Student Support

 **Instant Check System**

Check Your Readiness 544

Check Skills You'll Need 547, 555, 561, 568, 574, 582

Quick Check 548, 549, 550, 555, 556, 557, 562, 563, 569, 570, 576, 577, 583, 584, 585

Checkpoint Quiz 566, 580

Vocabulary 🔊

New Vocabulary 547, 555, 561, 568, 574

Vocabulary Tip 547, 550, 568, 571, 574, 575, 582

Vocabulary Review 591

GO Online

Active Math 558, 564, 570, 577

Homework Video Tutor 551, 559, 565, 572, 578, 586

Lesson Quizzes 551, 559, 565, 573, 579, 587

Vocabulary Quiz 591

Chapter Test 594

A Point in Time 553

Chapter 11

Sequences and Series

Student Support

☑ Instant Check System

Check Your Readiness 598

Check Skills You'll Need 600, 606, 612, 619, 626, 635

Quick Check 601, 602, 606, 607, 613, 614, 620, 621, 627, 628, 636, 637

Checkpoint Quiz 617, 631

Vocabulary 🔊

New Vocabulary 600, 606, 612, 619, 626, 635

Vocabulary Tip 606, 619, 621, 627

Vocabulary Review 641

GO Online

Video Tutor Help 607, 613, 621

Active Math 606, 614, 636

Homework Video Tutor 604, 608, 615, 623, 629, 638

Lesson Quizzes 605, 609, 615, 623, 631, 639

Vocabulary Quiz 641

Chapter Test 644

A Point in Time 617

☑ **Check Your Readiness** **598**

11-1 **Mathematical Patterns** **600**

11-2 **Arithmetic Sequences** **606**
• Extension: The Fibonacci Sequence, 611

11-3 **Geometric Sequences** **612**
• **Guided Problem Solving** Understanding Math Problems, 618

☑ **Checkpoint Quiz 1** **617**

11-4 **Arithmetic Series** **619**

11-5 **Geometric Series** **626**
• **Activity Lab** Geometry and Infinite Series, 625
• Extension: Mathematical Induction, 632
• **Activity Lab** Technology: Evaluating Series, 634

☑ **Checkpoint Quiz 2** **631**

11-6 **Area Under a Curve** **635**

Assessment and Test Prep
• **Test-Taking Strategies:** Using Estimation, 640
• Chapter Review, 641
• Chapter Test, 644
• **Standardized Test Prep:** Reading Comprehension, 645

Chapter 12

Probability and Statistics

Student Support

 Instant Check System

Check Your Readiness 646

Check Skills You'll Need 648, 654, 660, 668, 677, 685, 692

Quick Check 648, 649, 650, 651, 654, 655, 656, 660, 661, 662, 663, 664, 669, 670, 671, 672, 677, 678, 679, 680, 686, 687, 688, 692, 693, 694

Checkpoint Quiz 667, 691

Vocabulary 🔊

New Vocabulary 648, 654, 660, 668, 677, 685, 692

Vocabulary Tip 648, 649, 660, 662, 669, 670, 677, 693

Vocabulary Builder 684

Vocabulary Review 701

GO Online

Active Math 663, 688

Homework Video Tutor 652, 657, 665, 673, 681, 689, 696

Lesson Quizzes 653, 657, 665, 673, 681, 691, 697

Vocabulary Quiz 701

Chapter Test 704

Algebra at Work 683

 **Check Your Readiness** **646**

12-1 Probability Distributions **648**

12-2 Conditional Probability **654**
  • Extension: Comparing Conditional Probabilities, 659

12-3 Analyzing Data **660**

   Checkpoint Quiz 1 . . . . **667**

12-4 Standard Deviation **668**
  • **Guided Problem Solving** Understanding Math Problems, 675
  • **Activity Lab** Continuous Probability, 676

12-5 Working With Samples **677**
  • **Vocabulary Builder** Variable and Parameter, 684

12-6 Binomial Distributions **685**

  Checkpoint Quiz 2 . . . . **691**

12-7 Normal Distributions **692**
  • **Activity Lab** Technology: Area Under a Curve, 699
  • **Activity Lab** Applying Sequences, 706

Assessment and Test Prep
  • **Test-Taking Strategies:** Answering the Question Asked, 700
  • Chapter Review, 701
  • Chapter Test, 704
  • **Standardized Test Prep:** Cumulative Review, 705

Chapter 13

Periodic Functions and Trigonometry

Student Support

✓ Instant Check System

Check Your Readiness 708

Check Skills You'll Need 710, 718, 726, 734, 743, 749, 756, 763

Quick Check 711, 712, 713, 718, 719, 721, 722, 727, 728, 729, 734, 735, 736, 744, 745, 750, 751, 756, 757, 758, 759, 760

Checkpoint Quiz 733, 762

Vocabulary

New Vocabulary 710, 718, 726, 734, 743, 749, 756, 763

Vocabulary Tip 712, 718, 720, 726, 734, 735, 736, 749

Vocabulary Review 771

GO Online

Video Tutor Help 727, 757

Active Math 735, 744, 750, 758

Homework Video Tutor 714, 723, 731, 739, 747, 753, 761, 767

Lesson Quizzes 715, 723, 733, 741, 747, 753, 761, 769

Vocabulary Quiz 771

Chapter Test 774

A Point in Time 716

✓	**Check Your Readiness**	**708**
13-1	**Exploring Periodic Data**	**710**
13-2	**Angles and the Unit Circle**	**718**
	• Geometry Review: Special Right Triangles, 717	
13-3	**Radian Measure**	**726**
	• **Activity Lab** Hands-On: Measuring Radians, 725	
✓	**Checkpoint Quiz 1**	**733**
13-4	**The Sine Function**	**734**
	• **Activity Lab** Technology: Graphing Trigonometric Functions, 742	
13-5	**The Cosine Function**	**743**
13-6	**The Tangent Function**	**749**
	• **Guided Problem Solving** Understanding Math Problems, 755	
13-7	**Translating Sine and Cosine Functions**	**756**
✓	**Checkpoint Quiz 2**	**762**
13-8	**Reciprocal Trigonometric Functions**	**763**

Assessment and Test Prep
• **Test-Taking Strategies:** Using Mental Math, 770
• Chapter Review, 771
• Chapter Test, 774
• **Standardized Test Prep:** Reading Comprehension, 775

Trigonometric Identities and Equations

Student Support

☑ Instant Check System

Check Your Readiness 776

Check Skills You'll Need 778, 783, 792, 801, 808, 814, 821

Quick Check 779, 780, 783, 784, 785, 786, 793, 794, 795, 801, 802, 803, 809, 810, 815, 816, 817, 822, 823

Checkpoint Quiz 799, 820

Vocabulary

New Vocabulary 778, 792, 801, 808

Vocabulary Tip 779, 780, 784, 793, 798, 801, 802, 815

Vocabulary Review 827

GO Online

Video Tutor Help 794

Active Math 779, 817

Homework Video Tutor 781, 788, 797, 805, 811, 818, 824

Lesson Quizzes 781, 789, 799, 805, 811, 819, 825

Vocabulary Quiz 827

Chapter Test 830

End-of-Course Test 831

Algebra at Work 813

☑ **Check Your Readiness** 776

14-1 Trigonometric Identities 778

14-2 Solving Trigonometric Equations Using Inverses 783
  • **Activity Lab** Technology: Lissajous Figures, 791

14-3 Right Triangles and Trigonometric Ratios 792
  • **Guided Problem Solving** Understanding Word
                              Problems, 800

☑ **Checkpoint Quiz 1** 799

14-4 Area and the Law of Sines 801
  • **Extension:** The Ambiguous Case, 807

14-5 The Law of Cosines 808

14-6 Angle Identities 814

☑ **Checkpoint Quiz 2** 820

14-7 Double-Angle and Half-Angle Identities 821

  • **Activity Lab** Applying Trigonometry, 834

Assessment and Test Prep
  • **Test-Taking Strategies:** Answering Open-Ended Questions, 826
  • Chapter Review, 827
  • Chapter Test, 830
  • **Standardized Test Prep:** Cumulative Review, 831

Connect Your Learning
through problem solving, activities, and the Web

Applications: Real-World Applications

Careers
Agriculturist, 650
Air Traffic Controller, 579
Business Owner, 403
Carpenter, 318
Ceramic Artist, 752
Consumer Researcher, 349
Craftsman, 403
Custom Tailor, 285
Dispatcher, 671
Financial Planner, 627
Graphic Designer, 613
Groomer, 122
Hot-Air Balloonist, 78
Mason, 526
Microbiologist, 143
Neonatal Nurse, 692
Park Planner, 794
Picture Framer, 249
Pilot, 812
Psychologist, 444
Radio Broadcaster, 532
Smoke Jumper, 268
Sound Engineer, 740
Stadium Designer, 157
Support Personnel, 533
Video Game Programmer, 505

Consumer Issues
Advertising, 122, 351
Budgeting, 498
Consumer Issues, 349, 400
Consumer Spending, 691
Cost Analysis, 67
Discounts, 426
Estimation, 9, 172, 242, 397, 760, 761
Fees, 122, 126
Gas Mileage, 76, 499
Gold, 308
Interest, 442, 472
Jobs, 172
Manufacturing, 90, 179, 248, 251, 264, 286, 699
Marketing, 653, 689
Merchandising, 686

Money Management, 560
Packaging, 249, 310, 371, 395
Prices, 182
Product Design, 147
Purchasing, 164
Retail Sale, 172
Sales, 82, 164, 172, 226, 401
Savings, 50, 330, 443, 474, 609
Shopping, 126, 138, 217

Entertainment
Circus, 418
Eiffel Tower, 66
Entertainment, 82, 102, 204, 603
Ferris Wheel, 747
Musical, 50
Parks, 789, 794
Radio, 532
Telephones, 722

Food
Cooking, 104, 143
Food Preparation, 351
Nutrition, 81, 82, 153, 162, 218, 226

Money Matters
Banking, 122, 161, 615
Break-Even Point, 130
Business, 121, 180, 187, 188, 216, 225, 256, 294, 435, 505, 506, 535, 643
Coins, 265
Depreciation, 434
Earnings, 164, 674
Finance, 157, 604
Financial Planning, 627
Fuel Economy, 526
Fund-Raising, 67, 128, 136, 137, 607
Investing, 15, 22, 156, 164, 443, 472, 473, 482, 560, 644
Market Research, 650–651, 655
Production, 698
Profit, 141, 163, 403
Revenue, 28, 188, 248
Wage Policy, 507

Recreation
Automobiles, 80, 294, 409, 526, 731
Aviation, 77
Boats, 346, 372
Carpentry, 318
Ceramics, 752
Computer Use, 682
Crafts, 620
Egyptology, 793
Exercise, 205
Games, 49, 505, 697
Gardening, 271
Hot-air Ballooning, 78, 796
Internet Access, 129
Nature, 611
Physical Fitness, 231
Picture Framing, 249
Recreation, 6, 112
Rocketry, 797
Sailing, 805
Stamps, 242, 283, 341
Travel, 90, 213, 314
Unicycles, 247
Video Game Programming, 505
Woodworking, 249, 525

Sports
Baseball, 798
Basketball, 36, 506
Golf, 616
Gymnastics, 170
Hockey, 292
Racing, 809
Sports, 21, 44, 60, 119, 157, 178, 286, 288, 300, 355, 669, 811
Stadium Design, 157
Track and Field, 84, 666, 696

Applications: **Algebra at Work**

Acoustical Physicist, 813
Demographer, 412
Economist, 537

Landscape Architect, 251
Market Researcher, 683
Miniaturist, 77

Quality Control Engineer, 326
Radiologist, 151
Wildlife Biologist, 24

Applications: **A Point in Time**

Moon Landing, 475
Murals, 211

Pacemakers, 716
Sun's Movements, 617

Titanic, 553

Applications: **Interdisciplinary Connections**

Archaeology, 389, 442, 451, 467
Architecture, 197, 287, 510, 622
Art, 4, 58, 269, 270, 291
Astronomy, 467, 573, 588, 741, 778, 814
Biology, 41, 444, 473, 481, 693, 695, 748
Botany, 442
Chemistry, 61, 445, 448, 450, 453, 467, 480
Civil Engineering, 254
Ecology, 142
Economics, 123, 247, 401, 437
Electrical Engineering, 15
Engineering, 15, 254, 797
Geography, 150, 731, 732
Geology, 665

Geometry, 14, 15, 20, 22, 30, 32, 38, 42, 43, 48, 60, 62, 69, 73, 76, 83, 100, 128, 137, 150, 158, 159, 191, 192, 196, 197, 218, 227, 242, 264, 286, 295, 311, 317, 318, 324, 330, 331, 349, 356, 362, 372, 378, 402, 405, 410, 411, 426, 444, 490, 602, 604, 605, 610, 625, 731, 753, 754, 768, 797, 798, 805, 812
History, 158, 232, 250, 587, 719
Language Arts, 715
Literature, 208, 209, 210, 347
Medicine, 440, 692
Meteorology, 37, 130, 390, 652, 656, 657, 664, 665, 688
Microbiology, 143
Music, 139, 185, 467, 496, 519, 732, 740

Oceanography, 436, 661, 663
Physics, 15, 218, 241, 248, 249, 271, 295, 302, 377, 378, 383, 389, 396, 443, 474, 480, 482, 490, 492, 512, 519, 614, 630, 644, 774, 782, 786, 787, 812
Psychology, 136, 444
Science, 79
Seismology, 446, 449, 465, 696
Social Science, 649
Social Studies, 83
Sociology, 689
Statistics, 174, 535, 690
Weather, 37, 130, 390, 652, 656, 657, 664, 665, 688
Zoology, 436, 462, 466, 489

Activities

Adding Fractions—Extended, 514
Analyzing Data Spread, 668
Analyzing Graphs, 118
Analyzing Hyperbolas, 573
Angles in a Circle, 720
Arithmetic Series, 619
Binomial Probability, 685
Checking for Extraneous Solutions, 394
Counting Zeros, 341
Estimating Square Roots, 4
Factoring, 259
Finding a Minimum Value, 139
Finding the Line of Best Fit, 86
Generating a Pattern, 602
Geometric Sequences, 612
Graphs of Polynomial Functions, 306
Hands-On, 39, 531

Inverses, 406
Linear Inequalities, 101
Periodic Cycles, 710
Point-Slope Form, 64
Properties of Logarithms, 454
Right Triangle Ratios, 792
Technology, 118, 306, 394, 582, 778
Tournament Play, 432
Translating a Geometric Figure, 191
Translating Conic Sections, 582
Trigonometric Identities, 778
Using Matrices, 184
Using the Line of Best Fit to Estimate, 87
Using the Line of Best Fit to Predict, 86
Vertex Form, 252

Activities: Activity Labs

Applying Conic Sections: Martian Math, 596–597

Applying Exponential Functions: A Crowded House, 484–485

Applying Functions: Bridges, Beams, and Tension, 114–115

Applying Inequalities: Building a Business, 234–235

Applying Quadratic Functions: As the Ball Flies, 364–365

Applying Sequences: Training Day, 706–707

Applying Trigonometry: A Question of Balance, 834–835

Area Under a Curve, 699

Completing the Square, 281

Conic Sections, 546

Continuous Probability, 676

Evaluating Series, 634

Exponential and Logarithmic Inequalities, 476–477

Extraneous Solutions, 521

Fibonacci Sequence, 611

Finding a Line of Best Fit, 86–87

Fitting Exponential Curves to Data, 438

Geometry and Infinite Series, 625

Graphing Conic Sections, 554

Graphing Inverses, 413

Graphing Rational Functions, 494

Graphing Trigonometric Functions, 742

Linear and Exponential Models, 469

Linear Programming, 145

Lissajous Figures, 791

Measuring Radians, 725

Modeling Using Residuals, 244

Parametric Equations, 124

Pascal's Triangle, 352

Quadratic Inequalities, 296–297

Radical Inequalities, 420–421

Rational Inequalities, 528–529

Solving Quadratic Systems, 589

Solving Systems Using Tables, 132

Spreadsheets, 25

Using Parametric Equations, 567

Working with Matrices, 181

Writing Equations From Roots, 273

Writing Expressions From Tables, 11

Activities: Guided Problem Solving

Understanding Math Problems, 32, 107, 220, 581, 618, 675, 755

Understanding Word Problems, 131, 288, 333, 405, 453, 530, 800

GO Online

Throughout this book you will find links to the Prentice Hall Web site. Use the Web Codes provided with each link to gain direct access to online material. Here's how to *Go Online*:

1. Go to PHSchool.com
2. Enter the Web Code
3. Click Go!

Lesson Web Codes

Lesson Quiz Web Codes: There is an online quiz for every lesson. Access these quizzes with Web Codes aga-1407 through aga-1407 for Lesson 1-1 through Lesson 14-7. See page 91.

Lesson Quizzes
Web Code format: aga-0204
02 = Chapter 2   04 = Lesson 4

Homework Video Tutor Web Codes: For every lesson, there is additional support online to help students complete their homework. Access this homework help online with Web Codes age-0101 through age-1407 for Lesson 1-1 through Lesson 14-7. See page 9.

Homework Video Tutor
Web Code format: age-0605
06 = Chapter 6   05 = Lesson 5

Chapter Web Codes

Chapter	Vocabulary Quizzes	Chapter Tests	Activity Labs
1	agj-0151	aga-0152	
2	agj-0251	aga-0252	age-0253
3	agj-0351	aga-0352	
4	agj-0451	aga-0452	age-0453
5	agj-0551	aga-0552	
6	agj-0651	aga-0652	age-0653
7	agj-0751	aga-0752	
8	agj-0851	aga-0852	age-0853
9	agj-0951	aga-0952	
10	agj-1051	aga-1052	age-1053
11	agj-1151	aga-1152	
12	agj-1251	aga-1252	age-1253
13	agj-1351	aga-1352	
14	agj-1451	aga-1452	age-1453
End-of-Course		aga-1454	

Additional Web Codes

Video Tutor Help:
Use web code age-0775 to access engaging online instructional videos to help bring math concepts to life. See page 18.

Data Updates:
Use web code agg-9041 to get up-to-date government data for use in examples and exercises. See page 83.

Algebra at Work:
For information about each Algebra at Work feature, use web code agb-2031. See page 24.

Using Your Book for Success

Welcome to *Prentice Hall Algebra 2*. There are many features built into the daily lessons of this text that will help you learn the important skills and concepts you will need to be successful in this course. Look through the following pages for some study tips that you will find useful as you complete each lesson.

Getting Ready to Learn

Check Your Readiness

Complete the *Check Your Readiness* exercises to see what topics you may need to review before you begin the chapter.

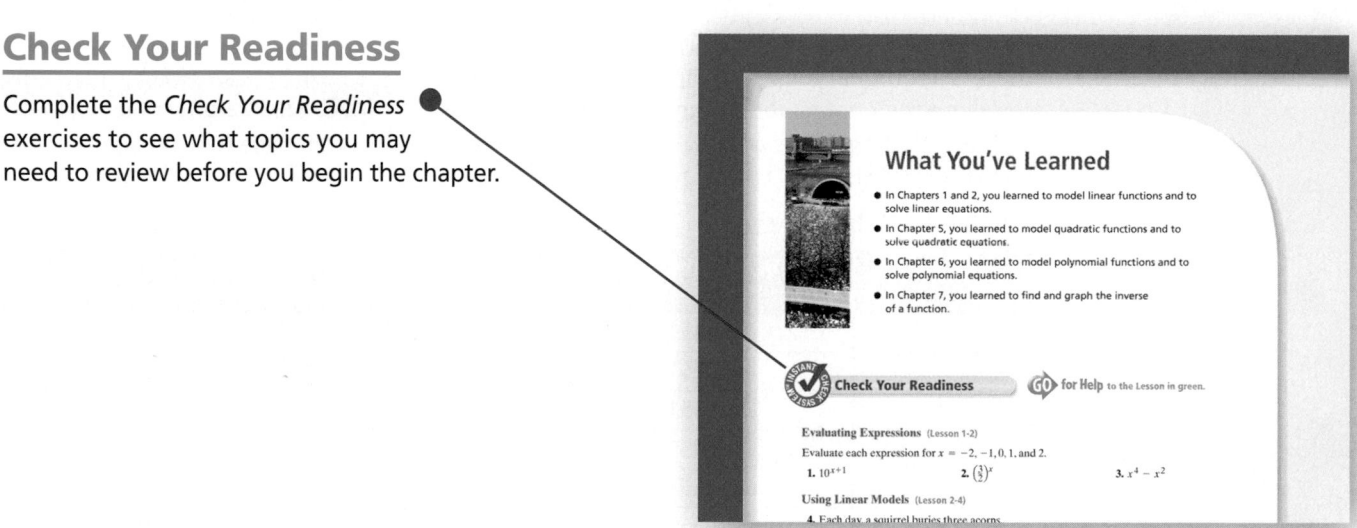

Check Skills You'll Need

Complete the *Check Skills You'll Need* exercises to make sure you have the skills needed to successfully learn the concepts in the lesson.

New Vocabulary

New Vocabulary is listed for each lesson so you can pre-read the text. As each term is introduced, it is highlighted in yellow.

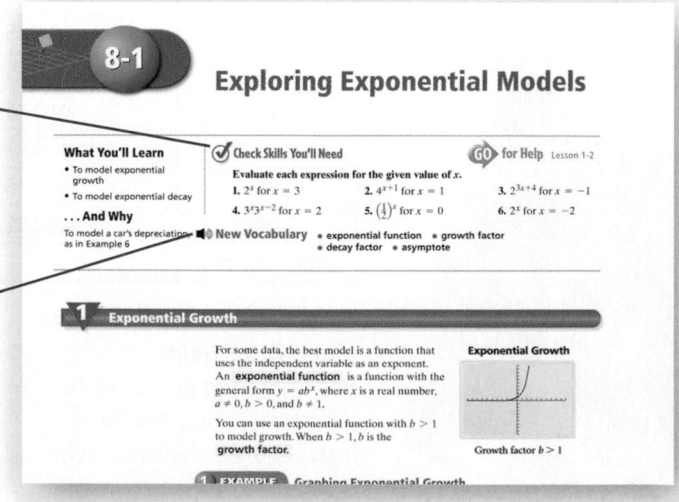

Built-In Help

Go for Help

Look for the green labels throughout your book that tell you where to "Go" for help. You'll see this built-in help in the lessons and in the homework exercises.

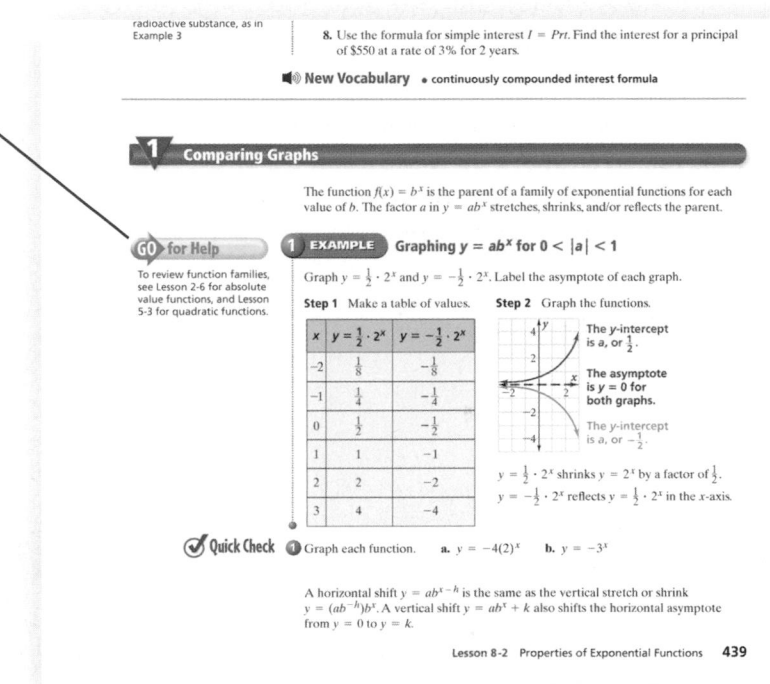

Video Tutor Help

Go online to see engaging videos to help you better understand important math concepts.

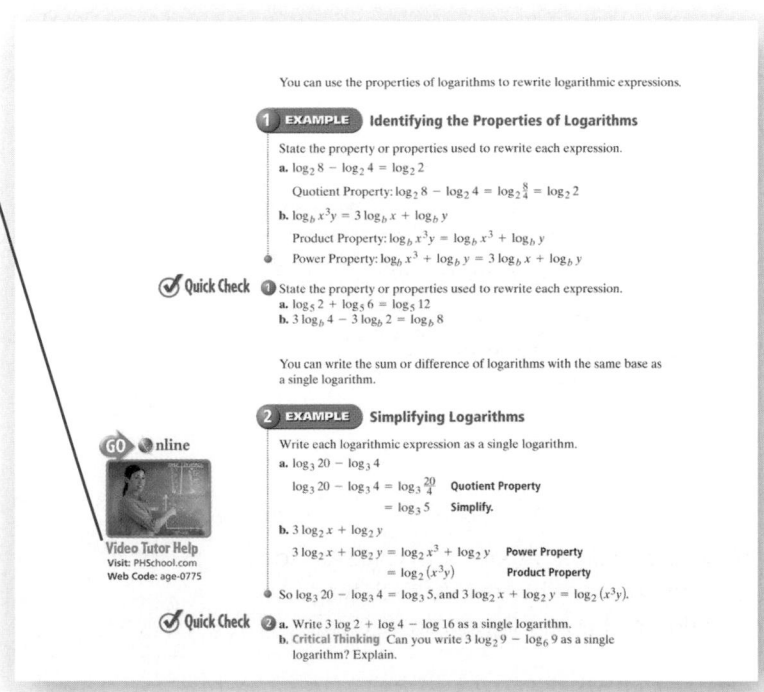

Understanding the Lesson

Quick Check

Every lesson includes numerous Examples, each followed by a *Quick Check* question that you can do on your own to see if you understand the skill being introduced. Check your progress with the answers at the back of the book.

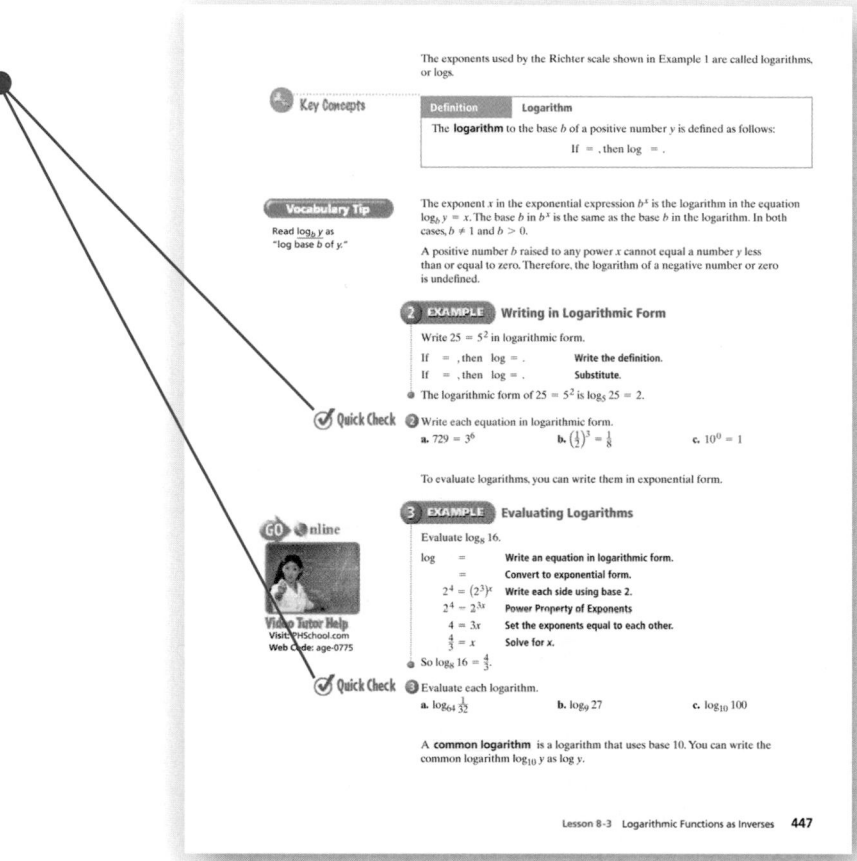

Understanding Key Concepts

Frequent *Key Concept* boxes summarize important definitions, formulas, and properties. Use these to review what you've learned.

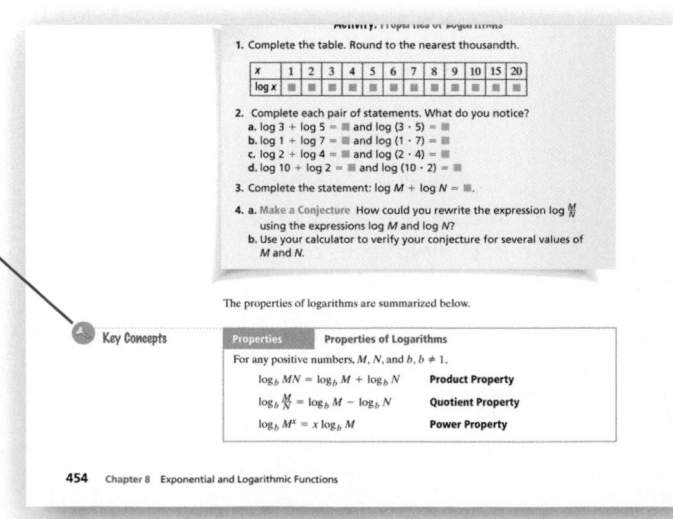

Online Active Math

Make math come alive with these online activities. Review and practice important math concepts with these engaging online tutorials.

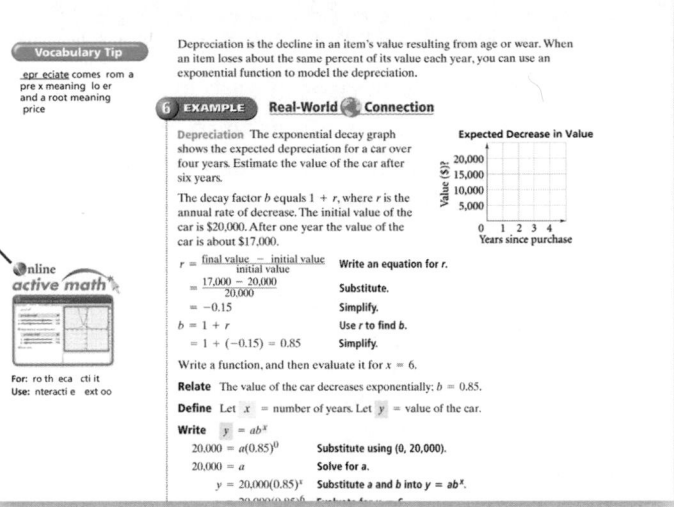

For: ro th eca cti it
Use: nteracti e ext oo

Vocabulary Tip

epr eciate comes rom a pre x meaning lo er and a root meaning price

Depreciation is the decline in an item's value resulting from age or wear. When an item loses about the same percent of its value each year, you can use an exponential function to model the depreciation.

6 EXAMPLE Real-World Connection

Depreciation The exponential decay graph shows the expected depreciation for a car over four years. Estimate the value of the car after six years.

Expected Decrease in Value

The decay factor b equals $1 + r$, where r is the annual rate of decrease. The initial value of the car is $20,000. After one year the value of the car is about $17,000.

$r = \dfrac{\text{final value} - \text{initial value}}{\text{initial value}}$ Write an equation for r.

$= \dfrac{17,000 - 20,000}{20,000}$ Substitute.

$= -0.15$ Simplify.

$b = 1 + r$ Use r to find b.

$= 1 + (-0.15) = 0.85$ Simplify.

Write a function, and then evaluate it for $x = 6$.

Relate The value of the car decreases exponentially; $b = 0.85$.

Define Let x = number of years. Let y = value of the car.

Write $y = ab^x$

$20,000 = a(0.85)^0$ Substitute using (0, 20,000).

$20,000 = a$ Solve for a.

$y = 20,000(0.85)^x$ Substitute a and b into $y = ab^x$.

Decay factor $b < 1$

4 EXAMPLE Analyzing a Function

Without graphing, determine whether the function $y = 14(0.95)^x$ represents exponential growth or exponential decay.

• In $y = 14(0.95)^x$, $b = 0.95$. Since $b < 1$, the function represents exponential decay.

✓ Quick Check ④ Without graphing, determine whether each function represents exponential growth or exponential decay.

a. $y = 100(0.12)^x$ **b.** $y = 0.2(5)^x$ **c.** $y = 16\left(\frac{1}{2}\right)^x$

Vocabulary Tip

s ptote   o es ro t e ree or   d *asymptotos,* eaning not eeting

An **asymptote** is a line that a graph approaches as x or y increases in absolute value.

5 EXAMPLE Graphing Exponential Decay

Graph $y = 24\left(\frac{1}{2}\right)^x$. Identify the horizontal asymptote.

Step 1 Make a table of values.

x	-3	-2	-1	0	1	2	3
y	192	96	48	24	12	6	3

Step 2 Graph the coordinates. Connect the points with a smooth curve.

Vocabulary Support

Understanding mathematical vocabulary is an important part of studying mathematics. *Vocabulary Tips* and *Vocabulary Builders* throughout the book help focus on the language of math.

Vocabulary Builder

Reasonable Context

One quick check of a solution to a real-world problem is determining whether the answer is *reasonable* for the given context. The *context* is the situational setting for the problem.

1 EXAMPLE Reasonableness of a Solution

The class had to solve a cubic equation to find an approximate radius of the hot air balloon. Here are some students' answers:

Ro: 5 ft   Sal: 15 ft   Tim: 25 ft   Una: 100 ft

Which answers are *unreasonable*?

Ro's answer is unreasonable because hot air balloons are much larger than the people who ride in them.

Una's answer is unreasonable because a balloon with a 100 ft radius would be two-thirds the size of a football field.

The context also helps you determine a reasonable domain and range for a function.

2 EXAMPLE Reasonable Domain and Range Values

The quadratic function $h(t) = -16t^2 + 96t + 112$ models the height in feet of a projectile at time t. Give a *reasonable* domain and range for the function h.

The function h is quadratic, so its mathematical domain is the set of real numbers. The graph opens downward, so the function

Practice What You've Learned

There are numerous exercises in each lesson that give you the practice you need to master the concepts in the lesson. Each practice set includes the following sections.

A: Practice by Example

Practice by Example exercises refer you back to the Examples in the lesson, in case you need help with completing these exercises.

B: Apply Your Skills

Apply Your Skills exercises combine skills from earlier lessons to offer you richer skill exercises and multi-step application problems.

C: Challenge

Challenge exercises give you an opportunity to solve problems that extend and stretch your thinking.

Homework Video Tutor

Go online to get help completing your homework! For every lesson, there is a narrated, interactive tutorial to help you review the lesson and understand key concepts.

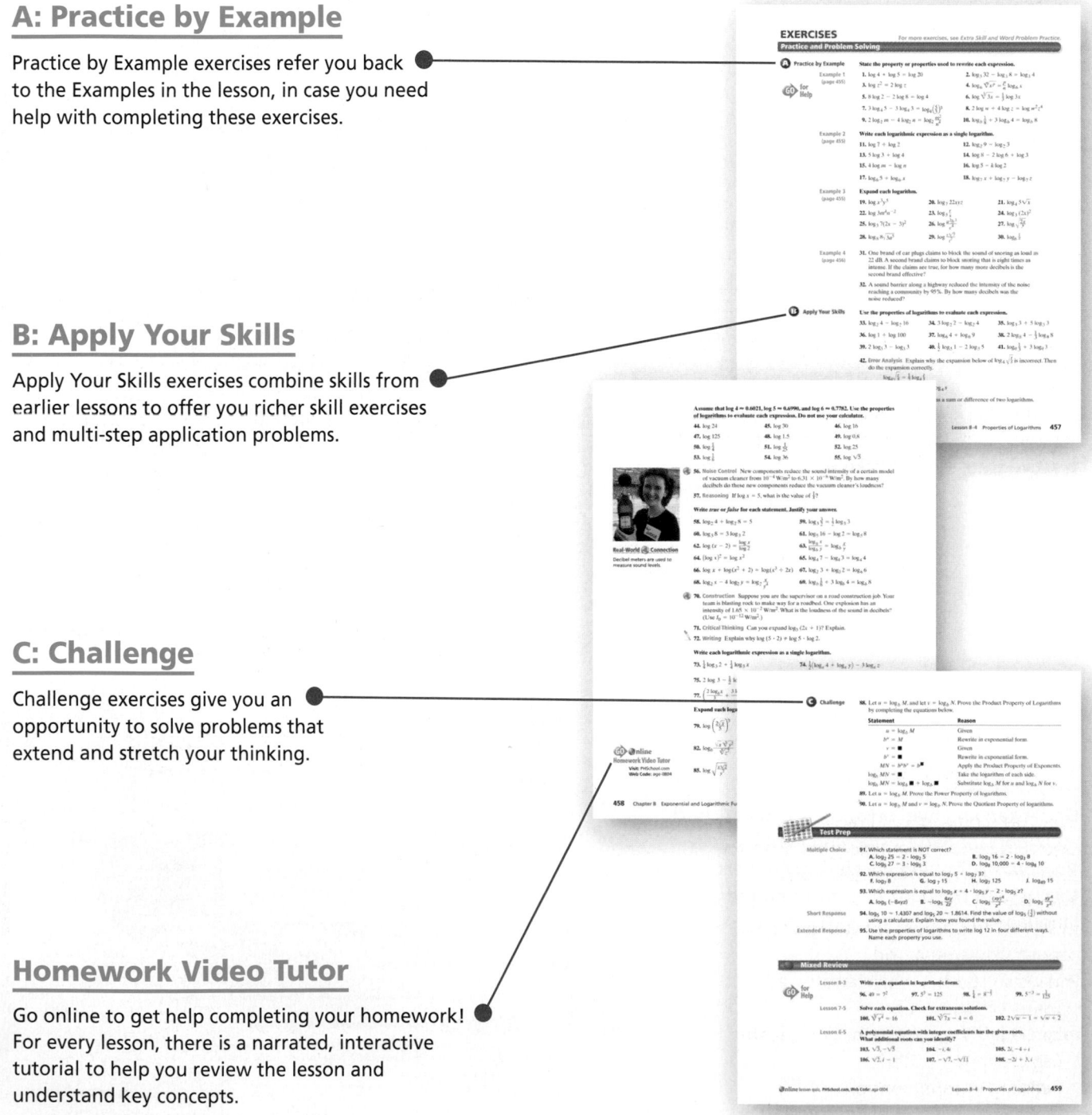

Preparing for Tests

Test-Taking Strategies

Test-Taking Strategies in every chapter teach you strategies to be successful and give you practice in the skills you need to pass state tests and national tests, including the SAT and ACT.

Standardized Test Prep

Standardized Test Prep pages in every chapter give you more opportunities to prepare for the tests you will have to take.

Test Item Formats

The Standardized Test Prep exercises in your book give you the practice you need to answer all types of test questions.
- Multiple Choice
- Gridded Response, for which you write your answer in a grid
- Short Response, which are scored using a 2-point rubric
- Extended Response, which are scored using a 4-point rubric
- Reading Comprehension

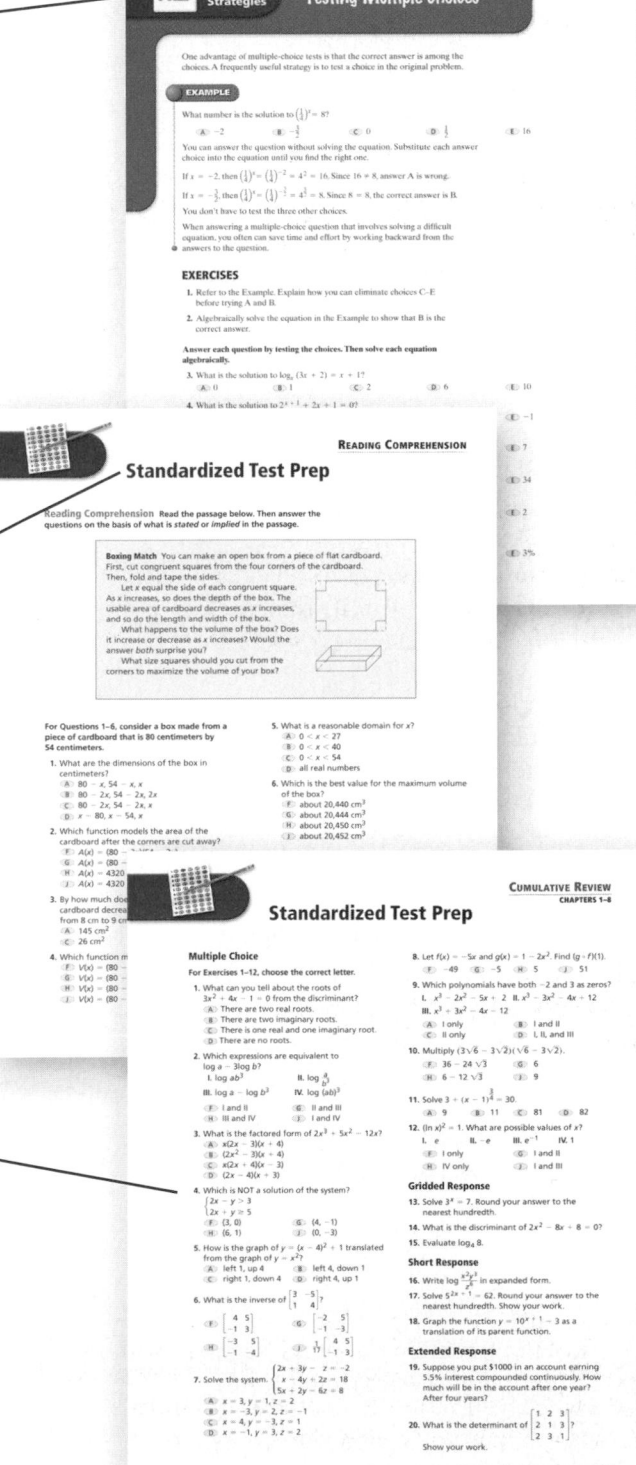

Beginning-Of-Course Diagnostic Test

1. Write the coordinates of each point A–E and name the quadrant or axis where each point lies.

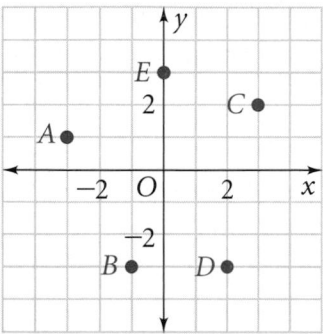

2. Add $6\frac{3}{5} + 2\frac{1}{8}$.

3. Simplify $6 - (-2)(4) + 3(-2)^2$.

4. Mika hiked 4 mi in 77 min. Use a proportion to find how many miles she will hike in 2 h if she hikes at the same rate.

5. Find the volume of the figure.

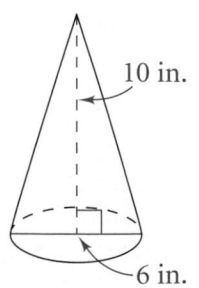

10 in.

6 in.

6. Find the midpoint of the segment with the endpoints $(-3, 4)$ and $(2, -6)$.

7. Display the data from the table in a circle graph.

U.S. Greenhouse Gas Emissions From Human Activities, 1999

Gas and Source	Emissions (teragrams of carbon dioxide equivalents)
Carbon dioxide (CO_2)	5558.1
Methane (CH_4)	619.6
Nitrous Oxide (N_2O)	432.6
Hydrofluorocarbons (HFCs), perfluorocarbons (PFCs), sulfer hexafluoride (SF_6)	135.7

SOURCE: *The World Almanac and Book of Facts, 2002*

8. Simplify $\dfrac{(3r^{-1}s^2t^3)^2}{27r^3st^{-2}}$. Use only positive exponents.

9. Simplify $\dfrac{x^3y^{-3}z^{-1}}{x^{-2}yz^2}$. Use only positive exponents.

10. Simplify $\sqrt{20} + \sqrt{80} - \sqrt{5}$.

11. Simplify $-\sqrt{\dfrac{4}{7}}$.

12. As of the year 2000, the highest wind speed recorded on the top of Mount Washington was 231 mi/h, which is about 298% of the highest wind speed recorded in Chicago. What was the highest wind speed recorded in Chicago as of the year 2000?
Source: *The World Almanac and Book of Facts, 2002*

13. Divide $4\frac{3}{4} \div 2\frac{1}{3}$.

14. Solve $3y - 2 > 5y$. Graph the solution.

15. Divide $\frac{x^4}{4} \div \frac{x^3}{20}$.

16. Alisha ran a total of 32 mi during three days of training for a marathon. On the second day of her training session, she ran 6 mi less than on the first day and 2 mi less than on the third day. How many miles did she run on the first day?

17. Write the product $(2.45 \times 10^3)(1.8 \times 10^5)$ in scientific notation. Round to the appropriate number of significant digits.

18. Let $\triangle ABC$ be an equilateral triangle with side length s. Estimate the percent that the area of the circle circumscribed about $\triangle ABC$ is of the area of the triangle. (It will be greater than 100%.) Recall that the distance from the circumcenter of the triangle to a vertex is equal to the radius of the circumscribed circle.

19. Solve $|4t - 3| = 6$.

20. Factor $2x^2 - 5x - 12$.

21. Graph $2x + 4y < 1$.

22. Find the distance between $(-3, -2)$ and $(1, 7)$. Round to the nearest tenth.

23. The vertices of $\triangle ABC$ are $A(-1, 2)$, $B(0, 3)$, and $C(3, 1)$. Determine the vertices A', B', and C' of the image of $\triangle ABC$ after a reflection across the x-axis.

24. How many ways can you roll two standard number cubes and get a sum of 9?

25. The formula $k = \frac{1}{2}mv^2$ relates the kinetic energy of a body to its mass m and speed v. Solve the formula for m.

26. Find the mean, median, and mode of the following data set.

$$-1 \quad -1 \quad 0 \quad 2 \quad 2 \quad 3 \quad 3 \quad 4 \quad 7 \quad 7 \quad 7$$

27. Find the area of a triangle with a base of 14 in. and a height of 6 in.

What You've Learned

- In your first course in algebra, you learned to add, subtract, multiply, and divide rational numbers. Rational numbers are the quotients of integers, and they include integers, positive and negative fractions, and positive and negative decimals.

- You have also learned to use the order of operations, which tells how to simplify expressions with grouping symbols, exponents, and operations.

- You have also learned to use algebraic expressions.

 **Check Your Readiness**   **for Help** to the Skills Handbook.

Adding Rational Numbers (Skills Handbook page 873)

Find each sum.

1. $6 + (-6)$ **2.** $-8 + 6$ **3.** $5.31 + (-7.40)$ **4.** $-1.95 + 10$

5. $7\frac{3}{4} + \left(-8\frac{1}{2}\right)$ **6.** $-2\frac{1}{3} + 3\frac{1}{4}$ **7.** $6\frac{2}{5} + \left(4\frac{3}{10}\right)$ **8.** $-1\frac{5}{6} + 5\frac{1}{3}$

Subtracting Rational Numbers (Skills Handbook page 873)

Find each difference.

9. $-28 - 14$ **10.** $61 - (-11)$ **11.** $-16 - (-25)$ **12.** $-6.2 - 3.6$

13. $-5\frac{2}{3} - \left(-2\frac{1}{3}\right)$ **14.** $-2\frac{1}{4} - 3\frac{1}{4}$ **15.** $2\frac{2}{3} - 7\frac{1}{3}$ **16.** $\frac{5}{2} - \frac{13}{4}$

Multiplying and Dividing Rational Numbers (Skills Handbook page 873)

Find each product or quotient.

17. $-3 \cdot 7$ **18.** $-2.1 \cdot (-3.5)$ **19.** $-\frac{2}{3} \div 4$ **20.** $-\frac{3}{8} \div \frac{5}{8}$

Using the Order of Operations (Skills Handbook page 873)

Simplify each expression.

21. $8 \cdot (-3) + 4$ **22.** $3 \cdot 4 - 8 \div 2$ **23.** $1 \div 2^2 - 0.54 + 1.26$

24. $9 \div (-3) - 2$ **25.** $5(3 \cdot 5 - 4)$ **26.** $1 - (1 - 5)^2 \div (-8)$

Tools of Algebra

LESSONS

1-1 Properties of Real Numbers

1-2 Algebraic Expressions

1-3 Solving Equations

1-4 Solving Inequalities

1-5 Absolute Value Equations and Inequalities

1-6 Probability

◀)) **Key Vocabulary**

- absolute value (p. 33)
- absolute value of a real number (p. 8)
- additive inverse (p. 7)
- algebraic expression (p. 12)
- coefficient (p. 13)
- compound inequality (p. 28)
- evaluate (p. 12)
- experimental probability (p. 40)
- extraneous solution (p. 34)
- multiplicative inverse (p. 7)
- opposite (p. 7)
- reciprocal (p. 7)
- sample space (p. 41)
- simulation (p. 40)
- solution of an equation (p. 18)
- term (p. 13)
- theoretical probability (p. 41)
- tolerance (p. 36)
- variable (p. 12)
- variable expression (p. 12)

What You'll Learn Next

- In Chapter 1, you will review and extend your knowledge of algebraic expressions and your skill in solving equations and inequalities.

- You will solve absolute value equations and inequalities by changing them to compound equations and inequalities.

- You will apply theoretical and experimental probabilities to real-world situations such as genetic inheritance.

Real-World Connection Applying what you learn, you will use algebraic expressions on page 13 to solve a problem involving elections.

Properties of Real Numbers

What You'll Learn

- To graph and order real numbers
- To identify and use properties of real numbers

... And Why

To classify the numbers used in managing an amusement park, as in Example 1

✓ **Check Skills You'll Need**

Simplify.

1. $-(-7.2)$

2. $1 - (-3)$

3. $-9 + (-4.5)$

4. $(-3.4)(-2)$

5. $-15 \div 3$

6. $\frac{-2}{5} + \frac{3}{-5}$

GO for Help Skills Handbook page 873

🔊 **New Vocabulary**
- opposite
- additive inverse
- reciprocal
- multiplicative inverse
- absolute value of a real number

---

1 Graphing and Ordering Real Numbers

Real-World Connection

Artists frequently use geometric figures in their work. Juan Gris (1887–1927) used right triangles in this portrait of Picasso.

Activity: Estimating Square Roots

1. Use the Pythagorean Theorem to calculate *PB, PC, PD,* and so on, in the figure below.

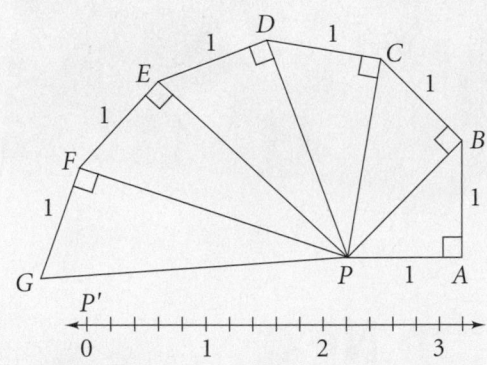

2. Copy the number line above. Mark point *B'* so that *P'B' = PB*. Similarly mark points *C', D',* and so on, on your number line.

3. Estimate the decimal coordinates of *B', C', D',* and so on. Copy and complete the table below.

Leg 1	1	$\sqrt{2}$	■	■	■	■
Leg 2	1	1	1	1	1	1
Hypotenuse	$\sqrt{2} \approx ?$	■	■	■	■	■

4. Evaluate each square root in the table using your calculator. Does the calculator give you exact answers? How do you know?

Algebra deals with operations and relations among numbers, including real numbers and imaginary numbers. Listed below are some of the subsets of the real numbers. Imaginary numbers will be introduced in Chapter 5.

 Key Concepts

Vocabulary Tip

$\sqrt{2}$ refers to the positive or <u>principal</u> <u>square</u> <u>root</u> of 2. The negative square root of 2 is written as $-\sqrt{2}$.

This diagram shows how the above sets of numbers are related.

Real Numbers   Examples: $-5, -\sqrt{3}, -\frac{1}{2}, 1, \sqrt{5}, \frac{8}{3}$

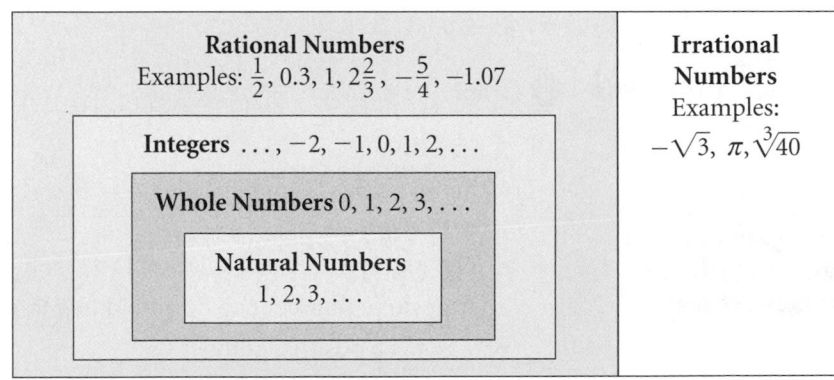

For example, the diagram shows the following:
- The set of whole numbers is a subset of the set of integers, the set of rational numbers, and the set of real numbers.
- The set of rational numbers and the set of irrational numbers do not intersect.
- Integers are not irrational numbers.
- The rational numbers and irrational numbers form the set of real numbers.

1 EXAMPLE Real-World Connection

Recreation Many mathematical relationships involving variables are related to amusement parks. Which set of numbers best describes the values for each variable?

a. the cost C in dollars of admission for n people

The cost C of admission is a rational number (such as $7.25), and the number n of people is a whole number.

b. the maximum speed s in meters per second on a roller coaster of height h in meters (Use the formula in the caption of the photograph.)

The height h is measured in rational numbers. Since the speed s is calculated using a formula with a square root, s is an irrational number unless h is the square of a rational number.

c. the park's profit (or loss) P in dollars for each week w of the year

The week number w is one of the first 52 natural numbers, and the profit (or loss) P is a rational number.

☑ **Quick Check** **1** The number r is the ratio of the number of adult tickets sold to the number of children's tickets sold. Which set of numbers best describes the values of r? Which set of numbers best describes the average cost c per family for tickets?

Real numbers are graphed as points on the number line.

2 EXAMPLE Graphing Numbers on the Number Line

Graph the numbers $-\frac{3}{2}, 1.\overline{7},$ and $\sqrt{5}$.

Since $-\frac{3}{2} = -1\frac{1}{2}, -\frac{3}{2}$ is between -1 and -2. Round $1.\overline{7}$ to 1.8. Use a calculator to find that $\sqrt{5} \approx 2.2$.

☑ **Quick Check** **2** Graph the numbers $-\sqrt{2}, 0.\overline{3},$ and $-2\frac{1}{4}$.

If a and b are real numbers, then $a = b, a < b,$ or $a > b$. There are several ways to prove that $a < b$:

- The graph of a is to the left of the graph of b on a number line.
- A positive number can be added to a to get b.
- $b - a$ is a positive number.

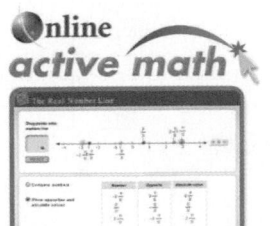
3 EXAMPLE Ordering Real Numbers

Compare $-\sqrt{0.25}$ and $-\sqrt{0.01}$. Use the symbols $<$ and $>$.

$-\sqrt{0.25} = -0.5,$ and $-\sqrt{0.01} = -0.1$. Since $-0.1 - (-0.5)$ is positive, $-0.5 < -0.1$. So $-\sqrt{0.25} < -\sqrt{0.01}$ and $-\sqrt{0.01} > -\sqrt{0.25}$.

☑ **Quick Check** **3** Compare $-\sqrt{0.08}$ and $-\sqrt{0.1}$ using the symbols $<$ and $>$.

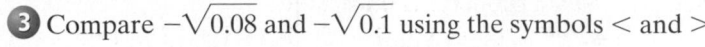

2 Properties of Real Numbers

The **opposite** or **additive inverse** of any number a is $-a$. The sum of opposites is 0.

The **reciprocal** or **multiplicative inverse** of any nonzero number a is $\frac{1}{a}$. The product of reciprocals is 1.

4 EXAMPLE   Finding Inverses

Find the opposite and the reciprocal of each number.

Vocabulary Tip

Read $-(-3.2)$ as "the opposite of negative 3.2."

a. -3.2

Opposite $-(-3.2) = 3.2$

Reciprocal $\frac{1}{-3.2} = \frac{10}{-32}$
$= -\frac{5}{16}$, or -0.3125

b. $\frac{3}{5}$

Opposite $-\left(\frac{3}{5}\right) = -\frac{3}{5}$

Reciprocal $\frac{1}{\frac{3}{5}} = 1 \cdot \frac{5}{3} = \frac{5}{3}$

 Quick Check **4** Find the opposite and the reciprocal of each number.

a. 400   **b.** $4\frac{1}{5}$ **c.** -0.002 **d.** $-\frac{4}{9}$

You can summarize the properties of real numbers in terms of addition and multiplication.

Key Concepts

Summary   Properties of Real Numbers

Let a, b, and c represent real numbers.

Property	Addition	Multiplication
Closure	$a + b$ is a real number.	ab is a real number.
Commutative	$a + b = b + a$	$ab = ba$
Associative	$(a + b) + c = a + (b + c)$	$(ab)c = a(bc)$
Identity	$a + 0 = a, 0 + a = a$	$a \cdot 1 = a, 1 \cdot a = a$
Inverse	$a + (-a) = 0$	$a \cdot \frac{1}{a} = 1, a \neq 0$
Distributive	$a(b + c) = ab + ac$	

5 EXAMPLE   Identifying Properties of Real Numbers

Which property is illustrated?

a. $6 + (-6) = 0$

Inverse Property of Addition

b. $(-4 \cdot 1) - 2 = -4 - 2$

Identity Property of Multiplication

 **Quick Check** **5** Which property is illustrated?

a. $(3 + 0) - 5 = 3 - 5$ **b.** $-5 + [2 + (-3)] = (-5 + 2) + (-3)$

The **absolute value of a real number** is its distance from zero on the number line.

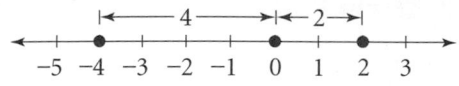

Find $|-4|, |0|,$ and $|-1 \cdot (-2)|$.

$|-1 \cdot (-2)| = |2|$ **Simplify within absolute value symbols first.**

Graph $-4, 0,$ and 2 on a number line.

Read |2| as "the absolute value of 2."

The distances from the origin are 4, 0, and 2. So,

$|-4| = 4$ $|0| = 0$ $|-1 \cdot (-2)| = |2| = 2$

Quick Check **6** **a.** Simplify $|-10|, |1.5|,$ and $|0 - 3|$.
   b. Critical Thinking For what values of x does $|x| = -x$?

EXERCISES

For more exercises, see *Extra Skill and Word Problem Practice.*

Practice and Problem Solving

Example 1
(page 6)

To which sets of numbers does each number belong?

1. 4   **2.** $\sqrt{6}$ **3.** π **4.** -6

5. 0   **6.** $0.\overline{6}$ **7.** $-\sqrt{0.04}$ **8.** $\sqrt{0.4}$

Which set of numbers best describes the values of each variable?

9. the number of times n a cricket chirps; the outdoor temperature T in tenths of a degree

10. the year y; the median selling price p for a house that year

11. the time t in seconds an object takes to fall d feet, where $t = \frac{\sqrt{d}}{4}$

Example 2
(page 6)

Graph each number on a number line.

12. 0   **13.** $-\sqrt{24}$ **14.** -2 **15.** $2\frac{1}{2}$ **16.** $-4\frac{2}{3}$

Example 3
(page 6)

Replace each ▪ with the symbol <, >, or = to make the sentence true.

17. -7 ▪ -9 **18.** 3 ▪ 3 **19.** 14 ▪ $\sqrt{14}$

20. $\sqrt{6}$ ▪ $\sqrt{10}$ **21.** 0 ▪ $0.\overline{3}$ **22.** 0.8 ▪ $\frac{4}{5}$

23. -18 ▪ -82 **24.** $0.72737475\ldots$ ▪ $0.73737373\ldots$

Compare each pair of numbers. Use < and >.

25. $-\frac{1}{4}, -\frac{1}{3}$ **26.** $0.075, 0.39$ **27.** $-2.\overline{3}, 2.\overline{1}$

28. $-5.2, -4.8$ **29.** $3.0\overline{4}, 3.4$ **30.** $0.4, \sqrt{0.4}$

31. $-4, -\sqrt{4}$ **32.** $\sqrt{5}, \sqrt{7}$ **33.** $-\sqrt{3}, -\sqrt{5}$

Example 4
(page 7)

Find the opposite and the reciprocal of each number.

34. 200 **35.** $3\frac{3}{5}$ **36.** -0.01 **37.** $-\frac{7}{2}$

38. $\sqrt{3}$ **39.** 2π **40.** -2.34 **41.** $\pi - 3$

Example 5
(page 7)

Name the property of real numbers illustrated by each equation.

42. $\pi(a + b) = \pi a + \pi b$ **43.** $-7 + 4 = 4 + (-7)$

44. $(2\sqrt{10}) \cdot \sqrt{3} = 2(\sqrt{10} \cdot \sqrt{3})$ **45.** $29\pi = \pi \cdot 29$

46. $-\sqrt{5} + 0 = -\sqrt{5}$ **47.** $\frac{4}{7} \cdot \frac{7}{4} = 1$

Example 6
(page 8)

Simplify each expression.

48. $|10.3|$ **49.** $|-0.06|$ **50.** $-|-25|$ **51.** $0.2|-8|$

52. $\left|-\frac{1}{3}\right|$ **53.** $|7 - 10|$ **54.** $|10 - 7|$ **55.** $|5| - |-7|$

B **Apply Your Skills**

Estimate the numbers graphed at the labeled points.

$$
\begin{array}{ccccccc}
A & B & C & D & E & F\ G\ H \\
\end{array}
$$

-5 -4 -3 -2 -1 0 1 2 3 4 5

56. point A **57.** point B **58.** point C **59.** point D

60. point E **61.** point F **62.** point G **63.** point H

64. Multiple Choice The length of a side of an equilateral triangle is 4. Which type of number best describes the length of the altitude of the triangle?
  Ⓐ whole number Ⓑ integer
  Ⓒ rational number Ⓓ irrational number

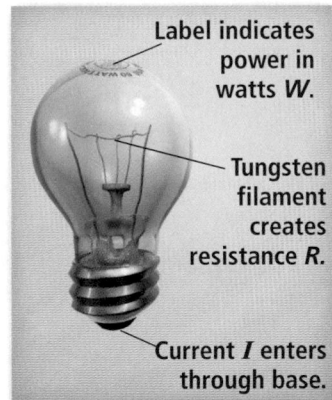

Label indicates power in watts *W.*

Tungsten filament creates resistance *R.*

Current *I* enters through base.

Electric Circuits The electric current I in amperes that flows through an appliance is given by the formula $I = \sqrt{\frac{W}{R}}$, where W is the power in watts and R is the resistance in ohms. Which sets of numbers contain the value of I for the given values of W and R?

65. $W = 100, R = 25$ **66.** $W = 100, R = 50$ **67.** $W = 500, R = 100$

68. $W = 50, R = 200$ **69.** $W = 250, R = 100$ **70.** $W = 240, R = 100$

Replace each ■ with the symbol $<$, $>$, or $=$ to make the sentence true.

71. $0 \ ■ \ -4$ **72.** $-4 \ ■ \ -9$ **73.** $-5.2 \ ■ \ -4.8$ **74.** $|-8| \ ■ \ |3|$

75. $|2| \ ■ \ |-6|$ **76.** $|7| \ ■ \ |-8|$ **77.** $-|6| \ ■ \ |6|$ **78.** $-|-6| \ ■ \ |-6|$

Reasoning Show that each statement is false by finding a counterexample (an example that makes the statement false).

79. The reciprocal of each whole number is a whole number.

80. The opposite of each natural number is a natural number.

81. There is no whole number that has an opposite that is a whole number.

82. There is no integer that has a reciprocal that is an integer.

83. The product of two irrational numbers is an irrational number.

84. Open-Ended Write an example of each of the 11 properties of real numbers listed on page 7.

Challenge   **Critical Thinking** Review the eleven properties on page 7. Which ones still hold true if *real numbers* is replaced by each of the following?

85. natural numbers   **86.** whole numbers   **87.** integers

88. rational numbers   **89.** irrational numbers

90. Writing Are there two integers with a product of -12 and a sum of -3? Explain.

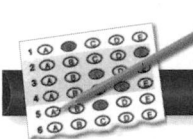

Test Prep

Multiple Choice   **91.** Which of the following is NOT a rational number?
   A. $\frac{\pi}{2\pi}$ **B.** $-\sqrt{144}$ **C.** 3.14   **D.**

92. If p is a multiple of 3 and q is a multiple of 5, which of the following is true?
   F. $p + q$ is even.   **G.** pq is odd.
   H. $5p + 3q$ is a multiple of 15.   **J.** $3p + 5q$ is a multiple of 15.

93. The number 8.09 belongs to which sets of numbers?
   A. natural numbers, real numbers
   B. irrational numbers, real numbers
   C. rational numbers, real numbers
   D. whole numbers, integers, rational numbers, real numbers

94. Which shows the numbers -3.5, -4.60, and $-3\frac{1}{4}$ in order from greatest to least?
   F. $-4.60, -3\frac{1}{4}, -3.5$ **G.** $-4.60, -3.5, -3\frac{1}{4}$
   H. $-3\frac{1}{4}, -4.60, -3.5$ **J.** $-3\frac{1}{4}, -3.5, -4.60$

95. What is the value of $|3 - 7| - |-11 + 3|$?
   A. -4 **B.** 4   **C.** 12   **D.** 24

Short Response   **96.** Explain why the *opposite of the reciprocal of 5* is the same as the *reciprocal of the opposite of 5*.

97. Are there any numbers that are their own reciprocals? Explain.

Mixed Review

Skills Handbook   **Simplify each expression.**
 **for Help**

   98. $3.6 + (-1.7)$ **99.** $1.2 - 5$ **100.** $(-3)(-9)$

   101. $0(-8)$ **102.** $-2.8 \div 7$ **103.** $-35 \div (-5)$

Skills Handbook   **Use the order of operations to simplify each expression.**

   104. $3 \div 4 + 6 \div 4$ **105.** $5[(2 + 5) \div 3]$

   106. $\frac{8 + 5 \cdot 2}{12}$ **107.** $(40 + 24) \div 8 - (2^2 - 1)$

   108. $40 + 24 \div 8 - 2^2 - 1$ **109.** $40 + 24 \div (8 - 2^2) - 1$

You can sometimes describe data in a table by writing an expression.

1 ACTIVITY

Study the polygons below. You can cut each polygon into triangles by connecting one vertex with each of the other nonadjacent vertices.

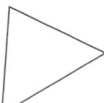 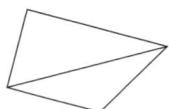 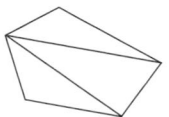 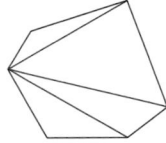

1. a. The sum of the angle measures for each triangle is 180. Fill in the data missing from the table.
  b. Describe the relationship between the number of sides in a polygon and the number of triangles.
  c. Describe the relationship between the number of triangles and the sum of the angle measures of the polygon.
  d. Complete the sentence: The sum of the angle measures of a polygon is the number of sides of the polygon less ? , times ? .
  e. The number of sides of a polygon is *n*. Write the number of triangles in terms of *n*.
  f. Write the sum of the angle measures of the *n*-sided polygon in terms of *n*.

Number of Sides	Number of Triangles	Sum of Angle Measures
3	1	180
4	2	360
5	3	■
6	4	■
7	■	■
8	■	1080
9	■	■

2 ACTIVITY

The diagrams below show arrangements of tables and chairs. Each small table can seat 6 people. When you join tables, you lose space for some chairs. So, an arrangement of two tables has 10 chairs rather than 12 chairs.

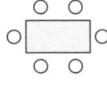 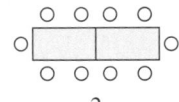 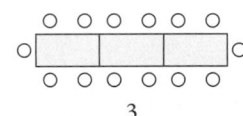 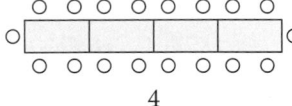

Number of tables: 1   2   3   4

2. a. Make a table that lists the number of tables and the number of chairs in each arrangement shown in the diagram.
  b. Find the number of chairs needed for arrangements of 5 tables and 6 tables.
  c. Write an expression for the number of chairs needed for *n* tables. (*Hint:* How many new chairs are needed for each new table?)

3. You can arrange the tables and chairs differently. One possible pattern is shown at the right. Write an expression for the number of chairs needed to make one large table out of *k* tables in this way.

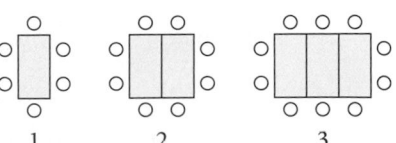

1   2   3

Algebraic Expressions

What You'll Learn

- To evaluate algebraic expressions
- To simplify algebraic expressions

. . . And Why

To use an expression for the number of voters in U.S. elections, as in Example 3

✓ **Check Skills You'll Need**

GO for Help Skills Handbook page 873

Use the order of operations to simplify each expression.

1. $8 \cdot 3 - 2 \cdot 4$

2. $8 - 4 + 6 \div 3$

3. $24 \div 12 \cdot 4 \div 3$

4. $3 \cdot 8^2 + 12 \div 4$

5. $27 + 18 \div 9 - 3^2 + 1$

6. $(40 + 24) \div 8 - (2^3 + 1)$

◀)) **New Vocabulary** • variable • algebraic expression • variable expression • evaluate • term • coefficient

---

1 Evaluating Algebraic Expressions

A **variable** is a symbol, usually a letter, that represents one or more numbers. An expression that contains one or more variables is an **algebraic expression** or a **variable expression.** When you substitute numbers for the variables in an expression and follow the order of operations, you **evaluate** the expression.

1 EXAMPLE Evaluating an Algebraic Expression

GO for Help

To review the order of operations, go to page 873.

Evaluate $a - 2b + ab$ for $a = 3$ and $b = -1$.

$$
\begin{aligned}
a - 2b + ab &= 3 - 2(-1) + 3(-1) && \text{Substitute 3 for } a \text{ and } -1 \text{ for } b. \\
&= 3 - (-2) + (-3) && \text{Multiply first.} \\
&= 3 + 2 + (-3) && \text{To subtract, add the opposite.} \\
&= 5 + (-3) && \text{Add from left to right.} \\
&= 2 && \text{Add.}
\end{aligned}
$$

✓ **Quick Check** ❶ Evaluate each expression for $x = 4$ and $y = -2$.
  a. $x + y \div x$ **b.** $3x - 4y + x - y$ **c.** $x + 2x \div y - 2y$

2 EXAMPLE Evaluating an Algebraic Expression with Exponents

Problem Solving Hint

Note that $-3^2 \neq (-3)^2$.
$-3^2 = -(3 \cdot 3) = -9$
$(-3)^2 = (-3)(-3) = 9$

Evaluate $-x^2 - 2(x + 1)$ for $x = 3$.

$$
\begin{aligned}
-x^2 - 2(x + 1) &= -3^2 - 2(3 + 1) && \text{Substitute 3 for } x. \\
&= -9 - 2(4) && \text{Simplify the power } 3^2. \text{ Add within the parentheses.} \\
&= -9 - 8 && \text{Multiply.} \\
&= -17 && \text{Subtract.}
\end{aligned}
$$

✓ **Quick Check** ❷ Evaluate each expression for $c = -3$ and $d = 5$.
  a. $c^2 - d^2$ **b.** $c(3 - d) - c^2$ **c.** $-d^2 - 4(d - 2c)$

---

12 Chapter 1 Tools of Algebra

In 1971, the U.S. voting age was lowered from 21 to 18.

 EXAMPLE Real-World Connection

Elections The expression $-0.3y + 61$ models the percent of eligible voters who voted in presidential elections from 1960 to 2000. In the expression, y represents the number of years since 1960. Find the approximate percent of eligible voters who voted in 1988.

Since $1988 - 1960 = 28$, $y = 28$ represents the year 1988.

$$-0.3y + 61 = -0.3(28) + 61 \quad \textbf{Substitute 28 for } y.$$
$$\approx 53$$

About 53% of the eligible voters voted in the 1988 presidential election.

✓ **Quick Check** ③ **a.** Assume that the model in Example 3 holds for future years. What percent of the eligible voters will vote in 2012? In 2020?

b. Critical Thinking Give some reasons that the model may not hold in future years.

---

2 Simplifying Algebraic Expressions

In an algebraic expression such as $-4x + 10$, the parts that are added are called terms. A **term** is a number, a variable, or the product of a number and one or more variables. The numerical factor in a term is the **coefficient.** Think of an expression such as $a - 2b$ as the sum $a + (-2b)$ to determine that the coefficient of b is -2.

$$\overbrace{7x^2 + 3y}$$ terms ... coefficients

Like terms have the same variables raised to the same powers.

Like terms: $3r^2$ and $-r^2$ $-2xy^3$ and $3xy^3$

You can simplify expressions by combining like terms using the basic properties on page 7 and other properties that can be derived from them. The simplified expressions are equivalent to the original expressions; that is, their values are equal for any replacement of the variables.

 Key Concepts

Summary	Properties for Simplifying Algebraic Expressions
Let a, b, and c represent real numbers.	
Definition of Subtraction	$a - b = a + (-b)$
Definition of Division	$a \div b = \frac{a}{b} = a \cdot \frac{1}{b}, b \neq 0$
Distributive Property for Subtraction	$a(b - c) = ab - ac$
Multiplication by 0	$0 \cdot a = 0$
Multiplication by -1	$-1 \cdot a = -a$
Opposite of a Sum	$-(a + b) = -a + (-b)$
Opposite of a Difference	$-(a - b) = b - a$
Opposite of a Product	$-(ab) = -a \cdot b = a \cdot (-b)$
Opposite of an Opposite	$-(-a) = a$

4 EXAMPLE Combining Like Terms

Simplify by combining like terms.

a. $3k - k$

$$
\begin{aligned}
3k - k &= 3k - 1k &&\textbf{Identity Property of Multiplication} \\
&= (3 - 1)k &&\textbf{Distributive Property} \\
&= 2k &&\textbf{Simplify.}
\end{aligned}
$$

b. $5z^2 - 10z - 8z^2 + z$

$$
\begin{aligned}
5z^2 - 10z - 8z^2 + z &= 5z^2 - 8z^2 + (-10z) + z &&\textbf{Commutative Property} \\
& &&\textbf{of Addition} \\
&= (5 - 8)z^2 + (-10 + 1)z &&\textbf{Distributive Property} \\
&= -3z^2 - 9z
\end{aligned}
$$

c. $-(m + n) + 2(m - 3n)$

$$
\begin{aligned}
-(m + n) + 2(m - 3n) & \\
= -m + (-n) + 2m + (-6n) &&\textbf{Opposite of a Sum, Distributive Property} \\
= -m + 2m + (-n) + (-6n) &&\textbf{Commutative Property of Addition} \\
= -1 \cdot m + 2m + (-1 \cdot n) + (-6n) &&\textbf{Multiplication by −1} \\
= (-1 + 2)m + [-1 + (-6)]n &&\textbf{Distributive Property} \\
= m - 7n
\end{aligned}
$$

✓ Quick Check **4** Simplify by combining like terms.

a. $2x^2 + 5x - 4x^2 + x - x^2$ **b.** $-2(r + s) - (2r + 2s)$

5 EXAMPLE Finding Perimeter

Multiple Choice Which expression represents the perimeter of the figure at the right?

(A) $8a + b$ (B) $6a + b$

(C) $6a + 2b$ (D) $4a + 3b$

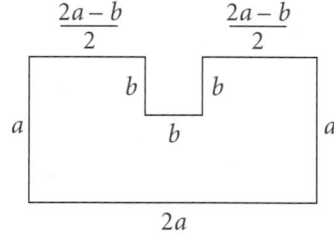

$$
\frac{2a - b}{2} + b + b + b + \frac{2a - b}{2} + a + 2a + a
$$

$$
= \frac{2a - b}{2} + \frac{2a - b}{2} + 3b + 4a
$$

$$
= \frac{2(2a - b)}{2} + 3b + 4a
$$

$$
= 2a - b + 3b + 4a
$$

$$
= 6a + 2b
$$

● The perimeter is $6a + 2b$. The correct choice is C.

Test-Taking Tip

You can check your answer, C, by substituting values. Let $a = 2$ and $b = 1$. The perimeter is 14. Also, $6a + 2b = 6(2) + 2(1)$
$= 14$.

✓ Quick Check **5** Find the perimeter of each figure. Simplify the answer.

a.

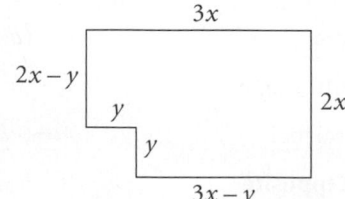

b.

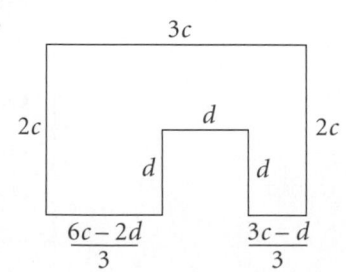

EXERCISES

For more exercises, see *Extra Skill and Word Problem Practice.*

Practice and Problem Solving

 Practice by Example

Examples 1 and 2
(page 12)

 **for Help**

Evaluate each expression for the given values of the variables.

1. $4a + 7b + 3a - 2b + 2a; a = -5$ and $b = 3$

2. $5y - 3z + 4y - 1z - 3y; y = 3$ and $z = -2$

3. $12a^2 - 3ab + 2b; a = -5$ and $b = 4$

4. $-k^2 - (3k - 5n) + 4n; k = -1$ and $n = -2$

5. $3y - (4y + 6x); x = 3$ and $y = -2$

6. $3(2c + d) - d; c = 5$ and $d = -1$

7. $-5(x + 2y) + 15(x + 2y); x = 7$ and $y = -7$

8. $4(2m - n) - 3(2m - n); m = -15$ and $n = -18$

Example 3
(page 13)

Physics The expression $16t^2$ models the distance in feet that an object falls during t seconds after being dropped. Find the distance an object falls during each time.

9. 0.25 second

10. 0.5 second

11. 2 seconds

12. 10 seconds

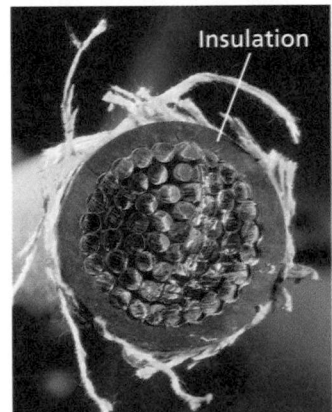

Insulation

Electrical Engineering The expression $0.01E + 0.003E^2$ gives the thickness in millimeters of the insulation needed for the high voltage cable shown at the left. E is the number of kilovolts carried by the cable. Find the thickness of insulation material needed for each voltage.

13. 1 kilovolt

14. 2 kilovolts

15. 10 kilovolts

16. 20 kilovolts

Investing The expression $1000(1.1)^t$ represents the value of a $1000 investment that earns 10% interest per year, compounded annually for t years. Find the value of a $1000 investment at the end of each period.

17. 2 years

18. 3 years

19. 4 years

20. 5 years

Example 4
(page 14)

Simplify by combining like terms.

21. $5a - a$

22. $5 + 10s - 8s$

23. $-5a - 4a + b$

24. $2a + 3b + 4a$

25. $6r + 3s + 2s + 4r$

26. $w + 3z + 5w + 2z$

27. $x^2 + x^2 + x$

28. $xy + 2x + x$

29. $0.5x - x$

30. $3(2x + 1) - 8$

31. $2(5y - 2) + x$

32. $3y - (4y + 6x)$

33. $7b - (3a - 8b)$

34. $5 + (4g - 7)$

35. $-(3x - 4y + z)$

Example 5
(page 14)

Geometry Find the perimeter of each figure. Simplify the answer.

36.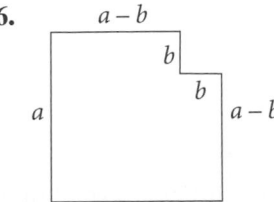

37.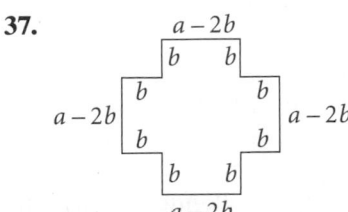

Lesson 1-2 Algebraic Expressions **15**

Evaluate each expression for the given value of the variable.

38. $|x| + |2x| - |x - 1|; x = 2$ **39.** $|2z + 3| + |5 - 3z|; z = -3$

40. $3|2a + 5| + 2|3 - a|; a = 4$ **41.** $6|4b - 5| + 3|2 - 2b|; b = -1$

42. $\dfrac{3(2x + 1) - 2(x - 3)}{x + 6}; x = -3$ **43.** $\dfrac{5(2k - 3) - 3(k + 4)}{3k + 2}; k = -2$

44. $y^2 + 3; y = \sqrt{7}$ **45.** $5c^3 - 6c^2 - 2c; c = -5$

46. Elections The expression $2.6y + 107$ models the number of eligible voters in millions in the United States from 1960 to 2000. In the expression, y represents the number of years since 1960.
  a. Find the approximate number of eligible voters in 1988.
  b. Assume that the model continues to hold for future years. How many eligible voters will there be in 2012? In 2020?
  c. The expression $-0.3y + 61$ models the *percent* of eligible voters who voted in presidential elections from 1960 to 2000. (See Example 3.) Write an expression that models the *number* of voters in presidential elections from 1960 to 2000.
  d. Use your model from (c) to find the approximate number of voters who voted for president in 1980.

Real-World 🌐 **Connection**

Each year, millions of U.S. citizens turn 18 and become eligible to vote. Unfortunately, fewer than half of them register.

Simplify by combining like terms.

47. $-a^2 + 2b^2 + \frac{1}{4}a^2$ **48.** $x + \frac{x^2}{2} + 2x^2 - x$ **49.** $\frac{y^2}{4} + \frac{y}{3} + \frac{y^2}{3} - \frac{y}{5}$

50. $-(2x + y) - 2(-x - y)$ **51.** $x(3 - y) + y(x + 6)$

52. $4(2x + y) - 2(2x + y)$ **53.** $\frac{1}{2}(x^2 - y^2) - \frac{5}{2}(x^2 - y^2)$

Match the property name with the appropriate equation.

54. Definition of Subtraction   **A.** $2(s - t) = 2s - 2t$

55. Definition of Division   **B.** $-(a - b) = (-1)(a - b)$

56. Distributive Property   **C.** $(7 - y) \div (2y) = \dfrac{7 - y}{2y}$

57. Multiplication by 0   **D.** $-[-(x - 10)] = x - 10$

58. Multiplication by -1 **E.** $-(2t - 11) = 11 - 2t$

59. Opposite of a Sum   **F.** $2t - 11 = 2t + (-11)$

60. Opposite of a Difference   **G.** $(4a^2 - 9a)(0) + 5a = 0 + 5a$

61. Opposite of a Product   **H.** $-[3 + (-y)] = -3 + [-(-y)]$

62. Opposite of an Opposite   **I.** $-(4z^2) = 4(-z^2)$

Justifying Steps Name the property used in each step of simplification.

63. $(3x + y) + x = 3x + (y + x)$
$\qquad = 3x + (x + y)$
$\qquad = (3x + x) + y$
$\qquad = (3x + 1x) + y$
$\qquad = (3 + 1)x + y$
$\qquad = 4x + y$

64. $2(5 + x) + 4(5 + x) = (2 + 4)(5 + x)$
$\qquad\qquad\qquad = 6(5 + x)$
$\qquad\qquad\qquad = 30 + 6x$

GO Online
Homework Video Tutor

Visit: PHSchool.com
Web Code: age-0102

C Challenge

65. Open-Ended Write four different expressions that simplify to $x^2 - x$. Each expression must have five terms.

66. Simplify $2(b - a) + 5(b - a)$ and explain each step in your simplification.

67. a. Evaluate the expression $2(2x^2 - x) - 3(x^2 - x) + x^2 - x$ for $x = 3$. Do *not* simplify the expression before evaluating it.

  b. Simplify the expression in (a) and then evaluate your answer for $x = 3$.

  c. Writing Explain why the values in (a) and (b) should be the same.

  d. Error Analysis A student simplified $2x(x - 6)$ to $2x^2 - 6x$. Should the student check his work by evaluating both expressions for $x = 0$? Explain.

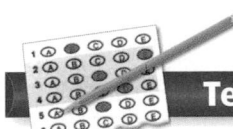

Test Prep

Multiple Choice

68. Which of the following expressions is NOT equivalent to the others?
  A. $3x - y - x - y$ **B.** $-2(x - y)$
  C. $2(x - y)$ **D.** $2x - 2y$

69. If xy is negative, which one of the following is possible?
  F. $x < y < 0$ **G.** $x < 0 < y$
  H. $x = y$ **J.** $0 \le x \le y$

70. Which factor in the term $-9x^2y$ is the coefficient?
  A. -9 **B.** 2 **C.** x^2 **D.** x^2y

71. Simplify $5a^2 + a^2 + 7a$.
  F. $5a^2 + 7a$ **G.** $6a^2 + 7a$ **H.** $12a^2$ **J.** $13a^3$

72. Which expression is equivalent to $-(p - q)$?
  A. $q - p$ **B.** $p + q$ **C.** $-p - q$ **D.** $p - q$

73. Which expression is equivalent to $4(2n - 1)$?
  F. $7n$ **G.** $8n$ **H.** $8n - 1$ **J.** $8n - 4$

74. Which expression has the greatest value for $x = -4$ and $y = 5$?
  A. $-3xy$ **B.** $3xy$ **C.** xy^2 **D.** x^2y

Short Response

75. For which values of x does $6x(x - 3) = 0$? Explain your answer.

76. Evaluate the expression $|x + 3| - |x - 6| + |x|$ for $x = -2$. Show your work.

77. Evaluate the expression $3(x^2 - 1) - x(x^2 - 1) - (2 - x)(x^2 - 1)$ for $x = 3$. Show your work.

Mixed Review

Lesson 1-1

Order the numbers from least to greatest.

78. $-1.5, -0.5, -\sqrt{2}, -1.4$ **79.** $|-4.3|, -4.3, -|3.4|, |-3.4|$

80. $-\frac{3}{8}, \frac{1}{2}, -\frac{3}{4}, -\frac{5}{6}$ **81.** $\sqrt{\frac{1}{4}}, \sqrt{\frac{1}{16}}, -\sqrt{\frac{1}{8}}, -\sqrt{\frac{1}{10}}$

Lesson 1-1

Replace each ■ with the symbol <, >, or = to make the sentence true.

82. $|-11|$ ■ $|9|$ **83.** $|11|$ ■ $|9|$ **84.** $|-11|$ ■ $|-9|$

85. $-|-7|$ ■ $|7|$ **86.** $-|7|$ ■ $|-7|$ **87.** $-|-7|$ ■ $-|7|$

1-3

Solving Equations

What You'll Learn

- To solve equations
- To solve problems by writing equations

... And Why

To solve a problem about aeronautics, as in Example 7

 Check Skills You'll Need

 GO for Help Lesson 1-2

Simplify each expression.

1. $5x - 9x + 3$

2. $2y + 7x + y - 1$

3. $10h + 12g - 8h - 4g$

4. $\frac{x}{3} + \frac{y}{3} + \frac{2y}{3} - y$

5. $(x + y) - (x - y)$

6. $-(3 - c) - 4(c - 1)$

New Vocabulary • solution of an equation

---

1 Solving Equations

An equation that contains a variable may be true for some replacements of the variable and false for others. A number that makes the equation true is a **solution of the equation.** You can use the properties of equality to solve equations.

Key Concepts

Summary	Properties of Equality
Let a, b, and c represent real numbers.	
Reflexive Property	$a = a$
Symmetric Property	If $a = b$, then $b = a$.
Transitive Property	If $a = b$ and $b = c$, then $a = c$.
Addition Property	If $a = b$, then $a + c = b + c$.
Subtraction Property	If $a = b$, then $a - c = b - c$.
Multiplication Property	If $a = b$, then $ac = bc$.
Division Property	If $a = b$ and $c \neq 0$, then $\frac{a}{c} = \frac{b}{c}$.
Substitution Property	If $a = b$, then b may be substituted for a in any expression to obtain an equivalent expression.

1 EXAMPLE Solving an Equation with a Variable on Both Sides

GO Online

Video Tutor Help

Visit: PhSchool.com
Web Code: age-0775

Solve $13y + 48 = 8y - 47$.

$$13y + 48 = 8y - 47$$
$$5y + 48 = -47 \quad \text{Subtract 8y from each side.}$$
$$5y = -95 \quad \text{Subtract 48 from each side.}$$
$$y = -19 \quad \text{Divide each side by 5.}$$

Check $13y + 48 = 8y - 47$
$$13(-19) + 48 \stackrel{?}{=} 8(-19) - 47$$
$$-199 = -199 \checkmark$$

✓ **Quick Check** ➊ Solve each equation. Check your answers.
  a. $8z + 12 = 5z - 21$ **b.** $2t - 3 = 9 - 4t$

➋ **EXAMPLE**   **Using the Distributive Property**

Vocabulary Tip

Literally, <u>to solve</u> means "to set apart." Think of solving an equation as setting apart the variable.

Solve $3x - 7(2x - 13) = 3(-2x + 9)$.

$3x - 7(2x - 13) = 3(-2x + 9)$

$3x - 14x + 91 = -6x + 27$ **Distributive Property**

$-11x + 91 = -6x + 27$ **Combine like terms.**

$-5x + 91 = 27$ **Add 6x to each side.**

$-5x = -64$ **Subtract 91 from each side.**

$x = \dfrac{64}{5}$, or 12.8   **Divide each side by −5.**

✓ **Quick Check** ➋ Solve each equation. Check your answers.
  a. $2(y - 3) + 6 = 70$ **b.** $6(t - 2) = 2(9 - 2t)$

When you have a formula or equation that has more than one variable, you can solve for any one of the variables.

➌ **EXAMPLE**   **Solving a Formula for One of Its Variables**

Geometry The formula for the area of a trapezoid is $A = \frac{1}{2}h(b_1 + b_2)$. Solve the formula for h.

$A = \frac{1}{2}h(b_1 + b_2)$

$2A = h(b_1 + b_2)$ **Multiply each side by 2.**

$\dfrac{2A}{b_1 + b_2} = h$ **Divide each side by $b_1 + b_2$.**

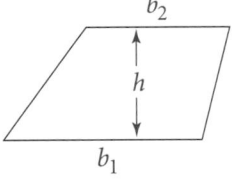

✓ **Quick Check** ➌ Solve the formula for the area of a trapezoid for b_1.

➍ **EXAMPLE**   **Solving an Equation for One of Its Variables**

Solve $\frac{x}{a} + 1 = \frac{x}{b}$ for x. Find any restrictions on a and b.

$\frac{x}{a} + 1 = \frac{x}{b}$

$ab\left(\frac{x}{a}\right) + ab(1) = ab\left(\frac{x}{b}\right)$ **Multiply each side by the least common denominator (LCD).**

$bx + ab = ax$ **Simplify.**

$ab = ax - bx$ **Collect terms with x on one side.**

$ab = (a - b)x$ **Distributive Property**

$x = \dfrac{ab}{a - b}$ **Divide each side by $a - b$.**

The denominators cannot be 0, so $a \neq 0$ and $b \neq 0$. Also $a - b \neq 0$, so $a \neq b$.

✓ **Quick Check** ➍ Solve each equation for x. Find any restrictions.
  a. $ax + bx - 15 = 0$ **b.** $d = \frac{2x}{a} + b$

You can write an equation to model and solve a real-world problem.

5 EXAMPLE **Real-World** **Connection**

Construction A dog kennel owner has 100 ft of fencing to enclose a rectangular dog run. She wants it to be 5 times as long as it is wide. Find the dimensions of the dog run.

Relate $2 \cdot$ width $+ 2 \cdot$ length $=$ perimeter

Define Let x = the width.

Then $5x$ = the length.

x

$5x$

Write $2x + 2(5x) = 100$

$$2x + 10x = 100 \quad \text{Multiply.}$$

$$12x = 100 \quad \text{Combine like terms.}$$

$$x = 8\tfrac{1}{3} \quad \text{Divide each side by 12.}$$

$$5x = 41\tfrac{2}{3} \quad \text{Find the length.}$$

The width is $8\tfrac{1}{3}$ ft and the length is $41\tfrac{2}{3}$ ft.

Check Is the answer reasonable? Since the dimensions are about 8 ft and 42 ft, and $2 \cdot 8 + 2 \cdot 42 = 100$, the answer is reasonable.

Real-World **Connection**

Some states regulate the minimum amount of floor space for animals in kennels.

Quick Check **5** A rectangle is twice as long as it is wide. Its perimeter is 48 cm. Find its dimensions.

Many geometry problems require writing and solving equations.

6 EXAMPLE **Using Ratios**

Geometry The lengths of the sides of a triangle are in the ratio $3 : 4 : 5$. The perimeter of the triangle is 18 in. Find the lengths of the sides.

Relate Perimeter equals the sum of the lengths of the three sides.

Define Let $3x$ = the length of the shortest side.
Then $4x$ = the length of the second side.
Then $5x$ = the length of the third side.

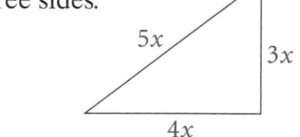

Write $18 = 3x + 4x + 5x$

$$18 = 12x \quad \text{Combine like terms.}$$

$$1.5 = x$$

$$3x = 3(1.5) \quad 4x = 4(1.5) \quad 5x = 5(1.5) \quad \textbf{Find the length of each side.}$$

$$= 4.5 \quad\quad\quad = 6 \quad\quad\quad = 7.5$$

The lengths of the sides are 4.5 in., 6 in., and 7.5 in.

Check Is the answer reasonable? Since $5 + 6 + 8 = 19$, the answer is reasonable.

Quick Check **6** The sides of a triangle are in the ratio $12 : 13 : 15$. The perimeter is 120 cm. Find the lengths of the sides of the triangle.

Real-World Connection

The F-117 is nearly invisible to radar. The faceted construction deflects most radar energy away from the radar receiver.

7 **EXAMPLE** **Real-World Connection**

Aeronautics Radar detected an unidentified plane 5000 mi away, approaching at 700 mi/h. Fifteen minutes later an interceptor plane was dispatched, traveling at 800 mi/h. How long did the interceptor take to reach the approaching plane?

Relate distance for interceptor + distance for approaching plane = 5000 mi

Define Let t = the time in hours for the interceptor.
Then $t + 0.25$ = the time in hours for the approaching plane.

Write $800t + 700(t + 0.25) = 5000$

$\ \ 800t + 700t + 175 = 5000$ **Distributive Property**

$\ 1500t = 4825$ **Solve for t.**

$\ t \approx 3.217$ or 3 h 13 min

Check Is the answer reasonable? In $3\frac{1}{4}$ h, the interceptor flies 2600 mi. In $3\frac{1}{2}$ h, the approaching plane flies 2450 mi. $2600 + 2450 \approx 5000$, so the answer is reasonable.

 **7** A space probe leaves Earth at the rate of 3 km/s. After 100 days, a radio signal is sent to the probe. Radio signals travel at the speed of light, about 3×10^5 km/s. About how long does the signal take to reach the probe?

EXERCISES

For more exercises, see *Extra Skill and Word Problem Practice*.

Practice and Problem Solving

A **Practice by Example**

 for Help

Example 1
(page 18)

Solve each equation. Check your answers.

1. $7w + 2 = 3w + 94$
2. $15 - g = 23 - 2g$
3. $43 - 3d = d + 9$
4. $5y + 1.8 = 4y - 3.2$
5. $6a - 5 = 4a + 2$
6. $7y + 4 = 3 - 2y$
7. $5c - 9 = 8 - 2c$
8. $4y - 8 - 2y + 5 = 0$

Example 2
(page 19)

9. $6(n - 4) = 3n$
10. $2 - 3(x + 4) = 8$
11. $5(2 - g) = 0$
12. $2(x + 4) = 8$
13. $6(t - 2) = 2(9t - 2)$
14. $4w - 2(1 - w) = -38$
15. $4(k + 5) = 2(9k - 4)$
16. $10(1 - 2y) = -5(2y - 1)$

Example 3
(page 19)

Solve each formula for the indicated variable.

17. $A = \frac{1}{2}bh$, for h
18. $s = \frac{1}{2}gt^2$, for g
19. $V = \ell wh$, for w
20. $I = prt$, for r
21. $S = 2\pi rh$, for r
22. $V = \pi r^2 h$, for h

Example 4
(page 19)

Solve each equation for x. Find any restrictions.

23. $ax + bx = c$
24. $bx - cx = -c$
25. $\frac{x}{a} + b = c$
26. $\frac{x}{a} - 5 = b$
27. $\frac{x - 2}{2} = m + n$
28. $\frac{2}{5}(x + 1) = g$

Write an equation to solve each problem.

29. Two buses leave Houston at the same time and travel in opposite directions. One bus averages 55 mi/h and the other bus averages 45 mi/h. When will they be 400 mi apart?

30. Two planes left an airport at noon. One flew east at a certain speed and the other flew west at twice the speed. The planes were 2700 mi apart in 3 h. How fast was each plane flying?

31. Geometry The length of a rectangle is 3 cm greater than its width. The perimeter is 24 cm. Find the dimensions of the rectangle.

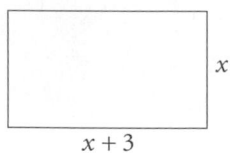

32. Geometry One side of a triangle is 1 in. longer than the shortest side and is 1 in. shorter than the longest side. The perimeter is 17 in. Find the dimensions of the triangle.

33. Geometry The sides of a rectangle are in the ratio $3 : 2$. What is the length of each side if the perimeter of the rectangle is 55 cm?

34. Geometry The sides of a triangle are in the ratio $3 : 4 : 5$. What is the length of each side if the perimeter of the triangle is 30 cm?

35. The sum of three consecutive integers is 90.
   a. Find the three numbers by letting x represent the first integer.
   b. Find the three numbers by letting x represent the second integer.

B Apply Your Skills

Solve each equation.

36. $0.2(x + 3) - 4(2x - 3) = 3.4$
37. $12 - 3(2w + 1) = 7w - 3(7 + w)$
38. $3(m - 2) - 5 = 8 - 2(m - 4)$
39. $7(a + 1) - 3a = 5 + 4(2a - 1)$
40. $\frac{x}{2} + \frac{x}{5} + \frac{x}{3} = 31$
41. $0.5\left(2x + \frac{3}{4}\right) - \frac{1}{3}(0.1 + x) = 1$

Solve each formula for the indicated variable.

42. $R(r_1 + r_2) = r_1 r_2$, for R
43. $R(r_1 + r_2) = r_1 r_2$, for r_2
44. $S = 2\pi r^2 + 2\pi rh$, for h
45. $h = vt - 5t^2$, for v
46. $v = s^2 + \frac{1}{2}sh$, for h
47. $A = \frac{1}{2}h(b_1 + b_2)$, for b_2

48. Geometry The measure of the supplement of an angle is 20° more than three times the measure of the original angle. Find the measures of the angles.

49. Geometry The measures of an angle and its complement differ by 22°. Find the measures of the angles.

50. Michael drove to a friend's house at a rate of 40 mi/h. He returned by the same route at a rate of 45 mi/h. The driving time for the round trip was 4 h. What is the distance Michael traveled?

51. Sports In the 2004 Olympics, a runner from Belarus won the gold medal in the 100-meter race. Her time was 10.93 seconds. In 1988, Florence Griffith Joyner of the United States set a world record of 10.49 seconds for the 100-meter race. If these two athletes had run in the same race with their respective times above, by how many meters would Griffith Joyner have won?

52. Investments Suppose you have $5000 to invest. A certificate of deposit (CD) earns 6% annual interest, while bonds, which are riskier, earn 8% annual interest. You decide to invest $2000 in a CD and the rest in bonds. How much interest will you have earned at the end of one year? Of two years, compounded annually?

53. Find 4 consecutive odd integers with a sum of 184.

54. Find 4 consecutive even integers such that the sum of the second and fourth is 76.

Solve for *x*. State any restrictions on the variables.

55. $\frac{x + a}{b} + b = a$

56. $bx + a = dx + c$

57. $cx - b = ax + d$

58. $a(x - 3) + 8 = b(x - 1)$

59. $c(x + 2) - 5 = b(x - 3)$

60. $a(3tx - 2b) = c(dx - 2)$

61. $b(5px - 3c) = a(qx - 4)$

62. $\frac{a}{b}(2x - 12) = \frac{c}{d}$

63. $\frac{3ax}{5} - 4c = \frac{ax}{5}$

64. $\frac{a - c}{x - a} = m$

 **Challenge**

65. a. The speed of sound in air *s*, in ft/s, is given by the formula $s = 1055 + 1.1t$, where *t* is the temperature in degrees Fahrenheit. Solve the formula for *t*.
  b. Find the Fahrenheit temperature at which the speed of sound is 1100 ft/s.
  c. The relationship between the temperature in degrees Fahrenheit *F* and degrees Celsius *C* is given by the formula $F = \frac{9}{5}C + 32$. Solve the formula for *C*.
  d. Find the Celsius temperature at which the speed of sound is 1100 ft/s.

66. There are 40 cows and chickens in the farmyard. One quiet afternoon, Jack counted and found that there were 100 legs in all. How many cows and how many chickens are there?
  a. Solve this problem by writing and solving an equation.
  b. Critical Thinking This problem can also be solved by reasoning. Suppose all 40 animals are chickens. How many legs would there be? How many too few legs is that? If one chicken is replaced by one cow, by how many would the number of legs be increased? How many cows would have to replace chickens to get the required 100 legs?
  c. Open-Ended Write a problem about the number of wheels in a group of bicycles and tricycles. Solve your problem.

67. Assume that *a*, *b*, and *c* are integers and $a \neq 0$.
  a. Proof Prove that the solution of the linear equation $ax - b = c$ must be a rational number.
  b. Writing Describe the values of *a*, *b*, and *c* for which the solutions of $ax^2 + b = c$ are rational.

68. A tortoise crawling at the rate of 0.1 mi/h passes a resting hare. The hare wants to rest another 30 min before chasing the tortoise at the rate of 5 mi/h. How many feet must the hare run to catch the tortoise?

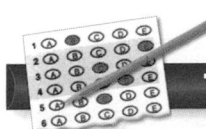

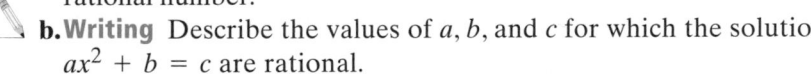 **Test Prep**

Gridded Response

69. What is the only value *z* for which $6z - 24 = 2z + 50$? Enter your answer as a decimal.

70. If 16 less than four times a number is 64, what is the number?

71. The measure of the supplement of an angle is 25° more than 7 times the measure of the angle. To the nearest tenth of a degree, what is the measure of the angle?

72. The sides of a rectangle are in the ratio 5 : 7, and its perimeter is 96 cm. What is the area of the rectangle in square centimeters?

Mixed Review

Go for Help

Lesson 1-2   **Evaluate each expression for $x = -4$ and $y = 3$.**

73. $x - 2y + 3$　　**74.** $x + x \div y$　　**75.** $3x - 4y - x$　　**76.** $x + 2y \div x$

Lesson 1-2   **Simplify each expression.**

77. $2x^2 + x + 5x^2 - 3x$　　**78.** $ab - a - 5a$　　**79.** $-(3x - y + 4x - y)$

80. $2(5x - 3) + x$　　**81.** $5 - 2(3x + 5)$　　**82.** $4r + 2s - (6r + 7s)$

✓ Checkpoint Quiz 1   Lessons 1-1 through 1-3

1. Simplify the expressions and arrange them in order from least to greatest.

$|4 - 11|$　　　　$0.1|-3|$　　　　$|1 - \frac{1}{3}|$　　　　$|3| - |4|$

2. What three properties of real numbers are needed to simplify $3x + (2 + 5x)$?

Simplify each expression.

3. $-(a + 2b) + 4(a + 2b) - 2(a + 2b)$　　**4.** $-3(a^2 + a + 1) - 4(-a^2 - a + 1)$

Solve each equation.

5. $2(4x + 1) = 3(4 + 2x)$　　　　　　**6.** $12 - 2(3x + 1) = 4x - 5$

7. $\frac{1}{2}(4b + 1) = 7 - \frac{1}{4}(6b - 2)$

Solve for the indicated variable. Find any restrictions.

8. $A = p(1 + rt)$, for r　　　　　　**9.** $8ax - b = 3b + ax$, for x

10. The perimeter of Sportsland Park is 624 yd. The length of the rectangular park is 8 yd more than 3 times the width. Find the dimensions of the park.

Algebra at Work

·································· Wildlife Biologist

Wildlife biologists can model changes in an animal population. An animal population increases rapidly when conditions are good. However, as the number of animals increases, the food supplies decrease. Hunger and disease then lower the population.

Wildlife biologists take a special interest in extremes of animal populations. If the population of one species becomes too large, it may reduce the population of another species. A continuing decrease may cause the species to become endangered or extinct.

Go Online
PHSchool.com   **For:** Information about wildlife biology
Web Code: agb-2031

Spreadsheets

FOR USE WITH LESSON 1-3

Suppose that you buy an electronic keyboard and sound system for $500 using a credit card. When you get your first monthly statement, the minimum payment is $25. The minimum payment is either $15 or 5% of your balance, whichever is greater. Interest is calculated at 1.8% per month. You pay the minimum each month.

ACTIVITY

You can examine the situation described above with a spreadsheet. Write cell formulas for row 3 of the spreadsheet.

	A	B	C	D	E	F	G
1	Month	Balance	Interest	Payment	New Balance	Total Interest	Total Paid
2	1	$500.00	$9.00	$25.00	$484.00	$9.00	$25.00
3	2	$484.00	$8.71	$24.20	$468.51	$17.71	$49.20
4	3	$468.51	$8.43	$23.43	$453.52	$26.15	$72.63

Month	$A3 = A2 + 1$	**Increase the month by 1.**
Balance	$B3 = E2$	**balance from the previous month**
Interest	$C3 = B3 \cdot 0.018$	**1.8% of the month's balance**
Payment	$D3 = B3 \cdot 0.05$	**5% of the month's balance**
New Balance	$E3 = B3 + C3 - D3$	**Add the interest and subtract the payment.**
Total Interest	$F3 = F2 + C3$	**Add the month's interest to the previous total interest.**
Total Paid	$G3 = G2 + D3$	**Add the month's payment to the previous total.**

EXERCISES

1. Create a spreadsheet for the situation in the Example.
   a. In which month will the minimum payment first be $15?
   b. After how many months will the balance reach zero?
   c. What is the total interest paid?
   d. What is the total amount you will pay?
   e. How many payments are required to reduce the balance to $400?
   f. Rewrite the right side of $E3 = B3 + C3 - D3$ in terms of B3.

2. Create a new spreadsheet for an account that charges 14.9% annual interest. Use a minimum payment of 10% or $20, whichever is greater. What is the total interest paid for the keyboard and sound system?

3. **Writing** Why is it better to pay off a credit card debt as soon as you can rather than pay just the minimum each month?

1-4

Solving Inequalities

What You'll Learn

- To solve and graph inequalities
- To solve and write compound inequalities

. . . And Why

To analyze quality control, as in Example 6

✓ **Check Skills You'll Need**

GO for Help Lessons 1-1 and 1-3

State whether each inequality is true or false.
1. $5 < 12$ **2.** $5 < -12$ **3.** $5 \geq 12$
4. $5 \leq -12$ **5.** $5 \leq 5$ **6.** $5 \geq 5$

Solve each equation.
7. $3x + 3 = 2x - 3$ **8.** $5x = 9(x - 8) + 12$

🔊 **New Vocabulary** • compound inequality

---

1 | Solving and Graphing Inequalities

As with an equation, the solutions of an inequality are the numbers that make it true.

An equation such as $-2x = 10$ has only one solution, -5. On the other hand, the inequality $-2x < 10$ is true for many values of x, such as -4.99, -1, and 100. The solutions of $-2x < 10$ are all the numbers x such that $x > -5$, as shown in the graph at the right.

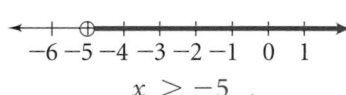

$x > -5$

GO for Help

To review the properties of equality, go to p. 18.

The properties for solving inequalities are similar to the properties for solving equations. The exception occurs when you multiply or divide each side by a negative quantity. Notice that you can obtain $x > -5$ from $-2x < 10$ by dividing each side by -2 and *reversing* the inequality symbol.

The following properties are for $\leq$. There are similar properties for $<$, $>$, and $\geq$.

Key Concepts

Property	Properties of Inequalities

Let a, b, and c represent real numbers.

Transitive Property   If $a \leq b$ and $b \leq c$, then $a \leq c$.

Addition Property   If $a \leq b$, then $a + c \leq b + c$.

Subtraction Property   If $a \leq b$, then $a - c \leq b - c$.

Multiplication Property   If $a \leq b$ and $c > 0$, then $ac \leq bc$.
                           If $a \leq b$ and $c < 0$, then $ac \geq bc$.

Division Property   If $a \leq b$ and $c > 0$, then $\frac{a}{c} \leq \frac{b}{c}$.

                     If $a \leq b$ and $c < 0$, then $\frac{a}{c} \geq \frac{b}{c}$.

← You must reverse the inequality symbol when c is negative.

1 **EXAMPLE** **Solving and Graphing Inequalities**

Solve each inequality. Graph the solution.

a. $3x - 12 < 3$

$3x - 12 < 3$

$\qquad 3x < 15$ **Add 12 to each side.**

$\qquad x < 5$ **Divide each side by 3.**

$$\xleftarrow{\quad} \underset{-1 \;\; 0 \;\; 1 \;\; 2 \;\; 3 \;\; 4 \;\; 5 \;\; 6}{\xrightarrow{\quad \overset{\oplus}{\quad} \quad}}$$ **Graph the solution.**

Check First check the boundary point: $3(5) - 12 = 3.$ ✓
Then check another point on the graph, such as 4: $3(4) - 12 < 3.$ ✓

b. $6 + 5(2 - x) \le 41$

$\qquad 6 + 10 - 5x \le 41$ **Distributive Property**

$\qquad 16 - 5x \le 41$ **Simplify.**

$\qquad -5x \le 25$ **Subtract 16 from each side.**

$\qquad x \ge -5$ **Divide each side by -5 and reverse the inequality.**

$$\xleftarrow{\quad} \underset{-6\;-5\;-4\;-3\;-2\;-1\;\;0\;\;1}{\xrightarrow{\quad \overset{\bullet}{\quad} \quad}}$$ **Graph the solution.**

Check First check the boundary point: $6 + 5[2 - (-5)] = 41.$ ✓
Then check another point, such as -4: $6 + 5[2 - (-4)] \le 41.$ ✓

 **Quick Check** ❶ Solve each inequality. Graph the solution.
a. $3x - 6 < 27$ **b.** $12 \ge 2(3n + 1) + 22$

Some inequalities have no solution, and some are true for all real numbers.

2 **EXAMPLE** **No Solutions or All Real Numbers as Solutions**

GO ◉**nline**

Video Tutor Help
Visit: PHSchool.com
Web Code: age-0775

Solve each inequality. Graph the solution.

a. $2x - 3 > 2(x - 5)$

$\qquad 2x - 3 > 2x - 10$ **Distributive Property**

$\qquad 2x > 2x - 7$ **Add 3 to each side.**

$\qquad 0 > -7$ **Subtract 2x from each side.**

The last inequality is always true, so $2x - 3 > 2(x - 5)$ is always true. All real numbers are solutions.

$$\xleftarrow{\quad} \underset{-3\;-2\;-1\;\;0\;\;1\;\;2\;\;3}{\xrightarrow{\qquad\qquad}}$$

b. $7x + 6 < 7(x - 4)$

$\qquad 7x + 6 < 7x - 28$ **Distributive Property**

$\qquad 6 < -28$ **Subtract 7x from each side.**

The last inequality is always false, so $7x + 6 < 7(x - 4)$ is always false. It has no solution.

 **Quick Check** ❷ **a.** Solve $2x < 2(x + 1) + 3$. Graph the solution.
      b. Solve $4(x - 3) + 7 \ge 4x + 1$. Graph the solution.
      c. Critical Thinking If possible, find values of a such that $2x + a > 2x$ has no solution. Then find values of a such that all real numbers are solutions.

3 EXAMPLE **Real-World** **Connection**

Revenue The band shown at the left agrees to play for $200 plus 25% of the ticket sales. Find the ticket sales needed for the band to receive at least $500.

Relate $200 + 25\%$ of ticket sales $\geq \$500$

Define Let x = ticket sales (in dollars).

Write $200 + 0.25x \geq 500$

$\qquad\qquad 0.25x \geq 300$ **Subtract 200 from each side.**

$\qquad\qquad\quad x \geq 1200$ **Divide each side by 0.25.**

● The ticket sales must be greater than or equal to $1200.

✓ Quick Check ❸ A salesperson earns a salary of $700 per month plus 2% of the sales. What must the sales be if the salesperson is to have a monthly income of at least $1800?

---

2   Compound Inequalities

●nline
active math

For: Inequalities Activity
Use: Interactive Textbook, 1-4

A **compound inequality** is a pair of inequalities joined by *and* or *or*.

Examples:
- $-1 < x$ and $x \leq 3$, which you can also write as $-1 < x \leq 3$
- $x < -1$ or $x \geq 3$

To solve a compound inequality containing *and*, find all values of the variable that make both inequalities true.

4 EXAMPLE **Compound Inequality Containing *And***

Graph the solution of $3x - 1 > -28$ and $2x + 7 < 19$.

$3x - 1 > -28$ and $2x + 7 < 19$

$\qquad 3x > -27 \qquad\qquad\quad 2x < 12$

$\qquad\quad x > -9$ and $x < 6$

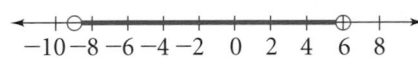

● This compound inequality can be rewritten as $-9 < x < 6$.

✓ Quick Check ❹ Graph the solution of $2x > x + 6$ and $x - 7 < 2$.

To solve a compound inequality containing *or*, find all values of the variable that make at least one of the inequalities true.

5 EXAMPLE **Compound Inequality Containing *Or***

Graph the solution of $4y - 2 \geq 14$ or $3y - 4 \leq -13$.

$4y - 2 \geq 14$ or $3y - 4 \leq -13$

$\qquad 4y \geq 16 \qquad\qquad\quad 3y \leq -9$

$\qquad\quad y \geq 4$ or $y \leq -3$

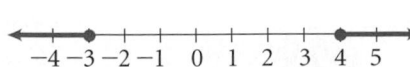

✓ Quick Check ❺ Solve the compound inequality $x - 1 < 3$ or $x + 3 > 8$. Graph the solution.

6 EXAMPLE Real-World Connection

Multiple Choice The ideal length of a bolt is 13.48 cm. The length can vary from the ideal by at most 0.03 cm. A machinist finds one bolt that is 13.67 cm long. By how much should the machinist decrease the length so the bolt can be used?

Ⓐ between 13.45 cm and 13.51 cm   Ⓑ between 13.64 cm and 13.70 cm

Ⓒ between 0.16 cm and 0.22 cm   Ⓓ between 0.13 cm and 0.19 cm

Test-Taking Tip

When you multiply by a negative number across a compound inequality, remember to reverse both inequality symbols.

Relate   minimum length $\leq$ final length $\leq$ maximum length

Define   Let x = number of centimeters to remove.

Write $13.48 - 0.03 \leq 13.67 - x \leq 13.48 + 0.03$

$\qquad\qquad 13.45 \leq 13.67 - x \leq 13.51$ **Simplify.**

$\qquad\qquad -0.22 \leq -x \leq -0.16$ **Subtract 13.67.**

$\qquad\qquad 0.22 \geq x \geq 0.16$ **Multiply by −1.**

The machinist must remove at least 0.16 cm and no more than 0.22 cm. The answer is C.

 **Quick Check** 6 The plans for a circular plastic part in a medical instrument require the diameter to be within 0.2 in. of 1.5 in. A machinist finds that the diameter is now 1.73 in. By how much should the machinist decrease the diameter?

EXERCISES

For more exercises, see *Extra Skill and Word Problem Practice.*

Practice and Problem Solving

Ⓐ Practice by Example

Examples 1 and 2
(page 27)

GO for Help

Solve each inequality. Graph the solution.

1. $-12 \geq 24x$ **2.** $-7k < 63$ **3.** $8a - 15 > 73$

4. $57 - 4t \geq 13$ **5.** $-18 - 5y \geq 52$

6. $14 - 4y \geq 38$ **7.** $4(x + 3) \leq 44$

8. $2(m - 3) + 7 < 21$ **9.** $4(n - 2) - 6 > 18$

10. $9(x + 2) > 9(x - 3)$ **11.** $6x - 13 < 6(x - 2)$

12. $-6(2x - 10) + 12x \leq 180$ **13.** $-7(3x - 7) + 21x \geq 50$

Example 3
(page 28)

Solve each problem by writing an inequality.

14. The length of a picture frame is 3 in. greater than the width. The perimeter is less than 52 in. Describe the dimensions of the frame.

15. The lengths of the sides of a triangle are in the ratio 5 : 6 : 7. Describe the length of the longest side if the perimeter is less than 54 cm.

16. Find the lesser of two consecutive integers with a sum greater than 16.

17. The cost of a field trip is $220 plus $7 per student. If the school can spend at most $500, how many students can go on the field trip?

Example 4
(page 28)

Solve each compound inequality. Graph the solution.

18. $2x > -10$ and $9x < 18$ **19.** $3x \geq -12$ and $8x \leq 16$

20. $6x \geq -24$ and $9x < 54$ **21.** $7x > -35$ and $5x \leq 30$

Example 5
(page 28)

Solve each compound inequality. Graph the solution.

22. $4x < 16$ or $12x > 144$ **23.** $3r > 3$ or $9x < 54$

24. $8x > -32$ or $-6x \le 48$ **25.** $9x \le -27$ or $4x \ge 36$

Example 6
(page 29)

Solve each problem by writing a compound inequality.

26. A baker needs between 40 lb and 50 lb of a flour-sugar mixture that contains ten times as much flour as sugar. What are the possible weights of flour the baker can use?

27. Between 15,000 yd^3 and 16,000 yd^3 of earth must be trucked away from a construction site. The trucks can remove 1000 yd^3 per day, and 10,500 yd^3 has already been removed. How many days are needed?

28. By how much should a machinist decrease the length of a rod that is 4.78 cm long if the length must be within 0.02 cm of 4.5 cm?

B Apply Your Skills

Solve each inequality. Graph the solution.

29. $2 - 3z \ge 7(8 - 2z) + 12$ **30.** $17 - 2y \le 5(7 - 3y) - 15$

31. $\frac{2}{3}(x - 12) \le x + 8$ **32.** $\frac{3}{5}(x - 12) > x - 24$

33. $3[4x - (2x - 7)] < 2(3x - 5)$ **34.** $6[5y - (3y - 1)] \ge 4(3y - 7)$

35. Writing Write a problem that can be solved using the inequality $x + 0.5x \le 60$.

36. Geometry The sum of the lengths of any two sides of a triangle is greater than the length of the third side. In $\triangle ABC$, $BC = 4$ and $AC = 8 - AB$. What can you conclude about AB?

GO for Help

For a guide to solving
Exercise 36, see page 32.

37. a. Error Analysis Suppose a classmate writes $y \le 20$ as the solution of $\frac{1}{2}(y - 16) \ge y + 2$. Prove that your classmate's answer is wrong by checking a number that is less than 20. Choose a number that makes the computation easy.
   b. Solve $\frac{1}{2}(y - 16) \ge y + 2$.

38. Construction A contractor estimated that her expenses for a construction project would be between $700,000 and $750,000. She has already spent $496,000. How much more can she spend and remain within her estimate?

Justifying Steps Justify each step by identifying the property used.

39. $3x \le 4(x - 1) - 8$
$3x \le 4x - 4 - 8$
$3x \le 4x - 12$
$-x \le -12$
$x \ge 12$

40. $\frac{1}{2}(y + 3) > \frac{1}{3}(4 - y)$
$3(y + 3) > 2(4 - y)$
$3y + 9 > 8 - 2y$
$5y + 9 > 8$
$5y > -1$
$y > -0.2$

Real-World Connection

Careers To bid on a job, a construction contractor must consider all the costs of running a business as well as the costs of materials and labor.

Solve each compound inequality. Graph the solutions.

41. $-6 < 2x - 4 < 12$ **42.** $11 < 3y + 2 < 20$

43. $-18 > 4x - 3 > -15$ **44.** $36 \ge 1 - 5z > -21$

45. $5a - 4 > 16$ or $3a + 2 < 17$ **46.** $6b + 3 < 15$ or $4b - 2 > 18$

47. $6c \le 18$ or $-5c \le 15$ **48.** $8d < -64$ and $5d > 25$

49. $4x \le 12$ or $-7x \le 21$ **50.** $15x > 30$ and $18x < -36$

Open-Ended Write an inequality with a solution that matches the graph. At least two steps should be needed to solve your inequality.

51. ←—+——●——+——+——+——+——+——→
     −3 −2 −1 0 1 2 3

52. ←—+——+——⊕——+——+——+——+——→
     −3 −2 −1 0 1 2 3

53. ←—+——⊕——+——+——⊕——+——+——→
     −3 −2 −1 0 1 2 3

54. ←—+——+——●——+——●——+——+——→
     −3 −2 −1 0 1 2 3

55. Critical Thinking Consider the compound inequality $x < 8$ and $x > a$.
   a. Are there any values of a such that all real numbers are solutions of the compound inequality? If so, what are they?
   b. Are there any values of a such that no real numbers are solutions of the compound inequality? If so, what are they?
   c. Repeat parts (a) and (b) for the compound inequality $x < 8$ or $x > a$.

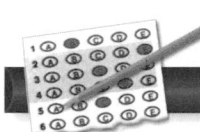

Test Prep

Multiple Choice

56. Which of the following statements are true?
  I. $-(-6) = 6$ and $-(-4) > -4$
  II. $-(-4) < 4$ or $-10 > 10 - 10$
  III. $5 + 6 = 11$ or $9 - 2 = 11$
  IV. $17 > 2$ or $6 < 9$

  A. I and II only
  B. I, II, and III only
  C. I, III, and IV only
  D. III and IV only

57. What is the solution of the inequality $8 - 3x < -3(1 + x) + 1$?
  F. all real numbers **G.** no real numbers **H.** $x > \frac{2}{3}$ **J.** $x < -\frac{11}{6}$

58. What is the solution of the compound inequality $2 < 2(x + 4) < 18$?
  A. all real numbers   **B.** no real numbers
  C. $-3 < x < 5$ **D.** $-4 < x < 5$

59. What is the solution of the compound inequality $\frac{x}{2} - 4 > 0$ or $\frac{x}{2} + 1 < 0$?
  F. all real numbers   **G.** no real numbers
  H. $x > 6$ or $x < 0$ **J.** $x > 8$ or $x < -2$

Short Response

60. What is the maximum number of 3- to 5-min songs that fill a 90-min CD? What is the minimum number? Explain your reasoning.

Extended Response

61. Fill each box with the word *and* or *or*, so that the solution of one compound inequality is *all real numbers* and the solution of the other is *no real numbers*. Justify each step of your solution.

    $x + 5 > 0$ ☐ $x - 3 < 0$ $x + 5 < 0$ ☐ $x + 5 > 0$

Mixed Review

Lesson 1-3

Solve each equation. Check your answers.

62. $7x - 6(11 - 2x) = 10$ **63.** $10x - 7 = 2(13 + 5x)$
64. $4y - \frac{1}{10} = 3y + \frac{4}{5}$ **65.** $0.4x + 1.18 = -3.1(2 - 0.01x)$

Lesson 1-2

Simplify each expression.

66. $(2a - 4) + (5a + 9)$ **67.** $3(x + 3y) - 5(x - y)$
68. $\frac{1}{3}(b + 12) - \frac{1}{4}(b + 12)$ **69.** $0.4(k - 0.1) + 0.5(3.3 - k)$

Understanding Math Problems Read the problem below. Then let Malik's thinking guide you through the solution. Check your understanding with the exercises at the bottom of the page.

Geometry The sum of the lengths of any two sides of a triangle is greater than the length of the third side. In $\triangle ABC$, $BC = 4$ and $AC = 8 - AB$. What can you conclude about AB?

What Malik Thinks	**What Malik Writes**
$\triangle ABC$ has three sides, so I can write three inequalities, each with AB.	$AC + BC > AB$ $AB + BC > AC$ $AB + AC > BC$
I also know that $BC = 4$ and $AC = 8 - AB$.	$BC = 4$ and $AC = 8 - AB$.
I can substitute for BC and AC in each of the three inequalities and simplify.	$(8 - AB) + 4 > AB$ $12 - AB > AB$ $12 > 2AB$
Here's the first inequality.	$6 > AB$, or $AB < 6$.
Here's the second.	$AB + 4 > 8 - AB$ $2AB > 4$ $AB > 2$, or $2 < AB$.
Here's the third.	$AB + (8 - AB) > 4$ $8 > 4$
I can combine $2 < AB$ and $AB < 6$ into a compound inequality.	$2 < AB < 6$

EXERCISES

The sum of the lengths of any two sides of a triangle is greater than the length of the third side. What can you conclude about AC in $\triangle ABC$?

1. $AB = 6$; $BC + 2AC = 18$

2. $BC = 7$; $AC = 2 + AB$

3. $AB + AC = 5$; $AC + BC = 4$

4. $BC + AC = 22$; $AB + BC = 12$

Absolute Value Equations and Inequalities

What You'll Learn

- To solve absolute value equations
- To solve absolute value inequalities

. . . And Why

To write specifications for a basketball, as in Example 6

✓ **Check Skills You'll Need**

 for Help Lessons 1-3 and 1-4

Solve each equation.

1. $5(x - 6) = 40$ **2.** $5b = 2(3b - 8)$ **3.** $2y + 6y = 15 - 2y + 8$

Solve each inequality.

4. $4x + 8 > 20$ **5.** $3a - 2 \geq a + 6$ **6.** $4(t - 1) < 3t + 5$

🔊 **New Vocabulary** • absolute value • extraneous solution • tolerance

---

1   Absolute Value Equations

The **absolute value** of a number is its distance from zero on the number line and distance is nonnegative. So the absolute value of a negative number such as -5 is its opposite, $-(-5)$. For $x < 0$, $|x| = -x$.

 Key Concepts

Definition	Algebraic Definition of Absolute Value
• If $x \geq 0$, then $|x| = x$.	• If $x < 0$, then $|x| = -x$.

An absolute value equation such as $|2y - 4| = 12$ has two solutions, since the expression $2y - 4$ can equal 12 or -12.

1 EXAMPLE   Solving Absolute Value Equations

Solve $|2y - 4| = 12$.

$|2y - 4| = 12$

$2y - 4 = 12$ or $2y - 4 = -12$ The value of $2y - 4$ can be 12 or -12 since $|12|$ and $|-12|$ both equal 12.

$2y = 16$ $2y = -8$ Add 4 to each side of both equations.

$y = 8$ or $y = -4$ Divide each side of both equations by 2.

Check $|2y - 4| = 12$

$|2(8) - 4| \stackrel{?}{=} 12$ $|2(-4) - 4| \stackrel{?}{=} 12$

$|12| = 12$ ✓ $|-12| = 12$ ✓

✓ **Quick Check**   1 Solve $|3x + 2| = 7$. Check your answer.

You will find it easier to solve a multi-step absolute value equation if you first isolate the absolute value expression on one side of the equation.

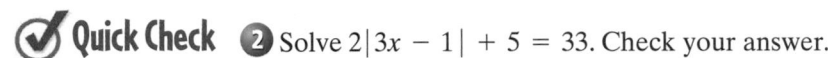 **EXAMPLE** Solving Multi-Step Absolute Value Equations

Solve $3|4w - 1| - 5 = 10$.

$$3|4w - 1| - 5 = 10$$

$\quad 3|4w - 1| = 15 \qquad$ **Add 5 to each side.**

$\quad\ \ |4w - 1| = 5 \qquad$ **Divide each side by 3.**

$\quad 4w - 1 = 5 \quad$ or $\quad 4w - 1 = -5 \qquad$ **Rewrite as two equations.**

$\qquad 4w = 6 \qquad\qquad\quad 4w = -4 \qquad$ **Add 1 to each side of both equations.**

$\qquad\quad w = \frac{3}{2} \quad$ or $\qquad w = -1 \qquad$ **Divide each side of both equations by 4.**

Check $\quad 3|4w - 1| - 5 = 10 \qquad\qquad 3|4w - 1| - 5 = 10$

$\qquad 3|4(\frac{3}{2}) - 1| - 5 \overset{?}{=} 10 \qquad 3|4(-1) - 1| - 5 \overset{?}{=} 10$

$\qquad\qquad 3|5| - 5 \overset{?}{=} 10 \qquad\qquad\quad 3|-5| - 5 \overset{?}{=} 10$

$\qquad\qquad\qquad 10 = 10 \checkmark \qquad\qquad\qquad 10 = 10 \checkmark$

 **Quick Check** ② Solve $2|3x - 1| + 5 = 33$. Check your answer.

The equation $|2x + 7| = -2$ has no solution because $|2x + 7|$ cannot be negative. It is important to check possible solutions in the original equation. One or more may be extraneous solutions.

Key Concepts

Definition	Extraneous Solution

An **extraneous solution** is a solution of an equation derived from an original equation that is not a solution of the original equation.

③ **EXAMPLE** Checking for Extraneous Solutions

Solve $|2x + 5| = 3x + 4$.

$$|2x + 5| = 3x + 4$$

$\quad 2x + 5 = 3x + 4 \quad$ or $\quad 2x + 5 = -(3x + 4) \qquad$ **Rewrite as two equations.**

$\qquad\ -x = -1 \qquad\qquad\quad 2x + 5 = -3x - 4 \qquad$ **Solve each equation.**

$\qquad\quad x = 1 \qquad\qquad\qquad\qquad 5x = -9$

$\qquad\quad x = 1 \qquad$ or $\qquad\qquad\quad x = -\frac{9}{5}$

Vocabulary Tip

Extraneous is pronounced ek-STRAY-nee-us.

Check $\quad |2x + 5| = 3x + 4 \qquad\qquad\quad |2x + 5| = 3x + 4$

$\qquad |2(1) + 5| \overset{?}{=} 3(1) + 4 \qquad |2(-\frac{9}{5}) + 5| \overset{?}{=} 3(-\frac{9}{5}) + 4$

$\qquad\qquad\quad |7| \overset{?}{=} 7 \qquad\qquad\qquad\quad |\frac{7}{5}| \overset{?}{=} -\frac{7}{5}$

$\qquad\qquad\quad 7 = 7 \checkmark \qquad\qquad\qquad\quad \frac{7}{5} \neq -\frac{7}{5}$

The only solution is 1. $-\frac{9}{5}$ is an extraneous solution.

 **Quick Check** ③ **a.** Solve $|2x + 3| = 3x + 2$. Check for extraneous solutions.

b. Solve $|x| = x - 1$. Check for extraneous solutions.

c. **Critical Thinking** Find a value for a such that $|x| = x + a$ has exactly one solution.

If $|x| > 3$, then x is more than 3 units from 0 on the number line.

$$-4\ -3\ -2\ -1\ \ 0\ \ 1\ \ 2\ \ 3\ \ 4$$

This is also the graph of $x < -3$ or $x > 3$. So the absolute value inequality $|x| > 3$ can be rewritten as the compound inequality $x < -3$ or $x > 3$.

4 EXAMPLE **Solving Absolute Value Inequalities, $|A| \ge b$**

Solve $|3x + 6| \ge 12$. Graph the solution.

$|3x + 6| \ge 12$

$3x + 6 \le -12$ or $3x + 6 \ge 12$ **Rewrite as a compound inequality.**

$3x \le -18$ $\qquad$ $3x \ge 6$

$x \le -6$ or $x \ge 2$

$$-7\ -6\ -5\ -4\ -3\ -2\ -1\ \ 0\ \ 1\ \ 2\ \ 3$$ **Graph the solution.**

✔ Quick Check **4** Solve $|2x - 3| > 7$. Graph the solution.

If $|x| < 2$, then x is less than 2 units from 0 on the number line.

$$-3\ -2\ -1\ \ 0\ \ 1\ \ 2\ \ 3$$

This is also the graph of $-2 < x < 2$. So the absolute value inequality $|x| < 2$ can be written as the compound inequality $-2 < x < 2$.

🔑 Key Concepts

Properties	Absolute Value Inequalities
Let k represent a positive real number.	
$|x| \ge k$ $\quad$ is equivalent to	$x \le -k$ or $x \ge k$.
$|x| \le k$ $\quad$ is equivalent to	$-k \le x \le k$.

When an absolute value is combined with other operations, first isolate the absolute value expression on one side of the inequality.

5 EXAMPLE **Solving Absolute Value Inequalities, $|A| < b$**

Solve $3|2x + 6| - 9 < 15$. Graph the solution.

$3|2x + 6| - 9 < 15$

$3|2x + 6| < 24$ **Isolate the absolute value expression. Add 9 to each side.**

$|2x + 6| < 8$ **Divide each side by 3.**

$-8 < 2x + 6 < 8$ **Rewrite as a compound inequality.**

$-14 < \quad 2x \quad < 2$ **Solve for x.**

$-7 < \quad x \quad < 1$

$$-8\ -7\ -6\ -5\ -4\ -3\ -2\ -1\ \ 0\ \ 1\ \ 2$$

GO▶ for Help

To review the properties of inequalities, go to p. 26.

✔ Quick Check **5** Solve $|5z + 3| - 7 < 34$. Graph the solution.

You can use absolute value inequalities and compound inequalities to specify allowable ranges in measurements. The difference between a desired measurement and its maximum and minimum allowable values is the tolerance. The **tolerance** equals one half of the difference between the maximum and the minimum values.

For example, if a manufacturing specification calls for a dimension d of 10 cm with a tolerance of 0.1 cm, then the allowable difference between d and 10 is less than or equal to 0.1. This specification can be expressed in the following ways.

$\|d - 10\| \leq 0.1$	**absolute value inequality**
$d - 10 \leq 0.1$ and $d - 10 \geq -0.1$	**equivalent compound inequality**
$-0.1 \leq d - 10 \leq 0.1$	**equivalent compound inequality**
$9.9 \leq d \leq 10.1$	**simplified compound inequality**

6 EXAMPLE   Real-World Connection

Basketball The specification for the circumference C in inches of a basketball for men is $29.5 \leq C \leq 30$. Write the specification as an absolute value inequality.

$\frac{30 - 29.5}{2} = \frac{0.5}{2} = 0.25$	**Find the tolerance.**
$\frac{29.5 + 30}{2} = 29.75$	**Find the average of the maximum and minimum values.**
$-0.25 \leq C - 29.75 \leq 0.25$	**Write an inequality.**
$\|C - 29.75\| \leq 0.25$	**Rewrite as an absolute value inequality.**

 **6** The specification for the circumference C in inches of a basketball for junior high school is $27.75 \leq C \leq 28.5$. Write the specification as an absolute value inequality.

EXERCISES

For more exercises, see *Extra Skill and Word Problem Practice*.

Practice and Problem Solving

A Practice by Example

Examples 1 and 2
(pages 33, 34)

Solve each equation. Check your answers.

1. $|3x| = 18$ **2.** $|-4x| = 32$ **3.** $|x - 3| = 9$

4. $2|3x - 2| = 14$ **5.** $|3x + 4| = -3$ **6.** $|2x - 3| = -1$

7. $|x + 4| + 3 = 17$ **8.** $|y - 5| - 2 = 10$ **9.** $|4 - z| - 10 = 1$

Example 3
(page 34)

Solve each equation. Check for extraneous solutions.

10. $|x - 1| = 5x + 10$ **11.** $|2z - 3| = 4z - 1$ **12.** $|3x + 5| = 5x + 2$

13. $|2y - 4| = 12$ **14.** $3|4w - 1| - 5 = 10$ **15.** $|2x + 5| = 3x + 4$

Example 4
(page 35)

Solve each inequality. Graph the solution.

16. $|x + 3| > 9$ **17.** $|x - 5| \geq 8$ **18.** $|y - 3| \geq 12$

19. $|2x + 1| \geq -9$ **20.** $3|2x + 1| \geq 21$ **21.** $|3z| - 4 > 8$

Example 5
(page 35)

22. $3|y - 9| < 27$ **23.** $|6y - 2| + 4 < 22$ **24.** $|3x - 6| + 3 < 15$

25. $\frac{1}{4}|x - 3| + 2 < 1$ **26.** $4|2w + 3| - 7 \leq 9$ **27.** $3|5t - 1| + 9 \leq 23$

Example 6
(page 36)

Write each specification as an absolute value inequality.

28. $1.3 \leq h \leq 1.5$ **29.** $50 \leq k \leq 51$ **30.** $27.25 \leq C \leq 27.75$

31. $50 \leq b \leq 55$ **32.** $1200 \leq m \leq 1300$ **33.** $0.1187 \leq d \leq 0.1190$

 Apply Your Skills

Solve each equation.

34. $-|4 - 8b| = 12$ **35.** $4|3x + 4| = 4x + 8$

36. $|3x - 1| + 10 = 25$ **37.** $\frac{1}{2}|3c + 5| = 6c + 4$

38. $5|6 - 5x| = 15x - 35$ **39.** $7|8 - 3h| = 21h - 49$

40. $2|3x - 7| = 10x - 8$ **41.** $6|2x + 5| = 6x + 24$

42. $\frac{1}{4}|4x + 7| = 8x + 16$ **43.** $\frac{2}{3}|3x - 6| = 4(x - 2)$

GO ●**nline**
Homework Video Tutor

Visit: PHSchool.com
Web Code: age-0105

Solve each inequality. Graph the solutions.

44. $|3x - 4| + 5 \leq 27$ **45.** $|2x + 3| - 6 \geq 7$

46. $-2|x + 4| < 22$ **47.** $2|4t - 1| + 6 > 20$

48. $|3z + 15| \geq 0$ **49.** $|-2x + 1| > 2$

50. $\frac{1}{9}|5x - 3| - 3 \geq 2$ **51.** $\frac{1}{11}|2x - 4| + 10 \leq 11$

52. $\left|\frac{x - 3}{2}\right| + 2 < 6$ **53.** $\left|\frac{x + 5}{3}\right| - 3 > 6$

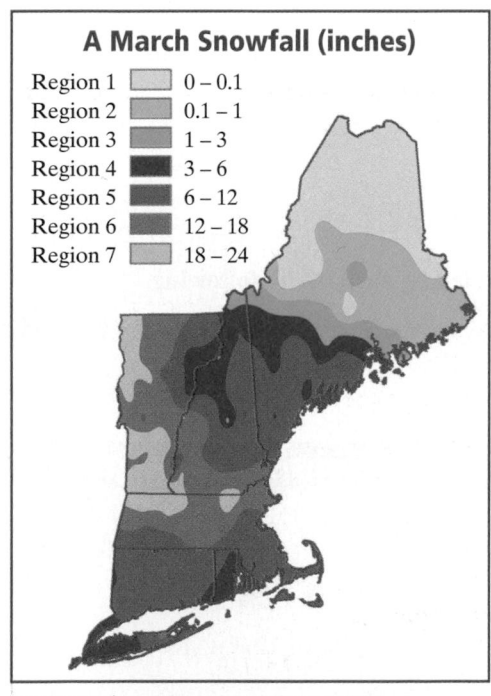

A March Snowfall (inches)

Region 1 ☐ 0 – 0.1
Region 2 ▨ 0.1 – 1
Region 3 ▨ 1 – 3
Region 4 ■ 3 – 6
Region 5 ▨ 6 – 12
Region 6 ▨ 12 – 18
Region 7 ☐ 18 – 24

Source: Northeast River Forecast Center/NOAA

54. Meteorology Write a compound inequality and an absolute value inequality for the snowfall in regions 1, 2, 3, and 4 in the figure at the left.

55. Multiple Choice The circumference of a basketball for college women must be from 28.5 in. to 29.0 in. Which absolute value inequality best represents the circumference of the ball?

Ⓐ $|C - 0.25| \geq 28.5$ Ⓑ $|C - 0.25| \leq 29.0$

Ⓒ $|C - 28.75| \leq 0.25$ Ⓓ $|C - 28.75| \geq 0.25$

56. Writing Describe the differences in the graphs of $|x| < a$ and $|x| > a$, where a is a positive real number.

57. Open-Ended Write an absolute value inequality for which every real number is a solution. Write an absolute value inequality that has no solution.

Write an absolute value inequality and a compound inequality for each length x with the given tolerance.

58. a length of 36.80 mm with a tolerance of 0.05 mm

59. a length of 9.55 mm with a tolerance of 0.02 mm

60. a length of 100 yd with a tolerance of 4 in.

 Challenge

Solve each equation for x.

61. $|ax| - b = c$ **62.** $|cx - d| = ab$ **63.** $a|bx - c| = d$

Graph each solution.

64. $|x| \geq 5$ and $|x| \leq 6$ **65.** $|x| \geq 6$ or $|x| < 5$ **66.** $|x - 5| \leq x$

Multiple Choice

67. Which number is a solution of $|x - 3| = x - 3$?

    A. -3 **B.** 0   **C.** 1   **D.** 3

68. What is the solution of the inequality $\left|\frac{3 - x}{2}\right| < 4$?

    F. $-5 < x < 11$ **G.** $-11 > x > -5$ **H.** $5 < x < 11$ **J.** $11 > x > -1$

69. Which of the following inequalities have the same solutions?

    I. $|5x - 7| \le 8$ **II.** $-8 \le 5x - 7$ or $5x - 7 \le 8$

   III. $8 \le 5x - 7$ and $5x - 7 \ge -8$ **IV.** $-8 \le 5x - 7$ and $5x - 7 \le 8$

    A. I and II   **B.** I and III   **C.** I and IV   **D.** I, III, and IV

70. Which number is a solution of $|9 - x| = 9 + x$?

    F. -3 **G.** 0   **H.** 3   **J.** 6

Short Response

71. Find all the integers that are solutions of $|x - 3| \le 5$. Show your work.

Extended Response

72. Solve $3|2x - 4| + 5 < 41$. Justify each step of your solution.

Mixed Review

Lesson 1-4

Solve each inequality. Graph the solution.

73. $5y - 10 < 20$ **74.** $-5(4s + 1) < 23$ **75.** $4a + 6 \ge 2a + 14$

76. $0.5x + 5 \ge x - 1$ **77.** $3(4x - 1) \ge 2(4 - x)$ **78.** $4(3t + 2) \le 43 + 7t$

Lesson 1-2

Evaluate each expression for the given value.

79. $3|4x - 6| - 2x^2$, for $x = -3$ **80.** $\frac{5r - r^2}{1 - 4r}$, for $r = 4$

Lesson 1-1

Name the property of real numbers illustrated by each of the following.

81. $16x + (-16x) = 0$ **82.** 5π is a real number.   **83.** $4(x - 9) = (x - 9)4$

Checkpoint Quiz 2   Lessons 1-4 through 1-5

Solve each inequality. Graph the solution.

1. $3x + 10 \le 25$ **2.** $8x + 15 > 15x - 24$

3. $5z > 2z - 18$ and $3 - 9z < 12$ **4.** $4w > 1 + 3w$ or $12w + 18 < 11w + 15$

5. $2|x + 4| \le 22$ **6.** $|2x| + 8 > 12$

Solve each equation.

7. $7|3 - 2y| = 56$ **8.** $\frac{1}{4}|4x + 2| = 1 - 2x$

9. Write and solve an inequality to find three consecutive whole numbers with a sum between 13 and 16.

10. Geometry The length of any side of a triangle is less than the sum of the lengths of the other two sides. In $\triangle PQR$, $PR = RQ + 4$ and $RQ < 11$. Write and solve an inequality for PQ.

Probability

What You'll Learn

- To find experimental probabilities
- To find theoretical probabilities

. . . And Why

To find the probabilities of inherited traits, as in Example 4

✓ **Check Skills You'll Need**

Write each number as a percent.

1. $\frac{3}{8}$

2. $1\frac{5}{6}$

3. 0.0043

4. $\frac{1}{400}$

5. 1.04

6. 3

GO for Help Skills Handbook page 870

🔊 **New Vocabulary**
- experimental probability
- simulation
- sample space
- theoretical probability

---

1 Experimental Probability

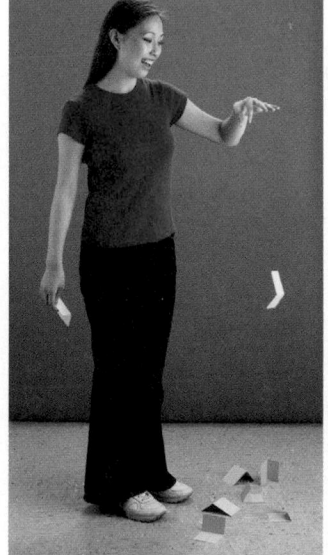

Hands-On Activity: Experimental Probability

Fold an index card slightly off center, as shown at the left. When you drop the card from a height of several feet, how will it land?

1. Drop the card 50 times. Record the number of times the card lands in each position.

2. What percent of the time does the card land on its short side? Find the percents for the other positions.

3. In what position is the card most likely to land? Least likely to land?

4. Suppose that you drop the card another 20 times. Predict how many times it will land in each position.

5. a. Drop the card another 20 times. Record your results.

   b. Compare the results with your prediction from Question 4. Are they close? How could you improve your prediction?

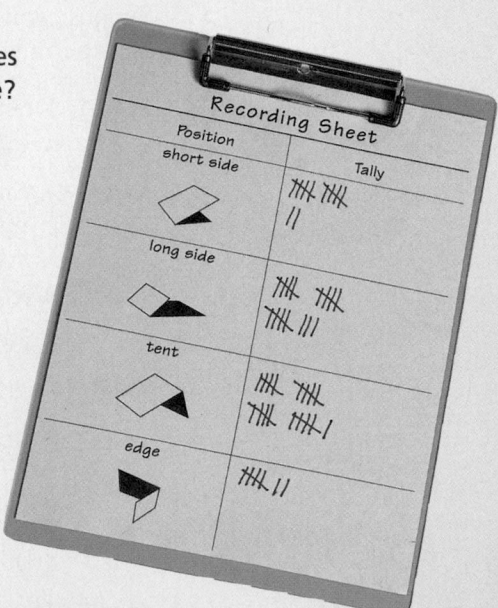

Probability measures how likely it is for an event to occur. You can express probabilities as percents (0% through 100%) or as real numbers (0 through 1).

The probability of an impossible event is 0 or 0%. The probability of a certain event, which must happen, is 1 or 100%.

When you gather data from observations, you can calculate an experimental probability. Each observation is called an experiment or a trial.

Key Concepts

Definition	Experimental Probability

experimental probability of event $= P(\text{event})$
$$= \frac{\text{number of times the event occurs}}{\text{number of trials}}$$

1 EXAMPLE Finding Experimental Probability

Vocabulary Tip

Read *P*(hit) as "probability of a hit."

When the University of Texas won college football's national championship in the 2006 Rose Bowl game, its quarterback completed 30 of 40 passes. Find the experimental probability of the quarterback completing a pass.

$P(\text{completion}) = \frac{30}{40} = 0.75$, or 75%

✓ Quick Check **1** In the same game, the University of Southern California quarterback completed 29 of 40 passes. Find the experimental probability of this player completing a pass.

When actual trials are difficult to conduct, you can find experimental probabilities by using a **simulation,** which is a model of one or more events.

2 EXAMPLE Using a Simulation

Suppose you take a true-or-false quiz and guess four answers at random. What is an experimental probability that you will get at least three correct answers?

rand
.8767044746
.7208728315
.6495877886
.3462435756
.8958229562
.4615208491

.1214849574
.5070685798
.5584414289
.9071019949
.1991062533
.4761581612
.4792397345

.6388889895
.5466561294
.2840659518
.2096111775
.7827769142
.7787959459
.6958584068

Step 1 Define how you will do the simulation.
- Generate random numbers on a calculator.
- Since you answer true or false at random, you have a 50% chance of guessing correctly on each question. So let half of the digits represent correct answers. For example, let even digits represent correct answers.
- Since there are four questions, group the random digits in groups of four. List 50 groups to represent taking the test 50 times.

Step 2 Conduct the simulation. Underline groups with at least three even digits.

8767	0447	4672	0872	8315	6495	8778	8634	6243	5756
8958	2295	6246	1520	8491	1214	8495	7450	7068	5798
5584	4142	8990	7101	9949	1991	0625	3347	6158	1612
4792	3973	4563	8888	9895	5466	5612	9428	4065	9518
2096	1117	7578	2776	9142	7787	9594	5969	5858	4068

Step 3 Interpret the simulation. Since 15 of the 50 groups represent at least three correct answers, $P(\text{at least 3 correct}) = \frac{15}{50} = 0.3$.

This experimental probability of getting at least three correct answers is 30%.

✓ Quick Check **2** What is the experimental probability of getting all four answers correct?

When you roll a number cube, the possible outcomes are 1, 2, 3, 4, 5, and 6. The set of all possible outcomes is called the **sample space.** You can calculate theoretical probability as a ratio of outcomes.

Key Concepts

Definition	**Theoretical Probability**

If a sample space has n equally likely outcomes and an event A occurs in m of these outcomes, then the **theoretical probability** of event A is $P(A) = \frac{m}{n}$.

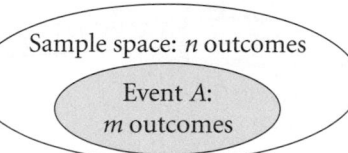
Sample space: n outcomes
Event A: m outcomes

3 **EXAMPLE** **Finding Theoretical Probability**

Find the theoretical probability of getting an even number when you roll a number cube.

The even outcomes are 2, 4, and 6.

3 outcomes result in an even number. → $\frac{3}{6}$ ← **6 equally likely outcomes are in the sample space.**

$= \frac{1}{2}$

 **Quick Check** **3** Find the theoretical probability of getting a prime number when you roll a number cube.

4 **EXAMPLE** **Real-World  Connection**

Biology Fold your hands so your fingers interlace. Do you naturally place your left or right thumb on top? Placing your left thumb on top is a dominant genetic trait.

When a parent has both a dominant and a recessive gene, then the two genes are equally likely to be passed to a child. If you have one or two dominant genes, you normally place your left thumb on top.

Suppose a child has parents who both have just one dominant gene. What is the theoretical probability that the child will naturally place the left thumb on top?

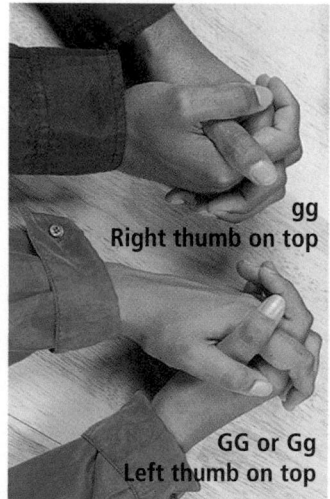

gg
Right thumb on top

GG or Gg
Left thumb on top

Make a table. Let G represent the dominant gene (left thumb on top). Let g represent the recessive gene (right thumb on top).

The sample space {GG, Gg, Gg, gg} contains four equally likely outcomes. Three outcomes have at least one G. So P(left thumb on top) $= \frac{3}{4}$.

		Gene from Mother	
		G	g
Gene from Father	G	GG	Gg
	g	Gg	gg

The theoretical probability that the child will naturally place the left thumb on top is $\frac{3}{4}$, or 75%.

 **Quick Check** **4** What is the theoretical probability that a child of the parents in Example 4 places the right thumb on top?

Sometimes you can use areas to find theoretical probability.

5 EXAMPLE **Finding Geometric Probability**

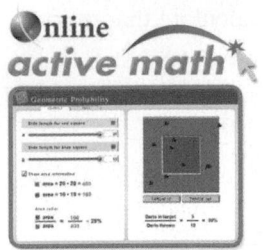

For: Probability Activity
Use: Interactive Textbook, 1-6

Geometry Suppose that all the points on the circular dartboard shown at the right are equally likely to be hit by a dart you have thrown. Find the probability of scoring at least ten points.

P(at least 10 points)

$$= \frac{\text{area of circle with radius } 2r}{\text{area of circle with radius } 4r}$$

$$= \frac{\pi(2r)^2}{\pi(4r)^2}$$

$$= \frac{4\pi r^2}{16\pi r^2} = \frac{1}{4}$$

Width of each ring = r.

● The theoretical probability of scoring at least ten points is $\frac{1}{4}$, or 25%.

✓ Quick Check **5** Use the dartboard from Example 5. Find each probability.
a. P(scoring 20 points)   **b.** P(scoring 5 points)

EXERCISES

For more exercises, see *Extra Skill and Word Problem Practice.*

Practice and Problem Solving

A **Practice by Example**

Example 1
(page 40)

1. A class tossed coins and recorded 161 heads and 179 tails. What is the experimental probability of heads? Of tails?

2. Another class rolled number cubes. Their results are shown in the table. What is the experimental probability of rolling each number?

Number	1	2	3	4	5	6
Occurrences	42	44	45	44	47	46

Example 2
(page 40)

For Exercises 3–5, define a simulation by telling how you represent correct answers, incorrect answers, and the quiz. Use your simulation to find each experimental probability.

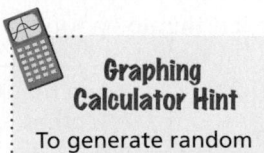
Graphing Calculator Hint

To generate random numbers, press
MATH ◀ 1 ENTER .

3. If you guess the answers at random, what is the probability of getting at least two correct answers on a five-question true-or-false quiz?

4. If you guess the answers at random, what is the probability of getting at least three correct answers on a five-question true-or-false quiz ?

5. A five-question multiple-choice quiz has five choices for each answer. What is the probability of correctly guessing at random exactly one correct answer? Exactly two correct answers? Exactly three correct answers? (*Hint:* You could let any two digits represent correct answers, and the other digits represent wrong answers.)

Example 3
(page 41)

A jar contains 30 red marbles, 50 blue marbles, and 20 white marbles. You pick one marble from the jar at random. Find each theoretical probability.

6. P(red)   7. P(blue)   8. P(not white)   9. P(red or blue)

A bag contains 36 red, 48 green, 22 yellow, and 19 purple blocks. You pick one block from the bag at random. Find each theoretical probability.

10. *P*(green)   **11.** *P*(purple)   **12.** *P*(not yellow)

13. *P*(green or yellow)   **14.** *P*(yellow or not green)

Example 4
(page 41)

For each situation, find the sample space and the theoretical probability that a child will naturally place the left thumb on top.

15. The father has gene pair gg and the mother has Gg.

16. The father has gene pair gg and the mother has GG.

Example 5
(page 42)

 Geometry **Suppose that a dart lands at random on the dartboard shown at the right. Find each theoretical probability.**

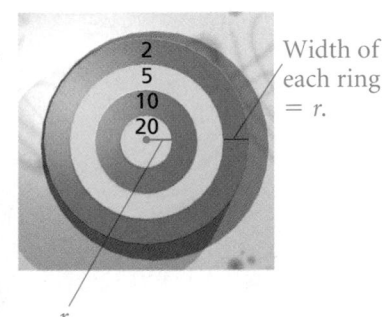

Width of each ring = *r*.

17. The dart lands in the bull's-eye.

18. The dart lands in a green region.

19. The dart scores at least 10 points.

20. The dart scores less than 10 points.

B **Apply Your Skills**

21. The common interpretation of Murphy's Law is, If something can go wrong, it will. Assume that Murphy's Law applies to the following situations, and estimate each probability as either 0 or 1.
a. *P*(your dog chews up your homework after you've finished it)
b. *P*(your teacher accepts your excuse for not having your homework)

22. Multiple Choice A caterer knows that, on average, there will be one broken egg in every 3 cartons. A carton contains 12 eggs. The caterer plans to serve 1200 eggs at a breakfast. What is the best estimate for the number of cartons the caterer should buy?

   Ⓐ 97 cartons   Ⓑ 100 cartons   Ⓒ 103 cartons   Ⓓ 112 cartons

Random Number Table		
31504	51648	40613
79321	80927	42404
15594	84675	68591
34178	00460	31754
49676	58733	00884
85400	72294	22551
22547	86066	93114
85211	07790	20890
21339	09414	51549
13843	18407	87043
34990	16214	46849
11390	01322	82656
45950	37521	77417

23. Use the random number table at the left to simulate tossing a coin 50 times. Find the experimental probability that the outcome of a coin toss is heads.

In a class of 147 students, 95 are taking math (M), 73 are taking science (S), and 52 are taking both math and science. One student is picked at random. Find each probability.

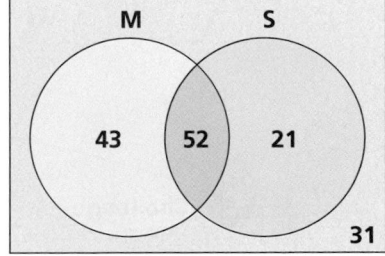

24. *P*(taking math or science or both)

25. *P*(not taking math)

26. *P*(taking math but not science)

27. *P*(taking neither math nor science)

Suppose you roll a number cube. Find each theoretical probability.

28. *P*(5)   **29.** *P*(an even number)

30. *P*(a number less than 5)   **31.** *P*(8)

32. *P*(a number greater than 5)   **33.** *P*(a number less than 8)

**Suppose you select a number at random from the sample space
{1, 2, 3, 4, 5, 6, 7, 8, 9}. Find each theoretical probability.**

34. P(the number is a multiple of 3)   **35.** P(the number is less than 5)

36. P(the number is prime)   **37.** P(the number is even)

38. Suppose you roll two number cubes.
    a. What is the sample space?
    b. How many outcomes are there?
    c. What is the theoretical probability of getting a sum of 12?
    d. What is the theoretical probability of getting a sum of 7?

39. Sports The batter's strike zone depends on the height and stance of the batter. Find the geometric probability that a baseball thrown at random within the batter's strike zone as shown in the figure below will be a high-inside strike. This is one of the hardest pitches to hit!

GO Online
Homework Video Tutor

Visit: PHSchool.com
Web Code: age-0106

40. a. Sports Team A has won one game and team B has won three games in a World Series. What is the experimental probability that team A wins the next game? That team B wins the next game?
    b. Critical Thinking Do you think that experimental probability is a good predictor of the winner of the next game? Explain.

41. Writing Explain what you would need to know to determine the theoretical probability that a five-digit postal ZIP code ends in 1.

42. Suppose you choose a two-digit number at random. What is the theoretical probability that its square root is an integer?

43. Assume that an event is neither certain nor impossible. Then the odds in favor of the event are the ratio of the number of favorable outcomes to the number of unfavorable outcomes.
    a. If the odds in favor of the event are a to b or $\frac{a}{b}$, what is the probability of the event?
    b. If the probability of the event is $\frac{a}{b}$, what are the odds in favor of the event?
    c. Would you rather play a game where your odds of winning are $\frac{1}{2}$, or a game where your probability of winning is $\frac{1}{2}$? Explain.

44. Open-Ended Use a telephone book. Select 50 telephone numbers at random and record the first three digits (the "exchange") of each number. Summarize your results using probability statements.

45. On a TV game show, you want to win a prize that is hidden behind one of three doors. You choose one door, but before it is opened the host opens another door and shows that the prize is not there. Now you can switch to the other unopened door or stick with your original choice.

   a. Find the experimental probability of winning the prize if you stick with your original choice. (*Hint:* Simulate the doors with index cards and the prize with a mark on one side of one card. One person can act as the host and another as the contestant.)

   b. Find the experimental probability of winning if you switch to the other door.

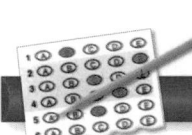

Test Prep

Multiple Choice

46. What is the theoretical probability of getting a 2 or a 3 when rolling a number cube?

   A. $\frac{1}{2}$ **B.** $\frac{1}{3}$ **C.** $\frac{1}{4}$ **D.** $\frac{1}{6}$

47. How many outcomes are in the sample space for rolling a number cube and tossing a coin?

   F. 2   **G.** 6   **H.** 12   **J.** 24

48. The random number table simulates an experiment where you toss a coin 90 times. Even digits represent heads and odd digits represent tails. What is the experimental probability, to the nearest percent, of the coin coming up heads?

   A. 45%   **B.** 50%

   C. 54%   **D.** 56%

Random Number Table		
31504	51648	40613
79321	80927	42404
15594	84675	68591
34178	00460	31754
49676	58733	00884
85400	72294	22551

Short Response

49. What is the sample space for spinning the spinner at the right twice? Are all the outcomes equally likely?

50. For the spinner at the right, what is the probability of spinning a 1 on both spins? Explain.

Extended Response

51. For the spinner at the right, which is more likely on two spins, an even sum or a sum that is not prime? Include all the steps of your solution.

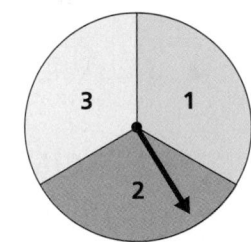

Mixed Review

Lesson 1-5

Solve each absolute value equation. Check your answers.

52. $|x + 3| = 9$ **53.** $|3x - 5| = 10$ **54.** $|2x + 7| + 3 = 22$

55. $|3x - 6| - 7 = 14$ **56.** $|2x + 3| - 9 = 14$ **57.** $|6 - 5x| = 18$

Lesson 1-5

Solve each absolute value inequality.

58. $2|x| - 3 \geq 5$ **59.** $|2x - 4| + 16 \leq 24$ **60.** $|3x - 5| - 2 > 0$

61. $|2x + 4| - 6 < 0$ **62.** $2|x + 3| \geq 10$ **63.** $6|x + 9| \leq 36$

Some tests require that you enter numerical answers in a grid. After finding an answer, write it in the top row of the grid. Then fill in the corresponding bubbles below.

EXAMPLE

A rabbit weighs one pound less than eight times the weight of a guinea pig. The rabbit weighs nine pounds. What is the weight in pounds of the guinea pig?

First find the answer by writing and solving an equation.

$8x - 1 = 9$

$8x = 10$

$x = \frac{10}{8} \text{ or } \frac{5}{4} \text{ or } 1.25$

Enter the answer in the grid. You could write it as $\frac{10}{8}$, as $\frac{5}{4}$, or as 1.25. Do not enter the answer as a mixed number. If you enter 1 1/4, it would be interpreted as $\frac{11}{4}$.

Note how to enter fraction bars and decimal points.

EXERCISES

Use a response grid to answer each question.

1. What is the value of $\frac{x^2 + 1}{2.5}$ when $x = 1.5$?

2. A music tape costs a dollar more than half the price of a CD. The music tape costs $5.99. What is the cost in dollars of the CD?

3. What is the solution of the equation $3(x - 1) - (x + 2) = 9$?

4. A number is selected at random from the sample space {10, 11, 12, 13, 14, 15}. What is the probability that the number is a multiple of 3?

5. Write a 4-digit number that is a multiple of both 5 and 6.

6. Write a rational number between $\sqrt{5}$ and $\sqrt{6}$.

7. 44.8 is what percent of 128?

8. The length of a picture frame must be at least 4.25 cm greater than the frame's width. The width is 19.5 cm. What is the minimum perimeter, in centimeters, of the picture frame?

Chapter Review

Vocabulary Review

🔊 absolute value (p. 33)
absolute value of a real
   number (p. 8)
additive inverse (p. 7)
algebraic expression (p. 12)
coefficient (p. 13)
compound inequality (p. 28)

evaluate (p. 12)
experimental probability (p. 40)
extraneous solution (p. 34)
multiplicative inverse (p. 7)
opposite (p. 7)
reciprocal (p. 7)
sample space (p. 41)

simulation (p. 40)
solution of an equation (p. 18)
term (p. 13)
theoretical probability (p. 41)
tolerance (p. 36)
variable (p. 12)
variable expression (p. 12)

Go Online
PHSchool.com
For: Vocabulary quiz
Web Code: agj-0151

Choose the correct vocabulary term to complete each sentence.

1. The opposite of a number is also called its _?_ .

2. The _?_ is the set of all possible outcomes of an experiment.

3. The _?_ makes an equation true.

4. A pair of inequalities joined by *and* or *or* is called a(n) _?_ .

5. _?_ is another name for a multiplicative inverse of a number.

6. The _?_ of an event is the ratio of occurrences to trials.

7. The _?_ of an event is the ratio of possible event outcomes to total possible outcomes.

8. A possible solution that does not satisfy the original equation is a(n) _?_ .

9. You can use a(n) _?_ to find experimental probabilities.

10. A number's distance from zero on the number line is its _?_ .

Skills and Concepts

1-1 Objectives

▼ To graph and order real numbers (p. 4)

▼ To identify and use properties of real numbers (p. 7)

The natural numbers, whole numbers, integers, rational numbers, and irrational numbers are all subsets of the real numbers. Each real number corresponds to a point on the number line. A real number's distance from zero on the number line is its absolute value.

For both addition and multiplication, real numbers satisfy the properties of closure, associativity, and commutativity. Real numbers have **additive inverses (opposites)**. Nonzero real numbers have **multiplicative inverses (reciprocals)**. They also have additive and multiplicative identities. Real numbers satisfy the Distributive Property.

To which sets of numbers does each number belong?

11. 8.1π **12.** -79 **13.** $\sqrt{121}$ **14.** $\sqrt{200}$ **15.** $12\frac{7}{8}$

Compare each pair of numbers. Use < or >.

16. $-\frac{2}{3}, -\frac{3}{2}$ **17.** $\sqrt{6}, 2.\overline{3}$ **18.** $0.45, 0.405$ **19.** $-7, |-7|$

Find the opposite and reciprocal of each number. Then graph all three numbers on a number line.

20. -3.4　　　　　**21.** $4 + \pi$　　　　　**22.** $1\frac{7}{8}$　　　　　**23.** $\sqrt{12}$

Open-Ended Write an equation that illustrates each property of real numbers.

24. The Identity Property of Multiplication

25. The Associative Property of Addition

26. The Distributive Property

27. The Commutative Property of Multiplication

28. The Identity Property of Addition

1-2 and 1-3 Objectives

▼ To evaluate algebraic expressions (p. 12)

▼ To simplify algebraic expressions (p. 13)

▼ To solve equations (p. 18)

▼ To solve problems by writing equations (p. 20)

You **evaluate** an **algebraic expression** by substituting numbers for the **variables**. You simplify an algebraic expression by combining like **terms**, using the appropriate properties. To find the **solutions of an equation**, use the properties of equality. To check for **extraneous solutions**, substitute in the original equation. Some equations may have no solutions. Some equations are true for all real numbers.

29. Evaluate $-x^2 + |x - 10|$ for $x = 2$.

30. Evaluate $3t(t + 2) - (3t^2 + 5t)$ for $t = 19$.

31. Simplify $-(3a - 2b) - 3(-a - b)$.

Solve each equation for *x*. State any restrictions.

32. $2x - 5 = 17$　　　　　　　　**33.** $8 - \frac{1}{2}x = 3$

34. $3x = 4x - 5$　　　　　　　　**35.** $0.1x + 1.4 = 1.2x - 3$

36. $\frac{7 - x}{3} = 5$　　　　　　　　**37.** $\frac{x + a}{b} = \frac{1}{a}$

Write an equation to solve each problem.

38. Geometry The lengths of the sides of a rectangle are in the ratio $5 : 3$. The perimeter of the rectangle is 32 cm. Find the length of each side.

39. Two planes left St. Louis for Los Angeles at the same time. After 4 h they were 700 mi apart. The slower plane traveled at 350 mi/h. What was the speed of the faster plane?

40. Geometry The measures of an angle and its supplement differ by 40°. Find the measures of the angles.

1-4 Objectives

▼ To solve and graph inequalities (p. 26)

▼ To solve and write compound inequalities (p. 28)

You can solve inequalities using properties that are similar to the properties for equations. An important difference is that multiplying or dividing each side of an inequality by a negative number reverses the inequality symbol. Just as with equations, some inequalities are true for all real numbers, and some have no solutions. If a **compound inequality** uses *and*, the solutions must satisfy both inequalities. If a compound inequality uses *or*, the solutions satisfy either one or both of the inequalities.

Solve each inequality. Graph the solution.

41. $4 - 5z \geq 2$ **42.** $2(5 - 3x) < x - 4(3 - x)$ **43.** $0.3(y - 2) > \frac{1}{2}(6 - y)$

Solve each compound inequality. Graph the solution.

44. $5 \leq 9 - 4x \leq 13$ **45.** $3 \geq 2x$ or $x - 4 > 2$ **46.** $6y > 2$ and $y - 5 \geq -2y$

47. A publisher estimates that the cost of publishing a book is from $980,000 to $1,240,000. So far, $824,150 has been spent. Use a compound inequality to describe the amount A that the publisher can still spend while remaining within the estimate.

1-5 Objectives

▼ To solve absolute value equations (p. 33)

▼ To solve absolute value inequalities (p. 35)

You can rewrite an equation or inequality that involves the absolute value of an **algebraic expression** as a compound sentence. You must consider both cases of the definition of absolute value. Check for **extraneous solutions.**

Solve each equation. Check for extraneous solutions.

48. $|2x + 8| = 3x + 7$ **49.** $|3x - 5| = 4 + 2x$ **50.** $|x - 4| + 3 = 1$

Solve each inequality. Graph the solution.

51. $|3x - 2| + 4 \leq 7$ **52.** $4|y - 9| > 36$ **53.** $\frac{2}{5}|3x - 3| - 4 > 2$

54. The specification for a length x is 43.6 cm with a tolerance of 0.1 cm. Write the specification as an absolute value inequality.

1-6 Objectives

▼ To find experimental probabilities (p. 39)

▼ To find theoretical probabilities (p. 41)

The probability of an event can be expressed as a number from 0% (impossible) to 100% (certain).

Experimental probability is the ratio of two numbers. The first is the observed number of times an experiment results in a particular event. The second is the number of trials. **Simulation** uses random numbers or other models to determine an experimental probability.

Theoretical probability in a sample space of equally likely outcomes is also the ratio of two numbers. The first is the number of outcomes corresponding to the particular event. The second is the number of elements in the sample space, which is the set of all possible outcomes. Geometric probability is computed as a ratio of areas.

Suppose you select a number at random from the sample space $\{-3, -2, -1, 0, 1, 2, 3, 4\}$. Find each probability.

55. P(a positive number)   **56.** P(a number less than 2)

57. P(an even number)   **58.** P(a multiple of 3)

59. Games You have won five games of checkers and your opponent has won three. What is the experimental probability of your winning?

60. Tests A five-question multiple-choice quiz has four choices for each answer. Find the experimental probability of getting exactly three correct answers if you guess the answers at random. Define a simulation using the random number table on page 43. Use your simulation to find the experimental probability.

Chapter Test

Go Online
PHSchool.com
For: Chapter Test
Web Code: aga-0152

 1. Writing Describe the relationships among these sets of numbers: natural numbers, whole numbers, integers, rational numbers, irrational numbers, and real numbers.

2. Justifying Steps Justify each step by identifying the property used.

$$t + 5(t + 1) = t + (5t + 5)$$
$$= (t + 5t) + 5$$
$$= (1t + 5t) + 5$$
$$= (1 + 5)t + 5$$
$$= 6t + 5$$

Evaluate each expression for $x = 5$.

3. $\frac{5}{3}(3x - 6) - (6 - 4x)$

4. $3(x^2 - 4) + 7(x - 2)$

5. $x - 2x + 3x - 4x + 5x$

Simplify each expression.

6. $a^2 + a + a^2$

7. $2x + 3y - 5x + 2y$

8. $5(a - 2b) - 3(a - 2b)$

9. $3[2(x - 3) + 2] + 5(x - 3)$

Solve each equation.

10. $4y - 6 = 2y + 8$

11. $3(2z + 1) = 35$

12. $5(3w - 2) - 7 = 23$

13. $t - 2(3 - 2t) = 2t + 9$

14. $5(s - 12) - 24 = 3(s + 2)$

15. $7(3 - 0.5k) = 3k - 5$

Solve each equation for x. State any restrictions.

16. $ax - bx = 2a$ **17.** $\frac{x}{c} + c = 4c$

18. $\frac{x - 5}{a} + 1 = b$ **19.** $ax + 2 = bx + c$

20. The lateral surface area of a cylinder is given by the formula $S = 2\pi rh$. Solve this equation for r.

Write an equation to solve each problem.

21. Savings Briana and her sister Molly both want to buy the same model bicycle. Briana needs $73 more before she can afford the bike. Molly needs $65 more. If they combine their money, they will have just enough to buy one bicycle that they could share. What is the cost of the bicycle?

22. Musical There is only one freshman in the cast of the high school musical. There are 6 sophomores and 11 juniors. One third of the cast are seniors. How many seniors are in the musical?

Solve each inequality or equation. Graph the solution.

23. $3x + 17 \geq 5$

24. $25 - 2x < 11$

25. $7t > 4t + 3(1 - t)$

26. $\frac{3}{8}x < -6$ or $5x > 2$

27. $2 < 10 - 4d < 6$

28. $4 - x = |2 - 3x|$

29. $|4x + 4| = 8x + 16$

30. $|5 - p| \leq 2$

31. $5|3w + 2| - 3 > 7$

Suppose you select a number at random from the sample space {5, 6, 7, 8, 9, 10, 11, 12, 13, 14}. Find each probability.

32. $P(\text{greater than } 10)$

33. $P(\text{multiple of } 30)$

34. $P(\text{less than } 7 \text{ or greater than } 10)$

35. $P(\text{integer})$

36. Open-Ended Your teacher selects at random two days out of every five days to give a "pop" quiz. Define a simulation to find the experimental probability that you will get a pop quiz on two consecutive days. Then use your simulation to find the probability.

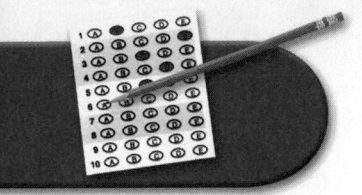

Standardized Test Prep

Reading Comprehension Read the passage below. Then answer the questions on the basis of what is *stated* or *implied* in the passage.

A-Frame Bookshelf Do-it-yourselfers can build large-capacity, self-supporting bookshelves that are easy to set up and break down. They are called A-frame bookshelves, because the frame and shelves form an A.

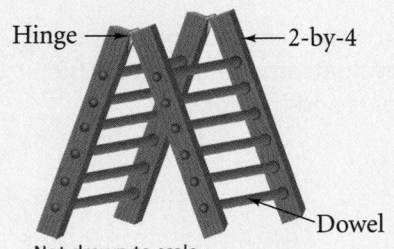

Hinge — 2-by-4

Dowel

Not drawn to scale

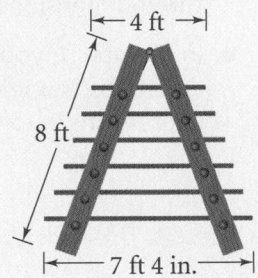

|← 4 ft →|

8 ft

|← 7 ft 4 in. →|

The frame uses four 2-by-4's, each 8 feet long. They are joined in pairs by a hinge. Holes are drilled through the 2-by-4's at 1-foot intervals. Round dowels, $\frac{3}{4}$ of an inch in diameter, connect the two parts of the frame. The shelves are fastened to the dowels. Each shelf is shorter than the one below it by the same amount. In the six-shelf unit shown above, the top shelf is 4 feet long and the bottom shelf is 7 feet 4 inches long.

1. What is the difference in length between each shelf and the one directly below it?
   - Ⓐ 4 in. Ⓑ 6 in. Ⓒ 8 in. Ⓓ $14\frac{2}{3}$in.

2. How far beyond each edge of the top shelf does each edge of the bottom shelf extend?
   - Ⓕ 4 in. Ⓖ 8 in.
   - Ⓗ 1 ft 8 in. Ⓙ 3 ft 6 in.

3. What is the total length of the shelves?
   - Ⓐ 29 ft 8 in. Ⓑ 32 ft
   - Ⓒ 33 ft 4 in. Ⓓ 34 ft

4. Suppose you can buy 2-by-4's in any length for $.29 per foot. About how much will you pay for the 2-by-4's for the bookcase?
   - Ⓕ $5 Ⓖ $10 Ⓗ $15 Ⓙ $20

5. Suppose the 2-by-4's are 2 in. thick, the shelves are 8 in. deep, and the dowels are cut flush with the front and back faces of the bookshelf. If the dowels are sold in 4-ft lengths, how many lengths would you have to buy for the bookcase?
   - Ⓐ 2 Ⓑ 3 Ⓒ 4 Ⓓ 12

For Questions 6–10, use the information below. Show your work.

A shorter bookshelf uses 2-by-4's that are 6 ft long, and has five shelves. The top shelf is 3 ft long and the bottom shelf is 6 ft 8 in. long.

6. What is the difference in length from each shelf to the one below it?

7. How much does the bottom shelf extend to the right beyond the right-most edge of the top shelf?

8. What is the total length of shelving in the bookshelf?

9. In a four-shelf bookshelf, the bottom shelf is 8 ft long. The top shelf is 5 ft $1\frac{1}{2}$ in. long. How long are the other two shelves?

10. Which is greater, the average length of the shelves in Questions 6–8 or the average length of the shelves in Question 9? How much greater is it?

What You've Learned

● In first-year algebra, you learned to interpret and solve problems algebraically.

● In geometry, you learned to analyze and manipulate two- and three-dimensional figures.

● In Chapter 1, you learned to represent relationships using variables. You learned to evaluate and simplify variable expressions involving integers and fractions.

 **Check Your Readiness**   **for Help** to the Lesson in green.

Graphing Numbers on the Number Line (Lesson 1-1)

Graph each group of numbers on a number line.

1. $2, -\frac{7}{4}, -1, \frac{15}{2}$
2. $0, \frac{2}{3}, -\sqrt{2}, -3$
3. $-\frac{5}{4}, \sqrt{7}, 2.\overline{6}, 4$

Simplifying Expressions (Lesson 1-2)

Simplify by combining like terms.

4. $7s - s$
5. $3a + b + a$
6. $xy - y + x$

7. $0.5g + g$
8. $4t - (t + 3t)$
9. $b - 2(1 + c - b)$

10. $5f - (5d - f)$
11. $2(h + 2g) - (g - h)$
12. $-(3z - 5) + z$

13. $(2 - d)g - 3d(4 + g)$
14. $5v - 3(2 - v)$
15. $7t - 3s(2 + t) + s$

Solving Absolute-Value Inequalities (Lesson 1-5)

Solve each absolute-value inequality. Graph the solution.

16. $|x - 3| < 5$
17. $|2a - 1| \geq 2a + 1$
18. $|3x + 4| > -4x - 3$

19. $|3x + 1| + 1 > 12$
20. $3|d - 4| \leq 13 - d$
21. $-\frac{1}{3}|f + 3| + 2 \geq -5$

Probability (Lesson 1-6)

A bag contains 12 red, 15 green, 10 yellow, 25 purple, and 2 black blocks. Find each theoretical probability for one block selected at random.

22. $P(\text{green})$
23. $P(\text{black})$
24. $P(\text{red or yellow})$

25. $P(\text{not red})$
26. $P(\text{not yellow})$
27. $P(\text{black or not red})$

Functions, Equations, and Graphs

Chapter 2

LESSONS

2-1 Relations and Functions

2-2 Linear Equations

2-3 Direct Variation

2-4 Using Linear Models

2-5 Absolute Value Functions and Graphs

2-6 Families of Functions

2-7 Two-Variable Inequalities

Key Vocabulary

- absolute value function (p. 88)
- constant of variation (p. 72)
- dependent variable (p. 62)
- direct variation (p. 72)
- domain (p. 56)
- function (p. 57)
- independent variable (p. 62)
- linear equation (p. 62)
- linear function (p. 62)
- linear inequality (p. 101)
- parent function (p. 93)
- point-slope form (p. 65)
- range (p. 56)
- relation (p. 55)
- slope (p. 64)
- slope-intercept form (p. 65)
- standard form (p. 63)
- translation (p. 93)
- vertical-line test (p. 57)
- x-intercept (p. 63)
- y-intercept (p. 63)

What You'll Learn Next

- In Chapter 2, you will move from simplifying variable expressions and solving one-variable equations and inequalities to working with two-variable equations and inequalities.

- You will learn how to represent function relationships by writing and graphing linear equations and inequalities.

- By graphing data and trend lines, you will understand how the slope of a line can be interpreted in real-world situations.

Activity Lab Applying what you learn, on pages 114–115 you will do activities involving bridges.

53

The Coordinate Plane

There is a one-to-one correspondence between the points in the coordinate plane and the set of ordered pairs (x, y), where x and y are real numbers. The first number is the x-coordinate, or abscissa. The abscissa gives the horizontal position of a point. The second number is the y-coordinate, or ordinate. The ordinate gives the vertical position of a point.

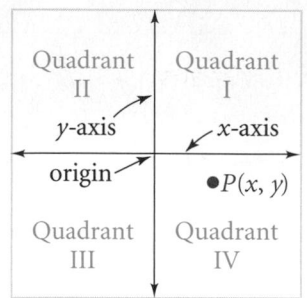

1 EXAMPLE **Graphing Points**

Graph $(4, 3)$ and $(-4, -3)$.

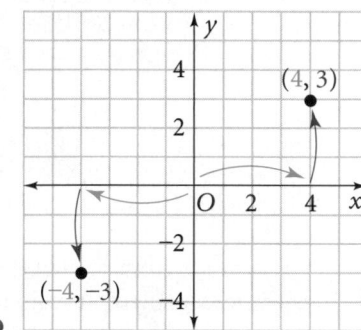

Graph and label each ordered pair.

You can write the coordinates of a point if you are given its graph.

2 EXAMPLE **Writing Coordinates**

Write the coordinates of each point in the graph.

The points are $A(2, 4)$, $B(3, 0)$, $C(-4, 0)$, $D(0, -3)$, $E(-5, 4)$, $F\left(4, \frac{1}{2}\right)$, $G(0, 0)$, and $H\left(-3, -3\frac{1}{2}\right)$.

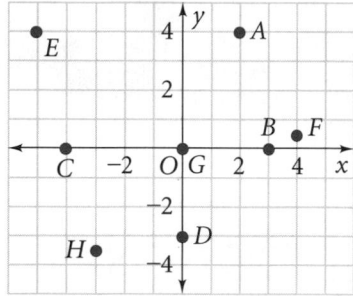

EXERCISES

Graph and label each ordered pair. Name the quadrant or axis where each point lies.

1. $(5, -2)$ **2.** $(-3, 4)$ **3.** $\left(-4, -2\frac{1}{2}\right)$

4. $\left(5\frac{1}{2}, 0\right)$ **5.** $(5, 2)$ **6.** $(0, -3)$

Write the coordinates of each point in the graph at the right.

7. C **8.** G **9.** J **10.** A

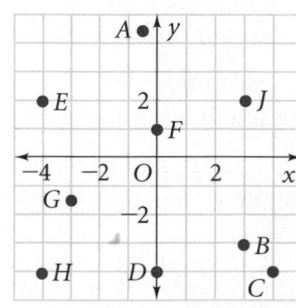

Relations and Functions

What You'll Learn

• To graph relations
• To identify functions

...And Why

To write a function for the area of a square, as in Example 6

Graph each ordered pair on the coordinate plane.

1. $(-4, -8)$ **2.** $(3, 6)$ **3.** $(0, 0)$ **4.** $(-1, 3)$ **5.** $(-6, 5)$

Evaluate each expression for $x = -1, 0, 2,$ and 5.

6. $x + 2$ **7.** $-2x + 3$ **8.** $2x^2 + 1$ **9.** $|x - 3|$

🔊 **New Vocabulary**   • relation   • domain   • range   • mapping diagram
• function   • vertical-line test   • function notation

---

1 Graphing Relations

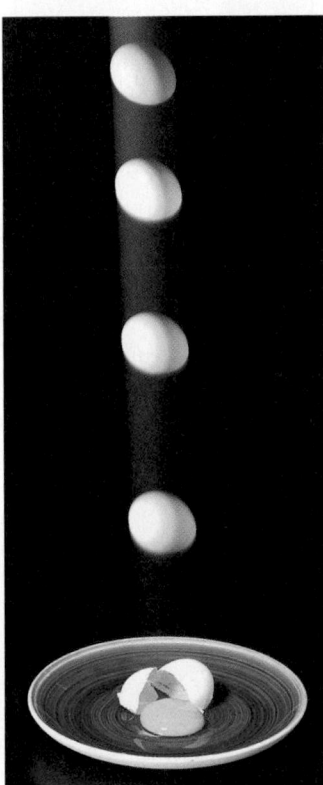

A camera recorded the egg's height at various times during its fall.

Suppose you use a motion detector to track an egg as it drops from 10 ft above the ground. The motion detector stores input values (times) and output values (heights). A **relation** is a set of pairs of input and output values. You can write a relation as a set of ordered pairs.

input (time in seconds) → {0   0.1   0.2   0.3   0.4}
                              ↓   ↓   ↓   ↓   ↓

relation → {(0, 10), (0.1, 9.8), (0.2, 9.4), (0.3, 8.6), (0.4, 7.4)}
              ↑   ↑   ↑   ↑   ↑

output (height in feet) → {10   9.8   9.4   8.6   7.4}

You can graph a relation on a coordinate plane.

1 EXAMPLE Graphing a Relation

Graph the relation $\{(-2, 4), (3, -2), (-1, 0), (1, 5)\}$.

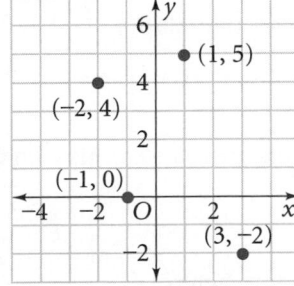

Graph and label each ordered pair.

✓ **Quick Check** ❶ Graph each relation.

a. $\{(0, 4), (-2, 3), (-1, 3), (-2, 2), (1, -3)\}$
b. $\{(-2, 1), (-1, 0), (0, 1), (1, 2)\}$

The **domain** of a relation is the set of all inputs, or *x*-coordinates of the ordered pairs. The **range** of a relation is the set of all outputs, or *y*-coordinates of the ordered pairs.

You can sometimes find the domain and range of a relation from its graph.

Backpacks or bookbags are used by 93% of students.

2 EXAMPLE **Finding Domain and Range**

Write the ordered pairs for the relation shown in the graph. Find the domain and range.

$\{(2, 4), (3, 4.5), (4, 7.5), (5, 7), (6, 5), (6, 7.5)\}$

The domain is $\{2, 3, 4, 5, 6\}$.

The range is $\{4, 4.5, 5, 7, 7.5\}$.

✓ **Quick Check** ❷ Find the domain and range of each relation.

a.
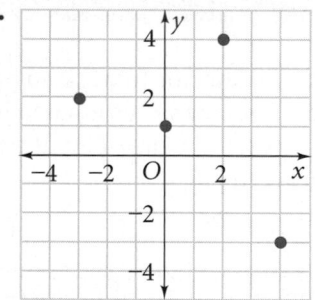

b.
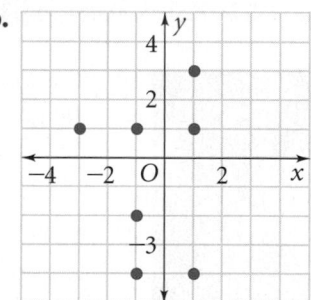

Another way to show a relation is to use a **mapping diagram,** which links elements of the domain with corresponding elements of the range. Write the elements of the domain in one region and the elements of the range in another. Draw arrows to show how each element from the domain is paired with elements from the range.

3 EXAMPLE **Making a Mapping Diagram**

Make a mapping diagram for the relation $\{(-1, -2), (3, 6), (-5, -10), (3, 2)\}$.

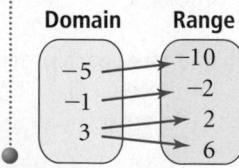

Pair the domain elements with the range elements.

✓ **Quick Check** ❸ Make a mapping diagram for each relation.

    a. $\{(0, 2), (1, 3), (2, 4)\}$

    b. $\{(2, 8), (-1, 5), (0, 8), (-1, 3), (-2, 3)\}$

A **function** is a relation in which each element of the domain is paired with exactly one element in the range.

4 EXAMPLE Identifying Functions

Determine whether each relation is a function.

a.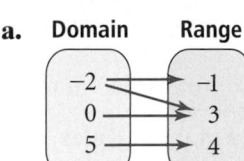

The element −2 of the domain is paired with both −1 and 3 of the range. The relation is *not* a function.

b.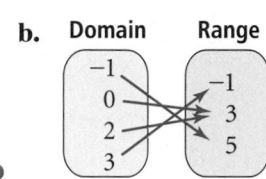

Each element of the domain is paired with exactly one element of the range. The relation is a function.

✓ **Quick Check** **4** Determine whether each relation is a function.

a. 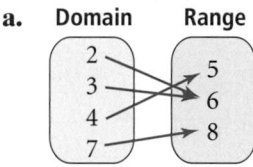   b.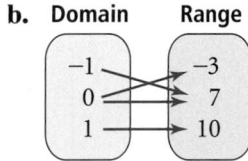

You can identify a function by its domain, its range, and the rule that relates the domain to the range. You can represent a function with a mapping diagram as in Example 4, part (b), or with a graph in the coordinate plane. Sometimes the graph of a function may be *discrete*, a collection of isolated points. Other times the graph may be *continuous*, an uninterrupted line or curve.

You can use the **vertical-line test** on the graph of a relation to tell whether the relation is a function. If a vertical line passes through at least two points on the graph, then one element of the domain is paired with more than one element of the range. The relation is *not* a function.

5 EXAMPLE Using the Vertical-Line Test

Use the vertical-line test to determine whether each graph represents a function.

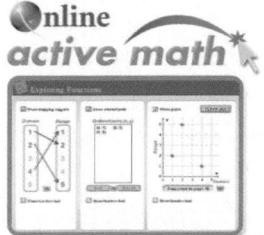

For: Exploring Functions Activity
Use: Interactive Textbook, 2-1

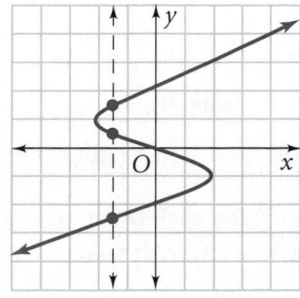

Vertical line
passes through

← 3 points   1 point →

← Not a function

A function →

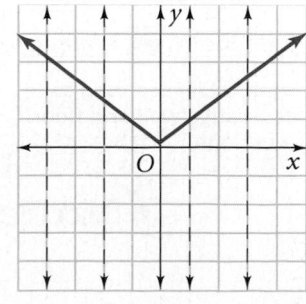

5 Use the vertical-line test to determine whether each graph represents a function.

a. 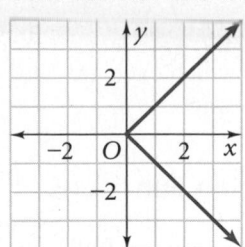 **b.** 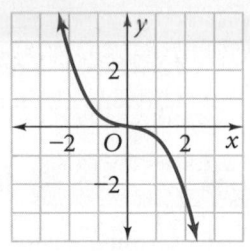 **c.**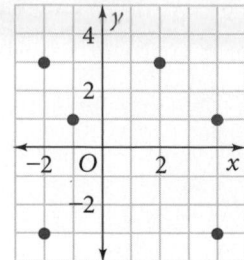

Video Tutor Help
Visit: PhSchool.com
Web Code: age-0775

A function rule expresses an output value in terms of an input value.

Examples of Function Rules

Input	Input	Input
↓	↓	↓
$y = 2x$	$f(x) = x + 5$	$C = \pi d$
↑	↑	↑
Output	Output	Output

You read the **function notation** $f(x)$ as "f of x" or "a function f of x." Note that $f(x)$ does *not* mean "f times x." When the value of x is 3, $f(3)$, read "f of 3," represents the value of the function at $x = 3$.

Input	Function	Output	Ordered Pair
5 ⟶	Subtract 1 ⟶	4	$(5, 4)$
a ⟶	Add 2 ⟶	$a + 2$	$(a, a + 2)$
3 ⟶	g ⟶	$g(3)$	$(3, g(3))$
x ⟶	f ⟶	$f(x)$	$(x, f(x))$

6 **EXAMPLE** **Real-World Connection**

Art The area of a square tile is a function of the length of a side of the square. Write a function rule for the area of a square. Evaluate the function for a square tile with side length 3.5 in.

Relate   area of a square   is   (side length)^2

Define Let s = the length of one side of the square tile.

Then $A(s)$ = the area of the square tile.

Write $A(s)$ = s^2

$A(3.5) = (3.5)^2$ **Substitute 3.5 for s.**

$= 12.25$ **Simplify.**

The area of a square tile with side length 3.5 in. is 12.25 in.^{2}.

Real-World Connection

Square tiles are used as decorative wall and floor coverings.

✓ **Quick Check** **6** Find $f(-3), f(0),$ and $f(5)$ for each function.

a. $f(x) = 3x - 5$ **b.** $f(a) = \frac{3}{4}a - 1$ **c.** $f(y) = -\frac{1}{5}y + \frac{3}{5}$

EXERCISES

For more exercises, see *Extra Skill and Word Problem Practice.*

Practice and Problem Solving

A Practice by Example

GO for
Help

Example 1
(page 55)

Graph each relation.

1. $\{(-1, 3), (-2, 1), (-3, -3), (-4, -5)\}$ 2. $\{(0, -2), (2, 0), (3, 1), (5, 3)\}$

3. $\left\{(-1, 0), \left(\frac{1}{2}, -1\right), \left(0, \frac{1}{2}\right), \left(-1, -\frac{1}{2}\right)\right\}$ 4. $\left\{\left(2\frac{1}{2}, 0\right), \left(-\frac{1}{2}, 0\right), (2, 0), (0, 0)\right\}$

Example 2
(page 56)

Write the ordered pairs for each relation. Find the domain and range.

5.
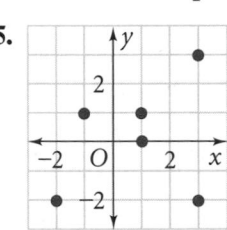

6.
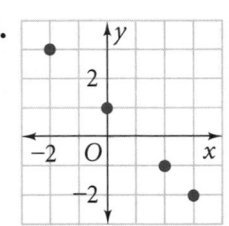

7.
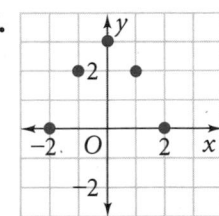

Example 3
(page 56)

Make a mapping diagram for each relation.

8. $\{(0, 0), (-1, -1), (-2, -8), (-3, -27)\}$ 9. $\{(-2, 8), (-1, 1), (0, 0), (1, 1), (2, 8)\}$

10. $\{(-\frac{1}{2}, 11), (0, 10), \left(\frac{1}{2}, 5\right), (1, 12)\}$ 11. $\{(5, 10), (10, 5), (15, 20), (20, 15)\}$

Example 4
(page 57)

Determine whether each relation is a function.

12. $\{(1, -2), (-2, 0), (-1, 2), (1, 3)\}$ 13. $\{(1, 1), (2, 2), (3, 5), (4, 10), (5, 15)\}$

14. $\left\{\left(17, \frac{15}{4}\right), \left(\frac{15}{4}, 17\right), \left(15, \frac{17}{4}\right), \left(\frac{17}{4}, 15\right)\right\}$ 15. $\left\{\left(-3, \frac{2}{5}\right), \left(-2, \frac{3}{5}\right), \left(\frac{3}{2}, -5\right), \left(5, \frac{2}{5}\right)\right\}$

Example 5
(page 57)

Use the vertical-line test to determine whether each graph represents a function.

16.
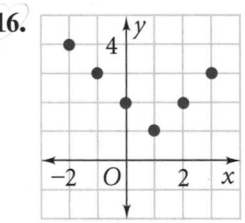

17.
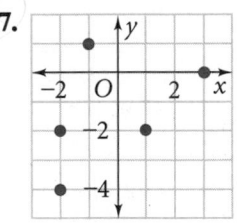

18.
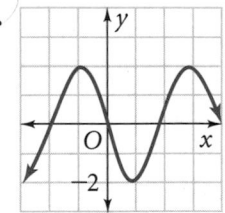

19.
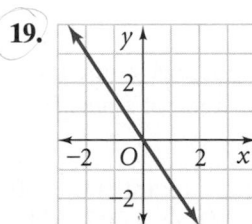

20.
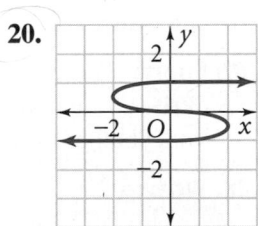

21.
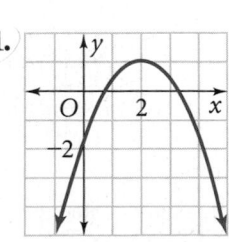

Example 6
(page 58)

For each function, find $f(-5)$, $f(-3)$, $f\left(\frac{1}{2}\right)$, and $f(4)$.

22. $f(a) = 2a + 3$ 23. $f(y) = -3y - 2$ 24. $f(z) = z + 9.5$

25. $f(x) = -x - 7$ 26. $f(d) = 1 - 4d$ 27. $f(x) = 2x - 3$

28. $f(h) = -6h - \frac{2}{3}$ 29. $f(x) = \frac{5}{6}x + \frac{1}{3}$ 30. $f(t) = \frac{1}{2}t - 2$

31. **Measurement** One meter equals about 39.37 in. Write a function rule for converting inches to meters. Evaluate the function for 59 in.

Graph each relation. Find the domain and range.

32. $\{(2,4),(3,5),(4,6),(5,7)\}$

33. $\{(-1,1),(-2,2),(-3,3),(-4,4)\}$

34. $\left\{\left(-\frac{1}{2},2\right),\left(2,\frac{1}{2}\right),\left(0,-\frac{1}{2}\right),\left(-\frac{1}{2},-2\right)\right\}$

35. $\left\{\left(\frac{3}{2},-\frac{1}{2}\right),\left(\frac{5}{2},\frac{1}{2}\right),\left(\frac{1}{2},\frac{1}{2}\right),\left(-\frac{3}{2},\frac{1}{2}\right)\right\}$

Find the domain and range of each relation and determine whether it is a function.

36. $\{(2,4),(4,8),(8,16)\}$

37. $\{(-1,2),(-2,5),(-2,7),(0,2),(9,2)\}$

38.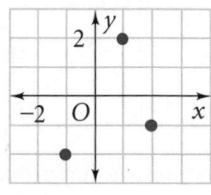

39.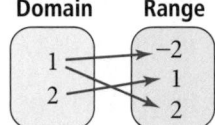

Match each relation with a model.

40. $\{(1,2),(-1,-2),(2,-1)\}$

41. $\{(2,1),(1,2),(1,-2)\}$

42. $\{(-1,2),(-2,1),(-1,-2)\}$

A.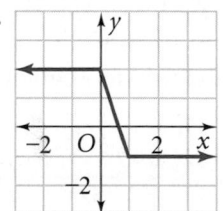

B.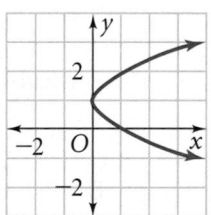

C.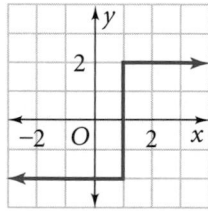

GO Online
Homework Video Tutor
Visit: PHSchool.com
Web Code: age-0201

Determine whether each graph represents *y* as a function of *x*.

43.

44.

45.

46. Geometry The volume of a cube is a function of the length of a side of the cube. Write a function for the volume of a cube. Find the volume of a cube with a side 13.5 cm long.

47. Sports The volume of a sphere is a function of the radius of the sphere. Write a function for the volume of a ball. Evaluate the function for a volleyball of radius 10.5 cm.

48. Writing Does the mapping diagram at the left represent a function? Explain.

49. Data Collection Draw a graph to show the relationship between the weight of a letter and the cost of postage. Is it a graph of a function? Explain.

Domain   Range

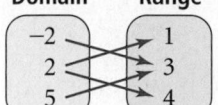

Suppose $f(x) = 2x + 5$ and $g(x) = -\frac{1}{3}x + 2$. Find each value. (*Hint:* For $2g(x)$, find $g(x)$ first, and then multiply the result by 2.)

50. $f(-4)$

51. $2g(7)$

52. $-2f(x+1)$

53. $\dfrac{f(1)}{g(3)}$

54. $\dfrac{f(-2)}{g(f(-2)+1)}$

C Challenge

For each relation, determine whether *y* is a function of *x*. Explain why or why not.

55. $y = 2x - 3$

56. $y^2 = x$

57. $x^2 = y - 3$

 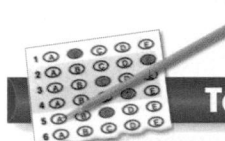
58. **Chemistry** The time required for a certain chemical reaction is related to the amount of catalyst present during the reaction. The domain of the relation is the number of grams of catalyst, and the range is the number of seconds required for a fixed amount of the chemical to react. The following relation is the data from several reactions: {(2, 180), (2.5, 6), (2.7, 0.05), (2.9, 0.001), (3.0, 6), (3.1, 15), (3.2, 37), (3.3, 176)}. Is the relation a function? If the domain and range were interchanged, would the relation be a function? Explain.

Suppose a and b are variables representing integers. Find the domain and range of each relation and determine whether it is a function. Justify your reasoning.

59.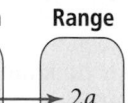

60.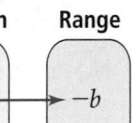

61.
Domain   Range

a ⟶ $2a$
   ⟶ $-2a$

Test Prep

Multiple Choice

62. Which graph models the relation {(−3, −1), (3, 1), (−3, 1), (3, −1)}?

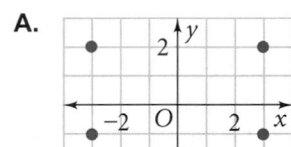

A.   B.   C.

63. Which relation is *not* a function?
 F. {(0, 9), (2, 3), (3, 2), (4, 1)}   **G.** {(3, 2), (4, 1), (0, 9), (3, 3)}
 H. {(0, 3), (2, 3), (3, 3), (4, 3)}   **J.** {(0, 3), (3, 2), (2, 4), (4, 6)}

Short Response

64. If $f(x) = -2x + 3$ and $g(x) = 4x - 3$, which is greater, $f(5)$ or $g(-2)$? Show your work.

Extended Response

65. Is the total surface area S of a cube a function of the edge c of the cube? If it is not a function, explain why not. If it is a function, write the function rule and then evaluate the function for a cube with edge 2.5 cm.

Mixed Review

Lesson 1-6

Find each probability for choosing a letter at random from the word *mathematics*.

66. $P(e)$ 67. $P(m)$ 68. $P(vowel)$ 69. $P(n)$

70. $P(a\ letter\ that\ occurs\ more\ than\ once)$ 71. $P(consonant)$ 72. $P(s\ or\ t)$

Lesson 1-5

Solve each equation or inequality. Graph the solution on a number line.

73. $|x - 4| = 10$ 74. $3 + |b| \leq 5$ 75. $|6 - y| > 0$

Skills Handbook

Find each percent of increase or decrease.

76. from 9 m to 10 m   77. from 1 gal to 1.5 gal   78. from 2 km to 1.5 km

---

Linear Equations

What You'll Learn

• To graph linear equations

• To write equations of lines

...And Why

To solve a transportation problem, as in Example 2

✓ **Check Skills You'll Need**

GO for Help Lesson 1-2

Evaluate each expression for $x = -2, 0, 1,$ and **4.**

1. $\frac{2}{3}x + 7$ **2.** $\frac{3}{5}x - 2$ **3.** $3x + 1$ **4.** $\frac{1}{2}x - 8$

🔊 **New Vocabulary**
• linear function   • linear equation
• dependent variable   • independent variable
• *x*-intercept   • *y*-intercept
• standard form of a linear equation   • slope
• point-slope form   • slope-intercept form

---

1   Graphing Linear Equations

A function whose graph is a line is a **linear function** . You can represent a linear function with a **linear equation,** such as $y = 3x + 2.$ A solution of a linear equation is any ordered pair (x, y) that makes the equation true.

You can write the solutions of the equation using set notation as $\{(x, y) \mid y = 3x + 2\}.$ Read the notation as "the set of ordered pairs x, y such that $y = 3x + 2.$" Because the value of y depends on the value of x, y is called the **dependent variable** and x is called the **independent variable.**

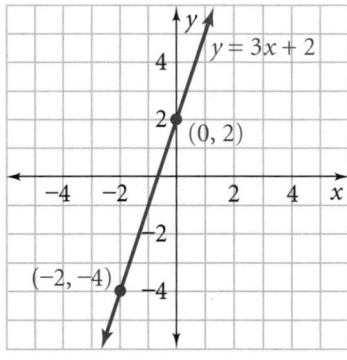

1 EXAMPLE   Graphing a Linear Equation

Graph the equation $y = \frac{2}{3}x + 3.$

Choose two values for x and find the corresponding values of $y.$ Plot the point for each ordered pair and complete the graph by drawing a line through the points.

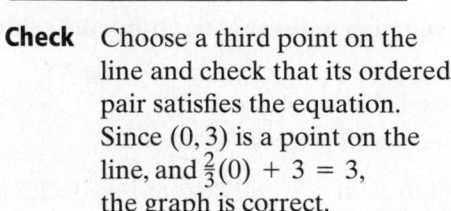

x	$\frac{2}{3}$x + 3	y	(x,y)
−3	$\frac{2}{3}(-3) + 3$	1	(−3, 1)
3	$\frac{2}{3}(3) + 3$	5	(3, 5)

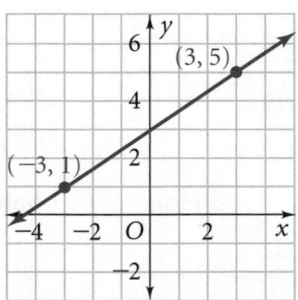

Check Choose a third point on the line and check that its ordered pair satisfies the equation. Since $(0, 3)$ is a point on the line, and $\frac{2}{3}(0) + 3 = 3,$ the graph is correct.

> **Problem Solving Hint**
>
> **Geometry** Since two points determine a line, you can use two points to graph a line. Check your line by finding a third point.

✓ **Quick Check** ① Graph each equation. Check your work.

  a. $y = \frac{3}{4}x$ **b.** $x + y = -2$ **c.** $y = -\frac{1}{2}x + \frac{1}{2}$

The **y-intercept** of a line is the point at which the line crosses the y-axis. You can use the same term to identify the y-coordinate of this point.

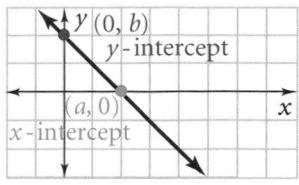

The **x-intercept** of a line is the point at which the line crosses the x-axis. You can use the same term to identify the x-coordinate of this point.

The **standard form of a linear equation** is $Ax + By = C$, where $A, B,$ and C are real numbers, and A and B are not both zero. You can graph a linear equation in standard form by finding the x- and y-intercepts.

② **EXAMPLE** Real-World ● Connection

Transportation The equation $3x + 2y = 120$ models the number of passengers who can sit in a train car, where x is the number of adults and y is the number of children. Graph the equation. Explain what the x- and y-intercepts represent. Describe the domain and the range.

Set x or y equal to zero to find each intercept.

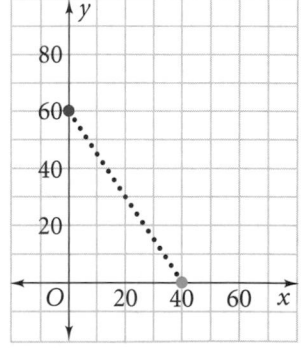

$$3x + 2y = 120 \qquad\qquad 3x + 2y = 120$$
$$3x + 2(0) = 120 \qquad\qquad 3(0) + 2y = 120$$
$$3x = 120 \qquad\qquad 2y = 120$$
$$x = 40 \qquad\qquad y = 60$$

Use the intercepts to graph the equation. The x-intercept is $(40, 0)$. When 40 adults are seated, no children can sit. The y-intercept is $(0, 60)$. When no adults are seated, 60 children can sit.

The number of passengers is a whole number. The situation is discrete. The domain is limited to the whole numbers 0 to 40; the range to the whole numbers 0 to 60.

✓ **Quick Check** ② **a.** Suppose the train system buys new train cars with molded plastic seats. The model changes to $x + y = 40$. Graph the equation and interpret the x- and y-intercepts.

  b. Explain how using molded seats changes the number of seated passengers.

Real-World ● Connection

In Japan, so many people ride public transportation that they need help getting into the trains.

Vocabulary Tip

The slope of a line is also the rate of change between two points on the line.

The **slope** of a nonvertical line is the ratio of the vertical change to a corresponding horizontal change. You can calculate slope by subtracting the corresponding coordinates of two points on the line.

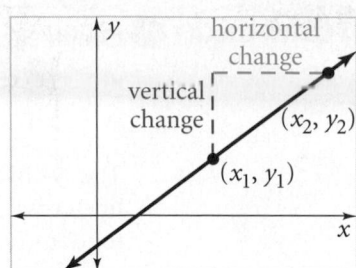

 **Key Concepts**

Definition	**Slope Formula**

$$\text{slope} = \frac{\text{vertical change (rise)}}{\text{horizontal change (run)}} = \frac{y_2 - y_1}{x_2 - x_1}, \text{where } x_2 - x_1 \neq 0$$

3 **EXAMPLE** **Finding Slope**

Find the slope of the line through the points $(3, 2)$ and $(-9, 6)$.

$\text{slope} = \dfrac{y_2 - y_1}{x_2 - x_1}$ **Use the slope formula.**

$\qquad = \dfrac{6 - 2}{-9 - 3}$ **Substitute (3, 2) for (x_1, y_1) and (−9, 6) for (x_2, y_2).**

$\qquad = \dfrac{4}{-12}$ **Subtract.**

$\qquad = -\dfrac{1}{3}$ **Simplify.**

The slope of the line is $-\dfrac{1}{3}$.

✓ **Quick Check** ❸ Find the slope of the line through each pair of points.
    a. $(-2, -2)$ and $(4, 2)$ **b.** $(0, -3)$ and $(7, -9)$

2 ◢ **Writing Equations of Lines**

Activity: Point-Slope Form

1. Make a table of values to graph each line.

    a. $y - 1 = -2(x - 2)$ **b.** $y - 2 = \frac{1}{3}(x - 1)$ **c.** $y - 5 = 3(x - 4)$

2. Find the slope of each line. Compare the slope of the line to the red number in the equation of the line. What do you notice?

3. Find the point on the graph of each line with an x-coordinate that is equal to the green number in the equation line. Then compare the y-coordinate of the point to the blue number in the equation of the line. What do you notice?

4. **Make a Conjecture** All three equations in Question 1 are in the form $y - y_1 = m(x - x_1)$. Make a conjecture about how you can use that form to help you graph an equation.

When you know the slope and a point on a line, you can use the **point-slope form** to write the equation of the line.

Definition	Point-Slope Form

The line through point (x_1, y_1) with slope m has the equation below.

$$y - y_1 = m(x - x_1)$$

4 EXAMPLE Writing an Equation Given the Slope and a Point

Write in standard form an equation of the line with slope $-\frac{1}{2}$ through the point $(8, -1)$.

$y - y_1 = m(x - x_1)$	Use the point-slope equation.
$y - (-1) = -\frac{1}{2}(x - 8)$	Substitute $-\frac{1}{2}$ for m, -1 for y_1, and 8 for x_1.
$y - (-1) = -\frac{1}{2}x - \left(-\frac{1}{2}\right)(8)$	Distributive Property
$y + 1 = -\frac{1}{2}x + 4$	Simplify.
$\frac{1}{2}x + y = 3$	Write in standard form.

✓ **Quick Check** ❹ Write in standard form the equation of each line.

a. slope 2, through $(4, -2)$ 　　　　**b.** slope $\frac{5}{6}$, through $(5, 6)$

When you know two points on a line, you can write an equation by using the point-slope equation combined with the slope formula.

5 EXAMPLE Writing an Equation Given Two Points

Write in point-slope form the equation of the line through $(1, 5)$ and $(4, -1)$.

$y - y_1 = m(x - x_1)$	Write the point-slope equation.
$y - y_1 = \frac{y_2 - y_1}{x_2 - x_1}(x - x_1)$	Substitute the slope formula for m.
$y - 5 = \frac{-1 - 5}{4 - 1}(x - 1)$	Substitute: $x_1 = 1$, $y_1 = 5$, $x_2 = 4$, $y_2 = -1$.
$y - 5 = \frac{-6}{3}(x - 1)$	Simplify.
$y - 5 = -2(x - 1)$	Write in point-slope form.

✓ **Quick Check** ❺ Write in point-slope form the equation of the line through each pair of points.
a. $(5, 0)$ and $(-3, 2)$ 　　**b.** $(-2, -1)$ and $(-10, 17)$ 　**c.** $(5, 1)$ and $(-4, -3)$

Another form of the equation of a line is **slope-intercept form,** which you can use to find slope by examining the equation.

Definition	Slope-Intercept Form

slope⌐　　⌐y-intercept

$$y = mx + b$$

6 EXAMPLE **Finding Slope Using Slope-Intercept Form**

Find the slope of $4x + 3y = 7$.

$4x + 3y = 7$

$\quad 3y = -4x + 7$ **Subtract 4x from each side.**

$\quad\ \ y = -\frac{4}{3}x + \frac{7}{3}$ **Write in slope-intercept form.**

● The slope of the line is $-\frac{4}{3}$.

✓ Quick Check **6** Find the slope of each line.

    a. $3x + 2y = 1$ **b.** $\frac{2}{3}x + \frac{1}{2}y = 1$ **c.** $Ax + By = C$

 Key Concepts

Summary	Equations of a Line	
Point-Slope Form	**Standard Form**	**Slope-Intercept Form**
$y - 2 = -3(x + 4)$	$3x + y = -10$	$y = -3x - 10$

The slopes of horizontal, vertical, perpendicular, and parallel lines have special properties.

Horizontal Line

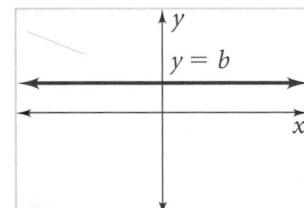

$m = 0$
y is constant.

Vertical Line

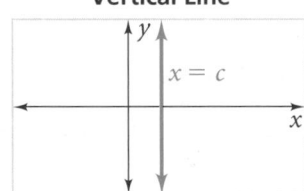

m is undefined.
x is constant.

Perpendicular Lines

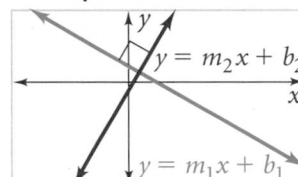

$m_1 \cdot m_2 = -1$
(In other words, m_2 is the negative reciprocal of m_1.)

Parallel Lines

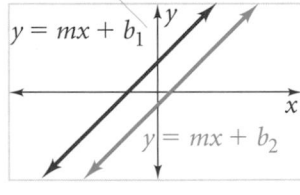

$m = m$
$b_1 \neq b_2$

Real-World 🌐 Connection

The steel girders of the Eiffel Tower model horizontal, vertical, perpendicular, and parallel lines.

Video Tutor Help
Visit: PHSchool.com
Web Code: age-0775
Also available on DVD

7 **EXAMPLE** **Writing an Equation of a Perpendicular Line**

Write an equation of the line through each point and perpendicular to $y = \frac{3}{4}x + 2$.
Graph all three lines.

a. $(0, 4)$

$m = -\left(\frac{1}{\frac{3}{4}}\right) = -\frac{4}{3}$ Find the negative reciprocal of $\frac{3}{4}$.

$y = mx + b$ Use slope-intercept form.

$y = -\frac{4}{3}x + 4$ Substitute: $m = -\frac{4}{3}$ and $b = 4$.

b. $(6, 1)$

$y = -\frac{4}{3}x + b$ Slope is $-\frac{4}{3}$.

$1 = -\frac{4}{3}(6) + b$ Substitute (6, 1) for (x, y).

$1 = -8 + b$ Simplify.

$9 = b$ Solve for b.

$y = -\frac{4}{3}x + 9$ Write the equation.

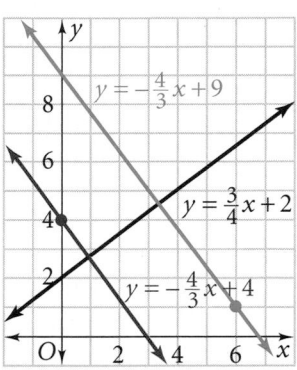

Quick Check **7** Write an equation for each line. Then graph the line.
  a. through $(-1, 3)$ and perpendicular to the line $y = 5x - 3$
  b. through $(2, 1)$ and parallel to the line $y = \frac{2}{3}x + \frac{5}{8}$
  c. vertical and through $(5, -3)$

EXERCISES

For more exercises, see *Extra Skill and Word Problem Practice.*

Practice and Problem Solving

 Practice by Example

Example 1
(page 62)

Graph each equation. Check your work.

1. $y = 2x$ **2.** $y = -3x - 1$ **3.** $y = 3x - 2$ **4.** $y = -4x + 5$

5. $5x - 2y = -4$ **6.** $-2x + 5y = -10$ **7.** $y - 3 = -2x$ **8.** $y + 4 = -3x$

Example 2
(page 63)

9. Cost Analysis The equation $y - 0.23x = 0$ relates the cost of operating a car to the number of miles driven, where x is the number of miles driven and y is the cost.
  a. Graph the equation and determine the domain and range.
  b. Explain what the x- and y-intercepts represent.
  c. Explain what 0.23 represents.

10. Fund-Raising The school glee club needs a total of $4500 for a trip to Omaha, Nebraska. To make money, members are selling baseball caps for $4.50 and sweatshirts for $12.50.
  a. Graph the equation $4.5x + 12.5y = 4500$, where x is the number of baseball caps and y is the number of sweatshirts sold.
  b. Explain the meaning of the x- and y-intercepts in terms of the fund-raising.

Example 3
(page 64)

Find the slope of the line through each pair of points.

11. $(1, 6)$ and $(8, -1)$ **12.** $(-3, 9)$ and $(0, 3)$ **13.** $(0, 0)$ and $(2, 6)$

14. $(-4, -3)$ and $(7, 1)$ **15.** $(-2, -1)$ and $(8, -3)$ **16.** $(1, 2)$ and $(2, 3)$

17. $\left(\frac{2}{3}, \frac{4}{7}\right)$ and $\left(\frac{2}{3}, \frac{11}{7}\right)$ **18.** $(-3, 5)$ and $(4, 5)$ **19.** $(-5, -7)$ and $(0, 10)$

Example 4
(page 65)

Write in standard form the equation of each line.

20. slope = 3; (1, 5)   **21.** slope = $\frac{5}{6}$; (22, 12)   **22.** slope = $-\frac{3}{5}$; (-4, 0)

23. slope = 0; (4, -2)   **24.** slope = -1; (-3, 5)   **25.** slope = 5; (0, 2)

Example 5
(page 65)

Write in point-slope form the equation of the line through each pair of points.

26. (-10, 3) and (-2, -5)   **27.** (1, 0) and (5, 5)   **28.** (-4, 10) and (-6, 15)

29. (0, -1) and (3, -5)   **30.** (7, 11) and (13, 17)   **31.** (1, 9) and (6, 2)

Example 6
(page 66)

Find the slope of each line.

32. $5x + y = 4$ **33.** $-3x + 2y = 7$ **34.** $-\frac{1}{2}x - y = \frac{3}{4}$

35. $Ax + By = C$ **36.** $Ax - By = C$ **37.** $y = 7$

Example 7
(page 67)

Write an equation for each line. Then graph the line.

38. through (-2, 1) and parallel to $y = -3x + 1$

39. through (-3, -1) and perpendicular to $y = -\frac{2}{5}x - 4$

40. through (-7, 10) and horizontal

41. through $\left(1, -\frac{2}{7}\right)$ and vertical

B **Apply Your Skills**

Graph each equation.

42. $y = -\frac{3}{5}x - \frac{12}{5}$ **43.** $y = -2x + 3$ **44.** $y = -x + 7$

45. $3y - 2x = -12$ **46.** $4x + 5y = 20$ **47.** $4x - 3y = -6$

48. $\frac{2}{3}x + \frac{y}{3} = -\frac{1}{3}$ **49.** $\frac{3}{5}y - \frac{x}{5} = -\frac{6}{5}$ **50.** $\frac{4}{5} = -\frac{1}{3}x - \frac{3}{4}y$

Find the slope of each line.

51. 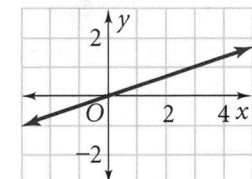   **52.** 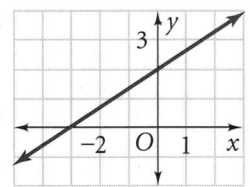   **53.**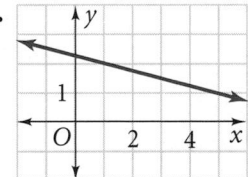

Find the slope and the intercepts of each line.

54. $f(x) = \frac{2}{3}x + 4$ **55.** $y = -x + 1000$ **56.** $y = 0.4 - 0.8x$

57. $g(x) = 54x - 1$ **58.** $x = -3$ **59.** $y = 0$

60. $-\frac{1}{3}x - \frac{2}{3}y = \frac{5}{3}$ **61.** $-Rx + Sy = -T$ **62.** $\frac{A}{D}x + \frac{B}{D}y = \frac{C}{D}$

Find the slope of the line through each pair of points.

63. $\left(\frac{3}{2}, -\frac{1}{2}\right)$ and $\left(-\frac{2}{3}, \frac{1}{3}\right)$ **64.** $\left(-\frac{1}{2}, -\frac{1}{2}\right)$ and (-3, -4)   **65.** $\left(0, \frac{1}{2}\right)$ and $\left(\frac{5}{7}, 0\right)$

Write an equation for each line. Each interval is 1 unit.

66. 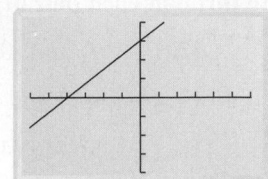   **67.** 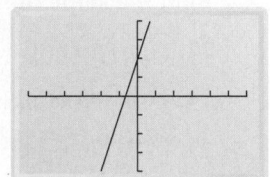   **68.**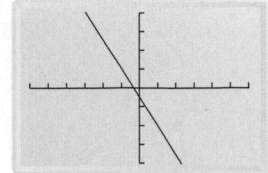

GO ●nline

Homework Video Tutor

Visit: PHSchool.com
Web Code: age-0202

Real-World Connection

You can download data from a motion detector to a computer to produce graphs of distance versus time.

Test-Taking Tip

On a graph that plots distance against time, be sure you understand exactly what distance is being modeled. In Exercise 69, it's the distance of the student *from* the detector.

69. Multiple Choice Three students moved away from or toward a motion detector, one at a time. Each graph shows distance from the detector as a function of time.

I. 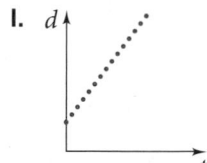 II. 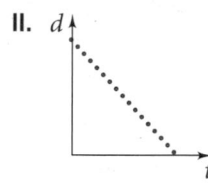 III.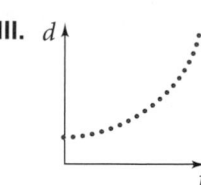

Which of the following statements is true?

- Ⓐ Student I was the only student who moved away from the detector.
- Ⓑ Student II was the only student who moved toward the detector.
- Ⓒ Student I was speeding up.
- Ⓓ Student II was slowing down.

70. Critical Thinking Most graphing calculators are designed to graph equations that are solved for y. What lines could not be graphed with this method?

Write an equation for each line. Then graph the line.

71. $m = 0$, through $(5, -1)$ **72.** $m = 2$, through $(1, 3)$

73. $m = \frac{5}{6}$, through $(-4, 0)$ **74.** $m = -\frac{3}{2}$, through $(0, -1)$

Write each equation in standard form.

75. $y = \frac{3}{2}x - 1$ **76.** $x + \frac{1}{3}y = \frac{2}{9}$ **77.** $-\left(\frac{1}{2}x + 2y\right) = \frac{2}{3}$

78. a. Open-Ended Write an equation of a line.
   b. Write an equation of the line parallel to the line you wrote in part (a) passing through the point $(0.5, 0.6)$.
   c. Write an equation of the line perpendicular to the line you wrote in part (a) passing through the point $\left(\frac{5}{3}, 2\right)$.
   d. Write an equation of the line parallel to the line you wrote in part (c) passing through the point $(-3, 1)$.
   e. Geometry Graph the lines from parts (a), (b), (c), and (d). If they form a polygon, describe it.

Ⓒ **Challenge**

Points that are on the same line are *collinear*. Use the definition of slope to determine whether the given points are collinear.

79. $(-2, 6), (0, 2), (1, 0)$ **80.** $(3, -5), (-3, 3), (0, 2)$

81. Write an equation of a line a through $(-1, 3)$ that is parallel to the line $y = 3x + 1$. Write an equation of a line b through $(-1, 3)$ that is perpendicular to line a. What is the intersection of line b and line $y = 3x + 1$?

Problem Solving Hint

The slopes of parallel lines are equal. The slopes of perpendicular lines are negative reciprocals.

82. Geometry Prove that the triangle with vertices $(3, 5)$, $(-2, 6)$, and $(1, 3)$ is a right triangle.

83. Geometry Prove that the quadrilateral with vertices $(2, 5)$, $(4, 8)$, $(7, 6)$, and $(5, 3)$ is a rectangle.

84. Critical Thinking Lines p, q, and r all pass through point $(-3, 4)$. Line p has slope 4 and is perpendicular to line q. Line r passes through Quadrants I and II only. Write an equation for each line. Then graph the three lines on the same coordinate plane.

Multiple Choice

85. Which equation represents a line through (3, 5) that is perpendicular to $y = 2x - 5$?
   A. $2y = -x + 13$ **B.** $2y = x + 13$
   C. $2y - x = 13$ **D.** $2y + x = -13$

86. For the equation $3x - 2y = 12$, which has value -6?
   F. the x-intercept   **G.** the y-intercept
   H. the slope   **J.** the origin

87. Which pair of equations represents perpendicular lines?
   A. $y = -\frac{3}{8}x + 12$ **B.** $y = -\frac{3}{8}x + 12$
         $(y - 1) = -\frac{3}{8}(x + 4)$ $3x + 8y = 20$

   C. $y = -\frac{3}{8}x + 12$ **D.** $y = -\frac{3}{8}x + 12$
         $(y - 1) = -\frac{8}{3}(x + 4)$ $(y - 1) = \frac{8}{3}(x + 4)$

Short Response

88. The line $(y - 1) = \frac{2}{3}(x + 1)$ contains point $H(a, -3)$. Find a. Show your work.

89. The point $(-8, k)$ is on the line with slope $-\frac{5}{8}$ and y-intercept 9. Explain how to find k.

Extended Response

90. A line passes through points $K(4, 4)$ and $W(-2, 10)$.
   a. Write an equation for the line in the form $Ax + By = C$. Show your work.
   b. Find the x- and y-intercepts.

Mixed Review

Lesson 2-1

Find the domain and range of each relation. Then decide whether it is a function.

91.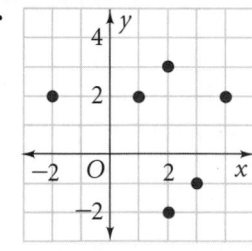

92.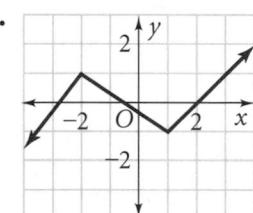

93.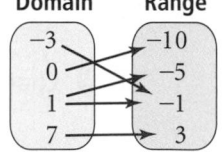

Lesson 1-1

Identify each demonstrated property (or properties) of real numbers.

94. $7.4 - 3.4 + 2.6 = 7.4 + 2.6 - 3.4$ **95.** $\frac{2}{5} + \frac{27}{5} \cdot \frac{5}{27} = \frac{2}{5} + 1$

96. $97(7) = 100(7) - 3(7)$ **97.** $21 + 19.7 - 19.7 = 21$

Skills Handbook **98. Commission** A fabric designer earns a 60% commission for works sold in a textile studio. The studio receives the other 40%. How much does the studio receive for selling a length of fabric that costs $15.65? How much does the designer receive?

Extension

Piecewise Functions

A piecewise function has different rules for different parts of its domain.

1 EXAMPLE Writing a Piecewise Function

Write a piecewise function to represent the graph at the right.

The graph has three distinct sections. The function needs a distinct rule for each of the three corresponding sections of the domain. Since $(-2, 3)$ and $(2, -5)$ both lie on two sections of the graph, arbitrarily assign each point to just one section.

When $x \leq -2$, the rule is $f(x) = x + 5$. When $-2 < x \leq 2$, the rule is $f(x) = -2x - 1$. When $x > 2$, the rule is $f(x) = 2x - 9$.

The piecewise function has three parts. $f(x) = \begin{cases} x + 5, & \text{if } x \leq -2 \\ -2x - 1, & \text{if } -2 < x \leq 2 \\ 2x - 9, & \text{if } x > 2 \end{cases}$

Some piecewise functions are step functions. Their graphs look like the steps of a staircase. One step function is the greatest integer function $f(x) = [x]$, where $[x]$ means the greatest integer less than or equal to x.

2 EXAMPLE Graphing a Piecewise Function

Graph the function $f(x) = [x]$.

Step 1 Choose an interval bounded by two consecutive integers. Make a table of values for the interval $0 \leq x \leq 1$.

x	0	0.25	0.5	0.75	1
f(x)	0	0	0	0	1

Each section of the graph ends at the y-value at which it starts. The left endpoint of each "step" is a closed circle. The right endpoint is an open circle.

Step 2 Graph the function.

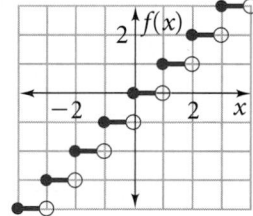

Use closed circles for included endpoints; use open circles for excluded endpoints.

EXERCISES

Graph each piecewise function.

1. $y = [x] + 2$

2. $f(x) = 3[x]$

3. $y = \begin{cases} x + 4, & \text{if } x \leq -2 \\ -x, & \text{if } x > -2 \end{cases}$

4. $f(x) = \begin{cases} -2x + 1, & \text{if } x < 3 \\ x - 8, & \text{if } x \geq 3 \end{cases}$

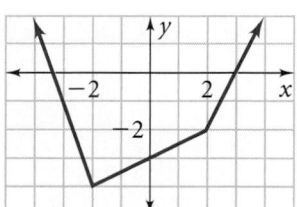

5. Write a piecewise function to represent the graph at the right.

6. Writing Explain how to graph a piecewise function.

Direct Variation

What You'll Learn

• To write and interpret direct variation equations

...And Why

To model a dripping faucet, as in Example 3

 **for Help** Lesson 1-3 and Skills Handbook page 872

Solve each equation for y.

1. $12y = 3x$ **2.** $12y = 5x$ **3.** $\frac{3}{4}y = 15$ **4.** $0.9y = 27x$ **5.** $5y = 35$

Tell whether each equation is true.

6. $\frac{1}{4} \overset{?}{=} \frac{2}{8}$ **7.** $\frac{2}{5} \overset{?}{=} \frac{6}{15}$ **8.** $\frac{9}{24} \overset{?}{=} \frac{12}{36}$ **9.** $\frac{20}{24} \overset{?}{=} \frac{30}{36}$

🔊 **New Vocabulary** • direct variation • constant of variation

---

1 Writing and Interpreting a Direct Variation

A linear function defined by an equation of the form $y = kx$, where $k \neq 0$, represents **direct variation**. As with any line, the slope k is constant.

When x and y are variables, you can write $k = \frac{y}{x}$, so the ratio $y : x$ equals the constant k, the **constant of variation**.

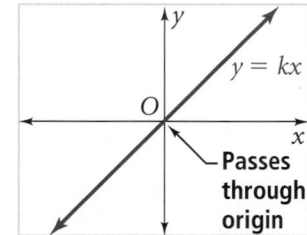

$y = kx$

Passes through origin

1 EXAMPLE   Identifying Direct Variation From a Table

Vocabulary Tip

You can describe direct variation as "y varies directly as x" or "y varies directly with x."

For each function, determine whether y varies directly with x. If so, find the constant of variation and write the equation.

a.

x	y
2	8
3	12
5	20

$\frac{y}{x} = \frac{8}{2} = \frac{12}{3} = \frac{20}{5} = 4$,

so y varies directly with x.

The constant of variation is 4.

The equation is $y = 4x$.

b.

x	y
1	4
2	7
5	16

Since $\frac{4}{1}, \frac{7}{2}$, and $\frac{16}{5}$ are not equal, $\frac{y}{x}$ is not constant.

y does *not* vary directly with x.

✓ **Quick Check** 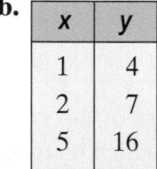 For each function, determine whether y varies directly with x. If so, find the constant of variation and write the equation.

a.

x	y
−6	−2
3	1
12	4

b.

x	y
−1	−2
3	4
6	7

c.

x	y
−9	5
3	$-1\frac{2}{3}$
6	$3\frac{5}{8}$

You can analyze an equation to determine whether it represents direct variation.

2 EXAMPLE **Identifying Direct Variation From an Equation**

For each function, determine whether y varies directly with x. If so, find the constant of variation.

a. $3y = 2x$
$3y = 2x$ is equivalent to $y = \frac{2}{3}x$, so y varies directly with x.
The constant of variation is $\frac{2}{3}$.

b. $y = 2x + 3$
Since you cannot write the equation in the form $y = kx$, y does *not* vary directly with x.

✓ **Quick Check** **2** For each function, determine whether y varies directly with x. If so, find the constant of variation.

a. $y = \frac{x}{2}$ **b.** $2y - 1 = x$ **c.** $\frac{5}{6}x = \frac{1}{3}y$ **d.** $7x + 4y = 10$

You can write an equation to solve a direct variation problem.

3 EXAMPLE **Real-World Connection**

Water Conservation A dripping faucet wastes a cup of water if it drips for three minutes. The amount of water wasted varies directly with the amount of time the faucet drips.

GO **Online**

Video Tutor Help
Visit: PhSchool.com
Web Code: age-0775

a. Find the constant of variation k and write an equation to model the direct variation.

Relate water wasted   varies directly   with time

Define Let w = number of cups of water wasted.
Let t = time in minutes the faucet drips.

Write w = k · t

$1 = k(3)$ **Substitute 1 for w and 3 for t.**
$\frac{1}{3} = k$ **Solve for k.**

The constant of variation k is $\frac{1}{3}$. The equation $w = \frac{1}{3}t$ models the direct variation.

b. Find how long the faucet must drip to waste $4\frac{1}{2}$ c of water.

$w = \frac{1}{3}t$ **Use the direct variation.**
$4\frac{1}{2} = \frac{1}{3}t$ **Substitute $4\frac{1}{2}$ for w.**
$\frac{9}{2}(3) = t$ **Solve for t.**
$13\frac{1}{2} = t$ **Simplify.**

The faucet must drip for $13\frac{1}{2}$ min to waste $4\frac{1}{2}$ c of water.

✓ **Quick Check** **3** **Geometry** The circumference of a circle varies directly with the diameter of the circle. The formula $C = \pi d$ relates the circumference to the diameter.
a. What is the constant of variation?
b. Find the diameter of a circle with circumference 105 cm to the nearest tenth.

You can use proportions to solve some direct variation problems. This can save time when the problem does not ask for the constant of variation.

4 EXAMPLE Using a Proportion

Suppose y varies directly with x, and $x = 27$ when $y = -51$. Find x when $y = -17$.

Let $(x_1, y_1) = (27, -51)$ and let $(x_2, y_2) = (x_2, -17)$.

$$\frac{y_1}{x_1} = \frac{y_2}{x_2}$$ Write a proportion.

$$\frac{-51}{27} = \frac{-17}{x_2}$$ Substitute.

$$-51(x_2) = 27(-17)$$ Write the cross products.

$$x_2 = \frac{27(-17)}{-51}$$ Solve for x_2.

$$x_2 = 9$$ Simplify.

✓ Quick Check **4** Find the missing value for each direct variation.
  a. If $y = 4$ when $x = 3$, find y when $x = 6$.
  b. If $y = 7$ when $x = 2$, find y when $x = 8$.
  c. If $y = 10$ when $x = -3$, find x when $y = 2$.
  d. If $y = 1$ when $x = 10$, find y when $x = 2$.

EXERCISES

For more exercises, see *Extra Skill and Word Problem Practice.*

Practice and Problem Solving

A Practice by Example

Example 1
(page 72)

For each function, determine whether y varies directly with x. If so, find the constant of variation and write the equation.

1.

x	y
2	4
4	8
16	32

2.

x	y
2	-6
4	-12
5	-15

3.

x	y
11	22
16	32
7	42

4.

x	y
27	9
30	10
60	20

5.

x	y
2	14
3	21
5	35

6.

x	y
3	9
4	13
7	23

7.

x	y
-2	4
-3	6
-5	10

8.

x	y
1	-2
3	-8
5	14

Example 2
(page 73)

Determine whether y varies directly with x. If so, find the constant of variation.

  9. $y = 12x$ **10.** $y = 6x$ **11.** $y = -2x$ **12.** $y = 4x + 1$

  13. $y = 4x - 3$ **14.** $y = -5x$ **15.** $y - 6x = 0$ **16.** $y + 3 = -3x$

Example 3
(page 73)

For each direct variation, find the constant of variation. Then find the value of y when $x = -5$.

  17. $y = 2$ when $x = 7$ **18.** $y = -5$ when $x = 3$

  19. $y = -2$ when $x = 2$ **20.** $y = -\frac{2}{3}$ when $x = -\frac{1}{3}$

  21. $y = 17$ when $x = -4$ **22.** $y = \frac{1}{2}$ when $x = -2$

23. Environment Suppose you work on a tree farm and you need to find the height of each tree. You know that the length of an object's shadow varies directly with its height. Refer to the diagram.

a. Find the constant of variation.

b. Write an equation to calculate the height of the tree.

c. Find the height of a tree with a shadow 8 ft 4 in. long.

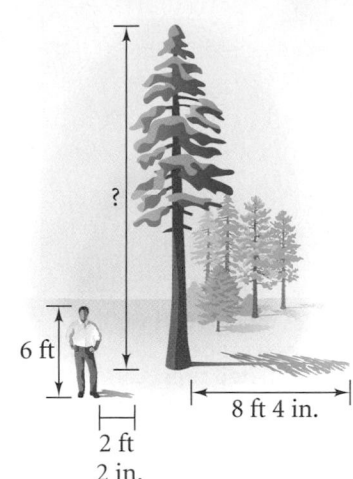

6 ft

?

8 ft 4 in.

2 ft 2 in.

Example 4
(page 74)

For Exercises 24–27, y varies directly with x.

24. If $y = 4$ when $x = -2$, find x when $y = 6$.

25. If $y = 6$ when $x = 2$, find x when $y = 12$.

26. If $y = 7$ when $x = 2$, find y when $x = 3$.

27. If $y = 5$ when $x = -3$, find y when $x = -1$.

B **Apply Your Skills**

For each function, determine whether y varies directly with x. If so, find the constant of variation and write the equation.

28.

x	y
9	6
12	8
15	10

29.

x	y
4	1
6	2
8	3

30.

x	y
23	24
55	56
66	67

31.

x	y
2	2.6
3	3.9
4	5.2

GO for Help

For Gridded Responses, see Test-Taking Strategies, page 46.

32. Gridded Response A speed of 60 mi/h is equal to a speed of 88 ft/s. Find the speed to the nearest mile per hour of an aircraft travelling 1000 ft/s.

Write an equation for a direct variation with a graph that passes through each point.

33. $(1, 2)$ **34.** $(-3, -7)$ **35.** $(2, -9)$ **36.** $(-0.1, 50)$

37. $(-5, -3)$ **38.** $(9, -1)$ **39.** $(7, 2)$ **40.** $(-3, 14)$

In Exercises 41–45, y varies directly with x.

41. If $y = 7$ when $x = 3$, find x when $y = 21$.

42. If $y = 25$ when $x = 15$, find x when $y = 10$.

43. If $y = 30$ when $x = -3$, find y when $x = -9$.

44. If $y = -20$ when $x = 2$, find y when $x = 14$.

45. If $y = 0.9$ when $x = 4.8$, find y when $x = 6.4$.

Determine whether a line with the given slope through the given point represents a direct variation. Explain.

46. $m = -1.7, (9, -9)$ **47.** $m = -\frac{5}{6}, \left(15, -12\frac{1}{2}\right)$ **48.** $m = \frac{7}{2}, \left(6\frac{1}{2}, 22\frac{3}{4}\right)$

Open-Ended In Exercises 49–51, choose a value of k within the given range. Then write and graph a direct variation using your value for k.

49. $0 < k < 1$ **50.** $3 < k < 4.5$ **51.** $-1 < k < -\frac{1}{2}$

It takes more effort for an engine to propel a car with underinflated tires. Cars with properly inflated tires get better gas mileage.

52. Gas Mileage Suppose you drive a car 392 mi on one tank of gas. The tank holds 14 gallons. The number of miles traveled varies directly with the number of gallons of gas you use.
  a. Write an equation that relates miles traveled to gallons of gas used.
  b. You only have enough money to buy 3.7 gallons of gas. How far can you drive before refueling?
  c. Last year you drove 11,700 mi. About how many gallons of gas did you use?
  d. Suppose the price of gas averaged $1.57 per gallon last year. Find the cost per mile.

53. Writing Suppose you use the origin to test whether a linear equation is a direct variation. Does this method work? Support your answer with an example.

54. Error Analysis Find the error in the following computation: If y varies directly with x^2, and $y = 2$ when $x = 4$, then $y = 3$ when $x = 9$.

 **Challenge**

In Exercises 55–58, y varies directly with x.

55. If x is doubled, what happens to y?

56. If x is halved, what happens to y?

57. If x is divided by 7, what happens to y?

58. If x is multiplied by 10, what happens to y?

59. If z varies directly with the product of x and y ($z = kxy$), then z is said to vary jointly with x and y.
  a. Geometry The area of a triangle varies jointly with its base and height. What is the constant of variation?
  b. Suppose q varies jointly with v and s, and $q = 24$ when $v = 2$ and $s = 3$. Find q when $v = 4$ and $s = 2$.
  c. Critical Thinking Suppose z varies jointly with x and y, and x varies directly with w. Show that z varies jointly with w and y.

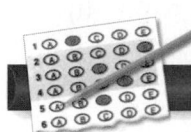

Test Prep

Multiple Choice

60. Which equation does NOT represent a direct variation?
  A. $y - 3x = 0$ **B.** $y + 2 = \frac{1}{2}x$ **C.** $\frac{y}{x} = \frac{2}{3}$ **D.** $y = \frac{x}{17}$

61. Suppose y varies directly with x. If x is 30 when y is 10, what is x when y is 9?
  F. 3   **G.** 27   **H.** 29   **J.** $\frac{300}{9}$

62. Suppose y varies directly with x. If x is -7 when y is 3, what is x when y is -5?
  A. $-11\frac{2}{3}$ **B.** $-4\frac{1}{5}$ **C.** $4\frac{1}{5}$ **D.** $11\frac{2}{3}$

63. Which equation represents the direct variation in the table at the right?
  F. $4y - 10x = 0$ **G.** $8x = 3y$
  H. $y + 8.1x = 0$ **J.** $10y = 27x$

x	3	4	9
y	8.1	10.8	24.3

Short Response

64. Do the values in the table below represent a direct variation? Explain.

x	4	5	7
y	13.1	16.3	22.6

Mixed Review

 Lesson 2-2

Use the given information to graph each line.

65. slope $= -\frac{3}{5}$, through $(-2, 5)$ **66.** slope $= -\frac{3}{2}$, through $(1, -4)$

67. slope $= -4$, through $(0, -1)$ **68.** slope $= -2$, $(-1, 6)$

Lesson 2-1

Graph each relation. Find the domain and range.

69. $\{(0, 1), (1, -3), (-2, -3), (3, -3)\}$ **70.** $\{(4, 0), (7, 0), (4, -1), (7, -1)\}$

71. $\{(1, -2), (2, -1), (4, 1), (5, 2)\}$ **72.** $\{(1, 7), (2, 8), (3, 9), (4, 10)\}$

Skills Handbook  **73. Aviation** On June 21, 2004, Simon Oliphant-Hope completed a record-setting helicopter trip around the world in 17 d 14 h 2 min 27 s. He spent 196.4 h in flight. What percent of the time was he not in the air?

✓ Checkpoint Quiz 1   Lessons 2-1 through 2-3

Find the *x*- and *y*-intercepts of each line.

1. $x - 3y = 9$ **2.** $y = 7x + 5$ **3.** $y = 6x$ **4.** $-4x + y = 10$

Write the equation of each line in slope-intercept form.

5. $2x - y = 9$ **6.** $4x = 2 + y$ **7.** $5y = -3x - 10$ **8.** $4x + 6y = 12$

9. a. A group of friends is going to the movies. Each ticket costs $7.00. Write an equation to model the total cost of the group's tickets.

     b. Graph the equation. Explain what the *x*- and *y*-intercepts represent.

     c. Writing Could the domain include fractions? Explain.

10. Which line is perpendicular to $3x + 2y = 6$?

     A. $4x - 6y = 3$ **B.** $y = -\frac{3}{2}x + 4$ **C.** $2x + 3y = 12$ **D.** $y = \frac{3}{2}x + 1$

Algebra at Work

· · · · · · · · · · · · · · · · · · · **Miniaturist**

People who make a career out of designing and creating miniature models of actual objects are called miniaturists. They apply direct variations to reproduce realistic models of items such as houses, stores, or scenes. Common scales used to create miniatures are the following.

* the one-inch scale (1 in. : 1 ft or 1 : 12)
* the half-inch scale (0.5 in. : 1 ft or 1 : 24)
* the quarter-inch scale (0.25 in. : 1 ft or 1 : 48)

Go Online
PHSchool.com   **For:** Information about careers in model design   **Web Code:** agb-2031

Using Linear Models

✓ **Check Skills You'll Need**

GO for Help   Lessons 2-1 and 2-2

Find the change in x and the change in y between each pair of points.

1. $(-0.2, 9)$ and $(3.4, 7.3)$ **2.** $(10, 17)$ and $(11.5, 13.5)$ **3.** $\left(0, \frac{3}{10}\right)$ and $\left(-1, \frac{2}{5}\right)$

Evaluate each function for the given values.

4. $f(x) = \frac{4}{3}x - 2$ for $x = -3, 0, \frac{1}{2}$ **5.** $g(x) = 3(2 - x)$ for $x = 0, \frac{1}{6}, 1$

◀)) **New Vocabulary**   • scatter plot   • trend line

---

1 Modeling Real-World Data

You can write linear equations to model real-world problems.

1 EXAMPLE   **Real-World** 🌐 **Connection**

Transportation Jacksonville, Florida has an elevation of 12 ft above sea level. A hot-air balloon taking off from Jacksonville rises 50 ft/min. Write an equation to model the balloon's elevation as a function of time. Graph the equation. Interpret the intercept at which the graph intersects the vertical axis.

Relate   balloon's elevation = rate · time + starting elevation

Define Let h = the balloon's elevation.

Let t = time (in minutes) since the hot-air balloon lifted off.

Write h =   50 · t +   12

An equation that models the balloon's elevation is $h = 50t + 12$.

Real-World 🌐 **Connection**

Careers Hot-air balloonists use mathematics to plot courses, calculate wind speed, and determine their air speed.

The h-intercept is $(0, 12)$.

The t-coordinate, 0, represents the time at the start of the trip.

The h-coordinate, 12, represents the elevation of the balloon at the start of the trip.

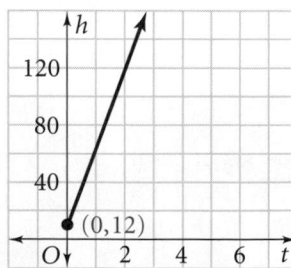

✓ **Quick Check** **1** Suppose a balloon begins descending at a rate of 20 ft/min from an elevation of 1350 ft.
  a. Write an equation to model the balloon's elevation as a function of time. What is true about the slope of this line?
  b. Graph the equation. Interpret the h-intercept.

You can use two data points from a linear relationship to write a model.

2 EXAMPLE **Real-World Connection**

Science A candle is 6 in. tall after burning for 1 h. After 3 h, it is $5\frac{1}{2}$ in. tall. Write a linear equation to model the height y of the candle after burning x hours.

Step 1 Identify the data points $(1, 6)$ and $\left(3, \frac{11}{2}\right)$ as (x_1, y_1) and (x_2, y_2).

Step 2 Find the slope of the line.

$$m = \frac{y_2 - y_1}{x_2 - x_1} \quad \text{Use the slope formula.}$$

$$m = \frac{\frac{11}{2} - 6}{3 - 1} \quad \text{Substitute.}$$

$$m = \frac{-\frac{1}{2}}{2} \quad \text{Simplify the numerator and denominator.}$$

$$m = -\frac{1}{4} \quad \text{Simplify.}$$

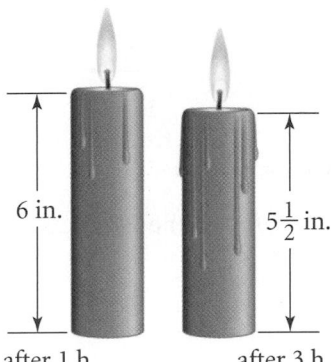

6 in.
$5\frac{1}{2}$ in.

after 1 h
after 3 h

Step 3 Use one of the points and the point-slope form to write an equation for the line.

$$y - y_1 = m(x - x_1) \quad \text{Use point-slope form.}$$

$$y - 6 = -\frac{1}{4}(x - 1) \quad \text{Substitute.}$$

$$y = -\frac{1}{4}x + 6\frac{1}{4} \quad \text{Solve for } y.$$

● An equation of the line that models the height of the candle is $y = -\frac{1}{4}x + 6\frac{1}{4}$.

✓ Quick Check **2** **a. Reasoning** What does the slope $-\frac{1}{4}$ represent?

b. What does the y-intercept $6\frac{1}{4}$ represent?

c. Another candle is 7 in. tall after burning for 1 h and 5 in. tall after burning for 2 h. Write a linear equation to model the height of the candle.

---

2 Predicting With Linear Models

You can use a linear model to make predictions.

3 EXAMPLE **Using a Linear Model**

Gridded Response Use the equation from Example 2. In how many hours will the candle be 4 in. tall?

$$y = -\frac{1}{4}x + 6\frac{1}{4} \quad \text{Write the equation.}$$

$$4 = -\frac{1}{4}x + 6\frac{1}{4} \quad \text{Substitute 4 for } y.$$

$$-4\left(4 - 6\frac{1}{4}\right) = x \quad \text{Solve for } x.$$

$$9 = x \quad \text{Simplify.}$$

The candle will be 4 in. tall after burning for 9 h.
● The answer is 9.

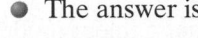

Test-Taking Tip

You can enter the 9 in any column of the grid.

✓ Quick Check **3** **a.** How tall will the candle be after burning for 11 h?

b. What was the original height of the candle?

c. When will the candle burn out?

A **scatter plot** is a graph that relates two different sets of data by plotting the data as ordered pairs. You can use a scatter plot to determine a relationship between the data sets.

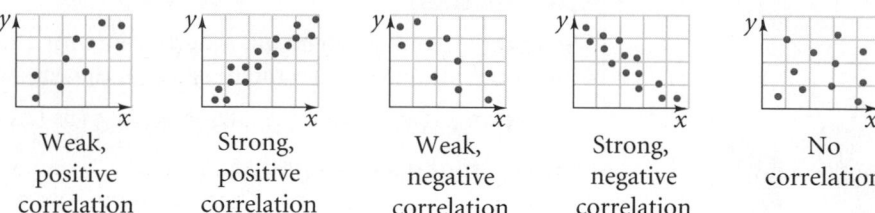

| Weak, positive correlation | Strong, positive correlation | Weak, negative correlation | Strong, negative correlation | No correlation |

A **trend line** is a line that approximates the relationship between the data sets of a scatter plot. You can use a trend line to make predictions.

4 EXAMPLE **Real-World Connection**

Automobiles A woman is considering buying the 1999 car shown in the photo. She researches prices for various years of the same model and records the data in a table.

Model Year	2000	2001	2002	2003	2004
Prices	$5784	$6810	$8237	$9660	$10,948
	$5435	$6207	$7751	$9127	$10,455

a. Let x represent the model year. (Use 1 for 2000, 2 for 2001, and so forth.) Let y be the price of the car. Draw a scatter plot. Decide whether a linear model is reasonable.

A linear model seems reasonable, since the points fall close to a line.

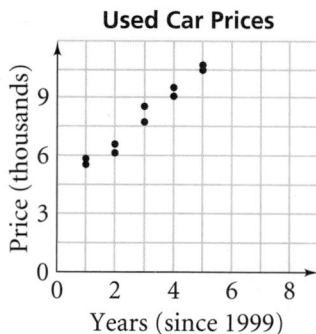

b. Draw a trend line. Write the equation of the line. Determine whether the asking price is reasonable.

Draw a line that has about the same number of data points above and below it. Use the slope and the y-intercept to find the equation of the line. Plot the data point for the asking price.

The equation of the trend line in the graph is $y = 1.3x + 4.1$. A fair price would be the value of y for $x = 0$, or about $4100.

The asking price of $4200 is reasonable.

✔ Quick Check **4** Graph each set of data. Decide whether a linear model is reasonable. If so, draw a trend line and write its equation.
a. $\{(-7.5, 19.75), (-2, 9), (0, 6.5), (1.5, 3), (4, -1.5)\}$
b. $\{(0, -3), (0.5, -2.5), (1, -1), (3.5, 21.5), (6, 69), (7, 35)\}$

EXERCISES

For more exercises, see *Extra Skill and Word Problem Practice.*

Practice and Problem Solving

 Practice by Example

Example 1
(page 78)

 **for Help**

1. A car enters an interstate highway 15 mi north of a city. The car travels due north at an average speed of 62.5 mi/h. Write an equation to model the car's distance *d* from the city after traveling for *h* hours. Graph the equation.

2. A pump removes 1000 gal of water from a pool at a constant rate of 50 gal/min.
   a. Write an equation to find the amount of water *y* in the pool after *t* minutes.
   b. Graph the equation and interpret the *t*- and *y*-intercepts.

3. A tree 5 ft tall grows an average of 8 in. each year. Write and graph an equation to model the tree's height *h* after *x* years.

Examples 2 and 3
(page 79)

For each situation, find a linear model and use it to make a prediction.

4. There are 2 leaves along 3 in. of an ivy vine. There are 14 leaves along 15 in. of the same vine. How many leaves are there along 6 in. of the vine?

5. An empty 5-gal water jug weighs 0.75 lb. With 3 c of water inside, the jug weighs 2.25 lb. Predict the weight of the jug with 5 c of water inside.

6. There are 55 blades of grass in 1 $in.^2$ of lawn. There are 230 blades of grass in 4 $in.^2$ of the same lawn. How many blades of grass are in 3 $in.^2$ of lawn?

7. A 2-mi cab ride costs $5.25. A 5-mi cab ride costs $10.50. How much does a 3.8-mi cab ride cost?

Example 4
(page 80)

Graph each set of data. Decide whether a linear model is reasonable. If so, draw a trend line and write its equation.

8. $\{(0, 11), (2, 8), (3, 7), (7, 2), (8, 0)\}$

9. $\{(1.2, 1), (2.5, 6), (2.5, 7.5), (4.1, 11), (7.9, 19)\}$

10. $\left\{ \left(-10, 3\frac{1}{2}\right), \left(-5\frac{1}{2}, 1\frac{1}{2}\right), \left(-\frac{1}{10}, -4\right), \left(3\frac{1}{2}, -7\frac{1}{2}\right), (12, -12) \right\}$

11. $\{(-15, 8), (-8, -7), (-3, 0), (0, 5), (7, -3)\}$

 Apply Your Skills

 12. **Measurement** The numbering system used in Europe for shoe sizes is different from the system used in the United States. Use the data in the table at the right to create a model for converting between systems.
   a. Graph the data. Is a linear model reasonable?
   b. Find the European equivalent of U.S. size 8.
   c. **Writing** Explain how to use a model to convert European sizes to U.S. sizes.

 13. **Nutrition** The table at the left shows the average daily energy requirements for male children and adolescents.
   a. Graph the data. Model the data with a linear equation.
   b. Estimate the daily energy requirements for a male 16 years old.
   c. **Reasoning** Do you think your model also applies to adult males? Explain.

Daily Energy Requirements for Males

Age (years)	Energy Needed (Calories)
1	1100
2	1300
5	1800
8	2200
11	2500
14	2800
17	3000

SOURCE: *Go Figure: The Numbers You Need for Everyday Life*

Women's Shoe Sizes

U.S. Size	European Size
1	31
3	34
5	36
7	39
9	41
11	44

SOURCE: *Sizes*

14. Sales Suppose you manufacture and sell tarps. The table displays your current sizes and prices.

Tarps

Size	Price	Size	Price
5 × 7 ft	$1.39	18 × 20 ft	$14.39
6 × 8 ft	$1.99	15 × 30 ft	$17.99
8 × 10 ft	$3.19	20 × 30 ft	$23.99
10 × 12 ft	$4.79	20 × 40 ft	$31.99
12 × 16 ft	$7.69	25 × 45 ft	$44.99
10 × 20 ft	$7.99	30 × 50 ft	$59.99
16 × 20 ft	$12.79	30 × 60 ft	$71.99

a. Draw a scatter plot showing the relationship between a tarp's area and its cost. Use area as the independent variable.

b. Use your scatter plot to develop a model relating the area of a tarp to its cost.

c. How good a model do you feel you have? Explain.

d. Is $7.00 a reasonable price for a tarp that measures 10 ft by 15 ft? Explain.

e. Using your model and the prices in the table, determine which tarp size varies the most from your predicted price. How great is the discrepancy between your model and the actual price?

Write an equation for each line.

15. through $(2, 2)$, y-intercept 10

16. x-intercept -2, y-intercept -6

17. y-intercept $-\frac{5}{2}$, x-intercept $-\frac{1}{3}$

18. through $(3.5, -2.3)$, x-intercept 5.1

19. Entertainment Refer to the diagram below. Suppose you are trying to decide whether to subscribe to cable service or just rent videos.

a. Write an equation to model the cost y of the cable service for 1 month.

b. Write a second equation to model the cost y of renting x movies from the video store. What is the slope? What is the y-intercept?

c. Open-Ended Suppose you currently rent 8 to 12 movies each month. Graph the two equations from parts (a) and (b). Interpret the graph. Use your interpretation to choose between the alternatives. Explain your reasoning.

20. Nutrition The table below shows the relationship between Calories and fat in various fast-food hamburgers.

Hamburger	A	B	C	D	E	F	G	H	I
Calories	720	530	510	500	305	410	440	320	598
Fat (g)	46	30	27	26	13	20	25	13	26

Source: *The Fat Counter*

a. Develop a model for the relationship between Calories and fat.

b. How much fat would you expect a 330–Calorie hamburger to have?

c. Error Analysis A student reports these estimates: 10 g of fat for a 200-Calorie hamburger and 36 g of fat for a 660-Calorie hamburger. Which estimate is *not* reasonable? Explain.

21. Data Analysis Is the population of a state related to the number of licensed drivers in that state? The table shows population and licensed-driver statistics from a recent year.

a. Which variable should be the independent variable?

b. Draw a scatter plot.

c. Draw a trend line.

d. The population of Michigan was approximately 10 million that year. About how many licensed drivers lived in Michigan that year?

 e. Writing Is the correlation between population and number of licensed drivers strong or weak? Explain.

State	Population (millions)	Licensed Drivers (millions)
Arkansas	2.7	2.0
Illinois	12.6	8.0
Kansas	2.7	1.9
Massachusetts	6.4	4.7
Pennsylvania	12.3	8.3
Texas	21.7	13.2

SOURCE: U.S. Census Bureau, National Highway Administration. Go to **www.PHSchool.com** for a data update. Web Code: agg-9041

22. Multiple Choice At a restaurant, Elena wants to leave a tip that is 15% of the bill B plus $1. Which linear model best describes the total T?

Ⓐ $T = 15B + 1$ Ⓑ $T = B + 15$

Ⓒ $T = 1.15B$ Ⓓ $T = 1.15B + 1$

A linear model for each situation passes through the origin. Find each missing value. Round your answer to the nearest tenth.

23. 47.5 min to jog 5 mi, ■ min to jog 11 mi

24. 8.5 gal of gas to drive 243.1 mi, 3 gal of gas to drive ■ mi

25. $9.45 to buy 7 lb of apples, $17.55 to buy ■ lb

Ⓒ Challenge **26. Social Studies** The table at the right shows per capita revenues and expenditures for selected states from a recent year.

a. Show the data on a scatter plot. Draw a trend line.

b. If a state collected revenue of $2000 per capita, how much would you expect it to spend per capita?

c. Ohio spent $3427 per capita during that year. According to your model, how much did it collect in taxes per capita?

State	Per Capita Revenue ($)	Per Capita Expenditure ($)
Arizona	2858	2926
Georgia	3023	3053
Maryland	3535	3573
Mississippi	3608	3710
New Mexico	4780	4587
Nevada	2753	2798
New York	4810	4676
Texas	2835	2723
Utah	3585	3725

SOURCE: U.S. Census Bureau. Go to **www.PHSchool.com** for a data update. Web Code: agg-9041

d. In that same year, New Jersey collected $3581 per capita in taxes and spent $4039 per capita. Does this information follow the trend? Explain.

> **Vocabulary Tip**
>
> Per <u>capita</u> means "for each person." <u>Capita</u> is a form of the Latin word for "head."

27. a. Use the first and last data points to find a linear model for the data in the table at the right.

x	−5	−2	−1	1	3	6
y	22	15	12	8	7	5

b. Use the middle two data points to find a linear model for the data.

c. Which model better represents the data? Can you find a third model that you think best represents the data? Explain.

 28. Geometry Write the equation of the perpendicular bisector of the segment with endpoints $(-3, 5)$ and $(7, 1)$.

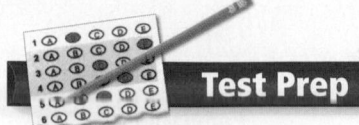
Gridded Response

Each set of three points is collinear. Find each missing x- or y-value to the nearest hundredth.

29. (2, 3.37), (10, 23.37), (4, y)

30. (6, 10.2), (1.5, 3.45), (x, 2.85)

31. (0.5, 1), (2.2, y), (1.6, 4.3)

32. (x, 0.8), (15, −0.4), (−4, 2.9)

Short Response

Use the newspaper article below for Exercises 34 and 35.

What's Harming Japan's Oysters?

A 1994 red tide killed off thousands of *akoya* oysters in Japan's Ago Bay. For years following the red tide, oysters continued to die, confounding pearl farmers and scientists alike. Scientists have suggested many possible causes, from a virus to pollutants.

Whatever the reason, in 1996, Japanese pearl farmers harvested only 56.6 tons of pearls from *akoya* oysters, down from 72.6 tons in 1993.

Source: *NOVA*, "The Perfect Pearl"

33. Use a linear model. Estimate the number of tons of pearls harvested in 2000.

34. In 2002, pearl farmers harvested 24 tons of pearls from akoya oysters. Use the harvests from 1996 and 2002 to estimate the 2000 harvest.

Mixed Review

Lesson 2-3

Find each constant of variation. Then find the value of y when $x = -5$.

35. $y = 27$ when $x = -10$

36. $y = -36$ when $x = 12$

37. $y = -\frac{2}{5}$ when $x = \frac{1}{3}$

38. $y = -\frac{21}{4}$ when $x = -\frac{5}{8}$

Lesson 2-1

Find the range of each function when the domain is $\{-3, -1, 0, 1.5, 4\}$.

39. $f(x) = 2x - 1$

40. $y = -(x - 5)$

41. $y = x^2 + 3$

42. $g(x) = \frac{x - 4}{2}$

43. $y = 100x + 1$

44. $y = 9 - 2x$

Skills Handbook

45. Track Svetlana Masterkova of Russia set a record for running the mile, in 4 minutes 12.56 seconds.
   a. Find Svetlana's rate in feet per second. How far did she run in 100 seconds?
   b. Write an equation that relates the distance she ran to time. Use feet per second as the unit.
   c. Calculate Svetlana's speed in miles per hour.

High-Use Academic Words

High-use academic words are words that you often see in textbooks and on tests. These words are not math vocabulary terms, but they are important for you to know to be successful in mathematics.

Words to Learn: Direction Words

Some words tell you what to do in a problem. You need to understand what these words are asking so that you give the correct answer.

Word(s)	Meaning
Explain (after a "yes-no" question)	"Yes" or "no" is only part of the correct answer. You must also write your reasons for your answer.
Determine whether	This is another form of a "yes-no" question. For a correct answer, you must show your process or support your "yes" or "no" response with evidence or reasons.

EXERCISES

1. If the fire alarm sounds, do you know what to do? Explain.

2. Determine whether physical education classes could be held outdoors today.

3. Suppose that a "yes-no" question asks you to "explain."

   a. Does a correct answer with poor reasons have any value? Explain.

   b. Does an incorrect answer with good reasons have any value? Explain.

The library keeps information on overdue-book returns. A five-day record is shown in the table.

4. Determine whether the overdue fines vary directly with the total number of days overdue.

5. Does the total number of days overdue vary directly with the number of overdue books returned? Explain.

6. In general, if x varies directly with y and y varies directly with z, does x vary directly with z? Explain.

7. Explain why the equation $y = 0.15x$ models the amount of fines from overdue books.

8. Word Knowledge Think about the word *model*.

   a. Choose the letter for how well you know the word.
     A. I know its meaning.
     B. I've seen it, but I don't know its meaning.
     C. I don't know it.

   b. Research Look up *model* in a dictionary or online. Write any definition that might apply to its use in mathematics.

   c. Write a sentence involving mathematics that uses the word *model*.

Overdue-Book Returns

Number of Books	Total Days Overdue	Overdue Fines ($)
21	32	4.80
12	20	3.00
30	44	6.60
9	16	2.40
18	28	4.20

The direct variation $y = 0.15x$ models the total fines y in dollars for x days of overdue books.

Finding a Line of Best Fit

Technology

FOR USE WITH LESSON 2-4

You can use your graphing calculator to display data sets, draw scatter plots, and draw a line to fit the data. The line is the linear regression line—a line of best fit. The LinReg feature on your calculator fits the model $y = ax + b$ to the data.

Go Online
PHSchool.com
For: Graphing calculator procedures
Web Code: age-2122

1 ACTIVITY Finding the LinReg Line of Best Fit

When a honeybee finds a source of food, it returns to the beehive and communicates to other bees the direction and distance of the source. The bee makes a loop, waggles its belly along a line, makes another loop, and then another waggle. The bee repeats its dance several times. The time for each cycle (one loop and waggle) reveals the approximate distance to the food source.

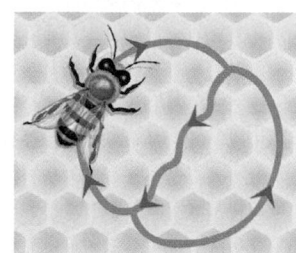

Distance to Food (km)	1.35	1.5	1.5	2	2.15	2.65	2.75	3.5	4	5	6
Cycle Time (seconds)	3.5	3.8	3.9	4.4	4.3	5	5.1	5.6	6	7	7.6

Enter the given data on your calculator. Show a scatter plot of the data. Find the LinReg line of best fit. Then show a graph of the line.

Step 1 Clear any existing lists, and clear any equations from Y= .

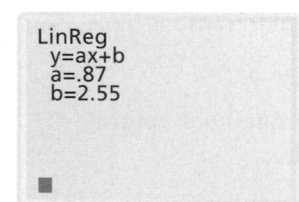

Step 2 Enter the data. Press STAT ENTER . Enter the x-values in L1 and the y-values in L2.

Step 3 Find the LinReg line of best fit. Press STAT ▶ 4 ENTER to find LinReg(ax+b) values. Press Y= VARS 5 ▶ ▶ 1 to enter the regression equation as Y1.

Step 4 Draw the graph. Use the STAT PLOT feature and press 1 ENTER to turn on Plot 1.

Use the ▼ key to move down the rows to select a scatter plot using L1 and L2. Press ZOOM 9 to show the scatter plot and the line of best fit.

2 ACTIVITY Using the Line of Best Fit to Predict

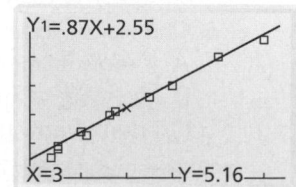

A bee finds food 3 km from the hive. Use the Activity 1 line of best fit and the CALC feature to predict the time of a waggle dance cycle.

With the graph shown, select the CALC feature. Press 1, then 3 ENTER to see the y-value for x = 3. A waggle dance cycle should take about 5.2 s.

A waggle dance cycle is 7.4 s. Use the line of best fit from Activity 1 and the TRACE feature to estimate the distance to the food source.

With the graph shown on the screen, press TRACE ▲. Then press ▶ or ◀ to get the y-value (shown on the screen) as close to 7.4 as possible. You may have to adjust the window dimension Xmax to allow for a large enough trace. The food source is approximately 5.6 km from the beehive.

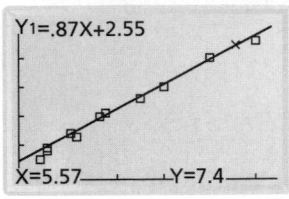

EXERCISES

In MODE , (second line), fix the number of decimal places to be 2. Then the slope and y-intercept values of the LinReg line will round to the nearest hundredth.

1. Find the LinReg line of best fit for this data set.
   $\{(-5, 6.3), (-4, 5.6), (-3, 4.8), (-2, 3.1), (-1, 2.5), (0, 1.0), (1, -1.4)\}$

2. **Health** Find the LinReg line of best fit for the National Health Expenditures data. Then predict national health expenditures for 2010. (*Hint:* You may have to expand the calculator window to include the year 2010 on the screen.)

Year	1997	1998	1999	2000	2001	2002
National Health Expenditures (billions of dollars)	1093	1150	1223	1309	1421	1553

3. **Congress** Find the LinReg line of best fit for the data below. Then estimate the number of U. S. Representatives for Texas. Texas's population for 2000 was 20.0 million.

State	AZ	CO	CT	GA	IL	MO	OH	RI	UT	WA	WI
Population (millions)	5.6	4.6	3.5	8.7	13	5.7	11	1.1	2.4	6.1	5.5
Representatives	8	7	5	13	19	9	18	2	3	9	8

4. There are different ways to find a line of best fit. The line of best fit found by the *least squares* method passes through the point $(\overline{x}, \overline{y})$, where $\overline{x}$ is the mean of the x-values of the data points (x, y), and $\overline{y}$ is the mean of the y-values.

   a. In MODE , change the number of fixed decimal places to 3. Use the data in the table below. Enter the numbers of teachers in L1. Enter the average salaries in L2. Find the LinReg line of best fit.

   Numbers and Average Salaries of Classroom Teachers

Year	1999	2000	2001	2002
Teachers (millions)	2.81	2.89	2.94	2.98
Average Salary (thousands of dollars)	40.5	41.8	43.4	44.6

   b. Calculate $\overline{x}$ and $\overline{y}$, the means for each data set. (To find $\overline{x}$, for example, press 2nd STAT ▶ ▶ 3 L1 ENTER .)

   c. Graph the LinReg line of best fit. Select the CALC feature. Press 1, enter the value of $\overline{x}$, and then press ENTER . Compare the y-value shown to $\overline{y}$.

   d. **Critical Thinking** Does $(\overline{x}, \overline{y})$ lie on the LinReg line of best fit? From this result can you conclude that the LinReg line of best fit and the least squares line of best fit are the same? are different? Explain.

Absolute Value Functions and Graphs

GO for Help   Lesson 2-2 and Skills Handbook page 879

What You'll Learn

• To graph absolute value functions

. . . And Why

To model distance, as in Example 4

✓ **Check Skills You'll Need**

Graph each equation for the given domain and range.

1. $y = x$ for real numbers x and $y \geq 0$

2. $y = 2x - 4$ for real numbers x and $y \geq 0$

3. $y = -x + 6$ for real numbers x and $y \leq 3$

◀》 **New Vocabulary**   • absolute value function   • vertex

---

1 Graphing Absolute Value Functions

A function of the form $f(x) = |mx + b| + c$, where $m \neq 0$, is an **absolute value function.** The related equation $y = |mx + b| + c$ is an absolute value equation in two variables. Graphs of absolute value equations in two variables look like angles.

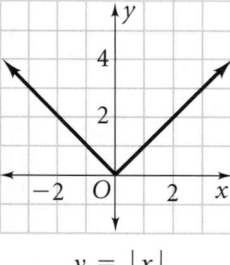

$$y = |x|$$

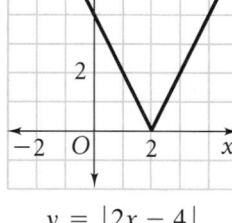

$$y = |2x - 4|$$

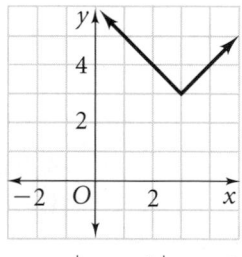

$$y = |x - 3| + 3$$

Vocabulary Tip

Vertex means "turning point."

The **vertex** of a function is a point where the function reaches a maximum or minimum. In general, the vertex of $y = |mx + b| + c$ is located at $\left(-\frac{b}{m}, c\right)$. In the middle graph above, the x-coordinate of the vertex is $-\left(\frac{-4}{2}\right) = 2$.

1 EXAMPLE   Graphing an Absolute Value Function

Graph $y = |3x + 12|$.

Evaluate the equation for several values of x, beginning with $x = -\frac{b}{m} = -\frac{12}{3} = -4$.

Make a table of values.

x	−6	−4	−3	−2
y	6	0	3	6

Graph the function.

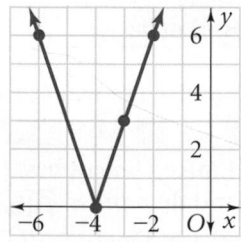

 **Quick Check** ❶ Graph each equation.

a. $y = |2x - 5|$ **b.** $y = -|x + 1| - 2$

You can use a graphing calculator to graph an absolute value equation.

Graphing Calculator Hint

For a calculator screen that shows x- and y-intervals of equal width, press ZOOM, and then select ZSquare.

❷ **EXAMPLE**   **Using a Graphing Calculator**

Graph $y = -|3x + 4| + 6$ on a graphing calculator.

Use the absolute value function.
Graph the equation
$Y1 = -abs(3X + 4) + 6$.

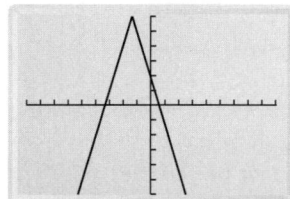

 **Quick Check** ❷ Graph each equation on a graphing calculator. Then sketch the graph.

a. $y = -|-x| + 5$ **b.** $y = 3 - \left|\frac{x}{2}\right|$

You can also graph an absolute value equation by first writing it as two linear equations with restricted domains.

❸ **EXAMPLE**   **Writing Two Linear Equations**

Graph $y = |x - 3| + 5$.

Step 1   Isolate the absolute value.
$$y = |x - 3| + 5$$
$$y - 5 = |x - 3|$$

Step 2   Use the definition of absolute value. Write one equation for $x - 3 \geq 0$ and a second equation for $x - 3 < 0$.

when $x - 3 \geq 0$	when $x - 3 < 0$
$y - 5 = x - 3$	$y - 5 = -(x - 3)$
$y = x + 2$	$y = -x + 8$

online active math*

For: Absolute Value Activity
Use: Interactive Textbook, 2-5

Step 3   Graph each equation for the appropriate domain.

When $x - 3 \geq 0$, or $x \geq 3$, $y = x + 2$.

When $x - 3 < 0$, or $x < 3$, $y = -x + 8$.

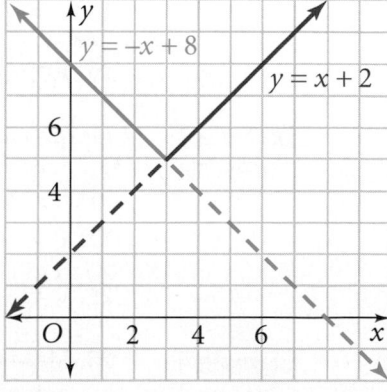

 **Quick Check** ❸ Graph each equation by writing two equations.

a. $y = \left|\frac{3}{2}x + 4\right| - 3$ **b.** $y = 2 - |x + 1|$

You can use absolute value functions to model time and distance problems. You can consider the time before you arrive at a destination to be negative.

4 EXAMPLE Real-World Connection

Travel Suppose you pass the Betsy Ross House halfway along your trip to school each morning. You walk at a rate of one city block per minute. Sketch a graph of your trip to school based on your distance and time from the Betsy Ross House.

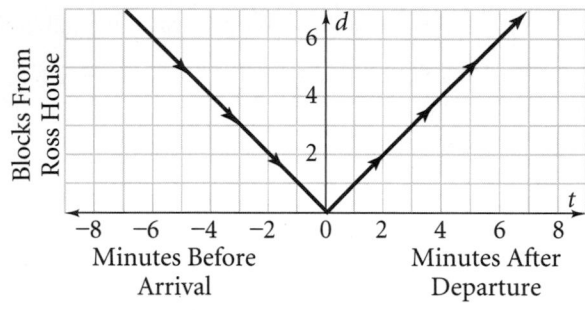

The equation $d = |t|$ models your distance from the Betsy Ross House.

 **Quick Check** 4 a. **Critical Thinking** Suppose you ride your bicycle to school at a rate of three city blocks per minute. How would the graph of your trip to school change?
   b. Sketch a new graph.

EXERCISES

For more exercises, see *Extra Skill and Word Problem Practice.*

Practice and Problem Solving

A **Practice by Example**

Example 1
(page 88)

 for Help

Make a table of values for each equation. Then graph the equation.

1. $y = |4x|$
2. $y = |4x| - 1$
3. $y = |4x - 1|$
4. $y = |-3x|$
5. $y = |-3x| + 2$
6. $y = |-3x + 2|$
7. $y = -|2x|$
8. $y = -|2x| + 5$
9. $y = -|2x + 5|$

Example 2
(page 89)

Graph each equation on a graphing calculator. Then sketch the graph.

10. $y = |x + 2| - 4$
11. $y = 4 - |x + 2|$
12. $y = 4|x + 2|$
13. $y = \frac{1}{3}|3 - 3x|$
14. $y = 3\left|\frac{1}{3} - \frac{1}{3}x\right|$
15. $y = \frac{3}{2}|x| - \frac{5}{2}$
16. $y = |x| + \frac{1}{2}|x|$
17. $y = \frac{1}{2}|x| - |x|$
18. $y = \frac{1}{2}\left|x - \frac{1}{2}\right|$

Example 3
(page 89)

Graph each equation by writing two linear equations.

19. $y = |x + 6|$
20. $y = |3x + 6|$
21. $y = |3x - 6|$
22. $y = -|x - 5|$
23. $y = |2x + 1|$
24. $y = \frac{3}{2}|3x - 1|$
25. $y = |x - 2| - 6$
26. $y = \left|\frac{1}{2}x - 4\right| + 4$
27. $y = \frac{1}{2}\left|\frac{1}{2}x + 2\right| - 2$

Example 4
(page 90)

28. **Manufacturing** The conveyor belt at a factory operates continuously 24 hours a day, carrying vitamin bottles and moving two feet each minute. Sketch a graph showing the distance in feet from the filling arm of one bottle on the conveyor belt before and after it is filled. Use the *x*-axis for time before and after the bottle is filled and the *y*-axis for distance from the filling arm.

Match each equation with its graph. Each interval is 1 unit.

29. $y = |3x| - 4$ **30.** $y = |3x - 4|$ **31.** $y = 3|x - 4|$ **32.** $y = |3x + 12|$

A.

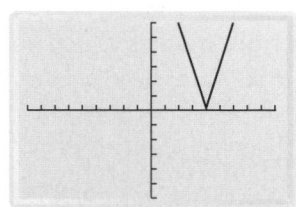

B.

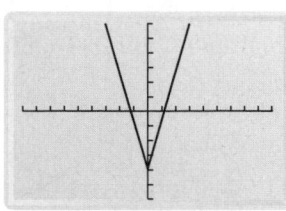

C.

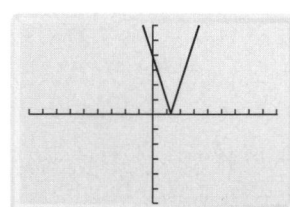

D.

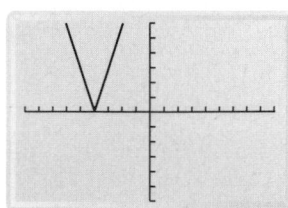

Problem Solving Hint

Before graphing, rewrite each absolute value equation as two linear equations with restricted domains.

Graph each absolute value equation.

33. $y = |4x + 2|$ **34.** $y = |-3x + 5|$ **35.** $y = |4 - 2x|$

36. $y = \left|-\frac{1}{4}x - 1\right|$ **37.** $y = \left|\frac{5}{2}x - 2\right|$ **38.** $y = \left|\frac{3}{2}x + 2\right|$

39. $y = |3x - 6| + 1$ **40.** $y = -|x - 3|$ **41.** $y = |2x + 6|$

42. $y = 2|x + 2| - 3$ **43.** $y = 6 - |3x|$ **44.** $y = 6 - |3x + 1|$

45. $y = -|-2x - 1| + 1$ **46.** $y = 2|x - 3|$ **47.** $y = -\frac{3}{2}\left|\frac{1}{2}x\right|$

48. $2y = \frac{1}{2}|x + 2|$ **49.** $\frac{1}{3}y - 3 = -|x + 2|$ **50.** $-3y = |3x - 6|$

51. Multiple Choice The graph at the right models a car traveling at a constant speed. Which equation best represents the relation shown in the graph?

   Ⓐ $y = |60x|$
   Ⓑ $y = |x + 60|$
   Ⓒ $y = |60 - x|$
   Ⓓ $y = |x| + 60$

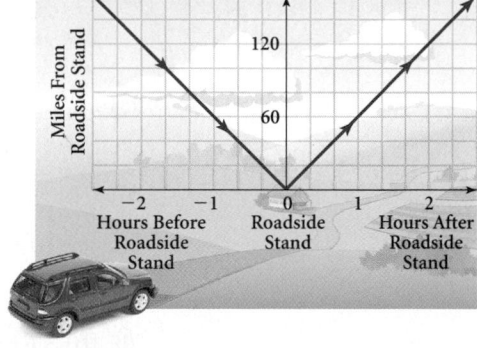

GO Online
Homework Video Tutor
Visit: PHSchool.com
Web Code: age-0205

52. a. Graph the equations $y = \left|\frac{1}{2}x - 6\right| + 3$ and $y = -\left|\frac{1}{2}x + 6\right| - 3$ on the same set of axes.

   b. Writing Describe the similarities and differences in the graphs.

C **Challenge** Graph each absolute value equation.

53. $y = |3x| - x\left|\frac{1}{3}\right|$ **54.** $y = x - |2x|$ **55.** $y = |2x| - x$

56. $y = \frac{1}{2}|x - 3| + 5$ **57.** $y = \frac{1}{2}|x| + 4|x - 1|$ **58.** $y = |x + 1| + |x|$

59. a. Open-Ended Find two absolute value equations with graphs that share a vertex.

   b. Find two absolute value equations with graphs that share part of a ray.

Multiple Choice

60. The graph at the right models which equation?
   A. $y = |3x - 1| + 2$ **B.** $y = |x - 1| - 2$
   C. $y = |x - 1| + 2$ **D.** $y = |3x - 3| - 2$

61. What is the vertex of $y = |x| - 5$?
   F. (5, 0)   **G.** (−5, 0)
   H. (0, 5)   **J.** (0, −5)

62. What is the vertex of $y = -|x| - 2$?
   A. (0, −2)   **B.** (0, 2)
   C. (2, 0)   **D.** (2, −2)

63. What is the vertex of $y = |x - 3| + 5$?
   F. (−3, 5)   **G.** (−3, 11)   **H.** (0, 5)   **J.** (3, 5)

64. Which pair of linear equations represents the equation $y = |x + 3| - 4$?
   A. $y = x + 1$ for $x \geq 3$ **B.** $y = x - 1$ for $x \geq 3$
      $y = x - 1$ for $x < 3$ $y = -x - 1$ for $x < 3$
   C. $y = x - 1$ for $x \geq -3$ **D.** $y = -x - 1$ for $x \geq -3$
      $y = -x - 7$ for $x < -3$ $y = -x + 7$ for $x < -3$

Short Response

65. Explain how to find the x-coordinate of the vertex of $y = |3x - 6|$.

Extended Response

66. How can you graph the equation $y = -|5x + 1|$ by writing two linear equations? Show both equations, and label the coordinates of the vertex in your graph.

Mixed Review

Lesson 2-4

Graph each set of data. Decide whether a linear model is reasonable. If so, draw a trend line and write its equation.

67. $\{(0, -5), (5, 25), (7, 44), (9, 70), (11, 90)\}$

68. $\{(-10, 0), (-4, 4), (-1, 6), (2, 8), (5, 10)\}$

69. $\{(-5, 6), (-1, 4), (0, 5), (3, 8), (4, 7)\}$

70. $\{(0, 7), (2, 6), (5, 4.5), (6, 4), (9, 2.5)\}$

Lesson 2-4

Find the slope of each line.

71. $3x + y = 1$ **72.** $5y - 20x = 6$ **73.** $y = \frac{-x}{9}$

74. $12x = 3y - 2$ **75.** $\frac{x}{2} + \frac{y}{3} = 1$ **76.** $0.1y = 0.5x + 0.1$

77. A tutor earns \$18 per hour. Write a function to model the tutor's earnings after h hours. What kind of function is this?

Lesson 1-3

Solve each equation.

78. $17x = 187$ **79.** $13c - 26 = 91$ **80.** $2(a - 6) + 11 = 25$

81. $7(b + 3) - 18(1 - b) = 103$ **82.** $6(m + 3) = 3(5 - m) + 66$

Families of Functions

What You'll Learn

- To analyze translations
- To analyze stretches, shrinks, and reflections

. . . And Why

To analyze a fabric design, as in Example 3

 Check Skills You'll Need

GO for Help Lessons 2-2 and 2-5

Graph each pair of functions on the same coordinate plane.

1. $y = x, y = x + 4$

2. $y = -2x, y = -2x - 3$

3. $y = |x|, y = |x| - 2$

4. $y = -|2x|, y = -|2x| + 1$

5. $y = |x|, y = |x - 1|$

6. $y = -\left|\frac{1}{2}x\right|, y = -\left|\frac{1}{2}x + 2\right|$

New Vocabulary • parent function • translation • stretch • shrink
  • reflection • transformation • parameter

---

1   Translations

Vocabulary Tip

Translate is a synonym for transfer.

Technology Activity: A Family of Functions

The four functions in each group are related. Graph each set of functions in the same viewing window. Explain how they are related.

1. $y_1(x) = |x|$ $y_2(x) = |x| + 2$ $y_3(x) = |x| + 4$ $y_4(x) = |x| - 2$

2. $y_1(x) = |x|$ $y_2(x) = |x + 2|$ $y_3(x) = |x + 4|$ $y_4(x) = |x - 2|$

3. $y_1(x) = |x|$ $y_2(x) = 2|x|$ $y_3(x) = 4|x|$ $y_4(x) = \frac{1}{2}|x|$

4. $y_1(x) = |x|$ $y_2(x) = -|x|$ $y_3(x) = 2|x|$ $y_4(x) = -2|x|$

Use the graphs from parts 1–4 to predict the graph of each function below. On graph paper and without plotting points, sketch what you think the graph of f should be. Then check your sketch on a graphing calculator.

5. $f(x) = |x + 4| - 2$

6. $f(x) = -2|x| + 4$

7. Sketch what you think the graph of $f(x) = -3|x + 2| - 1$ should be. Then check your sketch on a graphing calculator.

8. Considering all the functions in Exercises 1–7, which function would you call the simplest? Explain.

A family of functions is made up of functions with certain common characteristics.

A **parent function** is the simplest function with these characteristics. The equations of the functions in a family resemble each other. So do the graphs. Offspring of parent functions include translations, stretches, and shrinks.

A **translation** shifts a graph horizontally, vertically, or both. It results in a graph of the same shape and size but possibly in a different position.

The parent absolute value function is $y = |x|$. For a positive number k, $y = |x| \pm k$ is a vertical translation. To graph the function $y = |x| + k$, translate the graph of the parent function up k units. To graph the function $y = |x| - k$, translate the graph of the parent down k units.

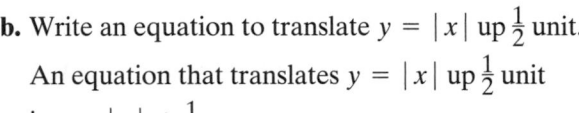 **Vertical Translation**

a. Describe the translation $y = |x| - 3$ and draw its graph.

$y = |x| - 3$ is a translation of $y = |x|$ by 3 units downward. Each y-value for $y = |x| - 3$ is 3 less than the corresponding y-value for $y = |x|$.

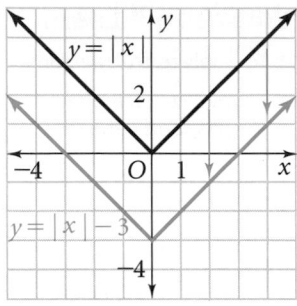

b. Write an equation to translate $y = |x|$ up $\frac{1}{2}$ unit.

An equation that translates $y = |x|$ up $\frac{1}{2}$ unit is $y = |x| + \frac{1}{2}$.

Real-World 🌐 **Connection**

Translations of two lines result in the diamond shapes in this window.

✓ **Quick Check** ➊ **a.** Describe the translation $y = |x| + 1$. Then draw the graphs of $y = |x|$ and $y = |x| + 1$ in the same coordinate plane.

b. Write an equation for the translation of $y = |x|$ down $\frac{1}{2}$ unit; Up 3.5 units.

Horizontal translations of the parent function $y = |x|$ share some of the characteristics of vertical translations.

For a positive number h, $y = |x \pm h|$ is a horizontal translation. To graph the function $y = |x - h|$, translate the graph of the parent function right h units. To graph the function $y = |x + h|$, translate the graph left h units.

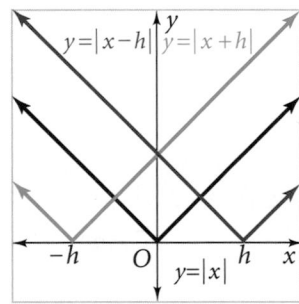

➋ **EXAMPLE** **Horizontal Translations**

a. The blue graph at the right is a translation of $y = |x|$. Write an equation for the graph.

The graph of $y = |x|$ is translated 5 units to the right. An equation for the graph is $y = |x - 5|$.

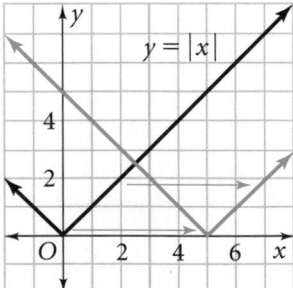

b. Describe the translation $y = |x + 3|$ and draw its graph.

$y = |x + 3|$ is a translation of $y = |x|$ by 3 units to the left.

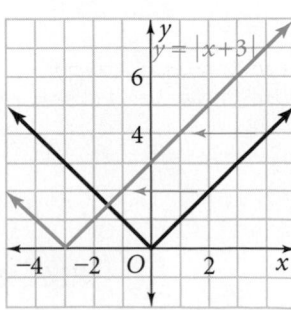

Quick Check **2** **a.** The graph is a translation of $y = |x|$.
Write an equation for the graph.
b. Describe the translation $y = |x - 1|$. Then draw
the graphs of $y = |x|$ and $y = |x - 1|$ in the same
coordinate plane.

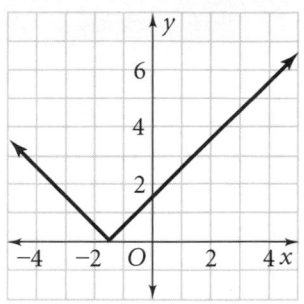

The parent absolute value function is $y = |x|$. For values h and k, $y = |x - h| + k$
is a combined translation of h units horizontally and k units vertically.

Key Concepts

Summary	The Family of Absolute Value Functions

Vertical Translation

Parent function:	$y = |x|$	$y = f(x)$
Translation up k units, $k > 0$:	$y = |x| + k$	$y = f(x) + k$
Translation down k units, $k > 0$:	$y = |x| - k$	$y = f(x) - k$

Horizontal Translation

Parent function:	$y = |x|$	$y = f(x)$
Translation right h units, $h > 0$:	$y = |x - h|$	$y = f(x - h)$
Translation left h units, $h > 0$:	$y = |x + h|$	$y = f(x + h)$

Combined Translation $y = |x - h| + k$ $y = f(x - h) + k$
(right h units, up k units)

3 **EXAMPLE** **Real-World** **Connection**

Fabric Design Describe possible translations of Figures A and B
in the Nigerian textile design below.

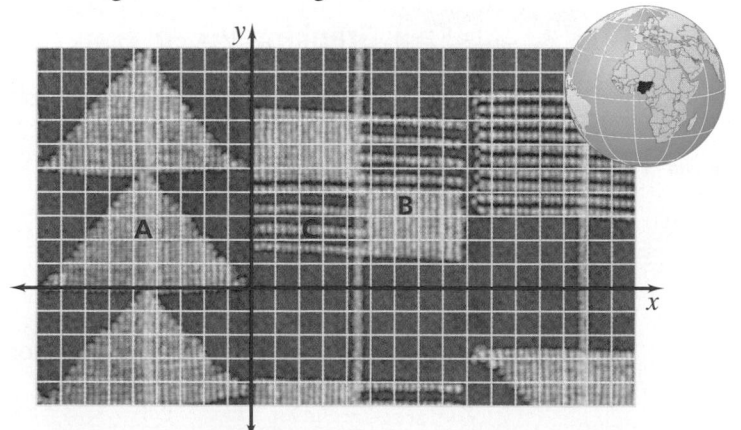

A translation of Figure A   A translation of Figure B
● 5 units up or 5 units down   about 5 units left and about 3 units up

 **Quick Check** **3** Describe a possible translation of Figure C in the textile design.

A vertical **stretch** multiplies all *y*-values by the same factor greater than 1, thereby stretching a graph vertically. A vertical **shrink** reduces *y*-values by a factor between 0 and 1, thereby compressing the graph vertically.

More formally, for the parent function $y = |x|$ and a number $a, a > 1, y = a|x|$ is a vertical stretch. For $0 < a < 1, y = a|x|$ is a vertical shrink.

4 EXAMPLE Graphing $y = a|x|$

a. Describe and then draw the graph of $y = 2|x|$.

$y = 2|x|$ is a vertical stretch of $y = |x|$ by a factor of 2. Each *y*-value for $y = 2|x|$ is twice the corresponding *y*-value for $y = |x|$.

Note that $(2, 2)$ lies on $y = |x|$, whereas $(2, 4)$ lies on $y = 2|x|$.

b. Write an equation for a vertical shrink of $y = |x|$ by a factor of $\frac{1}{2}$.

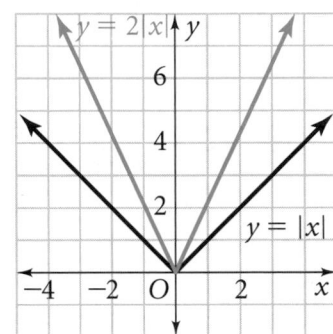

A vertical shrink of $y = |x|$ by a factor of $\frac{1}{2}$ is $y = \frac{1}{2}|x|$.

✓ **Quick Check** **4 a.** Describe the stretch or shrink $y = \frac{1}{3}|x|$. Then draw the graphs of $y = |x|$ and $y = \frac{1}{3}|x|$ in the same coordinate plane.
b. Write an equation for the vertical stretch of $y = |x|$ by a factor of 3.

A **reflection** in the *x*-axis changes *y*-values to their opposites. When you change the *y*-values of a graph to their opposites, the graph reflects across the *x*-axis.

For the parent function $y = |x|$, indeed for any function of the form $y = a|x|$, multiplying by –1 gives the reflection $y = -a|x|$, whose graph is a reflection of $y = a|x|$ across the *x*-axis.

5 EXAMPLE Graphing $y = -a|x|$

Multiple Choice Which equation describes the graph?

Ⓐ $y = \frac{1}{2}|x|$

Ⓑ $y = \frac{1}{2}x$

Ⓒ $y = -\frac{1}{2}|x|$

Ⓓ $y = -\frac{1}{2}x$

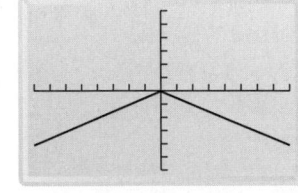

The parent function is $y = |x|$. This is a reflection across the *x*-axis of $y = \frac{1}{2}|x|$. The answer is C.

✓ **Quick Check** **5** A function is a vertical stretch of $y = |x|$ by a factor of 5. Write an equation for the reflection of the function across the *x*-axis.

What you have learned about the absolute value function extends to functions in general.

Each member of a family of functions is a **transformation,** or change, of a parent function. Algebraically, the transformations take the same form using **parameters,** like h, k, and a. Graphically, the results are similar—shifts, stretches, shrinks, and reflections of the parent function.

 Key Concepts

Summary	Families of Functions: Absolute Value Functions

Vertical Stretch or Shrink, and Reflection in x-axis

Parent function:	$y = \lvert x \rvert$	$y = f(x)$
Reflection in x-axis:	$y = -\lvert x \rvert$	$y = -f(x)$
Stretch $(a > 1)$ Shrink $(0 < a < 1)$ } by factor a:	$y = a\lvert x \rvert$	$y = af(x)$
Reflection in x-axis:	$y = -a\lvert x \rvert$	$y = -af(x)$

Combined Transformation	$y = a\lvert x - h \rvert + k$	$y = af(x - h) + k$

EXERCISES

For more exercises, see *Extra Skill and Word Problem Practice.*

Practice and Problem Solving

A **Practice by Example**

Example 1
(page 94)

 GO for Help

For each function, graph the function by translating the parent function.

1. $y = \lvert x \rvert - 3$ **2.** $y = \lvert x \rvert + 4\frac{1}{2}$ **3.** $y = \lvert x \rvert + 2$ **4.** $y = \lvert x \rvert - 6$

Write an equation for each vertical translation of $y = \lvert x \rvert$.

5. $\frac{2}{3}$ unit down   **6.** 4 units up   **7.** 2 units up

Example 2
(page 94)

For each function, identify the translation of the parent function. Then graph the function.

8. $y = \lvert x - 4 \rvert$ **9.** $y = \lvert x + 5 \rvert$ **10.** $y = \lvert x - 1 \rvert$ **11.** $y = \lvert x + 2 \rvert$

Write an equation for each horizontal translation of $y = \lvert x \rvert$.

12. 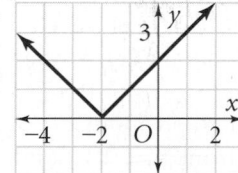   **13.** 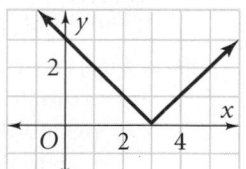   **14.**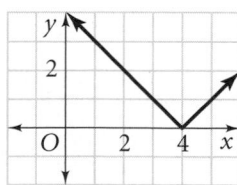

Example 3
(page 95)

Describe a possible translation for each figure.

15. 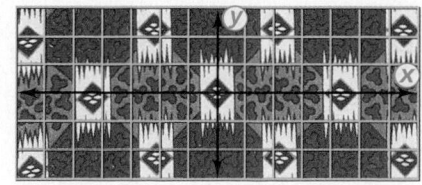   **16.**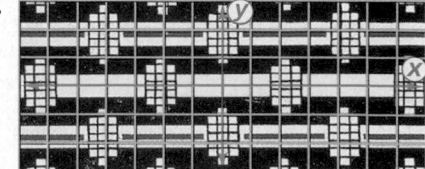

Example 4
(page 96)

Graph each function.

17. $y = 4|x|$ **18.** $y = \frac{1}{2}|x|$ **19.** $y = 2|x - 1|$

20. $y = \frac{1}{2}|x| + 2$ **21.** $y = 1.5|x| - 1$ **22.** $y = 0.5|x + 3|$

Write the equation for each graph. Each interval is 1 unit.

23. 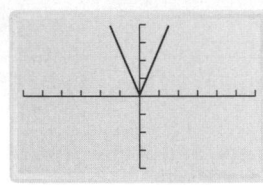   **24.** 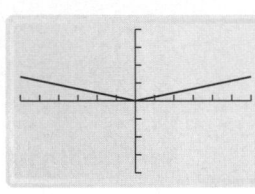   **25.**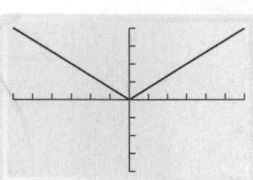

Example 5
(page 96)

26. 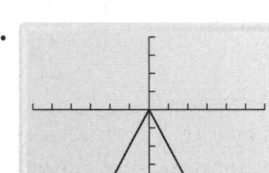   **27.** 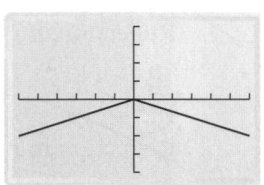   **28.**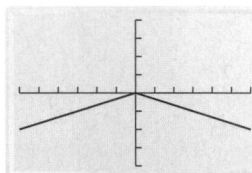

B Apply Your Skills

Describe each translation of $f(x) = |x|$ as *vertical*, *horizontal*, or *combined*. Then graph each translation.

29. $f(x) = |x| - 5$ **30.** $f(x) = |x - 5| + 3$ **31.** $f(x) = |x + 1|$

32. $f(x) = \left| x + \frac{1}{2} \right| - 4\frac{1}{2}$ **33.** $f(x) = |x| - 3$ **34.** $f(x) = |x - 3| - 6$

Write the equation for each graph. Each interval is 1 unit.

35. 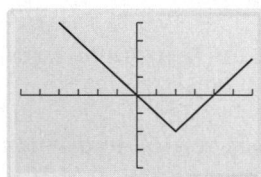   **36.** 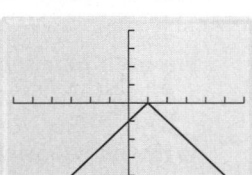   **37.**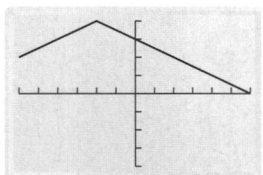

38. Data Analysis Suppose you plot data with years as the independent variable. What type of translation are you making when you start with $x = 0$ rather than a year such as 1998? Explain.

 39. Writing Explain why applying a vertical translation and then a horizontal translation produces the same result as applying a horizontal translation and then a vertical translation.

40. a. Graph the parent function $f(x) = x$ and the function $g(x) = 3x$ on a coordinate plane.
　　b. Translate the second graph 5 units up. Write an equation for the new line.
　　c. Translate the graph from part (b) 2 units right. Write an equation for the new line.
　　d. Which equation describes the line you graphed in part (c)?
　　　　A. $y = 3x + 5$ **B.** $y = 3x + 2$ **C.** $y = 3x - 2$
　　　　D. $y = 3(x - 5) + 2$ **E.** $y = 3(x - 2) + 5$
　　e. Critical Thinking Write the equation of the translation of $y = mx$ that has a graph passing through point (h, k).

41. Open-Ended Draw a figure in Quadrant I. Use a translation to move your figure into Quadrant III. Describe your translation.

GO Online
Homework Video Tutor

Visit: PHSchool.com
Web Code: age-0206

Each graph shows an absolute value function after a translation 4 units up and 3 units left. Write the equation of the original function.

42.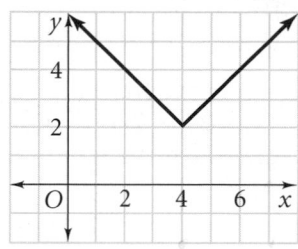

43.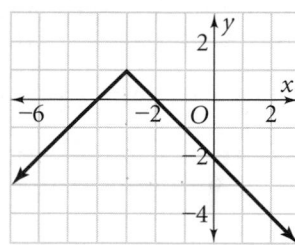

Write an equation for the translation so the graph has the given vertex.

44. $y = -|x|$; vertex $(-5, 0)$

45. $y = 2|x|$; vertex $(-4, 3)$

46. $y = |x|$; vertex (a, b)

47. $y = -|x|$; vertex (p, q)

Graph each pair of functions on the same coordinate plane. Describe the translation that takes the first function to the second function.

48. $y = |x + 1|, y = |x - 5|$

49. $y = |x| + 3, y = |x - 4|$

50. $y = |x - 3|, y = |x| + 1$

51. $y = |x + 1| - 1, y = |x - 2| + 2$

 **Challenge**

52. Suppose you are playing with a yo-yo, as shown at the right.
a. Sketch a graph of $h(t)$ to show the height h of the yo-yo above the floor over time t. At $t = 0$, the yo-yo leaves your hand.
b. Critical Thinking Should your graph be that of a function? Explain.
c. Suppose you demonstrate your yo-yo ability on an auditorium stage that is 5 ft above the floor. Describe the translation of the graph of $h(t)$ that represents the height of the yo-yo above the auditorium floor.
d. Choose a function $g(t)$ that represents the height of the yo-yo above the auditorium floor when you are on stage.
A. $g(t) = h(t + 5)$ **B.** $g(t) = h(t - 5)$
C. $g(t) = h(t) + 5$ **D.** $g(t) = h(t) - 5$

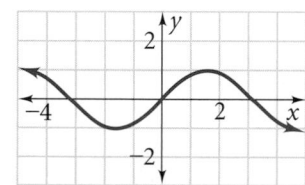
3 ft

53. Use the graph of the function $y = f(x)$ at the right. Sketch the graph of each function.
a. $f(x + 1)$
b. $f(x) - 2$
c. $f(x + 2) + 1$
d. $-2f(x)$

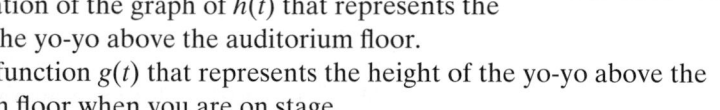

Test Prep

Multiple Choice

54. Which translation takes $y = |x + 2| - 1$ to $y = |x| + 2$?
A. 2 units right, 3 units down   **B.** 2 units left, 3 units up
C. 2 units right, 3 units up   **D.** 2 units left, 3 units down

55. The graph of which equation will NOT have a y-intercept of 5?
F. $y = |x| + 5$ **G.** $y = |x - 5|$ **H.** $y = |x - 5| + 5$ **J.** $y = |x + 5|$

56. The graph of $y = |x - 1|$ is translated 3 units left and 2 units down. What is the equation of the new graph?

A. $y = |x + 2| - 2$ **B.** $y = |x - 4| - 2$

C. $y = |x + 4| + 2$ **D.** $y = |x - 4| + 2$

Extended Response **57.** Start with the parent function of $y = |x + 3| - 2$. Explain how to describe the graph of $y = |x + 3| - 2$ as two consecutive translations of the parent function. Include graphs of the parent function and each translation.

Mixed Review

Lesson 2-5 Evaluate each function for five values of *x*. Then graph each function.

58. $f(x) = |x - 3| + 2$ **59.** $f(x) = |2x + 1| - 3$ **60.** $f(x) = \frac{1}{3}\left|\frac{1}{3}x - 3\right|$

Lesson 1-4 Solve each inequality. Graph each solution on a number line.

61. $x + 7 \le -3$ **62.** $2a + 6 > 15$ **63.** $7.5 - 3b < 12$

Lesson 1-3 **64. Geometry** Keiko, an orca whale who starred in a number of movies, moved into an outdoor pool with a volume of 281,250 cubic feet. The pool's surface is a 150 ft-by-75 ft rectangle. Write and solve an equation to find the depth of the pool.

✓ Checkpoint Quiz 2   Lessons 2-4 through 2-6

Graph each function.

1. $y = x - 5$ **2.** $y = |x + 1| + 4$ **3.** $f(x) = \frac{2}{3}x - 2$

4. $f(x) = |x| - 4$ **5.** $y = |2x - 1| - 2$ **6.** $y = 3x + 3$

Write an equation for each graph.

7.

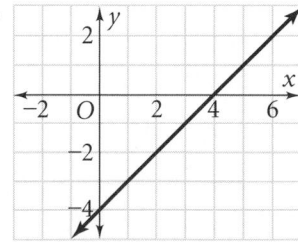

8.

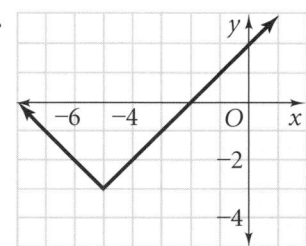

9. a. Use the table below. Model the relation with a scatter plot and a trend line.

    b. Predict the value of *y* when $x = 10$.

x	1.0	2.0	3.0	4.0	5.0	6.0	7.0
y	−1.5	0.0	1.5	2.0	2.5	3.5	4.0

10. The graph of $y = |x|$ is translated down 5 units and right 4 units. What is the equation of the new graph?

A. $y = |x + 4| + 5$ **B.** $y = |x + 4| - 5$

C. $y = |x - 4| + 5$ **D.** $y = |x - 4| - 5$

2-7

Two-Variable Inequalities

What You'll Learn

- To graph linear inequalities
- To graph absolute value inequalities

. . . And Why

To solve problems involving combinations, as in Example 2

 **Check Skills You'll Need**

GO for Help Lessons 1-4 and 1-5

Solve each inequality. Graph the solution on a number line.

1. $12p \leq 15$ **2.** $4 + t > 17$ **3.** $5 - 2t \geq 11$

Solve and graph each absolute value equation or inequality.

4. $|4c| = 18$ **5.** $|5 - b| = 3$ **6.** $|2h| \geq 7$

New Vocabulary • linear inequality

---

1   Graphing Linear Inequalities

Activity: Linear Inequalities

1. Graph the line $y = 2x + 3$ on graph paper.

2. a. Plot each point listed below.
$(-2, -3), (-2, -1), (-1, -1), (-1, 5), (0, 4), (0, 5), (1, 6), (2, 3), (2, 7)$
b. Classify each point as *on the line*, *above the line*, or *below the line*.

3. Are all the points that satisfy the inequality $y > 2x + 3$ *above*, *below*, or *on* the line?

Vocabulary Tip

$<$ less than
$\leq$ less than or equal to
$>$ greater than
$\geq$ greater than or equal to
$\neq$ not equal to

A **linear inequality** is an inequality in two variables whose graph is a region of the coordinate plane that is bounded by a line. To graph a linear inequality, first graph the boundary line. Then decide which side of the line contains solutions to the inequality and whether the boundary line is included.

$y > \frac{1}{2}x - 1$

For an inequality with $y <$ or $y \leq$, shade below the line.
For an inequality with $y >$ or $y \geq$, shade above the line.

A *dashed* boundary line indicates that the line is not part of the solution.

A *solid* boundary line indicates that the line is part of the solution.

Choose a test point above or below the boundary line. The test point $(0, 0)$ makes the inequality true. Shade the region containing this point.

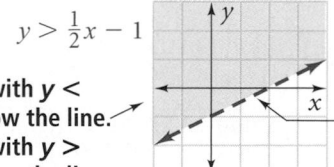

$2x + 3y \leq 6$

$(0, 0)$

1 EXAMPLE **Graphing a Linear Inequality**

Graph the inequality $y < \frac{1}{2}x - 3$.

Step 1 Graph the boundary line $y = \frac{1}{2}x - 3$. Since the inequality is *less than*, not *less than or equal to*, use a dashed boundary line.

Step 2 Since the inequality is *less than*, y-values must be less than those on the boundary line. Shade the region *below* the boundary line.

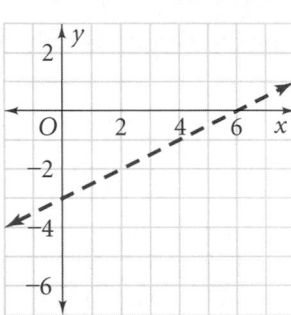

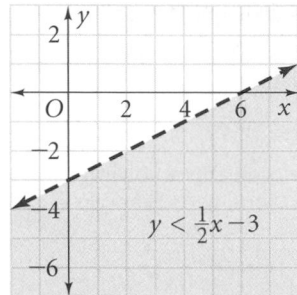

✓ **Quick Check** **1** Graph each inequality.
a. $4x + 2y \leq 4$ **b.** $y \geq 3x$ **c.** $\frac{x}{3} < -y + 2$

You can use linear inequalities to solve problems.

2 EXAMPLE **Real-World Connection**

Entertainment At least 35 performers of the Big Tent Circus are in the grand finale. Some pile into cars, while others balance on bicycles. Seven performers are in each car, and five performers are on each bicycle. Draw a graph showing all the combinations of cars and bicycles possible for the finale.

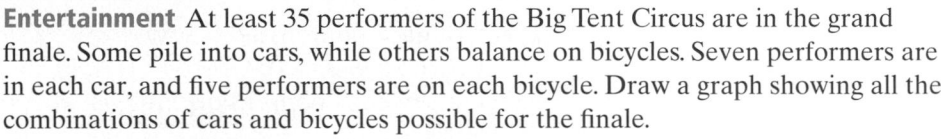

Relate the number of performers in cars plus the number of performers on bicycles is greater than or equal to 35

Define Let x = the number of cars.

Let y = the number of bicycles.

Write $7x$ + $5y$ ≥ 35

Step 1 Find the intercepts of the boundary line. Use the intercepts to graph the boundary line.

When $y = 0$, $7x + 5(0) = 35$.
$$7x = 35$$
$$x = 5$$

When $x = 0$, $7(0) + 5y = 35$.
$$5y = 35$$
$$y = 7$$

Graph the intercepts $(5, 0)$ and $(0, 7)$. Since the inequality is *greater than or equal to*, use a solid boundary line.

Step 2 Choose a test point not on the boundary line. The test point (6, 4) makes the inequality true. Shade the region containing (6, 4).

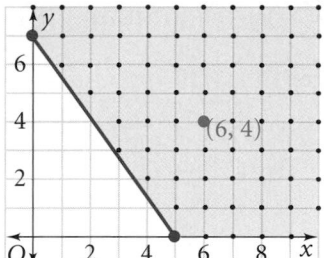

The numbers of cars x and bicycles y are whole numbers. The situation is discrete. In the shaded region, all points with whole number coordinates (shown by dots) represent possible combinations of cars and bicycles for the grand finale.

✓ **Quick Check** ② **a.** Find the minimum number of bicycles that will be needed if three cars are available. Then determine three other possible combinations of bicycles and cars.

b. Critical Thinking What inequalities describe the shaded region bounded by the x- and y-axes and the line in the graph above?

---

2   Graphing Two-Variable Absolute Value Inequalities

You can graph two-variable absolute value inequalities the same way you graph linear inequalities.

③ **EXAMPLE**   **Graphing Absolute Value Inequalities**

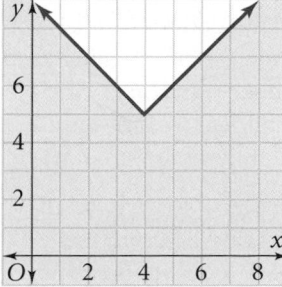

GO for Help

To review graphing absolute value functions, go to Lessons 2-5 and 2-6.

Graph each absolute value inequality.

a. $y \leq |x - 4| + 5$

Graph $y = |x - 4| + 5$.
Since the inequality is *less than or equal to*, the boundary is solid and the shaded region is below the boundary.

b. $-y + 3 > |x + 1|$

$-y > |x + 1| - 3$
$y < -|x + 1| + 3$

Graph $y = -|x + 1| + 3$.

Since the inequality is *less than*, the boundary is dashed and the shaded region is below the boundary.

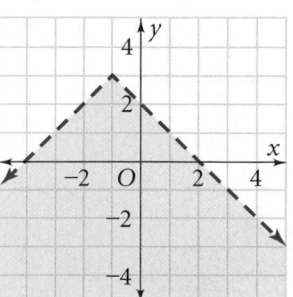

✓ **Quick Check** ③ Graph each absolute value inequality.

a. $y > -|x + 2| - 3$

b. $2y + 3 \leq -|x - 5|$

You can write an inequality by examining a graph.

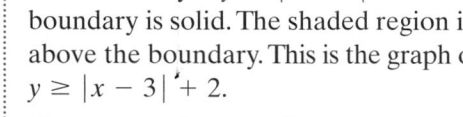 **4 EXAMPLE** Writing Inequalities

Multiple Choice The graph is the solution of which inequality?

Ⓐ $y > |x - 3| + 2$
Ⓑ $y < |x - 3| + 2$
Ⓒ $y \geq |x - 3| + 2$
Ⓓ $y \leq |x - 3| + 2$

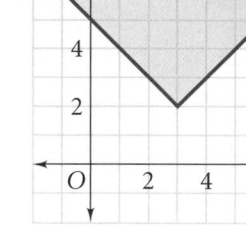

The boundary is $y = |x - 3| + 2$. The boundary is solid. The shaded region is above the boundary. This is the graph of $y \geq |x - 3| + 2$.

● The correct choice is C.

Test-Taking Tip

You can evaluate an inequality at a "test point" to check that a region corresponds to the solution of the inequality.

 **4** Write an inequality for each graph.

a.

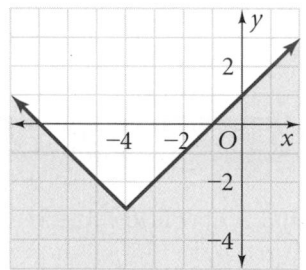

b.

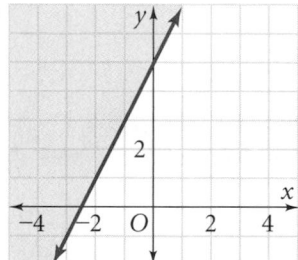

EXERCISES

For more exercises, see *Extra Skill and Word Problem Practice.*

Practice and Problem Solving

Ⓐ **Practice by Example**

Example 1
(page 102)

 for Help

Graph each inequality.

1. $y > 2x + 1$ **2.** $y < 3$ **3.** $x \leq 0$

4. $y \leq x - 5$ **5.** $2x + 3y \geq 12$ **6.** $2y \geq 4x - 6$

7. $y > \frac{2}{3}x + \frac{1}{3}$ **8.** $3x - 2y \leq 9$ **9.** $5x > -y + 3$

Example 2
(pages 102–103)

10. Cooking The time needed to roast a chicken depends on its weight. Allow at least 20 min/lb for a chicken weighing as much as 6 lb. Allow at least 15 min/lb for a chicken weighing more than 6 lb.
 a. Write two inequalities to represent the time needed to roast a chicken.
 b. Graph the inequalities.

Example 3
(page 103)

Graph each absolute value inequality.

11. $y \geq |2x - 1|$ **12.** $y \leq |3x| + 1$ **13.** $y \leq |4 - x|$

14. $y > |-x + 4| + 1$ **15.** $y - 7 > |x + 2|$ **16.** $y + 2 \leq \left|\frac{1}{2}x\right|$

17. $3 - y \geq -|x - 4|$ **18.** $1 - y < |2x - 1|$ **19.** $y + 3 \leq |3x| - 1$

Example 4
(page 104)

Write an inequality for each graph. The equation for the boundary is given.

20. $y = -x - 2$

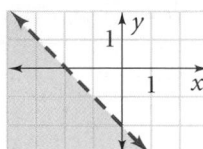

21. $5x + 3y = 9$

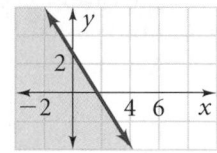

22. $2y = |2x + 6|$

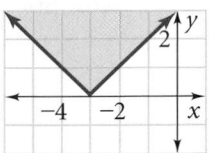

B **Apply Your Skills**

Graph each inequality on a coordinate plane.

23. $5x - 2y \geq -10$

24. $2x - 5y < -10$

25. $\frac{3}{4}x + \frac{2}{3}y > \frac{5}{2}$

26. $3(x - 2) + 2y \leq 6$

27. $0.5x + 1.2y < 6$

28. $-3x + 4y > -6$

29. $\frac{1}{2}x + \frac{2}{3}y \geq 1$

30. $|x - 1| > y + 7$

31. $y - |2x| \leq 21$

32. $\frac{2}{3}x + 2 \leq \frac{2}{9}y$

33. $0.25y - 1.5x \geq -4$

34. $8x - 4y \geq -3$

For a guide to solving
Exercise 35, see p. 107.

35. Open-Ended Write an inequality that has $(10, 15)$, $(-10, 20)$, $(-20, -25)$, and $(25, -10)$ as solutions.

Write an inequality for each graph.

36.

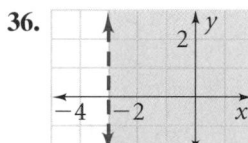

37.

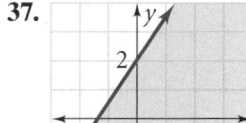

38.

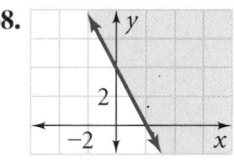

39.

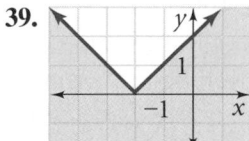

40.

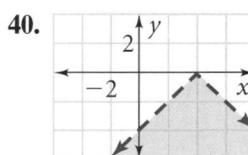

41.

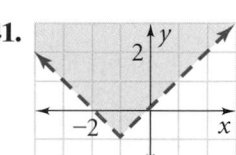

42. Multiple Choice Which graph best represents the solution of the inequality $y \geq 2|x - 1| - 2$?

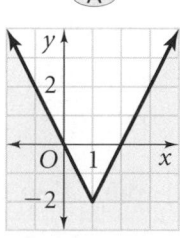

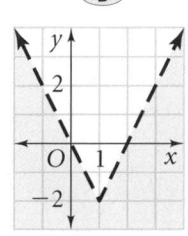

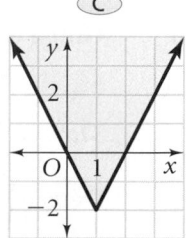

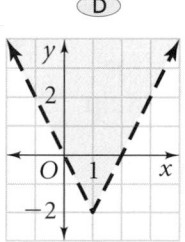

Go Online
Homework Video Tutor
Visit: PHSchool.com
Web Code: age-0207

C **Challenge**

43. Writing When you graph an inequality, you can often use the point $(0, 0)$ to test which side of the boundary line to shade. Describe a situation in which you could *not* use $(0, 0)$ as a test point.

Graph each inequality on a graphing calculator. Then sketch the graph.

44. $y \leq |x + 1| - |x - 1|$

45. $y > |x| + |x + 3|$

46. $y < |x - 3| - |x + 3|$

47. $y < 7 - |x - 4| + |x|$

Multiple Choice

48. The graph at the right shows
which inequality?

A. $y > |x + 4| - 4$
B. $y > |x - 4| + 4$
C. $y < |x + 4| - 4$
D. $y < |x - 4| + 4$

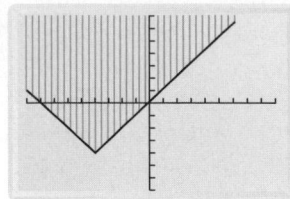

49. The graph of which inequality has its vertex at $\left(2\frac{1}{2}, -5\right)$?

F. $y < |2x - 5| + 5$
G. $y < |2x + 5| - 5$
H. $y > |2x + 5| - 5$
J. $y > |2x - 5| - 5$

50. Which inequality is NOT equivalent to the others?

A. $y \leq \frac{2}{3}x - 3$
B. $3y \leq 2x - 9$
C. $2x - 3y \geq 9$
D. $2x - 3y \leq 9$

51. The graph at the right shows
which inequality?

F. $y \leq -2.5x + 5$

G. $2.5x + y \geq 5$

H. $-2.5x + y < 5$

J. $5x + 2y \leq 5$

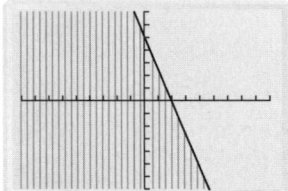

52. Which point(s) are solutions of the inequality $5x + 3y \geq 2$?

I. $(0, 0)$
II. $(-1, 0)$ and $\left(0, -\frac{2}{3}\right)$
III. $\left(0, \frac{2}{3}\right)$ and $\left(1, -\frac{2}{3}\right)$

A. I only
B. I and II
C. III only
D. II and III

Short Response

53. At least 300 tornadoes occur in the United States each year. Write an
inequality to model the number of tornadoes that could occur during the
next x years. Describe the domain and range of the inequality.

Mixed Review

Lesson 2-6

Graph each function by translating its parent function.

54. $y = 2x + 5$
55. $y = |x| - 3$
56. $f(x) = |x + 6|$

57. $f(x) = x - 2$
58. $y = |x + 2|$
59. $y = |x - 1| + 5$

Lesson 2-3

Determine whether y varies directly with x. If so, find the constant of variation.

60. $y = x + 1$
61. $y = 100x$
62. $5x + y = 0$
63. $y - 2 = 2x$

64. $x = \frac{y}{3}$
65. $-4 = y - x$
66. $y = -10x$
67. $xy = 1$

68. Commissions The amount of a commission is directly proportional to the
amount of a sale. A realtor received a commission of $13,500 on the sale of a
$225,000 house. How much would the commission be on a $130,000 house?

Lesson 2-2

Graph each pair of equations on the same coordinate plane.

69. $y = x, y = -x + 5$
70. $y = -2x + 1, y = 2x$
71. $y = 4x - 1, y = x$

Understanding Math Problems Read the problem below. Then let Carmen's thinking guide you through the solution. Check your understanding with the exercises at the bottom of the page.

Open-Ended Write an inequality that has $(10, 15)$, $(-10, 20)$, $(-20, -25)$, and $(25, -10)$ as solutions.

What Carmen Thinks

These points are not necessarily on the same line. I'll plot the points and see where they lie on the coordinate plane.

The problem asks me to write an inequality with these points as solutions. But the graph of a linear inequality has a boundary line with shading on one side. So, I'll have to choose a boundary line.

There are so many possibilities! I need only two points to draw a line, so I'll use $(-20, -25)$ and $(25, -10)$.

The boundary line is solid since the points lie on it. I can include the other two points in the solution set by shading above the boundary line.

Since I have two points, I can use point-slope form to write the equation of the boundary line.

I can substitute the values of $m, x,$ and y into my equation and simplify.

I need to write an inequality. I shaded above the line toward greater y-values, so the inequality includes "greater than." Since I used a solid boundary line, the inequality is "greater than or equal to."

What Carmen Writes

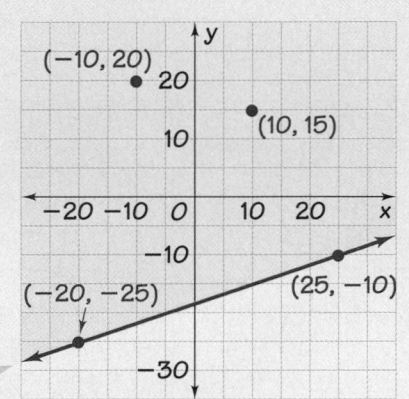

Boundary line through $(-20, -25)$ and $(25, -10)$ has slope $m = \dfrac{-10 - (-25)}{25 - (-20)}$.

$$y - y_1 = m(x - x_1)$$

$$y - (-25) = \frac{-10 - (-25)}{25 - (-20)}(x - (-20))$$

$$y + 25 = \frac{15}{45}(x + 20)$$

$$y = \tfrac{1}{3}(x + 20) - 25$$

$$y = \tfrac{1}{3}x - \frac{55}{3} \quad \text{equation of boundary line}$$

$$y \geq \tfrac{1}{3}x - \frac{55}{3} \quad \text{inequality}$$

EXERCISES

Write a different inequality that has the following ordered pairs as solutions.

1. $(10, 15), (-10, 20), (-20, -25), (25, -10)$ **2.** $(5, 2), (-2, 3), (-4, 5), (4, 9)$

Writing Short Responses

Short-response questions are usually worth two points. To get full credit you must not only give the correct answer, but also show your work or justify your reasoning.

EXAMPLE

A line parallel to $4x - 2y = 5$ passes through the point $(2, -3)$. Write the equation of the line in standard form, $Ax + By = C$.

Study the three responses below. Each received a different score.

2 points	1 point	0 points
$4x - 2y = 5$ $4x - 5 = 2y$ $y = 2x - \frac{5}{2}$ Slope is 2. $y + 3 = 2(x - 2)$ $y + 3 = 2x - 4$ $y = 2x - 7$ $2x - y = 7$	$4x - 2y = 5$ $-2y = 5 + 4x$ $y = -2x - \frac{5}{2}$ Slope is -2. $y = -2x + b$ $-3 = -4 + b$ $1 = b$ $y = -2x + 1$ $2x + y = 1$	$4x - 2y = -3$

In the 2-point response, the student found the correct answer and showed all the work.

In the 1-point response, the student made a computational error in the second line. The final answer is wrong, but still the student received a point because the rest of the work is correct.

In the 0-point response, the student gave an incorrect answer without showing any work. The answer is not far off, so the student probably would have received a point if some work had been shown.

EXERCISES

1. At the right is another response to the Example above. How many points does the response deserve? Explain your reasoning.

> The equation is
> $4x - 2y = k$
> $4(2) - 2(-3) = k$
> $14 = k$
> $4x - 2y = 14$

Answer each question. Show your work.

2. As an orange grows over a five-week period, there is a linear relationship between the volume of the orange and time. At the beginning of the period, the volume is about 34 cm^3. Four weeks later, the volume is about 50 cm^3. What is the volume at the end of the five-week period?

3. A line perpendicular to $x + 3y = 5$ passes through $(1, -1)$. What is the equation of the line in standard form?

Chapter Review

Vocabulary Review

🔊 absolute value function (p. 88)
constant of variation (p. 72)
dependent variable (p. 62)
direct variation (p. 72)
domain (p. 56)
function (p. 57)
function notation (p. 58)
independent variable (p. 62)
linear equation (p. 62)
linear function (p. 62)
linear inequality (p. 101)

mapping diagram (p. 56)
parameter (p. 97)
parent function (p. 93)
point-slope form (p. 65)
range (p. 56)
reflection (p. 96)
relation (p. 55)
scatter plot (p. 80)
shrink (p. 96)
slope (p. 64)

slope-intercept form (p. 65)
standard form (p. 63)
stretch (p. 96)
transformation (p. 97)
translation (p. 93)
trend line (p. 80)
vertex (p. 88)
vertical-line test (p. 57)
x-intercept (p. 63)
y-intercept (p. 63)

Go Online
PHSchool.com
For: Vocabulary quiz
Web Code: agj-0251

Choose the correct term to complete each sentence.

1. In the function $y = f(x)$, y is the (*dependent, independent*) variable.

2. All functions are (*relations, domains*).

3. The graph of a function is (*always, sometimes*) a line.

4. An equation of the form $y - y_1 = m(x - x_1)$ is in (*point-slope, slope-intercept*) form.

5. The vertex of the graph of an absolute value function is (*always, sometimes*) the lowest point on the graph.

Skills and Concepts

2-1 Objectives
▼ To graph relations (p. 55)
▼ To identify functions (p. 57)

A **relation** is a set of ordered pairs that can be represented by points in the coordinate plane or by a **mapping diagram.** The **domain** of a relation is the set of x-coordinates. The **range** is the set of y-coordinates.

When each element of the domain of a relation is paired with exactly one element of the range, the relation is a **function.** You can write a function using the notation $f(x)$, called **function notation.**

Determine whether each relation is a function. Find the domain and range.

6. $\{(5, 0), (8, 1), (1, 3), (5, 2), (3, 8)\}$

7. $\{(10, 2), (-10, 2), (6, 4), (5, 3), (-6, 7)\}$

8.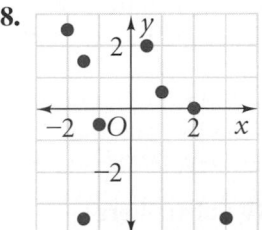

9.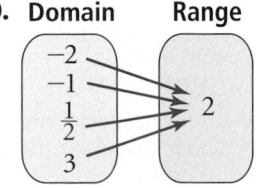

10.

For each function, find $f(-2)$, $f(-0.5)$, and $f(3)$.

11. $f(x) = -x + 4$

12. $f(x) = \frac{3}{8}x - 3$

13. $f(x) = -\frac{5}{12}x + 2$

2-2 Objectives
▼ To graph linear equations (p. 62)
▼ To write equations of lines (p. 64)

The graph of a **linear function** is a line. You can represent a linear function with a **linear equation.** In a function, the value of y depends on the value of x, so y is the **dependent variable** and x is the **independent variable.**

Given two points on a line, the **slope** of the line is the ratio of the difference of the y-coordinates to the corresponding difference of the x-coordinates. The slope equals the coefficient of x when you write a linear equation in **slope-intercept form.** You can also write a linear equation in **point-slope form** or **standard form.** You can use the slopes of lines to determine whether or not they are parallel, perpendicular, or horizontal. A vertical line has no slope.

Write in standard form an equation for each line.

14. slope $= -3$, through $(4, 0)$

15. through $(2, 3)$ and $(3, 5)$

Find the slope, x-intercept, and y-intercept of each line.

16. $4x - 2y = 3$

17. $Mx = Ny + P$

18. $5 - x = y$

19. a. Write an equation of the line parallel to $x + 2y = 6$ through $(8, 3)$.
b. Write an equation of the line perpendicular to $x + 2y = 6$ through $(8, 3)$.
c. Graph the three lines on the same coordinate plane.

2-3 Objectives
▼ To write and interpret direct variation equations (p. 72)

A linear equation of the form $y = kx$ represents a **direct variation.** The **constant of variation** is k. You can use proportions to solve some direct variation problems.

For each function, determine whether y varies directly with x. If so, find the constant of variation and write the equation.

20.

x	y
−2	3
0	4
2	7

21.

x	y
4	5
6	9
10	17

22.

x	y
0	0
1	1
5	5

Find each constant of variation. Then find the value of y when $x = -0.3$.

23. $y = 2$ when $x = -\frac{1}{2}$

24. $y = \frac{2}{3}$ when $x = 0.2$

25. $y = 7$ when $x = 2$

2-4 Objectives
▼ To write linear equations that model real-world data (p. 78)
▼ To make predictions from linear models (p. 79)

You can use mathematical models such as **scatter plots** to show relationships between data sets. You can use the models to make predictions. Sometimes you can draw a **trend line** to model the relation and make predictions.

 26. a. Data Analysis Draw a scatter plot of the data below.
b. Draw a trend line. Write its equation.
c. Estimate the number of cable TV subscribers in 2010.

Cable TV Subscribers

Year	1980	1985	1990	1995	2000
Millions of Subscribers	17.5	35.4	50.5	60.6	66.3

SOURCE: Television Bureau of Advertising

Draw a scatter plot of each set of data. Decide whether a linear model is reasonable. If so, draw a trend line and write its equation. Then predict the value of y when x is 15.

27.

x	3	4	5	7	8	9	10
y	5	7	9	10	10	11	13

28.

x	6	7	8	9	10	11	12
y	15.5	14.0	13.0	12.5	12.0	11.5	10.0

2-5 and 2-6 Objectives

▼ To graph absolute value functions (p. 88)

▼ To analyze translations (p. 93)

▼ To analyze stretches, shrinks, and reflections (p. 96)

The **absolute value function** $y = |x|$ has a graph in the shape of a V. It is the **parent function** for the family of functions of the form $y = a|x - h| + k$. The maximum or minimum point of the V is the **vertex** of the graph.

The value of h represents a horizontal translation of the parent graph by h units left (h is positive) or right (h is negative). The k represents a vertical translation of the graph by k units up (k is positive) or down (k is negative). The a represents a vertical stretch for $a > 1$; a vertical shrink for $0 < a < 1$. $y = -a|x|$ is a reflection of $y = a|x|$ in the x-axis.

Graph each equation by writing two linear equations.

29. $y = |x - 7|$ **30.** $y = -|x + 10|$ **31.** $y = \frac{1}{3}|2x + 6| + 2$

Write an equation for each translation of the graph of $y = |x|$.

32. 4 units up, 2 units right   **33.** vertex $(-3, 0)$

34. vertex $(5, 2)$ **35.** vertex $(4, 1)$

Graph each function.

36. $f(x) = |x| - 8$ **37.** $f(x) = 2|x - 5|$ **38.** $f(x) = \frac{1}{2}|x - 3| + 3$

39. $y = 3|x + 4|$ **40.** $y = -\frac{1}{4}|x - 2| + \frac{1}{2}$ **41.** $y = -2|x + 1| - 1$

2-7 Objectives

▼ To graph linear inequalities (p. 101)

▼ To graph absolute value inequalities (p. 103)

A **linear inequality** describes a region of the coordinate plane that has a boundary. To graph an inequality involving two variables, first graph the boundary. Then decide which side of the boundary contains solutions. Points on a dashed boundary are not solutions. Points on a solid boundary are solutions.

Graph each inequality.

42. $y \geq -2$ **43.** $y < 3x + 1$ **44.** $y \leq -|x - 5|$ **45.** $y > |2x + 1|$

46. Transportation An air cargo plane can transport as many as 15 regular shipping containers. One super-size container takes up the space of 3 regular containers.
   a. Write an inequality to model the situation.
   b. Describe the domain and range.
   c. Graph the inequality you wrote in part (a).

47. Open-Ended Write an absolute value inequality with a solid boundary that has solutions below the x-axis only.

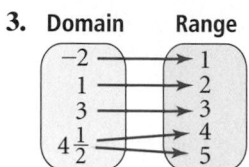

Chapter 2

Chapter Test

Go Online
PHSchool.com
For: Chapter test
Web Code: aga-0252

Find the domain and range. Graph each relation.

1. $\{(0,0), (1,-1), (2,-4), (3,-9), (4,-16)\}$

2. $\{(3,2), (4,3), (5,4), (6,5), (7,6)\}$

Determine whether each relation is a function.

3.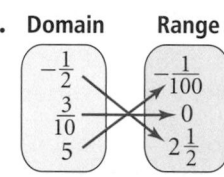

4.

Suppose $f(x) = 2x - 5$ and $g(x) = |-3x - 1|$. Find each value.

5. $f(3)$

6. $f(1) + g(2)$

7. $g(0)$

8. $g(2) - f(0)$

9. $f(-1) - g(3)$

10. $2g(-4)$

11. **Open-Ended** Graph a relation that is *not* a function. Find its domain and range.

Find the slope of each line.

12. through $(3,5)$ and $(1,1)$

13. $4x + 3y = 2$

14. through $(-0.5, 0.5)$, perpendicular to $y = -2x - 4$

Write in standard form an equation of the line with the given slope through the given point.

15. slope $= -3, (0,0)$

16. slope $= \frac{2}{5}, (6,7)$

17. slope $= 4, (-2,-5)$

18. slope $= -0.5, (0,6)$

Write in point-slope form an equation of the line through each pair of points.

19. $(0,0)$ and $(-4,7)$

20. $(-1,-6)$ and $(-2,10)$

21. $(3,0)$ and $(-1,-2)$

22. $(9,5)$ and $(8,2)$

23. **a. Open-Ended** Write an equation of a line with negative slope.
   b. Write an equation of the line perpendicular to the line from part (a) passing through $(-6,9)$.
   c. Write an equation of the line parallel to the line from part (b) passing through $(12,12)$.
   d. Write an equation of the line perpendicular to the line from part (c) passing through $(-1,-4)$.
   e. Graph the lines from parts (a), (b), (c), and (d). If they form a polygon, describe it.

For each direct variation, find the constant of variation. Then find the value of y when $x = -0.5$.

24. $y = 4$ when $x = 0.5$

25. $y = 2$ when $x = 3$

 26. **Transportation** The number of minutes a freight train takes to pass an intersection varies directly with the number of cars in the train. A 150-car train passes in 3 min. How long will a 210-car train take to pass?

Graph each function.

27. $y = 3x + 4$

28. $y = |5x - 3| + 1$

29. $y = -|x - 3| + 1$

30. $y = 3 - \frac{2}{5}x$

31. **Recreation** The table displays the amounts the Jackson family spent on vacations during the years 1996–2006.

Jackson Family Vacation Costs

Year	Cost	Year	Cost
1996	$1000	2002	$2750
1997	$1750	2003	$3200
1998	$1750	2004	$2900
1999	$2000	2005	$3100
2000	$2200	2006	$3300
2001	$2700		

a. Make a scatter plot of the data.
b. Draw a trend line. Write its equation.
c. Estimate the cost to the Jackson family of vacations in 2008.
d. **Writing** Explain how to use a trend line with a scatter plot.

Describe each transformation of the parent function $y = |x|$. Then, graph each function.

32. $y = |x| - 4$

33. $y = |x - 1| - 5$

34. $y = -|x + 4| + 3$

35. $y = 2|x + 1|$

36. $y = |x| + 5$

37. $y = -\frac{1}{2}|x + 2| - 3$

Graph each inequality.

38. $y \geq x + 7$

39. $y > |2x + 3| - 3$

40. $4x + 3y < 2$

41. $y \leq -|x + 1| - 2$

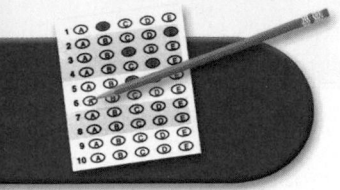

Standard Test Prep

Multiple Choice

For Exercises 1–13, choose the correct letter.

1. Which phrase could NOT describe $\sqrt{625}$?
   - Ⓐ whole number
   - Ⓑ irrational number
   - Ⓒ integer
   - Ⓓ rational number

2. Which value is in the solution set of $4 < -4x - 2 < 8$ and $3 > 4x + 2 > -10$?
   - Ⓕ -2
   - Ⓖ 0
   - Ⓗ 3
   - Ⓙ 4

3. Which point could NOT be on the graph of a function that includes $(5, 4)$, $(8, -1)$, $(7, 3)$, $(0, 5)$, and $(10, -2)$?
   - Ⓐ $(6, 4)$
   - Ⓑ $(10, 1)$
   - Ⓒ $(11, -1)$
   - Ⓓ $(9, 3)$

4. Which relations are functions?

   I. 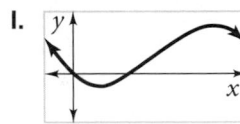 II.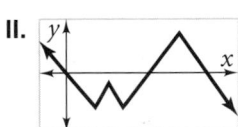

   III. 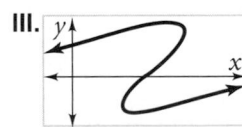 IV.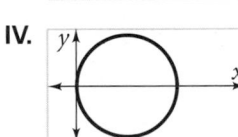

   - Ⓕ I and II
   - Ⓖ I and III
   - Ⓗ II and III
   - Ⓙ II and IV

5. Which lines are parallel?
   - I. $y = -2x + 1$
   - II. $y = x - 4$
   - III. $y = -x + 5$
   - IV. $y = 3 - 2x$
   - Ⓐ I and II
   - Ⓑ I and III
   - Ⓒ I and IV
   - Ⓓ II and III

6. Which values are solutions of $y < 2x + 3$?
   - I. $(0, 2)$
   - II. $(-1, 1)$
   - III. $(2, 0)$
   - Ⓕ I only
   - Ⓖ II only
   - Ⓗ I and III
   - Ⓙ II and III

7. Which line is perpendicular to $y = 2x - 4$?
   - Ⓐ $y = -2x + 4$
   - Ⓑ $y = -4 - 2x$
   - Ⓒ $y = -x - 2$
   - Ⓓ $y = -\frac{1}{2}x + 4$

8. Which equation is in standard form?
   - Ⓕ $x - y = 7$
   - Ⓖ $y = 3x - 1$
   - Ⓗ $x = 4y + 2$
   - Ⓙ $10 - 5x = 2y$

9. Which equation represents the graph of $y = -|4x|$ translated down 1 unit and right 5 units?
   - Ⓐ $y = -|4(x + 5)| - 1$
   - Ⓑ $y = -|4(x - 5)| - 1$
   - Ⓒ $y = -|4(x - 1)| + 5$
   - Ⓓ $y = -4|(x - 1)| - 5$

10. Solve $2|7 - x| < 2$ for x.
    - Ⓕ $6 < x < 8$
    - Ⓖ $x < 6$ or $x > 8$
    - Ⓗ $-8 < x < -6$
    - Ⓙ $x < 8$ or $x > 6$

11. Use the Addition Property of Equality to complete the statement: If $p = q$, then $x + p = \blacksquare$.
    - Ⓐ $p + x$
    - Ⓑ $x + 0$
    - Ⓒ $x + q$
    - Ⓓ $p + q$

12. A bag contains 18 red chips, 24 blue chips, 30 yellow chips, and 48 green chips. You pick a chip from the bag at random. Find the probability that the chip is red or green.
    - Ⓕ 37.5%
    - Ⓖ 45%
    - Ⓗ 55%
    - Ⓙ 66%

13. Which inequality has the same graph as $8 - y < |x + 3|$?
    - Ⓐ $y < -|x + 3| - 8$
    - Ⓑ $y < -|x + 3| + 8$
    - Ⓒ $y > -|x + 3| - 8$
    - Ⓓ $y > -|x + 3| + 8$

Gridded Response

14. What is the y-coordinate of the point through which the graph of every direct variation passes?

15. In one roll of two number cubes, what is the probability that the product of the faces is 12?

Short Response

16. Graph $y < |x + 3|$. Identify the parent function of the boundary and describe the translation.

17. Suppose y varies directly as x, and $y = 2$ when $x = -2$. Find the constant of variation. Then find the value of x when $y = 3$.

Extended Response

18. a. Write an equation of the line through $(-2, 6)$ with slope 2.
    b. Write an equation of the line through $(1, 1)$ perpendicular to the line in part (a).
    c. Graph the two lines on the same set of axes.

Bridges, Beams, and Tension

Applying Functions Even steel bends when heavy loads are applied to it. In designing bridges and other structures, civil engineers use functions to predict how much a beam will deflect, or bend, under a given load. They design bridges so that the stress from the combined weights of the bridge materials and the vehicles that cross the bridge, along with stress from winds, does not exceed allowable limits.

Communication Bridges Countries

Each note of the euro currency, which debuted in 12 countries in January 2002, has a bridge on the reverse side, symbolizing communication among the people of Europe and between Europe and the rest of the world.

Main cable
Length: 2332 m
Diameter: 92 cm

The Leonardo Bridge

Designed by Leonardo da Vinci in 1502 and constructed in 2000 near Oslo, Norway, the Leonardo Bridge is a pressed-bow construction. The middle section of the arch is only 65 cm thick. Toward the sides and bottom, the thickness increases by a factor of about seven, to 4.5 m.

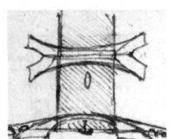

Activity

Materials: pencil and paper, graph paper, ruler, paper clips, two balsa wood dowels at least 55 cm long, 10 washers

- Lay the dowels side by side on a table so that they extend 25 cm over the edge. Place books on the dowels to hold them in place.

- Bend a paper clip into a hook to hold the washers. Suspend the paper clip from one of the dowels.

a. Add 1 washer at a time to the paper clip. Measure the amount of deflection of the end of the dowel by measuring the vertical distance between the dowels. Use a table to record the weight W in number of washers and the deflection v.

b. Reposition the dowels 15 cm over the edge of the table. Place 5 washers on the paper clip. Measure the deflection. Increase the length of the extension in 3-cm increments until the dowel extends 45 cm from the edge of the table. Record the length of the extension L and the deflection v in a table.

c. Using two different coordinate planes, graph the relationships from parts (a) and (b): deflection vs. weight and deflection vs. extension.

d. **Reasoning** In the functions below, k is a constant for the dowel tested, L is the length of the dowel extension, v is the deflection at the end of the dowel, and W is the weight of the load. Determine which function best describes a dowel's deflection in response to changes in load and length.

    A. $v = kLW$ **B.** $v = kL^2W$ **C.** $v = kLW^2$ **D.** $v = kL^2W^2$

The Golden Gate Bridge

The Golden Gate Bridge is named for the Golden Gate Strait, which is the entrance to San Francisco Bay from the Pacific Ocean. The bridge is 2.7 km long and 27.5 m wide, and when it carries a load it has a maximum downward deflection of 3.3 m.

Main tower
Height above water: 227 m
Height above roadway: 152 m

Go Online
PHSchool.com

For: Information about bridges
Web Code: age-0253

What You've Learned

- In Chapter 1, you learned to write and solve equations and inequalities in one variable.

- In Chapter 2, you learned to write and solve equations and inequalities in two variables.

- In Chapter 2, you learned to graph points and equations in two dimensions.

 **Check Your Readiness**

 for Help to the Lesson in green.

Combining Like Terms (Lesson 1-2)

Simplify by combining like terms.

1. $3x + (4x - 1)$ **2.** $12 - (p + 7)$ **3.** $(2z + 10) - 8z$ **4.** $(r - 1) - 3$

Solving and Graphing Inequalities (Lesson 1-4)

Solve each inequality. Graph the solutions on a number line.

5. $6a \leq 9$ **6.** $8b + 11 > 27$ **7.** $3(24 + 2c) < 0$ **8.** $5(0.2 + d) \leq -4$

Graphing Relations (Lesson 2-1)

Graph each relation on a coordinate plane.

9. $\{(0, 4), (-2, 1), (2, 7), (-4, 4), (4, 4)\}$ **10.** $\left\{ \left(0, \frac{1}{2}\right), \left(1, \frac{5}{2}\right), \left(2, \frac{9}{2}\right), \left(3, \frac{13}{2}\right), \left(4, \frac{17}{2}\right) \right\}$

Graphing Equations (Lesson 2-2)

Graph each equation on a coordinate plane.

11. $y = 4x + 1$ **12.** $-6y + x = 3$ **13.** $15x - 3y = 5$ **14.** $x = 2y - 7$

Writing a Linear Model (Lesson 2-4)

15. Each minute, a toll collector serves an average of six motorists. Write an equation to model the average number of motorists this toll collector assists as a function of time. Graph the equation.

Graphing Inequalities (Lesson 2-7)

Graph each inequality on a coordinate plane.

16. $y > 8x + 3$ **17.** $2y + x \leq -10$ **18.** $18x - 9y < 2$ **19.** $x \geq 4y - 5$

Linear Systems

Chapter 3

LESSONS

3-1 Graphing Systems of Equations

3-2 Solving Systems Algebraically

3-3 Systems of Inequalities

3-4 Linear Programming

3-5 Graphs in Three Dimensions

3-6 Systems with Three Variables

◀))) **Key Vocabulary**

• constraints (p. 139)
• coordinate space (p. 146)
• dependent system (p. 120)
• equivalent systems (p. 127)
• feasible region (p. 140)
• inconsistent system (p. 120)
• independent system (p. 120)
• linear programming (p. 139)
• linear system (p. 118)
• objective function (p. 139)
• ordered triples (p. 146)
• system of equations (p. 118)
• trace (p. 148)

What You'll Learn Next

● In Chapter 3, you will learn to solve systems of equations and inequalities in two variables algebraically and by graphing.

● You will learn to graph points and equations in three dimensions.

● You will learn to solve systems of equations in three variables.

Real-World Connection Applying what you learn, on page 143 you will solve a problem about planting trees.

3-1

Graphing Systems of Equations

What You'll Learn

- To solve a system by graphing

. . . And Why

To make predictions from data, as in Example 2

✓ Check Skills You'll Need

GO for Help Lesson 2-2

Graph each equation.

1. $y = 3x - 2$ **2.** $y = -x$ **3.** $y = -\frac{1}{2}x + 4$

Graph each equation. Use one coordinate plane for all three graphs.

4. $2x - y = 1$ **5.** $2x - y = -1$ **6.** $x + 2y = 2$

◀» New Vocabulary

- system of equations
- linear system
- independent system
- dependent system
- inconsistent system

---

1 Systems of Linear Equations

Technology Activity: Analyzing Graphs

1. Use a graphing calculator to graph each pair of equations.

   a. $y = x + 5$ **b.** $y = 3x + 2$ **c.** $y = -4x - 2$

   $y = -2x + 5$ $y = 3x - 1$ $y = \frac{8x + 4}{-2}$

2. For each pair, answer the following questions.
   a. Do the graphs have any points in common; if so, how many?
   b. Compare the slopes of the graphs. What is the relationship between the slopes and the number of points in common?

3. Copy and complete the table for the graphs of two linear equations.

Description of Lines	How Many Points of Intersection?	Equal Slopes? (yes/no)	Same y-intercepts? (yes/no)
intersecting	▪	▪	either
parallel	▪	▪	▪
coinciding	▪	▪	▪

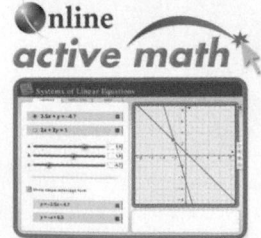

Online
active math

For: Linear Systems Activity
Use: Interactive Textbook, 3-1

A **system of equations** is a set of two or more equations that use the same variables. If the graph of each equation in a system of two variables is a line, then the system is a **linear system.**

A brace is used to keep the equations of a system together. $\begin{cases} y = x + 3 \\ y = -2x + 3 \end{cases}$

A solution of a system of equations is a set of values for the variables that makes all the equations true. You can solve some linear systems by graphing the equations. The points where both (or all) the graphs intersect represent solutions.

1 EXAMPLE Solving by Graphing

Multiple Choice Which ordered pair of numbers is the solution of the system?

$$\begin{cases} x + 2y = -7 \\ 2x - 3y = 0 \end{cases}$$

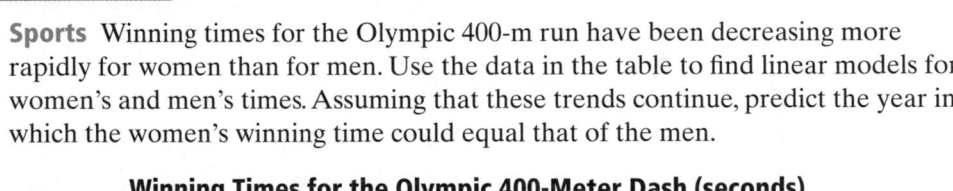

Ⓐ $(1, -4)$ Ⓑ $(-1, -3)$ Ⓒ $(-6, -4)$ Ⓓ $(-3, -2)$

Graph the equations and find the intersection. The solution appears to be $(-3, -2)$.

Check Show that $(-3, -2)$ makes both equations true.

$$x + 2y = -7 \qquad\qquad 2x - 3y = 0$$
$$-3 + 2(-2) \stackrel{?}{=} -7 \qquad 2(-3) - 3(-2) \stackrel{?}{=} 0$$
$$-3 - 4 \stackrel{?}{=} -7 \qquad\qquad -6 + 6 \stackrel{?}{=} 0$$
$$-7 = -7 ✔ \qquad\qquad\qquad 0 = 0 ✔$$

● The answer is D.

Quick Check ❶ Solve $\begin{cases} 2x + y = 5 \\ -x + y = 2 \end{cases}$ by graphing. Check your solution.

2 EXAMPLE Real-World 🌐 Connection

Sports Winning times for the Olympic 400-m run have been decreasing more rapidly for women than for men. Use the data in the table to find linear models for women's and men's times. Assuming that these trends continue, predict the year in which the women's winning time could equal that of the men.

Winning Times for the Olympic 400-Meter Dash (seconds)

Year	1968	1972	1976	1980	1984	1988	1992	1996	2000
Men's Time	43.86	44.66	44.26	44.60	44.27	43.87	43.50	43.49	43.84
Women's Time	52.03	51.08	49.29	48.88	48.83	48.65	48.83	48.25	49.11

SOURCE: *The World Almanac*

Step 1 Let $x =$ number of years since 1968.
Let $y =$ winning times in seconds.

Use the **LinReg** feature of a graphing calculator to find linear models.

Men's time: $y \approx -0.02433x + 44.43$
Women's time: $y \approx -0.08883x + 50.86$

Step 2 Graph each model. Use the Intersect feature on the graphing calculator. The two lines meet at about $(99.7, 42.0)$.

If the trends continue, the times for men and women
● will be equal about 100 years from 1968, in 2068.

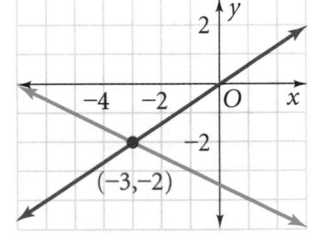

Intersection
X=99.72093 Y=42.00168

Real-World 🌐 Connection

Cathy Freeman won the 400-m run in the 2000 Olympics.

Quick Check ❷ **a.** Use the models in Example 2 to predict the winning times for the 400-m run at the Olympics in 2008 and in 2024.

b. Critical Thinking Example 2 assumes that current trends will continue. Explain why that assumption may not be valid.

You can classify a system of two linear equations by the number of solutions. A system that has a unique solution, as in Examples 1 and 2, is an **independent system.** However, not every system has a unique solution.

A **dependent system** does not have a unique solution. An **inconsistent system** is a system that has no solution.

 **Key Concepts**

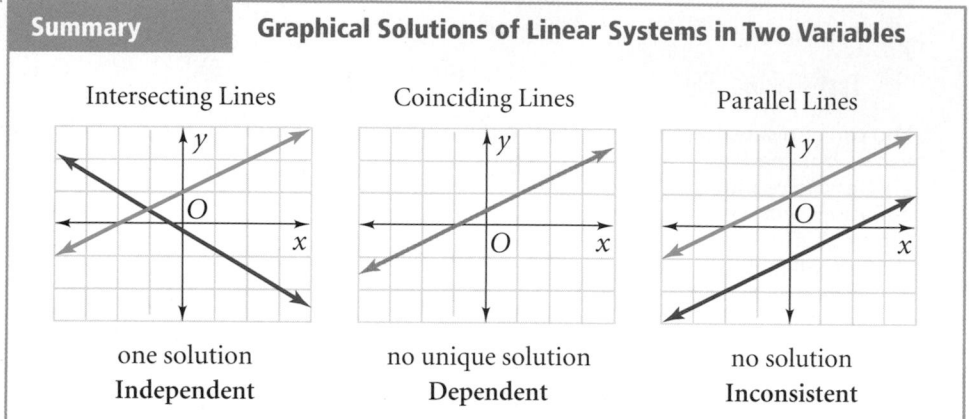

| **Summary** | **Graphical Solutions of Linear Systems in Two Variables** |

Intersecting Lines

Coinciding Lines

Parallel Lines

one solution
Independent

no unique solution
Dependent

no solution
Inconsistent

Video Tutor Help
Visit: PhSchool.com
Web Code: age-0775

You can also classify a system of equations without graphing. By comparing the slopes and y-intercepts of the equations, you can find the number of solutions.

3 EXAMPLE **Classifying Systems Without Graphing**

Classify the system without graphing. $\begin{cases} y = 2x + 3 \\ -2x + y = 1 \end{cases}$

$y = 2x + 3$ **Rewrite in slope-intercept form.** $\rightarrow$ $y = 2x + 1$

$m = 2, b = 3$ $\leftarrow$ **Find the slope and y-intercept.** $\rightarrow$ $m = 2, b = 1$

Since the slopes are the same, the lines could coincide. Compare the y-intercepts. Since the y-intercepts are different, the lines are parallel. There is no solution. The system is an inconsistent system.

✓ Quick Check **3** Without graphing, classify each system as *independent*, *dependent*, or *inconsistent*.

a. $\begin{cases} 3x + y = 5 \\ 15x + 5y = 2 \end{cases}$

b. $\begin{cases} y = 2x + 3 \\ -4x + 2y = 6 \end{cases}$

c. $\begin{cases} x - y = 5 \\ y + 3 = 2x \end{cases}$

EXERCISES

For more exercises, see *Extra Skill and Word Problem Practice.*

Practice and Problem Solving

A Practice by Example

Example 1
(page 119)

 **for Help**

Solve each system by graphing. Check your answers.

1. $\begin{cases} y = x - 2 \\ y = -2x + 7 \end{cases}$

2. $\begin{cases} y = -x + 3 \\ y = \frac{3}{2}x - 2 \end{cases}$

3. $\begin{cases} 2x + 4y = 12 \\ x + y = 2 \end{cases}$

4. $\begin{cases} x = -3 \\ y = 5 \end{cases}$

5. $\begin{cases} 2x - 2y = 4 \\ y - x = 6 \end{cases}$

6. $\begin{cases} 3x + y = 5 \\ x - y = 7 \end{cases}$

7. $\begin{cases} -5x + y = -9 \\ x + 3y = 21 \end{cases}$

8. $\begin{cases} y = x \\ y - 5x = 0 \end{cases}$

9. $\begin{cases} x = 10 \\ x = y - 10 \end{cases}$

Example 2
(page 119)

For Exercises 10–11, use your graphing calculator. Find linear models for each set of data. Use each model to predict the year in which the quantities will be equal.

10. **Annual U.S. Consumption of Vegetables**

Year	Broccoli (lb/person)	Cucumbers (lb/person)
1980	1.5	3.9
1985	2.6	4.4
1990	3.4	4.7
1995	4.3	5.6
1998	5.1	6.5
1999	6.5	6.8
2000	6.1	6.4

SOURCE: *Statistical Abstract of the United States.*
Go to www.PHSchool.com for a data update.
Web Code: agg-9041

11. **U.S. Life Expectancy at Birth**

Year	Men (years)	Women (years)
1970	67.1	74.7
1975	68.8	76.6
1980	70.0	77.4
1985	71.1	78.2
1990	71.8	78.8
1995	72.5	78.9
2000	74.3	79.7

SOURCE: U.S. Census Bureau.
Go to www.PHSchool.com for a data update.
Web Code: agg-9041

12. a. Business The spreadsheet shows the monthly revenue and monthly expenses for a new business. Find a linear model for monthly revenue and a linear model for monthly expenses.
b. Use the models to predict the month in which revenue will equal expenses.

	A	B	C
1	Month	Revenue	Expenses
2	Feb	8000	35000
3	Mar	12000	33000
4	Apr	13000	34000
5	May	18000	32000
6	Jun	20000	31000

Example 3
(page 120)

Without graphing, classify each system as *independent*, *dependent*, or *inconsistent*.

13. $\begin{cases} 7x - y = 6 \\ -7x + y = -6 \end{cases}$

14. $\begin{cases} -3x + y = 4 \\ x - \frac{1}{3}y = 1 \end{cases}$

15. $\begin{cases} 4x + 8y = 12 \\ x + 2y = -3 \end{cases}$

16. $\begin{cases} y = 2x - 1 \\ y = -2x + 5 \end{cases}$

17. $\begin{cases} x = 6 \\ x = -2 \end{cases}$

18. $\begin{cases} 2y = 5x + 6 \\ -10x + 4y = 8 \end{cases}$

19. $\begin{cases} x - 3y = 2 \\ 4x - 12y = 8 \end{cases}$

20. $\begin{cases} x + 4y = 12 \\ 2x - 8y = 4 \end{cases}$

21. $\begin{cases} 4x + 8y = -6 \\ 6x + 12y = -9 \end{cases}$

22. $\begin{cases} 4y - 2x = 6 \\ 8y = 4x - 12 \end{cases}$

23. $\begin{cases} y - x = 0 \\ y = -x \end{cases}$

24. $\begin{cases} 2y - x = 4 \\ \frac{1}{2}x - y = 2 \end{cases}$

B **Apply Your Skills**

Graph and solve each system. Where necessary, estimate the solution.

25. $\begin{cases} 3 = 4y + x \\ 4y = -x + 3 \end{cases}$

26. $\begin{cases} x - 2y + 1 = 0 \\ x + 4y - 6 = 0 \end{cases}$

27. $\begin{cases} 3x + 6y - 12 = 0 \\ x + 2y = 8 \end{cases}$

28. $\begin{cases} -x + 3y = 6 \\ 2x - y = 8 \end{cases}$

29. $\begin{cases} 3x + y = 3 \\ 2x - y = 7 \end{cases}$

30. $\begin{cases} 2x + 3y = 6 \\ 4x = 6y + 3 \end{cases}$

31. $\begin{cases} 10 - 3x = -3y \\ 2 = 2x + y \end{cases}$

32. $\begin{cases} 3x = -5y + 4 \\ 250 + 150x = 300 \end{cases}$

33. $\begin{cases} x + 3y = 6 \\ 6y + 2x = 12 \end{cases}$

34. $\begin{cases} 2y + x = 8 \\ y - 2x = -6 \end{cases}$

35. $\begin{cases} y = -2x + 6 \\ x - 3y = -6 \end{cases}$

36. $\begin{cases} -x - 2 = -2y \\ 2x - 4y - 4 = 0 \end{cases}$

37. Banking To pay your monthly bills, you can either open a checking account or use an online banking service. A local bank charges $3 per month and $.40 per check, while an online services charges a flat fee of $9 per month.

    a. Write and graph a system of linear equations to model the cost c of each service for b bills that you need to pay monthly.

    b. Find the point of intersection of the two linear models. What does this answer represent?

    c. If you pay about 12 bills per month, which service should you choose? Explain.

Classify each system without graphing.

38. $\begin{cases} 3x - 2y = 8 \\ 4y = 6x - 5 \end{cases}$
    39. $\begin{cases} 2x + 8y = 6 \\ x = -4y + 3 \end{cases}$
    40. $\begin{cases} 3a + 6b = 14 \\ -a + 2b = 3 \end{cases}$

41. $\begin{cases} 3m = -5n + 4 \\ n - \frac{6}{5} = -\frac{3}{5}m \end{cases}$
    42. $\begin{cases} -12x + 4y = 8 \\ y - 4 = 3x \end{cases}$
    43. $\begin{cases} -6y + 18 = 12x \\ 3y + 6x = 9 \end{cases}$

44. Fees Suppose you are going on vacation and leaving your dog in a kennel. The Bowowery charges $25 per day, which includes a one-time grooming treatment. The Poochpad charges $20 per day and a one-time fee of $30 for grooming.

    a. Write a system of equations to represent the cost c for d days that your dog will stay at a kennel.

    b. Using a graphing calculator, find the number of days for which the costs are the same.

    c. If your vacation is a week long, which kennel should you choose? Explain.

45. Advertising You and your business partner are mailing advertising flyers to your customers. You address 6 flyers each minute and have already done 80. Your partner addresses 4 flyers each minute and has already done 100. Graph and solve a system of equations to find when the two of you will have addressed equal numbers of flyers.

Open-Ended Write a second equation for each system so that the system will have the indicated number of solutions.

46. one
$\begin{cases} y = -3x + 2 \\ \underline{\quad ? \quad} \end{cases}$
    47. none
$\begin{cases} y = -4x - 6 \\ \underline{\quad ? \quad} \end{cases}$
    48. an infinite number
$\begin{cases} 3y = 6x + 7 \\ \underline{\quad ? \quad} \end{cases}$

49. Reasoning Is it possible for an inconsistent linear system to consist of two lines with the same y-intercept? Explain.

50. Writing Summarize the possible relationships for the y-intercepts, slopes, and number of solutions in a system of two linear equations of two variables.

Open-Ended Write a second equation for each system so that the system will have the indicated number of solutions.

51. infinite number of solutions
$\begin{cases} \frac{x}{4} + \frac{y}{3} = 1 \\ \underline{\quad ? \quad} \end{cases}$
    52. no solutions
$\begin{cases} 5x + 2y = 10 \\ \underline{\quad ? \quad} \end{cases}$

53. Write a system of linear equations with the solution set $\{(x, y) \mid y = 5x + 2\}$.

54. Critical Thinking Look back through the exercises on the previous two pages to find several dependent systems. What relationship exists between the equations in each system?

Real-World Connection

Groomers must be able to handle dogs of every breed and temperament.

GO Online
Homework Video Tutor
Visit: PHSchool.com
Web Code: age-0301

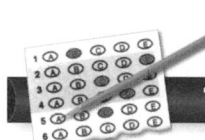
55. Economics Research shows that in a certain market only 2000 widgets can be sold at $8 each, but if the price is reduced to $3, then 10,000 can be sold.

a. Let p represent price and n represent the number of widgets. Identify the independent variable and the dependent variable.

b. Use the information above to write a linear *demand* equation.

c. A shop can make 2000 widgets for $5 each and 20,000 widgets for $2 each. Use this information to write a linear *supply* equation.

d. Find the equilibrium point where supply is equal to demand and profit is a maximum. Explain the meaning of the coordinates of this point within the context of the exercise.

Test Prep

Multiple Choice

56. Which is an equation for Line 2?

A. $3x - 5y = 15$ B. $3x + 5y = 3$

C. $3x + 5y = 15$ D. $5x + 3y = 15$

57. Which is NOT an equation for Line 1?

F. $y = x$ G. $x + y = 0$

H. $x - y = 0$ J. $y - x = 0$

58. Which point lies on both Line 1 and Line 2?

A. $(0, 0)$ B. $(1.875, 1.875)$

C. $(1.95, 1.95)$ D. $(2, 2)$

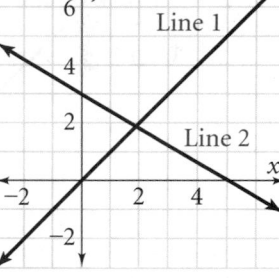

Exercises 56–58.

59. What is the solution of the system? $\begin{cases} 5x + 6y = -24 \\ -2x + 3y = 15 \end{cases}$

F. $(6, -1)$ G. $(6, 1)$ H. $(-6, 1)$ J. $(-6, -1)$

Short Response

60. Explain how you can use slopes to show that the system $\begin{cases} 2x - 5y = 23 \\ 3y - 7x = -8 \end{cases}$ is NOT inconsistent.

Extended Response

61. One equation of a system of equations is $2x - 3y = 5$.

a. Find a second equation such that the system is dependent.

b. Find a second equation such that the system is inconsistent.

Mixed Review

Lesson 2–7

Graph each inequality on a coordinate plane.

62. $3x - 4y \geq 16$ **63.** $-5x > 8y + 4$ **64.** $x < -4$

Lesson 2–2

Write an equation for each line.

65. $m = -\frac{2}{3}$; contains $(-9, 4)$ **66.** $m = 0$; contains $(3, 4)$

67. $m = 2$; contains $(-2, -3)$ **68.** $m = -\frac{1}{2}$; contains $(2, -6)$

Lesson 1–3

Solve each equation and check the solution.

69. $3n = -4(2 + n)$ **70.** $-4a + a = 7a - 6$ **71.** $\frac{x}{3} + 5 = \frac{1}{6}$

72. $4x - 2 = \frac{1}{2}x$ **73.** $\frac{r}{5} + 5 = r - 3$ **74.** $2(m - 3) = -4$

Parametric Equations

Parametric equations are equations that express the coordinates x and y as separate functions of a common third variable, called the parameter. You can use parametric equations to determine the position of an object over time.

ACTIVITY

Starting from a birdbath 3 ft above the ground, a bird takes flight. Let t equal time in seconds, x equal horizontal distance in feet, and y equal vertical distance in feet. The equations $x(t) = 5t$ and $y(t) = 8t + 3$ model the bird's distance from the base of the birdbath. Graph the equations. Describe the position of the bird at time $t = 3$.

Step 1 Press MODE . Change the function mode to Parametric.

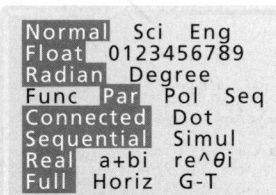

Step 2 Enter the equations.
(When you press Y= you will see a list of pairs of equations.)

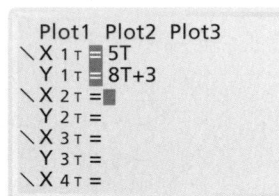

Step 3 Set the window values as shown.

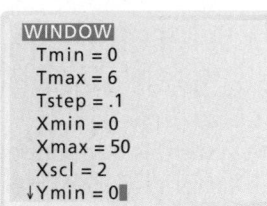

Step 4 Graph the equations. Press TRACE to find $t = 3$.

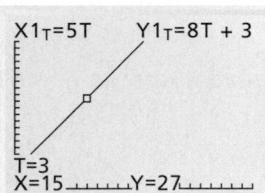

Three seconds after taking flight, the bird is 15 ft horizontally and 27 ft vertically from the base of the birdbath.

EXERCISES

Graph each pair of parametric equations. Set the window with the t-values at the right. Find the values of x and y at time $t = 3$.

1. $x(t) = t$
$y(t) = -t + 6$

2. $x(t) = -3t$
$y(t) = t - 6$

3. $x(t) = |t - 2|$
$y(t) = t + 2$

WINDOW
Tmin = -10
Tmax = 10
Tstep = .1
Xmin = -10
Xmax = 10
Xscl = 1
↓Ymin = -10▮

4. Writing Write a word problem involving the graph of $x(t) = 3t$ and $y(t) = 10t$. Interpret the x- and y-values at times $t = 0$, $t = 5$, and $t = -2$.

3-2
Solving Systems Algebraically

What You'll Learn

- To solve a system by substitution
- To solve a system by elimination

. . . And Why

To find the cost of joining a health club, as in Example 2

✓ **Check Skills You'll Need**

GO **for Help** Lessons 1-1 and 1-3

Find the additive inverse of each term.

1. 4   **2.** $-x$ **3.** $5x$ **4.** $8y$

Substitute $2y - 1$ for x in each equation. Solve for y.

5. $x + 2y = 3$ **6.** $y - 2x = 8$ **7.** $2y + 3x = -5$

◀》 **New Vocabulary** • equivalent systems

---

1   Solving Systems by Substitution

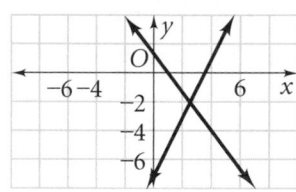

$$\begin{cases} 4x + 3y = 4 \\ 2x - y = 7 \end{cases}$$

Not every system can be solved easily by graphing. Consider the system at the left. Although you can graph each line easily, the exact point of intersection is not obvious. Substitution allows you to find exact solutions without using a graphing calculator.

1 EXAMPLE   Solving by Substitution

Solve the system by substitution. $\begin{cases} 4x + 3y = 4 \\ 2x - y = 7 \end{cases}$

Step 1 Solve for one of the variables. Solving the second equation for y is easiest.

$$2x - y = 7$$
$$y = 2x - 7$$

Step 2 Substitute the expression for y into the other equation. Solve for x.

$$4x + 3y = 4$$
$$4x + 3(2x - 7) = 4 \quad \textbf{Substitute for } \textbf{\textit{y}}.$$
$$4x + 6x - 21 = 4 \quad \textbf{Distributive Property}$$
$$4x + 6x = 25$$
$$x = 2.5$$

Step 3 Substitute the value of x into either equation. Solve for y.

$$y = 2x - 7$$
$$y = 2(2.5) - 7 \quad \textbf{Substitute for } \textbf{\textit{x}}.$$
$$y = -2$$

The solution is $(2.5, -2)$.

✓ **Quick Check** ❶ Solve each system by substitution. Check your answers.

     a. $\begin{cases} 2x - 3y = 6 \\ x + y = -12 \end{cases}$ **b.** $\begin{cases} 3x - y = 0 \\ 4x + 3y = 26 \end{cases}$

2 EXAMPLE **Real-World** 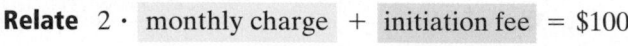 **Connection**

Fees Refer to the advertisement at the left. The cost of membership in a health club includes a monthly charge and a one-time initiation fee. Find the monthly charge and the initiation fee.

Relate 2 · monthly charge + initiation fee = $100

6 · monthly charge + initiation fee = $200

Define Let m = the monthly charge. Let f = the initiation fee.

Write $\begin{cases} 2m + f = 100 \\ 6m + f = 200 \end{cases}$

$2m + f = 100$ **Solve for one of the variables.**

$f = -2m + 100$

$6m + (-2m + 100) = 200$ **Substitute the expression for f into the other equation. Solve for m.**

$m = 25$

$2(25) + f = 100$ **Substitute the value of m into one of the equations. Solve for f.**

$f = 50$

● The monthly charge is $25, and the initiation fee is $50.

Health Club Membership Fees

2 months: $100
6 months: $200

 **Quick Check** ❷ **Shopping** You can buy CDs at a local store for $15.49 each. You can buy them at an online store for $13.99 each plus $6 for shipping. Solve a system of equations to find the number of CDs that you can buy for the same amount at the two stores.

---

2 **Solving Systems by Elimination**

You can solve a system of equations using the Addition Property of Equality. If the quantities you add contain a pair of additive inverses, you can eliminate a variable. You can also eliminate a variable by subtracting like terms.

3 EXAMPLE **Solving by Elimination**

Test-Taking Tip

You can grid the answer in columns 1–3 or columns 2–4.

Gridded Response Find the y-value in the solution of $\begin{cases} 4x - 2y = 7 \\ x + 2y = 3. \end{cases}$

$4x - 2y = 7$

$\underline{x + 2y = 3}$ **Two terms are additive inverses, so add.**

$5x \quad\quad = 10$

$x = 2$ **Solve for x.**

$x + 2y = 3$ **Choose one of the original equations.**

$2 + 2y = 3$ **Substitute for x.**

$y = \frac{1}{2}$ **Solve for y.**

● The solution is $\left(2, \frac{1}{2}\right)$. The y-value is $\frac{1}{2}$.

1	/	2	
	⦿	⦿	
⦿	⦿	⦿	⦿
	⓪	⓪	⓪
①	①	①	①
②	②	●	②
③	③	③	③
④	④	④	④
⑤	⑤	⑤	⑤
⑥	⑥	⑥	⑥
⑦	⑦	⑦	⑦
⑧	⑧	⑧	⑧
⑨	⑨	⑨	⑨

 **Quick Check** ❸ Solve each system by elimination.

a. $\begin{cases} 3x - 2y = 14 \\ 2x + 2y = 6 \end{cases}$

b. $\begin{cases} 4x + 9y = 1 \\ 4x + 6y = -2 \end{cases}$

126 Chapter 3 Linear Systems

To make two terms additive inverses, you may need to multiply one or both equations in a system by a nonzero number. In doing so, you create a system equivalent to the original one. **Equivalent systems** are systems that have the same solution(s).

Video Tutor Help
Visit: PhSchool.com
Web Code: age-0775

4 EXAMPLE Solving an Equivalent System

Solve the system below by elimination.
$$\begin{cases} 3x + 7y = 15 \\ 5x + 2y = -4 \end{cases}$$

To eliminate the y terms, make them additive inverses by multiplying.

① $3x + 7y = 15$	$6x + 14y = 30$	**Multiply ① by 2.**
② $5x + 2y = -4$	$\underline{-35x - 14y = 28}$	**Multiply ② by −7.**
	$-29x \quad\quad = 58$	**Add.**
	$x = -2$	**Solve for x.**

$$3x + 7y = 15 \quad \textbf{Choose an original equation.}$$
$$3(-2) + 7y = 15 \quad \textbf{Substitute the value of x.}$$
$$-6 + 7y = 15 \quad \textbf{Simplify.}$$
$$7y = 21$$
$$y = 3 \quad \textbf{Solve for y.}$$

● The solution is $(-2, 3)$.

 **Quick Check** ④ Explain how to solve the system in Example 4 by eliminating x.

Solving a system algebraically does not always result in a unique solution, as in Examples 3 and 4. You may get an equation that is always true, or one that is never true.

5 EXAMPLE Solving a System Without a Unique Solution

Solve each system by elimination.

a. $\begin{cases} 2x - y = 3 \\ -2x + y = -3 \end{cases}$
$\overline{0 = 0}$

b. $\begin{cases} 2x - 3y = 18 \\ -2x + 3y = -6 \end{cases}$
$\overline{0 = 12}$

Elimination gives an equation that is always true. The two equations in the system represent the same line. The system has an infinite number of solutions:
$\{(x, y) \mid y = 2x - 3\}.$

Elimination gives an equation that is always false. The two equations in the system represent parallel lines. The system has no solution.

For: Special Solutions Activity
Use: Interactive Textbook, 3-2

 **Quick Check** ⑤ Solve each system by substitution or elimination.

a. $\begin{cases} -3x + 5y = 7 \\ 6x - 10y = -14 \end{cases}$

b. $\begin{cases} -2x + 4y = 6 \\ -3x + 6y = 8 \end{cases}$

EXERCISES

For more exercises, see *Extra Skill and Word Problem Practice*.

Practice and Problem Solving

A Practice by Example

Example 1
(page 125)

GO for Help

Solve each system by substitution. Check your answers.

1. $\begin{cases} 4x + 2y = 7 \\ y = 5x \end{cases}$

2. $\begin{cases} 3c + 2d = 2 \\ d = 4 \end{cases}$

3. $\begin{cases} x + 12y = 68 \\ x = 8y - 12 \end{cases}$

4. $\begin{cases} 4p + 2q = 8 \\ q = 2p + 1 \end{cases}$

5. $\begin{cases} x + 3y = 7 \\ 2x - 4y = 24 \end{cases}$

6. $\begin{cases} x + 6y = 2 \\ 5x + 4y = 36 \end{cases}$

7. $\begin{cases} 3a + b = 3 \\ 2a - 5b = -15 \end{cases}$

8. $\begin{cases} t = 2r + 3 \\ 5r - 4t = 6 \end{cases}$

9. $\begin{cases} y = 2x - 1 \\ 3x - y = -1 \end{cases}$

10. $\begin{cases} 2m + 4n = 10 \\ 3m + 5n = 11 \end{cases}$

11. $\begin{cases} -6 = 3x - 6y \\ 4x = 4 + 5y \end{cases}$

12. $\begin{cases} r + s = -12 \\ 2r - 3s = 6 \end{cases}$

Example 2
(page 126)

13. **Fund-Raising** Suppose you have signed up for a bike-a-thon to raise money for charity. One person is sponsoring you at a rate of $.50 per mile. Each of the other sponsors plans to donate $15 no matter how far you bike.
   a. Write a system of equations to model the donation d for m miles biked.
   b. For how many miles will all sponsors donate the same amount?

14. **Transportation** A youth group with 26 members is going skiing. Each of the five chaperones will drive a van or a sedan. The vans can seat seven people, and the sedans can seat five people. How many of each type of vehicle could transport all 31 people to the ski area in one trip?

15. Suppose you have a part-time job delivering packages. Your employer pays you at a flat rate of $7 per hour. You discover that a competitor pays employees $2 per hour plus $.35 per delivery.
   a. Write a system of equations to model the pay p for d deliveries. Assume a four-hour shift.
   b. How many deliveries would the competitor's employees have to make in four hours to earn the same pay you earn in a four-hour shift?

16. A boat can travel 24 mi in 3 h when traveling with a current. Against the same current, it can travel only 16 mi in 4 h. Find the rate of the current and the rate of the boat in still water.

17. **Geometry** The measure of one acute angle of a right triangle is 30° more than twice the measure of the other acute angle. Find the measures of the angles.

Example 3
(page 126)

Solve each system by elimination.

18. $\begin{cases} x + y = 12 \\ x - y = 2 \end{cases}$

19. $\begin{cases} x + 2y = 10 \\ x + y = 6 \end{cases}$

20. $\begin{cases} 3a + 4b = 9 \\ -3a - 2b = -3 \end{cases}$

21. $\begin{cases} 4x + 2y = 4 \\ 6x + 2y = 8 \end{cases}$

22. $\begin{cases} 2w + 5y = -24 \\ 3w - 5y = 14 \end{cases}$

23. $\begin{cases} 3u + 3v = 15 \\ -2u + 3v = -5 \end{cases}$

24. $\begin{cases} x + 3y = 11 \\ x + 4y = 14 \end{cases}$

25. $\begin{cases} 5x + 3y = 30 \\ 3x + 3y = 18 \end{cases}$

26. $\begin{cases} x - 14 = -y \\ x - y = 2 \end{cases}$

27. $\begin{cases} 3x + 2y = 6 \\ 3x + 3 = y \end{cases}$

28. $\begin{cases} 5x - y = 4 \\ 2x - y = 1 \end{cases}$

29. $\begin{cases} 2r + s = 3 \\ 4r - s = 9 \end{cases}$

128 Chapter 3 Linear Systems

Examples 4, 5
(page 127)

Solve each system by elimination.

30. $\begin{cases} 4x - 6y = -26 \\ -2x + 3y = 13 \end{cases}$
31. $\begin{cases} 9a - 3d = 3 \\ -3a + d = -1 \end{cases}$
32. $\begin{cases} 2a + 3b = 12 \\ 5a - b = 13 \end{cases}$

33. $\begin{cases} 2x - 3y = 6 \\ 6x - 9y = 9 \end{cases}$
34. $\begin{cases} 20x + 5y = 120 \\ 10x + 7.5y = 80 \end{cases}$
35. $\begin{cases} 6x - 2y = 11 \\ -9x + 3y = 16 \end{cases}$

36. $\begin{cases} 2x - 3y = -1 \\ 3x + 4y = 8 \end{cases}$
37. $\begin{cases} 5x - 2y = -19 \\ 2x + 3y = 0 \end{cases}$
38. $\begin{cases} r + 3s = 7 \\ 2r - s = 7 \end{cases}$

39. $\begin{cases} y = 4 - x \\ 3x + y = 6 \end{cases}$
40. $\begin{cases} 3x + 2y = 10 \\ 6x + 4y = 15 \end{cases}$
41. $\begin{cases} 3m + 4n = -13 \\ 5m + 6n = -19 \end{cases}$

GO for Help

For a guide to solving
Exercise 42, see p. 131.

 42. **Elections** In a mayoral election, the number of votes for the incumbent was 25% more than the number for the opponent. Altogether, the two candidates received 5175 votes. How many votes did the incumbent mayor receive?

43. **Writing** Explain how you decide whether to use substitution or elimination to solve a system.

B **Apply Your Skills**

Solve each system.

44. $\begin{cases} 5x + y = 0 \\ 5x + 2y = 30 \end{cases}$
45. $\begin{cases} 2m = -4n - 4 \\ 3m + 5n = -3 \end{cases}$
46. $\begin{cases} 7x + 2y = -8 \\ 8y = 4x \end{cases}$

47. $\begin{cases} v = 9t + 300 \\ v = 7t + 400 \end{cases}$
48. $\begin{cases} 80x + 60y = 85 \\ 100x - 40y = 20 \end{cases}$
49. $\begin{cases} 2x + 3y = 0 \\ 7x = 3(2y) + 3 \end{cases}$

50. $\begin{cases} \frac{x}{3} + \frac{4y}{3} = 300 \\ 3x - 4y = 300 \end{cases}$
51. $\begin{cases} 0.02a - 1.5b = 4 \\ 0.5b - 0.02a = 1.8 \end{cases}$
52. $\begin{cases} 4y = 2x \\ 2x + y = \frac{x}{2} + 1 \end{cases}$

53. **Multiple Choice** The equation $3x - 4y = 2$ and which equation below form a system with no solutions?
   Ⓐ $2y = 1.5x - 2$
   Ⓑ $2y = 1.5x - 1$
   Ⓒ $3x + 4y = 2$
   Ⓓ $4y - 3x = -2$

For each system, choose the method of solving that seems easier to use. Explain why you made each choice.

54. $\begin{cases} 3x - 5y = 26 \\ -2x - 3y = -11 \end{cases}$
55. $\begin{cases} y = \frac{2}{3}x - 3 \\ -x + 3y = 18 \end{cases}$
56. $\begin{cases} 2m + 3n = 12 \\ -5m + n = -13 \end{cases}$

57. $\begin{cases} 3x - y = 5 \\ y = 4x + 2 \end{cases}$
58. $\begin{cases} 2x - 3y = 4 \\ 2x - 5y = -6 \end{cases}$
59. $\begin{cases} 6x - 3y = 3 \\ 5x - 5y = 10 \end{cases}$

GO Online

Homework Video Tutor

Visit: PHSchool.com
Web Code: age-0302

60. **Open-Ended** Write a system of equations in which both equations must be multiplied by a nonzero number before using elimination. Solve your system.

 61. **Internet Access** The ads at the left show the costs of Internet access for two companies.
   a. Write a system of equations to represent the cost c for t hours of access in one month for each company.
   b. Graph the system from part (a). Label each line.
   c. For how many hours of use will the costs for the companies be the same? How is this information represented on the graph?
   d. If you use the Internet about 20 hours each month, which company should you choose? Explain how you reached an answer.

62. Break-Even Point A theater production costs $40,000 plus $2800 per performance. A sold-out performance brings in $3675. How many sold-out performances will the production need to break even?

C Challenge **63. Weather** The equation $F = \frac{9}{5}C + 32$ relates temperatures on the Celsius and Fahrenheit scales. Does any temperature have the same number reading on both scales? If so, what is the number?

Find the value of *a* that makes each system a dependent system.

64. $\begin{cases} y = 3x + a \\ 3x - y = 2 \end{cases}$

65. $\begin{cases} 3y = 2x \\ 6y - a - 4x = 0 \end{cases}$

66. $\begin{cases} y = \frac{x}{2} + 4 \\ 2y - x = a \end{cases}$

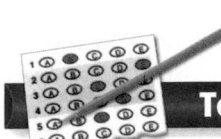

Gridded Response

Use the following system of equations for Exercises 67–70.

$$\begin{cases} 5x - 3y = 11 \\ -x + 12y = 3.5 \end{cases}$$

67. If you want to solve the system by eliminating *x* (with addition), by what would you multiply the second equation?

68. If you want to solve the system by eliminating *y* (with addition), by what would you multiply the first equation?

69. What is the value of *x* in the solution? Enter your answer as a decimal.

70. What is the value of *y* in the solution? Enter your answer as a decimal.

Use the following system of equations for Exercises 71–72.

$$\begin{cases} 4x - 10y = -3 \\ 12x + 5y = 12 \end{cases}$$

71. What is the value of *x* in the solution? Enter your answer as a fraction in simplest form.

72. What is the value of *y* in the solution? Enter your answer as a decimal.

Mixed Review

Lesson 3-1

Solve each system of equations by graphing.

73. $\begin{cases} y = 3x + 4 \\ 2y = 6x - 2 \end{cases}$

74. $\begin{cases} -3y = 9x + 1 \\ 6y = -18x - 2 \end{cases}$

75. $\begin{cases} 4x - y = -5 \\ -8x + 2y = 15 \end{cases}$

Lesson 2-6

Write an equation for each diagonal translation.

76. $y = x$, 4 units down, 3 units left

77. $y = |x|$, $\frac{1}{2}$ unit up, 2 units right

78. $y = 2x - 3$, 1 unit down, 1 unit right

79. $y = |x| + 2$, 4 units up, 2 units left

Lesson 1-1

80. What subset(s) of real numbers contain(s) 6?

81. The sum of the first and last of four consecutive odd integers is 48. What are the four integers?

Understanding Word Problems Read the problem below. Then let David's thinking guide you through the solution. Check your understanding with the exercises at the bottom of the page.

Elections In a mayoral election, the number of votes for the incumbent was 25% more than the number for the opponent. Altogether, the two candidates received 5175 votes. How many votes did the incumbent mayor receive?

What David Thinks

I'll restate the important information. In the first sentence, 25% more means the greater number is 1.25 times the lesser number.

The second sentence gives me the total number of votes.

What quantities are being used in the problem? I'll assign variables to the number of votes each received.

Now I can write a system of equations.

Great! The first equation defines the value of n. I'll solve the system by substituting $1.25p$ from the first equation into the second equation.

The problem asks me to find the number of incumbent votes. That's n. I'll use one of the original equations and substitute.

Now I'll write my answer as a sentence.

What David Writes

Incumbent received 25% more votes than opponent.

$$\text{incumbent's votes} = 1.25 \left(\text{opponent's votes} \right)$$

5175 votes total for both candidates.

$$\text{incumbent's votes} + \text{opponent's votes} = 5175$$

n = number of incumbent's votes
p = number of opponent's votes

$$\begin{cases} n = 1.25p \\ n + p = 5175 \end{cases}$$

$$n + p = 5175$$
$$1.25p + p = 5175$$
$$2.25p = 5175$$
$$p = 2300$$

$$n = 1.25p$$
$$n = 1.25(2300)$$
$$n = 2875$$

The incumbent mayor received 2875 votes.

EXERCISES

1. Two baseball cards together are worth $30. One card is worth 40% more than the other card. How much is the more expensive card worth?

2. A washer and dryer have the same retail price. The store discounts the washer by 10% and the dryer by 20%. The combined sale price for both appliances is $1020. What was the original price of each appliance?

Activity Lab

Solving Systems Using Tables

FOR USE WITH LESSON 3-2

To solve systems with tables, you compare numbers in the table lists.

ACTIVITY

A magnetic construction set has 38 bars. For a project, Carlos and Colleen need to make 7 regular polygons using the bars. Each polygon must be either a pentagon or a hexagon. Carlos wants to use all the bars. He can write two equations that represent the situation. Then he can solve the system using tables.

1. One equation relates the number of pentagons p and the number of hexagons h. What is that equation?

2. Another equation shows that the total number of bars used by p pentagons and h hexagons is 38. Write that equation.

3. Carlos made two tables side by side. One table lists the numbers of pentagons and hexagons that solve the first equation. The second table lists the numbers that solve the second equation. Build and complete the two tables.

Number of Pentagons	Number of Hexagons
0	7
1	6
2	

Number of Pentagons	Number of Hexagons
0	Not possible
1	

4. Find the rows in the two tables that list the same pairs of numbers.

5. How many polygons of each type do Carlos and Colleen need to make?

EXERCISES

A school track team is going to a track meet. The school has minivans that seat 8 passengers and minibuses that seat 12 passengers, in addition to the drivers in each case. The school wants to fill each vehicle used. There are 4 drivers who can drive any of the vehicles. There are 40 members on the team.

6. Write a system of equations that represents the situation.

7. Use tables to solve the system.

8. Explain what the solution of the system represents.

You can enter two equations as Y1 and Y2 in a graphing calculator. Then you can display a table showing X, Y1, and Y2. Decide how you can use such a table to solve each system of equations below. Then do so. (*Hint:* The screen at the right shows the table for Exercise 9.)

X	Y1	Y2
20.00	14.00	16.00
21.00	15.00	16.50
22.00	16.00	17.00
23.00	17.00	17.50
24.00	18.00	18.00
25.00	19.00	18.50
26.00	20.00	19.00
X=20		

9. $\begin{cases} y = x - 6 \\ y = \frac{1}{2}x + 6 \end{cases}$

10. $\begin{cases} y = 2x - 3 \\ y = -3x + 19.5 \end{cases}$

11. $\begin{cases} y = 1.5x \\ y = -0.75x + 9.75 \end{cases}$

3-3

Systems of Inequalities

What You'll Learn

- To solve systems of linear inequalities

... And Why

To model college entrance requirements, as in Example 3

✔ **Check Skills You'll Need**

GO for Help Lessons 1-4, 2-5, and 2-7

Solve each inequality.

1. $5x - 6 > 27$

2. $-18 - 5y \geq 52$

3. $-5(4x + 1) < 23$

Graph each inequality.

4. $y \leq 4x - 1$

5. $3y \geq 6x + 3$

6. $-5y + 2x > -5$

7. $y \leq |x|$

8. $y \geq |x + 3|$

9. $y < |x - 2| + 4$

---

1 Solving Systems of Inequalities

You can model a situation by writing a system of linear inequalities or a system that combines equations and inequalities.

1 EXAMPLE Solving a System by Using a Table

Classroom Management A science class has 6 computers for 20 students. Students have the option of using a computer program to investigate frog biology or using a computer and their graphing calculators to investigate the properties of heat transfer. Each frog lab must have 3 students in a group. Each heat lab must have 4 students in a group. In how many ways can you set up the lab groups?

Relate   number of frog lab groups + number of heat lab groups ≤ 6

3 · number of frog lab groups + 4 · number of heat lab groups = 20

Define Let f = the number of frog lab groups.

Let h = the number of heat lab groups.

Write $f + h \leq 6$

$3 f + 4 h = 20$

The situation is discrete. The replacement values for f and h must be whole numbers.

To solve the system $\begin{cases} f + h \leq 6 \\ 3f + 4h = 20 \end{cases}$

first make a table of values of f and h that solve the inequality.

f	h
0	6, 5, 4, 3, 2, 1, 0
1	5, 4, 3, 2, 1, 0
2	4, 3, 2, 1, 0
3	3, 2, 1, 0
4	2, 1, 0
5	1, 0
6	0

In that table look for values of f and h that solve the equation. Circle any that you find.

The only two whole number solutions of the system are $(0, 5)$ and $(4, 2)$.

There are two possible ways to set up the lab groups. You can assign all students to 5 heat lab groups, or you can assign them to 4 frog lab groups and 2 heat lab groups.

f	h
⓪	6, ⑤ 4, 3, 2, 1, 0
1	5, 4, 3, 2, 1, 0
2	4, 3, 2, 1, 0
3	3, 2, 1, 0
④	② 1, 0
5	1, 0
6	0

✓ Quick Check **❶** Use tables to solve each system. Assume that replacement values for the variables are whole numbers.

a. $\begin{cases} -x + y = 1 \\ x + 2y \le 20 \end{cases}$

b. $\begin{cases} x - y \ge 1 \\ 2x + 3y \le 21 \end{cases}$

You can solve a system of linear inequalities by graphing. Recall from Lesson 2-7 that when the variables represent real numbers, the solutions of an inequality include all the points on one side of a boundary line. Thus, for two inequalities, every point in the region of overlap of the two solutions is a solution of the system.

❷ EXAMPLE **Solving a System by Graphing**

Solve the system of inequalities. $\begin{cases} x - 2y < 6 \\ y \le -\frac{3}{2}x + 5 \end{cases}$

Graph each inequality. First graph the boundary lines. Then decide which side of each boundary line contains solutions and whether the boundary line is included.

Problem Solving Hint

After graphing a boundary line, test whether (0, 0) satisfies the inequality. If it does, shade the side of the line containing (0, 0).

$x - 2y < 6$

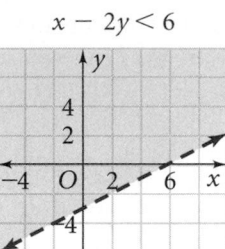

$y \le -\frac{3}{2}x + 5$

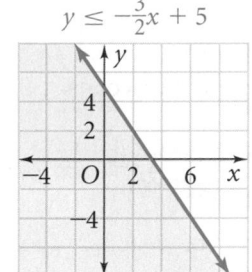

$\begin{cases} x - 2y < 6 \\ y \le -\frac{3}{2}x + 5 \end{cases}$

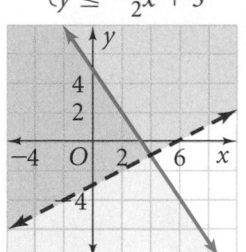

Every point in the red region above the dashed line is a solution of $x - 2y < 6$.

Every point in the blue region or on the solid line is a solution of $y \le -\frac{3}{2}x + 5$.

Every point in the purple region where the red and blue regions intersect is a solution of the system. For example, $(1, 1)$ is a solution.

Check Check $(1, 1)$ in both inequalities of the system.

$x - 2y < 6$ $y \le -\frac{3}{2}x + 5$

$1 - 2(1) < 6$ $1 \le -\frac{3}{2}(1) + 5$

$-1 < 6$ ✓ $1 \le \frac{7}{2}$ ✓

✓ Quick Check **❷** Solve each system of inequalities.

a. $\begin{cases} y \le -2x + 4 \\ x > -3 \end{cases}$

b. $\begin{cases} y \le 3x - 6 \\ y > -4x + 2 \end{cases}$

3 EXAMPLE Real-World  Connection

College Admissions An entrance exam has two parts, a verbal part and a mathematics part. You can score a maximum total of 1600 points. For admission, the school of your choice requires a math score of at least 600. Write a system of inequalities to model scores that meet the school's requirements. Then solve the system.

Relate verbal score + math score ≤ 1600

math score ≥ 600

Define Let x = the verbal score.

Let y = the mathematics score.

Write x + y ≤ 1600, or y ≤ 1600 − x

y ≥ 600

The system of inequalities is $\begin{cases} y \le 1600 - x \\ y \ge 600. \end{cases}$

Xmin = 0	Ymin = 10
Xmax = 1600	Ymax = 1600

Use a graphing calculator to graph the corresponding equations $y = 1600 - x$ and $y = 600$. Since the first inequality is ≤, shade below the first line. Since the second inequality is ≥, shade above the second line. The region of overlap is a graph of the solution.

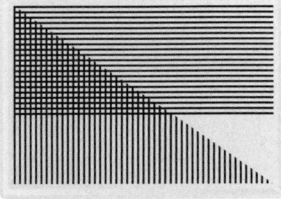

 **Quick Check** ❸ Another school requires a math score of at least 550 points and a total score of at least 1100 points. You can score up to 800 points on each part. Write and solve a system of inequalities to model scores that meet the school's requirements.

Some systems consist of linear and absolute value inequalities.

4 EXAMPLE Solving a Linear Absolute Value System

Solve the system of inequalities. $\begin{cases} y < 4 \\ y \ge |x - 3| \end{cases}$

$y < 4$

$y \ge |x - 3|$

$\begin{cases} y \ge |x - 3| \\ y < 4 \end{cases}$

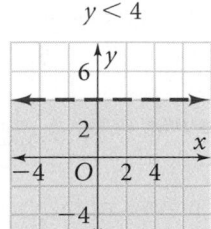 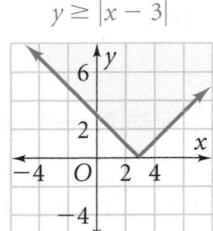 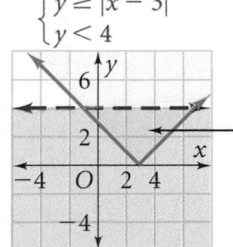

The region of overlap represents the solution.

 **Quick Check** ❹ Solve each system of inequalities.

a. $\begin{cases} y \ge x \\ y \le |x + 5| - 2 \end{cases}$

b. $\begin{cases} y \ge -2x + 4 \\ y \le |x - 4| \end{cases}$

c. **Critical Thinking** Write a system that includes an absolute value inequality but has no solutions.

Online
active math

For: Inequality Systems Activity
Use: Interactive Textbook, 3-3

EXERCISES

For more exercises, see *Extra Skill and Word Problem Practice.*

Practice and Problem Solving

 Practice by Example

Example 1
(page 133)

 **for Help**

Example 2
(page 134)

Find the whole number solutions of each system using tables.

1. $\begin{cases} y + 3x \le 8 \\ y - 3 > 2x \end{cases}$

2. $\begin{cases} x = y + 3 \\ x + y \le 12 \end{cases}$

3. $\begin{cases} x + y < 8 \\ 3x \le y + 6 \end{cases}$

Tell whether $(-3, 3)$ is a solution of each system.

4. $\begin{cases} y \ge x + 2 \\ 3y < -6x + 6 \end{cases}$

5. $\begin{cases} y - 2x \le 1 \\ y < -2x - 2 \end{cases}$

6. $\begin{cases} -2y + x \le 4 \\ 3y < -9x + 3 \end{cases}$

Solve each system of inequalities by graphing.

7. $\begin{cases} y \le 2x + 2 \\ y < -x + 1 \end{cases}$

8. $\begin{cases} y > -2 \\ x < 1 \end{cases}$

9. $\begin{cases} y \le 3 \\ y \le \frac{1}{2}x + 1 \end{cases}$

10. $\begin{cases} y \le 3x + 1 \\ -6x + 2y > 5 \end{cases}$

11. $\begin{cases} x + 2y \le 10 \\ x + y \le 3 \end{cases}$

12. $\begin{cases} -x - y \le 2 \\ y - 2x > 1 \end{cases}$

13. $\begin{cases} y > -2x \\ 2x - y \ge 2 \end{cases}$

14. $\begin{cases} c \ge d - 3 \\ c < \frac{1}{2}d + 3 \end{cases}$

15. $\begin{cases} 2x + y < 1 \\ -y + 3x < 1 \end{cases}$

Example 3
(page 135)

16. Fund-Raising You want to bake at least 6 and at most 11 loaves of bread for a bake sale. You want at least twice as many loaves of banana bread as nut bread. Write and graph a system of inequalities to model the situation.

17. Psychology A psychologist needs at least 40 subjects for her experiment. She cannot use more than 30 children. Write and graph a system of inequalities.

Example 4
(page 135)

Solve each system of inequalities by graphing.

18. $\begin{cases} y > 4 \\ y < |x - 1| \end{cases}$

19. $\begin{cases} y < -\frac{1}{3}x + 1 \\ y > |2x - 1| \end{cases}$

20. $\begin{cases} y > x - 2 \\ y \ge |x + 2| \end{cases}$

21. $\begin{cases} y \le -\frac{4}{3}x \\ y \ge -|x| \end{cases}$

22. $\begin{cases} 3y < -x - 1 \\ y \le |x + 1| \end{cases}$

23. $\begin{cases} y > -2 \\ y \le -|x - 3| \end{cases}$

24. $\begin{cases} -2x + y > 3 \\ y \le -|x + 4| \end{cases}$

25. $\begin{cases} 5y \ge 2x - 5 \\ y < |x + 3| \end{cases}$

26. $\begin{cases} y \ge -3x + 3 \\ y > |x + 2| \end{cases}$

27. $\begin{cases} -2y < 4x + 2 \\ y > |2x + 1| \end{cases}$

28. $\begin{cases} -x \ge 4 - y \\ y \ge |3x - 6| \end{cases}$

29. $\begin{cases} y \le x - 4 \\ y > |x - 6| \end{cases}$

 **Apply Your Skills**

In Exercises 30–39, identify the inequalities A, B, and C for which the given ordered pair is a solution.

A. $x + y \le 2$ **B.** $y \le \frac{3}{2}x - 1$ **C.** $y > -\frac{1}{3}x - 2$

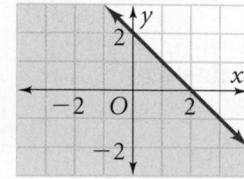 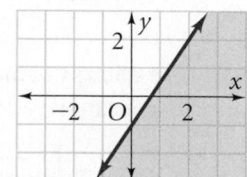 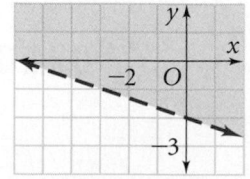

GO Online
Homework Video Tutor
Visit: PHSchool.com
Web Code: age-0303

30. $(0, 0)$ **31.** $(-2, -5)$ **32.** $(-2, 0)$ **33.** $(0, -2)$ **34.** $(-15, 15)$

35. $(3, 2)$ **36.** $(2, 0)$ **37.** $(-6, 0)$ **38.** $(4, -1)$ **39.** $(-8, -11)$

Real-World Connection

Bake sales are a popular way to raise money.

40. Fund-Raising Suppose the Student Council has asked you to form a committee to run a bake sale. The committee needs from 7 to 10 members. The number of seniors should be greater than the number of juniors.
   a. Write a system of inequalities to model the problem.
   b. Graph the system and list the combinations of juniors and seniors that may participate in the committee.
   c. Critical Thinking Explain why your list in part (b) is finite.

41. Open-Ended Write and graph a system of inequalities for which the solution is bounded by a dashed vertical line and a solid horizontal line.

42. Writing Explain how you determine where to shade when solving a system of inequalities.

Solve each system of inequalities by graphing.

43. $\begin{cases} x + y < 8 \\ x \geq 0 \\ y \geq 0 \end{cases}$

44. $\begin{cases} 2y - 4x \leq 0 \\ x \geq 0 \\ y \geq 0 \end{cases}$

45. $\begin{cases} y \geq -2x + 4 \\ x > -3 \\ y \geq 1 \end{cases}$

46. $\begin{cases} y \leq \frac{2}{3}x + 2 \\ y \geq |x| + 2 \end{cases}$

47. $\begin{cases} y < x - 1 \\ y > -|x - 2| + 1 \end{cases}$

48. $\begin{cases} 2x + y \leq 3 \\ y > |x + 3| - 2 \end{cases}$

C Challenge ▦ **Geometry** Write a system of inequalities to describe each shaded figure.

49.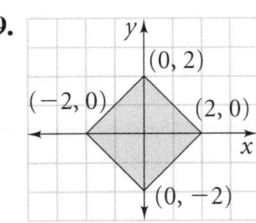

50.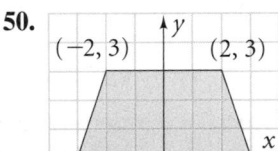

51.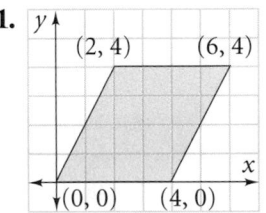

52. a. Graph the "bowtie" inequality, $|y| \leq |x|$.
   b. Write a system of inequalities to describe the graph shown at the right.

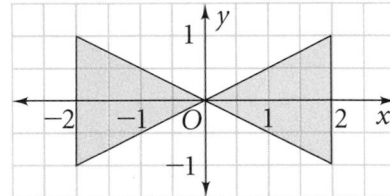

Test Prep

Multiple Choice

53. When you graph Inequality ① at the right, the boundary line should be __?__ and the shading should be __?__ the line.
   ① $\begin{cases} y < -2x + 3 \\ y \geq x - 4 \end{cases}$ ②
   A. dashed, above   **B.** dashed, below   **C.** solid, above   **D.** solid, below

54. When you graph Inequality ②, the boundary line should be __?__ and the shading should be __?__ the line.
   F. dashed, above   **G.** dashed, below   **H.** solid, above   **J.** solid, below

55. What is the x-value of the intersection of the boundary lines?
   A. $\frac{-7}{3}$ **B.** $\frac{-3}{7}$ **C.** $\frac{3}{7}$ **D.** $\frac{7}{3}$

Short Response

56. How would you test whether (2, −2) is a solution of the system?

Lesson 3-2

Solve each system by elimination or substitution.

57. $\begin{cases} y = 3x + 1 \\ 2x - y = 8 \end{cases}$
58. $\begin{cases} 3x + y = 4 \\ 2x - 4y = 7 \end{cases}$
59. $\begin{cases} -x + 5y = 3 \\ 2x - 10y = 4 \end{cases}$

60. $\begin{cases} 2x + 4y = -8 \\ -5x + 4y = 6 \end{cases}$
61. $\begin{cases} y - 3 = x \\ 4x + y = -2 \end{cases}$
62. $\begin{cases} 2 = 4y - 3x \\ 5x = 2y - 3 \end{cases}$

Lesson 2-3

For each function, *y* varies directly as *x*.

63. If $y = -6$ when $x = -2$, find *y* when $x = 3$.

64. If $y = -8$ when $x = 2$, find *x* when $y = 2$.

65. If $y = 4$ when $x = 7$, find *y* when $x = -14$.

66. If $y = 9$ when $x = 15$, find *x* when $y = 6$.

Lesson 1-5

Solve each equation. Check your answers.

67. $|2x + 5| = 6$
68. $|x + 7| = -2$

69. $3|x - 4| + 1 = 13$
70. $-2|x + 1| - 5 = -7$

71. $\frac{1}{2}|3x + 2| - 3 = 4$
72. $-|2x + 5| = -3$

Checkpoint Quiz 1   **Lessons 3-1 through 3-3**

Solve each system of equations.

1. $\begin{cases} 3x + 2y = 6 \\ x - 2y = 10 \end{cases}$
2. $\begin{cases} 4x + 7y = 28 \\ y = 2x - 14 \end{cases}$

3. $\begin{cases} 4x + 5y = -12 \\ 3x - 4y = 22 \end{cases}$
4. $\begin{cases} 3y - 2x = 7 \\ 2y - 2 = 4x \end{cases}$

5. The Village Inn offers two special packages. For two nights and three meals the cost is $158. For two nights and five meals the cost is $181. Write and solve a system of linear equations to find the costs per night and per meal.

 6. Smart Shopping An ordinary refrigerator costs $489 and has an estimated annual operating cost of $84. An energy-saving model costs $599, with an estimated annual cost of $61. After how many years will the costs to buy and to operate the two models be equal?

7. Each week you must do a minimum of 18 hours of homework. Participation in sports requires at least 12 hours per week. You have no more than 35 hours per week in total to devote to these activities.
a. Write a system of inequalities to model the situation.
b. Graph and solve the system.

Solve each system of inequalities by graphing.

8. $\begin{cases} y \leq -2 \\ y > |x + 1| \end{cases}$
9. $\begin{cases} 8x + 2y > 5 \\ x + 2y \leq -3 \end{cases}$
10. $\begin{cases} 4y < 3x - 1 \\ y > 2|x| - 3 \end{cases}$

Linear Programming

What You'll Learn

- To find maximum and minimum values
- To solve problems with linear programming

. . . And Why

To maximize profit, as in Example 2

✓ **Check Skills You'll Need**

GO for Help   Lessons 3-2 and 3-3

Solve each system of equations.

1. $\begin{cases} y = -3x + 3 \\ y = 2x - 7 \end{cases}$

2. $\begin{cases} x + 2y = 5 \\ x - y = -1 \end{cases}$

3. $\begin{cases} 4x + 3y = 7 \\ 2x - 5y = -3 \end{cases}$

Solve each system of inequalities by graphing.

4. $\begin{cases} x \geq 5 \\ y > -3x + 6 \end{cases}$

5. $\begin{cases} 3y > 5x + 2 \\ y \leq -x + 7 \end{cases}$

6. $\begin{cases} x + 3y < -6 \\ 2x - 3y \leq 4 \end{cases}$

◀)) **New Vocabulary**   • linear programming   • objective function   • constraints
• feasible region

---

1   Finding Maximum and Minimum Values

Activity: Finding a Minimum Value

Music Suppose you want to buy some tapes and CDs. You can afford as many as 10 tapes or 7 CDs. You want at least 4 CDs and at least 10 hours of recorded music. Each tape holds about 45 minutes of music, and each CD holds about an hour.

1. Write a system of inequalities to model the problem.
   Let x represent the number of tapes purchased.
   Let y represent the number of CDs purchased.

2. Graph your system of inequalities.

3. Does each ordered pair satisfy the system you have graphed?
   a. (4, 7)   b. (12, 7)   c. (7, 6)   d. (9, 4)   e. (10, 4)

Linear programming is a technique that identifies the minimum or maximum value of some quantity. This quantity is modeled with an **objective function.** Limits on the variables in the objective function are **constraints,** written as linear inequalities.

Vocabulary Tip

Constraints are sometimes referred to as restrictions.

The first paragraph of the Activity describes the constraints on buying tapes and CDs. Suppose you buy x tapes and y CDs. The constraints on x and y can be modeled with inequalities as follows.

as many as 10 tapes $x \leq 10$ at least 4 CDs $y \geq 4$

as many as 7 CDs $y \leq 7$ at least 10 hours $\frac{3}{4}x + y \geq 10$

Vocabulary Tip

<u>Feasible</u> means "doable" or "suitable."

The constraints form the system of inequalities at the right. The red region in the graph, the **feasible region,** contains all the points that satisfy all the constraints.

$$\begin{cases} x \leq 10 \\ y \leq 7 \\ y \geq 4 \\ \frac{3}{4}x + y \geq 10 \end{cases}$$

If you buy tapes at $8 each and CDs at $12 each, then the objective function for the total cost C is $C = 8x + 12y$. The blue line is the graph for the total cost $140. The green line is for the total cost $112.

Graphs of the objective function for various values of C are parallel lines. Lines closer to the origin represent lower costs. The graph closest to the origin that intersects the feasible region intersects it at the vertex $(8, 4)$. The graph of the objective function farthest from the origin that intersects the feasible region intersects it at the vertex $(10, 7)$. Graphs of an objective function that represent a maximum or minimum value intersect a feasible region at a vertex.

Key Concepts

Property	Vertex Principle of Linear Programming

If there is a maximum or a minimum value of the linear objective function, it occurs at one or more vertices of the feasible region.

---

1 EXAMPLE Testing Vertices

Test-Taking Tip

Remember to check the value of the objective function at *each* vertex when solving linear programming problems.

Multiple Choice What values of x and y maximize P for the objective function $P = 3x + 2y$?

Constraints $\begin{cases} y \geq \frac{3}{2}x - 3 \\ y \leq -x + 7 \\ x \geq 0, y \geq 0 \end{cases}$

Ⓐ $(2, 0)$ Ⓑ $(2, 6)$

Ⓒ $(4, 3)$ Ⓓ $(4, 4)$

Step 1
Graph the constraints.

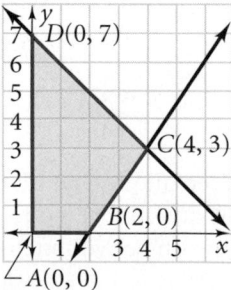

Step 2
Find coordinates for each vertex.

Vertex
$A(0, 0)$
$B(2, 0)$
$C(4, 3)$
$D(0, 7)$

Step 3
Evaluate P at each vertex.

$P = 3x + 2y$
$P = 3(0) + 2(0) = 0$
$P = 3(2) + 2(0) = 6$
$P = 3(4) + 2(3) = 18$
$P = 3(0) + 2(7) = 14$

• When $x = 4$ and $y = 3$, P has its maximum value of 18. The answer is C.

 **Quick Check** ❶ Use the constraints in Example 1 with the objective function $P = 2x + 3y$. Find the values of x and y that maximize and minimize P. Find the value of P at each point.

You can use linear programming to solve many real-world problems.

2 **EXAMPLE** **Real-World**  **Connection**

For: Linear Program Activity
Use: Interactive Textbook, 3-4

Profit Suppose you are selling cases of mixed nuts and roasted peanuts. You can order no more than a total of 500 cans and packages and spend no more than $600. How can you maximize your profit? How much is the maximum profit?

Mixed Nuts
12 cans per case

You pay ...... $24 per case
Sell at .... $3.50 per can

$18 profit per case!

Roasted Peanuts
20 packages per case

You pay ...... $15 per case
Sell at ... $1.50 per package

$15 profit per case!

Define Let x = number of cases of mixed nuts ordered.
Let y = number of cases of roasted peanuts ordered.
Let P = total profit.

Relate Organize the information in a table.

	Mixed Nuts	Roasted Peanuts	Total	
Number of Cases	x	y	$x + y$	
Number of Units	$12x$	$20y$	500	constraint
Cost	$24x$	$15y$	600	constraint
Profit	$18x$	$15y$	$18x + 15y$	objective

Write Write and simplify the constraints. Write the objective function.

$$\begin{cases} 12x + 20y \le 500 \\ 24x + 15y \le 600 \\ x \ge 0, y \ge 0 \end{cases} \Rightarrow \begin{cases} 3x + 5y \le 125 \\ 8x + 5y \le 200 \\ x \ge 0, y \ge 0 \end{cases} \qquad P = 18x + 15y$$

Step 1
Graph the constraints.

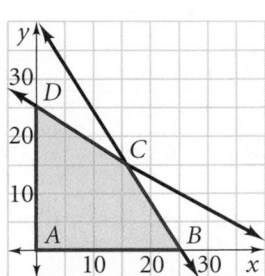

Step 2
Find the coordinates of each vertex.

Vertex
$A(0,0)$
$B(25,0)$
$C(15,16)$
$D(0,25)$

Step 3
Evaluate P at each vertex.

$P = 18x + 15y$
$P = 18(0) + 15(0) = 0$
$P = 18(25) + 15(0) = 450$
$P = 18(15) + 15(16) = 510$
$P = 18(0) + 15(25) = 375$

You can maximize your profit by selling 15 cases of mixed nuts and 16 cases of roasted peanuts. The maximum profit is $510.

 **Quick Check** **2** If you sell mixed nuts for $4.25 per can, what should you order to maximize profit?

EXERCISES

For more exercises, see *Extra Skill and Word Problem Practice.*

Practice and Problem Solving

 Practice by Example

Example 1
(page 140)

Find the values of x and y that maximize or minimize the objective function for each graph.

1.
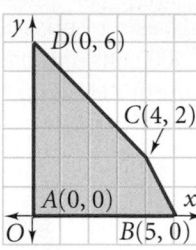
Maximum for
$P = 3x + 2y$

2.
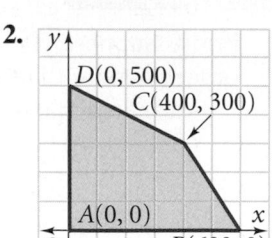
Maximum for
$P = 7x + 4y$

3.
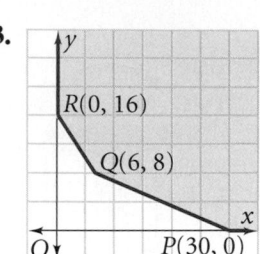
Minimum for
$C = 2x + 3y$

Graph each system of constraints. Name all vertices. Then find the values of x and y that maximize or minimize the objective function.

4. $\begin{cases} x \le 5 \\ y \le 4 \\ x \ge 0, y \ge 0 \end{cases}$

Maximum for
$P = 3x + 2y$

5. $\begin{cases} x + y \ge 8 \\ y \ge 5 \\ x \ge 0 \end{cases}$

Minimum for
$P = 3x + 2y$

6. $\begin{cases} x + y \le 8 \\ 2x + y \le 10 \\ x \ge 0, y \ge 0 \end{cases}$

Maximum for
$N = 100x + 40y$

7. $\begin{cases} x + y \ge 6 \\ x \le 8 \\ y \le 5 \end{cases}$

Minimum for
$C = x + 3y$

8. $\begin{cases} x + 2y \ge 8 \\ x \ge 2 \\ y \ge 0 \end{cases}$

Minimum for
$C = x + 3y$

9. $\begin{cases} 2 \le x \le 6 \\ 1 \le y \le 5 \\ x + y \le 8 \end{cases}$

Maximum for
$P = 3x + 2y$

Example 2
(page 141)

10. Ecology Teams chosen from 30 forest rangers and 16 trainees are planting trees. An experienced team consisting of two rangers can plant 500 trees per week. A training team consisting of one ranger and two trainees can plant 200 trees per week.

	Experienced Teams	Training Teams	Total
Number of Teams	x	y	$x + y$
Number of Rangers	$2x$	y	30
Number of Trainees	0	$2y$	16
Number of Trees Planted	$500x$	$200y$	$500x + 200y$

a. Write an objective function and constraints for a linear program that models the problem.

b. How many of each type of team should be formed to maximize the number of trees planted? How many trainees are used in this solution? How many trees are planted?

c. Find a solution that uses all the trainees. How many trees will be planted in this case?

11. Air Quality Trees in urban areas help keep air fresh by absorbing carbon dioxide. A city has $2100 to spend on planting spruce and maple trees. The land available for planting is 45,000 ft². How many of each tree should the city plant to maximize carbon dioxide absorption?

Facts for a Single Tree		
	Spruce	Maple
Planting Cost	$30	$40
Area Required	600 ft²	900 ft²
Carbon Dioxide Absorption	650 lb/yr	300 lb/yr

SOURCES: Auburn University and Anderson & Associates

B Apply Your Skills

12. Writing Explain why solving a system of linear equations is a necessary skill for linear programming.

13. Multiple Choice A biologist is developing two new strains of bacteria. Each sample of Type I bacteria produces four new viable bacteria, and each sample of Type II produces three new viable bacteria. Altogether, at least 240 new viable bacteria must be produced. At least 30, but not more than 60, of the original samples must be Type I. Not more than 70 of the samples can be Type II. A sample of Type I costs $5 and a sample of Type II costs $7. How many samples of Type II bacteria should be used to minimize cost?

- (A) 0
- (B) 30
- (C) 60
- (D) 70

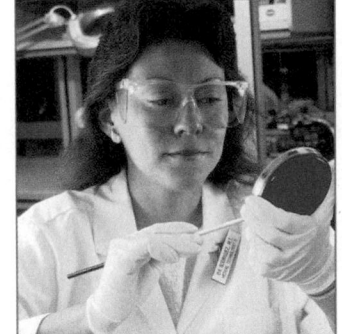

Real-World Connection

Careers A microbiologist studies microorganisms, such as bacteria and viruses, to determine their structure and function.

Graph each system of constraints. Name all vertices. Then find the values of x and y that maximize or minimize the objective function. Find the maximum or minimum value.

14. $\begin{cases} 3x + y \leq 7 \\ x + 2y \leq 9 \\ x \geq 0, y \geq 0 \end{cases}$

Maximum for
$P = 2x + y$

15. $\begin{cases} 25 \leq x \leq 75 \\ y \leq 110 \\ 8x + 6y \geq 720 \end{cases}$

Minimum for
$C = 8x + 5y$

16. $\begin{cases} x + y \leq 11 \\ 2y \geq x \\ x \geq 0, y \geq 0 \end{cases}$

Maximum for
$P = 3x + 2y$

17. $\begin{cases} 2x + y \leq 300 \\ x + y \leq 200 \\ x \geq 0, y \geq 0 \end{cases}$

Maximum for
$P = x + 2y$

18. $\begin{cases} 5x + y \geq 10 \\ x + y \geq 6 \\ x + 4y \geq 12 \\ x \geq 0, y \geq 0 \end{cases}$

Minimum for
$C = 10,000x + 20,000y$

19. $\begin{cases} 6 \leq x + y \leq 13 \\ x \geq 3 \\ y \geq 1 \end{cases}$

Maximum for
$P = 4x + 3y$

Homework Video Tutor

Visit: PHSchool.com
Web Code: age-0304

20. Cooking Baking a tray of corn muffins takes 4 c milk and 3 c wheat flour. A tray of bran muffins takes 2 c milk and 3 c wheat flour. A baker has 16 c milk and 15 c wheat flour. He makes $3 profit per tray of corn muffins and $2 profit per tray of bran muffins. How many trays of each type of muffin should the baker make to maximize his profit?

C Challenge

21. A vertex of a feasible region does not always have whole-number coordinates. Sometimes you may need to round coordinates to find the solution. Using the objective function and the constraints at the right, find the whole-number values of x and y that minimize C. Then find C for those values of x and y.

$C = 6x + 9y$
$\begin{cases} x + 2y \geq 50 \\ 2x + y \geq 60 \\ x \geq 0, y \geq 0 \end{cases}$

22. Open-Ended Write a system of constraints whose graphs determine a trapezoid. Write an objective function and evaluate it at each vertex.

23. Critical Thinking Sometimes two corners of a graph both yield the maximum profit. In this case, many other points may also yield the maximum profit. Evaluate the profit formula $P = x + 2y$ for the graph shown. Find four points that yield the maximum profit.

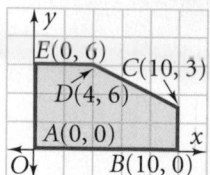

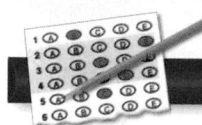

Multiple Choice

24. Which point maximizes $N = 4x + 3y$ and lies within the feasible region of the constraints at the right?

$$\begin{cases} y \leq 9 \\ 2x + 2y \leq 18 \\ x \leq 3 \end{cases}$$

A. (0, 0) **B.** (9, 0) **C.** (3, 6) **D.** (0, 9)

25. The vertices of a feasible region are (0, 0), (0, 2), (5, 2), and (4, 0). For which objective function is the maximum cost C found at the vertex (4, 0)?

F. $C = -2x + 3y$ **G.** $C = 2x + 7y$

H. $C = 4x - 3y$ **J.** $C = 5x + 3y$

Short Response

26. The figure at the right shows the feasible region for a system of constraints. This system includes $x \geq 0$ and $y \geq 0$. Find the remaining constraint(s).

Extended Response

27. What are the vertices of the feasible region bounded by the constraints at the right?

$$\begin{cases} x + y \leq 3 \\ 2x + y \leq 4 \\ x \geq 0, y \geq 0 \end{cases}$$

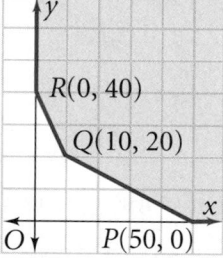

Mixed Review

Lesson 3-3

GO for Help

Solve each system of inequalities by graphing.

28. $\begin{cases} y < -2x + 8 \\ 3y \geq 4x - 6 \end{cases}$ **29.** $\begin{cases} x - 2y \geq 11 \\ 5x + 4y < 27 \end{cases}$ **30.** $\begin{cases} 2x + 6y > 12 \\ 3x + 9y \leq 27 \end{cases}$

31. $\begin{cases} 2y + x < 4 \\ y - 2x \geq 4 \end{cases}$ **32.** $\begin{cases} y + 5 \geq -2x \\ y - x \geq -2 \end{cases}$ **33.** $\begin{cases} 2y - 4x < 6 \\ 6x < 3y + 12 \end{cases}$

Lesson 2-4

34. Data Analysis Use the data below.

A Survey of Paperback Books: How Long and How Much?

Pages	326	450	246	427	208	339	367	445	404	465	378	265
Price ($)	7.50	7.99	6.99	7.99	6.99	7.95	7.50	7.95	7.95	7.99	7.99	6.99

a. Make a scatter plot of the data.
b. What kind of correlation do you see?
c. Find a linear model.
d. What price would you predict for a paperback containing 100 pages?

Lesson 1-2

Evaluate each expression for $a = 3$ and $b = -5$.

35. $2a + b$ **36.** $a - b$ **37.** $-4 + 2ab$ **38.** $a + \frac{3b}{a}$

39. $3(a - b)$ **40.** $4a - 2 + 3b$ **41.** $\frac{a - b}{2a}$ **42.** $b(2b - a)$

Activity Lab

Linear Programming

FOR USE WITH LESSON 3-4

You can solve linear programming problems with your graphing calculator.

Go Online
PHSchool.com
For: Graphing calculator procedures
Web Code: age-2109

ACTIVITY

Find the values of x and y that will maximize the objective function $P = 13x + 2y$ for the constraints at the right. What is the value of P at this maximum point?

$$\begin{cases} -3x + 2y \le 8 \\ -8x + y \ge -48 \\ x \ge 0, \ y \ge 0 \end{cases}$$

Step 1 Rewrite the first two inequalities to isolate y. Enter the inequalities.

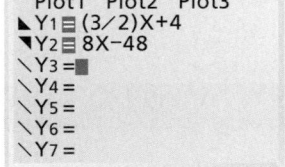

Step 2 Graph, using the window $0 \le x \le 12$, $0 \le y \le 20$.

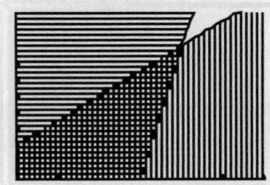

Step 3 Use the value option of **CALC** to find the upper left vertex. Press 0 ENTER.

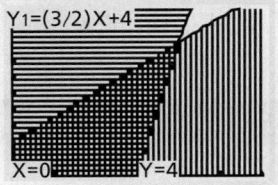

Step 4 Enter the expression for the objective function on the home screen. Press ENTER for the value of P at the vertex.

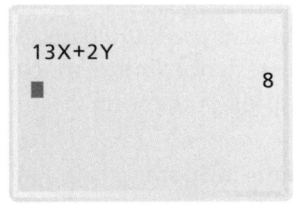

Step 5 Use the intersect option of **CALC** to find the upper right vertex. Go to the home screen and press ENTER for the value of P.

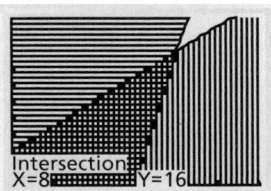

Step 6 Use the zero option of **CALC** to find the lower right vertex. Go to the home screen and press ENTER for the value of P.

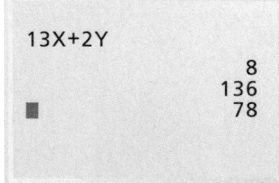

Compare the values of P for the coordinates of the three vertices you found. The objective function has a value of 0 for the vertex located at the origin. The maximum value 136 occurs when $x = 8$ and $y = 16$.

EXERCISES

Find the values of x and y that maximize or minimize the objective function.

1. $\begin{cases} 4x + 3y \ge 30 \\ x + 3y \ge 21 \\ x \ge 0, y \ge 0 \end{cases}$

Minimum for
$C = 5x + 8y$

2. $\begin{cases} 3x + 5y \le 35 \\ 2x + y \le 14 \\ x \ge 0, y \ge 0 \end{cases}$

Maximum for
$P = 3x + 2y$

3. $\begin{cases} x + y \ge 8 \\ x + 5y \ge 20 \\ x \ge 0, y \ge 2 \end{cases}$

Minimum for
$C = 3x + 4y$

4. $\begin{cases} x + 2y \le 24 \\ 3x + 2y \le 34 \\ 3x + y \le 29 \\ x \ge 0 \end{cases}$

Maximum for
$P = 2x + 3y$

Graphs in Three Dimensions

GO for Help   Lesson 2-2

What You'll Learn

- To graph points in three dimensions
- To graph equations in three dimensions

. . . And Why

To locate points on a virtual bicycle helmet, as in Example 2

✓ **Check Skills You'll Need**

Find the *x*- and *y*-intercepts of the graph of each linear equation.

1. $y = 2x + 6$

2. $2x + 9y = 36$

3. $3x - 8y = -24$

4. $4x - 5y = 40$

Graph each linear equation.

5. $y = 3x$

6. $y = -2x + 4$

7. $4y = 3x - 8$

8. $-3x - 2y = 7$

◀)) **New Vocabulary**   • coordinate space   • ordered triples   • trace

---

1   Graphing Points in Three Dimensions

Suppose you want to describe how to get from point *A* to point *B* along the grid shown at the right. You could say "Move down one unit, forward two units, and left three units," or "Move left three units, forward two units, and down one unit."

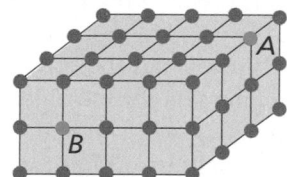

To describe positions in space, you need a three-dimensional coordinate system.

You have learned to graph on an *xy*-coordinate plane using ordered pairs. Adding a third axis, the *z*-axis, to the *xy*-coordinate plane creates **coordinate space.** In coordinate space you graph points using **ordered triples** of the form (x, y, z).

Real-World ● Connection

The global positioning system locates persons or objects in three dimensions.

Points in a Plane

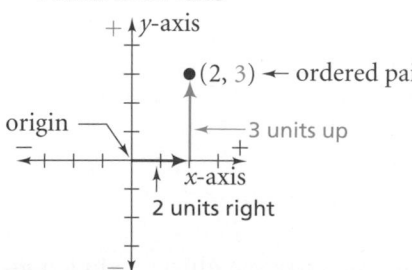

A two-dimensional coordinate system allows you to graph points in a plane.

Points in Space

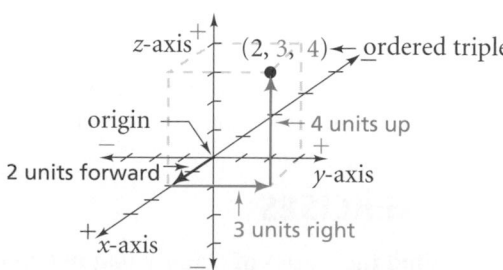

A three-dimensional coordinate system allows you to graph points in space.

In the coordinate plane, point $(2, 3)$ is two units right and three units up from the origin. In coordinate space, point $(2, 3, 4)$ is two units forward, three units right, and four units up.

1 EXAMPLE   Graphing in Coordinate Space

Graph each point in coordinate space.

a. $(0, 3, -2)$
Sketch the axes. From
the origin, move right 3 units
and down 2 units.

b. $(-2, -1, 3)$
Sketch the axes. From the origin,
move back 2 units, left 1 unit,
and up 3 units.

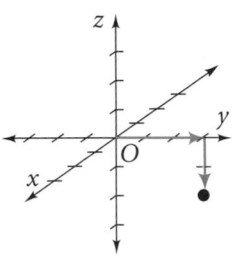

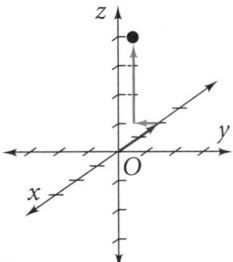

☑️ **Quick Check** ❶ Graph each point in coordinate space.
    a. $(0, -4, -2)$ **b.** $(-1, 1, 3)$ **c.** $(3, -5, 2)$ **d.** $(3, 3, -3)$

2 EXAMPLE   Real-World 🌐 Connection

Product Design Computers are used to
design three-dimensional objects. Programs
allow the designer to view the object from
different perspectives. Find coordinates for
points A, B, and C in the diagram below.

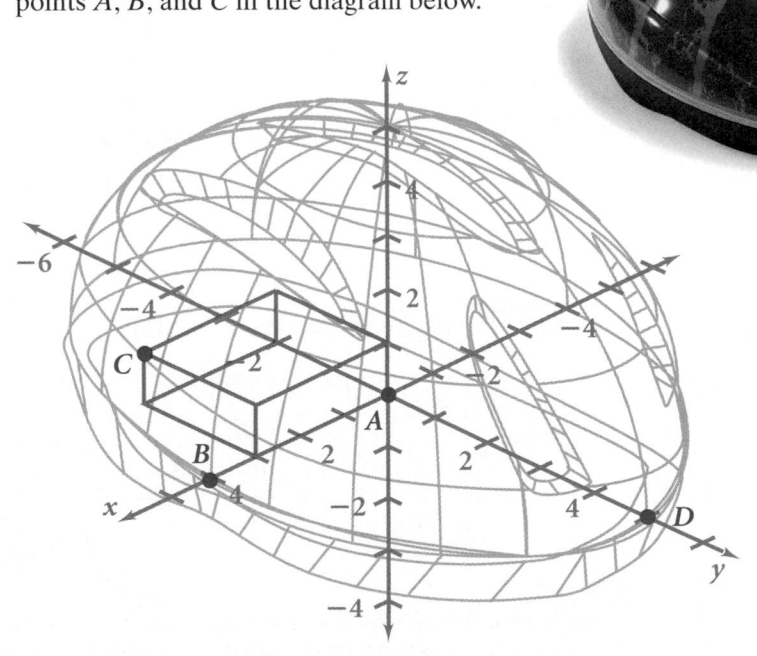

$A(0, 0, 0)$, $B(4, 0, 0)$, $C(3, -2, 1)$

☑️ **Quick Check** ❷ **a.** Find coordinates for point D in the diagram.
    b. Does the point $(-3, 2, 4)$ lie inside or outside the helmet? Explain.

The graph of an equation is a picture of all the solutions to the equation. In two dimensions, the graph of $3x - 2y = 6$ is a line. In three dimensions, the graph of $3x - 2y + z = 6$ is a plane, as shown at the right.

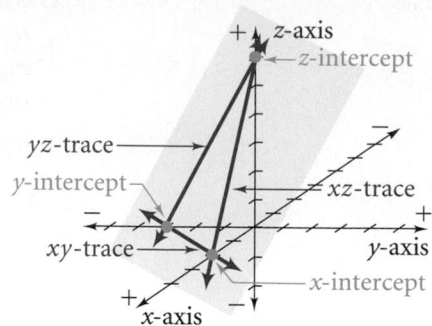

If the graph of a plane intersects one of the coordinate planes in a line, then the line is called a **trace**. For example, the xy-trace is the line in the xy-plane that contains the x- and the y-intercepts. The xz-trace and the yz-trace are defined similarly.

To sketch a plane, find the x-, y-, and z- intercepts. Then draw the traces and show the plane with shading.

3 **EXAMPLE**   **Sketching a Plane**

Sketch the graph of $2x + 3y + 4z = 12$.

Step 1 Find the intercepts.

$$2x + 3y + 4z = 12$$
$$2x + 3(0) + 4(0) = 12 \quad \textbf{To find the \textit{x}-intercept, substitute 0 for \textit{y} and \textit{z}.}$$
$$2x = 12$$
$$x = 6 \quad \textbf{The \textit{x}-intercept is 6.}$$
$$2(0) + 3y + 4(0) = 12 \quad \textbf{To find the \textit{y}-intercept, substitute 0 for \textit{x} and \textit{z}.}$$
$$3y = 12$$
$$y = 4 \quad \textbf{The \textit{y}-intercept is 4.}$$
$$2(0) + 3(0) + 4z = 12 \quad \textbf{To find the \textit{z}-intercept, substitute 0 for \textit{x} and \textit{y}.}$$
$$4z = 12$$
$$z = 3 \quad \textbf{The \textit{z}-intercept is 3.}$$

Step 2 Graph the intercepts.

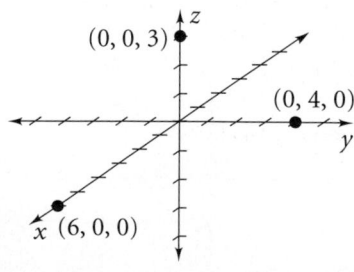

Step 3 Draw the traces. Shade the plane.

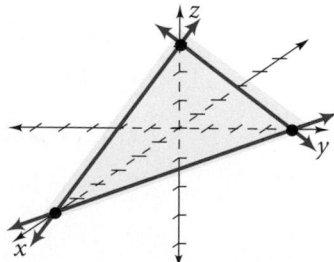

Each point on the plane represents a solution to $2x + 3y + 4z = 12$.

✓ **Quick Check** **3** Sketch the graph of each equation.
 a. $x + y + z = 5$ **b.** $2x - y + 3z = 6$ **c.** $x + 2y - z = -4$

EXERCISES

For more exercises, see *Extra Skill and Word Problem Practice*.

Practice and Problem Solving

 Practice by Example

Example 1
(page 147)

Describe the location of each point in coordinate space.

1. $(-1, 5, 0)$ **2.** $(3, -3, 4)$

3. $(2, 0, 5)$ **4.** $(-4, -7, -1)$

Graph each point in coordinate space.

5. $(5, 0, -2)$ **6.** $(0, 0, 4)$

7. $(10, -2, -5)$ **8.** $(-1, -1, -1)$

9. $(-4, -5, 3)$ **10.** $(25, 40, -30)$

11. $(1, 1, 0)$ **12.** $(0, -2, 2)$

Example 2
(page 147)

Find the coordinates of each point in the diagram.

13. A **14.** B **15.** C

16. D **17.** E **18.** F

Example 3
(page 148)

Sketch the graph of each equation.

19. $x + y + 2z = 4$ **20.** $x + y + z = 2$ **21.** $2x + 6y + z = 6$

22. $x - y - 4z = 8$ **23.** $-x + 3y + z = 6$ **24.** $2x - y - 5z = 10$

 **Apply Your Skills**

25. Writing While visiting friends in New York, you go to a concert. Explain how the seat information on your ticket at the right represents a point in three-dimensional coordinate space.

26. Multiple Choice Suppose you have $20 to spend on party decorations. Balloons are $.05 each, streamers are $.25 each, and noisemakers are $.40 each. Which equation best models this situation?

  Ⓐ $5b + 25s + 40n = 20$
  Ⓑ $20(b + s + n) = 0.05 + 0.25 + 0.4$
  Ⓒ $0.05b + 0.25s + 0.4n = 20$
  Ⓓ $0.05b + 0.25s + 0.4n + 20 = 0$

Sketch the graph of each equation.

27. $7x + 14y - z = 7$ **28.** $-3x + 5y + 10z = 15$

29. $32x + 16y - 8z = 32$ **30.** $-25x + 30y + 50z = 75$

31. $50x + 25y + 100z = 200$ **32.** $14x - 8y + 28z = 28$

GO Online
Homework Video Tutor
Visit: PHSchool.com
Web Code: age-0305

Sketch the graph of each equation and find the equation of each trace.

33. $6x + 6y - 12z = 36$ **34.** $-20x + 10y + 50z = 100$

35. $-12x - 32y - 48z = 96$ **36.** $25x + 125y - 25z = 125$

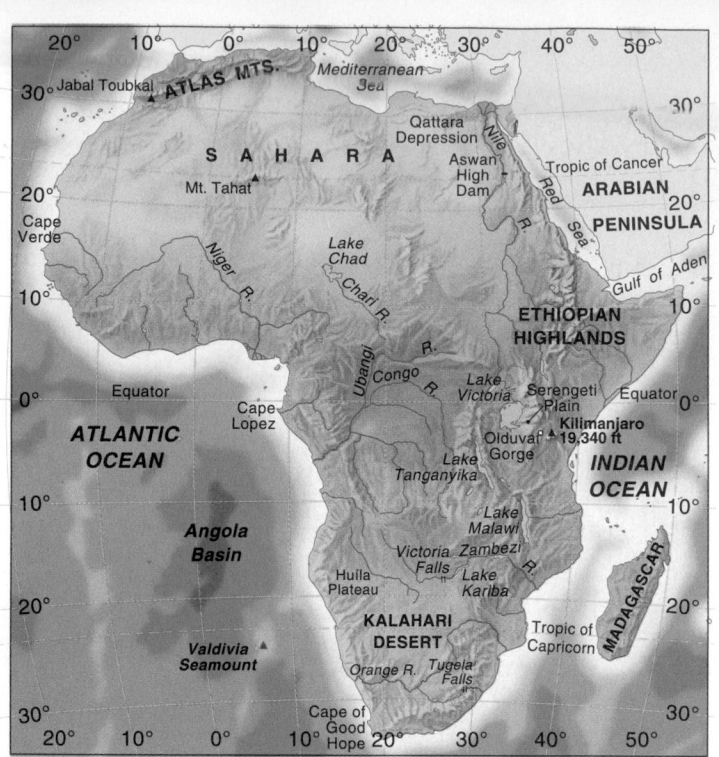

Geography Use the map to identify the geographic feature found at each location.

37. latitude 3° S
longitude 37° E
elevation 19,340 ft

38. latitude 23° N
longitude 5° E
elevation 9,573 ft

39. latitude 25° S
longitude 6° E
elevation −3,072 ft

40. latitude 15° N
longitude 18° W
elevation 0 ft

41. latitude 30° N
longitude 27° E
elevation −440 ft

42. latitude 13° N
longitude 14° E
elevation 919 ft

43. latitude 31° N
longitude 8° W
elevation 49,212 ft

44. latitude 18° S
longitude 25° E
elevation 2,927 ft

45. latitude 22° N
longitude 31° E
elevation 600 ft

46. latitude 1° S
longitude 33° E
elevation 3,720 ft

47. Error Analysis A student claims to find the x-intercept of a plane by substituting 0 for x in the equation of the plane. Explain the student's error.

 Challenge 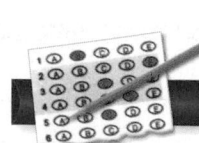 **48. a. Geometry** Use the Pythagorean Theorem to find the distance between $(1, 2, 4)$ and $(3, -2, 7)$. (*Hint:* Recall the Distance Formula.)
b. Make a Conjecture Make a conjecture about how to find the coordinates of the midpoint of a segment in coordinate space.

49. a. Critical Thinking Does every plane have three traces? Explain.
b. Must any two traces of a plane intersect? Explain.

Graph each equation in three-dimensional coordinate space.

50. $x = 3$ **51.** $2x + 3y = 6$ **52.** $y = 0$

Test Prep

Multiple Choice

53. Which point is NOT on the graph of $2x + 3y - z - 12 = 0$?
A. (6, 0, 0) **B.** (3, 3, 3) **C.** (0, 4, 0) **D.** (1, 1, 7)

54. Which point is NOT on the plane with equation $-2x - 3y + 5z = 7$?
F. (1, 2, 3) **G.** (−2, −3, 5) **H.** (−2, 4, 3) **J.** (−4, 2, 1)

55. What are the intercepts of $-3x + 5y - 2z = 60$?
A. $x = -180, y = 300, z = -120$ **B.** $x = -20, y = 12, z = -30$
C. $x = -3, y = 5, z = -2$ **D.** $x = -60, y = 60, z = -60$

56. What is the xy-trace of $2x - 4y + z = 8$?
F. $-4y + z = 8$ **G.** $x - 2y = 4$ **H.** $2x + z = 8$ **J.** $z = 8$

Short Response

57. What is the intersection of the xz-traces for the two planes $2x - 3y - 4z = -4$ and $x + 3y + z = 7$?
Explain each step of your answer.

GO for Help

Lesson 3-4

58. Maximize the objective function $P = x + 3y$ under the given constraints. At what vertex does this maximum value occur?

$$\begin{cases} x + y \le 5 \\ x + 2y \le 8 \\ x \ge 0, y \ge 0 \end{cases}$$

Lesson 2-7

Graph each inequality.

59. $y \le x - 3$ **60.** $3y - x > -4$ **61.** $2x - y \ge 0$

Lesson 1-6

62. Probability Your town has a drawing for 50 summer jobs. Including you, 150 students apply.
   a. What is the probability that you will get one of the jobs?
   b. You and a friend apply. What is the probability that you both get jobs?

✓ Checkpoint Quiz 2   Lessons 3-4 through 3-5

1. Find the values of x and y that minimize the objective function $C = 2x + 3y$ for the constraints at the right.

$$\begin{cases} y \ge x \\ x + y \le 32 \\ x \ge 5, y \ge 3 \end{cases}$$

 2. Agriculture A farmer has at most 400 acres and $45,000 available to grow corn and soybeans. Use the cost and profit information at the right to decide how many acres of each crop will maximize profit.

Cost and Profit for Corn and Soybeans

	Corn	Soybeans
Number of Acres	x	y
Cost	$100x$	$150y$
Profit	$60x$	$75y$

Graph each equation. Use traces and intercepts.

3. $3x + 2y + z = 6$ **4.** $x - y + z = 4$ **5.** $4x + y + z = 8$

Algebra at Work

·························· Radiologist

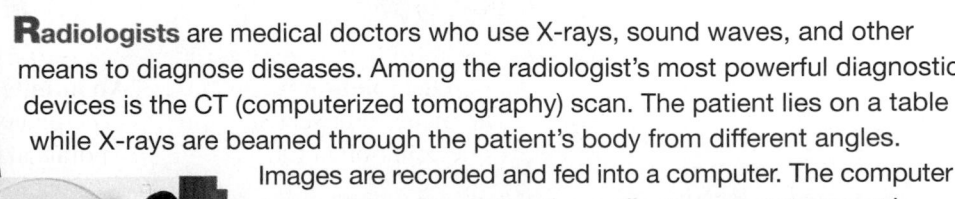

Radiologists are medical doctors who use X-rays, sound waves, and other means to diagnose diseases. Among the radiologist's most powerful diagnostic devices is the CT (computerized tomography) scan. The patient lies on a table while X-rays are beamed through the patient's body from different angles. Images are recorded and fed into a computer. The computer uses a three-dimensional coordinate system to record information and then to produce images of a cross section of the patient's body.

 **For:** Information about radiology
PHSchool.com Web Code: agb-2031

Systems With Three Variables

What You'll Learn

- To solve systems in three variables by elimination
- To solve systems in three variables by substitution

. . . And Why

To choose an investment strategy, as in Example 4

✓ **Check Skills You'll Need**

GO for Help   Lessons 3-1 and 3-2

Solve each system.

1. $\begin{cases} 2x - y = 11 \\ x + 2y = -7 \end{cases}$ 2. $\begin{cases} -x + 6y = 8 \\ 2x - 12y = -14 \end{cases}$ 3. $\begin{cases} 3x + 2y = -5 \\ 4x + 3y = -8 \end{cases}$

Let $y = 4x - 2$. Solve each equation for x.

4. $3x + y = 5$ 5. $x - 2y = -3$ 6. $4x + 3y = 2$

Determine whether the given ordered pair is a solution of each equation in the system.

7. $(1, 3)$ $\begin{cases} 2x + 5y = 17 \\ -4x + 3y = 5 \end{cases}$ 8. $(-4, 2)$ $\begin{cases} x + 2y = 0 \\ 3x - 2y = -16 \end{cases}$

1   Solving Three-Variable Systems by Elimination

You can represent systems of equations in three variables as graphs in three dimensions. As you learned in Lesson 3-5, the graph of any equation of the form $Ax + By + Cz = D$, where A, B, and C are not all zero, is a plane. The solutions of a three-variable system can be shown graphically as the intersections of planes.

GO for Help

To review solving systems in two variables by graphing, go to Lesson 3-1.

No solution
No point lies in all three planes.

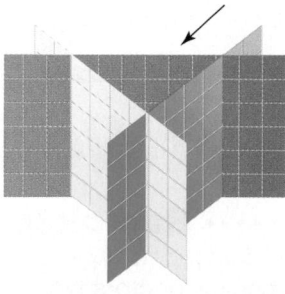

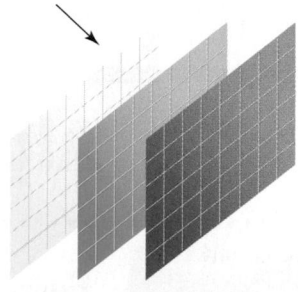

One solution
The planes intersect at one common point.

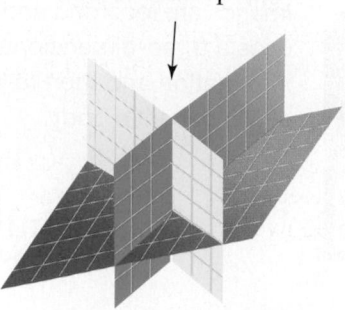

An infinite number of solutions
The planes intersect at all the points along a common line.

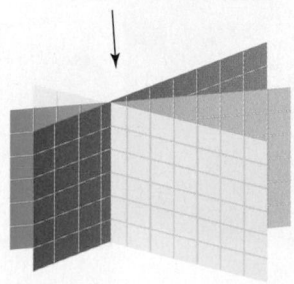

When the solution of a system of equations in three variables is represented by one point, you can write it as an ordered triple (x, y, z).

You can solve a system of three equations in three variables by working with the equations in pairs. You will use one of the equations *twice*.

1 EXAMPLE Solving by Elimination

Solve the system by elimination. The equations are numbered to make the procedure easy to follow.

$$\begin{array}{ll} ① & x - 3y + 3z = -4 \\ ② & 2x + 3y - z = 15 \\ ③ & 4x - 3y - z = 19 \end{array}$$

Step 1 Pair the equations to eliminate y because the y terms are already additive inverses.

$$\begin{array}{ll} ① & x - 3y + 3z = -4 \\ ② & 2x + 3y - z = 15 \\ ④ & 3x \qquad + 2z = 11 \end{array} \quad \textbf{Add.}$$

$$\begin{array}{ll} ② & 2x + 3y - z = 15 \\ ③ & 4x - 3y - z = 19 \\ ⑤ & 6x \qquad - 2z = 34 \end{array}$$

Step 2 Write the two new equations as a system. Solve for x and z.

$$\begin{array}{ll} ④ & 3x \qquad + 2z = 11 \\ ⑤ & 6x \qquad - 2z = 34 \\ & 9x \qquad\qquad = 45 \\ & x = 5 \end{array}$$

$$\begin{array}{ll} ④ & 3x + 2z = 11 \\ & 3(5) + 2z = 11 \\ & 2z = -4 \\ & z = -2 \end{array}$$

Substitute the value of x.

Step 3 Substitute the values for x and z into one of the original equations (①, ②, or ③) and solve for y.

$$\begin{array}{l} ① \quad x - 3y + 3z = -4 \\ 5 - 3y + 3(-2) = -4 \\ 5 - 3y - 6 = -4 \\ -3y = -3 \\ y = 1 \end{array}$$

The solution of the system is $(5, 1, -2)$.

Check Show that $(5, 1, -2)$ makes each equation true.

$$\begin{array}{lll} x - 3y + 3z = -4 & 2x + 3y - z = 15 & 4x - 3y - z = 19 \\ 5 - 3(1) + 3(-2) \stackrel{?}{=} -4 & 2(5) + 3(1) - (-2) \stackrel{?}{=} 15 & 4(5) - 3(1) - (-2) \stackrel{?}{=} 19 \\ 5 - 3 - 6 \stackrel{?}{=} -4 & 10 + 3 + 2 \stackrel{?}{=} 15 & 20 - 3 + 2 \stackrel{?}{=} 19 \\ -4 = -4 \checkmark & 15 = 15 \checkmark & 19 = 19 \checkmark \end{array}$$

 **Quick Check** ① Solve each system by elimination. Check your answers.

a. $$\begin{cases} 2x + y - z = 5 \\ 3x - y + 2z = -1 \\ x - y - z = 0 \end{cases}$$

b. $$\begin{cases} 2x - y + z = 4 \\ x + 3y - z = 11 \\ 4x + y - z = 14 \end{cases}$$

c. **Critical Thinking** Suppose, in a three-variable system, the coefficient of one of the variables in one of the equations is zero. When pairing the equations to solve the system, would you use that equation twice? Explain.

You can apply the method in Example 1 to any system of three equations in three variables. You may need to multiply one or more of the equations by a nonzero number to form an equivalent system.

Real-World Connection

You can use a system in three variables to model the amounts of vitamin C, potassium, and beta carotene in this three-fruit salad.

② EXAMPLE Solving an Equivalent System

Solve the system by elimination.
$$\begin{array}{r} ① \\ ② \\ ③ \end{array} \begin{cases} 2x + y - z = 5 \\ x + 4y + 2z = 16 \\ 15x + 6y - 2z = 12 \end{cases}$$

Step 1 Pair the equations to eliminate z.

$$\begin{array}{r} ① \\ ② \end{array} \begin{cases} 2x + y - z = 5 \\ x + 4y + 2z = 16 \end{cases}$$

$$\begin{array}{rl} 4x + 2y - 2z = 10 & \textbf{Multiply by 2.} \\ \underline{x + 4y + 2z = 16} \\ ④\; 5x + 6y \qquad = 26 \end{array}$$

$$\begin{array}{r} ② \\ ③ \\ ⑤ \end{array} \begin{array}{l} x + 4y + 2z = 16 \\ \underline{15x + 6y - 2z = 12} \\ 16x + 10y \qquad = 28 \end{array}$$

Step 2 Write the two new equations as a system. Solve for x and y.

$$\begin{array}{r} ④ \\ ⑤ \end{array} \begin{cases} 5x + 6y = 26 \\ 16x + 10y = 28 \end{cases}$$

$$\begin{array}{rl} 25x + 30y = 130 & \textbf{Multiply by 5.} \\ \underline{-48x - 30y = -84} & \textbf{Multiply by } -3. \\ -23x \qquad = 46 \\ x = -2 \end{array}$$

$$\begin{array}{rl} ④ & 5x + 6y = 26 \\ & 5(-2) + 6y = 26 \qquad \textbf{Substitute the value of } x. \\ & y = 6 \end{array}$$

Step 3 Substitute the values for x and y into one of the original equations (①, ②, or ③). Solve for z.

$$\begin{array}{rl} ① & 2x + y - z = 5 \\ & 2(-2) + 6 - z = 5 \\ & z = -3 \end{array}$$

The solution of the system is $(-2, 6, -3)$.

✓ Quick Check ❷ Solve the system by elimination. Check your answers.
$$\begin{cases} x + 4y - 5z = -7 \\ 3x + 2y + 3z = 7 \\ 2x + y + 5z = 8 \end{cases}$$

The graph illustrates the solution to Example 2. Each equation in the system represents a tilted plane. The graph of ① is red, the graph of ② is blue, and the graph of ③ is green. The three planes intersect at $(-2, 6, -3)$.

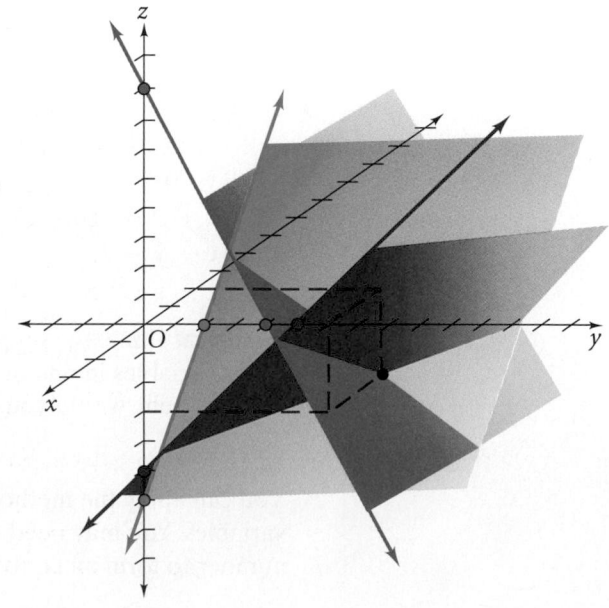

Solving Three-Variable Systems by Substitution

You can also use the substitution method to solve a system of three equations. Substitution is the best method to use when one of the equations can be solved easily for one variable.

GO for Help

To review the substitution method, go to Lesson 3-2.

3 EXAMPLE   Solving by Substitution

Solve the system by substitution.
$$\begin{array}{l} ① \\ ② \\ ③ \end{array} \begin{cases} x - 2y + z = -4 \\ -4x + y - 2z = 1 \\ 2x + 2y - z = 10 \end{cases}$$

Step 1 Choose one equation to solve for one of its variables.

① $x - 2y + z = -4$ **Solve the first equation for x.**
$$x - 2y = -z - 4$$
$$x = 2y - z - 4$$

Step 2 Substitute the expression for x into each of the other two equations.

② $\qquad -4x + y - 2z = 1$ $\qquad\qquad$ ③ $\qquad 2x + 2y - z = 10$

$-4(2y - z - 4) + y - 2z = 1$ **Simplify.** $2(2y - z - 4) + 2y - z = 10$

$\qquad -8y + 4z + 16 + y - 2z = 1 \qquad\qquad\qquad 4y - 2z - 8 + 2y - z = 10$

$\qquad\qquad -7y + 2z + 16 = 1 \qquad\qquad\qquad\qquad 6y - 3z - 8 = 10$

④ $\qquad\qquad -7y + 2z = -15$ $\qquad$ ⑤ $\qquad\qquad\qquad 6y - 3z = 18$

Step 3 Write the two new equations as a system. Solve for y and z.

$\begin{array}{l} ④ \\ ⑤ \end{array} \begin{cases} -7y + 2z = -15 \\ 6y - 3z = 18 \end{cases}$

$\qquad\qquad\qquad\qquad \begin{array}{r} -21y + 6z = -45 \\ \underline{12y - 6z = 36} \\ -9y = -9 \\ y = 1 \end{array}$ $\quad$ **Multiply by 3.**
$\quad$ **Multiply by 2.**

④ $\quad -7y + 2z = -15$

$\qquad -7(1) + 2z = -15$ **Substitute the value of y.**

$\qquad\qquad -7 + 2z = -15$

$\qquad\qquad\qquad 2z = -8$

$\qquad\qquad\qquad z = -4$

Step 4 Substitute the values for y and z into one of the original equations (①, ②, or ③). Solve for x.

① $\qquad\qquad x - 2y + z = -4$

$\qquad x - 2(1) + (-4) = -4$

$\qquad\qquad x - 2 - 4 = -4$

$\qquad\qquad\qquad x - 6 = -4$

$\qquad\qquad\qquad\qquad x = 2$

● The solution of the system is $(2, 1, -4)$.

✓ Quick Check ③ Solve each system by substitution. Check your answers.

a. $\begin{cases} x - 3y + z = 6 \\ 2x - 5y - z = -2 \\ -x + y + 2z = 7 \end{cases}$
$\qquad$ **b.** $\begin{cases} 3x + 2y - z = 12 \\ -4x + y - 2z = 4 \\ x - 3y + z = -4 \end{cases}$

Investment Options

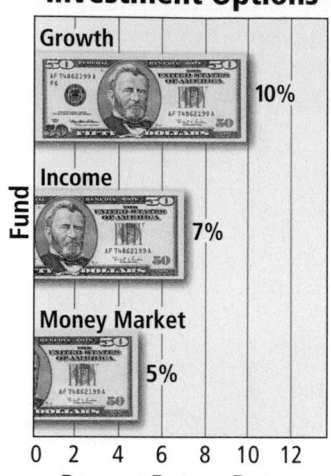

Fund

0 2 4 6 8 10 12
Percent Return Rate

4 EXAMPLE   **Real-World Connection**

Money Management Suppose you have saved $3200 from a part-time job and you want to invest your savings in a growth fund, an income fund, and a money market fund. Refer to the graph. To maximize your return, you decide to put twice as much money in the growth fund as in the money market fund. How should you invest the $3200 to get a return of $250 in one year?

Relate   growth fund + income fund + money market fund = 3200

   growth fund = 2 times money market fund

   10% of growth + 7% of income + 5% of money market = 250

Define   Let g = amount invested in a growth fund.

   Let i = amount invested in an income fund.

   Let m = amount invested in a money market fund.

Write
① $g + i + m = 3200$
② $g = 2m$
③ $0.10g + 0.07i + 0.05m = 250$

Step 1 Substitute $2m$ for g in equations ① and ③. Simplify.

① $g + i + m = 3200$	③ $0.10g + 0.07i + 0.05m = 250$
$2m + i + m = 3200$	$0.10(2m) + 0.07i + 0.05m = 250$
④ $\quad 3m + i = 3200$	⑤ $\quad 0.25m + 0.07i = 250$

Step 2 Write the two new equations as a system. Solve for m and i.

④ $\quad 3m + \quad i = 3200$ $3m + \quad i = 3200$
⑤ $\quad 0.25m + 0.07i = 250$ $3m + 0.84i = 3000$ **Multiply by 12.**

$\qquad\qquad\qquad\qquad\qquad\qquad 0.16i = 200$

$\qquad\qquad\qquad\qquad\qquad\qquad\qquad i = 1250$

④ $\qquad 3m + i = 3200$

$\quad 3m + 1250 = 3200$ **Substitute the value of i.**

$\qquad\qquad 3m = 1950$

$\qquad\qquad m = 650$

Step 3 Substitute the value of m into equation 2 and solve for g.

② $g = 2m$

$g = 2(650)$

$g = 1300$

You should invest $1300 in the growth fund, $1250 in the income fund, and $650 in the money market fund to get a return of $250 in one year.

✓ Quick Check **4** Suppose you discover that your growth fund, income fund, and money market fund return rates are better estimated at 12%, 6%, and 3% per year respectively. How should you invest the $3200 to get a return of $255 in one year?

You have learned how to solve systems of equations using the methods of graphing, elimination, and substitution. In Chapter 4, you will learn how to use matrices to solve systems of equations.

EXERCISES

For more exercises, see *Extra Skill and Word Problem Practice.*

Practice and Problem Solving

A **Practice by Example**

Examples 1 and 2
(pages 153 and 154)

GO for Help

Solve each system by elimination. Check your answers.

1. $\begin{cases} x - y + z = -1 \\ x + y + 3z = -3 \\ 2x - y + 2z = 0 \end{cases}$
2. $\begin{cases} x - y - 2z = 4 \\ -x + 2y + z = 1 \\ -x + y - 3z = 11 \end{cases}$
3. $\begin{cases} 2x - y + z = -2 \\ x + 3y - z = 10 \\ x + 2z = -8 \end{cases}$

4. $\begin{cases} a + b + c = -3 \\ 3b - c = 4 \\ 2a - b - 2c = -5 \end{cases}$
5. $\begin{cases} 6q - r + 2s = 8 \\ 2q + 3r - s = -9 \\ 4q + 2r + 5s = 1 \end{cases}$
6. $\begin{cases} x - y + 2z = -7 \\ y + z = 1 \\ x = 2y + 3z \end{cases}$

7. $\begin{cases} x + y + 2z = 3 \\ 2x + y + 3z = 7 \\ -x - 2y + z = 10 \end{cases}$
8. $\begin{cases} 3x - y + z = 3 \\ x + y + 2z = 4 \\ x + 2y + z = 4 \end{cases}$
9. $\begin{cases} x - 2y + 3z = 12 \\ 2x - y - 2z = 5 \\ 2x + 2y - z = 4 \end{cases}$

Examples 3 and 4
(pages 155 and 156)

Solve each system by substitution. Check your answers.

10. $\begin{cases} x + 2y + 3z = 6 \\ y + 2z = 0 \\ z = 2 \end{cases}$
11. $\begin{cases} 3a + b + c = 7 \\ a + 3b - c = 13 \\ b = 2a - 1 \end{cases}$
12. $\begin{cases} 5r - 4s - 3t = 3 \\ t = s + r \\ r = 3s + 1 \end{cases}$

13. $\begin{cases} 13 = 3x - y \\ 4y - 3x + 2z = -3 \\ z = 2x - 4y \end{cases}$
14. $\begin{cases} x + 3y - z = -4 \\ 2x - y + 2z = 13 \\ 3x - 2y - z = -9 \end{cases}$
15. $\begin{cases} x - 4y + z = 6 \\ 2x + 5y - z = 7 \\ 2x - y - z = 1 \end{cases}$

16. $\begin{cases} x - y + 2z = 7 \\ 2x + y + z = 8 \\ x - z = 5 \end{cases}$
17. $\begin{cases} x + y + z = 2 \\ x + 2z = 5 \\ 2x + y - z = -1 \end{cases}$
18. $\begin{cases} 5x - y + z = 4 \\ x + 2y - z = 5 \\ 2x + 3y - 3z = 5 \end{cases}$

19. **Finance** A company placed $1,000,000 in three different accounts. It placed part in short-term notes paying 4.5% per year, twice as much in government bonds paying 5%, and the rest in utility bonds paying 4%. The income after one year was $45,500. How much did the company place in each account?

20. **Sports** A stadium has 49,000 seats. Seats sell for $25 in Section A, $20 in Section B, and $15 in Section C. The number of seats in Section A equals the total number of seats in Sections B and C. Suppose the stadium takes in $1,052,000 from each sold-out event. How many seats does each section hold?

21. A change machine contains nickels, dimes, and quarters. There are 75 coins in the machine, and the value of the coins is $7.25. There are 5 times as many nickels as dimes. Find the number of coins of each type in the machine.

B **Apply Your Skills**

Find the number of solutions of each system.

22.
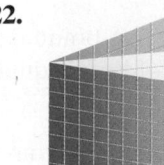

23.

24.
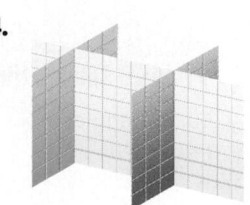

Solve each system.

25. $\begin{cases} x - 3y + 2z = 11 \\ -x + 4y + 3z = 5 \\ 2x - 2y - 4z = 2 \end{cases}$

26. $\begin{cases} x + 2y + z = 4 \\ 2x - y + 4z = -8 \\ -3x + y - 2z = -1 \end{cases}$

27. $\begin{cases} 4x - y + 2z = -6 \\ -2x + 3y - z = 8 \\ 2y + 3z = -5 \end{cases}$

28. $\begin{cases} 4A + 2U + I = 2 \\ 5A - 3U + 2I = 17 \\ A - 5U = 3 \end{cases}$

29. $\begin{cases} 4x - 2y + 5z = 6 \\ 3x + 3y + 8z = 4 \\ x - 5y - 3z = 5 \end{cases}$

30. $\begin{cases} 2\ell + 2w + h = 72 \\ \ell = 3w \\ h = 2w \end{cases}$

31. $\begin{cases} 3x + 2y - z = 17.8 \\ x - 3y + 2z = 7.9 \\ 2x + y - 3z = 3.9 \end{cases}$

32. $\begin{cases} x + 2y = 2 \\ 2x + 3y - z = -9 \\ 4x + 2y + 5z = 1 \end{cases}$

33. $\begin{cases} 3x + 2y + 2z = -2 \\ 2x + y - z = -2 \\ x - 3y + z = 0 \end{cases}$

34. $\begin{cases} 6x + y - 4z = -8 \\ \frac{y}{4} - \frac{z}{6} = 0 \\ 2x - z = -2 \end{cases}$

35. $\begin{cases} 4y + 2x = 6 - 3z \\ x + z - 2y = -5 \\ x - 2z = 3y - 7 \end{cases}$

36. $\begin{cases} 5z + 4y = 4 \\ 3x - 2y = 0 \\ x + 3z = -8 \end{cases}$

37. $\begin{cases} x + 6z = 12 \\ -2x + 3y = 6 \\ y - \frac{z}{2} = \frac{5}{2} \end{cases}$

38. $\begin{cases} 4x - y + z = -5 \\ -x + y - z = 5 \\ 2x - z - 1 = y \end{cases}$

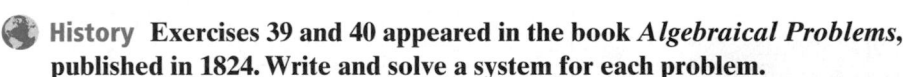

History Exercises 39 and 40 appeared in the book *Algebraical Problems*, published in 1824. Write and solve a system for each problem.

39. Ten apples cost a penny, and 25 pears cost two pennies. Suppose I buy 100 apples and pears for $9\frac{1}{2}$ pennies. How many of each shall I have?

40. A fish was caught whose tail weighed 9 lb. Its head weighed as much as its tail plus half its body. Its body weighed as much as its head and tail. What did the fish weigh?

41. Writing How do you decide whether substitution is the best method to solve a system in three variables?

GO Online
Homework Video Tutor
Visit: PHSchool.com
Web Code: age-0306

Challenge

42. Error Analysis A student says that the system consisting of $x = 0$, $y = 0$, and $z = 0$ has no solutions. Explain the student's error.

43. Geometry Refer to the regular five-pointed star at the right. Write and solve a system of three equations to find the measure of each labeled angle.

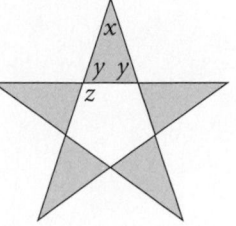

44. Open-Ended Write your own system having three variables. Begin by choosing the solution. Then write three equations that are true for your solution. Use elimination to solve the system.

Problem Solving Hint

Sum of angles in a pentagon: 540°

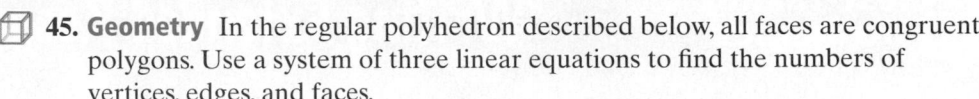 **45. Geometry** In the regular polyhedron described below, all faces are congruent polygons. Use a system of three linear equations to find the numbers of vertices, edges, and faces.

Every face has five edges and every edge is shared by two faces. Every face has five vertices and every vertex is shared by three faces. The sum of the number of vertices and faces is two more than the number of edges.

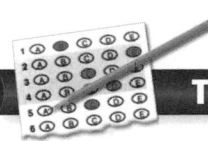

Test Prep

Multiple Choice

46. What is the solution of the system?
$$\begin{cases} -3x + 2y - z = 6 \\ 3x + y + 2z = 5 \\ 2x - 2y - z = -5 \end{cases}$$

A. $(6, 5, -3)$
B. $(1, 4, -1)$
C. $\left(0, \frac{17}{5}, \frac{4}{5}\right)$
D. no solution

47. What is the solution of the system?
$$\begin{cases} x + 3y - 2z = -8 \\ 3x - y + z = 11 \\ 2x + 4y + 2z = 14 \end{cases}$$

F. $(2, 0, 5)$
G. $(-8, 11, 14)$
H. $\left(-2, \frac{4}{3}, 5\right)$
J. no solution

48. What is the solution of the system?
$$\begin{cases} y = -2x + 10 \\ -x + y - 2z = -2 \\ 3x - 2y + 4z = 7 \end{cases}$$

A. $\left(3, -4, \frac{3}{2}\right)$
B. $\left(3, 16, \frac{15}{2}\right)$
C. $\left(-3, 16, \frac{15}{2}\right)$
D. $\left(3, 4, \frac{3}{2}\right)$

Short Response

49. Why is there no solution to the system? Explain your answer in terms of intersecting planes.
$$\begin{array}{l} ① \\ ② \\ ③ \end{array} \begin{cases} 2x - 3y + z = 5 \\ 2x - 3y + z = -2 \\ -4x + 6y - 2z = 10 \end{cases}$$

Mixed Review

Lesson 3-5

Graph each equation.

50. $x + y + 4z = 8$
51. $2x + 3y - z = 12$
52. $-3x + y + 5z = 15$
53. $-2x + 3y - z = 6$
54. $6x + 4y - 3z = -12$
55. $3x - 6y - 2z = 18$

Graph each equation.

Lesson 2-5

56. $y = |x + 4|$
57. $y = |3x - 2|$
58. $y = \left|\frac{1}{2}x + 3\right| - 2$
59. $y = |x - 2| + 1$
60. $y = |2x + 1|$
61. $y = |x + 3| - 2$

Lesson 1-4

Solve each inequality. Graph the solution on a number line.

62. $-4x + 3 \le 9$
63. $-(x + 4) - 3 \ge 11$
64. $2(3x - 1) < x - 7$
65. $6 - 2x > 2$
66. $3x + 2 < -x + 10$
67. $-2(x + 3) \ge x$

Writing Extended Responses

Extended-response questions usually are worth 4 points and have multiple parts. If you can't answer one part, you may be able to get partial credit for the other parts.

EXAMPLE

You plan to put a fence around a rectangular lot. The length of the lot must be at least 52 feet. The cost of the fence along the length of the lot is \$2 per foot, and the cost of the fence along the width is \$3 per foot. The total cost cannot exceed \$360.
a. Use two variables to write a system of inequalities that models the problem.
b. Graph the system, and shade the feasible region.
c. What is the maximum width of the lot if the length is 60 feet?

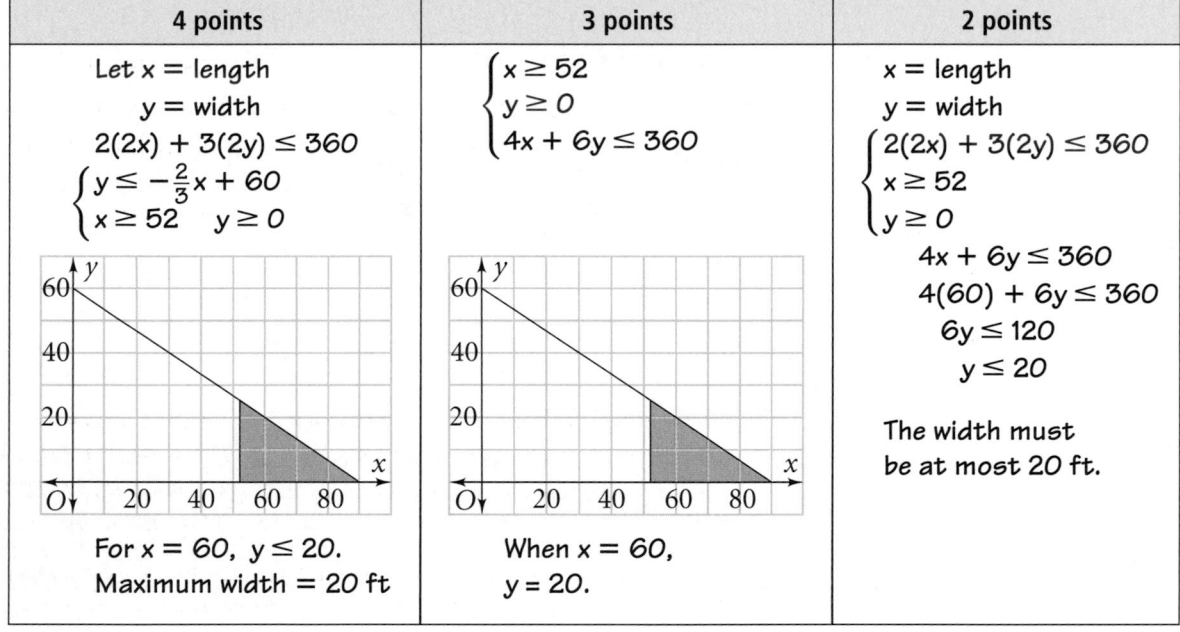

4 points	3 points	2 points
Let x = length y = width $2(2x) + 3(2y) \leq 360$ $\begin{cases} y \leq -\frac{2}{3}x + 60 \\ x \geq 52 \quad y \geq 0 \end{cases}$	$\begin{cases} x \geq 52 \\ y \geq 0 \\ 4x + 6y \leq 360 \end{cases}$	x = length y = width $\begin{cases} 2(2x) + 3(2y) \leq 360 \\ x \geq 52 \\ y \geq 0 \end{cases}$ $4x + 6y \leq 360$ $4(60) + 6y \leq 360$ $6y \leq 120$ $y \leq 20$ The width must be at most 20 ft.
For x = 60, $y \leq 20$. Maximum width = 20 ft	When x = 60, y = 20.	

The 4-point response gives a complete and correct answer to each part. The 3-point response lost credit for not showing all the work. The 2-point response does not include an answer for part (b), but answers the other parts correctly.

EXERCISES

1. What did the 3-point response to the Example leave out?

2. Open-Ended Describe a response to the Example that would deserve only 1 point.

3. Suppose the minimum length of the lot in the Example is changed to 60 feet, the cost of the fence along the width is changed to \$2 per foot, and the cost of the fence along the length is changed to \$1.50 per foot. Find the new answers to parts (a), (b), and (c). Show your work.

4. In Exercise 3, what is the maximum length of the lot if the width can be at most 36 ft?

Chapter Review

Vocabulary Review

🔊 constraints (p. 139)
coordinate space (p. 146)
dependent system (p. 120)
equivalent systems (p. 127)
feasible region (p. 140)

inconsistent system (p. 120)
independent system (p. 120)
linear programming (p. 139)
linear system (p. 118)
objective function (p. 139)

ordered triples (p. 146)
system of equations (p. 118)
trace (p. 148)

Match the vocabulary term in column 1 with the most appropriate phrase in column 2.

Go Online
PHSchool.com
For: Vocabulary quiz
Web Code: agj-0351

Column 1

1. dependent linear systems

2. equivalent systems

3. inconsistent linear systems

4. independent linear systems

5. three-variable systems

Column 2

A. have many solutions

B. have no solutions

C. have solutions that can be shown as the intersection of planes

D. have the same solutions

E. have unique solutions

Skills and Concepts

3-1 Objectives

▼ To solve a system by graphing (p. 118)

A **system of equations** is a set of two or more equations that use the same variables. The points where all the graphs intersect represent solutions. You must check the coordinates of the points of intersection in the original equations to be sure you have a solution. A **linear system** consists of linear equations.

An **independent system** has a unique solution while a **dependent system** does not have a unique solution. An **inconsistent system** has no solutions.

Solve each system by graphing.

6. $\begin{cases} y = 2x + 1 \\ y = 4x + 5 \end{cases}$

7. $\begin{cases} y = 3x - 2 \\ y = -2x + 8 \end{cases}$

8. $\begin{cases} y = 3x - 5 \\ 2y = 6x + 4 \end{cases}$

9. $\begin{cases} 3x + 2y = -6 \\ x - y = -2 \end{cases}$

10. $\begin{cases} 4x - y = 6 \\ -2x + 3y = 12 \end{cases}$

11. $\begin{cases} 12x + 3y = -9 \\ 4x + y = 7 \end{cases}$

Without graphing, classify each system as *independent*, *dependent*, or *inconsistent*.

12. $\begin{cases} 6x + 3y = 12 \\ y = -2x + 4 \end{cases}$

13. $\begin{cases} y = -x + 5 \\ x - y = -3 \end{cases}$

14. $\begin{cases} x + 2y = 2 \\ y = -0.5x - 2 \end{cases}$

 15. **Banking** Suppose a bank charges a monthly rate of $10 for your checking account. You can switch to a different account that charges $6 plus $.20 per check. For what number of checks is the cost of the two accounts the same?

3-2 Objectives

▼ To solve a system by substitution (p. 125)

▼ To solve a system by elimination (p. 126)

If you can easily solve one equation in a system of two equations for one of the variables, you can substitute that expression in the other equation. Then you can find the value of the other variable.

Otherwise, you can multiply one or both equations by a nonzero quantity to create two terms that are additive inverses. This creates an **equivalent system** of equations. Adding the two equations then eliminates one variable. Again, you can solve for the other variable.

In either case, you substitute the value of this second variable into either of the original equations to find the value of the first variable. Recall that some systems have an infinite number of solutions and some have no solutions.

Solve using substitution.

16. $\begin{cases} 3x + 5y = 10 \\ y = -4 \end{cases}$

17. $\begin{cases} 4x + 3y = 12 \\ x = 5y - 20 \end{cases}$

18. $\begin{cases} 8x + y = 17 \\ x + 4y = 37 \end{cases}$

Solve using elimination.

19. $\begin{cases} 2x + y = 13 \\ x - y = -4 \end{cases}$

20. $\begin{cases} 2x + 3y = 4 \\ 4x + 6y = 9 \end{cases}$

21. $\begin{cases} a + b = \frac{1}{3} \\ a - b = \frac{1}{4} \end{cases}$

 22. Nutrition Roast beef has 25 g of protein and 11 g of calcium per serving. A serving of mashed potatoes has 2 g of protein and 25 g of calcium. How many servings of each are needed to supply exactly 29 g of protein and 61 g of calcium?

3-3 Objectives

▼ To solve systems of linear inequalities (p. 133)

The solution of a system of inequalities is represented on a graph by the region of overlap of the inequalities. To solve a system by graphing, first graph the boundaries for each inequality. Then shade the regions of the plane containing the solutions for both inequalities.

Solve each system by graphing.

23. $\begin{cases} y < -x + 1 \\ y \geq \frac{3}{4}x - 6 \end{cases}$

24. $\begin{cases} x + y \leq 4 \\ y < 6 \end{cases}$

25. $\begin{cases} y > |x - 4| \\ y < \frac{1}{3}x \end{cases}$

26. For a community breakfast there should be at least three times as much regular coffee as decaffeinated coffee. A total of ten gallons is sufficient for the breakfast. Model this situation with a system of inequalities. Graph to solve the system.

3-4 Objectives

▼ To find maximum and minimum values (p. 139)

▼ To solve problems with linear programming (p. 141)

Linear programming is a technique used to find the maximum or minimum value of an **objective function**. Linear inequalities are **constraints** on the variables of the objective function. The solutions to the system of constraints are contained in the **feasible region**. The maximum or minimum value of the objective function occurs at a vertex of the feasible region.

Graph each system of constraints. Find all vertices. Then find the variable values that maximize or minimize the objective function.

27. $\begin{cases} x \le 8 \\ y \le 5 \\ x \ge 0, y \ge 0 \end{cases}$

Minimum for
$C = x + 5y$

28. $\begin{cases} x \ge 2 \\ y \ge 0 \\ 3x + 2y \ge 12 \end{cases}$

Minimum for
$C = 4x + y$

29. $\begin{cases} 3x + 2y \le 12 \\ x + y \le 5 \\ x \ge 0, y \ge 0 \end{cases}$

Maximum for
$P = 3x + 5y$

 30. Profit A lunch stand makes $.75 profit on each chef's salad and $1.20 profit on each Caesar salad. On a typical weekday, it sells between 40 and 60 chef's salads and between 35 and 50 Caesar salads. The total number sold has never exceeded 100 salads. How many of each type should be prepared in order to maximize profit?

3-5 Objectives

▼ To graph points in three dimensions (p. 146)

▼ To graph equations in three dimensions (p. 148)

You can plot **ordered triples** in **coordinate space.** To sketch a plane that is the graph of an equation in three variables, find the intercepts. To find the x-intercept, substitute 0 for y and z. Then find the other two intercepts. If the plane does not pass through the origin, connect the resulting intercepts on the three axes. These lines are called the **traces** of the plane.

Graph each point in coordinate space.

31. $(0, 2, 0)$ **32.** $(1, 0, 0)$ **33.** $(0, 0, 3)$ **34.** $(2, 3, 0)$ **35.** $(1, 0, 4)$

Find the coordinates of each point in the diagram at the right.

36. A

37. B

38. C

39. D

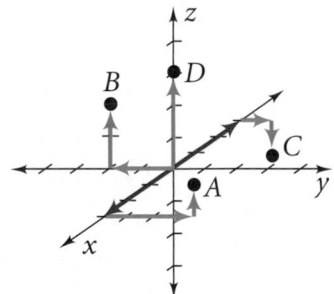

Sketch the graph of each equation.

40. $x - 2y + z = 4$ **41.** $10x - 4y - 5z = 20$ **42.** $2x + 6y + 3z = 18$

3-6 Objectives

▼ To solve systems in three variables by elimination (p. 152)

▼ To solve systems in three variables by substitution (p. 155)

You can solve systems of three equations in three variables using the technique of substitution you learned in Lesson 3-2.

Elimination with three equations in three variables involves pairing the equations. Use one equation twice. Then eliminate the same variable in both pairs. The result is a system of two equations in two variables. Proceed using the methods you learned in Lesson 3-2.

Solve each system.

43. $\begin{cases} x + y + z = 10 \\ 2x - y + z = 2 \\ -x + 2y - z = 5 \end{cases}$

44. $\begin{cases} x + 2y + z = 14 \\ y = z + 1 \\ x = -3z + 6 \end{cases}$

45. $\begin{cases} 3x + y - 2z = 22 \\ x + 5y + z = 4 \\ x = -3z \end{cases}$

Chapter Test

Go Online
PHSchool.com
For: Chapter test
Web Code: aga-0352

Classify each system without graphing. Then graph each system.

1. $\begin{cases} y = 5x - 2 \\ y = x + 4 \end{cases}$ 2. $\begin{cases} 3x + 2y = 9 \\ 3x + 2y = 4 \end{cases}$

Solve using substitution.

3. $\begin{cases} 3x + 2y = 9 \\ x + y = 4 \end{cases}$ 4. $\begin{cases} 0.3x - y = 0 \\ y = 2 + 0.25x \end{cases}$

Solve using elimination.

5. $\begin{cases} 3x - y = 1 \\ 2x + y = 14 \end{cases}$ 6. $\begin{cases} 4x - 2y = 3 \\ 2y - 4x = \frac{3}{2} \end{cases}$

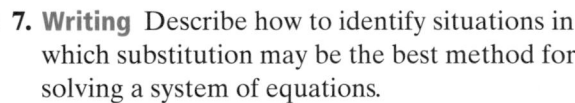 7. **Writing** Describe how to identify situations in which substitution may be the best method for solving a system of equations.

Graph each system.

8. $\begin{cases} 2x + y < 3 \\ x < y + 3 \end{cases}$ 9. $\begin{cases} 3y + 9x < 3 \\ y \geq 2 \end{cases}$

10. $\begin{cases} |x + 3| > y \\ y > 2x - 1 \end{cases}$ 11. $\begin{cases} y > -2x + 6 \\ y \leq \frac{1}{4}x - 3 \end{cases}$

Graph each system of constraints. Find all vertices. Evaluate the objective function at each vertex to find the maximum or minimum value.

12. $\begin{cases} x \leq 5 \\ y \leq 4 \\ x \geq 0, y \geq 0 \end{cases}$ 13. $\begin{cases} x + y \leq 8 \\ x + 2y \geq 6 \\ x \geq 0, y \geq 0 \end{cases}$

  Maximum for   Minimum for
  $P = 2x + y$ $C = x + 3y$

14. **Sales** A pizza shop makes $1.50 on each small pizza and $2.15 on each large pizza. On a typical Friday, it sells between 70 and 90 small pizzas and between 100 and 140 large pizzas. The shop can make no more than 210 pizzas in a day. How many of each size of pizza must be sold in order to maximize profit?

15. **Open-Ended** Write a system of constraints whose graph is a parallelogram.

Graph each point in coordinate space.

16. $(0, 5, 0)$ 17. $(-1, 0, 0)$ 18. $(1, 0, 4)$

19. $(3, 0, -1)$ 20. $(1, 4, -1)$ 21. $(2, -2, 3)$

Graph each equation. Use intercepts and traces.

22. $x + y + z = 6$ 23. $2x - 3y + z = 6$

24. $-2x + y - 5z = 10$ 25. $x - y + 2z = 8$

26. You are planning a party. You have $24 to spend on decorations. Balloons cost $.06 each, party favors cost $.48 each, and streamers cost $.08 each. Write and graph an equation for the number of each you can buy if you spend all the money.

Solve each system of equations.

27. $\begin{cases} x - y + z = 0 \\ 3x - 2y + 6z = 9 \\ -x + y - 2z = -2 \end{cases}$ 28. $\begin{cases} 2x + y + z = 8 \\ x + 2y - z = -5 \\ z = 2x - y \end{cases}$

Write a system of equations to solve each problem.

29. **Investing** A company invested $50,000 in three funds. After a year it had $54,500. The growth fund had a return rate of 12%, the income fund had a return rate of 8%, and the money market fund had a return rate of 5%. The company invested twice as much in the income fund as in the money market fund. How much did the company invest in each fund?

30. **Earnings** A student can make a weekly salary of $200 plus 15% commission on sales at the Radio Barn or a weekly salary of $300 plus 10% commission on sales at Woofer, Etc. For what amount of sales do these two jobs pay the same?

31. **Purchasing** To help passengers stranded by bad weather one winter, an airport made the purchases detailed below. Find the cost of a cot, a table, and a chair.

	Number of Cots	Number of Tables	Number of Chairs	Total Costs ($)
Nov	10	10	40	1950
Dec	20	0	20	1800
Jan	10	5	20	1350

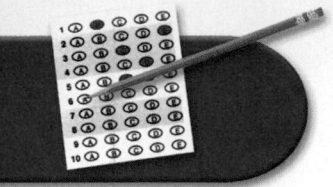

Standardized Test Prep

Reading Comprehension Read the passage below. Then answer the questions on the basis of what is *stated* or *implied* in the passage.

Hot and Cold Do you ever think about the math involved in filling a bathtub? Depending on the location and the season, the temperature of the cold water that enters a home may be 55°F. Some of the water goes to a water heater, where its temperature may be raised to 122°F.

Suppose you want a tub of 22 gallons of water at 78°F. You can write two equations, using *x* and *y* to represent the numbers of gallons of cold and hot water.

$x + y = 22$ The full tub contains 22 gal.

$55x + 122y = 22 \cdot 78$ *x* gal at 55° plus *y* gal at 122° is equivalent to 22 gal at 78°.

If you solve the system of equations, you find that you need about 14.4 gallons of cold water.

1. In the given system of equations, what does *x* represent?
   - A) the number of gallons of hot water
   - B) the number of gallons of cold water
   - C) the capacity of the tub
   - D) the temperature of the hot water

2. In the given system of equations, what is the value of *y*?
   - F) about 1716
   - G) about 22
   - H) about 14.4
   - J) about 7.6

3. Which equation results from solving for *x* in the first equation of the system and then substituting that result into the second equation of the system?
   - A) $55x + 122(22 - x) = 1716$
   - B) $55(22 - y) + 122y = 1716$
   - C) $x = \dfrac{1716 - 122y}{55}$
   - D) $y = \dfrac{1716 - 55x}{122}$

4. Suppose a tub with 22 gallons of water contains a mixture of *a* gallons of cold water at 60°F and *b* gallons of hot water at 120°F. The desired bath temperature is 80°F. Which of the following systems models the problem?

   - F) $a + b = 80$
     $60a + 120b = 22(80)$
   - G) $a + b = 120$
     $120a + 60b = 12(80)$
   - H) $a + b = 22$
     $60a + 120b = 22(80)$
   - J) $a + b = 22$
     $120a + 60b = 22(80)$

5. How many gallons of hot water are needed for the bath described in Question 4?
   - A) $7\frac{1}{3}$
   - B) 11
   - C) $14\frac{2}{3}$
   - D) $16\frac{1}{2}$

6. Suppose a tub with 21 gallons of water contains a mixture of cold water at 65°F and hot water at 128°F. The desired bath temperature is 82°F. Write a system of equations to model the volume *h* of hot water and the volume *c* of cold water needed for the bath.

7. Consider the bath described in Question 6.
   a. How many gallons of hot water are needed?
   b. How many gallons of cold water are needed?

What You've Learned

- In Chapter 1, you learned to represent relationships using variables. You learned to evaluate and simplify variable expressions involving integers and fractions.

- In Chapter 2, you learned to represent two-variable equations in a variety of ways. You learned to graph linear equations and inequalities.

- In Chapter 3, you learned to graph systems of equations and inequalities, including systems of three equations in three variables.

 **Check Your Readiness**

 for Help to the Lesson in green.

Evaluating Expressions (Lesson 1-2)

Evaluate $ad - bc$ for the given values of the variables.

1. $a = -1, b = -2, c = 5, d = 4$

2. $a = \frac{1}{2}, b = -1, c = -\frac{2}{3}, d = 2$

3. $a = 2, b = \frac{1}{2}, c = \frac{1}{4}, d = -\frac{1}{8}$

4. $a = -\frac{1}{3}, b = \frac{1}{2}, c = \frac{1}{4}, d = -\frac{2}{3}$

Solving Equations and Inequalities (Lessons 1-3 and 1-4)

Solve each equation or inequality. Check your answers.

5. $23 - x = 13 + 2x$

6. $\frac{x-1}{5} = -2$

7. $a + 17 = -3a$

8. $2y - 3 \leq 2y + 5$

9. $11 + 3t > -t$

10. $\frac{3s-2}{2} < s$

Graphing Equations (Lesson 2-2)

Graph each equation on a coordinate plane.

11. $3x - 2y = 4$

12. $-3x = y$

13. $-7x - 3y = 14$

14. $y = \frac{2}{3}x - 3$

15. $y = 2x - 1$

16. $2x - 3y = -6$

17. $-2x = 3y + 12$

18. $-2y - 4x = 15$

Solving Systems of Equations (Lessons 3-2 and 3-6)

Solve each system.

19. $\begin{cases} -2x + y = -5 \\ 4x + y = -2 \end{cases}$

20. $\begin{cases} 4x - y = -2 \\ -\frac{1}{2}x - y = 1 \end{cases}$

21. $\begin{cases} 3x + y = 5 \\ -x + y = 2 \end{cases}$

22. $\begin{cases} x + y + z = 10 \\ 2x - y = 5 \\ y - z = 15 \end{cases}$

23. $\begin{cases} -x + y + 2z = 16 \\ 2x - 2y - 2z = -16 \\ x + y = 0 \end{cases}$

24. $\begin{cases} -2x + 3y + z = 1 \\ x - 3z = 7 \\ -y + z = -5 \end{cases}$

Matrices

LESSONS

4-1 Organizing Data Into Matrices

4-2 Adding and Subtracting Matrices

4-3 Matrix Multiplication

4-4 Geometric Transformations with Matrices

4-5 2 × 2 Matrices, Determinants, and Inverses

4-6 3 × 3 Matrices, Determinants, and Inverses

4-7 Inverse Matrices and Systems

4-8 Augmented Matrices and Systems

◀)) **Key Vocabulary**

- augmented matrix (p. 222)
- determinant (p. 200)
- dilation (p. 192)
- equal matrices (p. 177)
- image (p. 192)
- matrix (p. 168)
- matrix addition (p. 174)
- matrix element (p. 169)
- matrix equation (p. 176)
- matrix multiplication (p. 184)
- preimage (p. 192)
- row operations (p. 223)
- scalar multiplication (p. 182)
- variable matrix (p. 214)
- zero matrix (p. 175)

What You'll Learn Next

- In Chapter 4, you will move from using matrices in organizing data to manipulating matrices through algebra.

- You will learn to represent real-world relationships by writing matrices and using operations such as addition and multiplication to develop new matrices.

- You will learn, by working with geometric figures, how matrices relate to graphic art.

Activity Lab Applying what you learn, on pages 234–235 you will do activities involving the profits and losses of a chocolate-making business.

Organizing Data Into Matrices

What You'll Learn

- To identify matrices and their elements
- To organize data into matrices

... And Why

To organize gymnastics data, as in Example 4

✓ **Check Skills You'll Need**

Use the table at the right.

1. How many units were imported to the United States in 1996? In 2000?

2. How many more units were imported in 1998 than in 1996?

3. How many more units were imported than exported in 2000?

4. Compare the percent increase of imports from 1996 to 2000 with the percent increase of exports from 1996 to 2000.

GO **for Help** Skills Handbook page 870.

U.S. Passenger Vehicles and Light Trucks Imports and Exports (millions)

	1996	1998	2000
Imports	4.678	5.185	6.964
Exports	1.295	1.331	1.402

SOURCE: U.S. Department of Commerce.
Go to **www.PHSchool.com** for a data update.
Web code: agg-9041

🔊 **New Vocabulary** • matrix • matrix element

1 Identifying Matrices

A **matrix** (plural: matrices) is a rectangular array of numbers written within brackets. You represent a matrix with a capital letter and classify it by its dimensions. The number of horizontal rows and the number of vertical columns determine the dimensions of a matrix.

Vocabulary Tip

When describing matrices, read $\times$ as "by." For example, read 2×3 as "two by three."

$$\begin{array}{c} \text{3 columns} \\ \downarrow \ \downarrow \ \downarrow \end{array}$$

$A = \begin{bmatrix} 2 & 3 & 4 \\ 6 & 7 & 0 \end{bmatrix} \begin{array}{l} \leftarrow \\ \leftarrow \end{array}$ 2 rows   **Matrix A is a 2 × 3 matrix.**

1 EXAMPLE Writing the Dimensions of a Matrix

Write the dimensions of each matrix.

a. $\begin{bmatrix} 4 & 6 & 5 \\ 2 & -3 & -7 \\ 1 & 0 & 9 \end{bmatrix}$

b. $\begin{bmatrix} -4 & \frac{1}{3} & -3 \end{bmatrix}$

c. $\begin{bmatrix} 1 \\ 2 \\ 0 \\ 0.5 \end{bmatrix}$

3 rows × 3 columns

This is a 3 × 3 matrix.

1 row × 3 columns

This is a 1 × 3 matrix.

4 rows × 1 column

This is a 4 × 1 matrix.

✓ **Quick Check** ❶ Write the dimensions of each matrix.

a. $\begin{bmatrix} 4 & 5 & 0 \\ -2 & 0.5 & 17 \end{bmatrix}$

b. $\begin{bmatrix} 8 & -3 & 15 \end{bmatrix}$

c. $\begin{bmatrix} 10 & 0 \\ 1 & -5 \\ -6.2 & 9 \end{bmatrix}$

Each number in a matrix is a **matrix element.** You can identify a matrix element by its position within the matrix. Use a lowercase letter with subscripts. The subscripts represent the element's row number and column number.

2 EXAMPLE **Identifying a Matrix Element**

Identify element a_{13} in matrix A below.

$$A = \begin{bmatrix} 17 & 24 & 3 \\ 10.4 & 12 & 15 \\ 9 & 30 & 15 \end{bmatrix}$$ **a_{13} is the element in the first row and the third column.**

● Element a_{13} is 3.

✔ **Quick Check** ② Use the matrix from Example 2. Identify each matrix element.
 a. a_{33} **b.** a_{11} **c.** a_{21} **d.** a_{12}

2 Organizing Statistical Data

Successful businesses must track great amounts of data in order to plan the best use of their resources. They use matrices to organize and compare statistical data.

3 EXAMPLE **Real-World**  **Connection**

Energy Energy is often measured in British thermal units (Btus). Write a matrix to represent the data below. Estimate the values from the graph.

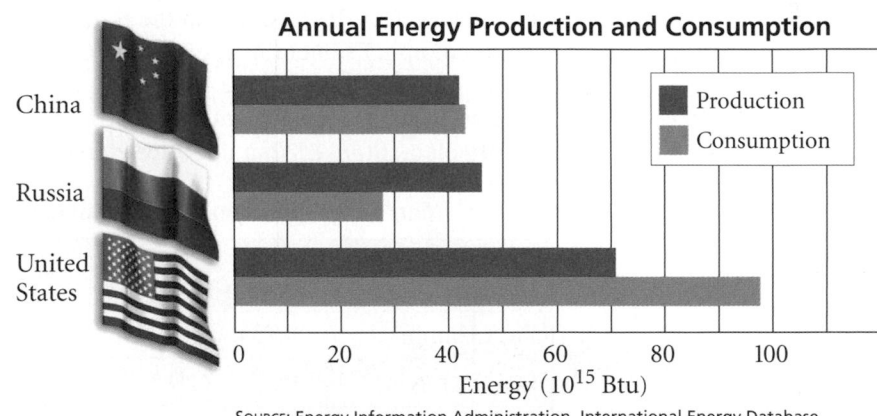

Annual Energy Production and Consumption

Source: Energy Information Administration, International Energy Database.
Go to **www.PHSchool.com** for a data update.
Web Code: agg-9041

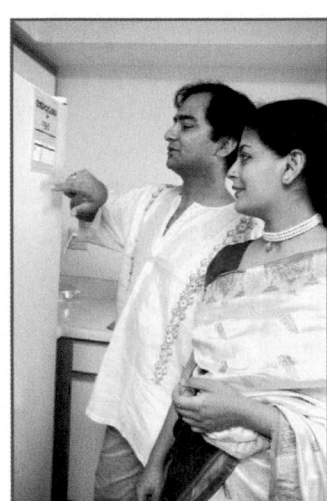

Real-World  **Connection**

New appliances have labels that tell how much energy the appliance uses each year.

Let each row represent a country and each column represent production or consumption levels.

$$\begin{array}{c} \\ \text{China} \\ \text{Russia} \\ \text{United States} \end{array} \begin{array}{cc} \text{Production} & \text{Consumption} \\ \begin{bmatrix} 42 & 43 \\ 46 & 28 \\ 71 & 98 \end{bmatrix} \end{array}$$

✔ **Quick Check** ③ **a.** Rewrite the matrix as a 2×3 matrix. Label the rows and columns.
 b. How could you modify your matrix to include data from other countries?
 c. Critical Thinking Explain the difference between a $c \times d$ matrix and a $d \times c$ matrix.

You can use matrices to show data from a table.

Gymnastics The table below shows scores from the 2004 Olympics in Athens, Greece.

U.S. Women's Olympic Gymnastics Team Qualifying Scores

Gymnast	Floor Exercise	Vault	Balance Beam	Uneven Bars
Mohini Bhardwaj	9.525	9.337	9.350	9.487
Courtney Kupets	9.400	9.350	9.550	9.637
Courtney McCool	9.250	9.350	9.112	9.575
Carly Patterson	9.500	9.512	9.725	9.600

SOURCE: Athens 2004 Olympic Games

Real-World Connection

In the vault, as in each of the other gymnastics events, a perfect individual score is 10.

a. Write a matrix W to represent the information. Use a 4×4 matrix.

Each column represents a different event.

$$W = \begin{array}{c} \text{M. Bhardwaj} \\ \text{C. Kupets} \\ \text{C. McCool} \\ \text{C. Patterson} \end{array} \begin{bmatrix} \overset{\text{Floor}}{\underset{\text{Exercise}}{\;}} & \text{Vault} & \overset{\text{Balance}}{\underset{\text{Beam}}{\;}} & \overset{\text{Uneven}}{\underset{\text{Bars}}{\;}} \\ 9.525 & 9.337 & 9.350 & 9.487 \\ 9.400 & 9.350 & 9.550 & 9.637 \\ 9.250 & 9.350 & 9.112 & 9.575 \\ 9.500 & 9.512 & 9.725 & 9.600 \end{bmatrix}$$

← Each row represents a different gymnast.

b. Which element represents Courtney McCool's score on the vault?

Courtney McCool's scores are in the third row. The vault scores are in the second column. Element w_{32} represents Courtney's score on the vault.

Quick Check ❹ **a.** Write a matrix M to represent the information from the table below.
b. Identify element m_{15}. What does this element represent?

Men's Olympic Gymnastics Individual Medal Winners, 2004

Gymnast	Floor Exercise	Pommel Horse	Still Rings	Vault	Parallel Bars	Horizontal Bars
Paul Hamm	9.725	9.700	9.587	9.137	9.837	9.837
Dae Eun Kim	9.650	9.537	9.712	9.412	9.775	9.725
Tae-Young Yang	9.512	9.650	9.725	9.700	9.712	9.475

SOURCE: Athens 2004 Olympic Games

EXERCISES

For more exercises, see *Extra Skill and Word Problem Practice*.

Practice and Problem Solving

Ⓐ Practice by Example

for Help

Example 1
(page 168)

State the dimensions of each matrix.

1. $\begin{bmatrix} 4 & -2 & 2 \\ 1 & 4 & 1 \\ 0 & 5 & -7 \end{bmatrix}$ **2.** $\begin{bmatrix} 1 \\ -9 \\ 5 \end{bmatrix}$ **3.** $\begin{bmatrix} 2 & \sqrt{5} \end{bmatrix}$ **4.** $\begin{bmatrix} 3 & 2 & 1 \\ 2 & 0 & -3 \end{bmatrix}$ **5.** $\begin{bmatrix} 2.5 \\ -3 \\ -1.6 \\ 10.0 \end{bmatrix}$

Example 2
(page 169)

Refer to matrices A and B at the right. Identify each matrix element.

$$A = \begin{bmatrix} 0 & -1 \\ 1.5 & 3 \\ 7 & -2 \end{bmatrix} \quad B = \begin{bmatrix} 6 & -3 & \frac{1}{2} \end{bmatrix}$$

6. a_{21} 7. b_{12} 8. a_{31}

9. b_{13} 10. a_{32} 11. a_{12}

Example 3
(page 169)

Use the graph below for Exercises 12 and 13.

12. Write a matrix to represent the data. Label the rows and columns.

13. Write a different matrix to represent the data. Label the rows and columns.

Example 4
(page 170)

14. **a.** Write a matrix H to represent the data in the table below.
    b. Find element h_{23}. What does this element represent?

Percent of Public Libraries Offering Programs

Location	Computer Instruction	Book Discussion	Parenting Skills	Employment Guidance
Urban	68	56	28	31
Suburban	59	50	24	18
Rural	49	34	15	12

SOURCE: U.S. National Center for Educational Statistics.
Go to **www.PHSchool.com** for a data update. Web Code: agg-9041

B Apply Your Skills

Use the table below for Exercises 15–17.

15. Display the data in a matrix A with columns representing years. Identify a_{23} and tell what it represents.

Manufacturer's Shipments of Recordings (millions)

Type	1998	1999	2000	2001	2002	2003
CDs	847.0	938.9	942.5	881.9	803.3	745.9
DVDs	0.5	2.5	3.3	7.9	10.7	17.5

SOURCE: Recording Industry Association of America.
Go to **www.PHSchool.com** for a data update. Web Code: agg-9041

16. Display the data in a matrix A with rows representing years. Identify a_{41} and tell what it represents.

17. State the dimensions of the matrices in Exercises 15 and 16.

18. **Error Analysis** A student identified element g_{32} from matrix G at the right as -3. What was the student's error?

$$G = \begin{bmatrix} 3 & 2.5 & 4.5 \\ 1.5 & 0 & -3 \\ -3 & 4.5 & 1.5 \end{bmatrix}$$

GO Online
Homework Video Tutor
Visit: PHSchool.com
Web Code: age-0401

19. **Writing** Describe the information necessary to make a matrix containing numerical data meaningful.

State the dimensions of each matrix. Identify the indicated element.

20. $\begin{bmatrix} 4 & 6 & 5 \\ 2 & -3 & -7 \\ 1 & 0 & 9 \end{bmatrix}, a_{23}$ 21. $\begin{bmatrix} -4 & 1 & -3 \\ 2 & 1 & 0 \end{bmatrix}, a_{12}$ 22. $\begin{bmatrix} 1 & 1 & 1 \\ 1 & 0 & 0 \\ 1 & 0 & 0 \end{bmatrix}, a_{32}$

23. $\begin{bmatrix} -4 & 8 & 12 \end{bmatrix}, a_{13}$ 24. $\begin{bmatrix} -5 \\ 4 \\ 3 \end{bmatrix}, a_{31}$ 25. $\begin{bmatrix} -16 & 24 \\ 8 & -2 \end{bmatrix}, a_{21}$

26. **Retail Sales** The graph shows August sales figures at a music store.

Music Store Sales, August

CDs Sold (vertical axis: 0, 50, 100, 150, 200)

Weeks: Week 1, Week 2, Week 3, Week 4

Legend: Rock, R & B, Rap, Classical

  a. **Estimation** Record the data in a table.
  b. Show the data in a matrix. What do the columns represent? What do the rows represent?

Challenge

27. **Jobs** The four tables display data from a study conducted by a school principal.
  a. Use the information to create four 2×2 matrices.
  b. How many boys in the school have part-time jobs?
  c. How many girls in the school have part-time jobs?
  d. What percent of the students with part-time jobs are girls?

Numbers of Students Who Work Part-time

9th Grade	Has Part-time Job	No Part-time Job
Boys	5	95
Girls	15	90

10th Grade	Has Part-time Job	No Part-time Job
Boys	35	65
Girls	30	55

11th Grade	Has Part-time Job	No Part-time Job
Boys	65	35
Girls	75	30

12th Grade	Has Part-time Job	No Part-time Job
Boys	70	25
Girls	65	45

28. **Transportation Costs** A computer accessory company makes computer carrying cases at four plants located in Atlanta, Boston, Chicago, and Denver. Represent the company's shipping costs in a matrix. Label the rows and columns.

Shipping Costs

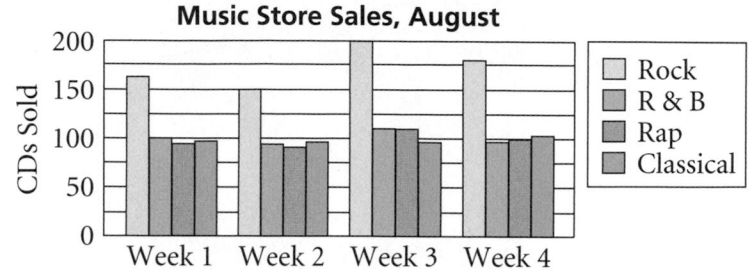

Atlanta to Boston $19
Atlanta to Chicago $12
Atlanta to Denver $23

Boston to Atlanta $19
Boston to Chicago $10
Boston to Denver $21

Chicago to Atlanta $12
Chicago to Boston $10
Chicago to Denver $15

Denver to Atlanta $23
Denver to Boston $21
Denver to Chicago $15

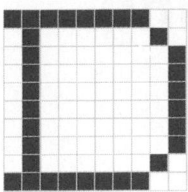

29. a. Open-Ended Using a 10×10 grid, create at least three different letters of the alphabet with a style similar to the one at the left.

b. Technology The tiny lights that make up a computer screen are called pixels. To make a letter, the computer tells the screen which pixels to light up. Represent each letter from part (a) by writing a matrix. Use 1 for a lit pixel and 0 for an unlit pixel.

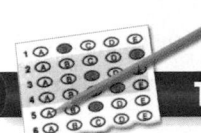

Test Prep

Multiple Choice

30. Which element in matrix $A = \begin{bmatrix} 5 & -2 & -\frac{1}{2} & 0 \end{bmatrix}$ is the number 0?

A. a_{40} **B.** a_4 **C.** a_{14} **D.** a_{41}

31. In which matrix is the value of a_{32} less than the value of a_{21}?

F. $\begin{bmatrix} -1 & 0 & 5 \\ 4 & 3 & -1 \\ -3 & 2 & 6 \end{bmatrix}$ **G.** $\begin{bmatrix} -1 & 5 & 0 \\ 3 & 4 & -1 \\ -3 & 6 & 2 \end{bmatrix}$ **H.** $\begin{bmatrix} 0 & 5 & -1 \\ -1 & 4 & 3 \\ 6 & 2 & -3 \end{bmatrix}$ **J.** $\begin{bmatrix} 0 & -1 & 5 \\ 0 & 3 & 4 \\ -3 & 1 & 6 \end{bmatrix}$

Extended Response

32. Anna made a table to show how much money she and two of her friends earned for summer chores.

a. Display the data in Anna's table in a matrix A with each row representing someone's earnings.

b. Rob made his own matrix, R, to show the earnings.

$$R = \begin{bmatrix} 12 & 20 & 15 \\ 35 & 40 & 55 \\ 40 & 0 & 70 \end{bmatrix}$$

What do values in the first column of matrix R represent?

Summer Earnings for Odd Jobs

	Weeding Gardens	Mowing Lawns	Pruning Bushes
Anna	$20	$40	$0
Rob	$12	$35	$40
Carla	$15	$55	$70

Mixed Review

Lesson 3-6

Solve each system.

33. $\begin{cases} 3x + 2y - 2z = -9 \\ 5x \quad\quad - 3z = -7 \\ x + 4y + 3z = 5 \end{cases}$ **34.** $\begin{cases} 2x + 3y + 4z = -1 \\ x - 2y + z = 9 \\ x + 4y - 2z = -12 \end{cases}$

Lesson 3-1

Solve each system by graphing.

35. $\begin{cases} 2x + y = 8 \\ x - 3y = -3 \end{cases}$ **36.** $\begin{cases} 2x + y = 7 \\ x + y = -5 \end{cases}$ **37.** $\begin{cases} x + 6y = 7 \\ 2x + 4y = -2 \end{cases}$

Lesson 2-3

Find the constant of variation for a direct variation that includes the given values.

38. $(2, 4)$ **39.** $(-1, 7)$ **40.** $(-4, -10)$ **41.** $(3, 5)$ **42.** $\left(\frac{1}{2}, 9\right)$

In each relation, y varies directly as x. Find y when $x = 9$.

43. $y = 6$ when $x = 4$ **44.** $y = 8$ when $x = 4$

Adding and Subtracting Matrices

What You'll Learn

• To add and subtract matrices

• To solve certain matrix equations

... And Why

To find SAT score totals, as in Example 1

 **Check Skills You'll Need**

GO for Help Skills Handbook page 873.

Simplify the elements of each matrix.

1. $\begin{bmatrix} 10 + 4 & 0 + 4 \\ -2 + 4 & -5 + 4 \end{bmatrix}$

2. $\begin{bmatrix} 5 - 2 & 3 - 2 \\ -1 - 2 & 0 - 2 \end{bmatrix}$

3. $\begin{bmatrix} -2 + 3 & 0 - 3 \\ 1 - 3 & -5 + 3 \end{bmatrix}$

4. $\begin{bmatrix} 3 + 1 & 4 + 9 \\ -2 + 0 & 5 + 7 \end{bmatrix}$

5. $\begin{bmatrix} 8 - 4 & -5 - 1 \\ 9 - 1 & 6 - 9 \end{bmatrix}$

6. $\begin{bmatrix} 2 + 4 & 6 - 8 \\ 4 - 3 & 5 + 2 \end{bmatrix}$

New Vocabulary • matrix addition • zero matrix • matrix equation • equal matrices

1 Adding and Subtracting Matrices

Sometimes you want to add or subtract matrices to get new information. You perform **matrix addition** on matrices with equal dimensions by adding the corresponding elements, which are elements in the same position in each matrix.

 **GO Online**

Video Tutor Help
Visit: PhSchool.com
Web Code: age-0775

Real-World Connection

Many schools have programs for students to help one another prepare for standardized tests.

1 EXAMPLE **Real-World Connection**

Statistics Use the data in the table.

a. Write two 2×4 matrices to represent the mean verbal and math SAT scores.

Verbal

	2000	2001	2002	2003
Male	507	509	507	512
Female	504	502	502	503

Math

	2000	2001	2002	2003
Male	533	533	534	537
Female	498	498	500	503

Mean SAT Scores

	Verbal		Math	
Year	Male	Female	Male	Female
2000	507	504	533	498
2001	509	502	533	498
2002	507	502	534	500
2003	512	503	537	503

SOURCE: College Entrance Examination Board

b. Find the combined mean SAT scores for each year in the table.

$$\begin{bmatrix} 507 & 509 & 507 & 512 \\ 504 & 502 & 502 & 503 \end{bmatrix} + \begin{bmatrix} 533 & 533 & 534 & 537 \\ 498 & 498 & 500 & 503 \end{bmatrix}$$

$$= \begin{bmatrix} 507 + 533 & 509 + 533 & 507 + 534 & 512 + 537 \\ 504 + 498 & 502 + 498 & 502 + 500 & 503 + 503 \end{bmatrix}$$

	2000	2001	2002	2003
$=$ Male	1040	1042	1041	1049
Female	1002	1000	1002	1006

 **Quick Check** ➊ Find each sum.

$$\textbf{a.} \begin{bmatrix} 1 & -2 & 0 \\ 3 & -5 & 7 \end{bmatrix} + \begin{bmatrix} 3 & 9 & -3 \\ -9 & 6 & 12 \end{bmatrix}$$

$$\textbf{b.} \begin{bmatrix} -12 & 24 \\ -3 & 5 \\ -1 & 10 \end{bmatrix} + \begin{bmatrix} -3 & 1 \\ 2 & -4 \\ -1 & 5 \end{bmatrix}$$

 Key Concepts

Definition	Matrix Addition

To add matrices A and B with the same dimensions, add corresponding elements.

$$A = \begin{bmatrix} a & b & c \\ d & e & f \end{bmatrix} \qquad B = \begin{bmatrix} r & s & t \\ u & v & w \end{bmatrix}$$

$$A + B = \begin{bmatrix} a & b & c \\ d & e & f \end{bmatrix} + \begin{bmatrix} r & s & t \\ u & v & w \end{bmatrix} = \begin{bmatrix} a+r & b+s & c+t \\ d+u & e+v & f+w \end{bmatrix}$$

 **Online
active math**

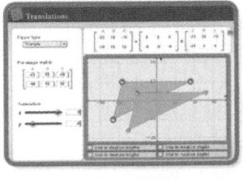

For: Matrix Addition Activity
Use: Interactive Textbook, 4-2

The additive identity matrix for the set of all $m \times n$ matrices is the **zero matrix** O, or $O_{m \times n}$, whose elements are all zeros. The opposite, or additive inverse, of an $m \times n$ matrix A is $-A$. $-A$ is the $m \times n$ matrix with elements that are the opposites of the corresponding elements of A.

➋ EXAMPLE Using Identity and Inverse Matrices

Find each sum.

$$\textbf{a.} \begin{bmatrix} 1 & 2 \\ 5 & -7 \end{bmatrix} + \begin{bmatrix} 0 & 0 \\ 0 & 0 \end{bmatrix}$$

$$= \begin{bmatrix} 1+0 & 2+0 \\ 5+0 & -7+0 \end{bmatrix}$$

$$= \begin{bmatrix} 1 & 2 \\ 5 & -7 \end{bmatrix}$$

$$\textbf{b.} \begin{bmatrix} 2 & 8 \\ -3 & 0 \end{bmatrix} + \begin{bmatrix} -2 & -8 \\ 3 & 0 \end{bmatrix}$$

$$= \begin{bmatrix} 2+(-2) & 8+(-8) \\ -3+3 & 0+0 \end{bmatrix}$$

$$= \begin{bmatrix} 0 & 0 \\ 0 & 0 \end{bmatrix}$$

 **Quick Check** ➋ Find each sum.

$$\textbf{a.} \begin{bmatrix} 14 & 5 \\ 0 & -2 \end{bmatrix} + \begin{bmatrix} -14 & -5 \\ 0 & 2 \end{bmatrix}$$

$$\textbf{b.} \begin{bmatrix} 0 & 0 & 0 \\ 0 & 0 & 0 \end{bmatrix} + \begin{bmatrix} -1 & 10 & -5 \\ 0 & 2 & -3 \end{bmatrix}$$

Some of the properties of real number addition also apply to matrix addition.

 Key Concepts

Properties	Matrix Addition

If A, B, and C are $m \times n$ matrices, then

$A + B$ is an $m \times n$ matrix.	Closure Property
$A + B = B + A$	Commutative Property of Addition
$(A + B) + C = A + (B + C)$	Associative Property of Addition
There exists a unique $m \times n$ matrix O such that $O + A = A + O = A$.	Additive Identity Property
For each A, there exists a unique opposite, $-A$. $A + (-A) = O$	Additive Inverse Property

You can define matrix subtraction by using the Additive Inverse Property.

 Key Concepts

Property	Matrix Subtraction

If two matrices, A and B, have the same dimensions, then $A - B = A + (-B)$.

3 EXAMPLE Subtracting Matrices

$A = \begin{bmatrix} 3 & 2 & 4 \\ -1 & 4 & 0 \end{bmatrix}$ and $B = \begin{bmatrix} 1 & 4 & 3 \\ -2 & 2 & 4 \end{bmatrix}$. Find $A - B$.

Vocabulary Tip

You can extend the meaning of <u>matrix</u> to describe a rectangular arrangement (rows and columns) of any objects.

Method 1 Use additive inverses.

$A - B = A + (-B) = \begin{bmatrix} 3 & 2 & 4 \\ -1 & 4 & 0 \end{bmatrix} + \begin{bmatrix} -1 & -4 & -3 \\ 2 & -2 & -4 \end{bmatrix}$ **Write the elements of $-B$.**

$= \begin{bmatrix} 3 + (-1) & 2 + (-4) & 4 + (-3) \\ -1 + 2 & 4 + (-2) & 0 + (-4) \end{bmatrix}$ **Add corresponding elements.**

$= \begin{bmatrix} 2 & -2 & 1 \\ 1 & 2 & -4 \end{bmatrix}$ **Simplify.**

Method 2 Use subtraction.

$A - B = \begin{bmatrix} 3 & 2 & 4 \\ -1 & 4 & 0 \end{bmatrix} - \begin{bmatrix} 1 & 4 & 3 \\ -2 & 2 & 4 \end{bmatrix}$

$= \begin{bmatrix} 3 - 1 & 2 - 4 & 4 - 3 \\ -1 - (-2) & 4 - 2 & 0 - 4 \end{bmatrix}$ **Subtract corresponding elements.**

$= \begin{bmatrix} 2 & -2 & 1 \\ 1 & 2 & -4 \end{bmatrix}$ **Simplify.**

✓ Quick Check **3** Find each difference.

a. $\begin{bmatrix} 6 & -9 & 7 \\ -2 & 1 & 8 \end{bmatrix} - \begin{bmatrix} -4 & 3 & 0 \\ 6 & 5 & 10 \end{bmatrix}$

b. $\begin{bmatrix} -3 & 5 \\ -1 & 10 \end{bmatrix} - \begin{bmatrix} -3 & 1 \\ 2 & -4 \end{bmatrix}$

 **Solving Matrix Equations**

A **matrix equation** is an equation in which the variable is a matrix. You can use the addition and subtraction properties of equality to solve matrix equations.

4 EXAMPLE Solving a Matrix Equation

Solve $X - \begin{bmatrix} 1 & 1 \\ 3 & 2 \end{bmatrix} = \begin{bmatrix} 0 & 1 \\ 8 & 9 \end{bmatrix}$ for the matrix X.

$X - \begin{bmatrix} 1 & 1 \\ 3 & 2 \end{bmatrix} = \begin{bmatrix} 0 & 1 \\ 8 & 9 \end{bmatrix}$

$X - \begin{bmatrix} 1 & 1 \\ 3 & 2 \end{bmatrix} + \begin{bmatrix} 1 & 1 \\ 3 & 2 \end{bmatrix} = \begin{bmatrix} 0 & 1 \\ 8 & 9 \end{bmatrix} + \begin{bmatrix} 1 & 1 \\ 3 & 2 \end{bmatrix}$ **Add $\begin{bmatrix} 1 & 1 \\ 3 & 2 \end{bmatrix}$ to each side of the equation.**

$X = \begin{bmatrix} 1 & 2 \\ 11 & 11 \end{bmatrix}$ **Simplify.**

✅ **Quick Check** ❹ Solve $X + \begin{bmatrix} -1 & 0 \\ 2 & 5 \end{bmatrix} = \begin{bmatrix} 10 & 7 \\ -4 & 4 \end{bmatrix}$.

Equal matrices are matrices with the same dimensions and equal corresponding elements.

5 EXAMPLE Determining Equal Matrices

Multiple Choice Which matrix is equal to matrix M? $\qquad M = \begin{bmatrix} -0.75 & \frac{1}{5} & 0 \\ \frac{1}{2} & -2 & 1.25 \end{bmatrix}$

Ⓐ $\begin{bmatrix} \frac{1}{2} & -2 & 1.25 \\ -0.75 & \frac{1}{5} & 0 \end{bmatrix}$ 　　　 Ⓑ $\begin{bmatrix} -\frac{3}{4} & 0.2 \\ 0.5 & -2 \end{bmatrix}$

Ⓒ $\begin{bmatrix} -\frac{3}{4} & 0.2 & 0 \\ 0.5 & \frac{-4}{2} & \frac{5}{4} \end{bmatrix}$ 　　　 Ⓓ $\begin{bmatrix} -0.75 & \frac{1}{2} \\ \frac{1}{5} & -2 \\ 0 & 1.25 \end{bmatrix}$

Matrix M is 2×3. Any matrix equal to it must have the same dimensions. Choice B is 2×2. Choice D is 3×2. You can eliminate choices B and D.

Choice A has first-row elements equal to second-row elements in M, but different from first-row elements in M. You can eliminate choice A.

Corresponding elements of M and choice C are equal.

$$-0.75 = -\frac{3}{4}, \quad \frac{1}{5} = 0.2, \quad 0 = 0; \qquad \frac{1}{2} = 0.5, \quad -2 = \frac{-4}{2}, \quad 1.25 = \frac{5}{4}$$

The answer is choice C.

✅ **Quick Check** ❺ Determine whether the two matrices in each pair are equal.

a. $\begin{bmatrix} 4 & 9 \\ 8 & 5 \end{bmatrix}, \begin{bmatrix} \frac{8}{2} & \frac{10}{2} \\ \frac{16}{2} & \frac{18}{2} \end{bmatrix}$ 　　　 **b.** $\begin{bmatrix} -2 & 3 \\ 5 & 0 \end{bmatrix}, \begin{bmatrix} -\frac{8}{4} & 6-3 \\ \frac{15}{3} & 4-4 \end{bmatrix}$

6 EXAMPLE Finding Unknown Matrix Elements

Solve the equation $\begin{bmatrix} 2x - 5 & 4 \\ 3 & 3y + 12 \end{bmatrix} = \begin{bmatrix} 25 & 4 \\ 3 & y + 18 \end{bmatrix}$ for x and y.

$$\begin{bmatrix} 2x - 5 & 4 \\ 3 & 3y + 12 \end{bmatrix} = \begin{bmatrix} 25 & 4 \\ 3 & y + 18 \end{bmatrix}$$

$2x - 5 = 25 \qquad\qquad 3y + 12 = y + 18$ 　　**Since the two matrices are equal, their**
$\qquad 2x = 30 \qquad\qquad\qquad 2y = 6$ 　　　　　　　　**corresponding elements are equal.**
$\qquad\quad x = 15 \qquad\qquad\qquad\quad y = 3$

The solutions are $x = 15$ and $y = 3$.

✅ **Quick Check** ❻ Solve each equation for x and y.

a. $\begin{bmatrix} x + 8 & -5 \\ 3 & -y \end{bmatrix} = \begin{bmatrix} 38 & -5 \\ 3 & 4y - 10 \end{bmatrix}$ 　　　 **b.** $[3x \quad 4] = [-9 \quad x + y]$

EXERCISES

For more exercises, see *Extra Skill and Word Problem Practice*.

Practice and Problem Solving

 Practice by Example

Example 1
(page 174)

 **for Help**

1. Sports The modern pentathlon is a grueling all-day competition. Each member of a team competes in five events: target shooting, fencing, swimming, horseback riding, and cross-country running. Here are scores for the U.S. women at the 2004 Olympic Games.

U.S. Women's Pentathlon Scores, 2004 Olympics

Event	Anita Allen	Mary Beth Iagorashvili
Shooting	952	760
Fencing	720	832
Swimming	1108	1252
Riding	1172	1144
Running	1044	1064

SOURCE: Athens 2004 Olympic Games

a. Write two 5×1 matrices to represent the individual scores for each event.
b. Find the total score for each woman.

Examples 2 and 3
(pages 175 and 176)

Find each sum or difference.

2. $\begin{bmatrix} 2 & -3 & 4 \\ 5 & 6 & -7 \end{bmatrix} + \begin{bmatrix} 0 & 0 & 0 \\ 0 & 0 & 0 \end{bmatrix}$

3. $\begin{bmatrix} 1 & 3 \\ 4 & 0 \end{bmatrix} + \begin{bmatrix} 0 & 5 \\ -1 & 2 \end{bmatrix} + \begin{bmatrix} 0 & -5 \\ 1 & -2 \end{bmatrix}$

4. $\begin{bmatrix} 6.4 & -1.9 \\ -6.4 & 0.8 \end{bmatrix} + \begin{bmatrix} -2.5 & -0.4 \\ 5.8 & 8.3 \end{bmatrix}$

5. $\begin{bmatrix} 6 & -3 \\ -7 & 2 \end{bmatrix} + \begin{bmatrix} -6 & 3 \\ 7 & -2 \end{bmatrix}$

6. $\begin{bmatrix} 5 & 4 & 3 \\ 1 & -2 & 6 \end{bmatrix} - \begin{bmatrix} 1 & 1 & 1 \\ 1 & 1 & 1 \end{bmatrix}$

7. $\begin{bmatrix} 2 & 1 & 2 \\ 1 & 2 & 1 \end{bmatrix} - \begin{bmatrix} 2 & 3 & 2 \\ 3 & 2 & 3 \end{bmatrix}$

8. $\begin{bmatrix} 0.5 & 9.5 \\ -3.5 & 5.5 \end{bmatrix} - \begin{bmatrix} 0.5 & 9.5 \\ -3.5 & 5.5 \end{bmatrix}$

9. $\begin{bmatrix} 1.5 & -1.9 \\ 0 & 4.6 \end{bmatrix} - \begin{bmatrix} 8.3 & -3.2 \\ 2.1 & 5.6 \end{bmatrix}$

Example 4
(page 176)

Solve each matrix equation.

10. $\begin{bmatrix} 1 & 2 \\ 2 & 1 \\ -3 & 4 \end{bmatrix} + X = \begin{bmatrix} 5 & -6 \\ 1 & 0 \\ 8 & 5 \end{bmatrix}$

11. $\begin{bmatrix} 2 & 1 & -1 \\ 0 & 2 & 1 \end{bmatrix} - X = \begin{bmatrix} 11 & 3 & -13 \\ 15 & -9 & 8 \end{bmatrix}$

12. $X - \begin{bmatrix} 1 & 4 \\ -2 & 3 \end{bmatrix} = \begin{bmatrix} 5 & -2 \\ 1 & 0 \end{bmatrix}$

13. $X + \begin{bmatrix} 6 & 1 \\ -2 & 3 \end{bmatrix} = \begin{bmatrix} 2 & 0 \\ -3 & 1 \end{bmatrix}$

Example 5
(page 177)

Determine whether the two matrices in each pair are equal. Justify your reasoning.

14. $\begin{bmatrix} -2 & 3 \\ 5 & 0 \end{bmatrix}, \begin{bmatrix} 2(-1) & 2(1.5) \\ 2(2.5) & 2(0) \end{bmatrix}$

15. $\begin{bmatrix} 4 \\ -6 \\ -8 \end{bmatrix}, \begin{bmatrix} \sqrt{16} & -6 & \sqrt{64} \end{bmatrix}$

Example 6
(page 177)

Find the value of each variable.

16. $\begin{bmatrix} 2 & 2 \\ -1 & 6 \end{bmatrix} - \begin{bmatrix} 4 & -1 \\ 0 & 5 \end{bmatrix} = \begin{bmatrix} x & y \\ -1 & z \end{bmatrix}$

17. $\begin{bmatrix} 2 & 4 \\ 8 & 12 \end{bmatrix} = \begin{bmatrix} 4x - 6 & -10t + 5x \\ 4x & 15t + 1.5x \end{bmatrix}$

B Apply Your Skills

Find each matrix sum or difference if possible. If not possible, explain.

$$A = \begin{bmatrix} 3 & 4 \\ 6 & -2 \\ 1 & 0 \end{bmatrix} \qquad B = \begin{bmatrix} -3 & 1 \\ 2 & -4 \\ -1 & 5 \end{bmatrix} \qquad C = \begin{bmatrix} 1 & 2 \\ -3 & 1 \end{bmatrix} \qquad D = \begin{bmatrix} 5 & 1 \\ 0 & 2 \end{bmatrix}$$

18. $A + B$ **19.** $B + D$ **20.** $C + D$ **21.** $B - A$ **22.** $C - D$

23. Multiple Choice You can put the pentathlon scores below into three matrices, one for each athlete. If you add the matrices, what does the sum matrix show?

U.S. Men's Pentathlon Scores, 2000 World Championship

Event	James Gregory	Velizar Iliev	Chad Senior
Shooting	1132	1072	1072
Fencing	760	910	610
Swimming	1173	1177	1285
Riding	1100	1100	1070
Running	1114	1118	1174

SOURCE: U.S. Modern Pentathlon Association

Real-World Connection

In the riding portion of the modern pentathlon, the athletes are given 20 min to get to know their horses before riding a 400-m course with 15 obstacles.

  A the total team score   **B** the team score for each event

  C each athlete's total score   **D** each athlete's score for each event

Solve each matrix equation for X.

24. $\begin{bmatrix} 1 & 2 & -3 \\ 2 & 1 & 3 \end{bmatrix} + X = \begin{bmatrix} 5 & 1 & 8 \\ -6 & 0 & 5 \end{bmatrix}$ **25.** $X - \begin{bmatrix} 4 & 12 \\ 75 & -1 \end{bmatrix} = \begin{bmatrix} 5 & 50 \\ 50 & -10 \end{bmatrix}$

26. Data Analysis Refer to the table.
 a. Find the total number of people participating in each activity.
 b. Find the difference between the numbers of males and females in each activity.
 c. Reasoning In part (b), does the order of the matrices matter? Explain.

U.S. Participation in Selected Leisure Activities (millions)

Activity	Male	Female
Movies	59.2	65.4
Exercise Programs	54.3	59.0
Sports Events	40.5	31.1
Home Improvement	45.4	41.8

SOURCE: U.S. National Endowment for the Arts.
Go to **www.PHSchool.com** for a data update.
Web-Code: agg-9041

27. Manufacturing The table below shows the number of beach balls produced during one shift at two manufacturing plants. Plant 1 has two shifts per day and Plant 2 has three shifts per day.

Beach Ball Production Per Shift

	1-color Plastic	1-color Rubber	3-color Plastic	3-color Rubber
Plant 1	500	700	1300	1900
Plant 2	400	1200	600	1600

GO nline
Homework Video Tutor
Visit: PHSchool.com
Web Code: age-0402

 a. Write matrices to represent one day's total output at the two plants.
 b. Use your results from part (a). Find the difference between production totals at the plants. Which plant produces more three-color plastic balls? Which plant produces more one-color rubber balls?

28. Writing Suppose A and B are two matrices with the same dimensions.
   a. Explain how to find $A + B$ and $A - B$.
   b. Explain how to find a matrix C such that $A + C = O$.

Solve each equation for each variable.

29. $\begin{bmatrix} 4b + 2 & -3 & 4d \\ -4a & 2 & 3 \\ 2f - 1 & -14 & 1 \end{bmatrix} = \begin{bmatrix} 11 & 2c - 1 & 0 \\ -8 & 2 & 3 \\ 0 & 3g - 2 & 1 \end{bmatrix}$
   30. $\begin{bmatrix} x^2 & 4 \\ -2 & y^2 \end{bmatrix} = \begin{bmatrix} 9 & 4 \\ -2 & 5y \end{bmatrix}$

31. $\begin{bmatrix} 4c & 2 - d & 5 \\ -3 & -1 & 2 \\ 0 & -10 & 15 \end{bmatrix} = \begin{bmatrix} 2c + 5 & 4d & g \\ -3 & h & f - g \\ 0 & -4c & 15 \end{bmatrix}$

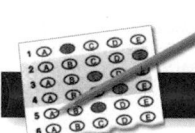 **Challenge**

32. Find the sum of $E = \begin{bmatrix} 3 \\ 4 \\ 7 \end{bmatrix}$ and the additive inverse of $G = \begin{bmatrix} -2 \\ 0 \\ 5 \end{bmatrix}$.

33. Prove that matrix addition is commutative for 2×2 matrices.

34. Prove that matrix addition is associative for 2×2 matrices.

Test Prep

Multiple Choice

Use matrices $A = \begin{bmatrix} 5 & 7 & 3 \\ -1 & 0 & -4 \end{bmatrix}$ and $C = \begin{bmatrix} -7 & 4 & 2 \\ 1 & -2 & -3 \end{bmatrix}$ for Exercises 35 and 36.

35. What is the sum $A + C$?
   A. The matrices cannot be added.
   B. $\begin{bmatrix} -2 & 11 & 5 \\ 0 & -2 & -7 \end{bmatrix}$
   C. $\begin{bmatrix} 12 & 3 & 1 \\ -2 & 2 & -1 \end{bmatrix}$
   D. $\begin{bmatrix} -35 & 28 & 6 \\ -1 & 0 & 12 \end{bmatrix}$

36. What is matrix Y if $Y - A = \begin{bmatrix} 1 & 0 & 1 \\ 0 & 1 & 0 \end{bmatrix}$?
   F. $\begin{bmatrix} 4 & 7 & 2 \\ -1 & -1 & -5 \end{bmatrix}$
   G. $\begin{bmatrix} 6 & 7 & 4 \\ -1 & 1 & -4 \end{bmatrix}$
   H. $\begin{bmatrix} -6 & 4 & 3 \\ 1 & -1 & -3 \end{bmatrix}$
   J. $\begin{bmatrix} -4 & -7 & -2 \\ 1 & 1 & 5 \end{bmatrix}$

Short Response

Find the value of each variable.

37. $\begin{bmatrix} x & y - 2 \\ z & w + 4 \end{bmatrix} + \begin{bmatrix} 2 & 5 \\ -2 & 4 \end{bmatrix} = \begin{bmatrix} 6 & 1 \\ 4 & 8 \end{bmatrix}$
   38. $\begin{bmatrix} x & 3 \\ x & -2 \end{bmatrix} + \begin{bmatrix} y & 6 \\ -y & 3 \end{bmatrix} = \begin{bmatrix} 6 & 9 \\ 4 & 1 \end{bmatrix}$

Mixed Review

 **GO for Help**

Lesson 4-1

39. Open-Ended Write a real-world problem that you can represent with a matrix. Write a matrix for the problem. Label the rows and columns.

Lesson 3-2

40. Business Your friend's mother plans to open a restaurant. The initial investment is $90,000. Weekly expenses will be about $8200. If the weekly income is about $8900, in how many weeks will she get back her investment?

Lesson 2-2

Find the slope and y-intercept of the graph of each function.

41. $y = 2x - 6$ **42.** $3y = 6 + 2x$ **43.** $-x - 2y = 12$ **44.** $y = 5x$

Working With Matrices

You can use a graphing calculator to work with matrices. First you need to enter the matrix into the calculator.

Go Online
PHSchool.com
For: Graphing calculator procedures
Web Code: age-2113

1 EXAMPLE

Enter matrix $A = \begin{bmatrix} -3 & 4 \\ 7 & -5 \\ 0 & -2 \end{bmatrix}$ into your graphing calculator. Select the **EDIT** option of

the **MATRIX** feature to edit matrix [A]. Specify a 3 × 2 matrix by pressing 3 **ENTER** 2 **ENTER** .

Enter the matrix elements one row at a time, pressing **ENTER** after each element. Then use the **QUIT** feature to return to the main screen.

```
NAMES  MATH  EDIT
1: [A]
2: [B]
3: [C]
4: [D]
5: [E]
```

```
MATRIX [A]   3  ×2
[ 0        0        ]
[ 0        0        ]
[ 0        0        ]

1,1= 0
```

```
MATRIX [A]   3  ×2
[ −3       4        ]
[ 7        −5       ]
[ 0        −2       ]

3,2= −2
```

You can use a graphing calculator to perform matrix operations.

2 EXAMPLE

Perform each operation for matrix $A = \begin{bmatrix} -3 & 4 \\ 7 & -5 \\ 0 & -2 \end{bmatrix}$ and matrix $B = \begin{bmatrix} 10 & -7 \\ 4 & -3 \\ -12 & 11 \end{bmatrix}$.

a. $A + B$

Use the **EDIT** option to select the matrices you want to add. Press **ENTER** to see the sum.

```
[A] + [B]
   [[ 7      −3    ]
    [ 11     −8    ]
    [ −12    9     ]]
```

b. $A - B$

Use the **EDIT** option to select the matrices you want to subtract. Press **ENTER** to see the difference.

```
[A] − [B]
   [[ −13    11    ]
    [ 3      −2    ]
    [ 12     −13   ]]
```

EXERCISES

Find each sum or difference.

1. $\begin{bmatrix} 0 & -3 \\ 5 & -7 \end{bmatrix} - \begin{bmatrix} -5 & 3 \\ 4 & 10 \end{bmatrix}$

2. $\begin{bmatrix} 3 & 5 & -7 \\ 0 & -2 & 0 \end{bmatrix} + \begin{bmatrix} -1 & 6 & 2 \\ -9 & 4 & 0 \end{bmatrix}$

3. $\begin{bmatrix} 3 \\ 5 \end{bmatrix} - \begin{bmatrix} -6 \\ 7 \end{bmatrix}$

4. $[3 \quad 5 \quad -8] + [-6 \quad 4 \quad 1]$

5. $\begin{bmatrix} 17 & 8 & 0 \\ 3 & -5 & 2 \end{bmatrix} - \begin{bmatrix} 4 & 6 & 5 \\ 2 & -2 & 9 \end{bmatrix}$

6. $[-9 \quad 6 \quad 4] + [-3 \quad 8 \quad 4]$

Matrix Multiplication

What You'll Learn

- To multiply a matrix by a scalar
- To multiply two matrices

...And Why

To calculate the gross income, as in Example 5

✓ **Check Skills You'll Need**

GO for Help Lesson 4-2

Find each sum.

1. $\begin{bmatrix} 3 & 5 \\ 2 & 8 \end{bmatrix} + \begin{bmatrix} 3 & 5 \\ 2 & 8 \end{bmatrix} + \begin{bmatrix} 3 & 5 \\ 2 & 8 \end{bmatrix}$

2. $\begin{bmatrix} -4 \\ 7 \end{bmatrix} + \begin{bmatrix} -4 \\ 7 \end{bmatrix} + \begin{bmatrix} -4 \\ 7 \end{bmatrix} + \begin{bmatrix} -4 \\ 7 \end{bmatrix} + \begin{bmatrix} -4 \\ 7 \end{bmatrix}$

3. $\begin{bmatrix} -1 & 3 & 4 \\ 0 & -2 & -5 \end{bmatrix} + \begin{bmatrix} -1 & 3 & 4 \\ 0 & -2 & -5 \end{bmatrix} + \begin{bmatrix} -1 & 3 & 4 \\ 0 & -2 & -5 \end{bmatrix} + \begin{bmatrix} -1 & 3 & 4 \\ 0 & -2 & -5 \end{bmatrix}$

🔊 **New Vocabulary** • scalar • scalar multiplication • matrix multiplication

1 Multiplying a Matrix by a Scalar

You can multiply a matrix by a real number.

$$3\begin{bmatrix} 3 & 5 \\ 2 & 8 \end{bmatrix} = \begin{bmatrix} 9 & 15 \\ 6 & 24 \end{bmatrix}$$

The real number factor (such as 3) is called a **scalar.**

Key Concepts

Definition	Scalar Multiplication

Scalar multiplication multiplies a matrix A by a scalar c. To find the resulting matrix cA, multiply each element of A by c.

1 EXAMPLE Real-World Connection

Prices Use the price list. The cafeteria plans to raise the cost of each beverage to one and a half times the current cost. How much will each beverage cost?

$$1.5\begin{bmatrix} 0.35 & 0.67 \\ 0.65 & 0.89 \\ 0.58 & 0.75 \end{bmatrix} = \begin{bmatrix} 1.5(0.35) & 1.5(0.67) \\ 1.5(0.65) & 1.5(0.89) \\ 1.5(0.58) & 1.5(0.75) \end{bmatrix}$$ **Multiply each element by 1.5.**

$$\approx \begin{bmatrix} 0.53 & 1.01 \\ 0.98 & 1.34 \\ 0.87 & 1.13 \end{bmatrix}$$ **Simplify.**

	SMALL	LARGE
LOWFAT MILK	$.35	$.67
ORANGE JUICE	$.65	$.89
TOMATO JUICE	$.58	$.75

Milk will cost $.53 and $1.01. Orange juice will cost $.98 and $1.34. Tomato juice will cost $.87 and $1.13.

✓ **Quick Check** ❶ Find $-3\begin{bmatrix} 15 & -12 & 10 & 0 \\ 20 & -10 & 7 & 0 \end{bmatrix}$.

You can find sums and differences of matrices multiplied by scalars.

 **EXAMPLE** **Using Scalar Products**

Find the difference $5A - 3B$ for $A = \begin{bmatrix} 2 & 3 & -7 \\ 1 & 4 & 5 \end{bmatrix}$ and $B = \begin{bmatrix} 3 & 0 & 6 \\ -1 & 8 & 2 \end{bmatrix}$.

$$5A - 3B = 5\begin{bmatrix} 2 & 3 & -7 \\ 1 & 4 & 5 \end{bmatrix} - 3\begin{bmatrix} 3 & 0 & 6 \\ -1 & 8 & 2 \end{bmatrix}$$

$$= \begin{bmatrix} 10 & 15 & -35 \\ 5 & 20 & 25 \end{bmatrix} - \begin{bmatrix} 9 & 0 & 18 \\ -3 & 24 & 6 \end{bmatrix} = \begin{bmatrix} 1 & 15 & -53 \\ 8 & -4 & 19 \end{bmatrix}$$

 Quick Check **2** Use matrices A and B from Example 2. Find each sum or difference.
a. $5B - 4A$ **b.** $A + 6B$

Key Concepts

Properties	Scalar Multiplication

If A, B, and O are $m \times n$ matrices and c and d are scalars, then

cA is an $m \times n$ matrix.	Closure Property
$(cd)A = c(dA)$	Associative Property of Multiplication
$c(A + B) = cA + cB$ $(c + d)A = cA + dA$	Distributive Property
$1 \cdot A = A$	Multiplicative Identity Property
$0 \cdot A = O$ and $cO = O$	Multiplicative Property of Zero

Vocabulary Tip

O is the <u>zero</u> <u>matrix</u>—the $m \times n$ matrix with every element zero.

You can use the properties of scalar multiplication to solve matrix equations.

3 **EXAMPLE** **Solving Matrix Equations with Scalars**

Solve $4X + 2\begin{bmatrix} 3 & 4 \\ -2 & 1 \end{bmatrix} = \begin{bmatrix} 10 & 0 \\ 4 & 2 \end{bmatrix}$.

$4X + 2\begin{bmatrix} 3 & 4 \\ -2 & 1 \end{bmatrix} = \begin{bmatrix} 10 & 0 \\ 4 & 2 \end{bmatrix}$

$4X + \begin{bmatrix} 6 & 8 \\ -4 & 2 \end{bmatrix} = \begin{bmatrix} 10 & 0 \\ 4 & 2 \end{bmatrix}$ **Scalar multiplication**

$4X = \begin{bmatrix} 10 & 0 \\ 4 & 2 \end{bmatrix} - \begin{bmatrix} 6 & 8 \\ -4 & 2 \end{bmatrix}$ **Subtract** $\begin{bmatrix} 6 & 8 \\ -4 & 2 \end{bmatrix}$ **from each side.**

$4X = \begin{bmatrix} 4 & -8 \\ 8 & 0 \end{bmatrix}$ **Simplify.**

$X = \frac{1}{4}\begin{bmatrix} 4 & -8 \\ 8 & 0 \end{bmatrix} = \begin{bmatrix} 1 & -2 \\ 2 & 0 \end{bmatrix}$ **Multiply each side by $\frac{1}{4}$ and simplify.**

Check $4X + 2\begin{bmatrix} 3 & 4 \\ -2 & 1 \end{bmatrix} = \begin{bmatrix} 10 & 0 \\ 4 & 2 \end{bmatrix}$

$4\begin{bmatrix} 1 & -2 \\ 2 & 0 \end{bmatrix} + 2\begin{bmatrix} 3 & 4 \\ -2 & 1 \end{bmatrix} \stackrel{?}{=} \begin{bmatrix} 10 & 0 \\ 4 & 2 \end{bmatrix}$ **Substitute.**

$\begin{bmatrix} 4 & -8 \\ 8 & 0 \end{bmatrix} + \begin{bmatrix} 6 & 8 \\ -4 & 2 \end{bmatrix} \stackrel{?}{=} \begin{bmatrix} 10 & 0 \\ 4 & 2 \end{bmatrix}$ **Multiply.**

$\begin{bmatrix} 10 & 0 \\ 4 & 2 \end{bmatrix} = \begin{bmatrix} 10 & 0 \\ 4 & 2 \end{bmatrix}$ ✓ **Simplify.**

 **Quick Check** ❸ Solve each matrix equation. Check your answer.

a. $2X = \begin{bmatrix} 4 & 12 \\ 1 & -4 \end{bmatrix} + \begin{bmatrix} -2 & 0 \\ 3 & 4 \end{bmatrix}$ **b.** $-3X + \begin{bmatrix} 7 & 0 & -1 \\ 2 & -3 & 4 \end{bmatrix} = \begin{bmatrix} 10 & 0 & 8 \\ -19 & -18 & 10 \end{bmatrix}$

2   Multiplying Matrices

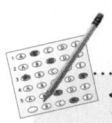

Test-Taking Tip

Read questions about tables carefully. Make sure you choose the correct rows, columns, and cells.

Activity: Using Matrices

Use the data in the table.

	Lunch 1	Lunch 2	Lunch 3
Cost per Lunch	$2.50	$1.75	$2.00
Number Sold	50	100	75

1. How much money did the cafeteria collect selling lunch 1? Selling lunch 2? Selling lunch 3?

2. a. How much did the cafeteria collect selling all three lunches?
   b. Explain how you used the data in the table to find your answer.

3. a. Write a 1 × 3 matrix to represent the cost of the lunches.
   b. Write a 3 × 1 matrix to represent the number of lunches sold.
   c. Writing Describe a procedure for using your matrices to find how much money the cafeteria collected from selling all three lunches. Use the words *row*, *column*, and *element*.

Graphing Calculator Hint

You can use the MATRIX feature of a graphing calculator to multiply matrices.

To perform **matrix multiplication,** multiply the elements of each *row* of the first matrix by the elements of each *column* of the second matrix. Add the products.

4 EXAMPLE   Multiplying Matrices

Find the product of $\begin{bmatrix} -1 & 0 \\ 3 & -4 \end{bmatrix}$ and $\begin{bmatrix} -3 & 3 \\ 5 & 0 \end{bmatrix}$.

Multiply a_{11} and b_{11}. Then multiply a_{12} and b_{21}. Add the products.

$\begin{bmatrix} -1 & 0 \\ 3 & -4 \end{bmatrix}\begin{bmatrix} -3 & 3 \\ 5 & 0 \end{bmatrix} = \begin{bmatrix} ? & \blacksquare \\ \blacksquare & \blacksquare \end{bmatrix}$ $(-1)(-3) + (0)(5) = 3$

The result is the element in the first row and first column.
Repeat with the rest of the rows and columns.

$\begin{bmatrix} -1 & 0 \\ 3 & -4 \end{bmatrix}\begin{bmatrix} -3 & 3 \\ 5 & 0 \end{bmatrix} = \begin{bmatrix} 3 & ? \\ \blacksquare & \blacksquare \end{bmatrix}$ $(-1)(3) + (0)(0) = -3$

$\begin{bmatrix} -1 & 0 \\ 3 & -4 \end{bmatrix}\begin{bmatrix} -3 & 3 \\ 5 & 0 \end{bmatrix} = \begin{bmatrix} 3 & -3 \\ ? & \blacksquare \end{bmatrix}$ $(3)(-3) + (-4)(5) = -29$

$\begin{bmatrix} -1 & 0 \\ 3 & -4 \end{bmatrix}\begin{bmatrix} -3 & 3 \\ 5 & 0 \end{bmatrix} = \begin{bmatrix} 3 & -3 \\ -29 & ? \end{bmatrix}$ $(3)(3) + (-4)(0) = 9$

The product of $\begin{bmatrix} -1 & 0 \\ 3 & -4 \end{bmatrix}$ and $\begin{bmatrix} -3 & 3 \\ 5 & 0 \end{bmatrix}$ is $\begin{bmatrix} 3 & -3 \\ -29 & 9 \end{bmatrix}$.

 **4 a.** Find the product of $\begin{bmatrix} -3 & 3 \\ 5 & 0 \end{bmatrix}$ and $\begin{bmatrix} -1 & 0 \\ 3 & -4 \end{bmatrix}$.

b. Critical Thinking Is matrix multiplication commutative? Explain.

 Key Concepts

Definition	Matrix Multiplication

To find element c_{ij} of the product matrix AB, multiply each element in the ith row of A by the corresponding element in the jth column of B, and then add.

5 EXAMPLE Real-World Connection

Real-World Connection

The music on an LP record (a) plays continuously as the stylus travels along the groove. The music on a CD (b) plays in discrete intervals read by a laser.

a   b

Gridded Response A used-record store sells tapes, LP records, and compact discs. The matrices show today's information. Find the store's gross income for the day, in dollars.

Prices

Tapes LPs CDs

$[\,\$8 \quad \$6 \quad \$13\,]$

Number of Items Sold

$\begin{array}{c} \text{Tapes} \\ \text{LPs} \\ \text{CDs} \end{array} \begin{bmatrix} 9 \\ 30 \\ 20 \end{bmatrix}$

Multiply each price by the number of items sold and add the products.

$$[\,8 \quad 6 \quad 13\,] \begin{bmatrix} 9 \\ 30 \\ 20 \end{bmatrix} = [\,8(9) + 6(30) + 13(20)\,] = [512]$$

● The store's gross income for the day was $512.

 Quick Check **5** Find each product if it exists.

a. $[\,12 \quad 3\,] \begin{bmatrix} 10 \\ -5 \end{bmatrix}$

b. $\begin{bmatrix} 10 \\ -5 \end{bmatrix} \begin{bmatrix} 12 & 3 \\ 0 & 0 \end{bmatrix}$

The product of two matrices A and B exists only if the number of *columns* of A is equal to the number of *rows* of B.

 **Key Concepts**

Property	Dimensions of a Product Matrix

If matrix A is an $m \times n$ matrix and matrix B is an $n \times p$ matrix, then the product matrix AB is an $m \times p$ matrix.

Example   **matrix A**   ·   **matrix B**

3 rows $\begin{bmatrix} 1 & 2 \\ 3 & 4 \\ 5 & 6 \end{bmatrix}$ 2 rows $\begin{bmatrix} 7 & 8 & 9 & 10 \\ 11 & 12 & 13 & 14 \end{bmatrix}$

2 columns   4 columns

equal

dimensions of product matrix

The dimensions of product matrix AB are 3×4.

6 **EXAMPLE** **Determining Whether a Product Matrix Exists**

Use matrices $G = \begin{bmatrix} 2 & 3 \\ -1 & 8 \\ 4 & 0 \end{bmatrix}$ and $H = \begin{bmatrix} 8 & 0 \\ 2 & -5 \end{bmatrix}$. Determine whether products *GH*

and *HG* are *defined* (exist) or *undefined* (do not exist).

Find the dimensions of each product matrix.

GH	*HG*
$(3 \times 2)(2 \times 2) \rightarrow 3 \times 2$	$(2 \times 2)(3 \times 2)$
↑ ↑ product	↑ ↑
equal matrix	*not* equal

Product *GH* is defined and is a 3×2 matrix. Product *HG* is undefined, because the number of columns of *H* is not equal to the number of rows of *G*.

✓ Quick Check **6** Let $R = \begin{bmatrix} 4 & -2 \\ 5 & -4 \end{bmatrix}$ and $S = \begin{bmatrix} 8 & 0 & -1 & 0 \\ 2 & -5 & 1 & 8 \end{bmatrix}$.

a. Determine whether products *RS* and *SR* are *defined* or *undefined*.
b. Find each defined product.

Matrix multiplication has some of the properties of real number multiplication.

🔑 Key Concepts

Properties	**Matrix Multiplication**

If *A*, *B*, and *C* are $n \times n$ matrices, then

AB is an $n \times n$ matrix.	Closure Property
$(AB)C = A(BC)$	Associative Property of Multiplication
$A(B + C) = AB + AC$ $(B + C)A = BA + CA$	Distributive Property
$OA = AO = O$, where *O* has the same dimensions as *A*.	Multiplicative Property of Zero

EXERCISES

For more exercises, see *Extra Skill and Word Problem Practice*.

Practice and Problem Solving

 **Practice by Example**

Examples 1 and 2
(pages 182 and 183)

 **for Help**

Use matrices *A*, *B*, *C*, and *D*. Find each product, sum, or difference.

$A = \begin{bmatrix} 3 & 4 \\ 6 & -2 \\ 1 & 0 \end{bmatrix}$ $B = \begin{bmatrix} -3 & 1 \\ 2 & -4 \\ -1 & 5 \end{bmatrix}$ $C = \begin{bmatrix} 1 & 2 \\ -3 & 1 \end{bmatrix}$ $D = \begin{bmatrix} 5 & 1 \\ 0 & 2 \end{bmatrix}$

1. $3A$ **2.** $4B$ **3.** $-3C$ **4.** $-D$

5. $A - 2B$ **6.** $3A + 2B$ **7.** $4C + 3D$ **8.** $2A - 5B$

Example 3
(page 183)

Solve each matrix equation. Check your answers.

9. $3\begin{bmatrix} 2 & 0 \\ -1 & 5 \end{bmatrix} - 2X = \begin{bmatrix} -10 & 5 \\ 0 & 17 \end{bmatrix}$ **10.** $5X - \begin{bmatrix} 1.5 & -3.6 \\ -0.3 & 2.8 \end{bmatrix} = \begin{bmatrix} 0.2 & 1.3 \\ -5.6 & 1.7 \end{bmatrix}$

Example 4
(page 184)

Find each product.

11. $\begin{bmatrix} -3 & 4 \\ 5 & 2 \end{bmatrix}\begin{bmatrix} 1 & 0 \\ 2 & -3 \end{bmatrix}$

12. $\begin{bmatrix} 1 & 0 \\ 2 & -3 \end{bmatrix}\begin{bmatrix} -3 & 4 \\ 5 & 2 \end{bmatrix}$

13. $\begin{bmatrix} 0 & 2 \\ -4 & 0 \end{bmatrix}\begin{bmatrix} 0 & 2 \\ -4 & 0 \end{bmatrix}$

14. $\begin{bmatrix} -3 & 5 \end{bmatrix}\begin{bmatrix} -3 \\ 5 \end{bmatrix}$

15. $\begin{bmatrix} -3 & 5 \end{bmatrix}\begin{bmatrix} -3 & 0 \\ 5 & 0 \end{bmatrix}$

16. $\begin{bmatrix} -3 & 5 \end{bmatrix}\begin{bmatrix} 0 & -3 \\ 0 & 5 \end{bmatrix}$

17. $\begin{bmatrix} 0 & -3 \\ 0 & 5 \end{bmatrix}\begin{bmatrix} -3 & 0 \\ 5 & 0 \end{bmatrix}$

18. $\begin{bmatrix} 1 & 0 \\ -1 & -5 \\ 0 & 3 \end{bmatrix}\begin{bmatrix} -1 & 0 \\ 0 & -1 \end{bmatrix}$

Example 5
(page 185)

19. **Business** A florist makes three special floral arrangements. One uses three lilies. The second uses three lilies and four carnations. The third uses four daisies and three carnations. Lilies cost $2.15 each, carnations cost $.90 each, and daisies cost $1.30 each.
   a. Write a matrix to show the number of each type of flower in each arrangement.
   b. Write a matrix to show the cost of each type of flower.
   c. Find the matrix showing the cost of each floral arrangement.

Example 6
(page 186)

Determine whether each product is defined or undefined.

$$F = \begin{bmatrix} 2 & 3 \\ 6 & 9 \end{bmatrix} \qquad G = \begin{bmatrix} -3 & 6 \\ 2 & -4 \end{bmatrix} \qquad H = \begin{bmatrix} -5 \\ 6 \end{bmatrix} \qquad J = \begin{bmatrix} 0 & 7 \end{bmatrix}$$

20. *FG*   21. *GF*   22. *FH*   23. *HF*   24. *GH*

25. *HG*   26. *FJ*   27. *JF*   28. *HJ*   29. *JH*

B **Apply Your Skills**

Mental Math Find each product.

30. $2\begin{bmatrix} -1 & 4 \\ 2 & 5 \end{bmatrix}$

31. $-1\begin{bmatrix} 9 & -7 & -4 \\ -8 & -2 & 3 \end{bmatrix}$

32. $0.5\begin{bmatrix} 3 & 14 \\ 7 & -4 \end{bmatrix}$

33. $\begin{bmatrix} -1 & 0 \\ 0 & -1 \end{bmatrix}\begin{bmatrix} -1 & 0 & 1 \\ 0 & -1 & 1 \end{bmatrix}$

34. $\begin{bmatrix} 1 & 0 \\ 0 & -1 \end{bmatrix}\begin{bmatrix} -1 & 0 \\ 0 & -1 \end{bmatrix}$

35. **Multiple Choice** Columns in matrix $A = \begin{bmatrix} 3 & 8 \\ 0 & 12 \end{bmatrix}$ show, respectively, the numbers of erasers and pencils sold. The rows show, respectively, the numbers sold on Monday and Tuesday. Matrix $B = \begin{bmatrix} 0.50 \\ 0.25 \end{bmatrix}$ shows the 50¢ cost of one eraser and the quarter cost of one pencil. What does the product AB show?
   Ⓐ the total paid for erasers on Monday and Tuesday and the total paid for pencils on Monday and Tuesday
   Ⓑ the total paid for erasers and pencils on Monday and the total paid for erasers and pencils on Tuesday.
   Ⓒ the total paid for pencils and erasers
   Ⓓ the cost of 1 pencil and 1 eraser

Find the dimensions of each product matrix. Then find each product.

36. $\begin{bmatrix} 5 & 7 & 0 \\ -\frac{4}{5} & 3 & 6 \\ 0 & -\frac{2}{3} & 4 \end{bmatrix}\begin{bmatrix} 2 & -1 \\ 1 & 1 \\ 0 & -1 \end{bmatrix}$

37. $\begin{bmatrix} 1 & 0 & 0 \\ 1 & 0 & -2 \\ 0 & 0 & 2 \\ -1 & 0 & 1 \end{bmatrix}\begin{bmatrix} a & 0 & b & 0 \\ 0 & c & 0 & d \\ e & 0 & 0 & f \end{bmatrix}$

For Exercises 38–45, use matrices D, E, and F shown below. Perform the indicated operations if they are defined. If an operation is not defined, label it undefined.

$$D = \begin{bmatrix} 1 & 2 & -1 \\ 0 & 3 & 1 \\ 2 & -1 & -2 \end{bmatrix} \qquad E = \begin{bmatrix} 2 & -5 & 0 \\ 1 & 0 & -2 \\ 3 & 1 & 1 \end{bmatrix} \qquad F = \begin{bmatrix} -3 & 2 \\ -5 & 1 \\ 2 & 4 \end{bmatrix}$$

38. DE **39.** $-3F$ **40.** $(DE)F$ **41.** $D(EF)$

42. $D - 2E$ **43.** $(E - D)F$ **44.** $(DD)E$ **45.** $(2D)(3F)$

 46. Business A hardware store chain displays prices in a 1×3 matrix and daily purchases at its three stores in a 3×3 matrix.

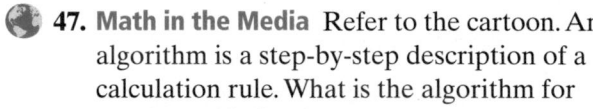

Prices

Hammers	Flashlights	Lanterns
[$3	$5	$7]

Number of Items Sold

	Store A	Store B	Store C
Hammers	10	9	8
Flashlights	3	14	6
Lanterns	2	5	7

a. Find the product of the two matrices. Explain what the product represents.
b. How would you find the total gross revenue from all three stores?
c. Find the total gross revenue from the flashlights sold at all three stores.

47. Math in the Media Refer to the cartoon. An algorithm is a step-by-step description of a calculation rule. What is the algorithm for matrix multiplication?

48. Open-Ended Find two 2×2 matrices X and Y, with not all elements equal, such that $XY = YX$.

 **49. Writing** Suppose A is a 2×3 matrix and B is a 3×2 matrix. Are AB and BA equal? Explain your reasoning. Include examples.

50. Revenue Write a matrix that represents the daily revenue from the play.

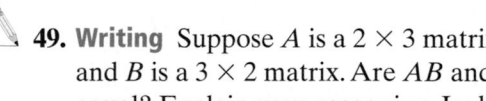

Ticket Prices		
Orchestra	Mezzanine	Balcony
$7.00	$6.00	$5.00

Number of Tickets Sold			
Location	Thursday	Friday	Saturday
Orchestra	150	130	160
Mezzanine	125	130	175
Balcony	60	52	80

Challenge

Solve for x and y.

51. $\begin{bmatrix} 2x & 1 \\ 2 & 0 \end{bmatrix} \begin{bmatrix} 1 & 3 \\ 2 & -y \end{bmatrix} = \begin{bmatrix} -4 & -9 \\ 2 & 6 \end{bmatrix}$ **52.** $\begin{bmatrix} 2x & 1 \\ 2 & 0 \end{bmatrix} \begin{bmatrix} 0 & 3 \\ 2x & -y \end{bmatrix} = \begin{bmatrix} -4 & -9 \\ 0 & 6 \end{bmatrix}$

For Exercises 53–56, use matrices P, Q, R, S, and I. Determine whether the two expressions in each pair are equal.

$$P = \begin{bmatrix} 3 & 4 \\ 1 & 2 \end{bmatrix} \quad Q = \begin{bmatrix} -1 & 0 \\ 3 & -2 \end{bmatrix} \quad R = \begin{bmatrix} 1 & 4 \\ -2 & 1 \end{bmatrix} \quad S = \begin{bmatrix} 0 & 1 \\ 2 & 0 \end{bmatrix} \quad I = \begin{bmatrix} 1 & 0 \\ 0 & 1 \end{bmatrix}$$

53. $(P + Q)R$ and $PR + QR$ **54.** $(P + Q)I$ and $PI + QI$

55. $(P + Q)(R + S)$ and $(P + Q)R + (P + Q)S$

56. $(P + Q)(R + S)$ and $PR + PS + QR + QS$

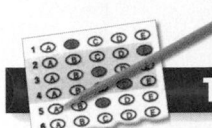
Multiple Choice

57. Which product is NOT defined?

A. $\begin{bmatrix} -1 \\ 2 \end{bmatrix}[-1 \ 2]$　　B. $\begin{bmatrix} -1 & 2 \\ -1 & 2 \end{bmatrix}[-1 \ 2]$　　C. $\begin{bmatrix} -1 & 2 \\ -1 & 2 \end{bmatrix}\begin{bmatrix} 2 & -1 \\ 2 & -1 \end{bmatrix}$　　D. $[-1 \ 2]\begin{bmatrix} -1 \\ 2 \end{bmatrix}$

58. Given $P = \begin{bmatrix} 4 & 3 & -2 \\ -1 & 0 & 5 \end{bmatrix}$ and $Q = \begin{bmatrix} 3 & -2 & -5 \\ -1 & -2 & -1 \end{bmatrix}$, what is $2P - 3Q$?

F. $\begin{bmatrix} 1 & -5 & 3 \\ 0 & -2 & 6 \end{bmatrix}$　　G. $\begin{bmatrix} 17 & 0 & 19 \\ -5 & 6 & 7 \end{bmatrix}$　　H. $\begin{bmatrix} -1 & 12 & 11 \\ 1 & 6 & 13 \end{bmatrix}$　　J. $\begin{bmatrix} 1 & 5 & 3 \\ 0 & 2 & 6 \end{bmatrix}$

Short Response

59. Solve $3Y + 2\begin{bmatrix} -1 & -3 \\ 2 & 5 \end{bmatrix} = \begin{bmatrix} 13 & -9 \\ 4 & 16 \end{bmatrix}$. Show the steps of your solution.

Extended Response

60. Given $M = \begin{bmatrix} -3 & 4 \\ 1 & -2 \end{bmatrix}$ and $N = \begin{bmatrix} 0 & 1 \\ -2 & 5 \end{bmatrix}$, does $M \times N = N \times M$? Explain.

Mixed Review

Lesson 4-2

Add or subtract.

61. $\begin{bmatrix} -1 & 2 \\ 0 & 17 \end{bmatrix} - \begin{bmatrix} 32 & 14 \\ 6 & -10 \end{bmatrix}$　　　　**62.** $\begin{bmatrix} 0 & -1 & 5 \\ 6 & 10 & 12 \end{bmatrix} + \begin{bmatrix} 9 & -5 & 7 \\ -4 & 10 & 0 \end{bmatrix}$

Lesson 3-4

Graph each system of constraints. Find all vertices. Then find the values of x and y that maximize or minimize the objective function.

63. $\begin{cases} x + y \le 3 \\ x \ge 0 \\ y \le 2 \end{cases}$
Maximize for
$P = 3x + 4y$.

64. $\begin{cases} x + 2y \le 8 \\ x \ge 2 \\ y \ge 0 \end{cases}$
Minimize for
$C = x + 3y$.

65. $\begin{cases} x + y \le 6 \\ 2x + y \le 10 \\ x \ge 0, y \ge 0 \end{cases}$
Maximize for
$P = 4x + y$.

Lesson 2-7

Graph each inequality.

66. $y < 4x - 1$　　　　**67.** $y \le -3x + 8$　　　　**68.** $y \ge |2x + 5| - 3$

Checkpoint Quiz 1　　　　**Lessons 4-1 through 4-3**

State the dimensions of each matrix. Identify the indicated element.

1. $\begin{bmatrix} 5 & 2 \\ -8 & 3 \\ 10 & 1 \end{bmatrix}; a_{32}$　　　　**2.** $\begin{bmatrix} 9 & 1 & 7 \\ 6 & -2 & 4 \end{bmatrix}; a_{22}$　　　　**3.** $\begin{bmatrix} 8 & 1 & 5 \\ 9 & 4 & 2 \\ 7 & 0 & 3 \end{bmatrix}; a_{13}$

Use matrices A, B, C, and D. Perform each operation.

$A = \begin{bmatrix} 3 & 1 \\ 5 & 7 \end{bmatrix}$　　　$B = \begin{bmatrix} 4 & 6 \\ 1 & 0 \end{bmatrix}$　　　$C = \begin{bmatrix} -5 & 3 \\ 1 & 9 \end{bmatrix}$　　　$D = \begin{bmatrix} 1.5 & 2 \\ 9 & -6 \end{bmatrix}$

4. $A + C$　　**5.** $B - A$　　**6.** $3D$　　**7.** BA　　**8.** $C(DB)$

 9. Writing How can you decide whether you can multiply two matrices?

10. Open-Ended Write a matrix equation with solution $\begin{bmatrix} 12 & 7 & -3 & 8 \\ 9 & 0 & -11 & 1 \end{bmatrix}$.

Geometric Transformations

Geometric patterns, such as those formed by geese flying south for the winter or tiles on a plane surface, can be described using geometric transformations. A transformation is a change made to a figure. There are four types.

A translation slides a figure a given distance and direction without changing its size or shape.

preimage

image

A rotation turns a figure through a given angle about a point called the center.

preimage

image

A reflection flips a figure over a given line called its axis of reflection.

preimage

image

A dilation enlarges or reduces a figure by a given scale factor.

image

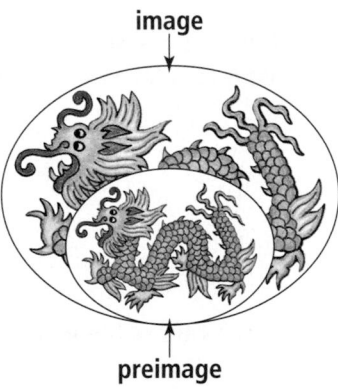

preimage

EXERCISES

Describe each transformation from the black figure (preimage) to the blue figure (image) as a *translation, rotation, reflection,* **or** *dilation.*

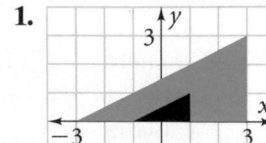

1.   2.   3.   4.

5. a. For Exercise 1, list the coordinates of the preimage vertices. Then list the coordinates of the image vertices.
   b. **Make a Conjecture** For the type of transformation you found, describe how the coordinates of the image relate to the coordinates of its preimage. Use other examples of that transformation to verify your conjecture.
   c. **Make More Conjectures** Repeat parts (a) and (b) for Exercises 2–4.

6. Open-Ended In a coordinate plane, draw a rectangle with center not at the origin. Then construct a dilation with center at the origin and scale factor 2.

4-4

Geometric Transformations with Matrices

What You'll Learn

- To represent translations and dilations with matrices
- To represent reflections and rotations with matrices

. . . And Why

To transform a photo, as in Example 2

✓ **Check Skills You'll Need**

GO **for Help** Lesson 2-6

Without using graphing technology, graph each function and its translation. Write the new function.

1. $y = x + 2$; left 4 units

2. $f(x) = \frac{1}{2}x + 2$; up 5 units

3. $g(x) = |x|$; right 3 units

4. $y = x$; down 2 units

5. $y = \frac{1}{3}|x - 3|$; down 2 units

6. $f(x) = -2|x|$; right 2 units

🔊 **New Vocabulary**
- image
- preimage
- dilation
- rotation
- center of rotation

---

1 **Translations and Dilations with Matrices**

Activity: Translating a Geometric Figure

Geometry In Chapter 2 you used vertical and horizontal translations to graph functions. A translation shifts a graph without changing its size or shape.

1. Draw the figure on a coordinate grid as shown.

2. Translate the figure 4 units right and 6 units down. Label the new figure.

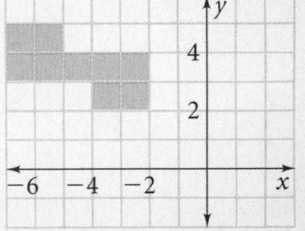

3. Identify the coordinates of the vertices of the original figure and the new figure.

4. How does the translation *4 units right and 6 units down* relate the coordinates of the new figure to the coordinates of the original figure?

5. Without graphing, identify the coordinates that result from a translation of the original figure 10 units right and 3 units up.

6. Suppose the original figure is translated so that two vertices have coordinates (0, 0) and (2, 0). Find two possible translations. Write the coordinates for the vertices of each translated figure.

7. **Critical Thinking** What translations of the original figure will result in a tessellation?

8. **Open-Ended** Design another simple figure that will tessellate the plane. Describe the translations needed to fill the plane.

Vocabulary Tip

A <u>tessellation</u> is a repeating pattern of figures that covers a plane, without gaps or overlaps.

You can write the vertices of a figure as a matrix. For example, the matrix below represents the vertices of figure $ABCD$.

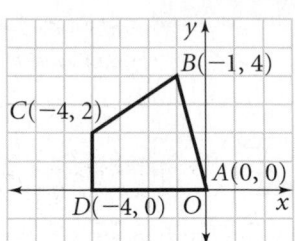

$$\begin{array}{c} \\ x\text{-coordinate} \\ y\text{-coordinate} \end{array} \begin{array}{cccc} A & B & C & D \\ \end{array} \\ \begin{bmatrix} 0 & -1 & -4 & -4 \\ 0 & 4 & 2 & 0 \end{bmatrix}$$

A change made to a figure is a transformation of the figure. The transformed figure is the **image**. The original figure is the **preimage**. A translation (Lesson 2–6) is a transformation that slides a figure without changing the size or shape of the figure. You can use matrix addition to translate all the vertices of a figure in one step.

1 EXAMPLE Translating a Figure

Geometry Quadrilateral $ABCD$ above has vertices $A(0,0)$, $B(-1,4)$, $C(-4,2)$, and $D(-4,0)$. Use a matrix to find the coordinates of the vertices of the image translated 6 units right and 2 units down. Then graph $ABCD$ and its image $A'B'C'D'$.

Vocabulary Tip

Read the notation
A' as "A prime,"
A'' as "A double prime,"
and so on. The prime symbol tells you that A' is related to A in some special way.

Vertices of the Quadrilateral　　　**Translation Matrix**　　　**Vertices of the Image**

Add 6 to each *x*-coordinate.

$$\begin{array}{cccc} A & B & C & D \\ \end{array} \\ \begin{bmatrix} 0 & -1 & -4 & -4 \\ 0 & 4 & 2 & 0 \end{bmatrix} \; + \; \begin{bmatrix} 6 & 6 & 6 & 6 \\ -2 & -2 & -2 & -2 \end{bmatrix} \; = \; \begin{array}{cccc} A' & B' & C' & D' \\ \end{array} \\ \begin{bmatrix} 6 & 5 & 2 & 2 \\ -2 & 2 & 0 & -2 \end{bmatrix}$$

Subtract 2 from each *y*-coordinate.

The vertices of the image are $A'(6,-2)$, $B'(5,2)$, $C'(2,0)$, and $D'(2,-2)$.

Graph both quadrilaterals.

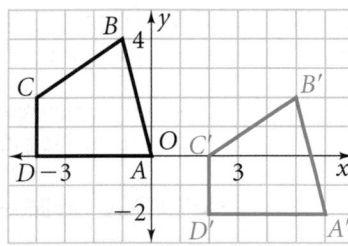

✓ Quick Check

1 **a. Critical Thinking** Explain how to translate quadrilateral $A'B'C'D'$ from Example 1 so that its image is quadrilateral $ABCD$.

b. What matrix would you use to translate the vertices of a pentagon 3 units left and 2 units up?

c. Use your answer to part (b) to translate the pentagon with vertices $(0,-5)$, $(-1,-1)$, $(-5,0)$, $(1,3)$, and $(4,0)$. Find the coordinates of the vertices of the image. Graph the preimage and the image.

Graphing Calculator Hint

Enter the preimage and translation matrices as [A] and [B]. Use matrix addition to find the coordinates of the image.

A **dilation** is a transformation that changes the size of a figure. When the center of the dilation is the origin, you can use scalar multiplication to find the coordinates of the vertices of an image. All dilations in this book are centered at the origin.

2 EXAMPLE **Real-World** **Connection**

Graphic Arts An artist sends you a photo electronically. You increase the photo dimensions by a factor of 1.2. Find the coordinates of the enlargement's vertices.

Write a matrix to represent the coordinates of the vertices, which are at $(0, 0)$, $(0, 5.875)$, $(9.75, 5.875)$, and $(9.75, 0)$. Then multiply by the factor 1.2.

$$1.2 \begin{bmatrix} 0 & 0 & 9.75 & 9.75 \\ 0 & 5.875 & 5.875 & 0 \end{bmatrix} = \begin{bmatrix} 0 & 0 & 11.7 & 11.7 \\ 0 & 7.05 & 7.05 & 0 \end{bmatrix}$$

● The new coordinates are $(0, 0)$, $(0, 7.05)$, $(11.7, 7.05)$, and $(11.7, 0)$.

 **Quick Check** ❷ The coordinates of the vertices of figure ABC are $A(-5, 0)$, $B(8, -1)$, and $C(4, 5)$. Find the coordinates of each image under the following dilations. Then graph each image and its preimage on the same coordinate plane.

a. 4 **b.** $\frac{1}{5}$ **c.** -1.5

---

2 **Reflections and Rotations with Matrices**

A reflection, or *flip,* is a transformation that results in symmetry on the coordinate plane. A reflection maps a point in the plane to its mirror image, using a specific line as the mirror. The lines used in this book are the *x*-axis (see Lesson 2-6), the *y*-axis, and the lines $y = x$ and $y = -x$.

You can use matrix multiplication to graph reflections in the coordinate plane.

 Key Concepts

Properties	**Matrices for Reflections in the Coordinate Plane**		
Reflection in the *y*-axis	Reflection in the *x*-axis	Reflection in the line $y = x$	Reflection in the line $y = -x$
$\begin{bmatrix} -1 & 0 \\ 0 & 1 \end{bmatrix}$	$\begin{bmatrix} 1 & 0 \\ 0 & -1 \end{bmatrix}$	$\begin{bmatrix} 0 & 1 \\ 1 & 0 \end{bmatrix}$	$\begin{bmatrix} 0 & -1 \\ -1 & 0 \end{bmatrix}$

3 EXAMPLE Reflecting a Figure

Reflect the triangle with coordinates $A(0, 0)$, $B(2, 5)$, and $C(-2, 3)$ in each line. Then graph each pair of triangles on the same coordinate plane.

a. y-axis

$$\begin{bmatrix} -1 & 0 \\ 0 & 1 \end{bmatrix} \begin{bmatrix} 0 & 2 & -2 \\ 0 & 5 & 3 \end{bmatrix} = \begin{bmatrix} 0 & -2 & 2 \\ 0 & 5 & 3 \end{bmatrix}$$

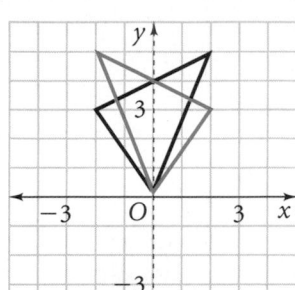

b. x-axis

$$\begin{bmatrix} 1 & 0 \\ 0 & -1 \end{bmatrix} \begin{bmatrix} 0 & 2 & -2 \\ 0 & 5 & 3 \end{bmatrix} = \begin{bmatrix} 0 & 2 & -2 \\ 0 & -5 & -3 \end{bmatrix}$$

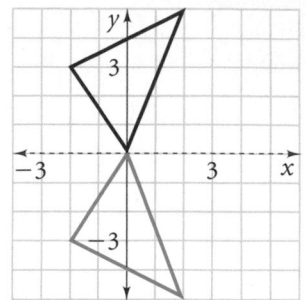

c. $y = x$

$$\begin{bmatrix} 0 & 1 \\ 1 & 0 \end{bmatrix} \begin{bmatrix} 0 & 2 & -2 \\ 0 & 5 & 3 \end{bmatrix} = \begin{bmatrix} 0 & 5 & 3 \\ 0 & 2 & -2 \end{bmatrix}$$

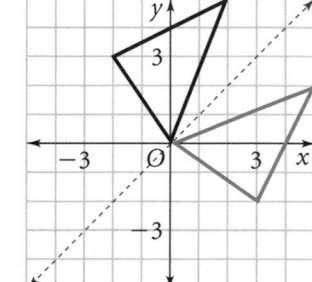

d. $y = -x$

$$\begin{bmatrix} 0 & -1 \\ -1 & 0 \end{bmatrix} \begin{bmatrix} 0 & 2 & -2 \\ 0 & 5 & 3 \end{bmatrix} = \begin{bmatrix} 0 & -5 & -3 \\ 0 & -2 & 2 \end{bmatrix}$$

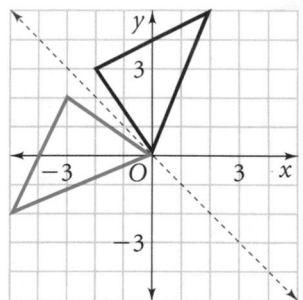

 Quick Check **3** Reflect the triangle with coordinates $D(-3, 0)$, $E(-4, 4)$, and $F(1, 1)$ in each line. Then graph each pair of triangles on the same coordinate plane.
a. y-axis **b.** x-axis **c.** $y = x$ **d.** $y = -x$

A **rotation** is a transformation that turns a figure about a fixed point called the **center of rotation.** You can rotate a figure as much as 360 degrees. In this book, all rotations are counterclockwise about the origin.

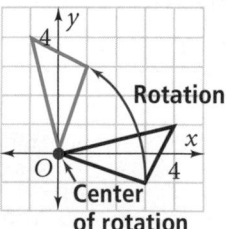

Key Concepts

Properties	Matrices for Rotations in the Coordinate Plane		
Rotation of 90°	Rotation of 180°	Rotation of 270°	Rotation of 360°
$\begin{bmatrix} 0 & -1 \\ 1 & 0 \end{bmatrix}$	$\begin{bmatrix} -1 & 0 \\ 0 & -1 \end{bmatrix}$	$\begin{bmatrix} 0 & 1 \\ -1 & 0 \end{bmatrix}$	$\begin{bmatrix} 1 & 0 \\ 0 & 1 \end{bmatrix}$

4 EXAMPLE **Rotating a Figure**

Rotate the triangle with coordinates $A(0, 0)$, $B(2, 5)$, and $C(-2, 3)$. Then graph each pair of triangles on the same coordinate plane.

a. 90°

$$\begin{bmatrix} 0 & -1 \\ 1 & 0 \end{bmatrix} \begin{bmatrix} 0 & 2 & -2 \\ 0 & 5 & 3 \end{bmatrix} = \begin{bmatrix} 0 & -5 & -3 \\ 0 & 2 & -2 \end{bmatrix}$$

b. 180°

$$\begin{bmatrix} -1 & 0 \\ 0 & -1 \end{bmatrix} \begin{bmatrix} 0 & 2 & -2 \\ 0 & 5 & 3 \end{bmatrix} = \begin{bmatrix} 0 & -2 & 2 \\ 0 & -5 & -3 \end{bmatrix}$$

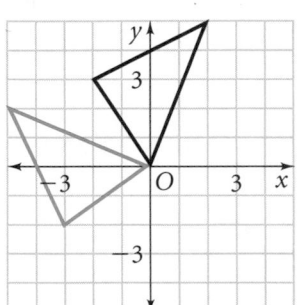

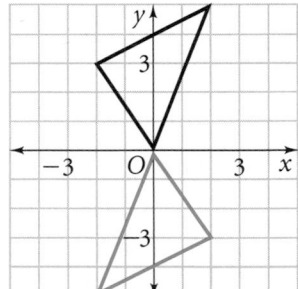

c. 270°

$$\begin{bmatrix} 0 & 1 \\ -1 & 0 \end{bmatrix} \begin{bmatrix} 0 & 2 & -2 \\ 0 & 5 & 3 \end{bmatrix} = \begin{bmatrix} 0 & 5 & 3 \\ 0 & -2 & 2 \end{bmatrix}$$

d. 360°

$$\begin{bmatrix} 1 & 0 \\ 0 & 1 \end{bmatrix} \begin{bmatrix} 0 & 2 & -2 \\ 0 & 5 & 3 \end{bmatrix} = \begin{bmatrix} 0 & 2 & -2 \\ 0 & 5 & 3 \end{bmatrix}$$

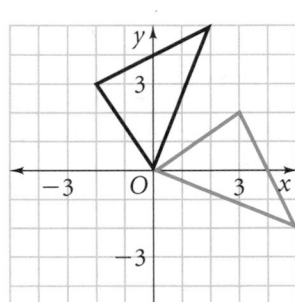

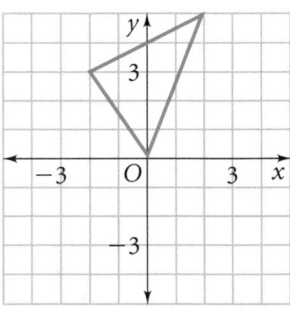

Real-World Connection

The windmill sails form a figure with 90° rotational symmetry.

Quick Check ④ Rotate the quadrilateral with coordinates $A(1, 1)$, $B(3, 1)$, $C(6, 4)$, and $D(1, 3)$. Then graph each pair of quadrilaterals on the same coordinate plane.

a. 90°　　　　**b.** 180°　　　　**c.** 270°　　　　**d.** 360°

EXERCISES

For more exercises, see *Extra Skill and Word Problem Practice.*

Practice and Problem Solving

Ⓐ Practice by Example

Example 1
(page 192)

Use matrix addition to find the coordinates of each image after a translation of 3 units left and 5 units up. If possible, graph each pair of figures on the same coordinate plane.

1. $A(1, -3)$, $B(1, 1)$, $C(5, 1)$, $D(5, -3)$

2. $G(0, 0)$, $H(4, 4)$, $I(4, -4)$, $J(8, 0)$

3. $J(-10, 2)$, $K(-16, a)$, $L(12, -5)$

4. $R(9, 3)$, $S(3, 6)$, $T(3, 3)$, $U(6, -3)$

Example 2
(page 193)

Graph each figure and its image after the given dilation.

5. $\begin{bmatrix} 0 & 2 & 5 & 8 \\ 0 & 4 & 5 & 1 \end{bmatrix}$, 2

6. $\begin{bmatrix} -7 & -3 & 4 \\ -5 & 4 & 0 \end{bmatrix}$, 0.5

7. $\begin{bmatrix} 0 & -2 & -5 \\ 0 & 0 & 5 \end{bmatrix}$, $\frac{9}{10}$

8. $\begin{bmatrix} -10 & -5 & 0 & 5 & 10 \\ 8 & 16 & 20 & 16 & 8 \end{bmatrix}$, $\frac{1}{4}$

9. $\begin{bmatrix} -8 & 2 & 3 & 1 & -2 \\ 6 & 4 & 0 & -4 & 0 \end{bmatrix}$, 1.5

Example 3
(page 194)

Graph each figure and its image after reflection in the given line.

10. $\begin{bmatrix} 0 & -3 & 5 \\ 0 & 1 & 2 \end{bmatrix}; y = x$ 　　11. $\begin{bmatrix} -1 & 0 & 5 \\ -1 & 5 & 0 \end{bmatrix}; y\text{-axis}$ 　　12. $\begin{bmatrix} -3 & -5 & -10 \\ 4 & 7 & 1 \end{bmatrix}, x\text{-axis}$

Find the coordinates of each image after reflection in the given line.

13. $\begin{bmatrix} 3 & 6 & 3 & 6 \\ -3 & 3 & 3 & -3 \end{bmatrix}; y = -x$ 　　14. $\begin{bmatrix} 0 & 4 & 8 & 6 \\ 0 & 4 & 4 & 2 \end{bmatrix}; x\text{-axis}$

15. $\begin{bmatrix} 1 & 2 & 3 & 4 & 2.5 \\ 3 & 2 & 2 & 3 & 5 \end{bmatrix}; y = x$ 　　16. $\begin{bmatrix} -1 & -2 & -4 & -6 & -2 \\ -4 & 0 & 0 & -3 & -4 \end{bmatrix}; x\text{-axis}$

Example 4
(page 195)

Graph each figure and its image after the given rotation.

17. $\begin{bmatrix} 0 & -3 & 5 \\ 0 & 1 & 2 \end{bmatrix}; 90°$ 　　18. $\begin{bmatrix} -1 & 0 & 5 \\ -1 & 5 & 0 \end{bmatrix}; 180°$ 　　19. $\begin{bmatrix} -5 & 6 & 0 \\ -1 & 2 & 4 \end{bmatrix}; 90°$

Find the coordinates of each image after the given rotation.

20. $\begin{bmatrix} 3 & 6 & 3 & 6 \\ -3 & 3 & 3 & -3 \end{bmatrix}; 270°$ 　　21. $\begin{bmatrix} 0 & 4 & 8 & 6 \\ 0 & 4 & 4 & 2 \end{bmatrix}; 360°$

22. $\begin{bmatrix} 1 & 2 & 3 & 4 & 2.5 \\ 3 & 2 & 2 & 3 & 5 \end{bmatrix}; 180°$ 　　23. $\begin{bmatrix} -1 & -2 & -4 & -6 & -2 \\ -4 & 0 & 0 & -3 & -4 \end{bmatrix}; 270°$

B Apply Your Skills 　 **Geometry** Each matrix represents the vertices of a polygon. Translate each figure 5 units left and 1 unit up. Express your answer as a matrix.

24. $\begin{bmatrix} -3 & -3 & 2 & 2 \\ -2 & -4 & -2 & -4 \end{bmatrix}$ 　25. $\begin{bmatrix} -3 & 0 & 3 & 0 \\ -9 & -6 & -9 & -12 \end{bmatrix}$ 　26. $\begin{bmatrix} 0 & 1 & -4 \\ 0 & 3 & 5 \end{bmatrix}$

For Exercises 27–34, use △ABC. Write the coordinates of each image in matrix form.

27. a dilation four times the original size
28. a translation 2 units left and 3 units down
29. a dilation half the original size
30. a translation 1 unit right and 7 units up
31. a rotation of 90°
32. a reflection in $y = x$
33. a rotation of 180°
34. a reflection in the x-axis

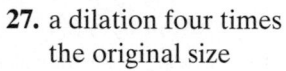

35. **Multiple Choice** What is true about $\begin{bmatrix} -3 & 0 \\ 0 & -3 \end{bmatrix}\begin{bmatrix} 1 & -2 & 4 \\ 1 & -1 & 2 \end{bmatrix}$ and $-3\begin{bmatrix} 1 & -2 & 4 \\ 1 & -1 & 2 \end{bmatrix}$

　Ⓐ They are equal matrices. 　　　　Ⓑ They are opposite matrices.
　Ⓒ Both are matrices for reflection. 　Ⓓ Neither product exists.

36. **Writing** Graph $\begin{bmatrix} 9 & 10 & 6 \\ 1 & -3 & -2 \end{bmatrix}$ and $2\begin{bmatrix} 9 & 10 & 6 \\ 1 & -3 & -2 \end{bmatrix}$. Compare the graphs.
　Generalize how a dilation changes a graph.

Vocabulary Tip

A <u>tessellation</u> is a repeating pattern of figures that covers a plane, without gaps or overlap.

37. **Geometry** Create a tessellation based on the quadrilateral $\begin{bmatrix} 0 & -3 & -5 & 0 \\ 1 & 3 & -1 & -1 \end{bmatrix}$.
　Translate the quadrilateral using $\begin{bmatrix} 5 & 5 & 5 & 5 \\ 2 & 2 & 2 & 2 \end{bmatrix}$ and $\begin{bmatrix} 3 & 3 & 3 & 3 \\ -4 & -4 & -4 & -4 \end{bmatrix}$.

38. **Writing** Explain why you might want to represent a transformation as a matrix.

Use matrices to represent the vertices of graph *f* and graph *g*. Name each transformation.

39.
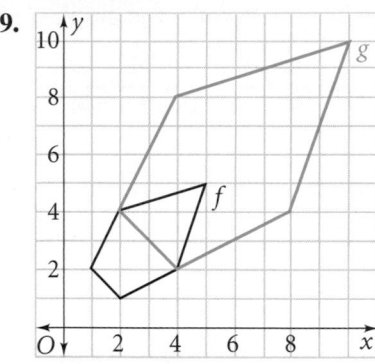

40.
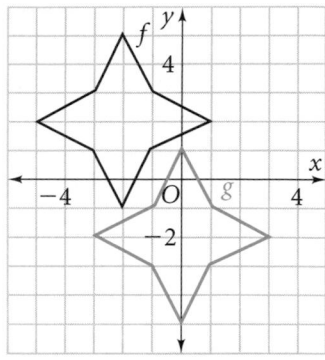

41.
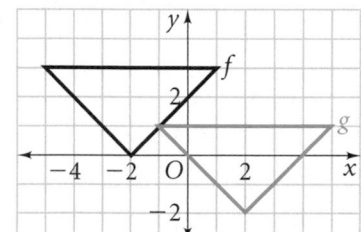

42.
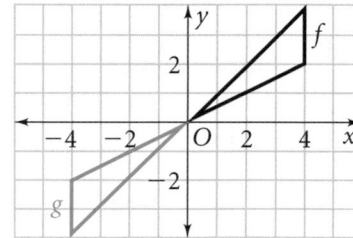

nline
Homework Video Tutor
Visit: PHSchool.com
Web Code: age-0404

Graph each triangle and its translation on the same coordinate plane.

43. $\begin{bmatrix} 0 & 2 & 3 \\ 0 & 0 & 5 \end{bmatrix}$; 3 units right, 4 units down **44.** $\begin{bmatrix} -5 & 3 & 4 \\ 5 & 1 & -4 \end{bmatrix}$; 2 units left, 5 units up

C Challenge 🌐 **45. Architecture** Use the pattern of brown tiles shown.

 a. Copy the graph. Mark scales on the axes so that the dimensions of the square tiles are 1 unit by 1 unit.

 b. Write a matrix for the translation of tile *ABCD* to tile *A′B′C′D′*. What are the coordinates of the vertices of the preimage and the image?

 c. A brown tile is 6 units right and 6 units down from tile *ABCD*. Write a matrix to represent the coordinates of its vertices.

 d. A tile has vertices at $(-6, 9)$, $(-6, 8)$, $(-7, 9)$, and $(-7, 8)$. What translation of tile *ABCD* results in these coordinates?

🔲 **Geometry** Each matrix represents the vertices of a polygon. Write a matrix to represent the vertices of the image after each transformation.

46. $\begin{bmatrix} -3 & 0.5 & -5 \\ 0 & 3 & 3 \end{bmatrix}$; dilation of 2 **47.** $\begin{bmatrix} 4 & 7 & 10 \\ 0 & 2 & 0 \end{bmatrix}$; rotation of 270°

48. $\begin{bmatrix} 17 & 6 & 6 & 2 \\ 5 & 10 & 2 & 6 \end{bmatrix}$; reflection in $y = x$ **49.** $\begin{bmatrix} 3 & 4.5 & 5 & 3.5 \\ 3 & 1.5 & 2 & 4 \end{bmatrix}$; rotation of 90°

50. Let the matrix $\begin{bmatrix} x \\ y \end{bmatrix}$ represent points on the graph $y = |x|$.

   a. Complete the table. Sketch the graph.

x	−3	−2	−1	0	1	2	3
y	■	■	■	■	■	■	■

   b. Critical Thinking What does the matrix addition $\begin{bmatrix} x \\ y \end{bmatrix} + \begin{bmatrix} -1 \\ 2 \end{bmatrix}$ represent?
Show your answer on your graph from part (a).

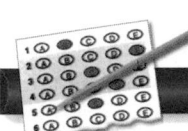

Test Prep

Multiple Choice

51. What are the coordinates of $X(5, 1)$, $Y(-5, -3)$, and $Z(-1, 3)$ reflected in the line $y = x$?
   A. $X'(-5, -1)$, $Y'(5, 3)$, $Z'(1, -3)$ **B.** $X'(1, 5)$, $Y'(-3, -5)$, $Z'(3, -1)$
   C. $X'(-1, -5)$, $Y'(3, 5)$, $Z'(-3, 1)$ **D.** $X'(5, 1)$, $Y'(-5, -3)$, $Z'(-1, 3)$

52. Reflection in which line takes the figure with vertices $A(0, 0)$, $B(-2, 4)$, $C(-4, 2)$, and $D(-3, 0)$ to $A'(0, 0)$, $B'(-2, -4)$, $C'(-4, -2)$, and $D'(-3, 0)$?
   F. x-axis   **G.** y-axis   **H.** $y = x$ **J.** $y = -x$

Short Response

53. Each vertex of the triangle at the right is transformed by *right 3, up 2* and then by *left 5, up 4*. What is a matrix for the combined transformation? What are the coordinates of the vertices of the final triangle?

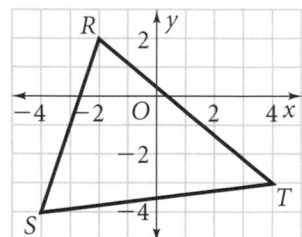

Extended Response

54. A quadrilateral has coordinates $\begin{bmatrix} 3 & 4 & -3 & -4 \\ 5 & 4 & -4 & -3 \end{bmatrix}$.
   a. Graph the quadrilateral.
   b. Find the product $\begin{bmatrix} 0 & -1 \\ 1 & 0 \end{bmatrix}\begin{bmatrix} 3 & 4 & -3 & -4 \\ 5 & 4 & -4 & -3 \end{bmatrix}$.
   c. Graph the result as a new quadrilateral.
   d. What is the relationship between the quadrilaterals in parts (a) and (c)?

Mixed Review

Lesson 4-3

If possible, find the dimensions of each product matrix; then find each product. If the product is not defined, explain why not.

55. $\begin{bmatrix} 1 & 0 & -5 \\ 2 & -1 & 6 \end{bmatrix}\begin{bmatrix} 2 & 4 & -2 \\ 0 & 10 & 4 \\ 0 & 1 & -7 \end{bmatrix}$ **56.** $\begin{bmatrix} 0 & 7 & k & 5 \\ 0 & 6 & 0 & 5 \end{bmatrix}\begin{bmatrix} 9 & -1 & 3 & 0 \\ 7 & 0 & 7 & 0 \end{bmatrix}$

Lesson 3-5

Graph each equation.

57. $x + y - z = 5$ **58.** $2x - y + 3z = 12$ **59.** $-x + 4y - z = -6$

Lesson 2-1

Make a mapping diagram for each relation. Determine whether it is a function.

60. $\{(-2, 4), (-1, 1), (0, 0), (1, 1), (2, 4)\}$ **61.** $\{(27, -2), (3, -1), (0, 0), (3, 1), (27, 2)\}$

62. $\{(-2, 15), (-1, 1), (0, -3), (1, 3), (2, 15)\}$ **63.** $\{(-3, 8), (-2, 1), (1, -2), (0, -1), (1, 4)\}$

4-5

2 × 2 Matrices, Determinants, and Inverses

What You'll Learn

- To evaluate determinants of 2 × 2 matrices and find inverse matrices
- To use inverse matrices in solving matrix equations

. . . And Why

To predict cell phone ownership, as in Example 5

✓ **Check Skills You'll Need**

GO **for Help** Skills Handbook page 873

Simplify each group of expressions.

1. a. $3(4)$ **b.** $2(6)$ **c.** $3(4) - 2(6)$

2. a. $3(-4)$ **b.** $2(-6)$ **c.** $3(-4) - 2(-6)$

3. a. $-3(-4)$ **b.** $2(-6)$ **c.** $-3(-4) - 2(-6)$

4. a. $-3(4)$ **b.** $-2(-6)$ **c.** $-3(4) - (-2)(-6)$

🔊 **New Vocabulary** • square matrix • multiplicative identity matrix
  • multiplicative inverse of a matrix • determinant

---

1   Evaluating Determinants of 2 × 2 Matrices

A **square matrix** is a matrix with the same number of columns as rows.

For any real number a, the number 1 is the multiplicative identity of a, since $a \cdot 1 = 1 \cdot a = a$. Square matrices also have a multiplicative identity.

 Key Concepts

Definition	**Multiplicative Identity Matrix**

For an $n \times n$ square matrix, the **multiplicative identity matrix** is an $n \times n$ square matrix I, or I_n, with 1's along the main diagonal and 0's elsewhere.

$$I_2 = \begin{bmatrix} 1 & 0 \\ 0 & 1 \end{bmatrix}, \qquad I_3 = \begin{bmatrix} 1 & 0 & 0 \\ 0 & 1 & 0 \\ 0 & 0 & 1 \end{bmatrix}, \qquad \text{and so forth}$$

If the product of the real numbers a and b is 1, then a and b are multiplicative inverses. Some, but not all, square matrices have multiplicative inverses.

 Key Concepts

Definition	**Multiplicative Inverse of a Matrix**

If A and X are $n \times n$ matrices, and $AX = XA = I$, then X is the multiplicative inverse of A, written A^{-1}.

$$AA^{-1} = A^{-1}A = I$$

If B is the multiplicative inverse of A, then A is the multiplicative inverse of B. To show that A and B are multiplicative inverses, show that $AB = I$ or that $BA = I$.

1 EXAMPLE Verifying Inverses

Show that B is the multiplicative inverse of A.

$$A = \begin{bmatrix} 2 & 3 \\ 1 & 2 \end{bmatrix} \qquad B = \begin{bmatrix} 2 & -3 \\ -1 & 2 \end{bmatrix}$$

$$AB = \begin{bmatrix} 2 & 3 \\ 1 & 2 \end{bmatrix}\begin{bmatrix} 2 & -3 \\ -1 & 2 \end{bmatrix} = \begin{bmatrix} 2(2) + 3(-1) & 2(-3) + 3(2) \\ 1(2) + 2(-1) & 1(-3) + 2(2) \end{bmatrix} = \begin{bmatrix} 1 & 0 \\ 0 & 1 \end{bmatrix}$$

$AB = I$, so B is the multiplicative inverse of A. A is also the multiplicative inverse of B.

Check $BA = \begin{bmatrix} 2 & -3 \\ -1 & 2 \end{bmatrix}\begin{bmatrix} 2 & 3 \\ 1 & 2 \end{bmatrix} = \begin{bmatrix} 2(2) + (-3)(1) & 2(3) + (-3)(2) \\ -1(2) + 2(1) & -1(3) + 2(2) \end{bmatrix} = \begin{bmatrix} 1 & 0 \\ 0 & 1 \end{bmatrix}$ ✔

✓ Quick Check **1** Show that the matrices are multiplicative inverses.

a. $\begin{bmatrix} 2 & 1 \\ 2.5 & 1 \end{bmatrix}$ and $\begin{bmatrix} -2 & 2 \\ 5 & -4 \end{bmatrix}$ **b.** $\begin{bmatrix} -2 & -5 \\ -3 & -8 \end{bmatrix}$ and $\begin{bmatrix} -8 & 5 \\ 3 & -2 \end{bmatrix}$

Every square matrix with real-number elements has a real-number determinant. Determinants can help you find inverses.

Write	**Read**	**Evaluate**
$\downarrow$	$\downarrow$	$\downarrow$
$A = \begin{bmatrix} a & b \\ c & d \end{bmatrix}$ $\det A = \begin{vmatrix} a & b \\ c & d \end{vmatrix}$	the determinant of A	$\begin{vmatrix} a & b \\ c & d \end{vmatrix} = ad - bc$

Key Concepts

Definition	**Determinant of a 2 × 2 Matrix**

The **determinant** of a 2 × 2 matrix $\begin{bmatrix} a & b \\ c & d \end{bmatrix}$ is $ad - bc$.

Symbols for the determinant of a matrix
$\downarrow \qquad \qquad \downarrow$

$\det A \qquad \begin{vmatrix} a & b \\ c & d \end{vmatrix}$

2 EXAMPLE Evaluating the Determinant of a 2 × 2 Matrix

Evaluate each determinant.

a. $\det \begin{bmatrix} -3 & 4 \\ 2 & -5 \end{bmatrix} = \begin{vmatrix} -3 & 4 \\ 2 & -5 \end{vmatrix} = (-3)(-5) - (4)(2) = 15 - 8 = 7$

b. $\det \begin{bmatrix} 2 & -3 \\ 3 & -2 \end{bmatrix} = \begin{vmatrix} 2 & -3 \\ 3 & -2 \end{vmatrix} = (2)(-2) - (-3)(3) = -4 - (-9) = 5$

c. $\det \begin{bmatrix} a & 0 \\ 0 & a \end{bmatrix} = \begin{vmatrix} a & 0 \\ 0 & a \end{vmatrix} = a^2 - 0 = a^2$

✓ Quick Check **2** Evaluate the determinant of each matrix.

a. $\begin{bmatrix} 4 & 2 \\ 4 & 2 \end{bmatrix}$ **b.** $\begin{bmatrix} 8 & 7 \\ 2 & 3 \end{bmatrix}$ **c.** $\begin{bmatrix} k & 3 \\ 3 - k & -3 \end{bmatrix}$

The following test will help you determine whether a 2 × 2 matrix has an inverse. The test will also help you find the inverse, if it exists.

Key Concepts

Property	Inverse of a 2 × 2 Matrix

Let $A = \begin{bmatrix} a & b \\ c & d \end{bmatrix}$. If $\det A = 0$, then A has no inverse.

If $\det A \neq 0$, then $A^{-1} = \frac{1}{\det A} \begin{bmatrix} d & -b \\ -c & a \end{bmatrix} = \frac{1}{ad-bc} \begin{bmatrix} d & -b \\ -c & a \end{bmatrix}$.

3 EXAMPLE Finding an Inverse Matrix

Determine whether each matrix has an inverse. If an inverse matrix exists, find it.

a. $M = \begin{bmatrix} -2 & 2 \\ 5 & -4 \end{bmatrix}$ $ad - bc = (-2)(-4) - (2)(5)$ **Find det M.**

$= -2$ **Simplify.**

Since $\det M \neq 0$, the inverse of M exists.

Change signs.

$M^{-1} = \begin{bmatrix} -2 & 2 \\ 5 & -4 \end{bmatrix}^{-1}$

Switch positions.

$= \frac{1}{\det M} \begin{bmatrix} -4 & -2 \\ -5 & -2 \end{bmatrix}$ **Use the determinant to write the inverse.**

$= \frac{1}{-2} \begin{bmatrix} -4 & -2 \\ -5 & -2 \end{bmatrix}$ **Substitute −2 for det M.**

$= \begin{bmatrix} 2 & 1 \\ 2.5 & 1 \end{bmatrix}$ **Multiply.**

b. $N = \begin{bmatrix} 3 & 9 \\ 2 & 6 \end{bmatrix}$ $ad - bc = (3)(6) - (9)(2)$ **Find det N.**

$= 0$ **Simplify.**

Since $\det N = 0$, the inverse of N does *not* exist.

Quick Check ❸ Determine whether each matrix has an inverse. If an inverse matrix exists, find it.

a. $\begin{bmatrix} 2 & 4 \\ 1 & 3 \end{bmatrix}$ **b.** $\begin{bmatrix} 0.5 & 2.3 \\ 3 & 7.2 \end{bmatrix}$

---

2   Using Inverse Matrices to Solve Equations

If the inverse of matrix A exists, you can use it to solve matrix equations of the form $AX = B$. Multiply each side of the equation by A^{-1} to find X.

$AX = B$

$A^{-1}(AX) = A^{-1}B$ **Multiply each side by A^{-1}.**

$(A^{-1}A)X = A^{-1}B$ **Associative Property of Multiplication**

$IX = A^{-1}B$ **definition of multiplicative inverse**

$X = A^{-1}B$ **definition of multiplicative identity**

4 EXAMPLE Solving a Matrix Equation

Solve $\begin{bmatrix} -2 & -5 \\ 1 & 3 \end{bmatrix} X = \begin{bmatrix} -2 \\ 2 \end{bmatrix}$ for the matrix X.

The matrix equation has the form $AX = B$. First find A^{-1}.

$A^{-1} = \dfrac{1}{ad - bc}\begin{bmatrix} d & -b \\ -c & a \end{bmatrix} = \dfrac{1}{-2(3) - (-5)1}\begin{bmatrix} 3 & 5 \\ -1 & -2 \end{bmatrix}$ **Use the definition of inverse.**

$\qquad\qquad\qquad = \begin{bmatrix} -3 & -5 \\ 1 & 2 \end{bmatrix}$ **Simplify.**

Use the equation $X = A^{-1}B$. $X = \begin{bmatrix} -3 & -5 \\ 1 & 2 \end{bmatrix}\begin{bmatrix} -2 \\ 2 \end{bmatrix}$ **Substitute.**

$\qquad\qquad\qquad = \begin{bmatrix} -3(-2) + -5(2) \\ 1(-2) + 2(2) \end{bmatrix} = \begin{bmatrix} -4 \\ 2 \end{bmatrix}$ **Multiply and simplify.**

Check $\begin{bmatrix} -2 & -5 \\ 1 & 3 \end{bmatrix} X = \begin{bmatrix} -2 \\ 2 \end{bmatrix}$ **Use the original equation.**

$\qquad\qquad \begin{bmatrix} -2 & -5 \\ 1 & 3 \end{bmatrix}\begin{bmatrix} -4 \\ 2 \end{bmatrix} \overset{?}{=} \begin{bmatrix} -2 \\ 2 \end{bmatrix}$ **Substitute.**

$\qquad\qquad \begin{bmatrix} -2(-4) + (-5)(2) \\ 1(-4) + 3(2) \end{bmatrix} \overset{?}{=} \begin{bmatrix} -2 \\ 2 \end{bmatrix}$ **Multiply.**

$\qquad\qquad\qquad\qquad \begin{bmatrix} -2 \\ 2 \end{bmatrix} = \begin{bmatrix} -2 \\ 2 \end{bmatrix}$ ✓   **Simplify.**

✓ Quick Check   **4** Solve each matrix equation in the form $AX = B$. Use the equation $X = A^{-1}B$.

a. $\begin{bmatrix} 3 & -4 \\ 4 & -5 \end{bmatrix} X = \begin{bmatrix} 0 & -22 \\ 0 & -28 \end{bmatrix}$ **b.** $\begin{bmatrix} 7 & 5 \\ 3 & 2 \end{bmatrix} X = \begin{bmatrix} -9 \\ -4 \end{bmatrix}$

You can use matrices to make predictions about trends.

5 EXAMPLE Real-World  Connection

Communications The diagram shows the trends in cell phone ownership over four consecutive years.

a. Write a matrix to represent the changes (or transitions) in cell phone use.

$\qquad\qquad$ From
$\qquad$ No cell   Cell

To $\quad$ No cell $\begin{bmatrix} 0.57 & 0.13 \\ 0.43 & 0.87 \end{bmatrix}$ **Write the percents**
$\qquad\quad$ Cell $\qquad\qquad\qquad$ **as decimals.**

b. In a stable population of 16,000 people, 9927 own cell phones, while 6073 do not. Assume the trends continue. Predict the number of people who will own cell phones next year.

No cell $\begin{bmatrix} 6073 \\ 9927 \end{bmatrix}$ **Write the information in a matrix.**
$\quad$ Cell

$\begin{bmatrix} 0.57 & 0.13 \\ 0.43 & 0.87 \end{bmatrix}\begin{bmatrix} 6073 \\ 9927 \end{bmatrix} \approx \begin{bmatrix} 4752 \\ 11{,}248 \end{bmatrix}$ **Use the transition matrix from part (a). Multiply.**

Next year, about 11,248 people in the population will own cell phones.

Real-World  Connection

Martin Cooper invented the portable cellular radio telephone in 1973.

c. Use the inverse of the matrix from part (a) to find the number of people who owned cell phones last year.

$$\begin{bmatrix} 0.57 & 0.13 \\ 0.43 & 0.87 \end{bmatrix}^{-1}\begin{bmatrix} 6073 \\ 9927 \end{bmatrix} = \begin{bmatrix} 9075 \\ 6925 \end{bmatrix}$$

Last year, 6925 people owned cell phones.

 **Quick Check** **5** **a. Critical Thinking** Find the percent of the population owning cell phones last year, this year, and next year. Estimate the percent two years from now.
b. Use the answer to Example 5, part (b), and the transition matrix to predict the number of people who will own cell phones two years from now.
c. Use the answer to Example 5, part (c), and the inverse of the transition matrix to estimate the number of people who owned cell phones two years ago.

EXERCISES

For more exercises, see *Extra Skill and Word Problem Practice*.

Practice and Problem Solving

A **Practice by Example**

 GO for Help

Example 1
(page 200)

Show that the matrices are multiplicative inverses.

1. $\begin{bmatrix} 3 & 2 \\ 4 & 3 \end{bmatrix}, \begin{bmatrix} 3 & -2 \\ -4 & 3 \end{bmatrix}$

2. $\begin{bmatrix} -3 & 7 \\ -2 & 5 \end{bmatrix}, \begin{bmatrix} -5 & 7 \\ -2 & 3 \end{bmatrix}$

3. $\begin{bmatrix} \frac{1}{5} & -\frac{1}{10} \\ 0 & \frac{1}{4} \end{bmatrix}, \begin{bmatrix} 5 & 2 \\ 0 & 4 \end{bmatrix}$

Example 2
(page 200)

Evaluate the determinant of each matrix.

4. $\begin{bmatrix} 7 & 2 \\ 0 & -3 \end{bmatrix}$

5. $\begin{bmatrix} 6 & 2 \\ -6 & -2 \end{bmatrix}$

6. $\begin{bmatrix} 0 & 0.5 \\ 1.5 & 2 \end{bmatrix}$

7. $\begin{bmatrix} \frac{1}{2} & \frac{2}{3} \\ \frac{3}{5} & \frac{1}{4} \end{bmatrix}$

8. $\begin{bmatrix} -1 & 3 \\ 5 & 2 \end{bmatrix}$

9. $\begin{bmatrix} -2 & 0 \\ 2 & -1 \end{bmatrix}$

10. $\begin{bmatrix} 5 & 3 \\ -2 & 1 \end{bmatrix}$

11. $\begin{bmatrix} 5 & 2 \\ 1 & 3 \end{bmatrix}$

12. $\begin{bmatrix} 2 & -1 \\ 5 & -4 \end{bmatrix}$

13. $\begin{bmatrix} -4 & 3 \\ 2 & 0 \end{bmatrix}$

Example 3
(page 201)

Determine whether each matrix has an inverse. If an inverse matrix exists, find it.

14. $\begin{bmatrix} 2 & -1 \\ 1 & 0 \end{bmatrix}$

15. $\begin{bmatrix} 2 & 3 \\ 1 & 1 \end{bmatrix}$

16. $\begin{bmatrix} 2 & 3 \\ 2 & 4 \end{bmatrix}$

17. $\begin{bmatrix} 1 & 3 \\ 2 & 0 \end{bmatrix}$

18. $\begin{bmatrix} 6 & -8 \\ -3 & 4 \end{bmatrix}$

19. $\begin{bmatrix} 4 & 8 \\ -3 & -2 \end{bmatrix}$

20. $\begin{bmatrix} -1.5 & 3 \\ 2.5 & -0.5 \end{bmatrix}$

21. $\begin{bmatrix} 1 & -2 \\ 3 & 0 \end{bmatrix}$

Example 4
(page 202)

Solve each matrix equation. If an equation cannot be solved, explain why.

22. $\begin{bmatrix} 12 & 7 \\ 5 & 3 \end{bmatrix} X = \begin{bmatrix} 2 & -1 \\ 3 & 2 \end{bmatrix}$

23. $\begin{bmatrix} 0 & -4 \\ 0 & -1 \end{bmatrix} X = \begin{bmatrix} 0 \\ 4 \end{bmatrix}$

24. $\begin{bmatrix} 5 & -3 \\ 4 & -2 \end{bmatrix} X = \begin{bmatrix} 5 \\ 10 \end{bmatrix}$

Example 5
(pages 202–203)

25. Data Analysis Use the information in the diagram.
a. Write a transition matrix to represent the changes in cable television subscribers.
b. In a stable population of 30,000 people, 20,000 people subscribe to cable television, while 10,000 do not. Predict the number of people who will subscribe to cable television next year.
c. Use the inverse of the matrix from part (a) to find the number of people who subscribed to cable television last year.

Evaluate each determinant.

26. $\begin{vmatrix} 4 & 5 \\ -4 & 4 \end{vmatrix}$ 27. $\begin{vmatrix} -3 & 10 \\ 6 & 20 \end{vmatrix}$ 28. $\begin{vmatrix} -\frac{1}{2} & 2 \\ -2 & 8 \end{vmatrix}$ 29. $\begin{vmatrix} 2 & 0 \\ 0 & 1 \end{vmatrix}$ 30. $\begin{vmatrix} 6 & 9 \\ 3 & 6 \end{vmatrix}$

Determine whether the matrices are multiplicative inverses. If they are not, explain why not.

31. $\begin{bmatrix} 2 & 0.5 \\ 5 & 1 \end{bmatrix}, \begin{bmatrix} -2 & 1 \\ 10 & -4 \end{bmatrix}$ 32. $\begin{bmatrix} -3 & 4 \\ 6 & -8 \end{bmatrix}, \begin{bmatrix} -1 & 0 \\ 5 & 2 \end{bmatrix}$ 33. $\begin{bmatrix} -2 & -5 \\ -2 & -4 \end{bmatrix}, \begin{bmatrix} -2.5 & 2 \\ 1 & -1 \end{bmatrix}$

GO **O**nline
Homework Video Tutor
Visit: PHSchool.com
Web Code: age-0405

Determine whether each matrix has an inverse. If an inverse matrix exists, find it. If it does not exist, explain why not.

34. $\begin{bmatrix} 1 & 4 \\ 1 & 3 \end{bmatrix}$ 35. $\begin{bmatrix} 4 & 7 \\ 3 & 5 \end{bmatrix}$ 36. $\begin{bmatrix} -3 & 11 \\ 2 & -7 \end{bmatrix}$ 37. $\begin{bmatrix} 2 & 0 \\ 0 & 2 \end{bmatrix}$

38. $\begin{bmatrix} 0 & 3 \\ 3 & 0 \end{bmatrix}$ 39. $\begin{bmatrix} -1 & 3 \\ 2 & 0 \end{bmatrix}$ 40. $\begin{bmatrix} 1 & 2 \\ 2 & 1 \end{bmatrix}$ 41. $\begin{bmatrix} 3 & 0 \\ 6 & 0 \end{bmatrix}$

Solve each matrix equation.

42. $\begin{bmatrix} 4 & 7 \\ 1 & 2 \end{bmatrix} X + \begin{bmatrix} 2 & 7 \\ -3 & 4 \end{bmatrix} = \begin{bmatrix} 6 & 2 \\ -2 & 3 \end{bmatrix}$ 43. $\begin{bmatrix} 1 & 9 \\ 6 & -6 \end{bmatrix} = \begin{bmatrix} -7 & -9 \\ 4 & 5 \end{bmatrix} X + \begin{bmatrix} 3 & 4 \\ 4 & -3 \end{bmatrix}$

 44. **Writing** Suppose $A = \begin{bmatrix} a & b \\ c & d \end{bmatrix}$ has an inverse. In your own words, describe how to switch or change the elements of A to write A^{-1}.

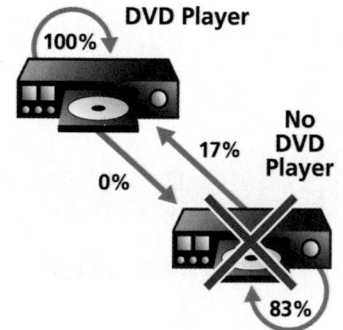
DVD Player
100%
17% No DVD Player
0%
83%

45. **Entertainment** Use the information in the diagram at the left.
   a. Write a transition matrix to represent the changes in DVD-player ownership.
   b. In a stable population of 30,000 people, 7000 people own DVD players, while 23,000 do not. Predict the number of people in the population who will own DVD players next year.
   c. Use the inverse of the matrix from part (a) to estimate the number of people in the population who owned DVD players last year.
   d. **Error Analysis** A student estimated that the number of people in the population who owned DVD players last year was 8434. What was the student's error?

 **C** Challenge

46. **Critical Thinking** Suppose $A = \begin{bmatrix} a & b \\ c & d \end{bmatrix}$. For what values of a, b, c, and d will A be its own inverse? (*Hint:* There is more than one correct answer.)

Solve each matrix equation.

47. $-2\begin{bmatrix} -2 & 0 \\ 0 & -1 \end{bmatrix} + \begin{bmatrix} 0 & -3 \\ 5 & -4 \end{bmatrix} X + \begin{bmatrix} 0 & -3 \\ 5 & -4 \end{bmatrix} = \begin{bmatrix} 19 & -27 \\ 10 & -24 \end{bmatrix}$

48. $\begin{bmatrix} 0 & -6 \\ 1 & 2 \end{bmatrix} - \begin{bmatrix} 5 & 2 \\ 4 & 3 \end{bmatrix} X - \begin{bmatrix} 2 & -26 \\ 3 & -18 \end{bmatrix} = \begin{bmatrix} 3 & 25 \\ 2 & 24 \end{bmatrix}$

49. **Critical Thinking** Explain why a 2×3 matrix does not have a multiplicative inverse.

50. Let $M = \begin{bmatrix} a & b \\ c & d \end{bmatrix}$ and $N = \begin{bmatrix} e & f \\ g & h \end{bmatrix}$. Prove that the product of the determinants of M and N equals the determinant of the matrix product MN.

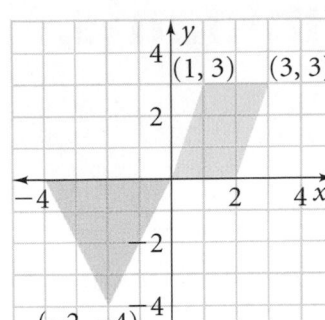

y
4 $(1, 3)$ $(3, 3)$
2
-4 2 4 x
-2
$(-2, -4)$ -4

51. a. Coordinate Geometry Find the area of the parallelogram at the left.

  b. Evaluate the determinant $\begin{vmatrix} 2 & 0 \\ 1 & 3 \end{vmatrix}$. Compare the value of the determinant to the area from part (a).

  c. Make a Conjecture Consider the triangle at the left to be half a parallelogram. Make a conjecture about its area and the value of

  $\frac{1}{2}\begin{vmatrix} -4 & 0 \\ -2 & -4 \end{vmatrix}$.

  d. Open-Ended Graph a different triangle with one vertex at the origin. Find the area of the triangle by writing and evaluating a determinant.

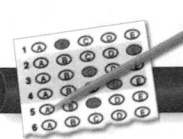

Test Prep

Gridded Response

52. What is the determinant of $\begin{bmatrix} -2 & -3 \\ 5 & 0 \end{bmatrix}$?

53. What is the determinant of $\begin{bmatrix} \frac{3}{10} & \frac{1}{5} \\ \frac{1}{8} & \frac{1}{3} \end{bmatrix}$? Enter your answer as a fraction.

54. If $A = \begin{bmatrix} 4 & 2 \\ -3 & -1 \end{bmatrix}$, and the inverse of A is $x\begin{bmatrix} -1 & -2 \\ 3 & 4 \end{bmatrix}$, what is the value of x? Enter your answer as a fraction.

55. If $B = \begin{bmatrix} 4 & -1 \\ 2 & 0 \end{bmatrix}$, what is det B^{-1}?

Mixed Review

Lesson 4-4

Each matrix represents the vertices of a polygon. Write a matrix to represent the vertices of the image after each transformation.

56. $\begin{bmatrix} 0 & 0 & 5 \\ 0 & -4 & 0 \end{bmatrix}$; rotation of 90°   **57.** $\begin{bmatrix} -2 & -5 & 0 \\ 0 & 3 & 5 \end{bmatrix}$; reflection in $y = x$

58. $\begin{bmatrix} 5 & 3 & 2 \\ 7 & 1 & 3 \end{bmatrix}$; 2 units left, 1 unit down   **59.** $\begin{bmatrix} -3 & -2 & -1 \\ 4 & 1 & 5 \end{bmatrix}$; dilation of 2

Lesson 3-6

Solve each system by substitution.

60. $\begin{cases} x = 5 \\ x - y + z = 5 \\ x + y - z = -5 \end{cases}$ **61.** $\begin{cases} x - 3y = 2z \\ x + 2y - z = 0 \\ x + y + z = 10 \end{cases}$ **62.** $\begin{cases} 3x + 3y - z = 9 \\ 2y = x - z \\ x - y + 5z = 9 \end{cases}$

Lesson 2-4   **63. a. Exercise** Suppose you begin a training program by walking 2 miles every day. During the first week, the walk takes you 40 minutes per day. Each week after that, you reduce your time by one minute. Write a linear model for the number of minutes you take to walk 2 miles in week w.

  b. Critical Thinking Can you continue to improve at the same rate? Explain.

3 × 3 Matrices, Determinants, and Inverses

✓ **Check Skills You'll Need**

GO for Help Skills Handbook page 873

Find the product of the red elements in each matrix.

1. $\begin{bmatrix} 2 & 3 & 0 \\ -1 & 3 & -2 \\ 4 & -3 & -4 \end{bmatrix}$

2. $\begin{bmatrix} 2 & 3 & 0 \\ -1 & 3 & -2 \\ 4 & -3 & -4 \end{bmatrix}$

3. $\begin{bmatrix} 2 & 3 & 0 \\ -1 & 3 & -2 \\ 4 & -3 & -4 \end{bmatrix}$

4. $\begin{bmatrix} 2 & 3 & 0 \\ -1 & 3 & -2 \\ 4 & -3 & -4 \end{bmatrix}$

5. $\begin{bmatrix} 2 & 3 & 0 \\ -1 & 3 & -2 \\ 4 & -3 & -4 \end{bmatrix}$

6. $\begin{bmatrix} 2 & 3 & 0 \\ -1 & 3 & -2 \\ 4 & -3 & -4 \end{bmatrix}$

1 Evaluating Determinants of 3 × 3 Matrices

As you learned in Lesson 4-5, the determinant of a matrix helps you to find an inverse matrix and solve a matrix equation.

 Key Concepts

Definition **The Determinant of a 3 × 3 Matrix**

The determinant of a 3 × 3 matrix $\begin{bmatrix} a_1 & b_1 & c_1 \\ a_2 & b_2 & c_2 \\ a_3 & b_3 & c_3 \end{bmatrix}$ is

$$\begin{vmatrix} a_1 & b_1 & c_1 \\ a_2 & b_2 & c_2 \\ a_3 & b_3 & c_3 \end{vmatrix} = (a_1 b_2 c_3 + a_2 b_3 c_1 + a_3 b_1 c_2) - (a_1 b_3 c_2 + a_2 b_1 c_3 + a_3 b_2 c_1)$$

Visualize the pattern this way:

$$\begin{matrix} a_1 & b_1 & c_1 \\ a_2 & b_2 & c_2 \\ a_3 & b_3 & c_3 \end{matrix} - \begin{matrix} a_1 & b_1 & c_1 \\ a_2 & b_2 & c_2 \\ a_3 & b_3 & c_3 \end{matrix}$$

1 EXAMPLE **Evaluating the Determinant of a 3 × 3 Matrix**

Evaluate the determinant of $F = \begin{bmatrix} -1 & 3 & 5 \\ 2 & -4 & 6 \\ 0 & 1 & -1 \end{bmatrix}$.

$$\begin{vmatrix} -1 & 3 & 5 \\ 2 & -4 & 6 \\ 0 & 1 & -1 \end{vmatrix} = [-1(-4)(-1) + 2(1)(5) + 0(3)(6)]$$
$$\quad - [-1(1)(6) + 2(3)(-1) + 0(-4)(5)]$$ **Use the definition.**

$$= [-4 + 10 + 0] - [-6 + (-6) + 0]$$ **Multiply.**

$$= 6 - (-12) = 18$$ **Simplify.**

The determinant of F is 18.

✓ Quick Check ❶ Evaluate each determinant.

a. $\begin{vmatrix} -3 & 4 & 0 \\ 2 & -5 & 1 \\ 0 & 2 & 3 \end{vmatrix}$ **b.** $\begin{vmatrix} 1 & -1 & 2 \\ 0 & 4 & 2 \\ 3 & -6 & 10 \end{vmatrix}$ **c.** $\begin{vmatrix} 2 & 0 & -1 \\ 0 & 0 & 0 \\ 1 & -5 & 3 \end{vmatrix}$

You can use a graphing calculator to evaluate the determinant of a 3×3 matrix.

2 EXAMPLE Using a Graphing Calculator

Enter matrix A into your graphing calculator. Use the matrix submenus to evaluate the determinant of A.

$$A = \begin{bmatrix} 1 & 7 & 2 \\ -1 & 1 & -2 \\ 1 & 1 & 1 \end{bmatrix}$$

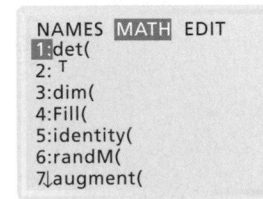

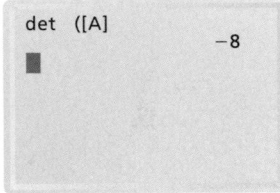

✓ Quick Check ❷ Use a graphing calculator to evaluate the determinant of $\begin{bmatrix} 13 & 21 & 11 \\ -2 & 4 & -1 \\ 17 & -2 & 0 \end{bmatrix}$.

2 Using Inverse 3 × 3 Matrices

You can test whether two 3×3 matrices are inverses by finding their product.

3 EXAMPLE Verifying Inverses

Determine whether the matrices are multiplicative inverses of each other.

a. $A = \begin{bmatrix} 1 & 5 & -1 \\ 1 & 0 & -1 \\ 1 & 0 & 0 \end{bmatrix}, B = \begin{bmatrix} 0 & 0 & 1 \\ 0.2 & -0.2 & 0 \\ 0 & -1 & 1 \end{bmatrix}$

$\begin{bmatrix} 1 & 5 & -1 \\ 1 & 0 & -1 \\ 1 & 0 & 0 \end{bmatrix}\begin{bmatrix} 0 & 0 & 1 \\ 0.2 & -0.2 & 0 \\ 0 & -1 & 1 \end{bmatrix} = \begin{bmatrix} 1 & 0 & 0 \\ 0 & 1 & 0 \\ 0 & 0 & 1 \end{bmatrix}$

Since $AB = I, A$ and B are multiplicative inverses.

b. $C = \begin{bmatrix} 3 & 4 & 1 \\ -2 & 0 & 2 \\ 1 & 5 & 3 \end{bmatrix}, D = \begin{bmatrix} 0 & 1 & 0 \\ 1 & 0 & 1 \\ 0 & 1 & 0 \end{bmatrix}$

$\begin{bmatrix} 3 & 4 & 1 \\ -2 & 0 & 2 \\ 1 & 5 & 3 \end{bmatrix}\begin{bmatrix} 0 & 1 & 0 \\ 1 & 0 & 1 \\ 0 & 1 & 0 \end{bmatrix} = \begin{bmatrix} 4 & 4 & 4 \\ 0 & 0 & 0 \\ 5 & 4 & 5 \end{bmatrix}$

Since $CD \neq I, C$ and D are not multiplicative inverses.

✓ Quick Check ❸ **a.** Verify that A and B are inverses by showing that $BA = I$.
   b. Verify that C and D are not inverses by showing that $DC \neq I$.

You can use 3×3 matrices to solve matrix equations.

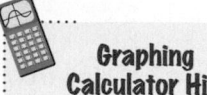

Graphing Calculator Hint

If a square matrix has no inverse, you will see ERR: SINGULAR MAT on the screen.

4 EXAMPLE Solving a Matrix Equation

Solve the matrix equation $\begin{bmatrix} 0 & 0 & 2 \\ 1 & 3 & -2 \\ 1 & -2 & 1 \end{bmatrix} X = \begin{bmatrix} 6 \\ -11 \\ 8 \end{bmatrix}$.

Let $A = \begin{bmatrix} 0 & 0 & 2 \\ 1 & 3 & -2 \\ 1 & -2 & 1 \end{bmatrix}$. Find A^{-1}.

```
[A]⁻¹
    [[  .1    .4    .6   ]
     [  .3    .2   -.2   ]
     [  .5     0     0  ]]
```

$X = \begin{bmatrix} 0.1 & 0.4 & 0.6 \\ 0.3 & 0.2 & -0.2 \\ 0.5 & 0 & 0 \end{bmatrix} \begin{bmatrix} 6 \\ -11 \\ 8 \end{bmatrix}$ ← **Use the equation**
$X = A^{-1}C$.
Multiply. →

```
[A]⁻¹[C]
    [[1 ]
     [-2]
     [3 ]]
```

$X = \begin{bmatrix} 1 \\ -2 \\ 3 \end{bmatrix}$

✓ Quick Check 4 **a.** Verify that A and A^{-1} are inverses.

b. Solve the matrix equation $\begin{bmatrix} 0 & 0 & 2 \\ 1 & 3 & -2 \\ 1 & -2 & 1 \end{bmatrix} X = \begin{bmatrix} 0 \\ -6 \\ 19 \end{bmatrix}$.

You can use 3×3 matrices to encode and decode messages.

5 EXAMPLE Real-World Connection

Cryptography Use the alphabet table and the encoding matrix E at the left.

a. Find the decoding matrix E^{-1}.

```
[E]⁻¹
    [[   1   -2    2    ]
     [   0    4   -2    ]
     [   1   -2    0   ]]
```

Use a graphing calculator.

A 26	N 13
B 25	O 12
C 24	P 11
D 23	Q 10
E 22	R 9
F 21	S 8
G 20	T 7
H 19	U 6
I 18	V 5
J 17	W 4
K 16	X 3
L 15	Y 2
M 14	Z 1

$E = \begin{bmatrix} 0.5 & 0.5 & 0.5 \\ 0.25 & 0.25 & -0.25 \\ 0.5 & 0 & -0.5 \end{bmatrix}$

b. Use the decoding matrix to decode $\begin{bmatrix} 22.5 & 26 & 15.5 \\ 0.25 & 9 & 7.75 \\ -4 & 9 & 3.5 \end{bmatrix}$.

$\begin{bmatrix} 1 & -2 & 2 \\ 0 & 4 & -2 \\ 1 & -2 & 0 \end{bmatrix} \begin{bmatrix} 22.5 & 26 & 15.5 \\ 0.25 & 9 & 7.75 \\ -4 & 9 & 3.5 \end{bmatrix} = \begin{bmatrix} 14 & 26 & 7 \\ 9 & 18 & 24 \\ 22 & 8 & 0 \end{bmatrix}$ **Use the decoding matrix from part (a). Multiply.**

In the result, 0 is a space-holder.
The numbers 14 26 7 9 18 24 22 8 correspond to the letters MATRICES.

✓ Quick Check 5 **Literature** Use the information from Example 5. Decode the matrix at the right, which gives the title of a Pablo Neruda poem. $\begin{bmatrix} 21 & 10.5 \\ 6 & 4.25 \\ 1 & 5 \end{bmatrix}$

Practice and Problem Solving

 Practice by Example

Example 1
(page 206)

 **for Help**

Evaluate the determinant of each matrix.

1. $\begin{bmatrix} 1 & 2 & 5 \\ 3 & 1 & 0 \\ 1 & 2 & 1 \end{bmatrix}$
2. $\begin{bmatrix} 1 & 4 & 0 \\ 2 & 3 & 5 \\ 0 & 1 & 0 \end{bmatrix}$
3. $\begin{bmatrix} -2 & 4 & 1 \\ 3 & 0 & -1 \\ 1 & 2 & 1 \end{bmatrix}$
4. $\begin{bmatrix} 2 & 3 & 0 \\ 1 & 2 & 5 \\ 7 & 0 & 1 \end{bmatrix}$

Example 2
(page 207)

Use a graphing calculator to evaluate the determinant of each 3 × 3 matrix.

5. $\begin{bmatrix} 1 & 0 & 0 \\ 0 & 1 & 0 \\ 0 & 0 & 1 \end{bmatrix}$
6. $\begin{bmatrix} 0 & -2 & -3 \\ 1 & 2 & 4 \\ -2 & 0 & 1 \end{bmatrix}$
7. $\begin{bmatrix} 12.2 & 13.3 & 9 \\ 1 & -4 & -17 \\ 21.4 & -15 & 0 \end{bmatrix}$

Example 3
(page 207)

Determine whether the matrices are multiplicative inverses.

8. $\begin{bmatrix} 1 & 2 & -1 \\ -1.5 & -3 & 1.75 \\ 0 & -1 & 0.5 \end{bmatrix}, \begin{bmatrix} 1 & 0 & 2 \\ 3 & 2 & -1 \\ 6 & 4 & 0 \end{bmatrix}$
9. $\begin{bmatrix} 2 & 2 & 2 \\ -2 & 2 & -2 \\ -2 & -2 & -2 \end{bmatrix}, \begin{bmatrix} 2 & 2 & 2 \\ -2 & 2 & -2 \\ -2 & -2 & -2 \end{bmatrix}$

Example 4
(page 208)

Solve each matrix equation.

10. $\begin{bmatrix} 5 & 1 & -4 \\ 2 & -3 & -5 \\ 7 & 2 & -6 \end{bmatrix} X = \begin{bmatrix} 5 \\ 2 \\ 5 \end{bmatrix}$
11. $\begin{bmatrix} 6 & 10 & -13 \\ 4 & -2 & 7 \\ 0 & 9 & -8 \end{bmatrix} X = \begin{bmatrix} 84 \\ 18 \\ 56 \end{bmatrix}$

Example 5
(page 208)

Literature Use the information from Example 5. Decode each title.

12. Emily Dickinson, $\begin{bmatrix} 23.5 & 12.5 \\ 4.75 & -0.25 \\ 6 & -3.5 \end{bmatrix}$
13. E. E. Cummings, $\begin{bmatrix} 18 & 14 & 17.5 \\ 0 & 3.5 & 8.75 \\ -3.5 & 2.5 & 4.5 \end{bmatrix}$

 Apply Your Skills

14. Multiple Choice If matrix A has an inverse, what must be true?

I. $AA^{-1} = I$ **II.** $A^{-1}A = I$ **III.** $A^{-1}I = A^{-1}$

(A) I only (B) II only (C) I and II only (D) I, II, and III

15. Cryptography Two members of the Hopewell High School math club share messages in code. They use the alphabet table from Example 5.
a. One of the students has lost her encoding matrix. Luckily, she remembers that the decoding matrix is
$$E^{-1} = \begin{bmatrix} 1 & -1 & 0 \\ 0 & 1 & -1 \\ 0 & 0 & 1 \end{bmatrix}.$$ Compute E to find the encoding matrix.
b. Use your answer to part (a) to encode the message MATH IS COOL.
c. Open-Ended Use the encoding matrix from part (a) to encode a short sentence. Use the decoding matrix to check your work.

Real-World Connection

During World War II, these Navajo code talkers transmitted messages in an unbreakable code.

Evaluate the determinant of each matrix.

16. $\begin{bmatrix} 0 & 2 & -3 \\ 1 & 2 & 4 \\ -2 & 0 & 1 \end{bmatrix}$
17. $\begin{bmatrix} 5 & 1 & 0 \\ 0 & 2 & -1 \\ -2 & -3 & 1 \end{bmatrix}$
18. $\begin{bmatrix} 4 & 6 & -1 \\ 2 & 3 & 2 \\ 1 & -1 & 1 \end{bmatrix}$
19. $\begin{bmatrix} -3 & 2 & -1 \\ 2 & 5 & 2 \\ 1 & -2 & 0 \end{bmatrix}$

Find the inverse of each matrix, if it exists.

20. $\begin{bmatrix} -2 & 1 & -1 \\ 2 & 0 & 4 \\ 0 & 2 & 5 \end{bmatrix}$ 21. $\begin{bmatrix} 2 & 0 & -1 \\ -1 & -1 & 1 \\ 3 & 2 & 0 \end{bmatrix}$ 22. $\begin{bmatrix} 0 & 0 & 2 \\ 1 & 4 & -2 \\ 3 & -2 & 1 \end{bmatrix}$ 23. $\begin{bmatrix} 1 & 2 & 6 \\ 1 & -1 & 0 \\ 1 & 0 & 2 \end{bmatrix}$

24. Writing Evaluate the determinant of each matrix. Describe any patterns.

a. $\begin{bmatrix} 1 & 2 & 3 \\ 1 & 2 & 3 \\ 1 & 2 & 3 \end{bmatrix}$ b. $\begin{bmatrix} -1 & -2 & -3 \\ -3 & -2 & -1 \\ -1 & -2 & -3 \end{bmatrix}$ c. $\begin{bmatrix} 1 & 2 & 3 \\ 2 & 3 & 1 \\ 1 & 2 & 3 \end{bmatrix}$ d. $\begin{bmatrix} -1 & 2 & -3 \\ 2 & -3 & -1 \\ -1 & 2 & -3 \end{bmatrix}$

Ⓒ Challenge

Literature Use the table and decoding matrix from Example 5. Decode each title.

25. Maya Angelou, $\begin{bmatrix} 26.5 & 28 & 15.5 & 16.5 & 13.5 \\ 0.25 & 2 & -3.25 & 8.25 & 6.75 \\ -6 & -6 & -6.5 & 6.5 & 9 \end{bmatrix}$

26. Oliver Wendell Holmes, $\begin{bmatrix} 19 & 24 & 24.5 & 18.5 & 26.5 & 13.5 & 19.5 & 20 \\ 6.5 & 8.5 & 3.25 & 1.75 & 10.25 & 2.75 & 9.75 & 10 \\ 0.5 & 6 & 2 & -7.5 & 9 & 5.5 & 13 & 7 \end{bmatrix}$

Solve each matrix equation.

27. $\begin{bmatrix} 7 & -5 & 3 \\ 0 & 1 & 3 \\ 8 & 4 & -2 \end{bmatrix} X + \begin{bmatrix} 5 \\ -9 \\ 0 \end{bmatrix} = \begin{bmatrix} 54 \\ -12 \\ 96 \end{bmatrix}$

28. $\begin{bmatrix} -1 & 0 & 2 \\ -6 & -5 & 0 \\ 1 & 4 & 1 \end{bmatrix} - \begin{bmatrix} -4 & 0 & 2 \\ 0 & 3 & 6 \\ 0 & 5 & 0 \end{bmatrix} X = \begin{bmatrix} -21 & 10 & 26 \\ -54 & 1 & -15 \\ 1 & 4 & -24 \end{bmatrix}$

Maya Angelou—poet, educator, historian, novelist, actress, and playwright

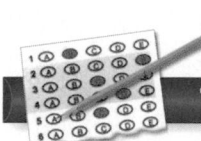

Test Prep

Multiple Choice

29. What is the determinant of $\begin{bmatrix} 5 & 0 & 0 \\ 0 & 5 & 0 \\ 0 & 0 & 5 \end{bmatrix}$?

   A. 5   **B.** 25   **C.** 125   **D.** 555

30. Which matrix has no inverse?

F. $\begin{bmatrix} 1 & 0 & 0 \\ 0 & 0 & 0 \\ 0 & 0 & 1 \end{bmatrix}$ **G.** $\begin{bmatrix} 1 & 0 & 1 \\ 0 & 1 & 0 \\ 0 & 0 & 1 \end{bmatrix}$ **H.** $\begin{bmatrix} 0 & 0 & 1 \\ 0 & -1 & 0 \\ 1 & 1 & 0 \end{bmatrix}$ **J.** $\begin{bmatrix} 1 & -1 & 0 \\ 0 & 0 & 1 \\ -1 & 0 & 1 \end{bmatrix}$

Short Response

31. What is the determinant of the identity matrix *I*?

32. The matrix *A* at the right has an inverse A^{-1}. What is the product AA^{-1}? Explain.

$A = \begin{bmatrix} 1 & 1 & 2 \\ 2 & -1 & 1 \\ 1 & 4 & -1 \end{bmatrix}$

33. Matrices *B* and *C* are inverses of each other.

$B = \begin{bmatrix} 1 & 1 & 0 \\ 0 & 2 & 1 \\ -2 & 0 & 2 \end{bmatrix}$ $C = \begin{bmatrix} 2 & -1 & 0.5 \\ -1 & 1 & -0.5 \\ 2 & -1 & 1 \end{bmatrix}$ $D = \begin{bmatrix} 2 \\ 0 \\ -1 \end{bmatrix}$

Solve the matrix equation $BX = D$.

GO **Online**
Homework Video Tutor
Visit: PHSchool.com
Web Code: age-0406

Lesson 4-5

Determine whether each matrix has an inverse. If an inverse matrix exists, find it.

34. $\begin{bmatrix} -9 & 3 \\ 4 & 2.5 \end{bmatrix}$
35. $\begin{bmatrix} 2 & 3 \\ 8 & 12 \end{bmatrix}$
36. $\begin{bmatrix} -3 & 4 \\ 9 & 10 \end{bmatrix}$
37. $\begin{bmatrix} 0 & -1 \\ -1 & 0 \end{bmatrix}$

Lesson 3-1

Solve each system of equations.

38. $\begin{cases} 2x + 2y = 10 \\ 3x - y = 4 \end{cases}$

39. $\begin{cases} -x + y + z = 5 \\ 2x + y - z = 2 \\ 3x + 2y + 4z = 0 \end{cases}$

✓ Checkpoint Quiz 2   Lessons 4-4 through 4-6

Use △ABC at the right. Find the coordinates of the image under each transformation.

1. a dilation of 2

2. a translation 3 units left and 3 units up

3. a rotation of 270°

4. a reflection in $y = -x$

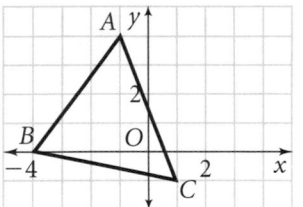

Solve each matrix equation.

5. $\begin{bmatrix} 0 & 3 \\ 5 & 0 \end{bmatrix} X = \begin{bmatrix} -12 & -15 \\ 10 & 15 \end{bmatrix}$
6. $\begin{bmatrix} -1 & 2 & 3 \\ 0 & 3 & 2 \\ 3 & -2 & 0 \end{bmatrix} X = \begin{bmatrix} 17 \\ 18 \\ 11 \end{bmatrix}$
7. $\begin{bmatrix} 4 & 5 \\ -1 & 5 \end{bmatrix} X = \begin{bmatrix} 32 \\ 42 \end{bmatrix}$

Evaluate the determinant of each matrix.

8. $\begin{bmatrix} -2 & 3 \\ 0 & 5 \end{bmatrix}$
9. $\begin{bmatrix} 0 & 5 & 4 \\ -1 & -1 & 3 \\ 2 & 5 & 0 \end{bmatrix}$
10. $\begin{bmatrix} -3 & 2 & 0 \\ 4 & 17 & 10 \\ 1 & -5 & -1 \end{bmatrix}$

⋯⋯ A Point in Time

1500   1600   1700   1800   1900   2000

An artist who paints murals creates a sketch and then uses a dilation of the sketch for the actual mural. Judith Francisca Baca is a muralist who serves as the artistic director of the Great Wall of Los Angeles. The 13-ft-by-2400-ft mural, which depicts California's multicultural history, has involved over 400 youths, 100 scholars, and 50 assisting artists.

Go Online
PHSchool.com
For: Information about murals
Web Code: age-2032

A finite graph is a set of points, called vertices, connected by curves, or paths.

You can use a matrix to describe a finite graph. A 1 indicates a path between two vertices or one vertex and itself. A 0 indicates that no path exists between two vertices or from one vertex to itself.

1 EXAMPLE

Write a matrix A to represent the finite graph. Explain the significance of element a_{41}.

$$A = \begin{array}{c} \\ N_1 \\ N_2 \\ N_3 \\ N_4 \end{array} \begin{array}{cccc} N_1 & N_2 & N_3 & N_4 \\ \left[\begin{array}{cccc} 0 & 1 & 1 & 0 \\ 1 & 0 & 1 & 1 \\ 1 & 1 & 0 & 0 \\ 0 & 1 & 0 & 0 \end{array}\right] \end{array}$$

← There is a path from N_2 to N_4.

Element a_{41} is 0. It indicates that there is no path between N_4 and N_1.

Directed graphs are finite graphs that indicate the direction of a path. The directed graph at the right below represents the information in the map.

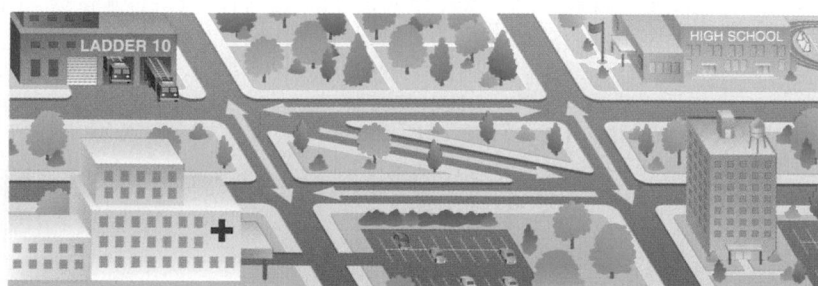

You can use a matrix to represent the information in a directed graph.

2 EXAMPLE

Write a matrix B to represent the information from the directed graph. Compare elements b_{12} and b_{21}.

$$B = \begin{array}{c} \textbf{From} \rightarrow \\ \\ \\ \\ \end{array} \begin{array}{c} \\ P \\ Q \\ S \\ T \end{array} \begin{array}{cccc} \textbf{To} \rightarrow P & Q & S & T \\ \left[\begin{array}{cccc} 0 & 1 & 0 & 1 \\ 0 & 0 & 1 & 1 \\ 1 & 1 & 0 & 0 \\ 1 & 0 & 1 & 0 \end{array}\right] \end{array}$$

Element b_{12} is 1, and element b_{21} is 0. The path between P and Q is one way from P to Q.

You can use information in a matrix to draw a directed graph.

3 EXAMPLE

Draw a directed graph to represent the information in the matrix.

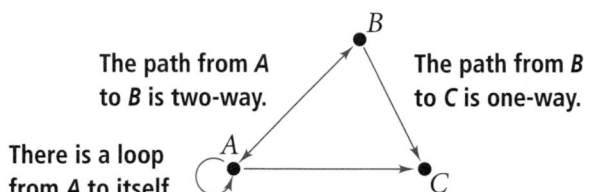

$$\begin{array}{c} \text{To} \to A \ B \ C \\ \begin{array}{c} A \\ \text{From} \to B \\ C \end{array} \begin{bmatrix} 1 & 1 & 1 \\ 1 & 0 & 1 \\ 0 & 0 & 0 \end{bmatrix} \end{array}$$

The path from A to B is two-way.

The path from B to C is one-way.

There is a loop from A to itself.

EXERCISES

Write a matrix to represent each finite or directed graph.

1.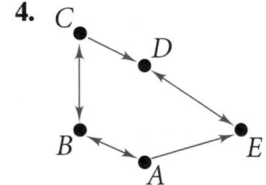

2.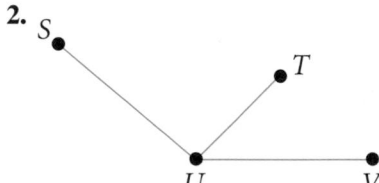

3.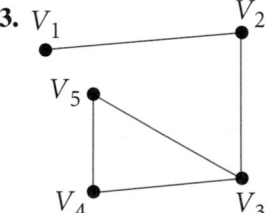

4.

5.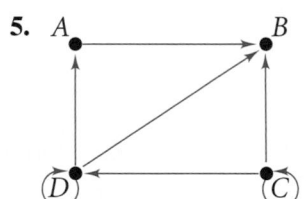

6.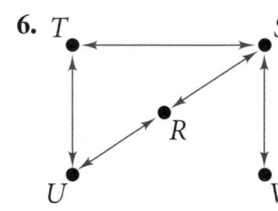

Draw a directed graph to represent the information in each matrix.

7.
$$\begin{array}{c} \quad\ J \ K \ L \ M \\ \begin{array}{c} J \\ K \\ L \\ M \end{array} \begin{bmatrix} 0 & 0 & 0 & 1 \\ 0 & 0 & 1 & 1 \\ 0 & 1 & 0 & 1 \\ 1 & 1 & 1 & 0 \end{bmatrix} \end{array}$$

8.
$$\begin{array}{c} \quad\ A \ B \ C \ D \\ \begin{array}{c} A \\ B \\ C \\ D \end{array} \begin{bmatrix} 0 & 0 & 1 & 1 \\ 1 & 1 & 0 & 0 \\ 0 & 1 & 0 & 1 \\ 1 & 0 & 1 & 0 \end{bmatrix} \end{array}$$

9.
$$\begin{array}{c} \quad\ N_1 \ N_2 \ N_3 \ N_4 \\ \begin{array}{c} N_1 \\ N_2 \\ N_3 \\ N_4 \end{array} \begin{bmatrix} 1 & 1 & 1 & 1 \\ 0 & 0 & 1 & 1 \\ 1 & 0 & 0 & 0 \\ 0 & 0 & 1 & 0 \end{bmatrix} \end{array}$$

10. Travel Alice and Becky live on Parkway East, at the intersections of Owens Bridge and Bay Bridge, respectively. Carl and David live on Parkway West, at the intersections of Bay Bridge and Owens Bridge, respectively. Parkway East is a one-way street running east. Parkway West is one way running west. Both bridges are two way.

a. Draw a directed graph indicating road travel between the houses.

b. Write a matrix T to represent the information in the directed graph.

c. Writing Calculate T^2. What does the new matrix model? Explain.

Inverse Matrices and Systems

GO for Help Lesson 3-6

What You'll Learn

- To solve systems of equations using inverse matrices

... And Why

To calculate business costs, as in Example 4

✓ **Check Skills You'll Need**

Solve each system.

1. $\begin{cases} 5x + y = 14 \\ 4x + 3y = 20 \end{cases}$

2. $\begin{cases} x - y - z = -9 \\ 3x + y + 2z = 12 \\ x = y - 2z \end{cases}$

3. $\begin{cases} -x + 2y + z = 0 \\ y = -2x + 3 \\ z = 3x \end{cases}$

🔊 **New Vocabulary** • coefficient matrix • variable matrix • constant matrix

---

1 Solving Systems of Equations Using Inverse Matrices

You can represent a system of equations with a matrix equation.

System of equations

$\begin{cases} x + 2y = 5 \\ 3x + 5y = 14 \end{cases}$

Matrix equation

$\begin{bmatrix} 1 & 2 \\ 3 & 5 \end{bmatrix}\begin{bmatrix} x \\ y \end{bmatrix} = \begin{bmatrix} 5 \\ 14 \end{bmatrix}$

Each matrix in an equation of the form $AX = B$ has a name.

Coefficient matrix A

$\begin{bmatrix} 1 & 2 \\ 3 & 5 \end{bmatrix}$

Variable matrix X

$\begin{bmatrix} x \\ y \end{bmatrix}$

Constant matrix B

$\begin{bmatrix} 5 \\ 14 \end{bmatrix}$

GO for Help

To review the definitions of *coefficient* and *variable*, go to Lesson 1-2.

1 EXAMPLE Writing a System as a Matrix Equation

Write the system $\begin{cases} -b + 2c = 4 \\ a + b - c = 0 \\ 2a + 3c = 11 \end{cases}$ as a matrix equation. Then identify the coefficient matrix, the variable matrix, and the constant matrix.

Matrix equation: $\begin{bmatrix} 0 & -1 & 2 \\ 1 & 1 & -1 \\ 2 & 0 & 3 \end{bmatrix}\begin{bmatrix} a \\ b \\ c \end{bmatrix} = \begin{bmatrix} 4 \\ 0 \\ 11 \end{bmatrix}$

Coefficient matrix

$\begin{bmatrix} 0 & -1 & 2 \\ 1 & 1 & -1 \\ 2 & 0 & 3 \end{bmatrix}$

Variable matrix

$\begin{bmatrix} a \\ b \\ c \end{bmatrix}$

Constant matrix

$\begin{bmatrix} 4 \\ 0 \\ 11 \end{bmatrix}$

✓ **Quick Check** ❶ Write each system as a matrix equation. Identify the coefficient matrix, the variable matrix, and the constant matrix.

a. $\begin{cases} 3x + 2y = 16 \\ y = 5 \end{cases}$

b. $\begin{cases} x - y + z = 0 \\ x - 2y - z = 5 \\ 2x - y + 2z = 8 \end{cases}$

Sometimes you can find the inverse of the coefficient matrix. Then you can use it to solve systems of equations quickly.

2 EXAMPLE Solving a System of Two Equations

Solve the system $\begin{cases} 2x + 3y = 11 \\ x + 2y = 6 \end{cases}$.

To review how to find the inverse of a 2 × 2 matrix, see page 201.

$\begin{bmatrix} 2 & 3 \\ 1 & 2 \end{bmatrix} \begin{bmatrix} x \\ y \end{bmatrix} = \begin{bmatrix} 11 \\ 6 \end{bmatrix}$ **Write the system as a matrix equation.**

$A^{-1} = \begin{bmatrix} 2 & -3 \\ -1 & 2 \end{bmatrix}$ **Find A^{-1}.**

$\begin{bmatrix} x \\ y \end{bmatrix} = A^{-1}B = \begin{bmatrix} 2 & -3 \\ -1 & 2 \end{bmatrix} \begin{bmatrix} 11 \\ 6 \end{bmatrix} = \begin{bmatrix} 4 \\ 1 \end{bmatrix}$ **Solve for the variable matrix.**

The solution of the system is $(4, 1)$.

Check	$2x + 3y = 11$	$x + 2y = 6$	**Use the original equations.**
	$2(4) + 3(1) \stackrel{?}{=} 11$	$4 + 2(1) \stackrel{?}{=} 6$	**Substitute.**
	$8 + 3 = 11 ✓$	$4 + 2 = 6 ✓$	**Simplify.**

 **2** Solve each system. Check your answers.

a. $\begin{cases} 5a + 3b = 7 \\ 3a + 2b = 5 \end{cases}$ b. $\begin{cases} x + 3y = 22 \\ 3x + 2y = 10 \end{cases}$

You can use a graphing calculator to solve a system of three equations.

3 EXAMPLE Solving a System of Three Equations

Solve the system $\begin{cases} 2x + y + 3z = 1 \\ 5x + y - 2z = 8 \\ x - y - 9z = 5 \end{cases}$.

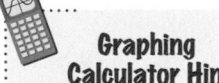

Graphing Calculator Hint

To select A^{-1}, use the MATRIX feature and the x^{-1} key.

Step 1 Write the system as a matrix equation.

$\begin{bmatrix} 2 & 1 & 3 \\ 5 & 1 & -2 \\ 1 & -1 & -9 \end{bmatrix} \begin{bmatrix} x \\ y \\ z \end{bmatrix} = \begin{bmatrix} 1 \\ 8 \\ 5 \end{bmatrix}$

Step 2 Enter the coefficient matrix as matrix A and the constant matrix as matrix B.

Step 3

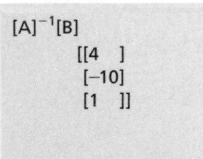

The solution is $(4, -10, 1)$.

 **3 a.** Check the solution from Example 3 in each of the original equations.

b. Solve the system $\begin{cases} x + y + z = 2 \\ 2x + y = 5 \\ x + 3y - 3z = 14 \end{cases}$. Check your solution.

There are many business applications for matrices of systems of equations.

$3.25

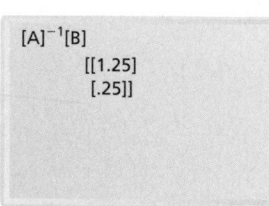

$4.75

4 EXAMPLE Real-World  Connection

Business A bead store has a sale on certain beads. Find the price of each size of bead.

Relate 2 large beads and 3 small beads cost $3.25.
3 large beads and 4 small beads cost $4.75.

Define Let x = the price of one large bead.
Let y = the price of one small bead.

Write $\begin{bmatrix} 2 & 3 \\ 3 & 4 \end{bmatrix} \begin{bmatrix} x \\ y \end{bmatrix} = \begin{bmatrix} 3.25 \\ 4.75 \end{bmatrix}$ **Write the system as a matrix equation.**

```
[A]⁻¹[B]
    [[1.25]
     [.25]]
```

Use a graphing calculator. Store the coefficient matrix as matrix A and the constant matrix as matrix B.

● The price of a large bead is $1.25. The price of a small bead is $.25.

✓ Quick Check **4** Suppose the sale is over, and the price of each package increases. The price of a package of two large beads and three small beads increases to $5.55. The price of a package of three large beads and four small beads increases to $8.05. Find the new price of each type of bead.

When the coefficient matrix of a system has an inverse, the system has a unique solution. Similarly, when the coefficient matrix does *not* have an inverse, the system does *not* have a unique solution. In that case, the system either has no solution or has an infinite number of solutions.

5 EXAMPLE Unique Solutions

Write the coefficient matrix for each system. Use it to determine whether the system has a unique solution.

Problem Solving Hint

$\det \begin{bmatrix} a & b \\ c & d \end{bmatrix} = ad - bc$

a. $\begin{cases} x + y = 3 \\ x - y = 7 \end{cases}$

$A = \begin{bmatrix} 1 & 1 \\ 1 & -1 \end{bmatrix}$; $\det A = \begin{vmatrix} 1 & 1 \\ 1 & -1 \end{vmatrix} = 1(-1) - 1(1) = -2$

Since $\det A \neq 0$, the matrix has an inverse, so the system has a unique solution.

b. $\begin{cases} x + 2y = 5 \\ 2x + 4y = 8 \end{cases}$

$A = \begin{bmatrix} 1 & 2 \\ 2 & 4 \end{bmatrix}$; $\det A = \begin{vmatrix} 1 & 2 \\ 2 & 4 \end{vmatrix} = 1(4) - 2(2) = 0$

Since $\det A = 0$, the matrix does not have an inverse and the system does *not* have a unique solution.

5 a. Determine whether the system $\begin{cases} 3x + 5y = 1 \\ 2x - y = -8 \end{cases}$ has a unique solution.

b. You can use an inverse matrix to solve a system of equations. What happens when you try to do this with a graphing calculator and the system does not have a unique solution?

EXERCISES

For more exercises, see *Extra Skill and Word Problem Practice.*

Practice and Problem Solving

A Practice by Example

Example 1
(page 214)

GO for Help

Write each system as a matrix equation. Identify the coefficient matrix, the variable matrix, and the constant matrix.

1. $\begin{cases} x + y = 5 \\ x - 2y = -4 \end{cases}$

2. $\begin{cases} y = 3x - 7 \\ x = 2 \end{cases}$

3. $\begin{cases} 3a + 5b = 0 \\ a + b = 2 \end{cases}$

4. $\begin{cases} x + 3y - z = 2 \\ x + 2z = 8 \\ 2y - z = 1 \end{cases}$

5. $\begin{cases} r - s + t = 150 \\ 2r + t = 425 \\ s + 3t = 0 \end{cases}$

6. $\begin{cases} x + 2y = 11 \\ 2x + 3y = 18 \end{cases}$

Examples 2 and 3
(page 215)

Solve each system of equations. Check your answers.

7. $\begin{cases} x + 3y = 5 \\ x + 4y = 6 \end{cases}$

8. $\begin{cases} p - 3q = -1 \\ -5p + 16q = 5 \end{cases}$

9. $\begin{cases} 300x - y = 130 \\ 200x + y = 120 \end{cases}$

10. $\begin{cases} x + 5y = -4 \\ x + 6y = -5 \end{cases}$

11. $\begin{cases} 2x + 3y = 12 \\ x + 2y = 7 \end{cases}$

12. $\begin{cases} 2x + 3y = 5 \\ x + 2y = 6 \end{cases}$

13. $\begin{cases} x + y + z = 4 \\ 4x + 5y = 3 \\ y - 3z = -10 \end{cases}$

14. $\begin{cases} 9y + 2z = 18 \\ 3x + 2y + z = 5 \\ x - y = -1 \end{cases}$

15. $\begin{cases} 9y + 2z = 14 \\ 3x + 2y + z = 5 \\ x - y = -1 \end{cases}$

Example 4
(page 216)

16. Shopping Suppose you want to fill nine 1-lb tins with a holiday snack mix. You plan to buy almonds for $2.45/lb, peanuts for $1.85/lb, and raisins for $.80/lb. You have $15 and want the mix to contain twice as much of the nuts as of the raisins by weight. How much of each ingredient should you buy?

 a. Writing Explain how each equation in the system at the right relates to the problem. What does each variable represent?

b. Solve the system.

$\begin{cases} x + y + z = 9 \\ 2.45x + 1.85y + 0.8z = 15 \\ x + y = 2z \end{cases}$

Example 5
(page 216)

Determine whether each system has a unique solution.

17. $\begin{cases} 20x + 5y = 240 \\ y = 20x \end{cases}$

18. $\begin{cases} 20x + 5y = 145 \\ 30x - 5y = 125 \end{cases}$

19. $\begin{cases} y = 2000 - 65x \\ y = 500 + 55x \end{cases}$

20. $\begin{cases} y = \frac{2}{3}x - 3 \\ y = -x + 7 \end{cases}$

21. $\begin{cases} 3x + 2y = 10 \\ 6x + 4y = 16 \end{cases}$

22. $\begin{cases} x + 2y + z = 4 \\ y = x - 3 \\ z = 2x \end{cases}$

B Apply Your Skills

Solve each matrix equation. If the coefficient matrix has no inverse, write *no unique solution.*

23. $\begin{bmatrix} 1 & 1 \\ 1 & 2 \end{bmatrix} \begin{bmatrix} x \\ y \end{bmatrix} = \begin{bmatrix} 8 \\ 10 \end{bmatrix}$

24. $\begin{bmatrix} 2 & -3 \\ -4 & 6 \end{bmatrix} \begin{bmatrix} a \\ b \end{bmatrix} = \begin{bmatrix} 1 \\ -2 \end{bmatrix}$

25. $\begin{bmatrix} 2 & 1 \\ 4 & 3 \end{bmatrix} \begin{bmatrix} x \\ y \end{bmatrix} = \begin{bmatrix} 10 \\ -2 \end{bmatrix}$

GO Online
Homework Video Tutor

Visit: PHSchool.com
Web Code: age-0407

Solve each system.

26. $\begin{cases} -3x + 4y = 2 \\ x - y = -1 \end{cases}$
 27. $\begin{cases} x + 2y = 10 \\ 3x + 5y = 26 \end{cases}$
 28. $\begin{cases} x - 3y = -1 \\ -6x + 19y = 6 \end{cases}$

29. $\begin{cases} x = 5 - y \\ 3y = z \\ x + z = 7 \end{cases}$
 30. $\begin{cases} -x = -4 - z \\ 2y = z - 1 \\ x = 6 - y - z \end{cases}$
 31. $\begin{cases} -b + 2c = 4 \\ a + b - c = -10 \\ 2a + 3c = 1 \end{cases}$

32. $\begin{cases} x + y + z = 4 \\ 4x + 5y = 4 \\ y - 3z = -9 \end{cases}$
 33. $\begin{cases} x + y + z = 4 \\ 4x + 5y = 3 \\ y - 3z = -10 \end{cases}$

34. $\begin{cases} -2w + x + y = 0 \\ -w + 2x - y + z = 1 \\ -2w + 3x + 3y + 2z = 6 \\ w + x + 2y + z = 5 \end{cases}$
 35. $\begin{cases} -2w + x + y = -2 \\ -w + 2x - y + z = -4 \\ -2w + 3x + 3y + 2z = 2 \\ w + x + 2y + z = 6 \end{cases}$

GO for Help

For a guide to solving
Exercise 36, see p. 220.

36. Coordinate Geometry The coordinates (x, y) of a point in a plane are the solution of the system $\begin{cases} 2x + 3y = 13 \\ 5x + 7y = 31 \end{cases}$. Find the coordinates of the point.

37. Geometry A rectangle is twice as long as it is wide. The perimeter is 840 ft. Find the dimensions of the rectangle.

 **Challenge**

Open-Ended Complete each system for the given number of solutions.

38. infinitely many

$\begin{cases} x + y = 7 \\ 2x + 2y = \blacksquare \end{cases}$

39. one solution

$\begin{cases} x + y + z = 7 \\ y + z = \blacksquare \\ z = \blacksquare \end{cases}$

40. no solution

$\begin{cases} x + y + z = 7 \\ y + z = \blacksquare \\ y + z = \blacksquare \end{cases}$

41. Physics When you mix hot and cold liquids, you can find the temperature of the mixture by using the formula $T = \frac{ah + bc}{a + b}$, where T is the temperature of the mixture, h is the temperature of the hot liquid, c is the temperature of the cold liquid, and a and b represent the amounts of hot and cold liquids. Suppose you mix hot tea and cold milk in a ratio $a : b$ of $9 : 1$, and find that the temperature of the mixture is 117°F. You then change the tea : milk ratio to $2 : 1$, and the temperature drops to 96°F. Find the initial temperatures of the tea and the milk.

42. Nutrition A caterer combines ingredients to make a paella, a Spanish fiesta dish. The paella weighs 18 lb, costs $29.50, and supplies 850 g of protein.
a. Write a system of three equations to find the weight of each ingredient.
b. Solve the system. How many pounds of each ingredient did she use?

Paella Nutrition Chart

Food	Cost/lb	Protein/lb
Chicken	$1.50	100 g
Rice	$.40	20 g
Shellfish	$6.00	50 g

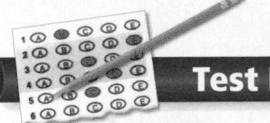

Test Prep

Multiple Choice

43. Which matrix equation represents the system $\begin{cases} 2x - 3y = -3 \\ -5x + y = 14 \end{cases}$?

A. $\begin{bmatrix} x \\ y \end{bmatrix}\begin{bmatrix} 2 & -3 \\ -5 & 1 \end{bmatrix} = \begin{bmatrix} -3 \\ 14 \end{bmatrix}$

B. $\begin{bmatrix} 2 & -3 \\ -5 & 1 \end{bmatrix}\begin{bmatrix} x \\ y \end{bmatrix} = \begin{bmatrix} -3 \\ 14 \end{bmatrix}$

C. $\begin{bmatrix} 2 & -3 \\ -5 & 1 \end{bmatrix}\begin{bmatrix} -3 \\ 14 \end{bmatrix} = \begin{bmatrix} x \\ y \end{bmatrix}$

D. $\begin{bmatrix} -3 \\ 14 \end{bmatrix}[x \ y] = \begin{bmatrix} 2 & -3 \\ -5 & 1 \end{bmatrix}$

44. What is the solution to the matrix equation $\begin{bmatrix} 3 & -1 \\ -1 & 2 \end{bmatrix}\begin{bmatrix} a \\ b \end{bmatrix} = \begin{bmatrix} 7 \\ -9 \end{bmatrix}$?

F. $a = 7, b = -9$ **G.** $a = 2, b = 1$ **H.** $a = \frac{7}{3}, b = -\frac{9}{2}$ **J.** $a = 1, b = -4$

Use the system $\begin{cases} 2x - 3y + z = 6 \\ x + 2y - 4z = 5 \\ -3x - 2y + 3z = -5 \end{cases}$ for Exercises 45–47.

45. Which matrix is the coefficient matrix for the system?

A. $\begin{bmatrix} 2 & 3 & 1 \\ 1 & 2 & 4 \\ 3 & 2 & 3 \end{bmatrix}$ **B.** $\begin{bmatrix} 2 & -3 & 1 & 6 \\ 1 & 2 & -4 & 5 \\ -3 & -2 & 3 & -5 \end{bmatrix}$ **C.** $\begin{bmatrix} 2 & -3 & 1 \\ 1 & 2 & -4 \\ -3 & -2 & 3 \end{bmatrix}$ **D.** $\begin{bmatrix} 6 \\ 5 \\ -5 \end{bmatrix}$

46. Which matrix is the constant matrix for the system?

F. $\begin{bmatrix} 2 & 3 & 1 \\ 1 & 2 & 4 \\ 3 & 2 & 3 \end{bmatrix}$ **G.** $\begin{bmatrix} 2 & -3 & 1 & 6 \\ 1 & 2 & -4 & 5 \\ -3 & -2 & 3 & -5 \end{bmatrix}$ **H.** $\begin{bmatrix} 2 & -3 & 1 \\ 1 & 2 & -4 \\ -3 & -2 & 3 \end{bmatrix}$ **J.** $\begin{bmatrix} 6 \\ 5 \\ -5 \end{bmatrix}$

47. What is the determinant of the coefficient matrix?
   A. -150 **B.** -27 **C.** 6 **D.** 29

Short Response

48. How can you write the three equations at the right as a matrix equation for a system? Explain your steps.

$2x - 3y + z + 10 = 0$
$x + 4y = 2z + 11$
$-2y + 3z + 7 = 3x$

Mixed Review

Lesson 4-6

Evaluate the determinant of each matrix.

49. $\begin{bmatrix} -1 & 3 & 7 \\ 5 & -4 & -2 \\ 0 & 2 & 10 \end{bmatrix}$ **50.** $\begin{bmatrix} 17 & 0 & 0 \\ 0 & 17 & 0 \\ 0 & 0 & 17 \end{bmatrix}$ **51.** $\begin{bmatrix} -3 & 0 & 5 \\ 5 & -3 & 2 \\ -3 & -5 & -2 \end{bmatrix}$

Lesson 4-2

Add or subtract.

52. $\begin{bmatrix} 5 & -3 \\ 4 & 11 \end{bmatrix} + \begin{bmatrix} 4 & 0 \\ -9 & 1 \end{bmatrix}$ **53.** $\begin{bmatrix} -1 & 2 & 0 \\ 10 & -5 & 15 \\ 17 & 3 & -4 \end{bmatrix} - \begin{bmatrix} 0 & 6 & -3 \\ 4 & -7 & 11 \\ -9 & 10 & -1 \end{bmatrix}$

Lesson 2-6

Describe each translation of $f(x) = |x|$ as *vertical*, *horizontal*, or *combined*. Then graph the translation.

54. $f(x) = |x + 4|$ **55.** $f(x) = |x| - 3$ **56.** $f(x) = |x - 5| + 3$

Understanding Math Problems Read the problem below. Then let Jaime's thinking guide you through the solution. Check your understanding with the exercises at the bottom of the page.

Coordinate Geometry The coordinates (x, y) of a point in a plane are the solution of the system $\begin{cases} 2x + 3y = 13 \\ 5x + 7y = 31 \end{cases}$. Find the coordinates of the point.

What Jaime Thinks

The problem tells me that the solution of this system is (x, y). I could graph the lines to see where they intersect, but that's not necessary when I can solve the system with matrices. I'll rewrite the system as a matrix equation.

To solve for the variable matrix that includes x and y, I should multiply each side of the equation by the inverse of the coefficient matrix. I'll use the formula on page 201.

Now that I have the inverse, I can multiply.

Something is wrong. I can't multiply the matrices on the right side of this equation because the dimensions don't match.

Oh!!! I have to multiply the inverse matrix on the left, because matrix multiplication is not commutative!

I'll rewrite the equation correctly. The result will be a 2×1 matrix.

This means the x-coordinate is 2 and the y-coordinate is 3. I'll write my answer in a sentence.

What Jaime Writes

$$\begin{cases} 2x + 3y = 13 \\ 5x + 7y = 31 \end{cases} \qquad \begin{bmatrix} 2 & 3 \\ 5 & 7 \end{bmatrix}\begin{bmatrix} x \\ y \end{bmatrix} = \begin{bmatrix} 13 \\ 31 \end{bmatrix}$$

Inverse of

$$\begin{bmatrix} 2 & 3 \\ 5 & 7 \end{bmatrix} = \frac{1}{(2)(7) - (5)(3)}\begin{bmatrix} 7 & -3 \\ -5 & 2 \end{bmatrix}$$

$$= -1\begin{bmatrix} 7 & -3 \\ -5 & 2 \end{bmatrix} = \begin{bmatrix} -7 & 3 \\ 5 & -2 \end{bmatrix}$$

$$\begin{bmatrix} -7 & 3 \\ 5 & -2 \end{bmatrix}\begin{bmatrix} 2 & 3 \\ 5 & 7 \end{bmatrix}\begin{bmatrix} x \\ y \end{bmatrix} = \begin{bmatrix} 13 \\ 31 \end{bmatrix}\begin{bmatrix} -7 & 3 \\ 5 & -2 \end{bmatrix}$$
$$\qquad\qquad\qquad\qquad\qquad\qquad 2 \times 1 \quad 2 \times 2$$
doesn't work!

$$\begin{bmatrix} -7 & 3 \\ 5 & -2 \end{bmatrix}\begin{bmatrix} 2 & 3 \\ 5 & 7 \end{bmatrix}\begin{bmatrix} x \\ y \end{bmatrix} = \begin{bmatrix} -7 & 3 \\ 5 & -2 \end{bmatrix}\begin{bmatrix} 13 \\ 31 \end{bmatrix}$$

$$\begin{bmatrix} x \\ y \end{bmatrix} = \begin{bmatrix} (-7)(13) + (3)(31) \\ (5)(13) + (-2)(31) \end{bmatrix} = \begin{bmatrix} 2 \\ 3 \end{bmatrix}$$

The coordinates of the point are (2, 3).

EXERCISES

1. The coordinates (x, y) of a point in a plane are the solution of the system $\begin{cases} 12x + 13y = 14 \\ 5x + 7y = 9 \end{cases}$. Find the coordinates of the point.

2. What difficulty would Jaime have with his solution process for a system that has no solutions? Infinitely many solutions?

4-8 Augmented Matrices and Systems

What You'll Learn

- To solve a system of equations using Cramer's Rule
- To solve a system of equations using augmented matrices

... And Why

To solve systems of three equations, as in Example 2

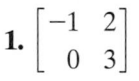 **Check Skills You'll Need**

GO for Help Lessons 4-5 and 4-6

Evaluate the determinant of each matrix.

1. $\begin{bmatrix} -1 & 2 \\ 0 & 3 \end{bmatrix}$

2. $\begin{bmatrix} 0 & 1 \\ -1 & 3 \end{bmatrix}$

3. $\begin{bmatrix} 2 & 1 \\ -1 & 5 \end{bmatrix}$

4. $\begin{bmatrix} 0 & 1 & -3 \\ 4 & 5 & -1 \\ -1 & 0 & 1 \end{bmatrix}$

5. $\begin{bmatrix} 3 & 4 & 5 \\ -1 & 2 & 0 \\ 0 & -1 & 1 \end{bmatrix}$

6. $\begin{bmatrix} 0 & 2 & -1 \\ 3 & 4 & 0 \\ -2 & -1 & 5 \end{bmatrix}$

New Vocabulary • Cramer's Rule • augmented matrix • row operations

---

1 Solving Systems Using Cramer's Rule

You can solve a system of linear equations that has a unique solution by using determinants and a pattern called Cramer's Rule.

 Key Concepts

Definition	**Cramer's Rule**

System

	Use the x- and y-coefficients. ↓	Replace the x-coefficients with the constants. ↓	Replace the y-coefficients with the constants. ↓

$$\begin{cases} ax + by = m \\ cx + dy = n \end{cases} \qquad D = \begin{vmatrix} a & b \\ c & d \end{vmatrix} \qquad D_x = \begin{vmatrix} m & b \\ n & d \end{vmatrix} \qquad D_y = \begin{vmatrix} a & m \\ c & n \end{vmatrix}$$

The solution of the system is $x = \dfrac{D_x}{D}$ and $y = \dfrac{D_y}{D}$, or $\left(\dfrac{D_x}{D}, \dfrac{D_y}{D} \right)$.

1 EXAMPLE Using Cramer's Rule

Use Cramer's Rule to solve the system $\begin{cases} 3x + 2y = 0 \\ x - y = -5 \end{cases}$.

Evaluate three determinants. Then find x and y.

$$D = \begin{vmatrix} 3 & 2 \\ 1 & -1 \end{vmatrix} = -5 \qquad D_x = \begin{vmatrix} 0 & 2 \\ -5 & -1 \end{vmatrix} = 10 \qquad D_y = \begin{vmatrix} 3 & 0 \\ 1 & -5 \end{vmatrix} = -15$$

$$x = \frac{D_x}{D} = \frac{10}{-5} = -2 \qquad y = \frac{D_y}{D} = \frac{-15}{-5} = 3$$

● The solution of the system is $(-2, 3)$.

 **Quick Check** ❶ Use Cramer's Rule to solve the system $\begin{cases} 3x + y = 5 \\ 2x + 3y = 8 \end{cases}$.

You can also use Cramer's Rule to solve a system of three equations.

2 EXAMPLE Using Cramer's Rule With Three Equations

Multiple Choice What is the value of x in the solution of the system at the right?

$$\begin{cases} y + 4z = 5 \\ x + y + z = 8 \\ 2x - 5y = 7 \end{cases}$$

Ⓐ -156 Ⓑ -26 Ⓒ 1 Ⓓ 6

$$D = \begin{vmatrix} 0 & 1 & 4 \\ 1 & 1 & 1 \\ 2 & -5 & 0 \end{vmatrix} = -26 \qquad \text{Evaluate the determinant.}$$

$$D_x = \begin{vmatrix} 5 & 1 & 4 \\ 8 & 1 & 1 \\ 7 & -5 & 0 \end{vmatrix} = -156 \qquad \text{Replace the } x\text{-coefficients with the constants and evaluate again.}$$

$$x = \frac{D_x}{D} = \frac{-156}{-26} = 6 \qquad \text{Find } x.$$

● The x-coordinate of the solution is 6. The answer is D.

Test-Taking Tip

When solving a system, make sure to match each value you find with the correct variable.

✓ Quick Check **2** **a. Critical Thinking** How would you modify the determinant D to find D_z?
b. Solve the system for y and z.

2 Solving Systems Using Augmented Matrices

Vocabulary Tip

<u>Augmented</u> means "increased in size" or "added to."

You can solve some linear systems by using an augmented matrix. An **augmented matrix** contains the coefficients and the constants from a system of equations. Each row of the matrix represents an equation.

3 EXAMPLE Writing an Augmented Matrix

Write an augmented matrix to represent the system. $\begin{cases} -6x + 2y = 10 \\ 4x = -20 \end{cases}$

System of equations $\begin{cases} -6x + 2y = 10 \\ 4x = -20 \end{cases}$

x-coefficients ↕   ↕ y-coefficients ↕ constants

Augmented matrix $\begin{bmatrix} -6 & 2 & | & 10 \\ 4 & 0 & | & -20 \end{bmatrix}$

↑ —— Draw a vertical bar to separate the coefficients from the constants.

An augmented matrix that represents the system is $\begin{bmatrix} -6 & 2 & | & 10 \\ 4 & 0 & | & -20 \end{bmatrix}$.

✓ Quick Check **3** Write an augmented matrix to represent each system.

a. $\begin{cases} x - 5y = 15 \\ 3x + 3y = 3 \end{cases}$ **b.** $\begin{cases} x + 2y + 3z = -4 \\ y - 2z = 8 \\ z = -3 \end{cases}$

An augmented matrix contains an entry of zero for any term missing from the system. You can write a system of equations from an augmented matrix.

4 **EXAMPLE** **Writing a System From an Augmented Matrix**

Write a system of equations for the augmented matrix $\begin{bmatrix} 6 & 0 & 3 \\ 1 & 1 & -5 \end{bmatrix}$.

Augmented matrix $\begin{bmatrix} 6 & 0 & \bigg| & 3 \\ 1 & 1 & \bigg| & -5 \end{bmatrix}$

x-coefficients $\updownarrow$ $\updownarrow$ y-coefficients $\updownarrow$ constants

System of equations $\begin{cases} 6x & + & & = & 3 \\ x & & y & = & -5 \end{cases}$

✓ **Quick Check** **4** Write a system of equations for each augmented matrix.

a. $\begin{bmatrix} 5 & 7 & -3 \\ 0 & -8 & 6 \end{bmatrix}$

b. $\begin{bmatrix} -1 & 0 & 3 & -4 \\ 7 & 2 & -1 & 0 \\ 0 & 1 & 2 & -3 \end{bmatrix}$

In Chapter 3 you learned how to solve systems of equations by using multiples of one or more of the equations to eliminate variables. You can do the same thing to an augmented matrix by using row operations.

🔑 **Key Concepts**

Definition	**Row Operations**

To solve a system of equations using an augmented matrix, you can use one or more of the following **row operations.**

- Switch any two rows.
- Multiply a row by a constant.
- Add one row to another.
- Combine one or more of these steps.

5 **EXAMPLE** **Using an Augmented Matrix**

Use an augmented matrix to solve the system $\begin{cases} x + 2y = -1 \\ 2x + 5y = -4 \end{cases}$.

$\begin{bmatrix} 1 & 2 & -1 \\ 2 & 5 & -4 \end{bmatrix}$ **Write an augmented matrix.**

$\begin{matrix} -2(1 & 2 & -1) \\ 2 & 5 & -4 \\ \hline 0 & 1 & -2 \end{matrix}$ **Multiply Row 1 by −2 and add it to Row 2.**

$\begin{bmatrix} 1 & 2 & -1 \\ 0 & 1 & -2 \end{bmatrix}$ **Write the new augmented matrix.**

$\begin{matrix} 1 & 2 & -1 \\ -2(0 & 1 & -2) \\ \hline 1 & 0 & 3 \end{matrix}$ **Multiply new Row 2 by −2 and add it to Row 1. Write the final augmented matrix.**

$\begin{bmatrix} 1 & 0 & 3 \\ 0 & 1 & -2 \end{bmatrix}$

The solution to the system is $(3, -2)$.

Check	$x + 2y = -1$	$2x + 5y = -4$	**Use the original equations.**
	$3 + 2(-2) \overset{?}{=} -1$	$2(3) + 5(-2) \overset{?}{=} -4$	**Substitute.**
	$3 + (-4) \overset{?}{=} -1$	$6 + (-10) \overset{?}{=} -4$	**Multiply.**
	$-1 = -1 ✓$	$-4 = -4 ✓$	**Simplify.**

✓ **Quick Check** **5** Solve $\begin{cases} x + y = -10 \\ -x + y = 20 \end{cases}$. Check your solution.

You can use augmented matrices and row operations to solve systems of three
equations. Graphing calculators have a feature that uses row operations to
simplify matrices.

6 EXAMPLE Using a Graphing Calculator

Use a graphing calculator to solve the system $\begin{cases} 2x + 3y - z = 11 \\ 3x - 2y + 4z = 10. \\ x + 4y - 2z = 8 \end{cases}$

Step 1 Enter the augmented
matrix as matrix A.

Step 2 Use the rref feature of your
graphing calculator.

```
[A]
[[  2   3   -1   11  ]
 [  3  -2    4   10  ]
 [  1   4   -2    8  ]]
```

```
rref([A])
[[  1   0   0   4  ]
 [  0   1   0   1  ]
 [  0   0   1   0  ]]
```

The simplified augmented matrix is equivalent to $\begin{cases} x = 4 \\ y = 1. \\ z = 0 \end{cases}$
The solution is $(4, 1, 0)$.

Partial Check

$2x + 3y - z = 11$	**Use the first equation.**
$2(4) + 3(1) - (0) \overset{?}{=} 11$	**Substitute.**
$8 + 3 - 0 \overset{?}{=} 11$	**Multiply.**
$11 = 11 \checkmark$	**Simplify.**

 **6 a.** Check the solution to Example 6 in the remaining two equations.

b. Use a graphing calculator to solve the system $\begin{cases} x + 4y - z = 4 \\ x - 2y + z = -2. \\ 5x - 3y + 8z = 13 \end{cases}$
Check your answer.

EXERCISES

For more exercises, see *Extra Skill and Word Problem Practice.*

Practice and Problem Solving

 Practice by Example

Examples 1 and 2
(pages 221 and 222)

Use Cramer's Rule to solve each system.

1. $\begin{cases} 2x + y = 4 \\ 3x - y = 6 \end{cases}$

2. $\begin{cases} 2x + y = 7 \\ -2x + 5y = -1 \end{cases}$

3. $\begin{cases} 2x + 4y = 10 \\ 3x + 5y = 14 \end{cases}$

4. $\begin{cases} y + 4z = 5 \\ x + y + z = 8 \\ 2x - 5y = 7 \end{cases}$

5. $\begin{cases} 2x + 3y + z = 5 \\ x + y - 2z = -2 \\ -3x + z = -7 \end{cases}$

Example 3
(page 222)

Write an augmented matrix for each system.

6. $\begin{cases} 3x - 4y = 17 \\ 8x + y = -3 \end{cases}$

7. $\begin{cases} 3x - 7y + 3z = -3 \\ x + y + 2z = -3 \\ 2x - 3y + 5z = -8 \end{cases}$

8. $\begin{cases} -x + 5y = -1 \\ x - 2y = 1 \end{cases}$

Example 4
(page 223)

Write a system of equations for each augmented matrix.

9. $\begin{bmatrix} 5 & 1 & | & -3 \\ -2 & 2 & | & 4 \end{bmatrix}$
10. $\begin{bmatrix} -1 & 2 & | & -6 \\ 1 & 1 & | & 7 \end{bmatrix}$
11. $\begin{bmatrix} 2 & 1 & 1 & | & 1 \\ 1 & 1 & 1 & | & 2 \\ 1 & -1 & 1 & | & -2 \end{bmatrix}$

Example 5
(page 223)

Use an augmented matrix to solve each system.

12. $\begin{cases} 2x - 2y = 15 \\ 4x + 4y = 10 \end{cases}$
13. $\begin{cases} 2x - 4y = 20 \\ 4x + 2y = -20 \end{cases}$
14. $\begin{cases} x + 2y = 3 \\ 4x + 2y = -6 \end{cases}$

15. $\begin{cases} x + 5y = -25 \\ 5x + y = 25 \end{cases}$
16. $\begin{cases} -x + 5y = 15 \\ 2x + 3y = 9 \end{cases}$
17. $\begin{cases} 3x + 6y = 2 \\ 2x - y = 3 \end{cases}$

Example 6
(page 224)

 Solve each system.

18. $\begin{cases} x + y + z = 2 \\ 2y - 2z = 2 \\ x - 3z = 1 \end{cases}$
19. $\begin{cases} x - y + z = 3 \\ x + 3z = 6 \\ y - 2z = -1 \end{cases}$
20. $\begin{cases} x + y - z = -1 \\ 3x + 4y - z = 8 \\ 6x + 8y - 2z = 16 \end{cases}$

21. $\begin{cases} x + y - z = 1 \\ 3x + 3y + z = 3 \\ 2x + 2y - 2z = 2 \end{cases}$
22. $\begin{cases} x + y = 1 \\ y + z = 2 \\ x - z = -1 \end{cases}$
23. $\begin{cases} x + z = -4 \\ y - z = 1 \\ x + y = -3 \end{cases}$

B **Apply Your Skills**

Use Cramer's Rule to solve each system.

24. $\begin{cases} 0.5x + 1.5y = 7 \\ 2.5x - 3.5y = -9 \end{cases}$
25. $\begin{cases} -1.2x - 0.3y = 2.1 \\ -0.2x + 0.8y = 4.6 \end{cases}$
26. $\begin{cases} \dfrac{x}{5} - \dfrac{2y}{5} = 4 \\ \dfrac{2x}{5} - \dfrac{3y}{5} = 5 \end{cases}$

27. $\begin{cases} \dfrac{x}{2} + \dfrac{y}{4} = 4 \\ \dfrac{x}{4} - \dfrac{3y}{8} = -2 \end{cases}$
28. $\begin{cases} 2x + 3y + 5z = 12 \\ 4x + 2y + 4z = -2 \\ 5x + 4y + 7z = 7 \end{cases}$

Use an augmented matrix to solve each system.

29. $\begin{cases} x + y + z = 1 \\ y - 3z = 4 \\ x - z = 2 \end{cases}$
30. $\begin{cases} x + y + z = 0 \\ y + 4z = -6 \\ 2x - 2z = 4 \end{cases}$
31. $\begin{cases} 2x + y = 8 \\ x + z = 5 \\ y - z = -1 \end{cases}$

 32. **Business** A manufacturer sells pencils and erasers in packages. The price of a package of five erasers and two pencils is $.23. The price of a package of seven erasers and five pencils is $.41. Find the price of one eraser and one pencil.

33. **Multiple Choice** Suppose you invested $5000 in three different funds for one year. The funds paid simple interest of 8%, 10%, and 7%, respectively. The total interest at the end of one year was $405. You invested $500 more at 10% than at 8%. How much did you invest in the 10% fund?
   (A) $150
   (B) $1000
   (C) $1500
   (D) $2500

34. **Open-Ended** Write and solve a system of three equations in three unknowns using Cramer's Rule.

Homework Video Tutor
Visit: PHSchool.com
Web Code: age-0408

Solve each system.

35. $\begin{cases} 2x - 3y + 2z = 10 \\ x + 3y + 4z = 14 \\ 3x - y + z = 9 \end{cases}$
36. $\begin{cases} 4x - y + z = 3 \\ x + 2y + z = 0 \\ 3x + 7y - 3z = 6 \end{cases}$
37. $\begin{cases} x + 2y + z = 4 \\ 3x + 6y + 3z = 2 \\ x - y + z = 3 \end{cases}$

Problem Solving Hint

1 gal = 4 qt = 8 pt

38. Colors A hardware store mixes paints in a ratio of two parts red to six parts yellow to make pumpkin orange. A ratio of five parts red to three parts yellow makes red-pepper red. A gallon of pumpkin orange sells for $25, and a gallon of red-pepper red sells for $28.
 a. Write a system of equations to model the situation.
 b. Solve the system.
 c. Find the cost of 1 qt of red paint and the cost of 1 qt of yellow paint.

39. Sales Refer to the signs below. Find the price per pound of each type of nut.

2 lb almonds
3 lb pecans
only $16

1 lb almonds
1 lb pecans
1 lb pistachios
only $12

3 lb pecans
2 lb pistachios
only $24

C **Challenge**

Solve using Cramer's Rule. (*Hint:* Start by substituting $m = \frac{1}{x}$ and $n = \frac{1}{y}$.)

40. $\begin{cases} \dfrac{4}{x} + \dfrac{1}{y} = 1 \\ \dfrac{8}{x} + \dfrac{4}{y} = 3 \end{cases}$

41. $\begin{cases} \dfrac{4}{x} - \dfrac{2}{y} = 1 \\ \dfrac{10}{x} + \dfrac{20}{y} = 0 \end{cases}$

 Solve each system.

42. $\begin{cases} w + x + y + z = 3 \\ -w + x - 2y + z = -2 \\ 2x - y + z = 1 \\ w + y - z = 2 \end{cases}$

43. $\begin{cases} 2x + 2y + z = 4 \\ w + y - z = -2 \\ w + x + y + z = 3 \\ -4w + z = 2 \end{cases}$

44. Nutrition While stranded on an island, the crew of a sailboat has access to only three sources of food, as shown in the table below. One of the crew members designs a daily diet to supply each person with 120 g of fat, 220 g of carbohydrates, and 80 g of protein.

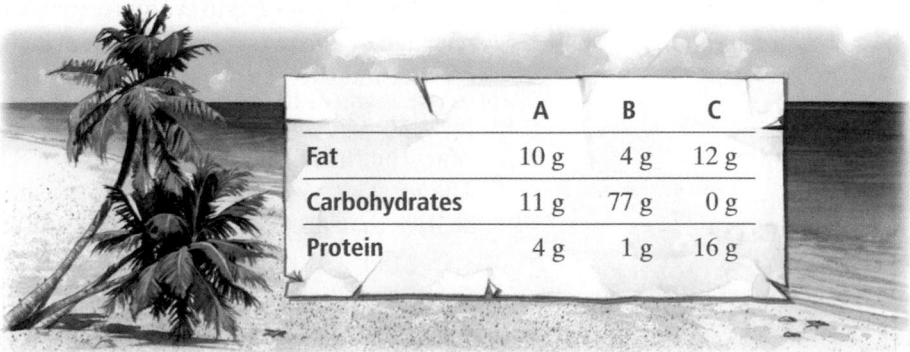

	A	B	C
Fat	10 g	4 g	12 g
Carbohydrates	11 g	77 g	0 g
Protein	4 g	1 g	16 g

 a. Write a system of three equations in three variables to find the number of portions of each food each person must have to meet the daily diet.
 b. Use an augmented matrix to solve the system of equations from part (a). Round each answer to the nearest tenth.
 c. **Writing** Suppose food C runs out. How would this change the number of portions of food required each day?

45. Geometry The perimeter of the rectangle at the right is 28 cm. The perimeter of each of the triangles is 24 cm. The diagonal of the rectangle is 2 cm longer than the longer side of the rectangle.

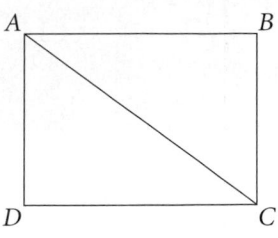

a. Write a system of three equations in three unknowns.
b. Simplify the system to a system of two equations in two unknowns.
c. Write an augmented matrix for the system in part (b).
d. Find the dimensions of the rectangle.
e. Find the length of the diagonal.

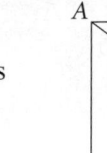

Test Prep

Multiple Choice Use the system $\begin{cases} 5x - 4y = -13 \\ -3x + 6y = 6 \end{cases}$ for Exercises 46 and 47.

46. Which is the determinant D_x?

A. $\begin{vmatrix} 5 & -4 \\ -3 & 6 \end{vmatrix}$ **B.** $\begin{vmatrix} -13 & -4 \\ 6 & 6 \end{vmatrix}$ **C.** $\begin{vmatrix} 5 & -13 \\ -3 & 6 \end{vmatrix}$ **D.** $\begin{vmatrix} 5 & 4 & -13 \\ -3 & 6 & 6 \end{vmatrix}$

47. What is the solution of the system?

F. $(-13, 6)$ **G.** $\left(-\frac{13}{5}, 1\right)$ **H.** $\left(-3, -\frac{1}{2}\right)$ **J.** $2x + 2y = -7$

Use the system $\begin{cases} 2x + y - 3z = -2 \\ 4x - 3y + 6z = 9 \\ -2x - 2y + 9z = 7 \end{cases}$ for Exercises 48 and 49.

48. What is the value of the determinant D_y?
A. -36 **B.** -24 **C.** -18 **D.** 36

49. What is the value of the determinant D_z?
F. -36 **G.** -24 **H.** -18 **J.** 36

Mixed Review

Lesson 4-7 Solve each system of equations by using the inverse of the coefficient matrix.

50. $\begin{cases} x + 4y + 3z = 3 \\ 2x - 5y - z = 5 \\ 3x + 2y - 2z = -3 \end{cases}$ **51.** $\begin{cases} x + y + z = -1 \\ y + 3z = -5 \\ x + z = -2 \end{cases}$

Lesson 3-3 Solve each system of inequalities by graphing.

52. $\begin{cases} 2x + y < 3 \\ -x - y \geq 1 \end{cases}$ **53.** $\begin{cases} 2x \leq 0 \\ -x + y > -1 \end{cases}$ **54.** $\begin{cases} x < 3 \\ y \geq -4 \\ -x + y < 5 \end{cases}$

Lesson 2-2 Write in point-slope form the equation of the line through each pair of points.

55. $(0, 1)$ and $(2, -5)$ **56.** $(-9, 3)$ and $(-4, -4)$ **57.** $(1, 8)$ and $(7, 2)$

Interpreting Data

A test item may give you a graph and ask you to choose a situation that best interprets the graph. Or it may give you a situation and ask you to choose a graph that best models the situation.

To make the choice, you must break down each situation to find the features that must be present in the graph.

EXAMPLE

In a research study, a rodent population remained stable for some time. It increased rapidly when a predator was removed. Then it declined rapidly as overpopulation caused a food shortage. Which graph best models this situation?

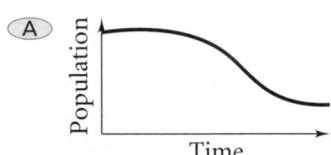
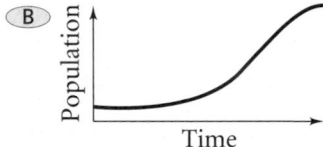
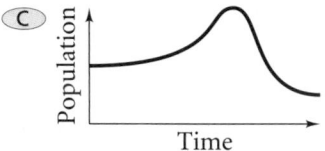

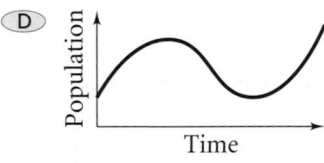
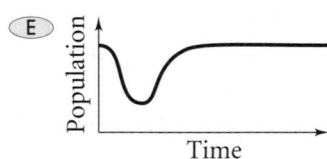

As time increases (from left to right), the correct graph must

- begin with a horizontal part to show a stable population.
- rise rapidly to show the predator's absence.
- fall rapidly to show the food shortage.

Only one graph has all three parts in the correct order. The answer is C.

EXERCISES

1. **Multiple Choice** A test item gives you the graph from choice E above. Which situation below best interprets this graph?
   - (A) An infection reduced the population of rodents. Then the population recovered and stabilized as the health of the remaining animals improved.
   - (B) The rodent population grew because food was abundant.
   - (C) The rodent population declined suddenly because of a mutant gene.
   - (D) The rodent birthrate steadily declined because of contaminated food.
   - (E) A flood displaced half the rodents. The remaining rodents moved to a different location during the year.

2. Repeat Exercise 1 for Graph A from the Example.

3. Describe a situation that fits Graph D from the Example.

Chapter Review

Vocabulary Review

augmented matrix (p. 222)
center of rotation (p. 194)
coefficient matrix (p. 214)
constant matrix (p. 214)
Cramer's Rule (p. 221)
determinant (p. 200)
dilation (p. 192)
equal matrices (p. 177)

image (p. 192)
matrix (p. 168)
matrix addition (p. 174)
matrix element (p. 169)
matrix equation (p. 176)
matrix multiplication (p. 184)
multiplicative identity matrix (p. 199)
multiplicative inverse matrix (p. 199)

preimage (p. 192)
rotation (p. 194)
row operations (p. 223)
scalar (p. 182)
scalar multiplication (p. 182)
square matrix (p. 199)
variable matrix (p. 214)
zero matrix (p. 175)

Choose the correct vocabulary term to complete each sentence.

1. A __?__ is a rectangular array of numbers.

2. Translations, dilations, reflections, and rotations are all __?__.

3. Cramer's Rule uses __?__ to solve a system of equations.

4. If corresponding elements of matrices are equal, the matrices are __?__.

5. The additive identity of a matrix is the __?__.

6. A __?__ consists of a coefficient matrix, a variable matrix, and a constant matrix.

7. An $n \times n$ matrix is called a __?__.

8. The image of a figure is a transformation of the __?__.

9. The product of a real number and a matrix is called a __?__.

10. A matrix is the inverse of another matrix if their product is the __?__.

Go Online
PHSchool.com
For: Vocabulary quiz
Web Code: agj-0451

Skills and Concepts

4-1 Objectives

▼ To identify matrices and their elements (p. 168)

▼ To organize data into matrices (p. 169)

It is often useful to organize data into matrices. A **matrix** is a rectangular array of numbers classified by its dimensions. An $m \times n$ matrix has m rows and n columns. A **matrix element** a_{ij} is in the ith row and jth column of matrix A.

State the dimensions of each matrix A. Identify the indicated element.

11. $\begin{bmatrix} 5 & 8 & -7 \\ 1 & 11 & 3 \end{bmatrix}; a_{13}$

12. $\begin{bmatrix} 3 & 1 \\ -5 & 0 \\ 7 & 6 \end{bmatrix}; a_{21}$

13. $\begin{bmatrix} 5 & 1 & -2 \\ 4 & -7 & 12 \\ 0 & 78 & 3 \end{bmatrix}; a_{32}$

Use the matrix at the right for Exercises 14–16.

14. How many points has Tamika scored?

15. How many three-point shots has Tran made?

16. What percent of Johanna's points were from one-point shots?

	1-pt Shots	2-pt Shots	3-pt Shots
Tamika	22	30	48
Johanna	21	31	48
Tran	21	29	50

To perform **matrix addition** or subtraction, add or subtract the corresponding elements in the matrices. To obtain the product of a matrix and a **scalar,** multiply each matrix element by the scalar. **Matrix multiplication** uses both multiplication and addition. The element in the ith row and jth column of the product of two matrices is the sum of the products of each element of the ith row of the first matrix and the corresponding element of the jth column of the second matrix. The first matrix must have the same number of columns as the second has rows.

Two matrices are **equal matrices** when they have the same dimensions and corresponding elements are equal. This principle is used to solve a **matrix equation.**

Solve each matrix equation for matrix X.

17. $[2 \quad -6 \quad 8] + [-1 \quad -2 \quad 4] = X$ **18.** $\begin{bmatrix} t \\ 6 \end{bmatrix} - \begin{bmatrix} 1 \\ 3 \end{bmatrix} = X$

19. $\begin{bmatrix} 7 & -1 \\ 0 & 8 \end{bmatrix} + X = \begin{bmatrix} 4 & 9 \\ -3 & 11 \end{bmatrix}$ **20.** $X - \begin{bmatrix} -7 & 13 & 5 \\ 31 & 0 & -4 \end{bmatrix} = \begin{bmatrix} 9 & -5 & 8 \\ 2 & 0 & -3 \end{bmatrix}$

Solve for each variable.

21. $\begin{bmatrix} x - 5 & 9 \\ 4 & t + 2 \end{bmatrix} = \begin{bmatrix} -7 & w + 1 \\ 8 - r & 1 \end{bmatrix}$ **22.** $\begin{bmatrix} -4 + t & 2y \\ r & w + 4 \end{bmatrix} = \begin{bmatrix} 2t & 11 \\ -2r + 12 & 9 \end{bmatrix}$

Use matrices $A, B, C,$ and D. Find each scalar product, sum, or difference, if possible. If an operation is not defined, label it *undefined*.

$A = \begin{bmatrix} 6 & 1 & 0 & 8 \\ -4 & 3 & 7 & 11 \end{bmatrix}$ $B = \begin{bmatrix} 1 & 3 \\ -2 & 4 \end{bmatrix}$ $C = \begin{bmatrix} -2 & 1 \\ 4 & 0 \\ 2 & 2 \\ 1 & 1 \end{bmatrix}$ $D = \begin{bmatrix} 5 & -2 \\ 3 & 6 \end{bmatrix}$

23. $3A$ **24.** $B - 2D$ **25.** AB **26.** BA **27.** $AC - BD$

A change made to a figure is a transformation. The original figure is the **preimage,** and the transformed figure is the **image.** A translation slides a figure without changing its size or shape. A **dilation** changes the size of a figure. You can use matrix addition to translate a figure and scalar multiplication to dilate a figure.

You can use multiplication by the appropriate matrix to perform transformations that are specific reflections or **rotations.** For example, to reflect a figure in the y-axis, multiply by $\begin{bmatrix} -1 & 0 \\ 0 & 1 \end{bmatrix}$. To rotate a figure 180°, multiply by $\begin{bmatrix} -1 & 0 \\ 0 & -1 \end{bmatrix}$.

For Exercises 28–35, use $\triangle ABC$ with vertices $A(3, 1)$, $B(-2, 0)$, and $C(1, 5)$. Write the coordinates of each image in matrix form.

28. a translation 1 unit right and 2 units down

29. a translation 3 units left and 4 units up

30. a reflection in the y-axis   **31.** a reflection in the line $y = x$

32. a rotation of 270°   **33.** a dilation half the original size

34. a dilation twice the original size   **35.** a rotation of 90°

4-5, 4-6 and 4-7 Objectives

▼ To evaluate determinants of 2 × 2 matrices and find inverse matrices (p. 199)

▼ To use inverse matrices in solving matrix equations (pp. 201 and 207)

▼ To evaluate determinants of 3 × 3 matrices (p. 206)

▼ To solve systems of equations using inverse matrices (p. 214)

A **square matrix** with 1's along its main diagonal and 0's elsewhere is the **multiplicative identity matrix,** I. If A and X are square matrices such that $AX = I$, then X is the **multiplicative inverse matrix** of A, A^{-1}.

You can use formulas to evaluate the determinants of 2 × 2 and 3 × 3 matrices.

$$\begin{vmatrix} a & b \\ c & d \end{vmatrix} = ad - bc \qquad \begin{vmatrix} a_1 & b_1 & c_1 \\ a_2 & b_2 & c_2 \\ a_3 & b_3 & c_3 \end{vmatrix} = \begin{aligned} & a_1 b_2 c_3 + a_2 b_3 c_1 + a_3 b_1 c_2 \\ & - a_1 b_3 c_2 - a_2 b_1 c_3 - a_3 b_2 c_1 \end{aligned}$$

You can use a calculator to find the inverse of a matrix. The inverse of a 2 × 2 matrix can be found by using its determinant.
$$\begin{bmatrix} a & b \\ c & d \end{bmatrix}^{-1} = \frac{1}{ad - bc} \begin{bmatrix} d & -b \\ -c & a \end{bmatrix}$$

You can use inverse matrices to solve some matrix equations.

You can also use inverse matrices to solve some systems of equations. When equations in a system are in standard form, the product of the **coefficient matrix** and the **variable matrix** equals the **constant matrix.** You solve the equation by multiplying both sides of the equation by the inverse of the coefficient matrix. If that inverse does not exist, the system does not have a unique solution.

Evaluate the determinant of each matrix, and find the inverse, if possible.

36. $\begin{bmatrix} 6 & 1 \\ 0 & 4 \end{bmatrix}$ 37. $\begin{bmatrix} 5 & -2 \\ 10 & -4 \end{bmatrix}$ 38. $\begin{bmatrix} 10 & 1 \\ 8 & 5 \end{bmatrix}$ 39. $\begin{bmatrix} 1 & 0 & 2 \\ -1 & 0 & 1 \\ -1 & -2 & 0 \end{bmatrix}$

Use an inverse matrix to solve each equation or system.

40. $\begin{bmatrix} 3 & 5 \\ 6 & 2 \end{bmatrix} X = \begin{bmatrix} -2 & 6 \\ 4 & 12 \end{bmatrix}$ 41. $\begin{cases} x - y = 3 \\ 2x - y = -1 \end{cases}$ 42. $\begin{bmatrix} 4 & 1 \\ 2 & 1 \end{bmatrix} \begin{bmatrix} x \\ y \end{bmatrix} = \begin{bmatrix} 10 \\ 6 \end{bmatrix}$

43. $\begin{bmatrix} -6 & 0 \\ 7 & 1 \end{bmatrix} X = \begin{bmatrix} -12 & -6 \\ 17 & 9 \end{bmatrix}$ 44. $\begin{cases} x + 2y = 15 \\ 2x + 4y = 30 \end{cases}$ 45. $\begin{cases} a + 2b + c = 14 \\ b = c + 1 \\ a = -3c + 6 \end{cases}$

46. **Physical Fitness** A club of 17 students is going on a canoe trip. The group of people on the trip includes 5 chaperones, one for each canoe. Some canoes hold 5 people, while some hold 4 people. How many of each kind of canoe should the group rent?

4-8 Objectives

▼ To solve a system of equations using Cramer's Rule (p. 221)

▼ To solve a system of equations using augmented matrices (p. 222)

Cramer's Rule for solving systems of equations uses determinants to solve for each variable. D is the determinant of the coefficient matrix. D_y is the determinant formed by replacing the coefficients of y in D with the constant terms.

You can also use **row operations** on an augmented matrix to solve a system.

Solve each system using Cramer's Rule. Check your answers by solving each system using an augmented matrix.

47. $\begin{cases} 2x - y = 15 \\ x + 3y = -17 \end{cases}$ 48. $\begin{cases} 3r + s - 2t = 22 \\ r + 5s + t = 4 \\ r = -3t \end{cases}$

History Use the table below for Exercises 1–3.

President	Years	Vetoes	Overrides
Kennedy	3	21	9
Johnson	5	30	0
Nixon	5.5	43	7
Ford	2.5	66	12
Carter	4	31	2
Reagan	8	78	9
G.H.W. Bush	4	46	1
Clinton	8	38	2

SOURCE: Congressional Research Service.
Go to **www.PHSchool.com** for a data update.
Web Code: agg-2041

1. Display the data in a matrix in which each row represents a president.

2. State the dimensions of the matrix.

3. Find and identify a_{32}.

Find each sum or difference.

4. $\begin{bmatrix} 4 & 7 \\ -2 & 1 \end{bmatrix} - \begin{bmatrix} -9 & 3 \\ 6 & 0 \end{bmatrix}$

5. $\begin{bmatrix} 4 & -5 & 1 \\ 10 & 7 & 4 \\ 21 & -9 & -6 \end{bmatrix} + \begin{bmatrix} -7 & -10 & 4 \\ 17 & 0 & 3 \\ -2 & -6 & 1 \end{bmatrix}$

Find each product.

6. $\begin{bmatrix} 2 & 6 \\ 1 & 0 \end{bmatrix}\begin{bmatrix} -1 & 5 \\ 3 & 1 \end{bmatrix}$

7. $2\begin{bmatrix} -8 & 5 & -1 \\ 0 & 9 & 7 \end{bmatrix}$

8. $\begin{bmatrix} 0 & 3 \\ -4 & 9 \end{bmatrix}\begin{bmatrix} -4 & 6 & 1 & 3 \\ 9 & -8 & 10 & 7 \end{bmatrix}$

Parallelogram $ABCD$ has coordinates $A(2, -1)$, $B(4, 3)$, $C(1, 5)$, and $D(-1, 1)$. Write a matrix for the vertices of its image after each transformation.

9. a dilation of size $\frac{2}{3}$

10. a translation right 2 units and down 4 units

11. a reflection in $y = x$ 12. a rotation of 270°

13. Graph parallelogram $ABCD$ and its image from Question 11 on the same coordinate plane.

14. **Open-Ended** Write a matrix that has no inverse.

15. **Writing** Explain how to determine whether two matrices can be multiplied and what the dimensions of the product matrix will be.

16. Find the value of each variable.
$\begin{bmatrix} x & 1 & y \\ 2 & 0 & 1 \end{bmatrix} = \begin{bmatrix} 1 - x & z & 2 \\ 2 + w & 4 - t & 1 \end{bmatrix}$

Find the determinant of each matrix.

17. $\begin{bmatrix} 1 & 0 & 0 \\ 0 & 1 & 0 \\ 0 & 0 & 1 \end{bmatrix}$
18. $\begin{bmatrix} 2 & 3 & 0 \\ -1 & 1 & 0 \\ 4 & 2 & 1 \end{bmatrix}$
19. $\begin{bmatrix} 8 & -3 \\ 2 & 9 \end{bmatrix}$

20. $\begin{bmatrix} 0 & 3 \\ x & t \end{bmatrix}$
21. $\begin{bmatrix} \frac{1}{2} & -1 \\ 3 & 0 \end{bmatrix}$

Find the inverse of each matrix, if it exists.

22. $\begin{bmatrix} 3 & 8 \\ -7 & 10 \end{bmatrix}$
23. $\begin{bmatrix} 0 & -5 \\ 9 & 6 \end{bmatrix}$
24. $\begin{bmatrix} \frac{1}{2} & -1 \\ 0 & 4 \end{bmatrix}$

25. $\begin{bmatrix} -8 & 4 & -11 \\ 5 & 2 & 9 \\ -5 & 6 & 2 \end{bmatrix}$
26. $\begin{bmatrix} 1 & 1 & 2 \\ 2 & 1 & 3 \\ 2 & 1 & 1 \end{bmatrix}$

Solve each matrix equation.

27. $\begin{bmatrix} 3 & -8 \\ 10 & 5 \end{bmatrix} - X = \begin{bmatrix} 2 & 8 \\ -1 & 12 \end{bmatrix}$

28. $\begin{bmatrix} 3 & 2 \\ -1 & 5 \end{bmatrix}X = \begin{bmatrix} -10 & -11 \\ 26 & -36 \end{bmatrix}$

29. $2X - \begin{bmatrix} -2 & 0 \\ 1 & 4 \end{bmatrix} = \begin{bmatrix} 5 & 10 \\ -15 & 9 \end{bmatrix}$

Solve each system using inverse matrices.

30. $\begin{cases} 2x - y = 5 \\ x + 4y = 7 \end{cases}$

31. $\begin{cases} x + 2y + z = -1 \\ 4x - y - z = -1 \\ 2z = -3y \end{cases}$

32. Solve $\begin{cases} -2x + 7y = 19 \\ x + 3y = 10 \end{cases}$ using Cramer's Rule.

33. Solve the system using an augmented matrix.
$\begin{cases} x + y + z = 9 \\ 4x + 3y - z = -6 \\ -x - y + 2z = 21 \end{cases}$

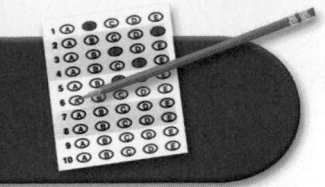

Standardized Test Prep

Multiple Choice

For Exercises 1–12, choose the correct letter.

1 Which number is irrational?

Ⓐ $8.\overline{12}$ Ⓑ $\sqrt{121}$ Ⓒ -5 Ⓓ $\sqrt{35}$

2. Which numbers are solutions of $\frac{5}{4}|2x - 9| = 5$?

Ⓕ $\frac{11}{8}, \frac{61}{8}$ Ⓖ $\frac{5}{2}, \frac{13}{2}$ Ⓗ $\frac{8}{5}, \frac{28}{5}$ Ⓙ $2, 7$

3. Which equation represents the *xy*-trace of $20x - 70y - 50z = 100$?

Ⓐ $2x - 7y = 10$ Ⓑ $-7y - 5z = 10$
Ⓒ $2x - 5z = 10$ Ⓓ $5z = -10$

4. Which ordered pair is *not* a solution of the system $\begin{cases} x + y \le -4 \\ 2x - y \ge -3 \end{cases}$?

Ⓕ $(1, 1)$ Ⓖ $(0, 3)$ Ⓗ $(-5, -1)$ Ⓙ $(3, 0)$

5. What is the solution of $\begin{cases} 2x - y = 4 \\ y = 2 - x \end{cases}$?

Ⓐ $(0, 2)$ Ⓑ $(2, 0)$
Ⓒ $(2, 4)$ Ⓓ $(0, -4)$

6. Suppose *y* varies directly with *x*. When *x* is 16, *y* is 10. What is *x* when *y* is –16?

Ⓐ -0.625 Ⓑ -1.6 Ⓒ -10 Ⓓ -25.6

7. What is the sum $\begin{bmatrix} 3 & 7 & -2 \\ 0 & 10 & 5 \end{bmatrix} + \begin{bmatrix} 6 & -8 & 1 \\ 9 & -4 & 11 \end{bmatrix}$?

Ⓐ $\begin{bmatrix} 9 & -1 & -1 \\ 9 & 6 & 16 \end{bmatrix}$ Ⓑ $\begin{bmatrix} 9 & 15 & -1 \\ 9 & 6 & 16 \end{bmatrix}$

Ⓒ $\begin{bmatrix} 9 & 15 & -3 \\ 9 & 6 & 16 \end{bmatrix}$ Ⓓ $\begin{bmatrix} -3 & 1 & -3 \\ -9 & 14 & -6 \end{bmatrix}$

8. Which equation has the solution $\begin{bmatrix} 1 & -2 & 0 \\ -5 & 4 & 7 \end{bmatrix}$?

Ⓕ $\begin{bmatrix} 7 & -2 & -3 \\ 0 & 1 & 8 \end{bmatrix} - X = \begin{bmatrix} 8 & -4 & -3 \\ -5 & 5 & 15 \end{bmatrix}$

Ⓖ $\begin{bmatrix} 10 & -8 & 12 \\ 4 & 0 & 5 \end{bmatrix} - \begin{bmatrix} -9 & -6 & 12 \\ -1 & -4 & -2 \end{bmatrix} = X$

Ⓗ $\begin{bmatrix} 0 & 6 & 5 \\ 2 & -1 & -9 \end{bmatrix} + X = \begin{bmatrix} 1 & 4 & 5 \\ -3 & 3 & -2 \end{bmatrix}$

Ⓙ $X - \begin{bmatrix} 3 & 7 & 4 \\ 8 & -6 & 1 \end{bmatrix} = \begin{bmatrix} 2 & -5 & 4 \\ -3 & 2 & 6 \end{bmatrix}$

9. Which equation represents a translation of the graph of $y = |x|$?

Ⓐ $y = -|x + 4|$ Ⓑ $y = |-x + 4|$
Ⓒ $y = |2x| + 4$ Ⓓ $y = 2|x - 2| + 4$

10. Which lines are perpendicular to $y = 3x - 8$?

I. $y = \frac{1}{3}x - 1$ **II.** $y = -\frac{1}{3}x + 1$
III. $y = 3x + 2$ **IV.** $y = 6x + 4$

Ⓕ I only   Ⓖ III and IV
Ⓗ I and II   Ⓙ II only

11. Which graph shows the solution of $8 < 4 - 2y < 15$?

Ⓐ ◄─┼─┼○┼─┼─┼○┼─┼─►
     -6 -4 -2 0
Ⓑ ◄─┼─┼○┼─┼─┼○┼─┼○┼─►
     0 2 4 6
Ⓒ ◄─┼○┼─┼─┼○┼─┼─┼─►
     -6 -4 -2 0
Ⓓ ◄─┼─┼○┼─┼─┼─┼○┼─►
     0 2 4 6

12. Find the domain of the relation $\{(3, -9), (2, 5), (-1, 6), (0, 0)\}$.

Ⓕ $\{-9, -1, 0, 2, 3, 5, 6\}$ Ⓖ $\{2, 3, 5, 6\}$
Ⓗ $\{-1, 0, 2, 3\}$ Ⓙ $\{-9, 0, 5, 6\}$

Gridded Response

13. What is the slope of the graph of $8x - 2y = 3$?

14. What is the value of $\begin{vmatrix} 7 & -1 \\ 3 & 2 \end{vmatrix}$?

Short Response

15. Write a matrix to translate $\begin{bmatrix} -1 & 4 & 5 \\ 0 & 7 & 2 \end{bmatrix}$ 7 units left and 2 units up. Use the matrix to find the coordinates of the image.

Extended Response

16. A dietitian wants to prepare a meal with 24 g of protein, 27 g of fat, and 20 g of carbohydrates using the three foods shown in the table.

Food	Protein	Fat	Carbohydrates
A	2 g/oz	3 g/oz	4 g/oz
B	3 g/oz	3 g/oz	1 g/oz
C	3 g/oz	3 g/oz	2 g/oz

a. Set up a matrix equation for the data.
b. Solve the matrix equation.
c. How many ounces of each food are needed?

Building a Business

Applying Inequalities The efficiency of a factory depends on how you divide limited resources among the products produced. The bad news is that in any factory you have a limited number of machines and raw materials available. The good news is that these limitations lead to inequalities that you can use to decide how to maximize your profits.

1 The cacao tree grows in tropical jungles. It produces melonlike fruits, each containing 20–40 cocoa beans.

3 The inside of the cocoa bean is ground into a concentrated chocolate liquid.

2 After roasting, cocoa beans pass through a machine that separates the shell from the inside of the bean.

Activity

You are in charge of a small private chocolate factory that makes two popular and profitable chocolate bars, Cocoa Bar and Choco-Lot. Your goal is to figure out how many of each type of chocolate bar you should produce each day to maximize your company's profits.

Here are a few key pieces of information:

- The success of your chocolate recipes lies in your use of two secret ingredients, referred to as Flavor A and Flavor B to protect the company's interests. The table shows the production rate and requirements of the flavors.

	Flavor A	Flavor B
Production rate	126 kg/day	136 kg/day
Cocoa Bar requirements	1.8 g/bar	4.0 g/bar
Choco-Lot requirements	2.8 g/bar	1.7 g/bar

- One machine wraps both candy bars. It can wrap 50,000 chocolate bars per day.

- Your profit on each Cocoa Bar bar is 14¢, and your profit on each Choco-Lot bar is 12¢.

a. Write inequalities to describe each objective and constraint.

b. Graph the inequalities you wrote in part (a).

c. Find the quantity of each chocolate bar you should manufacture to maximize your daily profit. Calculate the profit you will earn.

Chocolate Fondue

To make chocolate fondue, melt chocolate gently over low heat. Dip pieces of fruit in the melted chocolate.

4 Milk and sugar are mixed together before being added to the cocoa bean liquid.

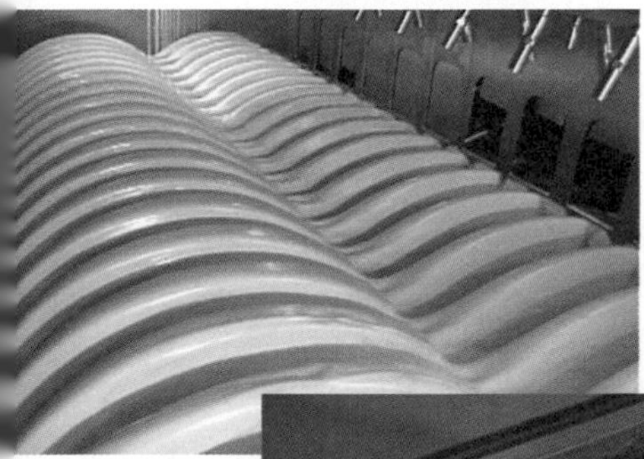

6 Any gritty particles are removed by machine.

7 The chocolate paste is ready to be cooled and molded.

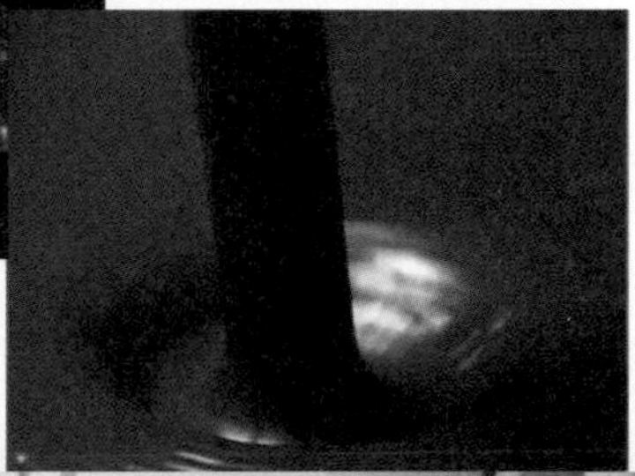

5 The cocoa, milk, and sugar mixture is dried to a powder and mixed with cocoa butter to make a chocolate paste.

White Chocolate

White chocolate is not a real chocolate, since it does not contain cocoa solids. A good white chocolate is made with cocoa butter as well as milk solids and sugar.

8 The molded chocolate takes a bumpy ride along a conveyor belt to eliminate air bubbles as it cools. It's ready for wrapping!

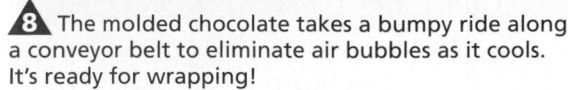

Go Online
PHSchool.com

For: Information about manufacturing
Web Code: age-0453

235

What You've Learned

- In Chapter 1, you learned to write and solve linear equations.
- In Chapter 2, you learned to graph linear functions.
- In Chapter 2, you learned to use linear functions to model real-world data.

 **Check Your Readiness**   **GO for Help** to the Lesson in green.

Simplifying Expressions (Lesson 1-2)

Simplify each expression.

1. $x^2 + 3x^2 - 5x$ **2.** $\frac{x^2}{2} - \frac{x^2}{3} + \frac{x^2}{5}$ **3.** $-6x(x + 2) - x(x + 1)$

Solving Linear Equations (Lesson 1-3)

Solve each equation. Check your answers.

4. $4 - 2x = x + 2$ **5.** $6x + 2.5 = 4x - 1.1$ **6.** $3(x - 1) = 8(2x - 2)$

Graphing Linear Functions (Lesson 2-2)

Graph each function.

7. $y = -5x - 1$ **8.** $y = 3x + 12$ **9.** $y = -6x + 6$

10. $2x - 3y = -4$ **11.** $-3x + 9y = -12$ **12.** $y - 1 = -4x$

Using Linear Models (Lesson 2-4)

Graph each set of ordered pairs. Decide whether a linear model is reasonable. If so, draw a trend line and write its equation.

13. $\{(0, 12), (2, 17), (4, 25), (6, 29), (8, 36)\}$

14. $\{(5.5, 16), (6.8, 18.4), (7.5, 19.3), (8, 20), (8.5, 20.8)\}$

15. Each second, a car that begins with a speed of 40 ft/s increases its speed by 6 ft/s. Write and graph an equation to model the car's speed at s seconds.

Graphing Translations (Lesson 2-6)

16. Identify the parent function of $y = |x - 5|$. Graph $y = |x - 5|$ by translating its parent function.

Quadratic Equations and Functions

LESSONS

5-1 Modeling Data with Quadratic Functions

5-2 Properties of Parabolas

5-3 Tranforming Parabolas

5-4 Factoring Quadratic Expressions

5-5 Quadratic Equations

5-6 Complex Numbers

5-7 Completing the Square

5-8 The Quadratic Formula

◀)) Key Vocabulary

- axis of symmetry (p. 239)
- completing the square (p. 282)
- complex number (p. 275)
- complex number plane (p. 275)
- difference of two squares (p. 263)
- discriminant (p. 291)
- factoring (p. 259)
- i (p. 274)
- imaginary number (p. 274)
- parabola (p. 239)
- perfect square trinomial (p. 262)
- Quadratic Formula (p. 289)
- quadratic function (p. 238)
- standard form of a quadratic function (p. 238)
- vertex form of a quadratic function (p. 252)
- zero of a function (p. 268)
- Zero Product Property (p. 267)

What You'll Learn Next

- In Chapter 5, you will learn to use quadratic functions to model real-world data.

- You will learn to graph and to solve quadratic equations.

- You will learn to graph complex numbers and to use them in solving quadratic equations.

Real-World Connection Applying what you learn, on page 269 you will solve a problem involving art.

Modeling Data With Quadratic Functions

✓ Check Skills You'll Need

GO for Help   Lessons 1-2 and 2-2

Evaluate each function for $x = -3, -1, 0, 1,$ and 3.

1. $f(x) = x$ 　　　　　　　　　　　**2.** $f(x) = x^2$

3. $f(x) = -x$ 　　　　　　　　　　**4.** $f(x) = -x^2$

5. $f(x) = \frac{1}{3}x^2$ 　　　　　　　　　**6.** $f(x) = -\frac{1}{3}x^2$

Write each equation in slope-intercept form.

7. $3x + 4y = 8$ 　　　**8.** $2x - y = -7$ 　　　**9.** $\frac{1}{2}x + 3y = 9$

🔊 **New Vocabulary**　• quadratic function　• standard form of a quadratic function　• parabola　• axis of symmetry　• vertex of a parabola

---

1　Quadratic Functions and Their Graphs

A **quadratic function** is a function that can be written in the standard form $f(x) = ax^2 + bx + c$, where $a \neq 0$. The domain of a quadratic function is all real numbers.

Key Concepts

Definition	Standard Form of a Quadratic Function
	$f(x) = \underset{\text{quadratic term}}{ax^2} + \underset{\text{linear term}}{bx} + \underset{\text{constant term}}{c}$

The condition $a \neq 0$ gives every quadratic function a quadratic term, but not necessarily a linear term or a constant term. If $a = 0$, then the function has no quadratic term, and it is not a quadratic function.

Vocabulary Tip

You can use the FOIL acronym to remember how to multiply.

1 EXAMPLE Classifying Functions

Determine whether each function is linear or quadratic. Identify the quadratic, linear, and constant terms.

a. $y = (2x + 3)(x - 4)$

$\quad = 2x^2 - 8x + 3x - 12$ 　　　**Multiply.**

$\quad = 2x^2 - 5x - 12$ 　　　　**Write in standard form.**

This is a quadratic function.
Quadratic term: $2x^2$
Linear term: $-5x$
Constant term: -12

b. $f(x) = 3(x^2 - 2x) - 3(x^2 - 2)$

$\quad = 3x^2 - 6x - 3x^2 + 6$

$\quad = -6x + 6$

This is a linear function.
Quadratic term: none
Linear term: $-6x$
Constant term: 6

1 Determine whether each function is linear or quadratic. Identify the quadratic, linear, and constant terms.

a. $f(x) = (x^2 + 5x) - x^2$ **b.** $f(x) = (x - 5)(3x - 1)$ **c.** $f(x) = x(x + 3)$

The graph of a quadratic function is a **parabola.** The **axis of symmetry** is the line that divides a parabola into two parts that are mirror images. The **vertex of a parabola** is the point at which the parabola intersects the axis of symmetry. The y-value of the vertex of a parabola represents the maximum or minimum value of the function.

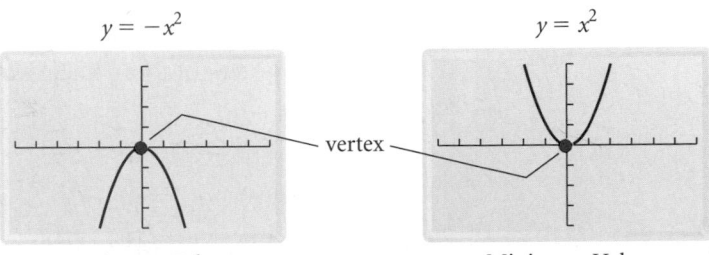

$y = -x^2$ $y = x^2$

vertex

Maximum Value Minimum Value

The axis of symmetry of the graph of a quadratic function is always a vertical line defined by the x-coordinate of the vertex. In each graph above, the axis of symmetry is the y-axis, $x = 0$.

Each point of the parabola has a corresponding point on its mirror image. Two corresponding points are the same distance from the axis of symmetry. In general the domain of a quadratic function is all real numbers.

Real-World Connection

Objects tossed into the air follow parabolic paths.

2 EXAMPLE **Points on a Parabola**

Below is the graph of $f(x) = 2x^2 - 8x + 8$. Identify the vertex, axis of symmetry, points P' and Q' corresponding to P and Q, and the range of $f(x)$.

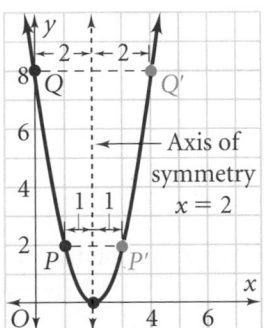

The vertex is $(2, 0)$.

The axis of symmetry is $x = 2$, the vertical line passing through the vertex.

$P(1, 2)$ is one unit to the left of the axis of symmetry. Corresponding point $P'(3, 2)$ is one unit to the right of the axis of symmetry.

$Q(0, 8)$ is two units to the left of the axis of symmetry. Corresponding point $Q'(4, 8)$ is two units to the right of the axis of symmetry.

The range of this function is all nonnegative real numbers.

2 Identify the vertex and the axis of symmetry of each parabola. Identify points corresponding to P and Q.

a.

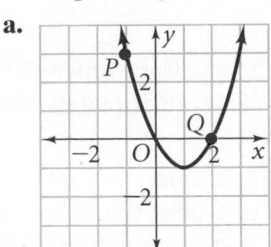

b.

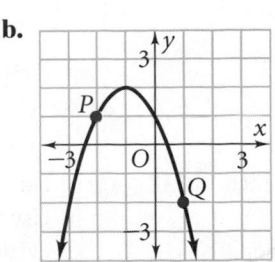

Given three noncollinear points, you can find a quadratic function whose graph passes through those points.

3 **EXAMPLE** **Fitting a Quadratic Function to 3 Points**

Find a quadratic function that includes the values in the table.

x	y
2	3
3	13
4	29

Substitute the values of x and y into $y = ax^2 + bx + c$. The result is a system of three linear equations.

$y = ax^2 + bx + c$

$3 = a(2)^2 + b(2) + c = 4a + 2b + c$ **Use (2, 3).**

$13 = a(3)^2 + b(3) + c = 9a + 3b + c$ **Use (3, 13).**

$29 = a(4)^2 + b(4) + c = 16a + 4b + c$ **Use (4, 29).**

Using one of the methods of Chapter 3, solve the system. $\begin{cases} 4a + 2b + c = 3 \\ 9a + 3b + c = 13 \\ 16a + 4b + c = 29 \end{cases}$

The solution is $a = 3, b = -5, c = 1$. Substitute these values into standard form.

$y = (3)x^2 + (-5)x + (1)$

● The quadratic function is $y = 3x^2 - 5x + 1$.

✓ **Quick Check** **3** Find a quadratic function with a graph that includes $(1, 0), (2, -3)$, and $(3, -10)$.

You can use the quadratic regression feature of a graphing calculator to model data with a quadratic function.

4 **EXAMPLE** **Real-World** Connection

Hydraulics The table at the left shows the height of a column of water as it drains from its container. Model the data with a quadratic function. Graph the data and the function. Use the model to estimate the water level at 35 seconds.

Elapsed Time	Water Level
0 s	120 mm
10 s	100 mm
20 s	83 mm
30 s	66 mm
40 s	50 mm
50 s	37 mm
60 s	28 mm

Step 1 Enter the data. Use **QuadReg**.

Step 2 Graph the data and the function.

Step 3 Use the table feature to find $f(35)$.

QuadReg
$y = ax^2 + bx + c$
$a = .0091666667$
$b = {}^-2.103571429$
$c = 120.3333333$
■

X	Y₁
29	67.039
30	65.476
31	63.932
32	62.406
33	60.898
34	59.409
35	57.937

$Y_1 = 57.9375$

An approximate model of the quadratic function is $y = 0.009167x^2 - 2.10x + 120$.
● At 35 seconds the water level is approximately 58 mm.

✓ **Quick Check** **4** **a.** Use the quadratic model to estimate the water level at 25 seconds.
    b. Use the quadratic model to predict the water level at 3 minutes.
    c. **Critical Thinking** Is your prediction in part (b) reasonable? Explain.

EXERCISES

For more exercises, see *Extra Skill and Word Problem Practice*.

Practice and Problem Solving

A Practice by Example

Example 1
(page 238)

for Help

Determine whether each function is linear or quadratic. Identify the quadratic, linear, and constant terms.

1. $y = x + 4$ **2.** $y = 2x^2 - (3x - 5)$ **3.** $y = 3x(x - 2)$

4. $f(x) = x^2 - 7$ **5.** $y = (x - 2)(x + 5)$ **6.** $g(x) = -7(x - 4)$

7. $h(x) = (3x)(2x) + 6$ **8.** $y = x(1 - x) - (1 - x^2)$ **9.** $f(x) = -x(2x + 8)$

Example 2
(page 239)

Identify the vertex and the axis of symmetry of each parabola.

10.
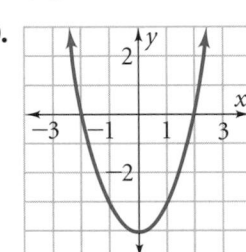

11.
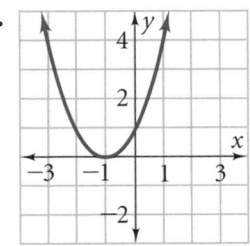

12.
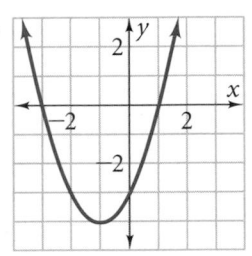

For each parabola, identify points corresponding to P and Q.

13.
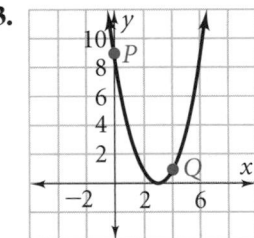

14.
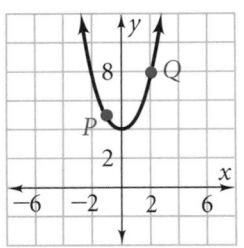

15.
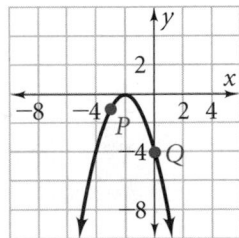

Example 3
(page 240)

Find a quadratic function that includes each set of values.

16. $(1, -2), (2, -2), (3, -4)$ **17.** $(1, -2), (2, -4), (3, -4)$ **18.** $(-1, 6), (1, 4), (2, 9)$

19.

x	−1	1	2
f(x)	−1	3	8

20.

x	−1	1	2
f(x)	17	17	8

Example 4
(page 240)

21. Physics A man throws a ball off the top of a building. The table shows the height of the ball at different times.
  a. Find a quadratic model for the data.
  b. Use the model to estimate the height of the ball at 2.5 seconds.

Height of a Ball

Time	Height
0 s	46 ft
1 s	63 ft
2 s	48 ft
3 s	1 ft

22. Communications The table shows the percent of U.S. houses with cable TV.
  a. Find a quadratic model using 1960 as year 0, 1970 as year 10, and so on.
  b. Use the model to estimate the percent of households with cable TV in 1995.

Television Cable Access

Year	1960	1970	1980	1990	2000
% of Households	0	7	20	56	68

SOURCE: *Time Almanac*

Determine whether a quadratic model exists for each set of values. If so, write the model.

23. $f(-2) = 16, f(0) = 0, f(1) = 4$ **24.** $f(0) = 5, f(2) = 3, f(-1) = 0$

25. $f(-1) = -4, f(1) = -2, f(2) = -1$ **26.** $f(-2) = 7, f(0) = 1, f(2) = 0$

Identify the vertex and the axis of symmetry for each function.

27. 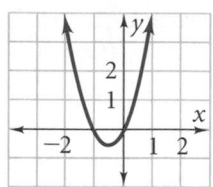   **28.** 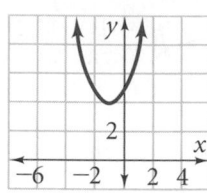   **29.**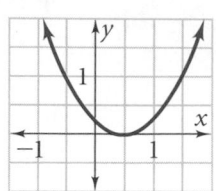

30. a. Geometry Copy and complete the table. It shows the total number of segments that can be drawn among x points, no three of which are collinear.

Number of points, *x*	2	3	■	■
Number of segments, *y*	1	3	■	■

     b. Write a quadratic model for the data.
     c. Predict the number of segments that can be drawn among ten points.

31. a. Postal Rates Find a quadratic model for the data. Use 1974 as year 0.

Price of First-Class Stamp

Year	1974	1978	1981	1983	1988	1995	2001	2002
Price (cents)	10	15	18	20	25	32	34	37

     b. Describe a reasonable domain and range for your model. (*Hint:* This is a discrete, real situation.)
     c. Estimation Estimate when first-class postage was 29¢.
     d. Use your model to predict when first-class postage will be 50¢. Explain why your prediction may not be valid.

The graph of each function contains the given point. Find the value of *c*.

32. $y = x^2 + c; (0, 3)$ **33.** $y = x^2 - c; (4, 8)$

34. $y = -5x^2 + c; (2, -14)$ **35.** $y = 2x^2 + c; \left(-\frac{3}{4}, -\frac{1}{4}\right)$

36. $y = -\frac{3}{4}x^2 + c; \left(3, -\frac{1}{2}\right)$ **37.** $y = (x + c)^2; (10, 0)$

38. Road Safety The table below gives the stopping distance for an automobile under certain road conditions.

Speed (mi/h)	20	30	40	50	55
Stopping Distance (ft)	17	38	67	105	127

     a. Find a linear model for the data.
     b. Find a quadratic model for the data.
     c. Writing Compare the models. Which is better? Explain.

39. Open-Ended Write three different quadratic functions, each with a graph that includes $(0, 0)$ and $(5, -1)$.

Real-World Connection

Aremy McCann won a stamp-design competition sponsored by the U.S. government.

GO Online
Homework Video Tutor
Visit: PHSchool.com
Web Code: age-0501

C **Challenge**

40. Critical Thinking What is the minimum number of data points you need to find a quadratic model for a data set? Explain.

41. How are the graphs of $y = x^2$ and $y = |x|$ similar? How are they different?

42. A parabola contains the points $(0, -4)$, $(2, 4)$, and $(4, 4)$. Find the vertex.

43. A model for the height of an arrow shot into the air is $h(t) = -16t^2 + 72t + 5$, where t is time and h is height. Without graphing, consider the function's graph.
   a. What can you learn by finding the graph's intercept with the h-axis?
   b. What can you learn by finding the graph's intercept(s) with the t-axis?

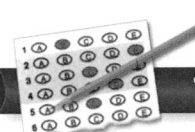

Test Prep

Multiple Choice

44. For which quadratic function is -3 the constant term?
   A. $y = (3x + 1)(-x - 3)$
   B. $y = x^2 - 3x + 3$
   C. $f(x) = (x - 3)(x - 3)$
   D. $g(x) = -3x^2 + 3x + 9$

45. The vertex of a parabola is $(3, 2)$. A second point on the parabola is $(1, 7)$. Which point is also on the parabola?
   F. $(-1, 7)$ **G.** $(3, 7)$ **H.** $(5, 7)$ **J.** $(3, -2)$

46. The graph of a quadratic function has vertex $(-3, -2)$. What is the axis of symmetry?
   A. $x = -3$ **B.** $x = 3$ **C.** $y = -2$ **D.** $y = 2$

47. Which function is NOT a quadratic function?
   F. $y = (x - 1)(x - 2)$
   G. $y = x^2 + 2x - 3$
   H. $y = 3x - x^2$
   J. $y = -x^2 + x(x - 3)$

Extended Response

48. What is the quadratic function with a graph that includes $(1, 6)$, $(2, 11)$, and $(3, 20)$? Find the function by writing and solving a system of equations. Write the function in standard form. Show all your work.

Mixed Review

GO **for Help**

Lesson 4-8  Write the augmented matrix for each system. Then solve the system.

49. $\begin{cases} 3x - y = 7 \\ 2x + 2y = 10 \end{cases}$

50. $\begin{cases} 3x + y - 2z = -3 \\ x - 3y - z = -2 \\ 2x + 2y + 3z = 11 \end{cases}$

Lesson 4-3 Find each product.

51. $\begin{bmatrix} 2 & -3 \end{bmatrix} \begin{bmatrix} 3 & -2 & 4 & 1 \\ 2 & 0 & -3 & 2 \end{bmatrix}$

52. $\begin{bmatrix} 3 & 10 \\ 1 & 5 \end{bmatrix} \begin{bmatrix} -7 & 2 \\ 8 & 4 \end{bmatrix}$

Lesson 3-2 Solve each system by elimination.

53. $\begin{cases} x + y = 7 \\ 5x - y = 5 \end{cases}$

54. $\begin{cases} 2x - 3y = -14 \\ 3x - y = 7 \end{cases}$

55. $\begin{cases} x - 3y = 2 \\ x - 2y = 1 \end{cases}$

Lesson 2-3 For each direct variation, find the value of y when $x = 2$.

56. $y = 2$ when $x = 5$ **57.** $y = 1$ when $x = 4$ **58.** $y = -2$ when $x = 4$

Modeling Using Residuals

FOR USE WITH LESSON 5-1

You can use more than one model for a set of data. You can determine which is a better model by analyzing the differences between the y-values of the data and the y-values of each model. These differences are called residuals. The better model will have residuals that are closer to zero.

ACTIVITY

The calculator screen shows the graphs of a linear model and a quadratic model for the data below. Which model better fits the data?

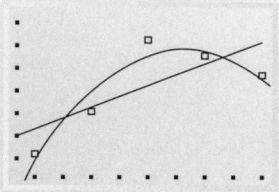

Participation in Backpacking or Wilderness Camp Activities

Year (1990 = 0)	1995	1997	1999	2001	2003
Millions of Participants	10.2	12.0	15.3	14.5	13.7

SOURCE: National Sporting Goods Association

Step 1 Press STAT ENTER to enter the data in L_1 and L_2. Then use the LinReg and QuadReg features to find linear and quadratic models.

Step 2 Enter the linear model as Y_1 and the quadratic model as Y_2.

Step 3 To find the residuals of the linear model and store the differences in L_3, enter L_2 − VARS ▶ 1 1 (L_1) STO▶ L_3 ENTER .

Step 4 Find the residuals of the quadratic model. Store the differences in L_4.

Step 5 Compare the residuals in L_3 and L_4. The values in L_4 are closer to zero, so the quadratic model is the better fit.

L2	L3	L4	2
10.2	−1.04	.28857	
12	−.19	−.8543	
15.3	2.16	.83143	
14.5	.41	−.2543	
13.7	−1.34	−.0114	
------	------	------	

L2(6) =

EXERCISES

For each set of data, find a linear model and a quadratic model. Which model is the better fit? Justify your reasoning.

1. **Money Spent in the U.S. on Personal Technology**

Year (0 = 1970)	0	10	20	22	24	26
Billions of Dollars	8.8	17.6	53.8	61.2	78.5	89.7

2. **Fishing Licenses Sold**

Year (0 = 1970)	0	5	10	15	20	25	30
Millions Sold	31.1	34.7	35.2	35.7	36.9	37.9	37.6

3. For each of Exercises 1 and 2, state whether the situation is discrete and describe a reasonable domain and range. Explain your responses.

Properties of Parabolas

What You'll Learn
• To graph quadratic functions
• To find maximum and minimum values of quadratic functions

. . . And Why
To maximize a company's revenue

✓ **Check Skills You'll Need**

GO **for Help** Lessons 2-2 and 2-5

Find the *y*-intercept of the graph of each function.

1. $y = 3x + 3$ **2.** $y = -2x - 1$ **3.** $4x - 3y = 12$

Find the vertex of the graph of each function.

4. $y = |-2x|$ **5.** $y = \left|-\frac{2}{3}x - 1\right|$ **6.** $y = |3x + 7|$

Graph each equation.

7. $y = -4x - 3$ **8.** $\frac{1}{2}x + y = -2$ **9.** $y = |5x - 5|$

---

1 Graphing Parabolas

The standard form of a quadratic function is $y = ax^2 + bx + c$ with $a \neq 0$. When $b = 0$, the function simplifies to $y = ax^2 + c$.

The graph of $y = ax^2 + c$ is a parabola with an axis of symmetry $x = 0$, the *y*-axis. The vertex of the graph is the *y*-intercept $(0, c)$.

Vocabulary Tip

The word <u>symmetry</u> comes from a prefix meaning "same" and a root meaning "measure."

1 EXAMPLE **Graphing a Function of the Form** $y = ax^2 + c$

Graph $y = -\frac{1}{2}x^2 + 2$.

Step 1 Graph the vertex, which is the *y*-intercept $(0, 2)$.

Step 2 Make a table of values to find some points on one side of the axis of symmetry $x = 0$. Graph the points.

x	1	2	3	4
y	$1\frac{1}{2}$	0	$-2\frac{1}{2}$	-6

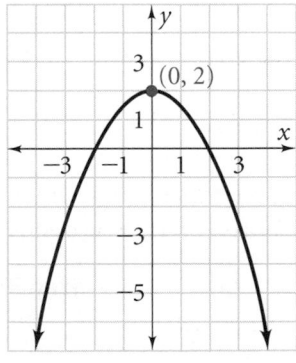

Step 4 Graph corresponding points on the other side of the axis of symmetry.

Step 5 Sketch the curve.

✓ **Quick Check** **1** **a.** Graph $y = 2x^2 - 4$.
 b. Graph $y = -5 + 3x^2$.
 c. **Reasoning** What are the coordinates of the vertex of the graph of a function in the form $y = ax^2$?

When $b \neq 0$ in the standard form of a quadratic function, $y = ax^2 + bx + c$, the values of both a and b affect the position of the axis of symmetry.

You can use the values of a, b, and c to find characteristics of the graph of a quadratic function.

Properties	**Graph of a Quadratic Function in Standard Form**

The graph of $f(x) = ax^2 + bx + c$ is a parabola when $a \neq 0$.

- When $a > 0$, the parabola opens up. When $a < 0$, the parabola opens down.
- The axis of symmetry is the line $x = -\frac{b}{2a}$.
- The x-coordinate of the vertex is $-\frac{b}{2a}$. The y-coordinate of the vertex is the y value of the function when $x = -\frac{b}{2a}$, or $y = f\left(-\frac{b}{2a}\right)$.
- The y-intercept is $(0, c)$.

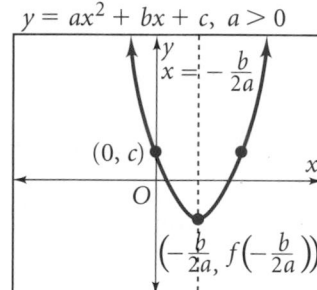

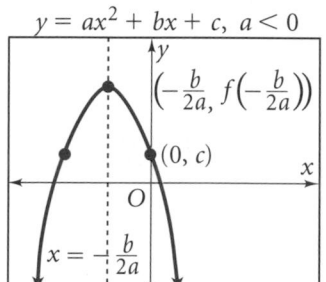

2 EXAMPLE **Graphing a Function of the Form $y = ax^2 + bx + c$**

Graph $y = x^2 - 2x - 3$. Label the vertex and the axis of symmetry.

Step 1 Find and graph the axis of symmetry.

$$x = -\frac{b}{2a} = -\frac{(-2)}{2(1)} = 1$$

Step 2 Find and graph the vertex. The x-coordinate of the vertex is $-\frac{b}{2a}$, or 1.

The y-coordinate is $y = (1)^2 - 2(1) - 3 = -4$. So the vertex is $(1, -4)$.

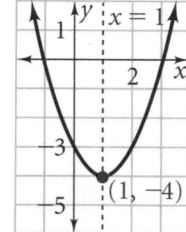

Since $a > 0$, the graph opens up.

Step 3 Find and graph the y-intercept and its reflection. Since $c = -3$, the y-intercept is $(0, -3)$ and its reflection is $(2, -3)$.

Step 4 Evaluate the function for another value of x, such as $y = (3)^2 - 2(3) - 3 = 0$. Graph $(3, 0)$ and its reflection $(-1, 0)$.

Step 5 Sketch the curve.

 **Quick Check** ❷ Graph each function. Label the vertex and the axis of symmetry.
  a. $y = -x^2 + 4x + 2$
  b. $y = -\frac{1}{3}x^2 - 2x - 3$

The y-coordinate of the vertex of a parabola represents the maximum or minimum value of a quadratic function.

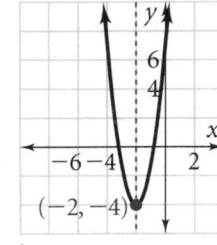

For: Quadratic Activity
Use: Interactive Textbook, 5-2

3 **EXAMPLE** **Finding a Minimum Value**

Graph $y = 3x^2 + 12x + 8$. What is the minimum value of the function?

Since $a > 0$, the graph of the function opens up, and the vertex represents the minimum value. Find the coordinates of the vertex.

$x = -\dfrac{b}{2a} = -\dfrac{12}{2(3)} = -2$ **Find the x-coordinate of the vertex.**

$y = 3(-2)^2 + 12(-2) + 8 = -4$ **Find the y-coordinate of the vertex.**

Graph the vertex and the axis of symmetry $x = -2$. Graph two points on one side of the axis of symmetry, such as $(0, 8)$ and $(-1, -1)$. Then graph corresponding points $(-4, 8)$ and $(-3, -1)$.

The minimum value of the function is -4.

✓ **Quick Check** **3** **a.** Graph $y = 2x^2 + 8x - 1$. Find the minimum value of the function.
    b. Critical Thinking What is the maximum value of the function?

You can find a maximum or minimum value without graphing the function.

4 **EXAMPLE** **Real-World 🌐 Connection**

Economics A company knows that $-2.5p + 500$ models the number it sells per month of a certain make of unicycle, where the price p can be set as low as $70 or as high as $120. Revenue from sales is the product of the price and the number sold. What price will maximize the revenue? What is the maximum revenue?

Relate   revenue equals price times number of unicycles sold

Define Let R = revenue. Let p = price of a unicycle.

        Let $-2.5p + 500$ = number of unicycles sold.

Write $R = p\ (-2.5p + 500)$

         $= -2.5p^2 + 500p$ **Write in standard form.**

Find the maximum value of the function. Since $a < 0$, the graph of the function opens down, and the vertex represents a maximum value.

$p = -\dfrac{b}{2a} = -\dfrac{500}{2(-2.5)} = 100$ **Find p at the vertex.**

$R = -2.5(100)^2 + 500(100)$ **Evaluate R for p = 100.**

$= 25{,}000$ **Simplify.**

A price of $100 will maximize revenue. The maximum revenue is $25,000.

Real-World 🌐 Connection

It generally takes 2–6 weeks of regular practice to learn to ride a unicycle.

✓ **Quick Check** **4** The number of widgets the Woodget Company sells can be modeled by $-5p + 100$, where p is the price of a widget. What price will maximize revenue? What is the maximum revenue?

EXERCISES

For more exercises, see *Extra Skill and Word Problem Practice*.

Practice and Problem Solving

A Practice by Example

Example 1
(page 245)

GO for Help

Graph each function.

1. $y = -x^2 + 1$ **2.** $y = -x^2 - 1$ **3.** $y = 2x^2 + 4$

4. $y = 3x^2 - 6$ **5.** $y = -\frac{1}{3}x^2 - 1$ **6.** $y = -5x^2 + 12$

7. $y = \frac{1}{2}x^2 + 3$ **8.** $y = \frac{1}{4}x^2 - 3$ **9.** $y = -2x^2 + \frac{3}{4}$

Example 2
(page 246)

Graph each function. Label the vertex and the axis of symmetry.

10. $y = x^2 + 2x + 1$ **11.** $y = -x^2 + 2x + 1$

12. $y = x^2 + 4x + 1$ **13.** $y = x^2 + 6x + 9$

14. $y = -x^2 - 3x + 6$ **15.** $y = 2x^2 + 4x$

16. $y = 4x^2 - 12x + 9$ **17.** $y = -6x^2 - 12x - 1$

18. $y = -\frac{3}{4}x^2 + 6x + 6$ **19.** $y = 3x^2 - 12x + 10$

20. $y = \frac{1}{2}x^2 + 2x - 8$ **21.** $y = -4x^2 - 24x - 36$

Example 3
(page 247)

Graph each function. If $a > 0$ find the minimum value. If $a < 0$ find the maximum value.

22. $y = -x^2 + 2x + 5$ **23.** $y = 3x^2 - 4x - 2$

24. $y = -2x^2 - 3x + 4$ **25.** $y = \frac{1}{3}x^2 + 2x + 5$

26. $y = -x^2 - x + 6$ **27.** $y = 2x^2 + 5$

Example 4
(page 247)

28. Revenue A model for a company's revenue is $R = -15p^2 + 300p + 12{,}000$, where p is the price in dollars of the company's product. What price will maximize revenue? Find the maximum revenue.

29. Physics The equation for the motion of a projectile fired straight up at an initial velocity of 64 ft/s is $h = 64t - 16t^2$, where h is the height in feet and t is the time in seconds. Find the time the projectile needs to reach its highest point. How high it will go?

30. Manufacturing The equation for the cost in dollars of producing automobile tires is $C = 0.000015x^2 - 0.03x + 35$, where x is the number of tires produced. Find the number of tires that minimizes the cost. What is the cost for that number of tires?

B Apply Your Skills

Sketch each parabola using the given information.

31. vertex $(3, 6)$, y-intercept 2   **32.** vertex $(-1, -4)$, y-intercept 3

33. vertex $(0, 5)$, point $(1, -2)$ **34.** vertex $(2, 3)$, point $(6, 9)$

35. Find a pair of numbers with a sum of 26 and a product that is a maximum. Find the maximum product.

36. Find two numbers with a difference of 10 and a product that is a minimum. Find the minimum product.

Match each function with its graph.

37. $y = x^2 + 4x + 1$ **38.** $y = -x^2 - 4x + 1$ **39.** $y = -\frac{1}{2}x^2 - 2x + 1$

A. 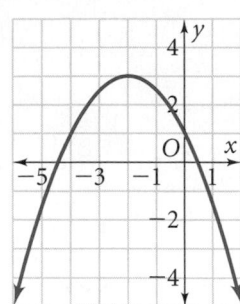   **B.** 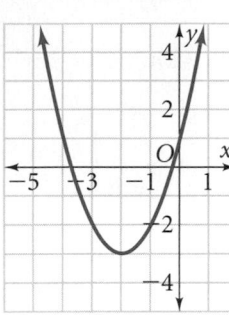   **C.**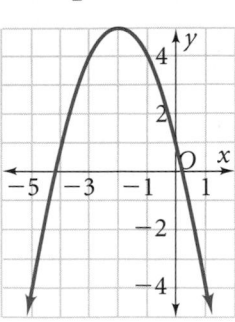

40. Open-Ended Write the equation of a parabola symmetric about $x = -10$.

41. Woodworking Suppose you want to frame a collage of pictures. You have a 9-ft strip of wood for the frame. What dimensions of the frame give you the maximum area for the collage? What is the maximum area?

42. Physics Suppose you throw a ball over a 10-ft fence. Barely clearing the fence, the ball reaches its highest point directly above the fence and lands 10 ft from the fence. Using the fence as the axis of symmetry, write a quadratic function that models the ball's height.

43. Packaging The bottom of a box is to be a rectangle with a perimeter of 36 cm. The box must be 4 cm high. What dimensions give the maximum volume?

For each function, the vertex of the function's graph is given. Find c.

44. $y = x^2 - 6x + c; (3, -4)$ **45.** $y = -3x^2 + 6x + c; (1, 0)$

46. $y = x^2 + 10x + c; (-5, -27)$ **47.** $y = c - x^2 - 2x; (-1, 3)$

Find the quadratic function $y = ax^2 + c$ with a graph that has the given points.

48. $(0, 2), (3, 5)$ **49.** $(0, -3), (1, -7)$ **50.** $\left(2, \frac{5}{2}\right), \left(0, -\frac{1}{2}\right)$

51. $(-3, 89), (2, 39)$ **52.** $(-2, -10), (4, -40)$ **53.** $(-1, 14), (4, 104)$

54. A rock club's profit from booking local bands depends on the ticket price. Using past receipts, the owners find that the profit p can be modeled by the function $p = -15t^2 + 600t + 50$, where t represents the ticket price in dollars.
   a. What price yields the maximum profit?
   b. What is the maximum profit?
   c. Open-Ended What price would you pay to see your favorite local band? How much profit would the club owner make using that ticket price?

55. Multiple Choice A town is planning a playground. It wants to fence in a rectangular space using an existing wall. What is the greatest area it can fence in using 100 ft of donated fencing?

   Ⓐ 1000 ft^2 Ⓑ 1250 ft^2
   Ⓒ 2500 ft^2 Ⓓ 10,000 ft^2

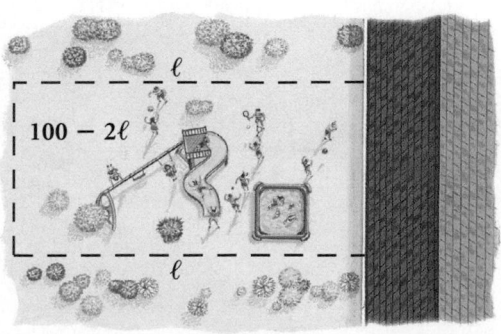

GO 🌐 nline
Homework Video Tutor
     Visit: PHSchool.com
     Web Code: age-0502

56. History Around 2500 B.C. in the Indus Valley of South Asia, the Harappan people built one of the first cities. The Harappans built rectangular houses that had open central courtyards surrounded by solid brick walls.
   a. Suppose you build a model of a Harappan house. For the outer walls you plan to use 2400 bricks. The walls of the model are 10 bricks high and 1 brick thick. Draw several possible floor plans.
   b. Find the dimensions of the floor plan that give the model of maximum area.

Each point lies on a parabola that has its vertex at (0, 1). Write the equation of the parabola. Indicate whether the graph opens up or down.

57. $(-3, 10)$	**58.** $(-1, 6)$	**59.** $(2, -1)$	**60.** $(4, -7)$
61. $(3, 4)$	**62.** $(5, -4)$	**63.** $(8, -15)$	**64.** $(-6, -2)$

— 10 ft —

65. Construction A construction worker places his toolbox on a board that rests on two cement posts 10 ft apart. The toolbox is halfway between the posts. Under the weight of the toolbox, the board sags by one quarter inch. Model the shape of the board in three different ways by writing a function whose graph satisfies each condition below.
   a. The origin of the graph corresponds to the position of the toolbox.
   b. The origin of the graph corresponds to the position of the post on the left.
   c. The origin of the graph corresponds to the position of the post on the right.

66. A student says that the graph of $y = ax^2 + bx + c$ gets wider as a increases.
   a. Error Analysis Use examples to show that the student is wrong.
   b. Writing Summarize the relationship between $|a|$ and the width of the graph of $y = ax^2 + bx + c$.

C **Challenge**

For each function, the vertex of the function's graph is given. Find a and b.

67. $y = ax^2 + bx - 27; (2, -3)$ **68.** $y = ax^2 + bx + 5; (-1, 4)$

69. $y = ax^2 + bx + 8; (2, -4)$ **70.** $y = ax^2 + bx; (-3, 2)$

The formula for the area enclosed by a parabola and the x-axis from x-intercepts x_1 to x_2 is $A = \frac{2}{3}h(x_2 - x_1)$, where h is the height. Find the enclosed area for each parabola.

71.
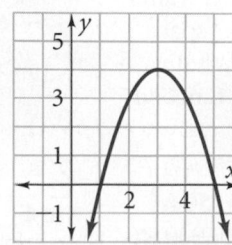

72.
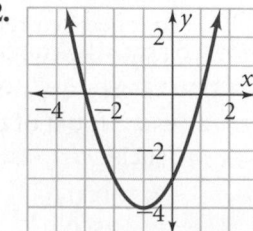

73.
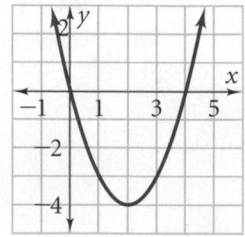

Multiple Choice

74. What is the vertex of $y = -2x^2 - 4x - 5$?
  A. $(-2, -3)$ **B.** $(1, -3)$ **C.** $(1, -11)$ **D.** $(-1, -3)$

75. What is the y-intercept of $y = (x + 1)^2 - 2$?
  F. $(0, -1)$ **G.** $(0, -3)$ **H.** $(0, 1)$ **J.** $(0, -2)$

76. What is the maximum area in square units of a rectangle with a perimeter of 128 units?
  A. 4096   **B.** 1024   **C.** 256   **D.** 32

77. The vertex of the graph of $y = -x^2 - 16x - 62$ lies in which quadrant?
  F. IV   **G.** III   **H.** II   **J.** I

78. What percent of nonzero integers have squares that are odd numbers?
  A. 25   **B.** 50   **C.** 75   **D.** 100

Short Response

79. Sketch the graph of $y = x^2 - 6x + 2$. Explain how to identify the vertex and two other points on the parabola.

for
Help

Lesson 5-1

80. Find a quadratic model for the values in the table.

x	0	5	10	15	20
y	17	39	54	61	61

Lesson 4-2

Solve each matrix equation.

81. $X + \begin{bmatrix} 0 & 4 \\ -2 & 1 \end{bmatrix} = \begin{bmatrix} 3 & 0 \\ 1 & 1 \end{bmatrix}$

82. $X - \begin{bmatrix} 3 & 3 \\ -2 & -1 \end{bmatrix} = \begin{bmatrix} 1 & 0 \\ 0 & 1 \end{bmatrix}$

Lesson 3-3 **83. Manufacturing** A new factory will require at least 40,000 ft² of storage space. No more than 25,000 ft² of the space will be covered with a roof. Write a system of inequalities to represent the constraints. Solve the system by graphing.

Algebra at Work
·····Landscape Architect

Landscape architects create outdoor environments for parks, office buildings, and homes. They plan walls, staircases, pools, walkways, and plantings. Landscape architects blend ideas from art, science, nature, and math in their work. They need training in all three areas before they begin their careers. For example, when planning a decorative fountain, an architect needs to predict the parabolic path of the spray. The height and distance of the spray depend on the speed of the water and the angle at which it exits a pipe. Basic principles of physics often help architects. By making adjustments to a model, they can plan the effect they want.

Go Online
PHSchool.com
For: Information about landscape architecture
Web Code: agb-2031

Transforming Parabolas

What You'll Learn

- To use the vertex form of a quadratic function

. . . And Why

To model a suspension bridge, as in Example 3

✓ **Check Skills You'll Need**

Identify the parent function of each function. Then graph the function by transforming the graph of the parent function.

1. $y = x + 2$ 2. $y = 3|x| + 2$ 3. $y = -|x + 1| - 1$

Write an equation for each translation.

4. $y = x$, 2 units down   5. $y = |x|$, 4 units up, 1 unit right

🔊 **New Vocabulary**   • vertex form of a quadratic function

1   Using Vertex Form

Activity: Vertex Form

1. Each function in the first column is written in standard form. In the second column, each function has been rewritten in vertex form. Use multiplication to verify that the functions in each row are equivalent.

Standard Form $y = ax^2 + bx + c$	$-\dfrac{b}{2a}$	Vertex Form $y = a(x - h)^2 + k$	h
$y = x^2 - 4x + 4$	■	$y = (x - 2)^2$	■
$y = x^2 + 6x + 8$	■	$y = (x + 3)^2 - 1$	■
$y = -3x^2 - 12x - 8$	■	$y = -3(x + 2)^2 + 4$	■
$y = 2x^2 + 12x + 19$	■	$y = 2(x + 3)^2 + 1$	■

2. a. **Patterns** Copy and complete the table.
   b. Compare the values of $-\dfrac{b}{2a}$ and h in each row. Write a formula to show the relationship between $-\dfrac{b}{2a}$ and h.

In Chapter 2, you learned to graph absolute value functions as transformations of their parent function $y = |x|$. Similarly, you can graph a quadratic function as a transformation of the parent function $y = x^2$.

To transform the graph of a quadratic function, you can use the **vertex form of a quadratic function,** $y = a(x - h)^2 + k$.

Key Concepts

Summary	The Family of Quadratic Functions

Vertical Stretch or Shrink, and/or Reflection in *x*-axis

Parent function: $\qquad\qquad\qquad\qquad\qquad\qquad\qquad\;\; y = x^2$
Reflection in *x*-axis: $\qquad\qquad\qquad\qquad\qquad\qquad\;\; y = -x^2$
Stretch ($a > 1$) or shrink ($0 < a < 1$) by factor *a*: $\;\; y = ax^2$
Reflection in *x*-axis: $\qquad\qquad\qquad\qquad\qquad\qquad\;\; y = -ax^2$

Vertex Form $\qquad\qquad\qquad\qquad\qquad\; \boldsymbol{y = a(x - h)^2 + k}$

The graph (and vertex) of $y = ax^2$ shifts
h units horizontally and *k* units vertically.

For $h > 0$, the graph shifts right.
For $h < 0$, the graph shifts left.
For $k > 0$, the graph shifts up.
For $k < 0$, the graph shifts down.

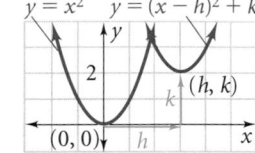

The vertex is (h, k), and the axis of symmetry is the line $x = h$.

Vocabulary Tip

Vertex means "turning point."

---

1 EXAMPLE Using Vertex Form to Graph a Parabola

Graph $y = -\frac{1}{2}(x - 2)^2 + 3$.

The vertex of $y = -\frac{1}{2}(x - 2)^2 + 3$ is 2 units right and 3 units up from the origin.
The axis of symmetry is $x = 2$.

Step 1 Graph the vertex $(2, 3)$. Draw the axis of symmetry $x = 2$.

Step 2 Find another point. When $x = 0$,
$y = -\frac{1}{2}(0 - 2)^2 + 3 = 1$. Graph $(0, 1)$.

Step 3 Graph the point $(4, 1)$. It is 2 units to the right of the axis of symmetry at $(4, 1)$.

Step 4 Sketch the curve.

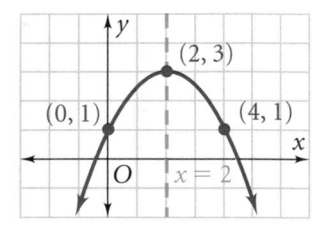

✓ Quick Check **1 a.** Graph $y = 2(x + 1)^2 - 4$.
b. In graphing the function in part (a), which method did you choose—stretching the parent function to graph $y = 2x^2$ and then translating the graph of $y = 2x^2$, or graphing the vertex and axis of symmetry? Explain your choice.

You can use the vertex form to write the equation of a parabola.

---

2 EXAMPLE Writing the Equation of a Parabola

Write the equation of the parabola at the right.

$y = a(x - h)^2 + k$ $\qquad$ **Use the vertex form.**
$y = a(x - 3)^2 + 4$ $\qquad$ **Substitute $h = 3$ and $k = 4$.**
$-4 = a(5 - 3)^2 + 4$ $\qquad$ **Substitute $(5, -4)$.**
$-8 = 4a$ $\qquad\qquad\quad$ **Simplify.**
$-2 = a$ $\qquad\qquad\quad$ **Solve for *a*.**

The equation of the parabola is $y = -2(x - 3)^2 + 4$.

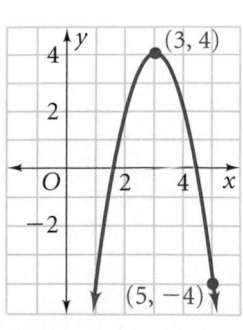

✓ **Quick Check** ❷ Use vertex form to write the equation of the parabola below.

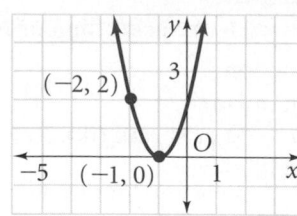

You can use vertex form to model real-world problems.

❸ EXAMPLE **Real-World 🌐 Connection**

Civil Engineering The photo shows the Verrazano–Narrows Bridge in New York, which has the longest span of any suspension bridge in the United States. A suspension cable of the bridge forms a curve that resembles a parabola. The curve can be modeled with the function $y = 0.0001432(x - 2130)^2$, where x and y are measured in feet.

The origin of the function's graph is at the base of one of the two towers that support the cable. How far apart are the towers? How high are they?

Start by drawing a diagram.

The function is in vertex form. Since $h = 2130$ and $k = 0$, the vertex is at $(2130, 0)$. The vertex is halfway between the towers, so the distance between the towers is $2(2130 \text{ ft}) = 4260 \text{ ft}$.

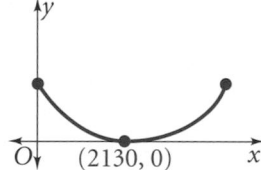

To find the tower's height, find y for $x = 0$.

$$y = 0.0001432(0 - 2130)^2$$
$$y = 0.0001432(-2130)^2$$
$$\approx 650$$

● The towers are 4260 ft apart and about 650 ft high.

✓ **Quick Check** ❸ Suppose the towers in Example 3 are 4000 ft apart and 600 ft high. Write a function that could model the curve of the suspension cable.

Both the vertex form and the standard form give useful information about a parabola. The standard form makes it easy to identify the y-intercept. The vertex form makes it easy to identify the vertex and the axis of symmetry, and to graph the parabola as a transformation of the parent function. The graph shows the relationship between the two forms.

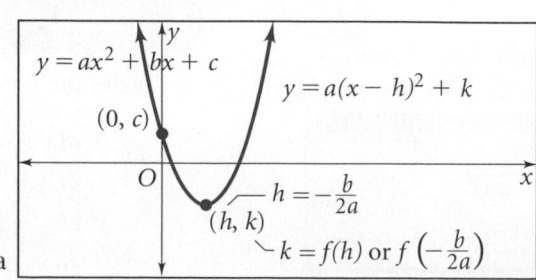

You can convert a function from standard form to vertex form.

4 EXAMPLE Converting to Vertex Form

Write $y = 2x^2 + 10x + 7$ in vertex form.

$x = -\dfrac{b}{2a}$ **Find the *x*-coordinate of the vertex.**

$= -\dfrac{10}{2(2)}$ **Substitute for *a* and *b*.**

$= -2.5$

$y = 2(-2.5)^2 + 10(-2.5) + 7$ **Find the *y*-coordinate of the vertex.**

$= -5.5$

The vertex is at $(-2.5, -5.5)$.

$y = a(x - h)^2 + k$ **Write the vertex form.**

$= 2(x - (-2.5))^2 - 5.5$ **Substitute for *a*, *h*, and *k*.**

$= 2(x + 2.5)^2 - 5.5$ **Simplify.**

● The vertex form of the function is $y = 2(x + 2.5)^2 - 5.5$.

✓ Quick Check ❹ Write $y = -3x^2 + 12x + 5$ in vertex form.

EXERCISES

For more exercises, see *Extra Skill and Word Problem Practice*.

Practice and Problem Solving

A Practice by Example

Example 1
(page 253)

Graph each function. Identify the axis of symmetry.

1. $y = (x - 1)^2 + 2$ **2.** $y = (x + 3)^2 - 4$

3. $y = 2(x - 2)^2 + 5$ **4.** $y = 2(x + 1)^2$

5. $y = -3(x + 7)^2 - 8$ **6.** $y = -\frac{1}{2}(x - 2)^2 + 1$

7. $y = (x - 5)^2 - 3$ **8.** $y = (x + 2)^2 - 3$

9. $y = -(x - 1)^2 + 4$ **10.** $y = 3(x + 5)^2 - 8$

11. $y = -(x - 7)^2 + 10$ **12.** $y = -4(x + 8)^2 - 6$

Example 2
(page 253)

Write the equation of each parabola in vertex form.

13.

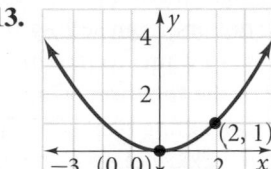

14.

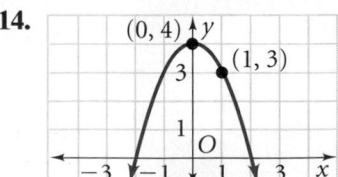

15.

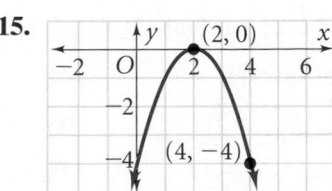

16.

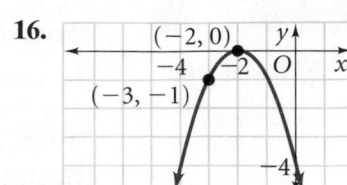

Write the equation of each parabola in vertex form.

17.
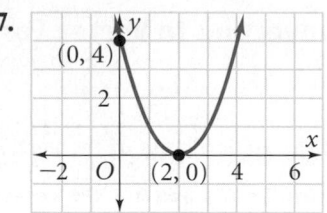

18.
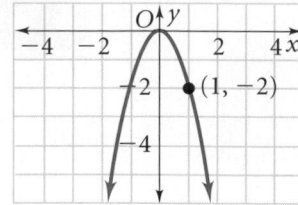

19.
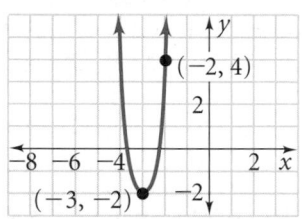

20.
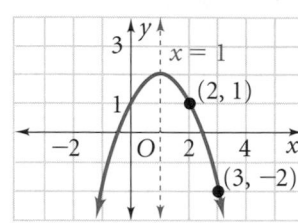

Example 3
(page 254)

Identify the vertex and the y-intercept of the graph of each function.

21. $y = -1.5(x + 20)^2$

22. $y = 0.1(x - 3.2)^2$

23. $y = 24(x + 5.5)^2$

24. $y = 0.0035(x + 1)^2 - 1$

25. $y = -(x - 4)^2 - 25$

26. $y = (x - 125)^2 + 125$

Example 4
(page 255)

Write each function in vertex form.

27. $y = x^2 - 4x + 6$

28. $y = x^2 + 2x + 5$

29. $y = 6x^2 - 10$

30. $y = -5x^2 + 12$

31. $y = 4x^2 + 7x$

32. $y = 2x^2 + x$

33. $y = 2x^2 - 5x + 12$

34. $y = -2x^2 + 8x + 3$

35. $y = \frac{9}{4}x^2 + 3x - 1$

B **Apply Your Skills**

Sketch each parabola. Identify the axis of symmetry.

36. $y = 2(x + 2)^2 - 3$

37. $y = -3(x - 2)^2$

38. $y = 5(x + 0.3)^2 - 10$

39. $y = -0.5(x - 2)^2 - 5$

Begin with the parent $y = x^2$ graph. Show how to transform it to graph each function below. Draw the final graph in a different color.

40. $y = -2(x + 1)^2 + 1$

41. $y = 0.2(x - 12)^2 - 3$

42. **Business** The Big Brick Bakery sells more bagels when it reduces its prices, but then its profit changes. The function $y = -1000(x - 0.55)^2 + 300$ models the bakery's daily profit in dollars, from selling bagels, where x is the price of a bagel in dollars. The bakery wants to maximize the profit.
 a. What is the domain of the function? Can x be negative? Explain.
 b. Find the daily profit for selling bagels for $.40 each; for $.85 each.
 c. What price should the bakery charge to maximize its profit from bagels?
 d. What is the maximum profit?

Write the equation of each parabola in vertex form.

Real-World **Connection**

Bagel sales in the United States total nearly $3 billion each year.

43. vertex $(1, 2)$, point $(2, -5)$

44. vertex $(3, 6)$, y-intercept 2

45. vertex $(-3, 6)$, point $(1, -2)$

46. vertex $(-2, 6)$, y-intercept 12

47. vertex $(-1, -4)$, y-intercept 3

48. vertex $(0, 5)$, point $(1, -2)$

49. vertex $\left(\frac{1}{10}, -\frac{9}{10}\right)$, y-intercept -1

50. vertex $\left(\frac{1}{4}, -\frac{3}{2}\right)$, point $(1, 3)$

Write each function in standard form.

51. $y = (5x + 6)^2 - 9$ **52.** $y = -(3x - 4)^2 + 6$ **53.** $y = 2x(x + 7) + 8x$

54. $y = \frac{1}{2}(x - 5)^2 + 5$ **55.** $y = -0.1(10x + 20)^2$ **56.** $y = (1 - 4x)^2 + 1$

 57. a. Technology Determine the axis of symmetry for each parabola defined by the spreadsheet values at the right.
    b. How could you use the spreadsheet columns to verify that the axes of symmetry are correct?
    c. Write functions in vertex form that model the data. Check that the axes of symmetry are correct.

	A	B
1	X1	Y1
2	1	−35
3	2	−15
4	3	−3
5	4	1
6	5	−3

	A	B
1	X2	Y2
2	1	10
3	2	2
4	3	2
5	4	10
6	5	26

 58. Writing Describe the family of quadratic functions whose members each have $(3, 4)$ as its vertex.

Determine whether each function is written in vertex form. If a function is not in vertex form, rewrite the function.

59. $y = -2x^2 + 35$ **60.** $y = -8x^2$ **61.** $y = -3x^2 - 2x + 1$

62. $y = -2(x + 1)^2 - 1$ **63.** $y = x^2 + 2x + 8$ **64.** $y = \frac{3}{10}x^2 - 1$

65. $y = -4x^2 + 6x + 3$ **66.** $y = 0.5x^2 + 10$ **67.** $y = 100x^2 - 40x + 10$

Determine a and k so both points are on the graph of the function.

68. $(0, 1), (2, 1); y = a(x - 1)^2 + k$ **69.** $(-3, 2), (0, 11); y = a(x + 2)^2 + k$

70. $(1, 11), (2, -19); y = a(x + 1)^2 + k$ **71.** $(-2, 6), (3, 1); y = a(x - 3)^2 + k$

72. $(-2, 10), (1, -34); y = 2a(x + 1)^2 + k$ **73.** $(4, 26), (5, -25); y = a(x - 30)^2 + k$

GO **Online**
Homework Video Tutor
Visit: PHSchool.com
Web Code: age-0503

74. Multiple Choice One parabola shown has equation $y = (x - 4)^2 + 2$. What is an equation for the other?
    A $y = -(x - 4)^2 + 2$ **B** $y = (x + 4)^2 - 2$
    C $y = (-x - 4)^2 + 2$ **D** $y = -(x + 4)^2 - 2$

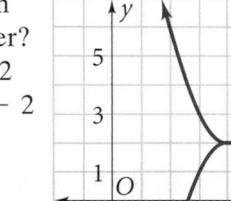

75. Open-Ended Write a quadratic function in vertex form for which the graph has a vertex at $(-2, 5)$. Rewrite the function in standard form.

76. Determine whether the function $f(x) = 0.25(2x - 15)^2 + 150$ has a maximum or a minimum value. Then find the value.

77. Critical Thinking Describe the differences between the graphs of $y = (x + 6)^2$ and $y = (x - 6)^2 + 7$.

C Challenge

78. a. In the function $y = ax^2 + bx + c, c$ represents the y-intercept. Find the value of the y-intercept in the function $y = a(x - h)^2 + k$.
    b. Under what conditions does k represent the y-intercept?

Find a quadratic function $y = a(x - h)^2$ for which the graph includes the given points.

79. $(-2, 1), (2, 1)$ **80.** $(-5, 2), (-1, 2)$ **81.** $(-1, -4), (7, -4)$

82. $(2, -1), (4, 0)$ **83.** $(-2, 18), (1, 0)$ **84.** $(1, -64), (-3, 0)$

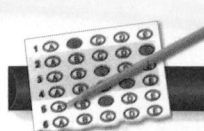

Test Prep

Gridded Response

Use the following information about quadratic functions for Exercises 85–90.

vertex form: $y = a(x - h)^2 + k$ standard form: $y = ax^2 + bx + c$

85. When $y = -3x^2 - 18x - 23$ is written in vertex form, what is the value of k?

86. When $y = 2(x - 3)(x + 5)$ is written in standard form, what is the value of b?

87. When $y = -2(x + 3)^2 + 25$ is written in standard form, what is the value of c?

88. For $y = 3x^2 - 7x + 5$, what is the x-value of the vertex? Enter your answer as an improper fraction in simplest form.

89. What is the y-coordinate of the vertex of $y = -2(x + 1)^2 + 3$?

90. How many units down must you shift the graph of $y = 3(x + 3)^2$ to get the graph of $y = 3(x + 3)^2 - 2$?

Mixed Review

GO for Help

Lesson 5-2

Graph each function.

91. $y = x^2 - 5$ **92.** $y = x^2 - 4x + 8$ **93.** $y = 3x^2 + 6x + 5$

Lesson 4-5

Solve each matrix equation.

94. $\begin{bmatrix} 0 & 1 \\ -1 & 2 \end{bmatrix} X = \begin{bmatrix} 20 \\ 10 \end{bmatrix}$ **95.** $\begin{bmatrix} -1 & 3 \\ 1 & -2 \end{bmatrix} X = \begin{bmatrix} 4 \\ -4 \end{bmatrix}$

Lesson 3-4

96. Find the maximum and minimum values of the objective function $P = 2x + y$, under the constraints at the right.

$\begin{cases} y \geq 2x - 2 & x \geq 0 \\ y \leq -x + 4 & y \geq 0 \end{cases}$

✓ Checkpoint Quiz 1   Lessons 5-1 through 5-3

Find a quadratic model in standard form for each set of values.

1. $(0, 3), (1, 10), (2, 19)$ **2.** $(-2, -15), (0, 1), (2, 1)$ **3.** $(0, 0), (1, -5), (2, 0)$

Graph each function.

4. $y = 4x^2 + 16x + 7$ **5.** $y = (x + 8)^2 - 3$ **6.** $y = -(x + 2)^2 - 7$

Determine whether each function has a maximum or minimum value. Then find the value.

7. $y = -x^2 + 6x + 5$ **8.** $y = \frac{1}{2}(x - 6)^2 + 7$

9. Rewrite the equation $y = -3x^2 - 6x - 8$ in vertex form. Identify the vertex and the axis of symmetry.

10. Open-Ended Write the equation of a parabola with a vertex at $(3, 2)$. Write the axis of symmetry and the coordinates of two other points on the graph.

258   Chapter 5   Quadratic Equations and Functions

5-4 Factoring Quadratic Expressions

What You'll Learn

- To find common and binomial factors of quadratic expressions
- To factor special quadratic expressions

. . . And Why

To model the cross section of a pipe, as in Example 8

✓ Check Skills You'll Need

GO for Help Lessons 1-2 and 5-1

Simplify each expression.

1. $x^2 + x + 4x - 1$ **2.** $6x^2 - 4(3)x + 2x - 3$ **3.** $4x^2 - 2(5 - x) - 3x$

Multiply.

4. $2x(5 - x)$ **5.** $(2x - 7)(2x - 7)$ **6.** $(4x + 3)(4x - 3)$

◀)) New Vocabulary   • factoring • greatest common factor (GCF) of an expression
                         • perfect square trinomial • difference of two squares

---

1   Finding Common and Binomial Factors

Activity: Factoring

1. Since $6 \cdot 3 = 18$, 6 and 3 make up a factor pair for 18.
   a. Find the other factor pairs for 18, including negative integers.
   b. Find the sum of the integers in each factor pair for 18.

2. a. Does 12 have a factor pair with a sum of -8? A sum of -9?
   b. Using all the factor pairs of 12, how many sums are possible?
   c. How many sums are possible for the factor pairs of -12?

Vocabulary Tip

One number is a <u>factor</u> of another if the first divides into the second with no remainder.

Factoring is rewriting an expression as the product of its factors. The **greatest common factor (GCF) of an expression** is a common factor of the terms of the expression. It's the common factor with the greatest coefficient and the greatest exponent. You can factor any expression that has a GCF not equal to 1.

1 EXAMPLE   Finding Common Factors

Factor each expression.

a. $4x^2 + 20x - 12$

$4x^2 + 20x - 12 = 4x^2 + 4(5x) - 4(3)$ **Factor out the GCF, 4.**

$= 4(x^2 + 5x - 3)$ **Rewrite using the Distributive Property.**

b. $9n^2 - 24n$

$9n^2 - 24n = 3n(3n) - 3n(8)$ **Factor out the GCF, 3n.**

$= 3n(3n - 8)$ **Rewrite using the Distributive Property.**

✓ Quick Check

1 Factor each expression.

a. $9x^2 + 3x - 18$ **b.** $7p^2 + 21$ **c.** $4w^2 + 2w$

Vocabulary Tip

A <u>monomial</u> is an expression with one term. A <u>binomial</u> has two terms, and a <u>trinomial</u> has three terms.

A quadratic trinomial is an expression in the form $ax^2 + bx + c$. You can factor many quadratic trinomials into two binomial factors. First find two factors with a product ac and a sum b. Then find common factors.

If ac and b are positive, then the factors of ac are both positive.

2 **EXAMPLE** **Factoring When $ac > 0$ and $b > 0$**

Factor $x^2 + 8x + 7$.

Step 1 Find factors with product ac and sum b.

Since $ac = 7$ and $b = 8$, find positive factors with product 7 and sum 8.

Factors of 7	1, 7
Sum of factors	8

These are the only positive factors of 7.

Step 2 Rewrite the term bx using the factors you found. Group the remaining terms and find the common factors for each group. After removing common factors from each group, you should find two identical binomials.

$x^2 + 8x + 7$

$x^2 + x + 7x + 7$ **Rewrite bx: $8x = x + 7x$.**

$x(x + 1) + 7(x + 1)$ **Find common factors.**

Step 3 Rewrite the expression as the product of two binomials.

$x(x + 1) + 7(x + 1)$

$(x + 1)(x + 7)$ **Rewrite using the Distributive Property.**

Check $(x + 1)(x + 7) = x^2 + 7x + x + 7$
$= x^2 + 8x + 7$ ✓

You can use algebra tiles to factor the expression in Example 2.

Quick Check **2** Factor each expression. Check your answers.
  a. $x^2 + 6x + 8$ **b.** $x^2 + 12x + 32$ **c.** $x^2 + 14x + 40$

If ac is positive and b is negative, then the factors of ac are both negative.

3 **EXAMPLE** **Factoring When $ac > 0$ and $b < 0$**

Factor $x^2 - 17x + 72$.

Step 1 Find factors with product ac and sum b.

Since $ac = 72$ and $b = -17$, find negative factors with product 72 and sum -17.

Factors of 72	−1, −72	−2, −36	−3, −24	−4, −18	−6, −12	−8, −9
Sum of factors	−73	−38	−27	−22	−18	−17

Step 2 Rewrite the term bx using the factors you found. Then find common factors and rewrite the expression as the product of two binomials.

$x^2 - 17x + 72$

$x^2 - 8x - 9x + 72$ **Rewrite bx.**

$x(x - 8) - 9(x - 8)$ **Find common factors.**

$(x - 9)(x - 8)$ **Rewrite using the Distributive Property.**

 **Quick Check** ❸ Factor each expression.

    a. $x^2 - 6x + 8$ **b.** $x^2 - 7x + 12$ **c.** $x^2 - 11x + 24$

Note in Example 3 that the factors of c, -9 and -8, appear in the binomials of the factored form, $(x - 9)(x - 8)$. That is also the case for the factors in Example 2, and it is the case whenever $a = 1$. So when $a = 1$, you can skip a few steps in factoring. See Example 4.

If ac is negative, then the factors of ac have different signs.

4 EXAMPLE   **Factoring When $ac < 0$**

Factor $x^2 - x - 12$.

Step 1 Find factors with product ac and sum b.

Since $ac = -12$ and $b = -1$, find factors with product -12 and sum -1.

Factors of −12	1, −12	−1, 12	2, −6	−2, 6	3, −4	−3, 4
Sum of factors	−11	11	−4	4	−1	1

Step 2 Since $a = 1$, you can write binomials using the factors you found.
$x^2 - x - 12$
● $(x - 4)(x + 3)$ **Use the factors you found.**

Quick Check ❹ Factor each expression.

    a. $x^2 - 14x - 32$ **b.** $x^2 + 3x - 10$ **c.** $x^2 + 4x - 5$

If ac is positive, as in Examples 2 and 3, then the factors of ac have the same sign. This is true even when $a \neq 1$.

5 EXAMPLE   **Factoring When $a \neq 1$ and $ac > 0$**

Factor $3x^2 - 16x + 5$.

Step 1 Find factors with product ac and sum b.

Since $ac = 15$ and $b = -16$, find negative factors with product 15 and sum -16.

Factors of 15	−1, −15	−3, −5
Sum of factors	−16	−8

Step 2 Rewrite the term bx using the factors you found. Then find common factors and rewrite the expression as the product of two binomials.
$3x^2 - 16x + 5$
$3x^2 - x - 15x + 5$ **Rewrite bx.**
$x(3x - 1) - 5(3x - 1)$ **Find common factors.**
● $(x - 5)(3x - 1)$ **Rewrite using the Distributive Property.**

 **Quick Check** ❺ Factor each expression. Check your answers.

    a. $2x^2 + 11x + 12$ **b.** $4x^2 + 7x + 3$ **c.** $2x^2 - 7x + 6$

Again, if ac is negative, then the factors of ac have different signs.

6 EXAMPLE Factoring When $a \neq 1$ and $ac < 0$

Factor $4x^2 - 4x - 15$.

Step 1 Find factors with product ac and sum b.

Since $ac = -60$ and $b = -4$, find factors with product -60 and sum -4.

Factors of −60	1, −60	−1, 60	2, −30	−2, 30	3, −20	−3, 20
Sum of factors	−59	59	−28	28	−17	17
Factors of −60	4, −15	−4, 15	5, −12	−5, 12	6, −10	−6, 10
Sum of factors	−11	11	−7	7	−4	4

Step 2 Rewrite the term bx using the factors you found. Then find common factors and rewrite the expression as the product of two binomials.

$4x^2 - 4x - 15$

$4x^2 + 6x - 10x - 15$ **Rewrite bx.**

$2x(2x + 3) - 5(2x + 3)$ **Find common factors.**

$(2x - 5)(2x + 3)$ **Rewrite using the Distributive Property.**

 **6** Factor each expression.
   a. $2x^2 + 7x - 9$ **b.** $3x^2 - 16x - 12$ **c.** $4x^2 + 5x - 6$

---

2   Factoring Special Expressions

A **perfect square trinomial** is the product you obtain when you square a binomial. An example is $x^2 + 10x + 25$, which can be written as $(x + 5)^2$. The first term and the third term of the trinomial are always positive, as they represent the squares of the two terms of the binomial. The middle term of the trinomial is two times the product of the terms of the binomial.

 **Key Concepts**

Property	Factoring Perfect Square Trinomials
$a^2 + 2ab + b^2 = (a + b)^2$	$a^2 - 2ab + b^2 = (a - b)^2$

7 EXAMPLE Factoring a Perfect Square Trinomial

Factor $9x^2 - 42x + 49$.

$9x^2 - 42x + 49 = (3x)^2 - 42x + 7^2$ **Rewrite the first and third terms as squares.**

$= (3x)^2 - 2(3x)(7) + 7^2$ **Rewrite the middle term to verify the perfect square trinomial pattern.**

$= (3x - 7)^2$ $a^2 - 2ab + b^2 = (a - b)^2$

 **7** Factor each expression.
   a. $4x^2 + 12x + 9$ **b.** $64x^2 - 16x + 1$ **c.** $25x^2 + 90x + 81$

An expression of the form $a^2 - b^2$ is defined as the **difference of two squares.**
It also follows a pattern that makes it easy to factor.

 Key Concepts

Property	Factoring a Difference of Two Squares
	$a^2 - b^2 = (a + b)(a - b)$

8 **EXAMPLE** **Real-World Connection**

Multiple Choice The photo shows the thin
ring that is the cross-section of the pipe.
Which expression gives the area of the
cross-section in completely factored form?

Ⓐ $\pi(3 + r)(3 - r)$ Ⓑ $\pi(3 - r)(3 - r)$

Ⓒ $\pi(9 - r^2)$ Ⓓ $9 - \pi r^2$

Relate   pipe's area   equals   the outer area

minus   the inner area

Define   Let r = inner radius in feet.

Write   area   = $\pi(3)^2$ − πr^2

$$\text{area} = \pi(3)^2 - \pi r^2$$
$$= \pi(3^2 - r^2)$$
$$= \pi(3 + r)(3 - r)$$

● The cross-sectional area is $\pi(3 + r)(3 - r)$ ft^2. The correct choice is A.

Test-Taking Tip

A correct solution to
the problem may not
be the correct answer
to the question asked.

✓ **Quick Check** **8** Factor each expression: **a.** $x^2 - 64$ **b.** $4a^2 - 49$

EXERCISES

For more exercises, see *Extra Skill and Word Problem Practice.*

Practice and Problem Solving

Ⓐ Practice by Example

Example 1
(page 259)

  **GO for Help**

Find the GCF of each expression. Then factor the expression.

1. $3a^2 + 9$ **2.** $25b^2 - 35$ **3.** $x^2 - 2x$

4. $5t^2 + 7t$ **5.** $14y^2 + 7y$ **6.** $27p^2 - 9p$

Factor each expression.

Example 2
(page 260)

7. $x^2 + 3x + 2$ **8.** $x^2 + 5x + 6$ **9.** $x^2 + 7x + 10$

10. $x^2 + 10x + 16$ **11.** $y^2 + 15y + 36$ **12.** $x^2 + 22x + 40$

Example 3
(page 260)

13. $x^2 - 3x + 2$ **14.** $x^2 - 13x + 12$ **15.** $r^2 - 11r + 18$

16. $x^2 - 10x + 24$ **17.** $d^2 - 12d + 27$ **18.** $x^2 - 13x + 36$

Example 4
(page 261)

19. $x^2 - 5x - 14$ **20.** $x^2 + x - 20$ **21.** $x^2 - 3x - 40$

22. $c^2 + 2c - 63$ **23.** $x^2 + 10x - 75$ **24.** $t^2 - 7t - 44$

Example 5
(page 261)

25. $3x^2 + 31x + 36$ **26.** $2x^2 - 19x + 24$ **27.** $5r^2 + 23r + 26$

28. $2m^2 - 11m + 15$ **29.** $5t^2 + 28t + 32$ **30.** $2x^2 - 27x + 36$

Example 6
(page 262)

Factor each expression.

31. $3x^2 + 7x - 20$ **32.** $5y^2 + 12y - 32$ **33.** $7x^2 - 8x - 12$

34. $2z^2 + z - 28$ **35.** $3x^2 + 8x - 16$ **36.** $28k^2 + 13k - 6$

Example 7
(page 262)

37. $x^2 + 2x + 1$ **38.** $t^2 - 14t + 49$ **39.** $x^2 - 18x + 81$

40. $4n^2 - 20n + 25$ **41.** $9x^2 + 48x + 64$ **42.** $81z^2 + 36z + 4$

43. $x^2 - 4$ **44.** $c^2 - 64$ **45.** $9x^2 - 1$

Example 8
(page 263)

46. Manufacturing Refer to the diagram at the right. A machine will cut a small square of plastic from a larger square. Write an expression for the remaining area. Factor the expression.

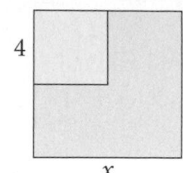

47. The area in square centimeters of a square mat is $25x^2 - 10x + 1$. Find the dimensions of the mat in terms of x.

B Apply Your Skills

48. The area of a rectangular cloth is $(6x^2 - 19x - 85)$ cm^2. The length is $(2x + 5)$ cm. Find the width.

49. Refer to the diagram at the right. Suppose you cut a small square from a square sheet of cardboard. Write an expression for the remaining area. Factor the expression.

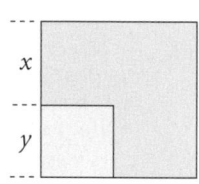

50. Interior Design Refer to the photo at the left. The area of the rug is $(x^2 - 11x + 28)$ ft^2. What is the width?

Factor each expression completely.

51. $9x^2 - 36$ **52.** $18z^2 - 8$ **53.** $12y^2 - 75$

54. $64t^2 - 16$ **55.** $12x^2 + 36x + 27$ **56.** $16x^2 - 80x + 100$

57. $2a^2 - 16a + 32$ **58.** $3x^2 - 24x - 27$ **59.** $18b^2 + 24b - 10$

60. $4n^2 - 20n + 24$ **61.** $3y^2 + 24y + 45$ **62.** $-x^2 + 5x - 4$

63. $4x^2 - 22x + 10$ **64.** $\frac{1}{2}x^2 - \frac{1}{2}$ **65.** $-6z^2 - 600$

 66. Geometry Express the volume of the shaded pipe at the right in completely factored form.

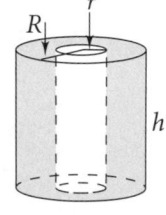

 67. Agriculture The area in square feet of a rectangular field is $x^2 - 120x + 3500$. The width in feet is $x - 50$. Find the length.

68. Writing Explain how to factor $3x^2 + 6x - 72$ completely.

69. Open-Ended Write a quadratic trinomial that can be factored, where $a \neq 1$, $ac > 0$, and $b < 0$. Factor the expression.

70. Error Analysis Find the error below. Then factor the expression correctly.

$2x^2 - 7x + 5$

$2x^2 - 5x - 2x + 5$

$x(2x - 5) + (2x - 5)$

$(x + 1)(2x - 5)$

GO Online
Homework Video Tutor
Visit: PHSchool.com
Web Code: age-0504

(x − 4) ft

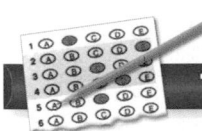

C **Challenge**   **71. Critical Thinking** Explain how to factor $4x^4 + 24x^3 + 32x^2$.

Factor each expression completely.

72. $0.25t^2 - 0.16$ **73.** $8100x^2 - 10{,}000$ **74.** $3600z^2 - 4900$

75. $(x + 3)^2 + 3(x + 3) - 54$ **76.** $(x - 2)^2 - 15(x - 2) + 56$

77. $6(x + 5)^2 - 5(x + 5) + 1$ **78.** $3(2a - 3)^2 + 17(2a - 3) + 10$

Test Prep

Multiple Choice   **79.** Which term is NOT a common factor of $4a^2c^2 + 2a^2c - 6ac^2$?
   A. $4c$ **B.** $2a$ **C.** $2ac$ **D.** ac

80. How can you write $(m - 5)(m + 4) + 8$ as a product of two binomials?
   F. $(m - 1)(m + 8)$ **G.** $(m - 4)(m + 3)$
   H. $(m + 8)(m + 8)$ **J.** $(m - 5)(8m + 32)$

81. What is the factored form of $4x^2 + 15x - 4$?
   A. $(2x + 2)(2x - 2)$ **B.** $(2x - 4)(2x + 1)$
   C. $(4x + 1)(x - 4)$ **D.** $(4x - 1)(x + 4)$

82. Which is a factored form of $0.81p^2 - 0.09$?
   F. $(0.9p + 0.045)(0.9p - 0.045)$ **G.** $(0.09p + 0.03)(0.09p - 0.03)$
   H. $(0.9p + 0.3)(0.9p - 0.3)$ **J.** $(0.9p + 0.81)(0.9p - 0.81)$

Short Response   **83.** Explain how to rewrite the expression $a^2 - 2ab + b^2 - 25$ as the product of two trinomial factors.

Extended Response   **84.** Suppose you hit a baseball and its flight takes a parabolic path. The height of the ball at certain times appears in the table below.

Time (s)	0.5	0.75	1	1.25
Height (ft)	10	10.5	9	5.5

   a. Find a quadratic model for the ball's height as a function of time.
   b. Write the quadratic function in factored form.

Mixed Review

 **GO** for Help

Lesson 5-3   **Write each function in vertex form.**

85. $y = x^2 - 2x + 1$ **86.** $y = -2x^2 + 2x + 5$ **87.** $y = 5x^2 - 1$

Lesson 4-6   **Evaluate each determinant.**

88. $\begin{vmatrix} 2 & -1 & 0 \\ 1 & 0 & 3 \\ 4 & -2 & 1 \end{vmatrix}$ **89.** $\begin{vmatrix} 1 & 5 & 0 \\ 3 & 3 & 5 \\ 0 & 1 & 2 \end{vmatrix}$ **90.** $\begin{vmatrix} 0 & 4 & 1 \\ 1 & 0 & 1 \\ 1 & 2 & 1 \end{vmatrix}$

Lesson 3-6 **91. Coins** The combined mass of a penny and a nickel and a dime is 9.8 g. Ten nickels and three pennies have the same mass as 25 dimes. Fifty dimes have the same mass as 18 nickels and 10 pennies. Write and solve a system of equations to find the mass of each type of coin.

Square Roots and Radicals

A radical symbol $\sqrt{}$ indicates a square root. The expression $\sqrt{16}$ means the principal, or positive, square root of 16. The expression $-\sqrt{16}$ means the negative square root of 16. In general, $\sqrt{x^2} = |x|$ for all real numbers x.

Properties	Square Roots

Multiplication Property of Square Roots

For any numbers $a \geq 0$ and $b \geq 0$, $\sqrt{ab} = \sqrt{a} \cdot \sqrt{b}$.

Division Property of Square Roots

For any numbers $a \geq 0$ and $b > 0$, $\sqrt{\dfrac{a}{b}} = \dfrac{\sqrt{a}}{\sqrt{b}}$.

You can use the properties of square roots to simplify radical expressions.

1 EXAMPLE Radical Expressions Containing Perfect Squares

Simplify $\sqrt{48}$.

$\sqrt{48} = \sqrt{16} \cdot \sqrt{3}$ **Multiplication Property of Square Roots**

$\phantom{\sqrt{48}} = 4\sqrt{3}$ **Simplify.**

2 EXAMPLE Denominators Containing Radical Expressions

Simplify $-\sqrt{\dfrac{5}{7}}$.

$-\sqrt{\dfrac{5}{7}} = -\dfrac{\sqrt{5}}{\sqrt{7}}$ **Division Property of Square Roots**

$\phantom{-\sqrt{\dfrac{5}{7}}} = -\dfrac{\sqrt{5}}{\sqrt{7}} \cdot \dfrac{\sqrt{7}}{\sqrt{7}}$ **Multiply both the numerator and the denominator by $\sqrt{7}$.**

$\phantom{-\sqrt{\dfrac{5}{7}}} = -\dfrac{\sqrt{35}}{\sqrt{49}}$ **Multiplication Property of Square Roots**

$\phantom{-\sqrt{\dfrac{5}{7}}} = -\dfrac{\sqrt{35}}{7}$ **Simplify.**

EXERCISES

Simplify each radical expression.

1. $\sqrt{18}$ **2.** $\sqrt{75}$ **3.** $-\sqrt{32}$ **4.** $\sqrt{\dfrac{3}{5}}$

5. $-\sqrt{\dfrac{7}{12}}$ **6.** $\sqrt{\dfrac{3}{8}}$ **7.** $-\sqrt{200}$ **8.** $5\sqrt{320}$

9. $(2\sqrt{27})^2$ **10.** $-\sqrt{10^4}$ **11.** $\sqrt{x^2y^2}$ **12.** $\sqrt{\dfrac{8}{x^2}}$

5-5

Quadratic Equations

GO for Help Lessons 5-2 and 5-4

What You'll Learn

- To solve quadratic equations by factoring and by finding square roots
- To solve quadratic equations by graphing

. . . And Why

To solve equations involving art, as in Example 5

✓ Check Skills You'll Need

Factor each expression.

1. $x^2 + 5x - 14$ **2.** $4x^2 - 12x$ **3.** $9x^2 - 16$

Graph each function.

4. $y = x^2 - 2x - 5$ **5.** $y = x^2 - 4x + 4$ **6.** $y = x^2 - 4x$

◀)) New Vocabulary

- standard form of a quadratic equation
- Zero-Product Property • zero of a function

---

1 Solving by Factoring and Finding Square Roots

The **standard form of a quadratic equation** is $ax^2 + bx + c = 0$, where $a \neq 0$. You can solve some quadratic equations in standard form by factoring the quadratic expression and then using the Zero-Product Property.

 Key Concepts

Property	Zero-Product Property
If $ab = 0$, then $a = 0$ or $b = 0$.	
Example If $(x + 3)(x - 7) = 0$, then $(x + 3) = 0$ or $(x - 7) = 0$.	

1 EXAMPLE Solving by Factoring

Solve $2x^2 - 11x = -15$.

$$2x^2 - 11x + 15 = 0 \qquad \text{Write in standard form.}$$
$$(x - 3)(2x - 5) = 0 \qquad \text{Factor the quadratic expression.}$$
$$x - 3 = 0 \quad \text{or} \quad 2x - 5 = 0 \qquad \text{Use the Zero-Product Property.}$$
$$x = 3 \qquad \text{or} \qquad x = \tfrac{5}{2} \qquad \text{Solve for } x.$$

The solutions are 3 and $\tfrac{5}{2}$.

Check
$$2x^2 - 11x = -15$$
$$2(3)^2 - 11(3) \overset{?}{=} -15$$
$$18 - 33 \overset{?}{=} -15$$
$$-15 = -15 \checkmark$$

$$2x^2 - 11x = -15$$
$$2\left(\tfrac{5}{2}\right)^2 - 11\left(\tfrac{5}{2}\right) \overset{?}{=} -15$$
$$\tfrac{25}{2} - \tfrac{55}{2} \overset{?}{=} -15$$
$$-15 = -15 \checkmark$$

 **Quick Check** **1** Solve each equation by factoring. Check your answers.

a. $x^2 + 7x = 18$ **b.** $2x^2 + 4x = 6$ **c.** $16x^2 = 8x$

You can solve an equation in the form $ax^2 = c$ by finding square roots.

2 EXAMPLE   Solving by Finding Square Roots

Solve $5x^2 - 180 = 0$.

$5x^2 - 180 = 0$

$\quad\quad 5x^2 = 180$ **Rewrite in the form $ax^2 = c$.**

$\quad\quad \dfrac{5x^2}{5} = \dfrac{180}{5}$ **Isolate x^2.**

$\quad\quad x^2 = 36$ **Simplify.**

$\quad\quad x = \pm 6$ **Find square roots.**

✓ Quick Check ❷ Solve each equation by finding square roots.
   a. $4x^2 - 25 = 0$ **b.** $3x^2 = 24$ **c.** $x^2 - \frac{1}{4} = 0$

3 EXAMPLE   Real-World  Connection

Firefighting Smoke jumpers are in free fall from the time they jump out of a plane until they open their parachutes. The function $y = -16t^2 + 1600$ models a jumper's height y in feet at t seconds for a jump from 1600 ft. How long is a jumper in free fall if the parachute opens at 1000 ft?

$\quad\quad\quad y = -16t^2 + 1600$

$\quad 1000 = -16t^2 + 1600$ **Substitute 1000 for y.**

$\quad -600 = -16t^2$ **Isolate t^2.**

$\quad\quad 37.5 = t^2$

$\quad\quad \pm 6.1 \approx t$ **Find square roots.**

The jumper is in free fall for about 6.1 seconds.

Check   Is the answer reasonable? The negative number -6.1 is also a solution to the equation. However, since a negative value for time has no meaning in this case, only the positive solution is reasonable.

Real-World  Connection

Careers Smoke jumpers are firefighters who parachute into areas near forest fires.

✓ Quick Check ❸ **a.** A smoke jumper jumps from 1400 ft. The function describing the height is $y = -16t^2 + 1400$. Using square roots, find the time during which the jumper is in free fall if the parachute opens at 1000 ft.
   b. Solve the equation in part (a) by factoring. Which method do you prefer—using square roots or factoring? Explain.

2 Solving by Graphing

Not every quadratic equation can be solved by factoring or by finding square roots. You can solve $ax^2 + bx + c = 0$ by graphing $y_1 = ax^2 + bx + c$—its related quadratic function. The value of y_1 is 0 where the graph intersects the x-axis. Each x-intercept is a **zero of the function** and a root of the equation.

You can also solve $ax^2 + bx + c = 0$ by displaying values of $y_1 = ax^2 + bx + c$ in a table. Scroll through the table to find where y_1 changes sign, effectively where the graph crosses the x-axis. Then "zoom-in" on the y_1 values by adjusting TblStart and Δ Tbl.

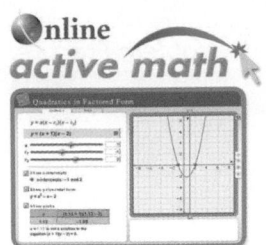
4 **EXAMPLE** Solving by Tables

Solve $x^2 - 5x + 2 = 0$.

Enter $y_1 = x^2 - 5x + 2$ in your graphing calculator. Use the TABLE window to see where y_1 changes sign. Change Δ Tbl to 0.01 and look again for the sign change. Continue this tabular zoom-in and find one solution to be $x \approx 0.44$.

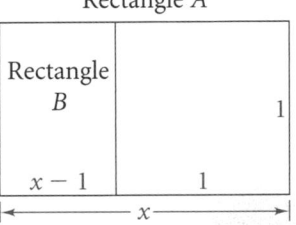

X	Y1
0	2
1	−2
2	−4
3	−4
4	−2
5	2
6	8

Y1 =X²−5X+2

X	Y1
.4	.16
.41	.1181
.42	.0764
.43	.0349
.44	−.0064
.45	−.0475
.46	−.0884

Y1 =X²−5X+2

Quick Check **4** In the first window above, the second sign change occurs between $x = 4$ and $x = 5$. Use tabular zoom-in to find the other solution to two decimal places.

5 **EXAMPLE** Solving by Graphing

Art Artists often use a golden rectangle in their work because forms based on it are visually pleasing. You can divide a golden rectangle into a square of side length one and a smaller rectangle that is similar to the original one. The ratio of the longer side to the shorter side of a golden rectangle is the golden ratio. Use the figure at the right to find the golden ratio.

Rectangle A

Rectangle B

$x - 1$ 1   1

x

Relate $\dfrac{\text{longer side of } A}{\text{shorter side of } A} = \dfrac{\text{longer side of } B}{\text{shorter side of } B}$

Define Let x = longer side of rectangle A. Then $x - 1$ = shorter side of rectangle B.

Write $\dfrac{x}{1} = \dfrac{1}{x - 1}$

$x^2 - x = 1$ **Find cross-products.**

$x^2 - x - 1 = 0$ **Write in standard form.**

Graph the function $y_1 = x^2 - x - 1$. Use "zero" in the CALC feature to find the positive solution.

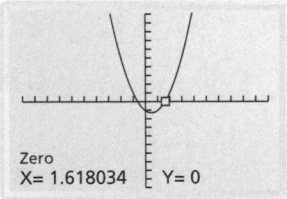

Zero
X= 1.618034   Y= 0

The ratio is about 1.62 : 1.

Quick Check **5** Solve each equation. When necessary, round to the nearest hundredth.
   a. $x^2 - 2x = 4$ **b.** $x^2 + \frac{1}{2}x - \frac{1}{4} = 0$

Real-World **Connection**

Francisco José de Goya y Lucientes (1746–1828) was a Spanish painter. In *Portrait of a Man,* Goya placed the most significant elements of the painting within golden rectangles.

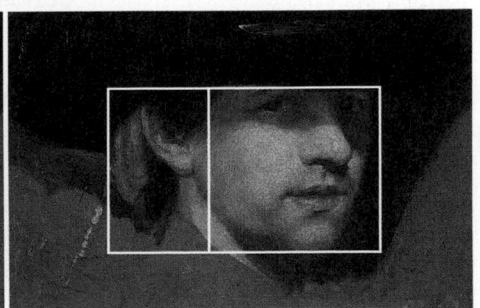

EXERCISES

For more exercises, see *Extra Skill and Word Problem Practice.*

Practice and Problem Solving

A Practice by Example

GO for Help

Example 1
(page 267)

Solve each equation by factoring. Check your answers.

1. $x^2 + 6x + 8 = 0$ **2.** $x^2 + 18 = 9x$ **3.** $2x^2 - x = 3$

4. $x^2 - 10x + 25 = 0$ **5.** $2x^2 + 6x = -4$ **6.** $3x^2 = 16x + 12$

Example 2
(page 268)

Solve each equation by finding square roots.

7. $5x^2 = 80$ **8.** $x^2 - 4 = 0$ **9.** $2x^2 = 32$

10. $9x^2 = 25$ **11.** $3x^2 - 15 = 0$ **12.** $5x^2 - 40 = 0$

Example 3
(page 268)

Solve each equation by factoring or by taking square roots.

13. $x^2 - 4x = 0$ **14.** $6x^2 + 4x = 0$ **15.** $12x^2 - 147 = 0$

16. $3x^2 = 48$ **17.** $2x^2 = 8x$ **18.** $4x^2 - 80 = 0$

19. Firefighters A smoke jumper jumps from a plane that is 1700 ft above the ground. The function $y = -16t^2 + 1700$ gives the jumper's height y in feet at t seconds.
 a. How long is the jumper in free fall if the parachute opens at 1000 ft?
 b. How long is the jumper in free fall if the parachute opens at 940 ft?

Example 4
(page 269)

Solve each equation using tables. Give each answer to at most two decimal places.

20. $x^2 + 5x + 3 = 0$ **21.** $x^2 - 7x = 11$ **22.** $2x^2 - x = 2$

Example 5
(page 269)

Solve each equation by graphing. Give each answer to at most two decimal places.

23. $6x^2 = -19x - 15$ **24.** $3x^2 - 5x - 4 = 0$ **25.** $5x^2 - 7x - 3 = 8$

26. $6x^2 + 31x = 12$ **27.** $1 = 4x^2 + 3x$ **28.** $\frac{1}{2}x^2 - x = 8$

29. $x^2 = 4x + 8$ **30.** $x^2 + 4x = 6$ **31.** $2x^2 - 2x - 5 = 0$

B Apply Your Skills

32. a. Art Verify that the Chinese painting at the right is a golden rectangle.
 b. What element in the painting divides it into a square and another golden rectangle?

33. Multiple Choice The period of a pendulum is the time the pendulum takes to swing back and forth. The function $\ell = 0.81t^2$ relates the length ℓ in feet of a pendulum to the time t in seconds that it takes to swing back and forth. The convention center in Portland, Oregon, has the longest pendulum in the United States. The pendulum's length is 90 ft. Find the period.

    Ⓐ 8.5 seconds   Ⓑ 10.5 seconds   Ⓒ 90 seconds   Ⓓ 111 seconds

34. Open-Ended Write an equation in standard form that you can solve by factoring and an equation that you cannot solve by factoring.

GO Online

Homework Video Tutor

Visit: PHSchool.com
Web Code: age-0505

35. Gardening Suppose you want to expand the garden shown at the right by planting a border of flowers. The border will be of the same width around the entire garden. The flowers you bought will fill an area of 276 ft². How wide should the border be?

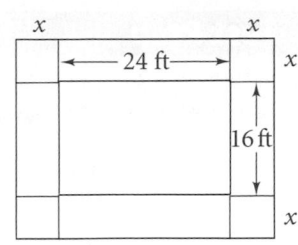

Solve each equation by factoring, by taking square roots, or by graphing. If necessary, round your answer to the nearest hundredth.

36. $x^2 + 6x + 5 = 45$ **37.** $x^2 - 11x + 24 = 0$ **38.** $3x^2 = 27$

39. $2x^2 - 5x - 3 = 0$ **40.** $x^2 + 2x = 6 - 6x$ **41.** $6x^2 + 13x + 6 = 0$

42. $2x^2 + 8x = 5x + 20$ **43.** $7x^2 - 243 = 0$ **44.** $3x^2 + 7x = 9$

45. $12x^2 - 154 = 0$ **46.** $x^2 + 4x = 0$ **47.** $x^2 = 8x - 7$

48. $x^2 + 2x = 15$ **49.** $x^2 + 11x + 10 = 0$ **50.** $4x^2 + 4x = 3$

51. $(x + 3)^2 = 9$ **52.** $2x^2 - 6x = 8$ **53.** $2x^2 + x - 28 = 0$

Critical Thinking The graphs of each pair of functions intersect. Find their points of intersection without using a calculator. (*Hint:* Solve as a system using substitution.)

54. $y = x^2$
$y = -\frac{1}{2}x^2 + \frac{3}{2}x + 3$

55. $y = x^2 - 2$
$y = 3x^2 - 4x - 2$

56. $y = -x^2 + x + 4$
$y = 2x^2 - 6$

 57. Writing Explain how you found the intersections in Exercises 54–56.

Open-Ended Write a quadratic equation with the given solutions.

58. 3 and 5   **59.** −3 and 2   **60.** −1 and −6   **61.** $\frac{1}{2}$ and $\frac{2}{3}$

Challenge

62. Matrices Find the possible values of x and y. (A matrix with exponent 2 means that you multiply the matrix by itself.)

$$\begin{bmatrix} x & 2 \\ 3 & y \end{bmatrix}^2 = \begin{bmatrix} 22 & 10 \\ 15 & \blacksquare \end{bmatrix}$$

63. Using tables, how might you recognize that a quadratic equation likely has exactly one solution? no solutions?

64. The equation $x^2 - 10x + 24 = 0$ can be written in factored form as $(x - 4)(x - 6) = 0$. How can you use this fact to find the vertex of the graph of $y = x^2 - 10x + 24$?

65. Physics Suppose you throw a ball straight up from the ground with a velocity of 80 ft/s. As the ball moves upward, gravity slows it. Eventually the ball begins to fall back to the ground. The height h of the ball after t seconds in the air is given by the quadratic function $h(t) = -16t^2 + 80t$.
a. How high does the ball go?
b. For how many seconds is the ball in the air before it hits the ground?

66. a. Let $a > 0$. Use algebraic or arithmetic ideas to explain why the lowest point on the graph of $y = a(x - h)^2 + k$ must occur when $x = h$.
b. Suppose that the function in part (a) is $y = a(x - h)^3 + k$. Is your reasoning still valid? Explain.

Multiple Choice

67. What are the values of x that satisfy the equation $3 - 27x^2 = 0$?

    A. $x = \pm 3$ **B.** $x = \pm\frac{1}{3}$

    C. $x = \frac{1}{9}$ or $x = -\frac{1}{9}$ **D.** $x = 2\sqrt{6}$ or $x = -2\sqrt{6}$

68. What are the solutions of the equation $6x^2 + 9x - 15 = 0$?

    F. $1, -15$ **G.** $1, -\frac{5}{2}$

    H. $-1, -5$ **J.** $3, \frac{5}{2}$

69. For which equation is -3 NOT a solution?

    A. $x^2 - 2x - 15 = 0$ **B.** $x^2 - 21 = 4x$

    C. $2x^2 + 12x = -18$ **D.** $9 + x^2 = 0$

70. What are the solutions of the equation $(2x - 7)^2 = 25$?

    F. $6, -6$ **G.** $6, 1$ **H.** $6, -1$ **J.** $-6, -1$

71. Find the sum of the solutions to the equation $x^2 + 2x - 15 = 0$.

    A. 8 **B.** -8 **C.** 2 **D.** -2

72. Find the product of the solutions to the equation $x^2 - 8x = 9$.

    F. 6 **G.** -6 **H.** 9 **J.** -9

73. Which equation has $-\frac{2}{5}$ as a solution?

    A. $(2x - 5)(x + 1) = 0$ **B.** $(2x + 5)(x + 1) = 0$

    C. $(5x - 2)(x + 1) = 0$ **D.** $(5x + 2)(x + 1) = 0$

74. How many times does the graph of $y = x^2 - 4x + 5$ cross the x-axis?

    F. 0 **G.** 1 **H.** 2 **J.** 33

75. The equation $x^2 - 3x + a = 0$ has two roots. One root of the equation is 2. What is the other root?

    A. -2 **B.** -1 **C.** 1 **D.** 3

Short Response

76. A quadratic equation has solutions 3 and -4. Write a possible equation.

77. One solution to the equation $x^2 + bx - 20 = 0$ is 5. Find the other solution.

Mixed Review

Lesson 5-4

Factor each expression.

78. $3x^2 - 4x + 1$ **79.** $25z^2 - 9$ **80.** $6s^2 + 9s$

Lesson 4-1

State the dimensions of each matrix. Identify the indicated element.

81. $\begin{bmatrix} 4 & 6 & 5 \\ 1 & -3 & 0 \\ 1 & 1 & 9 \end{bmatrix}; a_{13}$ **82.** $\begin{bmatrix} 4 & -1 & 6 \\ 2 & 0 & 0 \end{bmatrix}; a_{21}$ **83.** $\begin{bmatrix} -9 & 1 & -1 \\ 0 & 6 & 0 \\ 1 & 0 & -2 \end{bmatrix}; a_{32}$

Lesson 1-1

Name the property of real numbers illustrated by each equation.

84. $3(2x + y) = 6x + 3y$ **85.** $3x^2 + 7y = 7y + 3x^2$

86. $4(3x) = (4 \cdot 3)x$ **87.** $3 + (-3) = 0$

Writing Equations From Roots

You can use the Zero-Product Property to write a quadratic function from its zeros or a quadratic equation from its roots.

1 ACTIVITY

1. a. Write a nonzero linear function $f(x)$ that has a zero at $x = 3$.
   b. Write a nonzero linear function $g(x)$ that has a zero at $x = 2$.

2. a. For f and g from Part 1, write the product function $h(x) = f(x) \cdot g(x)$.
   b. What kind of function is $h(x)$?   **c.** Solve the equation $h(x) = 0$.

Mental Math **Write a quadratic function with zeros at each pair of values.**

3. 3 and 4   **4.** 2 and 2.5   **5.** -1 and $\frac{3}{2}$ **6.** 1 and -1 **7.** -6 and -6

Mental Math **Write a quadratic equation with each pair of values as roots.**

8. 2 and 1   **9.** 1.5 and 3   **10.** -2 and 2   **11.** 6 and 12   **12.** $\frac{1}{2}$ and -4

You can also use zeros or roots to write quadratic expressions in standard form.

2 ACTIVITY

13. a. Copy and complete the table. Write the product $(x - a)(x - b)$ in standard form for each pair a and b.
   b. Is there a pattern in the table? Explain.

14. a. If you know the roots, you can write a quadratic function or equation with a quadratic expression in standard form. Explain how.
   b. Demonstrate your method for each pair of values in Exercises 3–12.

a	b	$a + b$	ab	$(x - a)(x - b)$
2	3	5	6	$x^2 - 5x + 6$
-2	3	1	-6	■
2	-3	■	■	■
-2	-3	■	■	■
-5	-6	■	■	■
7	-12	■	■	■

EXERCISES

15. Explain how to write a quadratic equation that has 2 as its only root.

16. Write the equation $q(x) = 0$ suggested by each graph. Each tick mark is 1 unit.

a.
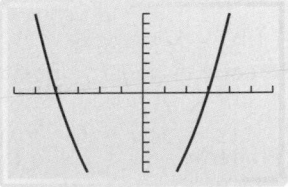

b.
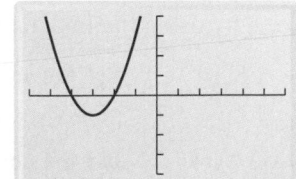

c.
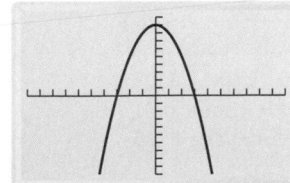

17. Describe the family of quadratic functions that have zeros at r and s. Sketch several members of the family in the coordinate plane.

18. True or False? The x-value of the vertex of a quadratic function with two zeros is the average of the zeros. Give a convincing argument.

5-6

Complex Numbers

What You'll Learn

- To identify and graph complex numbers
- To add, subtract, and multiply complex numbers

. . . And Why

To explore fractals, as in Example 8

✓ **Check Skills You'll Need** **for Help** Skills Handbook page 883

Simplify each expression. Assume variables are nonnegative.

1. $\sqrt{3^2 + 4^2}$ **2.** $\sqrt{(-2)^2 + 8^2}$ **3.** $\sqrt{5^2 + (-12)^2}$

4. $\sqrt{6^2 + 10^2}$ **5.** $\sqrt{x^2 + x^2}$ **6.** $\sqrt{(3x)^2 + (4x)^2}$

🔊 **New Vocabulary**   • i • imaginary number • complex numbers
• complex number plane
• absolute value of a complex number

---

1 Identifying Complex Numbers

When you learned to count, you used the natural numbers 1, 2, 3, and so on. Your number system has grown to include other types of numbers. You have used real numbers, which include both rational numbers such as $\frac{1}{2}$ and irrational numbers such as $\sqrt{2}$. Now your number system will expand to include numbers such as $\sqrt{-2}$.

The imaginary number **i** is defined as the number whose square is -1. So $i^2 = -1$ and $i = \sqrt{-1}$. An **imaginary number** is any number of the form $a + bi$, where a and b are real numbers, and $b \neq 0$.

 Key Concepts

Property	Square Root of a Negative Real Number

For any positive real number a, $\sqrt{-a} = i\sqrt{a}$.

Example $\sqrt{-4} = i\sqrt{4} = i \cdot 2 = 2i$
Note that $(\sqrt{-4})^2 = (i\sqrt{4})^2 = i^2\sqrt{4}^2 = -1 \cdot 4 = -4$ (not 4).

Video Tutor Help
Visit: PHSchool.com
Web Code: age-0775

1 EXAMPLE **Simplifying Numbers Using i**

Simplify $\sqrt{-8}$ by using the imaginary number i.

$\sqrt{-8} = i \cdot \sqrt{8}$ Use the Square Root Property of Negative Numbers.

$= i \cdot 2\sqrt{2}$ Simplify $\sqrt{8}$.

$= 2i\sqrt{2}$ Use the Commutative Property.

✓ **Quick Check** **1** Simplify each number by using the imaginary number i.

a. $\sqrt{-2}$ **b.** $\sqrt{-12}$ **c.** $\sqrt{-36}$

d. Now that $\sqrt{a}$ is defined for $a < 0$, explain why $\sqrt{a^2} \neq (\sqrt{a})^2$.

Imaginary numbers and real numbers together make up the set of **complex numbers.**

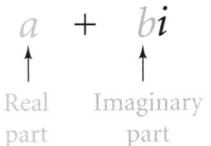

Key Concepts

Definition	Complex Numbers

A complex number can be written in the form $a + bi$, where a and b are real numbers, including 0.

$$\underset{\substack{\uparrow \\ \text{Real} \\ \text{part}}}{a} + \underset{\substack{\uparrow \\ \text{Imaginary} \\ \text{part}}}{bi}$$

2 EXAMPLE **Simplifying Imaginary Numbers**

Write the complex number $\sqrt{-9} + 6$ in the form $a + bi$.

$\sqrt{-9} + 6 = 3i + 6$ **Simplify the radical expression.**

$\phantom{\sqrt{-9} + 6} = 6 + 3i$ **Write in the form $a + bi$.**

✓ Quick Check **2** Write the complex number $\sqrt{-18} + 7$ in the form $a + bi$.

The diagram below shows the sets of numbers that are part of the complex number system, and examples of each set.

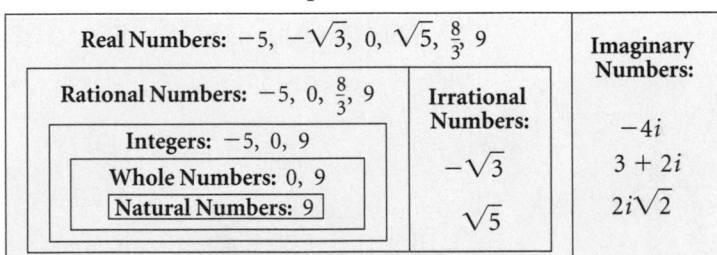

Complex Numbers

Real Numbers: $-5, -\sqrt{3}, 0, \sqrt{5}, \frac{8}{3}, 9$

Rational Numbers: $-5, 0, \frac{8}{3}, 9$

Integers: $-5, 0, 9$

Whole Numbers: $0, 9$

Natural Numbers: 9

Irrational Numbers: $-\sqrt{3}$ $\sqrt{5}$

Imaginary Numbers: $-4i$ $3 + 2i$ $2i\sqrt{2}$

You can use the **complex number plane** to represent a complex number geometrically. Locate the real part of the number on the horizontal axis and the imaginary part on the vertical axis. You graph $3 - 4i$ in the same way you would graph $(3, -4)$ on the coordinate plane.

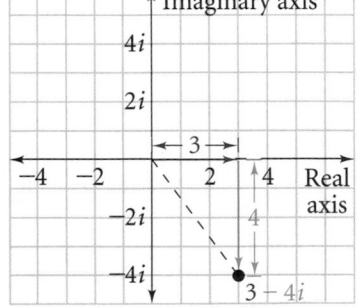

The **absolute value of a complex number** is its distance from the origin on the complex number plane. You can find the absolute value by using the Pythagorean Theorem. In general, $|a + bi| = \sqrt{a^2 + b^2}$.

Vocabulary Tip

Pythagorean Theorem:
$c^2 = a^2 + b^2$ and
$c = \sqrt{a^2 + b^2}$

3 EXAMPLE **Finding Absolute Value**

a. Find $|5i|$.

$5i$ is 5 units from the origin on the imaginary axis. So $|5i| = 5$.

b. Find $|3 - 4i|$.

$|3 - 4i| = \sqrt{3^2 + (-4)^2}$

$ = \sqrt{9 + 16} = 5$

✓ Quick Check **3** Find the absolute value of each complex number.

a. $|6 - 4i|$  **b.** $|-2 + 5i|$ **c.** $|4i|$

2 Operations With Complex Numbers

You can apply the operations of real numbers to complex numbers.

If the sum of two complex numbers is 0, then each number is the opposite, or additive inverse, of the other.

4 EXAMPLE Additive Inverse of a Complex Number

Find the additive inverse of $-2 + 5i$.

$-2 + 5i$

$-(-2 + 5i)$ **Find the opposite.**

$2 - 5i$ **Simplify.**

Quick Check 4 Find the additive inverse of each number.

a. $-5i$ **b.** $4 - 3i$ **c.** $a + bi$

To add or subtract complex numbers, combine the real parts and the imaginary parts separately.

5 EXAMPLE Adding Complex Numbers

Simplify the expression $(5 + 7i) + (-2 + 6i)$.

$(5 + 7i) + (-2 + 6i) = 5 + (-2) + 7i + 6i$ **Use commutative and associative properties.**

$= 3 + 13i$ **Simplify.**

Quick Check 5 Simplify each expression.

a. $(8 + 3i) - (2 + 4i)$ **b.** $7 - (3 + 2i)$ **c.** $(4 - 6i) + 3i$

For two imaginary numbers bi and ci, $(bi)(ci) = bc(i)^2 = bc(-1) = -bc$.

You can multiply two complex numbers of the form $a + bi$ by using the procedure for multiplying binomials.

6 EXAMPLE Multiplying Complex Numbers

a. Find $(5i)(-4i)$.

$(5i)(-4i) = -20i^2$ **Multiply the real numbers.**

$= -20(-1)$ **Substitute −1 for i^2.**

$= 20$ **Multiply.**

b. Find $(2 + 3i)(-3 + 5i)$.

$(2 + 3i)(-3 + 5i) = -6 + 10i - 9i + 15i^2$ **Multiply the binomials.**

$= -6 + 10i - 9i + 15(-1)$ **Substitute −1 for i^2.**

$= -21 + i$ **Simplify.**

Quick Check 6 Simplify each expression.

a. $(12i)(7i)$ **b.** $(6 - 5i)(4 - 3i)$ **c.** $(4 - 9i)(4 + 3i)$

Some quadratic equations have solutions that are complex numbers.

7 EXAMPLE Finding Complex Solutions

Solve $4x^2 + 100 = 0$.

$4x^2 + 100 = 0$

$\quad\quad 4x^2 = -100$ **Isolate x^2.**

$\quad\quad\quad x^2 = -25$

$\quad\quad\quad\ x = \pm\sqrt{-25}$ **Find square roots.**

$\quad\quad\quad\quad = \pm 5i$ **Simplify.**

Check $4x^2 + 100 = 0$

$\quad\quad 4(5i)^2 + 100 \stackrel{?}{=} 0$

$\quad\quad\quad\quad 4(25i^2) \stackrel{?}{=} -100$

$\quad\quad\quad\quad 4(-25) \stackrel{?}{=} -100$

$\quad\quad\quad\quad\quad -100 = -100 \ \checkmark$

$\quad\quad 4x^2 + 100 = 0$

$\quad 4(-5i)^2 + 100 \stackrel{?}{=} 0$

$\quad\quad\quad\quad 4(25i^2) \stackrel{?}{=} -100$

$\quad\quad\quad\quad 4(-25) = -100$

$\quad\quad\quad\quad\quad -100 = -100 \ \checkmark$

✓ Quick Check   **7** Solve each equation. Check your answers.
    a. $3x^2 + 48 = 0$ **b.** $-5x^2 - 150 = 0$ **c.** $8x^2 + 2 = 0$

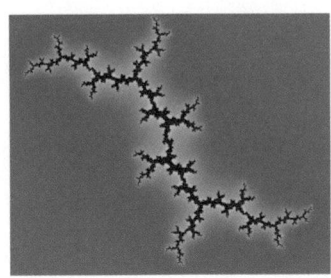

Functions of the form $f(z) = z^2 + c$ where c is a complex number generate fractal graphs on the complex plane like the one at the left. To test if z belongs to the graph, use 0 as the first input value and repeatedly use each output as the next input. If the output values do not become infinitely large, then z is on the graph.

8 EXAMPLE Real-World 🌐 Connection

Fractals Find the first three output values for $f(z) = z^2 + i$.

$f(z) = z^2 + i$

$f(0) = 0^2 + i$ **Use z = 0 as the first input value.**

$\quad\ = i$

$f(i) = i^2 + i$ **First output becomes second input. Evaluate for z = i.**

$\quad\ = -1 + i$

$f(-1 + i) = (-1 + i)^2 + i$ **Second output becomes third input. Evaluate for z = −1 + i.**

$\quad\quad\quad\quad = [(-1)^2 + (-1)(i) + (-1)(i) + (i)^2] + i$

$\quad\quad\quad\quad = (1 - 2i - 1) + i$

$\quad\quad\quad\quad = -i$ **Third output would be next input.**

The first three output values are i, $-1 + i$, and $-i$.

✓ Quick Check   **8** Find the first three output values for $f(z) = z^2 - 1 + i$.

EXERCISES

For more exercises, see *Extra Skill and Word Problem Practice*.

Practice and Problem Solving

 Practice by Example

 **for Help**

Example 1
(page 274)

Simplify each number by using the imaginary number *i*.

1. $\sqrt{-4}$　　2. $\sqrt{-7}$　　3. $\sqrt{-15}$　　4. $\sqrt{-81}$　　5. $\sqrt{-50}$

6. $\sqrt{-16}$　　7. $\sqrt{-32}$　　8. $3\sqrt{-9}$　　9. $-\sqrt{-100}$　　10. $\sqrt{-72}$

Example 2
(page 275)

Write each number in the form $a + bi$.

11. $2 + \sqrt{-3}$　　12. $\sqrt{-8} + 8$　　13. $6 - \sqrt{-28}$　　14. $\sqrt{-4} + 3$

15. $7 - \sqrt{-25}$　　16. $\sqrt{-1} + 2$　　17. $-\sqrt{-50} - 2$　　18. $\sqrt{-72} + 4$

Example 3
(page 275)

Find the absolute value of each complex number.

19. $|2i|$　　20. $|5 + 12i|$　　21. $|2 - 2i|$　　22. $|1 - 4i|$　　23. $|3 - 6i|$

Example 4
(page 276)

Find the additive inverse of each number.

24. $4i$　　25. $5 - 3i$　　26. $9 + i$　　27. $-3 - 2i$　　28. $-4 + 7i$

Example 5
(page 276)

Simplify each expression.

29. $(2 + 4i) + (4 - i)$　　30. $(-3 - 5i) + (4 - 2i)$　　31. $(7 + 9i) + (-5i)$

32. $6 - (8 + 3i)$　　33. $(12 + 5i) - (2 - i)$　　34. $(-6 - 7i) - (1 + 3i)$

Example 6
(page 276)

35. $(-2i)(5i)$　　36. $(4 - 3i)(5 + 2i)$　　37. $(8 + i)(2 + 7i)$

38. $(-6 - 5i)(1 + 3i)$　　39. $(-6i)^2$　　40. $(9 + 4i)^2$

Example 7
(page 277)

Solve each equation. Check your answers.

41. $x^2 + 25 = 0$　　42. $2x^2 + 1 = 0$　　43. $3s^2 + 2 = -62$

44. $x^2 = -7$　　45. $x^2 + 36 = 0$　　46. $-5x^2 - 3 = 0$

Example 8
(page 277)

Find the first three output values of each fractal-generating function. Use $z = 0$ as the first input value.

47. $z^2 - i$　　48. $f(z) = z^2 - 2i$　　49. $f(z) = z^2 + 1 - i$

 Apply Your Skills

Solve each equation.

50. $x^2 + 16 = -49$　　51. $x^2 - 30 = -79$　　52. $3x^2 + 1 = x^2 - 1$

 53. **Writing** In reality, is it possible for Mr. Milde's average to be an imaginary number? Explain.

ROBOTMAN by Jim Meddick

54. a. Name the complex number represented by each point on the graph at the right.
b. Find the additive inverse of each number.

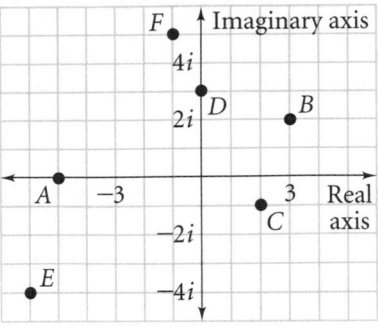

55. Multiple Choice In a complex number plane, what geometric figure describes the complex numbers with absolute value 10?

Ⓐ square   Ⓑ circle
Ⓒ line   Ⓓ two points

56. Solve $(x + 3i)(x - 3i) = 34$.

Simplify each expression.

57. $(8i)(4i)(-9i)$

58. $\left(2 + \sqrt{-1}\right) + \left(-3 + \sqrt{-16}\right)$

59. $\left(4 + \sqrt{-9}\right) + \left(6 - \sqrt{-49}\right)$

60. $\left(10 + \sqrt{-9}\right) - \left(2 + \sqrt{-25}\right)$

61. $\left(8 - \sqrt{-1}\right) - \left(-3 + \sqrt{-16}\right)$

62. $2i(5 - 3i)$

63. $-5(1 + 2i) + 3i(3 - 4i)$

64. $\left(3 + \sqrt{-4}\right)\left(4 + \sqrt{-1}\right)$

65. $\left(-2 + \sqrt{-9}\right)\left(6 + \sqrt{-25}\right)$

66. $\left(1 - \sqrt{-4}\right)\left(-3 - \sqrt{-25}\right)$

Homework Video Tutor
Visit: PHSchool.com
Web Code: age-0506

67. a. Copy and complete the table.
b. Number pairs such as p and q in the table are complex conjugates. Describe at least three patterns you see in complex conjugate pairs.

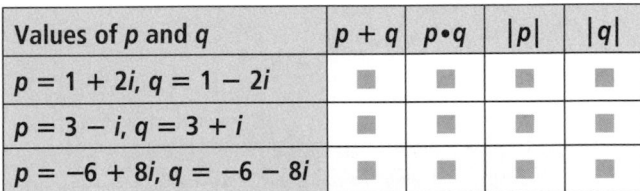

Values of p and q	$p + q$	$p \cdot q$	$\lvert p \rvert$	$\lvert q \rvert$
$p = 1 + 2i,\ q = 1 - 2i$	■	■	■	■
$p = 3 - i,\ q = 3 + i$	■	■	■	■
$p = -6 + 8i,\ q = -6 - 8i$	■	■	■	■

c. Plot each pair of conjugates. How are the points of each pair related?
d. True or false: The conjugate of an additive inverse is equal to the additive inverse of the conjugate. Explain your answer.

Two complex numbers $a + bi$ and $c + di$ are equal when $a = c$ and $b = d$. Solve each equation for x and y.

68. $2x + 3yi = -14 + 9i$ **69.** $3x + 19i = 16 - 8yi$ **70.** $-14 - 3i = 2x + yi$

71. Show that the product of a nonzero complex number $a + bi$ and its conjugate (as described in Exercise 67) is a real number.

72. Fractals The fractal at the left can be described by the function $f(z) = z^2 + c$. If $c = 0.383 + 0.11i$, find the first two output values of the function. Use $z = 0$ as the first input value.

73. For what real values of x and y is $(x + yi)^2$ an imaginary number?

74. Complex numbers can be used to generate interesting patterns. Here is a pattern generated by powers of $1 + 3i$.

$(1 + 3i)^1 = 1 + 3i$ and $1^2 + 3^2 = 10$
$(1 + 3i)^2 = -8 + 6i$ and $(-8)^2 + 6^2 = 10^2$
$(1 + 3i)^3 = -26 - 18i$ and $(-26)^2 + (-18)^2 = 10^3$
$(1 + 3i)^4 = 28 - 96i$ and $28^2 + (-96)^2 = 10^4$

Find the powers of $3 + 4i$ through $(3 + 4i)^5$. Generate and verify a similar pattern.

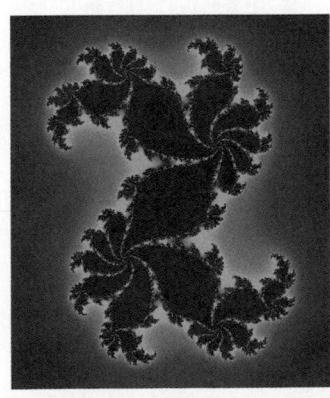

Exercise 72

75. Critical Thinking Graph $1 + 3i$ and $6 + 2i$. Also graph their sum. Draw the quadrilateral that has these three points and the origin as vertices. Repeat with other complex numbers. What do you notice?

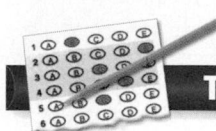

Test Prep

Multiple Choice

76. What is the number $\sqrt{-225} + 36$ when written in the form $a + bi$?

    A. $-15 + 6i$ **B.** $6 + 15i$ **C.** $6 - 15i$ **D.** $36 + 15i$

77. How can you rewrite the expression $(8 - 5i)^2$ in the form $a + bi$?

    F. $39 + 80i$ **G.** $39 - 80i$ **H.** $69 + 80i$ **J.** $69 - 80i$

78. What are the solutions of $-4x^2 - 72 = 0$?

    A. $\pm 2i\sqrt{3}$ **B.** $\pm 3i\sqrt{2}$ **C.** $\pm 2\sqrt{3}$ **D.** $\pm 3\sqrt{2}$

79. Which description of the graph of $y = ax^2 + bx + c$ is NOT possible?

    F. There are two x-intercepts, the vertex is below the x-axis, and $a > 0$.
    G. There is one x-intercept and the vertex is on the x-axis.
    H. There are two x-intercepts, the vertex is below the x-axis, and $a < 0$.
    J. There are no x-intercepts, the vertex is above the x-axis, and $a > 0$.

Extended Response

80. Use factoring to find all complex solutions to $x^4 - 16 = 0$. Show your work.

Mixed Review

GO for Help

Lesson 5-5	**Solve each equation using a graphing calculator.**

81. $2x^2 + 3x - 4 = 0$ **82.** $4x^2 + x = 1$ **83.** $x^2 = -7x - 8$

Lesson 5-2   **Graph each function.**

84. $y = -2(x + 1)^2 - 3$ **85.** $y = \frac{1}{2}(x - 4)^2 + 1$ **86.** $y = 3(x - 1)^2 - 5$

Lesson 3-5   **Graph each point in coordinate space.**

87. $(2, 0, -4)$ **88.** $(0, -3, 5)$ **89.** $(9, -1, 0)$

✓ Checkpoint Quiz 2   Lessons 5-4 through 5-6

Factor each quadratic expression.

    1. $2x^2 + x - 6$ **2.** $5x^2 - 45$ **3.** $4x^2 - 36x + 81$

Solve each equation.

    4. $(3x - 3)(2x + 8) = 0$ **5.** $x^2 - 2x + 1 = 0$ **6.** $x^2 + 121 = 0$

Find the absolute value of each number.

    7. $5 - 2i$ **8.** $9 - i$ **9.** $7 + 4i$

10. Can you solve the equation $x^2 + 7x + 14 = 0$ by graphing the related function $y = x^2 + 7x + 14$? Explain.

Completing the Square

Use tiles or draw a diagram. Copy the model below.

1. a. Add unit tiles until you have a complete square. How many tiles did you add?

    b. Write an expression to represent the sum of the areas of the tiles.

    c. Write an expression to represent the length times the width of the completed square.

    d. How do the six x-tiles in the model relate to the length of the sides of the completed square? To the number of unit tiles used?

2. Suppose the expression $x^2 + 8x + \blacksquare$ can also be modeled by a complete square of tiles.

    a. Draw a diagram or use tiles to find the missing value.

    b. What is the coefficient of x in the expression?

    c. Critical Thinking How can you use the coefficient of x to find the length of the completed square?

3. Suppose $x^2 - 4x + \blacksquare$ can be modeled by a complete square of tiles. Using red to represent negative values, draw a diagram or use tiles to find the missing value.

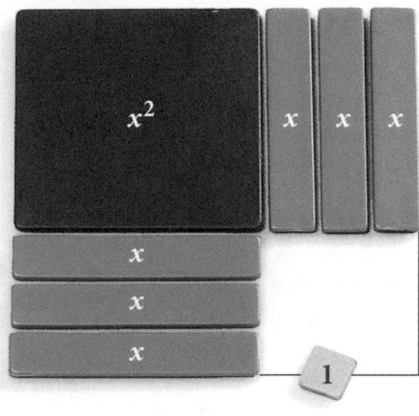

$x^2 + 6x + \blacksquare$

EXERCISES

Complete each square. Then write an expression that represents the sum of the areas of the tiles and an expression that represents the length times the width of the completed square.

1.

2.

3.

Assume that each expression can be modeled by a complete square of tiles. Find the missing value.

4. $x^2 + 14x + \blacksquare$ **5.** $x^2 + 20x + \blacksquare$

6. $x^2 + 10x + \blacksquare$ **7.** $x^2 + 100x + \blacksquare$

8. $x^2 + 32x + \blacksquare$ **9.** $x^2 - 8x + \blacksquare$

10. Make a Conjecture In Lesson 5-5, you solved quadratic equations by taking square roots. How could you use that method together with completing the square to solve $x^2 + 6x + 6 = 0$?

Completing the Square

What You'll Learn

- To solve equations by completing the square
- To rewrite functions by completing the square

. . . And Why

To find a price to maximize profit, as in Example 7

✓ **Check Skills You'll Need**

GO for Help Lesson 5-1 and page 266

Simplify each expression.

1. $(x - 3)(x - 3)$ **2.** $(2x - 1)(2x - 1)$

3. $(x + 4)(x + 4) - 3$ **4.** $\pm\sqrt{25}$

5. $\pm\sqrt{48}$ **6.** $\pm\sqrt{-4}$ **7.** $\pm\sqrt{\dfrac{9}{16}}$

🔊 **New Vocabulary** • completing the square

---

1 Solving Equations by Completing the Square

You can solve an equation in which one side is a perfect square trinomial by finding square roots.

1 EXAMPLE Solving a Perfect Square Trinomial Equation

Solve $x^2 + 10x + 25 = 36$.

$$x^2 + 10x + 25 = 36$$
$$(x + 5)^2 = 36 \qquad \text{Factor the trinomial.}$$
$$x + 5 = \pm 6 \qquad \text{Find square roots.}$$
$$x + 5 = 6 \quad \text{or} \quad x + 5 = -6 \qquad \text{Solve for } x.$$
$$x = 1 \quad \text{or} \qquad x = -11$$

Vocabulary Tip

Quadratic comes from the Latin word for "square."

✓ **Quick Check** **1** Solve $x^2 - 14x + 49 = 81$.

If one side of an equation is not a perfect square trinomial, you can rewrite the constant term to get a perfect square trinomial. The process of finding the last term of a perfect square trinomial is called **completing the square.** Use the following relationship to find the term that will complete the square.

$$x^2 + bx + \left(\frac{b}{2}\right)^2 = \left(x + \frac{b}{2}\right)^2$$

Video Tutor Help

Visit: PHSchool.com
Web Code: age-0775

2 EXAMPLE Completing the Square

Find the missing value to complete the square: $x^2 - 8x + \blacksquare$.

$$\left(\tfrac{b}{2}\right)^2 = \left(\tfrac{-8}{2}\right)^2 = 16 \qquad \text{Find } \left(\tfrac{b}{2}\right)^2. \text{ Substitute } -8 \text{ for } b.$$
$$x^2 - 8x + 16 \qquad \text{Complete the square.}$$

✓ **Quick Check** **2** Find the missing value to complete the square: $x^2 + 7x + \blacksquare$.

You can solve any quadratic equation by completing the square.

This stamp commemorates the 1200th birthday of al-Khwarizmi (780-850), who showed how to solve equations by completing the square. His book *Al-jabr w'al muqabala* gave algebra its name.

3 EXAMPLE   Solving by Completing the Square

Solve $x^2 - 12x + 5 = 0$.

$$\left(\frac{-12}{2}\right)^2 = 36 \qquad \text{Find } \left(\frac{b}{2}\right)^2.$$

$$x^2 - 12x = -5 \qquad \text{Rewrite so all terms containing } x \text{ are on one side.}$$

$$x^2 - 12x + 36 = -5 + 36 \qquad \text{Complete the square by adding 36 to each side.}$$

$$(x - 6)^2 = 31 \qquad \text{Factor the perfect square trinomial.}$$

$$x - 6 = \pm\sqrt{31} \qquad \text{Find square roots.}$$

$$x = 6 \pm \sqrt{31} \qquad \text{Solve for } x.$$

Check

$$x^2 - 12x + 5 \stackrel{?}{=} 0$$

$$(6 + \sqrt{31})^2 - 12(6 + \sqrt{31}) + 5 \stackrel{?}{=} 0$$

$$6^2 + 2(6\sqrt{31}) + (\sqrt{31})^2 - 72 - 12\sqrt{31} + 5 \stackrel{?}{=} 0$$

$$36 + 12\sqrt{31} + 31 - 72 - 12\sqrt{31} + 5 \stackrel{?}{=} 0$$

$$(36 + 31 - 72 + 5) + (12\sqrt{31} - 12\sqrt{31}) \stackrel{?}{=} 0$$

$$0 = 0 \checkmark$$

$$x^2 - 12x + 5 \stackrel{?}{=} 0$$

$$(6 - \sqrt{31})^2 - 12(6 - \sqrt{31}) + 5 \stackrel{?}{=} 0$$

$$6^2 - 2(6\sqrt{31}) + (\sqrt{31})^2 - 72 + 12\sqrt{31} + 5 \stackrel{?}{=} 0$$

$$36 - 12\sqrt{31} + 31 - 72 + 12\sqrt{31} + 5 \stackrel{?}{=} 0$$

$$(36 + 31 - 72 + 5) - (12\sqrt{31} - 12\sqrt{31}) \stackrel{?}{=} 0$$

$$0 = 0 \checkmark$$

 **Quick Check** ③ Solve each equation. Check your solution.
a. $x^2 + 4x - 4 = 0$ 　　　　　　　　**b.** $x^2 - 2x - 1 = 0$

By completing the square, you can solve equations that cannot be solved by factoring, finding square roots, or graphing.

4 EXAMPLE   Finding Complex Solutions

Solve $x^2 - 8x + 36 = 0$.

$$\left(\frac{-8}{2}\right)^2 = 16 \qquad \text{Find } \left(\frac{b}{2}\right)^2.$$

$$x^2 - 8x = -36 \qquad \text{Rewrite so all terms containing } x \text{ are on one side.}$$

$$x^2 - 8x + 16 = -36 + 16 \qquad \text{Complete the square by adding 16 to each side.}$$

$$(x - 4)^2 = -20 \qquad \text{Factor the perfect square trinomial.}$$

$$x - 4 = \pm\sqrt{-20} \qquad \text{Find square roots.}$$

$$x = 4 \pm 2i\sqrt{5} \qquad \text{Solve for } x \text{ and simplify.}$$

Quick Check ④ **a.** Check the solution to Example 4.
b. Try solving the same equation with a graphing calculator. Explain your results.
c. Solve $x^2 + 6x = -34$.

When the quadratic term has a coefficient that is not 1, you can still solve by completing the square. First divide each side of the equation by the coefficient.

⑤ EXAMPLE **Solving When $a \neq 1$**

Solve $5x^2 = 6x + 8$.

$$5x^2 = 6x + 8$$

$$x^2 = \tfrac{6}{5}x + \tfrac{8}{5} \qquad \text{Divide each side by 5.}$$

$$x^2 - \tfrac{6}{5}x = \tfrac{8}{5} \qquad \text{Rewrite so all terms containing } x \text{ are on one side.}$$

$$\left(\frac{-\tfrac{6}{5}}{2}\right)^2 = \left(-\tfrac{3}{5}\right)^2 = \tfrac{9}{25} \qquad \text{Find } \left(\tfrac{b}{2}\right)^2.$$

$$x^2 - \tfrac{6}{5}x + \tfrac{9}{25} = \tfrac{8}{5} + \tfrac{9}{25} \qquad \text{Complete the square by adding } \tfrac{9}{25} \text{ to each side.}$$

$$\left(x - \tfrac{3}{5}\right)^2 = \tfrac{49}{25} \qquad \text{Factor the perfect square trinomial.}$$

$$x - \tfrac{3}{5} = \pm\sqrt{\tfrac{49}{25}} \qquad \text{Find square roots.}$$

$$x = \tfrac{3}{5} \pm \tfrac{7}{5} \qquad \text{Solve for } x.$$

$$x = 2, -\tfrac{4}{5} \qquad \text{Simplify.}$$

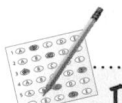

Test-Taking Tip

When you solve $x^2 = a$ by finding square roots, you get $|x| = \sqrt{a}$, which is equivalent to $x = \pm\sqrt{a}$. For speed, you can go from $x^2 = a$ to $x = \pm\sqrt{a}$.

✓ Quick Check **⑤** Solve each quadratic equation by completing the square.
a. $2x^2 + x = 6$ **b.** $2x^2 = 3x - 4$

2 Rewriting a Function by Completing the Square

In Lesson 5-3 you converted quadratic functions into vertex form by using $x = -\tfrac{b}{2a}$ to find the x-coordinate of the parabola's vertex. Then, by substituting for x, you found the y-coordinate of the vertex. Another way of rewriting a function is to complete the square.

Vocabulary Tip

Vertex form of a quadratic function:
$y = a(x - h)^2 + k$

When completing the square, you can work with just one side of the function equation. For example, $y = x^2 + 6x + 2$ is equivalent to $y = x^2 + 6x + 9 + 2 - 9$. When you add 9 to the right side of the equation, you must remember to subtract 9 to keep the equations equivalent.

⑥ EXAMPLE **Rewriting in Vertex Form**

Write $y = x^2 + 6x + 2$ in vertex form.

$$y = x^2 + 6x + 2$$

$$= x^2 + 6x + 3^2 + 2 - 3^2 \qquad \text{Complete the square. Add and subtract } 3^2 \text{ on the right side.}$$

$$= (x + 3)^2 + 2 - 9 \qquad \text{Factor the perfect square trinomial.}$$

$$= (x + 3)^2 - 7 \qquad \text{Simplify.}$$

The vertex form is $y = (x + 3)^2 - 7$.

✓ Quick Check **⑥** Write each equation in vertex form.
a. $y = x^2 - 10x - 2$ **b.** $y = x^2 + 5x + 3$

When the coefficient of the quadratic term is not 1, factor out the coefficient from the quadratic and linear terms. Remember that the factored coefficient is distributed to all terms within the parentheses.

7 EXAMPLE **Real-World** **Connection**

Gridded Response The profit P from handmade sweaters depends on the price s at which each sweater is sold. The function $P = -s^2 + 120s - 2000$ models the monthly profit from sweaters for one custom tailor. What is the maximum monthly profit, in dollars, determined by this model?

$$P = -s^2 + 120s - 2000$$

$$= -(s^2 - 120s) - 2000 \qquad \text{Factor out } -1.$$

$$= -[s^2 - 120s + (-60)^2] - 2000 + (-60)^2$$
$$\qquad\qquad\qquad\qquad\qquad \text{Complete the square.}$$

$$= -(s - 60)^2 - 2000 + 3600 \quad \text{Factor.}$$

$$= -(s - 60)^2 + 1600 \qquad \text{Simplify.}$$

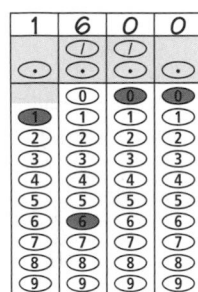

The quadratic function is in vertex form. The vertex is $(60, 1600)$. A price of \$60 per sweater gives a maximum monthly profit of \$1600.

Careers Custom tailors use math to design clothing and to calculate profit.

✓ **Quick Check** **7 a.** Use vertex form to find the vertex of $P = -\frac{1}{2}s^2 + 280s - 1200$.
   b. How do you know the vertex represents a maximum point?

EXERCISES

For more exercises, see *Extra Skill and Word Problem Practice*.

Practice and Problem Solving

A Practice by Example

Example 1
(page 282)

Solve each equation.

1. $x^2 + 6x + 9 = 1$ **2.** $x^2 - 4x + 4 = 100$ **3.** $x^2 - 2x + 1 = 4$

4. $x^2 + 8x + 16 = \frac{16}{9}$ **5.** $4x^2 + 4x + 1 = 49$ **6.** $x^2 - 12x + 36 = 25$

GO for Help

Example 2
(page 282)

Complete the square.

7. $x^2 + 18x + \blacksquare$ **8.** $x^2 - x + \blacksquare$ **9.** $x^2 - 24x + \blacksquare$

10. $x^2 + 20x + \blacksquare$ **11.** $m^2 - 3m + \blacksquare$ **12.** $x^2 + 4x + \blacksquare$

Examples 3 and 4
(page 283)

Solve each quadratic equation by completing the square.

13. $x^2 - 3x = 28$ **14.** $x^2 - 3x = 4$ **15.** $x^2 + 6x + 41 = 0$

16. $x^2 - 2x = -2$ **17.** $w^2 - 8w - 9 = 0$ **18.** $x^2 + 6x = -22$

19. $x^2 + 4 = 0$ **20.** $-x^2 - 2x = 5$ **21.** $6x - 3x^2 = -12$

Example 5
(page 284)

22. $2p^2 = 6p - 20$ **23.** $3x^2 - 12x + 7 = 0$ **24.** $4c^2 + 10c = -7$

25. $2x^2 + x - 28 = 0$ **26.** $9x^2 - 12x + 5 = 0$ **27.** $4x^2 + 4x = 3$

Example 6
(page 284)

Rewrite each equation in vertex form.

28. $y = x^2 + 4x - 7$ **29.** $y = -x^2 + 4x - 1$ **30.** $y = -2x^2 + 6x + 1$

31. $y = x^2 + 4x + 1$ **32.** $y = 2x^2 - 8x + 1$ **33.** $y = -x^2 - 2x + 3$

Example 7
(page 285)

Rewrite each equation in vertex form. Then find the vertex of the graph.

34. $y = -4x^2 - 5x + 3$ **35.** $y = \frac{1}{2}x^2 - 5x + 12$ **36.** $y = -\frac{1}{5}x^2 + \frac{4}{5}x + \frac{11}{5}$

37. Manufacturing An electronics company has a new line of portable radios with CD players. Their research suggests that the daily sales s for the new product can be modeled by $s = -p^2 + 120p + 1400$, where p is the price of each unit.
 a. Find the vertex of the graph of the function by completing the square.
 b. Describe a reasonable domain and range for the sales function. Explain.
 c. What price gives maximum daily sales? What are the maximum daily sales?

 38. Writing Explain the process of rewriting $x^2 + 8x + 11 = 0$ as $(x + 4)^2 = 5$.

For a guide to solving
Exercise 39, see page 288.

39. Sports The height of a punted football can be modeled with the quadratic function $h = -0.01x^2 + 1.18x + 2$. The horizontal distance in feet from the point of impact with the kicker's foot is x, and h is the height of the ball in feet.

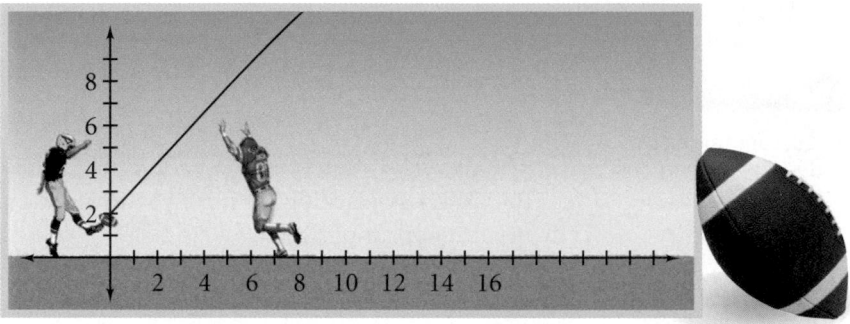

 a. Find the vertex of the graph of the function by completing the square.
 b. What is the maximum height of the punt?
 c. The nearest defensive player is 5 ft horizontally from the point of impact. How high must the player reach to block the punt?
 d. Suppose the ball was not blocked but continued on its path. How far down field would the ball go before it hit the ground?
 e. Critical Thinking The linear equation $h = 1.13x + 2$ could model the path of the football shown in the graph. Why is this not a good model?

B **Apply Your Skills**

Find the value of k that would make the left side of each equation a perfect square trinomial.

40. $x^2 + kx + 25 = 0$ **41.** $x^2 - kx + 100 = 0$ **42.** $x^2 - kx + 121 = 0$

43. $x^2 + kx + 64 = 0$ **44.** $x^2 - kx + 81 = 0$ **45.** $25x^2 - kx + 1 = 0$

46. $x^2 + kx + \frac{1}{4} = 0$ **47.** $9x^2 - kx + 4 = 0$ **48.** $36x^2 - kx + 1 = 0$

49. Geometry The table shows some possible dimensions of rectangles with a perimeter of 100 units. Complete the table.

Homework Video Tutor
Visit: PHSchool.com
Web Code: age-0507

Width	1	2	3	4	5	6	7	8	9	10
Length	49	48	■	■	■	■	■	■	■	■
Area	49	■	■	■	■	■	■	■	■	■

 a. Plot the points (width, area). Find a model for the data set.
 b. Find another point in the data set and use it to verify your model.
 c. What is a reasonable domain for this function? Explain.
 d. Find the maximum possible area. Find its dimensions.
 e. Find an equation for area in terms of width without using the table. Do you get the same equation as in part (a)? Explain.

Gateway Arch in St. Louis

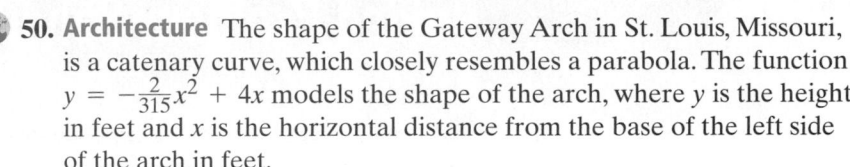

50. Architecture The shape of the Gateway Arch in St. Louis, Missouri, is a catenary curve, which closely resembles a parabola. The function $y = -\frac{2}{315}x^2 + 4x$ models the shape of the arch, where y is the height in feet and x is the horizontal distance from the base of the left side of the arch in feet.
  a. Graph the function and find its vertex.
  b. Describe a reasonable domain and range for the function. Explain.
  c. According to the model, what is the maximum height of the arch?
  d. What is the width of the arch at the base?

Solve each quadratic equation by completing the square.

51. $\frac{1}{3}x^2 + 8x - 3 = 0$ **52.** $\frac{1}{2}x^2 + 4x = 2$ **53.** $x^2 - \frac{1}{2}x = \frac{1}{3}$

54. $3x^2 + x = \frac{2}{3}$ **55.** $2x^2 - \frac{1}{2}x = \frac{1}{8}$ **56.** $x^2 + \frac{3}{4}x = \frac{1}{2}$

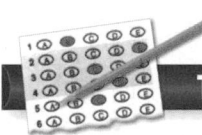 **Challenge**

Solve for x in terms of a.

57. $2x^2 - ax = 6a^2$ **58.** $3x^2 + ax = a^2$ **59.** $2a^2x^2 - 8ax = -6$

60. $4a^2x^2 + 8ax + 3 = 0$ **61.** $3x^2 + ax^2 = 9x + 9a$ **62.** $6a^2x^2 - 11ax = 10$

63. Solve $x^2 = (6\sqrt{2})x + 7$ by completing the square.

Test Prep

Multiple Choice

64. What can you add to $x^2 + 5x$ to get a perfect square trinomial?
  A.   **B.**   **C.** 25   **D.** 2.5x

65. How can you rewrite the equation $x^2 + 12x + 5 = 3$ so the left side of the equation is in the form $(x + a)^2$?
  F. $(x - 6)^2 = 28$ **G.** $(x + 6)^2 = 34$
  H. $(x + 6)^2 = 39$ **J.** $(x + 12)^2 = -2$

66. What are the solutions of the equation $x^2 + 10x + 40 = 5$?
  A. $10 \pm i$ **B.** $5 \pm i$ **C.** $-5 \pm i$ **D.** $-10 \pm i$

Short Response

67. Solve $14x = x^2 + 36$. Show your work.

Extended Response

68. List the steps for solving the equation $3x^2 - 6 = -7x$ by the method of completing the square. Explain each step.

Mixed Review

Lesson 5-6

Simplify each expression.

69. $(2 - 3i) + (-4 + 5i)$ **70.** $(7 + 3i) - (2 + i)$ **71.** $(4 - 9i)(3 + 8i)$

Lesson 5-1

Find a quadratic model for each set of data.

72. $(-4, 3), (-3, 3), (-2, 4)$ **73.** $\left(-1, \frac{1}{2}\right), (0, 2), (2, 2)$ **74.** $(0, 2), (1, 0), (2, 4)$

Lesson 4-8

Use Cramer's Rule to solve each system.

75. $\begin{cases} 2x + y = 4 \\ 3x - y = 6 \end{cases}$ **76.** $\begin{cases} 2x + y = 7 \\ -2x + 5y = -1 \end{cases}$ **77.** $\begin{cases} 2x + 4y = 10 \\ 3x + 5y = 14 \end{cases}$

Understanding Word Problems Read the problem below. Let the explanation guide you in using the formula. Check your understanding with the Exercises.

Sports The height of a punted football can be modeled with the quadratic function $h = -0.01x^2 + 1.18x + 2$. The horizontal distance in feet from the point of impact with the kicker's foot is x, and h is the height of the ball in feet.

  a. Find the vertex of the graph of the function by completing the square.
  b. What is the maximum height of the punt?
  c. The nearest defensive player is 5 ft horizontally from the point of impact. How high must the player reach to block the punt?

To understand a formula, identify the formula and its parts.

From the problem, the formula is
$h = -0.01x^2 + 1.18x + 2$.
The graph gives you other information.

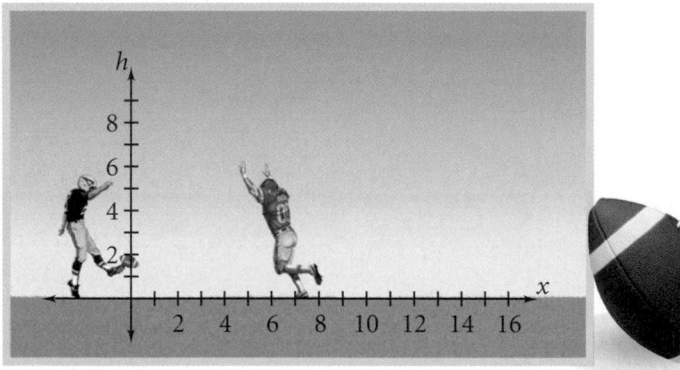

       height of the ball   horizontal distance from
                           the kicker's foot
        ↓   ↓   ↓
$$h = -0.01x^2 + 1.18x + 2$$
                         ↑
                     height at
                    time of kick

Part (a) of the problem asks you to find the vertex of the graph. By completing the square, you can get an equation in vertex form.

$h = -0.01(x - 59)^2 + 36.81$ **vertex form**
         ↑   ↑
  x-coordinate   *y*-coordinate

Since the y-coordinate of the vertex is 36.81, you know that the maximum height of the football is 36.81 ft. That answers part (b).

To block the punt, the defensive player must touch the football along its path. To answer part (c), find the height of the ball (and the height of the defensive player's hand) when it is horizontally 5 ft from the kicker, or when $x = 5$.

$h(5) = -0.01x^2 + 1.18x + 2$ **Use the formula.**
$\quad\quad = -0.01(5)^2 + 1.18(5) + 2$ **Substitute.**
$\quad\quad = 7.65$ **Simplify.**

The defensive player must reach 7.65 ft above the ground to block the punt.

EXERCISES

  1. What is the ball's height when it has traveled 20 yd (60 ft) downfield?

  2. How far downfield has the ball traveled when it reaches its maximum height?

  3. a. How far downfield has the ball traveled when it reaches a height of 6 ft?
     b. Reasoning Explain why part (a) has more than one answer.

The Quadratic Formula

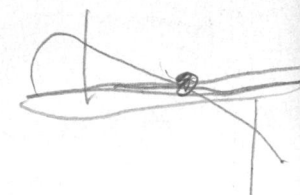

What You'll Learn

- To solve quadratic equations by using the Quadratic Formula
- To determine types of solutions by using the discriminant

. . . And Why

To investigate the motion of a field hockey ball, as in Example 5

Write each quadratic equation in standard form.

1. $y = 8 - 10x^2$ **2.** $y = (x + 2)^2 - 1$

3. $y = -2x(x - 1) + (x + 1)^2$ **4.** $y = (3x)^2 - (x - 1)^2$

Evaluate the expression $b^2 - 4ac$ for the given values of a, b, and c.

5. $a = 1, b = 6, c = 3$ **6.** $a = -5, b = 2, c = 4$

7. $a = 3, b = -6, c = 7$ **8.** $a = 2, b = 3, c = -10$

🔊 **New Vocabulary** • Quadratic Formula • discriminant

---

1 Using the Quadratic Formula

You can derive a formula for solving quadratic equations by completing the square. Below is the equation $2x^2 + 6x + 1 = 0$. Next to it is the general form of a quadratic equation, $ax^2 + bx + c = 0$. Each equation is solved for x.

$$2x^2 + 6x + 1 = 0 \qquad\qquad ax^2 + bx + c = 0$$

$$x^2 + 3x + \tfrac{1}{2} = 0 \qquad\qquad x^2 + \tfrac{b}{a}x + \tfrac{c}{a} = 0$$

$$x^2 + 3x = -\tfrac{1}{2} \qquad\qquad x^2 + \tfrac{b}{a}x = -\tfrac{c}{a}$$

$$x^2 + 2\left(\tfrac{3}{2}\right)x + \left(\tfrac{3}{2}\right)^2 = \left(\tfrac{3}{2}\right)^2 - \tfrac{1}{2} \qquad\qquad x^2 + 2\left(\tfrac{b}{2a}\right)x + \left(\tfrac{b}{2a}\right)^2 = \left(\tfrac{b}{2a}\right)^2 - \tfrac{c}{a}$$

$$\left(x + \tfrac{3}{2}\right)^2 = \tfrac{9}{4} - \tfrac{2}{4} \qquad\qquad \left(x + \tfrac{b}{2a}\right)^2 = \tfrac{b^2}{4a^2} - \tfrac{c}{a}$$

$$\left(x + \tfrac{3}{2}\right)^2 = \tfrac{7}{4} \qquad\qquad \left(x + \tfrac{b}{2a}\right)^2 = \tfrac{b^2 - 4ac}{4a^2}$$

$$x + \tfrac{3}{2} = \pm\sqrt{\tfrac{7}{4}} \qquad\qquad x + \tfrac{b}{2a} = \pm\sqrt{\tfrac{b^2 - 4ac}{4a^2}}$$

$$x = -\tfrac{3}{2} \pm \tfrac{\sqrt{7}}{2} \qquad\qquad x = -\tfrac{b}{2a} \pm \tfrac{\sqrt{b^2 - 4ac}}{2a}$$

$$x = \tfrac{-3 \pm \sqrt{7}}{2} \qquad\qquad x = \tfrac{-b \pm \sqrt{b^2 - 4ac}}{2a}$$

 Key Concepts

Theorem	**Quadratic Formula**

A quadratic equation written in standard form $ax^2 + bx + c = 0$ can be solved with the Quadratic Formula.

$$x = \frac{-b \pm \sqrt{b^2 - 4ac}}{2a}$$

1 EXAMPLE Using the Quadratic Formula

Use the Quadratic Formula to solve $3x^2 - 5x = 2$.

$3x^2 - 5x - 2 = 0$ **Write in standard form.**

$a = 3, b = -5, c = -2$ **Find the values of a, b, and c.**

$x = \dfrac{-b \pm \sqrt{b^2 - 4ac}}{2a}$ **Write the Quadratic Formula.**

$\quad = \dfrac{-(-5) \pm \sqrt{(-5)^2 - 4(3)(-2)}}{2(3)}$ **Substitute.**

$\quad = \dfrac{5 \pm \sqrt{25 - (-24)}}{6}$ **Simplify.**

$\quad = \dfrac{5 \pm \sqrt{49}}{6}$

$\quad = \dfrac{5 \pm 7}{6}$

$\quad = \dfrac{12}{6}$ or $\dfrac{-2}{6}$

$\quad = 2$ or $-\dfrac{1}{3}$

Check

$$3x^2 - 5x = 2 \qquad\qquad 3x^2 - 5x = 2$$

$$3(2)^2 - 5(2) \stackrel{?}{=} 2 \qquad 3\left(-\tfrac{1}{3}\right)^2 - 5\left(-\tfrac{1}{3}\right) \stackrel{?}{=} 2$$

$$12 - 10 \stackrel{?}{=} 2 \qquad\qquad \tfrac{1}{3} + \tfrac{5}{3} \stackrel{?}{=} 2$$

$$2 = 2 \checkmark \qquad\qquad\qquad 2 = 2 \checkmark$$

 **Quick Check** **1** Use the Quadratic Formula to solve $3x^2 - x = 4$. Check your solutions.

The Quadratic Formula will give you complex solutions that you cannot find by graphing or factoring.

2 EXAMPLE Finding Complex Solutions

Solve $2x^2 = -6x - 7$.

$2x^2 + 6x + 7 = 0$ **Write in standard form.**

$a = 2, b = 6, c = 7$ **Find the values of a, b, and c.**

$x = \dfrac{-(6) \pm \sqrt{(6)^2 - 4(2)(7)}}{2(2)}$ **Substitute.**

$\quad = \dfrac{-6 \pm \sqrt{36 - 56}}{4}$ **Simplify.**

$\quad = \dfrac{-6 \pm \sqrt{-20}}{4}$

$\quad = \dfrac{-6 \pm 2i\sqrt{5}}{4}$

$\quad = -\dfrac{3}{2} \pm \dfrac{i\sqrt{5}}{2}$

 **Quick Check** **2 a.** Use the Quadratic Formula to solve $-2x^2 = 4x + 3$.
     b. Graph the related quadratic function $y = 2x^2 + 4x + 3$. Explain why you cannot use the graph to find the solution.

In Lesson 5-5, you found an approximate value for the golden ratio by graphing the related function for the equation $x^2 - x - 1 = 0$. Now you can use the Quadratic Formula to find an exact value for the golden ratio.

 **3 EXAMPLE** Real-World 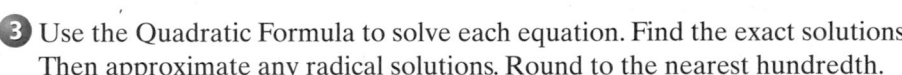 Connection

Art The golden ratio is the ratio of the longer side to the shorter side of a golden rectangle. Solve $x^2 - x - 1 = 0$ for x to find the exact value of the golden ratio.

$$x^2 - x - 1 = 0$$

$a = 1, b = -1, c = -1$ **Find the values of a, b, and c.**

$$x = \frac{-b \pm \sqrt{b^2 - 4ac}}{2a}$$ **Use the Quadratic Formula.**

$$= \frac{-(-1) \pm \sqrt{(-1)^2 - 4(1)(-1)}}{2(1)}$$ **Substitute for a, b, and c.**

$$= \frac{1 \pm \sqrt{5}}{2}$$ **Simplify.**

The golden ratio is $\frac{1 + \sqrt{5}}{2} : 1$, or simply $\frac{1 + \sqrt{5}}{2}$.

Check Is the answer reasonable? Since $\frac{1 - \sqrt{5}}{2}$ is a negative number, and a ratio of actual lengths cannot be negative, that answer is not reasonable. Since $\frac{1 + \sqrt{5}}{2} \approx 1.62$, which is the approximate value for the golden ratio found in Lesson 5-5, that answer is reasonable.

Real-World Connection

The golden ratio occurs in nature as well as in art. In sunflowers, the ratio of the number of clockwise spirals to the number of counterclockwise spirals approximates the golden ratio.

✓ Quick Check ❸ Use the Quadratic Formula to solve each equation. Find the exact solutions. Then approximate any radical solutions. Round to the nearest hundredth.

     a. $4x^2 = 8x - 3$ **b.** $x^2 + 4x = 41$

---

2   Using the Discriminant

Quadratic equations can have real or complex solutions. You can determine the type and number of solutions by finding the discriminant.

 Key Concepts

Definition	**Discriminant of a Quadratic Equation**

The **discriminant** of a quadratic equation in the form $ax^2 + bx + c = 0$ is the value of the expression $b^2 - 4ac$.

$$x = \frac{-b \pm \sqrt{b^2 - 4ac}}{2a} \quad \leftarrow \textbf{discriminant}$$

The table on the next page shows the relationships among the value of the discriminant, the solutions of a quadratic equation, and the graph of the related function. These relationships are true for real number values of a, b, and c.

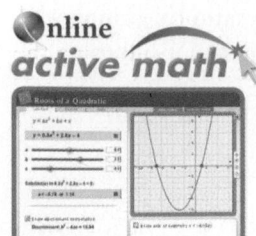
Value of the Discriminant	Type and Number of Solutions for $ax^2 + bx + c = 0$	Examples of Graphs of Related Functions $y = ax^2 + bx + c$
$b^2 - 4ac > 0$	two real solutions	two x-intercepts 
$b^2 - 4ac = 0$	one real solution	one x-intercept
$b^2 - 4ac < 0$	no real solution; two imaginary solutions	no x-intercept

4 EXAMPLE   Using the Discriminant

Determine the type and number of solutions of $x^2 + 6x + 8 = 0$.

$a = 1, b = 6, c = 8$ **Find the values of *a*, *b*, and *c*.**

$b^2 - 4ac = (6)^2 - 4(1)(8)$ **Evaluate the discriminant.**

$\quad\quad\quad = 4$ **Simplify.**

● Since the discriminant is positive, $x^2 + 6x + 8 = 0$ has two real solutions.

✓ Quick Check ④ Determine the type and number of solutions of each equation.
  a. $x^2 + 6x + 9 = 0$ **b.** $x^2 + 6x + 10 = 0$

5 EXAMPLE   Real-World 🌐 Connection

Real-World 🌐 Connection

A scoop is a field hockey pass that propels the ball from the ground into the air.

Multiple Choice Suppose a scoop releases a field hockey ball with an upward velocity of 34 ft/s. The function $h = -16t^2 + 34t$ models the height h in feet of the ball at time t in seconds. When will the ball reach a height of 20 ft?

   Ⓐ in 2 seconds   Ⓑ in 6 seconds   Ⓒ in 11 seconds   Ⓓ never

$\quad\quad h = -16t^2 + 34t$

$\quad\quad 20 = -16t^2 + 34t$ **Substitute 20 for *h*.**

$\quad\quad 0 = -16t^2 + 34t - 20$ **Write the equation in standard form.**

$a = -16, b = 34, c = -20$ **Find the values of *a*, *b*, and *c*.**

$b^2 - 4ac = (34)^2 - 4(-16)(-20)$ **Evaluate the discriminant.**

$\quad\quad\quad = 1156 - 1280$ **Simplify.**

$\quad\quad\quad = -124$

● Since the discriminant is negative, the equation $20 = -16t^2 + 34t$ has no real solutions. The ball will not reach a height of 20 ft. The answer is choice D.

✓ Quick Check ⑤ Will the ball in Example 5 ever reach a height of 15 ft? Explain.

You are now familiar with six methods of solving quadratic equations: finding square roots, factoring, using tables, graphing, completing the square, and using the Quadratic Formula. For $ax^2 = c$, finding square roots works best. The discriminant can help you decide how to solve equations that have an x-term.

Key Concepts

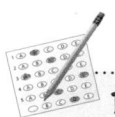

Test-Taking Tip

Learn to use a tool like the discriminant. It may not answer a test item but it could help you find an answer quickly.

Summary	Methods for Solving Quadratic Equations
Discriminant	**Methods**
positive square number	• factoring, tables, graphing, Quadratic Formula, or completing the square
positive nonsquare number	• for approximate solutions: tables, graphing, Quadratic Formula, or completing the square • for exact solutions: Quadratic Formula or completing the square
zero	• factoring, graphing, Quadratic Formula, or completing the square
negative	• Quadratic Formula or completing the square

EXERCISES

For more exercises, see *Extra Skill and Word Problem Practice*.

Practice and Problem Solving

A Practice by Example

Example 1
(page 290)

GO for Help

Solve each equation using the Quadratic Formula.

1. $x^2 - 4x + 3 = 0$ **2.** $x^2 + 8x + 12 = 0$ **3.** $2x^2 + 5x - 7 = 0$

4. $3x^2 + 2x - 1 = 0$ **5.** $x^2 + 10x = -25$ **6.** $2x^2 + 3x - 5 = 0$

7. $x^2 = 3x - 1$ **8.** $x^2 + 6x - 5 = 0$ **9.** $3x^2 - 4x - 2 = 0$

10. $8x^2 - 2x - 3 = 0$ **11.** $x(x - 5) = -4$ **12.** $9x^2 + 12x - 5 = 0$

Example 2
(page 290)

13. $x^2 - 6x + 11 = 0$ **14.** $x^2 = 2x - 5$ **15.** $x^2 + 3x + 5 = 0$

16. $2x^2 + 8x + 12 = 0$ **17.** $x^2 - 2x + 3 = 0$ **18.** $3x^2 + 4x + 10 = 0$

19. $-x^2 + 5x - 7 = 0$ **20.** $2x^2 = 7x - 8$ **21.** $15x^2 + 2x + 1 = 0$

Example 3
(page 291)

Solve each equation using the Quadratic Formula. Find the exact solutions. Then approximate any radical solutions. Round to the nearest hundredth.

22. $2x^2 - 5x - 3 = 0$ **23.** $3x^2 - 10x + 5 = 0$ **24.** $3x^2 + 4x - 3 = 0$

25. $6x^2 - 5x - 1 = 0$ **26.** $7x^2 - x - 12 = 0$ **27.** $5x^2 + 8x - 11 = 0$

28. $4x^2 + 4x = 22$ **29.** $2x^2 - 1 = 5x$ **30.** $2x^2 + x = \frac{1}{2}$

Examples 4 and 5
(page 292)

Evaluate the discriminant of each equation. Tell how many solutions each equation has and whether the solutions are real or imaginary.

31. $x^2 + 4x + 5 = 0$ **32.** $x^2 - 4x - 5 = 0$ **33.** $4x^2 + 20x + 25 = 0$

34. $2x^2 + x + 28 = 0$ **35.** $2x^2 + 7x - 15 = 0$ **36.** $6x^2 - 2x + 5 = 0$

37. $2x^2 + 7x = -6$ **38.** $x^2 - 12x + 36 = 0$ **39.** $x^2 = 8x - 16$

40. Business The weekly revenue for a company is $R = -3p^2 + 60p + 1060$, where p is the price of the company's product. Use the discriminant to find whether there is a price for which the weekly revenue would be $1500.

B **Apply Your Skills**

Solve each equation using any method. When necessary, round real solutions to the nearest hundredth. For imaginary solutions, write exact solutions.

41. $x^2 = 11x - 10$

42. $5x^2 = 210x$

43. $4x^2 + 4x = 3$

44. $2x^2 + 4x = 10$

45. $x^2 - 2x + 2 = 0$

46. $x^2 - 3x - 8 = 0$

47. $-3x^2 + 147 = 0$

48. $x^2 + 8x = 4$

49. $x^2 = 6x - 11$

50. $4x^2 - 4x - 3 = 0$

51. $\dfrac{x-3}{2} = \dfrac{6}{x-2}$

52. $\dfrac{x+2}{5} = \dfrac{3}{x+1}$

53. a. The area of a rectangle is 36 in.^{2}. The perimeter of the rectangle is 36 in. Write an equation using one variable to find the dimensions of the rectangle.
  b. Find the dimensions of the rectangle to the nearest hundredth of an inch.

54. Matrices Find the value of n in the determinant at the right.

55. Writing Summarize how to use the discriminant to analyze the types of solutions of a quadratic equation.

$$\begin{vmatrix} 2 & n & 4 \\ n & 2 & -1 \\ 4 & n & 7 \end{vmatrix} = -37$$

56. Air Pollution The function $y = 0.0721x^2 - 2.8867x + 117.061$ models the emissions of carbon monoxide in the United States since 1985. In the function, y represents the amount of carbon monoxide released in a year in millions of tons, and $x = 0$ represents the year 1985.
  a. How can you use a graph to estimate the year in which less than 100 million tons of carbon monoxide were released into the air?
  b. How can you use the Quadratic Formula to estimate the year in which less than 100 million tons of carbon monoxide were released into the air?
  c. Which method do you prefer? Explain why.

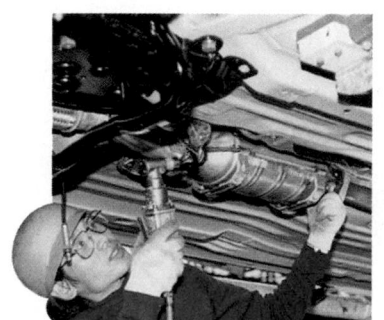

Real-World **Connection**

Automobiles are the primary source of carbon monoxide in the U.S. This worker is installing a catalytic converter, which decreases carbon monoxide emissions in cars.

Without graphing, tell how many x-intercepts each function has.

57. $y = -2x^2 + 3x - 1$

58. $y = 0.25x^2 + 2x + 4$

59. $y = x^2 + 3x + 5$

60. $y = -x^2 + 3x + 10$

61. $y = 3x^2 - 10x + 6$

62. $y = 10x^2 + 13x - 3$

63. Critical Thinking Determine the value(s) of k for which $3x^2 + kx + 12 = 0$ has each type of solution.
  a. exactly one real solution **b.** two imaginary solutions **c.** two real solutions

64. Open-Ended Find a value of k for which $x^2 + kx + 9 = 0$ has the given type of solution.
  a. two imaginary solutions **b.** two real solutions **c.** one real solution

65. Error Analysis After analyzing a quadratic equation with real coefficients, a student says that the equation has exactly one imaginary solution. Explain how you know that the student is wrong.

66. Use the discriminant to match each function with its graph.
  a. $f(x) = x^2 - 4x + 2$ **b.** $f(x) = x^2 - 4x + 4$ **c.** $f(x) = x^2 - 4x + 6$

I. 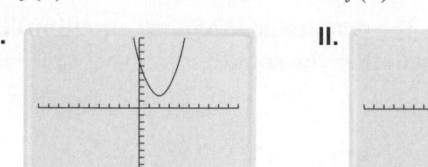 **II.** 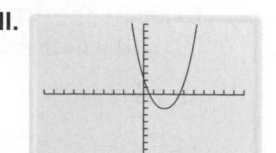 **III.**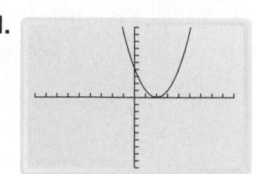

GO Online
Homework Video Tutor
Visit: PHSchool.com
Web Code: age-0508

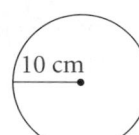

10 cm

 67. a. Geometry Write an equation to find the dimensions of a square that has the same area as the circle at the left.
  b. Find the length of a side of the square, to the nearest hundredth centimeter.

 68. Physics The equation $h = 80t - 16t^2$ models the height h feet reached in t seconds by an object propelled straight up from the ground.
  a. Will the object ever reach a height of 90 ft?
  b. Verify your answer to part (a) with a graph.
  c. For what values of t will the object be in the air?

C **Challenge**

Write a quadratic equation with the given solutions.

69. $\dfrac{3 + \sqrt{5}}{2}, \dfrac{3 - \sqrt{5}}{2}$ **70.** $\dfrac{-5 + \sqrt{13}}{2}, \dfrac{-5 - \sqrt{13}}{2}$ **71.** $\dfrac{5 + i\sqrt{3}}{2}, \dfrac{5 - i\sqrt{3}}{2}$

Use the Quadratic Formula to solve each equation for x in terms of a.

72. $2a^2x^2 - 6ax = -5$ **73.** $5a^2x^2 - 10ax = 12$ **74.** $x^2 + 2ax = 25a^2$

75. Use the Quadratic Formula to prove each statement.
  a. The sum of the solutions of the quadratic equation $ax^2 + bx + c = 0$ is $-\dfrac{b}{a}$.
  b. The product of the solutions of the quadratic equation $ax^2 + bx + c = 0$ is $\dfrac{c}{a}$.

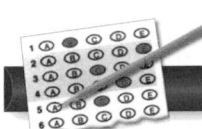

Test Prep

Multiple Choice

76. What is the discriminant of $qx^2 + rx + s = 0$?
  A. $|a + b|$ **B.** $q^2 - 4rs$ **C.** $r^2 - 4qs$ **D.** $s^2 - 4qr$

77. How many different real solutions are there for $2x^2 - 3x + 5 = 0$?
  F. 0   **G.** 1   **H.** 2   **J.** i

78. Which equation has $-3 \pm 5i$ as its solutions?
  A. $x^2 + 6x = -34$ **B.** $x^2 + 6x = -14$ **C.** $x^2 + 3x = 4$ **D.** $x^2 + 3x = 2$

Short Response

79. What is the discriminant of a quadratic equation, and what does its value tell you about the solution(s) of the equation?

Extended Response

80. Explain how you can use the Quadratic Formula to solve $3x^2 + 5 = x + 9$.

Mixed Review

Lesson 5-7

Solve by completing the square.

81. $x^2 - 8x - 20 - 0$ **82.** $2y^2 = 4y - 1$ **83.** $x^2 - 3x - 8 = 0$

Lesson 4-4

Each matrix represents vertices of a polygon. Translate each figure 3 units right and 2 units down. Express your answer as a matrix.

84. $\begin{bmatrix} 2 & 3 & -1 \\ -5 & 1 & 0 \end{bmatrix}$ **85.** $\begin{bmatrix} 0 & -3 & 1 & -5 \\ 2 & -1 & 4 & -2 \end{bmatrix}$

Lesson 4-3

Multiply.

86. $\begin{bmatrix} 0 & -3 \\ -3 & 1 \end{bmatrix}\begin{bmatrix} 4 & 0 \\ -9 & 1 \end{bmatrix}$ **87.** $\begin{bmatrix} 3 & 10 \\ 1 & 5 \end{bmatrix}\begin{bmatrix} -2 & 4 \\ -1 & 4 \end{bmatrix}$

Quadratic Inequalities

You can solve quadratic inequalities using graphs, tables, and algebraic methods. Indeed, the most effective way may be a combination of methods.

1 ACTIVITY

To find which of $x^2 - 12$ or $3x + 6$ is greater, enter the two functions as Y_1 and Y_2 in your graphing calculator, you could use the TABLE option to compare the two functions for various values of x, as shown below.

```
Plot1 Plot2 Plot3
\Y1 ▤ X² − 12
\Y2 ▤ 3X + 6
\Y3 =
\Y4 =
\Y5 =
\Y6 =
\Y7 =
```

```
TABLE SETUP
  TblStart=−10
  ∆Tbl=5
Indpnt: AUTO ASK
Depend: AUTO ASK
```

X	Y1	Y2
−10	88	−24
−5	13	−9
0	−12	6
5	13	21
10	88	36
15	213	51
20	388	66
X=−10		

1. For which values of x in the table is $x^2 - 12 > 3x + 6$?

2. For which values of x in the table is $x^2 - 12 < 3x + 6$?

3. Does this table tell you all values of x for which $x^2 - 12 < 3x + 6$? Explain.

4. In the TBLSET (TABLE SETUP) menu, change TblStart to -9 and ∆Tbl to 3. Display the table again. Does the table with this setup give you more information? Why?

You can compare functions more efficiently by making one side of the inequality 0.

5. Show that $x^2 - 12 < 3x + 6$ is equivalent to $x^2 - 3x - 18 < 0$.

6. Enter $x^2 - 3x - 18$ as Y_3 in your graphing calculator. Place the cursor on the = sign after Y_1 and press ENTER . This operation turns off the display of the equation Y_1. Turn off Y_2 as well, and then display the table. You will see the screen shown at the right. For which values of x in the table is $x^2 - 3x - 18 < 0$?

X	Y3	
−9	90	
−6	36	
−3	0	
0	−18	
3	−18	
6	0	
9	36	
X=9		

2 ACTIVITY

For a visual model, look at the same inequalities graphically. Turn off Y_3 and turn on Y_1 and Y_2. Begin by graphing the two functions in the original inequality as shown in the screens below.

```
Plot1 Plot2 Plot3
\Y1 ▤ X² − 12
\Y2 ▤ 3X + 6
\Y3 = X² − 3X − 18
\Y4 =
\Y5 =
\Y6 =
\Y7 =
```

```
WINDOW
  Xmin = −10
  Xmax = 10
  Xscl = 1
  Ymin = −20
  Ymax = 30
  Yscl = 5
  Xres = 1
```

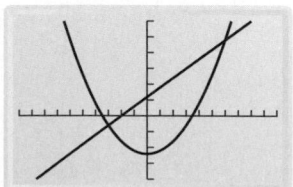

7. Which graph represents the function $f(x) = x^2 - 12$? Which graph represents $f(x) = 3x + 6$? How can you tell?

8. Use your calculator to find the values of x for which $x^2 - 12 < 3x + 6$ in this window.

9. Do you think there are values of x outside this window for which $x^2 - 12 < 3x + 6$? Explain.

Now turn off Y_1 and Y_2 and turn on Y_3. Graph Y_3 in the same window as above.

10. Use your calculator to find the values of x for which $x^2 - 3x - 18 < 0$. Are these the same values of x you found in Exercise 8?

11. Compare the strategy in Exercise 8 with the strategy in Exercise 10 for solving the inequality $x^2 - 12 < 3x + 6$ graphically. Is one easier than the other? Explain.

3 ACTIVITY

As an added tool, you can incorporate some algebra into the solution.

12. Factor the quadratic to find the two values of x for which $x^2 - 3x - 18 = 0$.

13. Shown at the left below is the graph of $y_3 = x^2 - 3x - 18$. What happens in this graph at the two x-values you found in Exercise 12?

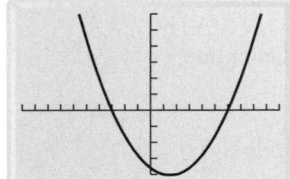 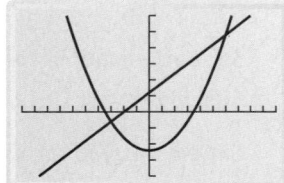

14. Shown at the right above is the graph of the functions $y_1 = x^2 - 12$ and $y_2 = 3x + 6$. What happens with these graphs at the two x-values you found in Exercise 12?

15. Tell how you can combine the algebra of Exercise 12 with the geometry of one of the graphs in Exercises 13 or 14 to give a complete solution of the inequality $x^2 - 12 < 3x + 6$.

EXERCISES

16. It is compelling to graph Y_1, Y_2, and Y_3 in the same window. When you do (see right), there is no relationship immediately apparent. However, based on your work above, what can you say is true about the graphs of Y_1, Y_2, and Y_3?

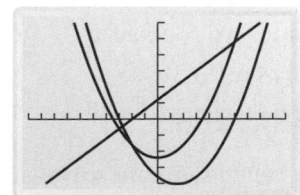

Here are some special quadratic inequalities to solve. You can use what you know about the family of quadratic functions to help solve some of them.

17. a. $x^2 - 2 < -x - 3$ **b.** $x^2 - 2 > -x - 3$ **18. a.** $x^2 < 2x^2$ **b.** $x^2 < \frac{1}{2}x^2$

19. a. $2(x - 2)(x + 3) < (x - 2)(x + 3)$ **20. a.** $-3x(x - 2) < (x - 2)(x - 4)$
     b. $-2(x - 2)(x + 3) < (x - 2)(x + 3)$ **b.** $-\frac{1}{3}x(x - 2) < (x - 2)(x - 4)$
                                             c. $-x(x - 2) < (x - 2)(x - 4)$

21. Let $y_1 = f(x)$ and $y_2 = g(x)$.
     a. Describe how you could use graphs to solve the inequality $f(x) < g(x)$.
     b. How are the solutions of $f(x) < g(x)$ and $f(x) > g(x)$ related?

22. Assume that f and g are discrete functions whose domains are whole numbers. Describe how you could use a table to solve the inequality $f(x) < g(x)$.

Using a Variable

You can solve many problems by defining a variable to represent an unknown quantity. Use the variable to write and solve an equation or inequality.

EXAMPLE

The two nonzero roots of the quadratic equation $x^2 - 9x + k = 0$ are in the ratio $2:1$. Find the roots and the value of k.

Since the roots are in the ratio $2:1$, define one root as $2r$ and the other root as r. Substituting each expression into the equation yields a system of two equations in two unknowns.

$$x^2 - 9x + k = 0 \qquad\qquad x^2 - 9x + k = 0$$
$$(2r)^2 - 9(2r) + k = 0 \quad \textbf{Substitute.} \quad (r)^2 - 9(r) + k = 0$$
$$4r^2 - 18r + k = 0 \quad \textbf{Simplify.} \quad r^2 - 9r + k = 0$$

$$4r^2 - 18r + k - (r^2 - 9r + k) = 0 - 0 \quad \textbf{Subtract equations to solve by elimination.}$$
$$3r^2 - 9r = 0 \qquad \textbf{Simplify.}$$
$$\frac{3r^2 - 9r}{r} = \frac{0}{r} \qquad \textbf{Since } r \neq 0, \textbf{ you can divide each side by } r.$$
$$3r - 9 = 0 \qquad \textbf{Simplify.}$$
$$3r = 9 \qquad \textbf{Solve for } r.$$
$$r = 3$$
$$2r = 6 \qquad \textbf{Find 2r.}$$

Now that you know r and $2r$, you can find k.

$$(3)^2 - 9(3) + k = 0 \qquad \textbf{Substitute into the original equation.}$$
$$9 - 27 + k = 0 \qquad \textbf{Simplify.}$$
$$k = 18 \qquad \textbf{Solve for } k.$$

● The nonzero roots of $x^2 - 9x + k = 0$ are 3 and 6, and $k = 18$.

EXERCISES

Write an equation to solve each problem. Clearly define the variables you use.

1. The nonzero roots of the equation $3x^2 - 4x + k = 0$ are in the ratio $3:1$. Find the roots and the value of k.

2. The roots of the equation $x^2 - 3x + k = 0$ differ by 2. Find the roots and the value of k.

3. The perimeter of a rectangle is 21 cm. Its area is 20 cm². Find the dimensions of the rectangle.

4. The point $(0, 0)$ is on the parabola $y = 5x - x^2$. What other point on the parabola has x- and y-coordinates that are equal?

5. The length of the diagonal of a rectangle is 5 ft. The rectangle's perimeter is 13 ft. Find the rectangle's dimensions. Round your answers to the nearest tenth.

Chapter Review

Vocabulary Review

🔊 absolute value of a complex number (p. 275)
axis of symmetry (p. 239)
completing the square (p. 282)
complex number (p. 275)
complex number plane (p. 275)
difference of two squares (p. 263)
discriminant (p. 291)
factoring (p. 259)

greatest common factor (GCF) of an expression (p. 259)
i (p. 274)
imaginary number (p. 274)
parabola (p. 239)
perfect square trinomial (p. 262)
Quadratic Formula (p. 289)
quadratic function (p. 238)

standard form of a quadratic equation (p. 267)
standard form of a quadratic function (p. 238)
vertex form of a quadratic function (p. 252)
vertex of a parabola (p. 239)
zero of a function (p. 268)
Zero Product Property (p. 267)

Choose the correct vocabulary term to complete each sentence.

1. The square of a binomial is a(n) _?_ .

2. Every quadratic equation can be solved with the _?_ .

Go Online
PHSchool.com
For: Vocabulary quiz
Web Code: agj-0551

3. The _?_ reveals a translation of a parent quadratic function.

4. A(n) _?_ is also an x-intercept of the graph of the function.

5. The _?_ completely determines the types of roots of a quadratic function.

Skills and Concepts

5-1 Objectives

▼ To identify quadratic functions and graphs (p. 238)

▼ To model data with quadratic functions (p. 240)

The **standard form of a quadratic function** is $f(x) = ax^2 + bx + c$, where $a \neq 0$. The quadratic term is ax^2. The graph of a **quadratic function** is a **parabola**.

The **axis of symmetry** is a line that divides a parabola into two mirror images. The **vertex of a parabola** is the point at the intersection of the parabola and its axis of symmetry. Corresponding points on the parabola are the same distance from the axis of symmetry.

You can find a quadratic model for a set of data by solving a system of three equations for a, b, and c, or by using the quadratic regression feature of a graphing calculator.

Determine whether each function is linear or quadratic. Identify the quadratic, linear, and constant terms.

6. $y = (3 - x)(2x + 1)$ **7.** $y = x - x^2 + 3$ **8.** $y = 3 - 4x$

Identify the vertex, the axis of symmetry, and the points corresponding to P and Q.

9. 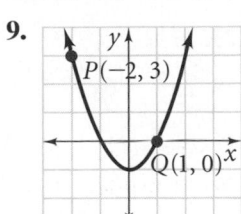   **10.** 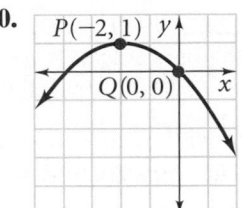   **11.**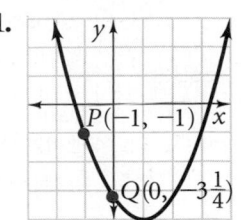

12. a. Sports Find a quadratic model for the attendance at women's college basketball games from 1995–1997 by solving three equations in a, b, and c.

b. Predict the year attendance will reach 12,000,000.

c. Use the quadratic regression feature of your calculator to find a model for all the data.

d. What does this regression model predict as the first year attendance will reach 12,000,000?

e. Find the maximum likely attendance.

Year	Attendance (thousands)
1995	4962
1996	5234
1997	6734
1998	7387
1999	8010
2000	8698

SOURCE: National Collegiate Athletic Association

5-2 and 5-3 Objectives

▼ To graph quadratic functions (p. 245)

▼ To find maximum and minimum values of quadratic functions (p. 247)

▼ To use the vertex form of a quadratic function (p. 252)

The parent function for the family of quadratic functions is $f(x) = x^2$. The constants a, b, and c characterize the graph of $y = ax^2 + bx + c$. The axis of symmetry is $x = -\frac{b}{2a}$, the vertex is at $\left(-\frac{b}{2a}, f\left(-\frac{b}{2a}\right)\right)$, and $f\left(-\frac{b}{2a}\right)$ is the maximum or minimum value. The **vertex form of a quadratic function** is $y = a(x - h)^2 + k$. The vertex is (h, k), the maximum or minimum value is k, and the axis of symmetry is the line $x = h$. If $a > 0$, the parabola opens up. If $a < 0$, it opens down.

Graph each function. Identify the vertex, y-intercept, and axis of symmetry.

13. $y = 2(x + 1)^2 - 4$ **14.** $y = (x - 5)^2$

15. $y = -(x - 2)^2 + 1$ **16.** $y = -x^2 + 7$

Write each function in vertex form. Find its maximum or minimum value.

17. $y = x^2 + x - 12$ **18.** $y = -x^2 + 2x + 2$

19. $y = 2x^2 + 8x - 3$ **20.** $y = -0.5x^2 + 5$

21. 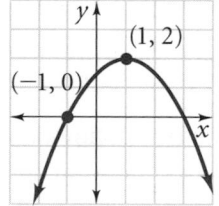 **22.** 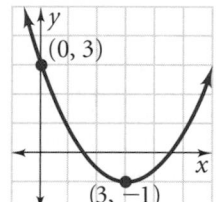 **23.**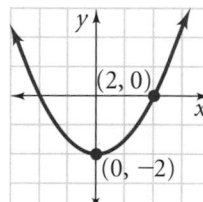

5-4 and 5-5 Objectives

▼ To find common and binomial factors of quadratic expressions (p. 259)

▼ To factor special quadratic expressions (p. 262)

▼ To solve quadratic equations by factoring and by finding square roots (p. 267)

▼ To solve quadratic equations by graphing (p. 268)

You can solve some quadratic equations by finding square roots of both sides or by finding the zeros of the related function. You can solve some quadratic equations in the **standard form of a quadratic equation** $ax^2 + bx + c = 0$ by **factoring** and using the **Zero Product Property**. For a **perfect square trinomial**, $ax^2 \pm 2abx + b^2 = (a \pm b)^2$. For the **difference of two squares**, $a^2 - b^2 = (a + b)(a - b)$. In all cases, first factor out the **greatest common factor (GCF)** of the expression.

Solve by factoring, taking square roots, or, if necessary, by graphing. Give exact radical answers. For answers found by graphing, round to the nearest hundredth.

24. $x^2 - 7x = 0$ **25.** $x^2 + 2x - 8 = 0$ **26.** $(x + 3)^2 = 9$

27. $4(x - 2)^2 = 32$ **28.** $2x^2 - 6x - 8 = 0$ **29.** $x^2 - 5x - 5 = 0$

30. $3x^2 - 14x + 8 = 0$ **31.** $x^2 - 3x - 4 = 0$ **32.** $x^2 + 8x + 16 = 0$

33. $x^2 - 6x + 9 = 0$ **34.** $4x^2 - 12x + 9 = 0$ **35.** $x^2 - 9 = 0$

36. $6x^2 - 13x - 5 = 0$ **37.** $4x^2 + 3 = -8x$ **38.** $3x^2 + 4x - 10 = 0$

▼ To identify and graph complex numbers (p. 274)

▼ To add, subtract, and multiply complex numbers (p. 276)

An **imaginary number** has the form $a + bi$, where $b \neq 0$. The imaginary number i is defined as $i^2 = -1$. A **complex number** has the form $a + bi$, where a and b are any real numbers. The **absolute value of a complex number** is its distance from the origin in the **complex number plane**. You graph $a + bi$ in the complex plane just as you graphed (a, b) in the coordinate plane. Complex numbers follow rules of operation like those of real numbers. Some quadratic equations have imaginary numbers as roots. Functions of complex numbers may be used to generate fractals.

Simplify each expression.

39. $\sqrt{-25}$　　　**40.** $\sqrt{-2} - 1$　　　**41.** $-4 - \sqrt{-1}$　　　**42.** $\sqrt{-27}$

43. $2\sqrt{-32} + 4$　　　**44.** $|3 - i|$　　　**45.** $|-2 + 3i|$　　　**46.** $|4i|$

47. $(3 + 4i) - (7 - 2i)$　　　**48.** $(5 - i)(9 + 6i)$

49. $(3 + 8i) + (5 - 2i)$　　　**50.** $(4 + 6i)(2 + i)$

Find the additive inverse of each number. Graph the number and its inverse.

51. $2 - i$　　　**52.** $-4 + 3i$　　　**53.** $-7 - 4i$　　　**54.** $-2i$

Solve each equation.

55. $x^2 + 2 = 0$　　　**56.** $x^2 = -5$

57. $3x^2 + 12 = 0$　　　**58.** $6x^2 + 4 = 0$

Find the first three outputs of each fractal-generating function. Begin with $z = 0$.

59. $f(z) = z^2 - i$　　　**60.** $f(z) = i - z^2$

5-7 and 5-8 Objectives

▼ To solve equations by completing the square (p. 282)

▼ To rewrite functions in vertex form by completing the square (p. 284)

▼ To solve quadratic equations by using the Quadratic Formula (p. 289)

▼ To determine types of solutions by using the discriminant (p. 291)

Completing the square is based on the relationship $x^2 + bx + \left(\frac{b}{2}\right)^2 = \left(x + \frac{b}{2}\right)^2$. You can use it to write a quadratic function in vertex form. If the coefficient of the quadratic term is not 1, you must factor out the coefficient from the variable terms.

You can solve any quadratic equation by using the Quadratic Formula.

If $ax^2 + bx + c = 0$, then $x = \frac{-b \pm \sqrt{b^2 - 4ac}}{2a}$.

The discriminant $b^2 - 4ac$ determines the number and type of solutions of the equation. If $b^2 - 4ac > 0$, the equation has two real solutions. If $b^2 - 4ac = 0$, the equation has one real solution. If $b^2 - 4ac < 0$, the equation has no real solutions and two imaginary solutions.

Solve each equation by completing the square.

61. $9x^2 + 6x + 1 = 4$　　　**62.** $x^2 + 3x = -25$　　　**63.** $x^2 - 2x + 4 = 0$

64. $-x^2 + x - 7 = 0$　　　**65.** $2x^2 + 3x = 8$　　　**66.** $4x^2 - x - 3 = 0$

Rewrite the equation in vertex form by completing the square. Find the vertex.

67. $y = x^2 + 3x - 1$　　　**68.** $y = 2x^2 - x - 1$　　　**69.** $y = x^2 + x + 2$

Determine the number and type of solutions. Solve using the Quadratic Formula.

70. $x^2 - 6x + 2 = 0$　　　**71.** $-2x^2 + 7x = 10$　　　**72.** $x^2 + 4 = 6x$

1. Write the equation of the parabola in standard form. Find the coordinates of the points corresponding to P, Q, and R.

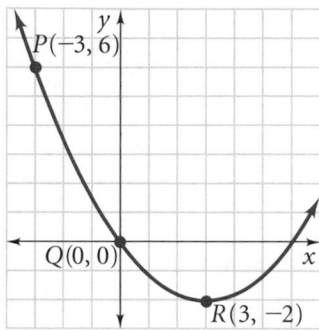

Sketch a graph of the parabola with the given vertex through the given point.

2. vertex $(0, 0)$, point $(-3, 3)$

3. vertex $(1, 5)$, point $(2, 11)$

Graph each quadratic function. Identify the axis of symmetry and the coordinates of the vertex.

4. $y = x^2 - 7$

5. $y = x^2 + 2x + 6$

6. $y = -x^2 + 5x - 3$

7. $y = -\frac{1}{2}x^2 - 8$

Simplify each expression.

8. $\sqrt{-16}$

9. $4\sqrt{-9} - 2$

10. $(4 - i) + (5 - 9i)$

11. $(2 + 3i)(8 - 5i)$

12. $(-3 + 2i) - (6 + i)$

13. $(7 - 4i)(10 - 2i)$

 14. **Physics** For a model rocket, the altitude h, in meters, as a function of time t, in seconds, is given by $h = 68t - 4.9t^2$. Find the maximum height of the rocket. How long does it take to reach the maximum height?

Find the additive inverse of each number.

15. $3 - 7i$

16. $-2 + i$

Graph each number on the complex plane. Then find its absolute value.

17. $7 - 2i$

18. $8i$

19. $4 + 8i$

20. 5

21. $6 - 4i$

22. $-2 + 3i$

 23. **Writing** Compare graphing a number on the complex plane to graphing a point on the coordinate plane. How are they similar? How are they different?

Solve each quadratic equation.

24. $x^2 - 25 = 0$

25. $x^2 + 5x - 24 = 0$

26. $x^2 + 8x - 9 = 0$

27. $3x^2 - 21x + 3 = 0$

28. $6x^2 = 9x$

29. $4x^2 + 4x + 4 = 0$

30. $5x^2 + x + 2 = 0$

31. $-3x^2 - 2x + 7 = 0$

32. $2x^2 + 6x + 12 = 0$

Write each function in vertex form. Sketch the graph of the function and label its vertex.

33. $y = x^2 - 6x + 5$

34. $y = -x^2 + 8x - 10$

35. $y = 2x^2 - 3x - 1$

36. $y = -\frac{1}{2}x^2 + 4x - 9$

Evaluate the discriminant of each equation. How many real and imaginary solutions does each have?

37. $x^2 + 6x - 7 = 0$

38. $3x^2 - x + 3 = 0$

39. $-2x^2 - 4x + 1 = 0$

40. $-x^2 + 6x - 9 = 0$

41. **Open-Ended** Sketch the graph of a quadratic function $f(x) = ax^2 + bx + c$ whose related quadratic equation $ax^2 + bx + c = 0$ has no real solutions.

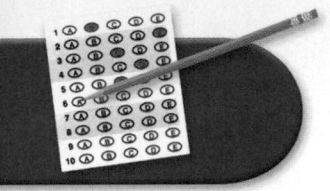

Standardized Test Prep

Reading Comprehension Read the passage below. Then answer the questions on the basis of what is *stated* or *implied* in the passage.

Dealing with Setbacks The boundary of a lot of land is called the property line. Many communities do not allow you to build up to the property line. Zoning laws may require a "setback" of several feet to ensure some distance between buildings and between a building and the property line.

Suppose the setback for a building is s feet on all four sides of a lot that has width 50 feet and length 60 feet. Then the maximum width of the building is $(50 - 2s)$ feet, and the maximum length of the building is $(60 - 2s)$ feet.

You can write and use functions in terms of s for the maximum area of the base of the building.

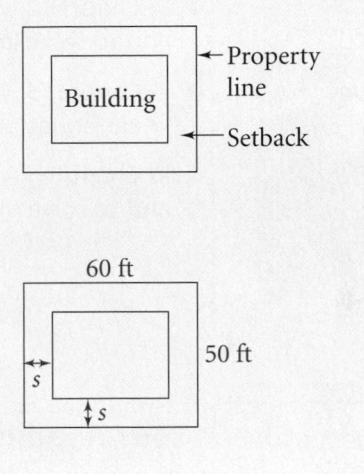

1. What is the area of the entire lot?
   - A 220 ft
   - B 2576 ft^2
   - C 3000 ft^2
   - D $(3000 - 4s^2)$ ft^2

2. Which function does NOT express the maximum area of the base of the building in terms of s?
   - F $A(s) = (50 - 2s)(60 - 2s)$
   - G $A(s) = 3000 - 220s + 4s^2$
   - H $A(s) = 4s^2 - 220s + 3000$
   - J $A(s) = 2[(50 - 2s) + (60 - 2s)]$

3. What is the maximum area of the base of the building when $s = 8$ ft?
   - A 64 ft^2
   - B 156 ft
   - C 1496 ft^2
   - D 2184 ft^2

4. What is the minimum area that is NOT occupied by the base of the building when $s = 6$ ft?
   - F 1176 ft^2
   - G 1824 ft^2
   - H 2376 ft^2
   - J 2856 ft^2

5. Suppose the building is set back five feet. Find the maximum area of the base of the building.

6. Suppose the maximum area of the base of the building is 2376 ft^2. What is the value of the setback?

7. Suppose the minimum area that is NOT occupied by the building is 1344 ft^2. What is the value of the setback?

8. Write a function for the perimeter of the base of the building in terms of s.

9. Suppose a lot is 30 feet by 90 feet. The setback is s feet. Write an expression for the maximum area of the base of the building.

10. Suppose a lot has length ℓ, width w, and setback s.
    a. Write an expression for the maximum area of the base of the building.
    b. Write an expression for the maximum perimeter of the base of the building.

11. A lot is 22 ft by 58 ft, and the setback on each side is s ft. Which formula expresses the maximum area of the base of the building in terms of s?
    - A $f(s) = 4s^2 - 160s + 1276$
    - B $f(s) = 1276 - 160s - 4s^2$
    - C $f(s) = (58 - s)(22 - s)$
    - D $f(s) = 1276 - s^2$

What You've Learned

- In Chapter 2, you learned to write and graph linear functions and to solve linear equations and inequalities.

- In Chapter 3, you learned to write, graph, and solve systems of linear equations and inequalities.

- In Chapter 5, you learned to write and graph quadratic functions and to solve quadratic equations.

 **Check Your Readiness**   **for Help** to the Lesson in green.

Finding models (Lesson 5-1)

Find a quadratic model for each set of values.

1. $(-1, 3), (0, 1), (2, 9)$ **2.** $(0, -1), (2, -2), (4, -5)$ **3.** $(-4, 75), (0, 3), (11, 300)$

Graphing functions (Lessons 2-2 and 5-2)

Graph each function.

4. $6x - 4y = -10$ **5.** $y = 3x^2 - 10x + 2$ **6.** $y = \frac{3}{4}(x^2 + 12) + 1$

Solving systems by graphing (Lesson 5-5)

 Solve each equation by graphing. Round to the nearest hundredth.

7. $1 = 4x^2 - 3x$ **8.** $\frac{1}{2}x^2 + x - 14 = 0$ **9.** $5x^2 + 30x = 12$

Solving equations algebraically (Lessons 5-5 and 5-8)

Solve each equation algebraically.

10. $x^2 - 5x - 36 = 0$ **11.** $2x^2 - 13x + 21 = 0$ **12.** $3x^2 - 4x = 3$

Finding the number and type of solutions (Lesson 5-8)

Evaluate the discriminant of each equation. Tell how many solutions each equation has and whether the solutions are real or imaginary.

13. $x^2 - 12x + 30 = 0$ **14.** $-4x^2 + 20x - 25 = 0$ **15.** $2x^2 = 8x - 8$

Finding probability (Lesson 1-6)

16. Suppose you select an integer from 100 to 200 at random. What is $P(\text{odd})$?

Polynomials and Polynomial Functions

6-1 Polynomial Functions

6-2 Polynomials and Linear Factors

6-3 Dividing Polynomials

6-4 Solving Polynomial Equations

6-5 Theorems About Roots of Polynomial Equations

6-6 The Fundamental Theorem of Algebra

6-7 Permutations and Combinations

6-8 The Binomial Theorem

What You'll Learn Next

- In Chapter 6, you will learn to write and graph polynomial functions and to solve polynomial equations.

- You will learn to use important theorems about the number of solutions to polynomial equations.

- You will learn to solve problems involving permutations, combinations, and binomial probability.

◀)) **Key Vocabulary**

- Binomial Theorem (p. 354)
- combination (p. 346)
- conjugates (p. 337)
- Factor Theorem (p. 315)
- Fundamental Theorem of Algebra (p. 341)
- Imaginary Root Theorem (p. 338)
- Irrational Root Theorem (p. 337)
- multiplicity (p. 316)
- Pascal's Triangle (p. 353)
- polynomial function (p. 307)
- Rational Root Theorem (p. 335)
- Remainder Theorem (p. 323)
- standard form of a polynomial (p. 307)
- synthetic division (p. 321)

Activity Lab Applying what you learn, on pages 364–365 you will do activities involving soccer.

Polynomial Functions

What You'll Learn

• To classify polynomials

• To model data using polynomial functions

... And Why

To model the world's gold production, as in Example 3

 Check Skills You'll Need

GO for Help   Lesson 1-2

Simplify each expression by combining like terms.

1. $3x + 5x - 7x$ **2.** $-8xy^2 - 2x^2y + 5x^2y$ **3.** $-4x + 7x^2 + x$

Find the number of terms in each expression.

4. $\frac{1}{2}bh$ **5.** $1 - x$ **6.** $4x^3 - x^2 - 9$

New Vocabulary   • polynomial • polynomial function • degree
• standard form of a polynomial • degree of a polynomial

---

1   Exploring Polynomial Functions

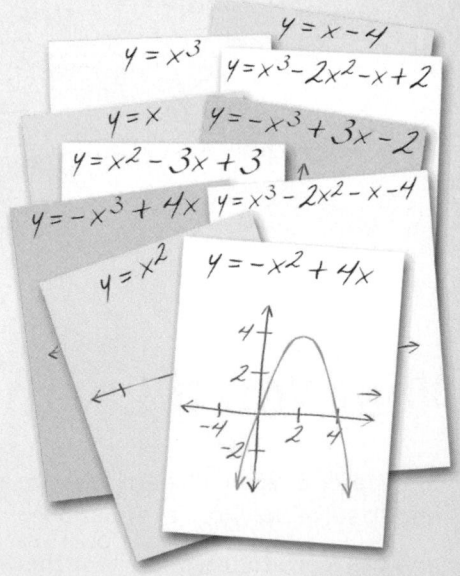

Technology Activity: Graphs of Polynomial Functions

• Use a graphing calculator to graph each equation listed at the right.

• Sketch each graph on a separate index card or sheet of paper. Label the graph with its equation.

• Sort the graphs into groups based on their shapes.

$y = x^3$
$y = x - 4$
$y = x^3 - 2x^2 - x + 2$
$y = x$
$y = -x^3 + 3x - 2$
$y = x^2 - 3x + 3$
$y = -x^3 + 4x$
$y = x^3 - 2x^2 - x - 4$
$y = x^2$
$y = -x^2 + 4x$

1. How are the graphs of the linear equations alike?

2. How are the graphs of the quadratic equations alike?

3. How are the graphs of the remaining equations alike? How are they different?

4. a. Estimate the x-intercept(s) of each graph. Write them on each card.

   b. Make a Conjecture Compare the number of x-intercepts of each graph and the greatest exponent found in its equation. What is the relationship?

A monomial is an expression that is either a real number, a variable, or a product of real numbers and variables with whole-number exponents. A **polynomial** is a monomial or the sum of monomials. For any polynomial, you can write the corresponding polynomial function, as shown below.

 Key Concepts

Definition	Polynomial Function

$P(x) = a_n x^n + a_{n-1} x^{n-1} + \ldots + a_1 x + a_0$ where n is a nonnegative integer and the coefficients $a_n, \ldots, a_0$ are real numbers.

Vocabulary Tip

The prefix <u>poly</u> means "many."

The exponent of the variable in a term determines the **degree** of that term. The terms in the polynomial shown below are in *descending order* by degree. This order demonstrates the **standard form of a polynomial.** A one-variable polynomial in standard form has no two terms with the same degree, since all like terms have been combined.

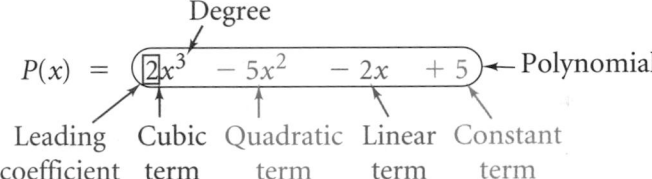

You can classify a polynomial by the number of terms it contains. A polynomial of more than three terms does not usually have a special name. You can also classify a polynomial by its degree. The **degree of a polynomial** is the largest degree of any term of the polynomial. The name assigned to each degree is listed below.

Degree	Name Using Degree	Polynomial Example	Number of Terms	Name Using Number of Terms
0	constant	6	1	monomial
1	linear	$x + 3$	2	binomial
2	quadratic	$3x^2$	1	monomial
3	cubic	$2x^3 - 5x^2 - 2x$	3	trinomial
4	quartic	$x^4 + 3x^2$	2	binomial
5	quintic	$-2x^5 + 3x^2 - x + 4$	4	polynomial of 4 terms

1 EXAMPLE **Classifying Polynomials**

Write each polynomial in standard form. Then classify it by degree and by number of terms.

a. $-7x + 5x^4$

$5x^4 - 7x$
The term with the largest degree is $5x^4$, so the polynomial is degree 4. It has two terms. The polynomial is a quartic binomial.

b. $x^2 - 4x + 3x^3 + 2x$

$3x^3 + x^2 - 2x$
The term with the largest degree is $3x^3$, so the polynomial is degree 3. It has three terms. The polynomial is a cubic trinomial.

 **Quick Check** ➊ Write each polynomial in standard form. Then classify it by degree and by number of terms.

a. $4x - 6x + 5$ **b.** $3x^3 + x^2 - 4x + 2x^3$ **c.** $6 - 2x^5$

You have already used lines and parabolas to model data. Sometimes you can fit data more closely by using a polynomial model of degree three or greater.

2 EXAMPLE Comparing Models

Using a graphing calculator, determine whether a linear model, a quadratic model, or a cubic model best fits the values in the table.

x	0	5	10	15	20
y	10.1	2.8	8.1	16.0	17.8

Enter the data. Use the LinReg, QuadReg, and CubicReg options of a graphing calculator to find the best-fitting model for each polynomial classification.

Graph each model and compare.

Linear model   **Quadratic model**   **Cubic model**

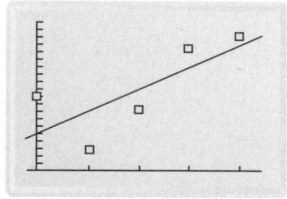 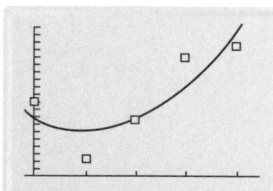 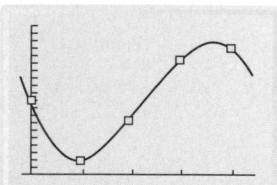

● The cubic model appears to best fit the given values.

✓ Quick Check ② Can you use the model in Example 2 to predict the value of *y* for *x* = 25? Explain.

Finding a close fit helps you estimate values between known data points.

3 EXAMPLE Real-World 🌐 Connection

Gold The table below shows world gold production for several years. Find a quartic function to model the data. Use it to estimate production in 1988.

World Gold Production

Year	1975	1980	1985	1990	1995	2000
Production (millions of troy ounces)	38.5	39.2	49.3	70.2	71.8	82.6

SOURCES: *The World Almanac* and *World Gold*

Real-World 🌐 Connection

The Federal Reserve stores gold in bars that weigh 400 troy ounces each.

Enter the data. Let 0 represent 1975. To find a quartic model, use the QuarticReg option of a graphing calculator. Graph the model.

```
QuarticReg
y=ax⁴+bx³+...+e
a=9.0333333E-4
b=-.0519296296
c=.9590277778
d=-3.898862434
↓e=38.85753968
```

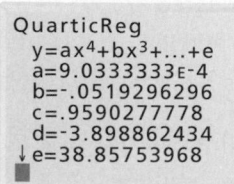

X	Y₁
7	42.915
8	46.157
9	49.519
10	52.875
11	56.12
12	59.168
13	61.959

X=13

The function $f(x) = 0.0009033x^4 - 0.05193x^3 + 0.959x^2 - 3.899x + 38.86$ is an approximate model for a quartic function.

To estimate gold production in 1988, you can use the Table option of a graphing calculator to find that $f(13) \approx 61.96$. According to the model, about 62 million troy ounces of gold were produced in 1988.

✓ **Quick Check** ❸ Use the quartic model in Example 3 to estimate gold production in 1997.

EXERCISES

For more exercises, see *Extra Skill and Word Problem Practice*.

Practice and Problem Solving

Ⓐ Practice by Example

Example 1
(page 307)

Write each polynomial in standard form. Then classify it by degree and by number of terms.

1. $7x + 3x + 5$ **2.** $5 - 3x$ **3.** $2m^2 - 3 + 7m$

4. $-x^3 + x^4 + x$ **5.** $-4p + 3p + 2p^2$ **6.** $5a^2 + 3a^3 + 1$

7. $-x^5$ **8.** $3 + 12x^4$ **9.** $6x^3 - x^3$

10. $7x^3 - 10x^3 + x^3$ **11.** $4x + 5x^2 + 8$ **12.** $x^2 - x^4 + 2x^2$

Example 2
(page 308)

Find a cubic model for each set of values.

13. $(-2, -7), (-1, 0), (0, 1), (1, 2), (2, 9)$ **14.** $(0, -12), (1, 10), (2, 4), (3, 42)$

15. $(-1, 2.5), (0, 1), (1, 1.5), (2, 13)$ **16.** $(-3, 91), (-2, 84), (-1, 93), (0, 100)$

17. Vital Statistics The data at the right indicate that the life expectancy for residents of the United States has been increasing. Recall that in Chapter 3 you found linear models for this data set.
   a. Find quadratic models for the data set.
   b. Find cubic models for the data set.
   c. Graph each model. Compare the quadratic and cubic models to determine whether one is a better fit.

Life Expectancy (years)

Year of Birth	Males	Females
1970	67.1	74.7
1980	70.0	77.4
1990	71.8	78.8
2000	74.3	79.7
2010	74.5	81.3

SOURCE: U.S. Bureau of the Census. Go to www.PHSchool.com for a data update. Web Code: agg-9041

Example 3
(pages 308–309)

Find a cubic model for each function. Then use your model to estimate the value of y when $x = 17$.

18. $(-1, -3), (0, 0), (1, -1), (2, 0)$ **19.** $(10, 0), (11, 121), (12, 288), (13, 507)$

20. $(10, 500), (14, 588), (16, 512), (20, 0)$ **21.** $(1, 91), (10, 95), (20, 260), (30, 365)$

22.

x	0	3	5	6	9	11	12	14	16	18	20
y	42	31	26	21	17	15	19	22	28	30	29

23.

x	0	2	3	6	8	10	12	14	16	18	20
y	4.1	6	15.7	21.1	23.6	23.1	24.7	24.9	23.9	25.2	29.5

Ⓑ Apply Your Skills

24. Open-Ended Write a third-degree polynomial function. Make a table of values and a graph. Find the x- and y-intercepts.

Write each polynomial in standard form. Then classify it by degree and by number of terms.

25. $8x - 4x + x^3$

26. $a^2 + a^3 - 4a^4$

27. 7

28. $2x(3x)$

29. $x^3(2 + x)$

30. $\dfrac{3x^5 + 4x}{6}$

 31. Packaging Design The diagram at the right shows a cologne bottle that consists of a cylindrical base and a hemispherical top.
 a. Write an expression for the cylinder's volume.
 b. Write an expression for the volume of the hemispherical top.
 c. Write a polynomial to represent the total volume.

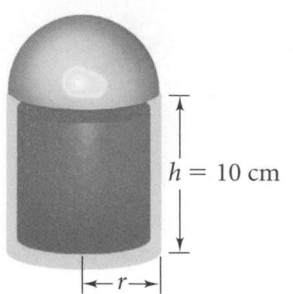

$h = 10$ cm

r

32. Writing Explain why cubic functions are useful for interpolating between known data points. Why are they often not reliable for extrapolating data?

Vocabulary Tip

To <u>interpolate</u> means to estimate a value inside the range of known values. To <u>extrapolate</u> means to estimate a value outside the range of known values.

Simplify. Classify each result by number of terms.

33. $(2c^2 + 9) - (3c^2 - 7)$

34. $(-8d^3 - 7) + (-d^3 - 6)$

35. $(7x^2 + 8x - 5) + (9x^2 - 9x)$

36. $(5x^3 - 6x + 8) - (3x^3 - 9)$

37. $(3a - 2b) + (6b - 2a)$

38. $(4x - 5y) - (4x + 7y)$

39. $(3x^2 - 6y - 1) + (5x^2 + 1)$

40. $(-a^2 - 3) - (3a - a^2 - 5)$

41. $(7x^3 + 9x^2 - 8x + 11) - (5x^3 - 13x - 16)$

42. $(-12x^3 + 5x - 23) - (4x^4 + 31 - 9x^3)$

43. $(30x^3 - 49x^2 + 7x) + (50x^3 - 75 - 60x^2)$

44. $(-3x^3 + 7x^2 - 8) - (-5x^3 + 9x^2 - 8x + 19)$

45. $(3a^2 - ab - 7) + (5a^2 + ab + 8) - (-2a^2 + 3ab - 9)$

Find each product. Classify the result by number of terms.

46. $x(2x)(4x + 1)$

47. $5x^2(6x - 2)$

48. $(2a - 5)(a^2 - 1)$

49. $b(b - 3)^2$

50. $(x - 2)^3$

51. $(x^2 + 1)^2$

52. $(2x + 5)^3 + 1$

53. $(a - b)^2(a + b)$

54. $(a - 1)^4$

55. $(s + 3)(4s - 1)(3s + 7)$

56. $(x + 1)(x - 1)(x + 2)$

57. $(2c - 3)(2c + 4)(2c - 1)$

58. $(s + t)(s - t)(s + t)(s - t)$

Homework Video Tutor

Visit: PHSchool.com
Web Code: age-0601

59. The table shows U.S. energy production for a number of years.
 a. Find a linear model, a cubic model, and a quartic model for the data set. Let 0 represent 1960.
 b. Graph each model. Compare the three models to determine which fits best.
 c. Use your answer to part (b) to estimate U.S. energy production in 1997.

U.S. Energy Production

Year	1960	1965	1970	1975	1980	1985	1990	1995	2000
Production ($\times 10^{15}$ Btu)	41.5	49.3	62.1	59.9	64.8	64.9	70.8	71.0	71.2

SOURCE: Energy Information Administration. Go to **www.PHSchool.com** for a data update.
Web Code: agg-9041

 **Challenge** **60. Geometry** Use the formula $V = \frac{\pi h}{3}(r^2 + rs + s^2)$ to find the volume of the truncated cone. Express your answer in scientific notation with the appropriate number of significant digits.

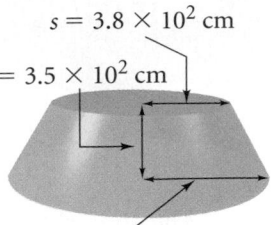

$s = 3.8 \times 10^2$ cm

$h = 3.5 \times 10^2$ cm

$r = 5.6 \times 10^2$ cm

61. Critical Thinking Recall that each family of functions has a simplest function called the parent function.
  a. Compare the graphs of $y = x^3$ and $y = x^3 + 4$. Describe how the graph of $y = x^3 + 4$ relates to the graph of $y = x^3$.
  b. Compare the graphs of $y = x^3$ and $y = 4x^3$. Describe how the graph of $y = 4x^3$ relates to the graph of $y = x^3$.
  c. Identify the parent function among the functions in parts (a) and (b).

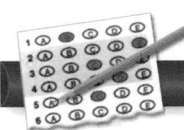

Test Prep

Multiple Choice

62. Which expression is a cubic polynomial?
  A. x^3 **B.** $3x + 3$ **C.** $2x^2 + 3x - 1$ **D.** $3x$

63. Which expression is a binomial?
  F. $2x$ **G.** $\frac{x}{2}$ **H.** $3x^2 + 2x + 4$ **J.** $x - 9$

64. What is the degree of the polynomial $5x + 4x^2 + 3x^3 - 5x$?
  A. 1   **B.** 2   **C.** 3   **D.** 4

65. Which expression is equivalent to $2x^4 - 3x + 6$?
  F. $(x^4 - 2x^2 + 3) - (x^4 - x^2 - 9)$ **G.** $2x^4 - 3(x + 6)$
  H. $(3x^4 - x + 3) + (3 - 2x - x^4)$ **J.** $x(2x^3 - 3x) + 6$

Short Response

66. Simplify $(9x^3 - 4x + 2) - (x^3 + 3x^2 + 1)$.

67. Simplify $x^2(3x^2 - 2x) - 3x^4$. Then name the polynomial by degree and the number of terms.

68. Why is finding the degree of a polynomial simplified when the polynomial is written in standard form?

Mixed Review

GO for Help

Lesson 5-8

Use the discriminant to find the number of real solutions.
69. $3x^2 + x - 6 = 0$ **70.** $5x^2 - 9 = 0$ **71.** $-x^2 + 2x - 8 = 0$

Lesson 5-3

72. Graph $f(x) = 3x^2 - 1$. Translate the graph right five units and down two units. What is the vertex of the new graph?

Lesson 4-4

Each matrix represents the vertices of a polygon. Translate each figure 3 units left and 2 units down. Express your answer as a matrix.

73. $\begin{bmatrix} 4 & 0 & 4 & 8 \\ -6 & -1 & 2 & -1 \end{bmatrix}$ **74.** $\begin{bmatrix} 5 & 0 & -3 \\ 7 & 0 & 2 \end{bmatrix}$ **75.** $\begin{bmatrix} 1 & 2 & 1 & 2 \\ -1 & -1 & -2 & -2 \end{bmatrix}$

End Behavior

FOR USE WITH LESSON 6-1

The end behavior of a graph describes the far left and the far right portions of the graph. The graphs of polynomial functions show four types of end behavior— *up and up, down and down, down and up,* and *up and down.*

Up and Up	Down and Down	Down and Up	Up and Down
(↖, ↗)	(↙, ↘)	(↙, ↗)	(↖, ↘)
Example	Example	Example	Example

$y = x^4 - 3x^3 + 5x$ $y = -x^2 + 6x$ $y = x^3$ $y = -0.3x^3 + 4x + 2$

You can determine *by inspection* the end behavior of the graph of a polynomial function in standard form. Look at the coefficient and degree of the leading term.

Right   If the leading coefficient is positive, then the graph rises to the right. If the leading coefficient is negative, then the graph falls to the right.

Left   If the degree of the polynomial is even, then the left behavior is the same as the right behavior. If the degree of the polynomial is odd, then the left behavior is the opposite of the right behavior.

EXAMPLE   **Describing End Behavior**

Determine by inspection the end behavior of the graph of each polynomial.

a. $y = 4x^3 - 3x$

The leading coefficient 4 is positive, so the graph rises to the right. The degree of the polynomial is 3, which is odd. The left behavior is opposite the right behavior, so the graph falls to the left. The end behavior is (↙, ↗).

b. $f(x) = -2x^4 + 8x^3 - 8x^2$

The leading coefficient –2 is negative, so the graph falls to the right. The degree of the polynomial is 4, which is even. The left behavior is the same as the right behavior, so the graph falls to the left. The end behavior is (↙, ↘).

EXERCISES

Determine by inspection the end behavior of the graph of each function.

1. $y = 3x + 2$

2. $y = 4x^3$

3. $g(t) = -t^2 + t$

4. $f(x) = 2x + x^5$

5. $g(x) = x^6$

6. $y = 3x^5 - 4x^4$

7. $y = -7x^8$

8. $f(x) = \frac{1}{2}x^4 - 2$

9. $y = -\frac{1}{2}x^3 + 4x^2 + x - 1$

10. $g(x) = x - x^3 + 5$

Polynomials and Linear Factors

GO for Help   Lessons 5-1 and 5-4

What You'll Learn

- To analyze the factored form of a polynomial
- To write a polynomial function from its zeros

. . . And Why

To find the dimensions of carry-on luggage, as in Example 3

✓ Check Skills You'll Need

Factor each quadratic expression.

1. $x^2 + 7x + 12$ **2.** $x^2 + 8x - 20$ **3.** $x^2 - 14x + 24$

Find each product.

4. $x(x + 4)$ **5.** $(x + 1)^2$ **6.** $(x - 3)^2(x + 2)$

🔊 **New Vocabulary**   • relative maximum   • relative minimum   • Factor Theorem   • multiple zero   • multiplicity

---

1   The Factored Form of a Polynomial

Just as you can rewrite a whole number as a product of its prime factors, you can write a polynomial as a product of its linear factors. Compare the factor trees for the whole number 6 and the quadratic expression $x^2 + 4x - 12$.

$$6$$
$$x^2 + 4x - 12$$

Prime factors → 2   3 $(x + 6)\ (x - 2)$ ← Linear factors

In the factor tree for the whole number 6, each branch ends with a prime number. Likewise, in the factor tree for the polynomial $x^2 + 4x - 12$, each branch ends with a "prime" linear factor. A linear factor is similar to a prime number in that it cannot be factored any further. Once a polynomial has been factored completely to its linear factors, it is in factored form.

1   EXAMPLE   Writing a Polynomial in Standard Form

Write the expression $(x + 1)(x + 2)(x + 3)$ as a polynomial in standard form.

$(x + 1)(x + 2)(x + 3) = (x + 1)(x^2 + 3x + 2x + 6)$ **Multiply $(x + 2)$ and $(x + 3)$.**

$= (x + 1)(x^2 + 5x + 6)$ **Simplify.**

$= x(x^2 + 5x + 6) + 1(x^2 + 5x + 6)$ **Distributive Property**

$= x^3 + 5x^2 + 6x + x^2 + 5x + 6$ **Multiply.**

$= x^3 + 6x^2 + 11x + 6$ **Simplify.**

The expression $(x + 1)(x + 2)(x + 3)$ is the factored form of $x^3 + 6x^2 + 11x + 6$.

✓ **Quick Check** ❶ Write the expression $(x + 1)(x + 1)(x + 2)$ as a polynomial in standard form.

You can sometimes use the GCF of the terms to help you factor a polynomial.

2 EXAMPLE Writing a Polynomial in Factored Form

Write $2x^3 + 10x^2 + 12x$ in factored form.

$$2x^3 + 10x^2 + 12x = 2x(x^2 + 5x + 6) \quad \textbf{Factor out the GCF, } 2x.$$
$$= 2x(x + 2)(x + 3) \quad \textbf{Factor } x^2 + 5x + 6.$$

Check $2x(x + 2)(x + 3) = 2x(x^2 + 5x + 6) \quad \textbf{Multiply } (x + 2)\,(x + 3).$
$$= 2x^3 + 10x^2 + 12x \checkmark \quad \textbf{Distributive Property}$$

✅ **Quick Check** ❷ Write $6x^3 - 15x^2 - 36x$ in factored form. Check by multiplication.

You can use polynomial functions to solve real-world problems. Consider the formula for volume: $V = $ depth $\cdot$ length $\cdot$ width. Each dimension can represent a linear factor of a polynomial function.

3 EXAMPLE Real-World 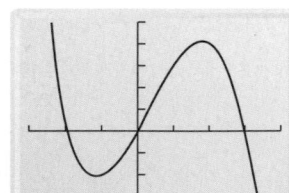 Connection

Travel Several popular models of carry-on luggage have a length 10 in. greater than their depth. To comply with airline regulations, the sum of the length, width, and depth may not exceed 40 in.

a. Assume that the sum of the length, width, and depth is 40 in. Graph the function relating volume V to depth x. Find the x-intercepts. What do they represent?

Relate   Volume $=$ ┃depth┃ $\cdot$ ┃length┃ $\cdot$ ┃width┃

Define   Let ┃x┃ $=$ depth. Then ┃$x + 10$┃ $=$ length, and
┃$40 - (\text{depth} + \text{length})$┃ $=$ width.

Write $V(x) = $ ┃x┃ (┃$x + 10$┃) (┃$40 - (x + x + 10)$┃)
$$= x(x + 10)(30 - 2x)$$

Graph the function for volume. The x-intercepts of the function are $x = 0, x = -10,$ and $x = 15$. These values of x produce a volume of zero.

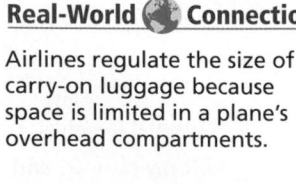

Xmin=-15
Xmax=20
Xscl=5
Ymin=-1500
Ymax=2500
Yscl=500

b. Describe a realistic domain.

The function has values over the set of all real numbers x. Since x represents the depth of the luggage, $x > 0$. Since the volume must be positive, $x < 15$. A realistic domain is $0 < x < 15$.

c. What is the maximum possible volume of a piece of luggage? What are the corresponding dimensions of the luggage?

Look for the greatest value of y that occurs within the domain $0 < x < 15$. Use the Maximum feature of a graphing calculator to find the maximum volume. A volume of approximately 2052 in.^{3} occurs for a depth of about 8.9 in. Then the length is about 18.9 in. and the width is about 12.2 in.

✅ **Quick Check** ❸ Suppose an airline raises the allowable sum of the luggage dimensions to 45 in. Find the maximum possible volume and the corresponding dimensions.

Real-World  Connection

Airlines regulate the size of carry-on luggage because space is limited in a plane's overhead compartments.

The maximum value in Example 3 is the greatest value of the points in a region of the graph. It is called a **relative maximum.** Similarly, a **relative minimum** is the least *y*-value among nearby points on a graph.

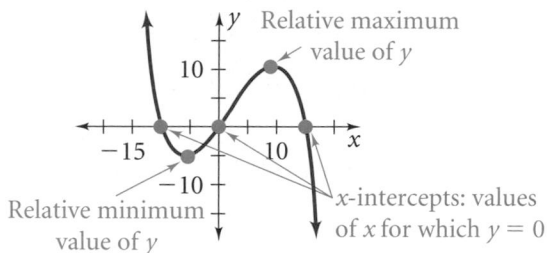

Recall that the *x*-intercepts of the graph of a function are called zeros because the value of the function is zero at each *x*-intercept.

2 Factors and Zeros of a Polynomial Function

Vocabulary Tip

Zero-Product Property: If a product equals zero, then at least one of its factors must equal zero.

If a polynomial is in factored form, you can use the Zero Product Property to find values that will make the polynomial equal zero.

4 EXAMPLE **Finding Zeros of a Polynomial Function**

Find the zeros of $y = (x - 2)(x + 1)(x + 3)$. Then graph the function.

Using the Zero Product Property, find a zero for each linear factor.

$$x - 2 = 0 \quad \text{or} \quad x + 1 = 0 \quad \text{or} \quad x + 3 = 0$$
$$x = 2 \qquad\qquad x = -1 \qquad\qquad x = -3$$

The zeros of the function are 2, −1, and −3. Now graph the function.

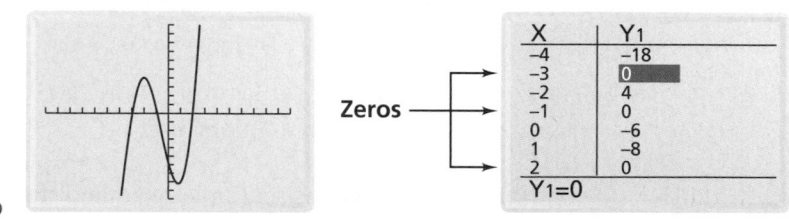

✓ Quick Check **4 a.** Find the zeros of the function $y = (x - 7)(x - 5)(x - 3)$.
b. Graph the function and label the zeros.

You can reverse the process and write linear factors when you know the zeros. The relationship between the linear factors of a polynomial and the zeros of a polynomial is described by the Factor Theorem.

 Key Concepts

Theorem	**Factor Theorem**

The expression $x - a$ is a linear factor of a polynomial if and only if the value *a* is a zero of the related polynomial function.

Online active math

For: Linear Factors Activity
Use: Interactive Textbook, 6-2

5 EXAMPLE Writing a Polynomial Function From its Zeros

Write a polynomial function in standard form with zeros at $-2, 3,$ and 3.

$$\begin{array}{ccc} -2 & 3 & 3 \end{array} \qquad \text{zeros}$$
$$\downarrow \quad\ \downarrow \quad\ \downarrow$$

$f(x) = (x + 2)(x - 3)(x - 3)$	**Write a linear factor for each zero.**
$= (x + 2)(x^2 - 6x + 9)$	**Multiply $(x - 3)$ and $(x - 3)$.**
$= x(x^2 - 6x + 9) + 2(x^2 - 6x + 9)$	**Distributive Property**
$= x^3 - 6x^2 + 9x + 2x^2 - 12x + 18$	**Distributive Property**
$= x^3 - 4x^2 - 3x + 18$	**Simplify.**

● The function $f(x) = x^3 - 4x^2 - 3x + 18$ has zeros at $-2, 3,$ and 3.

✓ Quick Check ⑤ **a.** Write a polynomial function in standard form with zeros at $-4, -2,$ and 1.
b. Write a polynomial function in standard form with zeros at $-4, -2,$ and 0.
c. Critical Thinking Explain why the zero at 0 produces more than one possible answer to part (b).

Vocabulary Tip

<u>Distinct</u> means "separate and different."

While the polynomial function in Example 5 has three zeros, it has only two distinct zeros: -2 and 3. If a linear factor of a polynomial is repeated, then the zero is repeated. A repeated zero is called a **multiple zero.** A multiple zero has a **multiplicity** equal to the number of times the zero occurs. In Example 5, the zero 3 has multiplicity 2.

6 EXAMPLE Finding the Multiplicity of a Zero

Find any multiple zeros of $f(x) = x^4 + 6x^3 + 8x^2$ and state the multiplicity.

$f(x) = x^4 + 6x^3 + 8x^2$
$f(x) = x^2(x^2 + 6x + 8)$ **Factor out the GCF, x^2.**
$f(x) = x^2(x + 4)(x + 2)$ **Factor $x^2 + 6x + 8$.**

Since you can rewrite x^2 as $(x - 0)(x - 0)$, or $(x - 0)^2$, the number 0 is a multiple zero of the function, with multiplicity 2.

✓ Quick Check ⑥ For each function, find any multiple zeros and state the multiplicity.
a. $f(x) = (x - 2)(x + 1)(x + 1)^2$ **b.** $y = x^3 - 4x^2 + 4x$

The Factor Theorem helps relate four key facts about a polynomial. These facts are equivalent—that is, if you know one of them, you know them all.

Key Concepts

Summary	Equivalent Statements about Polynomials
① -4 is a solution of $x^2 + 3x - 4 = 0$.	
② -4 is an x-intercept of the graph of $y = x^2 + 3x - 4$.	
③ -4 is a zero of $y = x^2 + 3x - 4$.	
④ $x + 4$ is a factor of $x^2 + 3x - 4$.	

EXERCISES
For more exercises, see *Extra Skill and Word Problem Practice*.

Practice and Problem Solving

 **Practice by Example**

Example 1
(page 313)

GO for Help

Write each expression as a polynomial in standard form.

1. $(x + 3)(x - 2)$ **2.** $(x + 3)(x + 4)(x + 5)$ **3.** $(x - 3)^2(x - 1)$

4. $x(x + 2)^2$ **5.** $x(x + 5)^2$ **6.** $x(x - 1)(x + 1)$

Example 2
(page 314)

Write each polynomial in factored form. Check by multiplication.

7. $x^3 - 36x$ **8.** $9x^3 + 6x^2 - 3x$ **9.** $10x^3 - 10x^2 + 15x$

10. $x^3 + 7x^2 + 10x$ **11.** $x^3 + 8x^2 + 16x$ **12.** $x^3 - 7x^2 - 18x$

Example 3
(page 314)

Find the relative maximum, relative minimum, and zeros of each function.

13. $f(x) = x^3 + 4x^2 - 5x$ **14.** $f(x) = -x^3 + 16x^2 - 76x + 96$

15. Metalwork A metalworker wants to make an open box from a sheet of metal, by cutting equal squares from each corner as shown.
   a. Write an expression for the length, width, and height of the open box.
   b. Use your answer from part (a) to write a function for volume. (*Hint*: Use factored form.)
   c. Graph the function. Find the maximum volume that can be contained by the box and the size of the square cut that produces this volume.

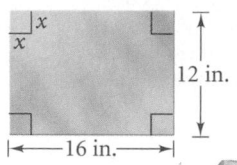

Example 4
(page 315)

Find the zeros of each function. Then graph the function.

16. $y = (x - 1)(x + 2)$ **17.** $y = (x - 2)(x + 9)$ **18.** $y = x(x + 5)(x - 8)$

19. $y = (x + 1)(x - 2)(x - 3)$ **20.** $y = (x + 1)(x - 1)(x - 2)$

Example 5
(page 316)

Write a polynomial function in standard form with the given zeros.

21. $x = 5, 6, 7$ **22.** $x = -2, 0, 1$ **23.** $x = -5, -5, 1$ **24.** $x = 3, 3, 3$

25. $x = 1, -1, -2$ **26.** $x = -1, -2, -3$ **27.** $x = 0, 0, 2$ **28.** $x = -\frac{1}{2}, 0, 4$

Example 6
(page 316)

Find the zeros of each function. State the multiplicity of multiple zeros.

29. $y = (x + 3)^3$ **30.** $y = x(x - 1)^3$ **31.** $y = 2x^3 + x^2 - x$

32. $y = 3x^3 - 3x$ **33.** $y = (x - 4)^2$ **34.** $y = (x - 2)^2(x - 1)$

35. $y = (2x + 3)(x - 1)^2$ **36.** $y = (x + 1)^2(x - 1)(x - 2)$

B **Apply Your Skills** **37. Geometry** A box has length $2x + 1$ units, width $x + 4$ units, and height $x + 3$ units. To build the box using $x^3, x^2, x,$ and unit (1) blocks, how many of each will you need?

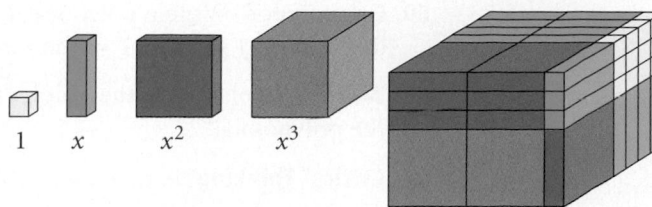

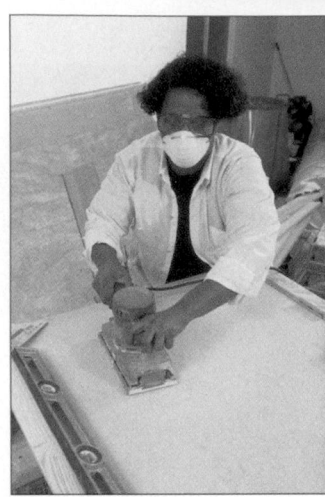

 38. Carpentry A carpenter hollowed out the interior of a block of wood as shown at the right.

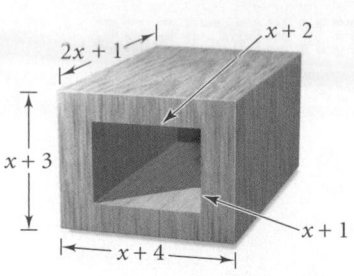

    a. Express the volume of the original block and the volume of the wood removed as polynomials in standard form.
    b. Write a polynomial for the volume of the wood remaining.

 39. Geometry A rectangular box is $2x + 3$ units long, $2x - 3$ units wide, and $3x$ units high. Express its volume as a polynomial.

 40. Measurement The volume in cubic feet of a CD holder can be expressed as $V(x) = -x^3 - x^2 + 6x$, or, when factored, as the product of its three dimensions. The depth is expressed as $2 - x$. Assume that the height is greater than the width.

    a. Factor the polynomial to find linear expressions for the height and the width.
    b. Graph the function. Find the x-intercepts. What do they represent?
    c. Describe a realistic domain for the function.
    d. Find the maximum volume of the CD holder.

Real-World Connection

Careers Carpenters use math to design and measure components of buildings, furniture, and art.

Write each function in standard form.

41. $y = (x + 1)(x - 4)(3 - 2x)$ **42.** $y = (x + 7)(5x + 2)(x - 6)^2$

Write each function in factored form. Check by multiplication.

43. $y = 3x^3 - 27x^2 + 24x$ **44.** $y = -2x^3 - 2x^2 + 40x$

45. $y = x^4 + 3x^3 - 4x^2$ **46.** $y = \frac{1}{2}x^3 - \frac{1}{8}x$

Find the relative maximum, relative minimum, and zeros of each function.

47. $y = 2x^3 - 23x^2 + 78x - 72$ **48.** $y = x^4 + 3x^3 - x^2 - 3x$

49. $y = 8x^3 - 10x^2 - x - 3$ **50.** $y = (x + 1)^4 - 1$

Write a polynomial function in standard form with the given zeros.

51. $5, -2, 0$ **52.** 7 multiplicity 3   **53.** $-2, -1, 3, 4$

For each function, determine the zeros. State the multiplicity of any multiple zeros.

54. $y = (x + 4)(x - 5)^3$ **55.** $f(x) = x^4 + 2x^3 + x^2$ **56.** $f(x) = x^3 - 36x$

57. Critical Thinking How can you find where the graph of a polynomial function crosses the y-axis?

58. A storage company needs to design a new storage box that has twice the volume of its largest box. Its largest box is 5 ft long, 4 ft wide, and 3 ft high. The new box must be formed by increasing each dimension by the same amount. Find the increase in each dimension.

59. Open-Ended Write a polynomial function with the following features: it has three distinct zeros; one of the zeros is 1; another zero has a multiplicity of 2.

 60. Writing Explain how the graph of a polynomial function can help you factor the polynomial.

61. Critical Thinking A polynomial function has a zero at $x = -2a$. Find one of its factors.

GO Online

Homework Video Tutor

Visit: PHSchool.com
Web Code: age-0602

C Challenge 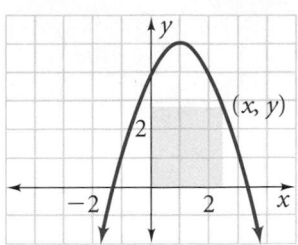 **62. Coordinate Geometry** The diagram at the right shows a rectangular region with one corner on the graph of $y = -x^2 + 2x + 4$.

a. Write a polynomial in standard form for the area A of the rectangular region.

b. Find the area of the rectangular region for $x = 2\frac{1}{2}$.

63. Find a fourth-degree polynomial function with zeros $1, -1, i,$ and $-i$. Write the function in both factored form and standard form.

64. a. Compare the graphs of $y = (x + 1)(x + 2)(x + 3)$ and $y = (x - 1)(x - 2)(x - 3)$. What transformation could you use to describe the change from one graph to the other?

b. Compare the graphs of $y = (x + 1)(x + 3)(x + 7)$ and $y = (x - 1)(x - 3)(x - 7)$. Does the transformation that you chose in part (a) still hold true? Explain.

c. Make a Conjecture What transformation could you use to describe the effect of changing the signs of the zeros of a polynomial function?

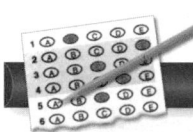

Test Prep

Multiple Choice

65. Which expression is the factored form of $x^3 + 2x^2 - 5x - 6$?

A. $(x + 1)(x + 1)(x - 6)$ **B.** $(x + 2)(2x - 5)(x - 6)$

C. $(x + 3)(x + 1)(x - 2)$ **D.** $(x - 3)(x - 1)(x + 2)$

66. What are the zeros of the polynomial function $y = (x - 3)(2x + 1)(x - 1)$?

F. $\frac{1}{2}, 1, 3$ **G.** $-1, 1, 3$ **H.** $-\frac{1}{2}, 1, 3$ **J.** $-3, \frac{1}{2}, 1$

67. Which polynomial function has zeros at $-4, 3,$ and 5?

A. $f(x) = (x + 4)(x + 3)(x + 5)$ **B.** $g(x) = (x + 4)(x - 3)(x - 5)$

C. $h(x) = (x - 4)(x - 3)(x - 5)$ **D.** $k(x) = (x - 4)(x + 3)(x + 5)$

Short Response

68. What is the factored form of $f(x) = x^4 + 8x^3 - 9x^2$?

Extended Response

69. What is the polynomial function, in standard form, whose zeros are $-2, 5,$ and 6, and whose leading coefficient is -2? Justify your reasoning.

Mixed Review

Lesson 6-1

Write each polynomial in standard form. Then classify it by degree and by number of terms.

70. $x^2 - 1 - 3x^5 + 2x^2$ **71.** $-2x^3 - 7x^4 + x^3$ **72.** $6x + x^3 - 6x - 2$

Lesson 5-4

Factor each expression.

73. $x^2 + 5x + 4$ **74.** $x^2 - 2x - 15$ **75.** $x^2 - 12x + 36$

Lesson 4-5

Evaluate the determinant of each matrix.

76. $A = \begin{bmatrix} 1 & -4 \\ 2 & 0 \end{bmatrix}$ **77.** $B = \begin{bmatrix} 5 & 3 \\ 2 & -1 \end{bmatrix}$ **78.** $C = \begin{bmatrix} 3 & -2 \\ 3 & -2 \end{bmatrix}$

6-3 Dividing Polynomials

What You'll Learn

- To divide polynomials using long division
- To divide polynomials using synthetic division

. . . And Why

To find the dimensions of a sarcophagus, as in Example 4

Check Skills You'll Need

GO for Help Lessons 5-1 and 6-1

Simplify each expression.

1. $(x + 3)(x - 4) + 2$

2. $(2x + 1)(x - 3)$

3. $(x + 2)(x + 1) - 11$

4. $-3(2 - x)(x + 5)$

Write each polynomial in standard form. Then list the coefficients.

5. $5x - 2x^2 + 9 + 4x^3$

6. $10 + 5x^3 - 9x^2$

7. $3x + x^2 - x + 7 - 2x^2$

8. $-4x^4 - 7x^2 + x^3 + x^4$

New Vocabulary • synthetic division • Remainder Theorem

1 Using Long Division

You can use polynomial division to help find all the zeros of a polynomial function. Division of polynomials is similar to numerical division.

Vocabulary Tip

$$6\overline{)24} \quad 4 \leftarrow \text{Quotient}, \; 24 \leftarrow \text{Dividend}, \; 6 \leftarrow \text{Divisor}$$

Recall that when a numerical division has a remainder of zero, as shown below, the divisor and quotient are both factors of the dividend.

$$\begin{array}{r} 7 \\ 8\overline{)56} \\ \underline{56} \\ 0 \end{array}$$

7 and 8 are factors of 56.

If numerical division leaves a nonzero remainder, as shown below, then neither the divisor nor the quotient is a factor of the dividend.

$$\begin{array}{r} 8 \\ 5\overline{)42} \\ \underline{40} \\ 2 \end{array}$$

Neither 5 nor 8 is a factor of 42.

Division serves as a test of whether one number is a factor of another.

The same is true for polynomial division. If you divide a polynomial by one of its factors, then you get another factor. When a polynomial division leaves a zero remainder, as shown below with monomials, you have factored the polynomial.

$$\begin{array}{r} 2x \\ x\overline{)2x^2} \\ \underline{2x^2} \\ 0 \end{array}$$

x and $2x$ are factors of $2x^2$.

To divide polynomials other than monomials, follow the same procedure you use to divide whole numbers.

1 EXAMPLE Polynomial Long Division

Divide $x^2 + 3x - 12$ by $x - 3$.

$$\begin{array}{r} x \\ x - 3 \overline{)x^2 + 3x - 12} \\ \underline{x^2 - 3x} \\ 6x - 12 \end{array}$$

Divide: $\frac{x^2}{x} = x$.

Multiply: $x(x - 3) = x^2 - 3x$.
Subtract: $x^2 + 3x - (x^2 - 3x) = 6x$. Bring down -12.

Repeat the process of dividing, multiplying, and subtracting.

$$\begin{array}{r} x + 6 \\ x - 3 \overline{)x^2 + 3x - 12} \\ \underline{x^2 - 3x} \\ 6x - 12 \\ \underline{6x - 18} \\ 6 \end{array}$$

Divide: $\frac{6x}{x} = 6$.

Multiply: $6(x - 3) = 6x - 18$.
Subtract: $6x - 12 - (6x - 18) = 6$.

The quotient is $x + 6$ with a remainder of 6, or simply $x + 6$, R 6.

Check Show that (divisor)(quotient) + remainder = dividend.

$$\begin{aligned} (x - 3)(x + 6) + 6 &= (x^2 + 6x - 3x - 18) + 6 \quad \textbf{Multiply } (x - 3)(x + 6). \\ &= x^2 + 3x - 12 \quad \textbf{Simplify.} \end{aligned}$$

Quick Check ❶ Divide $x^2 - 3x + 1$ by $x - 4$. Check your answer.

You can use polynomial long division to find the factors of a polynomial.

2 EXAMPLE Checking Factors

Determine whether $x + 4$ is a factor of each polynomial.

a. $x^2 + 6x + 8$

$$\begin{array}{r} x + 2 \\ x + 4 \overline{)x^2 + 6x + 8} \\ \underline{x^2 + 4x} \\ 2x + 8 \\ \underline{2x + 8} \\ 0 \end{array}$$

Since the remainder is zero,
$x + 4$ is a factor of $x^2 + 6x + 8$.

b. $x^3 + 3x^2 - 6x - 7$

$$\begin{array}{r} x^2 - x - 2 \\ x + 4 \overline{)x^3 + 3x^2 - 6x - 7} \\ \underline{x^3 + 4x^2} \\ -x^2 - 6x \\ \underline{-x^2 - 4x} \\ -2x - 7 \\ \underline{-2x - 8} \\ 1 \end{array}$$

Since the remainder $\neq 0$, $x + 4$ is
not a factor of $x^3 + 3x^2 - 6x - 7$.

Quick Check ❷ Determine whether each divisor is a factor of each dividend.
a. $(2x^2 - 19x + 24) \div (x - 8)$ **b.** $(x^3 - 4x^2 + 3x + 2) \div (x + 2)$

2 Using Synthetic Division

To divide by a linear factor, you can use a simplified process that is known as
synthetic division. In synthetic division, you omit all variables and exponents.
By reversing the sign in the divisor, you can add throughout the process instead
of subtracting.

3 EXAMPLE Using Synthetic Division

Vocabulary Tip

Synthetic division is sometimes called the method of detached coefficients.

Use synthetic division to divide $3x^3 - 4x^2 + 2x - 1$ by $x + 1$.

Step 1 Reverse the sign of the constant term in the divisor. Write the coefficients of the polynomial in standard form.

$$\text{Write} \quad x + 1 \overline{)\ 3x^3 - 4x^2 + 2x - 1}$$

$$\text{as} \quad \underline{-1}\ |\ 3 \quad -4 \quad\quad 2 \quad\quad -1$$

Step 2 Bring down the first coefficient.

$$\underline{-1}\ |\ 3 \quad -4 \quad 2 \quad -1 \ \longleftarrow \begin{array}{l}\text{Bring down the 3.}\\ \text{This begins the}\\ \text{quotient.}\end{array}$$
$$\overline{3 \quad \blacksquare \quad \blacksquare \quad \blacksquare}$$

Step 3 Multiply the first coefficient by the new divisor. Write the result under the next coefficient. Add.

$$\underline{-1}\ |\ 3 \quad -4 \quad 2 \quad -1 \ \longleftarrow \begin{array}{l}\text{Multiply 3 by } -1. \text{ Write}\\ \text{the result under } -4.\end{array}$$
$$\times \quad\quad -3$$
$$\overline{3 \quad -7 \quad \blacksquare \quad \blacksquare} \ \longleftarrow \text{Add } -4 \text{ and } -3.$$

Step 4 Repeat the steps of multiplying and adding until the remainder is found.

$$\underline{-1}\ |\ 3 \quad -4 \quad 2 \quad -1$$
$$\quad\quad\quad -3 \quad 7 \quad -9$$
$$\overline{3 \quad -7 \quad 9 \quad -10}$$
$$\quad\ 3x^2 - 7x + 9 \quad \text{Remainder}$$

● The quotient is $3x^2 - 7x + 9$, R -10.

 **Quick Check** ③ Use synthetic division to divide $x^3 + 4x^2 + x - 6$ by $x + 1$.

4 EXAMPLE Real-World  Connection

The volume in cubic feet of a sarcophagus (excluding the cover) can be expressed as the product of its three dimensions: $V(x) = x^3 - 13x + 12$. The length is $x + 4$.

a. Find linear expressions with integer coefficients for the other dimensions. Assume that the width is greater than the height.

$$\underline{-4}\ |\ 1 \quad\ 0 \quad -13 \quad\ 12 \qquad\qquad \begin{array}{l}\textbf{Divide. Use 0 as a place holder}\\ \textbf{for any missing term.}\end{array}$$
$$\quad\quad\quad -4 \quad 16 \quad -12$$
$$\overline{1 \quad -4 \quad\ 3 \quad\quad 0}$$
$$\quad x^2 \ - 4x + 3 \quad \text{Remainder}$$

$x^2 - 4x + 3 = (x - 1)(x - 3)$ **Factor the quotient.**

The width and the height are $x - 1$ and $x - 3$, respectively.

Real-World Connection

For the ancient Greeks, Romans, and Egyptians, a sarcophagus was a work of art created to honor a loved one. They decorated the stone tomb with elaborate inscriptions and ornaments.

b. If the length of the sarcophagus is 10 ft, what are the other two dimensions?

$x + 4 = 10$ **The length, $x + 4$, is 10.**

$x = 6$ **Find x.**

Since the width equals $x - 1$ and the height equals $x - 3$, the width is 5 ft and the height is 3 ft.

✓ **Quick Check** ④ **a.** Use synthetic division to divide $x^3 - 2x^2 - 5x + 6$ by $x + 2$.
b. Use your answer from part (a) to completely factor $x^3 - 2x^2 - 5x + 6$.

In Example 1, you saw that $x - 3$ is not a factor of $x^2 + 3x - 12$ because their quotient has a remainder of 6. If $x - 3$ were a factor of $x^2 + 3x - 12$, then 3 would be a zero of $P(x) = x^2 + 3x - 12$, and $P(3)$ would equal zero. You know that $P(3)$ does not equal zero, but what *does* it equal?

You can find $P(3)$ by substituting 3 for x.

$P(x) = x^2 + 3x - 12$
$P(3) = (3)^2 + 3(3) - 12$
$\quad\ = 6$

$P(3)$ equals the remainder in Example 1, because

dividend = divisor × quotient + remainder.

$P(x) = (x - 3)(x + 6) + 6$
$P(3) = (3 - 3)(3 + 6) + 6$
$\quad\ = 0(3 + 6) + 6$
$\quad\ = 6$

This relationship is defined by the **Remainder Theorem.**

 **Key Concepts**

Theorem	**Remainder Theorem**

If a polynomial $P(x)$ of degree $n \geq 1$ is divided by $(x - a)$, where a is a constant, then the remainder is $P(a)$.

You can use the Remainder Theorem to find values of $P(x)$.

⑤ **EXAMPLE**   **Evaluating a Polynomial by Synthetic Division**

Gridded Response Find $P(-4)$ for
$P(x) = x^4 - 5x^2 + 4x + 12$.

By the Remainder Theorem, $P(-4)$ equals the remainder when $P(x)$ is divided by $x - (-4)$.

```
-4│ 1    0    -5     4     12
        -4    16   -44    160
   ─────────────────────────────
    1   -4    11   -40    172
```

The remainder is 172, so $P(-4) = 172$.

✓ **Quick Check** ⑤ Use synthetic division to find $P(-1)$ for $P(x) = 2x^4 + 6x^3 - 5x^2 - 60$.

EXERCISES

For more exercises, see *Extra Skill and Word Problem Practice*.

Practice and Problem Solving

A Practice by Example

Example 1
(page 321)

Divide using long division. Check your answers.

1. $(x^2 - 3x - 40) \div (x + 5)$

2. $(3x^2 + 7x - 20) \div (x + 4)$

3. $(x^3 + 3x^2 - x + 2) \div (x - 1)$

4. $(2x^3 - 3x^2 - 18x - 8) \div (x - 4)$

5. $(9x^3 - 18x^2 - x + 2) \div (3x + 1)$

6. $(9x^2 - 21x - 20) \div (x - 1)$

7. $(x^2 - 7x + 10) \div (x + 3)$

8. $(x^3 - 13x - 12) \div (x - 4)$

Example 2
(page 321)

Determine whether each binomial is a factor of $x^3 + 4x^2 + x - 6$.

9. $x + 1$ **10.** $x + 2$ **11.** $x + 3$ **12.** $x - 3$

Example 3
(page 322)

Divide using synthetic division.

13. $(x^3 + 3x^2 - x - 3) \div (x - 1)$

14. $(x^3 - 4x^2 + 6x - 4) \div (x - 2)$

15. $(x^3 - 7x^2 - 7x + 20) \div (x + 4)$

16. $(x^3 - 3x^2 - 5x - 25) \div (x - 5)$

17. $(x^3 - 2x^2 - 5x + 6) \div (x - 1)$

18. $(-2x^3 + 5x^2 - x + 2) \div (x + 2)$

19. $(x^2 + 3) \div (x - 1)$

20. $(3x^3 + 17x^2 + 21x - 9) \div (x + 3)$

21. $(x^3 + 27) \div (x + 3)$

22. $(6x^2 - 8x - 2) \div (x - 1)$

Example 4
(pages 322–323)

Use synthetic division and the given factor to completely factor each polynomial function.

23. $y = x^3 + 2x^2 - 5x - 6; (x + 1)$

24. $y = x^3 - 4x^2 - 9x + 36; (x + 3)$

 25. Geometry Refer to the diagram. The volume in cubic inches of the decorative box can be expressed as the product of the lengths of its sides as $V(x) = x^3 + x^2 - 6x$. Write linear expressions with integer coefficients for the locker's length and height.

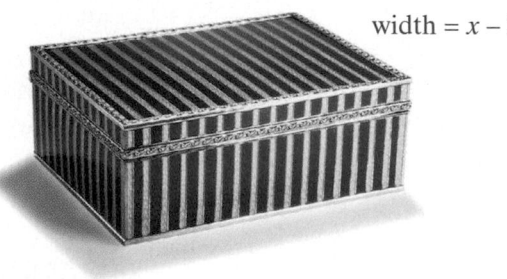

width = $x - 2$

Example 5
(page 323)

Use synthetic division and the Remainder Theorem to find $P(a)$.

26. $P(x) = x^3 + 4x^2 - 8x - 6; a = -2$

27. $P(x) = x^3 + 4x^2 + 4x; a = -2$

28. $P(x) = x^3 - 7x^2 + 15x - 9; a = 3$

29. $P(x) = x^3 + 7x^2 + 4x; a = -2$

30. $P(x) = 6x^3 - x^2 + 4x + 3; a = 3$

31. $P(x) = 2x^3 - x^2 + 10x + 5; a = \frac{1}{2}$

32. $P(x) = 2x^3 + 4x^2 - 10x - 9; a = 3$

33. $P(x) = 2x^4 + 6x^3 + 5x^2 - 45; a = -3$

B Apply Your Skills

34. Reasoning A polynomial $P(x)$ is divided by a binomial $x - a$. The remainder is zero. What conclusion can you draw? Explain.

35. Error Analysis A student represented the product of three linear factors as $x^3 - x^2 - 2x$. She used $x - 1$ as one of the factors. Use division to prove that the student made an error.

36. Open-Ended Write a polynomial division that has a quotient of $x + 3$ and a remainder of 2.

Divide.

37. $(2x^3 + 9x^2 + 14x + 5) \div (2x + 1)$ **38.** $(x^4 + 3x^2 + x + 4) \div (x + 3)$

39. $(x^5 + 1) \div (x + 1)$ **40.** $(x^4 + 4x^3 - x - 4) \div (x^3 - 1)$

41. $(3x^4 - 5x^3 + 2x^2 + 3x - 2) \div (3x - 2)$

Determine whether each binomial is a factor of $x^3 + x^2 - 16x - 16$.

42. $x + 2$ **43.** $x - 4$ **44.** $x + 1$

45. $x - 1$ **46.** $x - 2$ **47.** $x + 4$

Homework Video Tutor
Visit: PHSchool.com
Web Code: age-0603

Use synthetic division to determine whether each binomial is a factor of $3x^3 + 10x^2 - x - 12$.

48. $x + 3$ **49.** $x - 1$ **50.** $x + 2$ **51.** $x - 4$

Divide using synthetic division.

52. $(x^4 - 2x^3 + x^2 + x - 1) \div (x - 1)$ **53.** $(x^4 - 6x^2 - 27) \div (x + 2)$

54. $(x^4 - 5x^2 + 4x + 12) \div (x + 2)$ **55.** $\left(x^4 - \frac{9}{2}x^3 + 3x^2 - \frac{1}{2}x\right) \div \left(x - \frac{1}{2}\right)$

 **Challenge**

56. Reasoning Divide. Look for patterns in your answers.
 a. $(x^2 - 1) \div (x - 1)$ **b.** $(x^3 - 1) \div (x - 1)$ **c.** $(x^4 - 1) \div (x - 1)$
 d. Using the patterns, factor $x^5 - 1$.

57. Divide. Look for patterns in your answers.
 a. $(x^3 + 1) \div (x + 1)$ **b.** $(x^5 + 1) \div (x + 1)$ **c.** $(x^7 + 1) \div (x + 1)$
 d. Using the patterns, factor $x^9 + 1$.

58. Critical Thinking Explain why a polynomial of degree n, divided by a polynomial of degree 1, yields a quotient of degree $n - 1$ and a remainder that is a constant.

59. Use synthetic division to find $(x^2 + 4) \div (x - 2i)$.

60. Writing Suppose 3, -1, and 4 are zeros of a cubic polynomial function. Sketch a graph of the function. Could there be more than one graph? Explain.

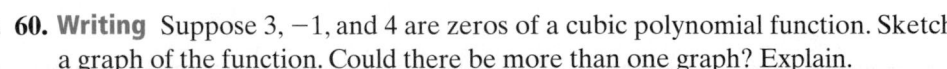

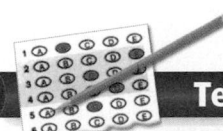

Test Prep

Multiple Choice

61. What is the remainder when $x^2 - 5x + 7$ is divided by $x + 1$?
 A. -13 **B.** -1 **C.** 1 **D.** 13

62. Which binomial is NOT a factor of $x^3 - x^2 - 17x - 15$?
 F. $x - 5$ **G.** $x + 1$ **H.** $x + 3$ **J.** $x + 5$

63. Which of the following, when multiplied by $x - 1$, results in a cubic polynomial whose standard form has three terms?
 A. $(x - 1)^2$ **B.** $x^2 - x$ **C.** $x^2 - 1$ **D.** $x - 1$

Short Response

64. One factor of $x^3 - 7x^2 - x + 7$ is $x - 1$. What are all the zeros of the related polynomial function? Show your work.

Lesson 6-2   Write a polynomial function in standard form with the given zeros.

65. $3, -5$ **66.** $0, 1, 8$ **67.** $-1, 2, 5$ **68.** 1, multiplicity 4

Lesson 5-6   Simplify each expression.

69. $(-4i)(6i)$ **70.** $(2 + i)(2 - i)$ **71.** $(4 - 3i)(5 + i)$

Lesson 4-6   Find the inverse of each matrix, if it exists.

72. $\begin{bmatrix} 1 & 0 & 3 \\ 1 & 1 & 0 \\ -1 & 0 & -1 \end{bmatrix}$ **73.** $\begin{bmatrix} 1 & 2 & 0 \\ 0 & 2 & -2 \\ 1 & 0 & 2 \end{bmatrix}$ **74.** $\begin{bmatrix} 2 & 1 & 0 \\ -1 & 1 & -2 \\ 3 & -2 & 4 \end{bmatrix}$

✓ Checkpoint Quiz 1   Lessons 6-1 through 6-3

1. Write a polynomial function with at least three zeros that are negative, one of which has multiplicity 2.

Write each polynomial in standard form. Then classify it by degree and by number of terms.

2. $-2x^3 + 6 - x^3 + 5x$ **3.** $\frac{1}{2}x + x^4 - 3x^2 + 2x$ **4.** $3(x - 1)(x + 4)$

For each function, determine the zeros and their multiplicity.

5. $y = (x - 2)^2(x - 1)$ **6.** $y = (2x + 1)(x - 4)$ **7.** $y = x^3(x - 3)(x + 1)^2$

Divide.

8. $(x^3 + 3x^2 + 3x + 1) \div (x + 1)$ **9.** $(2x^3 - 7x^2 + 7x - 2) \div (x - 2)$

10. Use synthetic division to find $P(4)$ for $P(x) = 2x^4 - 3x^2 + 4x - 1$.

Algebra at Work

······················· **Quality Control Engineer**

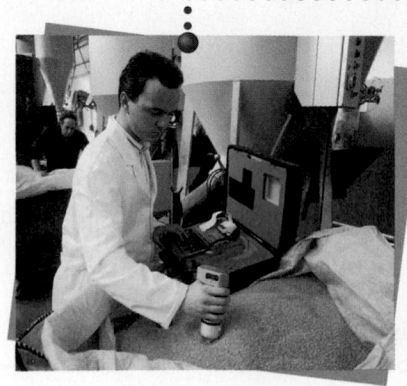

Quality control engineers establish procedures for assuring that products meet minimum standards of quality such as length or purity. Each product is sampled regularly. Data relating to each standard are collected and analyzed. All samples must fall within certain limiting parameters. Quality is further controlled by requiring that a significant portion of the samples fall within even stricter limiting parameters.

 **For:** Information about quality control
PHSchool.com   **Web Code:** agb-2031

6-4

Solving Polynomial Equations

What You'll Learn

- To solve polynomial equations by graphing
- To solve polynomial equations by factoring

. . . And Why

To calculate the dimensions of a portable kennel, as in Example 2

✔ **Check Skills You'll Need**

GO for Help Lessons 3-1 and 5-4

Graph each system. Find any points of intersection.

1. $\begin{cases} y = 3x + 1 \\ y = -2x + 6 \end{cases}$

2. $\begin{cases} -2x + 3y = 0 \\ x + 3y = 3 \end{cases}$

3. $\begin{cases} 2y = -x + 8 \\ x + 2y = -6 \end{cases}$

Factor each expression.

4. $x^2 - 2x - 15$

5. $x^2 - 9x + 14$

6. $x^2 + 6x + 5$

◀)) **New Vocabulary** • sum of cubes • difference of cubes

---

1 Solving Equations by Graphing

You can solve a polynomial equation by graphing each side of the equation separately and finding the x values at the point(s) of intersection.

Graphing Calculator Hint

You can also solve the equation in Example 1 by graphing the related function $y = x^3 + 3x^2 - x - 3$ and finding its zeros.

1 EXAMPLE Solving by Graphing

Solve $x^3 + 3x^2 = x + 3$ by graphing.

Step 1 Graph $y_1 = x^3 + 3x^2$ and $y_2 = x + 3$ on a graphing calculator.

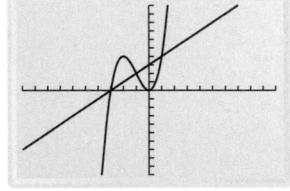

Step 2 Use the Intersect feature to find the x values at the points of intersection.

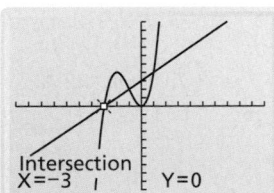
Intersection
X=-3   Y=0

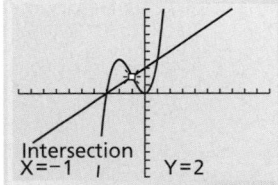
Intersection
X=-1   Y=2

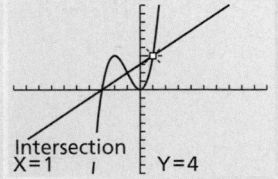
Intersection
X=1   Y=4

The solutions are $-3, -1,$ and 1.

Check Show that each solution makes the original equation a true statement.

$$x^3 + 3x^2 = x + 3 \qquad\qquad x^3 + 3x^2 = x + 3 \qquad\qquad x^3 + 3x^2 = x + 3$$

$$(-3)^3 + 3(-3)^2 \overset{?}{=} -3 + 3 \quad (-1)^3 + 3(-1)^2 \overset{?}{=} -1 + 3 \quad (1)^3 + 3(1)^2 \overset{?}{=} 1 + 3$$

$$-27 + 27 \overset{?}{=} -3 + 3 \qquad\qquad -1 + 3 \overset{?}{=} -1 + 3 \qquad\qquad 1 + 3 \overset{?}{=} 1 + 3$$

$$0 = 0 \checkmark \qquad\qquad\qquad 2 = 2 \checkmark \qquad\qquad\qquad 4 = 4 \checkmark$$

✔ **Quick Check** ① Graph and solve $x^3 - 2x^2 = -3$. Check your answers.

You can write and solve a polynomial equation that models a real-world situation.

2 EXAMPLE **Real-World Connection**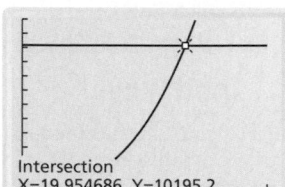

Pet Transportation The dimensions in inches of a portable kennel can be expressed as width x, length $x + 7$, and height $x - 1$. The volume is 5.9 ft^3. Find the portable kennel's dimensions.

$$5.9 \text{ ft}^3 \cdot \frac{12^3 \text{ in.}^3}{\text{ft}^3} = 10{,}195.2 \text{ in.}^3 \qquad \text{Convert the volume to cubic inches.}$$

$$V = \ell \cdot w \cdot h \qquad \text{Write the formula for volume.}$$

$$10{,}195.2 = (x + 7)x(x - 1) \qquad \text{Substitute.}$$

Graph $y_1 = 10{,}195.2$ and $y_2 = (x + 7)x(x - 1)$. Use the Intersect feature of the calculator. When $y = 10{,}195.2$, $x \approx 20$. So $x + 7 \approx 27$ and $x - 1 \approx 19$.

The dimensions of the portable kennel are about 27 in. by 20 in. by 19 in.

Real-World Connection

International regulations specify the allowable dimensions of pet transportation carriers.

 Quick Check ❷ Find the dimensions of a carrier with volume 7 ft^3, width x inches, length $(x + 3)$ inches, and height $(x - 2)$ inches.

---

2 Solving Equations by Factoring

Recall that a quadratic *difference of squares* has a special factoring pattern. A cubic **sum of cubes** and **difference of cubes** also have special factoring patterns.

🔑 **Key Concepts**

Properties	Sum and Difference of Cubes
	$a^3 + b^3 = (a + b)(a^2 - ab + b^2)$
	$a^3 - b^3 = (a - b)(a^2 + ab + b^2)$

You can verify the patterns by multiplying. Here are steps for the sum of cubes:

$$(a + b)(a^2 - ab + b^2) = a(a^2 - ab + b^2) + b(a^2 - ab + b^2)$$
$$= a^3 - a^2 b + ab^2 + a^2 b - ab^2 + b^3$$
$$= a^3 + b^3$$

3 EXAMPLE **Factoring a Sum or Difference of Cubes**

Multiple Choice If you factor $x^3 - 8$ in the form $(x - A)(x^2 + Bx + C)$, what is the value of A?

Ⓐ 2   Ⓑ −2   Ⓒ 4   Ⓓ −4

$$x^3 - 8 = (x)^3 - (2)^3 \qquad \text{Rewrite the expression as the difference of cubes.}$$
$$= (x - 2)(x^2 + 2x + (2)^2) \qquad \text{Factor.}$$
$$= (x - 2)(x^2 + 2x + 4) \qquad \text{Simplify.}$$

The answer is choice A.

Test-Taking Tip

Remembering patterns may help you find answers more quickly.

 **Quick Check** ❸ Factor $8x^3 - 1$.

In Chapter 5, you found the complex roots of quadratic equations. You can do the same with polynomial equations of higher degree.

4 EXAMPLE **Solving a Polynomial Equation**

Solve $27x^3 + 1 = 0$. Find all complex roots.

$27x^3 + 1 = (3x)^3 + (1)^3$ **Rewrite the cubic expression as the sum of cubes.**

$= (3x + 1)((3x)^2 - 3x + 1)$ **Factor.**

$= (3x + 1)(9x^2 - 3x + 1)$ **Simplify.**

Since $3x + 1$ is a factor, $x = -\frac{1}{3}$ is a root.

The quadratic expression $9x^2 - 3x + 1$ cannot be factored, so use the Quadratic Formula to solve the related quadratic equation $9x^2 - 3x + 1 = 0$.

$x = \dfrac{-b \pm \sqrt{b^2 - 4ac}}{2a}$ **Quadratic Formula**

$= \dfrac{-(-3) \pm \sqrt{(-3)^2 - 4(9)(1)}}{2(9)}$ **Substitute 9 for *a*, −3 for *b*, and 1 for *c*.**

$= \dfrac{3 \pm \sqrt{-27}}{18}$ **Use the Order of Operations.**

$= \dfrac{3 \pm 3i\sqrt{3}}{18}$ **Simplify.**

$= \dfrac{1 \pm i\sqrt{3}}{6}$

● The roots are $-\frac{1}{3}$ and $\dfrac{1 \pm i\sqrt{3}}{6}$.

Vocabulary Tip

$\sqrt{-1} = i$

✓ Quick Check ❹ Solve each equation.

    a. $x^3 + 8 = 0$ **b.** $27x^3 - 1 = 0$

You can sometimes factor a polynomial of higher degree by using the techniques you have used in solving polynomials of lower degree.

5 EXAMPLE **Factoring by Using a Quadratic Pattern**

Factor $x^4 - 2x^2 - 8$.

Step 1 You can write $x^4 - 2x^2 - 8$ in the pattern of a quadratic expression, so you can factor it like one. Make a temporary substitution of variables.

    $x^4 - 2x^2 - 8 = (x^2)^2 - 2(x^2) - 8$ **Rewrite in the pattern of a quadratic expression.**

               $= a^2 - 2a - 8$ **Substitute *a* for x^2.**

Step 2 Factor $a^2 - 2a - 8$.

    $a^2 - 2a - 8 = (a - 4)(a + 2)$

Step 3 Substitute back to the original variable.

    $(a - 4)(a + 2) = (x^2 - 4)(x^2 + 2)$ **Substitute x^2 for *a*.**

                    $= (x + 2)(x - 2)(x^2 + 2)$ **Factor completely.**

● The factored form of $x^4 - 2x^2 - 8$ is $(x + 2)(x - 2)(x^2 + 2)$.

✓ Quick Check ❺ Factor each expression.

    a. $x^4 + 7x^2 + 6$ **b.** $x^4 - 3x^2 - 10$

6 EXAMPLE **Solving a Higher-Degree Polynomial Equation**

Solve $x^4 - x^2 = 12$.

$$x^4 - x^2 = 12$$

$$x^4 - x^2 - 12 = 0 \quad \text{Rewrite so one side of the equation is equal to zero.}$$

$$(x^2)^2 - (x^2) - 12 = 0 \quad \text{Write in the form of a quadratic expression. Think of the expression as } a^2 - a - 12, \text{ which factors as } (a - 4)(a + 3).$$

$$(x^2 - 4)(x^2 + 3) = 0$$

$$(x - 2)(x + 2)(x^2 + 3) = 0$$

$x = 2$ or $x = -2$ or $x^2 = -3$ Use the Factor Theorem.

$\qquad\qquad x = \pm 2$ or $x = \pm\sqrt{-3}$ Solve for x.

$\qquad\qquad x = \pm 2$ or $x = \pm i\sqrt{3}$ Simplify.

● The solutions are $2, -2, i\sqrt{3}$, and $-i\sqrt{3}$.

✓ Quick Check **6** Solve $x^4 + 11x^2 + 18 = 0$.

EXERCISES

For more exercises, see *Extra Skill and Word Problem Practice*.

Practice and Problem Solving

 **Practice by Example**

Examples 1 and 2
(pages 327 and 328)

 **for Help**

Solve each equation by graphing. Check your answers.

1. $x^3 - 4x^2 - 7x = -10$ **2.** $3x^3 - 6x^2 - 9x = 0$ **3.** $4x^3 - 8x^2 + 4x = 0$

4. $6x^2 = 48x$ **5.** $x^3 + 3x^2 + 2x = 0$ **6.** $2x^3 + 5x^2 = 7x$

7. $4x^3 = 4x^2 + 3x$ **8.** $2x^4 - 5x^3 - 3x^2 = 0$ **9.** $x^2 - 8x + 7 = 0$

10. Savings The polynomial $1600x^3 + 1200x^2 + 800x$ represents your savings, with interest, from a summer job after three years. The annual interest rate equals $x - 1$. Find the interest rate needed so that you will have $4000 at the end of three years.

11. Geometry The volume V of a container is modeled by the function $V(x) = x^3 - 3x^2 - 4x$. Let $x, x + 1$, and $x - 4$ represent the width, the length, and the height respectively. The container has a volume of 70 ft³. Find the container's dimensions.

Example 3
(page 328)

Factor each expression.

12. $x^3 + 64$ **13.** $x^3 - 1000$ **14.** $125x^3 - 27$

Example 4
(page 329)

Solve each equation.

15. $x^3 - 27 = 0$ **16.** $x^3 + 64 = 0$ **17.** $x^3 - 125 = 0$

18. $2x^3 + 2 = 0$ **19.** $8x^3 - 1 = 0$ **20.** $64x^3 + 8 = 0$

Example 5
(page 329)

Factor each expression.

21. $x^4 - 8x^2 + 7$ **22.** $x^4 + 8x^2 - 20$ **23.** $x^4 - 7x^2 + 12$

24. $x^4 - 5x^2 + 4$ **25.** $x^4 - 1$ **26.** $4x^4 - 6x^2 + 2$

Example 6
(page 330)

Solve each equation.

27. $x^4 - 10x^2 + 9 = 0$ **28.** $x^4 - 8x^2 + 16 = 0$ **29.** $x^4 - 12x^2 - 64 = 0$

30. $x^4 + 7x^2 - 18 = 0$ **31.** $x^4 + 4x^2 - 12 = 0$ **32.** $x^4 + 8x^2 + 15 = 0$

B Apply Your Skills   Solve each equation by graphing. Where necessary, round to the nearest hundredth.

33. $x^3 - x^2 - 6x - 4 = 0$ **34.** $2x^4 + 18x^3 = 0$

35. $x^4 + 2x^3 - 7x^2 - 8x = -12$ **36.** $x^4 + x^3 = 4x^2 + 4x - 5$

37. $x^3 + 13x = 10x^2$ **38.** $x^3 - 6x^2 + 6x = 0$ **39.** $12x^3 = 60x^2 + 75x$

40. The product of three consecutive integers $n - 1, n$, and $n + 1$ is 210. Write and solve an equation to find the numbers.

41. Multiple Choice The chamber in the container below consists of a cylinder on top of a hemisphere. The chamber holds 500 cm^3. What is the radius of the chamber, to the nearest hundredth of a centimeter?

  Ⓐ 2.75 cm   Ⓑ 3.12 cm   Ⓒ 3.32 cm   Ⓓ 3.58 cm

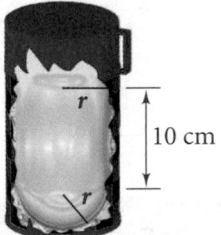

Real-World Connection

The vacuum bottle, or Dewar flask, was invented by the chemist James Dewar for storing liquefied gases.

Solve each equation.

42. $125x^3 + 216 = 0$ **43.** $81x^3 - 192 = 0$ **44.** $x^4 - 64 = 0$

45. $-2x^4 + 46x^2 = -100$ **46.** $27 = -x^4 - 12x^2$ **47.** $x^5 - 5x^3 + 4x = 0$

48. $x^4 - 100 = 0$ **49.** $5x^3 = 5x^2 + 12x$ **50.** $64 - x^3 = 0$

51. $x^3 - 6x^2 + 6x = 0$ **52.** $2x^3 = 5x^2 + 12x$ **53.** $3x^4 + 12x^2 - 15 = 0$

54. $x^3 + 3x^2 - 4x - 12 = 0$ **55.** $x^3 - 5x^2 + 3x + 9 = 0$

56. $4x^3 - 16x^2 + 12x = 0$ **57.** $2x^4 - 14x^3 + 12x^2 = 0$

58. $4x^4 - 2x^2 - 4 = 2$ **59.** $9x^4 - 9x^2 + 2 = 20$

60. Open-Ended To solve a polynomial equation, you can use any combination of graphing, factoring, and the Quadratic Formula. Write and solve an equation to illustrate each method.

For Exercises 61 and 62, write a polynomial function to describe each volume. Then graph your function to solve each problem.

GO for Help

For a guide to solving Exercise 61, see p. 333.

61. Geometry Suppose a 2-in. slice is cut from one face of the cheese block as shown. The remaining solid has a volume of 224 in.^{3}. Find the dimensions of the original block.

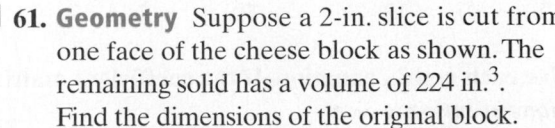

62. Geometry The width of a box is 2 m less than the length. The height is 1 m less than the length. The volume is 60 m^3. Find the length of the box.

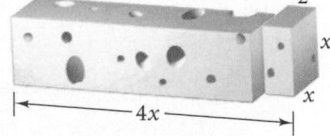

Homework Video Tutor
Visit: PHSchool.com
Web Code: age-0604

Graph each function to find the zeros. Rewrite the function with the polynomial in factored form.

63. $y = 2x^2 + 3x - 5$ **64.** $y = x^4 - 10x^2 + 9$ **65.** $y = x^3 - 3x^2 + 4$

66. $y = x^3 - 2x^2 - 5x + 6$ **67.** $y = x^3 + 2x^2 - 11x - 12$

68. Error Analysis A student claims that 1, 2, 3, and 4 are the zeros of a cubic polynomial function. Explain why the student is mistaken.

 Challenge

69. a. Open-Ended Write and solve a fourth-degree polynomial equation that includes the difference of squares.
   b. Critical Thinking Are all the roots real numbers? Justify your answer.

70. Writing From a large cube with edges a units long, you cut a smaller cube with edges three units long. Explain how the diagram at the right illustrates that $a^3 - 27 = (a - 3)(a^2 + 3a + 9)$.

71. a. The sum of two positive numbers is 4 and the sum of their cubes is 28. What is the sum of their squares?
   b. The product of two positive numbers is 96 and the sum of their squares is 208. What are the two numbers?

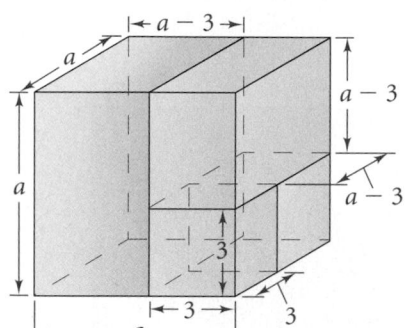

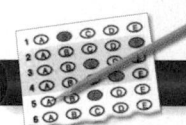 **Test Prep**

Multiple Choice

72. Which expression is a factor of $x^4 - 18x^2 + 81$?
   A. $x^2 - 9$ **B.** $x^2 + 6x - 9$ **C.** $x^2 - 6x - 9$ **D.** $x^2 + 9$

73. Which value is NOT a solution of $x^4 - 3x^2 - 54 = 0$?
   F. -3 **G.** 3   **H.** $-3i$ **J.** $-i\sqrt{6}$

Short Response

74. Show how you can rewrite $\frac{a^3}{b^6} + \frac{1}{8}$ as a sum of two cubes.

Extended Response

75. What are all the solutions to $8x^3 - 27 = 0$? Show your work.

Mixed Review

 **for Help**

Lesson 6-3

Divide.

76. $(x^3 - 2x^2 - 13x - 10) \div (x + 1)$ **77.** $(2x^3 - 7x^2 - 7x + 14) \div (x - 4)$

Lesson 5-5

Solve each equation by factoring or by taking square roots.

78. $n^2 - 4n = 12$ **79.** $n^2 + 1 = 37$ **80.** $2n^2 - 5n - 3 = 0$

Lesson 4-7

Solve each matrix equation. If the coefficient matrix has no inverse, write *no unique solution.*

81. $\begin{bmatrix} 2 & -1 \\ -3 & 2 \end{bmatrix} \begin{bmatrix} x \\ y \end{bmatrix} = \begin{bmatrix} 5 \\ -10 \end{bmatrix}$ **82.** $\begin{bmatrix} 1 & 4 \\ -2 & -8 \end{bmatrix} \begin{bmatrix} x \\ y \end{bmatrix} = \begin{bmatrix} 2 \\ -4 \end{bmatrix}$

Understanding Word Problems Read the problem below. Then let Ian's thinking guide you through the solution. Check your understanding with the exercises at the bottom of the page.

Geometry Suppose a 2-in. slice is cut from one face of the cheese block as shown. The remaining solid has a volume of 224 in.^{3}. Find the dimensions of the original block.

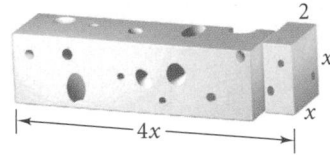

What Ian Thinks

From the diagram, it looks like the widths and heights of the two blocks are equal. I can subtract the amount cut off from the total length to find the length left.

The problem tells me that the volume of the leftover block is 224 in.^{3}. I can write a relationship, substitute, and simplify.

The polynomial equation is a cubic, and the problem asks me to solve by graphing. I'll graph two equations and find their intersection.

I'll enter the equations as Y_1 and Y_2, and I'll change my window values to accommodate a y-value of 224.

Next, I'll use the INTERSECT feature. When $y = 224$, $x = 4$. OK! Now I know x.

I can use x to find the dimensions of the original block.

What Ian Writes

$$\text{length of leftover block} = 4x - \text{length of cut block}$$
$$= 4x - 2$$

$$\text{volume of leftover block} = \ell wh = 224$$
$$V = (4x - 2)(x)(x) = 224$$
$$(4x - 2)(x^2) = 224$$
$$4x^3 - 2x^2 = 224$$

$$Y1 = 4x^3 - 2x^2$$
$$Y2 = 224$$

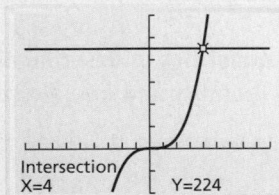

Intersection
X=4   Y=224

Xmin=–10
Xmax=10
Xscl=1
Ymin=–100
Ymax=300
Yscl=50

Width = Height = x = 4
Length = 4x = 4(4) = 16

The block of cheese measured
16 in. × 4 in. × 4 in.

EXERCISES

1. Slices of wood $\frac{1}{4}$-in. thick are cut from opposite sides of a cube of wood. The remaining solid has a volume of 151.25 in.^{3}. Find the dimensions of the original block of wood.

2. The water level in a fish tank is 4 in. from the top. The depth of the water is the same as the width of the tank, which is half of its length. The volume of the water in the tank is 4394 in.^{3}. What is the capacity of the fish tank?

Continuous and Discrete

Continuous and *discrete* are two rather sophisticated mathematics words that you can use in everyday conversations. Their mathematical and everyday meanings are compatible:

Continuous means unbroken.

Discrete means separate and distinct.

1 EXAMPLE

On a number line,
- real numbers are continuous,
- but integers are discrete.

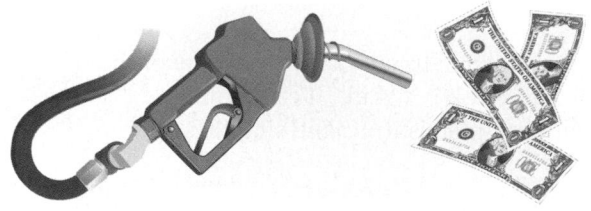

2 EXAMPLE

At the gas pump,
- gas pumped and value of gas are continuous;
- the amount you pay is discrete.

EXERCISES

Is the quantity continuous or discrete? Explain.

1. number of airplanes at an airport
2. altitude of an airplane
4. height of a growing flower

4. number of flowers in a garden
5. length of lead in a pencil
6. number of beans in a beanbag

You can use different quantities to describe different aspects of a situation. Name one continuous quantity and one discrete quantity for each situation.

7. a train ride between two cities
8. a soccer game

9. plowing a field
10. the weather today

Sometimes a situation itself can be described as continuous or discrete. Which word would you use to describe each situation below? Explain.

11. milk pouring into a glass
12. walking to school

13. bacteria living in a culture
14. Earth-to-sun distance

Is the mathematical object continuous or discrete? Explain.

15. the graph of a linear function
16. the graph of an absolute value function

17. a scatter plot of 100 data points
18. the zeros of a third-degree polynomial function

19. **Motion Pictures** Film editors watch for *continuity* from one scene to the next (both of which may have needed several "takes"). They want to avoid having a tennis racket suddenly switch from a left hand to a right hand or, worse yet, disappear entirely. Research and describe a continuity error found in a movie.

Theorems About Roots of Polynomial Equations

What You'll Learn

- To solve equations using the Rational Root Theorem
- To use the Irrational Root Theorem and the Imaginary Root Theorem

. . . And Why

To find all the roots of a polynomial equation, as in Example 2

GO for Help Lessons 1-1, 5-1, and 5-6

List all the integer factors of each number.

1. 12   **2.** 24   **3.** 36   **4.** 48

Multiply.

5. $(x - 5)(x^2 + 7)$ **6.** $(x + 2)(x + \sqrt{3})(x - \sqrt{3})$

Define each set of numbers.

7. rational   **8.** irrational   **9.** imaginary

🔊 **New Vocabulary**
- Rational Root Theorem
- Irrational Root Theorem
- Imaginary Root Theorem
- conjugates
- complex conjugates

---

1   The Rational Root Theorem

Vocabulary Tip

A polynomial equation has <u>roots</u>. A polynomial function has <u>zeros</u>.

You have learned several methods for finding the roots of a polynomial equation. Another method involves analyzing one or more integer coefficients of the polynomial in the equation.

Consider the equivalent equations $x^3 - 5x^2 - 2x + 24 = 0$ and $(x + 2)(x - 3)(x - 4) = 0$, which have $-2, 3$, and 4 as roots. The product of $2, 3$, and 4 is 24. Notice that all the roots are factors of the constant term, 24. In general, if the coefficients (including the constant term) in a polynomial equation are integers, then any integer root of the equation is a factor of the constant term.

A similar pattern applies to rational roots. Consider the equivalent equations $24x^3 - 22x^2 - 5x + 6 = 0$ and $\left(x + \frac{1}{2}\right)\left(x - \frac{2}{3}\right)\left(x - \frac{3}{4}\right) = 0$, which have $-\frac{1}{2}, \frac{2}{3}$, and $\frac{3}{4}$ as roots. The numerators $1, 2$, and 3 all are factors of the constant term, 6. The denominators $2, 3$, and 4 are factors of the leading coefficient, 24.

Both the constant term and the leading coefficient of a polynomial can play a key role in identifying the rational roots of the related polynomial equation. This role is expressed in the Rational Root Theorem.

 Key Concepts

Theorem	Rational Root Theorem

If $\frac{p}{q}$ is in simplest form and is a rational root of the polynomial equation $a_n x^n + a_{n-1} x^{n-1} + \ldots + a_1 x + a_0 = 0$ with integer coefficients, then p must be a factor of a_0 and q must be a factor of a_n.

You can use the Rational Root Theorem to find any rational roots of a polynomial equation with integer coefficients.

1 EXAMPLE Finding Rational Roots

Find the rational roots of $x^3 + x^2 - 3x - 3 = 0$.

Step 1 List the possible rational roots.

The leading coefficient is 1. The constant term is -3. By the Rational Root Theorem, the only possible rational roots of the equation have the form $\frac{\text{factor of } -3}{\text{factor of } 1}$.

The factors of -3 are ± 1 and ± 3. The factors of 1 are ± 1. The only possible rational roots are ± 1 and ± 3.

Step 2 Test each possible rational root.

Test 1: $x^3 + x^2 - 3x - 3 = (1)^3 + (1)^2 - 3(1) - 3$
$$= -4 \neq 0$$

Test 3: $x^3 + x^2 - 3x - 3 = (3)^3 + (3)^2 - 3(3) - 3$
$$= 24 \neq 0$$

Test -1: $x^3 + x^2 - 3x - 3 = (-1)^3 + (-1)^2 - 3(-1) - 3$
$$= 0 \quad \textbf{So } -1 \textbf{ is a root.}$$

Test -3: $x^3 + x^2 - 3x - 3 = (-3)^3 + (-3)^2 - 3(-3) - 3$
$$= -12 \neq 0$$

● The only rational root of $x^3 + x^2 - 3x - 3 = 0$ is -1.

✓ Quick Check ❶ Find the rational roots of $x^3 - 4x^2 - 2x + 8 = 0$.

You can often use the Rational Root Theorem to find all the roots of a polynomial equation.

2 EXAMPLE Using the Rational Root Theorem

Find the roots of $2x^3 - x^2 + 2x - 1 = 0$.

Step 1 List the possible rational roots.

The leading coefficient is 2. The constant term is -1. By the Rational Root Theorem, the only possible rational roots of the equation have the form $\frac{\text{factor of } -1}{\text{factor of } 2}$.

The factors of -1 are ± 1. The factors of 2 are ± 1 and ± 2. So the only possible rational roots are ± 1 and $\pm \frac{1}{2}$.

Step 2 Test each possible rational root until you find a root.

Test 1: $2x^3 - x^2 + 2x - 1 = 2(1)^3 - (1)^2 + 2(1) - 1$
$$= 2 \neq 0$$

Test $\frac{1}{2}$: $2x^3 - x^2 + 2x - 1 = 2\left(\frac{1}{2}\right)^3 - \left(\frac{1}{2}\right)^2 + 2\left(\frac{1}{2}\right) - 1$
$$= 0 \quad \textbf{So } \tfrac{1}{2} \textbf{ is a root.}$$

Step 3 Use synthetic division with the root you found in Step 2 to find the quotient.

$$
\begin{array}{r|rrrr}
\frac{1}{2} & 2 & -1 & 2 & -1 \\
& & 1 & 0 & 1 \\
\hline
& 2 & 0 & 2 & 0 \\
\end{array}
$$

$2x^2 \qquad\quad +2 \qquad$ Remainder

Step 4 Find the roots of $2x^2 + 2 = 0$.

$2x^2 + 2 = 0$

$2(x^2 + 1) = 0$ **Factor out the GCF, 2.**

$x^2 + 1 = 0$

$x^2 = -1$

$x = \pm i$

The roots of $2x^3 - x^2 + 2x - 1 = 0$ are $\frac{1}{2}, i,$ and $-i$.

 **② Find the roots of each equation.**

a. $x^3 - 2x^2 - 5x + 10 = 0$ **b.** $3x^3 + x^2 - x + 1 = 0$

---

2   Irrational Root Theorem and Imaginary Root Theorem

In Chapter 5 you learned to find irrational solutions to quadratic equations. For example, by the Quadratic Formula, the solutions of $x^2 - 4x - 1 = 0$ are $2 + \sqrt{5}$ and $2 - \sqrt{5}$. Number pairs of the form $a + \sqrt{b}$ and $a - \sqrt{b}$ are called **conjugates.**

You can often use conjugates to find the irrational roots of a polynomial equation.

 Key Concepts

Theorem	**Irrational Root Theorem**

Let a and b be rational numbers and let $\sqrt{b}$ be an irrational number. If $a + \sqrt{b}$ is a root of a polynomial equation with rational coefficients, then the conjugate $a - \sqrt{b}$ also is a root.

3 EXAMPLE   **Finding Irrational Roots**

A polynomial equation with integer coefficients has the roots $1 + \sqrt{3}$ and $-\sqrt{11}$. Find two additional roots.

By the Irrational Root Theorem, if $1 + \sqrt{3}$ is a root, then its conjugate $1 - \sqrt{3}$ is also a root. If $-\sqrt{11}$ is a root, then its conjugate $\sqrt{11}$ also is a root.

The additional roots are $1 - \sqrt{3}$ and $\sqrt{11}$.

 **③ a.** A polynomial equation with rational coefficients has the roots $2 - \sqrt{7}$ and $\sqrt{5}$. Find two additional roots.

b. Critical Thinking One of the roots of a polynomial equation is $4 - \sqrt{2}$. Can you be certain that $4 + \sqrt{2}$ also is a root of the equation? Explain.

Number pairs of the form $a + bi$ and $a - bi$ are **complex conjugates.** You can use complex conjugates to find an equation's imaginary roots.

 **Key Concepts**

Theorem	Imaginary Root Theorem

If the imaginary number $a + bi$ is a root of a polynomial equation with real coefficients, then the conjugate $a - bi$ also is a root.

4 EXAMPLE Finding Imaginary Roots

A polynomial equation with integer coefficients has the roots $3 - i$ and $2i$. Find two additional roots.

By the Imaginary Root Theorem, if $3 - i$ is a root, then its complex conjugate $3 + i$ also is a root. If $2i$ is a root, then its complex conjugate $-2i$ also is a root.

● The additional roots are $3 + i$ and $2i$.

✓ **Quick Check** ❹ **a.** If a polynomial equation with real coefficients has $3i$ and $-2 + i$ among its roots, then what two other roots must it have?
b. Critical Thinking Describe the degree of the equation.

You can often use the Irrational Root Theorem and the Imaginary Root Theorem to write a polynomial equation if you know some of its roots.

5 EXAMPLE Writing a Polynomial Equation from Its Roots

Find a third-degree polynomial equation with rational coefficients that has roots 3 and $1 + i$.

Step 1 Find the other root using the Imaginary Root Theorem.

Since $1 + i$ is a root, then its complex conjugate $1 - i$ also is a root.

Step 2 Write the factored form of the polynomial using the Factor Theorem.

$(x - 3)(x - (1 + i))(x - (1 - i))$

Step 3 Multiply the factors.

$(x - 3)[x^2 - x(1 - i) - x(1 + i) + (1 + i)(1 - i)]$ **Multiply $(x - (1 + i))$ $(x - (1 - i))$.**

$(x - 3)(x^2 - x + ix - x - ix + 1 - i^2)$ **Simplify.**

$(x - 3)(x^2 - x - x + 1 + 1)$

$(x - 3)(x^2 - 2x + 2)$ **Multiply.**

$x^3 - 5x^2 + 8x - 6$

A third-degree polynomial equation with rational coefficients and roots 3
● and $1 + i$ is $x^3 - 5x^2 + 8x - 6 = 0$.

✓ **Quick Check** ❺ **a.** Find a third-degree polynomial equation with rational coefficients that has roots -1 and $2 - i$.
b. Find a fourth-degree polynomial equation with rational coefficients that has roots i and $2i$.

EXERCISES

For more exercises, see *Extra Skill and Word Problem Practice*.

Practice and Problem Solving

 **Practice by Example**

Example 1
(page 336)

Use the Rational Root Theorem to list all possible rational roots for each polynomial equation. Then find any actual rational roots.

1. $x^3 - x^2 + 2x - 2 = 0$ **2.** $x^3 + 4x^2 + x - 6 = 0$

3. $x^3 + x^2 + 4x + 4 = 0$ **4.** $2x^3 - 9x^2 - 11x + 8 = 0$

5. $x^3 + 2x^2 - 8x - 16 = 0$ **6.** $x^4 + 2x^2 - 15 = 0$

Example 2
(pages 336–337)

Find the roots of each polynomial equation.

7. $x^3 - 2x^2 + 5x - 10 = 0$ **8.** $x^3 - 5x^2 + 7x - 35 = 0$

9. $2x^4 - 5x^3 - 17x^2 + 41x - 21 = 0$ **10.** $4x^3 + 16x^2 - 22x - 10 = 0$

11. $4x^4 - 37x^2 + 9 = 0$ **12.** $9x^4 + 3x^3 - 30x^2 + 6x + 12 = 0$

Examples 3 and 4
(pages 337 and 338)

A polynomial equation with rational coefficients has the given roots. Find two additional roots.

13. $\sqrt{5}$ and $-\sqrt{13}$ **14.** $4 - \sqrt{6}$ and $\sqrt{3}$ **15.** $1 - \sqrt{10}$ and $2 + \sqrt{2}$

16. $1 + i$ and $-5i$ **17.** $2 + 3i$ and $6i$ **18.** $4 - i$ and $3 + 7i$

Example 5
(page 338)

Find a third-degree polynomial equation with rational coefficients that has the given numbers as roots.

19. 1 and $3i$ **20.** -5 and $1 - i$ **21.** 2 and $-4i$

22. $3 + i$ and -3 **23.** $-2i$ and 6 **24.** -1 and $i + 1$

 **Apply Your Skills**

Use the Rational Root Theorem to list all possible rational roots for each polynomial equation. Then find any actual rational roots.

25. $12x^3 - 32x^2 + 25x - 6 = 0$ **26.** $10x^3 - 49x^2 + 68x - 20 = 0$

27. $6x^4 - 5x^3 - 65x^2 + 85x - 21 = 0$ **28.** $8x^3 - 28x^2 + 14x + 15 = 0$

Find a fourth-degree polynomial equation with integer coefficients that has the given numbers as roots.

29. $3 + i$ and $-2i$ **30.** $\sqrt{3}$ and $1 - i$ **31.** $3 + \sqrt{2}$ and $\sqrt{5}$

In each equation, *r*, *s*, and *t* represent integers. Indicate whether the statement is *sometimes*, *always*, or *never* true. Explain your answer.

32. A root of the equation $3x^3 + rx^2 + sx + 8 = 0$ is 5.

33. A root of the equation $3x^3 + rx^2 + sx + 8 = 0$ is -2.

34. If a is a root of $x^3 + rx^2 + sx + t = 0$, then a is a factor of t.

35. $\sqrt{5}$ and $-\sqrt{5}$ are roots of $x^3 + rx^2 + sx + t = 0$.

36. $2 + i$ and $-2 - i$ are roots of $x^3 + rx^2 + sx + t = 0$.

37. Multiple Choice A fourth-degree polynomial with integer coefficients has zeros at 1 and $3 + \sqrt{5}$. Which number CANNOT also be a zero of this polynomial?

Ⓐ 1 Ⓑ -3 Ⓒ $3 - \sqrt{5}$ Ⓓ $3 + \sqrt{2}$

GO Online
Homework Video Tutor
Visit: PHSchool.com
Web Code: age-0605

38. Error Analysis A student claims that $2i$ is the only imaginary root of a polynomial equation that has real coefficients. Explain the student's mistake.

39. Open-Ended Write a fourth-degree polynomial equation with integer coefficients that has two irrational roots and two imaginary roots.

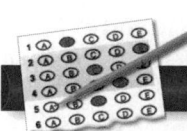 **Challenge**

40. a. Using *real* and *imaginary* as types of roots, list all possible combinations of root type for a fourth-degree polynomial equation.
  b. Repeat the process for a fifth-degree polynomial equation.
  c. Make a Conjecture Make a conjecture about the number of real roots of an odd-degree polynomial equation.

41. Writing A student states that $2 + \sqrt{3}$ is a root of $x^2 - 2x - (3 + 2\sqrt{3}) = 0$. The student claims that $2 - \sqrt{3}$ is another root of the equation by the Irrational Root Theorem. Explain how you would respond to the student.

42. What polynomial equation with complex coefficients and no multiple roots has $-4i$ and $2 + 3i$ as its only roots?

43. a. Find a polynomial equation in which $1 + \sqrt{2}$ is the only root.
  b. Find a polynomial equation with root $1 + \sqrt{2}$ of multiplicity 2.
  c. Find c such that $1 + \sqrt{2}$ is a solution of $x^2 - 2x + c = 0$.

Test Prep

Multiple Choice

44. Three roots of a polynomial equation with rational coefficients are $5 + \sqrt{3}$, -17, and $2 - \sqrt{4}$. Which number also is a root of the equation?
  A. 17   **B.** $2 + \sqrt{4}$ **C.** $4 - \sqrt{2}$ **D.** $5 - \sqrt{3}$

45. Two roots of a cubic polynomial equation with real coefficients are -3 and $-4i$. If the leading coefficient of the polynomial is 1, what is the equation?
  F. $x^3 - 3x^2 + 16x - 48 = 0$ **G.** $x^3 - 3x^2 - 16x + 48 = 0$
  H. $x^3 + 3x^2 + 16x + 48 = 0$ **J.** $x^3 + 3x^2 - 16x - 48 = 0$

Short Response

46. According to the Rational Root Theorem, what is the relationship between the polynomial equation $2x^4 - x^3 - 7x^2 + 3x + 3 = 0$ and rational roots of the form $\frac{p}{q}$, where $\frac{p}{q}$ is in simplest form?

Extended Response

47. A third-degree polynomial equation with rational coefficients has roots -4 and $-4i$. If the leading coefficient of the equation is $\frac{3}{2}$, what is the equation? Show your work.

Mixed Review

GO for Help

Lesson 6-4

Solve each equation.

48. $8x^3 + 27 = 0$ **49.** $x^4 - x^2 - 20 = 0$ **50.** $2x^4 - 50 = 0$

Lesson 5-7

Solve each equation by completing the square.

51. $x^2 - 6x - 7 = 0$ **52.** $p^2 + 4p = -8$ **53.** $4x^2 - 11 = 12x$

Lesson 4-8

Use Cramer's Rule to solve each system.

54. $\begin{cases} -3x + y = -7 \\ 5x + 2y = -3 \end{cases}$ **55.** $\begin{cases} x - 3y = -12 \\ 2x + 7y = 2 \end{cases}$ **56.** $\begin{cases} 2x - 8y = 10 \\ -3x + y = -15 \end{cases}$

The Fundamental Theorem of Algebra

What You'll Learn

- To use the Fundamental Theorem of Algebra in solving polynomial equations with complex roots

. . . And Why

To find all the zeros of a polynomial function, as in Example 2

GO for Help Lessons 5-8 and 6-1

Find the degree of each polynomial.

1. $3x^2 - x + 5$ **2.** $-x + 3 - x^3$ **3.** $-4x^5 + 1$

Solve each equation using the quadratic formula.

4. $x^2 + 16 = 0$ **5.** $x^2 - 2x + 3 = 0$ **6.** $2x^2 + 5x + 4 = 0$

🔊 **New Vocabulary**   • Fundamental Theorem of Algebra

---

1 The Fundamental Theorem of Algebra

Activity: Counting Zeros

In this activity you will find the solutions to polynomial equations, identify the types of solutions, and then count the number of solutions.

1. a. Find the solutions of $x^4 - 5x^2 + 4 = 0$.
    b. Identify each solution as *real* or *imaginary*.
    c. How many solutions are there?

2. a. Find the solutions of $x^4 + 7x^2 + 12 = 0$.
    b. Identify each solution as *real* or *imaginary*.
    c. How many solutions are there?

3. Make a conjecture about the number of zeros of a fourth-degree polynomial function, regardless of the types of zeros.

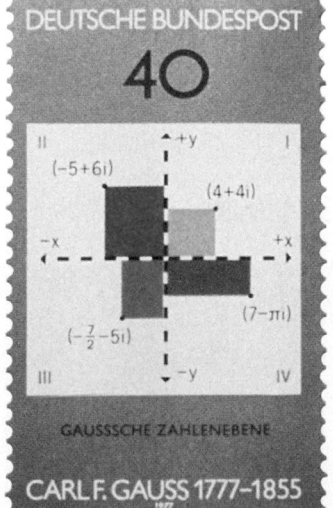

Real-World 🌐 Connection

Germany issued this stamp in honor of the bicentennial of the birth of Gauss.

You have solved polynomial equations and found that their roots are included in the set of complex numbers. That is, the roots have been integers, rational numbers, irrational numbers, and imaginary numbers. But can all polynomial equations be solved using complex numbers?

In 1799, the German mathematician Carl Friedrich Gauss (1777–1855) proved that the answer to this question is yes. The roots of every polynomial equation, even those with imaginary coefficients, are complex numbers. The answer is so important that his theorem is called the **Fundamental Theorem of Algebra.**

A corollary to the Fundamental Theorem of Algebra describes the relationship between the degree of a polynomial and the number of zeros of the related polynomial function.

Theorem   **Fundamental Theorem of Algebra**

If $P(x)$ is a polynomial of degree $n \geq 1$ with complex coefficients, then $P(x) = 0$ has at least one complex root.

Corollary

Including complex roots and multiple roots, an nth degree polynomial equation has exactly n roots; the related polynomial function has exactly n zeros.

Vocabulary Tip

A corollary of a theorem is itself a theorem. It may be easily and immediately deduced from the original theorem.

In other words, the corollary says that you can factor a polynomial of degree n into n linear factors. The number n includes multiple roots. For example, the equation $x^3 = 0$ should have three roots by the corollary to the Fundamental Theorem of Algebra. Since $x^3 = 0$ can be rewritten as $x \cdot x \cdot x = 0$ or $(x - 0)(x - 0)(x - 0) = 0$, the equation has three linear factors and three roots, all of which are zero.

1 EXAMPLE   Using the Fundamental Theorem of Algebra

For the equation $x^3 + 2x^2 - 4x - 6 = 0$, find the number of complex roots, the possible number of real roots, and the possible rational roots.

By the corollary to the Fundamental Theorem of Algebra, $x^3 + 2x^2 - 4x - 6 = 0$ has three complex roots.

By the Imaginary Root Theorem, the equation has either no imaginary roots or two imaginary roots (one conjugate pair). So the equation has either three real roots or one real root.

By the Rational Root Theorem, the possible rational roots of the equation are $\pm 1, \pm 2, \pm 3$, and ± 6.

✓ Quick Check **①** For the equation $x^4 - 3x^3 + x^2 - x + 3 = 0$, find the number of complex roots, the possible number of real roots, and the possible rational roots.

You can often find all the zeros of a polynomial function by using some combination of graphing, the Factor Theorem, polynomial division, the Remainder Theorem, and the Quadratic Formula.

2 EXAMPLE   Finding All Zeros of a Polynomial Function

Find the number of complex zeros of $f(x) = x^3 + x^2 - x + 2$. Find all the zeros.

By the corollary to the Fundamental Theorem of Algebra, there are three complex zeros. You can use synthetic division to find a rational zero.

Step 1 Find a rational root from the possible roots of ± 1 and ± 2. Use synthetic division to test each possible root until you get a remainder of zero.

$$
\begin{array}{r|rrrr}
-2 & 1 & 1 & -1 & 2 \\
   &   & -2 & 2 & -2 \\
\hline
   & 1 & -1 & 1 & 0 \\
   & \downarrow & \downarrow & \downarrow & \\
   & 1x^2 & -1x & +1 &
\end{array}
$$

So -2 is one of the roots.

Step 2 Since the expression $x^2 - x + 1$ cannot be factored, use the Quadratic Formula to solve the related quadratic equation $x^2 - x + 1 = 0$.

$$x = \frac{-b \pm \sqrt{b^2 - 4ac}}{2a}$$

$$x = \frac{-(-1) \pm \sqrt{(-1)^2 - 4(1)(1)}}{2(1)}$$

$$x = \frac{1 \pm \sqrt{-3}}{2}$$

$$x = \frac{1 \pm i\sqrt{3}}{2}$$

The polynomial function $f(x) = x^3 + x^2 - x + 2$ has one real zero of $x = -2$, and two complex zeros of $x = \frac{1 + i\sqrt{3}}{2}$ and $x = \frac{1 - i\sqrt{3}}{2}$.

✓ Quick Check **2** **a.** Find all zeros of $y = x^3 - 2x^2 + 4x - 8$.
b. Which zeros can you verify on a graphing calculator? Explain.

EXERCISES

For more exercises, see *Extra Skill and Word Problem Practice*.

Practice and Problem Solving

Ⓐ Practice by Example

Example 1
(page 342)

 **GO for Help**

For each equation, state the number of complex roots, the possible number of real roots, and the possible rational roots.

1. $x^3 + 4x^2 + 5x - 1 = 0$

2. $3x^2 - 7 = 0$

3. $-x^4 = 0$

4. $2x^5 - 4x^4 - 4x^2 + 5 = 0$

5. $x^7 - x^3 - 2x - 3 = 0$

6. $4x + 8 = 0$

7. $-2x^6 - x^2 + x - 7 = 0$

8. $x^{10} + x^8 - x^4 + 3x^2 - x + 1 = 0$

Example 2
(pages 342–343)

Find all the zeros of each function.

9. $y = 2x^3 + x^2 + 1$

10. $f(x) = x^3 - 3x^2 + x - 3$

11. $g(x) = x^3 - 5x^2 + 5x - 4$

12. $y = x^3 - 2x^2 - 3x + 6$

13. $y = x^4 - 6x^2 + 8$

14. $f(x) = x^4 - 3x^2 - 4$

15. $y = x^3 - 3x^2 - 9x$

16. $y = x^3 + 6x^2 + x + 6$

Ⓑ Apply Your Skills

For each equation, state the number of complex roots, the possible number of real roots, and the possible rational roots.

17. $2x^4 - x^3 + 2x^2 + 5x - 26 = 0$

18. $x^5 - x^3 - 11x^2 + 9x + 18 = 0$

19. $-12 + x + 10x^2 + 3x^3 = 0$

20. $4x^6 - x^5 - 24 = 0$

Find all the zeros of each function.

21. $y = x^3 - 4x^2 + 9x - 36$

22. $f(x) = x^3 + 2x^2 - 5x - 10$

23. $y = 2x^3 + 14x^2 + 13x + 6$

24. $y = 4x^3 + 9x^2 + 22x + 5$

25. $g(x) = x^3 - \frac{1}{2}x^2 + 20x - 10$

26. $y = 15x^3 - x^2 + 3x - 2$

GO ●nline
Homework Video Tutor
Visit: PHSchool.com
Web Code: age-0606

27. Open-Ended Write a polynomial function that has four possible rational zeros but no actual rational zeros.

Challenge **Graph each function. Approximate the real zeros to the nearest hundredth.**

28. $f(x) = x^4 + 3x^2 - 2$ **29.** $f(x) = x^4 + 2x^3 - 2x^2 + 4x - 8$

30. **Writing** Using the Rational Root Theorem, explain why the following statement is false: If a polynomial has no constant term, then the corresponding polynomial equation has only the number 0 as a possible rational root.

31. **Critical Thinking** Consider a polynomial with integer coefficients in which the leading coefficient is not equal to 1. Can the related polynomial equation have a rational root that is an integer? Explain.

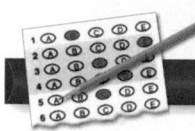

Test Prep

Multiple Choice   **32.** Which number is a root of $f(x) = x^3 + 6x^2 + 9x$ that has multiplicity 1?

     A. 3   **B.** 1   **C.** 0   **D.** −3

33. Three roots of a polynomial equation with real coefficients are 3, $5 - 3i$, and $-3i$. Which number MUST also be a root of the equation?

     I. −3   **II.** $5 + 3i$ **III.** $3i$

     F. II only   **G.** I and II only   **H.** II and III only   **J.** I, II, and III

34. One root of the equation $x^3 + x^2 - 2 = 0$ is 1. What are the other two roots?

     A. $1 \pm 2i$ **B.** $-1 \pm i$ **C.** $\pm 1 + 2i$ **D.** $\pm 1 - i$

35. A polynomial with real coefficients has 3, $2i$, and $-i$ as three of its zeros. What is the least possible degree of the polynomial?

     F. 3   **G.** 4   **H.** 5   **J.** 6

36. How many times does the graph of $x^3 + 27$ cross the x-axis?

     A. 0   **B.** 1   **C.** 2   **D.** 4

Short Response   **37.** Find all roots of the equation $x^4 = 256$. Show your work.

38. One root of the equation $x^4 - 4x^3 - 6x^2 + 4x + 5 = 0$ is −1.
     a. Find the number of complex roots.
     b. Find all the roots.

39. List the possible rational roots of the equation $x^4 - 2x^3 + 6x^2 - 2x + 5 = 0$. Do not solve the equation. Explain how you made your list.

Mixed Review

Lesson 6-5   **40.** Find a fourth-degree polynomial equation with integer coefficients that has $2i$ and $-3 + i$ as roots.

Lesson 5-8   **Solve each equation using the Quadratic Formula.**

     41. $x^2 - 6x + 9 = 0$ **42.** $2x^2 + 5x = -9$ **43.** $2(x^2 + 2) = 3x$

Lesson 5-1   **Find a quadratic model for each function.**

     44. $f(-1) = 0, f(2) = 3, f(1) = 4$ **45.** $f(-4) = 11, f(-5) = 5, f(-6) = 3$

Permutations and Combinations

✓ **Check Skills You'll Need**

GO for Help   Lesson 1-2

Simplify each expression.

1. $10 \cdot 9 \cdot 8 \cdot 7 \cdot 6$ **2.** $\frac{4 \cdot 3 \cdot 2}{6 \cdot 5}$ **3.** $\frac{7 \cdot 6 \cdot 5 \cdot 4 \cdot 3 \cdot 2 \cdot 1}{4 \cdot 3 \cdot 2 \cdot 1}$

Let $a * b = 2a(a + b)$. Evaluate each expression.

4. $3 * 4$ **5.** $2 * 7$ **6.** $5 * 1$ **7.** $6 * 10$

🔊 **New Vocabulary**   • permutation   • *n* factorial   • combination

---

1   Permutations

A **permutation** is an arrangement of items in a particular order. You can often find the number of permutations of some set of items by using the Multiplication Counting Principle.

You can use the Multiplication Counting Principle when you plan to choose all of the items of a particular set. Suppose you want to find the number of permutations for three items. There are three ways to choose the first item, two ways to choose the second item, and only one way to choose the third item. By the Multiplication Counting Principle, there are $3 \cdot 2 \cdot 1$ permutations.

Using factorial notation, you can write $3 \cdot 2 \cdot 1$ as 3!, read "three factorial."

 Key Concepts

Definition	*n* Factorial
For any positive integer $n, n! = n(n - 1) \cdot \ldots \cdot 3 \cdot 2 \cdot 1$. For $n = 0, n! = 1$.	

1 EXAMPLE Finding Permutations

Graphing Calculator Hint

To calculate factorials, press MATH and then choose the PRB menu and the ! option.

In how many different orders can ten dogs line up to be groomed?

Since all ten dogs are being groomed, you are using all the items from the original set. You can use the Multiplication Counting Principle or factorial notation.

There are ten ways to select the first dog in line, nine ways to select the next dog, and so on. The total number of permutations is $10 \cdot 9 \cdot \ldots \cdot 2 \cdot 1 = 10!$.

$10! = 3,628,800$

The ten dogs can line up in 3,628,800 different orders.

✓ **Quick Check** ❶ In how many ways can you arrange six trophies on a shelf?

Some permutations do not use all the items available in a set. You can still use the Multiplication Counting Principle or factorial notation. The relationship between permutations and factorials can be summarized with a formula.

Key Concepts

Definition	Number of Permutations

The number of permutations of n items of a set arranged r items at a time is $_nP_r$.

$$_nP_r = \frac{n!}{(n-r)!} \text{ for } 0 \le r \le n$$

Example $_{10}P_4 = \frac{10!}{(10-4)!} = \frac{10!}{6!} = 5040$

Real-World Connection

In how many ways can these boats finish first, second, and third?

2) EXAMPLE   Real-World Connection

Boating Seven yachts enter a race. First, second, and third places will be given to the three fastest yachts. How many arrangements of first, second, and third places are possible with seven yachts?

Method 1 Use the Multiplication Counting Principle.
$7 \cdot 6 \cdot 5 = 210$

Method 2 Use the permutation formula. Since there are seven yachts arranged three at a time, $n = 7$ and $r = 3$.

$$_7P_3 = \frac{7!}{(7-3)!} = \frac{7!}{4!} = 210$$

There are 210 possible arrangements of first, second, and third places.

✓ Quick Check **2** How many arrangements of first, second, and third places are possible with ten yachts?

2   Combinations

In Example 2, you found the number of ways in which three of seven yachts can finish first, second, and third in a race. Each yacht would have a unique place. Consider a situation in which the three fastest yachts win the race with equal status, that is, without first, second, and third places. In that case, the *order* in which the three winning yachts cross the finish line does not matter. A selection in which order does not matter is a **combination.**

As with permutations, you can calculate the number of combinations of n items chosen r at a time by using a formula.

Key Concepts

Definition	Number of Combinations

The number of combinations of n items of a set chosen r items at a time is $_nC_r$.

$$_nC_r = \frac{n!}{r!(n-r)!} \text{ for } 0 \le r \le n$$

Example $_5C_3 = \frac{5!}{3!(5-3)!} = \frac{5!}{3! \cdot 2!} = \frac{120}{6 \cdot 2} = 10$

3 EXAMPLE Finding Combinations

Evaluate $_{12}C_3$.

$$_{12}C_3 = \frac{12!}{3!(12-3)!}$$ Use the formula $_nC_r = \frac{n!}{r!(n-r)!}$.

$$= \frac{12!}{3! \cdot 9!}$$ Simplify.

$$= \frac{12 \cdot 11 \cdot 10 \cdot \cancel{9} \cdot \cancel{8} \cdot \cancel{7} \cdot \cancel{6} \cdot \cancel{5} \cdot \cancel{4} \cdot \cancel{3} \cdot \cancel{2} \cdot \cancel{1}}{3 \cdot 2 \cdot 1 \cdot \cancel{9} \cdot \cancel{8} \cdot \cancel{7} \cdot \cancel{6} \cdot \cancel{5} \cdot \cancel{4} \cdot \cancel{3} \cdot \cancel{2} \cdot \cancel{1}}$$ Simplify each factorial.

$$= \frac{12 \cdot 11 \cdot 10}{3 \cdot 2 \cdot 1}$$

$$= 220$$

 **3** Evaluate each expression.

    a. $_{10}C_5$ **b.** $_8C_2$ **c.** $_{25}C_7$

You can use a graphing calculator to find combinations.

4 EXAMPLE Real-World  Connection

Literature A reading list for a course in world literature has 20 books on it. In how many ways can you choose four books to read?

Relate   20 books   chosen   4 books at a time

Define   Let n = total number of books.

           Let r = number of books chosen at a time.

Write $_nC_r = {}_{20}C_4$

20 nCr 4

                        4845   Use the $_nC_r$ feature of your calculator.

You can choose four books in 4845 different ways.

 **4** Of the 20 books, in how many ways can you choose seven books? Twelve books?

5 EXAMPLE Real-World  Connection

Multiple Choice Ten candidates are running for three seats in the student government. You may vote for as many as three candidates. In how many ways can you vote for three or fewer candidates?

   Ⓐ 6   Ⓑ 120   Ⓒ 176   Ⓓ 216

You may vote for   3 people,   2 people,   1 person,   or none.

                      ↓   ↓   ↓   ↓

                 $_{10}C_3$ $_{10}C_2$ $_{10}C_1$ $_{10}C_0$

                  120   45   10   1

The total number of ways to vote is $120 + 45 + 10 + 1 = 176$.

There are 176 ways to cast your ballot. The correct choice is C.

The National Association of Student Councils has more than 18,000 member schools.

 **5** In how many ways can you vote for five or fewer people?

EXERCISES

For more exercises, see *Extra Skill and Word Problem Practice*.

Practice and Problem Solving

A **Practice by Example**

Example 1
(page 345)

GO for Help

Evaluate each expression.

1. $5!$ **2.** $10!$ **3.** $13!$ **4.** $5!3!$

5. $\frac{12!}{6!}$ **6.** $5(4!)$ **7.** $\frac{10!}{7!3!}$ **8.** $\frac{15!}{10!5!}$

9. Automobiles You should rotate tires on a car at regular intervals.
  a. In how many ways can four tires be arranged on a car?
  b. If the spare tire is included, how many arrangements are possible?

Example 2
(page 346)

Evaluate each expression.

10. $_8P_1$ **11.** $_8P_2$ **12.** $_8P_3$ **13.** $_8P_4$

14. $_3P_2$ **15.** $_5P_4$ **16.** $_9P_6$ **17.** $_5P_3$

18. Fifteen students ask to visit a college admissions counselor. Each visit includes one student. In how many ways can ten time slots be assigned?

19. How many different nine-player batting orders can be chosen from a baseball squad of 16?

20. The prom committee has four sites available for the banquet and three sites for the dance. How many arrangements are possible for the banquet and dance?

Examples 3 and 4
(page 347)

Evaluate each expression.

21. $_6C_2$ **22.** $_8C_5$ **23.** $_4C_4$ **24.** $_4C_3$

25. $_7C_3$ **26.** $3(_5C_4)$ **27.** $_6C_2 + _6C_3$ **28.** $\frac{_7C_4}{_9C_4}$

29. Sports How many different teams of 11 players can be chosen from a soccer squad of 16?

30. Suppose you find seven articles related to the topic of your research paper. In how many ways can you choose five articles to read?

Example 5
(page 347)

31. For a band camp, you can choose two or three roommates from a group of 25 friends. In how many ways can you choose?

32. A salad bar offers eight choices of toppings for lettuce. In how many ways can you choose four or five toppings?

B **Apply Your Skills**

Assume *a* and *b* are positive integers. Decide whether each statement is *true* or *false*. If it is true, explain why. If it is not true, give a counterexample.

33. $a! + b! = b! + a!$ **34.** $a!(b!c!) = (a!b!)c!$ **35.** $(a + b)! = a! + b!$

36. $(ab)! = a!b!$ **37.** $(a!)! = (a!)^2$ **38.** $(a!)^b = a^{(b!)}$

39. Multiple Choice A car door lock has a five-button keypad. Each button has two numerals. How many different five-button patterns are possible? You can use a button more than once.

| 1/2 | 3/4 | 5/6 | 7/8 | 9/0 |

The entry code 21914 uses the same button sequence as the code 11023.

Ⓐ 120   Ⓑ 720   Ⓒ 3125   Ⓓ 5555

Real-World 🌐 **Connection**

Careers Consumer researchers use formulas to compare and rate products.

40. Consumer Issues A consumer magazine rates televisions by identifying two levels of price, five levels of repair frequency, three levels of features, and two levels of picture quality. How many different ratings are possible?

41. Writing In how many ways is it possible to arrange the two numbers a and b in an ordered pair? Explain why such a pair is called an *ordered* pair.

Evaluate each expression.

42. $\dfrac{_{50}C_5}{_{50}C_{10}}$ **43.** $\dfrac{1}{3}(_{10}C_5)$ **44.** $\dfrac{_{25}C_2}{_{50}C_2}$ **45.** $\dfrac{_6C_2}{3}$

Indicate whether each situation involves a combination or a permutation.

46. 5 runners crossing the finish line   **47.** 12 books arranged on a shelf

48. 4 books pulled at random from a shelf

49. 3 flavors of juice selected from a variety pack

How many combinations of four can you make from each set?

50. 300 people in a club   **51.** {0, 1, 2, 3, 4, 5, 6, 7, 8, 9}

52. 25 baseball cards   **53.** a rose, a daisy, a peony, a daffodil, and a tulip

54. Each line in the [MODE] screen of a graphing calculator shows two or more choices. In how many different ways can you set the mode of this calculator?

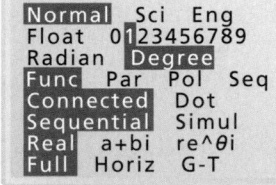

55. a. Geometry Eight points lie on a circle. How many triangles can you make using three of the points as vertices?
   b. How many pentagons can you make using five points as vertices?
   c. Reasoning Explain why your answers to parts (a) and (b) should be the same.

How many four-letter permutations can you form from the letters of each word?

56. MODEL   **57.** EQUATIONS   **58.** LINEAR   **59.** REAL

60. MATRICES   **61.** FORMULA   **62.** CONJUGATES   **63.** SUM

Open-Ended Write a problem that can be solved using each technique.

64. the Multiplication Counting Principle   **65.** a single factorial

66. the permutation formula   **67.** the combination formula

68. a. Refer to the cartoon below. How many different sets of answers are possible if the test includes eleven true-or-false questions?
   b. Do you agree with the statement in the last frame? Justify your answer.

69. a. The graph at the right shows the function $y = {}_xC_2$. Use it to graph the function $y = {}_xC_{x-2}$.
b. Critical Thinking Explain why the graph consists of discrete points rather than a continuous curve.

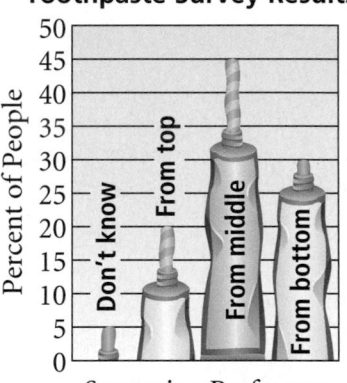

70. a. In how many ways can you choose three flags from a collection of seven different flags?
b. Once you choose three flags, in how many different orders can you arrange them?
✎ **c. Writing** You want to arrange three flags from a group of seven. Explain how you can use ${}_7C_3 \cdot 3!$ to create the permutation formula.

 71. In the sequence $1!, 2!, 3!, 4!, 5!, 6!, \ldots$, the first term that ends with a zero is $5!$.
a. Explain why $5!$ and all the terms following $5!$ end with a zero.
b. Find the number of zeros with which $100!$ ends.

72. Find a number n for which entering $n!$ in your calculator causes overflow error.

 73. Data Analysis The bar graph at the right shows the results of 40 responses to a survey.
a. How many people said they squeeze the toothpaste from the middle of the tube?
b. Use your answer to part (a). Find the number of possible combinations of five people who said they squeeze the toothpaste from the middle of the tube.
c. Suppose five people are chosen at random from all the people who responded to the survey. How many combinations of five people are possible?
d. Probability What is the probability that the five people selected at random all squeeze toothpaste from the middle of the tube?

Toothpaste Survey Results

(bar graph: Percent of People vs. Squeezing Preference, categories: Don't know, From top, From middle, From bottom)

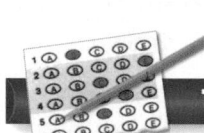

Test Prep

Gridded Response

74. Find the value of $7!$.

75. What is the value of $\frac{6!}{8!}$? Give your answer as a fraction in simplest terms.

76. What is the value of ${}_7C_2$?

77. Find the value of $(3 + 2)! - (4 - 2)!$.

78. How many ways are there to select 25 books from a collection of 27 books?

79. What is the value of the sum $\frac{2!}{3!} + \frac{3!}{4!} + \frac{4!}{5!}$? Express your answer to three decimal places.

80. A box has 10 items, and you select 3 of them. What is the value of $P - C$, if P represents the number of permutations possible when selecting 3 of the items, and C is the number of combinations possible when selecting 3 of the items?

for Help

Lesson 6-6

81. For the equation $12x^3 - 17x^2 + 3x + 2 = 0$, find the number of complex roots, the possible number of real roots, and the possible rational roots.

82. Find all the zeros of the function $f(x) = x^3 - 2x^2 + 6x - 12$.

Lesson 6-1

Write each polynomial in standard form. Then classify it by degree and by number of terms.

83. $-3x^2 + 6 - x^3$ **84.** $2(x - 1)^2 + 6$ **85.** $t^2 - 3t + 4t^2$

86. $-100 + x^4$ **87.** $x(x + 2)(x - 2)$ **88.** $(t^2 - t)^2$

Lesson 5-4

Factor each expression completely.

89. $4x^2 - 8x + 4$ **90.** $-x^2 - 6x - 9$ **91.** $3x^2 - 75$

Lesson 5-2

Determine whether the function has a maximum or minimum value. Then find the value.

92. $y = x^2 + 4x - 8$ **93.** $y = -2x^2 + 5x + 1$ **94.** $y = 4x^2 - 7$

 **Checkpoint Quiz 2**   **Lessons 6-4 through 6-7**

Solve each equation.

1. $x^3 - 2x^2 = 5x - 6$ **2.** $27x^3 - 1 = 0$ **3.** $x^4 - 4x^2 - 45 = 0$

Use the Rational Root Theorem to find all the roots of each equation.

4. $2x^3 + x^2 + x - 1 = 0$ **5.** $3x^3 + 4x^2 - 12x - 16 = 0$

6. Two roots of a polynomial equation with real coefficients are $3 - 5i$ and $\sqrt{2}$.
    a. Find two additional roots.
    b. Describe the degree of the polynomial.

7. How many roots does a fifth-degree polynomial equation have? Explain.

8. Evaluate each expression.
    a. $_4P_3 + {}_6P_5$ **b.** $_4C_3 + {}_6C_5$

 9. Food Preparation The students at a culinary arts school are learning to prepare seven different items. In how many ways can you choose each number of items?
    a. two items   **b.** three items   **c.** four items   **d.** five items

10. Advertising Use the ad and the telephone keypad shown below. Find the last seven digits of this phone number. How many seven-number arrangements can be made with these digits?

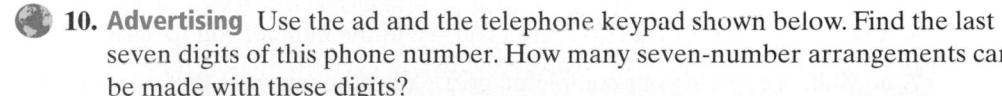

Call ☎ 1-DIAL VSW for information on Video Sales Worldwide.

Pascal's Triangle

Suppose you are standing at the corner of the grid shown below (point A1). You are allowed to travel down or to the right only.

The only way you can get to point A2 is by traveling down one unit. You can get to point B1 by traveling to the right one unit. The numbers of ways you can get to points A2, B1, and B2 are written next to these points.

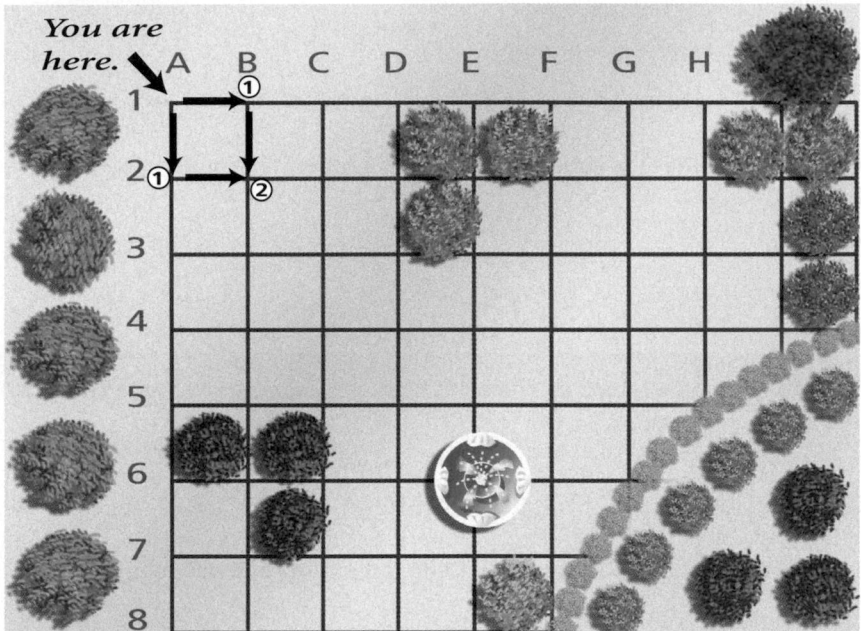

1. The number 2 is written next to point B2. What are the two different ways you can get from point A1 to point B2?

2. Copy the grid. Travel only down or to the right. In how many ways can you get from point A1 to point A3?

3. Use your copy of the grid from Exercise 2. In how many ways can you get from point A1 to point C2?

4. In how many ways can you get to the fountain at point E6 from your starting point at A1?

5. Mark the number of ways you can get to each point from point A1.

6. **Reasoning** Describe any patterns you see in the numbers on the grid.

7. **a.** Make a copy of your completed grid. Color the numbers that are multiples of 2. (You may need to extend the grid to see a pattern.)
   b. The pattern you see in part (a) is called the Sierpinski triangle. Find another way to describe how to obtain this pattern.

8. **Writing** The completed grid is called Pascal's Triangle. Rotate your copy of the grid 45° clockwise so that point A1 is at the top. Explain why the grid is called a triangle.

The Binomial Theorem

What You'll Learn

- To use Pascal's Triangle
- To use the Binomial Theorem

... And Why

To find probabilities associated with basketball, as in Example 4

✓ **Check Skills You'll Need**

GO for Help Lessons 5-1 and 6-7

Multiply.

1. $(x + 2)^2$ **2.** $(2x + 3)^2$ **3.** $(x - 3)^3$ **4.** $(a + b)^4$

Evaluate.

5. $_5C_0$ **6.** $_5C_1$ **7.** $_5C_2$ **8.** $_5C_3$ **9.** $_5C_4$

🔊 **New Vocabulary** • expand • Pascal's Triangle • Binomial Theorem

1   Binomial Expansion and Pascal's Triangle

You have learned to multiply binomials using the FOIL method and the Distributive Property. If you are raising a *single* binomial to a power, you have another option for finding the product.

Consider the expansion of several binomials. To **expand** a binomial being raised to a power, first multiply; then write the result as a polynomial in standard form.

$$(a + b)^2 = (a + b)(a + b) = a^2 + 2ab + b^2$$

$$(a + b)^3 = (a + b)(a + b)(a + b) = a^3 + 3a^2b + 3ab^2 + b^3$$

In the first case, the coefficients of the product are $1, 2, 1$. In the second case, they are $1, 3, 3, 1$. Notice that each set of coefficients matches a row of **Pascal's Triangle** below. Pascal's Triangle is a triangular array of numbers formed by first lining the border with 1's, and then placing the sum of two adjacent numbers within a row between and underneath the two original numbers.

Coefficients of an Expansion (Pascal's Triangle)

$$
\begin{array}{lcccccccc}
(a + b)^0 & & & & & 1 & & & \\
(a + b)^1 & & & & 1 & & 1 & & \\
(a + b)^2 & & & 1 & & 2 & & 1 & \\
(a + b)^3 & & 1 & & 3 & & 3 & & 1 \\
(a + b)^4 & 1 & & 4 & & 6 & & 4 & & 1 \\
(a + b)^5 & 1 & 5 & & 10 & & 10 & & 5 & & 1
\end{array}
$$

The earliest known version of Pascal's Triangle was developed between 300 and 200 B.C. by the Indian mathematician Halayudha. Although other cultures were aware of the triangle, it has been named for Blaise Pascal (1623−1662), a French mathematician.

Each row of Pascal's Triangle contains coefficients for the expansion of $(a + b)^n$. For example, when $n = 6$, you can find the coefficients for the expansion of $(a + b)^6$ in the row that begins $1, 6, 15, \ldots$

Real-World 🌐 **Connection**

In addition to his famous triangle, Pascal made many contributions to math, physics, and philosophy. In 1642 he built the first mechanical digital calculating machine.

1 EXAMPLE Using Pascal's Triangle

Use Pascal's Triangle to expand $(a + b)^6$.

Use the row that has 6 as its second number.

Pascal's Triangle

```
          1
        1   1
      1   2   1
    1   3   3   1
  1   4   6   4   1
 1  5  10  10  5  1
1  6  15 20 15  6  1
1 7 21 35 35 21 7 1
1 8 28 56 70 56 28 8 1
```

The exponents for a begin with 6 and decrease to 0.

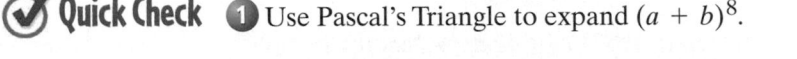

$$1a^6b^0 + 6a^5b^1 + 15a^4b^2 + 20a^3b^3 + 15a^2b^4 + 6a^1b^5 + 1a^0b^6$$

The exponents for b begin with 0 and increase to 6.

In simplest form, the expansion is
$$a^6 + 6a^5b + 15a^4b^2 + 20a^3b^3 + 15a^2b^4 + 6ab^5 + b^6.$$

✔ **Quick Check** ❶ Use Pascal's Triangle to expand $(a + b)^8$.

Sometimes the terms of the binomial have coefficients other than 1. You can still base the expansion to standard form on the pattern for $(a + b)^n$.

2 EXAMPLE Expanding a Binomial

Use Pascal's Triangle to expand $(x - 2)^3$.

First write the pattern for raising a binomial to the third power.

$$\begin{array}{cccc} 1 & 3 & 3 & 1 \\ \downarrow & \downarrow & \downarrow & \downarrow \end{array} \quad \text{coefficients from Pascal's Triangle}$$

$$(a + b)^3 = a^3 + 3a^2b + 3ab^2 + b^3$$

Since $(x - 2)^3 = (x + (-2))^3$, substitute x for a and -2 for b.

$$(x + (-2))^3 = x^3 + 3x^2(-2) + 3x(-2)^2 + (-2)^3$$
$$= x^3 - 6x^2 + 12x - 8$$

The expansion of $(x - 2)^3$ is $x^3 - 6x^2 + 12x - 8$.

✔ **Quick Check** ❷ Use Pascal's Triangle to expand $(x - 2)^4$.

2 The Binomial Theorem

You can also use combinations to help find the terms of a binomial expansion. For example, if you evaluate the combinations $_4C_0, {}_4C_1, {}_4C_2, {}_4C_3,$ and $_4C_4$, you can see a pattern. The results, 1, 4, 6, 4, and 1 match the row of Pascal's Triangle that you would use to expand $(a + b)^4$. You can use the **Binomial Theorem** as a general formula for expanding a binomial.

🔑 **Key Concepts**

Theorem	Binomial Theorem

For every positive integer n, $(a + b)^n =$
$$_nC_0a^n + {}_nC_1a^{n-1}b + {}_nC_2a^{n-2}b^2 + \ldots + {}_nC_{n-1}ab^{n-1} + {}_nC_nb^n$$

Notice that the sequence of exponents decreases for a while it increases for b.

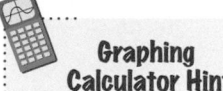

3 EXAMPLE Using the Binomial Theorem

Use the Binomial Theorem to expand $(g + h)^4$.

Write the pattern for raising a binomial to the fourth power.

$$(a + b)^4 = {}_4C_0a^4 + {}_4C_1a^3b + {}_4C_2a^2b^2 + {}_4C_3ab^3 + {}_4C_4b^4$$

Substitute g for a and h for b. Evaluate each combination.

$$(g + h)^4 = {}_4C_0g^4 + {}_4C_1g^3h + {}_4C_2g^2h^2 + {}_4C_3gh^3 + {}_4C_4h^4$$
$$= g^4 + 4g^3h + 6g^2h^2 + 4gh^3 + h^4$$

● The expansion of $(g + h)^4$ is $g^4 + 4g^3h + 6g^2h^2 + 4gh^3 + h^4$.

 **Quick Check** ③ Use the Binomial Theorem to expand each binomial.
a. $(v + w)^9$ **b.** $(c - 2)^5$

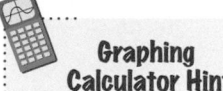

Graphing Calculator Hint

To evaluate a combination, use the MATH feature, the PRB menu, and the ${}_nC_r$ option.

You can use the Binomial Theorem to solve probability problems. Suppose an event has a probability of success p and a probability of failure q. Each term in the expansion of $(p + q)^n$ represents a probability. For example, ${}_{10}C_2\,p^8q^2$ represents the probability of exactly eight successes in ten trials.

4 EXAMPLE Real-World Connection

Sports Refer to the photo. Assume that Dawn's probability of success on any single shot is the same as her cumulative record to date. Find the probability that she will make exactly 6 out of 10 consecutive free throws.

Since you want 6 successes (and 4 failures), use the term containing p^6q^4. This term has the coefficient ${}_{10}C_4$.

$$
\begin{aligned}
\text{Probability (6 out of 10)} &= {}_{10}C_4\,p^6q^4 \\
&= \frac{10!}{4!\cdot 6!} \cdot (0.9)^6(0.1)^4 \qquad \text{The probability } p \text{ of success} = 90\%, \text{ or } 0.9.\\
&= 0.011160261 \qquad \text{Simplify.}
\end{aligned}
$$

Dawn Staley has about a 1% chance of making exactly 6 out of 10 consecutive free throws.

Real-World Connection

WNBA star Dawn Staley makes about 90% of the free throws she attempts.

 **Quick Check** ④ **a.** Find the probability that Dawn Staley will make exactly 9 out of 10 consecutive free throw attempts.
b. Find the probability that she will make exactly 10 out of 10 attempts.

EXERCISES
For more exercises, see *Extra Skill and Word Problem Practice*.

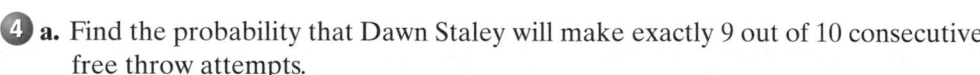

Practice and Problem Solving

 Practice by Example

Examples 1 and 2
(page 354)

 **for Help**

Use Pascal's Triangle to expand each binomial.

1. $(a + b)^3$ **2.** $(x - y)^2$ **3.** $(a + b)^4$

4. $(x - y)^5$ **5.** $(a - b)^6$ **6.** $(x - y)^7$

7. $(x + y)^8$ **8.** $(d + 1)^9$ **9.** $(x - 3)^3$

10. $(a + 3b)^4$ **11.** $(x - 2)^6$ **12.** $(x - 4)^8$

Example 3
(page 355)

Use the Binomial Theorem to expand each binomial.

13. $(x + y)^4$ **14.** $(w + 1)^5$ **15.** $(s - t)^2$ **16.** $(x - 1)^6$

17. $(x - y)^4$ **18.** $(p + q)^7$ **19.** $(x - 3)^5$ **20.** $(4 - x)^3$

Example 4
(page 355)

21. Probability A coin is tossed ten times. The probability of heads on each toss is 0.5. Evaluate each probability.
   a. exactly 5 heads **b.** exactly 6 heads **c.** exactly 7 heads

22. A calculator contains four batteries. With normal use, each battery has a 90% chance of lasting for one year. Find the probability that all four batteries will last a year.

B **Apply Your Skills**

Expand each binomial.

23. $(x + y)^7$ **24.** $(x - 5y)^8$ **25.** $(3x - y)^4$ **26.** $(x - 4y)^5$

27. $(7 - 2x)^6$ **28.** $(2x + 3y)^3$ **29.** $(x^2 + y^2)^2$ **30.** $(x^2 - 2y)^3$

31. $(x + 1)^6$ **32.** $(x - 1)^6$ **33.** $(x + 2)^5$ **34.** $(x - 2)^5$

35. $(2x + 3y)^4$ **36.** $(3x + 5y)^3$ **37.** $(2x - 2y)^6$ **38.** $(3x + 2y)^4$

39. $(2x + y)^5$ **40.** $(3x + y)^7$ **41.** $(x - 3y)^6$ **42.** $(x + 5y)^3$

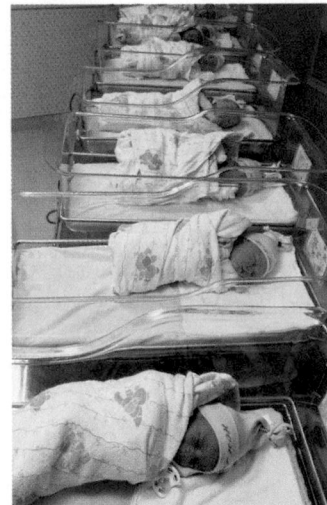

43. Genetics A family has five children. Assume that the probability of having a boy is 0.5. Write the term in the expansion of $(b + g)^5$ for each outcome described. Then evaluate each probability.
   a. exactly 3 boys **b.** exactly 4 boys **c.** exactly 4 girls

44. In the expansion of $(m + n)^9$, one of the terms contains m^3.
   a. What is the exponent of n in this term?
   b. What is the coefficient of this term?

45. Suppose $_8C_3 x^5 y^3$ is a term of a binomial expansion. Write the next term.

46. The term $126c^4 d^5$ appears in the expansion of $(c + d)^n$. Find n.

47. The coefficient of the second term in the expansion of $(r + s)^n$ is 7. Find the value of n, and write the complete term.

Find the specified term of each binomial expansion.

48. Third term of $(x + 3)^{12}$ **49.** Fourth term of $(x + 2)^5$

50. Second term of $(x + 3)^9$ **51.** Third term of $(x - 2)^{12}$

52. Twelfth term of $(2 + x)^{11}$ **53.** Seventh term of $(x - 2y)^6$

54. Eighth term of $(x - 2y)^{15}$ **55.** Third term of $(3x - 2)^9$

56. Seventh term of $(x^2 - 2y)^{11}$ **57.** Eighth term of $(x^2 + y^2)^{13}$

58. Writing Explain why the terms of $(a - 4)^6$ have alternating positive and negative signs.

 59. Geometry A cube has sides of length s. Suppose each of the dimensions of the cube is increased by 0.5.
   a. Write a binomial expression for the volume of the new cube.
   b. Expand the binomial.

60. Error Analysis A student claims that $_7C_5 p^2 q^4$ is a term in a binomial expansion. Explain the student's error.

Real-World **Connection**

Worldwide, about 51.4% of babies born are male.

GO Online
Homework Video Tutor
Visit: PHSchool.com
Web Code: age-0608

State the number of terms in each expansion and give the first two terms.

61. $(d + e)^{12}$ **62.** $(x - y)^{15}$ **63.** $(2a + b)^5$ **64.** $(x - 3y)^7$

C **Challenge**

65. a. Expand $(1 + i)^4$.
   b. Verify that $1 - i$ is a fourth root of -4 by repeating the process in part (a) for $(1 - i)^4$.

66. Verify that $-1 + \sqrt{3}i$ is a cube root of 8 by expanding $(-1 + \sqrt{3}i\,)^3$.

67. Open-Ended Write a probability problem for which $_5C_3(0.5)^2(0.5)^3$ is the solution.

68. a. Show that $(k + 1)! = (k + 1) \cdot k!$.
   b. Show that $_nC_k + {}_nC_{k + 1} = {}_{n + 1}C_{k + 1}$.
   c. Suppose $n = 4$ and $k = 2$. What entries in Pascal's Triangle are represented by $_nC_k, {}_nC_{k + 1}$, and $_{n + 1}C_{k + 1}$? Verify that the equation in part (b) is true for these entries.

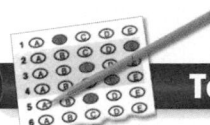

Test Prep

Multiple Choice

69. What is the expanded form of $(a - b)^3$?
   A. $a^3 + a^2b + ab^2 + b^3$ **B.** $a^3 + 3a^2b + 3ab^2 + b^3$
   C. $a^3 - a^2b + ab^2 - b^3$ **D.** $a^3 - 3a^2b + 3ab^2 - b^3$

70. What is the third term in the expansion of $(a - b)^7$?
   F. $-21a^5b^2$ **G.** $-7a^6b$ **H.** $7a^6b$ **J.** $21a^5b^2$

71. What is the coefficient of the third term in the expansion of $(2a - b)^5$?
   A. -80 **B.** 32 **C.** 40 **D.** 80

72. Which term in the expansion of $(2a - 3b)^6$ has coefficient 2160?
   F. second term **G.** third term
   H. fourth term **J.** fifth term

Short Response

73. One term of a binomial expansion is $_7C_2x^5y^2$. What is the term just before that term?

Extended Response

74. Explain how you can use the Binomial Theorem to find the sixth term in the expansion of $(2x - 3y)^7$.

Mixed Review

Lesson 6-7

for Help

Simplify each expression.

75. $_5P_2$ **76.** $4!$ **77.** $_7C_3$

78. $11!$ **79.** $\dfrac{7!}{3!(7 - 3)!}$ **80.** $_5C_2 + {}_5C_3$

Lesson 6-2

Find the relative maximum, relative minimum, and zeros of each function.

81. $f(x) = x^3 - 2x^2 - 11x + 12$ **82.** $f(x) = -x^3 - x^2 + 25x + 25$

Lesson 5-3

Write each function in vertex form.

83. $y = x^2 - 6x + 2$ **84.** $y = x^2 + 7x - 1$ **85.** $y = -4x^2 + 9$

Drawing a Diagram

A picture or a graph can help you solve a problem. If a test problem does not already have a diagram, you can draw one.

1 EXAMPLE

How many real and how many imaginary solutions does the equation $x^5 = x + 1$ have?

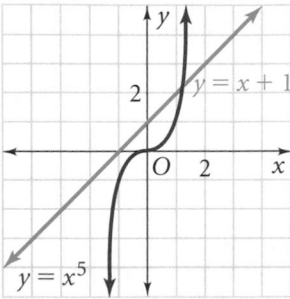

The question asks for the number of solutions, not the solutions themselves. Graph $y_1 = x^5$ and $y_2 = x + 1$. There is just one point of intersection. So the equation has just one real solution. Since the related function $y = x^5 - x - 1$ is a fifth-degree function with five zeros, the other four solutions must be imaginary.

● The equation $x^5 = x + 1$ has one real and four imaginary solutions.

2 EXAMPLE

In how many ways can a president, vice-president, and treasurer be selected from 5 people?

Method 1 Assign titles to people. Draw 5 spaces to represent the 5 people. Assign president (P) to the first person. Then you can assign vice-president (V) to any of the remaining 4, and treasurer (T) to any of the remaining 3. There are $4 \cdot 3$, or 12, ways to assign the titles V and T, if the first person is president. Since P can be assigned to 5 people, there are $5 \cdot 12$ ways to assign the titles.

$$P(\_ \ \_ \ \_ \ \_)$$
$$P \ V(\_ \ \_ \ \_)$$
$$P \ V \ T \ \_ \ \_$$

The answer is 60 ways.

Method 2 Assign people to titles. Draw 3 spaces to represent the 3 titles. Five people can be assigned to the first title, 4 to the second title, and 3 to the third title. There are $5 \cdot 4 \cdot 3$ ways to assign people to titles.

$$\underline{5} \ \_ \ \_$$
$$\underline{5} \ \underline{4} \ \_$$
$$\underline{5} \ \underline{4} \ \underline{3}$$

● Again, the answer is 60 ways.

EXERCISES

Find the number of real solutions.

1. $x + 3 = (x - 5)^2$ **2.** $x^4 = x - 10$ **3.** $x^3 = 5 - x$

4. In how many ways can two cars be assigned to two of six people, if no car can be assigned to more than one person, and no person can be assigned to more than one car?

5. Is it easier to draw a diagram that assigns 3 jobs to 3 of 100 people, or to draw a diagram that assigns 100 people to 3 jobs? Explain.

Chapter Review

Vocabulary Review

Binomial Theorem (p. 354)
combination (p. 346)
complex conjugates (p. 338)
conjugates (p. 337)
degree (p. 307)
degree of a polynomial (p. 307)
difference of cubes (p. 328)
expand (p. 353)
Factor Theorem (p. 315)

Fundamental Theorem of Algebra (p. 341)
Imaginary Root Theorem (p. 338)
Irrational Root Theorem (p. 337)
multiple zero (p. 316)
multiplicity (p. 316)
n factorial (p. 345)
Pascal's Triangle (p. 353)
permutation (p. 345)
polynomial (p. 307)

polynomial function (p. 307)
Rational Root Theorem (p. 335)
relative maximum (p. 315)
relative minimum (p. 315)
Remainder Theorem (p. 323)
standard form of a polynomial (p. 307)
sum of cubes (p. 328)
synthetic division (p. 321)

Choose the correct vocabulary word or phrase to complete each sentence.

1. The exponent of the variable in a term determines its   ? .

2. The   ?   has terms written in descending order by degree.

3. The number of appearances of a zero of a polynomial function describes the   ?   of that zero.

4. The numbers $a + bi$ and $a - bi$ are called   ? .

5. Order is not important when counting   ? .

Go Online
PHSchool.com

For: Vocabulary quiz
Web Code: agj-0651

Skills and Concepts

6-1 Objectives

▼ To classify polynomials (p. 306)

▼ To model data using polynomial functions (p. 308)

A **polynomial** is a monomial or a sum of monomials with whole-number exponents. The exponent of the variable in a term is the **degree** of that term. The **degree of a polynomial** is the largest degree of any term of the polynomial. When the terms of a polynomial are in descending order by degree, the polynomial is in standard form. You can classify a polynomial by the number of terms it contains or by its degree. A **polynomial function** in one variable can be written in the form $P(x) = a_n x^n + a_{n-1} x^{n-1} + \ldots + a_1 x + a_0$, where $n \geq 0$ and the coefficients $a_n, \ldots, a_0$ are complex numbers.

You can use a calculator to find cubic or quartic polynomial functions to model data, just as you have done with linear and quadratic polynomial functions.

Write each polynomial in standard form. Then classify it by degree and by number of terms.

6. $p^3 - 2p + 2p^3$ **7.** $3 - 5x^9$ **8.** $x - x^3 - x^5$

9. $3x + 2x^2 - x + 4x^3$ **10.** $5 + x + x^4 - x^2 + x^7$ **11.** s

12. Find both a cubic and a quartic model for the set of values. Graph each model. Compare the two models to determine which is a better fit.

x	1.2	1.4	1.6	1.8	2.0	2.2
y	3.1	−4.2	4.1	7.5	−8.9	10

Chapter 6   Chapter Review   **359**

6-2 and 6-3 Objectives

▼ To analyze the factored form of a polynomial (p. 313)

▼ To write a polynomial function from its zeros (p. 315)

▼ To divide polynomials using long division (p. 320)

▼ To divide polynomials using synthetic division (p. 321)

A polynomial can be factored into linear factors. The **Factor Theorem** states that the expression $x - a$ is a linear factor of a polynomial if and only if a is a zero of the related polynomial function. Then a is an x-intercept of the polynomial function and is a solution of the related polynomial equation.

If the zeros of a polynomial function are known, a polynomial function can be determined by finding the product of the corresponding linear factors. If $x - a$ is repeated as a factor k times, then a is a **multiple zero** of the polynomial—a zero of **multiplicity** k.

When you consider only neighboring points on a graph, the greatest y-value occurs at a **relative maximum** and the least y-value occurs at a **relative minimum.**

You can divide a polynomial by one of its factors to find another factor. When you divide by a linear factor, you can simplify this division by writing only the coefficients of each term. This process is called **synthetic division**. The **Remainder Theorem** guarantees that $P(a)$ is the remainder when $P(x)$ is divided by $x - a$.

Write each polynomial function in factored form. List the zeros of the function, and their multiplicity. Find any relative maximum or relative minimum values. Round to the nearest hundredth if necessary.

13. $f(x) = x^3 - x^2 - 12x$ **14.** $g(x) = 4 - x^2$ **15.** $y = x^3(x + 2)^4$

Write a polynomial function in standard form with the given zeros.

16. $-3, -2, 0, 2$ **17.** $1, 1, 2$ **18.** $-3, 0, 0, 1$ **19.** $-2, -2, -2$

Divide. Use both long division and synthetic division. Show your work.

20. $(x^3 + 3x^2 - 2x - 4) \div (x - 2)$ **21.** $(x^4 - x + 2) \div (x + 1)$

Use synthetic division and the given factor to completely factor each polynomial.

22. $x^3 - 3x^2 - x + 3; x + 1$ **23.** $x^3 - 4x^2 - 3x + 18; x - 3$

Use synthetic division and the Remainder Theorem to find $P(a)$.

24. $P(x) = x^4 + x^3 - x^2 - 2x; a = 3$ **25.** $P(x) = 4 - x - x^5; a = 2$

26. $P(x) = 5x^4 - x^2 + 1; a = -2$ **27.** $P(x) = x^3 - 8x^2 + 5x - 7; a = 1$

6-4 Objectives

▼ To solve polynomial equations by graphing (p. 327)

▼ To solve polynomial equations by factoring (p. 328)

You can solve polynomial equations by graphing or by factoring. The **sum of cubes** and the **difference of cubes** have factor formulas. Sometimes you can factor polynomial expressions of higher degree by rewriting the expression in the standard form of a quadratic equation.

Solve each equation by graphing. If necessary, round to the nearest hundredth.

28. $x^3 - 4x^2 + 5 = 0$ **29.** $x - 3 = 4 - x^2 + x^3$ **30.** $x^3 + x = 3x^2 - 3x^3$

31. $x^3 + x + 5 = 0$ **32.** $-5 = 2 - x^2 + x^3$ **33.** $x^3 + 4 = x^3 - 3x^2$

Factor the expression on the left side of each equation. Then solve each equation.

34. $x^3 - 8 = 0$ **35.** $4t^6 - t^4 = 0$ **36.** $8x^3 + 1 = 0$

37. $x^3 - 5x^2 + 4x = 0$ **38.** $x^3 - 2x^2 - 5x = 0$ **39.** $x^6 + 16x^3 + 64 = 0$

6-5 and 6-6 Objectives

▼ To solve equations using the Rational Root Theorem (p. 335)

▼ To use the Irrational Root Theorem and the Imaginary Root Theorem (p. 337)

▼ To use the Fundamental Theorem of Algebra (p. 341)

▼ To solve polynomial equations with complex zeros (p. 342)

The **Rational Root Theorem** identifies all possible rational roots of a polynomial equation with integer coefficients. A rational root of a polynomial equation is the quotient of a factor of the constant term and a factor of the leading coefficient.

Number pairs of the form $a + \sqrt{b}$ and $a - \sqrt{b}$ are called **conjugates,** while those of the form $a + bi$ and $a - bi$ are called **complex conjugates**. The **Irrational Root Theorem** states that irrational roots of a polynomial equation with rational coefficients occur in conjugate pairs. Similarly, the **Imaginary Root Theorem** states that imaginary roots of a polynomial equation with real coefficients occur in complex conjugate pairs.

The **Fundamental Theorem of Algebra** and its corollary assert that an nth degree polynomial equation, where $n \geq 1$, has exactly n complex roots.

For each equation, state the number of complex roots, the possible number of real roots, and the possible rational roots. Then find all the roots.

40. $x^3 - 6x^2 + 11x - 6 = 0$ **41.** $10x^4 - 13x^3 - 21x^2 + 10x + 8 = 0$

42. $x^4 - 6x^2 + 7 = 0$ **43.** $x^4 + 6x^3 + 13x^2 + 12x + 4 = 0$

44. $x^3 - 3x^2 + x + 5 = 0$ **45.** $x^4 - 2x^3 - 7x^2 + 18x - 18 = 0$

Write a polynomial equation of least possible degree, with integer coefficients, that has the given numbers as roots.

46. $2, i, -i$ **47.** $4 + \sqrt{2}, 4 - \sqrt{3}$ **48.** $3 + i, 2 - i$

49. $0, -2i, 3 + \sqrt{2}$ **50.** $1 + 2i, 3 - \sqrt{3}$ **51.** $\sqrt{5}, -\sqrt{7}$

6-7 and 6-8 Objectives

▼ To count permutations (p. 345)

▼ To count combinations (p. 346)

▼ To use Pascal's Triangle (p. 353)

▼ To use the Binomial Theorem (p. 354)

The notation $n!$, read **"n factorial,"** means $n(n - 1)(n - 2) \cdot \ldots \cdot 3 \cdot 2 \cdot 1$, and $0! = 1$.

A **permutation** is an arrangement of items in a particular order. You can count permutations using the Multiplication Counting Principle or factorial notation. To compute the number of permutations of n objects chosen r at a time, you can also use the formula $_nP_r = \frac{n!}{(n - r)!}$, for $0 \leq r \leq n$.

A selection in which order does not matter is a **combination**. The number of combinations of n objects chosen r at a time is $_nC_r = \frac{n!}{r!(n - r)!}$, for $0 \leq r \leq n$.

Use the **Binomial Theorem** to **expand** a binomial raised to a power. For $n \geq 0$, $(a + b)^n = {_nC_0}a^n + {_nC_1}a^{n-1}b + {_nC_2}a^{n-2}b^2 + \ldots + {_nC_{n-1}}ab^{n-1} + {_nC_n}b^n$. The coefficients in the expansion of $(a + b)^n$ are found in **Pascal's Triangle.** You can also use the Binomial Theorem to find probabilities when an event has only two possible outcomes.

Evaluate each expression.

52. $3(4!)$ **53.** $_4P_3$ **54.** $_7C_4$ **55.** $_5P_2 + {_5C_3}$ **56.** $\frac{_6C_3}{_5C_3}$

57. In how many ways can you arrange 5 different canisters in a row on a shelf?

58. Find the fourth term in the binomial expansion of $(2x + 3y)^6$.

59. A coin is tossed seven times. Find the probability of getting exactly four heads.

Chapter

6

Chapter Test

Go Online
PHSchool.com
For: Chapter Test
Web Code: aga-0652

Write each polynomial in standard form. Then classify it by degree and by number of terms.

1. $3x^2 - 7x^4 + 9 - x^4$

2. $11x^2 + \frac{3}{8}x - 3x^2$

3. $2x(x - 3)(x + 2)$

4. $(t - 2)(t + 1)(t + 1)$

Graph each function. Approximate the real zeros to the nearest hundredth.

5. $P(x) = -x^3 - x^2 + x$

6. $P(x) = (x + 1)(x + 2)(x^2 + 4x - 5)$

7. $f(x) = x^4 + 3x^3 - 1$

8. $g(x) = -x^6 - x^3 + 2$

9. $f(x) = x^3 - 3x^2 + 2$

Write a polynomial function with rational coefficients in standard form with the given zeros.

10. $x = 1, 2, \frac{3}{5}$

11. $x = -2, 0, \sqrt{3}$

12. $x = -4, -4, -4$

13. $x = -1, 1, 1$

14. $x = \sqrt{2}, -i$

15. $x = 3 + i, 1 - \sqrt{5}$

16. **Open-Ended** Write a polynomial function with real coefficients that has an imaginary zero and an irrational zero.

Solve each equation.

17. $(2x - 3)(3x + 2)(x + 2)(x + 2)\left(x - \frac{7}{8}\right) = 0$

18. $(x^2 - 3)(x^2 + 3x - 4) = 0$

19. $\left(x + \frac{2}{3}\right)(x^2 + 5x + 1) = 0$

20. $x^3 - 2x^2 + x = 0$

21. $x^3 + 3x^2 - 5x - 4 = 0$

Divide using long division.

22. $(x^2 + 3x - 4) \div (x - 1)$

23. $(x^3 + 7x^2 - 5x - 6) \div (x + 2)$

Divide using synthetic division.

24. $(3x^2 - 3x + 4) \div (x + 1)$

25. $(x^3 + x^2 + x - 14) \div (x + 2)$

Use synthetic division and the Remainder Theorem to find $P(a)$.

26. $P(x) = 6x^4 + 19x^3 - 2x^2 - 44x - 24; a = \frac{-2}{3}$

27. $P(x) = -x^3 - x^2 + x; a = 0$

28. $P(x) = 2x^3 - 2x^2 - 12x; a = 3$

29. $P(x) = x^4 + 3x^3 - 7x^2 - 9x + 12; a = 3$

30. $P(x) = x^3 + 3x^2 - 5x - 4; a = -1$

Evaluate each expression.

31. $6!$

32. $\frac{6!}{4!2!}$

33. $_7C_3$

34. $_5P_2$

35. $_{11}P_9$

36. $_9C_8$

37. $2(_5C_4) - _3C_2$

Indicate whether each situation involves a combination or a permutation. Then solve.

38. How many ways are there to select five actors from a troupe of nine to improvise a scene?

39. How many different three-student study groups can be formed from a class of 15?

40. You are looking for a new apartment. There are five apartments available. In how many ways can you inspect the apartments?

Use the Binomial Theorem to expand each binomial.

41. $(x + z)^5$

42. $(1 - 2t)^2$

43. A weighted coin has $P(\text{heads}) = \frac{2}{5}$. The coin is tossed seven times. Find the probability of getting exactly six heads.

44. **Writing** Describe how to use combinations to produce row n of Pascal's Triangle.

45. **Geometry** The volume V of a prism is modeled by $V = 2\ell^3 - 2\ell$, where ℓ is the length of the prism. The width of the prism equals $\ell - 1$. Find the height of the prism.

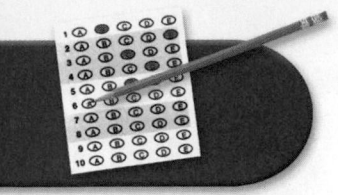

Standardized Test Prep

Multiple Choice

For Exercises 1–10, choose the correct letter.

1. For which function is 5 a zero?

Ⓐ $y = (x - 5)^2$ Ⓑ $y = (x + 5)^2$
Ⓒ $y = (x - 1)^2 + 5$ Ⓓ $y = (x + 1)^2 - 5$

2. The graph of which line is perpendicular to the graph of $y = 2x + 1$?

Ⓕ $y = \frac{1}{2}x + 7$ Ⓖ $x + 2y = 4$
Ⓗ $y = -2x - 5$ Ⓙ $x - 2y = 10$

3. What is the equation of the function $y = x^2$ translated 3 units up and 4 units left?

Ⓐ $y = (x - 3)^2 - 4$ Ⓑ $y = (x + 4)^2 + 3$
Ⓒ $y = (x - 4)^2 + 3$ Ⓓ $y = (x + 3)^2 - 4$

4. What is the axis of symmetry of the graph of a quadratic function with vertex at $(5, -1)$?

Ⓕ $x = 5$ Ⓖ $x = -5$
Ⓗ $y = -1$ Ⓙ $y = 1$

5. What is the solution of the matrix equation?

$$\begin{bmatrix} -1 & 0 & 2 \\ -3 & 1 & 1 \\ -5 & 4 & 0 \end{bmatrix} X = \begin{bmatrix} -0 & -1 & -20 \\ -2 & -2 & -27 \\ 22 & -5 & -22 \end{bmatrix}$$

Ⓐ $\begin{bmatrix} -1 & 3 & -2 \\ -1 & 0 & -1 \\ -7 & 2 & -6 \end{bmatrix}$ Ⓑ $\begin{bmatrix} -2 & -1 & 6 \\ -3 & -0 & 2 \\ -1 & -1 & 7 \end{bmatrix}$

Ⓒ $\begin{bmatrix} -2 & 3 & 1 \\ -1 & 0 & 1 \\ -6 & 2 & 7 \end{bmatrix}$ Ⓓ $\begin{bmatrix} -2 & 0 & -7 \\ -3 & 1 & -1 \\ -1 & 2 & -6 \end{bmatrix}$

6. Which relation is NOT a function?

Ⓕ $y = 3\sqrt{x} - 1$ Ⓖ $y = |x - 7|$
Ⓗ $y = \pm 3x$ Ⓙ $y = 1 - x^3$

7. Which is a factor of $x^4 + 2x^3 - 3x^2 - 4x + 4$?

   I. $x + 2$ II. $x - 1$ III. $x + 1$

Ⓐ I only   Ⓑ II only
Ⓒ I and II   Ⓓ II and III

8. Which ordered pair is a solution of this system?

$\begin{cases} y \le 2x + 3 \\ y > |x + 1| \\ y < -x + 4 \end{cases}$ I. $(0, 2)$
             II. $(1, -3)$
             III. $(-1, 4)$

Ⓕ II and III   Ⓖ II only
Ⓗ I and II   Ⓙ I only

9. At which point is the cost function $C = 3x + y$ minimized for the restrictions $x + y \ge 1$, $x \ge 0$, and $y \ge 0$?

Ⓐ $(3, 1)$ Ⓑ $(1, 0)$ Ⓒ $(0, 1)$ Ⓓ $(0, 0)$

10. What are the solutions of $x^3 + 4x^2 + x - 6 = 0$?

Ⓕ $-1, -2, 3$ Ⓖ $-1, 2, -3$
Ⓗ $1, -2, -3$ Ⓙ $-1, 2, 3$

11. Solve $|2 - 4x| + 9 < 19$.

Ⓐ $-3 < x < 2$ Ⓑ $-2 < x < 3$
Ⓒ $x < -3$ and $x > 2$ Ⓓ $x < -2$ and $x > 3$

12. Which expression is NOT equivalent to $(3 - (2 - x)) - 2(1 + x)$?

Ⓕ $1 + x$ Ⓖ $-x - 1$
Ⓗ $(1 + x) - (2 + 2x)$ Ⓙ $-(-(-1 - x))$

13. Which inequality has a graph that is shaded below the boundary?

Ⓐ $y < |x + 7| + 1$ Ⓑ $y + 4x > 20$
Ⓒ $x - y < -2$ Ⓓ $3y - 6x + 16 > -8$

14. For which system of equations can you eliminate the variable y by first multiplying one equation by 2 and then adding the equations?

Ⓕ $\begin{cases} 3x - 4y = 7 \\ x + 2y = 9 \end{cases}$ Ⓖ $\begin{cases} 2x + 6y = 1 \\ 2x - 4y = -3 \end{cases}$

Ⓗ $\begin{cases} x + y = 2 \\ x - y = 1 \end{cases}$ Ⓙ $\begin{cases} 2.5x + 6y = 0 \\ 5x - 9y = 14 \end{cases}$

Gridded Response

15. Find $7!$.

16. Find $_3P_2 - {_3}C_2$.

17. What is the coefficient of a^2b^3 in the expansion of $(a + b)^5$?

Short Response

18. An employer is selecting 4 out of 30 workers as employees of the month.

   a. Does this situation involve a combination or a permutation? Explain.
   b. How many different selections are possible?

Extended Response

19. Open-Ended Graph a polygon. Use matrices to find the image of the polygon after a reflection in the x-axis followed by a rotation of $90°$ counterclockwise. Show your work.

Activity Lab

As the Ball Flies

Applying Quadratic Functions Have you ever wondered how far a soccer player can kick a ball? Ignoring wind and air resistance, you can use a linear function and a quadratic function to describe the path of a soccer ball. These functions

depend on two factors that are within the soccer player's control: velocity of the kick (v_k) and angle of the kick (θ). A good high-school soccer player can kick the ball at speeds ranging from 50 to 60 mi/h. A strong professional player can kick the ball at nearly 80 mi/h.

Activity 1

a. Use the information in the diagram on the facing page to calculate the horizontal and vertical velocities of a ball kicked at a 35° angle with an initial velocity of 60 mi/h. Convert the velocities to ft/s.

b. The equations $x(t) = v_x t$ and $y(t) = v_y t + 0.5gt^2$ describe the x- and y-coordinates of a soccer ball as a function of time. (The gravitational constant g is described on the facing page.) Use the second equation to calculate the time the ball will take to complete its path.

c. Use the first equation to calculate how far the ball will travel horizontally from its original position.

The Soccer Ball

The easily recognized form of a soccer ball is due to its unique combination of pentagons and hexagons.

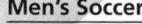

Men's Soccer

Jurgen Klinsmann is one of Germany's most successful strikers. He led his team to the 1996 European Championship.

In practice, air resistance and wind play a role in determining the ball's path, but these factors make the equations more complex.

A ball in flight follows a parabolic path.

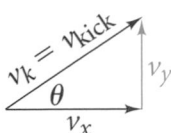

Vectors

The vectors at the left describe the initial velocity of the soccer ball as the combination of a vertical and a horizontal velocity.

$v_x = v_k \cos \theta$
$v_y = v_k \sin \theta$

Gravity

The constant g represents the acceleration of any object as a result of Earth's gravity. The value of g near the surface of Earth is about -32 ft/s^2.

Activity 2

a. Use the technique developed in Activity 1 to calculate the horizontal distance of the kick for angles in 5° increments from 5° to 90°. (You may find a spreadsheet helpful for making these calculations.)

b. Graph the horizontal distance of the kick as a function of the angle of the kick. Which angle gives the greatest distance?

Activity 3

Suppose you played soccer on the moon, where the gravitational acceleration is about one sixth of its value on Earth. What are the maximum height and maximum horizontal distance you could kick the ball by giving it an initial velocity of 48 mi/h?

The Women's World Cup
Cindy Parlow of the U.S. women's soccer team avoids a tackle in the 1999 final against China.

Go Online
PHSchool.com
For: Information about soccer
Web Code: age-0653

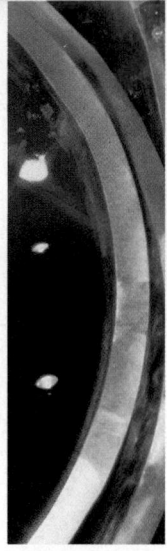

What You've Learned

- In Chapter 2, you learned about relations and functions and their domains and ranges. You also learned to draw graphs of relations and functions on the coordinate plane.

- In Chapter 5, you reviewed square roots and the multiplication and division of square roots. Then you used these skills in graphing and solving quadratic equations.

- In Chapter 6, you learned to graph polynomial functions and solve polynomial equations.

 **Check Your Readiness**

 **for Help** to the Lesson in green.

Multiplying Binomials (Lesson 6-2)

Multiply.

1. $(3y - 2)(y - 4)$ **2.** $(7a + 10)(7a - 10)$ **3.** $(x - 3)(x + 6)(x + 1)$

Simplifying Exponential Expressions (Skills Handbook p. 880)

Simplify each expression. Use only positive integer exponents.

4. $(3x^3)^2$ **5.** $(2b^{-2})(4b^5)$ **6.** $(xy^{-3})^2$ **7.** $\dfrac{18a^2}{3a^{-4}}$ **8.** $\dfrac{4ab^{-3}}{6a^2b^3}$

Solving by Factoring (Lessons 5-5 and 6-4)

Solve each equation by factoring.

9. $x^2 - 5x - 14 = 0$ **10.** $2x^2 - 11x + 15 = 0$ **11.** $3x^2 + 10x - 8 = 0$

12. $12x^2 - 12x + 3 = 0$ **13.** $8x^2 - 98 = 0$ **14.** $x^4 - 14x^2 + 49 = 0$

Finding the Domain and Range of Functions (Lesson 2-1)

Find the domain and range of each function.

15. $\{(1, 2), (2, 3), (3, 4), (4, 5)\}$ **16.** $\{(1, 2), (2, 2), (3, 2), (4, 2)\}$

17. $f(x) = -x - 1$ **18.** $f(x) = 2x^2 + 3$

Graphing Quadratic Functions (Lesson 5-3)

Graph each function.

19. $y = 2x^2 - 4$ **20.** $y = -3(x^2 + 1)$ **21.** $y = \frac{1}{2}(x - 3)^2 + 1$

22. $y = -(x + 4)^2 - 5$ **23.** $y = \frac{1}{4}(x + 2)^2 - 1$ **24.** $y = 7 - (5 - x)^2$

Radical Functions and Rational Exponents

LESSONS

7-1 Roots and Radical Expressions

7-2 Multiplying and Dividing Radical Expressions

7-3 Binomial Radical Expressions

7-4 Rational Exponents

7-5 Solving Square Root and Other Radical Equations

7-6 Function Operations

7-7 Inverse Relations and Functions

7-8 Graphing Square Root and Other Radical Functions

🔊 **Key Vocabulary**

- composite function (p. 399)
- index (p. 370)
- inverse functions (p. 409)
- inverse relation (p. 407)
- like radicals (p. 380)
- nth root (p. 369)
- principal root (p. 370)
- radical equation (p. 391)
- radical function (p. 415)
- radicand (p. 370)
- rational exponent (p. 385)
- rationalize the denominator (p. 376)
- square root equation (p. 391)
- square root function (p. 415)

What You'll Learn Next

- In Chapter 7, you will extend your knowledge of roots to include cube roots, fourth roots, fifth roots, and so on.

- You will learn to add, subtract, multiply, and divide radical expressions, including binomial radical expressions.

- You will solve radical equations, and graph translations of radical functions and their inverses.

Real-World Connection Applying what you learn, on page 386 you will solve a problem involving space travel.

Properties of Exponents

Exponents are used to indicate powers. Their properties are listed below. Assume throughout your work that no denominator is equal to zero and that m and n are integers.

- $a^0 = 1, a \neq 0$

- $a^{-n} = \dfrac{1}{a^n}$

- $a^m \cdot a^n = a^{m+n}$

- $\dfrac{a^m}{a^n} = a^{m-n}$

- $(ab)^n = a^n b^n$

- $\left(\dfrac{a}{b}\right)^n = \dfrac{a^n}{b^n}$

- $(a^m)^n = a^{mn}$

EXAMPLE

Simplify and rewrite each expression using only positive exponents.

a. $(7a^2)(-2a^{-5})$

$(7a^2)(-2a^{-5})$

$\quad = 7(-2)a^{2+(-5)}$

$\quad = -14a^{-3}$

$\quad = \dfrac{-14}{a^3}, \text{ or } -\dfrac{14}{a^3}$

b. $(-2x^{-1}y^2)^3$

$(-2x^{-1}y^2)^3$

$\quad = (-2)^3(x^{-1})^3(y^2)^3$

$\quad = -8x^{-3}y^6$

$\quad = \dfrac{-8y^6}{x^3}, \text{ or } -\dfrac{8y^6}{x^3}$

c. $\dfrac{2ab^5c^2}{a^3bc^2}$

$\dfrac{2ab^5c^2}{a^3bc^2}$

$\quad = 2a^{1-3}b^{5-1}c^{2-2}$

$\quad = 2a^{-2}b^4c^0$

$\quad = \dfrac{2b^4}{a^2}$

EXERCISES

Simplify each expression. Use only positive exponents.

1. $(3a^2)(4a^6)$

2. $(-4x^2)(-2x^{-2})$

3. $(4x^3y^5)^2$

4. $(2x^{-5}y^4)^3$

5. $\dfrac{8a^5}{2a^2}$

6. $\dfrac{6x^7y^5}{3x^{-1}}$

7. $\dfrac{(4x^2)^0}{2xy^5}$

8. $\left(\dfrac{3x^2}{2}\right)^2$

9. $(-6m^2n^2)(3mn)$

10. $(3x^4y^5)^{-3}$

11. $\dfrac{(2r^{-1}s^2t^0)^{-2}}{2rs}$

12. $x^5(2x)^3$

13. $\dfrac{x^4x^{-2}}{x^{-5}}$

14. $\dfrac{(12x^2y^6)^2}{8x^4y^7}$

15. $(4p^2q)(p^2q^3)$

16. $\dfrac{4x^3}{2x}$

17. $(p^2)^{-2}$

18. $\dfrac{-15x^4}{3x}$

19. $\dfrac{r^2s^3t^4}{r^2s^4t^{-4}}$

20. $\dfrac{xy^2}{2} \cdot \dfrac{6x}{y^2}$

21. $(s^2t)^3(st)$

22. $(3x^{-3}y^{-2})^{-2}$

23. $(h^4k^5)^0$

24. $\dfrac{s^2t^3}{r} \cdot \dfrac{sr^3}{t}$

25. Writing Write a numerical example for each property of exponents shown above. Which properties could be called distributive properties for exponents? Explain.

Roots and Radical Expressions

GO for Help Lesson 5-4

What You'll Learn

• To simplify *n*th roots

... And Why

To solve a packaging problem, as in Example 4

✓ Check Skills You'll Need

Write each number as a square of a number.

1. 25   **2.** 0.09   **3.** $\frac{4}{49}$

Write each expression as a square of an expression.

4. x^{10} **5.** x^4y^2 **6.** $169x^6y^{12}$

🔊 **New Vocabulary** • *n*th root • radicand • index • principal root

---

1   Roots and Radical Expressions

Since $5^2 = 25$, 5 is a square root of 25.

Since $5^3 = 125$, 5 is a cube root of 125.

Since $5^4 = 625$, 5 is a fourth root of 625.

Since $5^5 = 3125$, 5 is a fifth root of 3125.

This pattern leads to the definition of *n*th root.

 Key Concepts

Definition	**nth Root**

For any real numbers a and b, and any positive integer n, if $a^n = b$,

then a is an **nth root** of b.

Vocabulary Tip

The term <u>root</u> is used in more than one way in mathematics:
   root of an equation
   root of a number.

The roots of the equation $y^4 = 16$ are the fourth roots of 16.

Since $2^4 = 16$ and $(-2)^4 = 16$, both 2 and -2 are fourth roots of 16.

Since there is no real number x such that $x^4 = -16$, -16 has no real fourth root.

Since -5 is the only real number whose cube is -125, -5 is the only real cube root of -125.

Some roots, such as the square roots of 10, are irrational numbers. Nevertheless, there is a positive square root and a negative square root of 10.

Here is a summary of the number of possible real roots of a real number.

Type of Number	Number of Real *n*th Roots When *n* Is Even	Number of Real *n*th Roots When *n* Is Odd
positive	2	1
0	1	1
negative	none	1

1 EXAMPLE **Finding All Real Roots**

Find all the real roots.

a. the cube roots of 0.008, -1000, and $\frac{1}{27}$

Since $(0.2)^3 = 0.008$, 0.2 is the cube root of 0.008.
Since $(-10)^3 = -1000$, -10 is the cube root of -1000.
Since $\left(\frac{1}{3}\right)^3 = \frac{1}{27}$, $\frac{1}{3}$ is the cube root of $\frac{1}{27}$.

b. the fourth roots of 1, -0.0001, and $\frac{16}{81}$

Since $1^4 = 1$ and $(-1)^4 = 1$, 1 and -1 are fourth roots of 1.
There is no real number with a fourth power of -0.0001.
Since $\left(\frac{2}{3}\right)^4 = \frac{16}{81}$ and $\left(-\frac{2}{3}\right)^4 = \frac{16}{81}$, $\frac{2}{3}$ and $-\frac{2}{3}$ are fourth roots of $\frac{16}{81}$.

✓ Quick Check **1 a.** Find all the real fifth roots of 0, -1, and 32.
b. Find all the real square roots of 0.0001, -1, and $\frac{36}{121}$.

Vocabulary Tip

Like the word *radish*, radical comes from the Latin word for root.

A radical sign is used to indicate a root. The number under the radical sign is the **radicand.** The **index** gives the degree of the root.

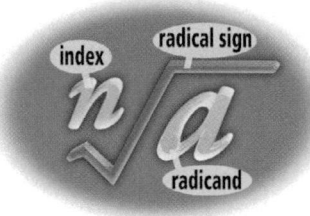

When a number has two real roots, the positive root is called the **principal root** and the radical sign indicates the principal root. The principal fourth root of 16 is written as $\sqrt[4]{16}$.

The principal fourth root of 16 is 2 because $\sqrt[4]{16}$ equals $\sqrt[4]{2^4}$. The other fourth root of 16 is written as $-\sqrt[4]{16}$, which equals -2.

2 EXAMPLE **Finding Roots**

Find each real-number root.

a. $\sqrt[3]{-8}$

$\sqrt[3]{-8} = \sqrt[3]{(-2)^3}$ **Rewrite -8 as the third power of a number.**

$\quad\quad = -2$ **Simplify.**

b. $\sqrt{-100}$

There is no real number whose square is -100.

✓ Quick Check **2** Find each real-number root.

a. $\sqrt[3]{-27}$ **b.** $\sqrt[4]{81}$ **c.** $\sqrt{49}$

Notice that when $x = 5$, $\sqrt{x^2} = \sqrt{5^2} = \sqrt{25} = 5 = x$,
and when $x = -5$, $\sqrt{x^2} = \sqrt{(-5)^2} = \sqrt{25} = 5 \ne x$.

 Key Concepts

Property	***n*th Root of a^n, $a < 0$**

For any negative real number a,
$$\sqrt[n]{a^n} = |a| \text{ when } n \text{ is even.}$$

3 EXAMPLE Simplifying Radical Expressions

Simplify each radical expression.

a. $\sqrt{4x^6}$

$$\sqrt{4x^6} = \sqrt{2^2(x^3)^2} = \sqrt{(2x^3)^2} = 2|x^3|$$

Absolute value symbols ensure that the root is positive when x is negative.

b. $\sqrt[3]{a^3b^6}$

$$\sqrt[3]{a^3b^6} = \sqrt[3]{a^3(b^2)^3} = \sqrt[3]{(ab^2)^3} = ab^2$$

Absolute value symbols must not be used here. If a is negative, then the radicand is negative and the root must also be negative.

c. $\sqrt[4]{x^4y^8}$

$$\sqrt[4]{x^4y^8} = \sqrt[4]{x^4(y^2)^4} = \sqrt[4]{(xy^2)^4} = |x|y^2$$

Absolute value symbols ensure that the root is positive when x is negative. They are not needed for y because y^2 is never negative.

✓ **Quick Check** ③ Simplify each radical expression. Use absolute value symbols when needed.

    a. $\sqrt{4x^2y^4}$ **b.** $\sqrt[3]{-27c^6}$ **c.** $\sqrt[4]{x^8y^{12}}$

Online active math

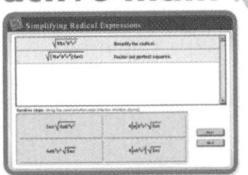

For: Simplifying Activity
Use: Interactive Textbook, 7-1

---

4 EXAMPLE Real-World Connection

Packaging A citrus grower wants to ship a select grade of oranges that weigh from 8 to 9 ounces in gift cartons. Each carton will hold three dozen oranges, in 3 layers of 3 oranges by 4 oranges.

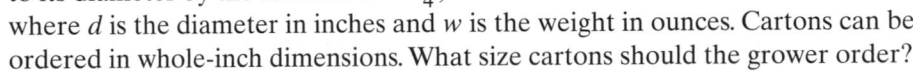

The weight of an orange is related to its diameter by the formula $w = \dfrac{d^3}{4}$, where d is the diameter in inches and w is the weight in ounces. Cartons can be ordered in whole-inch dimensions. What size cartons should the grower order?

Find the diameters of the oranges.

$8 \le$	w	≤ 9	**Write an inequality.**
$8 \le$	$\frac{d^3}{4}$	≤ 9	**Substitute for w in terms of d.**
$32 \le$	d^3	≤ 36	**Multiply by 4.**
$\sqrt[3]{32} \le$	$\sqrt[3]{d^3}$	$\le \sqrt[3]{36}$	**Take cube roots.**
$3.17 \le$	d	≤ 3.30	**The diameters range from 3.17 in. to 3.30 in.**

The length of a row of 4 of the largest oranges is 4(3.30 in.) = 13.2 in. The length of a row of 3 of the largest oranges is 3(3.30 in.) = 9.90 in. The grower should order cartons that are 14 in. long by 10 in. wide by 10 in. high to accommodate three dozen of the largest oranges.

Graphing Calculator Hint

Use the $\sqrt[3]{}$ feature in the MATH menu to find cube roots. For other roots, type the index first and then select the $\sqrt[x]{}$ feature.

✓ **Quick Check** ④ Use the formula in Example 4 to find the diameter of each orange.

    a. 3 oz   **b.** 5.5 oz   **c.** 6.25 oz

EXERCISES

For more exercises, see *Extra Skill and Word Problem Practice*.

Practice and Problem Solving

 Practice by Example

Example 1
(page 370)

 **for Help**

Find all the real square roots of each number.

1. 225　　　**2.** 0.0049　　　**3.** $-\frac{1}{121}$　　　**4.** $\frac{64}{169}$

Find all the real cube roots of each number.

5. -64　　　**6.** 0.125　　　**7.** $-\frac{27}{216}$　　　**8.** 0.000343

Find all the real fourth roots of each number.

9. 16　　　**10.** -16　　　**11.** 0.0081　　　**12.** $\frac{10,000}{81}$

Example 2
(page 370)

Find each real-number root.

13. $\sqrt{36}$　　　**14.** $-\sqrt{36}$　　　**15.** $\sqrt{-36}$　　　**16.** $\sqrt{0.36}$

17. $-\sqrt[3]{64}$　　　**18.** $\sqrt[3]{-64}$　　　**19.** $-\sqrt[4]{81}$　　　**20.** $\sqrt[4]{-81}$

Example 3
(page 371)

Simplify each radical expression. Use absolute value symbols when needed.

21. $\sqrt{16x^2}$　　　**22.** $\sqrt{0.25x^6}$　　　**23.** $\sqrt{x^8y^{18}}$　　　**24.** $\sqrt{64b^{48}}$

25. $\sqrt[3]{-64a^3}$　　　**26.** $\sqrt[3]{27y^6}$　　　**27.** $\sqrt[4]{x^8y^{12}}$　　　**28.** $\sqrt[5]{32y^{10}}$

Example 4
(page 371)

Geometry The formula for the volume of a sphere is $V = \frac{4}{3}\pi r^3$. Find the radius to the nearest hundredth of a sphere with each volume.

29. 10 in.^{3}　　　**30.** 20 ft^3　　　**31.** 0.45 cm^3　　　**32.** 0.002 mm^3

 Apply Your Skills

Find the two real-number solutions of each equation.

33. $x^2 = 100$　　　**34.** $x^4 = 1$　　　**35.** $x^2 = 0.25$　　　**36.** $x^4 = \frac{16}{81}$

37. Arrange the numbers $\sqrt[3]{-64}$, $-\sqrt[3]{-64}$, $\sqrt{64}$, and $\sqrt[6]{64}$ in order from least to greatest.

38. Boat Building Boat builders share an old rule of thumb for sailboats. The maximum speed K in knots is 1.35 times the square root of the length L in feet of the boat's waterline.
   a. A customer is planning to order a sailboat with a maximum speed of 8 knots. How long should the waterline be?
   b. How much longer would the waterline have to be to achieve a maximum speed of 10 knots?

Simplify each radical expression. Use absolute value symbols when needed.

39. $\sqrt[3]{0.125}$　　　**40.** $\sqrt[3]{\frac{8}{216}}$　　　**41.** $\sqrt[4]{0.0016}$　　　**42.** $\sqrt[4]{\frac{1}{256}}$

43. $\sqrt[4]{16c^4}$　　　**44.** $\sqrt[3]{81x^3y^6}$　　　**45.** $\sqrt{144x^3y^4z^5}$　　　**46.** $\sqrt[5]{y^{20}}$

47. $\sqrt[5]{-y^{20}}$　　　**48.** $\sqrt[5]{k^{15}}$　　　**49.** $\sqrt[5]{-k^{15}}$　　　**50.** $\sqrt{(x+3)^2}$

51. $\sqrt{(x+1)^4}$　　　**52.** $\sqrt[2n]{x^{2n}}$　　　**53.** $\sqrt[2n]{x^{4n}}$　　　**54.** $\sqrt[2n]{x^{6n}}$

55. Open-Ended Find three radical expressions that simplify to $-2x^2$.

56. Critical Thinking For what positive integers n is each of the statements true?
  a. If $x^n = b$, then x is an nth root of b.   **b.** If $x^n = b$, then $x = \sqrt[n]{b}$.

57. Writing Is 10 a first root of 10? Explain.

Tell whether each equation is true for all, some, or no values of the variable. Explain your answers.

58. $\sqrt{x^4} = x^2$ **59.** $\sqrt{x^6} = x^3$ **60.** $\sqrt[3]{x^8} = x^2$ **61.** $\sqrt[3]{x^3} = |x|$

 **Challenge**

Simplify each radical expression. n is an even number.

62. $\sqrt[n]{m^n}$ **63.** $\sqrt[n]{m^{2n}}$ **64.** $\sqrt[n]{m^{3n}}$ **65.** $\sqrt[n]{m^{4n}}$

Simplify each radical expression. n is an odd number.

66. $\sqrt[n]{m^n}$ **67.** $\sqrt[n]{m^{2n}}$ **68.** $\sqrt[n]{m^{3n}}$ **69.** $\sqrt[n]{m^{4n}}$

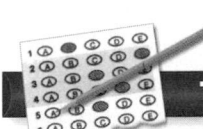

Test Prep

Multiple Choice

70. Which equation has more than one real-number solution?
  A. $x^2 = 0$ **B.** $x^2 = 1$ **C.** $x^2 = -1$ **D.** $x^3 = -1$

71. Which number is greatest?
  F. $\sqrt{0.5}$ **G.** $\sqrt[3]{0.5}$ **H.** $\sqrt[4]{0.5}$ **J.** $\sqrt[5]{0.5}$

72. Which statement is NOT true?
  A. $-3 = -\sqrt{9}$ **B.** $-3 = -\sqrt{-9}$
  C. $-3 = \sqrt[3]{-27}$ **D.** $-3 = -\sqrt[4]{81}$

73. Absolute value symbols are needed when you simplify some of these expressions. Which ones are they?
  I. $\sqrt[3]{-x^3y^6}$ **II.** $\sqrt{x^2y^4}$ **III.** $\sqrt[4]{x^8y^{12}}$ **IV.** $\sqrt{x^4y^6}$
  F. II and III only   **G.** II and IV only
  H. II, III and IV only   **J.** I, II, III and IV

Short Response

74. For what values of x and y does $\sqrt{x^2y^4}$ equal $\sqrt[3]{x^3y^6}$? Explain your answer.

Mixed Review

Lesson 6-8

Expand each binomial.

75. $(x + y)^5$ **76.** $(2 - 3y)^4$ **77.** $(3x - 5)^6$ **78.** $(2a - b)^7$

Lesson 6-2

Write each function in factored form. Check by multiplying.

79. $y = 4x^3 - 49x$ **80.** $y = 81x^2 + 36x + 4$

81. $y = 4x^3 + 8x^2 + 4x$ **82.** $y = 12x^3 + 14x^2 + 2x$

Lesson 5-3

Rewrite each equation in vertex form.

83. $y = 3x^2 - 7$ **84.** $y = -2x^2 + x - 10$ **85.** $y = \frac{x^2}{4} + 2x - 1$

Multiplying and Dividing Radical Expressions

GO for Help page 368

What You'll Learn

• To multiply radical expressions

• To divide radical expressions

. . . Any Why

To transform a famous formula, as in Example 6

✓ **Check Skills You'll Need**

Find each missing factor.

1. $150 = 5^2(\blacksquare)$
2. $54 = (\blacksquare)^3(2)$
3. $48 = 4^2(\blacksquare)$
4. $x^5 = (\blacksquare)^2(x)$
5. $3a^3b^4 = (\blacksquare)^3(3b)$
6. $75a^7b^8 = (\blacksquare)^2(3a)$

 **New Vocabulary** • rationalize the denominator

---

1 Multiplying Radical Expressions

To multiply radicals consider the following.

$\sqrt{16} \cdot \sqrt{9} = 4 \cdot 3 = 12$ and $\sqrt{16 \cdot 9} = \sqrt{144} = 12$.
So $\sqrt{16} \cdot \sqrt{9} = \sqrt{16 \cdot 9}$.

$\sqrt[3]{-8} \cdot \sqrt[3]{27} = -2 \cdot 3 = -6$ and $\sqrt[3]{-8 \cdot 27} = \sqrt[3]{-216} = -6$.
So $\sqrt[3]{-8} \cdot \sqrt[3]{27} = \sqrt[3]{-8 \cdot 27}$.

In general, the product of the principal nth roots of two numbers equals the principal nth root of their product.

🔑 **Key Concepts**

Property	**Multiplying Radical Expressions**
If $\sqrt[n]{a}$ and $\sqrt[n]{b}$ are real numbers, then $\sqrt[n]{a} \cdot \sqrt[n]{b} = \sqrt[n]{ab}$.	

1 EXAMPLE Multiplying Radicals

Multiply. Simplify if possible.

a. $\sqrt{2} \cdot \sqrt{8}$

$\sqrt{2} \cdot \sqrt{8} = \sqrt{2 \cdot 8} = \sqrt{16} = 4$

b. $\sqrt[3]{-5} \cdot \sqrt[3]{25}$

$\sqrt[3]{-5} \cdot \sqrt[3]{25} = \sqrt[3]{-125} = \sqrt[3]{(-5)^3} = -5$

c. $\sqrt{-2} \cdot \sqrt{8}$

The property for multiplying radicals does *not* apply. $\sqrt{-2}$ is not a real number.

✓ **Quick Check** ❶ Multiply. Simplify if possible.

a. $\sqrt{3} \cdot \sqrt{12}$ **b.** $\sqrt[3]{3} \cdot \sqrt[3]{-9}$ **c.** $\sqrt[4]{4} \cdot \sqrt[4]{-4}$

$2\sqrt[3]{3}$ is considered to be a simplified form of $\sqrt[3]{24}$. You can use the property for multiplying radical expressions to simplify some radical expressions.

2 EXAMPLE Simplifying Radical Expressions

Simplify each expression. Assume that all variables are positive. Then absolute value symbols are never needed in the simplified expression.

a. $\sqrt{72x^3}$

$$\sqrt{72x^3} = \sqrt{6^2 \cdot 2 \cdot x^2 \cdot x} \qquad \text{Factor into perfect squares.}$$
$$= \sqrt{6^2x^2} \cdot \sqrt{2x} \qquad \sqrt[n]{a} \cdot \sqrt[n]{b} = \sqrt[n]{ab}$$
$$= 6x\sqrt{2x} \qquad \text{Simplify.}$$

b. $\sqrt[3]{80n^5}$

$$\sqrt[3]{80n^5} = \sqrt[3]{2^3 \cdot 10 \cdot n^3 \cdot n^2} \qquad \text{Factor into perfect cubes.}$$
$$= \sqrt[3]{2^3n^3} \cdot \sqrt[3]{10n^2} \qquad \sqrt[n]{a} \cdot \sqrt[n]{b} = \sqrt[n]{ab}$$
$$= 2n\sqrt[3]{10n^2} \qquad \text{Simplify.}$$

✓ Quick Check **2** Simplify $\sqrt{50x^4}$ and $\sqrt[3]{18x^4}$. Assume that x is positive.

Simplify the products of radicals as much as possible.

3 EXAMPLE Multiplying Radical Expressions

Multiply and simplify $\sqrt[3]{54x^2y^3} \cdot \sqrt[3]{5x^3y^4}$. Assume that all variables are positive.

$$\sqrt[3]{54x^2y^3} \cdot \sqrt[3]{5x^3y^4} = \sqrt[3]{54x^2y^3 \cdot 5x^3y^4} \qquad \sqrt[n]{a} \cdot \sqrt[n]{b} = \sqrt[n]{ab}$$
$$= \sqrt[3]{3^3x^3(y^2)^3 \cdot 10x^2y} \qquad \text{Factor into perfect cubes.}$$
$$= \sqrt[3]{3^3x^3(y^2)^3} \cdot \sqrt[3]{10x^2y} \qquad \sqrt[n]{a} \cdot \sqrt[n]{b} = \sqrt[n]{ab}$$
$$= 3xy^2\sqrt[3]{10x^2y} \qquad \text{Simplify.}$$

✓ Quick Check **3** Multiply and simplify $3\sqrt{7x^3} \cdot 2\sqrt{21x^3y^2}$. Assume that all variables are positive.

2 Dividing Radical Expressions

To divide radicals, consider the following.

$$\frac{\sqrt{36}}{\sqrt{25}} = \frac{6}{5} \text{ and } \sqrt{\frac{36}{25}} = \sqrt{\left(\frac{6}{5}\right)^2} = \frac{6}{5}. \text{ So } \frac{\sqrt{36}}{\sqrt{25}} = \sqrt{\frac{36}{25}}.$$

In general, the quotient of the principal nth roots of two numbers equals the principal nth root of their quotient.

 **Key Concepts**

Property	Dividing Radical Expressions
If $\sqrt[n]{a}$ and $\sqrt[n]{b}$ are real numbers and $b \neq 0$, then $\dfrac{\sqrt[n]{a}}{\sqrt[n]{b}} = \sqrt[n]{\dfrac{a}{b}}$.	

4 EXAMPLE Dividing Radicals

Divide and simplify. Assume that all variables are positive.

a. $\dfrac{\sqrt[3]{32}}{\sqrt[3]{-4}}$

$$\dfrac{\sqrt[3]{32}}{\sqrt[3]{-4}} = \sqrt[3]{\dfrac{32}{-4}} = \sqrt[3]{-8} = -2$$

b. $\dfrac{\sqrt[3]{162x^5}}{\sqrt[3]{3x^2}}$

$$\dfrac{\sqrt[3]{162x^5}}{\sqrt[3]{3x^2}} = \sqrt[3]{\dfrac{162x^5}{3x^2}} = \sqrt[3]{54x^3} = \sqrt[3]{3^3 x^3 \cdot 2} = \sqrt[3]{3^3 x^3} \cdot \sqrt[3]{2} = 3x\sqrt[3]{2}$$

✓ Quick Check **4** Divide and simplify. Assume that all variables are positive.

a. $\dfrac{\sqrt{243}}{\sqrt{27}}$ b. $\dfrac{\sqrt{12x^4}}{\sqrt{3x}}$ c. $\dfrac{\sqrt[4]{1024x^{15}}}{\sqrt[4]{4x}}$

To **rationalize the denominator** of an expression, rewrite it so there are no radicals in any denominator and no denominators in any radical.

Rationalizing the denominator of a numerical expression makes it easier to calculate its decimal approximation. For example, $\dfrac{1}{\sqrt{2}} = \dfrac{\sqrt{2}}{2}$ and it is easier to divide by 2 than by $\sqrt{2}$.

5 EXAMPLE Rationalizing the Denominator

Rationalize the denominator of each expression. Assume that all variables are positive.

a. $\dfrac{\sqrt{2}}{\sqrt{3}}$

Method 1

$$\dfrac{\sqrt{2}}{\sqrt{3}} = \sqrt{\dfrac{2}{3}} = \sqrt{\dfrac{2 \cdot 3}{3 \cdot 3}} = \sqrt{\dfrac{6}{3^2}} = \dfrac{\sqrt{6}}{\sqrt{3^2}} = \dfrac{\sqrt{6}}{3}$$ Rewrite as a square root of a fraction. Then make the denominator a perfect square.

Method 2

$$\dfrac{\sqrt{2}}{\sqrt{3}} = \dfrac{\sqrt{2} \cdot \sqrt{3}}{\sqrt{3} \cdot \sqrt{3}} = \dfrac{\sqrt{6}}{3}$$ Multiply the numerator and denominator by $\sqrt{3}$ so the denominator becomes a whole number.

b. $\dfrac{\sqrt{x^3}}{\sqrt{5xy}}$

$$\dfrac{\sqrt{x^3}}{\sqrt{5xy}} = \dfrac{\sqrt{x^3} \cdot \sqrt{5xy}}{\sqrt{5xy} \cdot \sqrt{5xy}} = \dfrac{\sqrt{5x^4y}}{5xy} = \dfrac{x^2\sqrt{5y}}{5xy} = \dfrac{x\sqrt{5y}}{5y}$$

c. $\sqrt[3]{\dfrac{2}{3x}}$

$$\sqrt[3]{\dfrac{2}{3x}} = \sqrt[3]{\dfrac{2 \cdot 3^2 x^2}{3x \cdot 3^2 x^2}} = \sqrt[3]{\dfrac{18x^2}{3^3 x^3}} = \dfrac{\sqrt[3]{18x^2}}{3x}$$ Rewrite the fraction so the denominator is a perfect cube.

✓ Quick Check **5** Rationalize the denominator of each expression. Assume that the variables are positive.

a. $\sqrt{\dfrac{7}{5}}$ b. $\dfrac{\sqrt{2x^3}}{\sqrt{10xy}}$ c. $\dfrac{\sqrt[3]{4}}{\sqrt[3]{6x}}$

Einstein's famous formula $E = mc^2$ relates energy E, mass m, and the speed of light c. Express c in terms of E and m and rationalize the denominator.

$$E = mc^2$$

$$c^2 = \frac{E}{m}$$

$$c = \sqrt{\frac{E}{m}} = \sqrt{\frac{Em}{m^2}} = \frac{\sqrt{Em}}{\sqrt{m^2}} = \frac{\sqrt{Em}}{m}$$

 Quick Check **6** The formula $a = \frac{d}{t^2}$ relates the acceleration a of a moving object to the distance d it moves in the time t. Solve the formula for t and rationalize the denominator.

EXERCISES

For more exercises, see *Extra Skill and Word Problem Practice*.

Practice and Problem Solving

 **Practice by Example**

Example 1
(page 374)

 for Help

Multiply, if possible. Then simplify.

1. $\sqrt{8} \cdot \sqrt{32}$ **2.** $\sqrt[3]{4} \cdot \sqrt[3]{16}$ **3.** $\sqrt[3]{9} \cdot \sqrt[3]{-81}$ **4.** $\sqrt[4]{8} \cdot \sqrt[4]{32}$

5. $\sqrt{-5} \cdot \sqrt{5}$ **6.** $\sqrt[3]{-5} \cdot \sqrt[3]{-25}$ **7.** $\sqrt[3]{9} \cdot \sqrt[3]{-24}$ **8.** $\sqrt[3]{-12} \cdot \sqrt[3]{-18}$

Example 2
(page 375)

Simplify. Assume that all variables are positive.

9. $\sqrt{20x^3}$ **10.** $\sqrt[3]{81x^2}$ **11.** $\sqrt{50x^5}$ **12.** $\sqrt[3]{32a^5}$

13. $\sqrt[3]{54y^{10}}$ **14.** $\sqrt{200a^6b^7}$ **15.** $\sqrt[3]{-250x^6y^5}$ **16.** $\sqrt[4]{64x^3y^6}$

Example 3
(page 375)

Multiply and simplify. Assume that all variables are positive.

17. $\sqrt[3]{6} \cdot \sqrt[3]{16}$ **18.** $\sqrt{8y^5} \cdot \sqrt{40y^2}$

19. $\sqrt{7x^5} \cdot \sqrt{42xy^9}$ **20.** $4\sqrt{2x} \cdot 5\sqrt{6xy^2}$

21. $3\sqrt[3]{5y^3} \cdot 2\sqrt[3]{50y^4}$ **22.** $-\sqrt[3]{2x^2y^2} \cdot 2\sqrt[3]{15x^5y}$

Example 4
(page 376)

Divide and simplify. Assume that all variables are positive.

23. $\frac{\sqrt{500}}{\sqrt{5}}$ **24.** $\frac{\sqrt{48x^3}}{\sqrt{3xy^2}}$ **25.** $\frac{\sqrt{56x^5y^5}}{\sqrt{7xy}}$ **26.** $\frac{\sqrt[3]{250x^7y^3}}{\sqrt[3]{2x^2y}}$

Example 5
(page 376)

Rationalize the denominator of each expression. Assume that all variables are positive.

27. $\frac{\sqrt{x}}{\sqrt{2}}$ **28.** $\frac{\sqrt{5}}{\sqrt{8x}}$ **29.** $\frac{\sqrt[3]{x}}{\sqrt[3]{2}}$ **30.** $\sqrt[3]{\frac{5}{3x}}$

31. $\frac{\sqrt[4]{2}}{\sqrt[4]{5}}$ **32.** $\frac{15\sqrt{60x^5}}{3\sqrt{12x}}$ **33.** $\frac{\sqrt{3xy^2}}{\sqrt{5xy^3}}$ **34.** $\frac{\sqrt{5x^4y}}{\sqrt{2x^2y^3}}$

Example 6
(page 377)

35. Physics The formula $F = \frac{Gm_1m_2}{r^2}$ relates the gravitational force F between an object of mass m_1 and an object of mass m_2 separated by distance r. G is a constant known as the constant of gravitation. Solve the formula for r. Rationalize the denominator.

Apply Your Skills

36. a. Simplify $\dfrac{\sqrt{2} + \sqrt{3}}{\sqrt{75}}$ by multiplying the numerator and denominator by $\sqrt{75}$.

  b. Simplify the expression in (a) by multiplying by $\sqrt{3}$ instead of $\sqrt{75}$.

  c. Explain how you would simplify $\dfrac{\sqrt{2} + \sqrt{3}}{\sqrt{98}}$.

Simplify each expression. Rationalize all denominators. Assume that all variables are positive.

37. $\sqrt{5} \cdot \sqrt{40}$

38. $\sqrt[3]{4} \cdot \sqrt[3]{80}$

39. $\sqrt{x^5 y^5} \cdot 3\sqrt{2x^7 y^6}$

40. $5\sqrt{2xy^6} \cdot 2\sqrt{2x^3 y}$

41. $\sqrt{2}(\sqrt{50} + 7)$

42. $3(5 + \sqrt{21})$

43. $\sqrt{5}(\sqrt{5} + \sqrt{15})$

44. $\sqrt[3]{2x} \cdot \sqrt[3]{4} \cdot \sqrt[3]{2x^2}$

45. $\sqrt[3]{3x^2} \cdot \sqrt[3]{x^2} \cdot \sqrt[3]{9x^3}$

46. $\dfrac{\sqrt{5x^4}}{\sqrt{2x^2 y^3}}$

47. $\dfrac{5\sqrt{2}}{3\sqrt{7x}}$

48. $\dfrac{1}{\sqrt[3]{9x}}$

49. $\dfrac{10}{\sqrt[3]{5x^2}}$

50. $\dfrac{\sqrt[3]{14}}{\sqrt[3]{7x^2 y}}$

51. $\dfrac{3\sqrt{11x^3 y}}{-2\sqrt{12x^4 y}}$

52. $-2\left(\sqrt[3]{32} + \sqrt[3]{54}\right)$

53. $\dfrac{3 + \sqrt{5}}{\sqrt{5}}$

54. $\dfrac{\sqrt{3} - \sqrt{2}}{\sqrt{8}}$

55. Satellites The circular velocity v, in miles per hour, of a satellite orbiting Earth is given by the formula $v = \sqrt{\dfrac{1.24 \times 10^{12}}{r}}$, where r is the distance in miles from the satellite to the center of Earth. How much greater is the velocity of a satellite orbiting at an altitude of 100 mi than one orbiting at an altitude of 200 mi? (The radius of Earth is 3950 mi.)

56. Geometry A rectangular shelf is $\sqrt{440}$ cm by $\sqrt{20}$ cm. Find its area.

57. Error Analysis Explain the error in this simplification of radical expressions.
$\sqrt{-2} \cdot \sqrt{-8} = \sqrt{-2(-8)} = \sqrt{16} = 4$

58. Physics A freely falling object hit the ground in $\sqrt{18a^5}$ seconds. It fell h feet. Use the formula $h = 16t^2$ to find h in terms of a.

59. Writing Does $\sqrt{x^3} = \sqrt[3]{x^2}$ for all, some, or no values of x? Explain.

60. Open-Ended Of the equivalent expressions $\sqrt{\frac{2}{3}}$, $\frac{\sqrt{2}}{\sqrt{3}}$, and $\frac{\sqrt{6}}{3}$, which do you prefer to use for finding a decimal approximation with a calculator? Justify your reasoning.

Challenge

Simplify each expression. Rationalize all denominators. Assume that all variables are positive.

61. $\sqrt{\sqrt{16x^4 y^4}}$

62. $\sqrt[3]{\sqrt{64x^6 y^{12}}}$

63. $\sqrt{\sqrt[3]{8000}}$

64. $\sqrt[3]{x^{-1} y^{-2}}$

65. $\sqrt[5]{x^{-4} y}$

66. $\sqrt[6]{\dfrac{y^{-3}}{x^{-4}}}$

67. Critical Thinking When $\sqrt{x^a y^b}$ is simplified, the result is $\dfrac{1}{x^c y^{3d}}$, where c and d are positive integers. Express a in terms of c, and b in terms of d.

68. Critical Thinking In Example 3 you saw that $\sqrt[3]{54x^2 y^3} \cdot \sqrt[3]{5x^3 y^4}$ simplifies to $3xy^2 \sqrt[3]{10x^2 y}$, if you assume that all the variables are positive. Now assume that the variables represent any real numbers. What changes must be made in the answer? Explain.

Homework Video Tutor
Visit: PHSchool.com
Web Code: age-0702

Real-World 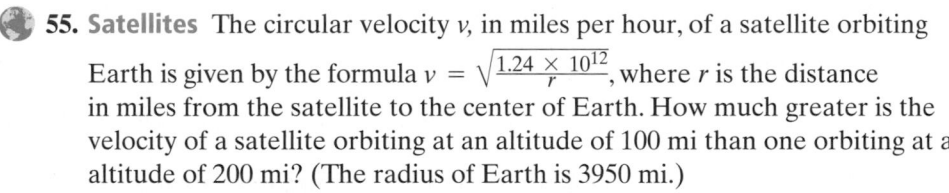 **Connection**

A satellite being launched from the cargo bay of the space shuttle

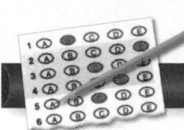

Multiple Choice

69. Which expression does NOT simplify to -10?

A. $-\sqrt[3]{1000}$

B. $\sqrt{25} \cdot \sqrt[3]{-8}$

C. $-\sqrt{25} \cdot \sqrt[5]{-32}$

D. $\sqrt[3]{-125} \cdot \sqrt[4]{16}$

70. How can you write $\sqrt[3]{\frac{5}{2xy}}$ with a rationalized denominator?

F. $\frac{\sqrt[3]{5}}{2xy}$

G. $\frac{\sqrt[3]{20}}{2xy}$

H. $\frac{\sqrt[3]{20x^2y^2}}{2xy}$

J. $\frac{\sqrt[3]{4x^2y^2}}{2xy}$

71. What is the simplified form of $\frac{3 - \sqrt{5}}{\sqrt{5}}$?

A. $\frac{3\sqrt{5} - 5}{5}$

B. $\frac{5\sqrt{3} - 5}{5}$

C. $\frac{3\sqrt{3} - \sqrt{15}}{5}$

D. $\frac{14 - 6\sqrt{5}}{5}$

72. To rationalize the denominator of $\sqrt[3]{\frac{2}{9}}$, by what number would you multiply the numerator and denominator of the fraction?

F. 2

G. 3

H. 6

J. 9

73. Which of the following expressions is in simplest form?

A. $\sqrt{20x^3}$

B. $\sqrt[3]{81x}$

C. $\sqrt{\frac{6}{2}}$

D. $\frac{\sqrt{2}}{5}$

Short Response

74. For what values of x is $\sqrt{x} \cdot \sqrt{-x}$ a real number? Explain.

Extended Response

75. Rationalize the denominator of $\sqrt[3]{\frac{3}{2x}}$. Explain your steps.

Mixed Review

 **for Help**

Lesson 7-1

Simplify each radical expression. Use absolute value symbols as needed.

76. $\sqrt{121a^{90}}$

77. $-\sqrt{81c^{48}d^{64}}$

78. $\sqrt[3]{-64a^{81}}$

79. $\sqrt[5]{32y^{25}}$

80. $\sqrt{0.25x^6}$

81. $\sqrt[7]{x^{14}y^{35}}$

82. $\sqrt[4]{16x^{36}y^{96}}$

83. $\sqrt{0.0064x^{40}}$

Lesson 6-3

Divide. Tell whether each divisor is a factor of the dividend.

84. $(y^3 - 64) \div (y + 4)$

85. $(x^3 + 27) \div (x + 3)$

86. $(6a^3 + a^2 - a + 4) \div (2a + 1)$

87. $(2x^4 - 3x^3 - 4x + 10) \div (x - 2)$

Lesson 5-7

Complete the square.

88. $x^2 + 10x + \blacksquare$

89. $x^2 - 10x + \blacksquare$

90. $x^2 + 11x + \blacksquare$

91. $x^2 - 11x + \blacksquare$

92. $x^2 - \frac{x}{3} + \blacksquare$

93. $x^2 + 0.3x + \blacksquare$

94. $x^2 - \frac{3}{4}x + \blacksquare$

95. $x^2 + \frac{3}{5}x + \blacksquare$

7-3

Binomial Radical Expressions

What You'll Learn

- To add and subtract radical expressions
- To multiply and divide binomial radical expressions

. . . And Why

To find the dimensions of a window design, as in Example 2

✓ **Check Skills You'll Need**  **for Help** Lesson 5-1 or Skills Handbook page 881

Multiply.

1. $(5x + 4)(3x - 2)$
2. $(-8x + 5)(3x - 7)$
3. $(x + 4)(x - 4)$
4. $(4x + 5)(4x - 5)$
5. $(x + 5)^2$
6. $(2x - 9)^2$

◀)) **New Vocabulary** • like radicals

1   Adding and Subtracting Radical Expressions

Like radicals are radical expressions that have the same index and the same radicand. To add or subtract like radicals, use the Distributive Property.

1 EXAMPLE   Adding and Subtracting Radical Expressions

Add or subtract if possible.

a. $5\sqrt[3]{x} - 3\sqrt[3]{x}$

$$5\sqrt[3]{x} - 3\sqrt[3]{x} = (5 - 3)\sqrt[3]{x} \quad \textbf{Distributive Property with like radicals}$$
$$= 2\sqrt[3]{x} \qquad \textbf{Simplify.}$$

b. $4\sqrt{2} + 5\sqrt{3}$

The radicals are not like radicals. They cannot be combined.

✓ **Quick Check** ❶ Add or subtract if possible.

a. $2\sqrt{7} + 3\sqrt{7}$ **b.** $7\sqrt[4]{5} - 2\sqrt[3]{5}$ **c.** $4\sqrt{xy} + 5\sqrt{xy}$

2 EXAMPLE   Real-World Connection

Gridded Response In the stained-glass window design at the left, the side of each small square is 5 in. Find the perimeter of the window to the nearest tenth of an inch.

The diagonal of a square with side s is $s\sqrt{2}$. So the window's height is $2(5\sqrt{2})$ in., or $10\sqrt{2}$ in. The length is $3(5\sqrt{2})$ in., or $15\sqrt{2}$ in. The perimeter is $2(10\sqrt{2} + 15\sqrt{2})$in., or $50\sqrt{2}$ in. To the nearest tenth of an inch, the perimeter is 70.7 in.

7	0	.	7
	⊘	⊘	
⊙	⊙	●	⊙
	⓪	⓪	⓪
①	①	①	①
②	②	②	②
③	③	③	③
④	④	④	④
⑤	⑤	⑤	⑤
⑥	⑥	⑥	⑥
●	⑦	⑦	●
⑧	⑧	⑧	⑧
⑨	⑨	⑨	⑨

✓ **Quick Check** ❷ Find the perimeter of the window if each small square is 6 in. on a side.

Simplify radicals before adding or subtracting so you can find all the like radicals.

Test-Taking Tip

A gridded response for an answer that contains a radical has to be an approximation.

3 EXAMPLE Simplifying Before Adding or Subtracting

Simplify $6\sqrt{18} + 4\sqrt{8} - 3\sqrt{72}$.

$$6\sqrt{18} + 4\sqrt{8} - 3\sqrt{72} = 6\sqrt{3^2 \cdot 2} + 4\sqrt{2^2 \cdot 2} - 3\sqrt{6^2 \cdot 2} \quad \text{Factor each radicand.}$$
$$= 6 \cdot 3\sqrt{2} + 4 \cdot 2\sqrt{2} - 3 \cdot 6\sqrt{2} \quad \text{Simplify each radical.}$$
$$= 18\sqrt{2} + 8\sqrt{2} - 18\sqrt{2} \quad \text{Multiply.}$$
$$= (18 + 8 - 18)\sqrt{2} \quad \text{Distributive Property}$$
$$= 8\sqrt{2}$$

✓ **Quick Check** ③ Simplify $\sqrt{50} + 3\sqrt{32} - 5\sqrt{18}$.

---

2 Multiplying and Dividing Binomial Radical Expressions

GO Online

Video Tutor Help
Visit: PHSchool.com
Web Code: age-0775

Multiply radical expressions that are in the form of binomials by using FOIL.

4 EXAMPLE Multiplying Binomial Radical Expressions

Multiply $(3 + 2\sqrt{5})(2 + 4\sqrt{5})$.

$$(3 + 2\sqrt{5})(2 + 4\sqrt{5}) = 3 \cdot 2 + 3 \cdot 4\sqrt{5} + 2 \cdot 2\sqrt{5} + 2\sqrt{5} \cdot 4\sqrt{5} \quad \text{Use FOIL.}$$
$$= 6 + 12\sqrt{5} + 4\sqrt{5} + 40 \quad \text{Multiply.}$$
$$= 6 + (12 + 4)\sqrt{5} + 40 \quad \text{Combine like radicals.}$$
$$= 46 + 16\sqrt{5}$$

✓ **Quick Check** ④ Multiply $(\sqrt{2} - \sqrt{3})^2$.

GO for Help

To review conjugates, go to Lesson 6-5.

Conjugates are expressions, such as $\sqrt{a} + \sqrt{b}$ and $\sqrt{a} - \sqrt{b}$, that differ only in the sign of the second terms. If a and b are rational numbers, then the product of these conjugates is a rational number.

Let a and b represent rational numbers.
$$(\sqrt{a} + \sqrt{b})(\sqrt{a} - \sqrt{b}) = (\sqrt{a})^2 - (\sqrt{b})^2 \quad \text{The product is the difference of squares.}$$
$$= a - b \quad \text{Simplify.}$$
The difference of the rational numbers a and b is a rational number. So the product of the conjugates is a rational number.

5 EXAMPLE Multiplying Conjugates

Multiply $(2 + \sqrt{3})(2 - \sqrt{3})$.

$$(2 + \sqrt{3})(2 - \sqrt{3}) = 2^2 - (\sqrt{3})^2 \quad (a + b)(a - b) = a^2 - b^2$$
$$= 4 - 3$$
$$= 1$$

✓ **Quick Check** ⑤ Multiply $(\sqrt{5} + \sqrt{2})(\sqrt{5} - \sqrt{2})$.

Sometimes you need to rationalize the denominator of a fraction when the denominator is a binomial radical expression. Multiply the numerator and denominator of the fraction by the conjugate of the denominator.

6 EXAMPLE Rationalizing Binomial Radical Denominators

Rationalize the denominator of $\dfrac{3 + \sqrt{5}}{1 - \sqrt{5}}$.

$$\frac{3 + \sqrt{5}}{1 - \sqrt{5}} = \frac{3 + \sqrt{5}}{1 - \sqrt{5}} \cdot \frac{1 + \sqrt{5}}{1 + \sqrt{5}} \qquad \mathbf{1 + \sqrt{5}} \text{ is the conjugate of } \mathbf{1 - \sqrt{5}}.$$

$$= \frac{(3 + \sqrt{5})(1 + \sqrt{5})}{(1 - \sqrt{5})(1 + \sqrt{5})} \qquad \text{Multiply.}$$

$$= \frac{3 + 3\sqrt{5} + \sqrt{5} + (\sqrt{5})^2}{1^2 - (\sqrt{5})^2} \qquad \text{Simplify.}$$

$$= \frac{8 + 4\sqrt{5}}{-4}$$

$$= \frac{8}{-4} + \frac{4\sqrt{5}}{-4}$$

$$= -2 - \sqrt{5}$$

✓ Quick Check ⑥ Rationalize the denominator of $\dfrac{6 + \sqrt{15}}{4 - \sqrt{15}}$.

EXERCISES

For more exercises, see *Extra Skill and Word Problem Practice.*

Practice and Problem Solving

A Practice by Example

Examples 1 and 2
(page 380)

Example 3
(page 381)

Example 4
(page 381)

Example 5
(page 381)

Example 6
(page 382)

Add or subtract if possible.

1. $5\sqrt{6} + \sqrt{6}$　　　**2.** $6\sqrt[3]{3} - 2\sqrt[3]{3}$　　　**3.** $4\sqrt{3} + 4\sqrt[3]{3}$

4. $3\sqrt{x} - 5\sqrt{x}$　　　**5.** $14\sqrt{x} + 3\sqrt{y}$　　　**6.** $7\sqrt[3]{x^2} - 2\sqrt[3]{x^2}$

Simplify.

7. $6\sqrt{18} + 3\sqrt{50}$　　　**8.** $14\sqrt{20} - 3\sqrt{125}$　　　**9.** $\sqrt{18} + \sqrt{32}$

10. $\sqrt[3]{54} + \sqrt[3]{16}$　　　**11.** $3\sqrt[3]{81} - 2\sqrt[3]{54}$　　　**12.** $\sqrt[4]{32} + \sqrt[4]{48}$

Multiply.

13. $(3 + \sqrt{5})(1 + \sqrt{5})$　　　　　**14.** $(2 + \sqrt{7})(1 + 3\sqrt{7})$

15. $(3 - 4\sqrt{2})(5 - 6\sqrt{2})$　　　　　**16.** $(\sqrt{3} + \sqrt{5})^2$

17. $(\sqrt{13} + 6)^2$　　　　　**18.** $(2\sqrt{5} + 3\sqrt{2})^2$

Multiply each pair of conjugates.

19. $(5 - \sqrt{11})(5 + \sqrt{11})$　　　　　**20.** $(4 - 2\sqrt{3})(4 + 2\sqrt{3})$

21. $(2\sqrt{6} + 8)(2\sqrt{6} - 8)$　　　　　**22.** $(\sqrt{3} + \sqrt{5})(\sqrt{3} - \sqrt{5})$

Rationalize each denominator. Simplify the answer.

23. $\dfrac{4}{1 + \sqrt{3}}$　　　**24.** $\dfrac{4}{3\sqrt{3} - 2}$　　　**25.** $\dfrac{5 + \sqrt{3}}{2 - \sqrt{3}}$　　　**26.** $\dfrac{3 + \sqrt{8}}{2 - 2\sqrt{8}}$

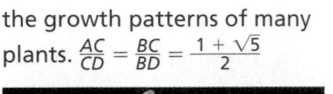

B **Apply Your Skills**

Simplify. Rationalize all denominators. Assume that all the variables are positive.

27. $\sqrt{72} + \sqrt{32} + \sqrt{18}$
28. $\sqrt{75} + 2\sqrt{48} - 5\sqrt{3}$

29. $5\sqrt{32x} + 4\sqrt{98x}$
30. $\sqrt{75} - 4\sqrt{18} + 2\sqrt{32}$

31. $4\sqrt{216y^2} + 3\sqrt{54y^2}$
32. $3\sqrt[3]{16} - 4\sqrt[3]{54} + \sqrt[3]{128}$

33. $(\sqrt{3} - \sqrt{7})(\sqrt{3} + 2\sqrt{7})$
34. $(2\sqrt{5} + 3\sqrt{2})(5\sqrt{5} - 7\sqrt{2})$

35. $(1 + \sqrt{72})(5 + \sqrt{2})$
36. $(2 - \sqrt{98})(3 + \sqrt{18})$

37. $(\sqrt{x} + \sqrt{3})(\sqrt{x} + 2\sqrt{3})$
38. $(2\sqrt{y} - 3\sqrt{2})(4\sqrt{y} - 5\sqrt{2})$

39. $\dfrac{4 + \sqrt{27}}{2 - 3\sqrt{27}}$
40. $\dfrac{4 + \sqrt{6}}{\sqrt{2} + \sqrt{3}}$

41. $\dfrac{5 - \sqrt{21}}{\sqrt{3} - \sqrt{7}}$
42. $\dfrac{3 + \sqrt[3]{2}}{\sqrt[3]{2}}$

43. $\dfrac{5 + \sqrt[4]{x}}{\sqrt[4]{x}}$
44. $\dfrac{4 - 2\sqrt[3]{6}}{\sqrt[3]{4}}$

Homework Video Tutor

Visit: PHSchool.com
Web Code: age-0703

Real-World Connection

The golden ratio is found in the growth patterns of many plants. $\dfrac{AC}{CD} = \dfrac{BC}{BD} = \dfrac{1 + \sqrt{5}}{2}$

45. The golden ratio is $\dfrac{1 + \sqrt{5}}{2}$. Find the difference between the golden ratio and its reciprocal.

46. **Critical Thinking** Describe the possible values of a such that $\sqrt{72} + \sqrt{a}$ can be simplified to a single term.

47. **Writing** Discuss the advantages and disadvantages of first simplifying $\sqrt{72} + \sqrt{32} + \sqrt{18}$ in order to estimate its decimal value.

48. **Physics** An object is moving at a speed of $(3 + \sqrt{2})$ ft/s. How long will it take the object to travel 20 ft?

49. **Open-Ended** Find two pairs of conjugates with a product of 3.

50. **Multiple Choice** The length of a rectangle is $(3 + \sqrt{5})x$. The height is $(1 + 2\sqrt{5})y$. Which expression best describes the area of a rectangle?

   Ⓐ $(4 + 3\sqrt{5})(x + y)$ Ⓑ $13xy$

   Ⓒ $(6 + 2\sqrt{5})x + (2 + 4\sqrt{5})y$ Ⓓ $(13 + 7\sqrt{5})xy$

C **Challenge**

Add or subtract.

51. $\dfrac{1}{1 - \sqrt{5}} + \dfrac{1}{1 + \sqrt{5}}$
52. $\dfrac{4}{\sqrt{5} - \sqrt{3}} - \dfrac{4}{\sqrt{5} + \sqrt{3}}$

53. For what values of a and b does $\sqrt{a} + \sqrt{b} = \sqrt{a + b}$?

54. **Error Analysis** A student used the steps shown below to simplify an expression. Find the student's error and explain why the step is incorrect.

$$\frac{1}{(1 - \sqrt{2})^2} = (1 - \sqrt{2})^{-2}$$
$$= 1^{-2} - (\sqrt{2})^{-2}$$
$$= \frac{1}{1^2} - \frac{1}{(\sqrt{2^2})} = \frac{1}{1} - \frac{1}{2} = \frac{1}{2}$$

55. In the expression $\sqrt[n]{x^m}$, m and n are positive integers and x is a real number. The expression can be simplified.
   a. If $x > 0$, what are the possible values for m and n?
   b. If $x < 0$, what are the possible values for m and n?
   c. If $x < 0$ and an absolute value symbol is needed in the simplified expression, what are the possible values of m and n?

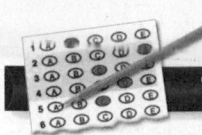
Multiple Choice

56. Which expression does NOT simplify to one term?

  A. $-4\sqrt{8} + \sqrt{18}$ B. $\sqrt{27} - \sqrt{8}$

  C. $\sqrt{32} + 3\sqrt{8}$ D. $\sqrt{12} - \sqrt{75}$

57. What is an expression for $\sqrt{20} - \sqrt{80} + \sqrt{125}$?

  F. $\sqrt{65}$ G. $13\sqrt{5}$ H. $11\sqrt{5}$ J. $3\sqrt{5}$

58. Which expression is NOT equal to 13?

  A. $(4 + \sqrt{3})(4 - \sqrt{3})$ B. $(5 - 2\sqrt{3})(5 + 2\sqrt{3})$

  C. $(6 + \sqrt{23})(6 - \sqrt{23})$ D. $(7 - \sqrt{6})(7 + \sqrt{6})$

59. How can you write $\dfrac{1 + \sqrt{3}}{5 - \sqrt{3}}$ with a rationalized denominator?

  F. -1 G. $-2 - 3\sqrt{3}$ H. $4 + 3\sqrt{3}$ J. $\dfrac{4 + 3\sqrt{3}}{11}$

60. Which of the following is equivalent to $(2 + 3\sqrt{5})(3 + 3\sqrt{5})$?

  A. 51 B. $6 + 9\sqrt{5}$ C. $6 + 24\sqrt{5}$ D. $51 + 15\sqrt{5}$

Short Response

61. Is the product $\left(1 - \sqrt[3]{8}\right)\left(1 + \sqrt[3]{8}\right)$ a rational number? Explain.

Extended Response

62. What is the value of $\dfrac{2}{5 + 2\sqrt{2}} - \dfrac{3}{5 - 2\sqrt{2}}$? Show your work.

Mixed Review

GO for Help

Lesson 7-2

Simplify each expression. Rationalize all denominators. Assume that all variables are positive.

63. $\sqrt[3]{3} \cdot \sqrt[3]{18}$ **64.** $\sqrt{3x} \cdot \sqrt{5x}$ **65.** $\dfrac{\sqrt{32}}{\sqrt{2}}$ **66.** $\dfrac{\sqrt{62}}{\sqrt{6}}$

67. $\sqrt[3]{2x^2} \cdot \sqrt[3]{4x}$ **68.** $\sqrt{7x} \cdot \sqrt{14x^3}$ **69.** $\dfrac{\sqrt{6m}}{\sqrt{2mn}}$ **70.** $\sqrt[3]{\dfrac{4}{5x}}$

Lesson 6-4

Solve each equation.

71. $2x^3 - 16 = 0$ **72.** $x^3 + 1000 = 0$ **73.** $125x^3 - 1 = 0$

74. $x^4 - 14x^2 + 49 = 0$ **75.** $25x^4 - 40x^2 + 16 = 0$ **76.** $81x^4 - 1 = 0$

✓ Checkpoint Quiz 1   Lessons 7-1 through 7-3

Simplify each radical expression. Use absolute value symbols when needed.

1. $\sqrt[4]{b^4c^8}$ **2.** $\sqrt[5]{x^5y^{10}}$ **3.** $\sqrt[3]{-a^3}$ **4.** $\sqrt[5]{-y^{10}}$

Simplify each expression. Rationalize all denominators. Assume that all variables are positive.

5. $\sqrt{8}(\sqrt{24} + 3\sqrt{8})$ **6.** $2\sqrt{5x^3} \cdot 3\sqrt{28x^3y^2}$

7. $4\sqrt[3]{81} - 3\sqrt[3]{54}$ **8.** $\dfrac{4\sqrt{2xy}}{9\sqrt{5x^2y}}$

9. $(\sqrt{5} + 2\sqrt{3})(\sqrt{5} - 2\sqrt{3})$ **10.** $\dfrac{5}{4\sqrt{7} + 5}$

Rational Exponents

Check Skills You'll Need

GO for **Help** page 368

Simplify.

1. 2^{-4}

2. $(3x)^{-2}$

3. $(5x^2y)^{-3}$

4. $2^{-2} + 4^{-1}$

5. $(2a^{-2}b^3)^4$

6. $(4a^3b^{-1})^{-2}$

🔊 **New Vocabulary** • rational exponent

---

1   Simplifying Expressions With Rational Exponents

Another way to write a radical expression is to use a **rational exponent.** See the examples at the right.

Like the radical form, the exponent form always indicates the principal root.

Radical form		Exponent form
$\sqrt{25}$	$=$	$25^{\frac{1}{2}}$
$\sqrt[3]{27}$	$=$	$27^{\frac{1}{3}}$
$\sqrt[4]{16}$	$=$	$16^{\frac{1}{4}}$

Vocabulary Tip

Exponent comes from the Latin word meaning "place outside."

1   EXAMPLE   Simplifying Expressions With Rational Exponents

Simplify each expression.

a. $125^{\frac{1}{3}}$

$$125^{\frac{1}{3}} = \sqrt[3]{125} \qquad \text{Rewrite as a radical.}$$
$$= \sqrt[3]{5^3} \qquad \text{Rewrite 125 as a cube.}$$
$$= 5 \qquad \text{Simplify.}$$

b. $5^{\frac{1}{2}} \cdot 5^{\frac{1}{2}}$

$$5^{\frac{1}{2}} \cdot 5^{\frac{1}{2}} = \sqrt{5} \cdot \sqrt{5} \qquad \text{Rewrite as radicals.}$$
$$= 5 \qquad \text{By definition, } \sqrt{5} \text{ is the number whose square is 5.}$$

c. $10^{\frac{1}{3}} \cdot 100^{\frac{1}{3}}$

$$10^{\frac{1}{3}} \cdot 100^{\frac{1}{3}} = \sqrt[3]{10} \cdot \sqrt[3]{100} \qquad \text{Rewrite as radicals.}$$
$$= \sqrt[3]{10 \cdot 100} \qquad \text{Property for multiplying radical expressions}$$
$$= \sqrt[3]{10^3} \qquad \text{Rewrite the radicand as a cube.}$$
$$= 10 \qquad \text{Simplify.}$$

✓ **Quick Check** ❶ Simplify each expression.

     a. $16^{\frac{1}{4}}$ **b.** $2^{\frac{1}{2}} \cdot 2^{\frac{1}{2}}$ **c.** $2^{\frac{1}{2}} \cdot 8^{\frac{1}{2}}$

A rational exponent may have a numerator other than 1. The property $(a^m)^n = a^{mn}$ shows how to rewrite an expression with an exponent that is an improper fraction.

$$25^{\frac{3}{2}} = 25^{(3 \cdot \frac{1}{2})} = (25^3)^{\frac{1}{2}} = \sqrt{25^3} \quad \text{or} \quad 25^{\frac{3}{2}} = 25^{(\frac{1}{2} \cdot 3)} = (25^{\frac{1}{2}})^3 = (\sqrt{25})^3$$

 Key Concepts

Definition	Rational Exponents

If the nth root of a is a real number and m is an integer, then

$$a^{\frac{1}{n}} = \sqrt[n]{a} \quad \text{and} \quad a^{\frac{m}{n}} = \sqrt[n]{a^m} = (\sqrt[n]{a})^m.$$ If m is negative, $a \neq 0$.

 **Converting to and From Radical Form**

a. Write the exponential expressions $x^{\frac{3}{5}}$ and $y^{-2.5}$ in radical form.

$$x^{\frac{3}{5}} = \sqrt[5]{x^3} \text{ or } (\sqrt[5]{x})^3 \qquad\qquad y^{-2.5} = y^{-\frac{5}{2}} = \frac{1}{\sqrt{y^5}} \text{ or } \frac{1}{(\sqrt{y})^5}$$

b. Write the radical expressions $\sqrt{a^3}$ and $(\sqrt[5]{b})^2$ in exponential form.

$$\sqrt{a^3} = a^{\frac{3}{2}} \qquad\qquad (\sqrt[5]{b})^2 = b^{\frac{2}{5}}$$

 **Quick Check** **2 a.** Write the expressions $y^{-\frac{3}{8}}$ and $z^{0.4}$ in radical form.

b. Write the expressions $\sqrt[3]{x^2}$ and $(\sqrt{y})^3$ in exponential form.

c. Critical Thinking Refer to the definition of rational exponents. Explain the need for the following restriction: If m is negative, $a \neq 0$.

3 EXAMPLE **Real-World**  **Connection**

Graphing Calculator Hint

Use the $\wedge$ key to enter an exponent. If the exponent is a fraction, enclose it in parentheses. For example, $729^{\frac{2}{3}}$ is entered as
729 $\wedge$ $(2 \div 3)$.

Space Travel Bone loss for astronauts on lengthy space voyages may be prevented with a bedlike apparatus that rotates to simulate the effect of gravity. In the formula $N = \dfrac{a^{0.5}}{2\pi r^{0.5}}$, N is the rate of rotation in revolutions per second, a is the simulated acceleration in m/s^2, and r is the radius of the apparatus in meters. How fast would an apparatus with a radius of 1.7 m have to rotate to simulate the acceleration of 9.8 m/s^2 that is due to Earth's gravity?

$$N = \frac{a^{0.5}}{2\pi r^{0.5}} \qquad \text{Write the formula.}$$

$$= \frac{9.8^{0.5}}{2\pi (1.7)^{0.5}} \qquad \text{Substitute for } a \text{ and } r.$$

$$\approx 0.382 \qquad \text{Use a calculator.}$$

The apparatus would have to rotate about 0.382 revolutions per second, or about 23 revolutions per minute.

 **Quick Check** **3** Calculate the rate of rotation needed for the apparatus in Example 3 to simulate a gravitational acceleration half as strong as Earth's.

All of the properties of integer exponents also apply to rational exponents. Here is a summary.

Key Concepts

GO for Help

Refer to the properties of integer exponents on p. 368.

Summary	Properties of Rational Exponents

Let m and n represent rational numbers. Assume that no denominator equals 0.

Property	Example
$a^m \cdot a^n = a^{m+n}$	$8^{\frac{1}{3}} \cdot 8^{\frac{2}{3}} = 8^{\frac{1}{3}+\frac{2}{3}} = 8^1 = 8$
$(a^m)^n = a^{mn}$	$\left(5^{\frac{1}{2}}\right)^4 = 5^{\frac{1}{2}\cdot4} = 5^2 = 25$
$(ab)^m = a^m b^m$	$(4 \cdot 5)^{\frac{1}{2}} = 4^{\frac{1}{2}} \cdot 5^{\frac{1}{2}} = 2 \cdot 5^{\frac{1}{2}}$
$a^{-m} = \dfrac{1}{a^m}$	$9^{-\frac{1}{2}} = \dfrac{1}{9^{\frac{1}{2}}} = \dfrac{1}{3}$
$\dfrac{a^m}{a^n} = a^{m-n}$	$\dfrac{\pi^{\frac{3}{2}}}{\pi^{\frac{1}{2}}} = \pi^{\frac{3}{2}-\frac{1}{2}} = \pi^1 = \pi$
$\left(\dfrac{a}{b}\right)^m = \dfrac{a^m}{b^m}$	$\left(\dfrac{5}{27}\right)^{\frac{1}{3}} = \dfrac{5^{\frac{1}{3}}}{27^{\frac{1}{3}}} = \dfrac{5^{\frac{1}{3}}}{3}$

You can simplify a number with a rational exponent by using the properties of exponents or by converting the expression to a radical expression.

GO Online

Video Tutor Help

Visit: PHSchool.com
Web Code: age-0775

4 EXAMPLE   Simplifying Numbers With Rational Exponents

Simplify each number.

a. $(-32)^{\frac{3}{5}}$

Method 1

$$(-32)^{\frac{3}{5}} = \left((-2)^5\right)^{\frac{3}{5}}$$
$$= (-2)^{5 \cdot \frac{3}{5}}$$
$$= (-2)^3$$
$$= -8$$

Method 2

$$(-32)^{\frac{3}{5}} = \left(\sqrt[5]{-32}\right)^3$$
$$= \left(\sqrt[5]{(-2)^5}\right)^3$$
$$= (-2)^3$$
$$= -8$$

b. $4^{-3.5}$

Method 1

$$4^{-3.5} = 4^{-\frac{7}{2}}$$
$$= \left(2^2\right)^{-\frac{7}{2}}$$
$$= 2^{2 \cdot -\frac{7}{2}}$$
$$= 2^{-7}$$
$$= \frac{1}{2^7}$$
$$= \frac{1}{128}$$

Method 2

$$4^{-3.5} = 4^{-\frac{7}{2}}$$
$$= \frac{1}{4^{\frac{7}{2}}}$$
$$= \frac{1}{(\sqrt{4})^7}$$
$$= \frac{1}{2^7}$$
$$= \frac{1}{128}$$

✔ Quick Check 4 Simplify each number.

a. $25^{-\frac{3}{2}}$ **b.** $32^{\frac{3}{5}}$ **c.** $(-32)^{\frac{4}{5}}$

To write an expression with rational exponents in simplest form, write every exponent as a positive number.

5 EXAMPLE **Writing Expressions in Simplest Form**

Write $\left(16y^{-8}\right)^{-\frac{3}{4}}$ in simplest form.

$$\left(16y^{-8}\right)^{-\frac{3}{4}} = \left(2^4 y^{-8}\right)^{-\frac{3}{4}}$$
$$= 2^{4 \cdot \left(-\frac{3}{4}\right)} \cdot y^{-8 \cdot \left(-\frac{3}{4}\right)}$$
$$= 2^{-3} y^6$$
$$= \frac{y^6}{2^3}$$
$$= \frac{y^6}{8}$$

✓ Quick Check **5** Write $\left(8x^{15}\right)^{-\frac{1}{3}}$ in simplest form.

EXERCISES

For more exercises, see *Extra Skill and Word Problem Practice*.

Practice and Problem Solving

A Practice by Example

Example 1
(page 385)

Simplify each expression.

1. $36^{\frac{1}{2}}$ **2.** $27^{\frac{1}{3}}$ **3.** $49^{\frac{1}{2}}$

4. $10^{\frac{1}{2}} \cdot 10^{\frac{1}{2}}$ **5.** $(-3)^{\frac{1}{3}} \cdot (-3)^{\frac{1}{3}} \cdot (-3)^{\frac{1}{3}}$ **6.** $3^{\frac{1}{2}} \cdot 12^{\frac{1}{2}}$

7. $2^{\frac{1}{2}} \cdot 32^{\frac{1}{2}}$ **8.** $3^{\frac{1}{3}} \cdot 9^{\frac{1}{3}}$ **9.** $3^{\frac{1}{4}} \cdot 27^{\frac{1}{4}}$

Example 2
(page 386)

Write each expression in radical form.

10. $x^{\frac{1}{6}}$ **11.** $x^{\frac{1}{5}}$ **12.** $x^{\frac{2}{7}}$ **13.** $y^{\frac{2}{5}}$

14. $y^{-\frac{9}{8}}$ **15.** $t^{-\frac{3}{4}}$ **16.** $x^{1.5}$ **17.** $y^{1.2}$

Write each expression in exponential form.

18. $\sqrt{-10}$ **19.** $\sqrt{7x^3}$ **20.** $\sqrt{(7x)^3}$ **21.** $\left(\sqrt{7x}\right)^3$

22. $\sqrt[3]{a^2}$ **23.** $\left(\sqrt[3]{a}\right)^2$ **24.** $\sqrt[4]{c^2}$ **25.** $\sqrt[3]{(5xy)^6}$

Example 3
(page 386)

The optimal height h of the letters of a message printed on pavement is given by the formula $h = \frac{0.00252d^{2.27}}{e}$. Here d is the distance of the driver from the letters and e is the height of the driver's eye above the pavement. All of the distances are in meters. Find h for the given values of d and e.

26. $d = 100$ m, $e = 1.2$ m   **27.** $d = 50$ m, $e = 1.2$ m

28. $d = 50$ m, $e = 2.3$ m   **29.** $d = 25$ m, $e = 2.3$ m

Example 4
(page 387)

Simplify each number.

30. $8^{\frac{2}{3}}$ **31.** $64^{\frac{2}{3}}$ **32.** $(-8)^{\frac{2}{3}}$ **33.** $(-32)^{\frac{6}{5}}$

34. $(32)^{-\frac{4}{5}}$ **35.** $4^{1.5}$ **36.** $16^{1.5}$ **37.** $10,000^{0.75}$

Example 5
(page 388)

Write each expression in simplest form. Assume that all variables are positive.

38. $\left(x^{\frac{2}{3}}\right)^{-3}$ **39.** $\left(x^{-\frac{4}{7}}\right)^7$ **40.** $\left(3x^{\frac{2}{3}}\right)^{-1}$ **41.** $5\left(x^{\frac{2}{3}}\right)^{-1}$

42. $\left(-27x^{-9}\right)^{\frac{1}{3}}$ **43.** $\left(-32y^{15}\right)^{\frac{1}{5}}$ **44.** $\left(\dfrac{x^3}{x^{-1}}\right)^{-\frac{1}{4}}$ **45.** $\left(\dfrac{x^2}{x^{-11}}\right)^{\frac{1}{3}}$

46. $\left(x^{\frac{1}{2}}y^{-\frac{2}{3}}\right)^{-6}$ **47.** $\left(x^{\frac{2}{3}}y^{-\frac{1}{6}}\right)^{-12}$ **48.** $\left(\dfrac{x^{\frac{1}{4}}}{y^{-\frac{3}{4}}}\right)^{12}$ **49.** $\left(\dfrac{x^{-\frac{2}{3}}}{y^{-\frac{1}{3}}}\right)^{15}$

 **Apply Your Skills**

Simplify each number.

50. $(-343)^{\frac{1}{3}}$ **51.** $(-243)^{\frac{1}{5}}$ **52.** $32^{1.2}$ **53.** $243^{1.2}$

54. $64^{3.5}$ **55.** $100^{4.5}$ **56.** $32^{-0.4}$ **57.** $64^{-0.5}$

58. $(-216)^{-\frac{2}{3}}$ **59.** $2(16)^{\frac{3}{4}}$ **60.** $-(-27)^{-\frac{4}{3}}$ **61.** $\dfrac{1000^{\frac{4}{3}}}{100^{\frac{3}{2}}}$

62. Archaeology The ratio R of radioactive carbon to nonradioactive carbon left in a sample of an organism that died T years ago can be approximated by the formula $R = A(2.7)^{-\frac{T}{8033}}$. Here A is the ratio of radioactive carbon to nonradioactive carbon in the living organism. What percent of A is left after 2000 years? After 4000 years? After 8000 years?

63. Multiple Choice The expression $0.036m^{\frac{3}{4}}$ is used in the study of fluids. Which best represents the value of the expression for $m = 46 \times 10^4$?

   Ⓐ 636   Ⓑ 1460   Ⓒ 1660   Ⓓ 16,600

64. Physics In the expression $PV^{\frac{7}{5}}$, P represents the pressure and V represents the volume of a sample of a gas. Evaluate the expression for $P = 6$ and $V = 32$.

Real-World Connection

Archaeologists estimate the ages of artifacts and fossils by using exponential functions.

Simplify each expression. Assume that all variables are positive.

65. $x^{\frac{2}{7}} \cdot x^{\frac{3}{14}}$ **66.** $y^{\frac{1}{2}} \cdot y^{\frac{3}{10}}$ **67.** $x^{\frac{3}{5}} \div x^{\frac{1}{10}}$ **68.** $y^{\frac{5}{7}} \div y^{\frac{3}{14}}$

69. $\dfrac{x^{\frac{2}{3}}y^{-\frac{1}{4}}}{x^{\frac{1}{2}}y^{-\frac{1}{2}}}$ **70.** $\dfrac{x^{\frac{1}{2}}y^{-\frac{1}{3}}}{x^{\frac{3}{4}}y^{\frac{1}{2}}}$ **71.** $\left(\dfrac{16x^{14}}{81y^{18}}\right)^{\frac{1}{2}}$ **72.** $\left(\dfrac{81y^{16}}{16x^{12}}\right)^{\frac{1}{2}}$

73. $\left(x^{\frac{1}{2}} \cdot x^{\frac{5}{12}}\right)^{\frac{1}{3}} \div x^{\frac{2}{3}}$ **74.** $\left(x^{\frac{3}{4}} \div x^{\frac{7}{8}}\right) \cdot x^{-\frac{1}{6}}$ **75.** $\left[\left(x^{-\frac{1}{2}}\right)^2\right]^{\frac{1}{3}}$ **76.** $\left[\left(\sqrt{x^3y^3}\right)^{\frac{1}{3}}\right]^{-1}$

77. Writing Explain why $(-64)^{\frac{1}{3}} = -64^{\frac{1}{3}}$ and $(-64)^{\frac{1}{2}} \neq -64^{\frac{1}{2}}$.

78. Error Analysis Explain why the following simplification is incorrect.
$$5\left(4 - 5^{\frac{1}{2}}\right) = 5(4) - 5\left(5^{\frac{1}{2}}\right) = 20 - 25^{\frac{1}{2}} = 15$$

79. Open-Ended Find three nonzero numbers a such that $a\left(4 + 5^{\frac{1}{2}}\right)$ is a rational number. Can a itself be a rational number? Explain.

80. a. Reasoning Show that $\sqrt[4]{x^2} = \sqrt{x}$ by using the definition of fourth root.

   b. Reasoning Show that $\sqrt[4]{x^2} = \sqrt{x}$ by rewriting $\sqrt[4]{x^2}$ in exponential form.

 **Challenge**

Exponents that are irrational numbers can be defined so that all the properties of rational exponents are also true for irrational exponents. Use those properties to simplify each expression.

81. $\left(7^{\sqrt{2}}\right)^{\sqrt{2}}$ **82.** $\dfrac{3^{3+\sqrt{5}}}{3^{1+\sqrt{5}}}$ **83.** $\dfrac{x^{4\pi}}{x^{2\pi}}$

84. $5^{2\sqrt{3}} \cdot 25^{-\sqrt{3}}$ **85.** $9^{\frac{1}{\sqrt{2}}}$ **86.** $\left(3^{2+\sqrt{2}}\right)^{2-\sqrt{2}}$

87. Weather Using data for the effect of temperature and wind on an exposed face, the National Weather Service uses the following formula.

$$\text{Wind Chill Index} = 35.74 + 0.6215T - 35.75V^{0.16} + 0.4275TV^{0.16}$$

T is the temperature in degrees Fahrenheit and V is the velocity of the wind in miles per hour. Frostbite occurs in about 15 minutes when the wind chill index is about -20. Find the wind speed that produces a wind chill index of -20 when the temperature is 5°F.

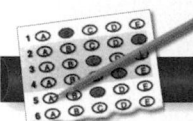

Test Prep

Multiple Choice

88. Which expression is NOT equivalent to $\sqrt[4]{4n^2}$?

A. $\left(4n^2\right)^{\frac{1}{4}}$ **B.** $2n^{\frac{1}{2}}$ **C.** $(2n)^{\frac{1}{2}}$ **D.** $\sqrt{2n}$

89. Which expression is NOT equivalent to $\sqrt[6]{81x^4y^8}$?

F. $\left(3xy^2\right)^{\frac{2}{3}}$ **G.** $(3x)^{\frac{2}{3}}y^{\frac{4}{3}}$ **H.** $\left(3x^2y^4\right)^{\frac{1}{3}}$ **J.** $\sqrt[3]{9x^2y^4}$

90. Which equation represents a property of exponents?

A. $(a^m)^n = a^{m+n}$ **B.** $\left(\dfrac{a}{b}\right)^m = \dfrac{a^m}{b}$ **C.** $a^{-m} = \dfrac{1}{a^m}$ **D.** $a^m \cdot a^n = a^{mn}$

91. Which expression is equivalent to $\left(\dfrac{1}{64}\right)^{-\frac{1}{6}}$?

F. $\left(\dfrac{1}{2}\right)^{-6}$ **G.** 4^3 **H.** 2   **J.** 64^6

92. Which expression is equivalent to $\left(n^{\frac{3}{2}} \div n^{-\frac{1}{6}}\right)^{-3}$?

A. n^{27} **B.** n^{-27} **C.** n^{-4} **D.** n^{-5}

93. Which number is closest to $(81n^2)^{0.75}$ for $n = 2$?

F. 45.4   **G.** 76.4   **H.** 243.0   **J.** 2061.9

Short Response

94. What is the value of x if $32^{0.8}x = 1$? Simplify the answer.

95. For $x > 0$ and $y > 0$, write $\sqrt{9x^5y^{-6}}$ in simplest form.

96. Find a nonzero number q such that $q\left(1 - \sqrt{2}\right)$ is a rational number. Explain.

Mixed Review

GO for Help

Lesson 7-3

Simplify. Rationalize all denominators.

97. $6\sqrt[3]{3} - 2\sqrt[3]{3}$ **98.** $3\sqrt{18} + 2\sqrt{72}$ **99.** $\left(\sqrt{5} - 1\right)\left(\sqrt{5} + 4\right)$

100. $\left(\sqrt{8} - \sqrt{7}\right)^2$ **101.** $\dfrac{2 + \sqrt{10}}{2 - 3\sqrt{5}}$ **102.** $\dfrac{-2 + \sqrt{8}}{-3 - \sqrt{2}}$

Lesson 5-4

Factor each expression.

103. $4x^3 - 8x^2 + 16x$ **104.** $x^2 + 4x + 4$ **105.** $x^2 - 18x + 81$

106. $16a^2 - 9b^2$ **107.** $25x^2 - 40xy + 16y^2$ **108.** $9x^2 + 48x + 64$

Solving Square Root and Other Radical Equations

What You'll Learn

- To solve square root and other radical equations

. . . And Why

To find the power from a circular solar cell, as in Example 3

✓ **Check Skills You'll Need**

GO for Help Lesson 5-5

Solve by factoring.
1. $x^2 = -x + 6$
2. $x^2 = 5x + 14$
3. $2x^2 + x = 3$
4. $3x^2 - 2 = 5x$
5. $4x^2 = -8x + 5$
6. $6x^2 = 5x + 6$

◀)) **New Vocabulary** • radical equation • square root equation

---

1 Solving Radical Equations

A **radical equation** is an equation that has a variable in a radicand (or a variable with a fractional exponent). If the radical has index 2, the equation is a **square root equation**. In this lesson, you may assume that all radicals have real-number values.

$3 + \sqrt{x} = 10$ **square root equation** $\sqrt{3} + x = 10$ **not a square root equation**

To solve a radical equation, isolate the radical on one side of the equation and then raise both sides of the equation to the same power.

If $\sqrt[n]{x} = k$, then $(\sqrt[n]{x})^n = k^n$ and $x = k^n$.

1 EXAMPLE Solving Square Root Equations

Solve $2 + \sqrt{3x - 2} = 6$.

$$2 + \sqrt{3x - 2} = 6$$
$$\sqrt{3x - 2} = 4 \qquad \text{Isolate the radical.}$$
$$(\sqrt{3x - 2})^2 = 4^2 \qquad \text{Square each side.}$$
$$3x - 2 = 16$$
$$3x = 18$$
$$x = 6$$

Check $2 + \sqrt{3x - 2} = 6$
$$2 + \sqrt{3(6) - 2} \stackrel{?}{=} 6$$
$$2 + \sqrt{16} \stackrel{?}{=} 6$$
$$2 + 4 \stackrel{?}{=} 6$$
$$6 = 6 \checkmark$$

✓ **Quick Check**  Solve $\sqrt{5x + 1} - 6 = 0$.

You can solve equations of the form $x^{\frac{m}{n}} = k$ by raising each side of the equation to the power $\frac{n}{m}$, the reciprocal of $\frac{m}{n}$. If the nth root of x is a real number, then $(x^{\frac{m}{n}})^{\frac{n}{m}} = |x|$.

2 EXAMPLE Solving Radical Equations With Rational Exponents

Solve $2(x - 2)^{\frac{2}{3}} = 50$.

$$2(x - 2)^{\frac{2}{3}} = 50$$

$$(x - 2)^{\frac{2}{3}} = 25 \qquad \text{Divide each side by 2.}$$

$$\left((x - 2)^{\frac{2}{3}}\right)^{\frac{3}{2}} = 25^{\frac{3}{2}} \qquad \text{Raise each side to the } \tfrac{3}{2} \text{ power.}$$

$$|x - 2|^1 = 25^{\frac{3}{2}} \qquad \text{Simplify.}$$

$$x - 2 = \pm\,125 \qquad \text{Simplify.}$$

$$x = 127 \text{ or } x = -123$$

Check
$$2(x - 2)^{\frac{2}{3}} = 50 \qquad\qquad 2(x - 2)^{\frac{2}{3}} = 50$$
$$2(127 - 2)^{\frac{2}{3}} \stackrel{?}{=} 50 \qquad\qquad 2(-123 - 2)^{\frac{2}{3}} \stackrel{?}{=} 50$$
$$2(5^3)^{\frac{2}{3}} \stackrel{?}{=} 50 \qquad\qquad 2(-125)^{\frac{2}{3}} \stackrel{?}{=} 50$$
$$2(5)^2 \stackrel{?}{=} 50 \qquad\qquad 2(-5)^2 \stackrel{?}{=} 50$$
$$50 = 50 \checkmark \qquad\qquad 50 = 50 \checkmark$$

✔ **Quick Check** ② Solve $2(x + 3)^{\frac{3}{2}} = 54$.

3 EXAMPLE Real-World  Connection

Real-World Connection

Solar cells convert sunlight directly into electricity. They power calculators, emergency road signs, satellites, and experimental vehicles.

Multiple Choice The power P in watts that a circular solar cell produces and the radius of the cell in centimeters are related by the square root equation

$r = \sqrt{\dfrac{P}{0.02\pi}}$. About how much power is produced by a cell with a radius of 10 cm?

Ⓐ 0.13 watt   Ⓑ 0.63 watt   Ⓒ 1.3 watts   Ⓓ 6.3 watts

$$r = \sqrt{\frac{P}{0.02\pi}}$$

$$10 = \sqrt{\frac{P}{0.02\pi}} \qquad \text{Substitute 10 for } r.$$

$$100 = \frac{P}{0.02\pi} \qquad \text{Square each side.}$$

$$100(0.02\pi) = P \qquad \text{Multiply each side by } 0.02\pi.$$

$$6.3 \approx P \qquad \text{Simplify. Round to one decimal place.}$$

A cell with radius 10 cm produces about 6.3 watts of power. The correct choice is D.

✔ **Quick Check** ③ How much power is produced by a cell with radius 20 cm? How does this compare with the power produced by a 10-cm cell?

Extraneous solutions can be introduced when you raise both sides of an equation to a power. So check all possible solutions in the original equation.

To review extraneous solutions, go to Lesson 1-5.

4 EXAMPLE Checking for Extraneous Solutions

Solve $\sqrt{x - 3} + 5 = x$. Check for extraneous solutions.

$$\sqrt{x - 3} + 5 = x$$

$\sqrt{x - 3} = x - 5$	Isolate the radical.
$(\sqrt{x - 3})^2 = (x - 5)^2$	Square each side.
$x - 3 = x^2 - 10x + 25$	Simplify.
$0 = x^2 - 11x + 28$	Combine like terms.
$0 = (x - 4)(x - 7)$	Factor.
$x - 4 = 0$ or $x - 7 = 0$	Zero Product Theorem
$x = 4$ or $x = 7$	

Check $\sqrt{x - 3} + 5 = x$ $\qquad\qquad$ $\sqrt{x - 3} + 5 = x$

$\qquad\quad$ $\sqrt{4 - 3} + 5 \stackrel{?}{=} 4$ $\qquad\qquad$ $\sqrt{7 - 3} + 5 \stackrel{?}{=} 7$

$\qquad\qquad\quad$ $\sqrt{1} + 5 \stackrel{?}{=} 4$ $\qquad\qquad\qquad$ $\sqrt{4} + 5 \stackrel{?}{=} 7$

$\qquad\qquad\qquad\quad$ $6 \neq 4$ $\qquad\qquad\qquad\qquad\quad$ $7 = 7$

● The only solution is 7.

Quick Check ④ Solve $\sqrt{5x - 1} + 3 = x$. Check for extraneous solutions.

If an equation contains two radical expressions (or two terms with rational exponents), isolate one of the radicals (or one of the terms).

5 EXAMPLE Solving Equations With Two Rational Exponents

Solve $(2x + 1)^{0.5} - (3x + 4)^{0.25} = 0$. Check for extraneous solutions.

$$(2x + 1)^{0.5} - (3x + 4)^{0.25} = 0$$

$(2x + 1)^{0.5} = (3x + 4)^{0.25}$	
$((2x + 1)^{0.5})^4 = ((3x + 4)^{0.25})^4$	Raise each side to the 4th power.
$(2x + 1)^2 = 3x + 4$	Simplify exponents.
$4x^2 + 4x + 1 = 3x + 4$	Simplify.
$4x^2 + x - 3 = 0$	Combine like terms.
$(4x - 3)(x + 1) = 0$	Factor.
$x = \frac{3}{4}$ or $x = -1$	Zero Product Theorem

Test-Taking Tip

When you check a solution on a test, use the equation printed on the test rather than the one you've written on your paper. You could have copied the equation incorrectly.

Check $(2x + 1)^{0.5} - (3x + 4)^{0.25} = 0$ $\qquad$ $(2x + 1)^{0.5} - (3x + 4)^{0.25} = 0$

$\quad$ $\left(2 \cdot \frac{3}{4} + 1\right)^{0.5} - \left(3 \cdot \frac{3}{4} + 4\right)^{0.25} \stackrel{?}{=} 0$ $\quad$ $(2(-1) + 1)^{0.5} - (3(-1) + 4)^{0.25} \stackrel{?}{=} 0$

$\qquad\qquad\qquad$ $\left(\frac{5}{2}\right)^{0.5} - \left(\frac{25}{4}\right)^{0.25} \stackrel{?}{=} 0$ $\qquad\qquad\qquad\qquad$ $(-1)^{0.5} - (1)^{0.25} \stackrel{?}{=} 0$

$\qquad\qquad\quad$ $\left(\frac{5}{2}\right)^{0.5} - \left(\left(\frac{5}{2}\right)^2\right)^{0.25} \stackrel{?}{=} 0$ $\qquad\qquad\qquad$ $(-1)^{0.5}$ is not a real number.

$\qquad\qquad\qquad\qquad$ $\left(\frac{5}{2}\right)^{0.5} - \left(\frac{5}{2}\right)^{0.5} = 0$

● The only solution is $\frac{3}{4}$.

Quick Check ⑤ Solve $\sqrt{3x + 2} - \sqrt{2x + 7} = 0$. Check for extraneous solutions.

Technology Activity: Checking for Extraneous Solutions

You can use a graphing calculator to check for extraneous solutions.

1. a. Solve $x = \sqrt{x + 7} + 5$. How many apparent solutions do you get?

b. Any or all of the apparent solutions may be extraneous. One way to find out is to let y_1 equal the left side of the equation and let y_2 equal the right side. Graph the two equations. In how many points do they intersect?

c. The x-values of the points of intersection are solutions of the original equation. Are any of the apparent solutions extraneous?

d. Substitute the apparent solutions in the original equation. Does this algebraic check agree with the calculator check?

2. Use a graphing calculator to determine the number of solutions of each equation.

a. $\sqrt{x} = x - 2$ **b.** $\sqrt{x^2 + 3} = 2x - 1$ **c.** $x + 8 = 4\sqrt{x + 5}$

EXERCISES

For more exercises, see *Extra Skill and Word Problem Practice.*

Practice and Problem Solving

A **Practice by Example**

Example 1
(page 391)

GO for Help

Solve.

1. $3\sqrt{x} + 3 = 15$

2. $4\sqrt{x} - 1 = 3$

3. $\sqrt{x + 3} = 5$

4. $\sqrt{3x + 4} = 4$

5. $\sqrt{2x + 3} - 7 = 0$

6. $\sqrt{6 - 3x} - 2 = 0$

Example 2
(page 392)

Solve.

7. $(x + 5)^{\frac{2}{3}} = 4$

8. $(x - 2)^{\frac{2}{3}} = 9$

9. $3(x - 2)^{\frac{3}{4}} = 24$

10. $3(x + 3)^{\frac{3}{4}} = 81$

11. $(x + 1)^{\frac{3}{2}} - 2 = 25$

12. $3 + (4 - x)^{\frac{3}{2}} = 11$

Example 3
(page 392)

13. Volume A spherical water tank holds 15,000 ft³ of water. Find the diameter of the tank. (*Hint:* $V = \frac{\pi}{6}d^3$)

14. Hydraulics The maximum flow of water in a pipe is modeled by the formula $Q = Av$, where A is the cross-sectional area of the pipe and v is the velocity of the water. Find the diameter of a pipe that allows a maximum flow of 50 ft³/min of water flowing at a velocity of 600 ft/min. Round your answer to the nearest inch.

Example 4
(page 393)

Solve. Check for extraneous solutions.

15. $\sqrt{11x + 3} - 2x = 0$

16. $(5x + 4)^{\frac{1}{2}} - 3x = 0$

17. $\sqrt{3x + 13} - 5 = x$

18. $\sqrt{x + 7} + 5 = x$

19. $(x + 3)^{\frac{1}{2}} - 1 = x$

20. $(5 - x)^{\frac{1}{2}} = x + 1$

Example 5
(page 393)

Solve. Check for extraneous solutions.

21. $\sqrt{3x} = \sqrt{x+6}$

22. $(x+5)^{\frac{1}{2}} - (5-2x)^{\frac{1}{4}} = 0$

23. $(7x+6)^{\frac{1}{2}} = (9+4x)^{\frac{1}{2}}$

24. $\sqrt{3x+7} = x-1$

25. $\sqrt{x+7} - x = 1$

26. $\sqrt{-3x-5} = x+3$

27. $(3x+2)^{\frac{1}{2}} - (2x+7)^{\frac{1}{2}} = 0$

28. $x+8 = (x^2+16)^{\frac{1}{2}}$

29. $(2x)^{\frac{1}{2}} = (x+5)^{\frac{1}{2}}$

30. $1 = (3+x)^{\frac{1}{2}}$

B **Apply Your Skills**

31. a. Form a pair of simultaneous equations by letting y_1 equal the left side and y_2 equal the right side of $\sqrt{5} - x = 1$. Graph the equations.
   b. Repeat part (a) with the equivalent equation $\sqrt{5} = x+1$.
   c. Repeat part (a) with the equivalent equation $\sqrt{5} - x - 1 = 0$.
   d. Writing Describe the similarities and differences among the graphs of the three sets of simultaneous equations.

32. a. Package Design The formula for the area A of a hexagon with a side s units long is $A = \frac{3s^2\sqrt{3}}{2}$. See the figure below. Solve the formula for s and rationalize the denominator.

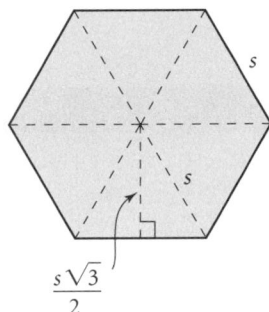 

   b. A package designer wants the hexagonal base of a hat box to have an area of about 200 in.^{2}. About how long is each side?
   c. What is the distance between opposite sides of the hat box?

33. Multiple Choice Your can find the area A of a square whose side is s units as $A = s^2$. Find the best estimate for the side of a square with an area of 32 m^2.

   Ⓐ 4.2 m   Ⓑ 5.7 m   Ⓒ 8.0 m   Ⓓ 16 m

Solve. Check for extraneous solutions.

34. $3\sqrt{2x} - 3 = 9$

35. $2(2x)^{\frac{1}{3}} + 1 = 5$

36. $\sqrt{2x-1} - 3 = 0$

37. $(2x+3)^{\frac{1}{2}} - 7 = 0$

38. $\sqrt{x^2+3} = x+1$

39. $(2x+3)^{\frac{3}{4}} - 3 = 5$

40. $2(x-1)^{\frac{4}{3}} + 4 = 36$

41. $x^{\frac{1}{2}} - (x-5)^{\frac{1}{2}} = 2$

42. $\sqrt{x} = \sqrt{x-8} + 2$

GO Online
Homework Video Tutor
Visit: PHSchool.com
Web Code: age-0705

For each equation, let Y1 = left side and Y2 = right side. Display a graphing calculator table of X, Y1, and Y2 values. Find where Y1 = Y2. Use the Technology Activity steps on page 394 to check that you've found all solutions.

43. $\sqrt{5x+1} - \sqrt{4x+3} = 0$

44. $\sqrt{x+10} + \sqrt{3-x} = 5$

45. $(3x+2)^{\frac{1}{2}} = 8(3x+2)^{-\frac{1}{2}}$

46. $\sqrt{4x-10} = 3\sqrt{x-5}$

47. $(x-9)^{\frac{1}{2}} + 1 = x^{\frac{1}{2}}$

48. $\sqrt{10x} - 2\sqrt{5x-25} = 0$

49. $(2x+1)^{\frac{1}{3}} = (2+3x)^{\frac{1}{3}}$

50. $(2x-1)^{\frac{1}{3}} = (x+1)^{\frac{1}{6}}$

51. Physics The velocity v of an object dropped from a tall building is given by the formula $v = \sqrt{64d}$, where d is the distance the object has dropped. Solve the formula for d.

52. Open-Ended Write an equation that has two radical expressions and no real roots.

 **Challenge**

Solve. Check for extraneous solutions.

53. $\sqrt{x + 1} + \sqrt{2x} = \sqrt{5x + 3}$ **54.** $\sqrt{x + \sqrt{2x}} = \sqrt{2x}$

55. $\sqrt{x + \sqrt{2x}} = 2$

56. $\sqrt{\sqrt{x + 25}} = \sqrt{x + 5}$

57. Critical Thinking Devise a plan to find the value of x.
$$x = \sqrt{2 + \sqrt{2 + \sqrt{2 + \ldots}}}$$

58. Critical Thinking You have solved equations containing square roots by squaring both sides. You were using the property that if $a = b$ then $a^2 = b^2$. Show that the following statements are *not* true for all real numbers.
a. If $a^2 = b^2$ then $a = b$.
b. If $a < b$ then $a^2 < b^2$.

Test Prep

Gridded Response

59. Solve $\sqrt{4x - 23} - 3 = 2$.

60. Solve $(x + 2)^{\frac{3}{4}} = 27$.

61. Solve $\sqrt{2x + 1} - \sqrt[4]{x + 11} = 0$.

62. Solve $5\sqrt{x} + 7 = 8$.

63. Solve $-\sqrt[3]{x} + 3 = 0$.

64. Solve $\sqrt{x + 2} = x$.

Mixed Review

Lesson 7-4

Simplify each expression.

65. $64^{\frac{2}{3}}$ **66.** $25^{1.5}$ **67.** $6^{\frac{1}{2}} \cdot 12^{\frac{1}{2}}$ **68.** $8^{\frac{1}{2}} \cdot 40^{\frac{1}{2}}$ **69.** $3^{\frac{1}{3}} \cdot 18^{\frac{1}{3}}$

70. $81^{-0.25}$ **71.** $4^{3.5}$ **72.** $125 \cdot 125^{-\frac{1}{3}}$ **73.** $32 \cdot 256^{-\frac{1}{2}}$ **74.** $100^{-\frac{3}{2}} \cdot 0.01^{\frac{3}{2}}$

Lesson 6-7

Evaluate each expression.

75. $_7P_1$ **76.** $_7P_3$ **77.** $_5P_3$ **78.** $_8P_4$ **79.** $_4P_4$

80. $_5C_2$ **81.** $_7C_5$ **82.** $_5C_5$ **83.** $_6C_5$ **84.** $_7C_1$

Lesson 5-5

Solve each equation by factoring.

85. $x^2 - 7x + 12 = 0$ **86.** $x^2 - 8x + 15 = 0$ **87.** $x^2 + 9x + 20 = 0$

88. $3x^2 + 8x + 4 = 0$ **89.** $9x^2 + 15x + 4 = 0$ **90.** $4x^2 + 11x + 6 = 0$

Radical Expressions in Formulas

You frequently need to use radical expressions in geometry formulas.

EXAMPLE

The cube at the right fits in (is inscribed in) the sphere. How much more than the cube does the sphere hold?

A. 25% more   **B.** 50% more   **C.** 100% more   **D.** 150% more

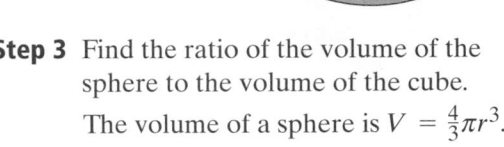

Step 1 Find k.

k is the diagonal of the square that is the base of the cube. Use the Pythagorean Theorem.

$$k^2 = e^2 + e^2$$
$$= 2e^2$$
$$k = e\sqrt{2}$$

Step 2 Find the radius of the sphere.

The diameter d of the sphere is also the diagonal of the cube and the hypotenuse of a right triangle with legs k and e.

$$d^2 = k^2 + e^2$$
$$= (e\sqrt{2})^2 + e^2$$
$$= 2e^2 + e^2$$
$$= 3e^2$$
$$d = e\sqrt{3}.$$

So the radius of the sphere is $\frac{d}{2}$ or $\frac{e\sqrt{3}}{2}$.

Step 3 Find the ratio of the volume of the sphere to the volume of the cube.

The volume of a sphere is $V = \frac{4}{3}\pi r^3$.

The volume of the cube is e^3.

$$\frac{\text{volume of sphere}}{\text{volume of cube}} = \frac{\frac{4}{3}\pi\left(\frac{e\sqrt{3}}{2}\right)^3}{e^3}$$
$$= \frac{4\pi \cdot 3e^3\sqrt{3}}{3 \cdot 8 \cdot e^3}$$
$$= \frac{\pi\sqrt{3}}{2} \approx 2.7$$

The sphere holds about 2.7 times as much as the cube, so it holds 1.7 times more, or 170% more than the cube. If you chose answer D, you are a very good estimator!

EXERCISES

1. a. The cube at the right is inscribed in a cylinder. Estimate the percent by which the volume of the cylinder exceeds the volume of the cube. Then compute the percent. (For the volume of a cylinder: $V = \pi r^2 h$.)

  b. Estimate the percent by which the surface area of the cylinder exceeds the surface area of the cube. Then compute the percent. (The formula for the surface area of a cylinder is S.A. $= 2\pi r^2 + 2\pi rh$.)

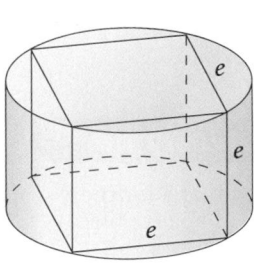

2. Estimate the percent by which the surface area of a sphere exceeds the surface area of its inscribed cube. Then compute the percent. (The formula for the surface area of a sphere is S.A. $= 4\pi r^2$.)

3. Estimate the percent by which the area and circumference of a circle exceed the area and perimeter of its inscribed square. Then compute the percents.

4. In the Example, suppose a smaller sphere is inscribed in the cube. Estimate the percent by which the volume of the outer sphere exceeds the volume of the inner sphere. Then compute the percent.

Function Operations

GO for Help Lesson 2-1

What You'll Learn

- To add, subtract, multiply, and divide functions
- To find the composite of two functions

...And Why

To find successive discounts, as in Example 4

✓ Check Skills You'll Need

Find the domain and range of each function.

1. $\{(0, -5), (2, -3), (4, -1)\}$ **2.** $\{(-1, 0), (0, 0), (1, 0)\}$

3. $f(x) = 2x - 12$ **4.** $g(x) = x^2$

Evaluate each function for the given value of x.

5. Let $f(x) = 3x + 4$. Find $f(2)$.   **6.** Let $g(x) = 2x^2 - 3x + 1$. Find $g(-3)$.

🔊 **New Vocabulary** • composite function

---

1   Operations With Functions

If an airplane has an airspeed of 415 mi/h, then $f(x) = 415x$ represents the distance traveled by the plane in still air in x hours. If the wind speed is 30 mi/h, then $g(x) = 30x$ represents the motion of the wind, and $f(x) + g(x) = 415x + 30x$ represents the distance traveled by the airplane flying with the wind.

You can add, subtract, multiply, and divide functions.

Key Concepts

Definition	**Function Operations**
Addition	$(f + g)(x) = f(x) + g(x)$
Multiplication	$(f \cdot g)(x) = f(x) \cdot g(x)$
Subtraction	$(f - g)(x) = f(x) - g(x)$
Division	$\left(\dfrac{f}{g}\right)(x) = \dfrac{f(x)}{g(x)}, g(x) \neq 0$

Vocabulary Tip

The <u>domain</u> of a function is the set of all possible inputs of the function.

The <u>range</u> of a function is the set of all possible outputs of the function.

The domains of the sum, difference, product, and quotient functions consist of the x-values that are in the domains of both f and g. However, the domain of a quotient function does not contain any x-value for which $g(x) = 0$.

1 EXAMPLE   Adding and Subtracting Functions

Let $f(x) = 3x + 8$ and $g(x) = 2x - 12$. Find $f + g$ and $f - g$ and their domains.

$(f + g)(x) = f(x) + g(x) = (3x + 8) + (2x - 12) = 5x - 4$

$(f - g)(x) = f(x) - g(x) = (3x + 8) - (2x - 12) = x + 20$

● The domain of both $f + g$ and $f - g$ is the set of real numbers.

✓ **Quick Check** **1** Let $f(x) = 5x^2 - 4x$ and $g(x) = 5x + 1$. Find $f + g$ and $f - g$ and their domains.

2 EXAMPLE **Multiplying and Dividing Functions**

Let $f(x) = x^2 - 1$ and $g(x) = x + 1$. Find $f \cdot g$ and $\dfrac{f}{g}$ and their domains.

$$(f \cdot g)(x) = f(x) \cdot g(x) = (x^2 - 1)(x + 1) = x^3 + x^2 - x - 1$$

$$\left(\dfrac{f}{g}\right)(x) = \dfrac{f(x)}{g(x)} = \dfrac{x^2 - 1}{x + 1} = \dfrac{(x + 1)(x - 1)}{x + 1} = x - 1, x \neq -1$$

The domains of f and g are the set of real numbers, so the domain of $f \cdot g$ is also.

The domain of $\dfrac{f}{g}$ does not include -1 because $g(-1) = 0$.

✓ **Quick Check** **2** Let $f(x) = 6x^2 + 7x - 5$ and $g(x) = 2x - 1$. Find $f \cdot g$ and $\dfrac{f}{g}$ and their domains.

2 Composition of Functions

The diagram below shows what happens when you apply one function $g(x)$ after another function $f(x)$.

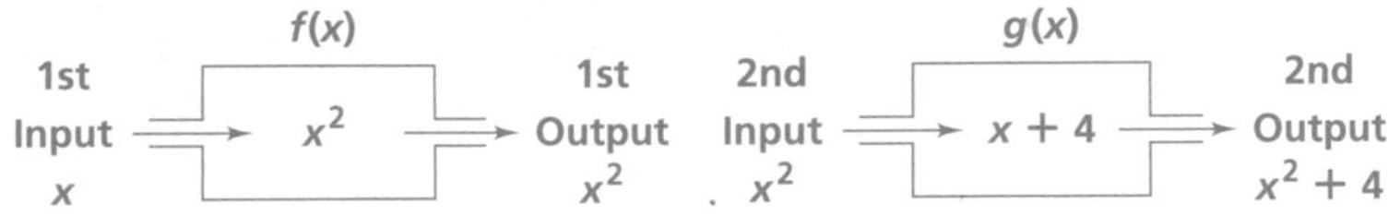

Vocabulary Tip

Composite means "put together."

The output from the first function becomes the input for the second function. When you combine two functions as in the diagram above, you form a **composite function.**

🔑 **Key Concepts**

Definition	**Composition of Functions**

The composition of function g with function f is written as $g \circ f$ and is defined as $(g \circ f)(x) = g(f(x))$. The domain of $g \circ f$ consists of the values a in the domain of f for which $f(a)$ is in the domain of g.

$$(g \circ f)(x) = g(f(x))$$

① Evaluate the inner function $f(x)$ first.

② Then use your result as the input of the outer function $g(x)$.

3 EXAMPLE **Composition of Functions**

Let $f(x) = x - 2$ and $g(x) = x^2$. Find $(g \circ f)(-5)$.

Method 1

$(g \circ f)(x) = g(f(x)) = g(x - 2) = (x - 2)^2$
$(g \circ f)(-5) = (-5 - 2)^2$
$\qquad\qquad = (-7)^2$
$\qquad\qquad = 49$

Method 2

$(g \circ f)(x) = g(f(x))$
$g(f(-5)) = g(-5 - 2)$
$\qquad\qquad = g(-7)$
$\qquad\qquad = (-7)^2 = 49$

✓ **Quick Check** **3 a.** Find $(f \circ g)(x)$ and evaluate $(f \circ g)(-5)$ for the functions f and g defined in Example 3.
b. Critical Thinking Is a composition of functions commutative? Explain.

4 EXAMPLE **Real-World Connection**

Consumer Issues Suppose you are shopping in the store in the photo. You have a coupon worth $5 off any item.

a. Use functions to model discounting an item by 20% and to model applying the coupon.

Let x = the original price.

Cost with 20% discount:
$$f(x) = x - 0.2x = 0.8x$$

Cost with a coupon for $5:
$$g(x) = x - 5$$

b. Use a composition of your two functions to model how much you would pay for an item if the clerk applies the discount first and then the coupon.

$$(g \circ f)(x) = g(f(x)) \quad \text{**applying the discount first**}$$
$$= g(0.8x)$$
$$= 0.8x - 5$$

c. Use a composition of your two functions to model how much you would pay for an item if the clerk applies the coupon first and then the discount.

$$(f \circ g)(x) = f(g(x)) \quad \text{**applying the coupon first**}$$
$$= f(x - 5)$$
$$= 0.8(x - 5)$$
$$= 0.8x - 4$$

d. How much more is any item if the clerk applies the coupon first?

$$(f \circ g)(x) - (g \circ f)(x) = (0.8x - 4) - (0.8x - 5) \quad \text{**Subtract the functions.**}$$
$$= 1$$

● Any item will cost $1 more.

✓ Quick Check **4** A store is offering a 10% discount on all items. In addition, employees get a 25% discount.
a. Write a composite function to model taking the 10% discount first.
b. Write a composite function to model taking the 25% discount first.
c. Suppose you are an employee. Which discount would you prefer to take first?

EXERCISES

For more exercises, see *Extra Skill and Word Problem Practice.*

Practice and Problem Solving

A **Practice by Example**

Examples 1 and 2
(pages 398 and 399)

for Help

Let $f(x) = 3x + 5$ and $g(x) = x^2$. **Perform each function operation.**

1. $f(x) + g(x)$ **2.** $g(x) - f(x)$ **3.** $f(x) - g(x)$

4. $f(x) \cdot g(x)$ **5.** $\dfrac{f(x)}{g(x)}$ **6.** $\dfrac{g(x)}{f(x)}$

7. $(f + g)(x)$ **8.** $(f - g)(x)$ **9.** $(g - f)(x)$

10. $(f \cdot g)(x)$ **11.** $\left(\dfrac{f}{g}\right)(x)$ **12.** $\left(\dfrac{g}{f}\right)(x)$

Let $f(x) = 2x^2 + x - 3$ and $g(x) = x - 1$. Perform each function operation and then find the domain.

13. $f(x) + g(x)$ **14.** $g(x) - f(x)$ **15.** $f(x) - g(x)$

16. $f(x) \cdot g(x)$ **17.** $\dfrac{f(x)}{g(x)}$ **18.** $\dfrac{g(x)}{f(x)}$

19. Let $f(x) = 9x$ and $g(x) = 3x$. Find $(f \cdot g)(x)$ and $\left(\dfrac{f}{g}\right)(x)$ and their domains.

Example 3
(page 399)

Use each diagram to find $(g \circ f)(x)$. Then evaluate $(g \circ f)(3)$ and $(g \circ f)(-2)$.

20.
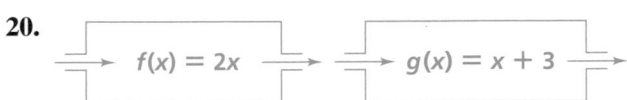

$f(x) = 2x$ $\longrightarrow$ $g(x) = x + 3$

21.

$f(x) = x^2$ $\longrightarrow$ $g(x) = |x + 5|$

Let $g(x) = 2x$ and $h(x) = x^2 + 4$. Evaluate each expression.

22. $(h \circ g)(1)$ **23.** $(h \circ g)(-5)$ **24.** $(h \circ g)(-2)$

25. $(g \circ h)(-2)$ **26.** $(g \circ h)(0)$ **27.** $(g \circ h)(-1)$

28. $(g \circ g)(3)$ **29.** $(h \circ h)(2)$ **30.** $(h \circ h)(-4)$

Let $f(x) = x^2$ and $g(x) = x - 3$. Find each value or expression.

31. $(g \circ f)(-2)$ **32.** $(f \circ g)(-2)$ **33.** $(g \circ f)(0)$

34. $(f \circ g)(0)$ **35.** $(g \circ f)(3.5)$ **36.** $(f \circ g)(3.5)$

37. $(f \circ g)\left(\dfrac{1}{2}\right)$ **38.** $(g \circ f)\left(\dfrac{1}{2}\right)$ **39.** $(f \circ g)(c)$

40. $(g \circ f)(c)$ **41.** $(f \circ g)(-a)$ **42.** $(g \circ f)(-a)$

Example 4
(page 400)

43. **Sales** A car dealer offers a 10% discount off the list price x for any car on the lot. At the same time, the manufacturer offers a $2000 rebate for each purchase of a car.
 a. Write a function $f(x)$ to represent the price after the discount.
 b. Write a function $g(x)$ to represent the price after the $2000 rebate.
 c. Suppose the list price of a car is $18,000. Use a composite function to find the price of the car if the discount is applied before the rebate.
 d. Suppose the list price of a car is $18,000. Use a composite function to find the price of the car if the rebate is applied before the discount.

Real-World Connection

International companies must often compute their costs in many currencies.

44. **Economics** Suppose the function $f(x) = 0.12x$ represents the number of U.S. dollars equivalent to x Chinese yuan and the function $g(x) = 9.14x$ represents the number of Mexican pesos equivalent to x U.S. dollars.
 a. Write a composite function that represents the number of Mexican pesos equivalent to x Chinese yuan.
 b. Find the value in Mexican pesos of an item that costs 15 Chinese yuan.

Let $f(x) = 2x + 5$ and $g(x) = x^2 - 3x + 2$. Perform each function operation.

45. $f(x) + g(x)$ **46.** $3f(x) - 2$ **47.** $g(x) - f(x)$

48. $-2g(x) + f(x)$ **49.** $f(x) - g(x) + 10$ **50.** $4f(x) + 2g(x)$

Let $f(x) = 3x^2 + 2x - 8$ and $g(x) = x + 2$. Perform each function operation and then find the domain.

51. $-f(x) + 4g(x)$ **52.** $f(x) - 2g(x)$ **53.** $f(x) \cdot g(x)$

54. $-3f(x) \cdot g(x)$ **55.** $\dfrac{f(x)}{g(x)}$ **56.** $\dfrac{5f(x)}{g(x)}$

 57. Writing Evaluate $(g \circ f)(3)$, when $f(x) = 2x$ and $g(x) = x + 1$. Explain what you do first and why.

Let $g(x) = 3x + 2$ and $f(x) = \dfrac{x - 2}{3}$. Find each value.

58. $f(g(1))$ **59.** $g(f(-4))$ **60.** $f(g(0))$ **61.** $g(f(2))$

GO for Help

For a guide to solving
Exercise 62a, see p. 405.

 62. Geometry You toss a pebble into a pool of water and watch the circular ripples radiate outward. You find that the function $r(x) = 12.5x$ describes the radius r in inches of a circle x seconds after it was formed. The function $A(x) = \pi x^2$ describes the area A of a circle with radius x.
a. Find $(A \circ r)(x)$ when $x = 2$. Interpret your answer.
b. Find the area of a circle 4 seconds after it was formed.

For each pair of functions, find $f(g(x))$ and $g(f(x))$.

63. $f(x) = 3x, g(x) = x^2$ **64.** $f(x) = x + 3, g(x) = x - 5$

65. $f(x) = 3x^2 + 2, g(x) = 2x$ **66.** $f(x) = \dfrac{x - 3}{2}, g(x) = 2x - 3$

67. $f(x) = -x - 7, g(x) = 4x$ **68.** $f(x) = \dfrac{x + 5}{2}, g(x) = x^2$

69. Open-Ended Write a function rule that approximates each value.
a. The amount you save is a percent of what you earn. (You choose the percent.)
b. The amount you earn depends on how many hours you work. (You choose the hourly wage.)
c. Write and simplify a composite function that expresses your savings as a function of the number of hours you work. Interpret your results.

 70. a. Technology Suppose $f(x) = 3x$ and $g(x) = x^2 + 3$. In the spreadsheet, values for x are in Column A. What do the formulas in B and C represent?

	A	B	C	D	E
1		=3*A1	=A1^2+3	▪	▪
2	0	▪	▪	▪	▪
3	5	▪	▪	▪	▪
4	10	▪	▪	▪	▪

GO Online
Homework Video Tutor
Visit: PHSchool.com
Web Code: age-0706

b. If the formulas in columns B and C are copied down the columns, what numbers will appear?
c. Find $(f \circ g)(x)$.
d. Complete column D for $(f \circ g)(x)$.
e. Find $(g \circ f)(x)$.
f. Complete column E for $(g \circ f)(x)$.

 71. Profit A craftsman makes and sells violins. The function $C(x) = 1000 + 700x$ represents his cost in dollars to produce x violins. The function $I(x) = 5995x$ represents the income in dollars from selling x violins.
 a. Write and simplify a function $P(x) = I(x) - C(x)$.
 b. Find $P(30)$, the profit earned when he makes and sells 30 violins.

72. Writing A salesperson earns a 3% bonus on weekly sales over $5000.

$$g(x) = 0.03x$$
$$h(x) = x - 5000$$

 a. Explain what each function above represents.
 b. Which composition, $(h \circ g)(x)$ or $(g \circ h)(x)$, represents the weekly bonus? Explain.

Let $f(x) = 3x - 2$ and $g(x) = x^2 + 1$. Perform each function operation and use the properties of real numbers to justify each step in simplifying your answer.

73. $(f + g)(x)$ **74.** $(f - g)(x)$ **75.** $(f \circ g)(x)$

 76. Grades Suppose your teacher offers to give the whole class a bonus if everyone passes the next math test. The teacher says she will (1) give everyone a 10-point bonus and (2) increase everyone's grade by 9% of their score.
 a. Let x represent the original test scores. Write statements (1) and (2) as the functions $f(x)$ and $g(x)$, respectively.
 b. Explain the meaning of $f(g(x))$. Evaluate $f(g(75))$.
 c. Explain the meaning of $g(f(x))$. Evaluate $g(f(75))$.
 d. Does $g(f(x)) = f(g(x))$?

C Challenge

Let $f(x) = x^4 + 2x^3 - 5x^2 - 10x$ and $g(x) = x^3 - 3x^2 - 5x + 15$. Perform each function operation and simplify, and then find the domain.

77. $f(x) \cdot g(x)$ **78.** $\dfrac{f(x)}{g(x)}$ **79.** $\dfrac{g(x)}{f(x)}$

Find each composition of functions. Simplify your answer.

80. Let $f(x) = \dfrac{1}{x}$. Find $f(f(x))$.

81. Let $f(x) = \dfrac{1}{x}$. Find $f(f(f(x)))$.

82. Let $f(x) = 1 - \dfrac{x}{2}$. Find $f(f(f(x)))$.

83. Let $f(x) = 2x - 3$. Find $\dfrac{f(1 + h) - f(1)}{h}, h \neq 0$.

84. Let $f(x) = 4x - 1$. Find $\dfrac{f(a + h) - f(a)}{h}, h \neq 0$.

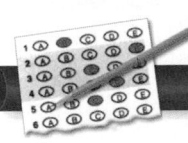

Test Prep

Multiple Choice

85. Let $f(x) = -4x + 1$ and $g(x) = 2x - 6$. Find $(g - f)(x)$.
 A. $6x - 5$ **B.** $6x - 7$ **C.** $-6x + 5$ **D.** $-6x + 7$

86. If $f(x) = 2x^2$ and $g(x) = 3x$, what is $(g \circ f)(x)$?
 F. $6x^2$ **G.** $9x^2$ **H.** $18x^2$ **J.** $8x^4$

87. Let $f(x) = 2x - 3$ and $g(x) = -x^2 - 1$. Find $(g \circ f)(x)$.
 A. $-2x^3 + 3x^2 - 2x + 3$ **B.** $-4x^2 + 12x - 10$
 C. $-x^2 + 2x - 4$ **D.** $-x^2 - 2x + 2$

80. If $(f \circ g)(x) = x^2 - 6x + 8$ and $g(x) = x - 3$, which expression could represent $f(x)$?

　　F. $x - 4$ 　　　　**G.** $x - 1$ 　　　　**H.** $x^2 - 1$ 　　　　**J.** $x^2 - 6x + 5$

89. Let $g(x) = x - 3$ and $h(x) = x^2 + 6$. Find $(h \circ g)(1)$.

　　A. -14 　　　　**B.** 4 　　　　**C.** 5 　　　　**D.** 10

90. If $f(x) = 3 - x$ and $g(x) = x^2 - 3$, which expression has the greatest value?

　　F. $(g \circ f)(-3)$ 　　**G.** $(f \circ g)(-3)$ 　　**H.** $(f \cdot g)(-3)$ 　　**J.** $(g - f)(-3)$

91. If $f(x) = x^2$ and $g(x) = x - 1$, which statement is true?

　　A. $(f \circ g)(x) \geq (g \circ f)(x)$ for all values of x.
　　B. $(f \circ g)(x) \leq (g \circ f)(x)$ for all values of x.
　　C. $(f \circ g)(x) = (g \circ f)(x)$ only for $x = 1$.
　　D. $(f \circ g)(x) \neq (g \circ f)(x)$ for any value of x.

Short Response　　**92.** Let $f(x) = 2x + 9$ and $g(x) = x - 6$. Find $(f \circ g)(-1)$. Show your work.

93. Let $g(x) = x^2 - 4$ and $h(x) = 4x - 6$. Find $\left(\dfrac{g}{h}\right)(x)$.

94. If $f(x) = 3x - 4$ and $g(x) = x + 3$, what does $(f \cdot g)(x)$ mean? What is $(f \cdot g)(x)$? Simplify the answer.

Mixed Review

Lesson 7-5　　**Solve. Check for extraneous solutions.**

　　95. $\sqrt{x^2 + 3} = x + 1$ 　　**96.** $x + 8 = (x^2 + 16)^{\frac{1}{2}}$ 　　**97.** $\sqrt{x^2 + 9} = x + 1$

　　98. $(x^2 - 9)^{\frac{1}{2}} - x = -3$ 　　**99.** $\sqrt{x^2 + 12} - 2 = x$ 　　**100.** $(3x)^{\frac{1}{2}} = (x + 6)^{\frac{1}{2}}$

Lesson 6-8　　**Expand each binomial.**

　　101. $(x + 4)^8$ 　　**102.** $(x + y)^6$ 　　**103.** $(2x - y)^4$ 　　**104.** $(2x - 3y)^7$

　　105. $(9 - 2x)^5$ 　　**106.** $(4x - y)^5$ 　　**107.** $(x^2 + x)^4$ 　　**108.** $(x^2 + 2y^3)^6$

Lesson 5-6　　**Simplify each expression.**

　　109. $(2 - 3\sqrt{-4}) + (4 + 2\sqrt{-16})$ 　　**110.** $3\sqrt{-50} - (2 - \sqrt{-32})$

　　111. $(6 + \sqrt{-20}) - (-7 - \sqrt{-45})$ 　　**112.** $(5 - \sqrt{-9})(2 - \sqrt{-36})$

✓ Checkpoint Quiz 2　　　　　　　　　　　　　Lessons 7-4 through 7-6

Simplify each expression.

　　1. $(-27x^3)^{\frac{4}{3}}$ 　　　　　　　　　　　　**2.** $(32y^5)^{-0.4}$

Solve each equation.

　　3. $\sqrt{3x + 1} - 4 = 0$ 　　　　　　　　　　**4.** $(5x + 2)^{\frac{2}{3}} = 9$

Solve each equation. Check for extraneous solutions.

　　5. $\sqrt{3x + 3} - 3 = 3x$ 　　　　　　　　　**6.** $(2 - x)^{0.5} - x = 4$

Let $f(x) = 2x + 3$ and $g(x) = x^2 - x$. Find each value.

　　7. $(f + g)\left(\frac{1}{2}\right)$ 　　**8.** $(f \cdot g)(1)$ 　　**9.** $\left(\frac{f}{g}\right)(2)$ 　　**10.** $(f \circ g)(5)$

Guided Problem Solving

FOR USE WITH PAGE 402, EXERCISE 62a

Understanding Word Problems Read the problem below. It has two parts. Let the explanations guide you through both solutions. Check your understanding with the exercises at the bottom of the page.

Geometry You toss a pebble into a pool of water and watch the circular ripples radiate outward. You find that the function $r(x) = 12.5x$ describes the radius r in inches of a circle x seconds after it was formed. The function $A(x) = \pi x^2$ describes the area A of a circle with radius x.

a. Find $(A \circ r)(x)$ when $x = 2$. Interpret your answer.

The problem uses function notation. Here is the way to read function notation.

Write $A(x)$ $\qquad$ $A(r(x))$ $\qquad$ $(A \circ r)(x) = A(r(x))$

Read A of x $\quad$ A of r of x $\quad$ The composition of A with r equals A of r of x.

Solve For $A(x) = \pi x^2$ and $r(x) = 12.5x$, find $(A \circ r)(2)$.

$$(A \circ r)(2) = A(r(2))$$

$$r(2) = 12.5(2) = 25 \quad \text{Find } r(2) \text{ first.}$$

$$A(25) = \pi(25)^2 \quad \begin{array}{l}\text{Use the output } r(2) = 25 \\ \text{as the input for } A(x).\end{array}$$

$$= 625\pi \approx 1963$$

$$r \qquad\qquad A$$
$$2 \rightarrow 12.5(2) \rightarrow 25 \rightarrow \pi(25)^2 \rightarrow 625\pi$$

To interpret your answer is to explain what your answer means in terms of the problem. The problem tells you that $A(x)$ is the area of a circle with radius x and that $r(x)$ is the radius of a circle x seconds after it was formed.

So $(A \circ r)(2)$ is the area of a circle after 2 seconds. The area is about 1963 in.^{2}.

b. Find the area of a circle 4 seconds after it was formed.

Similar to part (a), $(A \circ r)(4)$ is the area. Using part (a) as a guide,

$$(A \circ r)(4) = A(r(4))$$

$$r(4) = 12.5(4) = 50$$

$$A(50) = \pi(50)^2$$

$$= 2500\pi \approx 7854$$

The area of a circle after 4 seconds is about 7854 in.^{2}.

EXERCISES

1. You toss a pebble into a pool of water and watch the circular ripples radiate outward. You find that the function $r(x) = 12.5x$ describes the radius of the first circle r in inches after x seconds. The function $C(x) = 2\pi x$ describes the circumference C of a circle with radius x. Find $(C \circ r)(x)$ when $x = 3$. Interpret your answer.

2. A tanker leaks a small amount of crude oil into the bay. The function $d(x) = 2.3x$ models the length d, in kilometers, of the oval oil slick after x hours. $A(x) = \frac{3}{8}\pi x^2$ models the area of a slick x km long. Find the area of the oil slick after 10.5 hours.

Guided Problem Solving Understanding Word Problems **405**

Inverse Relations and Functions

- To find the inverse of a relation or function

...And Why

To estimate the speed of a car, as in Example 5

✓ **Check Skills You'll Need**

GO for Help Lesson 3-1

Graph each pair of functions on a single coordinate plane.

1. $y = x - 6$
$y = x + 6$

2. $y = \frac{x - 7}{2}$
$y = 2x + 7$

3. $y = 3x - 1$
$y = \frac{x + 1}{3}$

4. $y = 0.5x + 1$
$y = 2x - 2$

5. $y = -x + 4$
$y = \frac{-x + 4}{-1}$

6. $y = \frac{x + 4}{5}$
$y = 5x - 4$

🔊 **New Vocabulary** • inverse relation • inverse functions

---

1 The Inverse of a Function

Activity: Inverses

- Function f doubles the input and then subtracts 8. $f(x) = 2x - 8$
- Function g adds 8 to the input and then divides by 2. $g(x) = \frac{x + 8}{2}$

$$10 \xrightarrow{\quad f(x) \quad} 2x - 8 \xrightarrow{\quad} \xrightarrow{\quad g(x) \quad} \frac{x + 8}{2} \xrightarrow{\quad} ?$$

1. a. Find $f(10)$ and $g(f(10))$.
  b. Find $f(0)$ and $g(f(0))$.
  c. Find $f(-7)$ and $g(f(-7))$.
  d. Without computing, use the pattern in parts (a)–(c) to find $g(f(-1496))$.

$$6 \xrightarrow{\quad g(x) \quad} \frac{x + 8}{2} \xrightarrow{\quad} \xrightarrow{\quad f(x) \quad} 2x - 8 \xrightarrow{\quad} ?$$

2. a. Find $g(6)$ and $f(g(6))$.
  b. Find $g(0)$ and $f(g(0))$.
  c. Find $g(-32)$ and $f(g(-32))$.
  d. Without computing, use the pattern in parts (a)–(c) to find $f(g(\pi))$.

3. a. Interchange the x and y variables in $y = 2x - 8$ and solve for y.
  b. Graph your two equations in part (a) on the same coordinate axes. Fold your graph paper so the two lines coincide. How are the two graphs related?

If a relation pairs element a of its domain to element b of its range, the **inverse relation** pairs b with a. So, if (a, b) is an ordered pair of a relation, then (b, a) is an ordered pair of its inverse.

This diagram shows a relation r and its inverse.

The range of the relation is the domain of the inverse, and the domain of the relation is the range of the inverse.

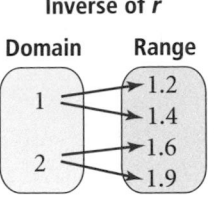

1 EXAMPLE Finding the Inverse of a Relation

a. Find the inverse of relation s.

Relation s

x	1	2	3	4
y	−1	0	1	1

Interchange the x and y values to get the inverse.

Inverse of Relation s

x	−1	0	1	1
y	1	2	3	4

b. Graph s and its inverse.

Relation s Reversing the Ordered Pairs   Inverse of s

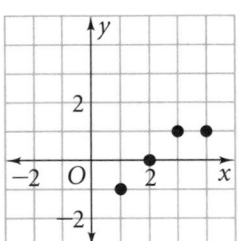
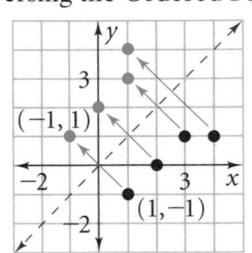
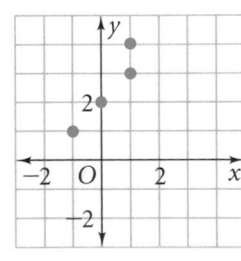

✓ Quick Check **1 a.** Describe how the line $y = x$ is related to the graphs of s and its inverse.
b. In Example 1, is relation s a function? Is the inverse of s a function?

As shown in Example 1, the graph of the inverse of a relation is the reflection in the line $y = x$ of the graph of the relation. If a relation or function is described by an equation in x and y, you can interchange x and y to get the inverse.

2 EXAMPLE Interchanging x and y

Find the inverse of $y = x^2 + 3$.

$$y = x^2 + 3$$
$$x = y^2 + 3 \quad \text{Interchange } x \text{ and } y.$$
$$x - 3 = y^2 \quad \text{Solve for } y.$$
$$\pm\sqrt{x - 3} = y \quad \text{Find the square root of each side.}$$

✓ Quick Check **2 a.** Does $y = x^2 + 3$ define a function? Is its inverse a function? Explain.
b. Find the inverse of $y = 3x - 10$. Is the inverse a function? Explain.

3 EXAMPLE Graphing a Relation and Its Inverse

Graph $y = x^2 + 3$ and its inverse, $y = \pm\sqrt{x - 3}$.

The graph of $y = x^2 + 3$ is a parabola that opens upward with vertex $(0, 3)$. The reflection of the parabola in the line $y = x$ is the graph of the inverse.

You can also find points on the graph of the inverse by reversing the coordinates of points on $y = x^2 + 3$.

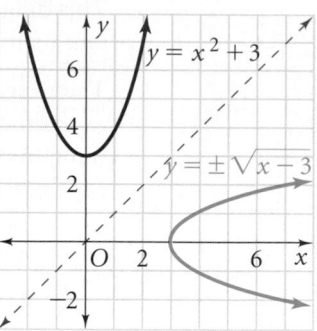

✓ Quick Check ③ Graph $y = 3x - 10$ and its inverse.

Vocabulary Tip

For a nonzero number x, x^{-1} is the multiplicative inverse of x, or $\frac{1}{x}$.

For a function f, f^{-1} is the relation that is the inverse of f.

The inverse of function f is denoted by f^{-1}. Read f^{-1} as "the inverse of f" or as "f inverse." The notation $f(x)$ is used for functions, but the relation f^{-1} may not even be a function.

4 EXAMPLE Finding an Inverse Function

Consider the function $f(x) = \sqrt{x + 1}$.

a. Find the domain and range of f.

Since the radicand cannot be negative, the domain is the set of numbers greater than or equal to -1. Since the principal square root is nonnegative, the range is the set of nonnegative numbers.

b. Find f^{-1}.

$$f(x) = \sqrt{x + 1}$$
$$y = \sqrt{x + 1} \qquad \text{Rewrite the equation using } y.$$
$$x = \sqrt{y + 1} \qquad \text{Interchange } x \text{ and } y. \text{ Since } x \text{ equals a principal square root, } x \geq 0.$$
$$x^2 = y + 1 \qquad \text{Square both sides.}$$
$$y = x^2 - 1 \qquad \text{Solve for } y.$$

So, $f^{-1}(x) = x^2 - 1$, $x \geq 0$.

Test-Taking Tip

If the graph of a function f does not have two points in line horizontally, then f^{-1} is also a function.

c. Find the domain and range of f^{-1}.

The domain of f^{-1} equals the range of f, which is the set of nonnegative numbers. Since $x^2 \geq 0$, $x^2 - 1 \geq -1$. Thus the range of f^{-1} is the set of numbers greater than or equal to -1. Note that the range of f^{-1} is the same as the domain of f.

d. Is f^{-1} a function? Explain.

For each x in the domain of f^{-1}, there is only one value of $f^{-1}(x)$. So f^{-1} is a function.

✓ Quick Check ④ Let $f(x) = 10 - 3x$. Find each of the following.
a. the domain and range of f **b.** f^{-1}
c. the domain and range of f^{-1} **d.** $f^{-1}(f(3))$
e. $f(f^{-1}(2))$

Functions that model real-life situations are frequently expressed as formulas with letters that remind you of the variables they represent. When finding the inverse of a formula, it would be very confusing to interchange the letters. Keep the letters the same and just solve the formula for the other variable.

5 EXAMPLE **Real-World** 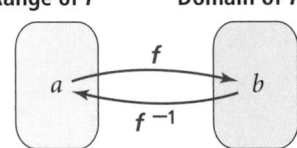 **Connection**

Multiple Choice The function $d = \frac{r^2}{24}$ is a model for the distance d in feet that a car with locked brakes skids in coming to a complete stop from a speed of r mi/h. Find the inverse of the function. What is the best estimate of the speed of a car that made skid marks 114 feet long?

   (A) 5 mi/h   (B) 12 mi/h   (C) 23 mi/h   (D) 52 mi/h

$d = \frac{r^2}{24}$

$r^2 = 24d$ **Solve for r. Do not interchange the variables.**

$r = \sqrt{24d}$ **Rate of speed must be positive.**

$ = \sqrt{24 \cdot 114}$ **Substitute 114 for d.**

$ \approx 52$ **Use a calculator.**

● The car was traveling about 52 mi/h. The correct choice is D.

Real-World  **Connection**

Many safe driving programs include experience with braking distance.

✓ **Quick Check** ⑤ The function $d = \frac{v^2}{64}$ is a model relating the distance d a stone has fallen in feet to its velocity v in feet per second (ft/s). Find the inverse of the function and use it to find the velocity of a stone that has fallen 30 ft.

If f and f^{-1} are both functions, and if f maps a to b, then f^{-1} must map b to a.

Domain of f Range of f
Range of f^{-1} Domain of f^{-1}

If f and f^{-1} are functions, they are called **inverse functions.** For inverse functions, $f^{-1}(f(x)) = x$ and $f(f^{-1}(x)) = x$.

Key Concepts

Property	Composition of Inverse Functions

If f and f^{-1} are inverse functions, then

$(f^{-1} \circ f)(x) = x$ and $(f \circ f^{-1})(x) = x.$

6 EXAMPLE **Composition of Inverse Functions**

For the function $f(x) = \frac{x - 7}{6}$, find $(f^{-1} \circ f)(374)$ and $(f \circ f^{-1})(-99\pi)$.

Since f is a linear function with nonzero slope, f^{-1} is also a linear function.

● So $(f^{-1} \circ f)(374) = 374$ and $(f \circ f^{-1})(-99\pi) = -99\pi$.

✓ **Quick Check** ⑥ For $f(x) = 5x + 11$, find $(f^{-1} \circ f)(777)$ and $(f \circ f^{-1})(-5802)$.

EXERCISES

For more exercises, see *Extra Skill and Word Problem Practice.*

Practice and Problem Solving

A Practice by Example

Example 1
(page 407)

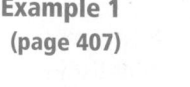

Find the inverse of each relation. Graph the given relation and its inverse.

1.
x	1	2	3	4
y	0	1	0	2

2.
x	1	2	3	4
y	0	1	2	3

3.
x	0	1	2	3
y	0	1	4	9

4.
x	−3	−2	−1	0
y	2	2	2	2

Example 2
(page 407)

Find the inverse of each function. Is the inverse a function?

5. $y = 3x + 1$ 6. $y = 2x - 1$ 7. $y = 4 - 3x$

8. $y = 5 - 2x^2$ 9. $y = x^2 + 4$ 10. $y = 3x^2 - 5$

11. $y = (x + 1)^2$ 12. $y = (3x - 4)^2$ 13. $y = (1 - 2x)^2 + 5$

Example 3
(page 408)

Graph each relation and its inverse.

14. $y = 2x - 3$ 15. $y = 3 - 7x$ 16. $y = -x$

17. $y = 3x^2$ 18. $y = -x^2$ 19. $y = 4x^2 - 2$

20. $y = (x - 1)^2$ 21. $y = (2 - x)^2$ 22. $y = (3 - 2x)^2 - 1$

Example 4
(page 408)

For each function f, find f^{-1} and the domain and range of f and f^{-1}. Determine whether f^{-1} is a function.

23. $f(x) = 3x + 4$ 24. $f(x) = \sqrt{x - 5}$

25. $f(x) = \sqrt{x + 7}$ 26. $f(x) = \sqrt{-2x + 3}$

27. $f(x) = 2x^2 + 2$ 28. $f(x) = -x^2 + 1$

Example 5
(page 409)

29. The formula for converting from Celsius to Fahrenheit temperatures is $C = \frac{9}{5}F + 32$.

    a. Find the inverse of the formula. Is the inverse a function?
    b. Use the inverse to find the Fahrenheit temperature that corresponds to 25°C.

30. **Geometry** The formula for the volume of a sphere is $V = \frac{4}{3}\pi r^3$.

    a. Find the inverse of the formula. Is the inverse a function?
    b. Use the inverse to find the radius of a sphere that has a volume of 35,000 ft^3.

Example 6
(page 409)

For Exercises 31–34, $f(x) = 10x - 10$. Find each value.

31. $(f^{-1} \circ f)(10)$ 32. $(f \circ f^{-1})(-10)$

33. $(f^{-1} \circ f)(0.2)$ 34. $(f \circ f^{-1})(d)$

B Apply Your Skills

Find the inverse of each function. Is the inverse a function?

35. $f(x) = 1.5x^2 - 4$ 36. $f(x) = \frac{3x^2}{4}$ 37. $f(x) = \sqrt{2x - 1} + 3$

38. $f(x) = (x + 1)^2$ 39. $f(x) = (2x - 1)^2$ 40. $f(x) = (x + 1)^2 - 1$

41. $f(x) = x^3$ 42. $f(x) = x^4$ 43. $f(x) = \frac{2x^2}{5} + 1$

Real-World  **Connection**

Water towers are tall because each foot of height provides 0.43 lb/in.² of pressure. A typical tower holds about a one-day supply for users.

44. Water Supply The velocity of the water that flows from an opening at the base of a tank depends on the height of water above the opening. The function $v(x) = \sqrt{2gx}$ models the velocity v in feet per second where g, the acceleration due to gravity, is about 32 ft/s² and x is the height in feet of the water. Find the inverse function and use it to find the depth of water when the flow is 40 ft/s, and when the flow is 20 ft/s.

45. Writing Explain how you can find the range of the inverse of $f(x) = \sqrt{x - 1}$ without finding the inverse itself.

46. A function consists of the pairs $(2, 3)$, $(x, 4)$ and $(5, 6)$. What values, if any, may x not assume?

For each function f, find f^{-1}, the domain and range of f and f^{-1}, and determine whether f^{-1} is a function.

47. $f(x) = -\sqrt{x}$ **48.** $f(x) = \sqrt{x} + 3$ **49.** $f(x) = \sqrt{-x + 3}$

50. $f(x) = \sqrt{x + 2}$ **51.** $f(x) = \frac{x^2}{2}$ **52.** $f(x) = \frac{1}{x^2}$

53. $f(x) = (x - 4)^2$ **54.** $f(x) = (7 - x)^2$ **55.** $f(x) = \frac{1}{(x + 1)^2}$

56. $f(x) = 4 - 2\sqrt{x}$ **57.** $f(x) = \frac{3}{\sqrt{x}}$ **58.** $f(x) = \frac{1}{\sqrt{-2x}}$

59. a. Copy the mapping diagram at the right. Complete it by writing members of the domain and range and connecting them with arrows so that r is a function and r^{-1} is not a function.
     b. Repeat part (a) so that r is not a function and r^{-1} is a function.

Relation r

Domain	Range

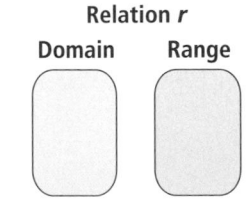

60. Critical Thinking Relation r has one element in its domain and two elements in its range. Is r a function? Is the inverse of r a function? Explain.

GO **nline**
Homework Video Tutor
Visit: PHSchool.com
Web Code: age-0707

61. Geometry Write a function that gives the length of the hypotenuse of an isosceles right triangle with side length s. Evaluate the inverse of the function to find the side length of an isosceles right triangle with a hypotenuse of 6 in.

62. Open-Ended Write a function f such that the graph of f^{-1} lies in Quadrants III and IV.

C **Challenge**

Find the inverse of each function. Is the inverse a function?

63. $f(x) = \frac{1}{5}x^3$ **64.** $f(x) = \sqrt[3]{x - 5}$ **65.** $f(x) = \frac{\sqrt[3]{x}}{3}$

66. $f(x) = (x - 2)^3$ **67.** $f(x) = \sqrt[4]{x}$ **68.** $f(x) = 1.2x^4$

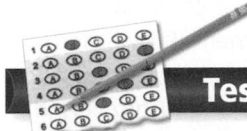 **Test Prep**

Multiple Choice

69. What is the inverse of $y = 5x - 1$?

     A. $y = 5x + 1$ **B.** $y = \frac{x + 1}{5}$ **C.** $y = \frac{x}{5} + 1$ **D.** $y = \frac{x}{5} - 1$

70. If $f(x) = 4x - 3$, what is $(f^{-1} \circ f)(10)$?

     F. $\frac{13}{4}$ **G.** 10   **H.** 37   **J.** $\frac{481}{4}$

71. What is the inverse of $y = x^2 - 3$?

  A. $y = \pm\sqrt{x} + 3$ **B.** $y = \pm\sqrt{x} - 3$

  C. $y = \pm\sqrt{x + 3}$ **D.** $y = \pm\sqrt{x - 3}$

Short Response

72. What is the inverse of $y = 4x^2 + 5$? For what values of x is the inverse a real number?

Extended Response

73. What is the inverse of $y = x^2 - 2x + 1$? Is the inverse a function? Explain.

Mixed Review

GO for Help

Lesson 7-6

Let $f(x) = 4x$, $g(x) = \frac{1}{2}x + 7$, and $h(x) = |-2x + 4|$. Simplify each function.

74. $(f \circ g)(x)$ **75.** $(g \circ f)(x)$ **76.** $(h \circ g)(x)$

77. $g(x) + g(x)$ **78.** $(h \circ (g \circ f))(x)$ **79.** $(f \circ g)(x) + h(x)$

Lesson 7-1

Find each indicated root if it is a real number.

80. $\sqrt[4]{16}$ **81.** $-\sqrt[4]{16}$ **82.** $\sqrt[4]{-16}$ **83.** $\sqrt[5]{243}$

84. $-\sqrt[5]{243}$ **85.** $\sqrt[5]{-243}$ **86.** $\sqrt[3]{0.064}$ **87.** $\sqrt[4]{810{,}000}$

Lesson 6-5

List all possible rational roots for each equation. Then use the Rational Root Theorem to find each root.

88. $2x^3 + 3x^2 - 8x - 12 = 0$ **89.** $3x^3 - 5x^2 - 4x + 4 = 0$

90. $3x^3 + 10x^2 - x - 12 = 0$ **91.** $2x^3 - 11x^2 - x + 30 = 0$

92. $x^3 - 6x^2 + 11x - 6 = 0$ **93.** $x^3 + 3x^2 - 4x - 12 = 0$

Algebra at Work

Demographer

Demographers study human populations. They collect, analyze, and present data relating to the basic life cycle: birth, marriage, divorce, family formation, employment, aging, migration, and death. Demographers draw on the related disciplines of sociology, economics, political science, anthropology, psychology, public health, and ecology.

  Demography is also concerned with the broader nature of social and economic change and its impact on the natural environment. It includes studying family structure, the role of women, and the value of children, as well as the social, cultural, and institutional context of demographic change. Demography is an essential component of many activities, such as planning government policies and market research.

For: Information about demography

PHSchool.com   **Web Code:** agb-2031

Graphing Inverses

You can graph inverses of functions on a graphing calculator by using the DrawInv feature or by using parametric equations. It takes more keystrokes to set up parametric equations, but once you do you can easily change from one function to another and quickly see the graphs of the new function and its inverse.

ACTIVITY

Graph $y = 0.3x^2 + 1$ and its inverse.

Method 1 Use the DrawInv feature.

Step 1   Press Y= and enter the equation. Press ZOOM 5 to see a graph of the function with equal x- and y-intervals.

Step 2   Press 2nd **DRAW** 8. You will see DrawInv followed by a flashing cursor. Select equation Y_1 by pressing VARS ▶ 1 1. Press ENTER to see the graph of the function and its inverse.

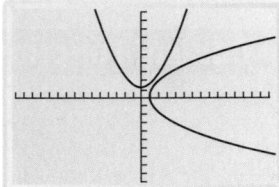

Method 2 Use parametric equations.

Step 1   Set to parametric mode. Press MODE, select **Par**, and press 2nd **QUIT**.

Step 2   Enter the given equation in parametric form. Press Y= and enter the equations $X_{1T} = T$ and $Y_{1T} = .3T^2 + 1$.

Step 3   Now use $X_{2T} = Y_{1T}$ and $Y_{2T} = X_{1T}$ to interchange the x- and y-values of the first parametric equation. Press Y= and move the cursor to follow $X_{2T} =$. Select Y_{1T} by pressing VARS ▶ 2 2. Enter the equation $Y_{2T} = X_{1T}$ in a similar fashion.

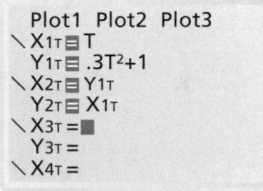

Step 4   Press ZOOM 5. Adjust the Window so that Tmin and Tmax approximately agree with Xmin and Xmax. Press GRAPH to see the graph of the function and its inverse.

EXERCISES

Graph each function and its inverse with a graphing calculator. Then sketch the graphs.

1. $y = x^2 - 5$ **2.** $y = (x - 3)^2$ **3.** $y = 0.01x^4$ **4.** $y = 0.5x^3 - 3$

5. Critical Thinking In Method 2, suppose you added a third pair of parametric equations that interchanged the x- and y-values of the second pair ($X_{3T} = Y_{2T}$ and $Y_{3T} = X_{2T}$). What would be the effect on the graphs? Explain.

6. Writing Change the parametric equation $X_{2T} = Y_{1T}$ in Method 2, Step 3 to $X_{2T} = -Y_{1T}$. Describe the graph that results.

7. Explain how, once you set up parametric equations, you can change from one function to another and quickly see the graphs of the new function and its inverse.

Graphing Square Root and Other Radical Functions

☑ **Check Skills You'll Need**

GO for Help Lesson 5-3

Graph each equation.

1. $y = (x + 2)^2$ **2.** $y = (x - 3)^2$ **3.** $y = -(x + 4)^2$

4. $y = -x^2 - 1$ **5.** $y = -(x + 1)^2 + 1$ **6.** $y = 3x^2 + 3$

🔊 **New Vocabulary** • radical function • square root function

---

1 Radical Functions

GO for Help

To review the vertical line test, go to Lesson 2-1.

A horizontal line can intersect the graph of $f(x) = x^2$ in two points. For example, $f(-2) = f(2)$. Therefore, a vertical line can intersect the graph of the inverse of $f(x) = x^2$ in two points, and f^{-1} is *not* a function.

$f(x) = x^2$

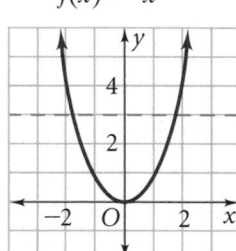

$f^{-1}(x) = \pm\sqrt{x}$

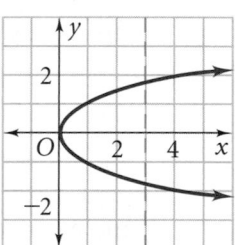

You can restrict the domain of f so that its inverse is a function.

$f(x) = x^2, x \geq 0$

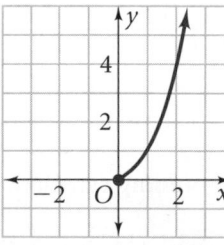

$f^{-1}(x) = \sqrt{x}$

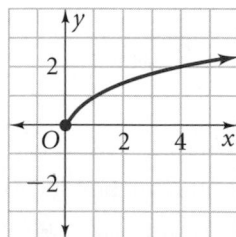

The inverse of $g(x) = x^3$ is a function.

$g(x) = x^3$

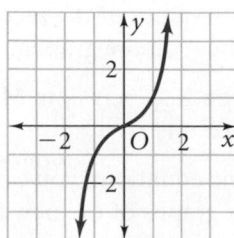

$g^{-1}(x) = \sqrt[3]{x}$

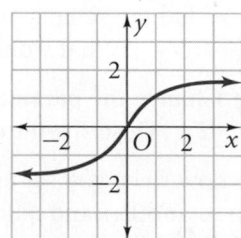

Inverses of functions of the form $y = x^n$ (with domains restricted as needed) form parent functions $y = \sqrt[n]{x}$ of families of **radical functions.** In particular, $f(x) = \sqrt{x}$ is the parent for the family of **square root functions.** Members of this family have the form $f(x) = a\sqrt{x - h} + k$.

 **Key Concepts**

Summary	Families of Radical Functions Including the Square Root Function	
	Square Root	**Radical**
Parent function:	$y = \sqrt{x}$	$y = \sqrt[n]{x}$
Reflection in x-axis:	$y = -\sqrt{x}$	$y = -\sqrt[n]{x}$
Stretch $(a > 1)$, shrink $(0 < a < 1)$ by factor a:	$y = a\sqrt{x}$	$y = a\sqrt[n]{x}$
Reflection in x-axis:	$y = -a\sqrt{x}$	$y = -a\sqrt[n]{x}$
Translation: Horizontal by h	$y = \sqrt{x - h}$	$y = \sqrt[n]{x - h}$
Vertical by k	$y = \sqrt{x} + k$	$y = \sqrt[n]{x} + k$
Combined:	$y = \sqrt{x - h} + k$	$y = \sqrt[n]{x - h} + k$

1 EXAMPLE **Translating Square Root Functions Vertically**

Graph $y = \sqrt{x} + 2$ and $y = \sqrt{x} - 1$.

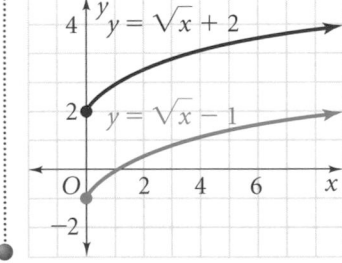

The graph of $y = \sqrt{x} + 2$ is the graph of $y = \sqrt{x}$ shifted up 2 units. The graph of $y = \sqrt{x} - 1$ is the graph of $y = \sqrt{x}$ shifted down 1 unit.

The domains of both functions are the set of nonnegative numbers, but their ranges differ.

✓**Quick Check** ❶ Graph $y = \sqrt{x} - 3$ and $y = \sqrt{x} + 3$.

The graph of $y = \sqrt{x - h}$ is a horizontal translation of $y = \sqrt{x}$. If h is positive, translate h units to the right. If h is negative, translate $|h|$ units to the left.

2 EXAMPLE **Translating Square Root Functions Horizontally**

Graph $y = \sqrt{x + 3}$ and $y = \sqrt{x - 2}$.

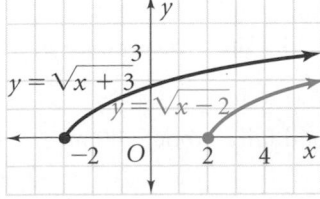

The graph of $y = \sqrt{x + 3}$ is the graph of $y = \sqrt{x}$ shifted left 3 units. The graph of $y = \sqrt{x - 2}$ is the graph of $y = \sqrt{x}$ shifted right 2 units.

The ranges of both functions are the set of nonnegative numbers, but their domains differ.

✓**Quick Check** ❷ Graph $y = \sqrt{x - 1}$ and $y = \sqrt{x + 4}$.

For the combined transformation $y = a\sqrt{x - h} + k$, a indicates a vertical stretch ($a > 1$) or shrink ($0 < a < 1$). A negative sign indicates reflection in the x-axis.

3 EXAMPLE Graphing Square Root Functions

Graph $y = -2\sqrt{x + 1} - 3$.

The graph of $y = -2\sqrt{x}$ is a stretch of $y = \sqrt{x}$ by a factor of 2 and a reflection across the x-axis (in black). Then translate left 1 unit and down 3 units.

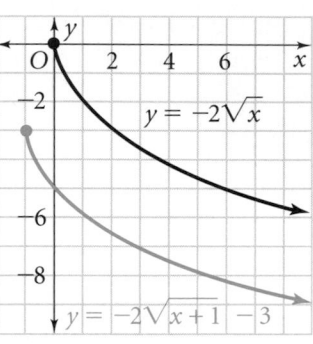

✓ **Quick Check** **3** Graph $y = \frac{1}{4}\sqrt{x - 2} - 4$.

The pattern for graphing square root functions applies to other radical functions.

4 EXAMPLE Graphing Cube Root Functions

Graph $y = 2\sqrt[3]{x + 3} - 1$.

The graph of $y = 2\sqrt[3]{x + 3} - 1$ is the graph of $y = 2\sqrt[3]{x}$ translated 3 units left and 1 unit down.

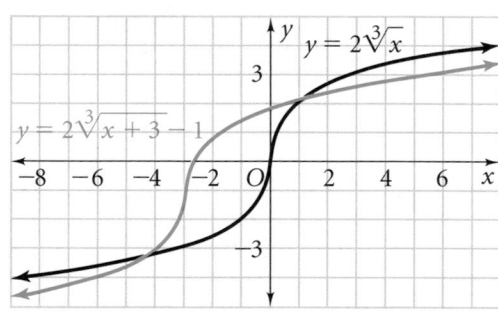

✓ **Quick Check** **4** Graph $y = 3 - \sqrt[3]{x + 1}$.

5 EXAMPLE Solving Square Root Equations by Graphing

Physics You can model the time t, in seconds, an object takes to reach the ground falling from height H, in meters, by $t(H) = \sqrt{\dfrac{2H}{g}}$. The value of g is 9.81 m/s^2. From what height does an object fall if it takes 7 seconds to reach the ground?

For $t = 7$, solve the equation $7 = \sqrt{\dfrac{2H}{9.81}}$.

Graph Y1 $= \sqrt{(2X/9.81)}$ and Y2 $= 7$. Adjust the window to find where the graphs intersect. Use the Intersect feature to find the x-coordinate of the intersection.

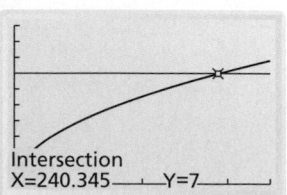

The height for a 7-second fall is about 240 m.

✓ **Quick Check** **5** How far does an object fall if it takes 3.5 seconds to reach the ground? How does this compare with the height of a 7-second fall?

For: Radical Functions Activity
Use: Interactive Textbook, 7-8

Sometimes you have to rewrite a radical function so you can graph it using transformations.

6 EXAMPLE **Rewriting Radical Functions**

Rewrite $y = \sqrt{4x - 12}$ to make it easy to graph using transformations. Describe the graph.

$$y = \sqrt{4x - 12} = \sqrt{4(x - 3)} = 2\sqrt{x - 3}$$

● The graph of $y = \sqrt{4x - 12}$ is the graph of $y = 2\sqrt{x}$ translated 3 units right.

✓ **Quick Check** ⑥ Rewrite $y = \sqrt[3]{8x - 24} + 3$ to make it easy to graph using transformations. Describe the graph.

EXERCISES

For more exercises, see *Extra Skill and Word Problem Practice*.

Practice and Problem Solving

Ⓐ Practice by Example

Examples 1 and 2
(page 415)

Graph each function.

1. $y = \sqrt{x} + 1$ **2.** $y = \sqrt{x} - 2$ **3.** $y = \sqrt{x} - 4$ **4.** $y = \sqrt{x} + 5$

5. $y = \sqrt{x - 3}$ **6.** $y = \sqrt{x + 1}$ **7.** $y = \sqrt{x + 6}$ **8.** $y = \sqrt{x - 4}$

Example 3
(page 416)

Graph each function.

9. $y = 3\sqrt{x}$ **10.** $y = -0.25\sqrt{x}$ **11.** $y = \frac{1}{3}\sqrt{x}$

12. $y = -\sqrt{x} - 1$ **13.** $y = -5\sqrt{x} + 2$ **14.** $y = -0.75\sqrt{x} + 3$

15. $y = -\sqrt{x - 3} + 2$ **16.** $y = \frac{1}{4}\sqrt{x + 2} - 1$ **17.** $y = 3\sqrt{x + 1} + 4$

Example 4
(page 416)

Graph each function.

18. $y = \sqrt[3]{x} + 5$ **19.** $y = \sqrt[3]{x} - 4$ **20.** $y = \sqrt[3]{x + 2} - 7$

21. $y = -\sqrt[3]{x + 3} - 1$ **22.** $y = 2\sqrt[3]{x - 6} - 9$ **23.** $y = \frac{1}{2}\sqrt[3]{x - 1} + 3$

24. Agriculture A center-pivot irrigation system can water from 1 to 130 acres of crop land. The length ℓ in feet of rotating pipe needed to irrigate A acres is given by the function $\ell = 117.75\sqrt{A}$.
a. Graph the equation on your calculator. Make a sketch of the graph.
b. Find the lengths of pipe needed to irrigate 40, 80, and 130 acres.

Example 5
(page 416)

🖩 **Solve each square root equation by graphing. Round the answer to the nearest hundredth if necessary. If there is no solution, explain why.**

25. $\sqrt{x - 3} = 12$ **26.** $\sqrt{2x - 3} = 4$ **27.** $3\sqrt{3 - x} = 10$

28. $2.5\sqrt{2x - 1.3} = -1$ **29.** $2\sqrt{x + 4} = 3\sqrt{x - 1}$ **30.** $\sqrt{2x + 5} = \sqrt{2 - x}$

Example 6
(page 417)

Rewrite each function to make it easy to graph using transformations of its parent function. Describe the graph.

31. $y = \sqrt{9x - 9}$ **32.** $y = -\sqrt{16x + 32}$ **33.** $y = -2\sqrt{49x + 49}$

34. $y = \sqrt[3]{64x + 128}$ **35.** $y = \sqrt{64x - 128} - 3$ **36.** $y = \sqrt[3]{27x - 54} + 1$

B **Apply Your Skills**

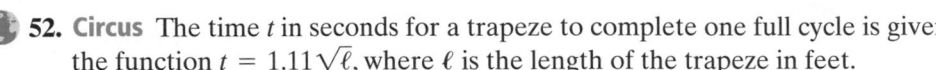

Graph. Find the domain and the range of each function.

37. $y = \sqrt{x} + 7$　　**38.** $y = \sqrt{x} - 6$　　**39.** $y = \sqrt{x - 6}$

40. $y = -3\sqrt{x} + 2$　　**41.** $y = -\frac{4}{5}\sqrt{x}$　　**42.** $y = 7 - \sqrt{2x - 1}$

43. $y = 4\sqrt[3]{x - 2} + 1$　　**44.** $y = \frac{1}{2}\sqrt{x - 1} + 3$　　**45.** $y = -3\sqrt[3]{x - 4} - 3$

46. $y = -\sqrt{x + \frac{1}{2}}$　　**47.** $y = -\sqrt[3]{8x} + 5$　　**48.** $y = -2\sqrt[3]{x - 4}$

49. $y = -1 - \sqrt{4x + 20}$　　**50.** $y = 4 - \sqrt[3]{x + 2.5}$　　**51.** $y = -3\sqrt{x - \frac{3}{4}} + 7$

52. Circus The time t in seconds for a trapeze to complete one full cycle is given by the function $t = 1.11\sqrt{\ell}$, where ℓ is the length of the trapeze in feet.
  a. Graph the equation on your calculator. Make a sketch of the graph.
  b. How long is a full cycle if the trapeze is 15 ft. long? 30 ft. long?

53. a. Graph $y = \sqrt{x - 2} - 2$.
  b. Find the domain and the range.
  c. At what coordinate point does the graph start?
  d. Critical Thinking What is the relationship of the point at which the graph starts to the domain and the range?

54. a. The graph of $y = \sqrt{x}$ is translated five units to the right and two units down. Write an equation of the translated function.
  b. The translated graph from part (a) is again translated, this time four units left and three units down. Write an equation of the translated function.

55. a. Graph $y = \sqrt{x - 2} + 1$ and $y = -\sqrt{x - 2} + 1$.
  b. Find the domain and the range of each function.

Real-World  **Connection**

The length of the pendulum formed by an aerialist on a trapeze depends on how far he hangs below the bar.

Rewrite each function to make it easy to graph using transformations of its parent function. Describe the graph.

56. $y = \sqrt{25x - 100} - 1$　　**57.** $y = \sqrt{36x + 108} + 4$　　**58.** $y = -\sqrt[3]{8x - 2}$

59. $y = \sqrt{\frac{x - 1}{4}} - 2$　　**60.** $y = 10 - \sqrt[3]{\frac{x + 3}{27}}$　　**61.** $y = \sqrt{\frac{x}{9} + 1} + 5$

62. Open-Ended Write a cube root function in which the vertical translation of $y = \sqrt[3]{x}$ is twice the horizontal translation.

63. Electronics The size of a television screen is the length of the screen's diagonal d in inches. The equation $d = \sqrt{2A}$ models the length of a diagonal of a television screen with area A.
  a. Graph the equation on your calculator.
  b. Suppose you want to buy a new television that has twice the area of your old television. Your old television has an area of 100 in.^{2}. What size screen should you buy?

64. Writing Explain the effect that a has on the graph of $y = a\sqrt{x}$.

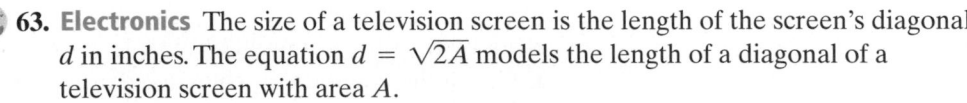

C **Challenge**

Rewrite each function to make it easy to graph using transformations of its parent function. Describe the graph. Find the domain and the range of each function.

65. $y = -\sqrt{2x + 8}$　　　　　　**66.** $y = -\sqrt{2(4x - 3)}$

67. $y = \sqrt{3x - 5} + 6$　　　　　**68.** $y = -3 - \sqrt{12x + 18}$

69. a. Graph $y = \sqrt{-x}$, $y = \sqrt{1-x}$, and $y = \sqrt{2-x}$.

b. Make a Conjecture How does the graph of $y = \sqrt{h-x}$ differ from the graph of $y = \sqrt{x-h}$?

70. For what positive integers n are the domain and range of $y = \sqrt[n]{x}$ the set of real numbers? Assume that x is a real number.

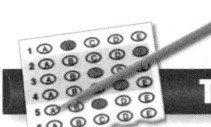

Test Prep

Multiple Choice

71. How is the graph of $y = \sqrt{x} + 7$ translated from the graph of $y = \sqrt{x}$?
A. shifted 7 units left   B. shifted 7 units right
C. shifted 7 units up   D. shifted 7 units down

72. How is the graph of $y = \sqrt{x} - 5$ translated from the graph of $y = \sqrt{x}$?
F. shifted 5 units left   G. shifted 5 units right
H. shifted 5 units up   J. shifted 5 units down

73. The graph of $y = -\sqrt{x}$ is shifted 4 units up and 3 units right. Which equation represents the new graph?
A. $y = -\sqrt{x-4} + 3$ B. $y = -\sqrt{x-3} + 4$
C. $y = -\sqrt{x+3} + 4$ D. $y = -\sqrt{x+4} + 3$

74. Which equation shows $y + 3 = \sqrt{\frac{x}{16} + 2}$ rewritten in the form $y = a\sqrt{x - h} + k$?
F. $y = \frac{3}{4}\sqrt{x - (-2)}$ G. $y = \frac{1}{4}\sqrt{x - (-2)} + (-3)$
H. $y = \frac{1}{4}\sqrt{x - (-32)} + (-3)$ J. $y = \frac{1}{8}\sqrt{x + 32} + (-3)$

Use the graph at the right with Exercises 75 and 76.

Short Response

75. How are the graphs of $f(x) = \sqrt{x-1}$ and $g(x) = \sqrt{x} - 1$ like the graph shown, and how are they different?

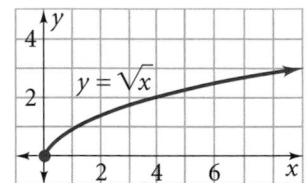

Extended Response

76. Compare the domains and ranges of the functions $f(x) = \sqrt{x-1}$ and $g(x) = \sqrt{x} - 1$.

Mixed Review

Lesson 7-7

Find the inverse of each function. Is the inverse a function?

77. $f(x) = 4x - 1$ **78.** $f(x) = \frac{2}{3}x - 3$ **79.** $f(x) = 2.4x^2 + 1$

80. $f(x) = \sqrt{x+3} - 4$ **81.** $f(x) = (2x + 1)^2$ **82.** $f(x) = 2x^3$

Lesson 7-2

Rationalize the denominator of each expression. Assume that all variables are positive.

83. $\dfrac{\sqrt{36x^3}}{\sqrt{12x}}$ **84.** $\sqrt[3]{\dfrac{3x}{2y}}$ **85.** $\dfrac{\sqrt[3]{x}}{\sqrt[3]{3y}}$ **86.** $\sqrt[5]{\dfrac{3x^3}{2y}}$

Lesson 5-8

Solve using the Quadratic Formula.

87. $5x^2 + x = 3$ **88.** $3x^2 + 9x = 27$ **89.** $x^2 - 9x + 15 = 0$

90. $x^2 + 10x + 11 = 0$ **91.** $x^2 - 12x + 25 = 0$ **92.** $8x^2 + 2x - 15 = 0$

Activity Lab

Technology

Radical Inequalities

FOR USE WITH LESSON 7-8

Solving radical inequalities can be challenging. The domain considerations can be subtle. Algebraic processes can introduce extraneous solutions.

1 ACTIVITY

Can a number be smaller than its own square root?

Many people rely on their number sense and answer "no" to this question. In their minds, they run through a table of values like the one shown here.

Plot1 Plot2 Plot3
\Y1 ≡ X
\Y2 ≡ √(X)
\Y3 =
\Y4 =
\Y5 =
\Y6 =
\Y7 =

X	Y1	Y2
0	0	0
1	1	1
2	2	1.4142
3	3	1.7321
4	4	2
5	5	2.2361
6	6	2.4495

X=0

1. Why is there no need to start this table with an x-value less than zero?

2. For the table above, $y_1 = x$ and $y_2 = \sqrt{x}$.
a. Enter a third function $Y_3 = Y_1 - Y_2$. What will this function show?
b. Turn off Y_1 and Y_2. Then view a table of Y_3 values. Scroll down. What happens to Y_3 values as the value of X increases?

3. In the table above and in your Y_3 table, the first two rows are unique. They may lead you to wonder what happens between $x = 0$ and $x = 1$.
a. To find out, go to TBLSET. Change ΔTbl to 0.2 and view a $Y_1 - Y_2$ table. How do the values of x and $\sqrt{x}$ compare for values of x between 0 and 1?
b. What would you expect to see in the Y_3 table? Check your conjecture.

In Exercise 3, you should have discovered some numbers that are smaller than their own square roots. But can you find them all? It helps to compare $Y_1 = X$ and $Y_2 = \sqrt{(X)}$ graphically.

4. a. Use the window settings shown at the right. Graph Y_1 and Y_2.
b. Give a convincing argument that only numbers between 0 and 1 are smaller than their own square roots.
c. What would you expect to see in a graph of Y_3? Check your conjecture. (*Hint:* You'll have to change your window settings.)

WINDOW
Xmin = 0
Xmax = 3
Xscl = 1
Ymin = 0
Ymax = 2
Yscl = 1
Xres = 1

2 ACTIVITY

A graphing calculator provides a practical way to solve radical inequalities. However, you must be careful to use appropriate table or window settings.

5. a. What are the domains of $Y_1 = f(x) = \sqrt{x - 3}$ and $Y_2 = g(x) = \sqrt{7 - x}$?
b. What are the only values of x that you have to consider to solve the radical inequality $\sqrt{x - 3} \leq \sqrt{7 - x}$? (*Hint:* Both expressions must be real numbers.)
c. Graph Y_1 and Y_2. Solve the inequality.
d. Let TblStart = 2 and ΔTbl = 1. Predict what a table will show, then check.

6. You can square both sides of the inequality $\sqrt{x-3} \le \sqrt{7-x}$ and simplify to $x \le 5$. Are there any x-values that satisfy $x \le 5$ but are not solutions of $\sqrt{x-3} \le \sqrt{7-x}$?

3 ACTIVITY

A **truth function** for an equation or inequality in x is a function whose domain is a set of real numbers and whose range is the two numbers 0 and 1. Domain values are the real numbers that can be used in place of x in the equation or inequality. If a value for x makes the equation or inequality true, the truth-function value is 1. Otherwise, it is 0.

You can solve an inequality graphically by viewing the graph of its truth function.

7. With your calculator in DOT mode, enter $Y_1 = \sqrt{x-3} \le \sqrt{7-x}$. (Find "$\le$" in the TEST menu.) Graph the truth function Y_1 as shown here.

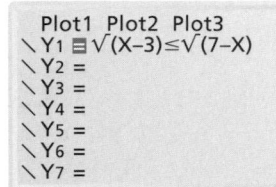
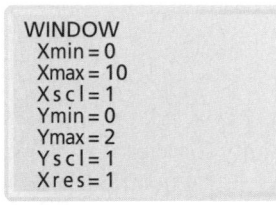
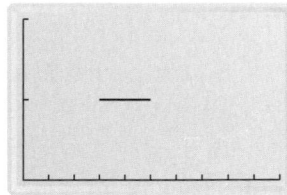

8. Explain how the screen on the right shows where $\sqrt{x-3} \le \sqrt{7-x}$ is true. Based on the graph, for what values of x is the inequality true? Does this agree with your result in Exercise 6(c)?

9. For what values of x is the inequality false? How can you tell from the graph?

10. Solve the inequality $\sqrt{8+x} + \sqrt{4x} \ge 3 + \sqrt{5-x}$ in two ways.
  a. by graphing it as a truth function
  b. by graphing and comparing the two related functions
  c. Compare your solutions from parts (a) and (b).

11. Solve the inequality $\sqrt{x} - \sqrt{x-3} \le \sqrt{6-x}$ in two ways.
  a. by graphing it as a truth function
  b. algebraically
  c. Explain why a truth function might be less useful for solving this inequality.

4 ACTIVITY

You can find the LOGIC menu next to the TEST menu. The **logical operators** in the LOGIC menu can help you find the domain of an equation or inequality—that is, the values of x to which the solutions of an equation or inequality are restricted.

12. Use the inequality $\sqrt{x} - \sqrt{x-3} \le \sqrt{6-x}$ from Exercise 11.
  a. For $\sqrt{x} - \sqrt{x-3} \le \sqrt{6-x}$ it must be true that $x \ge 0$, $x-3 \ge 0$, and $6-x \ge 0$. Why?
  b. The truth function Y_1 in the screen at the right uses the logical operator *and*. Explain why the graph of Y_1 will show the domain of the inequality $\sqrt{x} - \sqrt{x-3} \le \sqrt{6-x}$.
  c. How can graphing Y_1, $Y_2 = \sqrt{x} - \sqrt{x-3}$, and $Y_3 = \sqrt{6-x}$ in the same window help you solve the inequality $\sqrt{x} - \sqrt{x-3} \le \sqrt{6-x}$?

```
Plot1 Plot2 Plot3
\Y1 ▤X≥0 and X–3≥0
and 6–X≥0
\Y2 =
\Y3 =
\Y4 =
\Y5 =
\Y6 =
```

Finding Multiple Correct Answers

In some multiple-choice questions, there may be several correct answers.

1 EXAMPLE

Which of the following are true for all values of x?

   I. $\sqrt[3]{2^x} = \left(\sqrt[3]{2}\right)^x$ **II.** $\sqrt{x^2} = \sqrt[3]{x^3}$ **III.** $\sqrt{x^2 + 1} = |x| + 1$

  (A) I only   (B) III only   (C) I and II only   (D) I and III only   (E) II and III only

Determine whether each statement is true for all values of x.

Equation I $\sqrt[3]{2^x} = (2^x)^{\frac{1}{3}} = \left(2^{\frac{1}{3}}\right)^x = \left(\sqrt[3]{2}\right)^x$ *True*

Equation II $\sqrt{x^2} = |x| \neq x = \sqrt[3]{x^3}$ *False*

Equation III   Square each side to get
                           $x^2 + 1 = x^2 + 2|x| + 1$,
                           or $0 = 2|x|$, which is true only for $x = 0$.   *False*

● Only statement I is true for all values of x. The correct choice is A.

2 EXAMPLE

Which of the following are equal to x for all nonzero values of x?

   I. $\sqrt{x^2}$ **II.** $\sqrt[3]{x^3}$ **III.** $\dfrac{\sqrt[3]{x^4}}{\sqrt[3]{x}}$

  (A) I only   (B) II only   (C) I and II only   (D) II and III only   (E) I, II, and III

Rewrite each statement.

Expression I $\sqrt{x^2} = x$ only when x is positive.

Expression II $\sqrt[3]{x^3} = x$ for all values of x.

Expression III $\dfrac{\sqrt[3]{x^4}}{\sqrt[3]{x}} = \dfrac{x^{\frac{4}{3}}}{x^{\frac{1}{3}}} = x^{\frac{4}{3} - \frac{1}{3}} = x$ when $x \neq 0$.

● Expressions II and III are correct choices. The correct choice is D.

EXERCISES

1. Test each equation in Example 1 with $x = 2$ and $x = -2$. What do your results show about each of the three equations?

2. **Critical Thinking** Test each equation in Example 1 with $x = 0$ and $x = 1$. Explain whether these values help you answer the question.

3. Suppose Example 2 asked, "Which of the following are equal to x for some nonzero values of x?" What would be the correct answer choice?

4. Which of the following equations are true?

   I. $\left(\sqrt[4]{\sqrt{3}}\right)^8 = 3$ **II.** $\left(\sqrt[4]{\sqrt{3}}\right)^6 = 3$ **III.** $\dfrac{1}{\left(\frac{3}{5}\right)^{-1}} = \dfrac{5}{3}$

  (A) I only   (B) II only   (C) I and II only   (D) I and III only   (E) II and III only

Chapter Review

Vocabulary Review

composite function (p. 399)
index (p. 370)
inverse functions (p. 409)
inverse relation (p. 407)

like radicals (p. 380)
nth root (p. 369)
principal root (p. 370)
radical equation (p. 391)
radical function (p. 415)

radicand (p. 370)
rational exponent (p. 385)
rationalize the denominator (p. 376)
square root equation (p. 391)
square root function (p. 415)

Choose the correct vocabulary term to complete each sentence.

1. In the expression $\sqrt[3]{8}$, 8 is called the *(principal root, radicand)*.

2. In the expression $\sqrt[3]{8}$, 3 is called the *(principal root, index)*.

3. When you rewrite an expression so there are no radicals in any denominator and no denominators in any radical, you *(rationalize the denominator, compose two functions)*.

4. The expressions $\sqrt{x}$ and $\sqrt[5]{x}$ *(are, are not)* examples of like radicals.

5. The definition of *(rational exponents, inverse functions)* allows us to write $7^{\frac{2}{3}} = \sqrt[3]{7^2}$.

6. If $g(x) = x - 4$ and $h(x) = x^2$, $(g \circ h)(x) = x^2 - 4$ is a *(radical function, composite function)*.

7. To multiply expressions you sometimes add *(radicands, rational exponents)*.

8. If f and f^{-1} are *(composite functions, inverse functions)*, then $(f \circ f^{-1})(x) = x$ and $(f^{-1} \circ f)(x) = x$.

9. $(x - 7)^{\frac{1}{2}} + 2 = x$ is an example of *(a radical equation, an inverse relation)*.

10. The positive even root of a number is called the *(principal root, rational exponent)*.

Go Online
PHSchool.com

For: Vocabulary quiz
Web Code: agj-0751

Skills and Concepts

7-1 and 7-2 Objectives

▼ To simplify *n*th roots (p. 369)

▼ To multiply radical expressions (p. 374)

▼ To divide radical expressions (p. 375)

For any real numbers a and b, and any positive integer n, if $a^n = b$, then a is an *n*th root of b. The **principal root** of a number with two real roots is the positive root. The principal *n*th root of b is written as $\sqrt[n]{b}$. b is the **radicand** and n is the **index** of the radical.

For any negative real number a, $\sqrt[n]{a^n} = |a|$ when n is even.

If $\sqrt[n]{a}$ and $\sqrt[n]{b}$ are real numbers, then $\sqrt[n]{a} \cdot \sqrt[n]{b} = \sqrt[n]{ab}$, and, if $b \neq 0$, then $\dfrac{\sqrt[n]{a}}{\sqrt[n]{b}} = \sqrt[n]{\dfrac{a}{b}}$.

To **rationalize the denominator** of an expression, rewrite it so there are no radicals in any denominator and no denominators in any radical.

Find each indicated root if it is a real number.

11. $\sqrt{144}$ **12.** $\sqrt[3]{-0.064}$ **13.** $\sqrt[4]{7^4}$ **14.** $\sqrt{0.25}$ **15.** $-\sqrt[3]{27}$

Simplify each radical expression. Use absolute value symbols as needed.

16. $\sqrt{49x^2y^{10}}$ **17.** $\sqrt[3]{-64y^9}$ **18.** $\sqrt{(a-1)^4}$

19. $\sqrt[5]{243x^{15}}$ **20.** $\sqrt[3]{(y+3)^6}$ **21.** $\sqrt{32x^9y^5}$

Simplify each expression. Assume that all variables are positive.

22. $\sqrt{10} \cdot \sqrt{40}$ **23.** $\sqrt[3]{12} \cdot \sqrt[3]{36}$ **24.** $2\sqrt[3]{2x^2y} \cdot 5\sqrt[3]{6x^4y^4}$

25. $\sqrt{7x^3} \cdot \sqrt{14x}$ **26.** $\sqrt{5x^4y^3} \cdot \sqrt{45x^3y}$ **27.** $3\sqrt[4]{4x^3} \cdot \sqrt[4]{8xy^5}$

28. $\dfrac{\sqrt{128}}{\sqrt{8}}$ **29.** $\dfrac{\sqrt[3]{56y^5}}{\sqrt[3]{7y}}$ **30.** $\dfrac{\sqrt{75x^3}}{\sqrt{3x}}$ **31.** $\dfrac{\sqrt{216x^3y^2}}{\sqrt{2}}$ **32.** $\dfrac{\sqrt[3]{81a^8b^5}}{\sqrt[3]{3a^2b}}$

Simplify each expression. Rationalize all denominators. Assume that all variables are positive.

33. $\dfrac{\sqrt{8}}{\sqrt{6}}$ **34.** $\dfrac{\sqrt{3x^5}}{\sqrt{8x^2}}$ **35.** $\dfrac{\sqrt[3]{5}}{\sqrt[3]{x^4}}$ **36.** $\dfrac{\sqrt{2a^7b^2}}{\sqrt{32b^3}}$ **37.** $\dfrac{\sqrt[3]{6x^2y^4}}{2\sqrt[3]{5x^7y}}$

7-3 and 7-4 Objectives

▼ To add and subtract radical expressions (p. 380)

▼ To multiply and divide binomial radical expressions (p. 381)

▼ To simplify expressions with rational exponents (p. 385)

Like radicals have the same index and the same radicand. Use the distributive property to add or subtract them. Simplify radicals to find all the like radicals.

Use FOIL to multiply binomial radical expressions.

Binomials such as $a + b$ and $a - b$ are called conjugate expressions.

If the denominator of a fraction is a binomial radical expression, multiply both the numerator and denominator of the fraction by the conjugate of the denominator to rationalize the denominator.

The definition of **rational exponents** states that if the nth root of a is a real number and m is an integer, then $a^{\frac{1}{n}} = \sqrt[n]{a}$ and $a^{\frac{m}{n}} = \sqrt[n]{a^m} = \left(\sqrt[n]{a}\right)^m$. If m is negative, $a \neq 0$. The usual properties of exponents hold for rational exponents.

Simplify each expression.

38. $\sqrt{27} + \sqrt{75} - \sqrt{12}$ **39.** $(5 + \sqrt{3})(2 - \sqrt{3})$ **40.** $(7 - \sqrt{6})(7 + \sqrt{6})$

Simplify each expression. Rationalize all denominators. Assume that all variables are positive.

41. $\sqrt{2x} - \sqrt{8x} + \sqrt{18x}$ **42.** $\dfrac{6}{7 + 2\sqrt{3}}$ **43.** $\dfrac{\sqrt{2}}{1 - \sqrt{5}}$

Write each expression in radical form.

44. $3^{\frac{1}{5}}$ **45.** $x^{\frac{2}{3}}$ **46.** $2^{-\frac{3}{4}}$ **47.** $3^{0.2}$ **48.** $p^{-2.25}$

Simplify each expression. Assume that all variables are positive.

49. $(243)^{\frac{4}{5}}$ **50.** $36^{\frac{3}{2}}$ **51.** $\left(x^{\frac{3}{4}}\right)^{\frac{4}{3}}$ **52.** $x^{\frac{1}{6}} \cdot x^{\frac{2}{3}}$ **53.** $\left(x^{-\frac{3}{8}}y^{\frac{1}{4}}\right)^{16}$

To solve a **square root equation** or any **radical equation,** isolate a radical on one side of the equation. Then raise both sides of the equation to the same power. Check all possible solutions in the original equation to eliminate extraneous solutions.

Solve each equation. Check for extraneous solutions.

54. $\sqrt[3]{3x + 1} = -5$ **55.** $\sqrt{x + 7} = x + 1$ **56.** $x^{\frac{1}{2}} - 3 = 8$

7-6 and 7-7 Objectives

▼ To add, subtract, multiply, and divide functions (p. 398)

▼ To find the composite of two functions (p. 399)

▼ To find the inverse of a relation or function (p. 406)

The following are definitions of function operations.

Addition $(f + g)(x) = f(x) + g(x)$ Subtraction $(f - g)(x) = f(x) - g(x)$

Multiplication $(f \cdot g)(x) = f(x) \cdot g(x)$ Division $\left(\dfrac{f}{g}\right)(x) = \dfrac{f(x)}{g(x)}, g(x) \neq 0$

The composition of function g with function f is written as $g \circ f$ and is defined as $(g \circ f)(x) = g(f(x))$. The domain of the **composite function** $g \circ f$ consists of the values a in the domain of f such that $f(a)$ is in the domain of g.

If (a, b) is an ordered pair of a relation, then (b, a) is an ordered pair of its **inverse relation.** If a relation or function is described by an equation in x and y, you can interchange x and y to get the inverse. The inverse of a function is denoted by f^{-1}.

If f and f^{-1} are both functions, they are called **inverse functions,** and $(f^{-1} \circ f)(x) = x$ and $(f \circ f^{-1})(x) = x$.

Let $f(x) = 2x + 5$ and $g(x) = x^2 - 3x + 2$. Perform each function operation.

57. $(f + g)(x)$ **58.** $f(x) - g(x)$ **59.** $g(x) \cdot f(x)$ **60.** $(g - f)(x)$ **61.** $\dfrac{g(x)}{f(x)}$

Let $f(x) = x^2$ and $g(x) = x - 3$. Evaluate each expression.

62. $(g \circ f)(-2)$ **63.** $(f \circ g)(-2)$ **64.** $(f \circ g)(0)$ **65.** $(g \circ g)(7)$ **66.** $(f \circ g)(c)$

Find the inverse of each function. Is the inverse a function?

67. $y = 6x + 2$ **68.** $y = 2x^3 + 1$ **69.** $y = (x - 2)^4$ **70.** $y = \sqrt{x + 2}$

Let $f(x) = 3x + 1$. Find each value.

71. $(f^{-1} \circ f)(5)$ **72.** $(f^{-1} \circ f)(-5)$ **73.** $(f^{-1} \circ f)(6)$ **74.** $(f^{-1} \circ f)(t)$

7-8 Objective

▼ To graph square root and other radical functions (p. 414)

The parent function $f(x) = \sqrt{x}$ defines a family of **square root functions** $f(x) = a\sqrt{x - h} + k$. The graph of $f(x) = a\sqrt{x}$ is a stretch $(a > 0)$ or a shrink $(0 < a < 1)$ of the parent function. The graph of $y = a\sqrt{x - h} + k$ is a translation h units horizontally and k units vertically of $y = a\sqrt{x}$.

Graph each function.

75. $y = \sqrt{x} + 3$ **76.** $y = \sqrt{x - 1}$

77. $y = -3\sqrt{x} + 6$ **78.** $y = \sqrt{x + 7} - 2$

Simplify each radical expression. Use absolute value symbols when they are needed.

1. $\sqrt[3]{-0.027}$

2. $\sqrt{54x^3y^5}$

3. $\sqrt[5]{-64x^{14}y^{20}}$

4. $\sqrt{(x-2)^4}$

Simplify each expression. Rationalize all denominators. Assume that all variables are positive.

5. $\sqrt{7x^3} \cdot \sqrt{14x}$

6. $\sqrt{3y^3} \cdot \sqrt{4xy^4} \cdot \sqrt{6x^5y^2}$

7. $\dfrac{\sqrt{7x^4y}}{\sqrt{63xy^2}}$

8. $\dfrac{1-\sqrt{3x}}{\sqrt{6x}}$

9. $\sqrt{48} + 2\sqrt{75} + 5\sqrt{12}$

10. $\sqrt{98} + \sqrt{50} - \sqrt{5}$

11. $(3 + 2\sqrt{5})(1 - \sqrt{20})$

12. $(7 + \sqrt{3})(3 + 5\sqrt{3})$

13. $\dfrac{5}{3 - 2\sqrt{6}}$

14. $\dfrac{1 + \sqrt{3}}{\sqrt{3} - \sqrt{2}}$

Simplify each expression. Assume that all variables are positive.

15. $(125)^{-\frac{2}{3}}$

16. $x^{\frac{1}{6}} \cdot x^{\frac{1}{3}}$

17. $\left(\dfrac{8x^9y^3}{27x^2y^{12}}\right)^{\frac{2}{3}}$

Solve each equation. Check for extraneous solutions.

18. $\sqrt{x - 3} = x - 5$

19. $\sqrt{x + 4} = \sqrt{3x}$

20. $(3x + 4)^{\frac{1}{3}} = -5$

21. $x - 6 = (x - 4)^{\frac{1}{2}}$

Let $f(x) = x - 2$ and $g(x) = x^2 - 3x + 2$. Perform each function operation and then find the domain.

22. $g(x) - f(x)$

23. $-2g(x) + f(x)$

24. $\dfrac{g(x)}{f(x)}$

25. $-f(x) \cdot g(x)$

For each pair of functions, find $f(g(x))$ and $g(f(x))$.

26. $f(x) = x^2 - 2, g(x) = 4x + 1$

27. $f(x) = 2x^2 + x - 7, g(x) = -3x - 1$

 28. Writing Explain why -108 has no real 6th roots.

 29. Discounts While purchasing a pair of shoes on sale for 50% off, you noticed that the price on the cash register was only 25% off. The cashier then took another 25% off that price.
   a. Write a function $f(x)$ to represent the 50%-off price of the shoes.
   b. Write a function $g(x)$ to represent the price the cash register rang up the first time.
   c. Write a composite function to represent the price of the shoes after the cashier's solution to the problem.
   d. Compare the result of the cashier's solution to the correct price of the shoes.

Rewrite each function to make it easy to graph using a translation. Describe the graph.

30. $y = \sqrt{16x + 80} - 1$

31. $y = \sqrt{9x + 3}$

Graph. Find the domain and range of each function.

32. $y = 2\sqrt{x} + 3$

33. $y = \sqrt{2x + 3}$

34. $y = -\frac{1}{2}\sqrt{x} - 4$

35. $y = \sqrt{x + 3} - 4$

Let $f(x) = x^3 + 1$ and $g(x) = 7x - 4$. Find each value.

36. $f(g(-2))$

37. $g(f(3))$

38. $f(g(0))$

Find the inverse of each function. Is the inverse a function?

39. $f(x) = 3x^3 - 2$

40. $g(x) = \sqrt{x + 3} - 1$

41. $g(x) = \sqrt{2x + 1}$

42. $f(x) = \frac{1}{4}x^4$

43. a. Geometry For a sphere, $V = \frac{4}{3}\pi r^3$. Find the volume of a sphere with radius 4 in.
   b. Solve the formula in part (a) for r.
   c. Find to the nearest hundredth the radius of a sphere of volume 100 in.^{3}.

44. Open-Ended Write a relation rule that is not a function, but whose inverse is a function.

45. Measurement The time t in seconds for a swinging pendulum to complete one full cycle is given by the function $t = 0.2\sqrt{\ell}$, where ℓ is the length of the pendulum in cm. How long is a full cycle if the pendulum is 10 cm long? 20 cm long?

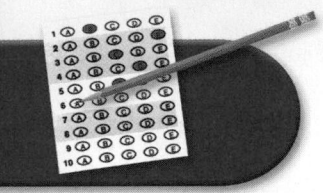

Standardized Test Prep

Reading Comprehension Read the passage below. Then answer the questions on the basis of what is *stated* or *implied* in the passage.

Boxing Match You can make an open box from a piece of flat cardboard. First, cut congruent squares from the four corners of the cardboard. Then, fold and tape the sides.

Let x equal the side length of each square. As x increases, so does the depth of the box. The usable area of cardboard decreases as x increases, and so do the length and width of the box.

What happens to the volume of the box? Does it increase or decrease as x increases? Would the answer *both* surprise you?

What size squares should you cut from the corners to maximize the volume of your box?

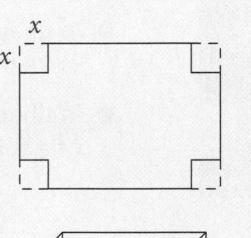

For Questions 1–6, consider a box made from a piece of cardboard that is 80 centimeters by 54 centimeters.

1. What are the dimensions of the box in centimeters?
   - Ⓐ $80 - x$, $54 - x$, x
   - Ⓑ $80 - 2x$, $54 - 2x$, $2x$
   - Ⓒ $80 - 2x$, $54 - 2x$, x
   - Ⓓ $x - 80$, $x - 54$, x

2. Which function models the area of the cardboard after the corners are cut away?
   - Ⓕ $A(x) = (80 - 2x)(54 - 2x)$
   - Ⓖ $A(x) = (80 - 2x)(54 - 2x) + 4x^2$
   - Ⓗ $A(x) = 4320 - 4x^2$
   - Ⓙ $A(x) = 4320 - 4(2x)^2$

3. By how much does the area of the cardboard decrease when x changes from 8 cm to 9 cm?
   - Ⓐ 145 cm^2
   - Ⓑ 68 cm^2
   - Ⓒ 26 cm^2
   - Ⓓ 17 cm^2

4. Which function models the volume of the box?
   - Ⓕ $V(x) = (80 - x)(54 - x)x$
   - Ⓖ $V(x) = (80 - x)(54 - x) + x$
   - Ⓗ $V(x) = (80 - 2x)(54 - 2x)x$
   - Ⓙ $V(x) = (80 - 2x) + (54 - 2x) + x$

5. What is a reasonable domain for x?
   - Ⓐ $0 < x < 27$
   - Ⓑ $0 < x < 40$
   - Ⓒ $0 < x < 54$
   - Ⓓ all real numbers

6. Which is the best value for the maximum volume of the box?
   - Ⓕ about 20,440 cm^3
   - Ⓖ about 20,444 cm^3
   - Ⓗ about 20,450 cm^3
   - Ⓙ about 20,452 cm^3

For Questions 7–9, consider a box made from a piece of cardboard that is 18 inches square.

7. Write a function that models the volume of the box.

8. What is a reasonable domain for x?

9. Find the maximum volume. Is this the maximum of the volume function? Explain.

10. **Open-Ended** Find the dimensions of three different rectangular pieces of cardboard you could use to make a box with volume 432 unit^3.

What You've Learned

- In Chapters 1 and 2, you learned to model linear functions and to solve linear equations.

- In Chapter 5, you learned to model quadratic functions and to solve quadratic equations.

- In Chapter 6, you learned to model polynomial functions and to solve polynomial equations.

- In Chapter 7, you learned to find and graph the inverse of a function.

 **Check Your Readiness**

 for Help to the Lesson in green.

Evaluating Expressions (Lesson 1-2)

Evaluate each expression for $x = -2, -1, 0, 1,$ and 2.

1. 10^{x+1} **2.** $\left(\frac{3}{2}\right)^x$ **3.** $x^4 - x^2$

Using Linear Models (Lesson 2-4)

4. Each day, a squirrel buries three acorns.
 a. Write and graph a function to model the number n of acorns the squirrel buries in d days.
 b. Use your function to find the number of acorns buried in four weeks.
 c. Suppose the squirrel had started out with nine acorns already buried. Explain how this would change your function and its graph.

Using Quadratic Models (Lesson 5-1)

Find a quadratic function to model each set of values. Then graph the function.

5. $\{(0,0), (2, -4), (3, -3)\}$ **6.** $\{(0,7), (2, 15), (5, 72)\}$

Graphing Transformations (Lesson 5-3)

Identify the parent function of each equation. Graph each equation as a transformation of its parent function.

7. $y = -(x - 1)^2 + 4$ **8.** $y = 3(x + 2)^2 - 1$

Graphing Inverse Functions (Lesson 7-7)

Graph each function and its inverse on a coordinate plane.

9. $y = -5x$ **10.** $y = \sqrt{5x + 12}$ **11.** $y = 2x^3$

Exponential and Logarithmic Functions

LESSONS

8-1 Exploring Exponential Models

8-2 Properties of Exponential Functions

8-3 Logarithmic Functions as Inverses

8-4 Properties of Logarithms

8-5 Exponential and Logarithmic Equations

8-6 Natural Logarithms

🔊 **Key Vocabulary**

- asymptote (p. 433)
- Change of Base Formula (p. 461)
- common logarithm (p. 447)
- continuously compounded interest formula (p. 441)
- decay factor (p. 433)
- exponential equation (p. 461)
- exponential function (p. 430)
- growth factor (p. 430)
- logarithm (p. 447)
- logarithmic equation (p. 463)
- logarithmic function (p. 448)
- natural logarithmic function (p. 470)

What You'll Learn Next

- In Chapter 8, you will learn to use exponential functions to model real-world data.

- You will learn to graph exponential functions and their inverses, logarithmic functions.

- You will learn to solve exponential and logarithmic equations.

Activity Lab Applying what you learn, on pages 484–485 you will do activities involving world population.

429

Exploring Exponential Models

What You'll Learn

- To model exponential growth
- To model exponential decay

...And Why

To model a car's depreciation, as in Example 6

✓ **Check Skills You'll Need**

GO for Help Lesson 1-2

Evaluate each expression for the given value of x.

1. 2^x for $x = 3$

2. 4^{x+1} for $x = 1$

3. 2^{3x+4} for $x = -1$

4. $3^x 3^{x-2}$ for $x = 2$

5. $\left(\frac{1}{2}\right)^x$ for $x = 0$

6. 2^x for $x = -2$

🔊 **New Vocabulary** • exponential function • growth factor
• decay factor • asymptote

---

1 Exponential Growth

For some data, the best model is a function that uses the independent variable as an exponent. An **exponential function** is a function with the general form $y = ab^x$, where x is a real number, $a \neq 0$, $b > 0$, and $b \neq 1$.

You can use an exponential function with $b > 1$ to model growth. When $b > 1$, b is the **growth factor**.

Exponential Growth

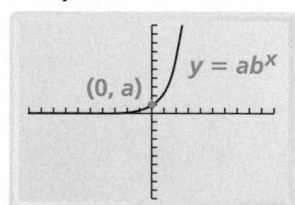

Growth factor $b > 1$

1 EXAMPLE Graphing Exponential Growth

Graph $y = 2^x$.

Step 1 Make a table of values.

x	2^x	y
−3	2^{-3}	$\frac{1}{8} = 0.125$
−2	2^{-2}	$\frac{1}{4} = 0.25$
−1	2^{-1}	$\frac{1}{2} = 0.5$
0	2^0	1
1	2^1	2
2	2^2	4
3	2^3	8

Step 2 Graph the coordinates. Connect the points with a smooth curve.

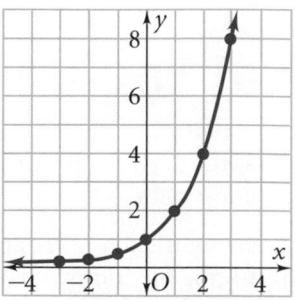

✓ **Quick Check** **1** Graph each function.

a. $y = 4(2)^x$

b. $y = 3^x$

You can use an exponential function to model population growth. If you know the rate of increase r, you can find the growth factor by using the equation $b = 1 + r$.

2 EXAMPLE Real-World Connection

Multiple Choice Refer to the graph. In 2000, the annual rate of increase in the U.S. population was about 1.24%. Suppose the rate of increase continues to be 1.24%. Which function best models U.S. population growth, in millions, after 2000?

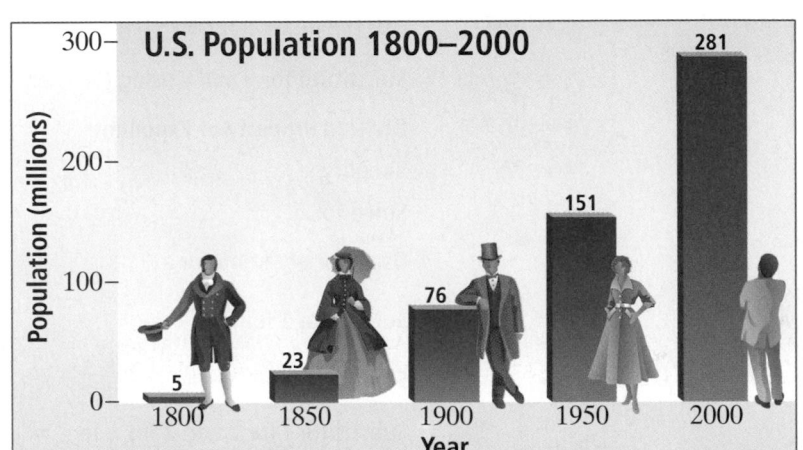

U.S. Population 1800–2000

SOURCE: U.S. Census Bureau. Go to www.PHSchool.com for a data update. Web Code: agg-9041

Ⓐ $281 + 1.0124^x$ Ⓑ $281(1.24)^x$ Ⓒ $281(1.024)^x$ Ⓓ $281(1.0124)^x$

First, find the growth factor.

$b = 1 + r$
$\quad = 1 + 0.0124$ **Substitute 1.24%, or 0.0124, for r.**
$\quad = 1.0124$ **Simplify.**

Then write a function.

Relate The population increases exponentially, so use the general form of an exponential function, $p(x) = ab^x$.

Define Let x = number of years after 2000.

          Let $p(x)$ = the population in millions.

Write $p(x) = a(1.0124)^x$

$281 = a(1.0124)^0$ **To find a, substitute the 2000 values: $p(x) = 281$, $x = 0$.**
$281 = a \cdot 1$ **Any nonzero number to the zero power equals 1.**
$281 = a$ **Simplify.**
$p(x) = 281(1.0124)^x$ **Substitute a and b into $p(x) = ab^x$.**

• The function $p(x) = 281(1.0124)^x$ models U.S. population growth. The answer is D.

✓ Quick Check ❷ **a.** Predict U.S. population in 2015 to the nearest million.
    b. Critical Thinking Explain why the model and your prediction may not be valid for 2015.
    c. Suppose the rate of population increase changes to 1.4%. Write a function to model population growth and use it to predict the 2015 population to the nearest million.

You can write an exponential function from two points on the function's graph.

3 EXAMPLE Writing an Exponential Function

Write an exponential function $y = ab^x$ for a graph that includes $(2, 2)$ and $(3, 4)$.

$y = ab^x$	Use the general form.
$2 = a \cdot b^2$	Substitute for x and y using $(2, 2)$.
$\frac{2}{b^2} = a$	Solve for a.
$y = ab^x$	Use the general form.
$4 = \frac{2}{b^2} b^3$	Substitute for x and y using $(3, 4)$ and for a using $\frac{2}{b^2}$.
$4 = 2b^{3-2}$	Division Property of Exponents
$4 = 2b$	Simplify.
$b = 2$	Solve for b.
$a = \frac{2}{b^2}$	Use your equation for a.
$a = \frac{2}{2^2}$	Substitute 2 for b.
$a = \frac{1}{2}$	Simplify.
$y = \frac{1}{2} \cdot 2^x$	Substitute $\frac{1}{2}$ for a and 2 for b in $y = ab^x$.

● The exponential function for a graph that includes $(2, 2)$ and $(3, 4)$ is $y = \frac{1}{2} \cdot 2^x$.

✓ **Quick Check** **3** Write an exponential function $y = ab^x$ for a graph that includes $(2, 4)$ and $(3, 16)$.

2 Exponential Decay

Real-World Connection

On a day in March, the NCAA announces the selection of 64 teams for its annual tournament.

Activity: Tournament Play

The National Collegiate Athletic Association (NCAA) holds an annual basketball tournament. The top 64 teams in Division I are invited to play each spring. When a team loses, it is out of the tournament.

1. How many teams are left in the tournament after the first round of basketball games?

2. a. Copy, complete, and extend the table until only one team is left.

After Round x	Number of Teams Left in Tournament (y)
0	64
1	■
2	■

b. Graph the points from your table on graph paper.

3. How many rounds are played in the tournament?

4. Does the graph represent a linear function? Explain.

5. How does the number of teams left in each round compare to the number of teams in the previous round?

You can use an exponential function with $0 < b < 1$ to model decay. When $b < 1$, b is a **decay factor.**

Exponential Decay

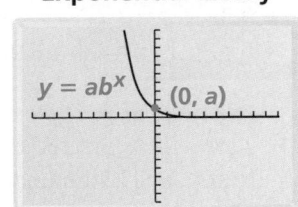

Decay factor $b < 1$

4 EXAMPLE **Analyzing a Function**

Without graphing, determine whether the function $y = 14(0.95)^x$ represents exponential growth or exponential decay.

● In $y = 14(0.95)^x$, $b = 0.95$. Since $b < 1$, the function represents exponential decay.

 **Quick Check** ④ Without graphing, determine whether each function represents exponential growth or exponential decay.

a. $y = 100(0.12)^x$ **b.** $y = 0.2(5)^x$ **c.** $y = 16\left(\frac{1}{2}\right)^x$

Vocabulary Tip

Asymptote comes from the Greek word *asymptotos,* meaning "not meeting."

An **asymptote** is a line that a graph approaches as x or y increases in absolute value.

5 EXAMPLE **Graphing Exponential Decay**

Graph $y = 24\left(\frac{1}{2}\right)^x$. Identify the horizontal asymptote.

Step 1 Make a table of values.

x	−3	−2	−1	0	1	2	3
y	192	96	48	24	12	6	3

Step 2 Graph the coordinates. Connect the points with a smooth curve.

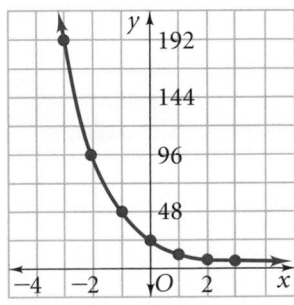

As x increases, y approaches 0.

● The asymptote is the x-axis, $y = 0$.

 **Quick Check** ⑤ Graph each decay function. Identify the horizontal asymptote.

a. $y = 24\left(\frac{1}{3}\right)^x$ **b.** $y = 100(0.1)^x$

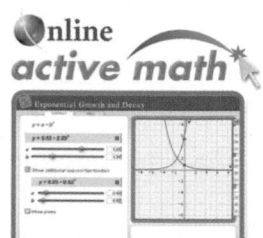
Vocabulary Tip

Depreciate comes from a prefix meaning "lower" and a root meaning "price."

Depreciation is the decline in an item's value resulting from age or wear. When an item loses about the same percent of its value each year, you can use an exponential function to model the depreciation.

6 EXAMPLE Real-World Connection

Depreciation The exponential decay graph shows the expected depreciation for a car over four years. Estimate the value of the car after six years.

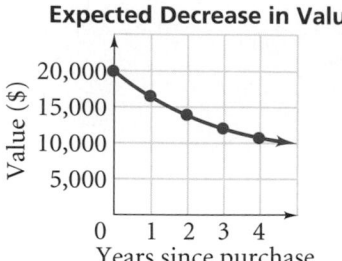

Expected Decrease in Value

The decay factor b equals $1 + r$, where r is the annual rate of decrease. The initial value of the car is $20,000. After one year the value of the car is about $17,000.

$r = \dfrac{\text{final value } - \text{ initial value}}{\text{initial value}}$ Write an equation for r.

$\quad = \dfrac{17{,}000 - 20{,}000}{20{,}000}$ Substitute.

$\quad = -0.15$ Simplify.

$b = 1 + r$ Use r to find b.

$\quad = 1 + (-0.15) = 0.85$ Simplify.

Write a function, and then evaluate it for $x = 6$.

Relate The value of the car decreases exponentially; $b = 0.85$.

Define Let x = number of years. Let y = value of the car.

Write $y = ab^x$

$20{,}000 = a(0.85)^0$ Substitute using (0, 20,000).

$20{,}000 = a$ Solve for a.

$\quad y = 20{,}000(0.85)^x$ Substitute a and b into $y = ab^x$.

$\quad y = 20{,}000(0.85)^6$ Evaluate for $x = 6$.

$\quad \approx 7542.99$ Simplify.

• The car's value after six years will be about $7540.

Quick Check ⑥ Estimate the value of the car from Example 6 after 10 years.

EXERCISES

For more exercises, see *Extra Skill and Word Problem Practice.*

Practice and Problem Solving

Ⓐ **Practice by Example**

Example 1
(page 430)

Graph each function.

1. $y = 6^x$ **2.** $y = 3(10)^x$ **3.** $y = 1000(2)^x$ **4.** $y = 9(3)^x$

5. $f(x) = 2(3)^x$ **6.** $s(t) = 1.5^t$ **7.** $y = 8(5)^x$ **8.** $y = 2^{2x}$

GO for Help

Example 2
(page 431)

9. Population The world population in 2000 was approximately 6.08 billion. The annual rate of increase was about 1.26%.
 a. Find the growth factor for the world population.
 b. Suppose the rate of increase continues to be 1.26%. Write a function to model world population growth.

Example 3
(page 432)

Write an exponential function $y = ab^x$ for a graph that includes the given points.

10. $(4, 8), (6, 32)$

11. $(2, 122.5), (3, 857.5)$

12. $(2, 18), (5, 60.75)$

13. $\left(-1, 8\frac{1}{3}\right), (2, 1.8)$

14. $(-3, 24), (-2, 12)$

15. $(0, 24), \left(3, \frac{8}{9}\right)$

Example 4
(page 433)

Without graphing, determine whether each function represents exponential growth or exponential decay.

16. $y = 129(1.63)^x$

17. $f(x) = 2(0.65)^x$

18. $y = 12\left(\frac{17}{10}\right)^x$

19. $y = 0.8\left(\frac{1}{8}\right)^x$

20. $f(x) = 4\left(\frac{5}{6}\right)^x$

21. $y = 0.45 \cdot 3^x$

22. $y = \frac{1}{100}\left(\frac{4}{3}\right)^x$

23. $f(x) = 2^{-x}$

Example 5
(page 433)

Graph each function.

24. $y = (0.75)^x$

25. $y = 2(0.5)^x$

26. $y = (0.25)^x$

27. $g(x) = 5(0.2)^x$

28. $f(x) = \left(\frac{1}{5}\right)^x$

29. $y = 81\left(\frac{1}{3}\right)^x$

30. $s(t) = \left(\frac{1}{10}\right)^t$

31. $y = \frac{1}{2}\left(\frac{1}{2}\right)^x$

Example 6
(page 434)

Write an exponential function for each graph. Evaluate the function for $x = 6$.

32.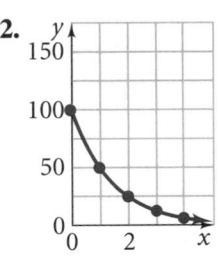

33.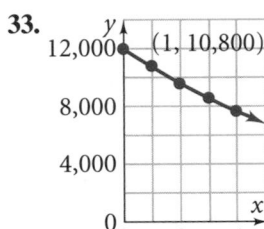

34.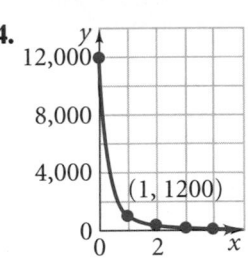

35. Business A computer valued at $6500 depreciates at the rate of 14.3% per year.
  a. Write a function that models the value of the computer.
  b. Find the value of the computer after three years.

B **Apply Your Skills**

For each function, find the percent increase or decrease that the function models.

36. $y = 1298(1.63)^x$

37. $y = 0.65(1.3)^x$

38. $f(x) = 2(0.65)^x$

39. $y = 12\left(\frac{17}{10}\right)^x$

40. $y = 0.8\left(\frac{1}{8}\right)^x$

41. $y = 16\left(\frac{1}{4}\right)^x$

42. Multiple Choice According to the projected growth rate, how will these regions rank from largest to smallest populations in 2015?

World's Largest Metropolitan Regions Outside the U.S.

Rank in 2000	City	2000 Population	Projected Average Annual Growth
1	Tokyo, Japan	34,450,000	0.51%
2	Mexico City, Mexico	18,066,000	1.47%
3	Mumbai (Bombay), India	17,099,000	1.39%
4	Saõ Paulo, Brazil	16,086,000	2.62%

SOURCE: United Nations, Department for Economic and Social Information and Policy Analysis

(A) Tokyo, Mexico City, São Paulo, Mumbai
(B) Tokyo, Mexico City, Mumbai, São Paulo
(C) Tokyo, Mumbai, São Paulo, Mexico City
(D) Tokyo, São Paulo, Mexico City, Mumbai

 43. Oceanography The function $y = 20 \cdot 0.975^x$ models the intensity of sunlight beneath the surface of the ocean. The output y represents the percent of surface sunlight intensity that reaches a depth of x feet. The model is accurate from about 20 feet to about 600 feet beneath the surface.
   a. Find the percent of sunlight 50 feet beneath the surface of the ocean.
   b. Find the percent of sunlight at a depth of 370 ft.

 44. a. Depreciation Each graph below shows the expected decrease in a car's value over the next five years. Write a function to model each car's depreciation. Determine which car will be worth more after 10 years.

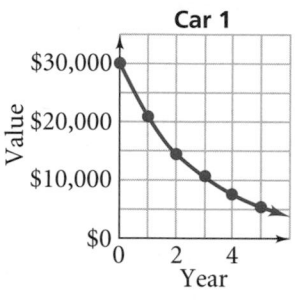

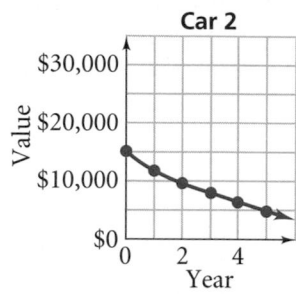

   b. Data Collection Find the initial value and the expected decrease in value of your favorite type of car. Write an exponential function to model the car's depreciation.

45. The population of a certain animal species decreases at a rate of 3.5% per year. You have counted 80 of the animals in the habitat you are studying.
   a. Write a function that models the change in the animal population.
    b. Graph the function. Estimate the number of years until the population first drops below 15 animals.

For each annual rate of change, find the corresponding growth or decay factor.

46. $+70\%$ **47.** $+500\%$ **48.** -75% **49.** -55%

50. $+12.5\%$ **51.** -0.1% **52.** $+0.1\%$ **53.** $+100\%$

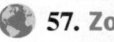
 54. Communications
Cellular phone usage grew about 22% each year from 1995 (about 34 million) to 2003. Write a function to model U.S. cellular phone usage over that time period.

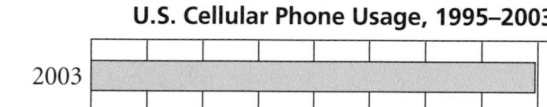

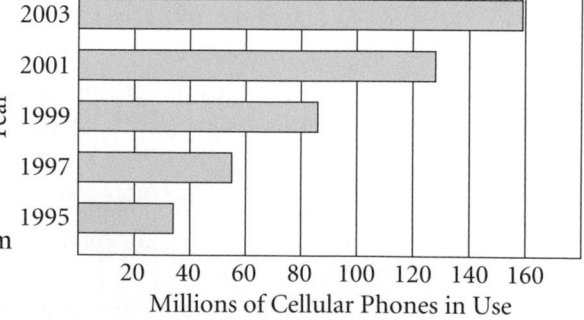

SOURCE: The CTIA Semi-Annual Wireless Survey

55. Open-Ended Write a problem that could be modeled with $y = 20(1.1)^x$.

C **Challenge**

56. The value of an industrial machine has a decay factor of 0.75 per year. After six years, the machine is worth $7500. What was the original value of the machine?

 57. Zoology Determine which situation best matches the graph.
   A. A population of 120 cougars decreases 98.75% yearly.
   B. A population of 125 cougars increases 1.25% yearly.
   C. A population of 115 cougars decreases 1.25% yearly.
   D. A population of 200 cougars decreases 50% yearly.

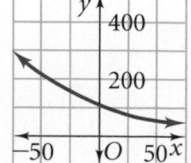

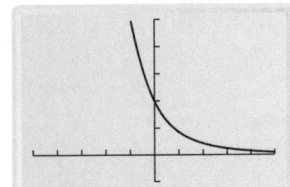

58. Critical Thinking Analyze the graph at the left to determine which function the graph represents. Explain your reasoning.

A. $y = \left(\frac{1}{3}\right)2^x$ **B.** $y = 2\left(\frac{1}{3}\right)^x$ **C.** $y = -2\left(\frac{1}{3}\right)^x$

59. Economics The table gives the 2003 gross domestic product and the real growth rate for several countries.

  a. Writing Explain how a negative growth rate affects the equation for an exponential model.
  b. Write a function for each country to model the GDP.
  c. Suppose the given real growth rates continue. Predict the gross domestic product for each country in 2008.

Domestic Product Growth Rates

Country	2003 Gross Domestic Product (billions)	2003 Real Growth Rate
Armenia	$11.8	9.9%
Canada	$958.7	1.7%
Germany	$2271	−0.1%
Venezuela	$117.9	−9.2%

SOURCE: CIA, *The World Factbook*

Test Prep

Multiple Choice

60. Which function represents exponential growth?
  A. $y = 35x^{1.35}$ **B.** $y = 35 \cdot (0.35)^x$
  C. $y = 35 \cdot (1.35)^x$ **D.** $y = 35 \div (1.35)^x$

61. Which function represents the value after x years of a delivery van that was purchased new for $17,500 and depreciates 11% each year?
  F. $y = -11(17{,}500)^x$ **G.** $y = 17{,}500(0.11)^x$
  H. $y = 17{,}500(0.89)^x$ **J.** $y = 17{,}500(1.11)^x$

62. What is the equation of the asymptote of $y = 15 \cdot \left(\frac{1}{3}\right)^x$?
  A. $y = 1$ **B.** $y = 0$ **C.** $y = x$ **D.** $y = \frac{1}{3}$

Short Response

63. Sketch the graph of the function $y = 2 \cdot \left(\frac{1}{4}\right)^x$.

Extended Response

64. Write an exponential equation in the form $y = ab^x$ for a graph that includes $(2, 54)$ and $\left(\frac{1}{2}, 2\right)$. Show your work.

Mixed Review

GO for Help

Lesson 7-8

Graph each function.

65. $y = \sqrt{x + 2}$ **66.** $y = -2\sqrt[3]{x} + 4$ **67.** $y = \sqrt{9x - 153} - 5$

Lesson 7-2

Simplify each expression.

68. $\sqrt{180n^5}$ **69.** $3\sqrt[3]{72r^5} \cdot 2\sqrt[3]{343r^3}$ **70.** $\dfrac{\sqrt{64x^4}}{\sqrt{144x^5}}$

Lesson 6-2

Construct a polynomial function with the given zeros.

71. $x = 0, 1, 4$ **72.** $x = -2, -1, 3$ **73.** $x = 5, 0, 2$

Lesson 5-2

Each point lies on a parabola with vertex (0, 2). Write the equation of the parabola.

74. $(1, 3)$ **75.** $(1, -3)$ **76.** $(-1, 4)$ **77.** $(2, 42)$

78. $(-2, 8)$ **79.** $(-1, 5)$ **80.** $(2, 0)$ **81.** $(2, -2)$

You can use your graphing calculator to fit an exponential curve to data and find the exponential function.

Go Online
PHSchool.com

For: Graphing calculator procedures
Web Code: age-2123

ACTIVITY

The table at the right shows the number of degrees above room temperature for a cup of coffee after x minutes of cooling. Graph the data. Find the best-fitting exponential function.

Step 1 Press STAT ENTER to enter the data in lists.

Step 2 Use the **STAT PLOT** feature to draw a scatter plot.

Step 3 Find the equation for the best-fitting exponential function. Press STAT ▶ 0 ENTER to use the **ExpReg** feature. The line of best fit can be approximated by $f(x) = 133.458 (0.942)^x$.

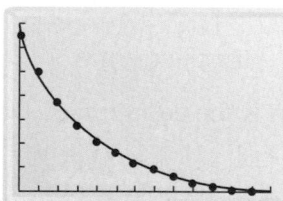

```
ExpReg
  y=a*b^x
  a=133.4584506
  b=.942405561
  r=-.9997925841
```

Step 4 Graph the function. Press Y= CLEAR VARS 5 ▶ ▶ ENTER to enter the **ExpReg** results. Press GRAPH to display the function and the scatter plot together.

Press ZOOM 9 to automatically adjust the window.

Cooling Coffee

Time (min)	°F Above Room Temperature
0	135
5	100
10	74
15	55
20	41
25	30
30	22
35	17
40	12
45	9
50	7
55	5
60	4

EXERCISES

Use a graphing calculator to find the exponential function that best fits each set of data. Graph each function. Sketch your graph.

1.

x	−3	−2	−1	0	1	2
y	50	25	12.5	6.25	3.13	1.56

2.

x	0	1	2	3	4	5
y	2	2.4	2.88	3.46	4.15	5

3.

x	1	2	3	4	5	6
y	1.2	4.8	19.2	76.8	307.2	1228.8

4.

x	−10	−9	−8	−7	−6	−5
y	0.03	0.07	0.14	0.27	0.55	1.09

5. Writing In the example above, the function appears to level off. Explain why this happens.

6. a. Find a linear function that models the data in Exercise 3.
   b. Which is a better fit, the linear function or the exponential function? Explain.

8-2

Properties of Exponential Functions

What You'll Learn

- To identify the role of constants in $y = ab^{cx}$
- To use e as a base

. . . And Why

To model the half-life of a radioactive substance, as in Example 3

✓ **Check Skills You'll Need**

GO for Help Lessons 2-6, 5-3, and 7-4

Write an equation for each translation.

1. $y = |x|$, 1 unit up, 2 units left
2. $y = -|x|$, 2 units down
3. $y = x^2$, 2 units down, 1 unit right
4. $y = -x^2$, 3 units up, 1 unit left

Write each equation in simplest form. Assume that all variables are positive.

5. $y = \left(x^{-\frac{5}{4}}\right)^4$
6. $y = \left(x^{-\frac{1}{7}}\right)^{-7}$
7. $y = \left(x^{\frac{5}{6}}\right)^6$

8. Use the formula for simple interest $I = Prt$. Find the interest for a principal of \$550 at a rate of 3% for 2 years.

🔊 **New Vocabulary** • continuously compounded interest formula

---

1 Comparing Graphs

The function $f(x) = b^x$ is the parent of a family of exponential functions for each value of b. The factor a in $y = ab^x$ stretches, shrinks, and/or reflects the parent.

GO for Help

To review function families, see Lesson 2-6 for absolute value functions, and Lesson 5-3 for quadratic functions.

1 EXAMPLE Graphing $y = ab^x$ for $0 < |a| < 1$

Graph $y = \frac{1}{2} \cdot 2^x$ and $y = -\frac{1}{2} \cdot 2^x$. Label the asymptote of each graph.

Step 1 Make a table of values.

x	$y = \frac{1}{2} \cdot 2^x$	$y = -\frac{1}{2} \cdot 2^x$
-2	$\frac{1}{8}$	$-\frac{1}{8}$
-1	$\frac{1}{4}$	$-\frac{1}{4}$
0	$\frac{1}{2}$	$-\frac{1}{2}$
1	1	-1
2	2	-2
3	4	-4

Step 2 Graph the functions.

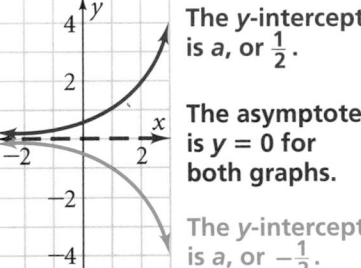

The y-intercept is a, or $\frac{1}{2}$.

The asymptote is $y = 0$ for both graphs.

The y-intercept is a, or $-\frac{1}{2}$.

$y = \frac{1}{2} \cdot 2^x$ shrinks $y = 2^x$ by a factor of $\frac{1}{2}$.

$y = -\frac{1}{2} \cdot 2^x$ reflects $y = \frac{1}{2} \cdot 2^x$ in the x-axis.

✓ **Quick Check**  Graph each function. **a.** $y = -4(2)^x$ **b.** $y = -3^x$

A horizontal shift $y = ab^{x-h}$ is the same as the vertical stretch or shrink $y = (ab^{-h})b^x$. A vertical shift $y = ab^x + k$ also shifts the horizontal asymptote from $y = 0$ to $y = k$.

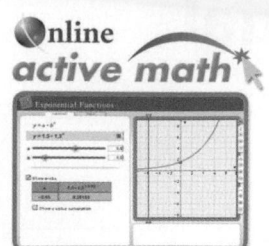

For: Exponential Activity
Use: Interactive Textbook, 8-2

2 **EXAMPLE** Translating $y = ab^x$

Graph the stretch $y = 8\left(\frac{1}{2}\right)^x$ and then the translation $y = 8\left(\frac{1}{2}\right)^{x+2} + 3$.

Step 1 Graph $y = 8\left(\frac{1}{2}\right)^x$. The horizontal asymptote is $y = 0$.

Step 2 For $y = 8\left(\frac{1}{2}\right)^{x+2} + 3$, $h = -2$ and $k = 3$. So shift the $y = 8\left(\frac{1}{2}\right)^x$ graph 2 units left and 3 units up. The horizontal asymptote is $y = 3$.

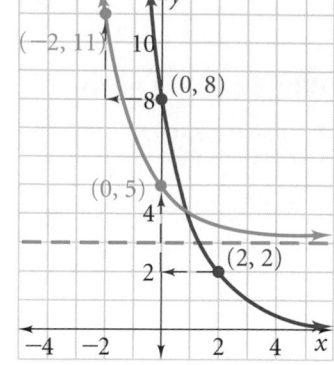

✓ **Quick Check** **2** Graph the stretch $y = 9(3)^x$ and then each translation.
   a. $y = 9(3)^{x+1}$
   b. $y = 9(3)^x - 4$
   c. $y = 9(3)^{x-3} - 1$

Some exponential functions are of the form $y = ab^{cx}$, where c is a nonzero constant.

3 **EXAMPLE** Real-World Connection

Medicine The half-life of a radioactive substance is the time it takes for half of the material to decay. A hospital prepares a 100-mg supply of technetium-99m, which has a half-life of 6 hours. Make a table showing the amount of technetium-99m that remains at the end of each 6-hour interval for 36 hours. Then write an exponential function to find the amount of technetium-99m that remains after 75 hours.

The amount of technetium-99m is reduced by one half each 6 hours.

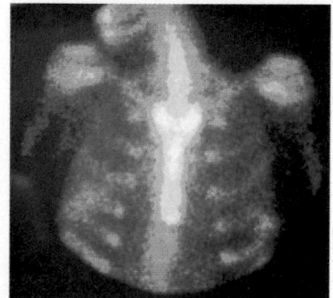

Real-World Connection

As technetium-99m decays, it emits low-energy gamma rays. The rays are detected by a gamma camera to produce images like the one above.

Number of 6-h Intervals	0	1	2	3	4	5	6
Number of Hours Elapsed	0	6	12	18	24	30	36
Technetium-99m (mg)	100	50	25	12.5	6.25	3.13	1.56

Relate The amount of technetium-99m is an exponential function of the number of half-lives. The initial amount is 100 mg. The decay factor is $\frac{1}{2}$. One half-life equals 6 h.

Define Let y = the amount of technetium-99m.

Let x = the number of hours elapsed. Then $\frac{1}{6}x$ = the number of half-lives.

Write $y = 100\left(\frac{1}{2}\right)^{\frac{1}{6}x}$

$y = 100\left(\frac{1}{2}\right)^{\frac{1}{6} \cdot 75}$ **Substitute 75 for x.**

$= 100\left(\frac{1}{2}\right)^{12.5}$ **Simplify.**

≈ 0.017 **Use a calculator.**

After 75 hours, about 0.017 mg of technetium-99m remains.

✓ **Quick Check** **3** Arsenic-74 is used to locate brain tumors. It has a half-life of 17.5 days. Write an exponential decay function for a 90-mg sample. Use the function to find the amount remaining after 6 days.

Key Concepts

Summary	Families of Exponential Functions
Parent function:	$y = b^x$
Stretch ($|a| > 1$) Shrink ($0 < |a| < 1$) Reflection ($a < 0$) in x-axis	$y = ab^x$
Translation (horizontal by h; vertical by k):	$y = b^{x-h} + k$
Combined:	$y = ab^{x-h} + k$

2 The Number e

At the right is part of the graph of the function $y = \left(1 + \frac{1}{x}\right)^x$. One of the graph's asymptotes is $y = e$, where e is an irrational number approximately equal to 2.71828.

Exponential functions with a base of e are useful for describing continuous growth or decay. Your graphing calculator has a key for e^x.

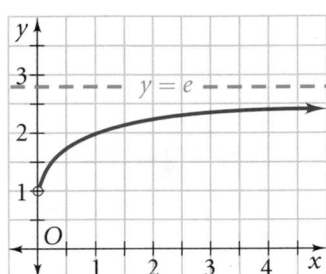

4 EXAMPLE Evaluating e^x

Graph $y = e^x$. Evaluate e^2 to four decimal places.

Step 1 Graph $y = e^x$.   **Step 2** Find y when $x = 2$.

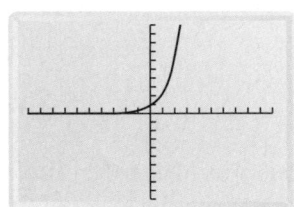   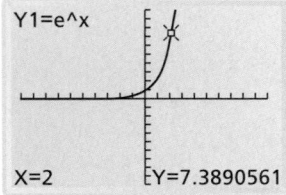

Graphing Calculator Hint

After graphing e^x, press [TRACE] 2 [ENTER] to find y for $x = 2$.

● The value of e^2 is about 7.3891.

 Quick Check ④ Use the graph of $y = e^x$ to evaluate each expression to four decimal places.

    a. e^4 **b.** e^{-3} **c.** $e^{\frac{1}{2}}$

In past courses, you studied simple and compound interest. The more frequently interest is compounded, the more quickly the amount in an account increases. The formula for *continuously* compounded interest uses the number e.

Key Concepts

Definition	Continuously Compounded Interest Formula

        amount in account   rate of interest (annual)

$$A = Pe^{rt} \longleftarrow \text{time in years}$$

principal

5 EXAMPLE   Real-World  Connection

Gridded Response Suppose you invest $1050 at an annual interest rate of 5.5% compounded continuously. How much money, to the nearest dollar, will you have in the account after five years?

$$A = Pe^{rt}$$
$$= 1050 \cdot e^{0.055(5)} \quad \text{Substitute 1050 for } P, \text{ 0.055 for } r, \text{ and 5 for } t.$$
$$= 1050 \cdot e^{0.275} \quad \text{Simplify.}$$
$$\approx 1050(1.316531) \quad \text{Evaluate } e^{0.275}.$$
$$\approx 1382.36 \quad \text{Simplify.}$$

● You will have about $1382 in the account.

✓ Quick Check ⑤ Suppose you invest $1300 at an annual interest rate of 4.3% compounded continuously. Find the amount you will have in the account after three years.

EXERCISES

For more exercises, see *Extra Skill and Word Problem Practice.*

Practice and Problem Solving

A Practice by Example

Example 1
(page 439)

Graph each function. Label the asymptote of each graph.

1. $y = -5^x$ **2.** $y = -\left(\frac{1}{2}\right)^x$ **3.** $y = -2(4)^x$ **4.** $y = -9(3)^x$

5. $y = -3(2)^x$ **6.** $y = -24\left(\frac{1}{2}\right)^x$ **7.** $y = -4^x$ **8.** $y = -\left(\frac{1}{3}\right)^x$

Example 2
(page 440)

Graph each function as a transformation of its parent function.

9. $y = 8^x + 5$ **10.** $y = 15\left(\frac{4}{3}\right)^x - 8$ **11.** $y = -(0.3)^{x-2}$

12. $y = -2(5)^{x+3}$ **13.** $y = 52\left(\frac{2}{13}\right)^{x-1} + 26$ **14.** $y = 9\left(\frac{1}{3}\right)^{x+7} - 3$

Example 3
(page 440)

15. Botany Phosphorus-32 is used to study a plant's use of fertilizer. It has a half-life of 14.3 days. Write the exponential decay function for a 50-mg sample. Find the amount of phosporus-32 remaining after 84 days.

16. Public Works Iodine-131 is used to find leaks in water pipes. It has a half-life of 8.14 days. Write the exponential decay function for a 200-mg sample. Find the amount of iodine-131 remaining after 72 days.

17. Archaeology Carbon-14 is used to determine the age of artifacts in carbon dating. It has a half-life of 5730 years. Write the exponential decay function for a 24-mg sample. Find the amount of carbon-14 remaining after 30 millennia (1 millennium = 1000 years).

Example 4
(page 441)

Use the graph of $y = e^x$ to evaluate each expression to four decimal places.

18. e^3 **19.** e^6 **20.** e^{-2} **21.** e^0 **22.** $e^{\frac{5}{2}}$ **23.** e^e

Example 5
(page 442)

Find the amount in a continuously compounded account for the given conditions.

24. principal: $2000
annual interest 5.1%
time: 3 yr

25. principal: $400
annual interest 7.6%
time: 1.5 yr

26. principal: $950
annual interest 6.5%
time: 10 yr

B Apply Your Skills

27. Find the value of a for which the graph of $y = ab^x$ is a horizontal line.

28. Find the value of b for which the graph of $y = ab^x$ is a horizontal line.

29. Assume that a is positive and $b \geq 1$. Describe the effects of $c < 0, c = 0$, and $c > 0$ on the graph of the function $y = ab^{cx}$.

Real-World Connection

A savings plan can be an important part of preparing for college.

30. Savings A student wants to save $8000 for college in five years. How much should be put into an account that earns 5.2% annual interest compounded continuously?

31. When $a < 0$ and $b > 1$, $y = ab^x$ models negative exponential growth.
  a. Open-Ended Write an exponential function that models negative growth.
  b. Give an example of a situation that could be modeled by your function.
  c. Critical Thinking Explain one difference between negative exponential growth and exponential decay.

The parent function for each graph below is of the form $y = ab^x$. Write the parent function. Then write a function for the translation indicated.

32.

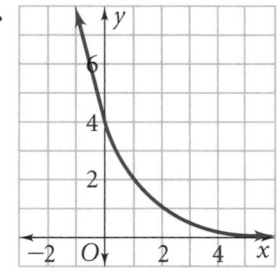

translation: left 4 units, up 3 units

33.

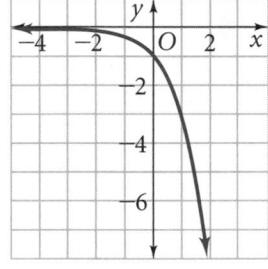

translation: right 8 units, up 2 units

34.

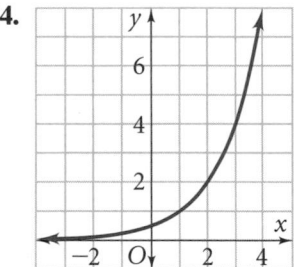

translation: right 6 units, down 7 units

35.

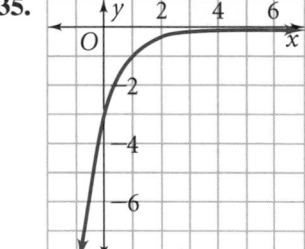

translation: left 5 units, down 1 unit

Vocabulary Tip

The <u>pascal</u> is the metric unit of pressure.

36. Physics At a constant temperature, the atmospheric pressure p in pascals is given by the formula $p = 101.3e^{-0.001h}$, where h is the altitude in meters. Find p at an altitude of 300 m.

37. Investment How long would it take to double your principal at an annual interest rate of 8% compounded continuously?

38. Writing Like a debt, a deficit is a negative amount of money. Explain how you would model a deficit that is growing exponentially. In $y = ab^{cx}$, would the values of a and c be positive or negative? Would the value of b be greater than 1 or less than 1?

39. Multiple Choice The gross domestic product, or GDP, of the United States was about $10.99 trillion in 2003. Assume that GDP grows 3.1% each year. Use an exponential model to find which percent best describes the GDP growth that occurs over 18 years.

Visit: PHSchool.com
Web Code: age-0802

(A) 19.0%   (B) 74.7%   (C) 129.1%   (D) 173.2%

40. Suppose you invest $2000 at an annual interest rate of 4.5%, compounded quarterly.
  a. How much will you have in the account after five years?
  b. Determine how much more you would have if the interest were compounded continuously.

41. An investor withdraws all $525 from an account that was neglected for 8 years. It earned 3.4% annual interest, compounded continuously. How much was the initial deposit?

Without graphing, determine whether each equation represents exponential growth or exponential decay.

42. $s(t) = 5e^t$

43. $y = \frac{1}{6}e^x$

44. $y = \left(\frac{1}{e}\right)^x$

45. $y = \frac{7}{5}\left(\frac{e}{2}\right)^x$

46. $f(x) = \left(\frac{e}{3.7}\right)^x$

47. $y = -70e^t$

C Challenge 🌎 **48. Biology** A new flu virus is introduced when a stranger visits an isolated village of 8000 people. Every infected person infects two more each day.
  a. Write an exponential function to model the number of *uninfected* people.
  b. Determine how many people remain uninfected after one week.
  c. After how many days will the entire population be infected?

🌎 **49. Psychology** Psychologists use an exponential model of the learning process, $f(t) = c(1 - e^{-kt})$, where c is the total number of tasks to be learned, k is the rate of learning, t is time, and $f(t)$ is the number of tasks learned.
  a. Suppose you move to a new school, and you want to learn the names of 30 classmates in your homeroom. If your learning rate for new tasks is 20% per day, how many complete names will you know after 2 days? After 8 days?
  b. Graph the function on your graphing calculator. How many days will it take to learn everyone's name? Explain.
  c. Open-Ended Does this function seem to describe your own learning rate? If not, how could you adapt it to reflect your learning rate?

Real-World 🌎 **Connection**

Careers Psychologists use models to evaluate and predict learning rates.

50. Work begins on digging a moat on the perimeter of a property. After the first weekend, the first worker recruits a friend to help. After every succeeding weekend, each moat-digger recruits another friend. One person can dig 15 m³ of dirt per weekend. The moat should be 4 m wide and 3 m deep, and it must lie entirely within the 60 m-by-70 m property.
  a. Geometry Determine the volume of dirt that must be removed for the moat.
  b. Write an exponential function to model the volume of dirt remaining to be shoveled after x weekends.
  c. On which weekend will the moat be completed?

Test Prep

Multiple Choice

51. How is the graph of $y = 4 \cdot \left(\frac{1}{2}\right)^{x-3}$ translated from the graph of $y = 4 \cdot \left(\frac{1}{2}\right)^x$?
  A. 3 units right   **B.** 3 units left   **C.** 3 units down   **D.** 3 units up

52. How is the graph of $y = 4 \cdot \left(\frac{1}{2}\right)^x + 3$ translated from the graph of $y = 4 \cdot \left(\frac{1}{2}\right)^x$?
  F. 3 units right   **G.** 3 units left   **H.** 3 units down   **J.** 3 units up

53. A savings account earns 4.62% annual interest, compounded continuously. After approximately how many years will a principal of $500 double?

    A. 2 years   **B.** 10 years   **C.** 15 years   **D.** 44 years

54. Sodium-24 has a half-life of 15 hours. How much sodium-24 will you have after 60 hours if your original sample is 64 mg?

    F. 4 mg   **G.** 16 mg   **H.** 32 mg   **J.** 64 mg

Short Response   **55.** How much should you invest in a continuously compounded account at an annual interest rate of 6% if you want exactly $8000 after four years? Show how you got your answer.

Mixed Review

Lesson 8-1   **Write an exponential equation $y = ab^x$ for a graph that includes the given points.**

56. $(0, 1), (1, 3)$ **57.** $(1, -8), (2, -32)$ **58.** $(0, -5), (2, -20)$

59. $(-1, 16), (3, 1)$ **60.** $(-3, 0.07), (-1, 7)$ **61.** $(2, 6400), (4, 4096)$

Lesson 7-3   **Simplify each expression.**

62. $5\sqrt{5} + \sqrt{5}$ **63.** $\sqrt[3]{4} - 2\sqrt[3]{4}$ **64.** $\sqrt{75} + \sqrt{125}$ **65.** $\sqrt[4]{32} + \sqrt[4]{128}$

66. $5\sqrt{3} - 2\sqrt{12}$ **67.** $3\sqrt{63} + \sqrt{28}$ **68.** $(3 - \sqrt{6})^2$ **69.** $\dfrac{-2 - 2\sqrt{5}}{1 - \sqrt{5}}$

Lesson 6-3   **Divide using either long division or synthetic division.**

70. $(x^2 - 3x - 1) \div x$ **71.** $(x^3 - 2x^2 - 5x + 6) \div (x - 1)$

72. $(x^3 + 4x^2 - x - 4) \div (x + 4)$ **73.** $(x^3 - 4x^2 - 4x - 5) \div (x - 5)$

74. $(13x^2 - 51x - 4) \div (x - 4)$ **75.** $(9x^3 - 18x^2 - x + 2) \div (3x + 1)$

Lesson 3-5   **Find the equations of the traces of each graph.**

76. $x - y + z = 5$ **77.** $x + y + 4z = -2$ **78.** $3x + 3y - 6z = 24$

79. $x - y + 2z = 8$ **80.** $3x + y + 9z = -18$ **81.** $-2x + y - 5z = 10$

✓ Checkpoint Quiz 1   Lessons 8-1 through 8-2

Identify each function as modeling either exponential growth or exponential decay. What percent of increase or decrease does the function model?

1. $y = 15(1.45)^x$ **2.** $y = 0.32(0.99)^x$ **3.** $y = 0.1(1.7)^x$ **4.** $y = 7.3(0.8)^x$

Graph each function.

5. $y = 3^x$ **6.** $y = 2^x + 1$ **7.** $y = (0.25)^x$ **8.** $y = 4^x - 5$

9. Open-Ended Describe a real-world problem that you could model with an exponential growth function.

10. Chemistry An element has a half-life of 30 hours. Write the exponential decay function for a 100-mg sample. Use the function to find the amount of the element remaining after 100 hours.

Logarithmic Functions as Inverses

What You'll Learn

- To write and evaluate logarithmic expressions
- To graph logarithmic functions

. . . And Why

To compare the acidities of milk and lemon juice, as in Example 4

Solve each equation.

1. $8 = x^3$ **2.** $x^{\frac{1}{4}} = 2$ **3.** $27 = 3^x$ **4.** $4^6 = 4^{3x}$

Graph each relation and its inverse on a coordinate plane.

5. $y = 5x$ **6.** $y = 2x^2$ **7.** $y = -x^3$ **8.** $y = \frac{1}{2}x$

🔊 **New Vocabulary** • logarithm • common logarithm • logarithmic function

---

1   Writing and Evaluating Logarithmic Expressions

The magnitude of an earthquake is a measure of the amount of energy released at its source. The Richter scale is an exponential measure of earthquake magnitude. An earthquake of magnitude 5 releases about 30 times as much energy as an earthquake of magnitude 4.

The Richter Scale

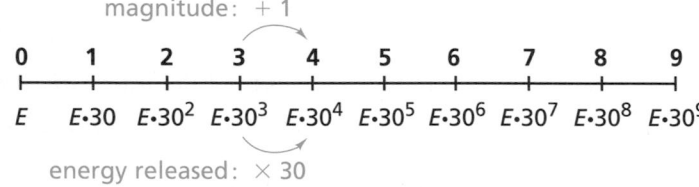

magnitude: $+1$

| 0 | 1 | 2 | 3 | 4 | 5 | 6 | 7 | 8 | 9 |

E $E\cdot30$ $E\cdot30^2$ $E\cdot30^3$ $E\cdot30^4$ $E\cdot30^5$ $E\cdot30^6$ $E\cdot30^7$ $E\cdot30^8$ $E\cdot30^9$

energy released: $\times 30$

Real-World 🌐 Connection

The earthquake that struck Washington in 2001 measured 6.8 on the Richter scale.

1 EXAMPLE   **Real-World 🌐 Connection**

Seismology In 1995, an earthquake in Mexico registered 8.0 on the Richter scale. In 2001, an earthquake of magnitude 6.8 shook Washington state. Compare the amounts of energy released in the two earthquakes.

$\dfrac{E \cdot 30^{8.0}}{E \cdot 30^{6.8}}$ **Write a ratio.**

$= \dfrac{30^{8.0}}{30^{6.8}}$ **Simplify.**

$= 30^{8.0 \,-\, 6.8}$ **Division Property of Exponents**

$= 30^{1.2}$ **Simplify.**

≈ 59.2 **Use a calculator.**

The earthquake in Mexico released about 59 times as much energy as the earthquake in Washington.

✓ **Quick Check** ❶ In 1997, an earthquake in Alabama registered 4.9 on the Richter scale. In 1999, one in California registered 7.0. Compare the energy released in the two quakes.

The exponents used by the Richter scale shown in Example 1 are called logarithms, or logs.

 Key Concepts

> **Definition**   **Logarithm**
>
> The **logarithm** to the base b of a positive number y is defined as follows:
>
> $$\text{If } y = b^x, \text{ then } \log_b y = x.$$

Read $\log_b y$ as
"log base b of y."

The exponent x in the exponential expression b^x is the logarithm in the equation $\log_b y = x$. The base b in b^x is the same as the base b in the logarithm. In both cases, $b \neq 1$ and $b > 0$.

A positive number b raised to any power x cannot equal a number y less than or equal to zero. Therefore, the logarithm of a negative number or zero is undefined.

2 EXAMPLE   **Writing in Logarithmic Form**

Write $25 = 5^2$ in logarithmic form.

   If $y = b^x$, then $\log_b y = x$.   **Write the definition.**

   If $25 = 5^2$, then $\log_5 25 = 2$.   **Substitute.**

●   The logarithmic form of $25 = 5^2$ is $\log_5 25 = 2$.

✓ **Quick Check**   **2** Write each equation in logarithmic form.

   a. $729 = 3^6$ **b.** $\left(\frac{1}{2}\right)^3 = \frac{1}{8}$ **c.** $10^0 = 1$

To evaluate logarithms, you can write them in exponential form.

3 EXAMPLE   **Evaluating Logarithms**

GO **⊙nline**

Video Tutor Help
Visit: PHSchool.com
Web Code: age-0775

Evaluate $\log_8 16$.

   $\log_8 16 = x$ **Write an equation in logarithmic form.**

      $16 = 8^x$ **Convert to exponential form.**

    $2^4 = (2^3)^x$ **Write each side using base 2.**

    $2^4 = 2^{3x}$ **Power Property of Exponents**

     $4 = 3x$ **Set the exponents equal to each other.**

     $\frac{4}{3} = x$ **Solve for x.**

●   So $\log_8 16 = \frac{4}{3}$.

✓ **Quick Check**   **3** Evaluate each logarithm.

   a. $\log_{64} \frac{1}{32}$ **b.** $\log_9 27$ **c.** $\log_{10} 100$

A **common logarithm** is a logarithm that uses base 10. You can write the common logarithm $\log_{10} y$ as $\log y$.

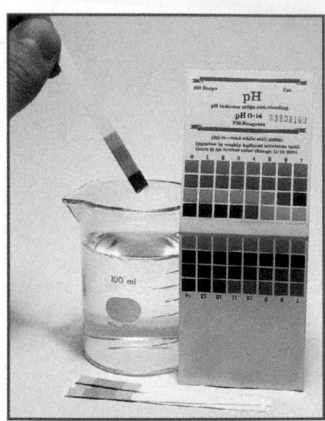

Scientists use common logarithms to measure acidity, which increases as the concentration of hydrogen ions in a substance increases. The pH of a substance equals $-\log[H^+]$, where $[H^+]$ is the concentration of hydrogen ions.

4 EXAMPLE **Real-World Connection**

Chemistry The pH of lemon juice is 2.3, while the pH of milk is 6.6. Find the concentration of hydrogen ions in each substance. Which substance is more acidic?

Lemon juice	Milk
$pH = -\log[H^+]$	$pH = -\log[H^+]$
$2.3 = -\log[H^+]$	$6.6 = -\log[H^+]$
$\log[H^+] = -2.3$	$\log[H^+] = -6.6$
$[H^+] = 10^{-2.3}$	$[H^+] = 10^{-6.6}$
$\approx 5.0 \times 10^{-3}$	$\approx 2.5 \times 10^{-7}$

The $[H^+]$ of lemon juice is about 5.0×10^{-3}. The $[H^+]$ of milk is about 2.5×10^{-7}.
● Lemon juice has a higher concentration of hydrogen ions, so it is more acidic.

✓ **Quick Check** ④ Find the concentration of hydrogen ions in seawater of pH 8.5.

2 Graphing Logarithmic Functions

A **logarithmic function** is the inverse of an exponential function. The graph shows $y = 10^x$ and $y = \log x$. Note that $(0, 1)$ and $(1, 10)$ lie on the graph of $y = 10^x$, and that $(1, 0)$ and $(10, 1)$ lie on the graph of $y = \log x$.

Recall that the graph of a function is symmetric to the graph of its inverse over the line $y = x$. You can graph $y = \log_b x$ as the inverse of $y = b^x$.

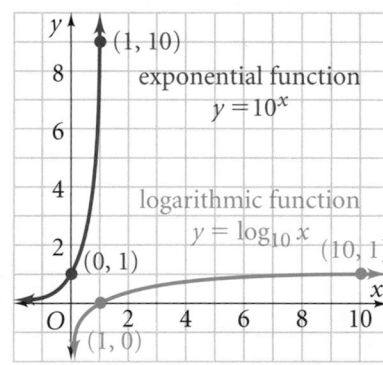

5 EXAMPLE Graphing a Logarithmic Function

Graph $y = \log_2 x$.

By the definition of logarithm, $y = \log_2 x$ is the inverse of $y = 2^x$.

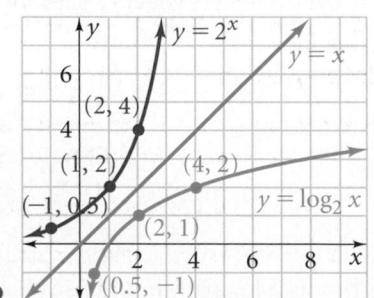

Step 1 Graph $y = 2^x$.

Step 2 Draw $y = x$.

Step 3 Choose a few points on $y = 2^x$. Reverse the coordinates and plot the points of $y = \log_2 x$.

✓ **Quick Check** ⑤ Graph $y = \log_3 x$.

The function $y = \log_b x$ is the inverse of $y = b^x$. Since $(0, 1)$ and $(1, b)$ are points on the graph of $y = b^x$, $(1, 0)$ and $(b, 1)$ are points on the graph of $y = \log_b x$. Since the x-axis is an asymptote for $y = b^x$, the y-axis is an asymptote for $y = \log_b x$. Using these facts, you can sketch the graph of $y = \log_b x$.

You can graph $y = \log_b (x - h) + k$ by translating the graph of $y = \log_b x$ horizontally by h and vertically by k.

 Key Concepts

Summary	Families of Logarithmic Functions
Parent function:	$y = \log_b x, b > 0, b \neq 1$
Stretch ($\lvert a \rvert > 1$) Shrink ($0 < \lvert a \rvert < 1$) Reflection ($a < 0$) in x-axis	$y = a \log_b x$
Translation (horizontal by h; vertical by k):	$y = \log_b(x - h) + k$
Combined:	$y = a \log_b (x - h) + k$

6 EXAMPLE Translating $y = \log_b x$

Graph $y = \log_6 (x - 2) + 3$.

Step 1 Make a table of values for the parent function.

x	$\log_6 x$	y
6	$\log_6 6 = 1$	1
1	$\log_6 1 = 0$	0
$\frac{1}{6}$	$\log_6 \frac{1}{6} = -1$	-1
$\frac{1}{36}$	$\log_6 \frac{1}{36} = -2$	-2
$\frac{1}{216}$	$\log_6 \frac{1}{216} = -3$	-3

Step 2 Graph the function by shifting the points from the table to the right 2 units and up 3 units.

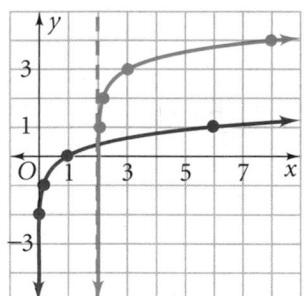

Vocabulary Tip

A parent function is the simplest function in a family of functions.

 **Quick Check** ⑥ Graph $y = \log_3 (x + 3)$.

EXERCISES

For more exercises, see *Extra Skill and Word Problem Practice*.

Practice and Problem Solving

 Practice by Example

Example 1
(page 446)

 **GO for Help**

Seismology In 1812, an earthquake of magnitude 7.9 shook New Madrid, Missouri. Compare the amount of energy released by that earthquake to the amount of energy released by each earthquake below.

1. magnitude 7.7 in San Francisco, California, in 1906

2. magnitude 9.5 in Valdivia, Chile, in 1960

3. magnitude 3.2 in Charlottesville, Virginia, in 2001

4. magnitude 6.9 in Kobe, Japan, in 1995

5. magnitude 9.2 in Prince William Sound, Alaska, in 1964

Example 2
(page 447)

Write each equation in logarithmic form.

6. $49 = 7^2$ **7.** $10^3 = 1000$ **8.** $625 = 5^4$ **9.** $\frac{1}{10} = 10^{-1}$

10. $8^2 = 64$ **11.** $4 = \left(\frac{1}{2}\right)^{-2}$ **12.** $\left(\frac{1}{3}\right)^3 = \frac{1}{27}$ **13.** $10^{-2} = 0.01$

Example 3
(page 447)

Evaluate each logarithm.

14. $\log_2 16$ **15.** $\log_4 2$ **16.** $\log_8 8$ **17.** $\log_4 8$

18. $\log_2 8$ **19.** $\log_{49} 7$ **20.** $\log_5 (-25)$ **21.** $\log_3 9$

22. $\log_2 2^5$ **23.** $\log_{\frac{1}{2}} \frac{1}{2}$ **24.** $\log 10,000$ **25.** $\log_5 125$

Example 4
(page 448)

The pH of each food is given. Find the concentration of hydrogen ions [H$^+$].

26. maple syrup, 5.2   **27.** lime juice, 2.2   **28.** egg white, 8.0

29. cider vinegar, 3.1   **30.** condensed milk, 6.3   **31.** soy sauce, 4.9

32. tomato juice, 4.0   **33.** watermelon, 5.4   **34.** mustard, 3.6

Examples 5 and 6
(pages 448 and 449)

Graph each logarithmic function.

35. $y = \log_4 x$ **36.** $y = \log_5 x$ **37.** $y = \log_8 x$

38. $y = \log_5 x + 1$ **39.** $y = \log_7 (x - 2)$ **40.** $y = \log_3 (x - 5) + 3$

 Apply Your Skills

Use your calculator to evaluate each logarithm to four decimal places. Then find the largest integer that is less than the value of the logarithm.

41. $\log 5$ **42.** $\log (6.1 \times 10^{-5})$ **43.** $\log 0.08$ **44.** $\log 200$

45. $\log \frac{1}{6}$ **46.** $\log 17.52$ **47.** $\log (1.3 \times 10^7)$ **48.** $\log \frac{13}{4}$

For a guide to solving
Exercise 49, see p. 453.

 49. Chemistry The pH scale ranges from 0 to 14. A pH level of 7 is neutral. A level greater than 7 is basic, and a level less than 7 is acidic. The table shows the hydrogen ion concentration [H$^+$] for selected foods. Find the pH of each item. Determine whether it is basic or acidic.

Approximate [H$^+$] of Foods

Food	[H$^+$]
Apple juice	3.2×10^{-4}
Buttermilk	2.5×10^{-5}
Cream	2.5×10^{-7}
Ketchup	1.3×10^{-4}
Shrimp sauce	7.9×10^{-8}
Strained peas	1.0×10^{-6}

50. Error Analysis Find the error in the following evaluation of $\log_{27} 3$. Then evaluate the logarithm correctly.

$$\log_{27} 3 = x$$
$$27 = x^3$$
$$3 = x$$
$$\log_{27} 3 = 3$$

 51. Writing Explain why the base b in $y = \log_b x$ cannot equal 1.

52. Open-Ended Write a logarithmic function of the form $y = \log_b x$. Find its inverse function. Graph both functions on one set of axes.

Homework Video Tutor
Visit: PHSchool.com
Web Code: age-0803

Write each equation in exponential form.

53. $\log_2 128 = 7$ **54.** $\log 0.0001 = -4$ **55.** $\log_7 16,807 = 5$

56. $\log_6 6 = 1$ **57.** $\log_4 1 = 0$ **58.** $\log_3 \frac{1}{9} = -2$

59. $\log_2 \frac{1}{2} = -1$ **60.** $\log 10 = 1$ **61.** $\log_2 8192 = 13$

62. Archaeology One method of dating artifacts is radiocarbon dating. The artifacts in the table were found at a dig site near Kit Carson, Colorado. An artifact's age t in years is $t = 1.904 \times 10^4 \cdot \log\left(\frac{13.7}{R}\right)$, where R is the number of beta radiation emissions per minute per gram of carbon in the artifact.

Beta Emissions of Artifacts

Object	Mass of Carbon (g)	Beta Emissions per Minute
Buffalo bone	400	1640 ± 30
Bone fragment	15	61.5 ± 1.5
Pottery shard	25	342 ± 7
Charcoal	10	41.0 ± 1.3
Spear shaft	250	1020 ± 30

a. For each artifact, use the range of beta emissions to find the artifact's maximum and minimum ages.

b. Critical Thinking Which artifact is significantly different in age from the others? Give two possible explanations for the difference.

63. Multiple Choice Which function or functions are the inverse of $y = -\log_{0.25} x$?

I. $y = 4^x$ **II.** $y = 4^{-x}$ **III.** $y = \left(\frac{1}{4}\right)^{-x}$

   Ⓐ II only   Ⓑ III only   Ⓒ I and III   Ⓓ II and III

Find the inverse of each function.

64. $y = \log_4 x$ **65.** $y = \log_{0.5} x$ **66.** $y = \log_{10} x$

67. $y = \log_2 2x$ **68.** $y = \log(x + 1)$ **69.** $y = \log 10x$

70. $y = \log(x - 2)$ **71.** $y = \log_5 x^2$ **72.** $y = \log_a(x - b)$

Graph each logarithmic function.

73. $y = \log 2x$ **74.** $y = 2\log_2 x$ **75.** $y = \log_4(2x + 3)$

Find the domain and the range of each function.

76. $y = \log_5 x$ **77.** $y = 3\log x$ **78.** $y = \log_2(x - 3)$

79. $y = 1 + \log x$ **80.** $y = \log(x - 2) + 1$ **81.** $y = \log_6(x + 1)$

82. $y = \log_8 x - 2$ **83.** $y = \log_2 x + \frac{1}{3}$ **84.** $y = \log(x - t)$

Ⓒ **Challenge** 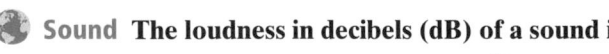 **Sound** The loudness in decibels (dB) of a sound is defined as $10 \log \frac{I}{I_0}$. I is the intensity of the sound. I_0 is 10^{-12}, the intensity of a barely audible sound. Complete the table.

Loudness of Sounds

	Type of Sound	Intensity (W/m²)	Loudness (dB)
	Pain-producing	1	120
85.	Jackhammer	10^{-2}	▮
86.	Busy street	10^{-5}	▮
87.	Conversation	10^{-6}	▮
88.	Whisper	10^{-10}	▮
89.	Rustle of leaves	10^{-11}	▮
	Barely audible sound	10^{-12}	0

90. Match each function with the graph of its inverse.

a. $y = \log_3 x$ **b.** $y = \log_2 4x$ **c.** $y = \log_{\frac{1}{2}} x$

I. 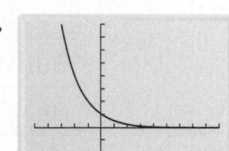   **II.** 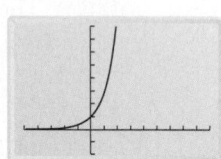   **III.**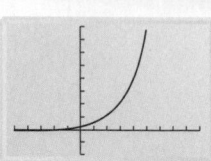

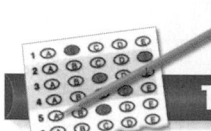

Test Prep

Multiple Choice

91. What is the ratio of $(65 \cdot 3^{17})$ to $(65 \cdot 3^{14})$?
   A. 17 to 14   **B.** 3 to 1   **C.** 9 to 1   **D.** 27 to 1

92. What is the logarithmic form of the exponential equation $2^4 = 16$?
   F. $\log_{16} 2 = 4$ **G.** $\log_{16} 4 = 2$ **H.** $\log_4 16 = 2$ **J.** $\log_2 16 = 4$

93. Which function is the inverse of $f(x) = 2^{x-1}$?
   A. $f^{-1}(x) = \log_2 (x - 1)$ **B.** $f^{-1}(x) = \log_2 (x + 1)$
   C. $f^{-1}(x) = \log_2 x - 1$ **D.** $f^{-1}(x) = \log_2 x + 1$

94. Which function is a shrink of $y = \log x$ by a factor of $\frac{1}{2}$?
   F. $\log \sqrt{x}$ **G.** $\log x^2$ **H.** $\log \left(x - \frac{1}{2}\right)$ **J.** $\log \left(x + \frac{1}{2}\right)$

95. Which of the following relationships is best represented by the graph at the right?
   A. $y = \log_4 (x - 1) + 5$
   B. $y = \log_4 (x - 2) - 2$
   C. $y = \log_4 (x + 2) - 2$
   D. $y = \log_4 (x - 1) - 1$

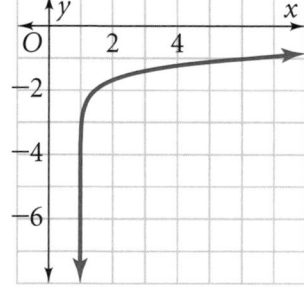

Short Response

96. Evaluate $\log_2 \frac{1}{32}$ without using a calculator. Show your work.

97. Solve the equation $\log_6 y = 3$.

98. Solve the equation $\log_b 9 = \frac{1}{2}$.

Mixed Review

Lesson 8-2

Sketch the graph of each function. Then locate the asymptote of the curve.

99. $y = 5^x - 100$ **100.** $y = -10(4)^{x+2}$ **101.** $y = -27(3)^{x-1} + 9$

Lesson 7-4

Write each expression in radical form.

102. $t^{\frac{2}{3}}$ **103.** $(16w^3)^{\frac{1}{2}}$ **104.** $z^{\frac{8}{5}}$ **105.** $x^{\frac{p}{n}}$

Lesson 6-4

Solve each equation by graphing. If necessary, round to the nearest thousandth.

106. $3x^2 + 18x + 24 = 0$ **107.** $1 - x = x^2 - 7x$ **108.** $x^4 = 7x^3 + 10x^2$

Lesson 5-4

Factor each expression.

109. $4x^2 - 8x + 3$ **110.** $\frac{1}{4}b^2 - 4$ **111.** $5x^2 + 13x - 6$

Understanding Word Problems Read the problem below. Let the explanations guide you through the use of the data table. Check your understanding with the exercise at the bottom of the page.

Chemistry The pH scale ranges from 0 to 14. A pH level of 7 is neutral. A level greater than 7 is basic, and a level less than 7 is acidic. The table shows the hydrogen ion concentration [H⁺] for selected foods. Find the pH of each item. Determine whether it is basic or acidic.

Approximate [H+] of Selected Foods

Food	[H+]
Apple Juice	3.2×10^{-4}
Buttermilk	2.5×10^{-5}
Cream	2.5×10^{-7}
Ketchup	1.3×10^{-4}
Shrimp Sauce	7.9×10^{-8}
Strained Peas	1.0×10^{-6}

A table is a tool for organizing data.

The title of the table indicates the type of data represented. →

Approximate [H+] of Selected Foods

Food	[H+]
Apple Juice	3.2×10^{-4}
Buttermilk	2.5×10^{-5}

← **Each row represents a different item. Row 1 contains data for apple juice.**

Each column represents a different category of data. Column 2 lists the [H⁺] of each food.

Now you can use the table.

$$pH = -\log [H^+]$$ **Refer to page 448 for the formula for pH.**
pH of apple juice $= -\log ([H^+]$ of apple juice$)$ **Use the formula.**
$$= -\log (3.2 \times 10^{-4})$$ **Substitute.**
$$\approx 3.49$$ **Simplify.**

Since the pH of apple juice is less than 7, it is acidic.

The problem asks you to find the pH and whether the item is basic or acidic. To organize the information, you can add two columns to the table.

Food	[H+]	pH	Acid or Base
Apple Juice	3.2×10^{-4}	3.49	Acid

EXERCISE

Copy and complete the table below.

[H+]	pH	Acid or Base
4.6×10^{-8}	■	■
3.7×10^{-3}	■	■
1.8×10^{-4}	■	■

Properties of Logarithms

What You'll Learn

- To use the properties of logarithms

. . . And Why

To relate sound intensity and decibel level, as in Example 4

Simplify each expression.

1. $\log_2 4 + \log_2 8$ **2.** $\log_3 9 - \log_3 27$ **3.** $\log_2 16 \div \log_2 64$

Evaluate each expression for $x = 3$.

4. $x^3 - x$ **5.** $x^5 \cdot x^2$ **6.** $\dfrac{x^6}{x^9}$ **7.** $x^3 + x^2$

---

1   Using the Properties of Logarithms

Activity: Properties of Logarithms

1. Complete the table. Round to the nearest thousandth.

x	1	2	3	4	5	6	7	8	9	10	15	20
log x	■	■	■	■	■	■	■	■	■	■	■	■

2. Complete each pair of statements. What do you notice?
   a. log 3 + log 5 = ■ and log (3 · 5) = ■
   b. log 1 + log 7 = ■ and log (1 · 7) = ■
   c. log 2 + log 4 = ■ and log (2 · 4) = ■
   d. log 10 + log 2 = ■ and log (10 · 2) = ■

3. Complete the statement: log M + log N = ■.

4. **a. Make a Conjecture** How could you rewrite the expression log $\frac{M}{N}$ using the expressions log M and log N?
   b. Use your calculator to verify your conjecture for several values of M and N.

The properties of logarithms are summarized below.

Key Concepts

Properties	Properties of Logarithms

For any positive numbers, M, N, and b, $b \neq 1$,

$$\log_b MN = \log_b M + \log_b N \qquad \textbf{Product Property}$$

$$\log_b \frac{M}{N} = \log_b M - \log_b N \qquad \textbf{Quotient Property}$$

$$\log_b M^x = x \log_b M \qquad \textbf{Power Property}$$

You can use the properties of logarithms to rewrite logarithmic expressions.

1 EXAMPLE Identifying the Properties of Logarithms

State the property or properties used to rewrite each expression.

a. $\log_2 8 - \log_2 4 = \log_2 2$

Quotient Property: $\log_2 8 - \log_2 4 = \log_2 \frac{8}{4} = \log_2 2$

b. $\log_b x^3 y = 3 \log_b x + \log_b y$

Product Property: $\log_b x^3 y = \log_b x^3 + \log_b y$

Power Property: $\log_b x^3 + \log_b y = 3 \log_b x + \log_b y$

✓ **Quick Check** **1** State the property or properties used to rewrite each expression.
a. $\log_5 2 + \log_5 6 = \log_5 12$
b. $3 \log_b 4 - 3 \log_b 2 = \log_b 8$

You can write the sum or difference of logarithms with the same base as a single logarithm.

2 EXAMPLE Simplifying Logarithms

Video Tutor Help
Visit: PHSchool.com
Web Code: age-0775

Write each logarithmic expression as a single logarithm.

a. $\log_3 20 - \log_3 4$

$$\log_3 20 - \log_3 4 = \log_3 \frac{20}{4} \quad \textbf{Quotient Property}$$
$$= \log_3 5 \quad \textbf{Simplify.}$$

b. $3 \log_2 x + \log_2 y$

$$3 \log_2 x + \log_2 y = \log_2 x^3 + \log_2 y \quad \textbf{Power Property}$$
$$= \log_2 (x^3 y) \quad \textbf{Product Property}$$

So $\log_3 20 - \log_3 4 = \log_3 5$, and $3 \log_2 x + \log_2 y = \log_2 (x^3 y)$.

✓ **Quick Check** **2** **a.** Write $3 \log 2 + \log 4 - \log 16$ as a single logarithm.
b. **Critical Thinking** Can you write $3 \log_2 9 - \log_6 9$ as a single logarithm? Explain.

You can sometimes write a single logarithm as a sum or difference of two or more logarithms.

3 EXAMPLE Expanding Logarithms

Vocabulary Tip

In mathematics, <u>to</u> <u>expand</u> means "to show the full form of."

Expand each logarithm.

a. $\log_5 \frac{x}{y}$

$= \log_5 x - \log_5 y$ **Quotient Property**

b. $\log 3r^4$

$= \log 3 + \log r^4$ **Product Property**
$= \log 3 + 4 \log r$ **Power Property**

✓ **Quick Check** **3** Expand each logarithm.
a. $\log_2 7b$
b. $\log \left(\frac{y}{3}\right)^2$
c. $\log_7 a^3 b^4$

Logarithms are used to model sound. The intensity of a sound is a measure of the energy carried by the sound wave. The greater the intensity of a sound, the louder it seems. This apparent loudness L is measured in decibels.

You can use the formula $L = 10 \log \frac{I}{I_0}$, where I is the intensity of the sound in watts per square meter (W/m^2). I_0 is the lowest-intensity sound that the average human ear can detect.

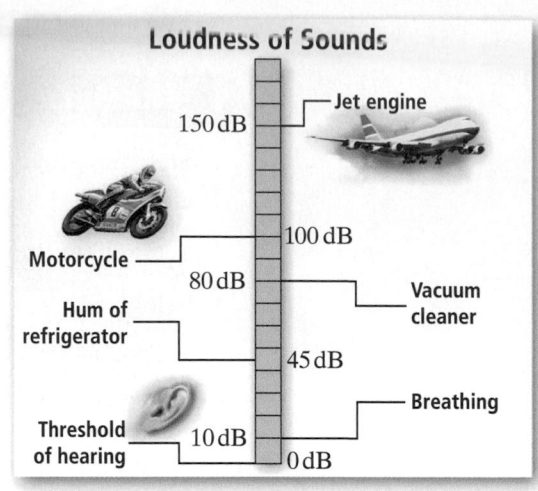

Loudness of Sounds

- Jet engine — 150 dB
- Motorcycle — 100 dB
- Vacuum cleaner — 80 dB
- Hum of refrigerator
- Breathing — 45 dB
- Threshold of hearing — 10 dB
- 0 dB

4 EXAMPLE **Real-World Connection**

Noise Control A shipping company has started flying cargo planes out of the city airport. Residents in a nearby neighborhood have complained that the cargo planes are too loud. Suppose the shipping company hires you to design a way to reduce the intensity of the sound by half. By how many decibels would the loudness of the sound be decreased?

Relate The reduced intensity is one half of the present intensity.

Define Let I_1 = present intensity.
Let I_2 = reduced intensity.
Let L_1 = present loudness.
Let L_2 = reduced loudness.

Write $I_2 = 0.5\, I_1$

$$L_1 = 10 \log \frac{I_1}{I_0}$$

$$L_2 = 10 \log \frac{I_2}{I_0}$$

$$L_1 - L_2 = 10 \log \frac{I_1}{I_0} - 10 \log \frac{I_2}{I_0} \qquad \text{Find the decrease in loudness } L_1 - L_2.$$

$$= 10 \log \frac{I_1}{I_0} - 10 \log \frac{0.5 I_1}{I_0} \qquad \text{Substitute } I_2 = 0.5 I_1.$$

$$= 10 \log \frac{I_1}{I_0} - 10 \log \left(0.5 \cdot \frac{I_1}{I_0} \right)$$

$$= 10 \log \frac{I_1}{I_0} - 10 \left(\log 0.5 + \log \frac{I_1}{I_0} \right) \qquad \text{Product Property}$$

$$= 10 \log \frac{I_1}{I_0} - 10 \log 0.5 - 10 \log \frac{I_1}{I_0} \qquad \text{Distributive Property}$$

$$= -10 \log 0.5 \qquad \text{Combine like terms.}$$

$$\approx 3.0 \qquad \text{Use a calculator.}$$

The decrease in loudness would be about three decibels.

Real-World Connection

The workers who direct planes at airports must wear ear protection.

Quick Check ④ Suppose the shipping company wants you to reduce the sound intensity to 25% of the original intensity. By how many decibels would the loudness be reduced?

EXERCISES

For more exercises, see *Extra Skill and Word Problem Practice.*

Practice and Problem Solving

A Practice by Example

Example 1
(page 455)

GO for Help

State the property or properties used to rewrite each expression.

1. $\log 4 + \log 5 = \log 20$

2. $\log_3 32 - \log_3 8 = \log_3 4$

3. $\log z^2 = 2 \log z$

4. $\log_6 \sqrt[n]{x^p} = \frac{p}{n} \log_6 x$

5. $8 \log 2 - 2 \log 8 = \log 4$

6. $\log \sqrt[3]{3x} = \frac{1}{3} \log 3x$

7. $3 \log_4 5 - 3 \log_4 3 = \log_4 \left(\frac{5}{3}\right)^3$

8. $2 \log w + 4 \log z = \log w^2 z^4$

9. $2 \log_2 m - 4 \log_2 n = \log_2 \frac{m^2}{n^4}$

10. $\log_b \frac{1}{8} + 3 \log_b 4 = \log_b 8$

Example 2
(page 455)

Write each logarithmic expression as a single logarithm.

11. $\log 7 + \log 2$

12. $\log_2 9 - \log_2 3$

13. $5 \log 3 + \log 4$

14. $\log 8 - 2 \log 6 + \log 3$

15. $4 \log m - \log n$

16. $\log 5 - k \log 2$

17. $\log_6 5 + \log_6 x$

18. $\log_7 x + \log_7 y - \log_7 z$

Example 3
(page 455)

Expand each logarithm.

19. $\log x^3 y^5$

20. $\log_7 22xyz$

21. $\log_4 5\sqrt{x}$

22. $\log 3m^4 n^{-2}$

23. $\log_5 \frac{r}{s}$

24. $\log_3 (2x)^2$

25. $\log_3 7(2x - 3)^2$

26. $\log \frac{a^2 b^3}{c^4}$

27. $\log \sqrt{\frac{2x}{y}}$

28. $\log_8 8\sqrt{3a^5}$

29. $\log \frac{s\sqrt{7}}{t^2}$

30. $\log_b \frac{1}{x}$

Example 4
(page 456)

31. One brand of ear plugs claims to block the sound of snoring as loud as 22 dB. A second brand claims to block snoring that is eight times as intense. If the claims are true, for how many more decibels is the second brand effective?

32. A sound barrier along a highway reduced the intensity of the noise reaching a community by 95%. By how many decibels was the noise reduced?

B Apply Your Skills

Use the properties of logarithms to evaluate each expression.

33. $\log_2 4 - \log_2 16$

34. $3 \log_2 2 - \log_2 4$

35. $\log_3 3 + 5 \log_3 3$

36. $\log 1 + \log 100$

37. $\log_6 4 + \log_6 9$

38. $2 \log_8 4 - \frac{1}{3} \log_8 8$

39. $2 \log_3 3 - \log_3 3$

40. $\frac{1}{2} \log_5 1 - 2 \log_5 5$

41. $\log_9 \frac{1}{3} + 3 \log_9 3$

42. Error Analysis Explain why the expansion below of $\log_4 \sqrt{\frac{t}{s}}$ is incorrect. Then do the expansion correctly.

$$\log_4 \sqrt{\frac{t}{s}} = \frac{1}{2} \log_4 \frac{t}{s}$$
$$= \frac{1}{2} \log_4 t - \log_4 s$$

43. Open-Ended Write $\log 150$ as a sum or difference of two logarithms.

Assume that $\log 4 \approx 0.6021$, $\log 5 \approx 0.6990$, and $\log 6 \approx 0.7782$. Use the properties of logarithms to evaluate each expression. Do not use your calculator.

44. $\log 24$ **45.** $\log 30$ **46.** $\log 16$

47. $\log 125$ **48.** $\log 1.5$ **49.** $\log 0.8$

50. $\log \frac{1}{4}$ **51.** $\log \frac{1}{25}$ **52.** $\log 25$

53. $\log \frac{1}{6}$ **54.** $\log 36$ **55.** $\log \sqrt{5}$

Real-World Connection

Decibel meters are used to measure sound levels.

56. Noise Control New components reduce the sound intensity of a certain model of vacuum cleaner from 10^{-4} W/m^2 to 6.31×10^{-6} W/m^2. By how many decibels do these new components reduce the vacuum cleaner's loudness?

57. Reasoning If $\log x = 5$, what is the value of $\frac{1}{x}$?

Write *true* or *false* for each statement. Justify your answer.

58. $\log_2 4 + \log_2 8 = 5$ **59.** $\log_3 \frac{3}{2} = \frac{1}{2} \log_3 3$

60. $\log_3 8 = 3 \log_3 2$ **61.** $\log_5 16 - \log 2 = \log_5 8$

62. $\log (x - 2) = \frac{\log x}{\log 2}$ **63.** $\frac{\log_b x}{\log_b y} = \log_b \frac{x}{y}$

64. $(\log x)^2 = \log x^2$ **65.** $\log_4 7 - \log_4 3 = \log_4 4$

66. $\log x + \log (x^2 + 2) = \log (x^3 + 2x)$ **67.** $\log_2 3 + \log_3 2 = \log_6 6$

68. $\log_2 x - 4 \log_2 y = \log_2 \frac{x}{y^4}$ **69.** $\log_b \frac{1}{8} + 3 \log_b 4 = \log_b 8$

70. Construction Suppose you are the supervisor on a road construction job. Your team is blasting rock to make way for a roadbed. One explosion has an intensity of 1.65×10^{-2} W/m^2. What is the loudness of the sound in decibels? (Use $I_0 = 10^{-12}$ W/m^2.)

71. Critical Thinking Can you expand $\log_3 (2x + 1)$? Explain.

72. Writing Explain why $\log (5 \cdot 2) \neq \log 5 \cdot \log 2$.

Write each logarithmic expression as a single logarithm.

73. $\frac{1}{4} \log_3 2 + \frac{1}{4} \log_3 x$ **74.** $\frac{1}{2}(\log_x 4 + \log_x y) - 3 \log_x z$

75. $2 \log 3 - \frac{1}{2} \log 4 + \frac{1}{2} \log 9$ **76.** $x \log_4 m + \frac{1}{y} \log_4 n - \log_4 p$

77. $\left(\frac{2 \log_b x}{3} + \frac{3 \log_b y}{4} \right) - 5 \log_b z$ **78.** $\frac{\log z - \log 3}{4} - 5 \frac{\log x}{2}$

Expand each logarithm.

79. $\log \left(\frac{2\sqrt{x}}{5} \right)^3$ **80.** $\log \frac{m^3}{n^4 p^{-2}}$ **81.** $\log 2 \sqrt{\frac{4r}{s^2}}$

82. $\log_b \frac{\sqrt{x} \sqrt[3]{y^2}}{\sqrt[5]{z^2}}$ **83.** $\log_4 \frac{\sqrt{x^5 y^7}}{zw^4}$ **84.** $\log \frac{\sqrt{x^2 - 4}}{(x + 3)^2}$

85. $\log \sqrt{\frac{x\sqrt{2}}{y^2}}$ **86.** $\log_3 \left[(xy)^{\frac{1}{3}} \div z^2 \right]^3$ **87.** $\log_7 \frac{\sqrt{r + 9}}{s^2 t^{\frac{1}{3}}}$

88. Let $u = \log_b M$, and let $v = \log_b N$. Prove the Product Property of Logarithms by completing the equations below.

Statement	Reason
$u = \log_b M$	Given
$b^u = M$	Rewrite in exponential form.
$v = \blacksquare$	Given
$b^v = \blacksquare$	Rewrite in exponential form.
$MN = b^u b^v = b^{\blacksquare}$	Apply the Product Property of Exponents.
$\log_b MN = \blacksquare$	Take the logarithm of each side.
$\log_b MN = \log_b \blacksquare + \log_b \blacksquare$	Substitute $\log_b M$ for u and $\log_b N$ for v.

89. Let $u = \log_b M$. Prove the Power Property of logarithms.

90. Let $u = \log_b M$ and $v = \log_b N$. Prove the Quotient Property of logarithms.

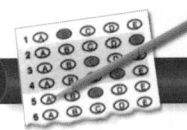

Test Prep

Multiple Choice

91. Which statement is NOT correct?
A. $\log_2 25 = 2 \cdot \log_2 5$
B. $\log_3 16 = 2 \cdot \log_3 8$
C. $\log_5 27 = 3 \cdot \log_5 3$
D. $\log_8 10{,}000 = 4 \cdot \log_8 10$

92. Which expression is equal to $\log_7 5 + \log_7 3$?
F. $\log_7 8$
G. $\log_7 15$
H. $\log_7 125$
J. $\log_{49} 15$

93. Which expression is equal to $\log_5 x + 4 \cdot \log_5 y - 2 \cdot \log_5 z$?
A. $\log_5 (-8xyz)$
B. $-\log_5 \frac{4xy}{2z}$
C. $\log_5 \frac{(xy)^4}{z^2}$
D. $\log_5 \frac{xy^4}{z^2}$

Short Response

94. $\log_5 10 \approx 1.4307$ and $\log_5 20 \approx 1.8614$. Find the value of $\log_5 \left(\frac{1}{2}\right)$ without using a calculator. Explain how you found the value.

Extended Response

95. Use the properties of logarithms to write log 12 in four different ways. Name each property you use.

Mixed Review

Lesson 8-3

Write each equation in logarithmic form.

96. $49 = 7^2$
97. $5^3 = 125$
98. $\frac{1}{4} = 8^{-\frac{2}{3}}$
99. $5^{-3} = \frac{1}{125}$

Lesson 7-5

Solve each equation. Check for extraneous solutions.

100. $\sqrt[3]{y^4} = 16$
101. $\sqrt[3]{7x} - 4 = 0$
102. $2\sqrt{w - 1} = \sqrt{w + 2}$

Lesson 6-5

A polynomial equation with integer coefficients has the given roots. What additional roots can you identify?

103. $\sqrt{3}, -\sqrt{5}$
104. $-i, 4i$
105. $2i, -4 + i$
106. $\sqrt{2}, i - 1$
107. $-\sqrt{7}, -\sqrt{11}$
108. $-2i + 3, i$

Reasonable Context

One quick check of a solution to a real-world problem is determining whether the answer is *reasonable* for the given context. The *context* is the situational setting for the problem.

1 EXAMPLE Reasonableness of a Solution

The class had to solve a cubic equation to find an approximate radius of the hot air balloon. Here are some students' answers:

Ro: 5 ft   Sal: 15 ft   Tim: 25 ft   Una: 100 ft

Which answers are *unreasonable*?

Ro's answer is unreasonable because hot air balloons are much larger than the people who ride in them.

Una's answer is unreasonable because a balloon with a 100 ft radius would be two-thirds the size of a football field.

The context also helps you determine a reasonable domain and range for a function.

2 EXAMPLE Reasonable Domain and Range Values

The quadratic function $h(t) = -16t^2 + 96t + 112$ models the height in feet of a projectile at time t. Give a *reasonable* domain and range for the function h.

The function h is quadratic, so its mathematical domain is the set of real numbers. The graph opens downward, so the function reaches a maximum value at its vertex where

$t = -\dfrac{b}{2a} = -\dfrac{96}{2(-16)} = 3$, and $h(3) = -16(3)^2 + 96(3) + 112 = 256$.

The mathematical range of the function is $h(t) \leq 256$.

There is not enough information—namely a context—to give a specific domain and range. You can state a reasonable assumed context, however, to give a reasonable domain and range:

Assuming the projectile starts and ends on the ground ($h = 0$), a reasonable domain is $-1 \leq t \leq 7$ and a reasonable range is $0 \leq h(t) \leq 256$.

EXERCISES

1. Two other student answers for the radius of the hot air balloon in Example 1 were 8 ft and 50 ft. Is either of these answers unreasonable? Explain.

For Example 2, there are situations possible in which the projectile could have begun its flight at $t = 0$, $t = 3.5$, or even $t = -2$. Give a context for which each set of values below would be a reasonable domain.

2. $0 \leq t \leq 7$ **3.** $0 \leq t \leq 8$ **4.** $0 \leq t \leq 6$ **5.** $3.5 \leq t \leq 7$ **6.** $-2 \leq t \leq 3$

7. Suppose an answer is reasonable in context. Does this provide a check that the answer is correct?

Exponential and Logarithmic Equations

What You'll Learn

- To solve exponential equations
- To solve logarithmic equations

. . . And Why

To model animal populations, as in Example 5

✓ **Check Skills You'll Need**

GO **for Help** Lessons 8-3 and 7-4

Evaluate each logarithm.

1. $\log_9 81 \cdot \log_9 3$
2. $\log 10 \cdot \log_3 9$
3. $\log_2 16 \div \log_2 8$
4. Simplify $125^{-\frac{2}{3}}$.

◀)) **New Vocabulary**
- exponential equation
- logarithmic equation
- Change of Base Formula

---

1 Solving Exponential Equations

An equation of the form $b^{cx} = a$, where the exponent includes a variable, is an **exponential equation**. If m and n are positive and $m = n$, then $\log m = \log n$. You can therefore solve an exponential equation by taking the logarithm of each side of the equation.

1 EXAMPLE Solving an Exponential Equation

Solve $7^{3x} = 20$.

$$7^{3x} = 20$$

$\log 7^{3x} = \log 20$ **Take the common logarithm of each side.**

$3x \log 7 = \log 20$ **Use the power property of logarithms.**

$x = \dfrac{\log 20}{3 \log 7}$ **Divide each side by 3 log 7.**

≈ 0.5132 **Use a calculator.**

Check $7^{3x} = 20$

$7^{3(0.5132)} \approx 20.00382 \approx 20$ ✓

✓ **Quick Check** ❶ Solve each equation. Round to the nearest ten-thousandth. Check your answers.
a. $3^x = 4$
b. $6^{2x} = 21$
c. $3^{x+4} = 101$

2 EXAMPLE Solving an Exponential Equation by Graphing

Solve $6^{2x} = 1500$.

Graph the equations $y_1 = 6^{2x}$ and $y_2 = 1500$. Find the point of intersection.

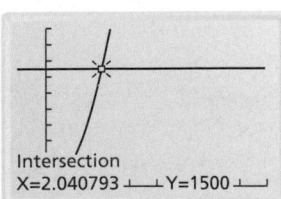

Intersection
X=2.040793   Y=1500

The solution is $x \approx 2.0408$.

✓ **Quick Check** ❷ Solve $11^{6x} = 786$ by graphing.

3 EXAMPLE Solving an Exponential Equation by Tables

Solve the equation $2(1.5^x) = 6$ to the nearest hundredth.

Enter $y_1 = 2(1.5^x) - 6$. Use tabular zoom-in to find the sign change, as shown at the right.

The solution is $x \approx 2.71$.

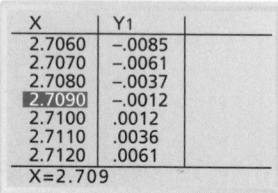

X	Y1
2.7060	−.0085
2.7070	−.0061
2.7080	−.0037
2.7090	−.0012
2.7100	.0012
2.7110	.0036
2.7120	.0061
X=2.709	

✓ Quick Check **3** Solve $11^{6x} = 786$ using tables. Compare your result with your solution in Quick Check 2.

4 EXAMPLE Real-World 🌐 Connection

Zoology Refer to the photo. Write an exponential equation to model the decline in the population. If the decay rate remains constant, in what year might only five peninsular bighorn sheep remain in the United States?

Step 1 Enter the data into your calculator. Let 0 represent the initial year, 1971.

Step 2 Use the **ExpReg** feature to find the exponential function that fits the data.

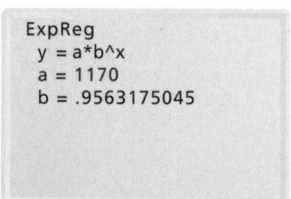

ExpReg
y = a*b^x
a = 1170
b = .9563175045

Real-World 🌐 Connection

The U.S. population of peninsular bighorn sheep was 1170 in 1971. By 1999, only 335 remained.

Step 3 Graph the function and the line $y = 5$.

Step 4 Find the point of intersection.

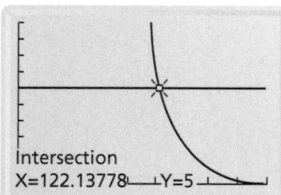

Intersection
X=122.13778   Y=5

The solution is $x \approx 122$, and $1971 + 122 = 2093$, so there may be only five peninsular bighorn sheep in 2093.

✓ Quick Check **4** The population of peninsular bighorn sheep in Mexico was approximately 6200 in 1971. By 1999, about 2300 remained. Determine the year by which only 200 peninsular bighorn sheep might remain in Mexico.

2 Solving Logarithmic Equations

To evaluate a logarithm with any base, you can use the **Change of Base Formula.**

 Key Concepts

Property	**Change of Base Formula**

For any positive numbers, M, b, and c, with $b \neq 1$ and $c \neq 1$,

$$\log_b M = \frac{\log_c M}{\log_c b}$$

5 **EXAMPLE** **Using the Change of Base Formula**

Use the Change of Base Formula to evaluate $\log_3 15$. Then convert $\log_3 15$ to a logarithm in base 2.

$$\log_3 15 = \frac{\log 15}{\log 3} \qquad \text{Use the Change of Base Formula.}$$

$$\approx 2.4650 \qquad \text{Use a calculator.}$$

$$\log_3 15 = \log_2 x \qquad \text{Write an equation.}$$

$$2.4650 \approx \log_2 x \qquad \text{Substitute } \log_3 15 \approx 2.4650.$$

$$x \approx 2^{2.4650} \qquad \text{Write in exponential form.}$$

$$\approx 5.5212 \qquad \text{Use a calculator.}$$

● The expression $\log_3 15$ is approximately equal to 2.4650, or $\log_2 5.5212$.

✓ Quick Check **5 a.** Evaluate $\log_5 400$ and convert it to a logarithm in base 8.
   b. Critical Thinking Consider the equation $2.465 \approx \log_2 x$ from Example 2. How could you solve the equation without using the Change of Base Formula?

An equation that includes a logarithmic expression, such as $\log_3 15 = \log_2 x$ in Example 5, is called a **logarithmic equation.**

6 **EXAMPLE** **Solving a Logarithmic Equation**

Solve $\log (3x + 1) = 5$.

Method 1 $\log (3x + 1) = 5$

$$3x + 1 = 10^5 \qquad \text{Write in exponential form.}$$

$$3x + 1 = 100{,}000$$

$$x = 33{,}333 \qquad \text{Solve for } x.$$

Method 2 Graph the equations $y_1 = \log (3x + 1)$ and $y_2 = 5$. Use Xmin = 30000, Xmax = 40000, Ymin = 4.9, Ymax = 5.1.

Find the point of intersection.

The solution is $x = 33{,}333$.

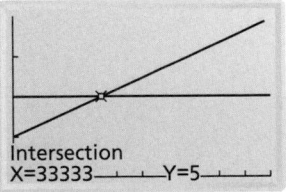

Method 3 Enter $y_1 = \log (3x + 1) - 5$. Use tabular zoom-in to find the sign change. Use the information from Methods 1 or 2 to help you with your TblSet values.

The solution is $x = 33{,}333$.

X	Y1
33330	−4E−5
33331	−3E−5
33332	−1E−5
33333	0.0000
33334	1.3E−5
33335	2.6E−5
33336	3.9E−5
Y1=0	

Check $\log (3x + 1) = 5$

$$\log (3 \cdot 33{,}333 + 1) \stackrel{?}{=} 5$$

$$\log 100{,}000 \stackrel{?}{=} 5$$

$$\log 10^5 = 5 \checkmark$$

✓ Quick Check **6** Solve $\log (7 - 2x) = -1$. Check your answer.

Sometimes the properties of logarithms will help solve an equation.

7 EXAMPLE Using Logarithmic Properties to Solve an Equation

Solve $2 \log x - \log 3 = 2$.

$2 \log x - \log 3 = 2$

$\log \left(\frac{x^2}{3}\right) = 2$ Write as a single logarithm.

$\frac{x^2}{3} = 10^2$ Write in exponential form.

$x^2 = 3(100)$ Multiply each side by 3.

$x = \pm 10\sqrt{3}$, or about ± 17.32

● Log x is defined only for $x > 0$, so the solution is $10\sqrt{3}$, or about 17.32.

✓ **Quick Check** ⑦ Solve $\log 6 - \log 3x = -2$.

EXERCISES

For more exercises, see *Extra Skill and Word Problem Practice.*

Practice and Problem Solving

A Practice by Example

Example 1
(page 461)

GO for Help

Solve each equation. Round to the nearest ten-thousandth. Check your answers.

1. $2^x = 3$ **2.** $4^x = 19$ **3.** $5^x = 81.2$ **4.** $3^x = 27.3$

5. $8 + 10^x = 1008$ **6.** $5 - 3^x = -40$ **7.** $9^{2y} = 66$ **8.** $4^{2z} = 40$

9. $14^{x+1} = 36$ **10.** $12^{y-2} = 20$ **11.** $25^{2x+1} = 144$ **12.** $2^{3x-4} = 5$

Example 2
(page 461)

Solve by graphing. Round to the nearest ten-thousandth.

13. $4^{7x} = 250$ **14.** $5^{3x} = 500$ **15.** $6^x = 4565$ **16.** $1.5^x = 356$

Example 3
(page 462)

Use a table to solve each equation. Round to the nearest hundredth.

17. $2^{x+3} = 512$ **18.** $3^{x-1} = 72$ **19.** $6^{2x} = 10$

20. $3^{x-2} = 12x - 1$ **21.** $4^{2x+1} = x^2$ **22.** $2^{2x-1} = 3^x$

Example 4
(page 462)

23. An investment of $2000 earns 5.75% interest, which is compounded quarterly. After approximately how many years will the investment be worth $3000?

24. The equation $y = 281(1.0124)^x$ models the U.S. population y, in millions of people, x years after the year 2000. Graph the function on your graphing calculator. Estimate when the U.S. population will reach 350 million.

Example 5
(page 463)

Use the Change of Base Formula to evaluate each expression. Then convert it to a logarithm in base 8.

25. $\log_2 9$ **26.** $\log_4 8$ **27.** $\log_3 54$ **28.** $\log_5 62$

29. $\log_3 33$ **30.** $\log_2 7$ **31.** $\log_5 510$ **32.** $\log_4 1.116$

Example 6
(page 463)

Solve each equation. Check your answers.

33. $\log 2x = -1$ **34.** $2 \log x = -1$ **35.** $\log (3x + 1) = 2$

36. $\log x + 4 = 8$ **37.** $\log 6x - 3 = -4$ **38.** $\log (x - 2) = 1$

39. $3 \log x = 1.5$ **40.** $2 \log (x + 1) = 5$ **41.** $\log (5 - 2x) = 0$

Example 7
(page 464)

Solve each equation.

42. $\log x - \log 3 = 8$ **43.** $\log 2x + \log x = 11$

44. $2 \log x + \log 4 = 2$ **45.** $\log 5 - \log 2x = 1$

46. $3 \log x - \log 6 + \log 2.4 = 9$ **47.** $\log (7x + 1) = \log (x - 2) + 1$

 **Apply Your Skills**

48. Consider the equation $2^{\frac{x}{3}} = 80$.
   a. Solve the equation by taking the logarithm in base 10 of each side.
   b. Solve the equation by taking the logarithm in base 2 of each side.
   c. Writing Compare your result in parts (a) and (b). What are the advantages of either method? Explain.

49. Seismology An earthquake of magnitude 7.9 occurred in 2001 in Gujarat, India. It was 11,600 times as strong as the greatest earthquake ever to hit Pennsylvania. Find the magnitude of the Pennsylvania earthquake. (*Hint*: Refer to the Richter Scale on page 446.)

Write an equation. Then solve the equation without graphing.

50. A parent raises a child's allowance by 20% each year. If the allowance is $8 now, when will it reach $20?

51. Protactinium-234m, a toxic radioactive metal with no known use, has a half-life of 1.17 minutes. How long does it take for a 10-mg sample to decay to 2 mg?

52. Multiple Choice As a town gets smaller, the population of its high school decreases by 12% each year. The student body has 125 students now. In how many years will it have about 75 students?
   (A) 4 years   (B) 7 years   (C) 10 years   (D) 11 years

Mental Math Solve each equation.

53. $2^x = \frac{1}{2}$ **54.** $3^x = 27$ **55.** $\log_9 3 = x$ **56.** $\log_4 64 = x$

57. $\log_8 2 = x$ **58.** $10^x = \frac{1}{100}$ **59.** $\log_7 343 = x$ **60.** $25^x = \frac{1}{5}$

Population Use this "Most Populous States" table for Exercises 61–63.

Most Populous States

Rank in 2000	State	2000 Population	Average Annual Percentage Increase Since 1990
1	California	33,871,648	1.30%
2	Texas	20,851,820	2.08%
3	New York	18,976,457	0.54%
4	Florida	15,982,378	2.13%

SOURCE: U.S. Census Bureau. Go to **www.PHSchool.com** for a data update. Web Code: agg-9041

61. a. Determine the growth factors for Florida and New York. Then write an equation to model each state's population growth.
   b. Estimate when Florida's population might exceed New York's population.

62. a. Determine the growth factors for Texas and California. Then write an equation to model each state's population growth.
   b. Estimate when Texas's population might exceed California's population.

63. Critical Thinking Is it likely that Florida's population will exceed that of Texas? Explain your reasoning.

Real-World Connection

Careers Seismologists use models to determine the source, nature, and size of seismic events.

64. Error Analysis What is wrong with the "proof" below that $2 = 1$?

$$2 = \frac{2}{1} = \frac{\log 10^2}{\log 10^1} = \log 10^{2-1} = \log 10^1 = 1$$

65. Open-Ended Write and solve a logarithmic equation.

66. Zoology Conservation efforts have increased the endangered Florida manatee population from 1465 in 1991 to 3276 in 2001. If this growth rate continues, when might there be 10,000 manatees? Explain the reasoning behind your choice of a model.

67. Consider the equation $a^x = b$.
  a. Solve the equation by using log base 10.
  b. Solve the equation by using log base a.
  c. Use your results in parts (a) and (b) to justify the Change of Base Formula.

Write each logarithm as the quotient of two common logarithms. Do not simplify the quotient.

68. $\log_7 2$ **69.** $\log_3 8$ **70.** $\log_5 140$ **71.** $\log_9 3.3$

72. $\log_4 3x$ **73.** $\log_6 (1 - x)$ **74.** $\log_x 5$ **75.** $\log_x (x + 1)$

Real-World 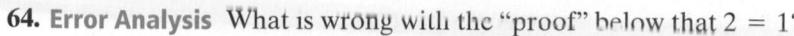 **Connection**

Many Florida manatees die after collisions with motorboats.

Acoustics In Exercises 76–78, the loudness measured in decibels (dB) is defined by loudness $= 10 \log \frac{I}{I_0}$, where I is the intensity and $I_0 = 10^{-12}$ W/m^2.

76. The human threshold for pain is 120 dB. Instant perforation of the eardrum occurs at 160 dB.
  a. Find the intensity of each sound.
  b. How many times as intense is the noise that will perforate an eardrum as the noise that causes pain?

77. The noise level inside a convertible driving along the freeway with its top up is 70 dB. With the top down, the noise level is 95 dB.
  a. Find the intensity of the sound with the top up and with the top down.
  b. By what percent does leaving the top up reduce the intensity of the sound?

78. A screaming child can reach 90 dB. A launch of the space shuttle produces sound of 180 dB at the launch pad.
  a. Find the intensity of each sound.
  b. How many times as intense as the noise from a screaming child is the noise from a shuttle launch?

Solve each equation. If necessary, round to the nearest ten-thousandth.

79. $8^x = 444$ **80.** $14^{9x} = 146$

81. $3^{7x} = 120$ **82.** $\frac{1}{2} \log x + \log 4 = 2$

83. $4 \log_3 2 - 2 \log_3 x = 1$ **84.** $\log x^2 = 2$

85. $9^{2x} = 42$ **86.** $\log_8 (2x - 1) = \frac{1}{3}$

87. $1.3^x = 7$ **88.** $\log (5x - 4) = 3$

89. $2.1^x = 9$ **90.** $12^{4-x} = 20$

91. $5^{3x} = 125$ **92.** $\log 4 + 2 \log x = 6$

Homework Video Tutor

93. $4^{3x} = 77.2$ **94.** $\log_7 3x = 3$

Visit: PHSchool.com
Web Code: age-0805

95. $3^x + 0.7 = 4.9$ **96.** $7^x - 1 = 371$

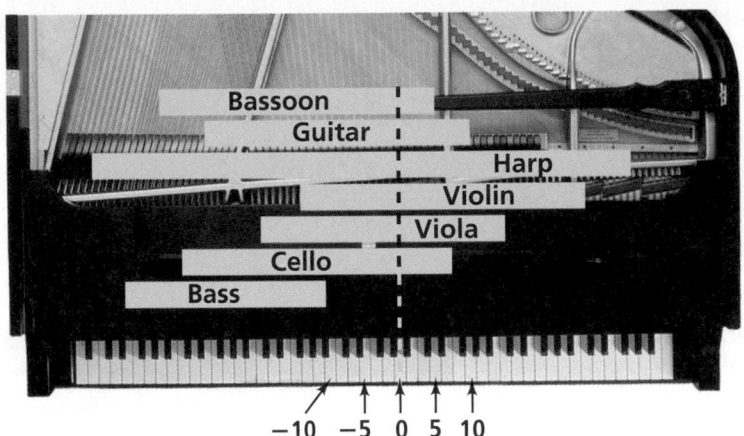

Bassoon
Guitar
Harp
Violin
Viola
Cello
Bass

−10 −5 0 5 10

C **Challenge** **97. Music** The pitch, or frequency, of a piano note is related to its position on the keyboard by the function $F(n) = 440 \cdot 2^{\frac{n}{12}}$, where F is the frequency of the sound wave in cycles per second and n is the number of piano keys above or below Concert A, as shown above. If $n = 0$ at Concert A, which of the instruments shown in the diagram can sound notes of the given frequency?

   a. 590   **b.** 120   **c.** 1440   **d.** 2093

98. Astronomy The brightness of an astronomical object is called its magnitude. A decrease of five magnitudes increases the brightness exactly 100 times. The sun is magnitude −26.7, and the full moon is magnitude −12.5. The sun is about how many times brighter than the moon?

99. Archaeology A scientist carbon-dates a piece of fossilized tree trunk that is thought to be over 5000 years old. The scientist determines that the sample contains 65% of the original amount of carbon-14. The half-life of carbon-14 is 5730 years. Is the reputed age of the tree correct? Explain.

Solve each equation.

100. $\log_7 (2x - 3)^2 = 2$ **101.** $\log_2 (x^2 + 2x) = 3$

102. $\log_4 (x^2 - 17) = 3$ **103.** $\frac{3}{2} \log_2 4 - \frac{1}{2} \log_2 x = 3$

104. In the formula $P = P_0(\frac{1}{2})^{\frac{h}{4795}}$, P is the atmospheric pressure in millimeters of mercury at elevation h meters above sea level. P_0 is the atmospheric pressure at sea level. If P_0 equals 760 mm, at what elevation is the pressure 42 mm?

105. Chemistry A technician found 12 mg of a radon isotope in a soil sample. After 24 hours, another measurement revealed 10 mg of the isotope.
   a. Estimate the length of the isotope's half-life to the nearest hour and to the nearest day.
   b. For each estimate, determine the amount of the isotope after two weeks.
   c. Compare your answers to part (b). Which is more accurate? Explain.

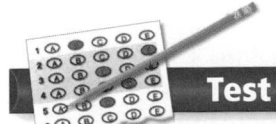

Test Prep

Gridded Response   Use a calculator to solve each equation. Enter each answer to the nearest hundredth.

   106. $7^{2x} = 75$ **107.** $11^{x-5} = 250$ **108.** $1080 = 15^{3x-4}$

Use the Change of Base Formula to solve each equation. Enter the answer to the nearest tenth.

109. $\log_5 x = \log_3 20$

110. $\log_9 x = \log_6 15$

Solve each equation.

111. $\log(1 + 3x) = 3$

112. $\log(x - 3) = 2$

Mixed Review

Lesson 8-4

Expand each logarithm.

113. $\log 2x^3 y^{-2}$

114. $\log_3 \frac{x}{y}$

115. $\log_2 (3x)^3$

116. $\log_3 7(2x - 3)^2$

117. $\log_4 5\sqrt{x}$

118. $\log_2 \left(\frac{5a}{b^2}\right)$

Lesson 7-6

Let $f(x) = 3x$ and $g(x) = x^2 - 1$. Perform each function operation.

119. $(f + g)(x)$

120. $(g - f)(x)$

121. $(f \cdot g)(x)$

Lesson 6-6

Find all the zeros of each function.

122. $y = x^3 - x^2 + x - 1$

123. $f(x) = x^4 - 16$

124. $f(x) = x^4 - 5x^2 + 6$

125. $y = 3x^3 - 21x - 18$

Lesson 1-3

Write an equation to solve each problem.

126. A customer at a hardware store mentions that he is buying fencing for a vegetable garden that is 12 ft longer than it is wide. He buys 128 ft of fencing. What is the width of the garden?

127. A bowler has an average of 133. In a set of games one night, her scores are 135, 127, 119, 142, and 156. What score must she bowl in the sixth game to maintain her average?

✓ Checkpoint Quiz 2   Lessons 8-3 through 8-5

Graph each logarithmic function.

1. $y = \log_6 x$

2. $y = \log(x - 2)$

Expand each logarithm.

3. $\log \frac{s^3}{r^5}$

4. $\log_6 (3xy)^2$

5. $\log_6 4\sqrt{x}$

Solve each equation.

6. $7 - 2^x = -1$

7. $\log 5x = 2$

8. $3 \log x = 9$

9. Evaluate the expressions below and order them from least to greatest.

2^3 $\log_2 3$ $\log_3 2$ 3^2 $\log 2$

 10. Writing Explain how to use the Change of Base Formula to rewrite $\log_2 10$ as a logarithmic expression with base 3.

Linear and Exponential Models

Technology

FOR USE WITH LESSON 8-5

Go Online
PHSchool.com
For: Graphing calculator procedures
Web Code: age-2117

You can transform an exponential function into a linear function by taking the logarithm of each side. Since linear models are easy to recognize, you can then determine whether an exponential function is a good model for a set of values.

$y = ab^x$	**Write the general form of an exponential function.**
$\log y = \log ab^x$	**Take the logarithm of each side.**
$\log y = \log a + x(\log b)$	**Product Property and Power Property**
$\log y = (\log b)x + \log a$	**Rewrite.**

If $\log b$ and $\log a$ are constants, then $\log y = (\log b)x + \log a$ is a linear equation in slope-intercept form. To confirm that $\log b$ is a constant, check that the graph of $\log y = (\log b)x + \log a$ is a line.

ACTIVITY

Determine whether an exponential function is a good model for the values in the table.

x	0	2	4	6	8	10
y	3.0	5.1	8.6	14.5	24.5	41.4

Step 1 Enter the values into ▮STAT▮ lists **L₁** and **L₂**. To enter the values of log *y*, place the cursor in the heading of **L₃** and press ▮LOG▮ **L₂** ▮ENTER▮.

Step 2 To graph log *y*, access the **STAT PLOT** feature and press 1. Then enter **L₃** next to Ylist:. Then press ▮ZOOM▮ 9.

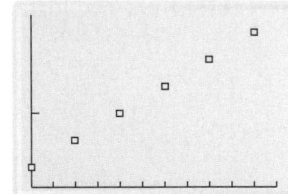

L1	L2	L3	1
0	3	0.47712	
2	5.1	0.70757	
4	8.6	0.9345	
6	14.5	1.1614	
8	24.5	1.3892	
10	41.4	1.617	

L1(1) = 0

Since the graph of $\log y = (\log b)x + \log a$ is linear, the slope log *b* is constant, and *b* also is constant. An exponential function therefore is a suitable model.

Step 3 Press ▮STAT▮ ▮▶▮ 0 ▮ENTER▮ to find the exponential function: $y = 3(1.3)^x$.

EXERCISES

For each set of values, determine whether an exponential function is a good model. If so, find the function.

1.

x	1	3	5	7	9
y	6	22	54	102	145

2.

x	−1	0	1	2	3
y	40.2	19.8	9.9	5.1	2.5

3. Writing Explain how you could determine whether a logarithmic function is a good model for a set of values.

Natural Logarithms

What You'll Learn

- To evaluate natural logarithmic expressions
- To solve equations using natural logarithms

. . . And Why

To model the velocity of a rocket, as in Example 2

Use your calculator to evaluate each expression to the nearest thousandth.

1. e^5 **2.** $2e^3$ **3.** e^{-2} **4.** $\frac{1}{e}$ **5.** $4.2e$

Solve.

6. $\log_3 x = 4$ **7.** $\log_{16} 4 = x$ **8.** $\log_{16} x = 4$

🔊 **New Vocabulary** • natural logarithmic function

---

 1   **Natural Logarithms**

In Lesson 8-2, you learned that the number $e \approx 2.71828$ can be used as a base for exponents. The function $y = e^x$ has an inverse, the **natural logarithmic function.**

🔑 **Key Concepts**

Definition	Natural Logarithmic Function

If $y = e^x$, then $\log_e y = x$, which is commonly written as $\ln y = x$.

The natural logarithmic function is the inverse, written as $y = \ln x$.

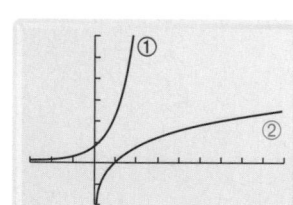

① $y = e^x$

② $y = \ln x$

Vocabulary Tip

In y means "the natural logarithm of y." The *l* stands for "logarithm" and the *n* stands for "natural."

The properties of common logarithms apply to natural logarithms also.

1 EXAMPLE   **Simplifying Natural Logarithms**

Write $3 \ln 6 - \ln 8$ as a single natural logarithm.

$3 \ln 6 - \ln 8 = \ln 6^3 - \ln 8$ **Power Property**

$\qquad\qquad\quad = \ln \frac{6^3}{8}$ **Quotient Property**

$\qquad\qquad\quad = \ln 27$ **Simplify.**

✓ **Quick Check** ❶ Write each expression as a single natural logarithm.

a. $5 \ln 2 - \ln 4$ **b.** $3 \ln x + \ln y$ **c.** $\frac{1}{4} \ln 3 + \frac{1}{4} \ln x$

Natural logarithms are useful because they help express many relationships in the physical world.

2 EXAMPLE Real-World Connection

Space A spacecraft can attain a stable orbit 300 km above Earth if it reaches a velocity of 7.7 km/s. The formula for a rocket's maximum velocity v in kilometers per second is $v = -0.0098t + c \ln R$. The booster rocket fires for t seconds and the velocity of the exhaust is c km/s. The ratio of the mass of the rocket filled with fuel to its mass without fuel is R. Suppose a rocket used to propel a spacecraft has a mass ratio of 25, an exhaust velocity of 2.8 km/s, and a firing time of 100 s. Can the spacecraft attain a stable orbit 300 km above Earth?

Let $R = 25, c = 2.8$, and $t = 100$. Find v.

$\begin{array}{ll} v = -0.0098t + c \ln R & \text{Use the formula.} \\ \quad = -0.0098(100) + 2.8 \ln 25 & \text{Substitute.} \\ \quad \approx -0.98 + 2.8(3.219) & \text{Use a calculator.} \\ \quad \approx 8.0 & \text{Simplify.} \end{array}$

The maximum velocity of 8.0 km/s is greater than the 7.7 km/s needed for a stable orbit. Therefore, the spacecraft can attain a stable orbit 300 km above Earth.

Real-World Connection

The space shuttle is launched into orbit.

 **Quick Check** **2 a.** A booster rocket for a spacecraft has a mass ratio of about 15, an exhaust velocity of 2.1 km/s, and a firing time of 30 s. Find the maximum velocity of the spacecraft. Can the spacecraft achieve a stable orbit 300 km above Earth?
  b. Critical Thinking Suppose a rocket, as designed, cannot provide enough velocity to achieve a stable orbit. Look at the variables in the velocity formula. What alterations could be made to the rocket so that a stable orbit could be achieved?

2 Natural Logarithmic and Exponential Equations

You can use the properties of logarithms to solve natural logarithmic equations.

3 EXAMPLE Solving a Natural Logarithmic Equation

Solve $\ln (3x + 5)^2 = 4$.

$\begin{array}{ll} \ln (3x + 5)^2 = 4 & \\ \quad (3x + 5)^2 = e^4 & \text{Rewrite in exponential form.} \\ \quad (3x + 5)^2 \approx 54.60 & \text{Use a calculator.} \\ \quad 3x + 5 \approx \pm \sqrt{54.60} & \text{Take the square root of each side.} \\ \quad 3x + 5 \approx 7.39 \text{ or } -7.39 & \text{Use a calculator.} \\ \quad \quad \quad x \approx 0.797 \text{ or } -4.130 & \text{Solve for } x. \end{array}$

Check $\ln (3 \cdot 0.797 + 5)^2 \overset{?}{=} 4 \qquad \ln (3 \cdot (-4.130) + 5)^2 \overset{?}{=} 4$

$\qquad\qquad \ln 54.6 \overset{?}{=} 4 \qquad\qquad\qquad\qquad \ln 54.6 \overset{?}{=} 4$

$\qquad\qquad 4.000 \approx 4 \checkmark \qquad\qquad\qquad\qquad 4.000 \approx 4 \checkmark$

 **Quick Check** **3** Solve each equation. Check your answers.
  a. $\ln x = 0.1$ **b.** $\ln (3x - 9) = 21$ **c.** $\ln \left(\frac{x + 2}{3}\right) = 12$

You can use natural logarithms to solve exponential equations.

4 EXAMPLE Solving an Exponential Equation

Use natural logarithms to solve $7e^{2x} + 2.5 = 20$.

$$7e^{2x} + 2.5 = 20$$

$7e^{2x} = 17.5$	Subtract 2.5 from each side.
$e^{2x} = 2.5$	Divide each side by 7.
$\ln e^{2x} = \ln 2.5$	Take the natural logarithm of each side.
$2x = \ln 2.5$	Simplify.
$x = \frac{\ln 2.5}{2}$	Solve for x.
$x \approx 0.458$	Use a calculator.

 **Quick Check** ④ Use natural logarithms to solve each equation.

a. $e^{x+1} = 30$ **b.** $e^{\frac{2x}{5}} + 7.2 = 9.1$

5 EXAMPLE Real-World  Connection

Multiple Choice An investment of $100 is now valued at $149.18. The interest rate is 8%, compounded continuously. About how long has the money been invested?

Ⓐ 2 years   Ⓑ 5 years   Ⓒ 7 years   Ⓓ 19 years

$A = Pe^{rt}$	Continuously compounded interest formula
$149.18 = 100e^{0.08t}$	Substitute 149.18 for A, 100 for P, and 0.08 for r.
$1.4918 = e^{0.08t}$	Divide each side by 100.
$\ln 1.4918 = \ln e^{0.08t}$	Take the natural logarithm of each side.
$\ln 1.4918 = 0.08t$	Simplify.
$\frac{\ln 1.4918}{0.08} = t$	Solve for t.
$5 \approx t$	Use a calculator.

The money has been invested for about five years. The answer is B.

Test-Taking Tip

If you perform an operation on one side of an equation, remember to perform the same operation on the other side.

 **Quick Check** ⑤ An initial investment of $200 is worth $315.24 after seven years of continuous compounding. Find the interest rate.

EXERCISES

For more exercises, see *Extra Skill and Word Problem Practice*.

Practice and Problem Solving

Ⓐ **Practice by Example**

Example 1
(page 470)

GO for Help

Write each expression as a single natural logarithm.

1. $3 \ln 5$ **2.** $\ln 9 + \ln 2$ **3.** $\ln 24 - \ln 6$

4. $4 \ln 8 + \ln 10$ **5.** $\ln 3 - 5 \ln 3$ **6.** $2 \ln 8 - 3 \ln 4$

7. $5 \ln m - 3 \ln n$ **8.** $\frac{1}{3}(\ln x + \ln y) - 4 \ln z$ **9.** $\ln a - 2 \ln b + \frac{1}{2} \ln c$

Example 2
(page 471)

Find the value of y for the given value of x.

10. $y = 15 + 3 \ln x$, for $x = 7.2$ **11.** $y = 0.05 - 10 \ln x$, for $x = 0.09$

For Exercises 12 and 13, use $v = -0.0098t + c \ln R$.

12. **Space** Find the velocity of a spacecraft whose booster rocket has a mass ratio of 20, an exhaust velocity of 2.7 km/s, and a firing time of 30 s. Can the spacecraft achieve a stable orbit 300 km above Earth?

13. A rocket has a mass ratio of 24 and an exhaust velocity of 2.5 km/s. Determine the minimum firing time for a stable orbit 300 km above Earth.

Example 3
(page 471)

Solve each equation. Check your answers.

14. $\ln 3x = 6$ 15. $\ln x = -2$ 16. $\ln (4x - 1) = 36$

17. $\ln (2m + 3) = 8$ 18. $\ln (t - 1)^2 = 3$ 19. $1.1 + \ln x^2 = 6$

20. $\ln \frac{x - 1}{2} = 4$ 21. $\ln 4r^2 = 3$ 22. $2 \ln 2x^2 = 1$

Example 4
(page 472)

Use natural logarithms to solve each equation.

23. $e^x = 18$ 24. $e^{2x} = 10$ 25. $e^{x + 1} = 30$

26. $e^{\frac{x}{5}} + 4 = 7$ 27. $e^{2x} = 12$ 28. $e^{\frac{x}{9}} - 8 = 6$

Example 5
(page 472)

29. **Investing** An initial deposit of $200 is now worth $331.07. The account earns 8.4% interest, compounded continuously. Determine how long the money has been in the account.

30. An investor sold 100 shares of stock valued at $34.50 per share. The stock was purchased at $7.25 per share two years ago. Find the rate of continuously compounded interest that would be necessary in a banking account for the investor to make the same profit.

 Apply Your Skills

Mental Math Simplify each expression.

31. $\ln e$ 32. $\ln e^2$ 33. $\ln e^{10}$ 34. $10 \ln e$

35. $\ln 1$ 36. $\frac{\ln e}{4}$ 37. $\frac{\ln e^2}{2}$ 38. $\ln e^{83}$

For Gridded Responses, see Test-Taking Strategies, page 46.

39. **Gridded Response** The battery power available to run a satellite is given by the formula $P = 50 e^{-\frac{t}{250}}$, where P is power in watts and t is time in days. For how many days can the satellite run if it requires 15 watts?

 40. **Space** Use the formula for maximum velocity $v = -0.0098t + c \ln R$. Find the mass ratio of a rocket with an exhaust velocity of 3.1 km/s, a firing time of 50 s, and a maximum shuttle velocity of 6.9 km/s.

Determine whether each statement is *always* true, *sometimes* true, or *never* true.

41. $\ln e^x > 1$ 42. $\ln e^x = \ln e^x + 1$ 43. $\ln t = \log_e t$

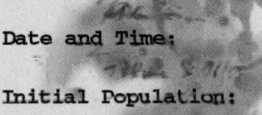

Antibiotic:

Date and Time:

Initial Population:

End Population:
 9200
Time Elapsed:
 21 hours
Rate of Decline:
 0.07

Biology For Exercises 44–46, use the formula $H = \left(\frac{1}{r}\right)(\ln P - \ln A)$. H is the number of hours, r is the rate of decline, P is the initial bacteria population, and A is the reduced bacteria population.

44. A scientist determines that an antibiotic reduces a population of 20,000 bacteria to 5000 in 24 hours. Find the rate of decline caused by the antibiotic.

45. A laboratory assistant tests an antibiotic that causes a rate of decline of 0.14. How long should it take for a population of 8000 bacteria to shrink to 500?

46. A scientist spilled coffee on the lab report shown at the left. Determine the initial population of the bacteria.

 **Savings** Suppose you invest $500 at 5% interest compounded continuously. Copy and complete the table to find how long it will take to reach each amount.

GO Online

Homework Video Tutor

Visit: PHSchool.com
Web Code: age-0808

	Amount (A)	Time (years)
47.	$600	■
48.	$700	■
49.	$800	■
50.	$900	■
51.	$1000	■
52.	$1100	■
53.	$1200	■
54.	$1300	■

Solve each equation.

55. $\ln x - 3 \ln 3 = 3$ **56.** $\ln (2x - 1) = 0$ **57.** $4e^{x+2} = 32$

58. $\ln (5x - 3)^{\frac{1}{3}} = 2$ **59.** $2e^{3x-2} + 4 = 16$ **60.** $2e^{x-2} = e^x + 7$

61. $\frac{1}{3} \ln x + \ln 2 - \ln 3 = 3$ **62.** $\ln (x + 2) - \ln 4 = 3$

C Challenge

63. Critical Thinking Can $\ln 5 + \log_2 10$ be written as a single logarithm? Explain.

64. In 2000, there were about 300 million Internet users. That number is projected to grow to 1 billion in 2005.
 a. Let t represent the time, in years, since 2000. Write a function of the form $y = ae^{ct}$ that models the expected growth in the population of Internet users.
 b. In what year might there be 500 million Internet users?
 c. In what year might there be 1.5 billion Internet users?
 d. Solve your equation for t.
 e. Writing Explain how you can use your equation from part (d) to verify your answers to parts (b) and (c).

 **65. Physics** The function $T(t) = T_r + (T_i - T_r)e^{kt}$ models Newton's Law of Cooling. $T(t)$ is the temperature of a heated substance t minutes after it has been removed from a heat (or cooling) source. T_i is the substance's initial temperature, k is a constant for that substance, and T_r is room temperature.
 a. The initial surface temperature of a beef roast is 236°F and room temperature is 72°F. If $k = -0.041$, how long will it take for this roast to cool to 100°F?
  b. Write and graph an equation that you can use to check your answer to part (a). Use your graph to complete the table below.

Temperature (°F)	225	200	175	150	125	100	75
Minutes Later	■	■	■	■	■	■	■

66. Open-Ended Write a real-world problem that you can answer using Newton's Law of Cooling. Then answer it.

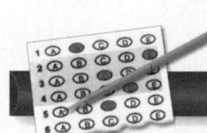 **Test Prep**

Multiple Choice

67. Which expression is equal to $3 \ln 4 - 5 \ln 2$?
 A. $\ln (-18)$ **B.** $\ln \left(\frac{6}{5}\right)$ **C.** $\ln 2$ **D.** $\ln 32$

68. What is the value of x if $17e^{4x} = 85$?

F. $\frac{5}{4}$ G. $\frac{\ln 85}{17 \cdot \ln 4}$ H. $\frac{\ln 5}{4}$ J. $\frac{\ln 85 - \ln 17}{\ln 4}$

69. An investment of $750 will be worth $1500 after 12 years of continuous compounding at a fixed interest rate. What is that interest rate?

A. 2.00% B. 5.78% C. 6.93% D. 200%

Extended Response **70.** The table shows the values of an investment after the given number of years of continuously compounded interest.

Years	0	1	2	3	4
Value	$500.00	$541.64	$586.76	$635.62	$688.56

a. What is the rate of interest?
b. Write an equation to model the growth of the investment.
c. To the nearest year, when will the investment be worth $1800?

Mixed Review

Lesson 8-5 **Solve each equation.**

71. $3^{2x} = 6561$ **72.** $7^x - 2 = 252$ **73.** $25^{2x+1} = 144$

74. $\log 3x = 4$ **75.** $\log 5x + 3 = 3.7$ **76.** $\log 9 - \log x + 1 = 6$

Lesson 7-7 **Find the inverse of each function. Is the inverse a function?**

77. $y = 5x + 7$ **78.** $y = 2x^3 + 10$ **79.** $y = -x^2 + 5$

Lesson 6-7 **80.** The Nut Shop carries 30 different types of nuts. The shop special is the Triple Play, a made-to-order mixture of any three different types of nuts. How many different Triple Plays are possible?

········ **A Point in Time**

1500   1600   1700   1800   1900   2000

The first manned moon landing on July 20, 1969, gave scientists a unique opportunity to test their theories about the moon's geologic history.

A logarithmic function was used to date lunar rocks. Radioactive rubidium-87 decays into stable strontium-87 at a fixed rate. The ratio r of the two isotopes in a sample can be measured and used in the equation $T = -h\frac{\ln(r+1)}{\ln 0.5}$, where T is the age in years and h is the half-life of rubidium-87, 4.7×10^{10} years. For the lunar sample, r was measured at 0.0588, giving an approximate age of 3.87 billion years.

 **For:** Information about space exploration
PHSchool.com **Web Code:** age-2032

Activity Lab

Technology

Exponential and Logarithmic Inequalities

FOR USE WITH LESSON 8-6

You can solve problems using exponential equations and inequalities.

1 ACTIVITY

Legend tells of a Roman general who was so successful in his campaigns that the emperor offered the general his choice of reward. The general asked the emperor for all the silver that he could carry out of the imperial treasury in one month. The emperor agreed, but offered a condition.

On the first day, the general would receive 1 silver denarius. On the second day, he would receive a coin valued at 2 denarii. Each day, the general was to come to the treasury and the treasurer would mint a special coin that would be twice as heavy and worth twice as much as the coin the general got a day earlier.

1. a. What function $V(x)$ gives the value of the coin that the general received on day x?
   b. What is the domain of this function?

One denarius coin weighed about 0.006 kg.

2. Write a function $M(x)$ that gives the mass of each coin in kilograms as a function of day x.

The largest object the general could carry or roll without help could weigh no more than 300 kg.

3. a. Use $M(x)$ from Exercise 2 to write an inequality that describes the mass of a coin that the general could carry or roll out of the treasury.
   b. Make a table of values of this function.
   c. Use the table to solve the inequality.

4. What is the total value of the coins that the general would receive?

2 ACTIVITY

Scientists are growing bacteria in a laboratory. They start with a known population of bacteria and measure how long it takes this population to double.

5. Sample A starts with 200,000 bacteria. The population doubles every hour. Write an exponential function that models the population in Sample A as a function of time in hours.

6. Sample B starts with 50,000 bacteria. The population doubles every half hour. Write an exponential function that models the population growth in Sample B as a function of time in hours.

7. a. Write an inequality that models the population in Sample B overtaking the population in Sample A.
   b. Use a graphing calculator to solve the inequality.

You can also use logarithmic equations and inequalities to solve problems.

3 ACTIVITY

Average barometric pressure varies with the altitude of a location. The greater the altitude is, the lower the pressure. The altitude A is measured in feet above sea level. The barometric pressure P is measured in inches of mercury (in. Hg). The altitude can be modeled by the function $A(P) = 90{,}000 - 26{,}500 \ln P$.

8. What is the reasonable domain of the function? What is the range of the function?

9. Use a graphing calculator to make a table of function values. Use TblStart = 30 and ΔTbl = −1.

10. Write an equation to find what average pressure the model predicts at sea level, or $A = 0$. Use your table to solve the equation.

11. Kilimanjaro is a mountain in Tanzania that formed from three extinct volcanoes. The base of the mountain is at 3000 ft above sea level. The peak is at 19,340 ft above sea level. On Kilimanjaro, $3000 \le A(P) \le 19{,}340$ is true for the altitude. Write an inequality from which you can find minimum and maximum values of normal barometric pressure on Kilimanjaro. Use a table and solve the inequality for P.

12. Denver, Colorado, is nicknamed the "Mile High City" because its elevation is about 1 mile, or 5280 ft, above sea level. The lowest point in Phoenix, Arizona, is 1070 ft above sea level. Write an inequality that describes the range of $A(P)$ as you drive from Phoenix to Denver. Then solve the inequality for P.

4 ACTIVITY

Carbon-14 is a radioisotope that is produced when cosmic radiation penetrates Earth's atmosphere. Plants absorb carbon-14 with carbon dioxide from the air. Animals ingest carbon-14 when they eat plants.

The concentration of carbon-14 in a living organism is the same as its concentration in the atmosphere. When an organism dies, it stops replacing carbon-14. The remaining carbon-14 begins to decay. Scientists use the ratio of the concentration of the remaining carbon-14 to its original concentration to estimate the age of organic material. Let r represent this ratio.

13. The age of a fossil $g(r)$, in years, can be modeled as a function of r as $g(r) = -5730 \log_2 r$ or $g(r) = -8266.64 \ln r$. What is the domain of the function? What is the range of the function?

14. Graph the function.

15. Describe the behavior of the function as r becomes very small.

16. A paleontologist found an animal bone fossil and measured r to be 0.01. What is the approximate age of the bone to the nearest thousand years?

17. Write an inequality that models the carbon-14 ratio in fossils that are more than 50,000 years old. Then solve the inequality by graphing the corresponding function on your calculator. What does your solution mean?

Testing Multiple Choices

One advantage of multiple-choice tests is that the correct answer is among the choices. A frequently useful strategy is to test a choice in the original problem.

EXAMPLE

What number is the solution to $\left(\frac{1}{4}\right)^x = 8$?

A -2 B $-\frac{3}{2}$ C 0 D $\frac{1}{2}$ E 16

You can answer the question without solving the equation. Substitute each answer choice into the equation until you find the right one.

If $x = -2$, then $\left(\frac{1}{4}\right)^x = \left(\frac{1}{4}\right)^{-2} = 4^2 = 16$. Since $16 \neq 8$, answer A is wrong.

If $x = -\frac{3}{2}$, then $\left(\frac{1}{4}\right)^x = \left(\frac{1}{4}\right)^{-\frac{3}{2}} = 4^{\frac{3}{2}} = 8$. Since $8 = 8$, the correct answer is B.

You don't have to test the three other choices.

When answering a multiple-choice question that involves solving a difficult equation, you often can save time and effort by working backward from the answers to the question.

EXERCISES

1. Refer to the Example. Explain how you can eliminate choices C–E before trying A and B.

2. Algebraically solve the equation in the Example to show that B is the correct answer.

Answer each question by testing the choices. Then solve each equation algebraically.

3. What is the solution to $\log_x (3x + 2) = x + 1$?

A 0 B 1 C 2 D 6 E 10

4. What is the solution to $2^{x+1} + 2x + 1 = 0$?

A 2 B 1 C 0 D $-\frac{1}{2}$ E -1

5. What is the solution to $\ln \sqrt{x + 2} + \ln \sqrt{3x + 4} = \ln 15$?

A -1 B 0 C 1 D 3 E 7

6. What is the solution to $\log (\log (3x - 2)) = 0$?

A $\frac{2}{3}$ B 1 C 2 D 4 E 34

7. What is the solution to $\log_x \frac{1}{2} = \frac{1}{2}$?

A $\frac{1}{4}$ B $\frac{1}{2}$ C 0 D 1 E 2

8. Use the formula for continuously compounded interest, $A = Pe^{rt}$, to find the annual interest rate for an $8000 investment that earns $410.17 in one year.

A 7% B 6% C 5% D 4% E 3%

Chapter Review

Vocabulary Review

 asymptote (p. 433)
Change of Base Formula (p. 462)
common logarithm (p. 447)
continuously compounded interest
  formula (p. 441)

decay factor (p. 433)
exponential equation (p. 461)
exponential function (p. 430)
growth factor (p. 430)
logarithm (p. 447)

logarithmic equation (p. 463)
logarithmic function (p. 448)
natural logarithmic function (p. 470)

Go Online
PHSchool.com
For: Vocabulary quiz
Web Code: agj-0851

Choose the correct term to complete each sentence.

1. In the exponential function $y = ab^x$, when $b > 1$, b is the __?__.

2. A __?__ is a logarithm that uses base 10.

3. The line $x = 2$ is a(n) __?__ of the function $f(x) = \dfrac{2}{x - 2}$.

4. The Change of Base Formula can be used to evaluate a __?__ with any base.

5. An __?__ can be solved by taking the logarithm of each side of the equation.

Skills and Concepts

8-1 Objectives

▼ To model exponential
  growth (p. 430)

▼ To model exponential
  decay (p. 432)

The general form of an **exponential function** is $y = ab^x$, where x is a real number, $a \neq 0$, $b > 0$, and $b \neq 1$. When $b > 1$, the function models exponential growth, and b is the **growth factor**. When $0 < b < 1$, the function models exponential decay, and b is the **decay factor**.

Determine whether each equation represents exponential growth or exponential decay. Find the rate of increase or decrease for each model. Graph each equation.

6. $y = 5^x$ **7.** $y = 2(4)^x$ **8.** $y = 0.2(3.8)^x$ **9.** $y = 3(0.25)^x$

Write an exponential equation whose graph passes through the given points.

10. $(1, 5), (2, 7)$ **11.** $(3, 1.5), (4, 15)$ **12.** $\left(-1, 6\frac{3}{4}\right), \left(2, \frac{1}{4}\right)$ **13.** $(-2, 9), (0, 1)$

Write an exponential function to model each situation. Find the value of each function after five years, to the nearest dollar.

14. A $12,500 car depreciates 9% each year.

15. A baseball card bought for $50 increases 3% in value each year.

Write an exponential equation for each graph. Evaluate the equation for $x = 4$.

16.

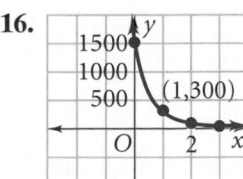

17.

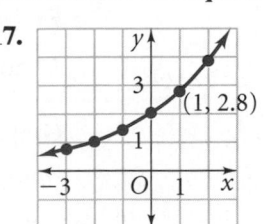

8-2 Objectives

▼ To identify the role of constants in $y = ab^{cx}$ (p. 439)

▼ To use e as a base (p. 441)

Exponential functions can be translated, stretched, shrunk, and reflected. The graph of $y = ab^{x-h} + k$ is the graph of $y = b^x$ stretched by a factor $|a|$, and translated $|h|$ units horizontally and $|k|$ units vertically.

The **continuously compounded interest** formula is $A = Pe^{rt}$, where P is the principal, r is the annual rate, and t is time in years.

Describe how the graph of each function relates to the graph of its parent function. Then graph each function.

18. $y = -3^x + 1$ **19.** $y = 8^x - 1$

20. $y = 2(2)^{x+1} + 3$ **21.** $y = -2\left(\frac{1}{3}\right)^{x-2}$

Find the amount in a continuously compounded account for the given conditions.

22. principal: $1000, annual interest rate: 4.8%, time: 2 yr

23. principal: $250, annual interest rate: 6.2%, time: 2.5 yr

24. principal: $500, annual interest rate: 8.5%, time: 3 yr

Evaluate to four decimal places.

25. e^1 **26.** e^{-1} **27.** e^5 **28.** $e^{-\frac{1}{2}}$

 29. Physics Radium has a half-life of 1620 years. Write the decay function for a 3-mg sample. Find the amount of radium remaining after 50 years.

8-3 Objectives

▼ To write and evaluate logarithmic expressions (p. 446)

▼ To graph logarithmic functions (p. 448)

If $y = b^x$, then $\log_b y = x$. The **logarithmic function** is the inverse of the exponential function, so the graphs of the functions are reflections of one another over the line $y = x$. Logarithmic functions can be translated, stretched, shrunk, and reflected.

When $b = 10$, the logarithm is called a **common logarithm**, which you can write as $\log y$.

 30. Chemistry The pH of a substance equals $-\log[\text{H}^+]$, where $[\text{H}^+]$ is the concentration of hydrogen ions. A sample of well water has a pH of 5.7. Find the concentration of hydrogen ions in the sample.

31. The concentration of hydrogen ions in water is 10^{-7}. Find the pH of water.

Write each equation in logarithmic form.

32. $6^2 = 36$ **33.** $2^{-3} = 0.125$

34. $3^3 = 27$ **35.** $10^{-3} = 0.001$

Evaluate each logarithm.

36. $\log_2 64$ **37.** $\log_3 \frac{1}{9}$ **38.** $\log 0.00001$ **39.** $\log_2 1$

Graph each logarithmic function.

40. $y = \log_3 x$ **41.** $y = \log(x + 2)$

42. $y = \log_2 2x$ **43.** $y = \log_5(x + 1)$

8-4 Objective

▼ To use the properties of logarithms (p. 454)

For any positive numbers, M, N, and b, $b \neq 1$, each of the following statements is true. Each can be used to rewrite a logarithmic expression.

- $\log_b MN = \log_b M + \log_b N$, by the Product Property
- $\log_b \frac{M}{N} = \log_b M - \log_b N$, by the Quotient Property
- $\log_b M^x = x \log_b M$, by the Power Property

Write each logarithmic expression as a single logarithm.

44. $\log 8 + \log 3$ **45.** $\log_2 5 - \log_2 3$

46. $4\log_3 x + \log_3 7$ **47.** $\log z - \log y$

Expand each logarithm. State the properties of logarithms that you use.

48. $\log_4 x^2 y^3$ **49.** $\log 4s^4 t$ **50.** $\log_3 \frac{2}{x}$ **51.** $\log (x + 3)^2$

52. Use the formula $L = 10 \log \frac{I}{I_0}$. Suppose the sound intensity of a fan must be reduced by one third. By how many decibels would the loudness be decreased?

8-5 Objectives

▼ To solve exponential equations (p. 461)

▼ To solve logarithmic equations (p. 463)

An equation in the form $b^{cx} = a$, where the exponent includes a variable, is called an **exponential equation**. You can solve exponential equations by taking the logarithm of each side of the equation. An equation that includes a logarithmic expression is called a **logarithmic equation**.

Solve each equation. Round your answers to the nearest hundredth.

53. $4^x = 27$ **54.** $3^x = 36$ **55.** $7^{x-3} = 25$ **56.** $5^x = 9$

Solve by graphing.

57. $5^{2x} = 25$ **58.** $3^{7x} = 160$ **59.** $6^{3x+1} = 215$ **60.** $0.5^x = 0.12$

Solve each logarithmic equation. Leave your answer in exact form.

61. $\log 3x = 1$ **62.** $\log_2 4x = 5$

63. $\log x = \log 2x^2 - 2$ **64.** $2\log_3 x = 54$

65. Convert $\log_2 7$ to a logarithm in base 5.

 66. Biology A culture of 10 bacteria is started, and the number of bacteria will double every hour. In about how many hours will there be 3,000,000 bacteria?

8-6 Objectives

▼ To evaluate natural logarithmic expressions (p. 470)

▼ To solve equations using natural logarithms (p. 471)

The inverse of $y = e^x$ is the **natural logarithmic function** $y = \log_e x = \ln x$. You solve natural logarithm equations in the same way as common logarithm equations.

Solve each equation.

67. $e^{3x} = 12$ **68.** $\ln x + \ln(x + 1) = 2$ **69.** $2 \ln x + 3 \ln 2 = 5$

70. $\ln 4 - \ln x = 10$ **71.** $4e^{(x-1)} = 64$ **72.** $3 \ln x + \ln 5 = 7$

73. Savings An initial investment of \$350 is worth \$429.20 after six years of continuous compounding. Find the interest rate.

Chapter Test

Go Online
PHSchool.com
For: Chapter Test
Web Code: aga-0852

Evaluate each function to the nearest hundredth for for $x = 0, 1, 2, 3, 4, 5$. Graph each function.

1. $y = 3(0.25)^x$

2. $f(x) = -(6)^x$

3. $y = 0.1(10)^x$

4. $f(x) = 100(2)^x$

5. Open-Ended Give an example of an exponential function that models exponential growth and an example of an exponential function that models exponential decay.

Write an exponential function of the form $y = ab^x$ that has a graph through the given points.

6. $(1, 1), (2, 3)$

7. $\left(-2, \frac{2}{25}\right), (1, 10)$

8. $\left(-3, \frac{1}{16}\right), (-1, 1)$

 9. Investment You put $1500 into an account earning 7% annual interest compounded continuously. How long will it be until you have $2000 in your account?

Describe how the graph of each function is related to the graph of its parent function.

10. $y = 3^x + 2$

11. $y = \left(\frac{1}{2}\right)^{x+1}$

12. $y = 5^{x-2} - 1$

13. $y = -(2)^{x+2}$

Evaluate each logarithm.

14. $\log_2 8$

15. $\log_7 7$

16. $\log_5 25$

17. $\log_3 27$

18. $\log_{11} 1$

19. $\log_4 256$

Graph each logarithmic function.

20. $y = \log_9 x$

21. $y = \log_3 (x - 1)$

22. $y = \frac{1}{2} \log_3 (x + 2)$

23. $y = 1 - \log_2 x$

Use the properties of logarithms to rewrite each logarithmic expression.

24. $\log_2 4 + 3 \log_2 9$

25. $3 \log a - 2 \log b$

26. $\log_7 \frac{a}{b}$

27. $\log 3x^3 y^2$

Use the properties of logarithms to evaluate each expression.

28. $\log_3 27 - \log_3 9$

29. $2 \log_2 64 + \log_2 2$

30. $-\log_4 \frac{1}{16} - \log_4 64$

31. $2 \log 5 + \log 40$

 32. Writing Show that solving the equation $3^{2x} = 4$ by taking common logarithms of both sides is equivalent to solving it by taking logarithms to the base 3 of both sides.

Solve each equation.

33. $\left(\frac{3}{4}\right)^x = 81$

34. $3^{x-1} = 24$

35. $\log 4x = 3$

36. $2 \log x = -4$

Use the Change of Base Formula to rewrite each expression using common logarithms.

37. $\log_3 16$

38. $\log_2 10$

39. $\log_7 8$

Use the properties of logarithms to simplify each equation and solve it. Round to thousandths.

40. $\ln 2 + \ln x = 1$

41. $\ln (x + 1) + \ln (x - 1) = 4$

42. $\ln (2x - 1)^2 = 7$

43. $3 \ln x - \ln 2 = 4$

 44. Physics Seawater absorbs light. In some instances, this relationship is modeled by $\ln I = \ln I_0 - 0.014d$. I_0 is the intensity of the light at the surface of the water, and I is the intensity at a depth of d cm. At what depth will the intensity of the light in the water be 25% of the surface intensity?

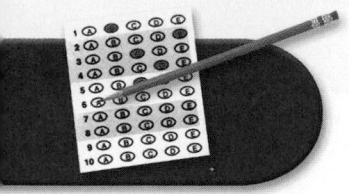
Standardized Test Prep

Multiple Choice

For Exercises 1–12, choose the correct letter.

1. What can you tell about the roots of
$3x^2 + 4x - 1 = 0$ from the discriminant?
- Ⓐ There are two real roots.
- Ⓑ There are two imaginary roots.
- Ⓒ There is one real and one imaginary root.
- Ⓓ There are no roots.

2. Which expressions are equivalent to
$\log a - 3\log b$?

I. $\log ab^3$ **II.** $\log \frac{a}{b^3}$

III. $\log a - \log b^3$ **IV.** $\log (ab)^3$

- Ⓕ I and II
- Ⓖ II and III
- Ⓗ III and IV
- Ⓙ I and IV

3. What is the factored form of $2x^3 + 5x^2 - 12x$?
- Ⓐ $x(2x - 3)(x + 4)$
- Ⓑ $(2x^2 - 3)(x + 4)$
- Ⓒ $x(2x + 4)(x - 3)$
- Ⓓ $(2x - 4)(x + 3)$

4. Which is NOT a solution of the system?
$$\begin{cases} 2x - y > 3 \\ 2x + y \geq 5 \end{cases}$$
- Ⓕ $(3, 0)$
- Ⓖ $(4, -1)$
- Ⓗ $(6, 1)$
- Ⓙ $(0, -3)$

5. How is the graph of $y = (x - 4)^2 + 1$ translated from the graph of $y = x^2$?
- Ⓐ left 1, up 4
- Ⓑ left 4, down 1
- Ⓒ right 1, down 4
- Ⓓ right 4, up 1

6. What is the inverse of $\begin{bmatrix} 3 & -5 \\ 1 & 4 \end{bmatrix}$?
- Ⓕ $\begin{bmatrix} 4 & 5 \\ -1 & 3 \end{bmatrix}$
- Ⓖ $\begin{bmatrix} -2 & 5 \\ -1 & -3 \end{bmatrix}$
- Ⓗ $\begin{bmatrix} -3 & 5 \\ -1 & -4 \end{bmatrix}$
- Ⓙ $\frac{1}{17}\begin{bmatrix} 4 & 5 \\ -1 & 3 \end{bmatrix}$

7. Solve the system. $\begin{cases} 2x + 3y - 2z = -2 \\ 2x - 4y + 2z = 18 \\ 5x + 2y - 6z = 8 \end{cases}$
- Ⓐ $x = 3, y = 1, z = 2$
- Ⓑ $x = -3, y = 2, z = -1$
- Ⓒ $x = 4, y = -3, z = 1$
- Ⓓ $x = -1, y = 3, z = 2$

8. Let $f(x) = -5x$ and $g(x) = 1 - 2x^2$. Find $(g \circ f)(1)$.
- Ⓕ -49
- Ⓖ -5
- Ⓗ 5
- Ⓙ 51

9. Which polynomials have both -2 and 3 as zeros?
- **I.** $x^3 - 2x^2 - 5x + 2$ **II.** $x^3 - 3x^2 - 4x + 12$
- **III.** $x^3 + 3x^2 - 4x - 12$
  - Ⓐ I only
  - Ⓑ I and II
  - Ⓒ II only
  - Ⓓ I, II, and III

10. Multiply $(3\sqrt{6} - 3\sqrt{2})(\sqrt{6} - 3\sqrt{2})$.
- Ⓕ $36 - 24\sqrt{3}$
- Ⓖ 6
- Ⓗ $6 - 12\sqrt{3}$
- Ⓙ 9

11. Solve $3 + (x - 1)^{\frac{3}{4}} = 30$.
- Ⓐ 9
- Ⓑ 11
- Ⓒ 81
- Ⓓ 82

12. $(\ln x)^2 = 1$. What are possible values of x?
- **I.** e **II.** $-e$ **III.** e^{-1} **IV.** 1
  - Ⓕ I only
  - Ⓖ I and II
  - Ⓗ IV only
  - Ⓙ I and III

Gridded Response

13. Solve $3^x = 7$. Round your answer to the nearest hundredth.

14. What is the discriminant of $2x^2 - 8x + 8 = 0$?

15. Evaluate $\log_4 8$.

Short Response

16. Write $\log \frac{x^2 y^3}{z^6}$ in expanded form.

17. Solve $5^{2x + 1} = 62$. Round your answer to the nearest hundredth. Show your work.

18. Graph the function $y = 10^{x + 1} - 3$ as a translation of its parent function.

Extended Response

19. Suppose you put $1000 in an account earning 5.5% interest compounded continuously. How much will be in the account after one year? After four years?

20. What is the determinant of $\begin{bmatrix} 1 & 2 & 3 \\ 2 & 1 & 3 \\ 2 & 3 & 1 \end{bmatrix}$?

Show your work.

Activity Lab

A Crowded House

Applying Exponential Functions The number of people in the world has more than tripled since 1900—from less than 2 billion to more than 6 billion. In 2000, an average of about 360,000 babies were born each day. That means that there were four babies born every second.

Old South Meeting House

Historical Site
Old South Meeting House, in Boston, Massachusetts, (left about 1903, right in 2002), was built in 1730. At the time, it was the tallest building in Boston. Note that the time on the clock is 1:43 in both photos.

Proportional Populations
These maps of China, the United States, and Australia are drawn so that their sizes are proportional to their populations.

United States, population about 284,500,000

China, population about 1,273,300,000

About one of every five people in the world lives in China.

Australia, population about 19,400,000

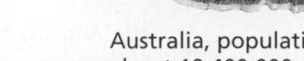

Population Densities

All cities are crowded, but some are more crowded than others. Hong Kong Island is so closely packed that if it were divided into tennis courts, there would be 25 people on each court. London would have only one person on each court.

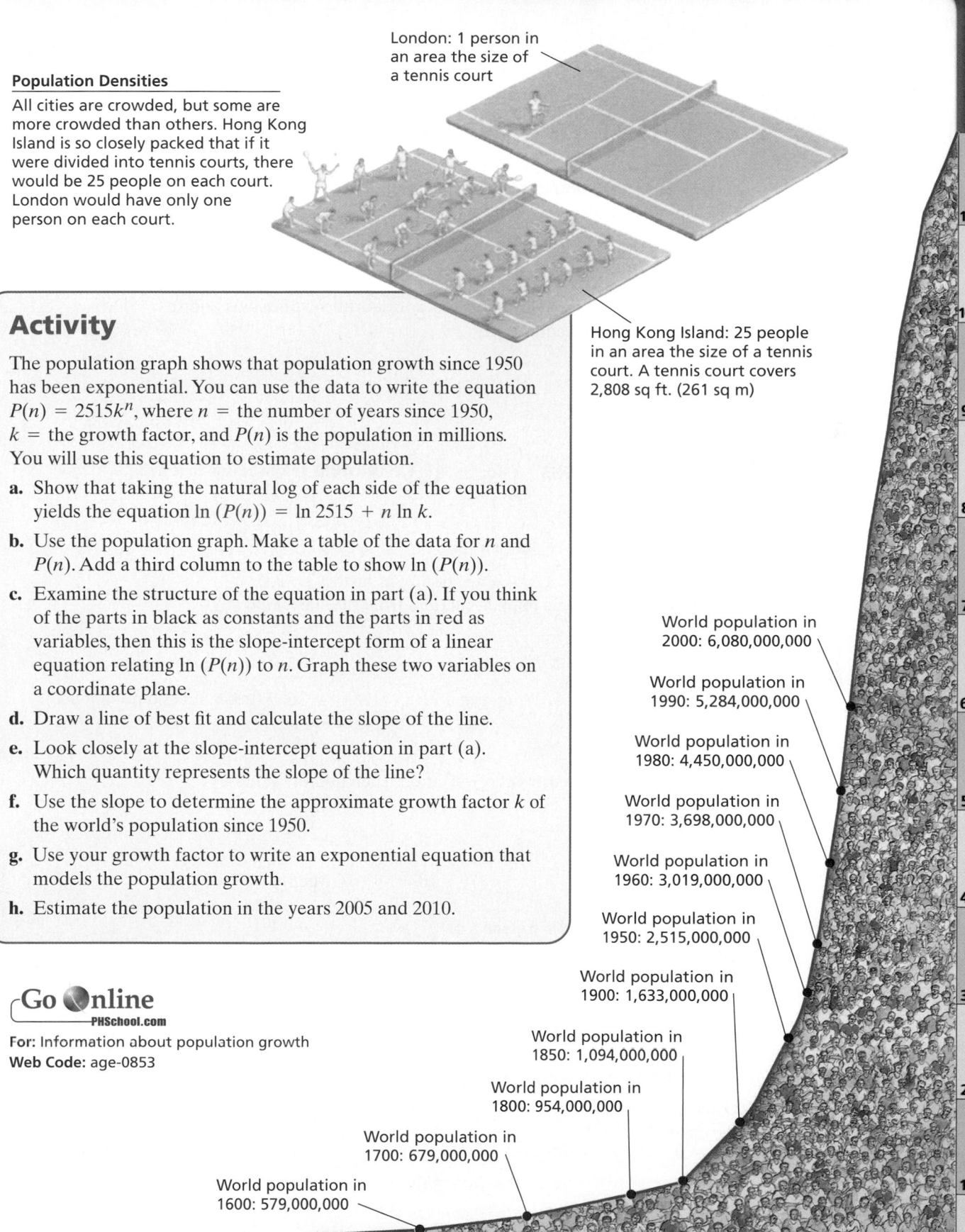

London: 1 person in an area the size of a tennis court

Hong Kong Island: 25 people in an area the size of a tennis court. A tennis court covers 2,808 sq ft. (261 sq m)

Activity

The population graph shows that population growth since 1950 has been exponential. You can use the data to write the equation $P(n) = 2515k^n$, where n = the number of years since 1950, k = the growth factor, and $P(n)$ is the population in millions. You will use this equation to estimate population.

a. Show that taking the natural log of each side of the equation yields the equation $\ln(P(n)) = \ln 2515 + n \ln k$.

b. Use the population graph. Make a table of the data for n and $P(n)$. Add a third column to the table to show $\ln(P(n))$.

c. Examine the structure of the equation in part (a). If you think of the parts in black as constants and the parts in red as variables, then this is the slope-intercept form of a linear equation relating $\ln(P(n))$ to n. Graph these two variables on a coordinate plane.

d. Draw a line of best fit and calculate the slope of the line.

e. Look closely at the slope-intercept equation in part (a). Which quantity represents the slope of the line?

f. Use the slope to determine the approximate growth factor k of the world's population since 1950.

g. Use your growth factor to write an exponential equation that models the population growth.

h. Estimate the population in the years 2005 and 2010.

Go Online
PHSchool.com

For: Information about population growth
Web Code: age-0853

World population in 2000: 6,080,000,000

World population in 1990: 5,284,000,000

World population in 1980: 4,450,000,000

World population in 1970: 3,698,000,000

World population in 1960: 3,019,000,000

World population in 1950: 2,515,000,000

World population in 1900: 1,633,000,000

World population in 1850: 1,094,000,000

World population in 1800: 954,000,000

World population in 1700: 679,000,000

World population in 1600: 579,000,000

1500 1600 1700 1800 1900 2000

What You've Learned

- In Chapter 1, you learned to find theoretical probabilities for random events.
- In Chapter 2, you learned to write and interpret direct variation equations to solve real-world problems.
- In Chapter 5, you learned to factor quadratic expressions and to solve quadratic equations.

 **Check Your Readiness** **for Help** to the Lesson in green.

Finding Theoretical Probabilities (Lesson 1-6)

A bookshelf contains 18 math books, 27 science books, 21 history books, and 15 grammar books. You pick one book at random from the shelf. Find each theoretical probability.

1. $P(\text{history})$ **2.** $P(\text{science})$ **3.** $P(\text{math or science})$

4. $P(\text{math or science or history})$ **5.** $P(\text{not grammar})$ **6.** $P(\text{not math and not science})$

Using Direct Variation (Lesson 2-3)

For each direct variation, find the constant of variation. Then find the value of y when $x = -3$.

7. $y = 4$ when $x = 3$ **8.** $y = 1$ when $x = -1.5$

9. $y = -5$ when $x = \frac{3}{2}$ **10.** $y = -16$ when $x = 7$

Factoring Quadratic Expressions (Lesson 5-4)

Factor each expression.

11. $x^2 + x - 6$ **12.** $4x^2 + 17x + 15$ **13.** $9x^2 - 25$

14. $x^2 - 12x + 36$ **15.** $3x^2 + 10x + 8$ **16.** $x^2 - 5x + 6$

Solving Quadratic Equations (Lesson 5-5)

Solve each equation.

17. $x^2 + 7x - 8 = 0$ **18.** $\frac{1}{4}x^2 + \frac{7}{2}x = -12$ **19.** $3x^2 = 18x - 24$

20. $9x^2 + 6x = 0$ **21.** $4x^2 + 16 = 34x$ **22.** $x^2 - 13x - 30 = 0$

Rational Functions

Chapter 9

LESSONS

9-1 Inverse Variation

9-2 The Reciprocal Function Family

9-3 Rational Functions and Their Graphs

9-4 Rational Expressions

9-5 Adding and Subtracting Rational Expressions

9-6 Solving Rational Equations

9-7 Probability of Multiple Events

◀)) **Key Vocabulary**

- branch (p. 495)
- complex fraction (p. 516)
- dependent events (p. 531)
- independent events (p. 531)
- inverse variation (p. 488)
- joint variation (p. 490)
- mutually exclusive events (p. 533)
- point of discontinuity (p. 501)
- rational function (p. 501)
- reciprocal function (p. 495)
- simplest form (p. 509)

What You'll Learn Next

- In Chapter 9, you will learn to use inverse variation and the graphs of inverse variations to solve real-world problems.

- You will learn to identify properties of rational functions.

- You will learn to simplify rational expressions and to solve rational equations.

Real-World Connection Applying what you learn, on page 515 you will solve a problem involving photography.

Inverse Variation

✓ Check Skills You'll Need

GO for Help Lesson 2-3

In Exercises 1–3, y varies directly with x.

1. Given that $x = 2$ when $y = 4$, find y when $x = 5$.

2. Given that $x = 1$ when $y = 5$, find y when $x = 3$.

3. Given that $x = 10$ when $y = 3$, find y when $x = 4$.

◀)) **New Vocabulary** • inverse variation • joint variation

---

1 Using Inverse Variation

In Chapter 2, you studied direct variation. You can model a direct variation with an equation of the form $y = kx$, where $k \neq 0$. You can model an **inverse variation** with any of the equations $xy = k$, $y = \frac{k}{x}$, or $x = \frac{k}{y}$, where $k \neq 0$. As with direct variation, k is the constant of variation.

The table and graph below show the times needed to ride a bike 24 miles at different rates.

Rate (mi/h)	Time (h)
3	8
6	4
12	2
24	1

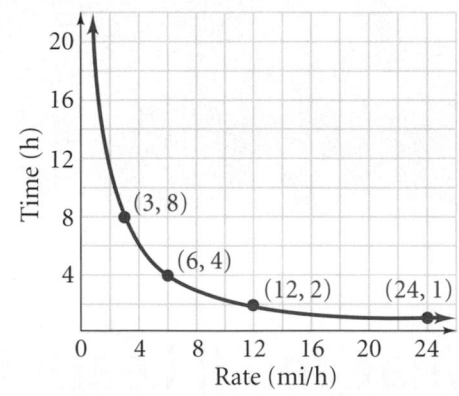

Notice that as the rate increases, the time decreases. Doubling the rate halves the time. The inverse variation $rt = 24$, or $t = \frac{24}{r}$, models this situation.

1 EXAMPLE Modeling Inverse Variation

Suppose that x and y vary inversely, and $x = 3$ when $y = -5$. Write the function that models the inverse variation.

Vocabulary Tip

You can describe an <u>inverse variation</u> as "y varies inversely as x" or as "y is inversely proportional to x."

$y = \dfrac{k}{x}$	x and y vary inversely.
$-5 = \dfrac{k}{3}$	Substitute the given values of x and y.
$-15 = k$	Find k.
$y = \dfrac{-15}{x}$	Use the value of k to write the function.

1 Suppose that x and y vary inversely, and $x = 0.3$ when $y = 1.4$. Write the function that models the inverse variation.

2 EXAMPLE **Identifying Direct and Inverse Variations**

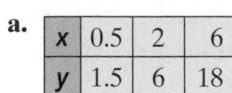

Is the relationship between the variables in each table a direct variation, an inverse variation, or neither? Write functions to model the direct and inverse variations.

a.

x	0.5	2	6
y	1.5	6	18

As x increases, y increases. Since each y-value is 3 times the corresponding x-value, y varies directly with x, the constant of variation is 3, and the function is $y = 3x$.

b.

x	0.2	0.6	1.2
y	12	4	2

As x increases, y decreases. The product of each pair of x- and y-values is 2.4. y varies inversely with x and the constant of variation is 2.4. So $xy = 2.4$ and the function is $y = \frac{2.4}{x}$.

c.

x	1	2	3
y	2	1	0.5

As x increases, y decreases, but this is not an inverse variation. Not all the products of x and y are the same ($2 \cdot 1 \neq 3 \cdot 0.5$). This is neither a direct variation nor an inverse variation.

For: Variation Activity
Use: Interactive Textbook, 9-1

✓ **Quick Check** **2** Is the relationship between the values in each table a direct variation, an inverse variation, or neither? Write functions to model the direct and inverse variations.

a.

x	0.8	0.6	0.4
y	0.9	1.2	1.8

b.

x	2	4	6
y	3.2	1.6	1.1

c.

x	1.2	1.4	1.6
y	18	21	24

3 EXAMPLE **Real-World 🌐 Connection**

Zoology Heart rates and life spans of most mammals are inversely related. Use the data to write a function that models this inverse variation. Use your function to estimate the average life span of a cat with a heart rate of 126 beats/min.

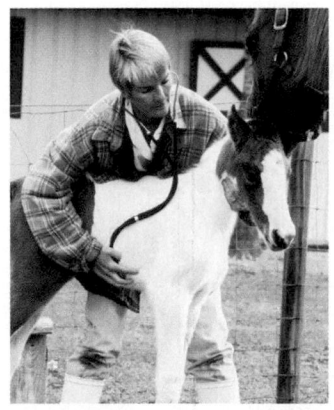

Real-World 🌐 Connection

Horses have a life span of about 30 years.

Heart Rate and Life Span

Mammal	Heart rate (beats/min)	Life span (min)
Mouse	634	1,576,800
Rabbit	158	6,307,200
Lion	76	13,140,000
Horse	63	15,768,000

SOURCE: *The Handy Science Answer Book*

Relate heart rate · life span = a constant

Define Let r = heart rate (beats/min).

Let s = life span (min).

Let k = constant of variation (beats in a life span).

Write $rs = k$

For each of the four mammals in the table, $rs \approx 1,000,000,000$.

$rs = 1,000,000,000$ **Substitute 1,000,000,000 for k.**

$126s = 1,000,000,000$ **Substitute 126 for r.**

$s \approx 8,000,000$

A cat's life span is about 8 million minutes, or about 15.2 years.

✓ **Quick Check** **3 a.** A squirrel's heart rate is 190 beats per minute. Estimate its life span.
  b. An elephant's life span is about 70 years. Estimate its average heart rate.

Quantities can vary with respect to each other in different ways. For example, y can vary directly with x^3 ($y = kx^3$) or inversely with x^2 ($y = \frac{k}{x^2}$).

It is possible for three or more variables to be related. When one quantity varies with respect to two or more other quantities, the result is a combined variation. For example, a variable z can vary directly with both x and y. You can model such a **joint variation** with the equation $z = kxy$, where $k \neq 0$.

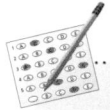

Vocabulary Tip

z varies <u>jointly</u> with x and y means z varies directly with the product of x and y.

Examples of Combined Variations

Combined Variation	Equation Form
z varies jointly with x and y.	$z = kxy$
z varies jointly with x and y and inversely with w.	$z = \frac{kxy}{w}$
z varies directly with x and inversely with the product wy.	$z = \frac{kx}{wy}$

Test-Taking Tip

Use dimensional analysis to check that a formula makes sense. For example, in.^{2} • in. = in.^{3} suggests that $V = Bh$ is correct.

4 EXAMPLE   <u>Real-World</u> Connection

Physics Newton's Law of Universal Gravitation is modeled by the formula $F = \frac{Gm_1m_2}{d^2}$. F is the gravitational force between two objects with masses m_1 and m_2, and d is the distance between the objects. G is the gravitational constant. Describe Newton's law as a combined variation.

$F = \dfrac{Gm_1m_2}{d^2}$ ← F varies jointly with the masses m_1 and m_2, and
          ← F varies inversely with the square of the distance d.

✓ Quick Check **④ Geometry** The formula for the area of a trapezoid is $A = \frac{1}{2}h(b_1 + b_2)$. Describe this relationship as a combined variation.

5 EXAMPLE   Finding a Formula

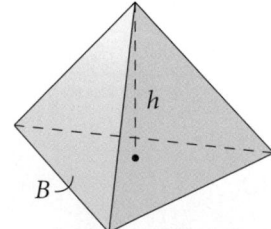

Multiple Choice The volume V of a tetrahedron varies jointly with its altitude h and base area B. A tetrahedron with a 5-cm altitude and 6-in.^{2} base has volume of 10 cm^3. Which formula models this joint variation?

  Ⓐ $V = 3Bh$ Ⓑ $V = \frac{1}{3}Bh$ Ⓒ $h = \frac{1}{12}VB$ Ⓓ $Vh = 5B$

$V = kBh$ **V varies jointly with B and h.**

$10 = k(6)(5)$ **Substitute given values for V, B, and h.**

$\frac{1}{3} = k$ **Solve for k.**

$V = \frac{1}{3}Bh$ **Substitute the value for k.**

The correct choice is B.

✓ Quick Check **⑤** The volume of a square pyramid with congruent edges varies directly as the cube of the length of an edge. The volume of a square pyramid with edge length 4 is $\frac{32\sqrt{2}}{3}$. Find the formula for the volume of a square pyramid with congruent edges.

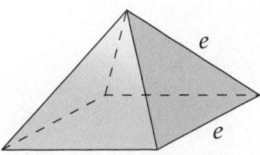

EXERCISES

For more exercises, see *Extra Skill and Word Problem Practice*.

Practice and Problem Solving

A Practice by Example

Example 1
(page 488)

Suppose that *x* and *y* vary inversely. Write a function that models each inverse variation.

1. $x = 1$ when $y = 11$ **2.** $x = -13$ when $y = 100$ **3.** $x = 1$ when $y = 1$

4. $x = 28$ when $y = -2$ **5.** $x = 1.2$ when $y = 3$ **6.** $x = 2.5$ when $y = 100$

Example 2
(page 489)

Is the relationship between the values in each table a direct variation, an inverse variation, or neither? Write equations to model the direct and inverse variations.

7.

x	3	8	10	22
y	15	40	50	110

8.

x	3	5	7	10.5
y	14	8.4	6	4

9.

x	0.5	2.1	3.5	11
y	1	4.2	7	22

10.

x	0.1	3	6	24
y	3	0.1	0.05	0.0125

11.

x	7	3	1	$\frac{1}{5}$
y	$\frac{1}{7}$	$\frac{1}{3}$	1	5

12.

x	10	12	20	23
y	2	$2\frac{2}{5}$	4	$5\frac{3}{5}$

Example 3
(page 489)

Suppose that *x* and *y* vary inversely. Write a function that models each inverse variation and find *y* when *x* = 10.

13. $x = 20$ when $y = 5$ **14.** $x = 20$ when $y = -4$ **15.** $x = 5$ when $y = -\frac{1}{3}$

Example 4
(page 490)

Describe the combined variation that is modeled by each formula.

16. $A = \pi r^2$ **17.** $A = 0.5bh$ **18.** $h = \frac{2A}{b}$ **19.** $V = \frac{Bh}{3}$

20. $V = \pi r^2 h$ **21.** $h = \frac{V}{\pi r^2}$ **22.** $V = \ell w h$ **23.** $\ell = \frac{V}{wh}$

Example 5
(page 490)

Write the function that models each variation. Find *z* when *x* = 4 and *y* = 9.

24. z varies directly with x and inversely with y. When $x = 6$ and $y = 2$, $z = 15$.

25. z varies jointly with x and y. When $x = 2$ and $y = 3$, $z = 60$.

26. z varies directly with the square of x and inversely with y. When $x = 2$ and $y = 4$, $z = 3$.

27. z varies inversely with the product of x and y. When $x = 2$ and $y = 4$, $z = 0.5$.

B Apply Your Skills

28. a. The spreadsheet shows data that could be modeled by an equation of the form $PV = k$. Estimate the value of k.
 b. Estimate P when $V = 62$.

Each ordered pair is from an inverse variation. Find the constant of variation.

29. $(6, 3)$ **30.** $(0.9, 4)$ **31.** $\left(\frac{3}{8}, \frac{2}{3}\right)$

32. $\left(\sqrt{2}, \sqrt{18}\right)$ **33.** $\left(\sqrt{3}, \sqrt{27}\right)$ **34.** $\left(\sqrt{8}, \sqrt{32}\right)$

	A	B
	P	V
1	P	V
2	140.00	100
3	147.30	95
4	155.60	90
5	164.70	85
6	175.00	80
7	186.70	75

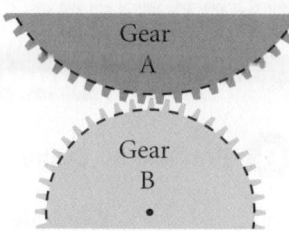

35. Mechanics Gear A drives Gear B. Gear A has a teeth and speed r_A in revolutions per minute (rpm). Gear B has b teeth and speed r_B. The quantities are related by the formula $ar_A = br_B$. Gear A has 60 teeth and speed 5400 rpm. Gear B has 45 teeth. Find the speed of Gear B.

Gear A

Gear B

36. Physics The force F of gravity on a rocket varies directly with its mass m and inversely with the square of its distance d from Earth. Write a model for this combined variation. $k\dfrac{m}{d^2}$

Each pair of values is from a direct variation. Find the missing value.

37. $(3, 7), (8, y)$ **38.** $(2, 5), (4, y)$ **39.** $(4, 6), (x, 3)$

40. $(9, 5), (x, 3)$ **41.** $(8.3, 7.1), (5, y)$ **42.** $(2.6, 4.5), (x, 6.3)$

Each pair of values is from an inverse variation. Find the missing value.

43. $(3, 7), (8, y)$ **44.** $(2, 5), (4, y)$ **45.** $(4, 6), (x, 3)$

46. $(9, 5), (x, 3)$ **47.** $(8.3, 7.1), (5, y)$ **48.** $(2.6, 4.5), (x, 6.3)$

49. Suppose that y varies inversely with the square of x, and $y = 50$ when $x = 4$. Find y when $x = 5$.

50. Suppose that c varies jointly with d and the square of g, and $c = 30$ when $d = 15$ and $g = 2$. Find d when $c = 6$ and $g = 8$.

51. Suppose that d varies jointly with r and t, and $d = 110$ when $r = 55$ and $t = 2$. Find r when $d = 40$ and $t = 3$.

52. Construction A concrete supplier sells premixed concrete in 300-ft³ truckloads. The area A that the concrete will cover is inversely proportional to the depth d of the concrete.
 a. Write a model for the relationship between the area and the depth of a truckload of poured concrete.
 b. What area will the concrete cover if it is poured to a depth of 0.5 ft? A depth of 1 ft? A depth of 1.5 ft?
 c. When the concrete is poured into a circular area, the depth of the concrete is inversely proportional to the square of the radius r. Write a model for this relationship.

Exercise 52

53. Suppose that y varies directly with x and inversely with z^2, and $x = 48$ when $y = 8$ and $z = 3$. Find x when $y = 12$ and $z = 2$.

54. Suppose that t varies directly with s and inversely with the square of r. How is the value of t changed when the value of s is doubled? Is tripled?

55. Suppose that x varies directly with the square of y and inversely with z. How is the value of x changed if the value of y is halved? Is quartered?

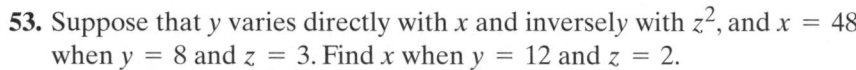

C Challenge   **56. Writing** Explain why 0 cannot be in the domain of an inverse variation.

57. Critical Thinking Suppose that (x_1, y_1) and (x_2, y_2) are values from an inverse variation. Show that $\dfrac{x_1}{x_2} = \dfrac{y_2}{y_1}$.

58. Open-Ended The height h of a cylinder varies directly with its volume V and inversely with the square of its radius r. Find at least four ways to change the volume and radius of a cylinder so that its height is quadrupled.

59. Health Health care professionals use the body mass index (BMI) to establish guidelines for determining any possible risks of their patients and for planning any useful preventative programs. The BMI varies directly with weight and inversely with the square of height. Use this portion of the BMI chart to determine the BMI formula.

Weights and Body Mass Index (BMI)

Height	Range of Weight (pounds)			
	BMI 19–24.9	BMI 25–29.9	BMI 30–39.9	BMI ≥ 40
5′6″	118–154	155–185	186–246	≥247
5′7″	121–158	159–190	191–254	≥255
5′8″	125–163	164–196	197–261	≥262
5′9″	128–168	169–202	203–269	≥270
5′10″	132–173	174–208	209–277	≥278
5′11″	136–178	179–214	215–285	≥286
6′0″	140–183	184–220	221–293	≥294

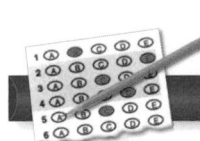 **Test Prep**

Multiple Choice

60. Which equation does NOT represent inverse variation between x and z?

A. $x = \dfrac{y}{z}$ **B.** $x = \dfrac{-15z}{y}$

C. $z = \dfrac{-15y}{x}$ **D.** $xz = 5y$

61. If p and q vary inversely, and $p = 10$ when $q = -4$, what is q when $p = -2$?

F. 20   **G.** $\dfrac{4}{5}$ **H.** $-\dfrac{4}{5}$ **J.** -20

62. Which equation shows that z varies directly with the square of x and inversely with the cube of y?

A. $z = \dfrac{x^2}{y^3}$ **B.** $z = \dfrac{x^3}{y^2}$ **C.** $z = \dfrac{y^2}{x^3}$ **D.** $z = \dfrac{y^3}{x^2}$

Short Response

63. Describe how the variables A and r vary in the formula for the area of a circle, $A = \pi r^2$.

Extended Response

64. Which data set shows inverse variation: (24.4, 4.8) and (9.6, 12.2), or (24.0, 4.5) and (18.0, 6.5)? Explain.

 **Mixed Review**

GO for Help

Lesson 8-6

Solve each equation.

65. $\ln 4 + \ln x = 5$ **66.** $\ln x - \ln 3 = 4$ **67.** $2 \ln x + 3 \ln 4 = 4$

Lesson 7-2

Multiply and simplify. Assume that all variables are positive.

68. $-5\sqrt{6x} \cdot 3\sqrt{6x^2}$ **69.** $3\sqrt[3]{4x^2} \cdot 7\sqrt[3]{12x^4}$ **70.** $\sqrt{5x^3} \cdot \sqrt{40xy^7}$

Lesson 7-1

Simplify each radical expression. Use absolute value bars where they are needed.

71. $\sqrt{x^{10}y^{100}}$ **72.** $\sqrt[3]{-64a^3b^6}$ **73.** $\sqrt[4]{64m^8n^4}$ **74.** $\sqrt[4]{x^4}$

You can use your graphing calculator to graph members of the reciprocal function family and other rational functions. It is sometimes preferable to use the Dot plotting mode rather than the Connected plotting mode. The Connected mode can join branches of a graph that should be separated. Try both modes to get the best graph.

EXAMPLE

Graph $y = \dfrac{4}{x-3} - 1.5$.

Step 1 Press the MODE key. Scroll down to highlight the word **Dot**. Then press ENTER.

Step 2 Enter the function. Use parentheses to enter the denominator accurately.

Step 3 Graph the function.

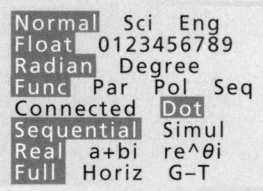

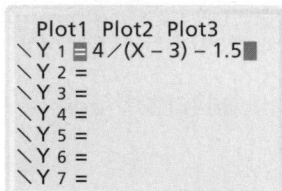

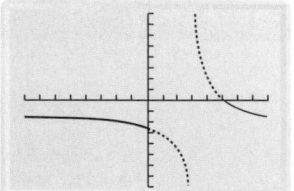

EXERCISES

1. a. Graph the parent reciprocal function $y = \frac{1}{x}$. Sketch the graph on paper.
  b. Examine both negative and positive values of x. Describe what happens to the y-values as x approaches zero.
  c. What happens to the y-values as x increases? As x decreases?

2. a. Change the mode on your graphing calculator to **Connected**. Graph the function from the example. Sketch the graph.
  b. Press the TRACE key and trace the function. What happens between $x \approx 2.9$ and $x \approx 3.2$?
  c. **Critical Thinking** How does your graph differ from the graph in the example? Explain the differences.

Use a graphing calculator to graph each function. Then sketch the graph.

3. $y = \dfrac{7}{x}$

4. $y = \dfrac{3}{x+4} - 2$

5. $y = \dfrac{x+2}{(x+1)(x+3)}$

6. $y = \dfrac{4x+1}{x-3}$

7. $y = \dfrac{2}{x-2}$

8. $y = \dfrac{1}{x+2} + 3$

9. $y = \dfrac{2x}{x+3}$

10. $y = \dfrac{x^2}{x^2-5}$

11. $y = \dfrac{20}{x^2+5}$

12. $y = \dfrac{1}{x-3} - 6$

13. $y = \dfrac{10}{x^2-5x-10}$

14. $y = \dfrac{x}{x^2-1}$

The Reciprocal Function Family

What You'll Learn

- To graph reciprocal functions
- To graph translations of reciprocal functions

. . . And Why

To analyze musical pitch and the size of the instrument, as in Example 3

GO for Help Lesson 2-6

Each of the following equations is a translation of $y = |x|$. Describe each translation.

1. $y = |x| + 2$

2. $y = |x + 2|$

3. $y = |x| - 3$

4. $y = |x - 3|$

5. $y = |x + 4| - 5$

6. $y = |x - 10| + 7$

🔊 **New Vocabulary**   • reciprocal function   • branch

---

1 Graphing Reciprocal Functions

Functions that model inverse variations belong to a family whose parent is the **reciprocal function** $f(x) = \frac{1}{x}$, where $x \neq 0$. The general form of a family member is $y = \frac{a}{x - h} + k$, with a single real number h missing from its domain.

The inverse variations $y = \frac{a}{x}$ are the stretches and shrinks of the parent reciprocal function.

1 EXAMPLE   Graphing an Inverse Variation

Sketch a graph of $y = \frac{6}{x}$, $x \neq 0$.

Make a table of values that includes positive and negative values of x.

x	−12	−6	−3	−2	−1	$-\frac{1}{2}$	$\frac{1}{2}$	1	2	3	6	12
y	$-\frac{1}{2}$	−1	−2	−3	−6	−12	12	6	3	2	1	$\frac{1}{2}$

Graph the points. Connect them with a smooth curve to the left of where $x = 0$ and another smooth curve to the right of where $x = 0$. Each part of the graph is called a **branch.**

The x-axis is a horizontal asymptote.

The y-axis is a vertical asymptote.

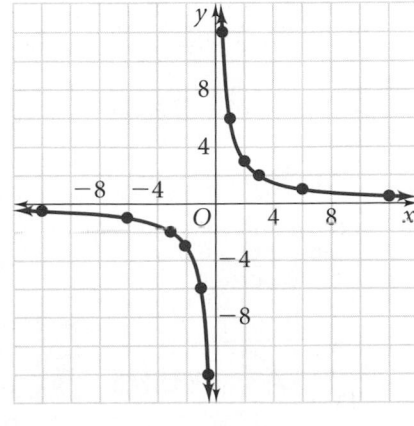

Vocabulary Tip

In a graph, a <u>branch</u> is a distinct part of a curve, just as, in nature, a branch is a distinct part of a river.

 **Quick Check** **1** Sketch a graph of $y = \frac{16}{x}$.

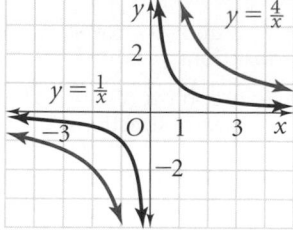

The branches of $y = \frac{1}{x}$ are in Quadrants I and III. Stretches of the parent function have the form $y = \frac{a}{x}$, where $a > 0$, and remain in Quadrants I and III. Their reflections, $y = \frac{-a}{x}$, are in Quadrants II and IV.

2 EXAMPLE Graphing Reciprocal Functions

Draw the graph of $f(x) = \frac{-4}{x}$. Describe properties of the graph.

The graph of $y = \frac{4}{x}$ is a stretch of $y = \frac{1}{x}$ by a factor of 4.

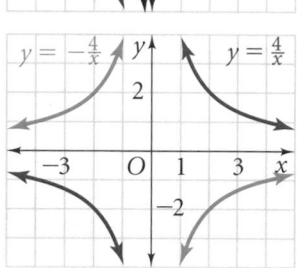

The graph of $y = \frac{-4}{x}$ is a reflection of $y = \frac{4}{x}$ in the x-axis.

The axes are asymptotes for each graph. Each graph is symmetric with respect to $y = x$ and $y = -x$.

✓ Quick Check ❷ Use a graphing calculator. Set $Xmin = -3$, $Xmax = 3$, $Ymin = -2$, and $Ymax = 2$. Draw and compare the graphs of $y = \frac{1}{x}$, $y = \frac{2}{x}$, $y = \frac{-2}{x}$, $y = \frac{0.5}{x}$, and $y = \frac{-0.5}{x}$.

A situation in which an increase in one quantity is related to a proportional decrease in another quantity suggests inverse variation.

3 EXAMPLE Real-World Connection

Music A musical pitch is determined by the frequency of vibration of the sound waves reaching the ear. The greater the frequency, the higher is the pitch. Frequency is measured in vibrations per second, or hertz (Hz).

The pitch y produced by a panpipe varies inversely with the length x of the pipe. The function $y = \frac{564}{x}$ models the inverse variation where x is the length in feet. Find the length of the pipe that produces a pitch of 277 Hz.

Graph the functions $y = \frac{564}{x}$ and $y = 277$. Use the **Intersect** feature.

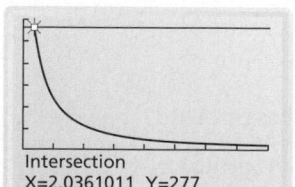

Xmin=0   Ymin=-75
Xmax=40   Ymax=300
Xscl=5   Yscl=50

Intersection
X=2.0361011 Y=277

The pipe should be about 2.0 ft long.

Real-World Connection

The length, not the diameter, of a panpipe or organ pipe determines its pitch.

✓ Quick Check ❸ **a.** Pitches of 247 Hz, 311 Hz, and 370 Hz form a musical chord. Find the length of pipe that will produce each pitch.
b. Writing The asymptotes of $y = \frac{564}{x}$ are $x = 0$ and $y = 0$. Explain why this makes sense in terms of the panpipe.

The graphs at the right show the parent function $y = \frac{1}{x}$ and two of its translations, $y = \frac{1}{x-1}$ and $y = \frac{1}{x+2}$.

The vertical asymptotes of the graphs are $x = 0$, $x = 1$, and $x = -2$.

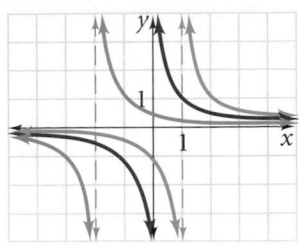

The graphs at the right show the parent function $y = \frac{1}{x}$ and two of its translations, $y = \frac{1}{x} + 1$ and $y = \frac{1}{x} - 2$.

The horizontal asymptotes of the graphs are $y = 0$, $y = 1$, and $y = -2$.

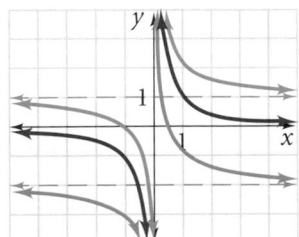

 Key Concepts

Summary	The Reciprocal Function Family

Parent function: $\qquad\qquad\qquad\qquad\qquad y = \frac{1}{x}, x \neq 0$

Stretch $(|a| > 1)$
Shrink $(0 < |a| < 1)$ $\qquad\qquad\qquad\qquad\qquad y = \frac{a}{x}$
Reflection $(a < 0)$ in x-axis

Translation (horizontal by h; vertical by k) with
vertical asymptote $x = h$, horizontal asymptote $y = k$: $\quad y = \frac{1}{x-h} + k$

Combined: $\qquad\qquad\qquad\qquad\qquad\qquad\qquad y = \frac{a}{x-h} + k$

You can use asymptotes to graph translations of the parent function.

4 EXAMPLE Graphing a Translation

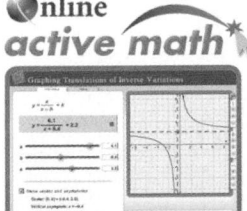

For: Translation Activity
Use: Interactive Textbook, 9-2

Sketch the graph of $y = \frac{1}{x-2} - 3$.

Step 1 Draw the asymptotes.
For $y = \frac{1}{x-2} + (-3)$,
$h = 2$ and $k = -3$.
The vertical asymptote is $x = 2$.
The horizontal asymptote is $y = -3$.

Step 2 Translate $y = \frac{1}{x}$.
The graph of $y = \frac{1}{x}$ includes $(1, 1)$ and $(-1, -1)$. Translate these points 2 units to the right and 3 units down to $(3, -2)$ and $(1, -4)$. Draw the branches through these points.

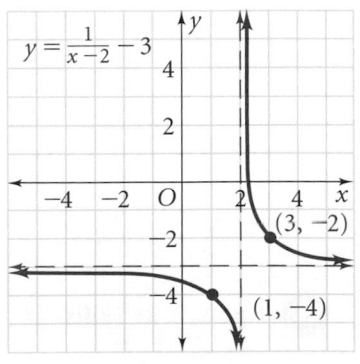

✓ **Quick Check** ④ Find the asymptotes and sketch the graph of $y = -\frac{1}{x+7} - 3$.

If you know the translations or asymptotes of a stretch or shrink, $y = \frac{a}{x}$, then you can write its equation.

5 EXAMPLE **Writing the Equation of a Transformation**

Write an equation for the translation of $y = \frac{5}{x}$ that has asymptotes at $x = -2$ and $y = 3$.

$y = \dfrac{5}{x - h} + k$ Use the general form of a translation.

$\quad = \dfrac{5}{x - (-2)} + 3$ Substitute -2 for h and 3 for k.

$\quad = \dfrac{5}{x + 2} + 3$ Simplify.

An equation for the translation is $y = \dfrac{5}{x + 2} + 3$.

✓ Quick Check **5** **a.** Write an equation for the translation of $y = -\frac{1}{x}$ that is 4 units left and 5 units up.
b. Check your work by graphing your solution to part (a).

EXERCISES

For more exercises, see *Extra Skill and Word Problem Practice*.

Practice and Problem Solving

 **Practice by Example**

 **for Help**

Example 1
(page 495)

Make a table of values. Then sketch a graph of each inverse variation.

1. $y = \frac{2}{x}$ **2.** $y = \frac{10}{x}$ **3.** $y = -\frac{10}{x}$

Example 2
(page 496)

Draw a graph of each function. Describe properties of the graph.

4. $y = \frac{0.2}{x}$ **5.** $y = \frac{-3}{x}$ **6.** $y = \frac{8}{x}$

7. $y = \frac{-5}{x}$ **8.** $y = \frac{100}{x}$ **9.** $y = \frac{-0.1}{x}$

Example 3
(page 496)

The weight P in pounds that a beam can safely carry is inversely proportional to the distance D in feet between the supports of the beam. For a certain type of wooden beam, $P = \frac{9200}{D}$. Use a graphing calculator and the Intersect feature to find the distance between supports that is needed to carry each given weight.

10. 500 lb   **11.** 1200 lb   **12.** 2400 lb   **13.** 5000 lb

Example 4
(page 497)

Sketch the asymptotes and the graph of each equation.

14. $y = \frac{1}{x} - 3$ **15.** $y = \frac{-2}{x} - 3$ **16.** $y = \frac{1}{x - 2} + 5$ **17.** $y = \frac{1}{x - 3} + 4$

18. $y = \frac{2}{x + 6} - 1$ **19.** $y = \frac{-10}{x + 1} - 8$ **20.** $y = \frac{1}{x} + 2$ **21.** $y = \frac{-8}{x + 5} - 6$

Example 5
(page 498)

Write an equation for the translation of $y = \frac{2}{x}$ that has the given asymptotes.

22. $x = 0$ and $y = 4$ **23.** $x = -2$ and $y = 3$ **24.** $x = 4$ and $y = -8$

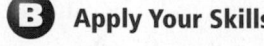 **Apply Your Skills** 🌐 **25. Budgeting** A high school spends $750 each year on student academic achievement awards. The amount spent per award depends on how many awards are given. Write and graph a function that models the relationship between the number a of awards given and the cost c of each award. What are a reasonable domain and range for the function?

26. Open-Ended Write an equation for a horizontal translation of $y = \frac{2}{x}$. Then write an equation for a vertical translation of $y = \frac{2}{x}$. Identify the horizontal and vertical asymptotes of the graph of each function.

Write each equation in the form $y = \frac{k}{x}$.

27. $y = \frac{1}{2x}$

28. $y = \frac{3}{4x}$

29. $y = -\frac{25}{3x}$

30. $xy = -0.01$

31. $3xy = 12$

32. $-7 = 5xy$

Sketch the graph of each function.

33. $xy = 3$

34. $xy + 5 = 0$

35. $3xy = 1$

36. $5xy = 2$

37. $10xy = -4$

38. $3xy = -17$

 39. Writing Explain how knowing the asymptotes of a translation of $y = \frac{k}{x}$ can help you graph the function. Include an example.

40. Multiple Choice The formula $p = \frac{69.1}{a + 2.3}$ models the relation between atmospheric pressure p in inches of mercury and altitude a in miles.

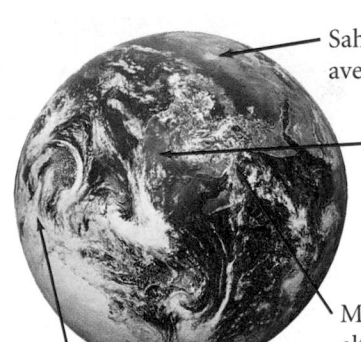

Sahara Desert average alt. 1500 ft

Kalahari Desert average alt. 3100 ft

Mt. Kilimanjaro alt. 19,340 ft

Vinson Massif alt. 16,860 ft

Use the data shown with the photo. At which location does the model predict the pressure to be about 23.93 in. of mercury?

Ⓐ Sahara Desert
Ⓑ Kalahari Desert
Ⓒ Mt. Kilimanjaro
Ⓓ Vinson Massif

Problem Solving Hint

1 mi = 5280 ft

Graph each pair of functions. Find the approximate point(s) of intersection.

41. $y = \frac{6}{x - 2}, y = 6$

42. $y = -\frac{1}{x - 3} - 6, y = 6.2$

43. $y = \frac{3}{x + 1}, y = -4$

44. $y = -\frac{2}{x^2}, y = -10$

45. $y = -\frac{1}{x - 4}, y = 4.2$

46. $y = \frac{4}{x^2} + 2, y = 9$

 47. a. Gasoline Mileage Suppose you drive an average of 10,000 miles each year. Your gasoline mileage (mi/gal) varies inversely with the number of gallons of gasoline you use each year. Write and graph a model for your average mileage m in terms of the gallons g of gasoline used.

b. After you begin driving on the highway more often, you use 50 gal less per year. Write and graph a new model to include this information.

c. Calculate your old and new mileage assuming that you originally used 400 gal of gasoline per year.

Homework Video Tutor
Visit: PHSchool.com
Web Code: age-0902

Ⓒ Challenge

Critical Thinking Compare each pair of graphs and find any points of intersection.

 48. $y = \frac{1}{x}$ and $y = \left|\frac{1}{x}\right|$

49. $y = \frac{1}{x}$ and $y = \frac{1}{x^2}$

50. $y = \left|\frac{1}{x}\right|$ and $y = \frac{1}{x^2}$

51. Find two reciprocal functions such that the minimum distance from the origin to the graph of each function is $4\sqrt{2}$.

52. Write each equation in the form $y = \frac{k}{x - b} + c$, and sketch the graph.

a. $y = \frac{2}{3x - 6}$ **b.** $y = \frac{1}{2 - 4x}$ **c.** $y = \frac{3 - x}{x + 2}$

d. $y = \frac{2x + 1}{2x - 1}$ **e.** $xy + 2x = 1$ **f.** $xy - y = 1$

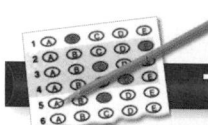

Test Prep

Multiple Choice

53. Which point is NOT on the graph of $y = -\frac{2}{x}$?

   A. $\left(-\frac{1}{2}, 4\right)$ **B.** $(-1, 2)$

   C. $(2, -1)$ **D.** $\left(8, -\frac{1}{16}\right)$

54. Which equation is a line of symmetry for $xy = -7$ and does NOT intersect the branches of the graph?

   F. $x = 0$ **G.** $y = 0$

   H. $y = x$ **J.** $y = -x$

55. What are the asymptotes of the graph of $y = \frac{10}{x - 5}$?

   A. $x = 0, y = 5$ **B.** $x = 5, y = 0$

   C. $x = 5, y = 10$ **D.** $x = 10, y = 5$

56. What are the asymptotes of the graph of $y = \frac{10}{x} + 5$?

   F. $x = 0, y = 5$ **G.** $x = 5, y = 5$

   H. $x = 5, y = 10$ **J.** $x = 10, y = 5$

57. What is an equation for the translation of $y = \frac{2}{x}$ that has asymptotes at $x = 3$ and $y = -5$?

   A. $y = \frac{2}{x - 3} - 5$ **B.** $y = \frac{2}{x + 3} + 5$

   C. $y = \frac{2}{x + 5} - 3$ **D.** $y = \frac{2}{x - 5} + 3$

Short Response

58. Explain how to find the asymptotes of $y = -\frac{3}{x - 2} + 11$.

Extended Response

59. Explain how to find an equation for the translation of $y = \frac{-3}{x}$ that has asymptotes at $x = -5$ and $y = -13$.

Mixed Review

Lesson 9-1

Describe the variation that is modeled by each formula.

60. $V = \frac{s^2 h}{3}$ **61.** $h = \frac{3V}{s^2}$ **62.** $B = \frac{3V}{h}$ **63.** $w = \frac{V}{\ell h}$ **64.** $b = \frac{2A}{h}$

Lesson 8-1

Identify each function as exponential growth or decay, and find the growth or decay factor.

65. $y = 3 \cdot 4^x$ **66.** $y = 0.1 \cdot 2^x$ **67.** $y = 5 \cdot (0.8)^x$ **68.** $y = 3 \cdot \left(\frac{1}{2}\right)^x$

Lesson 7-3

Multiply.

69. $\left(5\sqrt{3} - 2\right)^2$ **70.** $\left(\sqrt{3} + \sqrt{5}\right)\left(\sqrt{3} - \sqrt{5}\right)$

71. $\left(3\sqrt{5} + 2\sqrt{10}\right)\left(2\sqrt{5} + \sqrt{10}\right)$ **72.** $\left(4 + 2\sqrt{3}\right)\left(6 - 3\sqrt{3}\right)$

Rational Functions and Their Graphs

What You'll Learn

- To identify properties of rational functions
- To graph rational functions

. . . And Why

To find the average cost of producing CD-ROMs, as in Example 5

✓ **Check Skills You'll Need**

GO **for Help** Lessons 5-4 and 5-5

Factor.

1. $x^2 + 5x + 6$ **2.** $x^2 - 6x + 8$ **3.** $x^2 - 12x + 27$

4. $2x^2 + x - 28$ **5.** $2x^2 - 11x + 15$ **6.** $2x^2 - 19x + 24$

Solve.

7. $x^2 + x - 12 = 0$ **8.** $x^2 - 3x - 28 = 0$ **9.** $x^2 - 9x + 18 = 0$

🔊 **New Vocabulary** • rational function • point of discontinuity

---

1   Properties of Rational Functions

Members of the reciprocal function family are rational functions.

 Key Concepts

Definition	**Rational Function**

A **rational function** $f(x)$ is a function that can be written as

$$f(x) = \frac{P(x)}{Q(x)},$$

where $P(x)$ and $Q(x)$ are polynomial functions. The domain of $f(x)$ is all real numbers except those for which $Q(x) = 0$.

Vocabulary Tip

A <u>rational</u> <u>function</u> is a ratio of functions, just as a rational number is a ratio of numbers.

The graphs of the rational functions $y = \frac{-2x}{x^2 + 1}$, $y = \frac{1}{x^2 - 4}$, and $y = \frac{(x + 2)(x - 1)}{x + 1}$ are shown below.

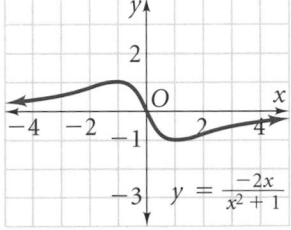 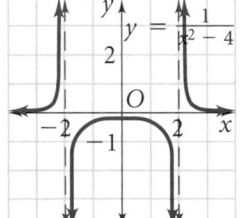 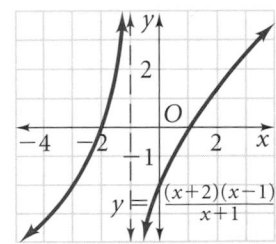

In the first rational function, there is no value of x that makes the denominator 0. The graph is continuous because it has no jumps, breaks, or holes in it. It can be drawn with a pencil that never leaves the paper.

In the second rational function, x cannot be 2 or -2. In the third, x cannot be -1. The last two graphs are discontinuous.

If a is a real number for which the denominator of a rational function f is zero, then a is not in the domain of f. The graph of f is not continuous at $x = a$ and the function has a **point of discontinuity** at $x = a$.

To find points of discontinuity, find the values of x that make the denominator 0.

① EXAMPLE Finding Points of Discontinuity

For each rational function, find any points of discontinuity.

a. $y = \dfrac{1}{x^2 + 2x + 1}$

The function is undefined at value(s) of x for which $x^2 + 2x + 1 = 0$.

$x^2 + 2x + 1 = 0$	**Set the denominator equal to zero.**
$(x + 1)(x + 1) = 0$	**Solve by factoring or using the Quadratic Formula.**
$x + 1 = 0$	**Zero Product Property**
$x = -1$	**Solve for x.**

There is a point of discontinuity at $x = -1$.

b. $y = \dfrac{-x + 1}{x^2 + 1}$

The function is undefined at value(s) of x for which $x^2 + 1 = 0$.

$x^2 + 1 = 0$	**Set the denominator equal to zero.**
$x^2 = -1$	**Solve for x.**
$x = \pm\sqrt{-1}$	

Since $\sqrt{-1}$ is not a real number, there is no real value for x for which the function $y = \dfrac{-x + 1}{x^2 + 1}$ is undefined. There is no point of discontinuity.

✓ Quick Check ① For each rational function, find any points of discontinuity.

a. $y = \dfrac{1}{x^2 - 16}$ **b.** $y = \dfrac{x^2 - 1}{x^2 + 3}$ **c.** $y = \dfrac{x + 1}{x^2 + 2x - 8}$

The graph of $y = \dfrac{x + 1}{(x - 1)(x + 2)}$ is shown at the right. The zeros of the denominator are 1 and -2. The graph has vertical asymptotes at those points.

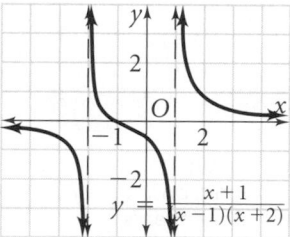

Graphing Calculator Hint

A hole in a graph is not displayed on a graphing calculator.

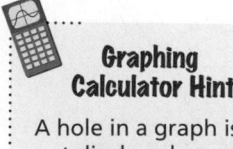

2 is a zero of both the numerator and the denominator of the rational function $y = \dfrac{(x - 2)(x + 1)}{x - 2}$. The graph of this function is the same as the graph of $y = x + 1$, except it has a hole at $x = 2$.

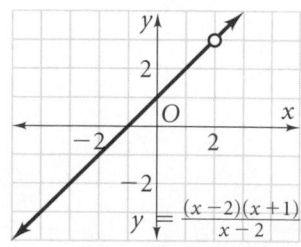

2 is a zero of both the numerator and the denominator of the rational function $y = \dfrac{x - 2}{(x - 2)(x - 1)}$. The graph of this function is the same as the graph of $y = \dfrac{1}{x - 1}$, except it has a hole at $x = 2$.

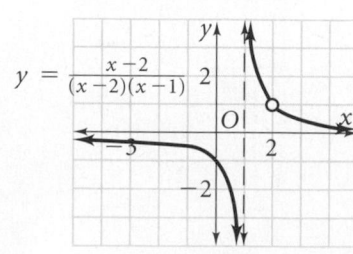

2 is a zero of both the numerator and the denominator of the rational function $y = \frac{x-2}{(x-2)^2}$.

The graph of this function is exactly the same as the graph of $y = \frac{1}{x-2}$. The vertical asymptote is $x = 2$ and there is no hole.

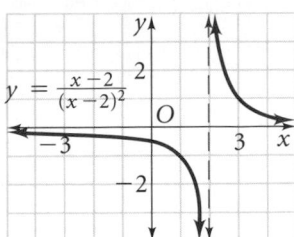

Key Concepts

Properties	Vertical Asymptotes

The rational function $f(x) = \frac{P(x)}{Q(x)}$ has a point of discontinuity for each real zero of $Q(x)$.

If $P(x)$ and $Q(x)$ have no common real zeros, then the graph of $f(x)$ has a vertical asymptote at each real zero of $Q(x)$.

If $P(x)$ and $Q(x)$ have a common real zero a, then there is a hole in the graph or a vertical asymptote at $x = a$.

2 EXAMPLE Finding Vertical Asymptotes

Describe the vertical asymptotes and holes for the graph of each rational function.

a. $y = \frac{x+1}{(x-2)(x-3)}$

Since 2 and 3 are the zeros of the denominator and neither is a zero of the numerator, $x = 2$ and $x = 3$ are vertical asymptotes.

b. $y = \frac{(x-2)(x-1)}{x-2}$

The graph of this function is the same as the graph of $y = x - 1$, except it has a hole at $x = 2$.

c. $y = \frac{(x-3)(x+4)}{(x-3)(x-3)(x+4)}$

The graph of this function is the same as the graph of $y = \frac{1}{x-3}$, except it has a hole at $x = -4$. The vertical asymptote is $x = 3$.

Quick Check ❷ Describe the vertical asymptotes and holes for the graph of each rational function.

a. $y = \frac{x-2}{(x-1)(x+3)}$ **b.** $y = \frac{x-2}{(x-2)(x+3)}$ **c.** $y = \frac{x^2-1}{x+1}$

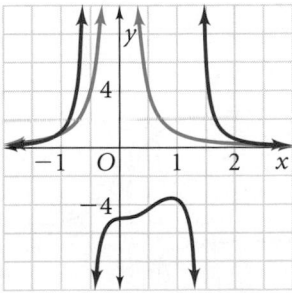

For the graphs of rational functions such as $y = \frac{1}{x}$ and $y = \frac{1}{x^2}$, the horizontal asymptote is $y = 0$. As shown at the left, when the absolute value of x is large, the graph of $y = \frac{2x^2 - x + 10}{5x^4 - 7x^3 + x^2 - 2}$ is very close to the graph of $y = \frac{1}{x^2}$. So $y = 0$ is the horizontal asymptote of both graphs.

In fact, $y = 0$ is the horizontal asymptote of the graph of any rational function, if the degree of the denominator is greater than the degree of the numerator.

If the degree of the numerator equals the degree of the denominator, then the horizontal asymptote can be found as shown in Example 3.

3 EXAMPLE Finding Horizontal Asymptotes

Find the horizontal asymptote of $y = \frac{3x + 5}{x - 2}$.

Divide the numerator by the denominator as shown at the right. The function $y = \frac{3x + 5}{x - 2}$ can be written as $y = \frac{11}{x - 2} + 3$. Its graph is a translation of $y = \frac{11}{x}$. The horizontal asymptote of the graph of $y = \frac{3x + 5}{x - 2}$ is $y = 3$.

$$
\begin{array}{r}
3 \\
x - 2 \overline{)\, 3x + 5} \\
\underline{3x - 6} \\
11
\end{array}
$$

✓ **Quick Check** ❸ Find the horizontal asymptote of the graph of each rational function.

a. $y = \frac{-2x + 6}{x - 1}$ **b.** $y = \frac{2x^2 + 5}{x^2 + 1}$

 Key Concepts

Properties	Horizontal Asymptotes

The graph of a rational function has at most one horizontal asymptote.

The graph of a rational function has a horizontal asymptote at $y = 0$ if the degree of the denominator is greater than the degree of the numerator.

If the degrees of the numerator and the denominator are equal, then the graph has a horizontal asymptote at $y = \frac{a}{b}$. a is the coefficient of the term of highest degree in the numerator and b is the coefficient of the term of highest degree in the denominator.

If the degree of the numerator is greater than the degree of the denominator, then the graph has no horizontal asymptote.

2 Graphing Rational Functions

You can use asymptotes to sketch the graphs of rational functions.

4 EXAMPLE Sketching Graphs of Rational Functions

active math

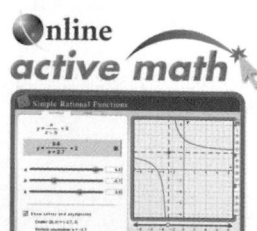

For: Rational Functions Activity
Use: Interactive Textbook, 9-3

Sketch the graph of $y = \frac{x + 2}{(x + 3)(x - 4)}$.

The degree of the denominator is greater than the degree of the numerator, so the y-axis is the horizontal asymptote. When $x > 4$, y is positive. So as x increases, the graph approaches the y-axis from above. When $x < -3$, y is negative. So as x decreases, the graph approaches the y-axis from below.

Since -2 is the zero of the numerator, the x-intercept is at -2. Since -3 and 4 are the zeros of the denominator, the vertical asymptotes are at $x = -3$ and $x = 4$.

Calculate the values of y for values of x near the asymptotes. Plot those points and sketch the graph.

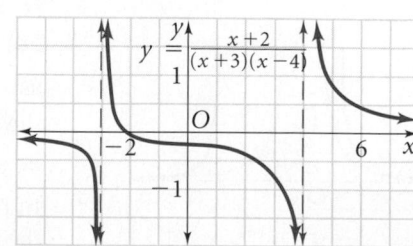

✓ **Quick Check** ❹ Sketch the graph of $y = \frac{x + 3}{(x - 1)(x - 5)}$.

 **EXAMPLE** Real-World 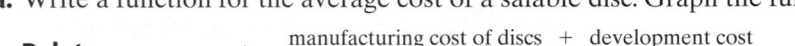 Connection

Business The CD-ROMs for a computer game can be manufactured for $.25 each. The development cost is $124,000. The first 100 discs are samples and will not be sold.

a. Write a function for the average cost of a salable disc. Graph the function.

Relate average cost = $\dfrac{\text{manufacturing cost of discs} + \text{development cost}}{\text{number of salable discs}}$

Define Let x = number of CD-ROMs produced.
Let y = average cost of one saleable disc.

Write $y = \dfrac{0.25x + 124{,}000}{x - 100}$

Graph the function. Adjust the viewing window.

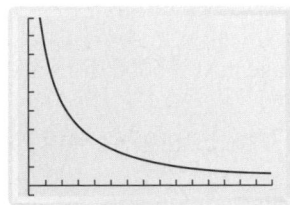

Xmin=0   Ymin=−10
Xmax=15000 Ymax=100
Xscl=1000   Yscl=10

b. What is the average cost if 2000 discs are produced? If 12,800 discs are produced?

Use the **CALC** feature to evaluate the function at $x = 2000$ and at $x = 12{,}800$. If 2000 discs are produced, the average cost will be about $65.53. If 12,800 discs are produced, the average cost will be about $10.02.

 Quick Check ⑤ **a. Critical Thinking** How could you find the number of discs that must be produced to bring the average cost under $8?
b. What is the vertical asymptote of the graph of the function in Example 5? What is the horizontal asymptote?
c. Describe how the asymptotes are related to the information given in Example 5.

EXERCISES

For more exercises, see *Extra Skill and Word Problem Practice.*

Practice and Problem Solving

 **A** **Practice by Example**

Find any points of discontinuity for each rational function.

Example 1
(page 502)

1. $y = \dfrac{2x^2 + 5}{x^2 - 2x}$
2. $y = \dfrac{x^2 + 2x}{x^2 + 2}$
3. $y = \dfrac{3x - 3}{x^2 - 1}$

4. $y = \dfrac{6 - 3x}{x^2 - 5x + 6}$
5. $y = \dfrac{x^2 + 5x + 6}{x^2 + 6x + 9}$
6. $y = \dfrac{x^2 + 4x + 3}{2x^2 + 5x - 7}$

7. $y = \dfrac{x^3 - 8}{x^3 - 8}$
8. $y = \dfrac{x^2}{x^2 + 1}$
9. $y = \dfrac{1}{2x^2 + 3x - 7}$

Example 2
(page 503)

Describe the vertical asymptotes and holes for the graph of each rational function.

10. $y = \dfrac{3}{x + 2}$
11. $y = \dfrac{x + 5}{x + 5}$
12. $y = \dfrac{x + 3}{(2x + 3)(x - 1)}$

13. $y = \dfrac{(x + 3)(x - 2)}{(x - 2)(x + 1)}$
14. $y = \dfrac{x^2 - 4}{x + 2}$
15. $y = \dfrac{x + 5}{x^2 + 9}$

16. $y = \dfrac{9 - x^2}{x^2 - 9}$
17. $y = \dfrac{2x^2}{2x^2 + 2}$
18. $y = \dfrac{6x^2 + x - 2}{3x^2 + 17x + 10}$

Example 3
(page 504)

Find the horizontal asymptote of the graph of each rational function.

19. $y = \dfrac{5}{x + 6}$

20. $y = \dfrac{x + 2}{2x^2 - 4}$

21. $y = \dfrac{x + 1}{x + 5}$

22. $y = \dfrac{x^2 + 2}{2x^2 - 1}$

23. $y = \dfrac{5x^3 + 2x}{2x^5 - 4x^3}$

24. $y = \dfrac{3x - 4}{4x + 1}$

Example 4
(page 504)

Sketch the graph of each rational function.

25. $y = \dfrac{x^2 - 4}{3x - 6}$

26. $y = \dfrac{4x}{x^3 - 4x}$

27. $y = \dfrac{x + 4}{x - 4}$

28. $y = \dfrac{x(x + 1)}{x + 1}$

29. $y = \dfrac{x + 6}{(x - 2)(x + 3)}$

30. $y = \dfrac{3x}{(x + 2)^2}$

Example 5
(page 505)

31. Business CDs can be manufactured for $.19 each. The development cost is $210,000. The first 500 discs are samples and will not be sold.
  a. Write a function for the average cost of a salable disc. Graph the function.
  b. What is the average cost if 5000 discs are produced? If 15,000 discs are produced?
  c. How many discs must be produced to bring the average cost under $10?
  d. What are the vertical and horizontal asymptotes of the graph of the function?

B **Apply Your Skills**

Find the vertical and horizontal asymptotes, if any, of the graph of each rational function.

32.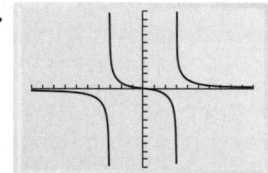

33.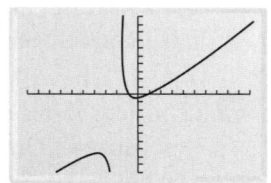

34.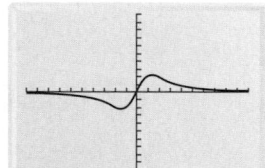

Sketch the graph of each rational function.

35. $y = \dfrac{2x + 3}{x - 5}$

36. $y = \dfrac{x^2 + 6x + 9}{x + 3}$

37. $y = \dfrac{4x^2 - 100}{2x^2 + x - 15}$

38. $y = -\dfrac{x}{(x - 1)^2}$

39. $y = \dfrac{2x}{3x - 1}$

40. $y = \dfrac{2}{x^2 - 4}$

41. Writing Describe the conditions that will produce a rational function with a graph that has no vertical asymptotes.

42. Basketball A basketball player has made 21 of her last 30 free throws—an average of 70%. To model the player's rate of success if she makes x more consecutive free throws, use the function $y = \dfrac{21 + x}{30 + x}$.
  a. Graph the function.
  b. Use the graph to find the number of consecutive free throws the player needs to raise her success rate to 75%.

43. Data Analysis The president of XYZ Company earns $200,000 a year. Each of the other x employees earns $20,000 a year.
  a. Write and graph a function that models the average salary of all employees of XYZ.
  b. What is the average salary if there are three employees? If there are 30 employees?
  c. Critical Thinking Is the average salary the best measure of the workers' pay? Explain. What other measure could you use?

44. Reasoning Look for a pattern in the sequence of shells below.

  a. Write a model for the number of purple shells $P(n)$ at each step n.
  b. Write a model for the number of red shells $R(n)$ at each step n.
  c. Write a model for the ratio of $P(n)$ to $R(n)$. Use it to predict the ratio
   of purple shells to red shells in the next figure. Verify your answer.

45. Wage Policy The graph below compares the average hourly wage for
  production workers and the minimum hourly wage from 1950 to 2000.

History of the Minimum Wage

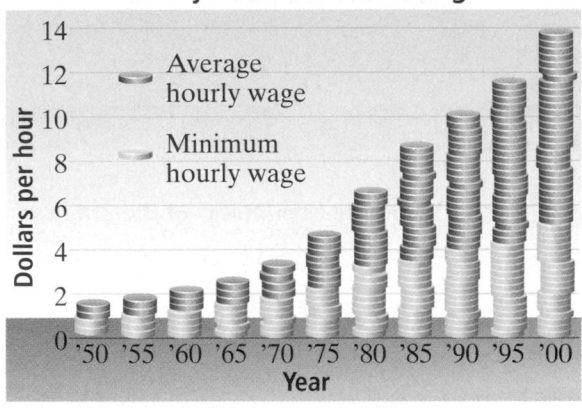

Source: Bureau of Labor Statistics.
Go to **www.PHSchool.com** for a data update.
Web Code: agg-9041

  a. How has the comparison of the minimum wage to the production workers'
   wage changed over the years?
  b. If the minimum wage and the production workers' wage are modeled by
   polynomials, what type of function would model their ratio?
  c. The quadratic function $M(x) = 0.00081x^2 + 0.049x + 0.68$ models the
   minimum wage, where x is the number of years since 1950. The quadratic
   function $A(x) = 0.0043x^2 + 0.04x + 1.21$ models the average wage. Write
   a model for the ratio of these two functions.
  d. Graph your model. If the present trends continue, when will the minimum
   wage decrease to 25% of the average wage?

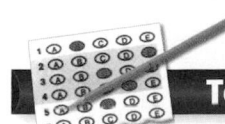

Test Prep

Multiple Choice

46. What are the points of discontinuity for $y = \dfrac{(2x + 3)(x - 5)}{(x + 5)(2x - 1)}$?

  A. $-5, 1$ **B.** $-\frac{3}{2}, 5$ **C.** $-5, \frac{1}{2}$ **D.** $5, -\frac{1}{2}$

47. How many points of discontinuity does the function $y = \dfrac{2x}{x^2 + 4}$ have?

  F. 0   **G.** 1   **H.** 2   **J.** 4

48. Which graph *cannot* be the graph of a rational function?

A.
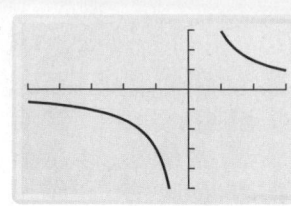

B.
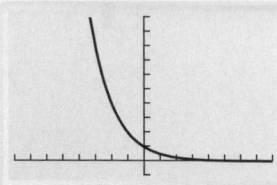

C.
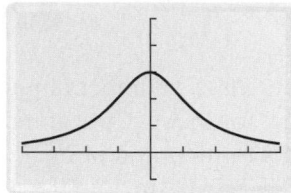

D.
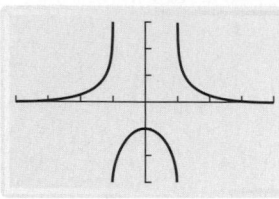

Short Response

49. Find the horizontal asymptote of $y = \frac{5x + 7}{x + 3}$ by dividing the numerator by the denominator. Explain your steps.

50. Find the points of discontinuity of $y = \frac{x(2x - 1)(x + 1)}{(x + 5)(x + 1)}$.

Mixed Review

Lesson 9-2

Find the asymptotes of the graph of each equation.

51. $y = \frac{3}{x} + 4$ **52.** $y = \frac{2}{x + 3}$ **53.** $y = \frac{-1}{x + 1} + 1$

54. $y = \frac{5}{x - 7} - 3$ **55.** $y = \frac{5}{2 - x}$ **56.** $y = \frac{-2}{5 - x} - 6$

Lesson 8-2

Describe how the graph of each function relates to the graph of $y = 4(0.8)^x$.

57. $y = 4(0.8)^{x-1}$ **58.** $y = 4(0.8)^x + 3$ **59.** $y = 4(0.8)^{x+1} - 5$

✓ Checkpoint Quiz 1   Lessons 9-1 through 9-3

If $z = 30$ when $x = 3$ and $y = 2$, write the function that models each relationship.

1. z varies jointly with x and y.

2. z varies directly with x and inversely with y.

3. z varies inversely with the product of x and y.

Explain how the graph of y_2 is related to the graph of y_1.

4. $y_1 = \frac{4}{x}$ and $y_2 = \frac{9}{x}$ **5.** $y_1 = \frac{1}{x}$ and $y_2 = \frac{1}{x} + 5$

6. $y_1 = \frac{1}{x - 1} + 2$ and $y_2 = \frac{1}{x + 1} - 2$

Sketch the graph of each rational function.

7. $y = \frac{x^2 - 9}{2x + 6}$ **8.** $y = \frac{3x}{x^3 - x}$ **9.** $y = \frac{x + 3}{x - 3}$ **10.** $y = \frac{x^2 - 2x}{x - 2}$

9-4

Rational Expressions

✓ Check Skills You'll Need

GO for Help 5-4 and Skills Handbook page 871

Factor.

1. $2x^2 - 3x + 1$ **2.** $4x^2 - 9$

3. $5x^2 + 6x + 1$ **4.** $10x^2 - 10$

Multiply or divide.

5. $\frac{3}{8} \cdot \frac{5}{6}$ **6.** $\frac{1}{2} \cdot \frac{4}{6}$ **7.** $\frac{8}{3} \cdot \frac{2}{16}$ **8.** $\frac{2}{5} \cdot \frac{3}{7}$

9. $\frac{5}{8} \div 4$ **10.** $\frac{3}{4} \div \frac{1}{2}$ **11.** $\frac{9}{16} \div \frac{3}{4}$ **12.** $\frac{5}{4} \div \frac{15}{8}$

🔊 **New Vocabulary** • simplest form

---

1 **Simplifying Rational Expressions**

A rational expression is in **simplest form** when its numerator and denominator are polynomials that have no common divisors.

In simplest form	Not in simplest form
$\dfrac{x}{x-1}$ $\dfrac{2}{x^2+3}$	$\dfrac{x}{x^2}$ $\dfrac{\frac{1}{x}}{x+1}$ $\dfrac{2(x-3)}{3(x-3)}$

You can simplify some expressions by dividing out common factors.

1 EXAMPLE   Simplifying Rational Expressions

Simplify $\dfrac{x^2 + 10x + 25}{x^2 + 9x + 20}$. State any restrictions on the variable.

$\dfrac{x^2 + 10x + 25}{x^2 + 9x + 20} = \dfrac{(x+5)(x+5)}{(x+4)(x+5)}$ **Factor the polynomials. Notice that $x \neq -4$ or -5.**

$= \dfrac{(x\cancel{+5})(x+5)}{(x+4)(x\cancel{+5})}$ **Divide out common factors.**

$= \dfrac{x+5}{x+4}$

The simplified expression is $\dfrac{x+5}{x+4}$ for $x \neq -4$ or -5. The restrictions on x are needed to prevent the denominator of the original expression from being zero.

✓ **Quick Check** **1.** Simplify each expression. State any restrictions on the variables.

a. $\dfrac{-27x^3y}{9x^4y}$ **b.** $\dfrac{-6 - 3x}{x^2 - 6x + 8}$ **c.** $\dfrac{2x^2 - 3x - 2}{x^2 - 5x + 6}$

2 EXAMPLE Real-World Connection

Architecture One factor in designing a structure is the need to maximize the volume (space for working) for a given surface area (material needed for construction). Compare the ratio of the volume to surface area of a cylinder with radius r and height r to a cylinder with radius r and height $2r$.

Use the formulas for volume and surface area of a cylinder.

$$\text{Volume } (V) = \pi r^2 h$$
$$\text{Surface Area (S.A.)} = 2\pi rh + 2\pi r^2$$

Cylinder with height r Cylinder with height $2r$

$\dfrac{V}{\text{S.A.}} = \dfrac{\pi r^2 h}{2\pi rh + 2\pi r^2}$	$\dfrac{V}{\text{S.A.}} = \dfrac{\pi r^2 h}{2\pi rh + 2\pi r^2}$ **Write a ratio.**
$= \dfrac{\pi r^2 (r)}{2\pi r(r) + 2\pi r^2}$	$= \dfrac{\pi r^2 (2r)}{2\pi r(2r) + 2\pi r^2}$ **Substitute for h.**
$= \dfrac{\pi r^3}{2\pi r^2 + 2\pi r^2}$	$= \dfrac{2\pi r^3}{4\pi r^2 + 2\pi r^2}$ **Simplify.**
$= \dfrac{\pi r^3}{4\pi r^2}$	$= \dfrac{2\pi r^3}{6\pi r^2}$ **Combine like terms.**
$= \dfrac{r}{4}$	$= \dfrac{r}{3}$ **Simplify.**

For a given radius, the ratio of volume to surface area is greater for the cylinder with a height of $2r$.

✓ Quick Check **2 a.** Find the ratio of volume to surface area of a cylinder whose height is $4r$.
     b. Critical Thinking Let mr be the height of a cylinder of radius r, with m a positive number. Describe how the ratio of volume to surface area changes as m changes.

---

2 Multiplying and Dividing Rational Expressions

You can use what you know about simplifying rational expressions when you multiply and divide them.

3 EXAMPLE Multiplying Rational Expressions

Multiply $\dfrac{2x^2 + 7x + 3}{x - 4}$ and $\dfrac{x^2 - 16}{x^2 + 8x + 15}$. State any restrictions on the variable.

$$\dfrac{2x^2 + 7x + 3}{x - 4} \cdot \dfrac{x^2 - 16}{x^2 + 8x + 15} = \dfrac{(2x + 1)(x + 3)}{x - 4} \cdot \dfrac{(x - 4)(x + 4)}{(x + 3)(x + 5)} \quad \textbf{Factor.}$$

$$= \dfrac{(2x + 1)(\overset{1}{\cancel{x + 3}})}{\underset{1}{\cancel{x - 4}}} \cdot \dfrac{(\overset{1}{\cancel{x - 4}})(x + 4)}{(\underset{1}{\cancel{x + 3}})(x + 5)} \quad \begin{array}{l}\textbf{Divide out}\\\textbf{common factors.}\end{array}$$

$$= \dfrac{(2x + 1)(x + 4)}{x + 5}$$

The product is $\dfrac{(2x + 1)(x + 4)}{x + 5}$ for $x \neq 4, -3,$ or -5.

✓ Quick Check **3** Multiply $\dfrac{a^2 - 4}{a^2 - 1}$ and $\dfrac{a + 1}{a^2 + 2a}$. State any restrictions on the variable.

For practice in dividing fractions, go to p. 871.

To divide rational expressions, remember to multiply by the reciprocal of the divisor, just as you did when dividing rational numbers.

4 EXAMPLE   **Dividing Rational Expressions**

Divide $\dfrac{4 - x}{(3x + 2)(x - 2)}$ by $\dfrac{5(x - 4)}{(x - 2)(7y - 5)}$. State any restrictions on the variables.

$$\dfrac{4 - x}{(3x + 2)(x - 2)} \div \dfrac{5(x - 4)}{(x - 2)(7y - 5)}$$

$$= \dfrac{4 - x}{(3x + 2)(x - 2)} \cdot \dfrac{(x - 2)(7y - 5)}{5(x - 4)}$$ Multiply by the reciprocal.

$$= \dfrac{\overset{1}{-(x - 4)}}{(3x + 2)\underset{1}{(x - 2)}} \cdot \dfrac{\overset{1}{(x - 2)}(7y - 5)}{5\underset{1}{(x - 4)}}$$ Divide out common factors.

$$= \dfrac{-1}{3x + 2} \cdot \dfrac{7y - 5}{5}$$ Rewrite the expression.

$$= \dfrac{-(7y - 5)}{5(3x + 2)}$$ Multiply.

The quotient is $\dfrac{-(7y - 5)}{5(3x + 2)}$ for $x \neq -\dfrac{2}{3}, 2$, or 4, and $y \neq \dfrac{5}{7}$.

Video Tutor Help

Visit: PHSchool.com
Web Code: age-0775

✓ **Quick Check** ❹ Divide $\dfrac{a^2 + 2a - 15}{a^2 - 16}$ by $\dfrac{a + 1}{3a - 12}$. State any restrictions on the variable.

EXERCISES

For more exercises, see *Extra Skill and Word Problem Practice.*

Practice and Problem Solving

A Practice by Example

Examples 1 and 2
(pages 509–510)

Simplify each rational expression. State any restrictions on the variable.

1. $\dfrac{2x}{4x^2 - 2x}$

2. $\dfrac{6c^2 + 9c}{3c}$

3. $\dfrac{b^2 - 1}{b - 1}$

4. $\dfrac{z^2 - 49}{z + 7}$

5. $\dfrac{2x + 10}{x^2 + 10x + 25}$

6. $\dfrac{x^2 + 8x + 16}{x^2 - 2x - 24}$

Example 3
(page 510)

Multiply. State any restrictions on the variables.

7. $\dfrac{4x^2}{5y} \cdot \dfrac{7y}{12x^4}$

8. $\dfrac{2x^4}{10y^2} \cdot \dfrac{5y^3}{4x^3}$

9. $\dfrac{8y - 4}{10y - 5} \cdot \dfrac{5y - 15}{3y - 9}$

10. $\dfrac{2x + 12}{3x - 9} \cdot \dfrac{2x - 6}{3x + 8}$

11. $\dfrac{x^2 - 4}{x^2 - 1} \cdot \dfrac{x + 1}{x^2 + 2x}$

12. $\dfrac{x^2 - 5x + 6}{x^2 - 4} \cdot \dfrac{x^2 + 3x + 2}{x^2 - 2x - 3}$

Example 4
(page 511)

Divide. State any restrictions on the variables.

13. $\dfrac{7x}{4y^3} \div \dfrac{21x^3}{8y}$

14. $\dfrac{3x^3}{5y^2} \div \dfrac{6x^5}{5y^3}$

15. $\dfrac{6x + 6y}{x - y} \div \dfrac{18}{5x - 5y}$

16. $\dfrac{3y - 12}{2y + 4} \div \dfrac{6y - 24}{4y + 8}$

17. $\dfrac{x^2}{x^2 + 2x + 1} \div \dfrac{3x}{x^2 - 1}$

18. $\dfrac{y^2 - 5y + 6}{y^3} \div \dfrac{y^2 + 3y - 10}{4y^2}$

Simplify each rational expression. State any restrictions on the variables.

19. $\dfrac{x^2 - 5x - 24}{x^2 - 7x - 30}$ 　　　**20.** $\dfrac{2y^2 + 8y - 24}{2y^2 - 8y + 8}$ 　　　**21.** $\dfrac{xy^3 - 9xy}{12xy^2 + 12xy - 144x}$

22. Write an expression for the area of the rectangle at the right.

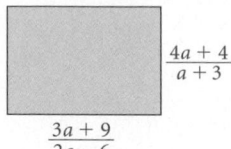

$\dfrac{4a + 4}{a + 3}$

$\dfrac{3a + 9}{2a - 6}$

23. Error Analysis A student claims that $x = 2$ is the only solution of the equation $\dfrac{x}{x - 2} = \dfrac{1}{2} + \dfrac{2}{x - 2}$. Is the student correct? Explain.

24. Open-Ended Write three rational expressions that simplify to $\dfrac{x}{x + 1}$.

25. Writing How can you tell whether a rational expression is in simplest form? Include an example with your explanation.

26. Industrial Design A storage tank will have a circular base of radius r and a height of r. The tank can be either cylindrical or hemispherical (half a sphere).

  a. Write and simplify an expression for the ratio of the volume of the hemispherical tank to its surface area (including the base). For a sphere, $V = \frac{4}{3}\pi r^3$ and S.A. $= 4\pi r^2$.

  b. Write and simplify an expression for the ratio of the volume of the cylindrical tank to its surface area (including the bases).

  c. Compare the ratios of volume to surface area for the two tanks.

  d. Compare the volumes of the two tanks.

Exercise 26

Multiply or divide. State any restrictions on the variable.

27. $\dfrac{a + 3}{a^2 + a - 12} \div \dfrac{a^2 - 9}{a^2 + 7a + 12}$ 　　　**28.** $\dfrac{b^2 - 25}{(b + 5)^2} \div \dfrac{2b + 10}{4b + 20}$

29. $\dfrac{6x^3 - 6x^2}{x^4 + 5x^3} \div \dfrac{3x^2 - 15x + 12}{2x^2 + 2x - 40}$ 　　　**30.** $\dfrac{2x^2 - 6x}{x^2 + 18x + 81} \cdot \dfrac{9x + 81}{x^2 - 9}$

31. $\dfrac{x^2 - x - 2}{2x^2 - 5x + 2} \div \dfrac{x^2 - x - 12}{2x^2 + 5x - 3}$ 　　　**32.** $\dfrac{2x^2 + 5x + 2}{4x^2 - 1} \cdot \dfrac{2x^2 + x - 1}{x^2 + x - 2}$

Simplify. State any restrictions on the variables.

33. $\dfrac{(x^2 - x)^2}{x(x - 1)^{-2}(x^2 + 3x - 4)}$ 　　　**34.** $\dfrac{2x + 6}{(x - 1)^{-1}(x^2 + 2x - 3)}$ 　　　**35.** $\dfrac{54x^3 y^{-1}}{3x^{-2}y}$

36. The width of the rectangle at the right is $\dfrac{a + 10}{3a + 24}$. Write an expression for the length of the rectangle.

$A = \dfrac{2a + 20}{6a + 15}$

37. Physics The acceleration of an object is a measure of how much its velocity changes in a given period of time.

$$\text{acceleration} = \frac{\text{final velocity} - \text{initial velocity}}{\text{time}}$$

Suppose you are riding a bicycle at 6 m/s. You step hard on the pedals and increase your speed to 12 m/s in about 5 s.

  a. Find your acceleration in m/s^2.

  b. A sedan can go from 0 to 60 mi/h in about 10 s. What is the acceleration in m/s^2? (*Hints:* 1 mi $\approx$ 1609 m; 1 h $=$ 3600 s.)

GO **Online**

Homework Video Tutor

Visit: PHSchool.com
Web Code: age-0904

C Challenge

38. a. Critical Thinking Simplify $\dfrac{(2x^n)^2 - 1}{2x^n - 1}$, where x is an integer and n is a positive integer. (*Hint:* Factor the numerator.)

  b. Use the result from part (a) to show that the value of the given expression is always an odd integer.

Use the fact that $\dfrac{\frac{a}{b}}{\frac{c}{d}} = \dfrac{a}{b} \div \dfrac{c}{d}$ to simplify each rational expression. State any restrictions on the variables.

39. $\dfrac{\frac{8x^2y}{x+1}}{\frac{6xy^2}{x+1}}$

40. $\dfrac{\frac{3a^3b^3}{a-b}}{\frac{4ab}{b-a}}$

41. $\dfrac{\frac{9m+6n}{m^2n^2}}{\frac{12m+8n}{5m^2}}$

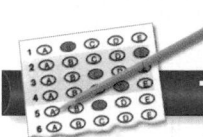

Test Prep

Multiple Choice

42. Which expression can be simplified to $\dfrac{x-1}{x-3}$?

   A. $\dfrac{x^2-x-6}{x^2-x-2}$ **B.** $\dfrac{x^2-2x+1}{x^2+2x-3}$

   C. $\dfrac{x^2-3x-4}{x^2-7x+12}$ **D.** $\dfrac{x^2-4x+3}{x^2-6x+9}$

43. Which expression is in simplest form?

   F. $\dfrac{x^2-x}{x^2-1}$ **G.** $\dfrac{x^2-1}{x^2+1}$

   H. $\dfrac{x^2-1}{x+1}$ **J.** $\dfrac{x+3}{x^2+4x+3}$

44. What is the product of $\dfrac{4x^2-1}{2x^2-5x-3}$ and $\dfrac{x^2-6x+9}{2x^2+5x-3}$?

   A. 1   **B.** $x-3$

   C. $x+3$ **D.** $\dfrac{x-3}{x+3}$

45. What are the restrictions on x when $\dfrac{x^2-x-2}{x^2-9}$ is divided by $\dfrac{x-8}{x^2+10x+25}$?

   F. $x \neq -3$ or -5 **G.** $x \neq 3, -3$, or -5
   H. $x \neq 3, -3, -5$, or 8 **J.** $x \neq 2, 9, 8$, or -25

Short Response

46. Let $f(x)$, $g(x)$, $h(x)$, and $k(x)$ be rational expressions. Explain how to find all the restrictions for $\dfrac{f(x)}{g(x)} \div \dfrac{h(x)}{k(x)}$.

47. The product of $\dfrac{x^2-11x+28}{x^2-2x-35}$ and a second rational expression $\dfrac{f(x)}{g(x)}$ is $\dfrac{x+4}{x+5}$. What is the second rational expression? Show each step of your work.

Mixed Review

Lesson 9-3

Describe the vertical asymptotes and holes for the graph of each rational function.

48. $y = \dfrac{x-3}{x-3}$ **49.** $y = \dfrac{x-1}{(3x+2)(x+1)}$ **50.** $y = \dfrac{(x-4)(x+5)}{(x+3)(x-4)}$

Lesson 8-3

Evaluate each logarithm.

51. $\log_4 64$ **52.** $\log_2 \dfrac{1}{32}$ **53.** $\log_5 5\sqrt{5}$ **54.** $\log_{16} 8$

Lesson 7-5

Solve each equation.

55. $\sqrt{x+3} - 1 = 4$ **56.** $\sqrt{7x+1} - \sqrt{6x+7} = 0$

9-5 Adding and Subtracting Rational Expressions

What You'll Learn

- To add and subtract rational expressions
- To simplify complex fractions

...And Why

To find the focal length of a camera lens, as in Example 1

Find the least common multiple of the two numbers.

1. 7, 21   **2.** 6, 10   **3.** 11, 17   **4.** 30, 105

Add or subtract.

5. $\frac{5}{19} + \frac{7}{38}$ **6.** $\frac{2}{15} + \frac{3}{25}$ **7.** $\frac{7}{24} - \frac{5}{36}$ **8.** $\frac{11}{12} - \frac{7}{45}$

◀)) **New Vocabulary**   • complex fraction

---

1   Adding and Subtracting Rational Expressions

Activity: Adding Fractions—Extended

1. Add. Simplify where possible.

   a. $\frac{2}{x} + \frac{3}{x}$ **b.** $\frac{4}{3x} + \frac{2}{3x}$ **c.** $\frac{3c}{2c-1} + \frac{5c+1}{2c-1}$

2. Explain the steps you followed in Question 1.

3. How is adding rational expressions similar to adding fractions?

To produce a clear photograph, light rays must be focused on the film. The focal length of a camera lens is the distance from the lens to the point where parallel rays of light are focused.

When you focus a camera, you change the distance from the lens to the film.

The lens equation is $\frac{1}{f} = \frac{1}{d_i} + \frac{1}{d_o}$.

f = focal length of the lens

d_i = distance from the lens to the film

d_o = distance from the lens to the object

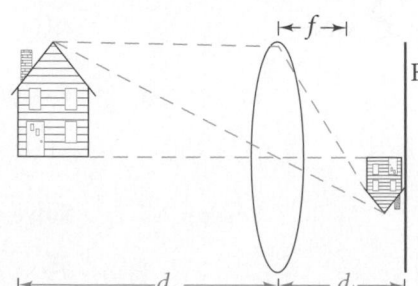

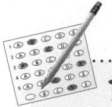

1 EXAMPLE **Real-World Connection**

Gridded Response An object is 15 cm from a camera lens. The object is in focus on the film when the lens is 10 cm from the film. Find the focal length of the lens in centimeters.

$\frac{1}{f} = \frac{1}{d_i} + \frac{1}{d_o}$ **Use the lens equation.**

$\frac{1}{f} = \frac{1}{10} + \frac{1}{15}$ **Substitute.**

$= \frac{3}{30} + \frac{2}{30}$ **Write equivalent fractions with the LCD.**

$= \frac{5}{30} = \frac{1}{6}$ **Add and simplify.**

● Since $\frac{1}{f} = \frac{1}{6}$, the focal length of the lens is 6 cm.

✓ Quick Check **①** Suppose an object is 20 cm from a camera lens. When the object is properly focused, the lens is 5 cm from the film. Find the focal length of the lens.

For practice in adding and subtracting fractions, go to p. 871.

To add or subtract rational expressions with different denominators, it is easiest to use the least common multiple of the denominators as a common denominator.

2 EXAMPLE **Finding Least Common Multiples**

Find the least common multiple of $4x^2 - 36$ and $6x^2 + 36x + 54$.

Step 1 Find the prime factors of each expression.

$4x^2 - 36 = 4(x^2 - 9) = (2)(2)(x - 3)(x + 3)$

$6x^2 + 36x + 54 = 6(x^2 + 6x + 9) = (2)(3)(x + 3)(x + 3)$

Step 2 Write each prime factor the greatest number of times it appears in either expression. Simplify where possible.

$(2)(2)(3)(x - 3)(x + 3)(x + 3) = 12(x - 3)(x + 3)^2$

● The least common multiple is $12(x - 3)(x + 3)^2$.

✓ Quick Check **②** Find the least common multiple of each pair of expressions.
a. $3x^2 - 9x - 30$ and $6x + 30$ **b.** $5x^2 + 15x + 10$ and $2x^2 - 8$

3 EXAMPLE **Adding Rational Expressions**

Simplify $\frac{1}{x^2 + 5x + 4} + \frac{5x}{3x + 3}$.

$\frac{1}{x^2 + 5x + 4} + \frac{5x}{3x + 3} = \frac{1}{(x + 1)(x + 4)} + \frac{5x}{3(x + 1)}$ **Factor the denominators.**

$= \frac{1}{(x + 1)(x + 4)} \cdot \frac{3}{3} + \frac{5x}{3(x + 1)} \cdot \frac{x + 4}{x + 4}$ **identity for multiplication**

$= \frac{3}{3(x + 1)(x + 4)} + \frac{5x(x + 4)}{3(x + 1)(x + 4)}$ **Multiply.**

$= \frac{3 + 5x(x + 4)}{3(x + 1)(x + 4)}$ **Add.**

$= \frac{5x^2 + 20x + 3}{3(x + 1)(x + 4)}$ **Simplify the numerator.**

Quick Check ❸ Simplify $\dfrac{1}{x^2 - 4x - 12} + \dfrac{3x}{4x + 8}$.

Video Tutor Help

Visit: PHSchool.com
Web Code: age-0775

❹ **EXAMPLE** **Subtracting Rational Expressions**

Simplify $\dfrac{7y}{5y^2 - 125} - \dfrac{4}{3y + 15}$.

$$\dfrac{7y}{5y^2 - 125} - \dfrac{4}{3y + 15} = \dfrac{7y}{5(y + 5)(y - 5)} - \dfrac{4}{3(y + 5)}$$ Factor the denominators.

$$= \dfrac{7y}{5(y + 5)(y - 5)} \cdot \dfrac{3}{3} - \dfrac{4}{3(y + 5)} \cdot \dfrac{5(y - 5)}{5(y - 5)}$$ identity for multiplication

$$= \dfrac{(3)(7y)}{(3)(5)(y + 5)(y - 5)} - \dfrac{(4)(5)(y - 5)}{(3)(5)(y + 5)(y - 5)}$$ Multiply.

$$= \dfrac{(3)(7y) - (4)(5)(y - 5)}{(3)(5)(y + 5)(y - 5)}$$ Simplify.

$$= \dfrac{y + 100}{15(y + 5)(y - 5)}$$ Simplify.

Quick Check ❹ Simplify each expression.

a. $\dfrac{-2}{3x^2 + 36x + 105} - \dfrac{3x}{6x + 30}$ **b.** $\dfrac{x}{3x^2 - 9x + 6} - \dfrac{2x + 1}{3x^2 + 3x - 6}$

2   Simplifying Complex Fractions

A **complex fraction** is a fraction that has a fraction in its numerator or denominator or in both its numerator and denominator. Here are some examples.

$$\dfrac{\frac{1}{x}}{y} \qquad\qquad \dfrac{3}{1 - \frac{1}{2y}} \qquad\qquad \dfrac{\frac{x - 2}{x} - \frac{2}{x + 1}}{\frac{3}{x - 1} - \frac{1}{x + 1}}$$

Problem Solving Hint

Note that the complex fractions below are *not* equivalent.

$$\dfrac{\frac{a}{b}}{c} \qquad \dfrac{a}{\frac{b}{c}}$$

To simplify a complex fraction such as $\dfrac{\frac{a}{b}}{\frac{c}{d}}$ you can multiply the numerator $\frac{a}{b}$ and denominator $\frac{c}{d}$ by their least common denominator (LCD) bd. Or you can divide the numerator $\frac{a}{b}$ by the denominator $\frac{c}{d}$.

❺ **EXAMPLE** **Simplifying Complex Fractions**

Simplify $\dfrac{\frac{1}{x} + 3}{\frac{5}{y} + 4}$.

Method I First find the LCD of all the rational expressions.

$$\dfrac{\frac{1}{x} + 3}{\frac{5}{y} + 4} = \dfrac{\left(\frac{1}{x} + 3\right) \cdot xy}{\left(\frac{5}{y} + 4\right) \cdot xy}$$ The LCD is *xy*. Multiply the numerator and denominator by *xy*.

$$= \dfrac{\frac{1}{x} \cdot xy + 3 \cdot xy}{\frac{5}{y} \cdot xy + 4 \cdot xy}$$ Use the Distributive Property.

$$= \dfrac{y + 3xy}{5x + 4xy}$$ Simplify.

Method 2 First simplify the numerator and denominator.

$$\frac{\frac{1}{x}+3}{\frac{5}{y}+4} = \frac{\frac{1}{x}+\frac{3x}{x}}{\frac{5}{y}+\frac{4y}{y}}$$ **Write equivalent expressions with common denominators.**

$$= \frac{\frac{1+3x}{x}}{\frac{5+4y}{y}}$$ **Add.**

$$= \frac{1+3x}{x} \div \frac{5+4y}{y}$$ **Divide the numerator fraction by the denominator fraction.**

$$= \frac{1+3x}{x} \cdot \frac{y}{5+4y}$$ **Multiply by the reciprocal.**

$$= \frac{(1+3x)y}{x(5+4y)}$$

$$= \frac{y+3xy}{5x+4xy}$$

 **Quick Check** ⑤ Simplify each complex fraction.

a. $\dfrac{\frac{1}{x}}{y}$ **b.** $\dfrac{3}{1-\frac{1}{2y}}$ **c.** $\dfrac{\frac{x-2}{x}-\frac{2}{x+1}}{\frac{3}{x-1}-\frac{1}{x+1}}$

EXERCISES

For more exercises, see *Extra Skill and Word Problem Practice*.

Practice and Problem Solving

A   **Practice by Example**

Example 1
(page 515)

The focal length f of a camera lens is 2 in. The lens equation is $\frac{1}{f} = \frac{1}{d_i} + \frac{1}{d_o}$, where d_i is the distance between the lens and the film and d_o is the distance between the lens and the object.

1. The object to be photographed is 10 ft away. How far should the lens be from the film?

2. The object to be photographed is 20 ft away. How far should the lens be from the film?

3. Critical Thinking Explain why one setting on the camera is used for photographing all objects that are more than 10 ft from the camera.

Example 2
(page 515)

Find the least common multiple of each pair of polynomials.

4. $9(x + 2)(2x - 1)$ and $3(x + 2)$ **5.** $x^2 - 1$ and $x^2 + 2x + 1$

6. $(x - 2)(x + 3)$ and $10(x + 3)^2$ **7.** $12x^2 - 6x - 126$ and $18x - 63$

8. $5y^2 - 80$ and $y + 4$ **9.** $x^2 - 32x - 10$ and $2x + 10$

Example 3
(page 515)

Simplify each sum.

10. $\dfrac{1}{2x} + \dfrac{1}{2x}$ **11.** $\dfrac{d-3}{2d+1} + \dfrac{d-1}{2d+1}$

12. $\dfrac{5y+2}{xy^2} + \dfrac{2x-4}{4xy}$ **13.** $\dfrac{5x}{x^2-9} + \dfrac{2}{x+4}$

14. $\dfrac{-3x}{x^2-9} + \dfrac{4}{2x-6}$ **15.** $\dfrac{5x}{x^2-x-6} + \dfrac{4}{x^2+4x+4}$

Example 4
(page 516)

Simplify each difference.

16. $\dfrac{-2}{x} - \dfrac{1}{x}$

17. $\dfrac{-5y}{2y - 1} - \dfrac{y + 3}{2y - 1}$

18. $\dfrac{y}{2y + 4} - \dfrac{3}{y + 2}$

19. $\dfrac{x}{3x + 9} - \dfrac{8}{x^2 + 3x}$

20. $\dfrac{3y}{y^2 - 25} - \dfrac{8}{y - 5}$

21. $\dfrac{2x}{x^2 - x - 2} - \dfrac{4x}{x^2 - 3x + 2}$

Example 5
(page 516)

Simplify each complex fraction.

22. $\dfrac{\frac{1}{x}}{\frac{2}{y}}$

23. $\dfrac{1 - \frac{1}{4}}{2 - \frac{3}{5}}$

24. $\dfrac{\frac{2}{x + y}}{3}$

25. $\dfrac{\frac{1}{3}}{\frac{3}{b}}$

26. $\dfrac{1}{1 + \frac{x}{y}}$

27. $\dfrac{3}{\frac{2}{x} + y}$

28. $\dfrac{\frac{2}{x + y}}{\frac{5}{x + y}}$

29. $\dfrac{\frac{3}{x - 4}}{1 - \frac{2}{x - 4}}$

30. $\dfrac{-3}{\frac{5}{x} + y}$

B **Apply Your Skills**

Add or subtract. Simplify where possible.

31. $\dfrac{3}{4x} - \dfrac{2}{x^2}$

32. $\dfrac{3}{x + 1} + \dfrac{x}{x - 1}$

33. $\dfrac{2x}{x^2 - 1} - \dfrac{1}{x^2}$

34. $\dfrac{4}{x^2 - 9} + \dfrac{7}{x + 3}$

35. $\dfrac{x + 2}{x - 1} - \dfrac{x - 3}{2x + 1}$

36. $\dfrac{x}{2x^2 - x} + \dfrac{1}{2x}$

37. $\dfrac{5x}{x^2 - x - 6} - \dfrac{4}{x^2 + 4x + 4}$

38. $3x + \dfrac{x^2 + 5x}{x^2 - 2}$

39. $4y - \dfrac{y + 2}{y^2 + 3y}$

40. $\dfrac{5y}{y^2 - 7y} - \dfrac{4}{2y - 14} + \dfrac{9}{y}$

41. **Open-Ended** Write two rational expressions whose sum is $\dfrac{x - 2}{x + 4}$.

 42. **Writing** Explain how factoring is used when adding or subtracting rational expressions. Include an example in your explanation.

43. **Error Analysis** How would you convince a student that $\dfrac{7x + 25}{x^2 - 9}$ is *not* the sum of $\dfrac{4}{x^2 - 9}$ and $\dfrac{7}{x + 3}$?

Simplify each complex fraction.

44. $\dfrac{\frac{2}{x} + \frac{3}{y}}{\frac{-5}{x} + \frac{7}{y}}$

45. $\dfrac{\frac{5}{x} - \frac{2}{y}}{\frac{-4}{x} - \frac{6}{y}}$

46. $\dfrac{1 + \frac{2}{x}}{2 + \frac{3}{2x}}$

47. $\dfrac{\frac{1}{xy} - \frac{1}{y^2}}{\frac{1}{x^2 y} - \frac{1}{xy^2}}$

48. $\dfrac{\frac{2}{x + 4} + 2}{1 + \frac{3}{x + 4}}$

49. $\dfrac{\frac{3}{x - 2} - 5}{2 - \frac{4}{x - 2}}$

50. **Open-Ended** Write two different complex fractions that simplify to $\dfrac{x - 2}{x + 4}$.

51. **Critical Thinking** What real numbers are not in the domain of function f? Explain.

$$f(x) = \dfrac{\dfrac{x + 1}{x + 2}}{\dfrac{x + 3}{x + 4}}$$

GO **Online**
Homework Video Tutor
Visit: PHSchool.com
Web Code: age-0905

Real-World 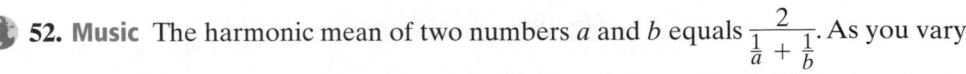 **Connection**

Shortening a guitar string to $\frac{1}{2}$ or $\frac{2}{3}$ its original length produces a sound in harmony with its original pitch.

52. Music The harmonic mean of two numbers a and b equals $\dfrac{2}{\frac{1}{a} + \frac{1}{b}}$. As you vary the length of a violin or guitar string, its pitch changes. If a full-length string is 1 unit long, then many lengths that are simple fractions produce pitches that harmonize, or sound pleasing together. The harmonic mean relates three lengths that produce harmonious sounds. For example, $\frac{1}{3}$ is the harmonic mean of $\frac{1}{2}$ and $\frac{1}{4}$, and strings of these lengths produce harmonious sounds. Find the harmonic mean for strings of lengths 1 and $\frac{1}{2}$, $\frac{3}{4}$ and $\frac{1}{2}$, and $\frac{3}{4}$ and $\frac{3}{5}$.

53. a. If you jog 12 mi at an average rate of 4 mi/h and walk the same route back at an average rate of 3 mi/h, you have traveled 24 mi in 7 h and your overall rate is $\frac{24}{7}$ mi/h. What is your overall average rate if you travel d mi at 3 mi/h and d mi at 4 mi/h?

b. Harmonic Mean Find the harmonic mean (see Exercise 52) of 3 and 4.

c. If you travel any distance at x mi/h and the same distance at y mi/h then your average rate for the trip is the harmonic mean of x and y. Find the average rate of speed if you travel to a distant city at 50 mi/h and return at 40 mi/h.

d. You travel to a city at x mi/h and the return trip is a mi/h faster. Express your average rate in terms of x and a.

 **Challenge**

54. Electricity The total resistance R for a parallel circuit with three bulbs is $R = \dfrac{1}{\frac{1}{R_1} + \frac{1}{R_2} + \frac{1}{R_3}}$.

a. Simplify the right side of the equation.

b. Find the total resistance R of a parallel circuit with bulbs that have resistances of 3 ohms, 2.5 ohms, and 2.5 ohms.

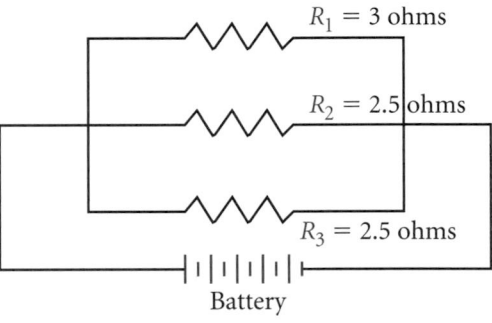

$R_1 = 3$ ohms

$R_2 = 2.5$ ohms

$R_3 = 2.5$ ohms

Battery

55. Physics Use the camera lens equation $\frac{1}{f} = \frac{1}{d_i} + \frac{1}{d_o}$, where d_i is the distance from the lens to the film and d_o is the distance from the lens to an object.

a. Solve the lens equation for f by taking the reciprocal of each side of the equation. Simplify the equation so it contains no complex fraction.

b. When an object is in focus, a lens is x cm from the object and $(2x + 1)$ cm from the film. Find the focal length of the lens.

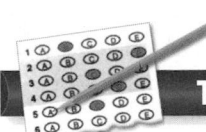 **Test Prep**

Multiple Choice

56. Find the least common multiple of $x^2 - 1$ and $x^2 - x$.

A. $x - 1$

B. $x(x - 1)(x + 1)$

C. $x(x - 1)^2(x + 1)$

D. $(x - 1)^2(x + 1)^2 x^2$

57. Which expression equals $\dfrac{1}{x^2 - 2x - 3} + \dfrac{1}{x^2 - 4x + 3}$?

F. $\dfrac{2x - 1}{(x - 1)(x + 3)(x + 1)}$

G. $\dfrac{2x + 1}{(x - 1)(x + 1)(x - 3)}$

H. $\dfrac{2x}{(x - 1)(x + 1)(x - 3)}$

J. $\dfrac{2x}{(x + 3)(x - 1)(x + 1)}$

58. Which expression equals $\dfrac{5x}{x^2 - 9} - \dfrac{4x}{x^2 + 5x + 6}$?

  A. $\dfrac{7x}{(x - 3)(x + 3)(x + 2)}$ **B.** $\dfrac{x^2 - 2x}{(x - 3)(x + 3)(x + 2)}$

  C. $\dfrac{x^2 + 22x}{(x - 3)(x + 3)(x + 2)}$ **D.** $\dfrac{9x^2 - 2x}{(x - 3)(x + 3)(x + 2)}$

59. Simplify $\dfrac{\frac{2}{x} - 5}{\frac{6}{x} - 3}$.

  F. $\dfrac{2 - 5x}{6 - 3x}$ **G.** $\dfrac{2 + 5x}{6 - 3x}$ **H.** $\dfrac{2x - 5}{6x + 3}$ **J.** $\dfrac{6 + 3x}{2 - 5x}$

Short Response   **60.** Find the least common denominator for the rational expressions $\dfrac{1}{x^2 - 5x - 6}$ and $\dfrac{1}{x^2 - 12x + 36}$. Show your work.

61. What are the asymptotes of the graph of $y = \dfrac{2x - 1}{x + 15}$?

Mixed Review

Lesson 9-4   **Divide. State any restrictions on the variables.**

62. $\dfrac{4x^3}{3y^4} \div \dfrac{16x^2}{9y^2}$ **63.** $\dfrac{7ax^3}{8by^2} \div \dfrac{14ax^4}{4by}$

64. $\dfrac{6x^2}{y} \div \dfrac{12x^4}{y^3}$ **65.** $\dfrac{3x^2 - 9x}{x - 2} \div \dfrac{x^2 - 9}{4x - 8}$

66. $\dfrac{3x - 6}{12x + 24} \div \dfrac{x^2 - 5x + 6}{3x^2 - 12}$ **67.** $\dfrac{5x + 15}{10x - 10} \div \dfrac{x^2 + 6x + 9}{3x^2 - 3}$

Lesson 8-4   **Write each expression as a single logarithm.**

68. $\log_3 y + 4 \log_3 t$ **69.** $7 \log_{10} p + \log_{10} q$ **70.** $\log_5 x - \frac{1}{5} \log_5 y$

Lesson 7-6   **Let $f(x) = x^2 + 1$ and $g(x) = 3x$. Find each value.**

71. $(g \circ f)(-3)$ **72.** $(f \circ g)(-3)$ **73.** $(g \circ f)\!\left(\tfrac{1}{2}\right)$ **74.** $(f \circ f)(3)$

✓ Checkpoint Quiz 2   Lessons 9-4 through 9-5

Simplify each expression.

1. $\dfrac{3x - 6}{5x - 20} \cdot \dfrac{x - 8}{5x - 10}$ **2.** $\dfrac{14x + 7}{4x - 6} \cdot \dfrac{8x - 12}{42x + 21}$

3. $\dfrac{y^2 - 25}{(y + 5)^2} \div \dfrac{2y - 10}{4y + 20}$ **4.** $\dfrac{y^2 - 25}{y^2 - 16} \div \dfrac{2y + 10}{y^2 - 4y}$

5. $\dfrac{8}{3x^3 y} + \dfrac{4}{9xy^3}$ **6.** $\dfrac{7}{5y + 25} + \dfrac{4}{3y + 15}$

7. $\dfrac{5x}{2y + 4} - \dfrac{6}{y^2 + 2y}$ **8.** $3x - \dfrac{x^2 + 5x}{x^2 - 2}$

9. $\dfrac{\frac{3}{2y}}{\frac{6}{8x}}$ **10.** $\dfrac{\frac{1}{x} + 3}{4 + \frac{5}{y}}$

Since division by zero is undefined, strange and illogical things can happen when division by zero sneaks unnoticed into algebraic procedures.

Does $2 = 1$? Study the proof below.

① $\qquad\qquad a = b$

② $\qquad\qquad a^2 = ab$

③ $\qquad\quad a^2 - b^2 = ab - b^2$

④ $\quad (a - b)(a + b) = b(a - b)$

⑤ $\qquad \dfrac{(a - b)(a + b)}{a - b} = \dfrac{b(a - b)}{a - b}$

⑥ $\qquad\qquad a + b = b$

⑦ $\qquad\qquad b + b = b$

⑧ $\qquad\qquad 2b = b$

⑨ $\qquad\qquad 2 = 1$

1. a. Describe each step of the proof.

   b. Check equation ① by replacing a and b with a number such as 3. Do the same for each of the other equations. Which equations are true?

   c. Equation ⑤ seems to be derived by using the Division Property of Equality: If $a = b$ and $c \neq 0$, then $\frac{a}{c} = \frac{b}{c}$. Explain why the property is not used correctly.

2. a. Justify each step of the solution to $\frac{1}{x^2} = \frac{2}{x}$.

   ① $\qquad\qquad \dfrac{1}{x^2} = \dfrac{2}{x}$

   ② $\qquad\qquad 2x^2 = x$

   ③ $\qquad\quad 2x^2 - x = 0$

   ④ $\qquad x(2x - 1) = 0$

   ⑤ $\quad x = 0 \text{ or } x = \dfrac{1}{2}$

   b. Check the solution $x = \frac{1}{2}$ in equations ④, ③, ②, and ①.

   c. Check the solution $x = 0$ in equations ④, ③, ②, and ①.

   d. How are the checks different? Explain.

   e. If equations ④ and ① have the same solutions, then you can work backward to derive equation ① from ④. What goes wrong when you try?

   f. Critical Thinking Explain why equation ③ can be derived from ②, and ② from ③, thereby ensuring that they have the same solutions.

   g. Equation ② is derived from equation ① using the Multiplication Property of Equality: If $a = b$ then $ac = bc$. Both sides of equation ① are multiplied by x^3 to obtain equation ②. Is there anything wrong with this step?

   h. Critical Thinking Explain why equation ② can be derived from ①, but ① cannot be derived from ②.

Solving Rational Equations

What You'll Learn

- To solve rational equations
- To use rational equations in solving problems

. . . And Why

To find the average speed of a bicycle trip, as in Example 3

✓ Check Skills You'll Need

GO for Help Skills Handbook page 871

Find the LCD of each pair of fractions.

1. $\dfrac{1}{3t}, \dfrac{1}{5t^2}$

2. $\dfrac{x}{2}, \dfrac{3x}{8}$

3. $\dfrac{4}{3h^2}, \dfrac{2h}{h^3}$

4. $\dfrac{4}{y+2}, \dfrac{3}{y-1}$

5. $\dfrac{z}{2z+1}, \dfrac{1}{z}$

6. $\dfrac{1}{k+2}, \dfrac{3k}{k^2-4}$

---

1 Solving Rational Equations

Extraneous solutions can be introduced when you multiply both sides of an equation by the same algebraic expression. An extraneous solution is a solution of the derived equation, but not of the original equation.

You must check all solutions of the derived equation in the original equation to find whether any of them are not solutions of the original equation.

1 EXAMPLE Solving Rational Equations

Solve $\dfrac{5}{2x-2} = \dfrac{15}{x^2-1}$. Check each solution.

$$\dfrac{5}{2x-2} = \dfrac{15}{x^2-1}$$

$5(x^2-1) = 15(2x-2)$	**Write the cross products.**
$5x^2 - 5 = 30x - 30$	**Distributive Property**
$5x^2 - 30x + 25 = 0$	**Write in standard form.**
$x^2 - 6x + 5 = 0$	**Divide each side by 5.**
$(x-1)(x-5) = 0$	**Factor.**
$x = 1$ or $x = 5$	**Zero-Product Property**

Problem Solving Hint

In a proportion, the cross products are equal.
If $\frac{a}{b} = \frac{c}{d}$, then $ad = cb$ $(b \neq 0, d \neq 0)$.

Check When $x = 1$, both denominators in the original equation are zero. The original equation is undefined at $x = 1$. So $x = 1$ is not a solution.

When 5 is substituted for x in the original equation, both sides equal $\frac{5}{8}$.

The solution is $x = 5$.

✓ Quick Check

❶ Solve each equation. Check each solution.

a. $\dfrac{-4}{5(x+2)} = \dfrac{3}{x+2}$

b. $\dfrac{-2}{x^2-2} = \dfrac{2}{x-4}$

GO Online

Video Tutor Help
Visit: PHSchool.com
Web Code: age-0775

When an equation has a sum or difference of two rational expressions, you can use the least common denominator (LCD) to simplify the equation.

2 EXAMPLE Solving Rational Equations

Solve $\frac{1}{2x} - \frac{2}{5x} = \frac{1}{2}$.

$$\frac{1}{2x} - \frac{2}{5x} = \frac{1}{2}$$

$10x\left(\frac{1}{2x} - \frac{2}{5x}\right) = 10x\left(\frac{1}{2}\right)$ **Multiply each side by the LCD, 10x.**

$\frac{10x}{2x} - \frac{10x(2)}{5x} = \frac{10x}{2}$ **Distributive Property**

$5 - 4 = 5x$ **Simplify.**

$x = \frac{1}{5}$

Since $\frac{1}{5}$ makes the original equation true, the solution is $x = \frac{1}{5}$.

✓ Quick Check **2** Solve $\frac{4}{x} - \frac{3}{x+1} = 1$. Check your solution.

---

2 **Using Rational Equations**

Real-World Connection

This high-performance bicycle has the aerodynamic design of a custom racing bicycle, but is practical enough for everyday riding.

3 EXAMPLE Real-World Connection

Aerodynamics The aerodynamic covering on this bicycle increases a cyclist's average speed by 10 mi/h. The time for a 75-mi trip is reduced by 2 h. What is the average speed for the trip using the aerodynamic covering?

Relate   speed with aerodynamic covering = speed without covering + 10

Define

	Distance (mi)	Rate (mi/h)	Time (h)
Without Covering	75	$\frac{75}{t}$	t
With Covering	75	$\frac{75}{t-2}$	$t-2$

Write $\frac{75}{t-2} = \frac{75}{t} + 10$

$$\frac{75}{t-2} = \frac{75}{t} + 10$$

$t(t-2)\left(\frac{75}{t-2}\right) = t(t-2)\left(\frac{75}{t}\right) + t(t-2)(10)$ **Multiply by the LCD, $t(t-2)$.**

$t(75) = (t-2)(75) + 10t(t-2)$ **Simplify.**

$75t = 75t - 150 + 10t^2 - 20t$ **Distributive Property**

$0 = 10t^2 - 20t - 150$ **Simplify.**

$0 = t^2 - 2t - 15$ **Divide each side by 10.**

$0 = (t-5)(t+3)$ **Factor.**

$t = 5$ or $t = -3$ The time must be positive, so $\frac{75}{t-2} = \frac{75}{5-2} = 25$.

The average speed with the aerodynamic covering is 25 mi/h.

✓ Quick Check **3** Rosa can jog 5 mi downhill in the same time it takes her to jog 3 mi uphill. She jogs downhill 4 mi/h faster than she jogs uphill. Find her jogging rate each way.

4 EXAMPLE   **Real-World Connection**

Volunteerism Tim can stuff envelopes three times as fast as his daughter Georgia. They have to stuff 5000 envelopes for a fund-raiser. Working together, Tim and Georgia can complete the job in about four hours. How many hours would it take each of them working alone?

Relate   Tim's rate   +   Georgia's rate   =   combined rate

Define

	Time (hr)	Rate (envelopes per hour)
Tim	x	$\dfrac{5000}{x}$
Georgia	$3x$	$\dfrac{5000}{3x}$
Combined	4	$\dfrac{5000}{4} = 1250$

Write $\dfrac{5000}{x} + \dfrac{5000}{3x}$ = 1250

Method 1   Use a graphing calculator. Graph $y_1 = \dfrac{5000}{x} + \dfrac{5000}{3x}$ and $y_2 = 1250$ in a window with Xmin = 3, Xmax = 10, Ymin = 0, and Ymax = 2000. Then use the INTERSECT feature to find the intersections of the two graphs. The graphs intersect at $x \approx 5.33$.

For help with solving equations by tables, see Lesson 5-5.

Method 2   Use a graphing calculator and $y_1 = \dfrac{5000}{x} + \dfrac{5000}{3x} - 1250$. Use the TABLE feature and "zoom in" on the point where the function changes sign. This occurs at $x \approx 5.33$.

Tim could stuff 5000 envelopes in about 5.33 hours.

• Georgia could stuff 5000 envelopes in 3(5.33) hours, or about 16 hours.

✓ **Quick Check**   **4 a.** Suppose Maria can stuff envelopes twice as fast as her friend Paco. Together, they can stuff 6750 envelopes in 4.5 hours. How long would it take each of them working alone?

      b. Suppose Adrian can weed the garden twice as fast as his son Phillip. Together they can weed the garden in 3 hours. How long would it take each of them working alone?

EXERCISES

For more exercises, see *Extra Skill and Word Problem Practice.*

Practice and Problem Solving

A   **Practice by Example**

Example 1
(page 522)

Solve each equation. Check each solution.

1. $\dfrac{x}{5} = \dfrac{x+3}{8}$ **2.** $\dfrac{1}{5x} = \dfrac{1}{9x}$ **3.** $\dfrac{4}{3x+3} = \dfrac{12}{x^2-1}$

4. $\dfrac{2}{x-1} = \dfrac{x+4}{3}$ **5.** $\dfrac{3}{x+1} = \dfrac{1}{x^2-1}$ **6.** $\dfrac{4}{2x-3} = \dfrac{x}{5}$

7. $\dfrac{3}{x} = \dfrac{12}{x+7}$ **8.** $\dfrac{10}{6x+7} = \dfrac{6}{2x+9}$ **9.** $\dfrac{2}{3x-5} = \dfrac{4}{x-15}$

Example 2
(page 523)

Solve each equation. Check each solution.

10. $\frac{1}{4} - x = \frac{x}{8}$

11. $\frac{y}{5} + \frac{y}{2} = 7$

12. $\frac{2x}{3} - \frac{1}{2} = \frac{2x + 5}{6}$

13. $\frac{3x - 2}{12} - \frac{1}{6} = \frac{1}{6}$

14. $\frac{1}{x} + \frac{x}{2} = \frac{x + 4}{2x}$

15. $\frac{11}{3x} - \frac{1}{3} = \frac{-4}{x^2}$

16. $\frac{3}{2x} - \frac{5}{3x} = 2$

17. $\frac{5x}{4} - \frac{3}{x} = \frac{1}{4}$

18. $\frac{2}{y} + \frac{1}{2} = \frac{5}{2y}$

19. $x + \frac{6}{x} = -5$

20. $\frac{1}{4x} - \frac{3}{4} = \frac{7}{x}$

21. $\frac{5}{2x} - \frac{2}{3} = \frac{1}{x} + \frac{5}{6}$

Examples 3 and 4
(pages 523 and 524)

22. Carlos can travel 40 mi on his motorbike in the same time it takes Paul to travel 15 mi on his bicycle. If Paul rides his bike 20 mi/h slower than Carlos rides his motorbike, find the speed for each bike.

23. A passenger train travels 392 mi in the same time that it takes a freight train to travel 322 mi. If the passenger train travels 20 mi/h faster than the freight train, find the speed of each train.

24. Shelley can paint a fence in 8 hours. Karen can do it in 4 hours. How long will it take them to do the job if they work together?

25. One pump can fill a tank with oil in 4 hours. A second pump can fill the same tank in 3 hours. If both pumps are used at the same time, how long will they take to fill the tank?

 **Apply Your Skills**

Solve each equation for the given variable.

26. $m = \frac{2E}{V^2}; E$

27. $\frac{c}{E} - \frac{1}{mc} = 0; E$

28. $\frac{m}{F} = \frac{1}{a}; F$

29. $\frac{1}{c} - \frac{c}{a^2 - b^2} = 0; c$

30. $\frac{\ell}{T^2} = \frac{g}{4\pi^2}; T$

31. $\frac{q}{m} = \frac{2V}{B^2 r^2}; B$

32. Anita and Fran have volunteered to contact every member of their organization by phone to inform them of an upcoming event. Fran can complete the calls in six days if she works alone. Anita can complete them in four days. How long will they take to complete the calls working together?

GO **for Help**

For a guide to solving
Exercise 32, see page 530.

33. **Multiple Choice** On the first four tests of the term your average is 84%. You think you can score 96% on each of the remaining tests. How many consecutive test scores of 96% would you need to bring your average up to 90% for the term?
    Ⓐ 1 　　　 Ⓑ 2 　　　 Ⓒ 3 　　　 Ⓓ 4

34. You are planning a school field trip to a local theater. It costs $60 to rent the bus. Each theater ticket costs $5.50.
    a. Write a function $c(x)$ to represent the cost per student if x students sign up.
    b. How many students must sign up if the cost is to be no more than $10 per student?

🌐 35. **Woodworking** A tapered cylinder is made by decreasing the radius of a rod continuously as you move from one end to the other. The rate at which it tapers is the taper per foot. You can calculate the taper per foot using the formula $T = \frac{24(R - r)}{L}$. The lengths $R, r,$ and L are measured in inches.

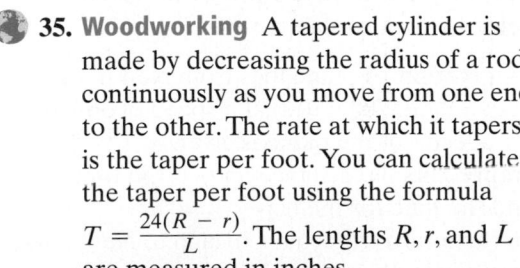

GO **Online**
Homework Video Tutor
Visit: PHSchool.com
Web Code: age-0906

    a. Solve this equation for L.
    b. Find L if $R = 4$ in.; $r = 3$ in.; and $T = 0.75, 0.85,$ and $0.95.$

36. **Fuel Economy** Suppose you drive an average of 15,000 miles per year, and your car gets 24 miles per gallon. Suppose gasoline costs $1.60 a gallon.
   a. How much money do you spend each year on gasoline?
   b. You plan to trade in your car for one that gets x more miles per gallon. Write an expression to represent the new yearly cost of gasoline.
   c. Write an expression to represent your savings on gasoline.
   d. Suppose you save $200 a year with the new car. How many miles per gallon does the new car get?

37. **Open-Ended** Write a rational equation that has the same solution as the question in the cartoon.

The Family Circus *by Bil Keane*

"What's 129 divided by 4?"

 38. **Industry** The average hourly wage $H(x)$ of workers in an industry is modeled by the function $H(x) = \frac{16.24x}{0.062x + 39.42}$, where x represents the number of years since 1970.
   a. In what year does the model predict that wages will be $25/h?
   b. **Critical Thinking** Is the prediction reasonable? Explain.

Solve each equation. Check each solution.

39. $\dfrac{15}{x} + \dfrac{9x - 7}{x + 2} = 9$

40. $\dfrac{2}{x + 2} - \dfrac{1}{x} = \dfrac{-4}{x(x + 2)}$

41. $\dfrac{1}{b + 1} + \dfrac{1}{b - 1} = \dfrac{2}{b^2 - 1}$

42. $c - \dfrac{c}{3} + \dfrac{c}{5} = 26$

43. $\dfrac{2}{x - 3} - \dfrac{4}{x + 3} = \dfrac{8}{x^2 - 9}$

44. $\dfrac{1}{8} + \dfrac{5x}{x + 2} = \dfrac{5}{2}$

45. $\dfrac{1}{x - 5} = \dfrac{x}{x^2 - 25}$

46. $\dfrac{k}{k + 1} + \dfrac{k}{k - 2} = 2$

47. $\dfrac{3}{x + 5} + \dfrac{2}{5 - x} = \dfrac{-4}{x^2 - 25}$

48. $\dfrac{5}{x + 2} = \dfrac{-1}{x^2 + 7x + 10} + \dfrac{3}{-x - 5}$

49. $\dfrac{5}{x^2 - 7x + 12} - \dfrac{2}{3 - x} = \dfrac{5}{x - 4}$

50. $\dfrac{10}{2y + 8} - \dfrac{7y + 8}{y^2 - 16} = \dfrac{-8}{2y - 8}$

51. $\dfrac{7x + 3}{x^2 - 8x + 15} + \dfrac{3x}{x - 5} = \dfrac{1}{3 - x}$

52. $\dfrac{2}{x + 3} - \dfrac{3}{4 - x} = \dfrac{2x - 2}{x^2 - x - 12}$

 53. **Landscape Design** Suppose you want to double the area of the patio shown at the right. Find the increase x of both the length and width of the patio.

54. **Writing** Write and solve a problem that can be modeled by a rational equation.

55. **Transportation** A plane flies from New York to Chicago (about 700 miles) at a speed of 360 mi/h.
   a. The speed s of the plane is given by $s = \dfrac{d}{t}$. d represents the distance and t is the time. Solve the equation for t.
   b. Find the time for the trip.
   c. On the return trip from Chicago to New York, a tail wind helps the plane move faster. Write an expression for the speed of the plane on the return trip. Let x represent the speed of the tail wind.
   d. The total flying time for the round trip is 3.5 h. Write a rational equation for the sum of the flying times. Find the speed x of the tail wind.

Real-World Connection

Careers Masons build patterns with brick or stone.

56. Open-Ended Write a rational equation that has the following.
  a. one solution   **b.** two solutions   **c.** no real solution

57. A salesman drove from his home to a nearby city at an average speed of 40 mi/h. He returned home at an average speed of 50 mi/h. What was his average speed for the entire trip?

58. An automatic pitching machine can pitch all its baseballs in $1\frac{1}{4}$ hours. One attendant can retrieve all the baseballs pitched by one machine in $3\frac{1}{2}$ hours. At least how many attendants working at the same rate should be hired so that the baseballs from 10 machines are all retrieved in less than 8 hours?

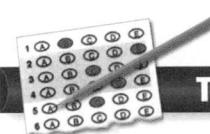

Test Prep

Multiple Choice

59. What are all the solutions of $\frac{3}{x^2 - 1} + \frac{4x}{x + 1} = \frac{1.5}{x - 1}$?

  A. 1, −1   **B.** 1, 0.375   **C.** 0.375   **D.** 0.375, 3

60. What is the solution of $x + \frac{1}{x} = -2$?

  F. 1 and −1   **G.** 0 only   **H.** $-\frac{1}{2}$ only   **J.** −1 only

61. How many roots does the equation $\frac{2}{x^2} + \frac{1}{x} = 0$ have?

  A. 0   **B.** 1   **C.** 2   **D.** 3

62. Solve $\frac{2}{x + 7} = \frac{x}{x^2 - 49}$.

  F. 14 only   **G.** 7 only   **H.** 7 or −7   **J.** −7 only

Short Response

63. A large snowplow can clear a parking lot in 4 hours. A small snowplow needs more time to clear the lot. Working together, they can clear the lot in 3 hours. How long would it take the small plow to clear the lot by itself? Show your work.

Extended Response

64. Solve and check the equation $\frac{x}{3x + 9} = \frac{x + 2}{x + 3}$. Show your work.

Mixed Review

 for Help

Lesson 9-5

Simplify each difference.

65. $\frac{3y + 1}{4y + 4} - \frac{2y + 7}{2y + 2}$ **66.** $\frac{5x}{2y + 4} - \frac{6}{y^2 + 2y}$ **67.** $\frac{x + 1}{2x - 2} - \frac{2x}{x^2 + 2x - 3}$

Lesson 8-5

Solve each equation.

68. $\log_{10} 0.001 = x$ **69.** $\log_3 27 = 3x + 6$

70. $\log_{0.1} (x + 1) = 3$ **71.** $\log_3 \frac{1}{9} = \frac{x}{3}$

Lesson 7-7

Find the inverse of each function. Is the inverse a function?

72. $y = 5 - 2x$ **73.** $y = x^2 + 1$ **74.** $y = x^3 - 4$

Rational Inequalities

You can multiply both sides of a rational inequality by the same algebraic expression just as you have done with equations. However, not only can you introduce extraneous solutions, you can also lose solutions!

1 ACTIVITY

1. Here is Alice's solution of the rational inequality $\frac{N}{4 - N} < 3$. Read it carefully.

$$\frac{N}{4 - N} < 3$$

$$N < 3(4 - N)$$

$$N < 12 - 3N$$

$$4N < 12$$

$$N < 3$$

Alice concluded that the solution consists of all integers less than 3. Or so it would seem. Does Alice's solution appear to be correct?

2. a. Choose an integer less than 3. Does it make the inequality true?
   b. Pick an integer greater than 4. Does it make the inequality true?
   c. What happens to the inequality when $N = 3$? $N = 4$?
   d. Make a conjecture about the solution based on your results in parts (a)–(c).

3. Enter the function $y_1 = x/(4 - x)$ in your graphing calculator. Set up a table as shown below. Scroll down through the table. All the x-values are integers greater than 3. Find one that fails to satisfy the inequality $\frac{N}{4 - N} < 3$. Does this finding agree with your results from Exercise 2?

```
Plot1  Plot2  Plot3
\Y1 ▤ X/(4 – X)
\Y2 =
\Y3 =
\Y4 =
\Y5 =
\Y6 =
\Y7 =■
```

```
TABLE SETUP
  TblStart=20
  ∆Tbl=5
Indpnt:  Auto  Ask
Depend:  Auto  Ask
```

X	Y1
20	−1.25
25	−1.19
30	−1.154
35	−1.129
40	−1.111
45	−1.098
50	−1.087

Y1=−1.25

2 ACTIVITY

It would appear that Alice's algebraic solution was only partially successful. It correctly concludes that any integer less than 3 satisfies the inequality. Unfortunately, it fails to identify other values that satisfy the inequality.

4. Error Analysis Alice made an error in one step in her solution. Where is the error? What erroneous assumption did Alice make?

5. What is the first change you would make to correct Alice's error.

6. Show how the assumption $N > 4$ leads to solutions of the inequality that Alice did not find. (*Hint:* What is important about the value of $4 - N$?)

7. Now, write a complete solution of the inequality $\frac{N}{4 - N} < 3$.

As you can see, the algebraic solution to the simple-looking rational inequality $\frac{N}{4-N} < 3$ is not all that simple. You might find it easier to solve this inequality (and other rational inequalities) graphically.

8. Graph two functions $y_1 = \frac{x}{4-x}$ and $y_2 = 3$ using the settings at the right. Explain how you can use the graph to solve the inequality $\frac{N}{4-N} < 3$.

```
WINDOW
Xmin = -4.7
Xmax = 9.4
Xscl = 1
Ymin = -8
Ymax = 5
Yscl = 1
Xres = 1■
```

9. Graph the function $y_3 = \frac{x}{4-x} - 3$ (or $y_3 = y_1 - y_2$) in the window used in Exercise 8. How can you use this graph to solve the inequality $\frac{N}{4-N} < 3$?

10. Show how to solve $\frac{N}{4-N} < 3$ by using y_1 and y_2 and tables, or y_3 and tables.

EXERCISES

Use the settings from Exercise 8. Solve each of 11–13 using your choice of two graphs (Exercise 8), one graph (Exercise 9), or tables (Exercise 10).

11. $\frac{2}{x-1} < x$

12. $x + 1 > \frac{x+5}{x+2}$

13. $\frac{2x}{(x-2)(x+3)} < 1$

14. For Exercises 11–13, check your work by using a different method to solve each inequality.

15. **Multiple Choice** Which graph can you use to solve the inequality $\frac{1}{x-2} < -3$

    (A)   (B)   (C)   (D)

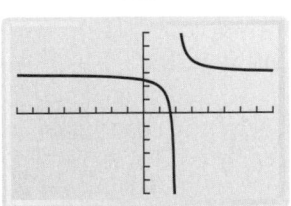 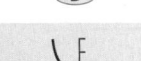 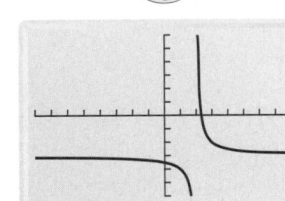 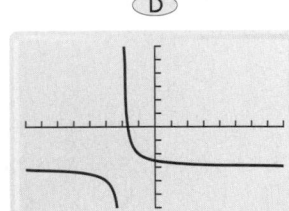

16. Mr. Huerta has 600 minutes per week to give individual help to students. He averages 20 min per student. If he reduces the time per student by t min to $(20 - t)$ min, he can meet with $\frac{600}{20-t}$ students. Write an inequality that describes each situation below and solve the inequality.

    a. How many fewer minutes per student will allow Mr. Huerta to work with at least 36 students?

    b. How many more minutes per student will allow Mr. Huerta to work with no more than 27 students?

17. The equation $d = rt$ relates the distance d you travel, the time t it takes to travel that distance, and the rate r at which you travel. So the time it takes is $t = \frac{d}{r}$. If you increase your rate by a to $r + a$, then it takes less time, $t = \frac{d}{r+a}$. In fact, the time you save by going at the faster rate is $T = \frac{d}{r} - \frac{d}{r+a}$.

    a. You normally take a 500-mi trip, averaging 45 mi/h. You want to increase the rate so that your travel time is at least 1 h shorter. Write an inequality that describes the situation.

    b. Solve your inequality in part (a).

Understanding Word Problems Read the problem below. Then let Ahmed's thinking guide you through the solution. Check your understanding with the exercises at the bottom of the page.

Anita and Fran have volunteered to contact every member of their organization by phone to inform them of an upcoming event. Fran can complete the calls in six days if she works alone. Anita can complete them in four days. How long will they take to complete the calls working together?

What Ahmed Thinks

I'll write the information in my own words.

Work problems involve rates. Even though I don't know the number of calls Fran and Anita are making, maybe I can just consider the entire job, or total amount of work, being done.

I'll define variables, t for time and w for work.

Now I can write an equation.

The variable w is going to cancel out of the equation, so I can just solve for t.

I can write my answer in a sentence now.

What Ahmed Writes

Fran can complete the work in 6 days.
Anita can complete the work in 4 days.

$$\text{rate} = \frac{\text{work being done}}{\text{time}}$$

$$\text{Fran's rate} = \frac{\text{work being done}}{\text{time}} = \frac{\text{total work}}{6}$$

$$\text{Anita's rate} = \frac{\text{work being done}}{\text{time}} = \frac{\text{total work}}{4}$$

w = total work
t = time working together

$$\text{Fran's rate} + \text{Anita's rate} = \text{combined rate}$$

$$\frac{\text{total work}}{6} + \frac{\text{total work}}{4} = \frac{\text{total work}}{\text{time together}}$$

$$\frac{w}{6} + \frac{w}{4} = \frac{w}{t}$$

$$\frac{1}{6} + \frac{1}{4} = \frac{1}{t}$$

$$2t + 3t = 12$$

$$5t = \frac{12}{5} = 2\frac{2}{5}$$

It will take Anita and Fran, working together, $2\frac{2}{5}$ days to complete all the calls.

EXERCISES

1. Charlene can wash a car in 15 minutes, and Robert can wash the same size car in 12 minutes. How long will it take them to wash a car if they work together?
2. It takes 12 min to fill a bathtub with the drain closed. If the tap is closed, it takes 20 min to drain the bathtub. How long does it take to fill the bathtub with both the tap and the drain open?

Probability of Multiple Events

What You'll Learn

- To find the probability of the event *A and B*
- To find the probability of the event *A or B*

. . . And Why

To solve problems involving radio call-in shows, as in Example 2

 **Check Skills You'll Need**

 **for Help** Lesson 1-6

A bag contains 24 green marbles, 22 blue marbles, 14 yellow marbles, and 12 red marbles. Suppose you pick one marble at random. Find each probability.

1. *P*(yellow)   **2.** *P*(not blue)   **3.** *P*(green or red)

4. Of 300 senior students at Taft High, 150 have taken physics, 192 have taken chemistry, and 30 have taken neither physics nor chemistry. How many students have taken both physics and chemistry?

New Vocabulary   • dependent events   • independent events
                       • mutually exclusive events

 Finding *P*(*A* and *B*)

Hands-On Activity: Multiple Events

- Work with a partner to analyze the game Primarily Odd.

- **Partner A:** Roll two standard number cubes. If the sum is either odd *or* a prime number, score a point.

- **Partner B:** Roll two standard number cubes. If the sum is both odd *and* a prime number, score a point.

- Alternate turns rolling the number cubes.

1. a. List all the possible outcomes of rolling two number cubes.
    b. How many outcomes result in an odd sum? Calculate the probability of getting an odd sum.
    c. How many outcomes result in a prime sum? Calculate the probability of getting a prime sum.

2. Predict which partner is more likely to score points in Primarily Odd. Justify your reasoning.

3. Play the game with your partner. Take 10 turns each. Keep track of each player's score. How do your results compare with the prediction you made in Question 2?

When the outcome of one event affects the outcome of a second event, the two events are **dependent events.** When the outcome of one event does *not* affect the outcome of a second event, the two events are **independent events.**

 **1 EXAMPLE** **Classifying Events**

Classify each pair of events as *dependent* or *independent*.

a. Roll a number cube. Then toss a coin.
Since the two events do not affect each other, they are independent.

b. Pick a flower from a garden. Then pick another flower from the same garden.
Picking the first flower affects the possible outcomes of picking the second flower. So the events are dependent.

 Quick Check **1** Suppose you select a marble from a bag of marbles. You replace the marble and then select again. Are your selections dependent or independent events? Explain.

You can find the probability that two independent events will both occur by multiplying probabilities.

Key Concepts

Property	**Probability of A and B**

If A and B are independent events, then $P(A \text{ and } B) = P(A) \cdot P(B)$.

Example: If $P(A) = \frac{1}{2}$ and $P(B) = \frac{1}{3}$, then $P(A \text{ and } B) = \frac{1}{2} \cdot \frac{1}{3} = \frac{1}{6}$.

2 EXAMPLE **Real-World 🌐 Connection**

Radio Suppose your favorite radio station is running a promotional campaign. Every hour, four callers chosen at random get to select two songs each. You call the station once after 7:00 A.M. and again after 3:00 P.M. What is the probability that you will be one of the four callers both times you call?

WKW Radio Statistics

Hour	Calls Received That Hour
7:00 A.M.	125
3:00 P.M.	200

Relate | probability of both events | is | probability of first event | times | probability of second event |

Define Event A = you are one of the four callers after 7:00 A.M. Then $P(A) = \frac{4}{125}$.

Event B = you are one of the four callers after 3:00 P.M. Then $P(B) = \frac{4}{200}$.

Write $P(A \text{ and } B) = P(A) \cdot P(B)$

$P(A \text{ and } B) = \frac{4}{125} \cdot \frac{4}{200}$

$= \frac{16}{25,000}$ **Multiply.**

$= \frac{2}{3125}$ **Simplify.**

The probability of being one of the four callers selected at random both times you call is $\frac{2}{3125}$, or 0.064%.

Real-World 🌐 Connection

Careers Radio broadcasters try to increase the size of their listening audience so they can increase their advertising rates.

 **Quick Check** **2** Suppose the radio station changes the promotional campaign. Now it chooses five callers at random each hour.
a. What is the probability of being one of the five callers after 7 A.M? After 3 P.M.?
b. Find the probability of being one of the five callers both times you call.

When two events cannot happen at the same time, the events are **mutually exclusive events.** If *A* and *B* are mutually exclusive events, then *P(A and B)* = 0.

3 EXAMPLE **Mutually Exclusive Events**

Are the events mutually exclusive? Explain.

a. rolling a 2 or a 3 on a number cube

Since you cannot roll a 2 and a 3 at the same time, the events are mutually exclusive.

b. rolling an even number or a multiple of 3 on a number cube

By rolling a 6, you can roll an even number and a multiple of 3 at the same time. So the events are not mutually exclusive.

 **Quick Check** **3** Are the events mutually exclusive? Explain.

a. rolling an even number and rolling a prime number on a number cube
b. rolling an even number and rolling a number less than 2 on a number cube

You need to determine whether events *A* and *B* are mutually exclusive before you can find the probability of (*A* or *B*).

Key Concepts

Property	**Probability of (*A or B*)**

If *A* and *B* are mutually exclusive events, then
$P(A \text{ or } B) = P(A) + P(B)$.

If *A* and *B* are not mutually exclusive events, then
$P(A \text{ or } B) = P(A) + P(B) - P(A \text{ and } B)$.

Many statistical measures are based on probabilities of the form *P(A or B)*.

4 EXAMPLE **Real-World Connection**

College Enrollment About 53% of U.S. college students are under 25 years old. About 21% of U.S. college students are over 34 years old. What is the probability that a U.S. college student chosen at random is under 25 or over 34?

Since a student cannot be under 25 and over 34, the events are mutually exclusive.

$P(\text{under 25 or over 34}) = P(\text{under 25}) + P(\text{over 34})$ **Use the *P(A or B)* formula for mutually exclusive events.**

$$= 0.53 + 0.21$$

$$= 0.74$$

The probability that a U.S. college student chosen at random is under 25 or over 34 is about 0.74, or about 74%.

 **Quick Check** **4** A U.S. college student is chosen at random. Find the probability for each age range of the student.

a. 25−34   **b.** 25−34 or over 34   **c.** 34 or under

When two events are *not* mutually exclusive, you need to subtract the probability of the common outcomes.

5 **EXAMPLE** **Probabilities of Events**

Multiple Choice Suppose you reach into the bowl at the left and select a piece of fruit at random. What is the probability that the fruit is an apple or green?

    Ⓐ $\frac{2}{9}$ Ⓑ $\frac{3}{9}$ Ⓒ $\frac{6}{9}$ Ⓓ $\frac{8}{9}$

$P(\text{apple or green}) = P(\text{apple}) + P(\text{green}) - P(\text{apple and green})$

$$= \frac{5}{9} + \frac{3}{9} - \frac{2}{9}$$

$$= \frac{6}{9}$$

The probability of picking a piece of fruit that is an apple or green is $\frac{6}{9}$, or $\frac{2}{3}$. The correct choice is C.

 Quick Check **5** Find each probability.   **a.** $P(\text{apple or red})$ **b.** $P(\text{green or citrus fruit})$

EXERCISES

For more exercises, see *Extra Skill and Word Problem Practice.*

Practice and Problem Solving

Ⓐ Practice by Example

Example 1
(page 532)

Classify each pair of events as *dependent* or *independent*.

1. A month is selected at random; a number from 1 to 30 is selected at random.

2. A month is selected at random; a day of that month is selected at random.

3. A letter of the alphabet is selected at random; one of the remaining letters is selected at random.

4. The color of a car is selected at random; the type of transmission is selected at random.

Example 2
(page 532)

Q and *R* are independent events. Find *P*(*Q* and *R*).

5. $P(Q) = \frac{1}{4}, P(R) = \frac{2}{3}$ **6.** $P(Q) = \frac{12}{17}, P(R) = \frac{3}{8}$

7. $P(Q) = 0.6, P(R) = 0.9$ **8.** $P(Q) = \frac{1}{3}, P(R) = \frac{6}{x}$

9. Suppose you have five books in your book bag. Three are novels, one is a biography, and one is a poetry book. Today you grab one book out of your bag without looking, and return it later. Tomorrow you do the same thing. What is the probability that you grab a novel both days?

Example 3
(page 533)

Two standard number cubes are tossed. State whether the events are mutually exclusive. Explain your reasoning.

10. The sum is a prime number; the sum is less than 4.

11. The numbers are equal; the sum is odd.

12. The product is greater than 20; the product is a multiple of 3.

Example 4
(page 533)

13. Population About 30% of the U.S. population is under 20 years old. About 17% of the population is over 60. What is the probability that a person chosen at random is under 20 or over 60?

S and T are mutually exclusive events. Find P(S or T).

14. $P(S) = \frac{5}{8}, P(T) = \frac{1}{8}$ **15.** $P(S) = \frac{3}{5}, P(T) = \frac{1}{3}$

16. $P(S) = 12\%, P(T) = 27\%$ **17.** $P(S) = \frac{1}{7}, P(T) = 60\%$

Example 5
(page 534)

A standard number cube is tossed. Find each probability.

18. P(3 or odd) **19.** P(4 or even)

20. P(even or less than 4) **21.** P(odd or greater than 2)

22. P(odd or prime) **23.** P(even or prime)

24. P(4 or less than 6) **25.** P(greater than 1 or less than 5)

B **Apply Your Skills**

Test-Taking Tip

In $P(C$ or $D)$, C or D means that C occurs by itself, D occurs by itself, or possibly both C and D occur together.

C and D are not mutually exclusive events. Copy and complete the table below to find each missing probability.

	P(C)	P(D)	P(C and D)	P(C or D)
26.	$\frac{4}{9}$	$\frac{4}{9}$	■	$\frac{5}{9}$
27.	$\frac{1}{2}$	$\frac{1}{3}$	$\frac{1}{4}$	■
28.	$\frac{2}{3}$	$\frac{3}{5}$	■	$\frac{13}{15}$
29.	$\frac{3}{7}$	$\frac{1}{4}$	$\frac{1}{8}$	■

30. Multiple Choice Suppose a number from 1 to 100 is selected at random. What is the probability that a multiple of 4 or 5 is chosen?

Ⓐ $\frac{1}{20}$ Ⓑ 0.36 Ⓒ $\frac{2}{5}$ Ⓓ 45%

Real-World 🌐 **Connection**

Careers Support personnel keep business and industry running smoothly.

🌐 **Statistics** **The graph at the right shows the types of jobs held by people in the United States. Find each probability.**

31. A person is in a service occupation.

32. A person is in service or sales.

33. A person is not in production or transportation.

34. A person is neither in sales nor in service, nor in managerial nor professional occupations.

35. A person is neither in service nor in sales.

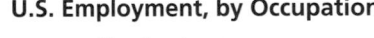

U.S. Employment, by Occupation

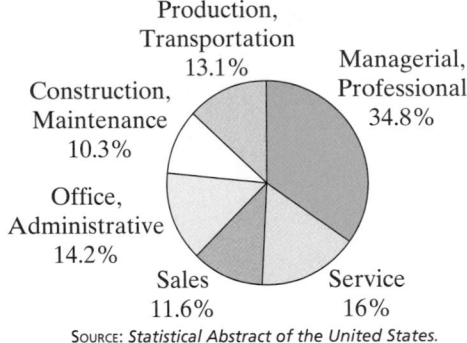

SOURCE: *Statistical Abstract of the United States.* Go to **www.PHSchool.com** for a data update. Web Code: agg-9041

A jar contains four blue marbles and two red marbles. Suppose you choose a marble at random, and do not replace it. Then you choose a second marble. Find the probability of each event.

36. You select a blue marble and then a red marble.

37. You select a red marble and then a blue marble.

38. One of the marbles you select is blue and the other is red.

39. Both of the marbles you select are red.

40. You select two red marbles or two blue marbles.

🌐 **nline**
Homework Video Tutor
Visit: PHSchool.com
Web Code: age-0907

H and J are not mutually exclusive events. Copy and complete the table below to find each missing probability.

	P(H)	P(J)	P(H and J)	P(H or J)
41.	$\frac{7}{11}$	$\frac{3}{11}$	■	$\frac{9}{11}$
42.	$\frac{1}{2}$	■	$\frac{1}{4}$	$\frac{2}{3}$
43.	■	$\frac{2}{5}$	$\frac{1}{5}$	$\frac{2}{3}$
44.	$\frac{2}{x}$	$\frac{3}{2x}$	$\frac{1}{x}$	■

45. Tests A multiple-choice test has four choices for each answer.
   a. What is the probability that a random guess on a question will yield the correct answer?
   b. Suppose you need to make a random guess on three of the ten test questions. What is the probability that you will answer all three correctly?

46. Open-Ended Describe two events that are not mutually exclusive. Estimate the probability of both events occurring.

47. Error Analysis Events F and G are mutually exclusive independent events. A student says that $P(F$ and $G)$ is greater than $P(F$ or $G)$. Explain how you can tell that the student is wrong.

C **Challenge**

Use the tables below for Exercises 48–50. One student from each school is chosen at random to be on a committee. Find each probability.

School A

Freshman	Sophomore	Junior	Senior
30%	27%	25%	18%

School B

Freshman	Sophomore	Junior	Senior
28%	28%	24%	20%

48. a junior from School A and a senior from School B

49. two juniors

50. a freshman or sophomore from School A and a senior from School B

51. Two number cubes are rolled. What is the probability that the sum is greater than 9 or less than 6?

52. Critical Thinking Tatyana has $x + 2$ pens in the pocket of her backpack. Samuel has $2x - 1$ pens in the pocket of his backpack.
   a. Tatyana has 2 blue pens. Find the probability that she pulls out a blue pen at random.
   b. Samuel has $x - 3$ blue pens. Find the probability that he pulls out a blue pen at random.
   c. Find the probability that both Tatyana and Samuel pull out blue pens at random.
   d. Find the probability that either Tatyana or Samuel pulls out a blue pen at random.

Use this information for Exercises 53–58.

Bag 1 contains 5 red marbles, 1 blue marble, 3 yellow marbles, and 2 green marbles. Bag 2 contains 1 red pencil, 3 red pens, 2 blue pencils, and 5 blue pens.

Gridded Response

53. One marble is drawn from bag 1. What is the probability that the marble is red or yellow?

54. One marble is drawn from bag 1. What is the probability that the marble is blue or not green?

55. One marble is drawn from bag 1. What is the probability that it is blue or yellow or green?

56. One item is drawn from bag 2. What is the probability that it is red?

57. One item is drawn from bag 2. What is the probability that it is a pen or a red pencil?

58. One item is drawn from bag 2. What is the probability that it is red or a pencil?

Mixed Review

for Help

Lesson 9-6

Solve each equation. Check your answer.

59. $\frac{1}{2} - x = \frac{x}{6}$

60. $\frac{2}{2x - 1} = \frac{x}{3}$

61. $\frac{3}{2x} - \frac{2}{3x} = 5$

Lesson 8-6

Solve each equation.

62. $\ln 2x = 3$

63. $\ln x + \ln 2 = 6$

64. $\ln x - \ln 4 = 5$

65. $\ln x^2 + 1 = 5$

66. $\ln x^2 + \ln x = 6$

67. $e^x = 12$

68. $e^{x+1} = 8$

69. $e^{x^2} = 3$

70. $2e^{2x} + 1 = 5$

Algebra at Work

·············· **Economist**

Economists study the relationship between the supply of a product and public demand for it. A supply curve shows that the number of units a manufacturer produces will increase as the price of the item increases. A demand curve shows that the number of units sold will decrease as the price increases. The curves cross at a point that establishes a stable equilibrium price.

Go Online
PHSchool.com
For: Information about economists
Web Code: agb-2031

Before you try to find the answer to a problem, you may be able to eliminate some answer choices. Cross out the answers you eliminate in the test booklet, NOT on the answer sheet.

1 EXAMPLE

What is the best approximation to $\sqrt{105} - \dfrac{3}{2 - \sqrt{27}}$?

   (A) -5.1 (B) 8.3 (C) 11.2 (D) 12.5 (E) 28.3

The denominator of $\dfrac{3}{2 - \sqrt{27}}$ is a negative number, so $\sqrt{105} - \dfrac{3}{2 - \sqrt{27}}$ is a positive number. Therefore, you can eliminate A.

Since $\sqrt{105}$ is close to 10, and $-\dfrac{3}{2 - \sqrt{27}}$ is a positive number close to 1, $\sqrt{105} - \dfrac{3}{2 - \sqrt{27}}$ is close to 11. You can eliminate B, D and E.

● The correct answer must be C.

2 EXAMPLE

Solve $\dfrac{2x}{x + 2} = 1 + \dfrac{x}{x - 2}$.

   (A) $x = \frac{2}{3}, x = -2,$ or $x = 2$

   (B) $x = \frac{2}{3}$

   (C) $x = 2$ or $x = -2$

   (D) $x = \frac{3}{2}$

   (E) $x = \frac{2}{3}$ or $x = \frac{3}{2}$

The equation has denominators $x + 2$ and $x - 2$. Since the denominators cannot equal zero, you know that x cannot equal -2 or 2. You can eliminate A and C.

EXERCISES

1. What is the correct answer to Example 2?

Explain how you can eliminate two or more choices for each problem.

2. Solve $\dfrac{x}{x - 4} + 2 = \dfrac{3x}{x + 1}$.

   (A) $x = \frac{8}{7}$ (B) $x = 1\frac{1}{2}$ (C) $x = 4, x = \frac{8}{7}$ (D) $x = \frac{7}{8}, x = -1$ (E) $x = \frac{7}{8}$

3. What is the best approximation to $\sqrt{50} + \dfrac{1}{\sqrt{5} - 3}$?

   (A) 5.66 (B) 5.76 (C) 7.06 (D) 7.66 (E) 7.67

4. A jar contains 3 red, 3 green, and 3 yellow chips. Two chips are drawn at random from the jar, without replacement. What is the probability that one chip is red and the other is green?

   (A) 0 (B) $\frac{2}{9}$ (C) $\frac{1}{4}$ (D) $\frac{2}{3}$ (E) 1

Chapter Review

Vocabulary Review

🔊 branch (p. 495)
complex fraction (p. 516)
dependent events (p. 531)
independent events (p. 531)

inverse variation (p. 488)
joint variation (p. 490)
mutually exclusive events (p. 533)
point of discontinuity (p. 501)

rational function (p. 501)
reciprocal function (p. 495)
simplest form (p. 509)

Go Online
PHSchool.com
For: Vocabulary quiz
Web Code: agj-0951

Choose the correct vocabulary term to complete each sentence.

1. Two events are __?__ if they cannot happen at the same time.

2. When the numerator and denominator of a rational expression are polynomials with no common divisors, the rational expression is in __?__.

3. When the outcome of one event does not affect the outcome of a second event, the two events are __?__.

4. A part of the graph of an inverse variation is called a(n) __?__.

5. If a is a zero of the denominator of a function, the function has a(n) __?__ at $x = a$.

Skills and Concepts

9-1 Objectives

▼ To use inverse variation (p. 488)

▼ To use joint and other variations (p. 490)

An equation in two variables of the form $xy = k$, $y = \frac{k}{x}$, or $x = \frac{k}{y}$, where $k \neq 0$, is an **inverse variation.** Extensions of direct and inverse variations to more complicated relationships are combined variations.

Suppose that x and y vary inversely. Write a function that models each inverse variation. Find y when $x = 5$.

6. $x = 10$ when $y = 15$ **7.** $x = 30$ when $y = 2$ **8.** $x = 6$ when $y = 30$

If possible, write direct or inverse variation equations to model each relation.

9.

x	3	4	8
y	24	18	9

10.

x	11	13	15
y	15	13	11

11.

x	5	7	9
y	30	42	54

Write the function that models each relationship. Find z when $x = 4$ and $y = 8$.

12. z varies jointly with x and y. When $x = 2$ and $y = 2$, $z = 7$.

13. z varies directly with x and inversely with y. When $x = 5$ and $y = 2$, $z = 10$.

14. z varies directly with the cube of x and inversely with y. When $x = 3$ and $y = 3$, $z = 9$.

Describe the variation modeled by each equation.

15. $R = kmn^2$ **16.** $W = \frac{k}{d^2}$ **17.** $P = \frac{kx}{y^2 z}$

9-2 Objectives

▼ To graph reciprocal functions (p. 495)

▼ To graph translations of reciprocal functions (p. 497)

The graph of an inverse variation has two parts called **branches**. The graph of $y = \frac{k}{x - b} + c$ is a translation of $y = \frac{k}{x}$ by b units horizontally and c units vertically. It has a vertical asymptote at $x = b$ and a horizontal asymptote at $y = c$.

Sketch the graph of each equation.

18. $y = \frac{1}{x}$ **19.** $y = \frac{-2}{x^2}$ **20.** $y = \frac{-1}{x} - 4$ **21.** $y = \frac{3}{x - 2} + 1$

Write an equation for the translation of $xy = 4$ that has the given asymptotes.

22. $x = 0, y = 3$ **23.** $x = 2, y = 2$ **24.** $x = -3, y = -4$

9-3 Objectives

▼ To identify properties of rational functions (p. 501)

▼ To graph rational functions (p. 504)

The rational function $f(x) = \frac{P(x)}{Q(x)}$ has a **point of discontinuity** for each real zero of $Q(x)$. If $P(x)$ and $Q(x)$ have no common factors, then the graph of $f(x)$ has a vertical asymptote when $Q(x) = 0$. If $P(x)$ and $Q(x)$ have a common real zero a, then there is a hole or a vertical asymptote at $x = a$.

If the degree of $Q(x)$ is greater than the degree of $P(x)$, then the graph of $f(x)$ has a horizontal asymptote at $y = 0$.

If $P(x)$ and $Q(x)$ have equal degrees, then there is a horizontal asymptote at $y = \frac{a}{b}$, where a and b are the coefficients of the terms of greatest degree in $P(x)$ and $Q(x)$.

If the degree of $P(x)$ is greater than the degree of $Q(x)$, then there is no horizontal asymptote.

25. A headset can be manufactured for \$.17. The development cost is \$150,000. Graph the function that represents the average cost of a headset. About how many must be manufactured to result in a cost of less than \$5 per headset?

Find any points of discontinuity for each rational function. Sketch the graph. Describe any vertical or horizontal asymptotes and any holes.

26. $y = \frac{2.5}{x + 7}$ **27.** $y = \frac{x - 1}{(x + 2)(x - 1)}$

28. $y = \frac{x^3 - 1}{x^2 - 1}$ **29.** $y = \frac{2x^2 + 3}{x^2 + 2}$

9-4 and 9-5 Objectives

▼ To simplify rational expressions (p. 509)

▼ To multiply and divide rational expressions (p. 510)

▼ To add and subtract rational expressions (p. 514)

▼ To simplify complex fractions (p. 516)

A rational expression is in **simplest form** when its numerator and denominator are polynomials that have no common divisors. To add or subtract rational expressions with different denominators, write each expression with the least common denominator.

A fraction that has a fraction in its numerator or denominator or in both is called a **complex fraction**. You can simplify a complex fraction by multiplying the numerator and denominator by the LCD of all the rational expressions.

Simplify each rational expression. State any restrictions on the variable.

30. $\frac{x^2 - 2x - 24}{x^2 + 7x + 12} \cdot \frac{x^2 - 1}{x - 6}$ **31.** $\frac{4x^2 - 2x}{x^2 + 5x + 4} \div \frac{2x}{x^2 + 2x + 1}$

32. What is the ratio of the volume of a sphere to its surface area?

33. A camera's focal length is 4 cm. If the lens is 6 cm from the film, what is the distance from the lens to an object that is in focus?

Simplify each expression.

34. $\dfrac{3x}{x^2 - 4} + \dfrac{6}{x + 2}$ **35.** $\dfrac{1}{x^2 - 1} - \dfrac{2}{x^2 + 3x}$ **36.** $\dfrac{2 - \frac{2}{3}}{3 - \frac{1}{2}}$ **37.** $\dfrac{\frac{1}{x + y}}{4}$

9-6 Objectives

▼ To solve rational equations (p. 522)

▼ To use rational equations in solving problems (p. 523)

Solving a rational equation often requires multiplying both sides by an algebraic expression. This may introduce an extraneous solution—a solution of a derived equation but not of the original equation. Check all possible solutions in the original equation.

Solve each equation. Check each solution.

38. $\dfrac{1}{x} = \dfrac{5}{x - 4}$ **39.** $\dfrac{2}{x + 3} - \dfrac{1}{x} = \dfrac{-6}{x(x + 3)}$ **40.** $\dfrac{1}{2} + \dfrac{x}{6} = \dfrac{18}{x}$

41. One pump can fill a water cistern twice as fast as a second pump. Working together, the two pumps can fill the cistern in 5 hours. Find how long it takes each pump to fill the cistern when working alone.

9-7 Objectives

▼ To find the probability of the event *A and B* (p. 531)

▼ To find the probability of the event *A or B* (p. 533)

When the occurrence of one event affects the probability of another event, the two events are **dependent events.** When the occurrence of one event does not affect the probability of another event, the two events are **independent events.** When two events cannot happen at the same time, the events are **mutually exclusive events.**

If A and B are independent, then $P(A \text{ and } B) = P(A) \cdot P(B)$.

If A and B are mutually exclusive, then $P(A \text{ and } B) = 0$.

If A and B are mutually exclusive, then $P(A \text{ or } B) = P(A) + P(B)$.

If A and B are not mutually exclusive, then
$P(A \text{ or } B) = P(A) + P(B) - P(A \text{ and } B)$.

Classify each pair of events as *dependent* or *independent*.

42. A student in your algebra class is selected at random. One of the remaining students is selected at random.

43. A number 1 through 6 is chosen by tossing a standard number cube. The same number cube is tossed again to select a number 1 through 6.

Two standard number cubes are tossed. State whether the events are mutually exclusive.

44. One of the numbers is 1 less than the other. The sum is odd.

45. The sum is greater than 10. Six is one of the numbers.

A standard number cube is tossed. Find each probability.

46. a 5 or a 6   **47.** an even number or a number greater than 4

48. an odd number or a number less than or equal to 5

Chapter Test

Go Online
PHSchool.com
For: Chapter Test
Web Code: aga-0952

Write a function that models each variation.

1. $x = 2$ when $y = -8$. y varies inversely with x.

2. $x = 0.2$ and $y = 3$ when $z = 2$. z varies jointly with x and y.

3. $x = \frac{1}{3}, y = \frac{1}{5}$, and $r = 3$ when $z = \frac{1}{2}$. z varies directly with x and inversely with the product of r^2 and y.

Is the relationship between the values in each table a direct variation, an inverse variation, or neither? Write an equation to model any direct or inverse variation.

4.
x	3	5	7	9
y	6	8	10	12

5.
x	4	6	8	10
y	10	8	6	4

6.
x	4	8	16	32
y	32	16	8	4

Graph the translation of $y = \frac{7}{x}$ with the given asymptotes. Write the equation of the translation.

7. $x = 1; y = 2$ 8. $x = -3; y = -2$

For each rational function, identify any holes, or horizontal or vertical asymptotes of its graph.

9. $y = \frac{x + 1}{x - 1}$ 10. $y = \frac{x + 3}{x + 3}$

11. $y = \frac{x - 2}{(x + 1)(x - 2)}$ 12. $y = \frac{2x^2}{x^2 - 4x}$

13. $y = \frac{1}{x + 2} - 3$ 14. $y = \frac{5}{x - 2} + 1$

15. $y = \frac{x^2 + 5}{x - 5}$ 16. $y = \frac{x + 2}{(x + 2)(x - 3)}$

Simplify each rational expression. State any restrictions on the variable.

17. $\frac{x^2 + 7x + 12}{x^2 - 9}$

18. $\frac{(x + 3)(2x - 1)}{x(x + 4)} \div \frac{(-x - 3)(2x + 1)}{x}$

19. **Open-Ended** Write a function whose graph has a horizontal asymptote but no vertical asymptote.

Find the least common multiple of each pair of polynomials.

20. $3x + 5$ and $9x^2 - 25$

21. $5(x + 3)(x + 1)$ and $2(x + 1)(x - 3)$

Simplify each sum or difference.

22. $\frac{x + 2}{(x - 3)(x + 1)} + \frac{(x - 1)(x + 2)}{x - 3}$

23. $\frac{x^2 - 1}{(x - 2)(3x - 1)} - \frac{x + 1}{x + 3}$

24. $\frac{x(x + 4)}{x - 2} + \frac{x - 1}{x^2 - 4}$

Simplify each complex fraction.

25. $\dfrac{\frac{2}{x}}{1 - \frac{1}{y}}$ 26. $\dfrac{3 - \frac{3}{4}}{\frac{1}{2} - \frac{1}{4}}$

Solve each equation. Check each solution.

27. $\frac{x}{2} = \frac{x + 1}{4}$ 28. $\frac{3}{x - 1} = \frac{4}{3x + 2}$

29. $\frac{3x}{x + 1} = 0$ 30. $\frac{3}{x + 1} = \frac{1}{x^2 - 1}$

31. $\frac{1}{x} + \frac{1}{3} = \frac{6}{x^2}$ 32. $\frac{1}{x} + \frac{x}{x + 2} = 1$

33. Almir can seal a driveway in 4 hours. Working together, he and Louis can seal it in 2.3 hours. How long would it take Louis to seal it working alone?

Two standard number cubes are tossed. State whether the events are mutually exclusive. Then find $P(A \text{ or } B)$.

34. A means their sum is 12; B means both are odd

35. A means they are equal; B means their sum is a multiple of 3

36. a. **Writing** Suppose you select a number at random from the set $\{90, 91, 92, \ldots, 99\}$. Event A is selecting a multiple of 3. Event B is selecting a multiple of 4. Are these two events mutually exclusive? Explain.
   b. Find $P(A \text{ and } B)$.
   c. Find $P(A \text{ or } B)$.

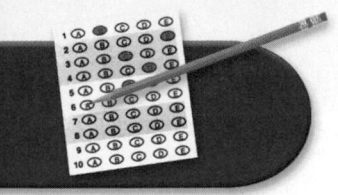

Standardized Test Prep

Reading Comprehension Read the passage below. Then answer the questions on the basis of what is *stated* or *implied* in the passage.

Payback Buying a house is the biggest investment most people ever make. So it's important to know how mortgage loans work.

Suppose you borrow $80,000 for a 30-year mortgage with an annual interest rate of 7.8%. The bank calculates a *monthly* interest rate ($7.8\% \div 12 = 0.0065$) and uses it to calculate a monthly payment of $575.90. Each month, the bank adds the monthly interest to the current principal to get the balance, and then subtracts the payment to get the new principal.

End of Month	Current Principal	Amount of Interest	Balance	Payment	New Principal
1	80,000.00	520.00	80,520.00	575.90	79,944.10
2	79,944.10	519.64	80,463.74	575.90	79,887.84
3	79,887.84	519.27	80,407.11	575.90	79,831.21

You can calculate the monthly payment for any mortgage with the formula $P = \dfrac{A \cdot m(1 + m)^{12y}}{(1 + m)^{12y} - 1}$. P is the monthly payment, A is the amount borrowed, m is the monthly interest rate, and y is the length of the mortgage in years.

If you know the monthly payment you want to make, you can use the formula $A = \dfrac{P\left[(1 + m)^{12y} - 1\right]}{m(1 + m)^{12y}}$ to find the total amount you can borrow.

---

1. For the mortgage loan described above, what will be the 4th month's balance after the interest is added to the principal?

   Ⓐ $518.90
   Ⓑ $575.90
   Ⓒ $79,744.21
   Ⓓ $80,350.11

2. If the annual interest for a loan is 8.55%, what is the monthly interest rate?

   Ⓕ 8.8375%
   Ⓖ 7.125
   Ⓗ 0.07125%
   Ⓙ 0.007125

3. Consider a 15-year mortgage for $65,000 with an annual interest rate of 6%. Rewrite the formula $P = \dfrac{A \cdot m(1 + m)^{12y}}{(1 + m)^{12y} - 1}$ by substituting values for A, m, and y.

4. To the nearest cent, what is the monthly payment for a 15-year mortgage loan of $65,000 with an annual interest rate of 6%?

5. To the nearest cent, what is the monthly payment for a 15-year mortgage loan of $65,000 with an annual interest rate of 7.5%?

6. Suppose you want to make a monthly mortgage payment of $675.00. To the nearest hundred dollars, what is the most you can borrow for a 25-yr mortgage with an annual interest rate of 7.2%?

7. Show how to derive the formula

   $A = \dfrac{P\left[(1 + m)^{12y} - 1\right]}{m(1 + m)^{12y}}$ from the

   formula $P = \dfrac{A \cdot m(1 + m)^{12y}}{(1 + m)^{12y} - 1}$.

What You've Learned

- In Chapter 5, you learned to write and graph the equation of a parabola.

- In Chapter 5, you also learned to rewrite a quadratic equation by completing the square.

- In Chapter 8, you learned to locate the asymptote of the graph of an exponential function.

 **Check Your Readiness**

 **GO for Help** to the Lesson in green.

Identifying Quadratic Functions (Lesson 5-1)

Determine whether each function is linear or quadratic. Identify the quadratic, linear, and constant terms.

1. $y = 6x - x^2 + 1$ **2.** $f(x) = -2(3 + x)^2 + 2x^2$ **3.** $y = 2x - y - 13$

4. $y = 4x(7 - 2x)$ **5.** $g(x) = -2x^2 - 3(x - 2)$ **6.** $y = x - 2(x + 5)$

Graphing Quadratic Functions (Lesson 5-2)

Graph each function.

7. $y = -x^2$ **8.** $y = \frac{1}{3}x^2$ **9.** $y = 2x^2 + 5$ **10.** $y = x^2 + 6x + 8$

Completing the Square (Lesson 5-7)

Complete the square.

11. $x^2 + 8x + $ ■ **12.** $x^2 - 5x + $ ■ **13.** $x^2 + 14x + $ ■

Rewrite each function in vertex form. Then graph the function.

14. $y = x^2 + 6x + 7$ **15.** $y = 2x^2 - 4x + 10$ **16.** $y = -3x^2 + x$

Solving Polynomial Equations (Lesson 6-5)

Find all the roots of each polynomial equation.

17. $2x^3 - x^2 + 10x - 5 = 0$ **18.** $2x^3 - 5x^2 + 4x - 1 = 0$

Graphing Exponential Decay (Lesson 8-1)

Sketch the graph for each decay function. Label the asymptote.

19. $y = 8\left(\frac{1}{2}\right)^x$ **20.** $y = 2(0.4)^x$ **21.** $y = \left(\frac{3}{4}\right)^x$

Quadratic Relations and Conic Sections

LESSONS

10-1 Exploring Conic Sections

10-2 Parabolas

10-3 Circles

10-4 Ellipses

10-5 Hyperbolas

10-6 Translating Conic Sections

What You'll Learn Next

- In Chapter 10, you will learn to use conic sections to model real-world problems.

- You will learn to graph parabolas, circles, ellipses, and hyperbolas.

- You will learn to identify the equation of a specific conic section by completing the square.

🔊 **Key Vocabulary**

- center (p. 561)
- circle (p. 561)
- conic section (p. 547)
- co-vertices (p. 568)
- directrix (p. 555)
- ellipse (p. 568)
- focus of a parabola (p. 555)
- focus of an ellipse (p. 568)
- focus of a hyperbola (p. 575)
- hyperbola (p. 575)
- major axis (p. 568)
- minor axis (p. 568)
- radius (p. 561)
- standard form of an equation of a circle (p. 561)
- transverse axis (p. 575)
- vertices of an ellipse (p. 568)
- vertices of a hyperbola (p. 575)

Activity Lab Applying what you learn, on pages 596–597 you will do activities involving planetary exploration.

A conic section is a special curve formed by the intersection of a cone and a plane. You can use paper cutouts to investigate conic sections.

Step 1 Draw two circular areas, each one measuring four inches in diameter. Cut out each circular area, and then cut it in half. Roll each half into a cone and secure it with tape.

Step 2 Trace the three templates below onto a sheet of paper. Cut out the parts corresponding to the white areas. The remaining parts corresponding to the blue areas are the templates. Label each one.

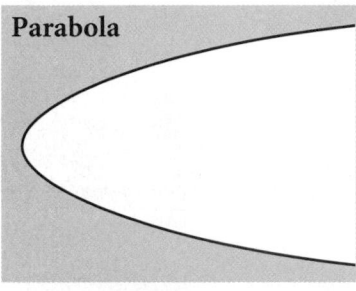

Parabola

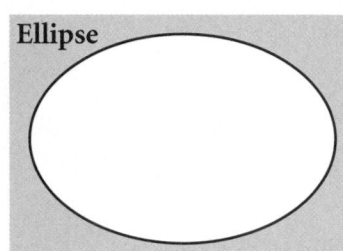

Ellipse

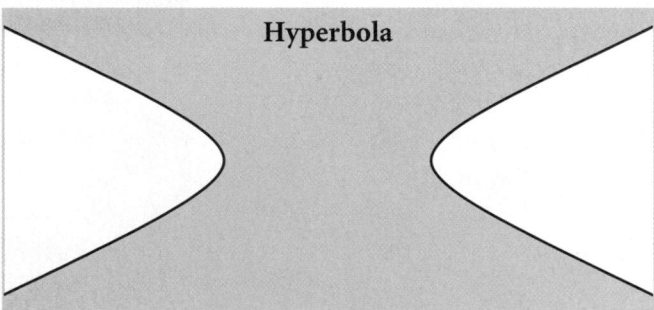

Hyperbola

Step 3 Make a fourth template for a circle. Use a compass or a coin of any size to draw the circle.

Step 4 Fit each template around the cones so that the template stays flat, like a plane. The ellipse is shown at the right. Sketch each result.

EXERCISES

1. a. The template for a hyperbola has two parts. Explain how you must position the cones to use this template as a model of a hyperbola.
  b. Suppose you tried to fit your other three templates around a double cone. Would the results change? Explain.

2. a. Fold the template for each curve so that two halves coincide. In how many ways can you do this for each of the four templates?
  b. How many axes of symmetry does each template have?

3. Which templates have rotational symmetry? Explain.

Exploring Conic Sections

What You'll Learn

• To graph conic sections

• To identify conic sections

...And Why

To analyze Moiré patterns, as in Example 5

Find the x- and y-intercepts of the graph of each function.

1. $y = 3x + 6$ **2.** $2y = -x - 3$

3. $3x - 4y = -12$ **4.** $y = x^2 - 4$

5. $y = (x - 3)^2$ **6.** $y = -4x^2 + 1$

🔊 **New Vocabulary** • conic section

---

1   Graphing Equations of Conic Sections

Vocabulary Tip

Cone comes from the Indo-European word for "sharpen." Section comes from the word for "cut."

A **conic section** is a curve formed by the intersection of a plane and a double cone. By changing the inclination of the plane, you can create a circle, a parabola, an ellipse, or a hyperbola. You can use lines of symmetry to graph a conic section.

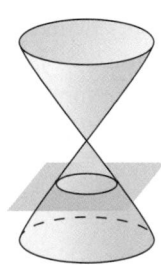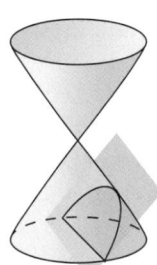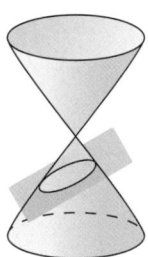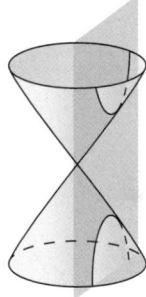

1 EXAMPLE   Graphing a Circle

Graph the equation $x^2 + y^2 = 25$. Describe the graph and its lines of symmetry. Then find the domain and range.

Make a table of values.

x	-5	-4	-3	0	3	4	5
y	0	± 3	± 4	± 5	± 4	± 3	0

The photograph shows a double cone of illuminated smoke being intersected by a laser to produce a circle.

Plot the points and connect them with a smooth curve.

The graph is a circle of radius 5. Its center is at the origin. Every line through the center is a line of symmetry.

Recall from Chapter 2 that you can use set notation to describe a domain or a range. In this example, the domain is $\{x \mid -5 \leq x \leq 5\}$. The range is $\{y \mid -5 \leq y \leq 5\}$.

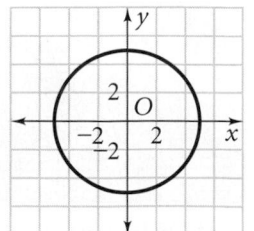

✓ **Quick Check** **1** **a.** Graph the functions $y = \sqrt{25 - x^2}$ and $y = -\sqrt{25 - x^2}$ on the same screen. Compare this graph to the one in Example 1.

b. Explain how you can get the equations in part (a) from $x^2 + y^2 = 25$.

c. **Critical Thinking** Why is there no point on the graph of Example 1 with an x-coordinate of 6?

An ellipse is similar to a circle, but it has only two lines of symmetry.

2 **EXAMPLE** **Graphing an Ellipse**

Graph the equation $9x^2 + 16y^2 = 144$. Describe the graph and the lines of symmetry. Then find the domain and range.

Make a table of values.

x	−4	−3	0	3	4
y	0	±2.0	±3	±2.0	0

Plot the points and connect them with a smooth curve.

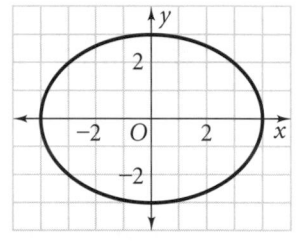

The graph is an ellipse. The center is at the origin. It has two lines of symmetry, the x-axis and the y-axis.

The domain is $\{x \mid -4 \le x \le 4\}$.
The range is $\{y \mid -3 \le y \le 3\}$.

Here the laser intersects the smoke to produce an ellipse.

✓ **Quick Check** **2** **a.** How far are the x-intercepts from the center of the ellipse? How far are the y-intercepts from the center? Describe how an ellipse differs from a circle.

b. The point $(1, 2.9)$ is an approximation of a point on the graph of Example 2. Use symmetry to find three other approximate points on the ellipse.

c. Graph the equation $2x^2 + y^2 = 18$. Describe the graph and give the coordinates of the x- and y-intercepts.

Not all conic sections consist of one smooth curve. Note the unique shape of the hyperbola.

3 **EXAMPLE** **Graphing a Hyperbola**

Graph the equation $x^2 - y^2 = 9$. Describe the graph and its lines of symmetry. Then find the domain and range.

Make a table of values.

x	−5	−4	−3	−2	−1	0	1	2	3	4	5
y	±4	±2.6	0	—	—	—	—	—	0	±2.6	±4

Plot the points and connect them with smooth curves.

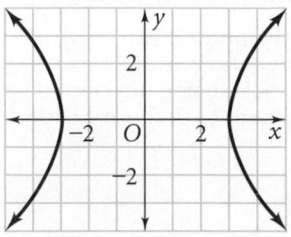

The graph is a hyperbola that consists of two branches. Its center is at the origin. It has two lines of symmetry, the x-axis and the y-axis.

The domain is $\{x \mid x \le -3 \text{ or } x \ge 3\}$. The range is all real numbers.

Here the laser intersects the smoke to produce a hyperbola.

 **3** **a.** Does the graph in Example 3 represent a function? Explain.

b. In the table in Example 3, why is the y-value undefined when $x = -2, -1, 0, 1,$ or 2?

c. Critical Thinking What two lines does each branch of this hyperbola get very close to? What are these lines called?

2 Identifying Conic Sections

The center and the intercepts are important points to identify on the graph of some conic sections.

4 EXAMPLE Identifying Graphs of Conic Sections

Identify the center and intercepts of each conic section. Then find the domain and range. In part (b), each interval on the graph represents one unit.

a.

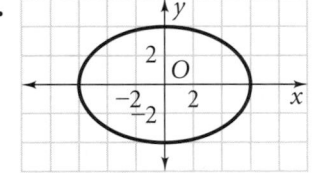

The center of the ellipse is $(0, 0)$. The x-intercepts are $(-6, 0)$ and $(6, 0)$, and the y-intercepts are $(0, -4)$ and $(0, 4)$. The domain is $\{x \mid -6 \le x \le 6\}$, and the range is $\{y \mid -4 \le y \le 4\}$.

b.

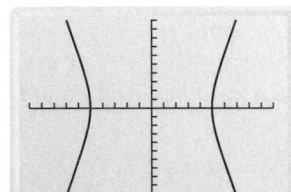

The center of the hyperbola is $(0, 0)$. The x-intercepts are $(-5, 0)$ and $(5, 0)$, and there are no y-intercepts. The domain is $\{x \mid x \ge 5 \text{ or } x \le -5\}$, and the range is all real numbers.

 **Quick Check** **4** Identify the center and intercepts of the conic section. Then find the domain and range. Each interval represents one unit.

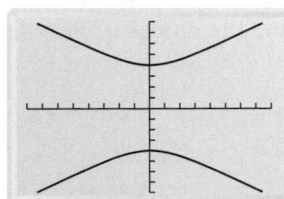

You will study each conic section in detail later in this chapter. Even before you learn the details of the equations of conic sections, you can match the equations with their graphs.

5 EXAMPLE **Real-World** 🌐 **Connection**

Design Moiré patterns are formed when two patterns, such as arrays of dots or lines, overlap to produce a third, unintended pattern. Moiré patterns cause problems for printers and video technicians. Describe each unintended pattern. Match it with one of these possible equations: $x^2 - y^2 = 1$, $x^2 + y^2 = 16$, or $9x^2 + 25y^2 = 225$.

Vocabulary Tip

Moiré is a French word meaning "watered" or "wavy."

a.

b.

c.

a. Ellipse: The equation $9x^2 + 25y^2 = 225$ represents a conic section with two sets of intercepts, $(\pm 5, 0)$ and $(0, \pm 3)$. Since the intercepts are not equidistant from the center, the equation models an ellipse.

b. Hyperbola: The equation $x^2 - y^2 = 1$ represents a conic section with one set of intercepts, $(\pm 1, 0)$, so the equation must model a hyperbola.

c. Circle: The equation $x^2 + y^2 = 16$ represents a conic section with two sets of intercepts, $(\pm 4, 0)$ and $(0, \pm 4)$. Since each intercept is 4 units from the center, the equation models a circle.

 **Quick Check** **5 a.** **Critical Thinking** What similarities do you notice among the three equations in Example 5?
b. What differences do you notice?

EXERCISES

For more exercises, see *Extra Skill and Word Problem Practice.*

Practice and Problem Solving

 Practice by Example

Examples 1, 2, and 3
(pages 547 and 548)

 **for Help**

Graph each equation. Identify the conic section and describe the graph and its lines of symmetry. Then find the domain and range.

1. $3y^2 - x^2 = 25$

2. $2x^2 + y^2 = 36$

3. $x^2 + y^2 = 16$

4. $3y^2 - x^2 = 9$

5. $4x^2 + 25y^2 = 100$

6. $x^2 + y^2 = 49$

7. $x^2 - y^2 + 1 = 0$

8. $x^2 - 2y^2 = 4$

9. $6x^2 + 6y^2 = 600$

10. $x^2 + y^2 - 4 = 0$

11. $6x^2 + 24y^2 - 96 = 0$

12. $4x^2 + 4y^2 - 20 = 0$

13. $x^2 + 9y^2 = 1$

14. $4x^2 - 36y^2 = 144$

15. $4y^2 - 36x^2 = 1$

16. $36x^2 + 4y^2 = 144$

Example 4
(page 549)

Identify the center and intercepts of each conic section. Give the domain and range of each graph. On graphing calculator screens, each interval represents one unit.

17.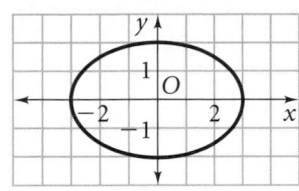

18.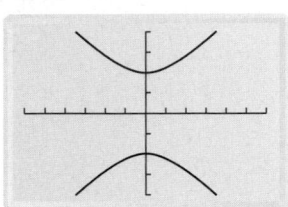

19.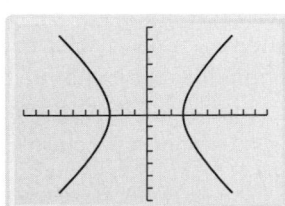

20.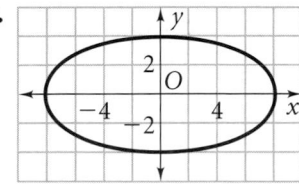

21.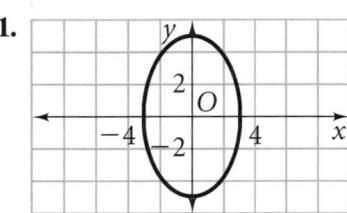

22.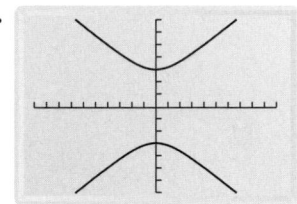

Example 5
(page 550)

Match each equation with a graph in Exercises 17–22.

23. $x^2 - y^2 = 9$

24. $4x^2 + 9y^2 = 36$

25. $y^2 - x^2 = 4$

26. $x^2 + 4y^2 = 64$

27. $25x^2 + 9y^2 = 225$

28. $y^2 - x^2 = 9$

B Apply Your Skills

Graph each equation. Describe the graph and its lines of symmetry. Then find the domain and range.

29. $9x^2 - y^2 = 144$

30. $11x^2 + 11y^2 = 44$

31. $-8x^2 + 32y^2 - 128 = 0$

32. $25x^2 + 16y^2 - 320 = 0$

33. **Light** The light emitted from a lamp with a shade forms a shadow on the wall. Explain how you could turn the lamp in relation to the wall so that the shadow cast by the shade forms each conic section.
   a. hyperbola   **b.** parabola   **c.** ellipse   **d.** circle

34. **a. Writing** Describe the relationship between the center of a circle and the axes of symmetry of the circle.
   b. Make a Conjecture Where is the center of an ellipse or a hyperbola located in relation to the axes of symmetry? Verify your conjectures with examples.

Graph each circle so that the center is at the origin. Then write the equation.

35. radius 6   36. radius $\frac{1}{2}$ 37. diameter 8   38. diameter 2.5

GO Online
Homework Video Tutor
Visit: PHSchool.com
Web Code: age-1001

39. **Multiple Choice** The sharpened part of the pencil at the right meets each painted surface in a curved path. What is the best name for such a path?
   Ⓐ circle   Ⓑ ellipse   Ⓒ parabola   Ⓓ hyperbola

Mental Math Each given point is on the graph of the given equation. Use symmetry to find at least one more point on the graph.

40. $(2, -4), y^2 = 8x$

41. $(-\sqrt{2}, 1), x^2 + y^2 = 3$

42. $(2, 2\sqrt{2}), x^2 + 4y^2 = 36$

43. $(-2, 0), 9x^2 + 9y^2 - 36 = 0$

44. $(-3, -\sqrt{51}), 6y^2 - 9x^2 - 225 = 0$

45. $(0, \sqrt{7}), x^2 + 2y^2 = 14$

46. Open-Ended Describe any other figures you can imagine that can be formed by the intersection of a plane and other shapes.

 **Challenge**

47. a. Graph the equation $xy = 16$. Use both positive and negative values for x.
   b. Which conic section does the equation appear to model?
   c. Identify any intercepts and lines of symmetry.
   d. Does your graph represent a function? If so, rewrite the equation using function notation.

 48. An xy term has an interesting effect on the graph of a conic section. Sketch the graph of each conic section below using your graphing calculator.
   (*Hint:* To solve for y, you will need to complete a square.)
   a. $4x^2 + 2xy + y^2 = 9$
   b. $4x^2 + 2xy - y^2 = 9$

 49. Sound An airplane flying faster than the speed of sound creates a cone-shaped pressure disturbance in the air. This is heard by people on the ground as a sonic boom. What is the shape of the path on the ground?

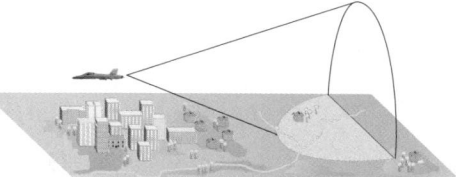

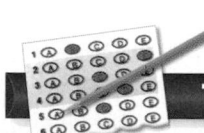

Test Prep

Multiple Choice

50. The graph of which equation of a circle contains all the points in the table below?

x	-3	0	3
y	0	±3	0

A. $x^2 + y^2 - 4 = 0$ **B.** $x^2 + y^2 = 25$
C. $x^2 + y^2 = 36$ **D.** $6x^2 + 6y^2 = 54$

51. The graph of which ellipse contains all the points in the table below?

x	-4	-2	0	2	4
y	0	±√3	±2	±√3	0

F. $x^2 + 4y^2 = 16$ **G.** $4x^2 + 16y^2 = 144$
H. $4x^2 + 25y^2 = 64$ **J.** $9x^2 + y^2 = 81$

52. Which point is NOT on the graph of $4x^2 - y^2 = 4$?
   A. $(-2, -2\sqrt{3})$ **B.** $(-1, 0)$ **C.** $(1, 0)$ **D.** $(2, 2)$

53. Which equation does NOT represent a line of symmetry for the circle with equation $x^2 + y^2 = 100$?
   F. $x = 0$ **G.** $y = \frac{1}{2}x$ **H.** $y = x$ **J.** $y = x + 1$

54. Which equation represents a line of symmetry for the ellipse with equation $x^2 + 9y^2 = 9$?
   A. $y = -x$ B. $y = 0$ C. $y = x$ D. $xy = 1$

Short Response   **55.** The graph of the equation $x^2 + y^2 = 121$ is a circle. Describe the graph and its lines of symmetry. Find the domain and the range.

Mixed Review

Lesson 9-7

A standard number cube is tossed. Find each probability.

56. $P(5$ or greater than $3)$ **57.** $P(\text{even or } 6)$

58. $P(\text{even or } 7)$ **59.** $P(\text{prime or } 2)$

Lesson 9-1

Suppose z varies jointly with x and y. Write a function that models each relationship. Find the value of z when $x = -2$ and $y = 3$.

60. $z = -5$ when $x = -1$ and $y = -1$ **61.** $z = 72$ when $x = 3$ and $y = -6$

62. $z = 32$ when $x = 0.1$ and $y = 8$ **63.** $z = 5$ when $x = -4$ and $y = 2.5$

Lesson 8-1

Write an exponential equation $y = ab^x$ whose graph passes through the given points.

64. $(-1, 2)$ and $(3, 32)$ **65.** $\left(0, \frac{1}{2}\right)$ and $(2, 8)$ **66.** $(1, 6)$ and $(2, 12)$

67. $\left(0, \frac{1}{3}\right)$ and $(2, 3)$ **68.** $\left(-1, \frac{2}{3}\right)$ and $(2, 18)$ **69.** $\left(-1, \frac{1}{8}\right)$ and $(4, 4)$

Lesson 6-8

Expand each binomial.

70. $(x - y)^3$ **71.** $(p + q)^6$ **72.** $(x - 2)^4$ **73.** $(3 - x)^5$

A Point in Time

1500   1600   1700   1800   1900   2000

Titanic was the largest passenger liner that had yet been built. On its maiden voyage in 1912, it struck an iceberg and sank. More than 1500 people died.

In 1985 a French and American team searched for *Titanic*. Research vessels combed the area with sonar. Transmitters aboard each ship sent out powerful spherical sound waves. Each wave reflected off any object in a half-mile-wide strip of ocean floor and returned to a receiver. The receiver then converted the echo to a picture of the object and calculated its depth. Two months after the search began, *Titanic* was discovered lying in two sections at a depth of some 13,000 feet.

Drawing not to scale

Go Online   **For:** Information about *Titanic*
PHSchool.com   **Web Code:** age-2032

You can use your graphing calculator to graph relations that are not functions.

Go Online
PHSchool.com

For: Graphing calculator procedures
Web Code: age-2110

ACTIVITY

Graph the ellipse $\frac{x^2}{16} + \frac{y^2}{9} = 1$.

Step 1 Solve the equation for y.

$$\frac{x^2}{16} + \frac{y^2}{9} = 1$$

$$\frac{y^2}{9} = 1 - \frac{x^2}{16}$$

$$y^2 = 9\left(1 - \frac{x^2}{16}\right)$$

$$y = \pm 3\sqrt{1 - \frac{x^2}{16}}$$

Step 2 Enter the equations as Y_1 and Y_2.

Step 3 Select a square window.

Step 4 Graph.

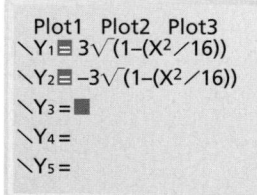

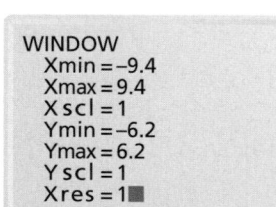

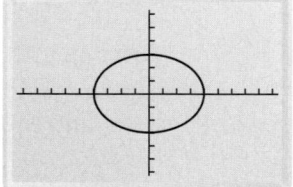

EXERCISES

Graph each conic section.

1. $x^2 + y^2 = 25$

2. $4x^2 + y^2 = 16$

3. $9x^2 - 16y^2 = 144$

4. $x^2 - y^2 = 3$

5. $\frac{x^2}{4} - \frac{y^2}{9} = 1$

6. $x^2 + \frac{y^2}{4} = 16$

7. a. Graph the functions $y = \sqrt{\frac{81}{4} - x^2}$ and $y = -\sqrt{\frac{81}{4} - x^2}$.
  b. Estimate the x-intercepts and find the y-intercepts.
  c. Adjust the window to $-9.3 \le x \le 9.5$. Verify the x-intercepts.
  d. What conic section does the graph represent?

Graph each conic section. Find the x- and y-intercepts.

8. $4x^2 + y^2 = 25$

9. $x^2 + y^2 = 30$

10. $9x^2 - 4y^2 = 72$

11. Writing Explain how to use a graphing calculator to graph the relation $x = |y - 3|$.

12. Critical Thinking Which conic sections can you graph using only one function? Explain.

Parabolas

What You'll Learn

- To write the equation of a parabola
- To graph parabolas

...And Why

To model a solar collector, as in Example 3

Solve for *c*.

1. $\frac{1}{8} = \frac{1}{c}$ **2.** $\frac{1}{8} = \frac{1}{2c}$ **3.** $\frac{1}{12} = \frac{1}{4c}$ **4.** $2 = \frac{1}{4c}$

Find the distance between the given points.

5. $(2, 3)$ and $(4, 1)$ **6.** $(4, 6)$ and $(3, -2)$ **7.** $(-1, 5)$ and $(2, -3)$

◀)) **New Vocabulary**   • focus of a parabola   • directrix

---

1   Writing the Equation of a Parabola

In Chapter 5 you learned that a parabola is the graph of a quadratic equation. By definition, a parabola is the set of all points in a plane that are the same distance from a fixed line and a fixed point not on the line. The fixed point is the **focus of a parabola.** The fixed line is the **directrix.** The line through the focus and perpendicular to the directrix is the axis of symmetry.

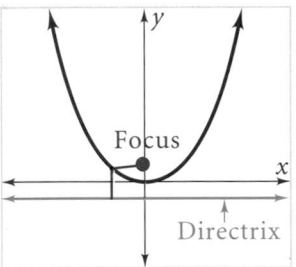

1 EXAMPLE   Using the Definition of a Parabola

Write an equation for a graph that is the set of all points in the plane that are equidistant from the point $F(0, 3)$ and the line $y = -3$.

You need to find all points $P(x, y)$ such that FP and the distance from P to the given line are equal.

Problem Solving Hint

The distance between $P_1(x_1, y_1)$ and $P_2(x_2, y_2)$ is $\sqrt{(x_2 - x_1)^2 + (y_2 - y_1)^2}$.

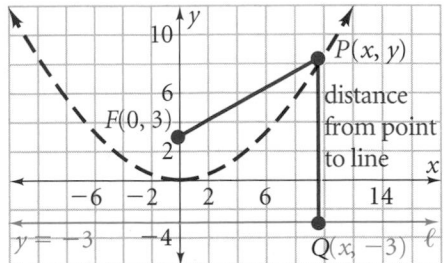

$$FP = PQ$$
$$\sqrt{(x - 0)^2 + (y - 3)^2} =$$
$$\sqrt{(x - x)^2 + (y - (-3))^2}$$
$$x^2 + (y - 3)^2 = 0^2 + (y + 3)^2$$
$$x^2 + y^2 - 6y + 9 = y^2 + 6y + 9$$
$$x^2 = 12y$$
$$y = \frac{1}{12}x^2$$

● An equation of the set of all points equidistant from $F(0, 3)$ and $y = -3$ is $y = \frac{1}{12}x^2$.

✓ **Quick Check**   ❶ Write an equation for a graph that is the set of all points in the plane that are equidistant from the point $F(2, 0)$ and the line $x = -2$.

In Chapter 5 you learned about the special relationship between the value of a and the graph of a quadratic function in the form $y = ax^2$. Now you will learn about the relationship between the value of a and the graph of a quadratic relation in the form $y = ax^2$ or $x = ay^2$.

If c is the distance from the vertex to the focus of a parabola, then $|a| = \frac{1}{4c}$.

Consider any parabola with equation $y = ax^2$ and vertex at the origin.

GO for Help

To review graphing parabolas, go to Lesson 5-2.

If $a > 0$, then
- the parabola opens upward
- the focus is at $(0, c)$
- the directrix is $y = -c$

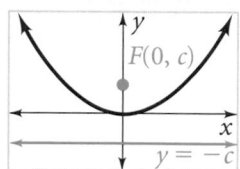

If $a < 0$, then
- the parabola opens downward
- the focus is at $(0, -c)$
- the directrix is at $y = c$

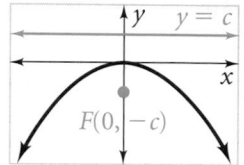

Consider any parabola with equation $x = ay^2$.

If $a > 0$, then
- the parabola opens to the right
- the focus is at $(c, 0)$
- the directrix is at $x = -c$

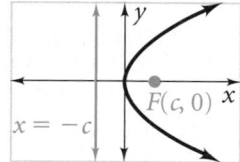

If $a < 0$, then
- the parabola opens to the left
- the focus is at $(-c, 0)$
- the directrix is at $x = c$

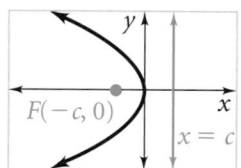

You can use the information above to write an equation of a parabola.

2 EXAMPLE Writing the Equation of a Parabola

Test-Taking Tip

When you identify or graph a relation, be sure you correctly match the equation variables and the graph variables.

Multiple Choice Which equation represents a parabola with a vertex at the origin and a focus at $(-5, 0)$?

(A) $y = \frac{1}{20}x^2$ (B) $x = \frac{1}{20}y^2$ (C) $y = -\frac{1}{20}x^2$ (D) $x = -\frac{1}{20}y^2$

Step 1 Determine the orientation of the parabola. Make a sketch. Since the focus is located to the left of the vertex, the parabola must open to the left. Use $x = ay^2$.

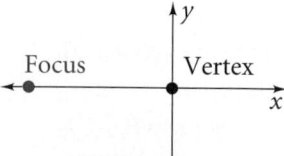

Step 2 Find a.

$|a| = \frac{1}{4c}$

$= \frac{1}{4(5)}$ **Since the focus is a distance of 5 units from the vertex, c = 5.**

$= \frac{1}{20}$

Since the parabola opens to the left, a is negative. So $a = -\frac{1}{20}$.

An equation for the parabola is $x = -\frac{1}{20}y^2$. The correct choice is D.

✓ Quick Check ❷ Write an equation of a parabola with a vertex at the origin and a focus at $\left(\frac{1}{2}, 0\right)$.

You can find the equation of a parabola that models a real-world situation.

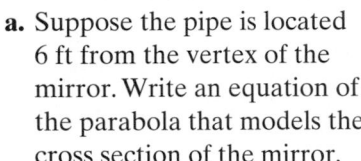 **EXAMPLE** <u>Real-World</u> **Connection**

Solar Energy In some solar collectors, a mirror with a parabolic cross section is used to concentrate sunlight on a pipe, which is located at the focus of the mirror.

a. Suppose the pipe is located 6 ft from the vertex of the mirror. Write an equation of the parabola that models the cross section of the mirror.

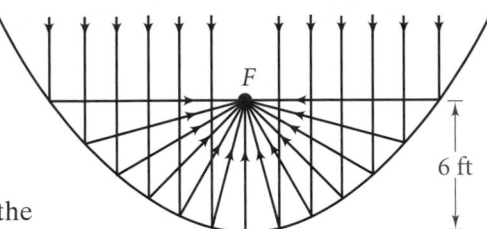

The distance from the vertex to the focus is 6 ft, so $c = 6$. Find the value of a.

$$a = \frac{1}{4c}$$

$$= \frac{1}{4(6)}$$

$$= \frac{1}{24} \quad \text{Since the parabola opens upward, } a \text{ is positive.}$$

The equation of the parabola is $y = \frac{1}{24}x^2$.

b. Suppose you stretch the equation of the mirror (and the mirror itself upward) by a factor of 2 to become $y = \frac{1}{12}x^2$. How should you move the pipe so that it remains at the focus?

In $a = \frac{1}{4c}$, if a doubles, the value of c must halve. The distance to the focus would change from 6 ft to 3 ft.

Quick Check ❸ Suppose the pipe is located 8.25 ft from the vertex of the mirror. Write an equation of the parabola to model the cross section of the mirror.

Graphing Parabolas

You can use the value of a to identify the focus and directrix of a parabola.

❹ **EXAMPLE** **Identifying Focus and Directrix**

Identify the focus and the directrix of the graph of the equation $y = -\frac{1}{16}x^2$.

The parabola is of the form $y = ax^2$, so the vertex is at the origin and the parabola has a vertical axis of symmetry. Since $a < 0$, the parabola opens downward.

$$|a| = \frac{1}{4c}$$

$$\left|-\frac{1}{16}\right| = \frac{1}{4c} \quad \text{Substitute } -\frac{1}{16} \text{ for } a.$$

$$4c = 16 \quad \text{Solve for } c.$$

$$c = 4$$

The focus is at $(0, -4)$. The equation of the directrix is $y = 4$.

Quick Check ❹ Identify the focus and the directrix of the graph of the equation $y = \frac{1}{12}x^2$.

You can use the focus and directrix to graph the equation of a parabola.

5 EXAMPLE **Graphing the Equation of a Parabola**

Identify the vertex, the focus, and the directrix of the graph of the equation $y^2 - 4x - 4y + 16 = 0$. Then graph the parabola.

$$y^2 - 4x - 4y + 16 = 0$$

$$4x = y^2 - 4y + 16 \qquad \text{Solve for } x, \text{ since } x \text{ is in only one term.}$$

$$4x = (y^2 - 4y + 4) + 16 - 4 \qquad \text{Complete the square in } y.$$

$$x = \tfrac{1}{4}(y^2 - 4y + 4) + 4 - 1 \qquad \text{Divide both sides of the equation by 4.}$$

$$x = \tfrac{1}{4}(y - 2)^2 + 3 \qquad \text{vertex form}$$

The parabola is of the form $x = a(y - k)^2 + h$. This is a translation of $x = ay^2$. All of the graph's features—axis of symmetry, vertex, focus, and directrix—translate with the parabola. The parabola has a horizontal axis of symmetry. $a > 0$, so the parabola opens to the right. Its vertex is at $(h, k) = (3, 2)$.

$$|a| = \tfrac{1}{4c}$$

$$\left|\tfrac{1}{4}\right| = \tfrac{1}{4c} \qquad \text{Substitute } \tfrac{1}{4} \text{ for } a.$$

$$4c = 4 \qquad \text{Solve for } c.$$

$$c = 1$$

The focus is at $(4, 2)$. The directrix is $x = 2$.

Locate one or more points on the parabola. Select a value for y, such as 4. The point on the parabola with a y-value of 4 is $(4, 4)$. Use the symmetric nature of a parabola to find the corresponding point, $(4, 0)$.

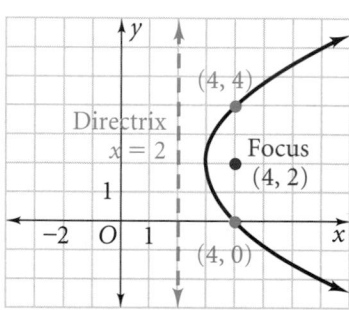

✓ Quick Check **5** Identify the vertex, the focus, and the directrix of the graph of $x^2 + 6x + 3y + 12 = 0$. Then graph the equation.

EXERCISES

For more exercises, see *Extra Skill and Word Problem Practice.*

Practice and Problem Solving

A Practice by Example

Example 1
(page 555)

Write an equation for a graph that is the set of all points in the plane that are equidistant from the given point and the given line.

1. $F(0, 2), y = -2$ **2.** $F(0, -1), y = 1$ **3.** $F(-3, 0), x = 3$

4. $F(0, -8), y = 8$ **5.** $F(0, 4), y = 0$ **6.** $F\left(\tfrac{1}{2}, 0\right), x = -\tfrac{1}{2}$

Example 2
(page 556)

Write an equation of a parabola with a vertex at the origin and the given focus.

7. focus at $(6, 0)$ **8.** focus at $(0, -4)$ **9.** focus at $(0, 7)$

10. focus at $(-1, 0)$ **11.** focus at $(2, 0)$ **12.** focus at $(0, -5)$

Example 3
(page 557)

Write an equation of a parabola opening upward with a vertex at the origin.

13. focus 1.5 units from vertex   **14.** focus $\tfrac{1}{8}$ of a unit from vertex

15. Optics A cross section of a flashlight reflector is a parabola. The bulb is located at the focus. Suppose the bulb is located $\frac{1}{4}$ in. from the vertex of the reflector. Model a cross section of the reflector by writing an equation of a parabola that opens upward and has its vertex at the origin. What is an advantage of this parabolic design?

Example 4
(page 557)

Identify the focus and the directrix of the graph of each equation.

16. $y = \frac{1}{4}x^2$ **17.** $y = x^2$ **18.** $y = -\frac{1}{8}x^2$ **19.** $x = \frac{1}{2}y^2$

20. $y = \frac{1}{2}x^2$ **21.** $x = \frac{1}{36}y^2$ **22.** $x = -\frac{1}{18}y^2$ **23.** $y = -2x^2$

Example 5
(page 558)

Identify the vertex, the focus, and the directrix of each graph. Then sketch the graph.

24. $x = \frac{1}{24}y^2$ **25.** $y = -\frac{1}{4}x^2$ **26.** $x = \frac{1}{12}y^2$

27. $y^2 - 25x = 0$ **28.** $x^2 = 4y$ **29.** $x^2 = -4y$

30. $(x - 2)^2 = 4y$ **31.** $-8x = y^2$ **32.** $(x + 2)^2 = y - 4$

33. $y^2 - 6x = 18$ **34.** $x^2 + 24y - 8x = -16$ **35.** $y^2 - 12x + 2y = -37$

B **Apply Your Skills**

Write an equation of a parabola with a vertex at the origin.

36. directrix $x = -3$ **37.** focus at $(0, 100)$ **38.** directrix $y = 5$

39. focus at $(-7, 0)$ **40.** directrix $x = 9$ **41.** directrix $y = 2.8$

42. Earth Science The equation $d = \frac{1}{10}s^2$ relates the depth d (in meters) of the ocean to the speed s (in meters per second) at which tsunamis travel. Graph the equation.

Use the information in each graph to write the equation for the graph.

43.
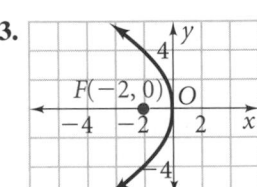

44.

45.
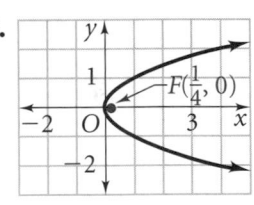

Real-World **Connection**

Tsunamis are ocean waves that result from an undersea earthquake. As the waves approach shallow water, their height increases and their speed decreases.

Graph each equation.

46. $y^2 - 8x = 0$ **47.** $y^2 - 8y + 8x = -16$ **48.** $2x^2 - y + 20x = -53$

49. $x^2 = 12y$ **50.** $y = 4(x - 3)^2 - 2$ **51.** $(y - 2)^2 = 4(x + 3)$

Write an equation of a parabola with a vertex at (1, 1).

52. directrix $y = -\frac{1}{2}$ **53.** directrix $x = \frac{3}{2}$ **54.** focus at $(1, 0)$

55. Open-Ended Write an equation for a parabola that opens to the left. Give the focus and directrix of the parabola.

56. Writing Explain how to find the distance from the focus to the directrix of the parabola $x = 2y^2$.

57. Multiple Choice The focus of a parabola is at $(-3, 3)$. The vertex is at $(0, 3)$. What is the equation of the parabola?

Ⓐ $y - 3 = \frac{1}{12}x^2$ Ⓑ $x = -\frac{1}{12}(y - 3)^2$

Ⓒ $y = -\frac{1}{12}(x - 3)^2$ Ⓓ $x = \frac{1}{12}(y + 3)^2$

GO Online
Homework Video Tutor
Visit: PHSchool.com
Web Code: age-1002

 **Challenge**

58. Critical Thinking Use the definition of a parabola to show that the parabola with vertex (h, k) and focus $(h, k + c)$ has the equation $(x - h)^2 = 4c(y - k)$.

59. Modeling Draw a cross section of a parabolic mirror modeled by the equation $y = 0.002323x^2$.

60. a. What part of a parabola is modeled by the function $y = -\sqrt{x}$?
   b. State the domain and range for the function in part (a).

61. The directrix of a parabola is the line $y = -2$. The focus is the point $(0, 2)$.
   a. Suppose the directrix remains fixed, but the focus is shifted along the y-axis farther away from the directrix. Explain what happens to the vertex and the shape of the parabola.
   b. Suppose the focus moves along the y-axis toward the directrix. Explain what happens to the vertex and the shape of the parabola.
   c. What would happen if the focus moved down all the way to the directrix?

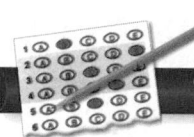

Test Prep

Multiple Choice

62. What is the distance from $P(2, -5)$ to the line $y = -8$?
   A. -6 **B.** 3   **C.** 5   **D.** 10

63. Which point is equidistant from $F(0, 5)$ and the line $y = -5$?
   F. $(-10, 5)$ **G.** $(-5, 0)$ **H.** $(0, 1)$ **J.** $(10, 10)$

64. Which equation represents a parabola that opens to the left?
   A. $x = -2y^2$ **B.** $x = 2y^2$ **C.** $y = -2x^2$ **D.** $y = 2x^2$

65. Which equation represents a parabola that opens downward?
   F. $x = -2y^2$ **G.** $x = 2y^2$ **H.** $y = -2x^2$ **J.** $y = 2x^2$

Short Response

66. What is the equation of a parabola that is the set of all points that are equidistant from $F(0, 4)$ and the line $y = -4$?

67. Find the focus and the directrix of the parabola with equation $y = \frac{1}{36}x^2$.

Mixed Review

 **for Help**

Lesson 10-1

Graph each equation.

68. $x^2 + y^2 = 64$ **69.** $x^2 + 9y^2 = 9$ **70.** $4x^2 - 9y^2 = 36$

Lesson 9-2

Find the asymptotes of the graph of each equation.

71. $y = \frac{3}{x}$ **72.** $y = \frac{1}{x} + 4$ **73.** $y = \frac{4}{x + 1}$

74. $y = -\frac{1}{x - 1}$ **75.** $y = \frac{5}{x + 5} + 2$ **76.** $y = \frac{2}{x - 3} - 1$

Lesson 8-2 **77. Investing** Suppose you have a continuously compounding account with a beginning principal of $3,800 and an interest rate of 8.1%. What is the balance after 4 years?

10-3

Circles

What You'll Learn

- To write and graph the equation of a circle
- To find the center and radius of a circle and use it to graph the circle

. . . And Why

To model gears in machinery, as in Example 3

✓ Check Skills You'll Need **for Help** Lesson 5-7 and Skills Handbook page 883

Simplify.

1. $\sqrt{16}$ **2.** $\sqrt{49}$ **3.** $\sqrt{20}$ **4.** $\sqrt{48}$ **5.** $\sqrt{72}$

Find the missing value to complete the square.

6. $x^2 - 2x + \blacksquare$ **7.** $x^2 + 4x + \blacksquare$ **8.** $x^2 - 6x + \blacksquare$

◀)) New Vocabulary • circle • center • radius
• standard form of an equation of a circle

---

1   Writing the Equation of a Circle

Real-World ⊕ Connection

People of many cultures use circular dwellings, like those shown above in Mali, to maximize volume for a given surface area.

A **circle** is the set of all points in a plane that are a distance r from a given point, called the **center**. The distance r is the **radius** of the circle.

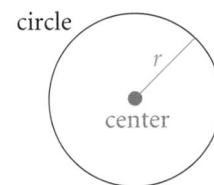

In the coordinate plane, if r is the radius of a circle with a center at the origin, then the equation of the circle can be written in the form $x^2 + y^2 = r^2$.

Not every circle has its center at the origin. You can use the distance formula to find an equation of a circle with a radius r and a center at the point (h, k).

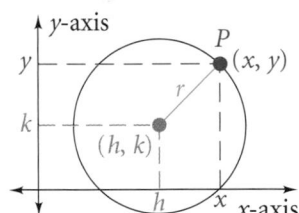

Let (x, y) be any point on the circle. The distance from (h, k) to (x, y) is the radius.

$d = \sqrt{(x_2 - x_2)^2 + (y_2 - y_1)^2}$ **Distance Formula**

$r = \sqrt{(x - h)^2 + (y - k)^2}$ **Substitute r for d, (h, k) for (x_1, y_1), and (x, y) for (x_2, y_2).**

$r^2 = (x - h)^2 + (y - k)^2$ **Square each side.**

This derivation leads to a definition.

 Key Concepts

Definition	**Standard Form of an Equation of a Circle**

The standard form of an equation of a circle with center (h, k) and radius r is

$$(x - h)^2 + (y - k)^2 = r^2.$$

You can use the center and the radius of a circle to write an equation for a circle.

1 EXAMPLE **Writing the Equation of a Circle**

Write an equation of a circle with center $(-4, 3)$ and radius 4.

$(x - h)^2 + (y - k)^2 = r^2$ **Use the standard form of the equation of a circle.**

$(x - (-4))^2 + (y - 3)^2 = 4^2$ **Substitute −4 for *h*, 3 for *k*, and 4 for *r*.**

$(x + 4)^2 + (y - 3)^2 = 16$ **Simplify.**

An equation for the circle is $(x + 4)^2 + (y - 3)^2 = 16$.

Check Solve the equation for *y* and enter both functions into your graphing calculator.

$$(x + 4)^2 + (y - 3)^2 = 16$$
$$(y - 3)^2 = 16 - (x + 4)^2$$
$$y - 3 = \pm \sqrt{16 - (x + 4)^2}$$
$$y = 3 \pm \sqrt{16 - (x + 4)^2}$$

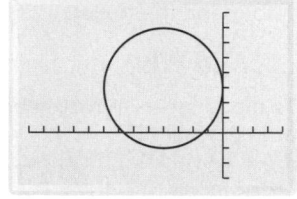

Graphing Calculator Hint

When graphing a conic section, press ZOOM 5 to select a square window. The standard window makes a circle look like an ellipse.

✓ **Quick Check** ❶ Write an equation for a circle with center at $(5, -2)$ and radius 8. Check your answer.

You can use parameters *h* and *k* to translate the circle $x^2 + y^2 = r^2$ with center $(0, 0)$ to the circle $(x - h)^2 + (y - k)^2 = r^2$ with center (h, k). Translate to the right when *h* is positive; to the left when *h* is negative. Translate up when *k* is positive; down when *k* is negative.

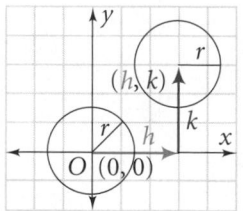

2 EXAMPLE **Using Translations to Write an Equation**

Write an equation for the translation of $x^2 + y^2 = 9$ four units left and three units up. Then graph the translation.

$(x - h)^2 + (y - k)^2 = r^2$ **Use standard form.**

$(x - (-4))^2 + (y - 3)^2 = 9$ **Substitute −4 for *h*, 3 for *k*, and 9 for r^2.**

$(x + 4)^2 + (y - 3)^2 = 9$ **Simplify.**

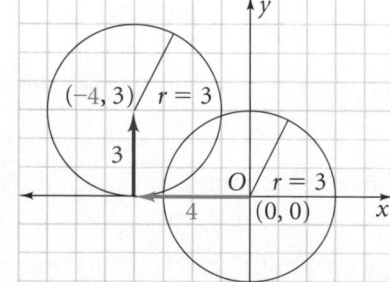

✓ **Quick Check** ❷ Write an equation for each translation.
    a. $x^2 + y^2 = 1$; left 5 and down 3   **b.** $x^2 + y^2 = 9$; right 2 and up 3

You can write an equation of a circle to model a real-world situation.

3 EXAMPLE Real-World 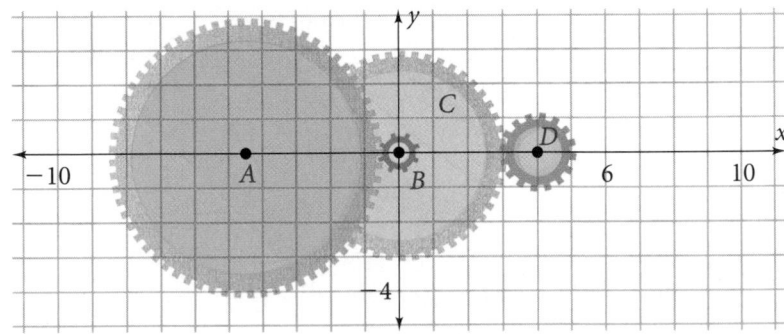 Connection

Machinery The diagram below shows four gears in a motor assembly. Gear B rotates 8 times for each rotation of gear A. Gears B and C share the same shaft, with centers at the origin. The radius of gear C is 6 times the radius of gear B. The radius of gear D is $\frac{1}{3}$ the radius of gear C. Write the equation of the circle that represents each gear.

Real-World Connection

Gears change the rate of rotation of different parts of a machine. The gears shown above are part of a printing press.

Make a table. Let the radius of gear $B = \frac{1}{2}$. The radius of gear A must be 8 times the radius of gear B, or 4.

Gear	(h, k)	r	Equation
A	$\left(-4\frac{1}{2}, 0\right)$	4	$\left(x + \frac{9}{2}\right)^2 + y^2 = 16$
B	$(0, 0)$	$\frac{1}{2}$	$x^2 + y^2 = \frac{1}{4}$
C	$(0, 0)$	3	$x^2 + y^2 = 9$
D	$(4, 0)$	1	$(x - 4)^2 + y^2 = 1$

✓ Quick Check ③ Write the equation of a circle for a gear that is the same size as gear D and has center $(0, -4)$.

2 Using the Center and Radius of a Circle

You can find the center and radius of a circle by rewriting the equation in the standard form of a circle.

4 EXAMPLE Finding the Center and Radius

Find the center and radius of the circle with equation $(x - 16)^2 + (y + 9)^2 = 144$.

$$(x - h)^2 + (y - k)^2 = r^2 \qquad \text{Write the standard form.}$$
$$(x - 16)^2 + (y + 9)^2 = 144 \qquad \text{Write the equation.}$$
$$(x - 16)^2 + (y - (-9))^2 = 12^2 \qquad \text{Rewrite the equation in standard form.}$$
$$h = 16 \qquad k = -9 \qquad r = 12 \qquad \text{Find } h, k, \text{ and } r.$$

The center of the circle is $(16, -9)$. The radius is 12.

✓ Quick Check ④ Find the center and radius of the circle with equation $(x + 8)^2 + (y + 3)^2 = 121$.

You can use the center and the radius to graph a circle.

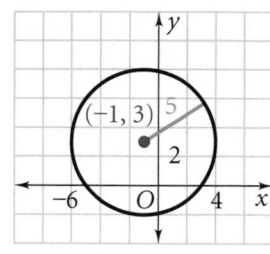
5 **EXAMPLE** **Graphing a Circle Using Center and Radius**

Graph $(x + 1)^2 + (y - 3)^2 = 25$.

$$(x - h)^2 + (y - k)^2 = r^2 \qquad \text{Find the center and the radius of the circle.}$$
$$(x - (-1))^2 + (y - 3)^2 = 25$$
$$h = -1 \qquad\qquad k = 3 \qquad r^2 = 25, \text{ or } r = 5$$

Draw the center $(-1, 3)$ and
radius 5. Draw a smooth curve.

Quick Check **5** Graph $(x - 4)^2 + (y + 2)^2 = 49$.

EXERCISES

For more exercises, see *Extra Skill and Word Problem Practice.*

Practice and Problem Solving

A Practice by Example

Write an equation of a circle with the given center and radius. Check your answers.

Example 1
(page 562)

1. $(0, 0), 10$ **2.** $(-4, -6), 7$ **3.** $(2, 3), 4.5$ **4.** $(-6, 10), 1$

5. $(1, -3), 10$ **6.** $(-5, -1), 6$ **7.** $(-3, 0), 8$ **8.** $(-1.5, -3), 2$

GO for Help

Example 2
(page 562)

Write an equation for each translation.

9. $x^2 + y^2 = 9$; down 1   **10.** $x^2 + y^2 = 1$; left 1

11. $x^2 + y^2 = 25$; right 2 and down 4   **12.** $x^2 + y^2 = 81$; left 1 and up 3

13. $x^2 + y^2 = 100$; down 5   **14.** $x^2 + y^2 = 49$; right 3 and up 2

15. $x^2 + y^2 = 20$; left 6 and up 1   **16.** $x^2 + y^2 = 50$; right 5

Example 3
(page 563)

Write an equation for each circle. Each interval represents one unit.

17.

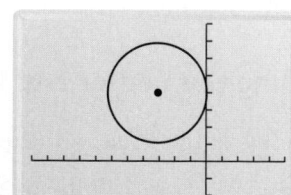

18.

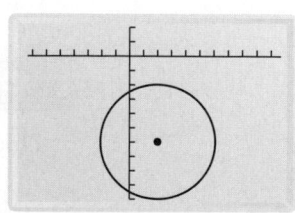

Example 4
(page 563)

For each equation, find the center and radius of the circle.

19. $(x - 1)^2 + (y - 1)^2 = 1$ **20.** $(x + 2)^2 + (y - 10)^2 = 4$

21. $(x - 3)^2 + (y + 1)^2 = 36$ **22.** $(x + 3)^2 + (y - 5)^2 = 81$

23. $x^2 + (y + 3)^2 = 25$ **24.** $(x + 6)^2 + y^2 = 121$

25. $(x + 2)^2 + (y + 4)^2 = 256$ **26.** $(x - 3)^2 + (y - 7)^2 = 96$

Example 5
(page 564)

Use the center and the radius to graph each circle.

27. $(x + 9)^2 + (y + 2)^2 = 100$ **28.** $(x + 4)^2 + (y - 4)^2 = 4$

29. $(x - 6)^2 + y^2 = 64$ **30.** $(x - 1)^2 + (y + 3)^2 = 16$

31. $x^2 + y^2 = 9$ **32.** $(x + 3)^2 + (y - 9)^2 = 49$

33. $(x - 7)^2 + (y - 1)^2 = 100$ **34.** $x^2 + (y + 4)^2 = 144$

B   **Apply Your Skills**

Write the equation of the circle that passes through the given point and has a center at the origin. (*Hint:* You can use the distance formula to find the radius.)

35. $(0, 4)$ **36.** $(0, -3)$ **37.** $(-5, 0)$ **38.** $(\sqrt{3}, 0)$ **39.** $(4, -3)$

40. $(-5, -12)$ **41.** $(12, -5)$ **42.** $(-2, 3)$ **43.** $(1, -5)$ **44.** $(-6, -4)$

Use the given information to write an equation of the circle.

45. radius 7, center $(-6, 13)$ **46.** area 25π, center $(5, -3)$

47. center $(-2, 7.5)$, circumference 3π **48.** center $(1, -2)$, through $(0, 1)$

49. center $(2, 1)$, through $(6, 4)$ **50.** center $(6, 4)$, through $(2, 1)$

51. translation of $(x - 1)^2 + (y + 3)^2 = 36$, 2 units left and 4 units down

52. Multiple Choice Which equation models the circular fountain at the right?

   Ⓐ $(x - 24)^2 + (y - 22)^2 = 100$

   Ⓑ $(x + 22)^2 + (y + 24)^2 = 100$

   Ⓒ $(x - 24)^2 + (y - 22)^2 = 10$

   Ⓓ $(x + 24)^2 + (y + 22)^2 = 10$

53. Open-Ended Write two functions that together represent a circle.

54. Error Analysis A student claims that the circle $(x + 7)^2 + (y - 7)^2 = 8$ is a translation of the circle $x^2 + y^2 = 8$, 7 right and 7 down. What is the student's mistake?

Find the center and the radius of each circle.

55. $x^2 + y^2 = 2$ **56.** $x^2 + (y + 1)^2 = 5$

57. $x^2 + y^2 = 14$ **58.** $x^2 + (y - 4)^2 = 11$

59. $(x + 5)^2 + y^2 = 18$ **60.** $(x + 2)^2 + (y + 4)^2 = 50$

61. $(x + 3)^2 + (y - 5)^2 = 38$ **62.** $x^2 + 2x + 1 + y^2 = 4$

63. $x^2 + y^2 - 6x - 2y + 4 = 0$ **64.** $x^2 + y^2 - 4y - 16 = 0$

GO Online
Homework Video Tutor
Visit: PHSchool.com
Web Code: age-1003

Graph each pair of equations. Identify the conic section represented by the graph. Then write the equation of the conic section.

65. $y = 3 + \sqrt{16 - (x - 4)^2}$ **66.** $y = -2 + \sqrt{x - 3}$

      $y = 3 - \sqrt{16 - (x - 4)^2}$ $y = -2 - \sqrt{x - 3}$

C   **Challenge**

67. Reasoning Let $P(x, y)$ be any point on the circle with center $(0, 0)$ and radius r. Choose a method for proving that $x^2 + y^2 = r^2$.

68. a. Writing Explain why $x^2 + y^2 = 0$ does not represent a circle.
  b. Critical Thinking What does the equation represent?

69. The table gives the diameters of four planets.
  a. Use a center of $(0, 0)$ to graph a circle that represents the size of each planet.
  b. Write an equation representing the circular cross section through the center of each planet.

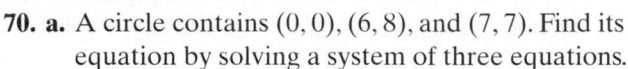

Planet	Diameter (miles)
Pluto	1430
Mercury	3031
Mars	4222
Earth	7926

70. a. A circle contains $(0, 0)$, $(6, 8)$, and $(7, 7)$. Find its equation by solving a system of three equations.
  b. Several parabolas contain the three points of part (a), but only one is described by a quadratic function. Find that function.

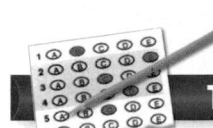

Test Prep

Gridded Response

71. What is the radius of the circle with equation $(x + 5)^2 + (y - 3)^2 = 144$?

72. What is the radius of the circle with equation $(x - 2)^2 + 3 + (y + 1)^2 = 7$?

73. Circle A has equation $(x + 5)^2 + y^2 = 169$. The diameter of circle B is one fourth as long as the diameter of circle A. What is the radius of circle B?

74. What is the distance between $T(9, -5)$ and the center of the circle with equation $(x - 6)^2 + (y + 1)^2 = 10$?

75. Find the distance between the centers of the circles with equations $(x - 5)^2 + (y - 1)^2 = 16$ and $(x + 1)^2 + (y - 9)^2 = 49$.

76. What is the area of the circle whose equation is $(x + 1)^2 + (y + 1)^2 = 1$? Round your answer to the nearest hundredth.

Mixed Review

Lesson 10-2
77. Write an equation of a parabola opening left with vertex $(0, 0)$ and focus $(-3, 0)$.

Lesson 9-3
For each rational function, find any points of discontinuity.

78. $y = \dfrac{2}{x + 1}$ **79.** $y = \dfrac{1}{x^2 - 5x + 6}$ **80.** $y = \dfrac{2x - 1}{x^2 + 4}$

Lesson 8-3
Evaluate each logarithm.

81. $\log_2 16$ **82.** $\log_5 25$ **83.** $\log_3 \dfrac{1}{27}$

84. $\log 10{,}000$ **85.** $\log_{36} 6$ **86.** $\log_{100} 100$

Checkpoint Quiz 1   Lessons 10-1 through 10-3

Identify the vertex, focus, and directrix of each parabola. Then graph the parabola.

1. $y = 3x^2$ **2.** $x = 4(y + 2)^2$ **3.** $y + 1 = (x - 3)^2$

4. Write an equation in standard form of the circle with center $(-6, 3)$ and radius 8.

5. What translation of $x^2 + y^2 = 18$ results in $(x + 4)^2 + (y - 6)^2 = 18$?

Using Parametric Equations

The graphing calculator program below uses parametric equations (Activity Lab, page 124) to graph a circle. To enter the program, use the [PRGM] **NEW** menu. Name your program **CIRCLE**.

Note that you find the **Disp**, **Prompt**, and **DispGraph** features in the [PRGM] **I/O** menu, and X_{1T} and Y_{1T} in the [VARS] **Y-Vars Parametric** menu. You can find **Par** and **Radian** under [MODE], and **Tmin**, **Tmax**, and **Tstep** in the [VARS] **Window T/θ** menu.

Use [ALPHA] keys to enter words, quotation marks, and variables H, K, R, and T.

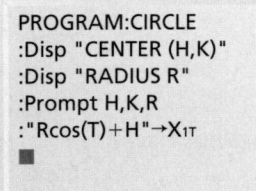

```
PROGRAM:CIRCLE
:Disp "CENTER (H,K)"
:Disp "RADIUS R"
:Prompt H,K,R
:"Rcos(T)+H"→X₁T
■
```

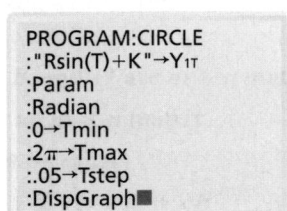

```
PROGRAM:CIRCLE
:"Rsin(T)+K"→Y₁T
:Param
:Radian
:0→Tmin
:2π→Tmax
:.05→Tstep
:DispGraph■
```

The screens below show the program being run for a circle with a center at $(-2, 3)$ and a radius of 5. Enter appropriate square-window values with the calculator in function mode. Then choose the program from the [PRGM] **EXEC** menu.

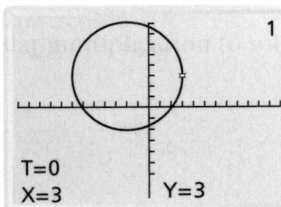

```
WINDOW
  Xmin=-12
  Xmax=12
  Xscl=1
  Ymin=-8
  Ymax=8
  Yscl=1
  Xres=1■
```

```
prgmCIRCLE
CENTER (H,K)
RADIUS R
H=?-2
K=?3
R=?5■
```

```
                    1

T=0
X=3        Y=3
```

Note that you can trace to find the coordinates of points on the circle.

EXERCISES

Use your program to graph each circle. Use an appropriate square window for each graph.

1. center $(0, 2)$, radius 4

2. center $(5, -2)$, radius 5

3. center $(-1, 3)$, radius 8

4. $(x - 2)^2 + (y + 1)^2 = 25$

5. $(x + 4)^2 + (y - 3)^2 = 100$

6. $x^2 + (y + 2)^2 = 49$

7. $(x - 1)^2 + (y + 2)^2 = 36$

8. $(x - 6)^2 + y^2 = 100$

9. Open-Ended Use [TRACE] to find four points in Quadrant III that lie on the circle described by the equation $(x + 5)^2 + (y - 2)^2 = 16$.

10. Writing Describe how to change your program to work in degrees and plot a point every 5° of rotation.

Go Online
PHSchool.com
For: Graphing calculator procedures
Web Code: age-2119

Ellipses

What You'll Learn

- To write the equation of an ellipse
- To find the foci of an ellipse and to graph an ellipse

... And Why

To model NASA's Transonic Tunnel, as in Example 2

✓ Check Skills You'll Need

GO for Help Lesson 5-5 and Skills Handbook page 874

Solve each equation.

1. $27 = x^2 + 11$ 2. $x^2 = 48$ 3. $84 = 120 - x^2$

Evaluate each expression for $a = 3$ and $b = 5$.

4. $a^2 + b^2$ 5. $a^2 - b^2$ 6. $b^2 - 2a^2$

◀)) New Vocabulary

- ellipse
- focus of an ellipse
- major axis
- vertices of an ellipse
- minor axis
- co-vertices

---

1 Writing the Equation of an Ellipse

Ellipses play an important role in science. For example, the planets follow elliptical, not circular, orbits around the sun.

 Key Concepts

Definition	**Ellipse**

An **ellipse** is a set of points P in a plane such that the sum of the distances from P to two fixed points F_1 and F_2 is a given constant k.

$$PF_1 + PF_2 = k, \text{ where } k > F_1F_2$$

Vocabulary Tip

Ellipse comes from a Greek word for "smaller." The cutting plane of an ellipse makes a smaller angle with the base than does the side of the cone. See p. 547.

Each fixed point F is a **focus of an ellipse** (plural: foci). The **major axis** is the segment that contains the foci and has its endpoints on the ellipse. The endpoints of the major axis are **vertices of an ellipse.** The midpoint of the major axis is the center of the ellipse. The **minor axis** is perpendicular to the major axis at the center. The endpoints of the minor axis are **co-vertices.**

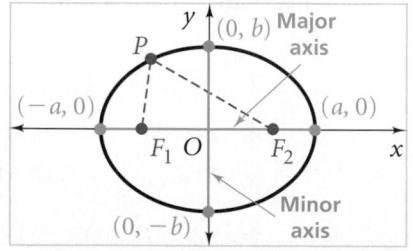

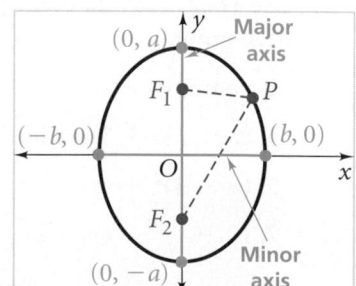

$$\frac{x^2}{a^2} + \frac{y^2}{b^2} = 1$$

major axis: horizontal
vertices: $(\pm a, 0)$
co-vertices: $(0, \pm b)$

← standard forms of an equation of an ellipse, with center at the origin and $a > b > 0$ →

$$\frac{x^2}{b^2} + \frac{y^2}{a^2} = 1$$

major axis: vertical
vertices: $(0, \pm a)$
co-vertices: $(\pm b, 0)$

You can write the equation of an ellipse with a center at the origin if you know an x-intercept and a y-intercept.

1 EXAMPLE **Writing the Equation of an Ellipse**

Write an equation in standard form of an ellipse that has a vertex at $(0, 5)$, a co-vertex at $(2, 0)$, and a center at the origin.

Since $(0, 5)$ is a vertex of the ellipse, the other vertex is at $(0, -5)$, and the major axis is vertical. Since $(2, 0)$ is a co-vertex, the other co-vertex is at $(-2, 0)$, and the minor axis is horizontal. So $a = 5, b = 2, a^2 = 25$, and $b^2 = 4$.

$\dfrac{x^2}{b^2} + \dfrac{y^2}{a^2} = 1$ **standard form of an equation of an ellipse with a vertical major axis**

$\dfrac{x^2}{4} + \dfrac{y^2}{25} = 1$ **Substitute 4 for b^2 and 25 for a^2.**

● An equation of the ellipse is $\dfrac{x^2}{4} + \dfrac{y^2}{25} = 1$.

✓ Quick Check ❶ Write an equation in standard form for an ellipse that has a vertex at $(0, -6)$, a co-vertex at $(3, 0)$, and a center at the origin.

You can write an equation for an ellipse with a center at the origin if you know the length of both axes.

2 EXAMPLE **Real-World Connection**

Aerodynamics Scientists used the Transonic Tunnel at NASA Langley Research Center, Virginia, to study the dynamics of air flow. The elliptical opening of the Transonic Tunnel is 82 ft wide and 58 ft high. Find an equation of the ellipse.

Imagine a large coordinate grid placed over the elliptical opening. Since the widest part of the ellipse is horizontal and the width is 82 ft, place the vertices at $(\pm 41, 0)$. Place the co-vertices at $(0, \pm 29)$.

So $a = 41, b = 29, a^2 = 1681$, and $b^2 = 841$.

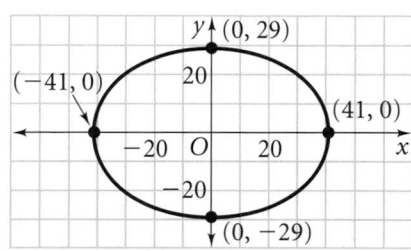

$\dfrac{x^2}{a^2} + \dfrac{y^2}{b^2} = 1$ **standard form for an ellipse with a horizontal major axis**

$\dfrac{x^2}{1681} + \dfrac{y^2}{841} = 1$ **Substitute 1681 for a^2 and 841 for b^2.**

● An equation of the ellipse is $\dfrac{x^2}{1681} + \dfrac{y^2}{841} = 1$.

✓ Quick Check ❷ Find an equation of an ellipse centered at the origin that is 12 units wide and 30 units high.

Real-World Connection

The guide vanes in the elliptical opening of the Transonic Tunnel allow a smooth flow of air through the passageway.

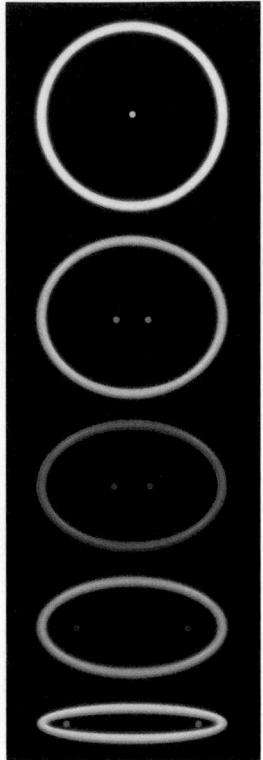

The figure above shows the relationship between the center of a circle and the foci of an ellipse.

The foci are important points in an ellipse. For example, the sun is at a focus, not at the center, of Earth's orbit around the sun.

The foci of an ellipse are always on the major axis at c units from the center.

There is an important and useful relationship among $a, b,$ and c: $c^2 = a^2 - b^2$.

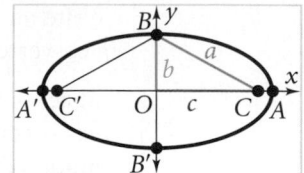

You can use the relationship to find the foci of an ellipse.

3 **EXAMPLE** **Finding the Foci of an Ellipse**

Find the foci of the ellipse with the equation $25x^2 + 9y^2 = 225$. Graph the ellipse.

$25x^2 + 9y^2 = 225$

$\dfrac{x^2}{9} + \dfrac{y^2}{25} = 1$ **Write in standard form.**

Since $25 > 9$ and 25 is with y^2, the major axis is vertical, $a^2 = 25$, and $b^2 = 9$.

$c^2 = a^2 - b^2$ **Find c.**

$\quad = 25 - 9$ **Substitute 25 for a^2 and 9 for b^2.**

$\quad = 16$

$c = 4$

The major axis is vertical, so the coordinates of the foci are $(0, \pm c)$. The foci are $(0, 4)$ and $(0, -4)$.

● The vertices are $(0, \pm 5)$. The co-vertices are $(\pm 3, 0)$.

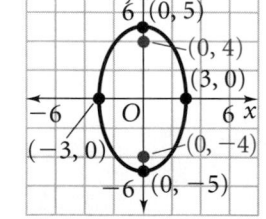

☑ **Quick Check** ❸ Find the foci of the ellipse with the equation $x^2 + 9y^2 = 9$. Graph the ellipse.

You can use the relationship among $a, b,$ and c to write the equation of an ellipse.

4 **EXAMPLE** **Using the Foci of an Ellipse**

For: Ellipse Activity
Use: Interactive Textbook, 10-4

Write an equation of the ellipse with foci at $(\pm 7, 0)$ and co-vertices at $(0, \pm 6)$.

Since the foci have coordinates $(\pm 7, 0)$, the major axis is horizontal.

Since $c = 7$ and $b = 6, c^2 = 49$ and $b^2 = 36$.

$c^2 = a^2 - b^2$ **Use the equation to find a^2.**

$49 = a^2 - 36$ **Substitute 49 for c^2 and 36 for b^2.**

$a^2 = 85$ **Simplify.**

$\dfrac{x^2}{85} + \dfrac{y^2}{36} = 1$ **Substitute 85 for a^2 and 36 for b^2.**

● An equation of the ellipse is $\dfrac{x^2}{85} + \dfrac{y^2}{36} = 1$.

☑ **Quick Check** ❹ Write an equation of the ellipse with foci at $\left(0, \pm\sqrt{17}\right)$ and co-vertices at $(\pm 8, 0)$.

EXERCISES

For more exercises, see *Extra Skill and Word Problem Practice*.

Practice and Problem Solving

 Practice by Example

Example 1
(page 569)

 for Help

Write an equation of an ellipse in standard form with center at the origin and with the given vertex and co-vertex.

1. $(4, 0), (0, 3)$ **2.** $(0, 1), (2, 0)$ **3.** $(3, 0), (0, -1)$ **4.** $(0, 6), (1, 0)$

5. $(0, -7), (4, 0)$ **6.** $(-6, 0), (0, 5)$ **7.** $(-9, 0), (0, -2)$ **8.** $(0, 5), (-3, 0)$

Example 2
(page 569)

Find an equation of an ellipse for each given height and width. Assume that the center of the ellipse is $(0, 0)$.

9. $h = 1\,\text{m}, w = 3\,\text{m}$ **10.** $h = 32\,\text{ft}, w = 16\,\text{ft}$ **11.** $h = 20\,\text{ft}, w = 12\,\text{ft}$

12. $h = 10\,\text{cm}, w = 7\,\text{cm}$ **13.** $h = 14\,\text{yd}, w = 28\,\text{yd}$ **14.** $h = 8\,\text{ft}, w = 2\,\text{ft}$

15. $h = 15\,\text{ft}, w = 32\,\text{ft}$ **16.** $h = 40\,\text{mi}, w = 60\,\text{mi}$ **17.** $h = 5\,\text{m}, w = 2\,\text{m}$

Example 3
(page 570)

Find the foci for each equation of an ellipse. Then graph the ellipse.

18. $\dfrac{x^2}{4} + \dfrac{y^2}{9} = 1$ **19.** $\dfrac{x^2}{9} + \dfrac{y^2}{25} = 1$ **20.** $\dfrac{x^2}{81} + \dfrac{y^2}{49} = 1$

21. $\dfrac{x^2}{100} + \dfrac{y^2}{36} = 1$ **22.** $\dfrac{x^2}{64} + \dfrac{y^2}{100} = 1$ **23.** $3x^2 + y^2 = 9$

24. $x^2 + 4y^2 = 16$ **25.** $\dfrac{x^2}{225} + \dfrac{y^2}{144} = 1$ **26.** $\dfrac{x^2}{256} + \dfrac{y^2}{121} = 1$

Example 4
(page 570)

Write an equation of an ellipse for the given foci and co-vertices.

27. foci $(\pm 6, 0)$, co-vertices $(0, \pm 8)$ **28.** foci $(0, \pm 8)$, co-vertices $(\pm 8, 0)$

29. foci $(\pm 5, 0)$, co-vertices $(0, \pm 8)$ **30.** foci $(0, \pm 4)$, co-vertices $(\pm 2, 0)$

31. foci $(\pm 14, 0)$, co-vertices $(0, \pm 7)$ **32.** foci $(\pm 17, 0)$, co-vertices $(0, \pm 15)$

 Apply Your Skills

Find the foci for each equation of an ellipse.

33. $4x^2 + 9y^2 = 36$ **34.** $16x^2 + 4y^2 = 64$ **35.** $36x^2 + 4y^2 = 144$

36. $25x^2 + 4y^2 = 100$ **37.** $36x^2 + 8y^2 = 288$ **38.** $25x^2 + 24y^2 = 600$

39. $25x^2 + 16y^2 + 150x = 160y - 225$ **40.** $2x^2 + 8x + y^2 + 4 = 0$

> **Vocabulary Tip**
>
> Eccentric means "out of center."

41. The eccentricity of an ellipse is a measure of how nearly circular it is. Eccentricity is defined as $\frac{c}{a}$, where c is the distance from the center to a focus and a is the distance from the center to a vertex.
   a. Find the eccentricity of an ellipse with foci $(\pm 9, 0)$ and vertices $(\pm 10, 0)$. Sketch the graph.
   b. Find the eccentricity of an ellipse with foci $(\pm 1, 0)$ and vertices $(\pm 10, 0)$. Sketch the graph.
   c. Describe the shape of an ellipse that has an eccentricity close to 0.
   d. Describe the shape of an ellipse that has an eccentricity close to 1.

42. Multiple Choice Which equation represents the ellipse with foci on the x-axis, major axis 9 units long, minor axis 4 units long, and center at the origin?

   A $\dfrac{x^2}{4} + \dfrac{y^2}{9} = 1$ **B** $\dfrac{x^2}{20.25} + \dfrac{y^2}{4} = 1$ **C** $\dfrac{x^2}{9} + \dfrac{y^2}{4} = 1$ **D** $\dfrac{x^2}{4} + \dfrac{y^2}{20.25} = 1$

43. a. Critical Thinking An ellipse has foci very close to the center. Its minor axis has length 2. Explain why its shape is close to that of a circle.
   b. Is a circle also an ellipse? Explain.

Write an equation for each ellipse.

44.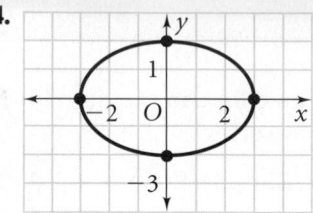

45.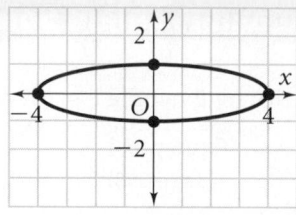

46.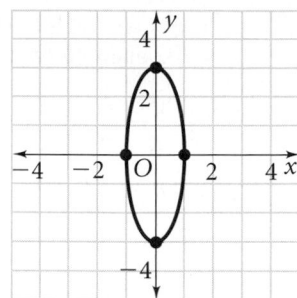

47.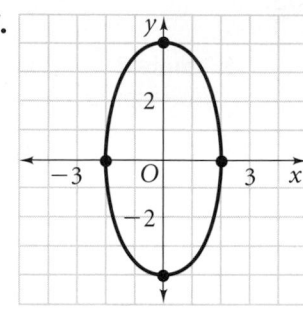

48. Error Analysis A student claims that an ellipse has vertices at $(\pm 3, 0)$ and co-vertices at $(0, \pm 7)$. What is the student's error?

49. Open-Ended Find a real-world design that uses ellipses. Place a coordinate grid over the design and write an equation of the ellipse.

Write an equation of an ellipse in standard form with center at the origin and with the given characteristics.

50. focus $(1, 0)$, width 4

51. $a = 5$, $b = 2$, width 10

52. vertex $(-11, 0)$, co-vertex $(0, 9)$

53. height 29, width 53

54. focus $(-5, 0)$, co-vertex $(0, -12)$

55. $c^2 = 68$, vertex $(0, -18)$

56. focus $(0, 3\sqrt{2})$, height 19

57. focus $(10\sqrt{3}, 0)$, width 40

58. focus $(2, 0)$, x-intercept 4

59. focus $(0, 3)$, y-intercept 5

60. focus $(0, -5)$, y-intercept 8

61. focus $(3, 0)$, x-intercept -6

62. $a = 3$, $b = 2$, width 4

63. $a = 2\sqrt{5}$, $b = 3\sqrt{2}$, width $6\sqrt{2}$

64. Draw an ellipse by placing two tacks in a piece of graph paper laid over a piece of cardboard. Place a loop of string around the tacks. With your pencil keeping the string taut, draw around the tacks. Mark the center of your ellipse $(0, 0)$ and draw the x- and y-axes.

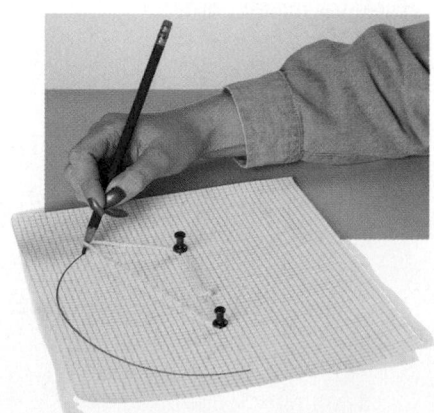

GO Online
Homework Video Tutor
Visit: PHSchool.com
Web Code: age-1004

  a. Where are the vertices and co-vertices of your ellipse?
  b. Where are the foci?
  c. Write the equation of your ellipse.

C Challenge  **65. Writing** The area of a circle is πr^2. The area of an ellipse is πab. Explain the connection.

66. Astronomy The sun is at a focus of Earth's elliptical orbit.
   a. Find the distance from the sun to the other focus.
   b. Refer to Exercise 41 for the definition of eccentricity. What is the eccentricity of the orbit?
   c. Write an equation of Earth's orbit. Assume that the major axis is horizontal.

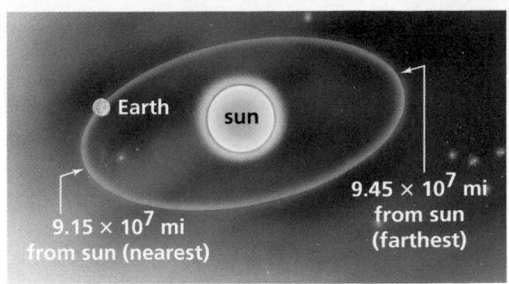

Earth sun

9.15×10^7 mi from sun (nearest)

9.45×10^7 mi from sun (farthest)

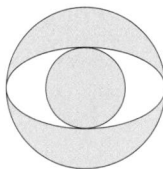 **67.** An ellipse and two circles share a center. The major axis of the ellipse is twice as long as its minor axis. The diameter of the larger circle is the same length as the major axis of the ellipse. The diameter of the smaller circle is the same length as the minor axis of the ellipse. The area of an ellipse is πab. Compare the areas of the blue and white regions at the left.

 68. Acoustics In "whispering galleries" a sound made at one focus can be clearly heard at the other focus, even though very little can be heard by someone in between. Suppose an elliptical room measures 320 ft long and 150 ft wide. How far would the listener have to be from the source of the sound in order to hear it?

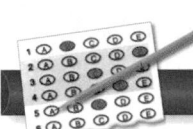

Test Prep

Multiple Choice

69. The point $A(-10, 0)$ is on the ellipse with equation $\frac{x^2}{100} + \frac{y^2}{64} = 1$. What is the sum of the distances $AF_1 + AF_2$, where F_1 and F_2 are the foci?
   A. 10   **B.** 12   **C.** 14   **D.** 20

70. What is the length of the major axis on the graph of $\frac{x^2}{100} + \frac{y^2}{64} = 1$?
   F. 12   **G.** $2\sqrt{41}$ **H.** 16   **J.** 20

71. What is the length of the minor axis of the graph of $\frac{x^2}{100} + \frac{y^2}{64} = 1$?
   A. 12   **B.** $2\sqrt{41}$ **C.** 16   **D.** 20

Short Response

72. Explain how to find an equation for the ellipse, centered at the origin, that is 50 units wide and 40 units high.

Mixed Review

Lesson 10-3

Write an equation of a circle with the given center and radius.

73. center $(2, -3)$, radius 6   **74.** center $(-4, 7)$, radius 11

Lesson 9-4

Simplify each expression. What are the restrictions on the variable?

75. $\dfrac{3x}{6x^2 - 9x^5}$ **76.** $\dfrac{x^2 - 36}{x^2 + 5x - 6}$ **77.** $\dfrac{x^2 - 3x - 10}{x^3 + 8}$

Lesson 8-4

Write each logarithmic expression as a single logarithm.

78. $\log 3 + \log 5$ **79.** $\log_3 12 - \log_3 2$ **80.** $3 \log 2 - \log 4$

81. $5 \log 2 + \log 10$ **82.** $\log x - \log y$ **83.** $k \log 5 - \log 4$

10-5

Hyperbolas

What You'll Learn

• To graph hyperbolas

• To find and use the foci of a hyperbola

. . . And Why

To write an equation that models the path of Voyager 2 around Saturn, as in Example 3

 **Check Skills You'll Need**  **for Help** Lesson 2-2 and Skills Handbook page 874

Write an equation of a line in slope-intercept form using the given information.

1. rise -5, run 2, through the origin   **2.** through $(3, 1)$ and $(9, 3)$

Solve each equation for y.

3. $\frac{x^2}{4} - \frac{y^2}{16} = 1$ **4.** $\frac{y^2}{9} - \frac{x^2}{25} = 1$ **5.** $\frac{x^2}{36} - \frac{y^2}{81} = 1$

New Vocabulary • hyperbola • transverse axis • focus of a hyperbola • vertices of a hyperbola

---

1 ▸ Graphing Hyperbolas Centered at the Origin

Vocabulary Tip

Hyperbola comes from a Greek word for "greater." The cutting plane of a hyperbola makes a greater angle with the base than does the side of the cone. See p. 547.

Activity: Analyzing Hyperbolas

1. The diagram below shows the shape of a hyperbola. Measure the distances to the nearest millimeter to complete the table.

2. **Make a Conjecture** What is the relationship between the distances from the points F_1 and F_2 to any point on the hyperbola?

Distance	P_1	P_2	P_3	...
Distance From F_1	■	■	■	■
Distance From F_2	■	■	■	■
$|PF_1 - PF_2|$	■	■	■	■

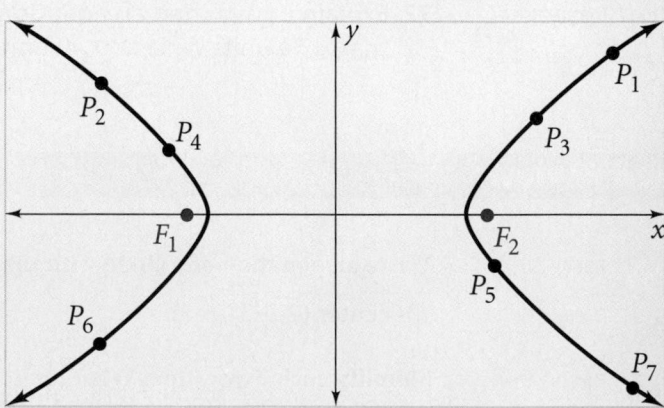

Hyperbolas play an important role in science and navigation. Some comets follow hyperbolic paths.

 **Key Concepts**

Definition	Hyperbola

A **hyperbola** is a set of points P in a plane such that the absolute value of the difference between the distances from P to two fixed points F_1 and F_2 is a constant k.

$$|PF_1 - PF_2| = k, \text{where } k < F_1F_2.$$

Each fixed point F is a **focus of a hyperbola.** The segment that lies on the line containing the foci and has endpoints on a hyperbola is the **transverse axis.** The endpoints are the **vertices of a hyperbola.** The midpoint of the segment is the center of a hyperbola.

Below are the standard forms of the equation of a hyperbola centered at $(0, 0)$.

$$\frac{x^2}{a^2} - \frac{y^2}{b^2} = 1$$

standard form of an equation of a hyperbola with a horizontal transverse axis

Vocabulary Tip

An <u>asymptote</u> is a line that a graph approaches.

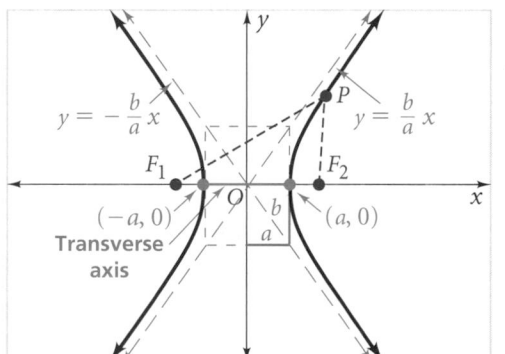

foci: F_1, F_2

vertices: $(\pm a, 0)$

asymptotes: $y = \pm \frac{b}{a} x$

x-intercepts: $\pm a$

y-intercepts: none

$$\frac{y^2}{a^2} - \frac{x^2}{b^2} = 1$$

standard form of an equation of a hyperbola with a vertical transverse axis

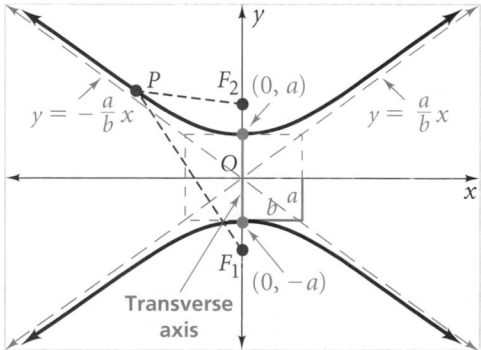

foci: F_1, F_2

vertices: $(0, \pm a)$

asymptotes: $y = \pm \frac{a}{b} x$

x-intercepts: none

y-intercepts: $\pm a$

To graph a hyperbola, use the standard form of the equation to find the values of a and b. You can use a and b to find and graph the vertices and to draw a central rectangle that is used to guide the graph.

Draw the asymptotes through the diagonals of the central rectangle. Then draw the branches of the hyperbola through the vertices so they approach the asymptotes.

1 **EXAMPLE** Graphing a Hyperbola

Graph $9x^2 - 25y^2 = 225$.

$$9x^2 - 25y^2 = 225$$

$$\frac{x^2}{25} - \frac{y^2}{9} = 1 \qquad \text{Rewrite the equation in standard form.}$$

The equation is of the form $\frac{x^2}{a^2} - \frac{y^2}{b^2} = 1$, so the transverse axis is horizontal. Since $a^2 = 25$ and $b^2 = 9, a = 5$ and $b = 3$.

Step 1 Graph the vertices. Since the transverse axis is horizontal, the vertices lie on the x-axis. The coordinates are $(\pm a, 0)$, or $(\pm 5, 0)$.

Step 2 Use the values of a and b to draw the central rectangle. The lengths of its sides are $2a$ and $2b$, or 10 and 6.

Step 3 Draw the asymptotes. The equations of the asymptotes are $y = \pm\frac{b}{a}x$ or $y = \pm\frac{3}{5}x$. The asymptotes contain the diagonals of the central rectangle.

Step 4 Sketch the branches of the hyperbola through the vertices so they approach the asymptotes.

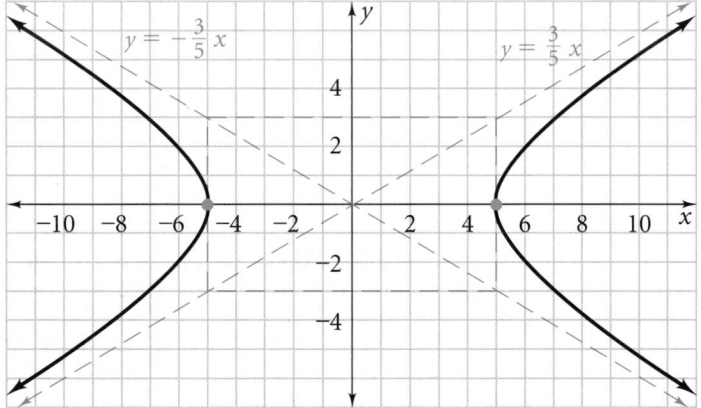

✓ **Quick Check** ❶ Graph the hyperbola with equation $\frac{y^2}{16} - \frac{x^2}{9} = 1$.

2 **Using the Foci of a Hyperbola**

Use $(\pm c, 0)$ for the coordinates of the foci if the transverse axis is horizontal or $(0, \pm c)$ if it is vertical.

The distance between the foci, $2c$, is also the length of the diagonal of the central rectangle.

You can find the value of c using the Pythagorean Theorem.

$$c^2 = a^2 + b^2$$

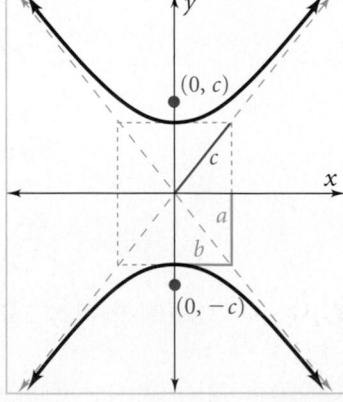

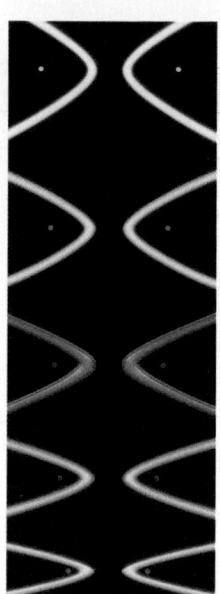

The figures above show how the shape of a hyperbola changes with decreased distances between the foci and the vertices.

Online active math

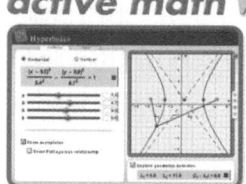

For: Hyperbola Activity
Use: Interactive Textbook, 10-5

2 EXAMPLE Finding the Foci of a Hyperbola

Find the foci of the graph $\frac{x^2}{36} - \frac{y^2}{4} = 1$. Draw the graph.

The equation is in the form $\frac{x^2}{a^2} - \frac{y^2}{b^2} = 1$, so the transverse axis is horizontal; $a^2 = 36$ and $b^2 = 4$.

$c^2 = a^2 + b^2$ **Use the Pythagorean Theorem.**

$ = 36 + 4$ **Substitute 36 for a^2 and 4 for b^2.**

$c = \sqrt{40} \approx 6.3$ **Find the square root of each side of the equation.**

The foci $(\pm c, 0)$ are approximately $(-6.3, 0)$ and $(6.3, 0)$. The vertices $(\pm a, 0)$ are $(6, 0)$ and $(-6, 0)$. The asymptotes are the lines $y = \pm\frac{b}{a}x$, or $y = \pm\frac{1}{3}x$.

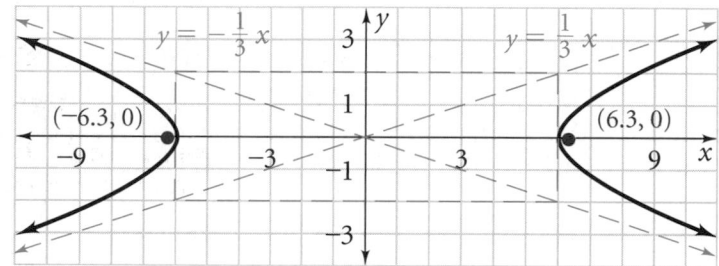

 **Quick Check** ② Find the foci of $\frac{x^2}{25} - \frac{y^2}{9} = 1$. Draw the graph.

You can use the value of c to write the equation of a hyperbola.

3 EXAMPLE Real-World Connection

Space As a spacecraft approaches a planet, the gravitational pull of the planet changes the spacecraft's path to a hyperbola that diverges from its asymptote. Find an equation that models the path of Voyager 2 around Saturn, given that $a = 332,965$ km and $c = 492,788.2$ km.

Assume that the center of the hyperbola is at the origin and that the transverse axis is horizontal. The equation will be in the form $\frac{x^2}{a^2} - \frac{y^2}{b^2} = 1$.

$c^2 = a^2 + b^2$ **Use the Pythagorean Theorem.**

$(492,788.2)^2 = (332,965)^2 + b^2$ **Substitute.**

$b^2 = (492,788.2)^2 - (332,965)^2$ **Solve for b^2.**

$ \approx 1.320 \times 10^{11}$ **Use a calculator.**

$\frac{x^2}{1.109 \times 10^{11}} - \frac{y^2}{1.320 \times 10^{11}} = 1$ **Substitute a^2 and b^2.**

The path of Voyager 2 around Saturn can be modeled by

$\frac{x^2}{1.109 \times 10^{11}} - \frac{y^2}{1.320 \times 10^{11}} = 1$.

Quick Check ③ Find an equation that models the path of Voyager 2 around Jupiter, given that $a = 2,184,140$ km and $c = 2,904,906.2$ km.

EXERCISES

For more exercises, see *Extra Skill and Word Problem Practice*.

Practice and Problem Solving

A Practice by Example

Example 1
(page 576)

Graph each equation.

1. $\frac{x^2}{16} - \frac{y^2}{4} = 1$

2. $\frac{y^2}{169} - \frac{x^2}{16} = 1$

3. $\frac{x^2}{25} - \frac{y^2}{36} = 1$

4. $x^2 - 4y^2 = 4$

5. $36y^2 - 9x^2 = 324$

6. $25x^2 - 16y^2 = 400$

7. $9x^2 - 49y^2 = 441$

8. $25x^2 - 35y^2 = 875$

9. $81y^2 - 9x^2 = 729$

Example 2
(page 577)

Find the foci of each hyperbola. Then draw the graph.

10. $\frac{y^2}{81} - \frac{x^2}{16} = 1$

11. $\frac{y^2}{49} - \frac{x^2}{64} = 1$

12. $\frac{x^2}{121} - \frac{y^2}{144} = 1$

13. $\frac{x^2}{64} - \frac{y^2}{36} = 1$

14. $\frac{y^2}{25} - \frac{x^2}{100} = 1$

15. $\frac{x^2}{36} - \frac{y^2}{169} = 1$

16. $4y^2 - 25x^2 = 100$

17. $36x^2 - 8y^2 = 288$

18. $14y^2 - 28x^2 = 448$

Example 3
(page 577)

For Exercises 19–21, find the equation of a hyperbola with the given values. Assume that the transverse axis is horizontal.

19. $a = 263, c = 407$

20. $b = 100, c = 500$

21. $a = 13{,}872, c = 19{,}043$

22. Find an equation that models the path of Voyager 2 around Jupiter, given that $a = 1{,}362{,}450$ km and $c = 1{,}543{,}781$ km.

B Apply Your Skills

Write the equation of a hyperbola with the given foci and vertices.

23. foci $(\pm 5, 0)$, vertices $(\pm 3, 0)$

24. foci $(0, \pm 13)$, vertices $(0, \pm 5)$

25. foci $(0, \pm 2)$, vertices $(0, \pm 1)$

26. foci $(\pm\sqrt{5}, 0)$, vertices $(\pm 2, 0)$

Graph each equation.

27. $5x^2 - 12y^2 = 120$

28. $16x^2 - 20y^2 = 560$

29. $\frac{y^2}{20} - \frac{x^2}{5} = 1$

Write the equation of a hyperbola from the given information. Graph the equation. Place the center of each hyperbola at the origin of the coordinate plane.

30. Transverse axis is vertical and is 9 units; central rectangle is 9 units by 4 units.

31. Perimeter of central rectangle is 16 units; vertices are at $(0, 3)$ and $(0, -3)$.

For a guide to solving Exercise 32, see p. 581.

32. (Distance from the center of a hyperbola to a focus)$^2 = 96$; endpoints of the transverse axis are at $\left(-\sqrt{32}, 0\right)$ and $\left(\sqrt{32}, 0\right)$.

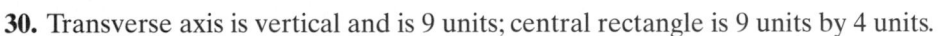 Solve each equation for *y*. Graph each relation on your graphing calculator.
 Use the TRACE feature to locate the vertices.

33. $x^2 - 2y^2 = 4$

34. $x^2 - y^2 = 1$

35. $3x^2 - y^2 = 2$

36. Rewrite the equation $4x^2 - 9y^2 = 36$ in standard form. Then write the equation for a translation right 3 units and down 5 units. Draw the graph of each.

37. **Open-Ended** Choose two points on an axis to be the vertices of a hyperbola. 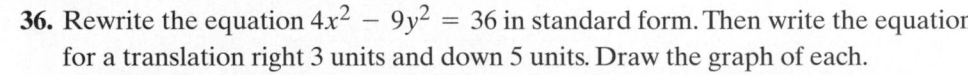 Choose two other points on the same axis to be the foci. Write the equation of your hyperbola and draw its graph.

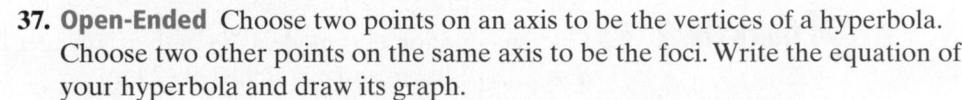

Online
Homework Video Tutor

Visit: PHSchool.com
Web Code: age-1005

38. List the properties of a hyperbola that allow you to sketch its graph.

39. Writing Describe the similarities and differences between hyperbolas and ellipses.

Find the vertices and the asymptotes of each hyperbola.

40. $y^2 - x^2 = 1$ **41.** $x^2 - 9y^2 = 1$ **42.** $y^2 - 4x^2 = 64$

43. $16x^2 - 25y^2 = 400$ **44.** $9y^2 - 36x^2 = 144$ **45.** $25x^2 - 49y^2 = 1225$

46. a. Prove that the hyperbola $\frac{y^2}{a^2} - \frac{x^2}{b^2} = 1$ never intersects its asymptotes.

     b. Is $\frac{y^2}{16} - \frac{x^2}{9} = 4$ a hyperbola? Is $\frac{y^2}{16} - \frac{x^2}{9} = -1$ a hyperbola? Explain.

 **Challenge** **47. Air Traffic Control** Suppose you are an air traffic controller directing the pilot of a plane on a hyperbolic flight path. You and another air traffic controller from a different airport send radio signals to the pilot simultaneously. The two airports are 48 km apart. The pilot's instrument panel tells him that the signal from your airport always arrives 100 μs (microseconds) before the signal from the other airport.

     a. To which airport is the plane closer?

     b. If the signals travel at a rate of 300 m/μs, what is the difference in distances from the plane to the two airports?

     c. Write the equation of the flight path. (*Hint: k = 2a*)

     d. Draw the hyperbola. Which branch represents the flight path?

Real-World Connection

Careers Air traffic controllers coordinate the flow of air traffic by the use of radar and visual observation.

48. The function $y = \sqrt{x^2 - 9}$ represents part of a hyperbola. The tables at the right show the coordinates of several points on the graph.

     a. Explain why ERROR appears for some entries.

     b. Describe the relationship between the x- and y-coordinates as x gets larger.

     c. Critical Thinking Do you think that the x- and y-coordinates will ever be equal? Explain.

     d. Make a Conjecture What are the equations of the asymptotes of this hyperbola? Verify your answer by drawing the complete graph.

X	Y1
0	ERROR
1	ERROR
2	ERROR
3	0
4	2.6458
5	4
6	5.1962
X=0	

X	Y1
10	9.5394
20	19.774
30	29.85
40	39.887
50	49.91
60	59.925
70	69.936
X=10	

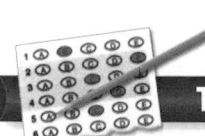

Test Prep

Multiple Choice **49.** Which hyperbola has (± 6, 0) as its x-intercepts?

     A. $y^2 - x^2 = 36$ **B.** $\frac{y^2}{36} - \frac{x^2}{49} = 1$ **C.** $\frac{x^2}{25} - \frac{y^2}{36} = 1$ **D.** $\frac{x^2}{36} - \frac{y^2}{4} = 1$

50. Which hyperbola does NOT have (0, ± 4) as its y-intercepts?

     F. $y^2 - x^2 = 16$ **G.** $4y^2 - 16x^2 = 64$

     H. $\frac{x^2}{25} - \frac{y^2}{16} = 1$ **J.** $\frac{y^2}{16} - \frac{x^2}{9} = 1$

51. What are the x-intercepts of $\frac{y^2}{25} - \frac{x^2}{49} = 1$?

     A. (± 7, 0)   **B.** (± 5, 0)   **C.** (0, ± 5)   **D.** none

Short Response **52.** What is the standard form of an equation of a hyperbola? Explain how to rewrite $25x^2 - 49y^2 = 1225$ in standard form.

Read the article below. Then complete Exercises 53 and 54.

Jupiter Bound: Voyager on its Way . . .

Voyager 1 explored the outer planets of our solar system. Its path was a hyperbola that depended on the planet that was closest.

The table below gives the distance c from each planet to the center of the hyperbola and the distance a from the vertex of the hyperbola to

the center of the hyperbola. At each vertex, Voyager 1's path was directly between a planet and the center of the hyperbola.

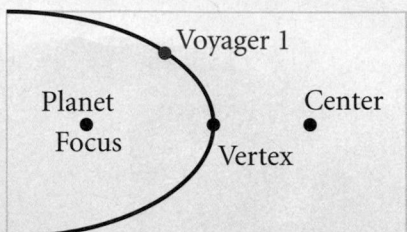

	Jupiter	Saturn
a	1,092,356 km	166,152 km
c	1,441,909.92 km	219,320.64 km

53. Write an equation of the path taken by Voyager 1 around Jupiter.

54. Write an equation of the path taken by Voyager 1 around Saturn.

Mixed Review

Lesson 10-4

Find the vertices and co-vertices of each ellipse.

55. $\frac{x^2}{34} + \frac{y^2}{25} = 1$

56. $3x^2 + 2y^2 = 6$

57. $25x^2 + 16y^2 = 1600$

Lesson 9-5

Simplify each expression.

58. $\frac{1}{5x} + \frac{1}{10x}$

59. $\frac{2x}{x^2 - 2x - 3} - \frac{7}{x^2 - 9}$

60. $\frac{4}{2x - 6} + \frac{x + 1}{x - 3}$

Lesson 8-5

Solve each equation.

61. $8^{2x} = 4$

62. $\log 8x = 3$

63. $2 \log_3 x - \log_3 4 = 2$

✓ Checkpoint Quiz 2   Lessons 10-4 through 10-5

Write an equation for each ellipse with the given foci and co-vertices.

1. foci $(\pm 3, 0)$
co-vertices $(0, \pm 4)$

2. foci $(0, \pm 2)$
co-vertices $(\pm 5, 0)$

3. foci $(0, \pm 7)$
co-vertices $(\pm 10, 0)$

Find the foci for each conic section. Then draw the graph.

4. $\frac{x^2}{16} - \frac{y^2}{49} = 1$

5. $\frac{y^2}{100} - \frac{x^2}{36} = 1$

6. $\frac{x^2}{4} - \frac{y^2}{81} = 1$

7. $\frac{y^2}{25} - \frac{x^2}{64} = 1$

Write an equation for a hyperbola centered at the origin with the given characteristics.

8. horizontal transverse axis, $a = 11, c = 15$

9. vertices $(\pm 4, 0)$, perimeter of central rectangle 28 units

10. Transverse axis is vertical, 16 units long; central rectangle is 16 units by 7 units.

Understanding Math Problems Read the problem below. Then let Michelle's thinking guide you through the solution. Check your understanding with the exercise at the bottom of the page.

Write the equation of a hyperbola from the given information. Graph the equation. Place the center of the hyperbola at the origin of the coordinate plane.

(Distance from the center of a hyperbola to a focus)^2 = 96; endpoints of the transverse axis are at $\left(-\sqrt{32}, 0\right)$ and $\left(\sqrt{32}, 0\right)$.

What Michelle Thinks

There is a lot of information here. I'll start with the second part. The endpoints of the transverse axis of a hyperbola are its vertices.

I know that the hyperbola opens horizontally, because the transverse axis lies on the x-axis. The vertices are at $(-a, 0)$ and $(a, 0)$, so I know the value of a^2.

Now I'll work on the first part of the given information. The distance from the center to the focus is c, which is also half the length of the diagonal of the central rectangle. I'll draw what I know so far.

Knowing c will help me find b! I can use the Pythagorean Theorem.

I'm ready to fill in the rest of the standard form of the equation for the hyperbola. Then I'll graph the hyperbola.

What Michelle Writes

Vertices: $\left(-\sqrt{32}, 0\right)$ and $\left(\sqrt{32}, 0\right)$

The transverse axis is horizontal, so the equation will look like $\dfrac{x^2}{a^2} - \dfrac{y^2}{b^2} = 1$.

$a = \sqrt{32}$, so $a^2 = 32$.

c = distance from center to focus
  = half length of diagonal

$c^2 = 96$, so $c = \sqrt{96}$

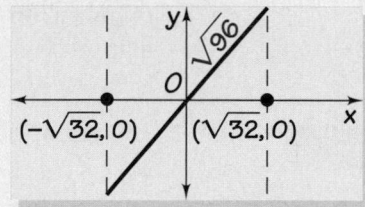

$b^2 = c^2 - a^2 = 96 - 32 = 64$

Equation:
$\dfrac{x^2}{32} - \dfrac{y^2}{64} = 1$

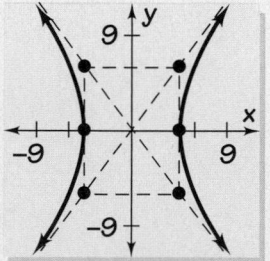

EXERCISE

Write the equation of a hyperbola from the given information. Graph the equation. Place the center of the hyperbola at the origin of the coordinate plane.

(Distance from the center of a hyperbola to a focus)^2 = 40; endpoints of the transverse axis are at $(-4, 0)$ and $(4, 0)$.

Translating Conic Sections

What You'll Learn

- To write the equation of a translated conic section
- To identify a translated conic section from an equation

. . . Any Why

To explore the LORAN navigation system, as in Example 3

✓ **Check Skills You'll Need**  **for Help** Lesson 5-3

Name the parent function for the equations in Exercises 1–4. Describe each equation as a translation of the parent function.

1. $y = x^2 + 4$

2. $y = (x - 3)^2 - 2$

3. $y - 1 = x^2$

4. $y = (x + 5)^2 + 6$

Rewrite each equation in vertex form.

5. $y = x^2 - 6x + 1$

6. $y = x^2 + 10x - 7$

7. $y = 2x^2 + 8x + 5$

8. $y = 4x^2 - 12x + 3$

---

1   Writing Equations of Translated Conic Sections

Vocabulary Tip

A <u>translation</u> shifts a graph horizontally, vertically, or both.

Technology Activity: Translating Conic Sections

1. Examine the calculator screen at the right. Describe the relationship between the two ellipses. How are they similar? How are they different?

2. The equation of ellipse ① is $\frac{x^2}{36} + \frac{y^2}{16} = 1$. Use what you know about translations to write the equation of ellipse ②.

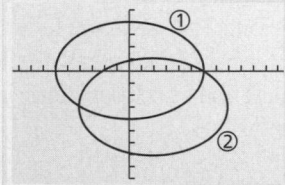

Xmin=−9   Ymin=−9
Xmax=12   Ymax=5
Xscl=1   Yscl=1

3. The graph at the right shows the hyperbola with equation $\frac{x^2}{9} - \frac{y^2}{4} = 1$. Write the equation of the hyperbola that has been shifted four units left and one unit up.

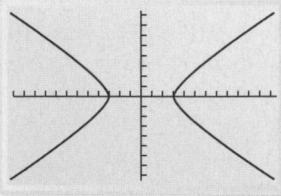

Xmin=−12   Ymin=−8
Xmax=12   Ymax=8
Xscl=1   Yscl=1

Just as you have translated parabolas in Chapter 5 and circles in Lesson 10-3, you can also use parameters h and k to translate ellipses and hyperbolas. A translated ellipse or hyperbola has center (h, k).

Summary	Families of Conic Sections

Conic Section	Standard Form of Equation	
Parabola	Vertex $(0,0)$ $y = ax^2$ $x = ay^2$	Vertex (h, k) $y - k = a(x - h)^2$ or $y = a(x - h)^2 + k$ $x - h = a(y - k)^2$ or $x = a(y - k)^2 + h$
Circle	Center $(0,0)$ $x^2 + y^2 = r^2$	Center (h, k) $(x - h)^2 + (y - k)^2 = r^2$
Ellipse	Center $(0,0)$ $\dfrac{x^2}{a^2} + \dfrac{y^2}{b^2} = 1$ $\dfrac{x^2}{b^2} + \dfrac{y^2}{a^2} = 1$	Center (h, k) $\dfrac{(x - h)^2}{a^2} + \dfrac{(y - k)^2}{b^2} = 1$ $\dfrac{(x - h)^2}{b^2} + \dfrac{(y - k)^2}{a^2} = 1$
Hyperbola	Center $(0,0)$ $\dfrac{x^2}{a^2} - \dfrac{y^2}{b^2} = 1$ $\dfrac{y^2}{a^2} - \dfrac{x^2}{b^2} = 1$	Center (h, k) $\dfrac{(x - h)^2}{a^2} - \dfrac{(y - k)^2}{b^2} = 1$ $\dfrac{(y - k)^2}{a^2} - \dfrac{(x - h)^2}{b^2} = 1$

1 EXAMPLE   Writing the Equation of a Translated Ellipse

Write an equation of an ellipse with center $(-3, -2)$, vertical major axis of length 8, and minor axis of length 6.

The length of the major axis is $2a$. So $2a = 8$ and $a = 4$. The length of the minor axis is $2b$. So $2b = 6$ and $b = 3$. Since the center is $(-3, -2)$, $h = -3$ and $k = -2$.

The major axis is vertical, so the equation has the form $\dfrac{(x - h)^2}{b^2} + \dfrac{(y - k)^2}{a^2} = 1$.

$\dfrac{(x - (-3))^2}{3^2} + \dfrac{(y - (-2))^2}{4^2} = 1$ **Substitute −3 for h and −2 for k.**

The equation of the ellipse is $\dfrac{(x + 3)^2}{9} + \dfrac{(y + 2)^2}{16} = 1$.

Check   Solve the equation for y and graph both equations.

$$\frac{(x + 3)^2}{9} + \frac{(y + 2)^2}{16} = 1$$
$$16(x + 3)^2 + 9(y + 2)^2 = 144$$
$$9(y + 2)^2 = 144 - 16(x + 3)^2$$
$$(y + 2)^2 = \tfrac{1}{9}(144 - 16(x + 3)^2)$$
$$y + 2 = \pm\sqrt{\tfrac{1}{9}(144 - 16(x + 3)^2)}$$
$$y = -2 \pm \tfrac{1}{3}\sqrt{144 - 16(x + 3)^2}$$

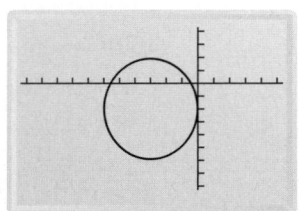

Quick Check **1** Write an equation of an ellipse with center $(1, -4)$, horizontal major axis of length 10, and minor axis of length 4. Check your answer.

2 EXAMPLE Writing the Equation of a Translated Hyperbola

Write an equation of a hyperbola with vertices $(0, 1)$ and $(6, 1)$, and foci $(-1, 1)$ and $(7, 1)$.

Draw a sketch. The center is the midpoint of the line joining the vertices. Its coordinates are $(3, 1)$.

Problem Solving Hint

The midpoint of the segment joining (x_1, y_1) and (x_2, y_2) is $\left(\dfrac{x_1 + x_2}{2}, \dfrac{y_1 + y_2}{2}\right)$.

The distance between the vertices is $2a$ and the distance between the foci is $2c$. $2a = 6$, so $a = 3$; $2c = 8$, so $c = 4$.

Find b^2 using the Pythagorean Theorem.

$c^2 = a^2 + b^2$

$16 = 9 + b^2$

$b^2 = 7$

The transverse axis is horizontal. The equation has form $\dfrac{(x - h)^2}{a^2} - \dfrac{(y - k)^2}{b^2} = 1$.

The equation of the hyperbola is $\dfrac{(x - 3)^2}{9} - \dfrac{(y - 1)^2}{7} = 1$.

✓ Quick Check **2** Write an equation of a hyperbola with vertices $(2, -1)$ and $(2, 7)$, and foci $(2, 10)$ and $(2, -4)$.

3 EXAMPLE Real-World 🌐 Connection

Navigation Some ships navigate using LORAN. The ship's equipment calculates the difference between the arrival times of simultaneously broadcast radio signals. The difference in arrival times indicates how much closer the ship is to one transmitter than to the other. The navigator then locates the ship on a hyperbola shown in red. The process is repeated using a second pair of transmitters to locate the ship on a hyperbola shown in blue.

All points on hyperbola #25800 as shown in the diagram are 48 mi closer to one transmitter than the other. The transmitters, at the foci, are 200 mi apart and are located at $(0, 0)$ and $(200, 0)$. Find the equation of hyperbola #25800.

Real-World 🌐 Connection

LORAN stands for *long range navigation*. It uses simultaneously broadcast radio signals from three transmitters to locate the ship's position at the intersection of the red and the blue hyperbolas.

Step 1 Find c. Since the foci are 200 mi apart, $2c = 200$, $c = 100$, and the center of the hyperbola is at $(100, 0)$.

Step 2 Find a by calculating the difference in the distances from the vertex at $(a + 100, 0)$ to the two foci.

$48 = (a + 100) - [200 - (a + 100)]$

$\quad = 2a$

$24 = a$

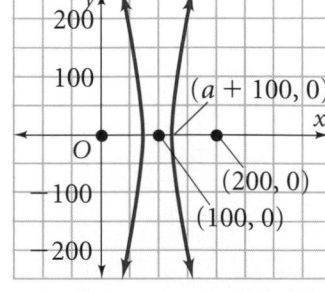

Step 3 Find b^2.

$c^2 = a^2 + b^2$

$(100)^2 = (24)^2 + b^2$

$10{,}000 = 576 + b^2$

$b^2 = 9424$

The equation of the hyperbola is $\dfrac{(x - 100)^2}{24^2} - \dfrac{y^2}{9424} = 1$ or $\dfrac{(x - 100)^2}{576} - \dfrac{y^2}{9424} = 1$.

✓ Quick Check **3** Use the information from Example 3. Find the equation of the hyperbola with all points 56 mi closer to one transmitter than the other.

To review completing the square, go to page 281 and Lesson 5-7.

The equation $Ax^2 + Bxy + Cy^2 + Dx + Ey + F = 0$ is the general equation for all conic sections, where A and C are not both equal to zero. To determine which conic section the equation represents, write the equation in standard form by completing the square for the x- and y-terms.

4 **EXAMPLE** **Identifying a Translated Conic Section**

Multiple Choice Identify the conic section with equation $4x^2 + y^2 - 24x + 6y + 9 = 0$.

Ⓐ circle; center $(3, -3)$ Ⓑ ellipse; foci $(3, -3 - 3\sqrt{3})$ and $(3, -3 + 3\sqrt{3})$
Ⓒ circle; center $(-3\sqrt{3}, 3\sqrt{3})$ Ⓓ ellipse; foci $(0, 3)$ and $(0, -3)$

Complete the square for the x- and y-terms to write the equation in standard form.

$$4x^2 + y^2 - 24x + 6y + 9 = 0$$

$$4x^2 - 24x + y^2 + 6y = -9 \qquad \text{Group the } x\text{- and } y\text{-terms.}$$

$$4(x^2 - 6x + \blacksquare) + (y^2 + 6y + \blacksquare) = -9 \qquad \text{Complete the square.}$$

$$4(x^2 - 6x + (-3)^2) + (y^2 + 6y + 3^2) = -9 + 4(-3)^2 + 3^2 \qquad \begin{array}{l}\text{Add } 4(-3)^2 \text{ and } 3^2 \\ \text{to each side.}\end{array}$$

$$4(x^2 - 6x + 9) + (y^2 + 6y + 9) = -9 + 36 + 9 \qquad \text{Simplify.}$$

$$4(x - 3)^2 + (y + 3)^2 = 36 \qquad \begin{array}{l}\text{Write the trinomials} \\ \text{as binomials squared.}\end{array}$$

$$\frac{4(x - 3)^2}{36} + \frac{(y + 3)^2}{36} = 1 \qquad \text{Divide each side by 36.}$$

$$\frac{(x - 3)^2}{9} + \frac{(y + 3)^2}{36} = 1 \qquad \text{Simplify.}$$

The equation represents an ellipse. The center is $(3, -3)$. The major axis is vertical. Since $b^2 = 9, b = 3$. Since $a^2 = 36, a = 6$.

$$c^2 = a^2 - b^2 = 36 - 9$$
$$= 27$$
$$c = 3\sqrt{3}$$

The distance from the center of the ellipse to the foci is $3\sqrt{3}$. Since the ellipse is centered at $(3, -3)$ and the major axis is vertical, the foci are located $3\sqrt{3}$ above and below this center. The foci are at $(3, -3 + 3\sqrt{3})$ and $(3, -3 - 3\sqrt{3})$. The correct choice is B.

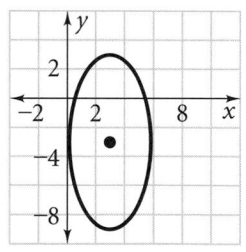

Test-Taking Tip

For equivalent equations, remember to add the same quantity to both sides.

✓ Quick Check ❹ Identify the conic section represented by $x^2 + y^2 - 12x + 4y = 8$. Sketch the graph.

EXERCISES

For more exercises, see *Extra Skill and Word Problem Practice.*

Practice and Problem Solving

Ⓐ **Practice by Example**

 for Help

Example 1
(page 583)

Write an equation of an ellipse with the given characteristics. Check your answers.

1. center $(-2, 1)$, horizontal major axis of length 6, minor axis of length 4

2. center $(5, 3)$, vertical major axis of length 12, minor axis of length 8

3. center $(0, -4)$, horizontal major axis of length 12, minor axis of length 10

4. center $(3, -6)$, vertical major axis of length 14, minor axis of length 6

Example 2
(page 584)

Write an equation of a hyperbola with the given characteristics.

5. vertices $(1, -3)$ and $(-7, -3)$, foci $(2, -3)$ and $(-8, -3)$

6. vertices $(4, -1)$ and $(4, -5)$, foci $(4, 3)$ and $(4, -9)$

7. vertices $(2, 2)$ and $(-4, 2)$, foci $(6, 2)$ and $(-8, 2)$

8. vertices $(-1, 4)$ and $(-1, -6)$, foci $(-1, 8)$ and $(-1, -10)$

9. vertices $(0, -2)$ and $(0, 4)$, foci $(0, 6)$ and $(0, -4)$

Example 3
(page 584)

For Exercises 10–11, find the equation of each hyperbola described.

10. All points on the hyperbola are 72 units closer to one focus than the other. The foci are located at $(0, 0)$ and $(300, 0)$.

11. All points on the hyperbola are 88 units closer to one focus than the other. The foci are located at $(0, 0)$ and $(350, 0)$.

Example 4
(page 585)

Identify the conic section represented by each equation by writing the equation in standard form. For a parabola, give the vertex. For a circle, give the center and the radius. For an ellipse or a hyperbola, give the center and the foci. Sketch the graph.

12. $x^2 - 8x - y + 19 = 0$ **13.** $x^2 + y^2 + 12x = 45$

14. $3x^2 + 6x + y^2 - 6y = -3$ **15.** $x^2 + y^2 - 2x + 6y = 3$

16. $y^2 - x^2 + 6x - 4y = 6$ **17.** $x^2 - 4y^2 - 2x - 8y = 7$

18. $x^2 + y^2 + 14y = -13$ **19.** $y^2 - 2x - 4y = -10$

20. $4x^2 + 9y^2 + 16x - 54y = -61$ **21.** $x^2 - y^2 + 6x + 10y = 17$

22. $x^2 + 4y^2 - 2x - 15 = 0$ **23.** $9x^2 - 4y^2 - 24y = 72$

 **Apply Your Skills**

24. A conic section centered at the origin is translated. Describe the translation that would produce the equation $x^2 - 2y^2 + 6x - 7 = 0$.

25. Critical Thinking Use the equation $Ax^2 + Bxy + Cy^2 + Dx + Ey + F = 0$ to identify the shape of the graph that results in each case.
a. $A = C = D = E = 0, B \neq 0, F \neq 0$
b. $A = B = C = 0, D \neq 0, E \neq 0, F \neq 0$

26. Multiple Choice How does the translation of an ellipse affect the lengths of its axes?
Ⓐ Both increase in length. Ⓑ Both decrease in length.
Ⓒ Both stay the same length. Ⓓ One increases; the other decreases.

 27. Writing Describe how the translation of a hyperbola affects the equations of its asymptotes.

28. Critical Thinking Campbell claims that $\frac{x^2}{10} + \frac{y^2}{10} = 1$ represents an ellipse. Monique disagrees. Whom do you support? Give a reasoned argument.

Write an equation for each conic section. Then sketch the graph.

29. circle with center $(-6, 9)$ and radius 9

30. ellipse with center $(3, 2)$, vertices $(9, 2)$ and $(-3, 2)$, and co-vertices $(3, 5)$ and $(3, -1)$

31. parabola with vertex $(2, -3)$ and focus $(2, 5)$

32. hyperbola with center $(6, -3)$, one focus $(6, 0)$, and one vertex $(6, -1)$

Homework Video Tutor
Visit: PHSchool.com
Web Code: age-1006

Write the equation of each graph. In Exercise 35, each interval represents one unit.

33.
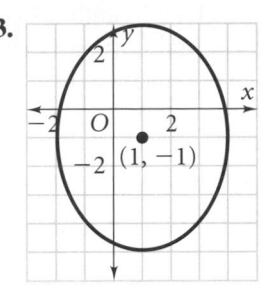

34.
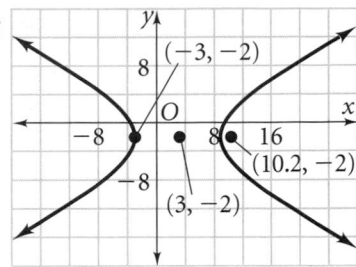

35.
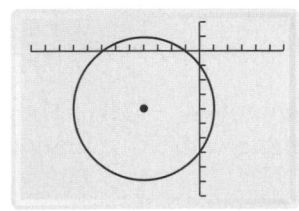

36.
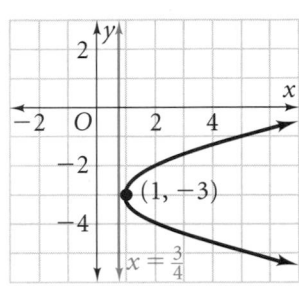

The graph of each equation is to be translated 3 units right and 5 units up. Write each new equation.

37. $(x - 5)^2 + (y + 3)^2 = 4$

38. $\dfrac{(x - 3)^2}{64} + \dfrac{(y + 3)^2}{36} = 1$

39. $y = 4x^2$

40. $9x^2 + 3x + 10 = 16y^2 + 154 + 3x$

41. $\dfrac{(x - 2)^2}{36} - \dfrac{(y - 3)^2}{25} = 1$

42. $\dfrac{(x - 3)^2}{4} + \dfrac{(y - 4)^2}{9} = 1$

43. $9x^2 + 16y^2 + 18x = 64y + 71$

44. $x^2 + 4y^2 + 6x - 7 = 0$

45. $x^2 - 16y^2 - 2x + 128y = 271$

46. $(x - 5)^2 = 12(y - 6)$

47. $25x^2 + 16y^2 + 150x = 160y - 225$

48. $x^2 - y^2 + 6x + 10y = 17$

 **Graph each pair of functions. Identify the conic section represented by the graph and write each equation in standard form.**

49. $y = \sqrt{36 - 4x^2}$
$y = -\sqrt{36 - 4x^2}$

50. $y = \sqrt{4x^2 - 36}$
$y = -\sqrt{4x^2 - 36}$

51. $y = \sqrt{4x^2 + 36}$
$y = -\sqrt{4x^2 + 36}$

52. $y = \sqrt{36 - x^2}$
$y = -\sqrt{36 - x^2}$

53. $y = 0.5\sqrt{36 - x^2}$
$y = -0.5\sqrt{36 - x^2}$

54. $y = \sqrt{x - 4}$
$y = -\sqrt{x - 4}$

Ⓒ Challenge

55. **Open-Ended** On a graphing calculator, create a design using three translated quadratic relations.

56. **History** Some symbols of the writing system of the Ejagham, people who lived in Nigeria and Cameroon, are shown. The symbol for marriage consists of two parabolic shapes. Reproduce this symbol on a graphing calculator. What equations did you use?

57. Consider equations of the form $Ax^2 + By^2 + Cx + Dy + E = 0$.
   a. What must be true about A and B for the graph of the equation to be a circle? To be an ellipse? To be a hyperbola? To be a parabola?
   b. Suppose $A = 1$ and $B = 1$. Must the graph be a circle? Explain.
   c. Suppose $A = 1$, $B = -1$, and $C = D = E = 0$. Describe the graph.

Real-World Ⓒ Connection

This Nigerian cloth combines writing symbols and patterns.

58. Astronomy The dimensions of the elliptical orbits of three planets are given in millions of kilometers in the table. The sun is at one focus. The other focus is on the positive x-axis.

a. Write an equation for each orbit and draw the curves on your graphing calculator. (Remember to adjust the viewing window.)

b. Reasoning Which orbit is most circular? Justify your reasoning.

Planet	a	b
Earth	149.60	149.58
Mars	227.9	226.9
Mercury	57.9	56.6

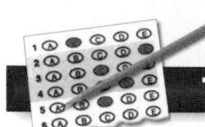

Test Prep

Multiple Choice

59. An ellipse with center $(-4, -2)$ has a horizontal major axis of length 6 and a minor axis of length 4. Which equation represents the ellipse?

A. $\dfrac{(x-4)^2}{4} - \dfrac{(y-2)^2}{9} = 1$

B. $\dfrac{(x+2)^2}{9} - \dfrac{(y+4)^2}{4} = 1$

C. $\dfrac{(x+4)^2}{9} + \dfrac{(y+2)^2}{4} = 1$

D. $\dfrac{(x+4)^2}{4} + \dfrac{(y+2)^2}{9} = 1$

60. The foci of a hyperbola are $(0, -4)$ and $(0, 8)$. Which additional information would allow you to write an equation for the hyperbola?

F. location of the center

G. location of one vertex

H. midpoint of transverse axis

J. distance from the center to a focus

61. Which of the following is an equation of a parabola?

A. $2x^2 - 5y^2 + 4x - 36 = 0$

B. $2x^2 - 5y + 4x - 36 = 0$

C. $2x^2 + 2y^2 + 4x - 12y - 36 = 0$

D. $2x^2 + 5y^2 - 36 = 0$

62. Which conic section is represented by the equation $x^2 + y^2 = 6x - 14y - 9$?

F. circle **G.** ellipse **H.** parabola **J.** hyperbola

63. Which of the conic sections have more than one focus?

I. circle II. parabola III. ellipse IV. hyperbola

A. I and III **B.** II and III **C.** I and II **D.** III and IV

Short Response

64. What are the coordinates of the foci of $4x^2 - 24x = 64 - 25y^2$?

65. A parabola with vertex at the origin and focus at $(-1, 0)$ is translated 3 units to the right and 4 units up. What is the equation of the translated parabola? Show your work.

Mixed Review

GO for Help

Lesson 10-5

Find the foci of each hyperbola. Draw the graph.

66. $\dfrac{x^2}{49} - \dfrac{y^2}{36} = 1$

67. $8y^2 - 6x^2 = 72$

68. $4y^2 - 100x^2 = 400$

Lesson 9-6

Solve each equation. Check your answers.

69. $\dfrac{1}{3x+1} = \dfrac{1}{x^2-3}$

70. $\dfrac{2}{x+2} = \dfrac{6}{x^2-4}$

71. $\dfrac{5}{x^2-x} + \dfrac{3}{x-1} = 6$

Lesson 8-6

Simplify each expression.

72. $\ln e$

73. $2 \ln e$

74. $\ln e^3$

75. $4 \ln e^2$

Activity Lab

Solving Quadratic Systems

In Chapter 3 you solved systems of linear equations algebraically and graphically. You can use the same methods to solve systems that include quadratic equations.

1 ACTIVITY — Solving Algebraically

Solve the system algebraically. $\begin{cases} x^2 - y^2 = 9 \\ x^2 + 9y^2 = 169 \end{cases}$

$$x^2 - y^2 = 9$$
$$\underline{x^2 + 9y^2 = 169}$$
$$-10y^2 = -160 \quad \text{Subtract like terms to eliminate the } x^2 \text{ terms.}$$
$$y = 4 \text{ or } y = -4 \quad \text{Solve for } y.$$

$$x^2 - (4)^2 = 9 \qquad \text{Substitute the values of } y \text{ into} \qquad x^2 - (-4)^2 = 9$$
$$x^2 = 25 \qquad \text{one of the original equations.} \qquad x^2 = 25$$

$$x = 5 \text{ or } x = -5 \quad \text{Solve for } x. \qquad\qquad x = 5 \text{ or } x = -5$$

● The ordered pairs $(5, 4), (-5, 4), (5, -4)$, and $(-5, -4)$ are solutions to the system.

2 ACTIVITY — Solving Graphically

Solve the system by graphing. $\begin{cases} x^2 + y^2 = 36 \\ y = (x - 2)^2 - 3 \end{cases}$

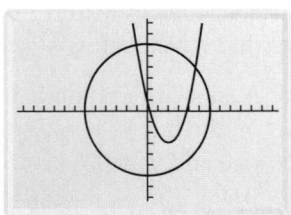

$$x^2 + y^2 = 36$$
$$y = \pm\sqrt{36 - x^2} \quad \text{Solve the first equation for } y.$$

Graph the equations and find the point(s) of intersection.
● The solutions are approximately $(-1.0, 5.9)$ and $(4.6, 3.8)$.

EXERCISES

Solve each quadratic system.

1. $\begin{cases} x^2 + 64y^2 = 64 \\ x^2 + y^2 = 64 \end{cases}$
2. $\begin{cases} 2x^2 - y^2 = 2 \\ x^2 + y^2 = 25 \end{cases}$
3. $\begin{cases} 9x^2 + 25y^2 = 225 \\ y = -x^2 + 5 \end{cases}$
4. $\begin{cases} 4x^2 + 4y^2 = 100 \\ 3x^2 + 3y^2 = 27 \end{cases}$

5. a. Writing The system that consists of $y = -3x + 6$ and $y = x^2 - 4x$ is a linear-quadratic system. How would you solve the system algebraically? Graphically?
   b. Solve the system in part (a).

Identify each system as linear-quadratic or quadratic-quadratic. Then solve.

6. $\begin{cases} y = x - 1 \\ x^2 + y^2 = 25 \end{cases}$
7. $\begin{cases} 9x^2 + 4y^2 = 36 \\ x^2 - y^2 = 4 \end{cases}$
8. $\begin{cases} -x + y = 4 \\ y = x^2 - 4x + 2 \end{cases}$
9. $\begin{cases} 4x^2 + 25y^2 = 100 \\ y = x + 2 \end{cases}$

10. $\begin{cases} y^2 = 5x - 3 \\ 3x^2 - 3y^2 = 1 \end{cases}$
11. $\begin{cases} y = 3x + 1 \\ x^2 + y^2 = 3 \end{cases}$
12. $\begin{cases} (x - 1)^2 = (y + 2)^2 \\ y = 2x^2 - 4 \end{cases}$
13. $\begin{cases} x^2 + y^2 = 25 \\ (x - 3)^2 + (y - 3)^2 = 100 \end{cases}$

Some multiple-choice questions cannot be solved. If so, then one of the answer choices will be *cannot be determined*. Be careful, however. Sometimes the answer choice *cannot be determined* is included as a distractor.

1 EXAMPLE

Find an equation of a circle that passes through the points $(0,0)$, $(1,0)$ and $(2,0)$.

A. $(x-1)^2 + y^2 = 1$
B. $\left(x - \frac{1}{2}\right)^2 + y^2 = \frac{1}{4}$
C. $\left(x - \frac{3}{2}\right)^2 + y^2 = \frac{1}{4}$
D. cannot be determined

Since the y-coordinates of all three points are zero, the points are collinear. A circle cannot pass through three collinear points. The correct answer is D.

2 EXAMPLE

Which of the following completely describes the graphs of $(x-d)^2 + (y-d)^2 = 2d^2$?

A. circles of radius d with centers on the line $y = x$
B. circles with centers (d, d)
C. circles with centers on the line $y = x$ and passing through $(0,0)$
D. cannot be determined

The standard form of an equation of a circle is $(x - h)^2 + (y - k)^2 = r^2$, where (h, k) is the center of the circle and r is the radius. So the equation in Example 2 describes circles that have centers at (d, d) and have radius $\sqrt{2d^2}$, or $|d|\sqrt{2}$.

Eliminate choice A, since the radius is incorrect. Since the centers of the circles are (d, d), they all lie on the line $y = x$. Choices B and C could be correct. Test choice C by substituting $x = 0$ and $y = 0$.

$(0 - d)^2 + (0 - d)^2 \stackrel{?}{=} 2d^2$ **Substitute (0, 0) for x and y.**
$(-d)^2 + (-d)^2 \stackrel{?}{=} 2d^2$ **Simplify.**
$2d^2 = 2d^2$

The circles pass through the point $(0, 0)$. The correct answer is C. Choice D is a distractor.

EXERCISES

If the answer to an exercise can be determined, write the answer. If not, write *cannot be determined* **and explain your reasoning.**

1. Find the radius of the circle defined by $x^2 + y^2 - 4x - 2y + 14 = 0$.

2. Find the number of points of intersection of the graphs of $y = x^2$ and $y = 2ax - a^2$.

3. Given that $x^2 - y^2 = 12$, find y when $x = 3$.

4. The focus of a parabola is $(0, 3)$. Find the equation of the directrix.

Chapter Review

Vocabulary Review

🔊 center (p. 561)
circle (p. 561)
conic section (p. 547)
co-vertices (p. 568)
directrix (p. 555)
ellipse (p. 568)

focus of a parabola (p. 555)
focus of an ellipse (p. 568)
focus of a hyperbola (p. 575)
hyperbola (p. 575)
major axis (p. 568)
minor axis (p. 568)

radius (p. 561)
standard form of an equation of a
  circle (p. 561)
transverse axis (p. 575)
vertices of an ellipse (p. 568)
vertices of a hyperbola (p. 575)

Go Online
PHSchool.com
For: Vocabulary quiz
Web Code: agj-1051

Choose the correct vocabulary term to complete each sentence.

1. In the definition of a parabola, the fixed line is the __?__ .

2. The vertices of an ellipse are on its __?__ .

3. $(x - h)^2 + (y - k)^2 = r^2$ is the __?__ .

4. The distance from a point on a circle to its center is the __?__ of the circle.

5. The vertices of a hyperbola are on its __?__ .

Skills and Concepts

10-1 Objectives

▼ To graph conic sections (p. 547)

▼ To identify conic sections (p. 549)

A **conic section** is a curve formed by the intersection of a plane and a double cone. Circles, ellipses, parabolas, and hyperbolas are all conic sections.

Graph each equation. Identify the conic section and describe the graph and its lines of symmetry. Then find the domain and range.

6. $\frac{x^2}{49} + \frac{y^2}{121} = 1$ **7.** $x^2 + y^2 = 4$ **8.** $\frac{x^2}{25} - \frac{y^2}{4} = 1$ **9.** $x = 2y^2 + 5$

Identify the center, the intercepts, and the domain and range of each graph.

10. 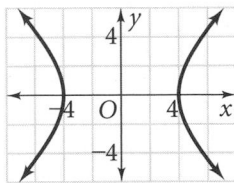   **11.**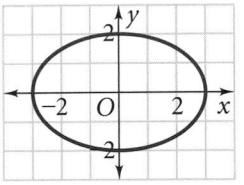

10-2 Objectives

▼ To write the equation of a parabola (p. 555)

▼ To graph parabolas (p. 557)

In a plane, a parabola is the set of all points that are the same distance c from a fixed line, the **directrix,** and a fixed point not on the line, the **focus.**

For $y = ax^2$ when $a > 0$, the parabola opens upward. The focus is $(0, c)$ and the directrix is $y = -c$. When $a < 0$, the parabola opens downward. The focus is $(0, -c)$ and the directrix is $y = c$. For $x = ay^2$, when $a > 0$, the parabola opens to the right. The focus is $(c, 0)$ and directrix is $x = -c$. When $a < 0$, the parabola opens to the left. The focus is $(-c, 0)$ and the directrix is $x = c$. Always, $|a| = \frac{1}{4c}$.

Write an equation for a graph that is the set of all points in the plane that are equidistant from the given point and the given line.

12. $F(0, 3), y = -1$ **13.** $F(-2, 0), x = 4$

Write an equation of a parabola with a vertex at the origin and the given focus.

14. focus at $(5, 0)$ **15.** focus at $(0, -5)$ **16.** focus at $(0, 6)$

Write an equation of a parabola opening upward with a vertex at the origin.

17. focus is 2.5 units from the vertex   **18.** focus is $\frac{1}{12}$ of a unit from the vertex

Find the focus and the directrix of the graph of each equation. Sketch the graph.

19. $y = 5x^2$ **20.** $x = 2y^2$ **21.** $x = -\frac{1}{8}y^2$

▼ To write and graph the equation of a circle (p. 561)

▼ To find the center and radius of a circle and use it to graph the circle (p. 563)

In a plane, a **circle** is the set of all points at a given distance, the **radius** r, from a given point, the **center** (h, k). The **standard form of an equation of a circle** is $(x - h)^2 + (y - k)^2 = r^2$.

Write an equation in standard form of the circle with the given center and radius.

22. center $(0, 0)$, radius 4   **23.** center $(8, 1)$, radius 5

Write an equation for each translation of $x^2 + y^2 = r^2$ with the given radius.

24. left 3 units, up 2 units; radius 10   **25.** right 5 units, down 3 units; radius 8

Write an equation for each circle. Each interval represents one unit.

26.
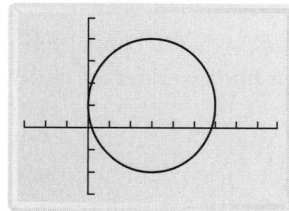

27.
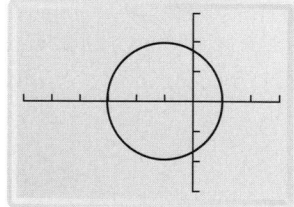

Find the center and the radius of each circle. Sketch the graph.

28. $(x - 1)^2 + y^2 = 64$ **29.** $(x + 7)^2 + (y + 3)^2 = 49$

▼ To write the equation of an ellipse (p. 568)

▼ To find the foci of an ellipse, and to graph an ellipse (p. 570)

In a plane, an **ellipse** is the set of all points P, the sum of whose distances to two fixed points, the **foci**, is constant. The **major axis** is the segment that contains the foci and has endpoints called the **vertices of an ellipse**. The **minor axis** is perpendicular to the major axis and has endpoints called the **co-vertices**.

There are two standard forms of an ellipse centered at the origin. If $\frac{x^2}{a^2} + \frac{y^2}{b^2} = 1$, the major axis is horizontal with vertices $(\pm a, 0)$ and co-vertices $(0, \pm b)$, where $a > b > 0$.

If $\frac{x^2}{b^2} + \frac{y^2}{a^2} = 1$, the major axis is vertical with vertices $(0, \pm a)$ and co-vertices $(\pm b, 0)$. In either case, you can find the foci c using the relationship $c^2 = a^2 - b^2$.

Write an equation of an ellipse in standard form with a center at the origin and with the given characteristics.

30. foci $(\pm 1, 0)$, co-vertices $(0, \pm 4)$

31. vertex $(0, \sqrt{29})$, co-vertex $(-5, 0)$

32. focus $(0, 1)$, vertex $(0, \sqrt{10})$

33. foci $(\pm 2, 0)$, co-vertices $(0, \pm 6)$

34. Write the equation of an ellipse centered at the origin with height 8 units and width 16 units.

35. Graph $\frac{x^2}{4} + \frac{y^2}{9} = 1$. Identify the foci.

10-5 Objectives

▼ To graph hyperbolas (p. 574)

▼ To find and use the foci of a hyperbola (p. 576)

In a plane, a **hyperbola** is the set of all points P such that difference between the distances from P to two fixed points, the **foci**, is constant. The foci lie on the line containing the **transverse axis**. Each branch of a hyperbola intersects the transverse axis at a **vertex of the hyperbola**. Each branch approaches the two asymptotes, which contain the diagonals of the central rectangle.

There are two standard forms of hyperbolas centered at the origin. If $\frac{x^2}{a^2} - \frac{y^2}{b^2} = 1$, the asymptotes are $y = \pm \frac{b}{a}x$, the transverse axis is horizontal with vertices $(\pm a, 0)$, and the foci are $(\pm c, 0)$. If $\frac{y^2}{a^2} - \frac{x^2}{b^2} = 1$, the asymptotes are $y = \pm \frac{a}{b}x$, the transverse axis is vertical with vertices $(0, \pm a)$, and the foci are $(0, \pm c)$. In either case, you can find the value of b using the relationship $c^2 = a^2 + b^2$.

Find the foci of each hyperbola. Draw the graph.

36. $\frac{x^2}{36} - \frac{y^2}{225} = 1$

37. $\frac{y^2}{400} - \frac{x^2}{169} = 1$

38. $\frac{x^2}{121} - \frac{y^2}{81} = 1$

39. Find an equation that models the path of a spacecraft around a planet if $a = 107{,}124$ and $c = 213{,}125.9$.

10-6 Objectives

▼ To write the equation of a translated conic section (p. 582)

▼ To identify the equation of a translated conic section (p. 585)

You can substitute $(x - h)$ for x and $(y - k)$ for y to translate graphs of an ellipse or a hyperbola. A translated ellipse or hyperbola has center (h, k).

Write an equation of a conic section with the given characteristics.

40. an ellipse with center $(3, -2)$, vertical major axis of length 6; minor axis of length 4

41. a hyperbola with vertices $(3, 3)$ and $(9, 3)$, foci $(1, 3)$ and $(11, 3)$

42. All points on the hyperbola are 81 units closer to one focus than the other. The foci are at $(0, 0)$ and $(155, 0)$.

Identify the conic section represented by each equation by writing the equation in standard form. For a parabola, give the vertex. For a circle, give the center and the radius. For an ellipse or a hyperbola, give the center and the foci. Sketch the graph.

43. $-x^2 + y^2 + 4y - 16 = 0$

44. $x^2 + y^2 + 3x - 4y - 9 = 0$

45. $x^2 + x - y - 42 = 0$

46. $2x^2 + 3y^2 - 4x + 12y - 20 = 0$

Chapter Test

Go Online
PHSchool.com
For: Chapter Test
Web Code: aga-1052

Identify the center and intercepts of each conic section. Give the domain and range of each graph.

1.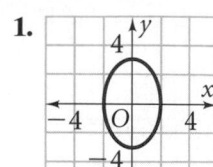

2.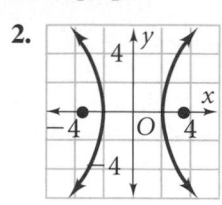

3.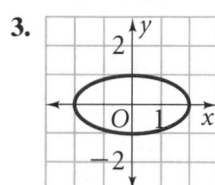

4.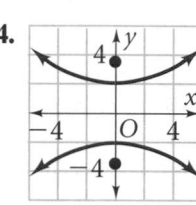

5. **Writing** Explain how you can tell what kind of conic section a quadratic equation describes without graphing the equation.

Identify the focus and the directrix of the graph of each equation.

6. $y = 3x^2$

7. $x = -2y^2$

8. $x + 5y^2 = 0$

9. $9x^2 - 2y = 0$

Write an equation of a parabola with a vertex at the origin and the given characteristic.

10. focus at $(0, -2)$

11. focus at $(3, 0)$

12. directrix $x = 7$

13. directrix $y = -1$

Find the center and radius of the circle. Sketch the circle.

14. $(x - 2)^2 + (y - 3)^2 = 36$

15. $(x + 5)^2 + (y + 8)^2 = 100$

16. $(x - 1)^2 + (y + 7)^2 = 81$

17. $(x + 4)^2 + (y - 10)^2 = 121$

Find an equation of an ellipse for each given height and width. Assume that the center of the ellipse is $(0, 0)$.

18. height 10 units, width 16 units

19. height 2 units, width 12 units

20. height 9 units, width 5 units

Find the foci for each ellipse. Sketch the ellipse.

21. $\frac{x^2}{81} + \frac{y^2}{36} = 1$

22. $\frac{x^2}{25} + \frac{y^2}{121} = 1$

23. $x^2 + \frac{y^2}{49} = 1$

24. $4x^2 + y^2 = 4$

25. **Critical Thinking** What is the shape of an ellipse whose height and width are equal?

Find the foci for each hyperbola. Sketch the hyperbola.

26. $\frac{x^2}{144} - \frac{y^2}{100} = 1$

27. $\frac{y^2}{169} - \frac{x^2}{400} = 1$

28. $\frac{x^2}{64} - \frac{y^2}{4} = 1$

29. $y^2 - \frac{x^2}{225} = 1$

30. **Open-Ended** Write the equation of a hyperbola with a transverse axis on the x-axis.

Write an equation of an ellipse with the given characteristics.

31. center $(0, 0)$, vertex $(4, 0)$, co-vertex $(0, -3)$

32. center $(-2, 7)$, horizontal major axis of length 8, minor axis of length 6

33. center $(3, -2)$, vertical major axis of length 12, minor axis of length 10

Write an equation of a hyperbola with the given characteristics.

34. vertices $(\pm 3, 7)$, foci $(\pm 5, 7)$

35. vertices $(2, \pm 5)$, foci $(2, -7), (2, 7)$

36. vertices $(-3, -1), (-5, -1)$, foci $(0, -1), (-8, -1)$

Identify the conic section represented by each equation. If it is a parabola, give the vertex. If it is a circle, give the center and radius. If it is an ellipse or a hyperbola, give the center and foci. Sketch the graph.

37. $3y^2 - x - 6y + 5 = 0$

38. $x^2 + y^2 - 4x - 6y + 4 = 0$

39. $4x^2 + y^2 - 16x - 6y + 9 = 0$

40. $4x^2 - y^2 - 16x + 6y - 9 = 0$

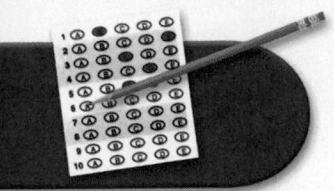
Standardized Test Prep

Multiple Choice

For Exercises 1–14, choose the correct letter.

1. Which equation represents a circle with center $(-3, 8)$ and radius 12?

- Ⓐ $(x - 8)^2 + (y + 3)^2 = 144$
- Ⓑ $(x - 8)^2 - (y + 3)^2 = 144$
- Ⓒ $(x + 3)^2 + (y - 8)^2 = 144$
- Ⓓ $(x - 3)^2 - (y - 8)^2 = 144$

2. Which function has a growth factor of 1.25?

- Ⓕ $y = 1.25x$
- Ⓖ $y = 4.1(1.25)^x$
- Ⓗ $y = 1.25(3.7)^x$
- Ⓙ $y = 1.25(0.9)^x$

3. What is the product $\dfrac{x^2(x - 2)}{x + 4} \cdot \dfrac{2(2x + 8)}{x^3 - x^2}$?

- Ⓐ $\dfrac{x^4(x - 1)(x - 2) - 4(x + 4)^2}{x^2(x - 1)(x + 4)}$
- Ⓑ $\dfrac{12x^4 + 14x^3 - 32x^2}{x^4 + 2x^3 - 4x^2}$
- Ⓒ $\dfrac{x^4(x - 1)(x - 2)}{4(x + 4)^2}$
- Ⓓ $\dfrac{4(x - 2)}{x - 1}$

4. The equation $y = (x - 4)^2$ represents which conic section?

- Ⓕ circle
- Ⓖ ellipse
- Ⓗ parabola
- Ⓙ hyperbola

5. Which events are dependent?
  - **I.** spinning a spinner three times
  - **II.** choosing three students from a class
  - **III.** tossing two coins and a number cube

- Ⓐ I only
- Ⓑ II only
- Ⓒ III only
- Ⓓ I and II

6. The graph below represents which function?

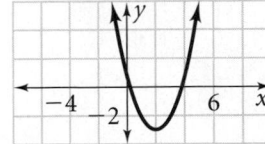

- Ⓕ $y = \dfrac{x^2 - 4}{x + 4}$
- Ⓖ $y = x^2 - 4x + 1$
- Ⓗ $y = |x + 4|$
- Ⓙ $y = x^3 + x^2 - 4$

7. Which equation has roots $-3, 0, 1,$ and 2?

- Ⓐ $x^4 - 7x^2 + 6x = 0$
- Ⓑ $x^4 - 6x^3 + 11x - 6x = 0$
- Ⓒ $x^4 - 4x^3 + x^2 - 6x = 0$
- Ⓓ $x^4 - 7x^2 - 6 = 0$

8. Solve $4x^2 - 64 = 0$.

- Ⓕ $x = \pm 2$
- Ⓖ $x = \pm 4$
- Ⓗ $x = \pm 8$
- Ⓙ $x = \pm 16$

9. Solve $4(9 - x)^{0.5} - 6 = 10$.

- Ⓐ 7
- Ⓑ -7
- Ⓒ 5
- Ⓓ -5

10. For what value of c is $x^2 - 5x + c$ a square of a binomial?

- Ⓕ 25
- Ⓖ -25
- Ⓗ $\dfrac{25}{4}$
- Ⓙ $-\dfrac{25}{4}$

11. What is the complete solution of $\log (6x - 9) = 2 \log x$?

- Ⓐ 3
- Ⓑ -3
- Ⓒ $-3, 3$
- Ⓓ $1, 3$

12. Evaluate $\log_3 81$.

- Ⓕ 2
- Ⓖ 3
- Ⓗ 4
- Ⓙ 9

13. Identify the directrix of the graph of $6x = x^2 + 8y + 9$.

- Ⓐ $x = 2$
- Ⓑ $y = 2$
- Ⓒ $x = -4$
- Ⓓ $y = -4$

14. Find the distance between the foci of the ellipse with the equation $\dfrac{x^2}{36} + \dfrac{(y - 2)^2}{100} = 1$.

- Ⓕ 4
- Ⓖ 8
- Ⓗ 12
- Ⓙ 16

Gridded Response

15. Simplify $\dfrac{1 - \frac{1}{8}}{2 - \frac{3}{4}}$.

16. A and B are independent but not mutually exclusive events. $P(A) = \frac{1}{4}$ and $P(B) = \frac{1}{5}$. Find $P(A \text{ or } B)$.

Short Response

17. Find $\begin{bmatrix} 1 & 0 \\ 0 & 2 \\ 1 & 3 \end{bmatrix} + \begin{bmatrix} 2 & 1 \\ 1 & 3 \\ 0 & 0 \end{bmatrix}$.

18. Find the zeros of the function $y = x^2 - 2x$. Show your work.

Extended Response

19. a. Write an equation of a line perpendicular to $y = 3x + 2$.
  b. Write an equation of a line parallel to $y = 3x + 2$.

20. Find $\dfrac{x + 4}{x^2 + 6x + 8} \div \dfrac{x^2 - 16}{x^2 + 8x + 12}$. What are the restrictions on the variable?

Activity Lab

Martian Math

Applying Conic Sections Even though we haven't discovered life on Mars, we know a lot of other things about the planet. Mars has a day about 25 hours long, a pattern of seasons similar to Earth's, and polar icecaps. Mars also has surface temperatures that rarely rise above freezing and almost no oxygen in its atmosphere. Mars is often called the Red Planet because red deserts cover its surface.

Activity 1

a. Mars travels in an elliptical orbit with the sun at one of its foci. Use the data from the diagram to calculate $a, b,$ and c of this elliptical orbit.

b. Point P is the midpoint between Mars' closest and farthest distances to the sun. Use your values of a and b to write an equation of the elliptical orbit of Mars relative to a coordinate system drawn through point P (y-axis in gray). Use distances in millions of kilometers.

c. It is also useful to define Mars' motion relative to the sun. Imagine a new coordinate system (y-axis in black) with its origin at the center of the sun. Rewrite your equation for the ellipse in this new coordinate system.

d. **Critical Thinking** Explain how the eccentricity of a planet's orbit can affect its annual weather cycle.

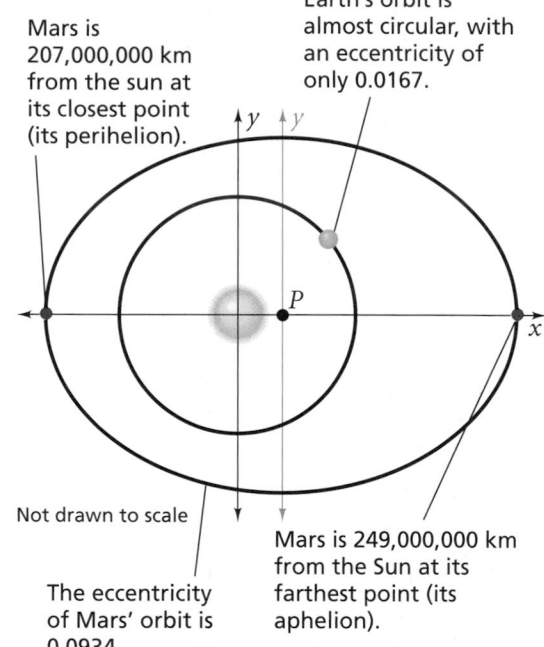

Mars is 207,000,000 km from the sun at its closest point (its perihelion).

Earth's orbit is almost circular, with an eccentricity of only 0.0167.

Not drawn to scale

The eccentricity of Mars' orbit is 0.0934.

Mars is 249,000,000 km from the Sun at its farthest point (its aphelion).

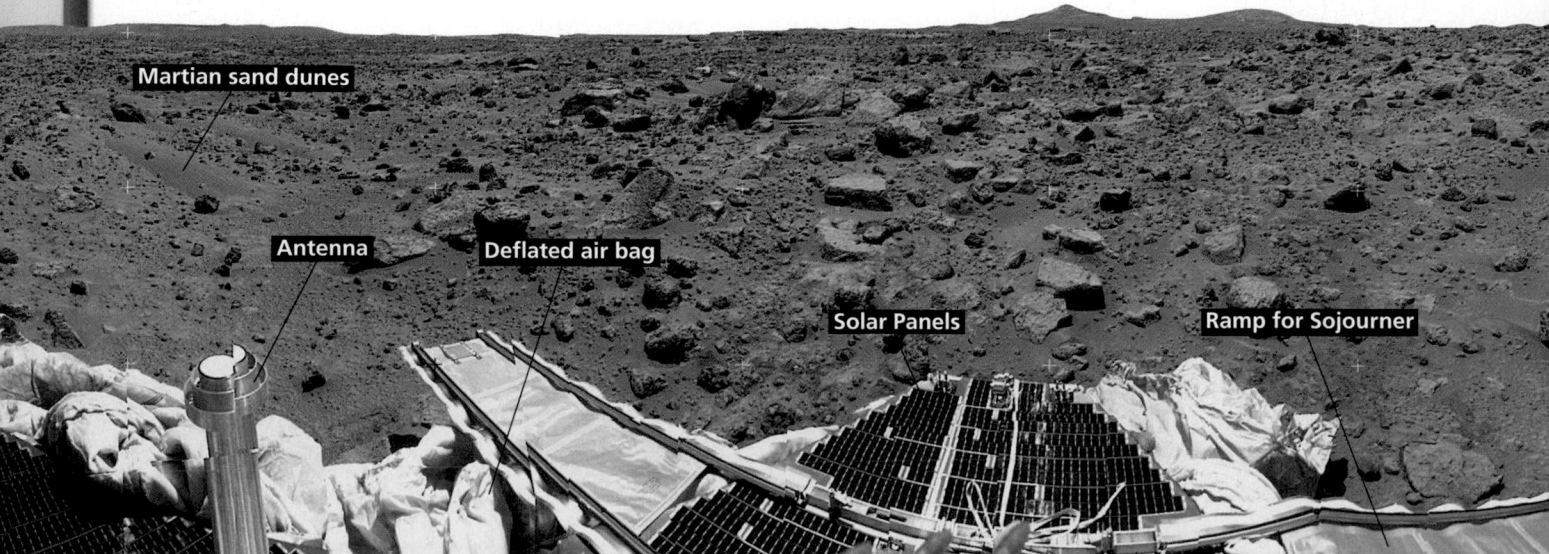

Martian sand dunes

Antenna

Deflated air bag

Solar Panels

Ramp for Sojourner

Activity 2

Astronauts who walked on the moon felt as if they weighed about one sixth of their weight on Earth. This is because the weight of an object is determined by the gravitational attraction between the object and the planet (or moon) it's on. You can use the following formula to estimate the weight of an object on the surface of any of the planets: gravitational force $= \dfrac{GmM}{r^2}$, where G = universal gravitational constant, m = mass of the object, M = mass of the planet, and r = radius of the planet. For a given object, G and m remain constant, so the force of gravity depends only on the variables M and r.

a. Use the data below. Write a ratio to determine the factor by which you would multiply the weight of a 150-lb person on Earth to find his or her weight on Mars.

b. Find the person's weight on Mars.

c. Repeat parts (a) and (b) for two other planets.

Man on the Moon
On July 20, 1969, U.S. astronauts first set foot on the moon.

Mercury
mass: 5788 Mercurys = 1 Jupiter
radius: 2439 km

Venus
mass: 393 Venuses = 1 Jupiter
radius: 6052 km

Saturn
mass: 3.3 Saturns = 1 Jupiter
radius: 60,268 km

Mars
mass: 2894 Marses = 1 Jupiter
radius: 3397 km

Earth
mass: 317 Earths = 1 Jupiter
radius: 6378 km

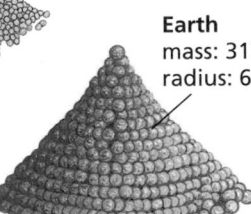

Jupiter
mass: 1 Jupiter
radius: 71,942 km

Go Online
PHSchool.com

For: Information about Mars
Web Code: age-1053

Sojourner rover

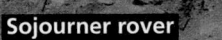

Bouncing to a Stop

The Pathfinder Probe parachuted onto Mars inside a giant "beach ball"—a set of air bags designed to cushion the probe's landing. The probe bounced 15 times across the rocky ground and rolled to a stop. Its airbags deflated. Three panels then folded out like petals, exposing the probe's instruments and the Sojourner rover to the Martian landscape.

What You've Learned

- In Chapter 2, you learned to evaluate functions in function notation.
- In Chapter 5, you learned to use parabolas for graphing quadratic functions.
- In Chapter 7, you learned to evaluate radical expressions.
- In Chapter 9, you learned to simplify complex fractions, which are fractions that have fractions in the numerator or denominator or in both the numerator and denominator.

 **Check Your Readiness**   **for Help** to the Lesson in green.

Evaluating Functions (Lesson 2-1)

For each function, find $f(1), f(2), f(3)$, and $f(4)$.

1. $f(x) = 2x + 7$
2. $f(x) = 5x - 4$
3. $f(x) = 0.2x + 0.7$

4. $f(x) = -5x + 3$
5. $f(x) = 4x - \frac{2}{3}$
6. $f(x) = -3x - 9$

Graphing Quadratic Functions (Lesson 5-2)

Graph each function.

7. $y = x^2 + 3$
8. $y = -\frac{1}{2}x^2 + 2$
9. $y = 4x^2 - 1$

10. $y = 2x^2 - 7x + 3$
11. $y = -4x^2 + 8x + 5$
12. $y = x^2 + 3x + 4$

Evaluating Radical Expressions (Lesson 7-1)

Find each real-number root.

13. $\sqrt{16}$
14. $-\sqrt{16}$
15. $\sqrt{0.16}$
16. $\sqrt{2500}$

Simplify each radical expression. Use absolute value symbols as needed.

17. $\sqrt{25x^4}$
18. $-\sqrt{0.09y^8}$
19. $\sqrt{x^6y^{10}}$
20. $\sqrt{121y^{24}}$

Simplifying Complex Fractions (Lesson 9-5)

Simplify each complex fraction.

21. $\dfrac{1 - \frac{1}{3}}{\frac{1}{2}}$
22. $\dfrac{\frac{1}{3} + \frac{1}{6}}{\frac{2}{3}}$
23. $\dfrac{1}{1 - \frac{2}{5}}$
24. $\dfrac{1 - \frac{3}{8}}{2 + \frac{1}{4}}$

Sequences and Series

LESSONS

11-1 Mathematical Patterns

11-2 Arithmetic Sequences

11-3 Geometric Sequences

11-4 Arithmetic Series

11-5 Geometric Series

11-6 Area Under a Curve

🔊 **Key Vocabulary**

- arithmetic mean (p. 607)
- arithmetic sequence (p. 606)
- arithmetic series (p. 620)
- circumscribed rectangles (p. 635)
- common difference (p. 606)
- common ratio (p. 612)
- converge (p. 627)
- diverge (p. 627)
- explicit formula (p. 602)
- geometric mean (p. 614)
- geometric sequence (p. 612)
- geometric series (p. 626)
- inscribed rectangles (p. 635)
- limit (p. 621)
- recursive formula (p. 602)
- sequence (p. 600)
- series (p. 619)
- term (p. 600)

What You'll Learn Next

- In Chapter 11, you will learn to identify and generate arithmetic sequences and geometric sequences.

- You will learn to evaluate arithmetic series and geometric series.

- You will use rectangles to approximate the area under a curve.

Real-World Connection Applying what you learn, on page 635 you will solve a problem involving the speed of a falcon.

599

11-1

Mathematical Patterns

What You'll Learn

- To identify mathematical patterns
- To use a formula for finding the *n*th term of a sequence

. . . And Why

To predict the height of a bouncing ball, as in Example 2

Find the next two numbers of each pattern. Then write a rule to describe the pattern.

1. $1, 3, 5, 7, 9, 11, \ldots$

2. $-2, -4, -6, -8, -10, -12, \ldots$

3. $0.2, 1, 5, 25, 125, 625, \ldots$

4. $50, 45, 40, 35, 30, 25, \ldots$

5. $512, 256, 128, 64, 32, 16, \ldots$

6. $2, 5, 8, 11, 14, 17, \ldots$

7. $16, 32, 64, \ldots$

8. $-3, -7, -11, -15, \ldots$

🔊 **New Vocabulary**   • sequence   • term   • recursive formula   • explicit formula

1   Identifying Mathematical Patterns

Activity: Generating a Pattern

Suppose each student in your math class has a phone conversation with every other member of the class. What is the minimum number of calls required?

Instead of actually making the calls, you can represent telephone conversations by drawing diagrams like the ones below.

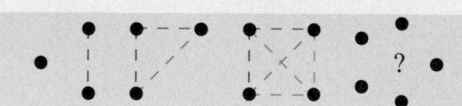

1. How many calls are necessary for two people to have a conversation?

2. How many calls are necessary for everyone to talk to everyone else in a group of three people? In a group of four people?

3. Use a diagram to find the number of calls needed for five people.

4. **Reasoning** Which of the following expressions represents the pattern for numbers of telephone calls?

   A. $2n - 3$ **B.** $n(n - 1) - 5$ **C.** $\dfrac{n(n - 1)}{2}$

5. Use the expression from Question 4 to find the number of calls needed for a group of seven students.

6. How many calls would be needed for your class?

Sometimes steps in a process form a pattern. You can describe some patterns with a **sequence**, or ordered list of numbers. Each number in a sequence is a **term**.

When you apply the construction from Example 1 to an equilateral triangle, you form the Koch snowflake.

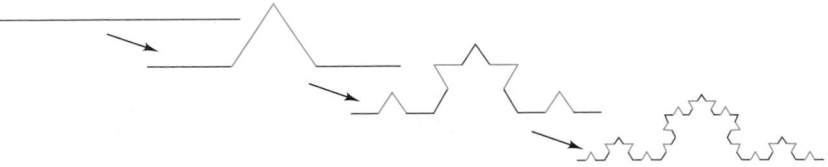

a. To create one side of the Koch snowflake, replace each _____ with _⌃_. Draw the first four figures of the pattern.

b. Write the number of segments in each figure above as a sequence.

$1, 4, 16, 64, \ldots$

c. Predict the next term of the sequence. Explain your choice.

Each term is 4 times the preceding term. The next term is $64 \cdot 4$, or 256. There will be 256 segments in the next figure in the pattern.

✓ **Quick Check** ❶ Describe the pattern formed. Find the next three terms.
a. $27, 34, 41, 48, \ldots$ **b.** $243, 81, 27, 9, \ldots$

Sometimes you can find the next term in a sequence by using a pattern from the terms that come before it.

2 EXAMPLE **Real-World 🌐 Connection**

Multiple Choice Suppose you drop a handball from a height of 10 ft. After the ball hits the floor, it rebounds to 85% of its previous height. About how high will the ball rebound after its fourth bounce?

Ⓐ 10 ft   Ⓑ 8.5 ft   Ⓒ 6.1 ft   Ⓓ 5.2 ft

Original height of ball: 10 ft →

After 1st bounce: 85% of $10 = 0.85(10) = 8.5 \rightarrow$

After 2nd bounce: $0.85(8.5) = 7.225 \rightarrow$

After 3rd bounce: $0.85(7.225) \approx 6.141 \rightarrow$

After 4th bounce: $0.85(6.141) \approx 5.220 \rightarrow$

The ball will rebound about 5.2 ft after the fourth bounce. The correct choice is D.

✓ **Quick Check** ❷ **a.** About how high will the ball rebound after the seventh bounce?
b. After what bounce will the rebound height be less than 2 ft?

You can use a variable, such as a, with positive integer subscripts to represent the terms in a sequence.

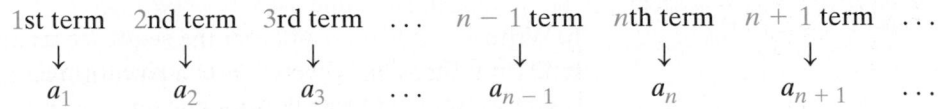

1st term	2nd term	3rd term	...	$n-1$ term	nth term	$n+1$ term	...
↓	↓	↓		↓	↓	↓	
a_1	a_2	a_3	...	a_{n-1}	a_n	a_{n+1}	...

A **recursive formula** defines the terms in a sequence by relating each term to the ones before it. The pattern in Example 2 was recursive because the height of the ball after each bounce was 85% of its previous height. The recursive formula that describes the ball's height is $a_n = 0.85a_{n-1}$, where $a_1 = 10$.

3 **EXAMPLE** **Using a Recursive Formula**

a. Describe the pattern that allows you to find the next term in the sequence $2, 4, 6, 8, 10, \ldots$ Write a recursive formula for the sequence.

The terms of the sequence are the even numbers. Add 2 to a term to find the next term. A recursive formula is $a_n = a_{n-1} + 2$, where $a_1 = 2$.

b. Find the sixth and seventh terms in the sequence.

Since $a_5 = 10$, $a_6 = 10 + 2 = 12$, and $a_7 = 12 + 2 = 14$.

c. Find the value of term a_9 in the sequence.

Term a_9 is the ninth term. $a_9 = a_8 + 2 = (a_7 + 2) + 2 = (14 + 2) + 2 = 18$

✓ **Quick Check** **3** Find terms a_{11} and a_{15} in the sequence.

Sometimes you can find the value of a term of a sequence without knowing the preceding term. Instead, you can use the number of the term to calculate its value. A formula that expresses the nth term in terms of n is an **explicit formula.**

4 **EXAMPLE** **Real-World 🌐 Connection**

Geometry The spreadsheet below shows the perimeters of squares with sides from 1 to 6 units long. The numbers in each row form a sequence.

	A	B	C	D	E	F	G	H
1		a1	a2	a3	a4	a5	a6	. . .
2	Length of a Side	1	2	3	4	5	6	. . .
3	Perimeter	4	8	12	16	20	24	. . .

a. For each sequence, find the next term (a_7) and the twenty-fifth term (a_{25}).

In the sequence in row 2, each term is the same as its subscript. Therefore, $a_7 = 7$ and $a_{25} = 25$.
In the sequence in row 3, each term is 4 times its subscript. Therefore, $a_7 = 4(7) = 28$ and $a_{25} = 4(25) = 100$.

b. Write an explicit formula for each sequence.

The explicit formula for the sequence in row 2 is $a_n = n$. The explicit formula for the sequence in row 3 is $a_n = 4n$.

✓ **Quick Check** **4 a.** Write the first six terms in the sequence showing the areas of the squares in Example 4. Then find a_{20}.
b. Write an explicit formula for the sequence from part (a).
c. **Critical Thinking** Given the recursive formula $a_n = a_{n-1} + 3$, can you find the fourth term in the sequence? Explain.

EXERCISES

For more exercises, see *Extra Skill and Word Problem Practice*.

Practice and Problem Solving

A Practice by Example

Examples 1 and 2
(page 601)

Describe each pattern formed. Find the next three terms.

1. $80, 77, 74, 71, 68, \ldots$ **2.** $4, 8, 16, 32, 64, \ldots$ **3.** $0, 3, 7, 12, 18, \ldots$

4. $1, 4, 7, 10, 13, \ldots$ **5.** $100, 10, 1, 0.1, 0.01, \ldots$ **6.** $\frac{1}{2}, \frac{1}{4}, \frac{1}{8}, \frac{1}{16}, \frac{1}{32}, \ldots$

7. $4, -8, 16, -32, 64, \ldots$ **8.** $1, 2, 6, 24, 120, \ldots$ **9.** $0, 1, 0, \frac{1}{3}, 0, \frac{1}{5}, \ldots$

Fractal Geometry Draw the first four figures of the sequence described.

10. —————— is replaced by ⎯⎦⎺⎣⎯ .   **11.**  is replaced by △ △ .

Example 3
(page 602)

Write a recursive formula for each sequence. Then find the next term.

12. $-2, -1, 0, 1, 2, \ldots$ **13.** $43, 41, 39, 37, 35, \ldots$ **14.** $40, 20, 10, 5, \frac{5}{2}, \ldots$

15. $6, 1, -4, -9, \ldots$ **16.** $144, 36, 9, \frac{9}{4}, \ldots$ **17.** $\frac{1}{2}, \frac{1}{4}, \frac{1}{8}, \frac{1}{16}, \frac{1}{32}, \ldots$

Example 4
(page 602)

Write an explicit formula for each sequence. Then find a_{12}.

18. $4, 5, 6, 7, 8, \ldots$ **19.** $\frac{1}{2}, \frac{1}{3}, \frac{1}{4}, \frac{1}{5}, \frac{1}{6}, \ldots$ **20.** $4, 7, 10, 13, 16, \ldots$

21. $3, 7, 11, 15, 19, \ldots$ **22.** $-2\frac{1}{2}, -2, -1\frac{1}{2}, -1, \ldots$ **23.** $2, 5, 10, 17, 26, \ldots$

B Apply Your Skills

Decide whether each formula is *explicit* or *recursive*. Then find the first five terms of each sequence.

24. $a_n = 2a_{n-1} + 3$, where $a_1 = 3$ **25.** $a_n = \frac{1}{2}(n)(n-1)$

26. $(n-5)(n+5) = a_n$ **27.** $a_n = -3a_{n-1}$, where $a_1 = -2$

28. $a_n = -4n^2 - 2$ **29.** $a_n = 2n^2 + 1$

30. $a_n = 5n$ **31.** $a_n = a_{n-1} - 17$, where $a_1 = 340$

Real-World 🌐 Connection

Bryan Berg built a 24-ft 4-in. 127-story freestanding house of cards.

32. Entertainment Suppose you are building a tower of cards with levels as displayed below. Complete the table, assuming the pattern continues.

Levels	1	2	3	4	5
Cards Needed	2	7	■	■	■

Find the next two terms in each sequence. Write a formula for the *n*th term. Identify each formula as *explicit* or *recursive*.

33. $5, 8, 11, 14, 17, \ldots$ **34.** $3, 6, 12, 24, 48, \ldots$ **35.** $1, 8, 27, 64, 125, \ldots$

36. $4, 16, 64, 256, 1024, \ldots$ **37.** $49, 64, 81, 100, 121, \ldots$ **38.** $-1, 1, -1, 1, -1, 1, \ldots$

39. $-16, -8, -4, -2, \ldots$ **40.** $-75, -68, -61, -54, \ldots$ **41.** $21, 13, 5, -3, \ldots$

42. Suppose the cartoon at the right included one sheep to the left and another sheep to the right of the three shown. What "names" would you give these sheep?

WHEN MATHEMATICIANS CAN'T SLEEP

43. Writing Explain the difference between a recursive formula and an explicit formula.

44. a. Open-Ended Write four terms of a sequence of numbers that you can describe both recursively and explicitly.
   b. Write a recursive formula and an explicit formula for your sequence.
   c. Find the 20th term of the sequence by evaluating one of your formulas. Use the other formula to check your work.

Use the given rule to write the 4th, 5th, 6th, and 7th terms of each sequence.

45. $a_1 = -1, a_n = a_{n-1} + n^2$

46. $a_1 = -2, a_n = 3(a_{n-1} + 2)$

47. $a_n = (n + 1)^2$

48. $a_n = 2(n - 1)^3$

49. $a_n = \dfrac{n^2}{n + 1}$

50. $a_n = \dfrac{n + 1}{n + 2}$

51. Geometry Suppose you are stacking boxes in levels that form squares. The numbers of boxes in successive levels form a sequence. The figure at the left shows the top four levels as viewed from above.
   a. How many boxes of equal size would you need for the next lower level?
   b. How many boxes of equal size would you need to add three levels?
   c. Suppose you are stacking a total of 285 boxes. How many levels will you have?

C Challenge

Use each recursive formula to write an explicit formula for the sequence.

52. $a_1 = 10, a_n = 2a_{n-1}$

53. $a_1 = -5, a_n = a_{n-1} - 1$

54. $a_1 = -2, a_n = \frac{1}{2}a_{n-1}$

55. $a_1 = 1, a_n = a_{n-1} + 4$

56. Finance Use the information in the ad.
   a. Suppose you start a savings account at Mun e-Bank. Write both a recursive formula and an explicit formula for the amount of money you would have in the bank at the end of any week.
   b. How much money would you have in the bank after four weeks?
   c. Assume the bank pays interest every four weeks. To calculate your interest, multiply the balance at the end of the four weeks by 0.005. Then add that much to your account on the last day of the four-week period. Write a recursive formula for the amount of money you have after each interest payment.
   d. Critical Thinking What is the bank's annual interest rate?

Mun e-Bank is offering a **GREAT** deal right now!

Start a savings club account by depositing only $25 today and $5 a week starting next week.

See how easy it is to save!

57. Geometry The triangular numbers form a sequence. The diagram represents the first three triangular numbers: 1, 3, and 6.

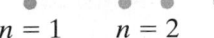

$n = 1 \quad n = 2 \quad n = 3$

a. Find the fifth and sixth triangular numbers.

b. Write a recursive formula for the nth triangular number.

c. Is the explicit formula $a_n = \frac{1}{2}(n^2 + n)$ the correct formula for this sequence? How do you know?

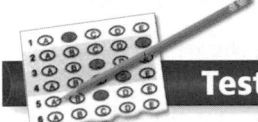

Test Prep

Multiple Choice

58. What is the difference between the third term in the sequence whose recursive formula is $a_1 = -5$, $a_n = 2a_{n-1} + 1$ and the third term in the sequence whose recursive formula is $a_1 = -3$, $a_n = -a_{n-1} + 3$?

   A. 2   **B.** 14   **C.** 20   **D.** 32

59. What is a recursive formula for the sequence whose explicit formula is $a_n = (n + 1)^2$?

   F. $a_1 = 1$, $a_n = (a_{n-1} + 1)^2$ **G.** $a_1 = 4$, $a_n = \left(\sqrt{a_{n-1}} + 1\right)^2$

   H. $a_1 = n$, $a_n = a_{n-1} + n$ **J.** $a_1 = n^2$, $a_n = (a_{n-1})^2 + 1$

Use the figure below for Exercises 60–62.

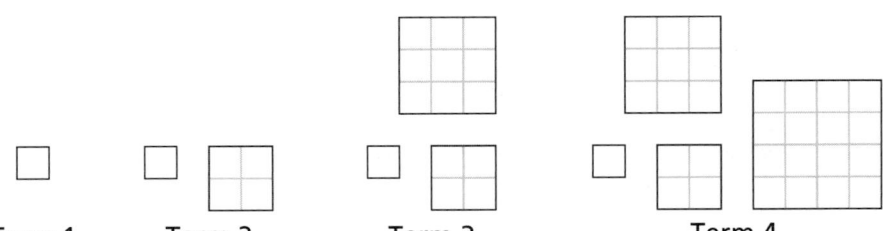

Term 1   Term 2   Term 3   Term 4

60. How many 1×1 squares are in the sixth term of the sequence?

   A. 21   **B.** 36   **C.** 91   **D.** 441

61. Which expressions represent the first three terms of the sequence?

   F. $1^2, 2^2, 3^2, \ldots$ **G.** $1, 1 + 2, 1 + 2 + 3, \ldots$

   H. $1^2, (1 + 2)^2, (1 + 2 + 3)^2, \ldots$ **J.** $1^2, 1^2 + 2^2, 1^2 + 2^2 + 3^2, \ldots$

Short Response

62. Write a recursive formula for the sequence in the figure above. Explain your reasoning.

Mixed Review

Lesson 10-6

The graph of each equation is translated 2 units left and 3 units down. Write each new equation.

63. $(x + 2)^2 + (y - 1)^2 = 5$ **64.** $\dfrac{(x - 1)^2}{36} + \dfrac{(y - 1)^2}{36} = 1$

Lesson 9-1

Each point is from an inverse variation. Write an equation to model the data.

65. $(1, 20)$ **66.** $(5, 2)$ **67.** $(9, 13)$ **68.** $(-3, -9)$

69. $(2, 5)$ **70.** $(-6, -12)$ **71.** $\left(\frac{1}{2}, -\frac{1}{2}\right)$ **72.** $(-10, -10)$

Arithmetic Sequences

What You'll Learn

- To identify and generate arithmetic sequences

...And Why

To determine the amount of money raised during a fund-raiser, as in Example 2

✓ **Check Skills You'll Need**

GO for Help   Skills Handbook p. 866

Describe the pattern in each sequence. Use at least one of the words *add*, *subtract*, or *difference*.

1. $10, 8, 6, 4, 2, 0, \ldots$

2. $100, 117, 134, 151, 168, \ldots$

3. $\frac{5}{7}, \frac{8}{7}, \frac{11}{7}, 2, \ldots$

4. $-\frac{1}{4}, -\frac{1}{2}, -\frac{3}{4}, -1, -\frac{5}{4}, -\frac{3}{2}, \ldots$

🔊 **New Vocabulary**   • arithmetic sequence   • common difference
• arithmetic mean

---

1 Identifying and Generating Arithmetic Sequences

Vocabulary Tip

The stress in the noun <u>arithmetic</u> is on the second syllable (uh RITH muh tik). The stress in the adjective <u>arithmetic</u> is on the third syllable (ar ith MET ik).

In an **arithmetic sequence,** the difference between consecutive terms is constant. This difference is called the **common difference.** The common difference can be positive (the terms of the sequence are increasing in value) or negative (the terms of the sequence are decreasing in value).

1 EXAMPLE   **Identifying an Arithmetic Sequence**

Is the given sequence arithmetic?

a. $2, 4, 8, 16, \ldots$

$2, \qquad 4, \qquad 8, \qquad 16, \ldots$

$\quad +2 \qquad\quad +4 \qquad\quad +8$

$4 - 2 = 2 \quad 8 - 4 = 4 \quad 16 - 8 = 8$

There is no common difference. This is *not* an arithmetic sequence.

Online active math

For: Sequences Activity
Use: Interactive Textbook, 11-2

b. the golf ball pattern at the right

$6, \qquad 12, \qquad 18, \ldots$

$\quad +6 \qquad\quad +6$

$12 - 6 = 6 \quad 18 - 12 = 6$

The common difference is 6. The dots on the golf ball form an arithmetic sequence.

✓ **Quick Check**   **1** Is the given sequence arithmetic? If so, identify the common difference.
a. $2, 5, 7, 12, \ldots$ **b.** $48, 45, 42, 39, \ldots$

You can use an explicit formula to find the value of the *n*th term of an arithmetic sequence when the previous term is unknown.

Property	Arithmetic Sequence Formulas

Recursive Formula   **Explicit Formula**

a_1 = a given value, $a_n = a_{n-1} + d$ $a_n = a_1 + (n-1)d$

In these formulas, a_n is the nth term ($n > 1$), a_1 is the first term, n is the number of the term, and d is the common difference.

Real-World Connection

The AIDSRide raises money for AIDS services in locations across the United States.

2 EXAMPLE Real-World Connection

Fund-Raising Suppose you participate in a bike-a-thon for charity. The charity starts with $1100 in donations. Each participant must raise at least $35 in pledges. What is the minimum amount of money raised if there are 75 participants?

Find the 76th term of the sequence 1100, 1135, 1170, ...

$a_n = a_1 + (n-1)d$	**Use the explicit formula.**
$a_{76} = 1100 + (76 - 1)(35)$	**Substitute $a_1 = 1100$, $n = 76$, and $d = 35$.**
$= 1100 + (75)(35)$	**Subtract within parentheses.**
$= 3725$	**Simplify.**

With 75 participants, the bike-a-thon will raise a minimum of $3725.

 **Quick Check** **2 a. Critical Thinking** In Example 2, why find the value of the 76th term, not the 75th term?
b. Use the explicit formula to find the 25th term in the sequence 5, 11, 17, 23, 29, . . .

Video Tutor Help
Visit: PHSchool.com
Web Code: age-0775

The **arithmetic mean** of any two numbers is the average of the two numbers.

$$\text{arithmetic mean} = \frac{\text{sum of two numbers}}{2}$$

For any three sequential terms in an arithmetic sequence, the middle term is the arithmetic mean of the first and third terms.

Graphs of arithmetic sequences are linear. Two terms of an arithmetic sequence and their arithmetic mean lie on the same line.

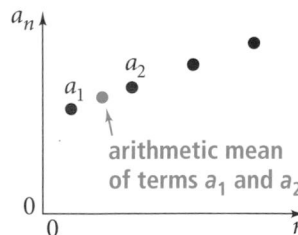

arithmetic mean of terms a_1 and a_2

You can use the arithmetic mean to find a missing term of an arithmetic sequence.

3 EXAMPLE Using the Arithmetic Mean

Find the missing term of the arithmetic sequence 84, ■, 110.

$\text{arithmetic mean} = \dfrac{84 + 110}{2}$ **Write the average.**

$= 97$ **Simplify.**

The missing term is 97.

 **Quick Check** **3 a.** Find the missing term of the arithmetic sequence 24, ■, 57.
b. Write an expression for the arithmetic mean of a_6 and a_7.

EXERCISES

For more exercises, see *Extra Skill and Word Problem Practice.*

Practice and Problem Solving

 Practice by Example

Example 1
(page 606)

Is the given sequence arithmetic? If so, identify the common difference.

1. $1, 4, 9, 16, \ldots$ **2.** $10, 20, 30, 40, \ldots$

3. $1, 1, 2, 3, 5, 8, \ldots$ **4.** $0, 1, 3, 6, 10, \ldots$

5. $-21, -18, -15, -12, \ldots$ **6.** $97, 86, 75, 64, \ldots$

7. $3, 7, 11, 15, \ldots$ **8.** $100, 10, 1, 0.1, \ldots$

9. $\frac{1}{2}, \frac{1}{4}, \frac{1}{8}, \frac{1}{16}, \ldots$ **10.** $-5, 5, -5, 5, -5, \ldots$

Example 2
(page 607)

Find the 32nd term of each sequence.

11. $34, 37, 40, 43, \ldots$ **12.** $-9, -8.7, -8.4, \ldots$

13. $0.1, 0.5, 0.9, 1.3, \ldots$ **14.** $0.0023, 0.0025, 0.0027, \ldots$

15. $101, 105, 109, 113, \ldots$ **16.** $213, 201, 189, 177, \ldots$

17. $3, 1, -1, -3, \ldots$ **18.** $23, 30, 37, 44, \ldots$

19. $9, 4, -1, -6, -11, \ldots$ **20.** $13, 17, 21, 25, \ldots$

Example 3
(page 607)

Find the missing term of each arithmetic sequence.

21. $-16, \blacksquare, 1, \ldots$ **22.** $14, \blacksquare, 28, \ldots$

23. $\ldots 5, \blacksquare, 21, \ldots$ **24.** $\frac{13}{2}, \blacksquare, \frac{51}{2}, \ldots$

25. $101, \blacksquare, -115, \ldots$ **26.** $203, \blacksquare, 1117, \ldots$

27. $25, \blacksquare, -10, \ldots$ **28.** $\ldots 65, \blacksquare, -60, \ldots$

29. $\ldots a_{10}, \blacksquare, a_{12}, \ldots$ **30.** $\ldots 99, \blacksquare, 66, \ldots$

 Apply Your Skills

Find the arithmetic mean a_n of the given terms.

31. $a_{n-1} = 7, a_{n+1} = 1$ **32.** $a_{n-1} = 4, a_{n+1} = -3$

33. $a_{n-1} = 21, a_{n+1} = 5$ **34.** $a_{n-1} = 100, a_{n+1} = 140$

35. $a_{n-1} = -18, a_{n+1} = -21$ **36.** $a_{n-1} = 0.3, a_{n+1} = 1.9$

37. $a_{n-1} = 9, a_{n+1} = -11$ **38.** $a_{n-1} = \frac{3}{5}, a_{n+1} = 1$

39. $a_{n-1} = r, a_{n+1} = s$ **40.** $a_{n-1} = r, a_{n+1} = r + s$

41. $a_{n-1} = -2x, a_{n+1} = 2x$ **42.** $a_{n-1} = x + 3, a_{n+1} = 3x - 1$

43. Error Analysis A student claims that the next term of the arithmetic sequence $0, 2, 4, \ldots$ is 8. What error did the student make?

44. a. Open-Ended Use your calculator to generate an arithmetic sequence with a common difference of -7. How could you use a calculator to find the 6th term? The 8th term? The 20th term?

     b. Critical Thinking Explain how your answer to part (a) relates to the explicit formula $a_n = a_1 + (n - 1)d$.

45. Writing Describe some advantages and some disadvantages of a recursive formula and an explicit formula.

Find the 17th term of each sequence.

46. $a_{16} = 18$, $d = 5$

47. $a_{16} = 18$, $d = -3$

48. $a_{16} = 18$, $d = \frac{1}{2}$

49. $a_{18} = 18$, $d = -4$

50. $a_{18} = 18$, $d = 12$

51. $a_{18} = 18$, $d = -11$

Write an explicit and a recursive formula for each sequence.

52. $2, 4, 6, 8, 10, \ldots$

53. $0, 6, 12, 18, 24, \ldots$

54. $-5, -4, -3, -2, -1, \ldots$

55. $-4, -8, -12, -16, -20, \ldots$

56. $-2, 5, 12, 19, 26, 33, \ldots$

57. $27, 15, 3, -9, -21, \ldots$

58. $-5, -3.5, -2, -0.5, 1, \ldots$

59. $-32, -20, -8, 4, 16, \ldots$

60. $1, 1\frac{1}{3}, 1\frac{2}{3}, 2, \ldots$

61. $0, \frac{1}{8}, \frac{1}{4}, \frac{3}{8}, \ldots$

Real-World Connection

San Francisco's historic cable cars move by gripping and releasing a moving steel cable under the street.

62. Transportation Suppose a trolley stops at a certain intersection every 14 min. The first trolley of the day gets to the stop at 6:43 A.M. How long do you have to wait for a trolley if you get to the stop at 8:15 A.M.? At 3:20 P.M.?

Find the missing terms of each arithmetic sequence. (*Hint:* The arithmetic mean of the first and fifth terms is the third term.)

63. $2, \blacksquare, \blacksquare, \blacksquare, -22, \ldots$

64. $10, \blacksquare, \blacksquare, \blacksquare, -11.6, \ldots$

65. $1, \blacksquare, \blacksquare, \blacksquare, -35, \ldots$

66. $\ldots \frac{13}{5}, \blacksquare, \blacksquare, \blacksquare, \frac{37}{5}, \ldots$

67. $17, \blacksquare, \blacksquare, \blacksquare, 17, \ldots$

68. $660, \blacksquare, \blacksquare, \blacksquare, 744, \ldots$

69. $\ldots -17, \blacksquare, \blacksquare, \blacksquare, 1, \ldots$

70. $\ldots a + 1, \blacksquare, \blacksquare, \blacksquare, a + 17, \ldots$

71. Savings In February you start a holiday savings account with a deposit of $20. You increase each monthly deposit by five dollars until the end of the year.
 a. Write the amount in the account after each deposit.
 b. Write a recursive formula for the sequence of balances.
 c. How much money will you have saved by the end of the year?

Graph the arithmetic sequence generated by each formula over the domain $1 \leq n \leq 10$.

72. $a_1 = -60$, $a_n = a_{n-1} + 9$

73. $a_n = 50 - 7n$

74. Critical Thinking Suppose you turn the water on in an empty bathtub with vertical sides. After 20 s, the water has reached a level of 1.15 in. You then leave the room. You want to turn the water off when the level in the bathtub is 8.5 in. How many minutes later should you return? (*Hint:* Begin by identifying two terms of an arithmetic sequence.)

 **Challenge**

75. The arithmetic mean of two terms in an arithmetic sequence is 42. One term is 30. Find the other term.

76. The arithmetic mean of two terms in an arithmetic sequence is -6. One term is -20. Find the other term.

77. In an arithmetic sequence with $a_1 = 4$ and $d = 9$, which term is 184?

78. In an arithmetic sequence with $a_1 = 2$ and $d = -2$, which term is -82?

Given two terms of each arithmetic sequence, find a_1 and d.

79. $a_3 = 5$ and $a_5 = 11$ **80.** $a_4 = 8$ and $a_7 = 20$

81. $a_3 = 32$ and $a_7 = -8$ **82.** $a_{10} = 17$ and $a_{14} - 34$

83. $a_4 = -34.5$ and $a_5 = -12.5$ **84.** $a_4 = -2.4$ and $a_6 = 2$

Find the indicated term of each arithmetic series.

85. $a_1 = k, d = k + 4; a_9$ **86.** $a_1 = k + 7, d = 2k - 5; a_{11}$

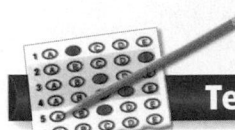

Test Prep

Multiple Choice

87. Which arithmetic sequence DOES NOT include the term 33?
     A. 1, 5, 9, 13, . . .   **B.** 1, 11, 21, . . .
     C. 3, 9, 15, . . .   **D.** 85, 72, 59, . . .

88. Which arithmetic sequence includes the term 27?
     I. $a_1 = 7, a_n = a_{n-1} + 5$ **II.** $a_n = 3 + (n-1)4$ **III.** $a_n = 57 - 6n$
     F. I only   **G.** I and II only   **H.** II and III only   **J.** I, II, and III

89. The arithmetic mean of the monthly salaries of two people is $2955. One person earns $2760 per month. What is the monthly salary of the other person?
     A. $2857.50   **B.** $3150   **C.** $5520   **D.** $5715

90. What is the 30th term of the sequence 7, 16, 25, 34, . . . ?
     F. 277   **G.** 270   **H.** 268   **J.** 261

Short Response

91. Explain how to use the arithmetic mean to find the missing terms in the arithmetic sequence 15, ■, ■, ■, 47, . . .

Extended Response

92. Find the 100th term of the arithmetic sequence 3, 10, 17, 24, 31, . . . Explain your steps.

Mixed Review

Lesson 11-1

GO for Help

Decide whether each formula is *explicit* or *recursive*. Then find the first five terms of each sequence.

93. $a_1 = -2, a_n = a_{n-1} - 5$ **94.** $a_n = 3n(n+1)$

95. $a_n = n^2 - 1$ **96.** $a_1 = -121, a_n = a_{n-1} + 13$

Lesson 10-6

Find the foci of each ellipse.

97. $\frac{x^2}{4} + \frac{y^2}{9} = 1$ **98.** $\frac{x^2}{36} + \frac{y^2}{4} = 1$

99. $\frac{(x-1)^2}{121} + \frac{y^2}{100} = 1$ **100.** $\frac{(x-1)^2}{64} + \frac{(y-3)^2}{25} = 1$

Lesson 7-2   **101. Geometry** The formula for volume V of a sphere with radius r is $V = \frac{4}{3}\pi r^3$. Find the radius of a sphere as a function of its volume. Rationalize the denominator.

One famous mathematical sequence is the Fibonacci sequence. You can find each term of the sequence using addition, but the sequence is not arithmetic. The recursive formula for the Fibonacci sequence is $F_n = F_{n-2} + F_{n-1}$, with $F_1 = 1$ and $F_2 = 1$.

You can use the formula to generate the first five terms of the sequence.

$F_1 = 1$

$F_2 = 1$

$F_3 = F_1 + F_2 = 1 + 1 = 2$

$F_4 = F_2 + F_3 = 1 + 2 = 3$

$F_5 = F_3 + F_4 = 2 + 3 = 5$

The first five terms of the Fibonacci sequence are $1, 1, 2, 3, 5$.

1. Nature The numbers of the Fibonacci sequence are often found in other areas, especially in nature. Which term of the Fibonacci sequence does each picture represent?

  a.   **b.**   **c.**   **d.**

2. a. Describe a recursive rule for constructing Pascal's Triangle at the right. How is your rule similar to the process for generating the Fibonacci sequence? (*Hint:* How can you find the numbers in the last row?)

  b. Find "diagonals" in Pascal's Triangle by starting with the first 1 in each row and moving one row up and one number to the right. For example, the diagonal starting in the fifth row is $1, 3, 1$. The diagonal starting in the sixth row is $1, 4, 3$. For each diagonal, write the sum of its entries. What pattern do the sums form?

```
          1
        1 1
       1 2 1
      1 3 3 1
     1 4 6 4 1
   1 5 10 10 5 1
 1 ■ ■ ■ ■ ■ ■
```

3. a. Generate the first ten terms of the Fibonacci sequence.

  b. Find the sum of the first ten terms of the Fibonacci sequence. Divide the sum by 11. What do you notice?

  c. Open-Ended Choose two numbers other than 1 and 1. Generate a Fibonacci-like sequence from them. Write the first ten terms of your sequence, find the sum, and divide the sum by 11. What do you notice?

  d. Make a Conjecture What is the sum of the first ten terms of any Fibonacci-like sequence?

4. a. Study the pattern at the right. Write the next line.

  b. Without calculating, use the pattern to predict the sum of squares of the first ten terms of the Fibonacci sequence.

  c. Verify the prediction you made in part (b).

$$1^2 + 1^2 = 2 = 1 \cdot 2$$
$$1^2 + 1^2 + 2^2 = 6 = 2 \cdot 3$$
$$1^2 + 1^2 + 2^2 + 3^2 = 15 = 3 \cdot 5$$
$$1^2 + 1^2 + 2^2 + 3^2 + 5^2 = 40 = 5 \cdot 8$$

5. Make a table with four columns, as shown as the right. Begin with $n = 2$ and complete the first 8 rows. Make a conjecture suggested by the numbers in the third and fourth columns.

n	F_n	$(F_n)^2$	$F_{n-1} \cdot F_{n+1}$

Geometric Sequences

11-3

✓ Check Skills You'll Need

GO for Help Lesson 11-1

Find the next term in each sequence.

1. 1, 2, 4, 8, . . .

2. 336, 168, 84, 42, . . .

3. 0.1, 1, 10, 100, . . .

4. 900, 300, 100, . . .

🔊 **New Vocabulary** • geometric sequence • common ratio • geometric mean

---

1 **Identifying and Generating Geometric Sequences**

Activity: Geometric Sequences

• Make a large right isosceles triangle out of colored paper.

• Cut the triangle into two congruent isosceles triangles.

• Place one triangle on top of the other and repeat the previous step.

1. Complete the sequence for the numbers of triangles below.

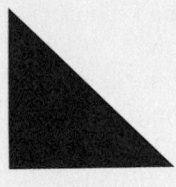  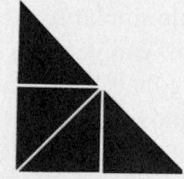 

$a_1 = \blacksquare$ $a_2 = \blacksquare$ $a_3 = \blacksquare$ $a_4 = \blacksquare$

2. Is the sequence in Question 1 arithmetic? Explain why or why not.

3. a. Find the sixth term, a_6, of the sequence.
   b. Write a formula for a_6 in terms of a_5.
   c. Write a general formula for a_n in terms of a_{n-1}.

4. a. Open-Ended Generate two sequences by multiplying by a constant factor. Write each sequence.
   b. Write a recursive formula for each sequence. What do these formulas and the formula for a_n from Question 3 have in common?
   c. Graph all three sequences. Then sketch each graph.
   d. Compare all three graphs. Write a description of the pattern.

Graphing Calculator Hint

Enter the values of n and a_n into lists. Then use the **STAT** and **2nd** STAT PLOT features to graph the sequences.

In a **geometric sequence,** the ratio between consecutive terms is constant. This ratio is called the **common ratio.** Unlike in an arithmetic sequence, the difference between consecutive terms varies.

① **EXAMPLE** **Identifying a Geometric Sequence**

Is the given sequence geometric? If so, identify the common ratio.

a. 5, 15, 45, 135, . . .

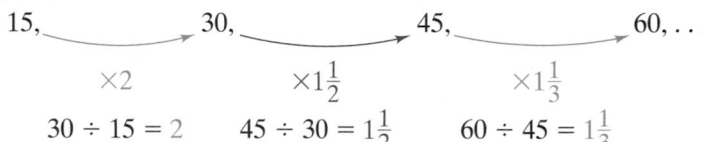

$$5, \qquad 15, \qquad 45, \qquad 135, \ldots$$
$$\times 3 \qquad \times 3 \qquad \times 3$$
$$15 \div 5 = 3 \quad 45 \div 15 = 3 \quad 135 \div 45 = 3$$

There is a common ratio of 3. This is a geometric sequence.

b. 15, 30, 45, 60, . . .

$$15, \qquad 30, \qquad 45, \qquad 60, \ldots$$
$$\times 2 \qquad \times 1\frac{1}{2} \qquad \times 1\frac{1}{3}$$
$$30 \div 15 = 2 \quad 45 \div 30 = 1\frac{1}{2} \quad 60 \div 45 = 1\frac{1}{3}$$

There is no common ratio. This is *not* a geometric sequence.

 Quick Check ① **a.** Write the first ten terms of the geometric sequence from Example 1. Explain how you found the tenth term in the sequence, a_{10}.
b. Is the sequence 6, −24, 96, −384, . . . *arithmetic, geometric,* or *neither?* Explain.
c. Is the sequence 8, 20, 32, 44, . . . *arithmetic, geometric,* or *neither?* Explain.

🔑 **Key Concepts**

Property	**Geometric Sequence Formulas**

Recursive Formula   **Explicit Formula**

$a_1 =$ a given value, $a_n = a_{n-1} \cdot r$ $a_n = a_1 \cdot r^{n-1}$

In these formulas, a_n is the nth term, a_1 is the first term, n is the number of the term, and r is the common ratio.

Real-World 🌐 Connection

Careers Graphic designers use math to lay out pages of books and magazines.

As with an arithmetic sequence, you can use an explicit formula to find the value of the nth term when the previous term is unknown.

② **EXAMPLE** **Real-World 🌐 Connection**

Design Suppose you want a reduced copy of a photograph. The actual length of the photograph is 10 in. The smallest size the copier can make is 64% of the original. Find the length of the photograph after five reductions at 64%.

For five reductions, you need to find the 6th term of the geometric sequence 10, 6.4, . . .

$$\begin{aligned} a_n &= a_1 \cdot r^{n-1} & &\text{Use the explicit formula.} \\ a_6 &= 10 \cdot 0.64^{6-1} & &\text{Substitute } a_1 = 10, n = 6, \text{ and } r = 0.64. \\ &= 10 \cdot 0.64^5 & &\text{Simplify the exponent.} \\ &\approx 1.07 & &\text{Use a calculator.} \end{aligned}$$

After five reductions of 64%, the photograph is about 1 in. long.

 **Quick Check** ② Find the 19th term in each sequence.
a. 11, 33, 99, 297, . . .   **b.** 20, 17, 14, 11, 8, . . .

The graphs of arithmetic and geometric sequences have different shapes.

To review exponential curves, go to Lesson 8–2.

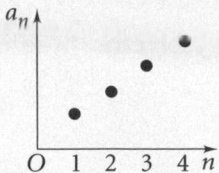

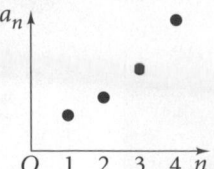

Arithmetic graphs are linear.   Geometric graphs are exponential.

You can find the **geometric mean** of any two positive numbers by taking the positive square root of the product of the two numbers.

$$\text{geometric mean} = \sqrt{\text{product of the two numbers}}$$

You can use the geometric mean to find a missing term of a geometric sequence.

3 EXAMPLE Real-World Connection

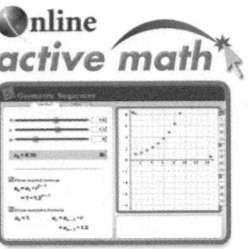

For: Sequences Activity
Use: Interactive Textbook, 11-3

Physics When a child swings without being pushed, air resistance causes the length of the arc of the swing to decrease geometrically. Find the missing arc length.

Find the geometric mean of the two arc lengths.

$$\begin{aligned}\text{geometric mean} &= \sqrt{8 \cdot 6\tfrac{1}{8}}\\ &= \sqrt{49}\\ &= 7\end{aligned}$$

8 ft
■ ft
$6\tfrac{1}{8}$ ft

On the second swing, the length of the arc is 7 ft.

 **Quick Check** ❸ Find the missing term of each geometric sequence. It could be the geometric mean or its opposite.
a. $20, ■, 80, \ldots$ **b.** $3, ■, 18.75, \ldots$ **c.** $28, ■, 5103, \ldots$

EXERCISES

For more exercises, see *Extra Skill and Word Problem Practice.*

Practice and Problem Solving

 Practice by Example

Example 1
(page 613)

 for Help

Is the sequence geometric? If so, find the common ratio and the next two terms.

1. $1, 2, 4, 8, \ldots$

2. $1, 2, 3, 4, \ldots$

3. $1, -2, 4, -8, \ldots$

4. $-1, 1, -1, 1, \ldots$

5. $10, 4, 1.6, 0.64, \ldots$

6. $7, 0.7, 0.07, 0.007, \ldots$

7. $18, -6, 2, -\tfrac{2}{3}, \ldots$

8. $1, \tfrac{1}{2}, \tfrac{1}{3}, \tfrac{1}{4}, \ldots$

9. $10, 15, 22.5, 33.75, \ldots$

10. $2, -10, 50, -250, \ldots$

11. $-1, -6, -36, -216, \ldots$

12. $\tfrac{1}{2}, \tfrac{1}{4}, \tfrac{1}{6}, \tfrac{1}{8}, \ldots$

Example 2
(page 613)

Write the explicit formula for each sequence. Then generate the first five terms.

13. $a_1 = 5, r = -3$ **14.** $a_1 = 0.0237, r = 10$ **15.** $a_1 = \frac{1}{2}, r = \frac{2}{3}$

16. $a_1 = 1, r = 0.5$ **17.** $a_1 = 100, r = -20$ **18.** $a_1 = 7, r = 1$

19. $a_1 = 1024, r = 0.5$ **20.** $a_1 = 4, r = 0.1$ **21.** $a_1 = 10, r = -1$

Example 3
(page 614)

Find the missing term of each geometric sequence. It could be the geometric mean or its opposite.

22. 5, ■, 911.25, . . . **23.** 9180, ■, 255, . . . **24.** $\frac{2}{5}$, ■, $\frac{8}{45}$, . . .

25. 3, ■, 0.75, . . . **26.** 5, ■, 2.8125, . . . **27.** 12, ■, 3, . . .

 Apply Your Skills

Identify each sequence as *arithmetic*, *geometric*, or *neither*. Then find the next two terms.

28. 45, 90, 180, 360, . . . **29.** 25, 50, 75, 100, . . . **30.** 3, −3, 3, −3, . . .

31. 30, 35, 40, 45, . . . **32.** −5, 10, −20, 40, . . . **33.** 2, 1, 0.5, 0.25, . . .

34. 5, 6, 8, 11, 15, . . . **35.** 2, 2, 2, 2, . . . **36.** 1, 4, 9, 16, . . .

Find the missing terms of each geometric sequence. (*Hint:* The geometric mean of the first and fifth terms is the third term. Some terms might be negative.)

37. 19,683; ■; ■; ■; 243; . . . **38.** 2.5, ■, ■, ■, 202.5, . . .

39. 12.5, ■, ■, ■, 5.12, . . . **40.** −4, ■, ■, ■, $-30\frac{3}{8}$, . . .

 **GO for Help**

For a guide to solving
Exercise 37, see p. 618.

41. a. Open-Ended Choose two positive numbers. Find their geometric mean.
  b. Find the common ratio for a geometric sequence that includes the terms from part (a) in order from least to greatest or from greatest to least.
  c. Find the 9th term of the geometric sequence from part (b).
  d. Find the geometric mean of the term from part (c) and the first term of your sequence. What term of the sequence have you just found?

For the geometric sequence 3, 12, 48, 192, . . . , find the indicated term.

42. 5th term **43.** 7th term **44.** 10th term

45. 14th term **46.** 17th term **47.** nth term

Find the 10th term of each geometric sequence.

48. $a_9 = 8, r = \frac{1}{2}$ **49.** $a_{11} = 8, r = \frac{1}{2}$

50. $a_9 = -5, r = -\frac{1}{2}$ **51.** $a_{11} = -5, r = -\frac{1}{2}$

52. $a_9 = -\frac{1}{3}, r = \frac{1}{2}$ **53.** $a_{11} = -\frac{1}{3}, r = \frac{1}{2}$

 nline
Homework Video Tutor
Visit: PHSchool.com
Web Code: age-1103

54. Writing Describe the similarities and differences between a common difference and a common ratio.

 **Challenge** 🌐 **55. Banking** Copy and complete the table below. Use the geometric mean. Assume compound interest is earned and no withdrawals are made.

Period 1	$140.00	$600.00	$25.00	$57.50	$100.00	$250.00
Period 2	■	■	■	■	■	■
Period 3	$145.64	$627.49	$32.76	$60.37	$111.98	$276.55

56. Golf Each of the putts misses the hole and continues past it for half the distance.

    a. Write a sequence to represent the ball's distance from the hole before each of his first six putts.

    b. Is this sequence geometric? Explain your reasoning.

    c. Write a recursive formula for the sequence.

57. Critical Thinking How are the formulas for a geometric sequence similar to the formulas for an arithmetic sequence?

58. Suppose a balloon is filled with 5000 cm^3 of helium. It then loses one fourth of its helium each day.

    a. Write the geometric sequence that shows the amount of helium in the balloon at the start of each day for five days.

    b. What is the common ratio of the sequence?

    c. How much helium will be left in the balloon at the start of the tenth day?

    d. Graph the sequence. Then sketch the graph.

    e. Critical Thinking How does the common ratio affect the shape of the graph?

Find a_1 for a geometric sequence with the given terms.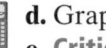

59. $a_5 = 112$ and $a_7 = 448$ **60.** $a_9 = \frac{1}{2}$ and $a_{12} = \frac{1}{16}$

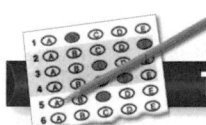

Test Prep

Multiple Choice

61. Which geometric sequence DOES NOT include the term 100?

    A. 5, 10, 20, . . .   **B.** 337.5, 225, 150, . . .

    C. $a_1 = 25, a_n = 2a_{n-1}$ **D.** $a_n = 4 \cdot 5^n$

62. What is the product of the geometric mean of 2 and 32 and the geometric mean of 1 and 4?

    F. 16   **G.** 19   **H.** 32   **J.** 256

63. Find the common ratio in the geometric sequence 4, 10, 25, 62.5, . . .

    A. 0.4   **B.** 2.5   **C.** 15   **D.** 25

64. What is the geometric mean of 8 and 18?

    F. 12   **G.** 13   **H.** 26   **J.** 36

65. Find the missing term in the geometric sequence 8, ■, 0.5, −0.125, . . .

    A. 2   **B.** −2   **C.** 4   **D.** −4

66. The first term of a geometric sequence is 1 and its common ratio is 6. What is the sixth term?

    F. 31   **G.** 3176   **H.** 7776   **J.** 46,656

Short Response

67. The first term of a geometric sequence is −1. The common ratio is −5. Find the eighth term in the sequence.

68. The sixth term in a geometric sequence is 120. The seventh term is 40. What is the first term in the sequence?

69. Which is greater, the geometric mean of 4 and 16 or the arithmetic mean of 4 and 16? Show your work.

Extended Response
70. In a geometric sequence, $a_1 = 3$ and $a_4 = 192$. Explain how to find a_2 and a_3.

Mixed Review

Lesson 11-2 Write an explicit and a recursive formula for each arithmetic sequence.

71. $-3, 0, 3, 6, \ldots$ **72.** $17, 8, -1, \ldots$ **73.** $-2, -13, -24, \ldots$

Lesson 10-3 Write an equation of the circle with the given center and radius. Graph the circle.

74. center $(0, 0)$, radius 3 **75.** center $(-3, 1)$, radius 5 **76.** center $(1, 1)$, radius 2

Lesson 9-3 Find the vertical asymptotes of each function.

77. $y = \frac{x-3}{x+3}$ **78.** $y = \frac{x-3}{x+1}$ **79.** $y = \frac{x-3}{x(x-1)}$

✓ Checkpoint Quiz 1   Lessons 11-1 through 11-3

Identify each sequence as *arithmetic* or *geometric*. Then find the common difference or common ratio.

1. $15, 30, 45, 60, \ldots$ **2.** $2, 6, 18, 54, \ldots$ **3.** $37, 34, 31, 28, 25, \ldots$

4. $700, 350, 175, 87.5, \ldots$ **5.** $8, -4, 2, -1, 0.5, \ldots$ **6.** $4, 2, 0, -2, -4, \ldots$

Find the fifth term of each sequence.

7. $a_1 = 100, a_n = \frac{1}{2}a_{n-1}$ **8.** $a_1 = 2, a_n = 3a_{n-1} - 2$ **9.** $a_n = -n + 6$

10. Writing Explain how to compute the arithmetic mean and the geometric mean of two terms of a sequence.

A Point in Time

1000 1200 1400 1600 1800 2000

In 1276, the Chinese astronomer Guo Shoujing built a device to study the sun. A hole in the tower of his observatory faced due south. At noon, a horizontal pole in the tower cast a shadow on a low wall that extended north from the building. Guo Shoujing learned about the sun's movements by studying the geometric pattern of the shadows on the wall.

Go Online
PHSchool.com
For: Information about techniques for measuring the sun's position
Web Code: age-2032

Understanding Math Problems Read the problem below. Then let Wanda's thinking guide you through the solution. Check your understanding with the exercises at the bottom of the page.

Find the missing terms of the geometric sequence. (*Hint:* The geometric mean of the first and fifth terms is the third term. Some terms might be negative.)

$19{,}683;$ ■; ■; ■; $243;$ …

What Wanda Thinks	What Wanda Writes
In this geometric sequence, the numbers decrease.	$19{,}683;$ ■; ■; ■; $243;$ …
	1st term $= 19{,}683$
The hint tells me information about terms in the sequence. I'll label the terms.	2nd term $=$ ■ 3rd term $=$ ■ 4th term $=$ ■ 5th term $= 243$
The hint says that the geometric mean of the first and fifth terms is the third term. That makes sense, because the third term is the middle term. I'll write that relationship and substitute.	Geometric mean of 1st and 5th terms is 3rd term 3rd term $= \sqrt{19{,}683 \cdot 243}$ 3rd term $= \sqrt{4{,}782{,}969}$
Perfect. I have the third term in the sequence.	3rd term $= 2187$
I can rewrite the sequence to include the third term.	$19{,}683;$ ■; $2187;$ ■; $243;$ …
	2nd term $= \pm\sqrt{19{,}683 \cdot 2187} = \pm 6561$
Now I can find the 2nd and 4th terms in the same way, because they are between terms I know.	4th term $= \pm\sqrt{2187 \cdot 243} = \pm 729$
I'll rewrite the sequence with the missing terms filled in.	The sequence is $19{,}683;\ 6561;\ 2187;\ 729;\ 243;$ … or $19{,}683;\ -6561;\ 2187;\ -729;\ 243;$ …

EXERCISES

Find the missing terms of each geometric sequence.

1. $12{,}312;$ ■; ■; ■; $152;$ …

2. $1.7;$ ■; ■; ■; $11{,}153.7;$ …

3. $-100;$ ■; ■; ■; $-0.16;$ …

4. $5040;$ ■; ■; ■; $\frac{35}{9};$ …

5. Critical Thinking Explain why, in the worked example above, the second and fourth terms can be both positive or both negative but the third term must be positive.

11-4 Arithmetic Series

What You'll Learn

- To write and evaluate arithmetic series
- To use summation notation

. . . And Why

To find the number of stitches in a cross-stitch pattern, as in Example 2

✓ **Check Skills You'll Need** ⬤ **for Help** Lesson 11-1

Find each sum.

1. $2 + 3.5 + 5 + 6.5 + 8$

2. $-17 + (-13) + (-9) + (-5) + (-1) + 3$

Write an explicit formula for each sequence.

3. $4, 6, 8, 10, 12, \ldots$ **4.** $1, 4, 7, 10, 13, 16, \ldots$

5. $-17, -23, -29, -35, \ldots$ **6.** $10, 1, -8, -17, \ldots$

🔊 **New Vocabulary** • series • arithmetic series • limit

---

1 ▸ Writing and Evaluating Arithmetic Series

Activity: Arithmetic Series

Use the sequence 1, 2, 3, 4, . . . , 97, 98, 99, 100 to answer each question.

1. Is it *arithmetic, geometric,* or *neither?* Justify your reasoning.

2. a. Add the first and last terms of the sequence and write down the answer. Then add the second and next-to-last terms. Continue adding terms until you get to the middle of the sequence.
   b. Reasoning What patterns do you notice in your answers to part (a)?

3. Use your answer to Question 2 to find the sum of the terms of the sequence.

4. a. Describe a short method for finding the following sum.
   $5 + 10 + 15 + 20 + 25 + 30 + 35 + 40 + 45 + 50$
   b. Find the sum.

Vocabulary Tip

<u>Ellipsis</u> points, as used here, indicate that the pattern continues.

A **series** is the expression for the sum of the terms of a sequence. Finite sequences and series have terms that you can count individually from 1 to a final whole number n. Infinite sequences and series continue without end. You indicate an infinite sequence or series with ellipsis points.

Finite sequence	**Finite series**
$6, 9, 12, 15, 18$	$6 + 9 + 12 + 15 + 18$

Infinite sequence	**Infinite series**
$3, 7, 11, 15, \ldots$	$3 + 7 + 11 + 15 + \ldots$

1 EXAMPLE   **Writing and Evaluating a Series**

Use the finite sequence 2, 11, 20, 29, 38, 47. Write the related series. Then evaluate the series.

   Related series → $2 + 11 + 20 + 29 + 38 + 47 = 147$ ← **Add to evaluate.**

● The sum of the terms of the sequence is 147.

✓ **Quick Check** **1** Write the related series for each finite sequence. Then evaluate the series.
   a. 0.3, 0.6, 0.9, 1.2, 1.5, 1.8, 2.1, 2.4, 2.7, 3.0   **b.** 100, 125, 150, 175, 200, 225

An **arithmetic series** is a series whose terms form an arithmetic sequence. When a sequence has many terms, or when you know only the first and last terms of the sequence, you can use a formula to evaluate the related series quickly.

🔑 **Key Concepts**

Property	**Sum of a Finite Arithmetic Series**

The sum S_n of a finite arithmetic series $a_1 + a_2 + a_3 + \ldots + a_n$ is

$$S_n = \frac{n}{2}(a_1 + a_n)$$

where a_1 is the first term, a_n is the nth term, and n is the number of terms.

2 EXAMPLE   **Real-World** 🌎 **Connection**

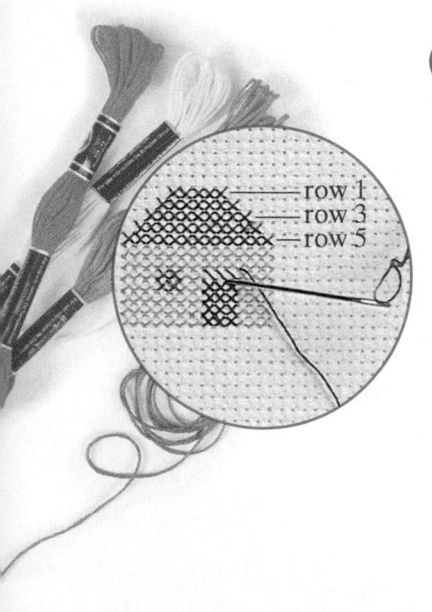
row 1
row 3
row 5

Crafts Embroidery such as cross-stitch frequently decorates table linens and clothing, although it was originally used to strengthen and repair woven fabric.

Several rows of cross-stitches make up the green roof. Find the total number of green cross-stitches in the roof.

Relate $\boxed{\text{sum of the series}}$ is $\dfrac{\boxed{\text{number of terms}}}{2}$ times $\left(\boxed{\text{the first term}} \text{ plus } \boxed{\text{the last term}} \right)$

Define   Let $\boxed{S_n}$ = total number of cross-stitches,

   and let $\boxed{n}$ = the number of rows.

   Then $\boxed{a_1}$ = the number of cross-stitches in the first row,

   and $\boxed{a_n}$ = the number of cross-stitches in the last row.

Write $S_n = \frac{n}{2}(\boxed{a_1} + \boxed{a_n})$ **Use the formula.**

   $= \frac{5}{2}(5 + 13)$ **Substitute $n = 5$, $a_1 = 5$, and $a_n = 13$.**
   $= 2.5(18)$ **Simplify.**
   $= 45$ **Multiply.**

● There are 45 cross-stitches in the green roof.

✓ **Quick Check** **2** Suppose the pattern from Example 2 extends to 14 rows of cross-stitches.
   a. Find the 14th term of the sequence.
   b. Use the formula to find the value of the series to the 14th term.

2 Using Summation Notation

Vocabulary Tip

Σ is the Greek capital letter <u>sigma</u>, the equivalent of the English letter S (for summation).

You can use the summation symbol Σ to write a series. Then you can use limits to indicate how many terms you are adding. **Limits** are the least and greatest integral values of n.

upper limit, greatest value of n ———————— explicit formula for the sequence

$$\sum_{n=1}^{3} (5n + 1)$$

lower limit, least value of n ————

3 EXAMPLE Writing a Series in Summation Notation

Use summation notation to write the series $3 + 6 + 9 + \ldots$ for 33 terms.

$3 \cdot 1 = 3, 3 \cdot 2 = 6, 3 \cdot 3 = 9, \ldots$ **The explicit formula for the sequence is 3n.**

$3 + 6 + 9 + \ldots + 99 = \sum_{n=1}^{33} 3n$ **The lower limit is 1 and the upper limit is 33.**

✓ **Quick Check** ③ Use summation notation to write each series for the specified number of terms.
  a. $1 + 2 + 3 + \ldots ; n = 6$
  b. $3 + 8 + 13 + 18 + \ldots ; n = 9$

To expand a series from summation notation, you can substitute each value of n into the explicit formula and add the results.

4 EXAMPLE Finding the Sum of a Series

GO ⬤nline

Video Tutor Help
Visit: PHSchool.com
Web Code: age-0775

Use the series $\sum_{n=1}^{3} (5n + 1)$.

a. Find the number of terms in the series.
  Since the values of n are 1, 2, and 3, there are three terms in the series.

b. Find the first and last terms of the series.
  The first term of the series is $5n + 1 = 5(1) + 1 = 6$.
  The last term of the series is $5n + 1 = 5(3) + 1 = 16$.

c. Evaluate the series.

$\sum_{n=1}^{3} (5n + 1) = (5(1) + 1) + (5(2) + 1) + (5(3) + 1)$ **Substitute.**

$= 6 + 11 + 16$ **Simplify within parentheses.**

$= 33$ **Add.**

⬤ The sum of the series is 33.

✓ **Quick Check** ④ For each sum, find the number of terms, the first term, and the last term. Then evaluate the series.

a. $\sum_{n=1}^{10} (n - 3)$ **b.** $\sum_{n=1}^{4} \left(\frac{1}{2}n + 1\right)$ **c.** $\sum_{n=2}^{5} n^2$

EXERCISES

For more exercises, see *Extra Skill and Word Problem Practice.*

Practice and Problem Solving

 A **Practice by Example**

Example 1
(page 620)

 **for Help**

Write the related series for each finite sequence. Then evaluate each series.

1. $21, 18, 15, 12, 9, 6, 3$

2. $-5, -15, -25, -35, -45$

3. $100, 99, 98, \ldots, 95$

4. $0.5, 0.25, 0, \ldots, -0.75$

5. $17.3, 19.6, 21.9, 24.2, 26.5$

6. $4.5, 5.6, 6.7, \ldots, 11.1$

Example 2
(page 620)

Each sequence has eight terms. Evaluate each related series.

7. $\frac{1}{2}, \frac{3}{2}, \frac{5}{2}, \ldots, \frac{15}{2}$

8. $1, -1, -3, \ldots, -13$

9. $5, 13, 21, \ldots, 61$

10. $-3.5, -1.25, 1, \ldots, 12.25$

11. $1765, 1414, 1063, \ldots, -692$

12. $-13, -14.5, -16, \ldots, -23.5$

Example 3
(page 621)

Use summation notation to write each arithmetic series for the specified number of terms.

13. $2 + 4 + 6 + \ldots; n = 4$

14. $8 + 9 + 10 + \ldots; n = 8$

15. $5 + 6 + 7 + \ldots; n = 7$

16. $1 + 4 + 7 + 10 + \ldots; n = 11$

17. $7 + 14 + 21 + \ldots; n = 15$

18. $(-3) + (-6) + (-9) + \ldots; n = 5$

Example 4
(page 621)

For each sum, find the number of terms, the first term, and the last term. Then evaluate the series.

19. $\displaystyle\sum_{n=1}^{5} (2n - 1)$

20. $\displaystyle\sum_{n=1}^{5} (-2n - 1)$

21. $\displaystyle\sum_{n=3}^{8} (7 - n)$

22. $\displaystyle\sum_{n=1}^{5} (0.2n - 0.2)$

23. $\displaystyle\sum_{n=2}^{10} \frac{4n}{3}$

24. $\displaystyle\sum_{n=5}^{10} (20 - n)$

B **Apply Your Skills**

Tell whether each list is a *sequence* or a *series*. Then tell whether it is *finite* or *infinite*.

25. $1, 2, 4, 8, 16, 32, \ldots$

26. $1, 0.5, 0.25, 0.125, 0.0625$

27. $5 + 10 + \ldots + 25$

28. $-0.5 - 0.25 - 0.125 - \ldots$

29. $\frac{4}{3}, \frac{7}{3}, \frac{10}{3}, \frac{13}{3}, \frac{16}{3}, \ldots$

30. $2.3 + 4.6 + 9.2 + 18.4$

31. Architecture A 20-row theater has three sections of seating. In each section, the number of seats in a row increases by one with each successive row. The first row of the middle section has 10 seats. The first row of each of the two side sections has 4 seats.

 a. Find the total number of chairs in each section. Then find the total seating capacity of the theater.

 b. Write an arithmetic series to represent each section.

 c. After every five rows, the ticket price goes down by $5. Front-row tickets cost $60. What is the total amount of money generated by a full house?

Real-World **Connection**

The seats in a theater are staggered so people don't block the view of those in the row behind them.

32. a. Consider the finite arithmetic series $10 + 13 + 16 + \ldots + 31$. How many terms are in it? Explain.

 b. Evaluate the series.

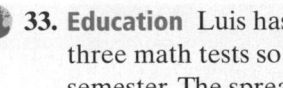 **33. Education** Luis has taken three math tests so far this semester. The spreadsheet shows his grades.

	A	B	C	D	
1	Student Name	Test 1	Test 2	Test 3	
2	Luis Ortez	75	79	83	
3	Marie Bova	78	85	84	
4	Lasheha Brown	87	82	91	

a. Suppose his test grades continue to improve at the same rate. What will be his grade on the fifth (and final) test?

b. What will his test average be for this grading period? (Assume each test is worth 100 points.)

34. a. A supermarket displays cans in a triangle. Write an explicit formula for the sequence of the number of cans.

b. Use summation notation to write the related series for a triangle with 10 cans in the bottom row.

c. Suppose the triangle had 17 rows. How many cans would be in the 17th row?

d. Critical Thinking Could the triangle have 110 cans? 140 cans? Justify your reasoning.

Evaluate each series to the given term.

35. $2 + 4 + 6 + 8 + \ldots$; 10th term

36. $-5 - 25 - 45 - \ldots$; 9th term

37. $2 + 3 + 4 + 5 + \ldots$; 100th term

38. $\frac{5}{2} + 1 - \frac{1}{2} - 2 - \ldots$; 8th term

39. $0.17 + 0.13 + 0.09 + 0.05 + \ldots$; 12th term

40. $1500 + 1499 + 1498 + 1497 + \ldots$; 1000th term

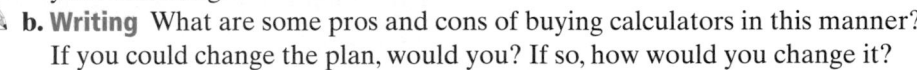 **41. Technology** A school committee has decided to spend a large portion of its annual technology budget on graphing calculators. This year, the technology coordinator bought 75 calculators, and plans to buy 25 new calculators each year from now on.

a. Suppose the school committee has decided that each student in the school should have access to a graphing calculator within seven years. The school population is 500. Will the technology coordinator meet this goal? Explain your reasoning.

b. Writing What are some pros and cons of buying calculators in this manner? If you could change the plan, would you? If so, how would you change it?

42. a. Open-Ended Write two explicit formulas for arithmetic sequences.

b. Write the first five terms of each related series.

c. Use summation notation to rewrite each series.

d. Evaluate each series.

C Challenge

Use the values of a_1 and S_n to find the value of a_n.

43. $a_1 = 4$ and $S_{40} = 6080$; a_{40}

44. $a_1 = -6$ and $S_{50} = -5150$; a_{50}

Find a_1 for each arithmetic series.

45. $S_8 = 440$ and $d = 6$

46. $S_{30} = 240$ and $d = -2$

47. Evaluate S_{10} for the series $x + (x + y) + (x + 2y) + \ldots$

48. Evaluate S_{15} for the series $3x + (3x - 2y) + (3x - 4y) + \ldots$

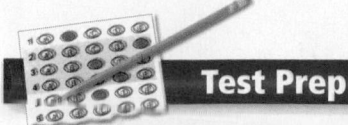
Multiple Choice

49. Which expression represents the sum $10 + 20 + 30 + 40$?

      I. $\displaystyle\sum_{n=1}^{4} 10n$ **II.** $\displaystyle\sum_{n=10}^{40} 10n$ **III.** $10\left(\displaystyle\sum_{n=1}^{4} n\right)$

    A. I and II only   **B.** I and III only   **C.** II and III only   **D.** I, II, and III

50. What is the value of $\displaystyle\sum_{n=1}^{5} (2n - 3)$?

    F. 6   **G.** 15   **H.** 17   **J.** $10n - 15$

51. Which expression defines the series $14 + 20 + 26 + 32 + 38 + 44 + 50$?

    A. $\displaystyle\sum_{n=2}^{8} (7n - 1)$ **B.** $\displaystyle\sum_{n=3}^{8} (6n - 4)$ **C.** $\displaystyle\sum_{n=3}^{9} (6n - 4)$ **D.** $\displaystyle\sum_{n=8}^{14} (n + 6)$

52. Which expression represents a series with 12 terms?

    F. $\displaystyle\sum_{n=3}^{12} 12n$ **G.** $\displaystyle\sum_{n=3}^{14} \left(\dfrac{n+4}{2}\right)$ **H.** $\displaystyle\sum_{n=9}^{21} (3n - 6)$ **J.** $\displaystyle\sum_{n=1}^{11} \dfrac{n}{2}$

53. Which expression represents the sum of the finite series $13 + 10 + 7 + 4$?

    I. $\displaystyle\sum_{n=1}^{4} (16 - 3n)$ **II.** $\displaystyle\sum_{n=3}^{6} (22 - 3n)$ **III.** $\displaystyle\sum_{n=1}^{4} (4 + 3n)$

    A. I and II   **B.** I and III   **C.** II and III   **D.** I, II, and III

54. The first term of an arithmetic series is 123. The common difference is 12, and the sum 1320. How many terms are in the series?

    F. 10   **G.** 9   **H.** 8   **J.** 7

Short Response

55. Write an expression for the sum of a 6-term arithmetic sequence with first term of 3 and a common difference of 4. Then find the sum.

56. Evaluate the series $\displaystyle\sum_{n=1}^{40} \left(10 - \dfrac{n}{2}\right)$ Show your work.

57. The 30th term of a finite arithmetic series is 4.4. The sum of the first 30 terms is 78. What is the first term of the series?

Mixed Review

GO for Help

Lesson 11-3

Write the explicit formula for each geometric sequence. Then generate the first three terms.

58. $a_1 = 1, r = 2$ **59.** $a_1 = 1, r = 5$ **60.** $a_1 = -1, r = -1$

61. $a_1 = 3, r = \dfrac{3}{2}$ **62.** $a_1 = -7, r = 0.1$ **63.** $a_1 = 20, r = -0.5$

Lesson 10-1

Graph each equation. Describe each graph and its lines of symmetry. Give the domain and range for each graph.

64. $x^2 + 3y^2 = 36$ **65.** $x^2 - y^2 = 25$ **66.** $x^2 + y^2 = 4$

Lesson 9-4

Simplify each rational expression.

67. $\dfrac{x^2 + 4x + 3}{x^2 - 3x - 4}$ **68.** $\dfrac{c^2 - 8c + 12}{c^2 - 11c + 30}$ **69.** $\dfrac{3z^4 + 36z^3 + 60z^2}{3z^3 - 3z^2}$

Geometry and Infinite Series

You can use geometric figures to model some infinite series.

1 ACTIVITY Modeling an Infinite Series

Geometry Draw a geometric figure to model the series.
$$\frac{1}{2} + \left(\frac{1}{2}\right)^2 + \left(\frac{1}{2}\right)^3 + \ldots + \left(\frac{1}{2}\right)^n + \ldots$$

Use a square grid. Shade one half of the grid. Then shade one half of the remaining area. Continue until the grid is full.

So the series

$$\frac{1}{2} + \left(\frac{1}{2}\right)^2 + \left(\frac{1}{2}\right)^3 + \ldots + \left(\frac{1}{2}\right)^n + \ldots$$

● appears to have a sum of 1.

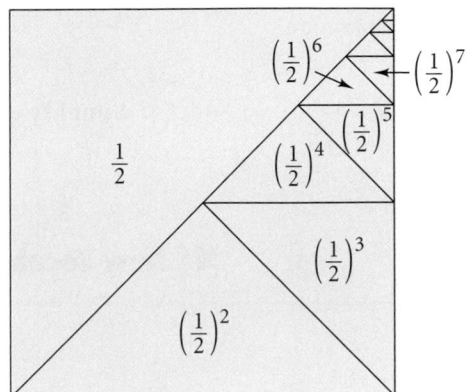

You can write an infinite series from a geometric model.

2 ACTIVITY Writing an Infinite Series

Geometry Write the series modeled by the trapezoids. Estimate the sum of the series. Explain your reasoning.

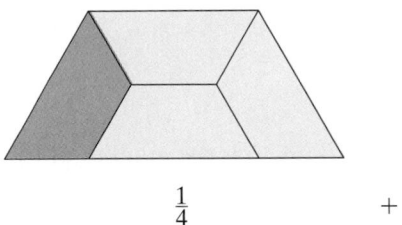 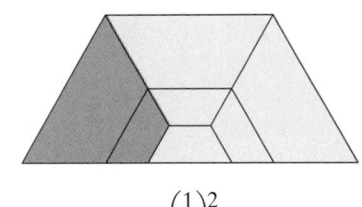 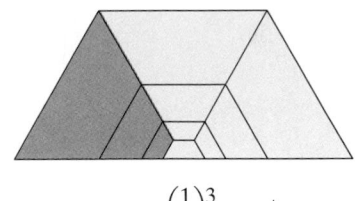

$$\frac{1}{4} \quad + \quad \left(\frac{1}{4}\right)^2 \quad + \quad \left(\frac{1}{4}\right)^3 \quad + \ldots$$

The red area approaches one third of the figure.
● So the series $\frac{1}{4} + \left(\frac{1}{4}\right)^2 + \left(\frac{1}{4}\right)^3 + \ldots + \left(\frac{1}{4}\right)^n + \ldots$ appears to have a sum of $\frac{1}{3}$.

EXERCISES

1. a. Write the series modeled by the figure at the right.
  b. Evaluate the series. Explain your reasoning.

2. Draw a figure to model the series. Begin with a 10×10 square.
$$\frac{1}{5} + \left(\frac{1}{5}\right)^2 + \left(\frac{1}{5}\right)^3 + \ldots + \left(\frac{1}{5}\right)^n + \ldots$$

3. Make a Conjecture Consider the series
$$\frac{1}{c} + \left(\frac{1}{c}\right)^2 + \left(\frac{1}{c}\right)^3 + \ldots + \left(\frac{1}{c}\right)^n + \ldots$$
What is the sum of the series? Explain your reasoning.

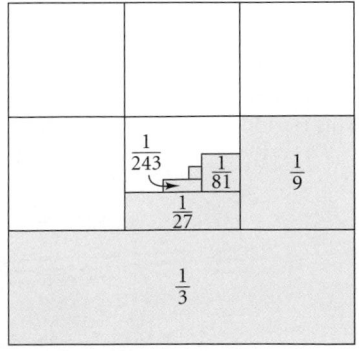

Geometric Series

11-5

What You'll Learn

- To evaluate a finite geometric series
- To evaluate an infinite geometric series

...And Why

To find the length of a chambered nautilus shell, as in Example 4

✓ Check Skills You'll Need

GO for Help   Lesson 9-5

Find each sum or difference.

1. $100 + 50 + 25 + \frac{25}{2} + \frac{25}{4}$

2. $3 + 9 + 27 + 81$

3. $-2 + 4 - 8 + 16 - 32$

4. $-5 - 10 - 20 - 40$

Simplify each fraction.

5. $\dfrac{1 - \frac{1}{5}}{\frac{1}{3}}$

6. $\dfrac{1}{1 - \frac{1}{4}}$

7. $\dfrac{\frac{1}{2} - \frac{1}{3}}{\frac{1}{4}}$

8. $\dfrac{2 + \frac{1}{16}}{\frac{1}{3}}$

🔊 **New Vocabulary** • geometric series • converge • diverge

---

1 Evaluating a Finite Geometric Series

A **geometric series** is the expression for the sum of the terms of a geometric sequence. As with arithmetic series, you can use a formula to evaluate a finite geometric series.

 Key Concepts

Property	**Sum of a Finite Geometric Series**

The sum S_n of a finite geometric series $a_1 + a_2 + a_3 + \ldots + a_n, r \neq 1$, is

$$S_n = \frac{a_1(1 - r^n)}{1 - r}$$

where a_1 is the first term, r is the common ratio, and n is the number of terms.

---

1 EXAMPLE Using the Geometric Series Formula

Use the formula to evaluate the series $3 + 6 + 12 + 24 + 48 + 96$.

The first term is 3, and there are six terms in the series.

The common ratio is $\frac{6}{3} = \frac{12}{6} = \frac{24}{12} = \frac{48}{24} = \frac{96}{48} = 2$.

So $a_1 = 3, r = 2$, and $n = 6$.

GO for Help

For more practice with ratios, see Skills Handbook p. 872.

$S_n = \dfrac{a_1(1 - r^n)}{1 - r}$ **Write the formula.**

$S_6 = \dfrac{3(1 - 2^6)}{1 - 2}$ **Substitute $a_1 = 3$, $r = 2$, and $n = 6$.**

$= \dfrac{-189}{-1} = 189$ **Simplify.**

● The sum of the series is 189.

✓ **Quick Check** ① Identify a_1, r, and n for each series. Then evaluate each series.

    a. $-45 + 135 - 405 + 1215 - 3645$ **b.** $\frac{1}{3} + \frac{1}{9} + \frac{1}{27} + \frac{1}{81}$

You can use the formula to solve problems involving geometric series.

② EXAMPLE   Real-World Connection

Financial Planning In March, the Floyd family starts saving for a vacation at the end of August. The Floyds expect the vacation to cost $1375. They start with $125. Each month they plan to deposit 20% more than the previous month. Will they have enough money for their trip?

Relate $S_n = \dfrac{a_1(1 - r^n)}{1 - r}$ Write the formula for the sum of a geometric series.

Define S_n = total amount saved

       $a_1 = 125$ initial amount

       $r = 1.2$ common ratio

       $n = 6$ number of months (March through August)

Write $S_6 = \dfrac{125(1 - 1.2^6)}{1 - 1.2}$ Substitute.

           $= 1241.24$ Simplify.

The final balance will be $1241.24. The Floyds will *not* have enough money for their trip in August.

Real-World Connection

Careers Financial planners use math to help families plan savings for college, retirement, and vacations.

✓ **Quick Check** ② **a.** **Reasoning** Explain how the common ratio 1.2 was found.

    b. Suppose each month the Floyds deposit 25% more than the previous month. Describe how this changes the problem.

    c. At this rate of saving, will they have enough money for their trip? Explain.

2   Evaluating an Infinite Geometric Series

In some cases you can evaluate an infinite geometric series. When $|r| < 1$, the series **converges,** or gets closer and closer, to the sum S. When $|r| \geq 1$, the series **diverges,** or approaches no limit.

③ EXAMPLE   Determining Divergence and Convergence

Decide whether each infinite geometric series *diverges* or *converges*. State whether the series has a sum.

Vocabulary Tip

In $\sum\limits_{n=1}^{\infty}$, the symbol for infinity ∞ indicates that the series continues without end.

a. $1 - \frac{1}{3} + \frac{1}{9} - \ldots$

    $a_1 = 1, a_2 = -\frac{1}{3}$

    $r = -\frac{1}{3} \div 1 = -\frac{1}{3}$

    Since $|r| < 1$, the series converges, and the series has a sum.

b. $\sum\limits_{n=1}^{\infty} 5(2)^{n-1}$

    $a_1 = 5(2^0) = 5, a_2 = 5(2^1) = 10$

    $r = 10 \div 5 = 2$

    Since $|r| \geq 1$, the series diverges, and the series does not have a sum.

✓ **Quick Check** ③ Determine whether each infinite series converges or diverges.

    a. $1 + \frac{1}{5} + \frac{1}{25} + \ldots$ **b.** $4 + 8 + 16 + \ldots$

Key Concepts

| **Definition** | **Sum of an Infinite Geometric Series** |

An infinite geometric series with $|r| < 1$ converges to the sum

$$S = \frac{a_1}{1 - r}$$

where a_1 is the first term and r is the common ratio.

You can use the sum formula to evaluate some infinite geometric series.

 **4 EXAMPLE** **Real-World Connection**

27 mm

Multiple Choice The length of the outside shell of each closed chamber of a chambered nautilus is 0.9 times the length of the larger chamber next to it. What is the best estimate for the total length of the outside shell for the enclosed chambers?

- (A) 24.3 mm
- (B) 30 mm
- (C) 243 mm
- (D) 270 mm

The outside edge of the largest enclosed chamber is 27 mm long, so $a_1 = 27$.

$$S = \frac{a_1}{1 - r} \quad \textbf{Use the formula.}$$

$$= \frac{27}{1 - 0.9} \quad \textbf{Substitute.}$$

$$= 270 \quad \textbf{Simplify.}$$

The estimate for the length is 270 mm. The correct choice is D.

 **Quick Check** ④ Evaluate each infinite geometric series.

a. $1 + \frac{1}{2} + \frac{1}{4} + \frac{1}{8} + \dots$

b. $3 - \frac{3}{2} + \frac{3}{4} - \frac{3}{8} + \dots$

EXERCISES

For more exercises, see *Extra Skill and Word Problem Practice*.

Practice and Problem Solving

  **Practice by Example**

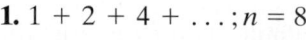 **Evaluate the finite series for the specified number of terms.**

Examples 1 and 2
(pages 626 and 627)

1. $1 + 2 + 4 + \dots; n = 8$ **2.** $4 + 12 + 36 + \dots; n = 6$

GO for Help

3. $3 + 6 + 12 + \dots; n = 7$ **4.** $7 - 35 + 175 - \dots; n = 5$

5. $-5 - 10 - 20 - \dots; n = 11$ **6.** $-\frac{1}{6} + 1 - 6 + 36 - \dots; n = 5$

7. $\frac{1}{2} + \frac{1}{4} + \frac{1}{8} + \dots; n = 8$ **8.** $1 - 3 + 9 - 27 + \dots; n = 8$

Example 3
(page 627)

Decide whether each infinite geometric series *diverges* or *converges*. State whether each series has a sum.

9. $1 + \frac{1}{4} + \frac{1}{16} + \dots$ **10.** $1 - \frac{1}{2} + \frac{1}{4} - \dots$ **11.** $4 + 2 + 1 + \dots$

12. $1 + 2 + 4 + \dots$ **13.** $6 + 18 + 54 + \dots$ **14.** $-54 - 18 - 6 - \dots$

15. $1 - 1 + 1 - \dots$ **16.** $1 + \frac{1}{5} + \frac{1}{25} + \dots$ **17.** $\frac{1}{4} + \frac{1}{2} + 1 + 2 + \dots$

Example 4
(page 628)

Evaluate each infinite geometric series.

18. $1.1 + 0.11 + 0.011 + \ldots$

19. $1.1 - 0.11 + 0.011 - \ldots$

20. $1 - \frac{1}{5} + \frac{1}{25} - \frac{1}{125} + \ldots$

21. $3 + 1 + \frac{1}{3} + \frac{1}{9} + \ldots$

22. $3 + 2 + \frac{4}{3} + \frac{8}{9} + \ldots$

23. $3 - 2 + \frac{4}{3} - \frac{8}{9} + \ldots$

B **Apply Your Skills**

Determine whether each series is *arithmetic* or *geometric*. Then evaluate the finite series for the specified number of terms.

24. $2 + 4 + 8 + 16 + \ldots; n = 10$

25. $2 + 4 + 6 + 8 + \ldots; n = 20$

26. $-5 + 25 - 125 + 625 - \ldots; n = 9$

27. $6.4 + 8 + 10 + 12.5 + \ldots; n = 7$

28. $1 + 2 + 3 + 4 + \ldots; n = 1000$

29. $81 + 27 + 9 + 3 + \ldots; n = 200$

 30. Communications Many companies use a telephone chain to notify employees of a closing due to bad weather. Suppose the first person in the chain calls four people. Then each of these people calls four others, and so on.
   a. Make a tree diagram to show the first three stages in the telephone chain. How many calls are made at each stage?
   b. Write the series that represents the total number of calls made through the first six stages.
   c. How many employees have been notified after stage six?

 31. The graph shows the sum of the first n terms in the series with $a_1 = 20$ and $r = 0.9$.
   a. Write the first four terms of the series.
   b. Use the graph to evaluate the series to the 47th term.
   c. Write and evaluate the formula for the sum of the series.
   d. Graph the sum using the window values shown. Use the graph to verify your answer to part (c).

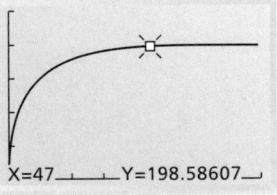

X=47   Y=198.58607

Xmin=0   Ymin=0
Xmax=94   Ymax=250
Xscl=10   Yscl=50

Evaluate each infinite series that has a sum.

32. $\displaystyle\sum_{n=1}^{\infty} \left(\frac{1}{5}\right)^{n-1}$

33. $\displaystyle\sum_{n=1}^{\infty} 3\left(\frac{1}{4}\right)^{n-1}$

34. $\displaystyle\sum_{n=1}^{\infty} \left(-\frac{1}{3}\right)^{n-1}$

35. $\displaystyle\sum_{n=1}^{\infty} 7(2)^{n-1}$

36. $\displaystyle\sum_{n=1}^{\infty} (-0.2)^{n-1}$

37. $\displaystyle\sum_{n=1}^{\infty} 2(1.2)^{n-1}$

38. A bouncing ball reaches heights of 16 cm, 12.8 cm, and 10.24 cm on three consecutive bounces.
   a. If the ball started at a height of 25 cm, how many times has it bounced when it reaches a height of 16 cm?
   b. Write a geometric series for the downward distances the ball travels from its release at 25 cm.
   c. Write a geometric series for the upward distances the ball travels from its first bounce.
   d. Find the total vertical distance the ball travels before it comes to rest.

GO **Online**
Homework Video Tutor
Visit: PHSchool.com
Web Code: age-1105

39. Open-Ended Write an infinite geometric series that converges to 3. Use the formula to evaluate the series.

40. a. A classmate uses the formula for the sum of an infinite geometric series to evaluate $1 + 1.1 + 1.21 + 1.331 + \ldots$ and gets -10. Is your classmate's answer reasonable? Explain.
  b. Error Analysis What did your classmate fail to check before using the formula?

Critical Thinking Find the specified value for each infinite geometric series.

41. $a_1 = 12, S = 96$; find r.

42. $S = 12, r = \frac{1}{6}$; find a_1.

43. Writing Suppose you are to receive an allowance each week for the next 26 weeks. Would you rather receive (a) $1000 per week or (b) 2¢ the first week, 4¢ the second week, 8¢ the third week, and so on for the 26 weeks? Justify your answer.

44. The sum of an infinite geometric series is twice its first term.
  a. Error Analysis A student says the common ratio of the series is $\frac{3}{2}$. What is the student's error?
  b. Find the common ratio of the series.

 **Challenge**

Technology Create a spreadsheet to evaluate the first n terms of each series. Determine whether each infinite series converges to a sum. If so, estimate the sum.

45. $\displaystyle\sum_{n=1}^{\infty} \frac{1}{2^n}$

46. $\displaystyle\sum_{n=1}^{\infty} \frac{100}{n}$

47. $\displaystyle\sum_{n=1}^{\infty} \frac{1}{(n-1)!}$

48. Physics Because of friction and air resistance, each swing of a pendulum is a little shorter than the previous one. The lengths of the swings form a geometric sequence. Suppose the first swing of a pendulum has a length of 100 cm and the return swing is 99 cm.
  a. On which swing will the arc first have a length less than 50 cm?
  b. Find the total distance traveled by the pendulum until it comes to rest.

49. a. Show that the infinite geometric series $0.142857 + 0.000000142857 + \ldots$ has a sum of $\frac{1}{7}$.
  b. Find the fraction form of the repeating decimal $0.428571428571\ldots$

50. The function $S(n) = \dfrac{10(1 - 0.8^n)}{0.2}$ represents the sum of the first n terms of an infinite geometric series.
  a. What is the domain of the function?
  b. Find $S(n)$ for $n = 1, 2, 3, \ldots, 10$. Sketch the graph of the function.
  c. Find the sum S of the infinite geometric series.

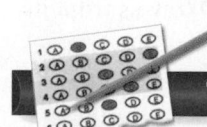

Test Prep

Gridded Response

51. What is the common ratio for the geometric series $\displaystyle\sum_{n=1}^{10} 7\left(\frac{4}{7}\right)^{n-1}$? Enter your answer as a fraction.

52. What is the common ratio in a geometric series if $a_2 = \frac{2}{5}$ and $a_5 = \frac{16}{135}$? Enter your answer as a fraction.

53. Evaluate the infinite geometric series $\frac{2}{5} + \frac{4}{25} + \frac{8}{125} + \ldots$ Enter your answer as a fraction.

54. Find the sum of the two infinite series $\sum\limits_{n=1}^{\infty} \left(\frac{2}{3}\right)^{n-1}$ and $\sum\limits_{n=1}^{\infty} \left(\frac{2}{3}\right)^{n}$.

55. Evaluate the sum $\sum\limits_{n=1}^{3} \left(\frac{1}{n+1}\right)^{2}$. Enter your answer as a decimal to the nearest hundredth.

56. Car 1 cost $22,600 when new and depreciated 14% each year for 5 years. The same year, Car 2 cost $17,500 when new and depreciated 7% each year for 5 years. To the nearest dollar, what was the difference in the values of the two cars after 5 years?

Mixed Review

Lesson 11-4

Evaluate each series to the given term.

57. $12.5 + 15 + 17.5 + 20 + 22.5 + \ldots$; 7th term

58. $-100 - 95 - 90 - 85 - \ldots$; 11th term

59. $-17 - 11 - 5 + 1 + 7 + 13 + \ldots$; 25th term

Lesson 10-2

Identify the focus and directrix of each parabola. Then graph the parabola.

60. $y = \frac{1}{16}x^2$ **61.** $x = -\frac{1}{4}y^2$ **62.** $x^2 = -9y$

Lesson 9-5

Add or subtract. Simplify where possible.

63. $\frac{7}{2c} - \frac{2}{c^2}$ **64.** $\frac{5}{y+3} + \frac{15}{y-3}$

65. $\frac{4}{x^2 - 36} + \frac{x}{x-6}$ **66.** $\frac{15}{3-d} - \frac{-3}{9-d^2}$

✓ Checkpoint Quiz 2   Lessons 11-4 through 11-5

Determine whether each series is *arithmetic* or *geometric*. Then evaluate the finite series for the specified number of terms.

1. $1 + 3 + 5 + 7 + \ldots$; $n = 30$ **2.** $1 + 3 + 9 + 27 + \ldots$; $n = 10$

3. $-4 - 2 - 1 - 0.5 - \ldots$; $n = 7$ **4.** $500 + 380 + 260 + 140 + \ldots$; $n = 6$

5. $120 + 60 + 30 + 15 + \ldots$; $n = 8$ **6.** $-175 - 50 + 75 + 200 + \ldots$; $n = 12$

Evaluate each infinite geometric series.

7. $\sum\limits_{n=1}^{\infty} \left(\frac{1}{15}\right)^{n-1}$ **8.** $\sum\limits_{n=1}^{\infty} 2(0.5)^{n-1}$

9. Open-Ended Write a finite geometric series with a sum less than 1.

10. Critical Thinking Can an infinite arithmetic series converge? Explain. Do not consider the series $0 + 0 + \ldots = 0$.

Consider the pattern in the following statements.

1	= 1
1 + 3	= 4
1 + 3 + 5	= 9
1 + 3 + 5 + 7	= 16
1 + 3 + 5 + 7 + 9	= 25

If this pattern continues without end, then the statement

$$1 + 3 + 5 + 7 + \ldots + (2n - 1) = n^2$$

is true for all positive integers n.

The general statement above is true for the first several values of n. There is, however, no number of examples that would prove it true for all positive integers. To prove such a statement true for all positive integers, you can use a method called mathematical induction.

Theorem	**Principle of Mathematical Induction**

Let S be a statement involving a positive integer n.

Then S is true for all positive integers if the following two conditions hold.

1. S is true for $n = 1$.

2. For any positive integer k, if S is true for k, then S is true for $k + 1$.

The principle of mathematical induction is like a chain reaction in an infinite line of dominoes. Proving that a statement is true for $n = 1$ is like knocking over the first domino. Knowing that if the statement is true for any value of k then it will be true for $k + 1$ is like knowing that if any domino is knocked over the one after it will be knocked over also.

EXAMPLE **Using Mathematical Induction**

Prove that the following statement is true for all positive integers n.

$1 + 3 + 5 + \ldots + (2n - 1) = n^2$

Proof First show that the statement is true for $n = 1$.

$2n - 1 = n^2$	**Use the statement.**
$2(1) - 1 \stackrel{?}{=} 1^2$	**Substitute 1 for n.**
$2 - 1 \stackrel{?}{=} 1^2$	**Multiply.**
$1 = 1 ✓$	**Simplify.**

The statement is true for $n = 1$.

Next, assume that the statement is true for k.

$$1 + 3 + 5 + \ldots + (2k - 1) = k^2$$

From this assumption, prove that the statement is true for $k + 1$.

$1 + 3 + 5 + \ldots + [2(k + 1) - 1] \overset{?}{=} (k + 1)^2$	**Write the statement for $k + 1$.**
$1 + 3 + 5 + \ldots + (2k + 1) \overset{?}{=} (k + 1)^2$	**Simplify the left side.**
$1 + 3 + 5 + \ldots + (2k - 1) + (2k + 1) \overset{?}{=} (k + 1)^2$	**Rewrite to show the odd number preceding $(2k + 1)$.**
$k^2 + (2k + 1) \overset{?}{=} (k + 1)^2$	**Substitute from the assumption.**
$(k + 1)^2 = (k + 1)^2 \checkmark$	**Factor the left side.**

The proof shows that conditions 1 and 2 of the principle of mathematical induction are true. By the principle, then, $1 + 3 + 5 + \ldots + (2n - 1) = n^2$ is true for all positive integers, which is what we wanted to prove.

EXERCISES

1. Test the statement from the example to verify that it is true for $n = 6, 7$, and 8.

2. Complete the mathematical induction steps below to prove that
$$2 + 4 + 6 + \ldots + 2n = n(n + 1)$$
is true for all positive integers n.
   a. Show that the statement is true for $n = 1$.
   b. What statement will you assume to be true?
   c. What statement will you prove true using the assumption from part (b)?
   d. Express the sum in your statement from part (c) in terms of what you assumed. Then substitute and simplify to complete the proof.

Use mathematical induction to prove that each statement is true for all positive integers n.

3. $\dfrac{1}{1 \cdot 2} + \dfrac{1}{2 \cdot 3} + \dfrac{1}{3 \cdot 4} + \ldots + \dfrac{1}{n(n + 1)} = \dfrac{n}{n + 1}$

4. $1 + 2 + 3 + \ldots + n = \dfrac{n(n + 1)}{2}$

5. $1 + 4 + 7 + \ldots + (3n - 2) = \dfrac{n(3n - 1)}{2}$

6. $\dfrac{1}{2} + \left(\dfrac{1}{2}\right)^2 + \left(\dfrac{1}{2}\right)^3 + \left(\dfrac{1}{2}\right)^4 + \ldots + \left(\dfrac{1}{2}\right)^n = 1 - \left(\dfrac{1}{2}\right)^n$

7. $n^2 + n$ is divisible by 2.

8. $1 \cdot 2 + 2 \cdot 3 + 3 \cdot 4 + \ldots + n(n + 1) = \dfrac{n(n + 1)(n + 2)}{3}$

9. $1^2 + 2^2 + 3^2 + \ldots + n^2 = \dfrac{n(n + 1)(2n + 1)}{6}$

10. $a_1 + a_1r + a_1r^2 + a_1r^3 + \ldots + a_1r^{n-1} = \dfrac{a_1(1 - r^n)}{1 - r}, r \neq 1$

(This is the formula for the sum of a finite geometric series, page 626.)

11. $1^3 + 2^3 + 3^3 + \ldots + n^3 = (1 + 2 + 3 + \ldots + n)^2$

You can use a graphing calculator to evaluate finite series.

1 ACTIVITY Using the Sum Feature

Find the sum of the terms of the sequence: 15, 30, 45, 60, 75, 90, 105.

Step 1 Enter the sequence in a list. Exit using **QUIT**.

Step 2 Select 5 from the **MATH** menu of the **LIST** feature.

Step 3 Enter the list number. Press **ENTER**.

L1	L2	L3
15	-------	-------
30		
45		
60		
75		
90		
105		

L1(7)=105

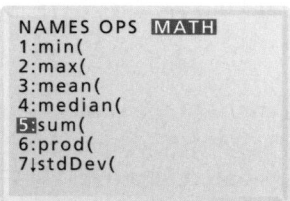

NAMES OPS **MATH**
1:min(
2:max(
3:mean(
4:median(
5:sum(
6:prod(
7↓stdDev(

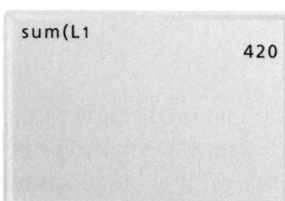

sum(L1
420

The sum of the series $15 + 30 + 45 + \ldots + 105$ is 420.

2 ACTIVITY Evaluating a Finite Series

Use your graphing calculator to evaluate $\sum_{n=1}^{5} \frac{n^2}{2}$.

Step 1 Access the **SUM** feature (Step 2 above).

Step 2 Select 5 from the **OPS** menu of the **LIST** feature.

Step 3 Enter the explicit formula, N, the lower limit, the upper limit, and 1 (to increase N by 1 each time). Press **ENTER**.

sum(■

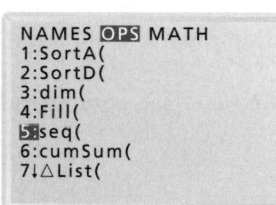

NAMES **OPS** MATH
1:SortA(
2:SortD(
3:dim(
4:Fill(
5:seq(
6:cumSum(
7↓△List(

sum(seq (N2/2,N,1
,5,1)
27.5

The value of $\sum_{n=1}^{5} \frac{n^2}{2}$ is 27.5.

EXERCISES

Evaluate each series.

1. $595 + 495 + 395 + 295$

2. $3 + 9 + 27 + 81$

3. $4 + 2 + 1 + \ldots + \frac{1}{8}$

4. $\sum_{n=1}^{5} (2n^2 - 5)$

5. $\sum_{x=1}^{5} 2^x$

6. $\sum_{n=1}^{5} -\sqrt{n^2}$

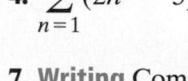

7. Writing Compare the methods in Activities 1 and 2. When would you use the method from Activity 1? When would you use the method from Activity 2? Explain.

Area Under a Curve

What You'll Learn

• To find area under a curve

. . . And Why

To estimate the distance traveled by a peregrine falcon, as in Example 1

Find the area of a rectangle with the given length and width.

1. $\ell = 4$ ft, $w = 1$ ft

2. $\ell = 5.5$ m, $w = 0.5$ m

3. $\ell = 6.2$ cm, $w = 0.1$ cm

4. $\ell = 9\frac{1}{2}$ in., $w = 3\frac{5}{8}$ in.

🔊 **New Vocabulary**   • inscribed rectangles   • circumscribed rectangles

---

1 Finding Area Under a Curve

You can easily calculate the exact area under part of a line parallel to the x-axis, but it is not so easy to calculate the exact area under part of a curve. You can use rectangles to estimate the area under a curve and analyze data.

Inscribed rectangles are completely under the curve. The approximation is less than the area.

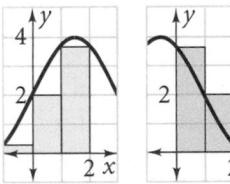

Circumscribed rectangles are partially above the curve. The approximation is greater than the area.

1 EXAMPLE   Real-World Connection

Data Analysis The curve at the right approximates the speed of a peregrine falcon during the first 20 s of a high-speed dive.

a. What does the area under the curve represent?

$$\text{area} = \frac{\text{meters}}{\text{second}} \cdot \text{seconds} \qquad \textbf{Use dimensional analysis.}$$

$$= \text{meters} \qquad \textbf{Simplify.}$$

The area under the curve approximates the total distance traveled by the peregrine falcon.

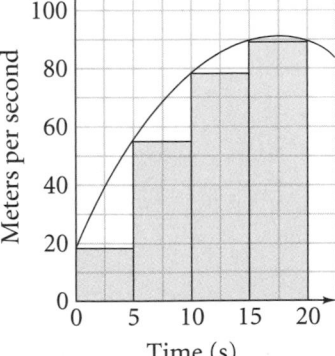

b. Use inscribed rectangles 5 units wide to estimate the area under the curve.

Width of each rectangle ⌐   ⌐ Total area

$$5(18) + 5(54) + 5(78) + 5(89) = 1195$$

↑   ↑   ↑   ↑

Value of curve at upper edge of each rectangle

The area under the curve is about 1195 units². The peregrine falcon traveled about 1195 m during the first 20 s of its dive. The estimate is low because inscribed rectangles were used.

Real-World Connection

Adult peregrine falcons can reach speeds of 200 mi/h in a dive.

① The graph at the right shows the curve from Example 1, but it shows circumscribed rectangles.

a. Estimate the area under the curve using circumscribed rectangles. How does your answer differ from the answer to Example 1?

b. Critical Thinking Find the mean of the answer using inscribed rectangles and the answer using circumscribed rectangles. Of the three answers, which is likely the most accurate? Explain.

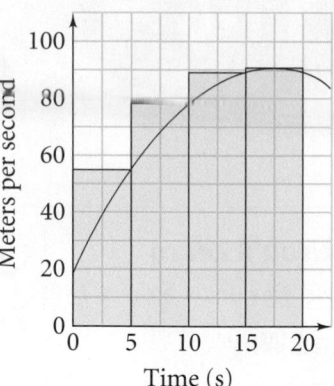

You can use summation notation to represent the area of a series of rectangles and to approximate the area under the curve $f(x)$. Let a_n represent the x-value of a point on the base of the nth rectangle.

$$A = \sum_{n=1}^{b} (w)f(a_n)$$

number of rectangles

width of each rectangle ⎯⎯⎯⎯ ⎣⎯ function value at a_n

The expression $f(a_n)$ gives the height of the nth rectangle.

② **EXAMPLE** **Using a Sum to Estimate Area Under a Curve**

For: Area Under a Curve Activity
Use: Interactive Textbook, 11-6

Estimate the area under the curve $f(x) = -x^2 + 5$ for the domain $0 \le x \le 2$ by evaluating the sum A.

$$A = \sum_{n=1}^{4} (0.5)f(a_n)$$

Evaluate the function at the right side of each rectangle.

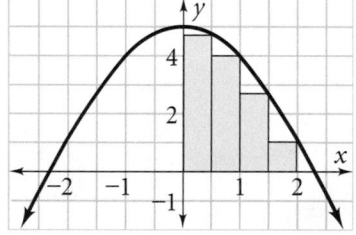

$a_1 = 0.5, a_2 = 1, a_3 = 1.5, a_4 = 2$ **Use the x-values on the right side of each rectangle.**

$A = 0.5f(0.5) + 0.5f(1) + 0.5f(1.5) + 0.5f(2)$ **Add the areas of the rectangles.**

$= 0.5(4.75 + 4 + 2.75 + 1)$ **total area = width of each rectangle · sum of the heights**

$= 0.5(12.5)$ **Add within parentheses.**

$= 6.25$ **Simplify.**

● The indicated area is about 6.25 units^2.

✓ **Quick Check** **②** **a.** Sketch the graph from Example 2 and draw circumscribed rectangles for the domain $0 \le x \le 2$.

b. Critical Thinking To find the area using these rectangles, you should evaluate the function at the left side of each rectangle. Explain why.

c. Use the circumscribed rectangles to write and evaluate a sum that approximates the area under the curve for the domain $0 \le x \le 2$. Compare your answer to the answer in Example 2.

You can use a graphing calculator to find the exact area under a curve.

3 EXAMPLE Using a Graphing Calculator

Graph the function $f(x) = -2x^2 + 5$. Find the area under the curve for the domain $-1 \le x \le 1.5$.

Step 1 Input the equation. Adjust the window values.

Step 2 Access the $\int f(x)dx$ feature from the CALC menu.

Step 3 Use the lower limit of $x = -1$.

Step 4 Use the upper limit of $x = 1.5$.

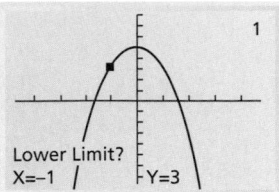

Xmin=–4.7   Ymin=–7
Xmax=4.7   Ymax=8
Xscl=1   Yscl=1

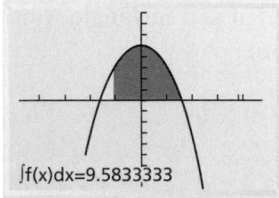

$\int f(x)dx=9.5833333$

Graphing Calculator Hint

To move the cursor by tenths along the x-axis, set your x window values to multiples of 4.7 or press ZOOM 4.

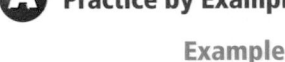

● The area under the curve between $x = -1$ and $x = 1.5$ is about 9.583 units^2.

✓ Quick Check ③ Use the equation from Example 3 and a graphing calculator. Find the area under the curve for each domain.
a. $0 \le x \le 1$ **b.** $-1 \le x \le 1$ **c.** $-1.5 \le x \le 0$

EXERCISES

For more exercises, see *Extra Skill and Word Problem Practice.*

Practice and Problem Solving

A Practice by Example

Example 1
(page 635)

GO for Help

Given each set of axes, what does the area under the curve represent?

1. y-axis: production rate, x-axis: time

2. y-axis: rate of growth, x-axis: time

3. y-axis: miles per gallon, x-axis: gallons

4. y-axis: distance traveled per year, x-axis: years

5. y-axis: price per pound of gold, x-axis: pounds of gold

Use the given rectangles to estimate area under the curve.

6.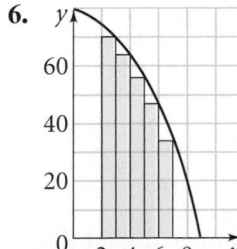

7.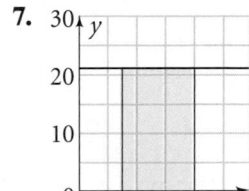

8.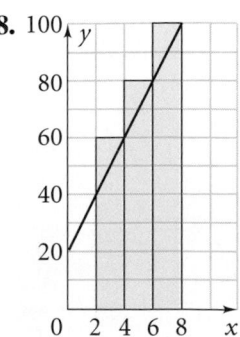

Example 2
(page 636)

Write and evaluate a sum to estimate the area under each curve for the domain $0 \le x \le 2$.
a. Use inscribed rectangles 1 unit wide.
b. Use circumscribed rectangles 1 unit wide.

9. $f(x) = \frac{1}{2}x^2$ **10.** $y = -x^2 + 5$ **11.** $g(x) = x^2 + 1$

12. $y = -x^2 + 4$ **13.** $y = \frac{2}{3}x^2 + 5$ **14.** $h(x) = 5x^2$

15. $y = 4 - \frac{1}{4}x^2$ **16.** $h(x) = -(x-2)^2 + 5$ **17.** $y = (x-2)^2 + 2$

Example 3
(page 637)

 **Find the area under each curve for the domain $0 \le x \le 1$.**

18. $y = -x^2 + 2$ **19.** $f(x) = x + 2$ **20.** $y = x^3$

21. $y = -x^4 + 2x^3 + 3$ **22.** $y = x^5 - x^2 + 2.5$ **23.** $y = -(x-1)^3 + 3$

B   **Apply Your Skills**

Graph each curve. Use inscribed rectangles to approximate the area under the curve for the interval and rectangle width given.

24. $y = x^2 + 1, 1 \le x \le 3, 0.5$ **25.** $y = 3x^2 + 2, 2 \le x \le 4, 1$

26. $y = x^2, 3 \le x \le 5, 0.5$ **27.** $y = 2x^2, 3 \le x \le 5, 1$

28. $y = x^3, 1 \le x \le 3, 0.25$ **29.** $y = x^2 + 4, -2 \le x \le 2, 0.5$

GO Online
Homework Video Tutor
Visit: PHSchool.com
Web Code: age-1106

30. a. Graph the curve $y = \frac{1}{3}x^3$.
   b. Use inscribed rectangles to approximate the area under the curve for the interval $0 \le x \le 3$ and rectangle width of 1 unit.
   c. Repeat part (b) using circumscribed rectangles.
   d. Find the mean of the areas you found in parts (b) and (c). Of the three estimates, which best approximates the area for the interval? Explain.

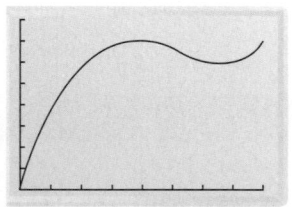

31. The graph at the left approximates the speed of a car as it enters a highway from a stopped position and merges with traffic. The x-axis represents time in seconds, and the y-axis represents miles per hour.
   a. Copy the graph. Use inscribed rectangles half the width of a grid square to estimate the total distance the car traveled in 50 s.
   b. Writing How does your choice of inscribed or circumscribed rectangles in part (a) affect your area estimate?

Xmin: 0   Ymin: 0
Xmax: 200   Ymax: 70
Xscl: 25   Yscl: 10

 **Evaluate the area under each curve for $-1 \le x \le 2$.**

32. $f(x) = -x^2 + 4$ **33.** $y = (x - 0.5)^2 + 1.75$ **34.** $g(x) = 2 + 3x^2$

35. $y = \sqrt{1 + x}$ **36.** $g(x) = 2^x + 1$ **37.** $y = x^3 + 2$

38. $y = -(x - 1)^2 + 4\frac{1}{3}$ **39.** $h(x) = \sqrt{x^2}$ **40.** $f(x) = -x^4 + 2x^3 + 3$

41. Open-Ended Write equations for three curves that are positive for $1 \le x \le 3$. Use your graphing calculator to find the area under each curve for this domain.

C   **Challenge**

42. Approximate the area under the curve $f(x) = x^2$ for the interval $0 \le x \le 4$ by evaluating each sum. Use inscribed rectangles.

   a. $\displaystyle\sum_{n=1}^{8} (0.5)f(a_n)$ **b.** $\displaystyle\sum_{n=1}^{4} (1)f(a_n)$

   c. Which estimate is closer to the actual area under the curve? Explain.

43. a. Graph $y = \frac{1}{4}x^3 + 1$ and $y = 1$ over the domain $-4.7 \le x \le 4.7$.
   b. Critical Thinking Evaluate the area under each curve for the interval $-1.5 \le x \le 1.5$. What do you notice? Explain.

44. Critical Thinking Use your graphing calculator to find the area of the triangle with vertices $(-3, 0), (-1, 3),$ and $(1, 0)$. (*Hint:* First find the function whose graph makes a peak at $(-1, 3)$.)

45. a. Write the equation $\frac{x^2}{25} + \frac{y^2}{9} = 1$ in calculator-ready form.
   b. Graph the top half of the ellipse. Calculate the area under the curve for the interval $-5 \leq x \leq 5$.
   c. Use symmetry to find the area of the entire ellipse.
   d. Open-Ended Find the area of another symmetric shape by graphing part of it. Sketch your graph and show your calculations.

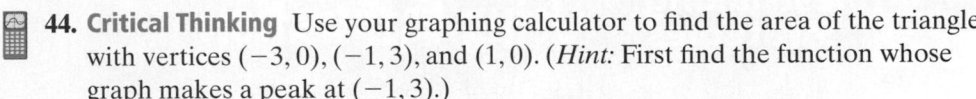

Test Prep

Multiple Choice

Use the graph of $f(x) = \sqrt{x} + 2$ for Exercises 46–49.

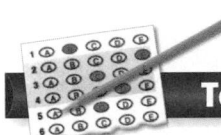

46. Which series represents the area of four inscribed rectangles?
   A. $(1)(2) + (1)(3) + (1)(3.4) + (1)(3.7)$
   B. $(1)(3) + (1)(3.4) + (1)(3.7) + (1)(4)$
   C. $(1 + 2 + 3 + 4)(0 + 1 + 2 + 3)$
   D. $(1 + 2 + 3 + 4)(3 + 3.4 + 3.7 + 4)$

47. Which series represents the area of four circumscribed rectangles?
   F. $(1)(2) + (1)(3) + (1)(3.4) + (1)(3.7)$
   G. $(1)(3) + (1)(3.4) + (1)(3.7) + (1)(4)$
   H. $(1 + 2 + 3 + 4)(0 + 1 + 2 + 3)$
   J. $(1 + 2 + 3 + 4)(3 + 3.4 + 3.7 + 4)$

48. Which of the following is the most accurate value of the area under $f(x) = \sqrt{x} + 2$ for $0 \leq x \leq 4$?
   A. 12.1   **B.** 14.1   **C.** 16.1   **D.** 24.0

49. Which expression does NOT represent a reasonable estimate of the area under $f(x) = \sqrt{x} + 2$ for $0 \leq x \leq 4$?
   F. $\sum_{n=1}^{4} f(a_n)$ **G.** $\sum_{n=1}^{5} (0.2)f(a_n)$ **H.** $\sum_{n=1}^{8} (0.5)f(a_n)$ **J.** $\sum_{n=1}^{10} (0.4)f(a_n)$

Short Response

50. The area under a curve is estimated using inscribed rectangles and circumscribed rectangles. Explain why the mean of these two values might be a more accurate estimate than either one.

Mixed Review

GO for **Help**

Lesson 11-5

Determine whether the sum of each infinite geometric series exists.

51. $4 + 2 + 1 + \frac{1}{2} + \frac{1}{4} + \ldots$ **52.** $-972 - 324 - 108 - \ldots$

Lesson 10-5

Write the equation of each hyperbola in standard form. Sketch the graph.

53. $9x^2 - 16y^2 = 144$ **54.** $x^2 - 25y^2 = 25$ **55.** $16x^2 - 10y^2 = 160$

Lesson 9-6

Solve each equation. Check your solution.

56. $\frac{x}{4} = \frac{x-3}{8}$ **57.** $\frac{5}{2-x} = \frac{4}{2x+1}$ **58.** $\frac{x}{x+1} - \frac{x}{x-3} = 9$

Estimating the answer to a test question may help you eliminate one or more answers, find the answer, or check your answer.

1 EXAMPLE

A ball drops from a height of 2 m. After it hits the floor, it rebounds to 60% of its previous height. Find the total distance the ball travels before it comes to rest.

    Ⓐ 3 m   Ⓑ 3.5 m   Ⓒ 5 m   Ⓓ 10 m   Ⓔ 20 m

Estimate the distance the ball travels before the second bounce. The ball rebounds about one-half its previous height, so it travels down 2 m, then up about 1 m, and then down about 1 m. Since $2 + 1 + 1 = 4$, the ball travels about 4 m before the second bounce. You can eliminate answer choices A and B.

Since the distance the ball travels on each bounce models a geometric sequence with $r < 1$, the final answer will be closer to 4 than to 10. The answer is C.

2 EXAMPLE

A student jogs 3.8 mi around a local reservoir five afternoons a week. The student claims to have run about 990 mi around the reservoir last year. Is the student correct? Explain.

$3.8 \cdot 5 \cdot 52 \approx 4 \cdot 5 \cdot 50$ **distance · days per week · weeks per year**

        $= 20 \cdot 50 = 1000$ **Simplify and multiply.**

The student ran about 1000 mi around the reservoir last year. The student is correct.

EXERCISES

1. A square is inscribed in a circle. The square has side length 4 cm. What is the best estimate for the area of the circle?

    Ⓐ 50 cm^2 Ⓑ 25 cm^2 Ⓒ 16 cm^2 Ⓓ 15 cm^2 Ⓔ 12 cm^2

2. Which is the best approximation of the area of the region between the graph of $y = (x - 1)^2$, the x-axis, and the y-axis?

    Ⓐ 2 units^2 Ⓑ 1.5 units^2 Ⓒ 1 units^2 Ⓓ 0.8 units^2 Ⓔ 0.5 units^2

3. Which estimate is closest to the sum $1 + \frac{1}{4} + \frac{1}{16} \cdots + \frac{1}{1024}$?

    Ⓐ 2.00   Ⓑ 1.50   Ⓒ 1.33   Ⓓ 0.5   Ⓔ 0.33

Estimate the answer to each problem.

4. Suppose your aunt gives you $100 on your birthday, along with a promise to give you one half the previous year's amount each year until the amount reaches 1¢. What is the total amount of money that your aunt will give you?

5. If two numbers a and b are approximately equal, their arithmetic mean and their geometric mean are approximately equal. Use this fact to estimate the value of $\sqrt{56}$.

Chapter Review

Vocabulary Review

arithmetic mean (p. 607)
arithmetic sequence (p. 606)
arithmetic series (p. 620)
circumscribed rectangles (p. 635)
common difference (p. 606)
common ratio (p. 612)

converge (p. 627)
diverge (p. 627)
explicit formula (p. 602)
geometric mean (p. 614)
geometric sequence (p. 612)
geometric series (p. 626)

inscribed rectangles (p. 635)
limit (p. 621)
recursive formula (p. 602)
sequence (p. 600)
series (p. 619)
term (p. 600)

Go Online
PHSchool.com

For: Vocabulary quiz
Web Code: agj-1151

Choose the correct vocabulary term to complete each sentence.

1. When using Σ to write a series, you can use __?__ to indicate how many terms you are adding.

2. Using __?__ to approximate the area under a curve will result in an approximation that is greater than the area.

3. An ordered list of terms is a __?__ .

4. If an infinite geometric series __?__ , then it must have a sum.

5. There is a __?__ between consecutive terms in a geometric sequence.

Skills and Concepts

11-1 Objectives

▼ To identify mathematical patterns (p. 600)

▼ To use a formula for finding the nth term of a sequence (p. 602)

A **sequence** is an ordered list of numbers called **terms**. A **recursive formula** gives the first term and defines the other terms in a sequence by relating each term to the one before it. An **explicit formula** expresses the nth term in a sequence in terms of n, where n is a positive integer.

Write a recursive formula for each sequence. Then find the next three terms.

6. $5, 22, 39, 56, \ldots$ 7. $1, -7, 49, -343, \ldots$ 8. $-2, 7, 16, 25, \ldots$

Write an explicit formula for each sequence. Then find a_{12}.

9. $1, 4, 7, 10, \ldots$ 10. $2, 4, 8, 16, \ldots$ 11. $-24, -6, 24, 66, \ldots$

 12. **Writing** Explain how you decide whether a formula is explicit or recursive.

11-2 Objectives

▼ To identify and generate arithmetic sequences (p. 606)

In an **arithmetic sequence,** the difference between consecutive terms is constant. The difference is the **common difference.** A recursive formula for an arithmetic sequence is $a_n = a_{n-1} + d$, given a_1. An explicit formula for an arithmetic sequence is $a_n = a_1 + (n-1)d$. In each case, a_n is the nth term, a_1 is the first term, n is the number of the term, and d is the common difference. The **arithmetic mean** of any two numbers (or terms in a sequence) is the average of the two numbers.

$$\text{arithmetic mean} = \frac{\text{sum of two numbers}}{2}$$

Is each given sequence arithmetic? If so, identify the common difference and find the 32nd term of the sequence.

13. $2, 4, 7, 10, 13, \ldots$ **14.** $3, 18, 33, 48, \ldots$ **15.** $7, 10, 13, 16, \ldots$

Find the missing term(s) of each arithmetic sequence.

16. $1, \blacksquare, 9, \ldots$ **17.** $104, \blacksquare, 99, \ldots$ **18.** $-4.6, \blacksquare, -5.2, \ldots$

19. $-1, \blacksquare, 11, \ldots$ **20.** $-13, \blacksquare, \blacksquare, \blacksquare, -3, \ldots$ **21.** $2, \blacksquare, \blacksquare, \blacksquare, -0.4, \ldots$

Find a_n, the arithmetic mean of the given terms.

22. $a_{n-1} = 7, a_{n+1} = 15$ **23.** $a_{n-1} = -2, a_{n+1} = 3$

 24. Writing Explain how you can determine if a sequence is arithmetic.

11-3 Objectives

▼ To identify and generate geometric sequences (p. 612)

In a **geometric sequence,** the ratio of consecutive terms is constant. The ratio is the **common ratio.** You can use recursive or explicit formulas to express a geometric sequence.

A recursive formula for a geometric sequence is $a_n = a_{n-1} \cdot r$, given a_1. An explicit formula for a geometric sequence is $a_n = a_1 \cdot r^{n-1}$. In each case, a_n is the nth term, a_1 is the first term, n is the number of the term, and r is the common ratio.

You can find the geometric mean of two positive numbers by taking the positive square root of the product of the two numbers.

$$\text{geometric mean} = \sqrt{\text{product of two numbers}}$$

The middle term of any three consecutive terms in a geometric sequence is the geometric mean of the first and third terms.

Is the given sequence geometric? If so, identify the common ratio, write the explicit formula for the sequence, and find the next two terms.

25. $1, \frac{1}{2}, \frac{1}{4}, \frac{1}{8}, \ldots$ **26.** $1, 3, 5, 7, \ldots$ **27.** $3, 3.6, 4.32, 5.184, \ldots$

Find the missing term(s) of each geometric sequence.

28. $3, \blacksquare, 12, \ldots$ **29.** $60, \blacksquare, \frac{20}{3}, \ldots$ **30.** $0.004, \blacksquare, 0.4, \ldots$

31. $-20, \blacksquare, \blacksquare, \blacksquare, -1.25, \ldots$ **32.** $-\frac{1}{6}, \blacksquare, \blacksquare, \blacksquare, -2\frac{2}{3}, \ldots$ **33.** $1, \blacksquare, \blacksquare, \blacksquare, 150\frac{1}{16}, \ldots$

11-4 Objectives

▼ To write and evaluate arithmetic series (p. 619)

▼ To use summation notation (p. 621)

A **series** is the expression for the sum of the terms of a sequence. Whether the sequence is finite or infinite determines whether the series is finite or infinite.

An **arithmetic series** is the expression for the sum of the terms of an arithmetic sequence. The sum S_n of the first n terms of an arithmetic series is $S_n = \frac{n}{2}(a_1 + a_n)$.

You can use a summation symbol, Σ, and **limits** to write a series. Limits are the least and greatest integral values of n.

Use summation notation to write each arithmetic series for the specified number of terms. Then evaluate the sum.

34. $10 + 7 + 4 + \ldots; n = 5$ **35.** $50 + 55 + 60 + \ldots; n = 7$

36. $6 + 7.4 + 8.8 + \ldots; n = 11$ **37.** $21 + 19 + 17 + \ldots; n = 8$

Find the number of terms in each series, the first term, and the last term. Then evaluate the sum.

38. $\displaystyle\sum_{n=1}^{3} (17n - 25)$

39. $\displaystyle\sum_{n=2}^{10} \left(\tfrac{1}{2}n + 3\right)$

40. $\displaystyle\sum_{n=5}^{15} \left(-\tfrac{2}{3}n\right)$

 41. Business Deanna Jones opened a video rental store this year with 400 tapes. She plans to buy 150 new tapes each year from now on. Deanna expects to have 1300 tapes available during her fifth year in business. At her current purchasing rate, will she reach her goal? Explain.

11-5 Objectives

▼ To evaluate a finite geometric series (p. 626)

▼ To evaluate an infinite geometric series (p. 627)

A **geometric series** is the sum of the terms of a geometric sequence. The sum S_n of the first n terms of a geometric series is $S_n = \dfrac{a_1(1 - r^n)}{1 - r}$.

You can find the sum of some infinite geometric series. When $|r| < 1$, the series gets closer and closer, or **converges,** to $S = \dfrac{a_1}{1 - r}$. When $|r| \geq 1$, the series **diverges,** or approaches no limit.

Evaluate the finite series for the specified number of terms.

42. $3 + 1 + \tfrac{1}{3} + \ldots ; n = 7$

43. $1 + 2 + 4 + \ldots ; n = 5$

44. $80 - 40 + 20 - \ldots ; n = 8$

45. $12 + 2 + \tfrac{1}{3} + \ldots ; n = 4$

Decide whether each infinite geometric series *converges* or *diverges*. Then state whether each series has a sum, and if it does, find the sum.

46. $150 + 30 + 6 + \ldots$

47. $2.2 + 2.42 + 2.662 + \ldots$

48. $-10 - 20 - 40 - \ldots$

49. $\tfrac{2}{3} + \tfrac{4}{9} + \tfrac{8}{27} + \ldots$

11-6 Objective

▼ To find the area under a curve (p. 635)

You can approximate the area under a curve by using **inscribed rectangles** or **circumscribed rectangles.** If you use inscribed rectangles, the approximation is less than the area under the curve. If you use circumscribed rectangles, the approximation is greater than the area under the curve. You can use summation notation to represent the area of a series of rectangles and the approximate area under a curve $f(x)$:

$$A = \sum_{n=1}^{b} (w)f(a_n),$$

where b is the number of rectangles, w is the width of each rectangle, a_n is the x-value of a point on the base of the nth rectangle, and $f(a_n)$ is the function value at a_n.

Write and evaluate a sum to approximate the area under each curve for the domain $0 \leq x \leq 2$.

a. Use inscribed rectangles 1 unit wide.
b. Use circumscribed rectangles 1 unit wide.
c. Use a graphing calculator to find the area under the curve.

50. $y = x^2$

51. $y = x^3 + 1$

52. $y = -2x^2 + 8$

53. $y = -x + 5$

54. $y = x^3 + 4$

55. $y = x^2 + 3$

Go Online
PHSchool.com
For: Chapter Test
Web Code: aga-1152

Write a recursive and an explicit formula for each sequence. Then find a_{12}.

1. $7, 13, 19, 25, 31, \ldots$ **2.** $10, 20, 40, 80, 160, \ldots$

3. After one month at a new job, you have saved $50. You decide to save $5 more each month.
  a. Write an explicit formula to model the amounts you save each month.
  b. How much will you save in the sixth month?

Determine whether each sequence is *arithmetic*, *geometric*, or *neither*. Then find the tenth term.

4. $23, 27, 31, 35, 39, \ldots$ **5.** $-12, -5, 2, 9, 16, \ldots$

6. $-5, 15, -45, 135, -405, \ldots$

Find the arithmetic mean a_n of the given terms.

7. $a_{n-1} = 4, a_{n+1} = 12$

8. $a_{n-1} = -11, a_{n+1} = 23$

9. Open-Ended Write an arithmetic sequence. Then write an explicit formula for it.

Determine whether each sequence is *arithmetic* or *geometric*. Then identify the common difference or the common ratio.

10. $1620, 540, 180, 60, 20, \ldots$

11. $78, 75, 72, 69, 66, 63, 60, \ldots$

12. $\frac{3}{32}, \frac{3}{16}, \frac{3}{8}, \frac{3}{4}, \frac{3}{2}, 3, 6, \ldots$

In Exercises 13–16, a_1 is the first term of a sequence, r is a common ratio, and d is a common difference. Write the first five terms.

13. $a_1 = 2, r = -2$ **14.** $a_1 = 3, d = 7$

15. $a_1 = -100, r = \frac{1}{5}$ **16.** $a_1 = 19, d = -4$

Find the missing term of each geometric sequence.

17. $2, \blacksquare, 0.5, \ldots$ **18.** $2, \blacksquare, 8, \ldots$

Find the sum of each infinite geometric series.

19. $0.5 + 0.05 + 0.005 + \ldots$

20. $1 - \frac{1}{2} + \frac{1}{4} - \ldots$ **21.** $6 + 5 + \frac{25}{6} + \ldots$

Determine whether each series is *arithmetic* or *geometric*. Then evaluate the finite series for the specified number of terms.

22. $2 + 7 + 12 + \ldots; n = 8$

23. $5000 + 1000 + 200 + \ldots; n = 15$

24. $1 + 0.01 - 0.98 - \ldots; n = 5$

For each sum, find the number of terms, the first term, and the last term. Then evaluate the sum.

25. $\sum_{n=1}^{5} (3n + 1)$ **26.** $\sum_{n=1}^{8} \frac{2n}{3}$

27. $\sum_{n=4}^{10} (0.8n - 0.4)$ **28.** $\sum_{n=2}^{6} (-2)^{n-1}$

29. Critical Thinking How can you tell whether or not a geometric series converges? Include examples of both types of series. Evaluate the series that converges.

30. Investments A diamond is purchased for $2500. Suppose its value increases 5% each year. Find the value of the diamond after 8 years.

31. Physics A ball on a pendulum moves 40 cm on its first swing. On each succeeding swing back or forth it moves 90% of the distance of the previous swing. Write the first four terms of the sequence of swing lengths.

Given each set of axes, what does the area under the curve represent?

32. y-axis: miles per hour, x-axis: hours

33. y-axis: pounds per in.^{2}, x-axis: in.^{2}

34. y-axis: dollars per gallon, x-axis: gallons

Use left endpoints in the given interval and inscribed rectangles 1 unit wide to approximate the area under the curve $y = f(x)$.

35. $y = 2x^2; 0 \le x \le 2$ **36.** $y = x^3; 1 \le x \le 3$

37. $y = x^2 + 1; -1 \le x \le 2$

38. Writing Explain how you could use circumscribed and inscribed rectangles to estimate the area under a curve.

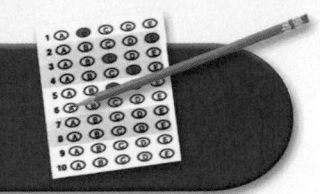
Standardized Test Prep

Reading Comprehension Read the passage below. Then answer the questions on the basis of what is *stated* or *implied* in the passage.

Arcs To cut an arc-topped shape from a rectangular board, carpenters may choose a circular arc or an elliptical arc.

Suppose the length of the board is $2m$ and the height is n.

For a circular arc, the carpenter can find the radius of the circle by using the formula $r = \frac{m^2 + n^2}{2n}$. Using a tack at the center C, and a piece of string of length r, the carpenter can draw a circular arc through points P, T, and Q.

For an elliptical arc, the carpenter can find points A and B on $\overline{PQ}$ that are $\sqrt{m^2 - n^2}$ units from point Z. Using tacks at A and B and a piece of string of length $2m$, the carpenter can draw an elliptical arc through points P, T, and Q.

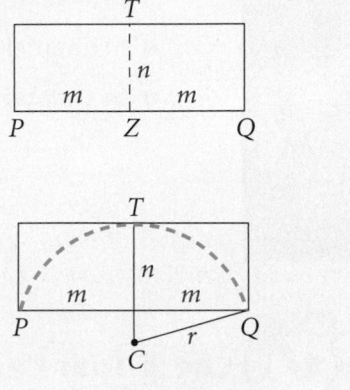

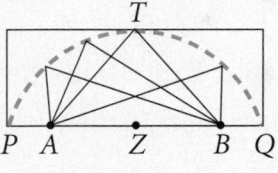

1. What is the value of PQ?
   - (A) $m + n$
   - (B) $2n$
   - (C) $2m$
   - (D) $\sqrt{m^2 + n^2}$

2. For a circular arc, what is the distance from point C to point Z?
   - (F) r
   - (G) $r - n$
   - (H) $r - m$
   - (J) $\frac{m^2 + n^2}{2n}$

3. Suppose $m = 21$ in. and $n = 7$ in. For a circular arc, what length of string should the carpenter use?
   - (A) 19.8 in.
   - (B) 22.1 in.
   - (C) 28 in.
   - (D) 35 in.

4. Suppose $\overline{PQ}$ is on the x-axis of a coordinate system and $\overline{TZ}$ is on the y-axis. What are the coordinates of the foci of the ellipse needed to draw an elliptical arc?
   - (F) $(m, 0)$ and $(-m, 0)$
   - (G) $(0, n)$ and $(0, -n)$
   - (H) $(\sqrt{m^2 + n^2}, 0)$ and $(-\sqrt{m^2 + n^2}, 0)$
   - (J) $(\sqrt{m^2 - n^2}, 0)$ and $(-\sqrt{m^2 - n^2}, 0)$

5. Suppose $m = 70$ cm and $n = 9$ cm. For an elliptical arc, what length of string should the carpenter use?
   - (A) 18 cm
   - (B) 70.58 cm
   - (C) 140 cm
   - (D) 276.72 cm

6. Use the Pythagorean Theorem and a diagram of a circular arc to derive the formula $r = \frac{m^2 + n^2}{2n}$.

7. A carpenter wants to cut the largest possible circular arc-topped shape from a board that is 40 in. by 12 in. Find the length of string the carpenter should use.

8. Using a board the same size as the one in Question 7, a carpenter wants to cut the largest possible elliptical arc-topped shape. What length of string should the carpenter use? Where should the carpenter attach the string?

9. A board is 30 in. by 15 in. Compare the largest circular and elliptical arc-topped shapes that can be cut from the board.

What You've Learned

- In Chapter 1, you learned to find theoretical and experimental probabilities.
- In Chapter 6, you learned to use the Binomial Theorem.
- In Chapter 9, you learned to find the probability of multiple events.

 **Check Your Readiness**   **for Help** to the Lesson in green.

Evaluating Expressions (Lesson 6-7)

Evaluate each expression.

1. $5!$

2. $6!$

3. $4! \cdot 3!$

4. $_5C_5$

5. $_6C_1$

6. $_7C_4$

Expanding Binomials (Lesson 6-8)

Use Pascal's Triangle or the Binomial Theorem to expand each binomial.

7. $(a + b)^5$

8. $(j + 3k)^3$

9. $(m + 0.7)^2$

10. $(0.2 + t)^6$

Finding Real Roots (Lesson 7-1)

Find the real square roots of each number. Round to the nearest thousandth.

11. $\frac{1}{100}$

12. $\frac{1}{200}$

13. $\frac{1}{250}$

14. $\frac{1}{391}$

15. $\frac{1}{435}$

16. $\frac{1}{757}$

Finding Probability (Lesson 9-7)

A and B are independent events. Find $P(A \text{ and } B)$.

17. $P(A) = 0.4, P(B) = 0.2$

18. $P(A) = 0.25, P(B) = 0.5$

19. $P(A) = 0.85, P(B) = 0.10$

20. Find $P(A \text{ or } B)$ for the events in Exercise 19.

 21. Data Analysis While processing a day's worth of new checkbook orders, a data entry operator notices that thirty percent of customers prefer the leather checkbook cover to the vinyl checkbook cover. Twenty percent prefer script lettering on their checks to any other kind of lettering. Find the probability that an order selected at random is for a leather checkbook cover with script lettering on the checks.

Probability and Statistics

LESSONS

12-1 Probability Distributions

12-2 Conditional Probability

12-3 Analyzing Data

12-4 Standard Deviation

12-5 Working With Samples

12-6 Binomial Distributions

12-7 Normal Distributions

🔊 **Key Vocabulary**

- binomial probability (p. 687)
- box-and-whisker plot (p. 662)
- conditional probability (p. 654)
- cumulative probability (p. 648)
- interquartile range (p. 669)
- margin of error (p. 679)
- measures of central tendency (p. 660)
- measures of variation (p. 669)
- normal distribution (p. 692)
- outlier (p. 664)
- percentile (p. 663)
- probability distribution (p. 649)
- quartiles (p. 662)
- sample (p. 677)
- sample proportion (p. 677)
- standard deviation (p. 669)
- standard normal curve (p. 693)
- z-score (p. 671)

What You'll Learn Next

- In Chapter 12, you will learn to make and use a probability distribution to conduct a simulation.

- You will learn to use formulas, tree diagrams, and normal distributions to find the probability of an event.

- You will learn to use measures of central tendency and measures of variation to compare data in real-world problems.

Applying what you learn, on pages 706–707 you will do activities involving trains.

Probability Distributions

What You'll Learn

- To make a probability distribution
- To use a probability distribution in conducting a simulation

... And Why

To conduct market research, as in Example 5

✓ Check Skills You'll Need

 **for Help** Lesson 1-6

Suppose you roll a standard number cube. State whether each set represents a sample space for the outcomes.

1. $\{1, 2, 3, 4, 5, 6\}$ **2.** $\{$less than $3, 4, 5, 6\}$ **3.** $\{$even, prime$\}$

Find each probability for two tosses of a number cube.

4. $P(4 \text{ and } 3)$ **5.** $P(\text{two odd numbers})$ **6.** $P(\text{two integers})$

◀)) New Vocabulary

- frequency table
- cumulative probability
- probability distribution

---

1   Making a Probability Distribution

A **frequency table** is a list of the outcomes in a sample space and the number of times each outcome occurs.

1 EXAMPLE   Making a Frequency Table

Vocabulary Tip

Scalene comes from the Latin word for uneven.

Below are three types of triangles: equilateral, isosceles, and scalene. Make a frequency table. For isosceles, use triangles with exactly two congruent sides.

Step 1 Count the number of each type.

Equilateral	ЛЖГ I
Isosceles	ЛЖГ ЛЖГ I
Scalene	ЛЖГ III
Total number of triangles: 25

Step 2 Make a table.

Type	Number
Equilateral	6
Isosceles	11
Scalene	8
Total	25

✓ Quick Check

1 The triangles in Example 1 can also be described as acute, right, and obtuse. Make a frequency table using those categories.

Probability over a continuous range of events is **cumulative probability.** You can use a frequency table to find cumulative probability.

Social Science Use the frequency table. Find the probability that an elderly person living alone will have contact with his or her children more than once a week.

Contact Between Children and Elderly Who Live Alone

How Often Contact Is Made	Number of Elderly
7 times per week	680
2–6 times per week	276
1 time per week	236
Less than 1 time per week	199
Total	1391

SOURCE: *Statistical Handbook on the American Family*

$P(\text{7 times per week}) = \frac{680}{1391}$

$P(\text{2}-\text{6 times per week}) = \frac{276}{1391}$

Find the experimental probability for each event in the table that represents contact more than once a week.

$\frac{680}{1391} + \frac{276}{1391} = \frac{956}{1391} \approx 0.687$

Add to find cumulative probability.

● The probability of contact more than once a week is about 0.687, or 68.7%.

✓ **Quick Check** **2** Find $P(\text{once a week or more})$.

A **probability distribution** is a function that gives the probability of each event in a sample space. You can use a table or a graph to show a probability distribution.

3 **EXAMPLE** Probability Distributions

Suppose you roll two number cubes. Show the probability distribution for the sum of the numbers.

Method 1 Make a frequency table. Then extend the table to include probabilities.

Rolling Two Number Cubes

Sum	2	3	4	5	6	7	8	9	10	11	12
Frequency	1	2	3	4	5	6	5	4	3	2	1
Probability	$\frac{1}{36}$	$\frac{2}{36}$	$\frac{3}{36}$	$\frac{4}{36}$	$\frac{5}{36}$	$\frac{6}{36}$	$\frac{5}{36}$	$\frac{4}{36}$	$\frac{3}{36}$	$\frac{2}{36}$	$\frac{1}{36}$

← There are 36 possible outcomes.

← Divide to find the probability.

Method 2 Draw a graph.

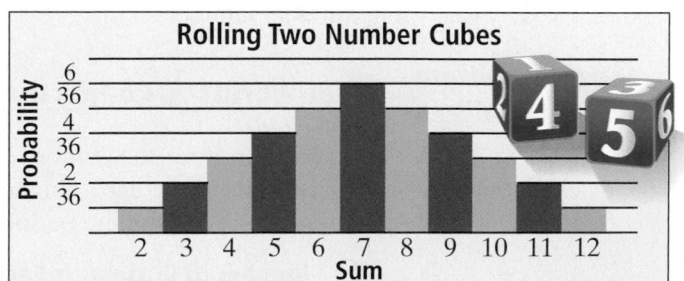

Rolling Two Number Cubes

✓ **Quick Check** **3** Use a table or a graph to show the probability distribution for the roll of one number cube.

A situation may be described by more than one sample space. In that case, each sample space has its own probability distribution.

Real-World Connection

Careers Agriculturists experiment to grow different types of crops.

4 EXAMPLE Real-World Connection

Genetics Use the information in the chart of inherited gene pairs. Graph the probability distribution for each sample space.

Inherited Gene Pairs From Two Hybrid Corn Plants

		Parent Plant	
		G	**w**
Parent Plant	**G**	GG	Gw
	w	Gw	ww

GG = dominant gene pair (green plant)
Gw = hybrid gene pair (green plant)
ww = recessive gene pair (white plant)

a. Genotype Distribution
{GG, Gw, ww}

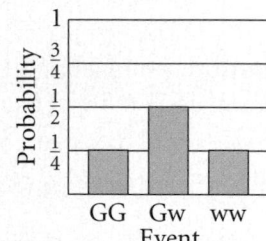

b. Plant Color Distribution
{green, white}

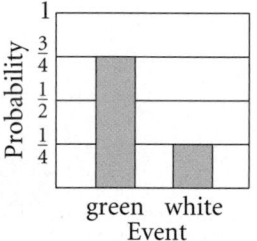

✓ Quick Check

4 a. Critical Thinking Which probability distribution would be more useful to a farmer who wants to avoid raising white corn plants? Explain.

b. Make a probability distribution table for each sample space in Example 4.

2 Using a Probability Distribution

You can design a simulation based on a probability distribution. First, use the probabilities to assign numbers to each event in the sample space. For example, if $P(\text{event}) = 0.15$, assign 15 out of 100 numbers to that event. Then you can conduct trials by generating random numbers.

5 EXAMPLE Real-World Connection

Market Research At a certain store, the number of customers c who arrive at the checkout counters each minute varies according to the distribution below. Simulate the number of customers over a ten-minute period.

Number of Customers Each Minute

c	0	1	2	3	4	5	6
P(c)	0.15	0.24	0.28	0.17	0.09	0.05	0.02

Step 1 Define how the simulation will be done. Use random numbers. Assign numbers from 1 to 100 to the events, based on the probability of each event. Use cumulative probabilities to help you assign the numbers.

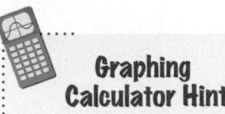
Event	Probability	Cumulative Probability	Assigned Numbers
0	0.15	0.15	01–15
1	0.24	0.39	16–39
2	0.28	0.67	40–67
3	0.17	0.84	68–84
4	0.09	0.93	85–93
5	0.05	0.98	94–98
6	0.02	1.00	99–100

Since $P(0) = 0.15$, assign 15 numbers to this outcome.

There are 17 numbers from 68 to 84.

Step 2 Conduct the simulation. Model a ten-minute period by generating ten random numbers from 1 to 100.

Minute →	1st	2nd	3rd	4th	5th	6th	7th	8th	9th	10th
Random numbers →	81	29	83	93	18	9	40	97	47	16
Number of customers →	3	1	3	4	1	0	2	5	2	1

The random number 9 is assigned to the outcome 0 customers.

Step 3 Interpret the simulation. Based on this simulation, a total of 22 customers would arrive at checkout counters over a ten-minute period.

 **Quick Check** **5** Conduct a simulation for Example 5 over a 20-minute period.

EXERCISES

For more exercises, see *Extra Skill and Word Problem Practice.*

Practice and Problem Solving

 **Practice by Example**

Example 1
(page 648)

for Help

In the game Rock-Paper-Scissors, the scissors cut the paper, the rock dulls the scissors, and the paper covers the rock. Use the results below for Exercises 1 and 2.

Rock-Paper-Scissors

Player 1	**R**	**S**	**P**	P	**S**	R	S	**S**	R	P	**S**	S	R	**S**	**P**	P	**R**	S
Player 2	S	P	R	**S**	P	**P**	**R**	R	S	R	**S**	**R**	**R**	P	P	R	**S**	S

R = Rock   P = Paper   S = Scissors   **Bold** = Winner

1. Make a frequency table for the objects played: rock, paper, or scissors.

2. Make a frequency table for the winning players: Player 1, Player 2, or tie.

Example 2
(page 649)

The table shows the frequency of responses to editorials. Find each probability.

Number of Responses	0	1	2	3	4	5	6 or more	Total
Number of Editorials	20	30	56	38	34	16	6	200

3. $P(5$ or more responses$)$ **4.** $P($at most 4 responses$)$ **5.** $P(0-2$ responses$)$

Example 3
(page 649)

6. Use a table and a graph to show the probability distribution for the spinner {red, green, blue, yellow}.

7. Use a table and a graph to show the probability distribution for the number of days {28, 29, 30, 31} in each of 48 consecutive months.

Example 4
(page 650)

Suppose you roll two number cubes. Graph the probability distribution for each sample space.

8. {sum of numbers even, sum of numbers odd}

9. {both numbers even, both numbers odd, one number even and the other odd}

Example 5
(pages 650–651)

 10. Design and conduct a simulation to determine the ages of 20 licensed drivers chosen at random in the United States.

Licensed Drivers in the United States, by Age

a	< 20	20–29	30–39	40–49	50–59	60–69	70–79	≥ 80
P(a)	0.048	0.175	0.199	0.211	0.167	0.102	0.066	0.032

SOURCE: U.S. Department of Transportation. Go to **www.PHSchool.com** for a data update. Web Code: agg-9041

11. Design and conduct a simulation to determine the size and type of 30 cars purchased from U.S. car dealerships.

U.S. Car Sales by Vehicle Size and Type

t	Luxury	Large	Midsize	Small
P(t)	0.165	0.076	0.527	0.232

SOURCE: Ward's Communications

 Apply Your Skills

Graph the probability distribution described by each function.

12. $P(x) = \frac{x}{10}$ for $x = 1, 2, 3,$ and 4

13. $P(x) = \frac{2x + 1}{15}$ for $x = 1, 2,$ and 3

 14. **Weather** Refer to the table at the left.
   a. Make a table showing the probability distribution for weather in Dayton.
   b. Define the independent and dependent variables.
   c. Find the probability that a day in Dayton will include rain or snow.

15. **Data Collection** Find weather data for a city near you. Draw a graph to show the probability distribution of weather conditions.

16. a. **Transportation** Sometimes a probability distribution is shown as a circle graph. Define the independent and dependent variables in the distribution at the right.
   b. Draw the distribution as a bar graph.
   c. Find P(the tank is at least half full when a driver buys gas).

Weather Conditions in Dayton, Ohio

Type of Weather	Days Per Year
Clear	82
Partly Cloudy	118
Mostly Cloudy	34
Rain	75
Light Snow (< 1.5 in.)	45
Snow (≥ 1.5 in.)	11
Total	365

SOURCE: *The USA Today Weather Almanac*

How Full is the Tank When People Buy Gas?

47% 16% 12% 25%

$\frac{3}{4}$ Full
$\frac{1}{2}$ Full
$\frac{1}{4}$ Full
Almost Empty

SOURCE: *The First Really Important Survey of American Habits*

17. **Writing** In a simulation, how do equally likely outcomes help you represent the probability distribution?

18. **Odds** The odds in favor of an event equal the ratio of the number of times the event occurs to the number of times the event does not occur. The odds in favor of event A are 1 : 4. The odds in favor of event B are 2 : 3. The odds in favor of event C are 1 : 3. The odds in favor of event D are 3 : 17. Graph the probability distribution of events A, B, C, and D.

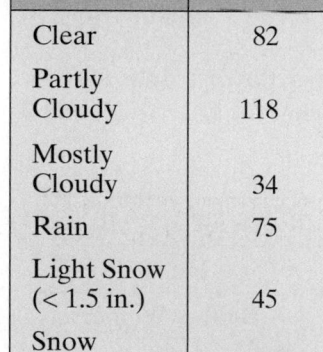

Homework Video Tutor

Visit: PHSchool.com
Web Code: age-1201

19. **Safety** The table shows data for 911 calls in a town.

 a. Conduct a simulation for the number of 911 calls over a 24-hour period.

b. If there are two response teams available, and each response takes about an hour, how many callers in your simulation have to wait?

c. Find P(caller will have to wait).

d. **Critical Thinking** Use your simulation to determine whether additional response teams are needed for this town. Explain your reasoning.

Probability Distribution for Number of 911 Calls Each Hour

c	P(c)
0	0.21
1	0.30
2	0.18
3	0.13
4	0.09
5	0.05
6	0.03
7	0.01

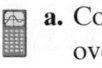 20. **Marketing** A company includes instant-win tickets with 10,000,000 of its products. Of the prizes offered, one is a large cash prize, 1,600,000 are small cash prizes, and the other prizes are free samples of the company's products.

a. Find the theoretical probability of winning each type of prize.

b. Design and conduct a simulation to determine the prizes for 100 products.

c. Find the experimental probability for winning each type of prize.

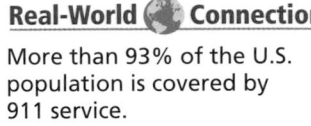

Real-World Connection

More than 93% of the U.S. population is covered by 911 service.

Test Prep

Multiple Choice

The table shows the number of cities in a region of the U.S. that are served by the given number of airlines. Use the table for Exercises 21–22.

Number of Airlines	Number of Cities
1	27
2	14
3	15
4	18
5	14
6	11

21. What is the probability that a city chosen at random is served by exactly 4 airlines?

A. $\frac{1}{18}$ B. $\frac{4}{21}$ C. $\frac{2}{11}$ D. $\frac{2}{9}$

22. What is the probability that a city chosen at random is served by at least 1 airline?

F. 0   G. $\frac{1}{99}$ H. $\frac{3}{11}$ J. 1

Extended Response

23. A spinner has 4 sections labeled A, B, C, and D. Can the spinner be designed so $P(A) = \frac{1}{12}$, $P(B) = \frac{1}{6}$, $P(C) = \frac{1}{3}$, and $P(D) = \frac{5}{12}$? If so, explain how.

Mixed Review

GO for Help

Lesson 11-6   **Find the area under each curve for the domain $0 \le x \le 1$.**

24. $y = 3$ 25. $y = 4x + 2$ 26. $y = 4x^3 + 1$

Lesson 10-6   **Sketch the graph of each equation.**

27. $x^2 - 4y^2 + 2x + 24y = 51$ 28. $20y^2 - 40y - x = -25$

Lesson 9-7   **Classify each pair of events as *dependent* or *independent*.**

29. Choose one item from a buffet. Then choose a different item from the buffet.

30. Choose a size for your drink. Then select a flavor.

Conditional Probability

What You'll Learn

- To find conditional probabilities
- To use formulas and tree diagrams

... And Why

To find the probability of school closings after snowfall, as in Example 4

✓ **Check Skills You'll Need**

GO for Help   Lesson 9-7

A spinner has four equal sections that are red, blue, green, and yellow. Find each probability for two spins.

1. P(blue, then blue)
2. P(red, then yellow)
3. P(not yellow, then green)
4. P(not blue, then not red)
5. P(at least one green)
6. P(neither spin red)

◀)) **New Vocabulary**   • conditional probability

---

1 Finding Conditional Probabilities

A **conditional probability** contains a condition that may limit the sample space for an event. You can write a conditional probability using the notation $P(B \mid A)$, read "the probability of event B, given event A."

1 EXAMPLE   Finding Conditional Probability

The table shows the results of a class survey. Find P(did a chore | male).

The condition *male* limits the sample space to 15 possible outcomes. Of the 15 males, 7 did a chore. Therefore, P(did a chore | male) equals $\frac{7}{15}$.

Did you do a household chore last night?

	Yes	No	
Male	7	8	← 15 males
Female	7	6	← 13 females

✓ **Quick Check** **1** Use the data in Example 1 to find P(female | did a chore).

2 EXAMPLE   Real-World  Connection

Multiple Choice Americans recycle increasingly more materials through municipal waste collection each year. The table shows recycling data for a recent year. Find the probability that a sample of recycled waste was paper.

Ⓐ 16 %
Ⓑ 28%
Ⓒ 36%
Ⓓ 54%

Test-Taking Tip

When using tables, mark on the table to help you keep track of the data you need.

Municipal Waste Collected (millions of tons)

Material	Recycled	Not Recycled
Paper	36.7	45.1
Metal	6.3	11.9
Glass	2.4	10.1
Plastic	1.4	24.0
Other	21.2	70.1

SOURCE: U.S. Environmental Protection Agency.
Go to **www.PHSchool.com** for a data update.
Web Code: agg-9041

The given condition limits the sample space to *recycled* waste. A favorable outcome is recycled paper.

$$P(\text{paper} \mid \text{recycled}) = \frac{36.7}{36.7 + 6.3 + 2.4 + 1.4 + 21.2}$$

$$\approx 0.54$$

The probability that the recycled waste was paper is about 54%. The correct choice is D.

 Quick Check ❷ Find the probability that a sample of recycled waste was plastic.

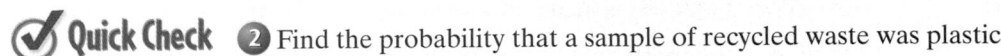

2 Using Formulas and Tree Diagrams

You can use a formula to find conditional probability.

🔑 **Key Concepts**

Property	Conditional Probability Formula

For any two events A and B from a sample space with $P(A) \neq 0$,

$$P(B \mid A) = \frac{P(A \text{ and } B)}{P(A)}$$

Using the formula, you can calculate a conditional probability from other probabilities.

❸ EXAMPLE Real-World 🌐 Connection

Market Research Researchers asked shampoo users whether they apply shampoo directly to the head, or indirectly using a hand. Find the probability that a respondent applies shampoo directly to the head, given that the respondent is female.

Applying Shampoo

	Directly Onto Head	Into Hand First
Male	2	18
Female	6	24

Relate $P(\text{female}) = \frac{30}{50}$

$P(\text{female} \textit{ and } \text{applies directly to head}) = \frac{6}{50}$

Define Let A = female.

Let B = applies directly to head.

Write $P(B \mid A) = \dfrac{P(A \text{ and } B)}{P(A)}$

$= \dfrac{\frac{6}{50}}{\frac{30}{50}}$ **Substitute.**

$= \frac{6}{30} = \frac{1}{5}$ **Simplify.**

The probability that a respondent applies shampoo directly to the head, given that the respondent is female, is $\frac{1}{5}$, or 20%.

 **Quick Check** ❸ Eighty percent of an airline's flights depart on schedule. Seventy-two percent of its flights depart and arrive on schedule. Find the probability that a flight that departs on time also arrives on time.

You can use tree diagrams to solve problems involving conditional probabilities.

Real-World Connection

During some winters, Buffalo gets more than 100 inches of snow.

4 EXAMPLE Making a Tree Diagram

A student in Buffalo, New York, made the observations below.

- Of all snowfalls, 5% are heavy (at least 6 in.).
- After a heavy snowfall, schools are closed 67% of the time.
- After a light (less than 6 in.) snowfall, schools are closed 3% of the time.

Find the probability that the snowfall is light and the schools are open.

Make a tree diagram. Use H for heavy snowfall, L for light snowfall, C for schools closed, and O for schools open. Find $P(L \text{ and } O)$.

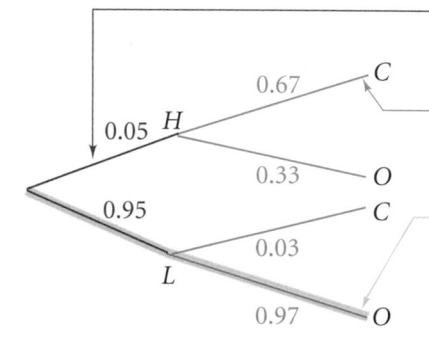

Each first branch represents a simple probability. $P(H) = 0.05$

Each second branch represents a conditional probability. $P(C|H) = 0.67$

The highlighted path represents $P(L \text{ and } O)$.
$$P(L \text{ and } O) = P(L) \cdot P(O|L)$$
$$= 0.95 \cdot 0.97$$
$$= 0.9215$$

● The probability that the snowfall is light and the schools are open is about 92%.

 **4** Find P(schools open, given heavy snow).

EXERCISES

For more exercises, see *Extra Skill and Word Problem Practice.*

Practice and Problem Solving

 Practice by Example

Example 1
(page 654)

Use the table to find each probability.

1. P(has diploma)

2. P(has diploma and experience)

3. P(has experience | has diploma)

4. P(has no diploma | has experience)

Characteristics of Job Applicants

		Has Experience	
		Yes	No
Has High School Diploma	Yes	54	27
	No	5	4

Example 2
(pages 654–655)

Use the table below to find each probability.

5. P(The recipient is male.)

6. P(The degree is a bachelor's.)

7. P(The recipient is female, given that the degree is advanced.)

8. P(The degree is *not* an associate's, given that the recipient is male.)

Projected Number of Degree Recipients in 2010 (thousands)

Degree	Male	Female
Associate's	245	433
Bachelor's	598	858
Advanced	293	376

SOURCE: U.S. National Center for Education Statistics

Example 3
(page 655)

Use the survey results below for Exercises 9 and 10.

9. Find the probability that a respondent has a pet, given that the respondent has had a pet.

10. Find the probability that a respondent has never had a pet, given that the respondent does not have a pet now.

> 39% have a pet now and have had a pet.
>
> 61% do not have a pet now.
>
> 86% have had a pet.
>
> 14% do not have a pet now and have never had a pet.

Example 4
(page 656)

11. Make a tree diagram based on the survey results below . Then find P(a female respondent is left-handed) and P(a respondent is both male and right-handed).
    - Of all the respondents, 17% are male.
    - Of the male respondents, 33% are left-handed.
    - Of female respondents, 90% are right-handed.

12. A football team has a 70% chance of winning when it doesn't snow, but only a 40% chance of winning when it snows. Suppose there is a 50% chance of snow. Make a tree diagram to find the probability that the team will win.

 **Apply Your Skills**

13. Suppose A and B are independent events, with $P(A) = 0.60$ and $P(B) = 0.25$. Find each probability.
    a. $P(A \text{ and } B)$
    b. $P(A \mid B)$
    c. What do you notice about $P(A)$ and $P(A \mid B)$?
    d. **Critical Thinking** One way to describe A and B as independent events is *The occurrence of B has no effect on the probability of A.* Explain how the answer to part (c) illustrates this relationship.

🌐 **Surveys Conduct a survey in your class. Then find each probability.**

14. P(left-handed $\mid$ left shoe)

15. P(left-handed $\mid$ not the right shoe)

16. P(left shoe $\mid$ right-handed)

17. P(first shoe picked up $\mid$ right-handed)

18. P(don't know)

Which Shoe Do You Put on First?		Dominant Hand	
		Right	Left
First Shoe Put On	Right	■	■
	Left	■	■
	First One Grabbed	■	■
	Don't Know	■	■

 **On**line
Homework Video Tutor
Visit: PHSchool.com
Web Code: age-1202

🌐 **Weather Use probability notation to describe the chance of each event. Let S, C, W, and R represent sunny, cloudy, windy, and rainy weather, respectively.**

19. cloudy weather

20. sunny and windy weather

21. rainy weather if it is windy

22. windy weather if it is sunny

 **Challenge**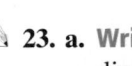

23. a. **Writing** Explain which branches of the tree diagram at the right represent conditional probabilities. Give a specific example.
    b. Are the event of having a license and the event of being an adult independent events? Justify your answer.
    c. **Open-Ended** Estimate probabilities for each branch of the tree diagram for your city or town. Then find $P(L)$.

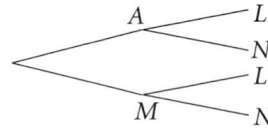

A = adult (21 or older)
M = minor (under 21)
L = licensed driver
N = not licensed to drive

24. Critical Thinking Sixty percent of a company's sales representatives have completed training seminars. Of these, 80% have had increased sales. Overall, 56% of the representatives (whether trained or not) have had increased sales. Use a tree diagram to find the probability of increased sales, given that a representative has not been trained.

Test Prep

Multiple Choice

A school library classifies its books as hardback or paperback, fiction or nonfiction, and illustrated or nonillustrated. Use the table at the right for Exercises 25–27.

		Illustrated	Non-illustrated
Hardback	Fiction	420	780
	Nonfiction	590	250
Paperback	Fiction	150	430
	Nonfiction	110	880

25. What is the probability that a book selected at random is a paperback, given that it is illustrated?

A. $\frac{260}{3610}$ B. $\frac{150}{1270}$ C. $\frac{260}{1270}$ D. $\frac{110}{150}$

26. What is the probability that a book selected at random is nonfiction, given that it is a nonillustrated hardback?

F. $\frac{250}{2040}$ G. $\frac{780}{1030}$ H. $\frac{250}{1030}$ J. $\frac{250}{780}$

27. What is the probability that a book selected at random is a paperback?

A. $\frac{1}{1570}$ B. $\frac{260}{1310}$ C. $\frac{1570}{2040}$ D. $\frac{1570}{3610}$

Short Response

28. In a library, the probability that a book is a hardback, given that it is illustrated, is 0.40. The probability that the book is hardback *and* illustrated is 0.20. Find the probability that a book is illustrated.

Mixed Review

Lesson 12-1

29. Consider a February that is not in a leap year. Graph the probability distribution for the sample space {weekdays, weekend days}.

Lesson 11-1  **30. Construction** An earthmover purchased for $600,000 loses 18% of its value each year. What is the value of the earthmover after one year? After three years?

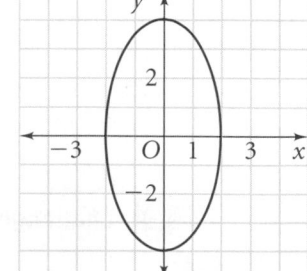

Lesson 10-1

31. Identify the center and intercepts of the conic section at the right. Then find the domain and range.

Lesson 8-5

Solve each equation. If necessary, round to the nearest thousandth.

32. $2^x = 4$ **33.** $4^{2x} = 10$ **34.** $4^{x+1} = 28$

35. $7 - 3^x = -38$ **36.** $\log x = -1$

37. $2 \log x = 1$ **38.** $\log (2x + 2) = 2$

Comparing Conditional Probabilities

FOR USE WITH LESSON 12-2

You can use a tree diagram like the one at the right to find the conditional probability $P(P \mid D)$, which is the probability that a person with a disease will test positive for it. In this case, $P(P \mid D) = 0.99$.

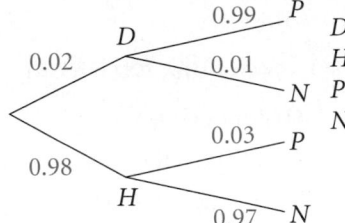

D = person has the disease
H = person is healthy
P = person tests positive
N = person tests negative

Scientists also look at $P(H \mid P)$, the probability of a "false positive," which is the probability that a person who tests positive is actually healthy. Since this probability is not found on a branch in the diagram, you must use the formula for conditional probability.

EXAMPLE

Use the tree diagram above to find $P(H \mid P)$.

Since $P(H \mid P) = \dfrac{P(H \text{ and } P)}{P(P)}$, find $P(H \text{ and } P)$ and $P(P)$.

$$P(H \text{ and } P) = 0.98 \cdot 0.03 \qquad P(P) = P(D \text{ and } P) \text{ or } P(H \text{ and } P)$$
$$= 0.0294 \qquad\qquad = 0.02 \cdot 0.99 + 0.98 \cdot 0.03 = 0.0492$$

So $P(H \mid P) = \dfrac{P(H \text{ and } P)}{P(P)}$

$\qquad = \dfrac{0.0294}{0.0492}$ **Substitute.**

$\qquad \approx 0.598$ **Simplify.**

● About 60% of the people who test positive do not actually have the disease.

EXERCISES

Use the tree diagram in the Example to find each probability.

1. $P(N)$ **2.** $P(H \text{ and } N)$ **3.** $P(H \mid N)$ **4.** $P(D \mid N)$

5. Transportation You can take Bus 65 or Bus 79 to get to work. You take the first bus that arrives. The probability that Bus 65 arrives first is 75%. There is a 40% chance that Bus 65 picks up passengers along the way. There is a 60% chance that Bus 79 picks up passengers. Your bus picked up passengers. What is the probability that it was Bus 65?

The tree diagram relates snowfall and school closings. Find each probability.

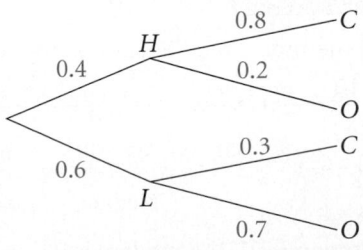

H = heavy snowfall
L = light snowfall
C = schools closed
O = schools open

6. $P(C)$ **7.** $P(H \text{ and } O)$

8. $P(H \mid C)$ **9.** $P(L \mid O)$

10. $P(L \mid C)$ **11.** $P(H \mid O)$

12. Writing Explain the difference in meaning between $P(P \mid D)$ and $P(D \mid P)$ for the test in the Example. Compare the values of $P(P \mid D)$ and $P(D \mid P)$. What is the best use for this test? Explain.

Analyzing Data

What You'll Learn

- To calculate measures of central tendency
- To draw and interpret box-and-whisker plots

. . . And Why

To analyze a set of water temperatures, as in Example 2

Check Skills You'll Need   **GO for Help** Lesson 1-1

Order each set of values from least to greatest. Then find the middle value.

1. 0.2 0.3 0.6 1.2 0.7 0.9 0.8   **2.** 11 23 15 17 21 18 21

3. 7.8 2.6 3.9 15.6 9.1 11.7 10.4   **4.** 76 89 80 82 86 84 86

New Vocabulary • measures of central tendency • mean • median • mode • bimodal • quartiles • box-and-whisker plot • percentiles • outlier

---

1 Measures of Central Tendency

Statistics is the study of data analysis and interpretation. The mean, the median, and the mode are single, central values that help describe a set of data. They are called **measures of central tendency**.

Key Concepts

	Definition	Measures of Central Tendency	
Measure	**Definition**	**Example, using {1, 2, 2, 3, 5, 5}**
Mean	$\dfrac{\text{sum of the data values}}{\text{number of data values}}$	$\dfrac{1 + 2 + 2 + 3 + 5 + 5}{6} = \dfrac{18}{6} = 3$
Median	middle value *or* mean of the two middle values	$\dfrac{2 + 3}{2} = 2.5$
Mode	most frequently occurring value	2 and 5

A **bimodal** data set has two modes. If a data set has more than two modes, then the modes are probably not statistically useful. If no value occurs more frequently than any other, then there is no mode.

1 EXAMPLE Finding Measures of Central Tendency

Vocabulary Tip

Read $\bar{x}$ as "the mean of x" or "x bar."

Find the mean, median, and mode for these values: 98, 95, 99, 97, 89, 92, 97, 62, 90.

$\bar{x} = \dfrac{98 + 95 + 99 + 97 + 89 + 92 + 97 + 62 + 90}{9} = \dfrac{819}{9} = 91$ **Use the symbol $\bar{x}$ to designate the mean.**

62 89 90 92 95 97 97 98 99   **Find the median and the mode by ordering the values numerically.**

Median   Mode

The mean is 91, the median is 95, and the mode is 97.

Quick Check **1** Find the mean, median, and mode for these values: 2.4, 4.3, 3.7, 3.9, 2.8, 5.4, 2.8.

You can use a graphing calculator to find the measures of central tendency.

2 EXAMPLE **Real-World Connection**

Oceanography Find the mean, the median, and the mode of all the water temperatures listed for the eastern coast of the Gulf of Mexico.

Gulf of Mexico Eastern Coast Water Temperatures (°F)

Location	J	F	M	A	M	J	J	A	S	O	N	D
Pensacola, Florida	56	58	63	71	78	84	85	86	82	74	65	58
St. Petersburg, Florida	62	64	68	74	80	84	86	86	84	78	70	64
Key West, Florida	69	70	75	78	82	85	87	87	86	82	76	72
Dauphin Island, Alabama	51	53	60	70	75	82	84	84	80	72	62	56
Grand Isle, Louisiana	61	61	64	70	77	83	85	85	83	77	70	65

Step 1 Use the STAT feature to enter the data as L1 in your graphing calculator.

Step 2 Use the LIST feature to access the MATH menu. Find the mean.

```
NAMES OPS MATH
1:min(
2:max(
3:mean(
4:median(
5:sum(
6:prod(
7↓stdDev(
```

```
mean (L1)
              73.65
```

Step 3 Return to the same menu to find the median.

```
NAMES OPS MATH
1:min(
2:max(
3:mean(
4:median(
5:sum(
6:prod(
7↓stdDev(
```

```
mean (L1)
              73.65
median (L1)
              75
```

Step 4 Use the STAT PLOT feature to access **Plot 1**. Choose the histogram, L1, and

```
Plot1 Plot2 Plot3
On Off
Type: ⊾ ⊿ ⊞
      ⊶ ⊞ ⊾
Xlist: L1
Freq: 1
```

```
WINDOW
Xmin = 50
Xmax = 90
Xscl = 1
Ymin = −2
Ymax = 8
Yscl = 1
Xres = 1
```

Frequency 1 options. Then enter an appropriate viewing window.

Step 5 Graph the data. Use the TRACE feature to move the cursor to the highest points of the graph.

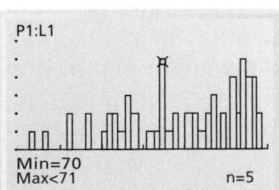

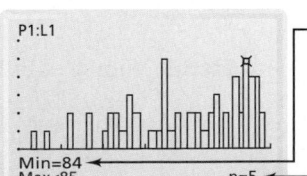

On the screen, the mode appears as the minimum value for the cursor. The modes are 70 and 84.

The modes both occur five times in the data.

● The mean is 73.65°F, the median is 75°F, and the modes are 70°F and 84°F.

✓ Quick Check ❷ Find the mean, median, and mode for the water temperatures in Grand Isle, Louisiana.

If you arrange data in increasing order, then the median divides the data set into two equal parts. You can use the median of each of the parts to divide the set further, into four equal parts. The values separating the four parts are called **quartiles.** Quartiles are shown below for the 12 water temperatures from Pensacola in Example 2.

Median of lower part (Q_1) = 60.5   Median of upper part (Q_3) = 83

56   58   58   63   65   71   74   78   82   84   85   86

Median of data set (Q_2) = 72.5

Vocabulary Tip

Quartiles are sometimes called "hinges."

The values Q_1, Q_2, and Q_3 are the first, second, and third quartiles. A **box-and-whisker plot** is a method of displaying data that uses quartiles to form the center box and the minimum and maximum values to form the whiskers.

Minimum Q_1 Q_2 Q_3 Maximum

50   60   70   80   90

3 **EXAMPLE**   **Making a Box-and-Whisker Plot**

Make a box-and-whisker plot for these values: 84, 79, 90, 73, 95, 88, 92, 81, 67.

Step 1 Find the quartile values, the minimum value, and the maximum value.

67 73 79 81 84 88 90 92 95

Q_2 = median = 84

When the median is a value of the data set, it is removed for the calculation of Q_1 and Q_3.

67 73 79 81   88 90 92 95

$Q_1 = \dfrac{73 + 79}{2} = 76$ $Q_3 = \dfrac{90 + 92}{2} = 91$

The minimum value is 67, and the maximum value is 95.

Step 2 Draw a number line for the base of your box-and-whisker plot. Above the number line, plot the three quartiles, the minimum value, and the maximum value.

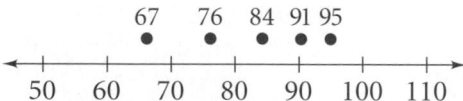

67   76   84 91 95

50   60   70   80   90   100   110

Step 3 Finish your box-and-whisker plot by drawing a box through Q_1 and Q_3, a vertical line through the median, and line segments from the box outward to the minimum and maximum values.

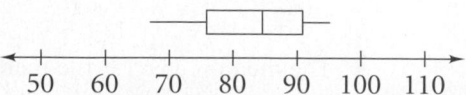

50   60   70   80   90   100   110

Quick Check ③ Make a box-and-whisker plot for these values: 34, 36, 47, 45, 28, 31, 29, 40.

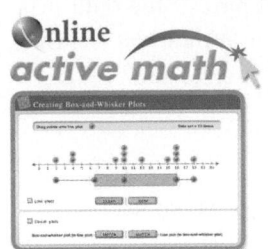

For: Box Plot Activity
Use: Interactive Textbook, 12-3

4 EXAMPLE Real-World Connection

Oceanography Use a graphing calculator to find the quartiles of the water temperature data in Example 2.

Use the **STAT PLOT** feature to select a box-and-whisker plot. Enter the window values. Graph the box-and-whisker plot.

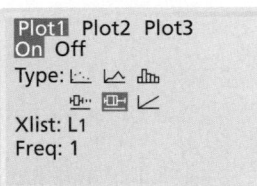
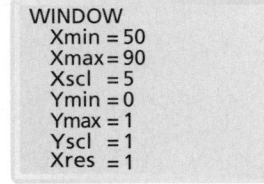
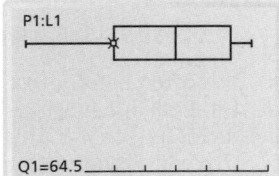

Use the **TRACE** feature to find the quartiles: $Q_1 = 64.5$, $Q_2 = 75$, and $Q_3 = 83.5$.

✓ Quick Check  Use the data for just the summer months, as shown in the graph below. Find the quartiles by graphing the box-and-whisker plot.

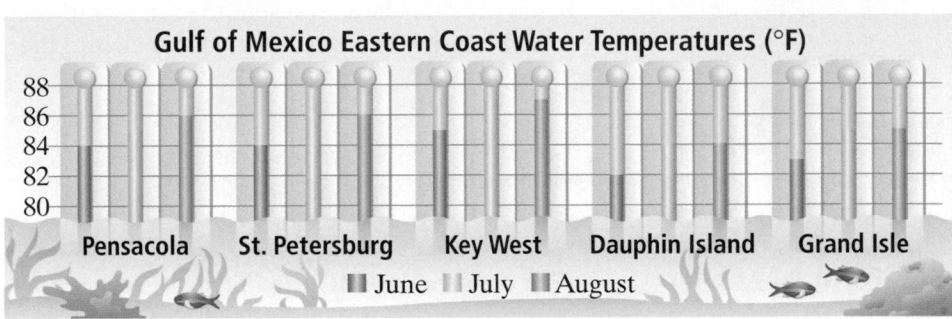

Gulf of Mexico Eastern Coast Water Temperatures (°F)

Pensacola   St. Petersburg   Key West   Dauphin Island   Grand Isle

■ June   ■ July   ■ August

Let x be a value from a data set. A **percentile** is a number from 0 to 100 that you can associate with x to indicate the percent of the data that are less than or equal to x. If x is at the 63rd percentile, then 63% of the data are less than or equal to x.

5 EXAMPLE Using Percentiles

Find the values at the 20th and 65th percentiles for the values below.
54 98 45 87 98 64 21 61 71 82 93 65 62 98 87 24 65 97 31 47

Step 1 Order the values.

21 24 31 45 47 54 61 62 64 65 65 71 82 87 87 93 97 98 98 98

Step 2 Find the number of values that fall below the 20th percentile and the number that fall below the 65th percentile.

Of the 20 values, 20% should fall below the 20th percentile and 65% should fall below the 65th percentile.

$20 \cdot 20\% = 20 \cdot 0.20 = 4$ $20 \cdot 65\% = 20 \cdot 0.65 = 13$

Since 47 is greater than 4 values, 47 is at the 20th percentile.   Since 87 is greater than 13 values, 87 is at the 65th percentile.

The value at the 20th percentile is 47 and the value at the 65th percentile is 87.

✓ Quick Check  Find the value at each percentile for the data in Example 5.
a. 0th percentile   **b.** 45th percentile   **c.** 55th percentile

An **outlier** is an item of data with a value substantially different from the rest of the items in the data set. Sometimes an outlier is an important part of the data. At other times it can represent a false reading. When you think an outlier has resulted from an error, you may remove it from the data set.

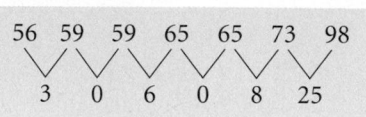 **Identifying an Outlier**

Multiple Choice Which is an outlier for this set of values: 56 65 73 59 98 65 59?

  Ⓐ 42   Ⓑ 65   Ⓒ 98   Ⓓ 59

         56 59 59 65 65 73 98   **Order the data.**

           3   0   6   0   8   25   **Find the differences between adjacent values.**

● 98 is substantially different, so 98 is an outlier. The correct choice is C.

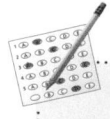
☑ **Quick Check**   ❻ **a.** Suppose the values in Example 6 are measurements of the water temperature of a lake. Would you discard the outlier? Explain.

         b. Suppose the data represent the number of customers in a small restaurant each night during one week. Would you discard the outlier? Explain.

EXERCISES

For more exercises, see *Extra Skill and Word Problem Practice*.

Practice and Problem Solving

Ⓐ **Practice by Example**

Examples 1 and 2
(pages 660 and 661)

Find the mean, median, and mode of each set of values.

1. 5 9 1 2 7 3 1 8 8 1 3   **2.** 307 309 323 304 390 398

3. 475 722 499 572 402 809 499 828 405 499 800 422 672 800

Examples 3 and 4
(pages 662 and 663)

 **for Help**

Make a box-and-whisker plot for each set of values.

4. 12 11 15 12 19 20 19   **5.** 120 145 133 105 117 150

6. 49 57.5 58 49.2 62 22.2 67 52.1 77 99.9 80 51.7 64

7. Weather The table shows the high temperatures for one day at different locations on the island of Maui, Hawaii. Make a box-and-whisker plot of the data.

| High Temperatures on Maui | |
Location	Temperature
Kahului	88°F
Kihei	85°F
Lahaina	86°F
Hana	82°F
Haleakala	66°F
Kula	75°F

Example 5
(page 663)

Find the values at the 30th and 90th percentiles for each set of values.

8. 6283 5700 6381 6274 5700 5896 5972 6075 5993 5581

9. 7 12 3 14 17 20 5 3 17 4 13 2 15 9 15 18 16 9 1 6

Example 6
(page 664)

Identify the outlier of each set of values.

10. 3.4 4.5 2.3 5.9 9.8 3.3 2.1 3.0 2.9

11. 17 21 19 10 15 19 14 0 11 16

Dilbert

B **Apply Your Skills**

12. a. What percent of the customers in the cartoon are exactly the median age?
  b. Must one item from a data set fall exactly at the median? Explain.
  c. Can the company do anything about the shocking discovery? Explain.

13. Meteorology On May 3, 1999, 59 tornadoes hit Oklahoma in the largest tornado outbreak ever recorded in the state. Sixteen of these were classified as strong (F2 or F3) or violent (F4 or F5).
  a. Make a box-and-whisker plot of the data for length of path.
  b. Identify the outliers. Remove them from the data set and make a revised box-and-whisker plot.
  c. Writing How does the removal of the outliers affect the box-and-whisker plot? How does it affect the median of the data set?

Identify the outlier of each set of values. Then describe how its value affects the mean of the data.

14. 947 757 103 619 661 582 626 900 869 728 1001 596 515

15. 87 104 381 215 174 199 233 186 142 228 9 53 117 129

For Exercises 16–18, use the set of values below.
1 1 1 1 1 1 2 3 5 8 13 21 34 55 89 89 89 89 89 89

16. At what percentile is 1?   **17.** At what percentile is 34?

18. Error Analysis A student claims that 89 is at the 100th percentile. Explain the student's error.

19. Geology The table below shows the number of major earthquakes (magnitude 7.0 or greater) worldwide in the ten-year period from 1991 through 2000.

Major Earthquakes Worldwide (Magnitude 7.0 and Greater)

Year	1991	1992	1993	1994	1995	1996	1997	1998	1999	2000
Earthquakes	11	23	16	15	25	22	20	16	23	18

SOURCE: U.S. Geological Survey National Earthquake Information Center

a. Find the mean and the median of the numbers of annual earthquakes.
b. Do the data include an outlier that you should discard? Explain.
c. Compare the box-and-whisker plots at the right. One shows the data above. The other shows worldwide earthquake data from 1900 through 2000. What conclusions can you draw about recent earthquakes? Justify your reasoning.

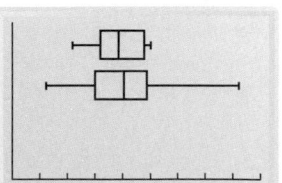

Xmin = 0   Ymin = 0
Xmax = 45   Ymax = 1
Xscl = 5   Yscl = 1

Major Tornadoes in Oklahoma, May 3, 1999

Length of Path (miles)	Intensity
6	F3
9	F3
4	F2
37	F5
7	F2
12	F3
8	F2
7	F2
15	F4
39	F4
1	F2
22	F3
15	F3
8	F2
13	F3
2	F2

SOURCE: National Oceanic & Atmospheric Administration

GO Online
Homework Video Tutor
Visit: PHSchool.com
Web Code: age-1203

20. Critical Thinking Which measure better represents a data set with several outliers—the mean or the median? Justify your answer.

21. Track and Field The table shows the 36 best qualifying distances for the shot put events for both men and women during the 2004 Olympics.

2004 Olympic Qualifying Distances for Shot Put (meters)

Men	21.15	20.78	20.65	20.61	20.53	20.45	20.37	20.32	20.11
	20.06	20.06	20.04	19.69	19.68	19.67	19.60	19.55	19.50
	19.46	19.41	19.40	19.38	19.31	19.25	19.14	19.09	19.09
	19.07	19.04	19.02	19.02	18.91	18.89	18.67	18.52	18.44
Women	19.69	19.10	18.90	18.79	18.65	18.61	18.57	18.52	18.38
	18.33	18.16	18.03	18.00	17.99	17.89	17.78	17.44	17.34
	17.28	17.22	17.17	17.11	16.90	16.58	16.49	16.47	16.45
	16.35	15.99	15.91	15.86	15.33	15.20	15.06	14.88	14.60

a. Using the same number line base for both plots, make a box-and-whisker plot for the men's results and another for the women's results.

b. Writing Compare your box-and-whisker plots. Describe any conclusions you can draw about Olympic-level male and female shot-putters.

Real-World Connection

The "shot" in shot put refers to cannonballs. For centuries, soldiers used them in throwing contests.

22. a. Government Make a box-and-whisker plot for the data from each of the three types of elections shown in the table below.

Voter Turnout (percent of voting-age population)

Presidential Year	1976	1980	1984	1988	1992	1996	2000
Voting for President	53.5	52.8	53.3	50.3	55.1	48.9	51.2
Voting for Representatives	48.9	47.6	47.8	44.9	50.8	45.7	47.2
Non-Presidential Year	1978	1982	1986	1990	1994	1998	2002
Voting for Representatives	34.9	38.0	33.5	33.1	36.6	32.7	34.2

SOURCE: U.S. Census Bureau. Go to **www.PHSchool.com** for a data update.
Web Code: agg-9041

b. Writing How does a Presidential election in the United States affect the voter turnout rate in elections for the House of Representatives? Use your box-and-whisker plots to describe any effect that you see.

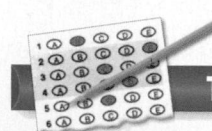

Test Prep

Multiple Choice

A person checked for e-mail four times each day. The table shows the number of new e-mails she received each time she checked during 5 days.

Day 1	Day 2	Day 3	Day 4	Day 5
6, 3, 1, 5	5, 3, 7, 2	6, 7, 3, 2	8, 2, 6, 9	7, 7, 6, 11

23. Which value is the greatest?
   A. the mean number of e-mails for checks made on days 1–3
   B. the mean number of e-mails for checks made on days 2–4
   C. the mean number of e-mails for checks made on days 2–3
   D. the median number of e-mails for checks made on days 3–4

24. Which of the given sets of data has the greatest median?
   F. 1, 1, 2, 3, 4, 5, 6, 7, 8, 8   **G.** 1, 2, 3, 4, 5, 6, 7, 8, 9, 10
   H. 4, 4, 4, 5, 5, 5, 5, 5, 5, 4, 4   **J.** 1, 2, 3, 4, 5, 6, 7, 8

25. Which statement(s) is (are) true?

    I. The mean number of e-mails for checks made over the 5 days was 5.3.
    II. The mean number of e-mails for checks made on day 5 was 7.75.
    III. The median number of e-mails for checks made over the 5 days was 6.5.

    A. I only   **B.** I and II only   **C.** II and III only   **D.** I, II, and III

Short Response   **26.** Describe how you could find the scores at the 20th and 60th percentiles in a set of 80 scores.

Extended Response   **27.** Draw a box-and-whisker plot for this set of values: 123, 127, 127, 142, 118, 131, 137, 125, 131.

Mixed Review

Lesson 12-2   **Of all the respondents to a survey, 59% are girls. Of the girls, 61% read horror stories. Of the boys, 49% read horror stories.**

28. Find P(boy and reads horror stories).   **29.** Find P(reads horror stories).

Lesson 11-2   **Is the sequence arithmetic? If so, identify the common difference.**

30. $16, 7, -2, \ldots$ **31.** $34, 51, 68, \ldots$ **32.** $2, 2.2, 2.22, \ldots$ **33.** $1, 1, 1, \ldots$

Lesson 10-2   **Graph each equation.**

34. $y^2 - x - 2y + 1 = 0$ **35.** $x^2 + 4x + 144y + 4 = 0$

Checkpoint Quiz 1   Lessons 12-1 through 12-3

In a poll, gymnasts were asked, "How many seconds long was your longest handstand on the balance beam?" Use the results below for Exercises 1 and 2.

Longest Handstand

Duration (seconds)	0–2	3–5	6–10	11–20	21–30	31–60	> 60	Total
Number of Respondents	14	27	19	18	13	15	24	130

1. Graph the probability distribution.   **2.** Find $P(6-30$ seconds$)$.

 3. Writing Could the function $P(x) = \frac{x - 2}{2}$ for $x = 1, 2, 3,$ or 4, represent a probability distribution? Explain.

Use the table at the right to find each probability.

4. $P($teacher $\mid$ yes$)$ **5.** $P($no $\mid$ teacher$)$

6. $P($student $\mid$ no$)$ **7.** $P($yes $\mid$ student$)$

Find the mean, median, and mode of each data set.

8. 7 4 9 3 5 4 4 7 9 10 3 1 8

9. 1.2   2.1   4.6   2.5   9.7   6.2   2.6   2.4   3.1   3.8

Did You Eat Breakfast Today?

	Yes	No
Teachers	12	20
Students	45	23

10. Open-Ended Write a data set that includes an outlier. Make a box-and-whisker plot of your data set with and without the outlier.

Standard Deviation

What You'll Learn

• To find the standard deviation of a set of values

• To use standard deviation in real-world situations

. . . And Why

To analyze energy demand, as in Example 3

Simplify each expression. If necessary, round to the nearest hundredth.

1. $\frac{34.3}{7}$

2. $\frac{6}{2.4}$

3. $8.4 \cdot 1.25$

4. $12 - 6 \cdot 0.5$

5. $\frac{1}{3}[(2 - 6)^2 + (7 - 6)^2 + (8 - 6)^2]$

6. $\sqrt{\frac{1}{2}(4 - 3)^2 + (5 + 3)^2}$

🔊 **New Vocabulary**   • measures of variation   • range of a set of data   • interquartile range   • standard deviation   • z-score

---

1   Finding Standard Deviation

Activity: Analyzing Data Spread

1. a. Find the mean, the median, and the mode of each set of data.

Set 1	77	78	79	80	80	81	82	83
Set 2	20	60	70	80	80	90	100	140
Set 3	50	60	70	80	80	90	100	110
Set 4	20	30	40	80	80	120	130	140

b. Are the sets the same? Explain.

2. Find the difference between the greatest and least values in each set of data. What do these differences tell you about each set of data?

3. Find the quartiles of each set of data.

4. For each set, half of the data lie between Q_1 and Q_3. The value $Q_3 - Q_1$ gives you an idea of how the data are spread out. Find $Q_3 - Q_1$ for each set of data.

5. a. Give an example of two sets of data that are spread out differently, though the differences between their extreme values are the same.

b. Give an example of two sets of data that are spread out differently, though their values of $Q_3 - Q_1$ are the same.

6. a. Summarize the similarities and differences among the four sets in terms of central tendency and spread. Which is the most spread-out set? Which is the least? Explain.

b. Make box-and-whisker plots of the four sets of data. Do the plots support your conclusions from part (a)?

Statisticians use several **measures of variation** to describe how the data in a data set are spread out.

The **range of a set of data** is the difference between the greatest and least values. The **interquartile range** is the difference between the third and first quartiles.

1 EXAMPLE Real-World  Connection

Thirteen men qualified for the 2002 U.S. Men's Alpine Ski Team. Find the range and the interquartile range of their ages at the time of qualification: 27, 28, 29, 23, 25, 26, 26, 28, 22, 23, 23, 21, 25.

$$\text{greatest value} - \text{least value} = 29 - 21 \qquad \textbf{Find the range.}$$
$$= 8$$

Median
↓
21 22 23 23 23 25 **25** 26 26 27 28 28 29   **Find the median.**
        ↑   ↑
$Q_1 = 23$ $Q_3 = \dfrac{27 + 28}{2} = 27.5$ **Find Q_1 and Q_3.**

$$Q_3 - Q_1 = 27.5 - 23 \qquad \textbf{Find the interquartile range.}$$
$$= 4.5$$

● The range is 8 years. The interquartile range is 4.5 years.

✓ **Quick Check** **1 a.** Seventeen women qualified for the 2002 U.S. Women's Alpine Ski Team. Find the range and the interquartile range of their ages: 24, 30, 29, 21, 22, 22, 28, 21, 16, 17, 25, 22, 21, 18, 19, 18, 19.

b. Critical Thinking Can the variation, or spread, in two sets of data be different, even though they have the same range? Give an example.

c. Can the variation in two sets of data be different, even though they have the same interquartile range? Give an example.

Another measure of variation is the **standard deviation,** a measure of how much the values in a data set vary, or deviate, from the mean. The Greek letter σ (sigma) represents standard deviation.

You can use the following procedure to calculate standard deviation.

 Key Concepts

Summary	**Finding Standard Deviation**

- Find the mean of the data set: $\overline{x}$.

- Find the difference between each value and the mean: $x - \overline{x}$.

- Square each difference: $(x - \overline{x})^2$.

- Find the average (mean) of these squares: $\dfrac{\sum (x - \overline{x})^2}{n}$.

- Take the square root to find the standard deviation:

$$\sigma = \sqrt{\dfrac{\sum (x - \overline{x})^2}{n}}.$$

Real-World  Connection

By age 29, skier Paul Casey Puckett had made the U.S. Olympic teams of 1992, 1994, 1998, and 2002.

Vocabulary Tip

The Greek letter <u>sigma</u> (σ or Σ) corresponds to the English letter s. In the notation used in the Summary, Σ means "summation."

2 EXAMPLE Finding the Standard Deviation

Find the mean and the standard deviation for the values: 48.0, 53.2, 52.3, 46.6, 49.9.

$$\bar{x} = \frac{48.0 + 53.2 + 52.3 + 46.6 + 49.9}{5} = 50.0$$ **Find the mean.**

Organize the next steps in a table.

x	$\bar{x}$	$x - \bar{x}$	$(x - \bar{x})^2$
48.0	50.0	−2.0	4.00
53.2	50.0	3.2	10.24
52.3	50.0	2.3	5.29
46.6	50.0	−3.4	11.56
49.9	50.0	−0.1	0.01

Sum: 31.1

$$\sigma = \sqrt{\frac{\sum (x - \bar{x})^2}{n}}$$ **Find the standard deviation.**

$$= \sqrt{\frac{31.1}{5}} \approx 2.5$$

The mean is 50.0, and the standard deviation is about 2.5.

✓ **Quick Check** **2** Find the mean and the standard deviation for these values: 50, 60, 70, 80, 80, 90, 100, 110.

Standard deviation is like a custom-made measuring stick for the variation in a set of data. A small standard deviation (compared to actual data values) indicates that the data are clustered tightly around the mean. As the data become more spread out, the standard deviation increases.

3 EXAMPLE Real-World Connection

Vocabulary Tip

The watt is the metric unit of measurement for power. One million watts of power delivered for one hour results in one megawatt-hour (MWh).

Energy Find the mean and the standard deviation of the data for daily energy demand in a small town during August.

Daily Energy Demand During August (MWh)

Sun.	Mon.	Tues.	Wed.	Thurs.	Fri.	Sat.
		53	52	47	50	39
33	40	41	44	47	49	43
39	47	49	54	53	46	36
33	45	45	42	43	39	33
33	40	40	41	42		

Step 1 Use the STAT feature to enter the data as L1.

Step 2 Use the CALC menu of STAT to access the 1-Var Stats option.

```
1-Var Stats
  x̄=43.16129032          ← mean
  Σx=1338
  Σx²=58872
  Sx=6.116081394
  σx=6.016626288         ← standard
  ↓n=31                      deviation
```

The mean is about 43.2 MWh; the standard deviation is about 6.0 MWh.

✓ **Quick Check** ③ Find the mean and standard deviation for this data set: 2 mm, 3 mm, 4 mm, 6 mm, 7 mm, 9 mm, 10 mm, 12 mm, 13 mm, 14 mm.

2 Using Standard Deviation

In a data list, every value falls within some number of standard deviations of the mean. When a value falls within one standard deviation of the mean, it is in the range of values from one standard deviation below the mean to one standard deviation above. For example, if the mean is 50 and the standard deviation is 10, then a value x within one standard deviation of the mean must be in the range $40 \le x \le 60$.

4 EXAMPLE   Real-World 🌐 Connection

Energy Use the energy demand data from Example 3. Within how many standard deviations of the mean do all of the values fall? How might the company supplying power to the town use this information?

Step 1 Draw a number line. Plot the data values and the mean.

Step 2 Mark off intervals of 6.0 on either side of the mean.

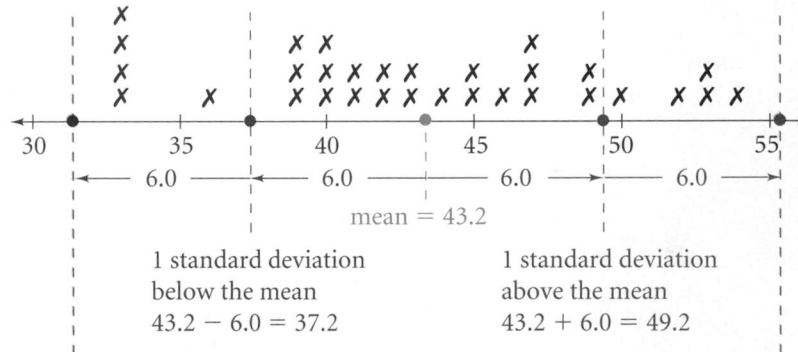

1 standard deviation below the mean
43.2 − 6.0 = 37.2

1 standard deviation above the mean
43.2 + 6.0 = 49.2

2 standard deviations below the mean
43.2 − 2(6.0) = 31.2

2 standard deviations above the mean
43.2 + 2(6.0) = 55.2

All of the values fall within two standard deviations of the mean. Therefore, the power company can expect that the daily demand on most days in August will fall within two standard deviations of the mean.

✓ **Quick Check** ④ **a.** Within how many standard deviations of the mean for August is a demand of 38.5 MWh?

b. In May, the mean daily energy demand is 35.8 MWh, with a standard deviation of 3.5 MWh. The power company prepares for any demand within three standard deviations of the mean. Are they prepared for a demand of 48 MWh? Explain.

The **z-score** is the number of standard deviations that a value is from the mean. In Example 4, the value 49.2 is one standard deviation above the mean, so it has a z-score of 1. The value 37.2, which is one standard deviation below the mean, has a z-score of −1.

 **EXAMPLE** Finding the *z*-score

A set of values has a mean of 85 and a standard deviation of 6. Find the *z*-score of the value 76.

$$z\text{-score} = \frac{\text{value } - \text{ mean}}{\text{standard deviation}}$$

$$= \frac{76 - 85}{6} \quad \textbf{Substitute.}$$

$$= \frac{-9}{6} \quad \textbf{Simplify.}$$

$$= -1.5$$

✓ **Quick Check** ⑤ Use the mean and standard deviation from Example 5. Find the value that has a *z*-score of 2.5.

EXERCISES

For more exercises, see *Extra Skill and Word Problem Practice.*

Practice and Problem Solving

 **Practice by Example**

Example 1 (page 669)

Find the range and the interquartile range of each set of values.

1. 5 6 7 3 4 5 6 7 8

2. 56 78 125 34 67 91 20

3. 724 786 670 760 300 187 190 345 456 732 891 879 324

Examples 2 and 3 (page 670)

Find the mean and the standard deviation for each set of values.

4. 78 90 456 673 111 381 21

5. 13 15 17 18 12 21 10

6. The Dow Jones Industrial average for the last 24 weeks of 1994:

3735.04	3764.50	3747.02	3768.71	3755.11	3881.05
3885.58	3874.81	3933.35	3831.75	3843.19	3797.43
3910.47	3891.30	3930.66	3807.52	3801.47	3815.26
3708.27	3745.62	3691.11	3807.19	3833.43	3834.44

7. The Dow Jones Industrial average for the last 24 weeks of 2004:

9962.22	10,139.71	9815.33	9825.35	10,110.14	10,195.01
10,260.20	10,313.07	10,284.46	10,047.24	10,192.65	10,055.20
9933.38	9757.81	10,027.47	10,387.54	10,539.01	10,456.91
10,522.23	10,592.21	10,543.22	10,649.92	10,827.12	10,783.01

Example 4 (page 671)

Determine the whole number of standard deviations that includes all data values.

8. The mean price of the nonfiction books on a best-sellers list is $25.07; the standard deviation is $2.62.
$26.95, $22.95, $24.00, $24.95, $29.95, $19.95, $24.95, $24.00, $27.95, $25.00

9. The mean length of Beethoven's nine symphonies is 37 minutes; the standard deviation is 12 minutes.
27 min, 30 min, 47 min, 35 min, 30 min, 40 min, 35 min, 22 min, 65 min

Example 5 (page 672)

A data set has mean 25 and standard deviation 5. Find the *z*-score of each value.

10. 39   **11.** 18   **12.** 125   **13.** 25   **14.** 11

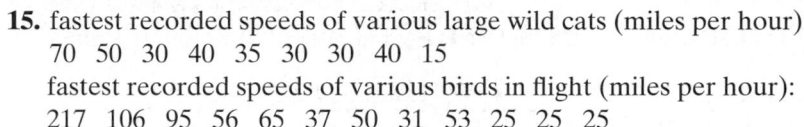

B Apply Your Skills 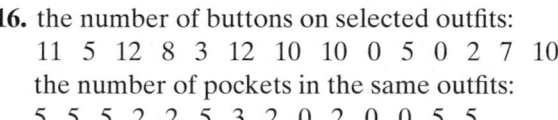 **Find the standard deviation for each data set. Use the standard deviations to compare each pair of data sets.**

15. fastest recorded speeds of various large wild cats (miles per hour):
70 50 30 40 35 30 30 40 15
fastest recorded speeds of various birds in flight (miles per hour):
217 106 95 56 65 37 50 31 53 25 25 25

16. the number of buttons on selected outfits:
11 5 12 8 3 12 10 10 0 5 0 2 7 10
the number of pockets in the same outfits:
5 5 5 2 2 5 3 2 0 2 0 0 5 5

Income Use the chart at the right for Exercises 17−20.

17. Find the mean income for each year.

18. **Writing** Use the range of the data for each year to describe how farm income varied from 2001 to 2002.

19. Find the standard deviation for each year. In which year did farm income cluster more tightly around the mean?

20. Which state's 2001 income has a z-score of about 1.4?

Farm Income in Midwestern States (millions of dollars)

State	2001	2002
Iowa	10,653	10,834
Kansas	7979	7862
Minnesota	7537	7478
Missouri	4723	4402
Nebraska	9221	9589
North Dakota	2938	3223
South Dakota	3897	3779

SOURCE: U.S. Department of Agriculture

Real-World Connection

The fastest wild cat is the cheetah, which can run as fast as 70 mi/h.

For a guide to solving Exercise 21, see p. 675.

21. **a. Energy** Find the mean and the standard deviation for daily energy usage during ten days in June: 51.8 MWh, 53.6 MWh, 54.7 MWh, 51.9 MWh, 49.3 MWh, 52.0 MWh, 53.5 MWh, 51.2 MWh, 60.7 MWh, 59.3 MWh.
    b. How many items in the data set fall within one standard deviation of the mean? Within two standard deviations? Within three standard deviations?

 Another measure of variation is *variance*, **which equals** σ^2. **Find the variance and the standard deviation of each data set.**

22. 12 h 3 h 2 h 4 h 5 h 7 h

23. 60 m 40 m 35 m 45 m 39 m

24. $6.99 $5.50 $7.10 $9.22 $8.99

25. 0.7 g 0.84 g 0.9 g 0.8 g 0.69 g

26. **Critical Thinking** From your results in Exercises 22–25, which do you think is a better measure of variation—variance or standard deviation? Explain.

27. **Error Analysis** Minh says that the data below fall within three standard deviations of the mean. Marsha disagrees, saying that the data fall within six standard deviations of the mean. With whom do you agree? Explain.

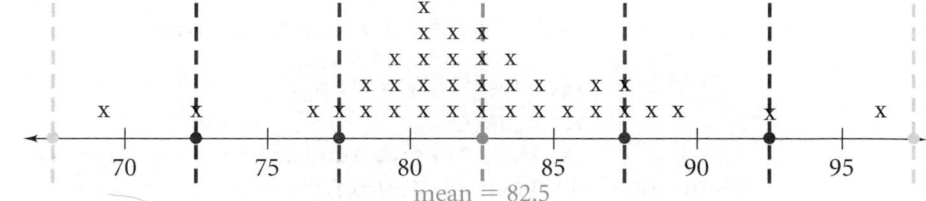

mean = 82.5

28. a. Data Collection Make a table showing the number of siblings of each student in the class.

   b. Find the mean and standard deviation of the data.

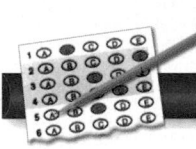

Challenge

29. a. Use the table at the left to find the range, the mean, and the standard deviation of the ages for each team.

   b. Critical Thinking For two data sets, does the set with the larger range necessarily have the larger standard deviation? Support your answer with your results from part (a).

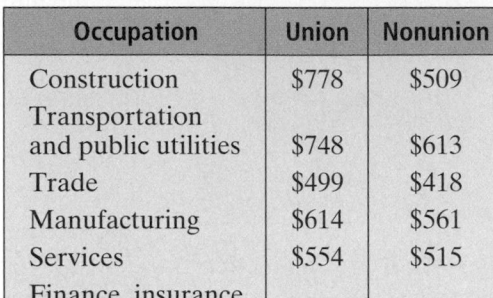

Ages of the Members of the 2000 U.S. Olympic Soccer Teams

Men		Women	
23	32	32	29
29	23	29	22
23	23	32	28
22	23	25	23
21	18	22	22
19	22	20	24
20	23	32	25
23	21	29	27
26	22	24	22

30. Earnings The table at the right shows the median weekly earnings of union and nonunion workers in various occupations.

   a. Find the mean and the range of the data for union workers and for nonunion workers.

   b. Find the standard deviation for each set of data.

   c. Within how many standard deviations of the mean are earnings of $395 for union workers? For nonunion workers?

   d. Writing Compare the wages of union and nonunion workers. Use your results from parts (a) through (c).

Workers' Median Weekly Earnings, 1999

Occupation	Union	Nonunion
Construction	$778	$509
Transportation and public utilities	$748	$613
Trade	$499	$418
Manufacturing	$614	$561
Services	$554	$515
Finance, insurance, and real estate	$582	$599
Mining	$710	$735

SOURCE: U.S. Bureau of Labor Statistics.
Go to www.PHSchool.com for a data update.
Web Code: agg-9041

Test Prep

Gridded Response

For Exercises 31–32, use the following bowling scores for six members of a bowling team: 175, 210, 180, 195, 208, 196.

31. What is the mean of the scores?

32. What is the standard deviation of the scores?

33. At a second bowling tournament, the mean of all the scores was 205, with a standard deviation of 14. What was the z-score for a score of 282?

34. At the second tournament, a participant had a z-score of -2.5. What was the participant's bowling score?

Mixed Review

Lesson 12-3

Make a box-and-whisker plot for each set of values.

35. 25, 25, 30, 35, 45, 45, 50, 55, 60, 60   **36.** 20, 23, 25, 36, 37, 38, 39, 50, 52, 55

Lesson 11-3

Find the missing positive term in each geometric sequence.

37. 64, ■, 4, . . .   **38.** 20, ■, 0.05, . . .   **39.** 29, ■, 65.25, . . .

Lesson 10-3

Graph each circle.

40. $(x - 2)^2 + (y + 1)^2 = 36$ **41.** $(x - 1)^2 + (y - 1)^2 = 4$

Understanding Math Problems Read the problem below. Let the explanation guide you through analyzing the data. Check your understanding by solving the exercises at the bottom of the page.

a. Energy Find the mean and the standard deviation for daily energy usage during ten days in June: 51.8 MWh, 53.6 MWh, 54.7 MWh, 51.9 MWh, 49.3 MWh, 52.0 MWh, 53.5 MWh, 51.2 MWh, 60.7 MWh, 59.3 MWh.

To find the mean, add the data entries and divide by the number of entries.

$$\bar{x} = \frac{51.8 + 53.6 + 54.7 + 51.9 + 49.3 + 52.0 + 53.5 + 51.2 + 60.7 + 59.3}{10} = 53.8$$

The mean energy usage for 10 days is 53.8 MWh.

To simplify finding standard deviation, enter the data into a table.

x	51.8	53.6	54.7	51.9	49.3	52.0	53.5	51.2	60.7	59.3
$\bar{x}$					53.8					
$x - \bar{x}$	−2.0	−0.2	0.9	−1.9	−4.5	−1.8	−0.3	−2.6	6.9	5.5
$(x - \bar{x})^2$	4.00	0.04	0.81	3.61	20.25	3.24	0.09	6.76	47.61	30.25

Now use the definition of standard deviation.

$$\sigma = \sqrt{\frac{\sum (x - \bar{x})^2}{n}}$$

$$= \sqrt{\frac{116.66}{10}}$$

$$\approx 3.4$$

The standard deviation is about 3.4 MWh.

b. How many items in the data set fall within one standard deviation of the mean? Within two standard deviations? Within three standard deviations?

Look at the $x - \bar{x}$ row in your table. Compare its values with the following.

$$1\sigma \approx 3.4 \qquad 2\sigma \approx 6.8 \qquad 3\sigma \approx 10.2$$

7 items are within 1σ of the mean, 9 items are within 2σ, and 10 items are within 3σ.

EXERCISES

Find the mean and the standard deviation of the data. List entries that are more than two standard deviations from the mean.

1. 1.1, 1.8, 2.1, 0.7, 1.8, 0.5, 0.9, 2.9, 5.0, 2.1

2. 122, 94, 111, 95, 137, 56, 89, 115, 119, 125

3. 1635, 1247, 1689, 1496, 1571, 1836, 1652

4. −0.6, 0.8, 1.1, 0.3, −0.8, −0.3, −1.6, 0.8, 0.4, −0.1

Most of the probability examples you study in this chapter are about discrete situations. These situations involve whole numbers of people, test scores, money amounts, and so on. You can apply probabilities to continuous situations as well.

ACTIVITY

A traffic signal is green for 20 seconds out of every minute. Find the probability that the signal will be green when you turn the corner and first see it.

You can model the signal's color intervals by using a number line.

Let an interval of 60 represent one cycle of green, yellow, and red. Inside that interval, an interval of 20 represents a green light. You come across the signal at a random point in time, so

$$P(\text{green}) = \frac{\text{time light is green}}{\text{total time of cycle}} = \frac{20}{60} = \frac{1}{3}$$

EXERCISES

1. The traffic signal is green when you first see it. What is the probability that it will turn yellow within 5 seconds?

2. The traffic signal is red when you first see it. What do you need to know to find the probability that it will not turn green for another 15 seconds?

The following continuous situations involve functions and conic sections that you have studied to this point. For each, assume that you pick real numbers a and b at random between 0 and 10. Find the probability of each of the following.

3. The line $y = ax$ intersects the segment joining $(0, 10)$ and $(5, 10)$. See graph at the right.

4. The circle $(x - a)^2 + (y - b)^2 = 1$ lies entirely within a square with opposite vertices $(0, 0)$ and $(10, 10)$.

5. The ellipse $\frac{x}{a^2} + \frac{y}{b^2} = 1$ has a vertical major axis.

6. The hyperbola $\frac{x}{a^2} - \frac{y}{b^2} = 1$ has a horizontal transverse axis.

7. The interval from 4 to 6 is a part of the domain of the function $y = \sqrt{x - a} + b$.

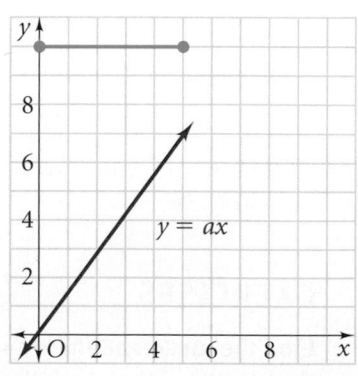

8. The function $y = ab^x$ models growth.

9. The function $y = \frac{1}{x - a} + b$ has a horizontal asymptote.

10. The point (a, b) is in the upper triangle formed by the diagonals of a square whose sides lie on the axes and the lines $x = 10$ and $y = 10$.

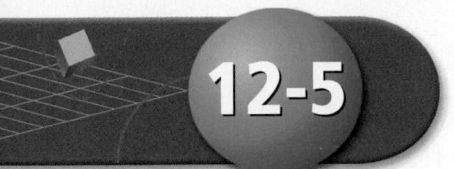

Working With Samples

What You'll Learn
- To find sample proportions
- To find the margin of error

... And Why
To analyze data from a poll, as in Example 5

✓ Check Skills You'll Need   GO for Help Lesson 7-1

Simplify each expression.

1. $\frac{1}{\sqrt{4}}$ 2. $-\frac{1}{\sqrt{9}}$ 3. $\frac{1}{\sqrt{36}}$

4. $-\frac{1}{\sqrt{121}}$ 5. $\frac{1}{\sqrt{50}}$ 6. $-\frac{1}{\sqrt{81}}$

■)) **New Vocabulary**   • sample   • sample proportion   • random sample
                          • margin of error

---

1 Sample Proportions

Suppose you want to know what percent of all teenagers recognize the word that means "to pass the summer in a state of slumber." Since it is too costly and time consuming to ask every teenager, use a sample. A **sample** gathers information from only part of a population.

Using any sample, you can find a sample proportion. The **sample proportion** is the ratio $\frac{x}{n}$, where x is the number of times an event occurs in a sample of size n.

> ### Word Wise
> Which word means "to pass the summer in a state of slumber"?
>
> A. stridulate
> B. ruminate
> C. estivate
> D. somnambulate

1 EXAMPLE Finding the Sample Proportion

In a sample of 350 teenagers, 294 have never made a snow sculpture. Find the sample proportion for those who have never made a snow sculpture. Write the answer as a percent.

sample proportion $= \frac{x}{n}$ **Write the formula.**

$= \frac{294}{350}$ **Substitute 294 for x and 350 for n.**

$= 0.84$ **Simplify.**

● The sample proportion is 84%.

✓ **Quick Check** ❶ In a poll of 1085 voters, 564 favor Candidate A. Find the sample proportion for those who favor Candidate A.

Samples vary in how well they reflect the entire population. In a **random sample,** all members of the population are equally likely to be chosen.

Vocabulary Tip

Bias means "slant."

When a part of a population is overrepresented or underrepresented in a sample, the sample is biased. A random sample can help avoid bias in gathering data.

2 EXAMPLE   Real-World Connection

Public Opinion A news program reports on a proposed school dress code. The purpose of the program is to find out what percent of the population in its viewing area favors the dress code. Identify any bias in each sampling method.

a. Viewers are invited to call the program and express their preferences.

The people who decide to call in may over- or underrepresent some views. For example, members of a group favoring the new dress code might encourage its members to call in. This type of sample is called a "self-selected" sample.

b. A reporter interviews people on the street near the local high school.

This is a "convenience" sample, since it is convenient for the reporter to stay in one place. Because the location is near the school, students may be overrepresented in the sample and the results will be biased.

c. During the program, 300 people are selected at random from the viewing area. Then each person is contacted.

This sampling method contains the least bias. It is a random sample.

✓ Quick Check **2 a.** Suppose the 350 teenagers in Example 1 all live in Florida. Is there bias in this sample? Explain.

b. Critical Thinking The only way to know a true population proportion is to poll every person in the population. Such a poll is no longer a sample, but a census. Describe a situation in which a sample is unsatisfactory and a census is required.

2 Sample Size and Margin of Error

The size of a sample affects its reliability. With a small sample size, you are likely to get a wide range of sample proportions. For example, in some samples, no one will recognize the word that means "to pass the summer in a state of slumber." In other samples, everyone will recognize *estivate*. With larger sample sizes, you are less likely to have a sample containing an "all or nothing" result.

The Law of Large Numbers states that the variation in a data set decreases as the sample size increases. By comparing the variation in samples, you can get an idea of their relative sizes.

3 EXAMPLE   Comparing Sample Sizes

Each graph below shows the sample proportions for 20 samples. Match each graph to the most likely sample size.

a. 20 people per sample   **b.** 5 people per sample

Distributions of Sample Proportions

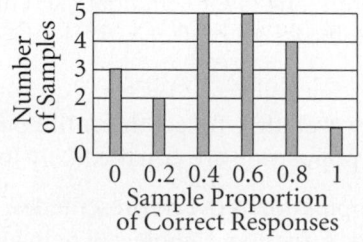

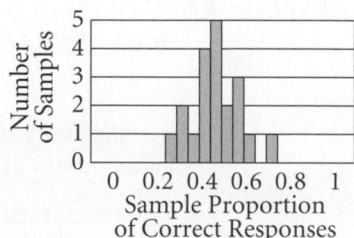

a. The graph on the right shows less variation, so it is more likely to be based on samples of a larger size, 20 people per sample.

b. The graph on the left shows more variation, so it is more likely to be based on 5 people per sample.

 **Quick Check** ❸ A science class measured the heights of blades of grass behind the school. The class took three samples. Use the information in the table below to decide which sample most likely was the greatest in size. Explain your reasoning.

Sample	Standard Deviation (in.)
A	1.45
B	1.09
C	1.26

A sample proportion should be reported with an estimate of error, called the **margin of error.** The margin of error is based on the standard deviation in graphs like those in Example 3. The larger the sample size, the smaller the margin of error.

Key Concepts

Property   **Margin of Error Formula**

When a random sample of size n is taken from a large population, the sample proportion has a margin of error of approximately $\pm \frac{1}{\sqrt{n}}$.

4 EXAMPLE **Using the Margin of Error**

A poll reports that 56% of voters favor Candidate B, with a margin of error of $\pm 3\%$. Estimate the number of voters in the poll.

$$\text{margin of error} = \pm \frac{1}{\sqrt{n}} \qquad \textbf{Write the formula.}$$

$$\pm \sqrt{n} = \frac{1}{\text{margin of error}} \qquad \textbf{Rewrite the equation.}$$

$$= \frac{1}{0.03} \qquad \textbf{Substitute 0.03 for margin of error.}$$

$$\approx 33.33 \qquad \textbf{Simplify.}$$

$$n \approx 1111 \qquad \textbf{Square each side.}$$

The poll included about 1100 voters.

 **Quick Check** ❹ Estimate the sample size for each margin of error.
a. $\pm 10\%$ **b.** $\pm 4\%$ **c.** $\pm 2\%$

You can use the margin of error to determine the likely range for the true population proportion. The graph below shows the range for the population in Example 4.

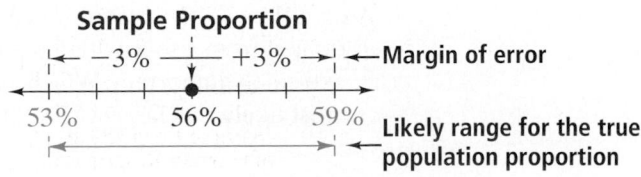

5 EXAMPLE   Real-World  Connection

Genetics A survey of 2580 students found that 9% are left-handed.

a. Find the margin of error for the sample.

$$\text{margin of error} = \pm\frac{1}{\sqrt{n}} \qquad \textbf{Use the formula.}$$

$$= \pm\frac{1}{\sqrt{2580}} \qquad \textbf{Substitute.}$$

$$\approx \pm 0.0197 \qquad \textbf{Use a calculator.}$$

The margin of error is about ±2%.

b. Use the margin of error to find an interval that is likely to contain the true population proportion.

The margin of error forms an interval with the sample proportion at its midpoint.

Sample Proportion

|← −2% —+2% →|

7%   9%   11%

The proportion of students who are left-handed is likely to be from 7% to 11%.

Real-World Connection

Some retail businesses cater to left-handers.

✓ **Quick Check** **5** In a poll of 123 students, 87 have never ridden a ferry. Find the sample proportion, the margin of error, and the interval likely to contain the true population proportion.

EXERCISES

For more exercises, see *Extra Skill and Word Problem Practice*.

Practice and Problem Solving

A **Practice by Example**

Example 1
(page 677)

For each sample, find the sample proportion. Write it as a percent.

1. 837 out of 1150 insurance applicants have no citations on their driving record.

2. 27 out of 60 shoppers prefer generic brands when available.

3. 532 out of 580 households own a color television set.

Example 2
(page 678)

Identify any bias in each sampling method.

4. A supermarket wants to find the proportion of shoppers who use reduced-price coupons. A manager interviews every shopper entering the greeting card aisle.

5. A maintenance crew wants to estimate how many of 3000 air filters in an office building need replacing. The crew examines five filters chosen at random on each floor of the building.

6. The student government wants to find out how many students have after-school jobs. A pollster interviews students selected at random as they board buses at the end of the school day.

Example 3
(pages 678–679)

7. In a survey, teenagers were asked the importance of "making your own things." The response scale ranged from 1 to 5, with 5 being extremely important. Which sample most likely was largest? Explain.

Sample	Score	Standard Deviation
A	3.6	1.2
B	3.8	1.0
C	3.8	0.5

8. The table below shows the results of a poll asking students, "How many hours a week would you say you spend doing academic homework?" Which sample most likely was smaller? Explain.

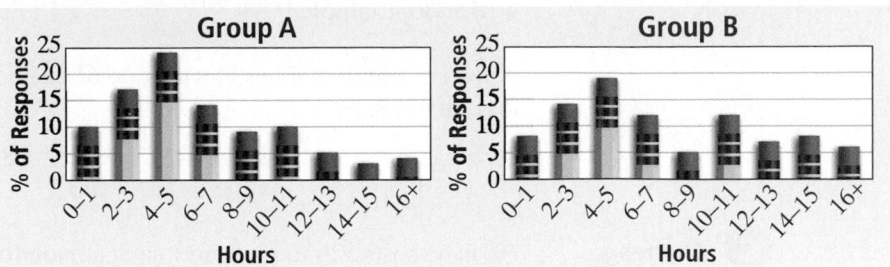

Example 4
(page 665)

Find the margin of error for the sample proportion, given each sample of size *n*.

9. $n = 200$ **10.** $n = 800$ **11.** $n = 1200$

Find the sample size that produces each margin of error.

12. ±8%   **13.** ±5%   **14.** ±1%

Example 5
(page 666)

For each situation, find the margin of error for the sample. Then find an interval likely to contain the true population proportion.

15. Of 750 teenagers polled, 59% think boys and girls are portrayed as equals on television.

16. Of 400 teenagers surveyed, 62% do not plan to stay in their community after finishing their education.

B   **Apply Your Skills**    **Surveys** **For each sample, find (a) the sample proportion, (b) the margin of error, and (c) the interval likely to contain the true population proportion.**

17. In a random sample of 408 grocery shoppers, 258 prefer one large trip per week to several smaller ones.

18. Of 500 teenagers surveyed, 460 would like to see adults in their community do more to solve drug problems.

19. In a survey of 32 people, 30 return a milk carton to the refrigerator immediately after using it.

20. In a survey of 16 people, one person never locks his car.

21. Writing Write a news article describing the sample proportion and margin of error for the poll results shown at the right.

22. Reasoning How is the margin of error affected if you double the sample size? Explain.

23. a. Data Collection Write a survey question to find out the number of students at your school who plan to continue their education after high school
    b. Describe the sampling method you would use.
    c. Conduct your survey.

Homework Video Tutor
Visit: PHSchool.com
Web Code: age-1205

24. Critical Thinking A sample proportion provides an estimate for the percent of an entire population that favors an event. Is a sample proportion an experimental or a theoretical probability? Explain.

dailypoll
Do you save more than 5% of your income?
◯ yes   ◯ no

dailypoll
Results:
yes **370**
no **583**

25. Computer Use An online advertisement asks you to participate in a survey. The survey asks how much time you spend online each week. Identify any bias in this method. If appropriate, suggest a method more likely to produce a random sample.

An event occurs x times in a sample of size n. Find its sample proportion and margin of error.

26. $x = 96$ **27.** $x = 20$ **28.** $x = 100$ **29.** $x = 273$
$n = 900$ $n = 64$ $n = 250$ $n = 435$

 Challenge

30. a. It costs \$20 to interview each person for a survey. Find the cost to obtain a $\pm 3\%$ margin of error.
     b. Critical Thinking Find the cost to obtain a $\pm 2\%$ margin of error. Why do you think polls with smaller margins of error are rare?

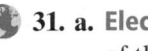 **31. a. Elections** A poll of 150 voters shows that a candidate is preferred by 56% of the voters while 44% prefer the opponent. Should the candidate be concerned? Explain.
     b. A later poll of 600 voters shows the candidate is preferred by 55% of the voters. Should this candidate feel more or less confident, given the results of the second poll? Explain.

Exercise 32

32. Wildlife Wild animal populations are often estimated through the use of the capture−tag−recapture method. Several animals are captured, tagged, and released back into the wild. The animals continue to roam freely. Then, some time later at the same site, several more animals are captured, and the number of tagged animals is recorded. An estimate of the population can then be calculated. This method of estimation assumes that the fraction of tagged animals in the second sample is equivalent to the fraction of tagged animals in the entire population.

$$\frac{\text{tagged animals in second sample}}{\text{animals in second sample}} = \frac{\text{tagged animals in population}}{\text{population } (P)}$$

Use the formula above to predict the black bear population of the northern coastal plain of South Carolina. Researchers tagged fourteen black bears in the fall and captured eleven bears the following summer. Of the eleven bears, three were tagged.

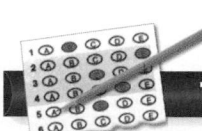

Test Prep

Multiple Choice

33. In a sample of 625 airline travelers, 485 collected "airline miles" toward free trips. What does the number $\frac{140}{625}$ represent?
   A. the probability that a passenger collects airline miles
   B. the sample proportion of the travelers who do not collect airline miles
   C. the sample proportion of the travelers who collect airline miles
   D. the margin of error for the sample

34. A random sample of people answered the question "Do you collect airline miles?" The margin of error for the sample was $\pm 2\%$. The sample proportion of people who answered no was $\frac{3}{10}$. How many people in the sample answered no?
   F. 15   **G.** 225   **H.** 750   **J.** 2500

35. A research group had a stack of survey responses. The number of respondents was more than 5000 and fewer than 5500. When the researchers divided the respondents into 13 equal groups, there were no extra respondents. Similarly, there were no extra respondents when they divided the responses into 7 equal groups or 11 equal groups. How many respondents were there?

A. 1001   **B.** 5005   **C.** 5031   **D.** 500,500

Short Response   **36.** What is the margin of error for a random sample of size 3600? Show your work.

Extended Response   **37.** In a poll of 2750 airline travelers, 138 said they never check their luggage when they fly. Find the sample proportion, the margin of error, and the interval likely to contain the true population proportion.

Mixed Review

Lesson 12-4

Find the mean and the standard deviation for each data set.

38. 0 km, 1 km, 1 km, 1 km, 2 km, 2 km, 2 km, 3 km, 3 km, 4 km, 5 km, 10 km

39. 1 oz, 1 oz, 2 oz, 2 oz, 3 oz, 4 oz, 5 oz, 6 oz, 8 oz, 9 oz, 10 oz, 10 oz, 12 oz, 20 oz

Lesson 11-4

Use summation notation to write each arithmetic series for the specified number of terms.

40. $3 + 8 + 13 + \ldots; n = 5$ **41.** $41 + 33 + 25 + \ldots; n = 8$

42. $-14 + (-8) + (-2) + \ldots; n = 6$ **43.** $-27 + (-21) + (-15) + \ldots; n = 10$

Lesson 10-4

Find the equation of each ellipse centered at the origin.

44. height: 20 units
width: 6 units

45. height: 12 units
width: 10 units

46. height: 24 units
width: 36 units

Algebra at Work

••••••••••••••••••••••••••••••• Market Researcher

When questions arise about consumer products or services, a market researcher gathers statistical information to help answer the questions. The information a market researcher collects and analyzes helps companies improve their products and make decisions about their customer base. Quantitative research allows a market researcher to analyze data from a large population of potential customers. Market research strategies for gathering information include the following.

- mail surveys
- telephone surveys
- focus groups
- in-person interviews

For: Information about market research
PHSchool.com   **Web Code:** agb-2031

Variable and Parameter

For the equation $y = mx + b$, you may have heard x and y described as variables and m and b as parameters. In other situations, however, x and y may be parameters and m and b may be variables. At this time, you can perhaps better understand the distinction between *variable* and *parameter* by considering examples than by reading definitions of these terms.

EXAMPLE The Family of Quadratic Functions

Distinguish between the variable x and the parameters a, h, and k as they appear in $f(x) = a(x - h)^2 + k$, the vertex form of a quadratic function.

The variable x represents any value in the domain of the function f. Since the domain of a quadratic function is the set of real numbers, x represents any real number.

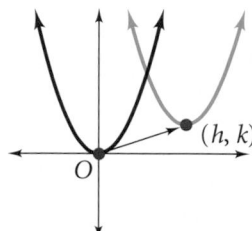

The parameters a, h, and k represent real numbers, but they are constant for any specific quadratic function. They give that function the stretch and translation characteristics that relate it to the parent quadratic function $y = x^2$.

EXERCISES

Describe the values given to the quadratic parameters in each vertex-form quadratic function below.

1. $f(x) = 2(x - 3)^2 + 4$ **2.** $g(x) = -(x + 1)^2 - 2$ **3.** $h(x) = -x^2 + 1$

4. You may not have noticed, but the "parent" exponential function $y = b^x$ is itself a family of functions, with each parent defined by the value of the parameter b. (That's why the Key Concepts Summary on page 441 uses the plural "Families" in its title "Families of Exponential Functions.")

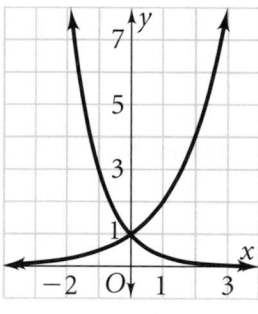

  a. What parameter values give the two parent exponential functions shown in the graph?

  b. Describe the domain of the parameter b for the exponential function $y = b^x$.

5. The function $V(k) = x^2 + k$ pairs a number k with a member of the family of quadratic functions. In other words, the inputs for V are the parameter values k; the outputs are quadratic functions. Describe this set of quadratic functions by their common characteristics.

The domain of each function is a set of real-number parameter values. The outputs are functions. Describe each set of outputs by their common characteristics.

6. $T(h) = (x - h)^2$ **7.** $S(a) = ax^2$ **8.** $V(k) = -x^2 + k$

9. $R(h) = \sqrt{x - h}$ **10.** $L(b) = \log_b x$ **11.** $V(h) = \pi r^2 h$

12. Probability Suppose k and n are whole numbers with $1 \le k \le n$.

  a. If you choose one number at random from 1 through n, what is $P(\text{choosing } k)$?

  b. For this situation, you can think of k as a variable and n as a parameter. How is your answer to part (a) affected by the value of the parameter n?

Binomial Distributions

What You'll Learn

- To find binomial probabilities
- To use binomial distributions

. . . And Why

To find the probability of winning a prize, as in Example 2

Evaluate each expression.

1. $_4C_2$ **2.** $_3C_3$ **3.** $_5C_2$

Use the binomial theorem to expand each binomial.

4. $(x + 2)^3$ **5.** $(w - y)^4$

6. $(m + n)^3$ **7.** $(t + 3s)^4$

8. $(a + 2b)^5$ **9.** $(p + q)^6$

🔊 **New Vocabulary** • binomial experiment • binomial probability

---

1   Finding Binomial Probabilities

Activity: Binomial Probability

1. Examine the situations described in the chart below. What do the situations printed in blue have in common?

| receive a numerical grade |
| receive a pass/fail grade |
| wear soccer, running, basketball, or street shoes |
| wear shoes with cleats or no cleats |
| guess on a matching test |
| guess on a true/false test |

Problem Solving Hint

You can use a coin, a number cube, or random numbers to conduct a simulation.

2. Suppose you guess each answer on a ten-question true-or-false test. Are you likely to get 70% or more right?
   a. Design and conduct a simulation for this situation.
   b. Run your simulation 10 times. Make a frequency table of the scores.
   c. Find P(70% or more right).

A **binomial experiment** has three important features:

- The situation involves repeated trials.

- Each trial has two possible outcomes (success or failure).

- The probability of success is constant throughout the trials. (The trials are independent.)

1 EXAMPLE **Designing a Binomial Experiment**

Suppose that you guess the answers to three questions of a multiple-choice test. Each question has five choices, with one correct choice.

a. Describe a trial for this situation. How many trials are there?

Each guess is a trial. Since you are guessing three times, there are three trials.

b. Describe a success. What is the probability of success on any single trial?

Each correct answer is a success. Since there are five possible answers, all of them equally likely, the probability of success on any single trial is 0.2.

c. Design and conduct a simulation to determine the probability of getting at least two answers correct. Run the simulation 10 times.

Assign each number from 1 to 5 to an outcome, based on each outcome's probability. Let 1 represent a correct response. Let 2−5 represent incorrect responses. Generate random numbers from 1 to 5.

Simulation	1	2	3	4	5	6	7	8	9	10
Number Generated, Trial 1	2	4	2	5	5	2	1	5	1	2
Number Generated, Trial 2	1	1	5	4	4	5	1	4	5	1
Number Generated, Trial 3	1	3	1	2	2	5	4	2	3	2
Number of Correct Guesses	2	1	1	0	0	0	2	0	1	1

Two of the simulations result in two or more correct guesses. So the experimental probability of getting at least two answers correct is $\frac{2}{10}$, or 20%.

✓ Quick Check **1** Run the simulation an additional 15 times. Use the results of all 25 simulations to find the experimental probability of getting at least two answers correct.

You can use a tree diagram to analyze binomial probabilities.

2 EXAMPLE **Real-World 🌐 Connection**

Merchandising As part of a promotion, a store is giving away scratch-off cards. Prizes are awarded on 40% of the game cards. Suppose you have three cards. Find the probability that exactly two of the three cards will reveal a prize.

Each card represents a trial with a probability of success of 0.4. The probability of failure is 0.6. The tree diagram below shows the probabilities along each path.

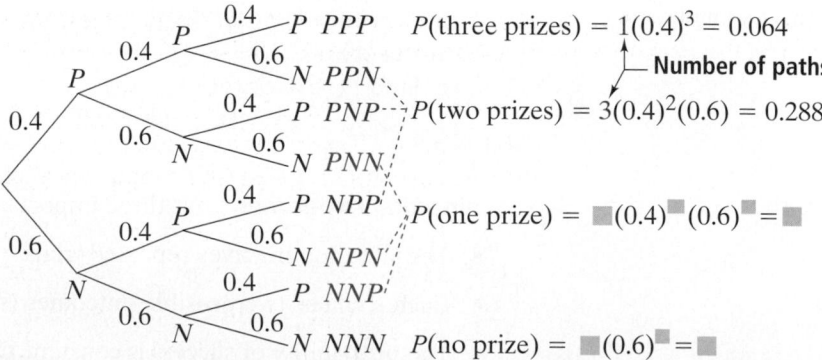

$P(\text{three prizes}) = 1(0.4)^3 = 0.064$

— **Number of paths**

$P(\text{two prizes}) = 3(0.4)^2(0.6) = 0.288$

$P(\text{one prize}) = \blacksquare(0.4)^\blacksquare(0.6)^\blacksquare = \blacksquare$

$P(\text{no prize}) = \blacksquare(0.6)^\blacksquare = \blacksquare$

The probability that exactly two of three cards will reveal a prize is 0.288.

 **Quick Check** ② **a.** Complete the tree diagram in Example 2 by finding the probability of receiving one prize and the probability of receiving no prize.
b. Verify your work by adding the probabilities for three, two, one, and no prizes. What answer should you get?

The relationships you have seen are summarized in the following formula.

 Key Concepts

Definition	Binomial Probability

Suppose you have repeated independent trials, each with a probability of success p and a probability of failure q (with $p + q = 1$). Then the probability of x successes in n trials is the following product.

$$_nC_x p^x q^{n-x}$$

③ EXAMPLE **Real-World Connection**

Quality Control A calculator contains four batteries. With normal use, each battery has a 90% chance of lasting for one year. What is the probability that all four batteries will last a year?

Relate This is a binomial experiment.

• There are four batteries.

• Each battery may succeed or fail.

• The probability of success is 0.9 for each battery.

Define Let $n = 4$.   Let $x = 4$.
Let $p = 0.9$.   Let $q = 0.1$.

Write $_nC_x p^x q^{n-x} = \,_4C_4(0.9)^4(0.1)^0$ **Substitute.**
$= (1)(0.9)^4(1)$ **Simplify.**
$= 0.6561$ **Simplify.**

```
(4 nCr 4) *0.9^4*0.1^0
                  .6561
```

The probability that all four batteries will last one year is about 66%.

> **Graphing Calculator Hint**
>
> $_nCr = \dfrac{n!}{r!(n-r)!}$
> On a graphing calculator, use
> MATH and nCr in the PRB menu.

 **Quick Check** ③ Find the probability of x successes in n trials for the given probability of success p on each trial.
a. $x = 2, n = 5, p = 0.25$ **b.** $x = 8, n = 10, p = 0.7$

---

2 Using a Binomial Distribution

To find the full probability distribution for a binomial experiment, expand the binomial $(p + q)^n$. For example, suppose you guess on four questions of a five-choice multiple choice test. For four questions, $n = 4, p = 0.2$, and $q = 0.8$.

$$
\begin{array}{ccccccccc}
& & \text{4 correct} & & \text{3 correct} & & \text{2 correct} & & \text{1 correct} & & \text{0 correct} \\
(p + q)^4 & = & 1p^4 & + & 4p^3q & + & 6p^2q^2 & + & 4pq^3 & + & 1q^4 \\
& = & (0.2)^4 & + & 4(0.2)^3(0.8) & + & 6(0.2)^2(0.8)^2 & + & 4(0.2)(0.8)^3 & + & (0.8)^4 \\
& = & 0.0016 & + & 0.0256 & + & 0.1536 & + & 0.4096 & + & 0.4096
\end{array}
$$

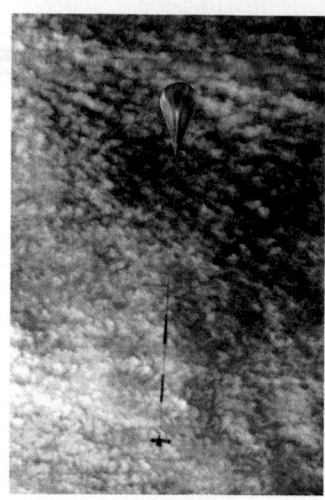

Real-World  Connection

Teardrop-shaped balloons collect weather data.

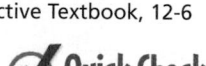
Online active math

For: Probability Activity
Use: Interactive Textbook, 12-6

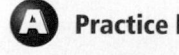 **Quick Check**

Of course, you can display a binomial distribution as a graph.

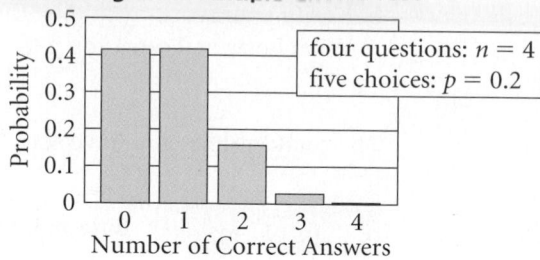

Guessing on a Multiple-Choice Test

four questions: $n = 4$
five choices: $p = 0.2$

4 EXAMPLE **Real-World  Connection**

Weather A scientist hopes to launch a weather balloon on one of the next three mornings. For each morning, there is a 40% chance of suitable weather. What is the probability that there will be at least one morning with suitable weather?

Use the expansion for $(p + q)^n$, with $n = 3, p = 0.4$, and $q = 0.6$.

3 successes	2 successes	1 success	0 successes

$$(p + q)^3 = \quad 1p^3 \quad + \quad 3p^2q \quad + \quad 3pq^2 \quad + \quad 1q^3$$
$$= \quad (0.4)^3 + 3(0.4)^2(0.6) + 3(0.4)(0.6)^2 + (0.6)^3$$
$$= \quad 0.064 \quad + \quad 0.288 \quad + \quad 0.432 \quad + \quad 0.216$$

$P(\text{at least 1 success}) = P(1 \text{ success}) + P(2 \text{ successes}) + P(3 \text{ successes})$
$$= 0.432 + 0.288 + 0.064$$
$$= 0.784$$

● The probability of at least one morning with suitable weather is about 78%.

4 One survey found that 80% of respondents eat corn on the cob in circles rather than from side to side. Assume that this sample accurately represents the population. What is the probability that, out of five people you know, at least two of them eat corn on the cob in circles?

EXERCISES

For more exercises, see *Extra Skill and Word Problem Practice.*

Practice and Problem Solving

A Practice by Example

Example 1
(page 686)

 **GO for Help**

For each situation, describe a trial and a success. Then design and run a simulation to find the probability.

1. On a true-or-false test, you guess the answers to five questions. Find the probability of guessing the correct answers to exactly three of the five questions.

2. A poll shows that 40% of the voters in a city favor passage of a bond issue to finance park improvements. If ten voters are selected at random, find the probability that exactly four of them will vote in favor of it.

3. A plant production line has a 90% probability of not experiencing a breakdown during an eight-hour shift. Find the probability that three successive shifts will not have a breakdown.

Example 2
(page 686)

Suppose you guess on a true-or-false test. Use a tree diagram to find each probability.

4. P(4 correct in 4 guesses)
5. P(1 correct in 4 guesses)
6. P(3 correct in 4 guesses)
7. P(6 correct in 4 guesses)

Example 3
(page 687)

Find the probability of x successes in n trials for the given probability of success p on each trial.

8. $x = 3, n = 8, p = 0.3$
9. $x = 4, n = 8, p = 0.3$
10. $x = 5, n = 10, p = 0.5$
11. $x = 5, n = 10, p = 0.1$

Example 4
(page 688)

Use the binomial expansion of $(p + q)^n$ to calculate and graph each binomial distribution.

12. $n = 6, p = 0.3$
13. $n = 6, p = 0.5$
14. $n = 6, p = 0.9$

 **Apply Your Skills**

 Marketing A fruit company guarantees that 90% of the pineapples it ships will be ripe within four days. Find each probability for a case containing 12 pineapples.

15. All 12 are ripe within four days.
16. At least 10 are ripe within four days.

17. No more than 9 are ripe within four days.

 Sociology A study shows that 50% of the families in a community watch television during dinner. Suppose you select 10 families at random from this population. Find each probability.

18. P(5 of the 10 families watch television during dinner)

19. P(6 of the 10 families watch television during dinner)

20. P(at least 5 of the 10 families watch television during dinner)

21. Writing Explain how a binomial experiment is related to a binomial expansion.

 22. Quality Control A company claims that 99% of its cereal boxes have at least as much cereal by weight as the amount stated on the box.
  a. At a quality control checkpoint, one box out of a random sample of ten boxes falls short of its stated weight. What is the probability of this happening due to chance variation in box weights?
  b. Suppose three of ten boxes fail to have the claimed weight. What would you conclude? Explain why.

23. Data Collection Use the current winning percentage of a local sports team as its probability of success. Find the team's probability of winning at least three of any five games.

24. Genetics About 11% of the general population is left-handed. At a school with an average class size of 30, each classroom contains four left-handed desks. Does this seem adequate? Justify your answer.

25. For a group of 40 people, what is the probability that exactly three people in the group will celebrate their birthdays on a Wednesday this year?
  a. Find the probability by using the binomial probability formula.
  b. Find the probability by designing and running a simulation.
  c. Compare your results for parts (a) and (b). Explain any discrepancy.

26. Open-Ended Describe a binomial experiment that can be solved using the expression $_7C_2(0.6)^2(0.4)^5$.

Real-World  **Connection**

Manufacturers ensure the quality of their products by inspecting raw materials, machinery, and procedures, as well as finished products.

GO **Online**
Homework Video Tutor
Visit: PHSchool.com
Web Code: age-1206

Statistics A multiple-choice test has ten questions. Each question has five choices, with only one correct.

27. Statisticians consider a "rare" event to have less than a 5% chance of occurring. According to this standard, what grades would be rare on this test if you guess? Justify your answer.

28. Design and conduct a simulation to model this situation. Gather results of simulations from your classmates. Do these results confirm the grades you identified as rare in Exercise 27? Explain.

29. Enter the binomial probability formula as shown. Set the window and table shown. (To get integer values of x, you may need to adjust your window.)

Plot1 Plot2 Plot3	WINDOW	TABLE SETUP
\Y₁◼ (7 nCr X) * 0.5^X*	Xmin = -1.7	TblStart = 0
0.5^(7–X)	Xmax = 7.7	ΔTbl = 1
\Y₂=	Xscl = 1	Indpnt: Auto Ask
\Y₃=	Ymin = -.2	Depend: Auto Ask
\Y₄=	Ymax = .5	
\Y₅=	Yscl = .1	
\Y₆=	Xres = 1	

a. Examine the graph of $y = {_7}C_x(0.5)^x(0.5)^{7-x}$. Describe any symmetry you see in the graph.

b. Verify the symmetry by displaying values of the function in table form.

c. Change the graph to $y = {_7}C_x(0.6)^x(0.4)^{7-x}$. Does this graph have any symmetry? Explain.

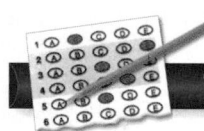

Test Prep

30. Four percent of the tenants in an apartment building live alone. Suppose five tenants are selected randomly. Which expression represents $P(\text{all live alone})$?
A. $(0.04)^5$ **B.** $(0.4)^5$ **C.** $(0.96)^5$ **D.** $(5)^{0.04}$

31. A survey shows that 60% of the adults floss their teeth every day. In a random sample of ten adults, what is the probability that exactly six floss every day?
F. 11%   **G.** 25%   **H.** 60%   **J.** 100%

32. A multiple-choice quiz contains five questions, each with three answer choices. You select all five answer choices at random. What is the best estimate of the probability that you will get at least four answers correct?
A. 4.1%   **B.** 4.5%   **C.** 13.2%   **D.** 46.1%

Short Response

33. A family is planning a four-day campout. The weather forecast shows a 20% chance of rain for each of the four days. Find the probability, to the nearest hundredth, that there will be no rain on at least three of the four days.

34. Evaluate ${_n}C_x p^x q^{n-x}$ for $n = 7$, $x = 4$, $p = 0.2$, and $q = 0.8$. Round your answer to the nearest thousandth.

Extended Response

35. A bank of track lights contains several bulbs. The chance that some number of the bulbs will last for at least 2 years is given by the expression ${_5}C_2(0.15)^2 (0.85)^3$.
a. What is the number of bulbs in the track?
b. How many bulbs should last at least 2 years?
c. What is the probability that all the bulbs will last at least 2 years?

Lesson 12-5

36. The table contains information from a study of the prices of comparable airline tickets. Which sample most likely was greater in size, A or B? Explain.

Sample	Standard Deviation
A	$10.81
B	$3.97

Lesson 11-5

Find the sum of each geometric series to the given term.

37. $8 + 12 + 18 + \ldots; n = 8$

38. $20 + (-2) + 0.2 + \ldots; n = 12$

39. $729 + 243 + 81 + \ldots; n = 9$

40. $\frac{1}{16} + \frac{1}{4} + 1 + \ldots; n = 6$

Lesson 10-5

Find the equation of a hyperbola with horizontal transverse axis, centered at the origin, for the given a and c values.

41. $a = 897$ units, $c = 1024$ units

42. $a = 20$ units, $c = 29$ units

Lesson 5-4

Factor each expression.

43. $x^2 + 6x + 9$

44. $x^2 + x - 6$

45. $x^2 - 7x + 10$

46. $3x^2 + 12x + 9$

47. $2x^2 - x - 6$

48. $5x^2 + 5x - 10$

Checkpoint Quiz 2   **Lessons 12-4 through 12-6**

Calculate the mean, range, and standard deviation for each set of data.

1. 34 36 29 45 34 25

2. 12 9 10 11 14 10

3. 1 5 2 1 4 1 3 2

4. A set of values has a mean of 300 and a standard deviation of 60. What value has a z-score of -1.2?

5. A survey on the Web site of an online CD store includes the question, "Who is your favorite singer?"
  a. Explain why the results of the survey may be biased.
  b. Open-Ended Suggest a way to make the survey an unbiased representation of the population of your high school.

 6. Consumer Spending In a survey of 683 car owners selected at random, 235 reported paying cash for their first car.
  a. Find the sample proportion.
  b. Find the margin of error.
  c. Find an interval likely to contain the true population proportion.

7. Determine the sample size that produces a margin of error of $\pm 20\%$.

8. Seventy percent of the time, a friend of yours is more than 10 minutes late to meet you for a movie. What is the probability that your friend will be more than 10 minutes late to meet you for all of the next three movies you see?

Each trial of an experiment has a probability of success p. Find the probability of x successes in n trials.

9. $p = 0.8, x = 4, n = 5$

10. $p = 0.4, x = 4, n = 5$

Normal Distributions

✓ **Check Skills You'll Need**

GO for Help Lesson 12-4

Find the numbers that are one and two standard deviations above and below each given mean. Write these numbers from least to greatest.

1. $\bar{x} = 12, \sigma = 2$ **2.** $\bar{x} = 16.7, \sigma = 1$ **3.** $\bar{x} = 7, \sigma = 1.5$

4. $\bar{x} = 22, \sigma = 1.7$ **5.** $\bar{x} = 17.5, \sigma = 0.9$ **6.** $\bar{x} = 33.1, \sigma = 1.2$

🔊 **New Vocabulary**   • normal distribution   • standard normal curve

---

1   Using a Normal Distribution

A **normal distribution** shows data that vary randomly from the mean. The pattern the data form is a bell-shaped curve called a normal curve.

1 EXAMPLE   Real-World 🌐 Connection

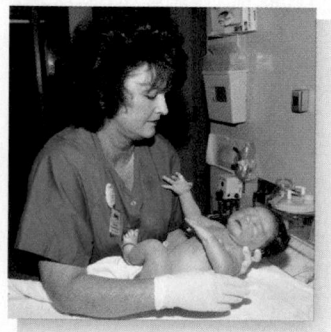

Real-World 🌐 Connection

Careers Neonatal nurses specialize in the nursing care of newborns and babies up to 30 days old.

Medicine The bar graph below gives the birth weights of a population of 100 babies. The red curve shows how the weights are normally distributed about the mean, 3250 g. Estimate the percent of babies weighing 2500–3999 g.

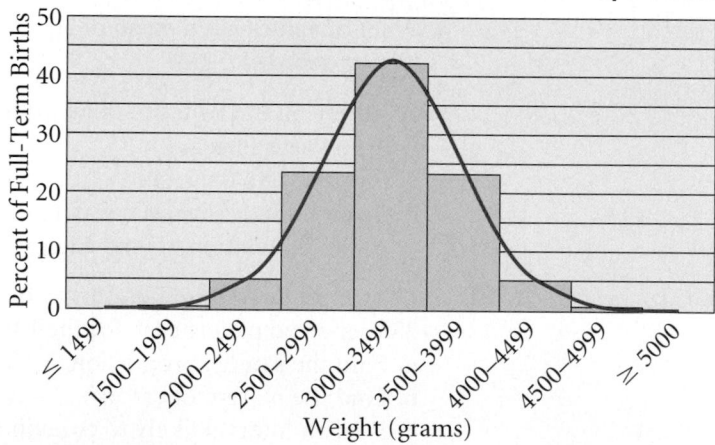

Full-Term Birth Weight Distribution for a Population

Estimate and add the percents for 2500–2999, 3000–3499, and 3500–3999.

$23\% + 42\% + 23\% = 88\%$

● About 88% of the babies weigh 2500–3999 g.

✓ **Quick Check** ❶ **a.** Estimate the percent of babies weighing less than 3500 g.

b. The standard deviation in birth weights is about 500 g. Estimate the percent of babies whose birth weights are within 1.5 standard deviations of the mean.

Every normal curve has a symmetric bell shape. When outcomes are normally distributed, you can sketch the graph of the distribution.

2 EXAMPLE **Real-World Connection**

Biology Refer to the photo. For the given population of sharks, the standard deviation of the jaw widths is 2.8 inches. Sketch a normal curve showing the jaw widths at one, two, and three standard deviations from the mean.

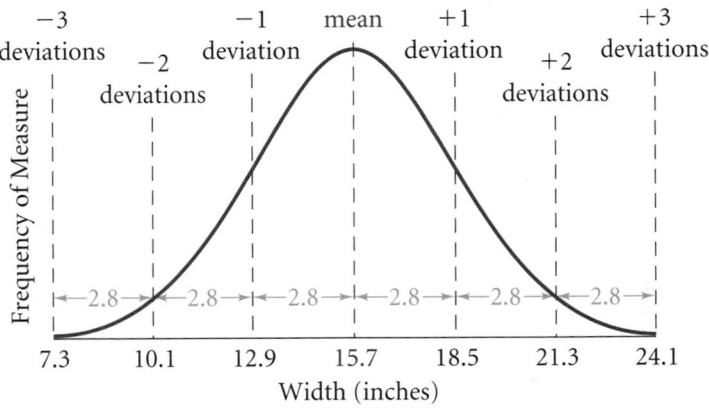

Distribution of Jaw Widths for Great White Sharks

✓ **Quick Check** ❷ Suppose the mean in Example 2 is 15.4 inches and the standard deviation is 3.1 inches. Sketch a normal curve showing the jaw widths at one, two, and three standard deviations from the mean.

2 Using the Standard Normal Curve

When you show a probability distribution as a bar graph, the height of the bar for each outcome indicates the probability. For a normal curve, however, the area between the curve and the *x*-axis represents the probability.

The **standard normal curve** is a normal distribution centered on the *y*-axis. The mean of the standard normal curve is 0. The standard deviation is 1.

The Standard Normal Curve

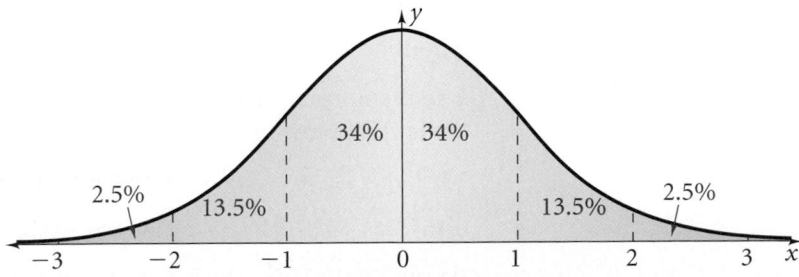

Every normal curve contains the same probability distribution. When a data set is normally distributed, about 68% of the data fall within one standard deviation of the mean. About 95% of the data fall within two standard deviations of the mean. To find the values that are two standard deviations away from the mean, find the values that have *z*-scores of −2 and 2.

3 EXAMPLE **Using the Standard Normal Curve**

In a survey, the responses to the question "How much time do you spend at meals in one week?" were normally distributed. The mean was 13 h; the standard deviation was 3 h.

a. What values are one standard deviation from the mean?

Values that are one standard deviation from the mean have z-scores of -1 and 1.

$$z\text{-score} = \frac{\text{value} - \text{mean}}{\text{standard deviation}}$$

$$-1 = \frac{v - 13}{3} \qquad\qquad 1 = \frac{u - 13}{3}$$

$$v = 10 \qquad\qquad\qquad u = 16$$

The values 10 h and 16 h are one standard deviation away from the mean.

b. What percent of the responses would you expect to find from 10 h to 16 h?

The responses are normally distributed, and 10 h and 16 h are the values that are one standard deviation from the mean. Since 68% of the data are within one standard deviation of the mean, 68% should be values from 10 h to 16 h.

 **3 a.** Suppose there were 100 responses to the survey question. How many responses would you expect to be values from 10 h to 16 h?

b. Of 100 responses, how many would you expect to be values from 16 h to 19 h?

4 EXAMPLE **Real-World** 🌐 **Connection**

Education In a university lecture class with 174 students, the final exam scores have a mean of 68.5 and a standard deviation of 7.3. The grades on the exams are all whole numbers, and the grade pattern follows a normal curve.

a. About how many students receive grades from one to two standard deviations above the mean.

Use the normal curve. About 13.5% of the students receive grades from one to two standard deviations above the mean.

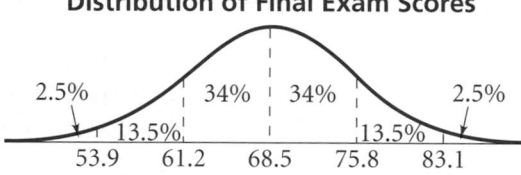

Distribution of Final Exam Scores

2.5%   34% | 34%   2.5%
13.5%   13.5%
53.9   61.2   68.5   75.8   83.1

$0.135(174) = 23.49$ **Find the number of students that corresponds to 13.5%.**

About 23 students receive grades from one to two standard deviations above the mean.

b. About how many students receive grades of 61 or below.

Use the normal curve from part (a). A grade of 61 is about one standard deviation below the mean.

$13.5\% + 2.5\% = 16\%$ **Find the % at least 1 standard deviation below the mean.**

$0.16(174) = 27.84$ **Find the number of students.**

About 28 students receive grades of 61 or below.

 **4 a.** Suppose there are 140 students in the class in Example 4. About how many would receive grades from 69 to 75?

b. Writing How do you know that in a class of 140 students, about 22 students receive grades of 76 or higher?

EXERCISES

For more exercises, see *Extra Skill and Word Problem Practice*.

Practice and Problem Solving

A Practice by Example

Example 1
(page 692)

for
Help

Biology The heights of men in a survey are distributed normally about the mean. Use the graph for Exercises 1–4.

Heights of Men Ages 25–34

1. About what percent of men aged 25 to 34 are 69–71 inches tall?

2. About what percent of men aged 25 to 34 are less than 70 inches tall?

3. Suppose the survey included data on 100 men. About how many would you expect to be 69–71 inches tall?

4. The mean of the data is 70, and the standard deviation is 2.5. About what percent of men are within one standard deviation of the mean in height?

Example 2
(page 693)

Sketch a normal curve for each distribution. Label the *x*-axis values at one, two, and three standard deviations from the mean.

5. mean = 45, standard deviation = 5   6. mean = 45, standard deviation = 10

7. mean = 45, standard deviation = 2   8. mean = 45, standard deviation = 3.5

Examples 3 and 4
(page 694)

A set of data with a mean of 62 and a standard deviation of 5.7 is normally distributed. Find each value, given its distance from the mean.

9. +3 standard deviations   10. −1 standard deviation

A set of data has a normal distribution with a mean of 50 and a standard deviation of 8. Find the percent of data within each interval.

11. from 42 to 58   12. greater than 34   13. less than 50

14. **Test Scores** The scores on an exam are normally distributed, with a mean of 85 and a standard deviation of 5. What percent of the scores are from 85 to 95?

B Apply Your Skills

15. The numbers of paper clips in a truckload of boxes are normally distributed, with a mean of 100 and a standard deviation of 5. Find the probability that a box will *not* contain from 95 to 105 clips.

16. **Writing** In a class of 25, one student receives a grade of 100 on a test. The grades are distributed approximately normally, with a mean of 78 and a standard deviation of 5. Do you think the student's grade is an outlier? Explain.

17. a. From the table at the right, select the set of values that appears to be distributed normally.
  b. Using the set you chose in part (a), make a histogram of the values.
  c. Sketch a normal curve over your graph.

18. Track To qualify as a contestant in a race, a runner has to be in the fastest 16% of all applicants. The running times are normally distributed, with a mean of 63 min and a standard deviation of 4 min. To the nearest minute, what is the qualifying time for the race?

19. Agriculture To win a prize, a tomato must be greater than 4 in. in diameter. The diameters of a crop of tomatoes grown in a special soil are normally distributed, with a mean of 3.2 in. and a standard deviation of 0.4 in. Find the probability that the crop will contain a winning tomato.

Set 1	Set 2	Set 3
1	5	5
10	7	6
5	7	9
19	7	1
2	4	1
7	11	5
1	7	11
7	7	1
2	7	10
10	9	4
6	7	2
9	7	8

A normal distribution has a mean of 100 and a standard deviation of 10. Find the probability that a value selected at random is in the given interval.

20. from 80 to 100   **21.** from 70 to 130   **22.** from 90 to 120

23. at least 100   **24.** at most 110   **25.** at least 80

26. Two tomato plants were chosen from two groups of plants grown in different soils. Each sample plant produced 23 tomatoes. The mean number of tomatoes for plants in the first soil was 17, with a standard deviation of 5. The mean number of tomatoes for plants in the second soil was 18, with a standard deviation of 6. Determine which plant, if either, is in the top 16% of its group.

27. In a set of data, the value that is -3 standard deviations from the mean is 86. The value that is $+1$ standard deviation from the mean is 250.
  a. Find the mean.
  b. Find the standard deviation.
  c. Find an interval with an end value of 250 that contains about 81.5% of the data.

28. Seismology The table below shows the number of earthquakes worldwide in 2000.
  a. Draw a histogram to represent the data.
  b. Does the histogram approximate a normal curve? Explain.

GO Online
Homework Video Tutor
Visit: PHSchool.com
Web Code: age-1207

Worldwide Earthquakes in 2000

Magnitude	Number	Magnitude	Number
0.1–0.9	6	5.0–5.9	1318
1.0–1.9	1028	6.0–6.9	157
2.0–2.9	3728	7.0–7.9	14
3.0–3.9	4741	8.0–8.9	4
4.0–4.9	8114	≥9.0	0

SOURCE: U.S. Geological Survey

29. Critical Thinking Jake and Elena took the same standardized test, but with different groups of students. They both received a score of 87. In Jake's group, the mean was 80 and the standard deviation was 6. In Elena's group, the mean was 76 and the standard deviation was 4. Did either student score in the top 10% of his or her group? Explain.

C Challenge **30. Quality Control** Tubs of Better Butter weigh 1.0 lb each, with a standard deviation of 0.06 lb. At a quality control checkpoint, 12 of the tubs taken as samples weighed less than 0.88 lb. Assume that the weights of the samples were normally distributed. How many tubs of butter were taken as samples?

31. Games In the Japanese game pachinko, a player launches small steel balls from the bottom of a playing frame to the top. The balls then fall through pins and bounce around haphazardly. They land in slots at the bottom of the game and form a normal distribution. If a ball falls into a specially marked slot, the player wins additional balls with which to play again in the next round. If a ball does not fall into a marked slot, the player loses that ball.

a. Suppose that all slots between one and two standard deviations from the center are marked. When a ball lands in one of the marked slots, you win the ball back along with two others. If you begin with 200 balls, how many balls should you have after one round?

b. Suppose that there are two sets of marked slots. One set is within one standard deviation of the center and the other set is more than two standard deviations from the center. When a ball lands in one of the slots in the first set, you win the ball back. When a ball lands in one of the slots in the second set, you win the ball back, along with four others. If you begin with 1000 balls, how many balls should you have after one round?

c. Open-Ended Using your knowledge of normal distributions, design a pachinko game with both winning and losing slots in which you would theoretically have the same number of balls after each round as when you started. You can adjust the number of balls at the beginning of the game, the placement of the winning slots, and the number balls won per slot.

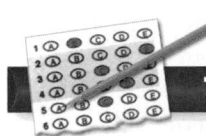

Test Prep

Multiple Choice

For a daily airline flight between two cities, the number of pieces of checked luggage has a mean of 380 and a standard deviation of 20. Use this information for Exercises 32–33.

32. On what percent of the flights would you expect from 340 to 420 pieces of checked luggage?
  A. 34% **B.** 47.5% **C.** 68% **D.** 95%

33. What number of pieces of checked luggage is 3 standard deviations above the mean?
  F. 60 **G.** 97.5 **H.** 440 **J.** 1140

34. A set of data is normally distributed with a mean of 44 and a standard deviation of 3.2. Which statements are NOT true?
  I. 68% of the values are between 37.6 and 50.4
  II. 13.5% of the values are less than 40.8
  III. 5% of the values are lower than 37.6 or higher than 50.4
  A. I and II only **B.** I and III only **C.** II and III only **D.** I, II, and III

Short Response

35. Distribution A has 50 data values with mean 40 and standard deviation 2.4. Distribution B has 30 data values with mean 40 and standard deviation 2.8. Which distribution has more data values at or below 40? Show your work.

Read the article below. Then answer Exercises 36–38.

College Entrance Exam Results for 2000

In 2000, over 1.2 million students across the country took college entrance exams. The average score on the verbal section showed no improvement over the average scores of the previous four years. The average score on the mathematics section was three points higher than the previous year's average.

Section	Mean	Standard Deviation
Math	505	111
Verbal	514	113

36. What is the probability that a student's score on the verbal section is from 401 to 514?

37. What is the probability that a student's score on the math section is greater than 727?

38. Both Susanna's math score and her verbal score were more than one standard deviation above the mean, but less than two standard deviations above the mean. What are the lower and upper limits of Susanna's combined score?

Mixed Review

Lesson 12-6 39. **Production** A plant production line has a 95% probability of not experiencing a breakdown during a six-hour shift. The plant managers want to know the probability that four successive shifts will not have a breakdown. Design and run a simulation to find the probability. Include an explanation of what constitutes a trial and a success.

Lesson 11-6 **For each set of axes, what does the area under the curve represent?**

40. y-axis: tons of garbage generated per year, x-axis: years

41. y-axis: bus passengers per hour, x-axis: hours

Lesson 10-6 42. **Coordinate Geometry** Write the equation of a circle centered at $(4, -5)$ with radius 7.

Open-Ended **Write the equation of a conic section with the given characteristics.**

43. an ellipse with a major axis 8 units long

44. a hyperbola with an asymptote at $y = -x$

Lesson 9-1 **Suppose that x and y vary inversely. Write a function to model inverse variation.**

45. $x = 1$ when $y = 5$ 46. $x = -1$ when $y = 10$ 47. $x = -3$ when $y = 3$

48. $x = 25$ when $y = -5$ 49. $x = 1.8$ when $y = -6$ 50. $x = 7.5$ when $y = 50$

Area Under a Curve

Technology

FOR USE WITH LESSON 12-7

Statisticians use the function $f(x) = \frac{1}{\sqrt{2\pi}}e^{-\frac{x^2}{2}}$ to model data such as height or birth weight. You can use the area under the graph of the function to find probabilities.

ACTIVITY

In a given population, the weights of babies are normally distributed about the mean, 3250 g. The standard deviation is 500 g. Find the probability that a baby chosen at random weighs from 2250 g to 4250 g.

Step 1 Find the z-scores of the lower and upper limits.

$$z\text{-score} = \frac{\text{value} - \text{mean}}{\text{standard deviation}}$$

$$z_1 = \frac{2250 - 3250}{500} = \frac{-1000}{500} = -2$$

$$z_2 = \frac{4250 - 3250}{500} = \frac{1000}{500} = 2$$

Step 2 Enter $f(x) = \frac{1}{\sqrt{2\pi}}e^{-\frac{x^2}{2}}$ as Y_1. Adjust the window values.

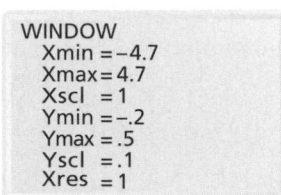

Step 3 Use the **CALC** feature and press 7 to access the $\int f(x)dx$ feature. Move the cursor until the lower limit is $x = -2$. Press ENTER. Move the cursor until the upper limit is $x = 2$. Press ENTER.

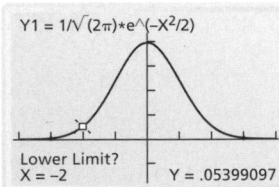 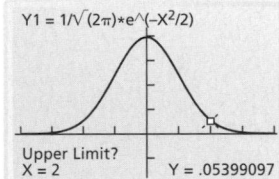 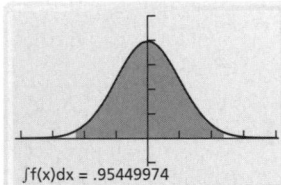

The area under the curve from $x = -2$ to $x = 2$ is about 0.95. So the probability that a baby weighs from 2250 g to 4250 g is about 95%.

EXERCISES

Use the data and the function in the example. Find the probability that the weight of a baby chosen at random falls within each interval.

1. 3150–4150 g   **2.** 4300–4500 g   **3.** less than 1800 g   **4.** more than 4550 g

5. For Exercises 1–4, estimate the number of babies within each interval from a population of 2400 babies.

 6. Manufacturing A battery company manufactures batteries having life spans that are normally distributed, with a mean of 45 months and a standard deviation of 5 months. Find the probability that a battery chosen at random will have each life span.
     a. 45–52 months   **b.** 48–50 months

When answering a question, be sure to answer the question that is asked. Read the question carefully and identify the quantity that you are asked to find. Some answer choices are answers to related questions, so you have to be careful that you are answering the right question.

EXAMPLE

There are five puppies in a litter. If the probability that a puppy is male is 0.5, what is the probability that at most one puppy in the litter is male?

    Ⓐ 0.15625   Ⓑ 0.1875   Ⓒ 0.5   Ⓓ 0.8125   Ⓔ 0.96875

The problem is asking for the probability of "at most" one male puppy. Do not confuse this with "exactly" or "at least" one male puppy.

$$\begin{aligned} P(\text{at most one male puppy}) &= P(\text{no male puppies}) + P(\text{exactly 1 male puppy}) \\ &= {}_5C_0(0.5)^0(0.5)^5 + {}_5C_1(0.5)^1(0.5)^4 \\ &= 0.03125 + 0.15625 = 0.1875 \end{aligned}$$

The correct answer is B.

Choices A and E are answers to related, but different, questions.

$$P(\text{exactly one male puppy}) = {}_5C_1(0.5)^1(0.5)^4 = 0.15625$$

$$\begin{aligned} P(\text{at least one male puppy}) &= P(\text{exactly 1 male}) + \ldots + P(\text{exactly 5 males}) \\ &= {}_5C_1(0.5)^1(0.5)^4 + \ldots + {}_5C_5(0.5)^5(0.5)^0 \\ &= 0.15625 + \ldots + 0.03125 \\ &= 0.96875 \end{aligned}$$

EXERCISES

Identify the quantity that is being asked for. Then answer the question.

1. A box contains four quarters. Exactly two of the quarters have the American eagle on the back. Suppose you draw two quarters with replacement at random from the box.
   a. What is the probability that both have the American eagle on the back?
   b. What is the probability that neither has the American eagle on the back?
   c. What is the probability that at least one has the American eagle on the back?

2. In a survey, 28% of respondents say they are left-handed, 64% say they are right-handed, and 8% say they are ambidextrous. If the ambidextrous people are omitted, about what percent of those remaining are left-handed?
     Ⓐ 28%   Ⓑ 30%   Ⓒ 32%   Ⓓ 34%   Ⓔ 36%

3. A student conducted a survey at school and found that 75% of the boys and 65% of the girls like to watch hockey games. There are an equal number of boys and girls in the school. If someone does not like to watch hockey games, what is the approximate probability that the person is a boy?
     Ⓐ 25%   Ⓑ 42%   Ⓒ 48%   Ⓓ 55%   Ⓔ 75%

Chapter Review

Vocabulary Review

- bimodal (p. 660)
- binomial experiment (p. 685)
- binomial probability (p. 687)
- box-and-whisker plot (p. 662)
- conditional probability (p. 654)
- cumulative probability (p. 648)
- frequency table (p. 648)
- interquartile range (p. 669)
- margin of error (p. 679)

- mean (p. 660)
- measures of central tendency (p. 660)
- measures of variation (p. 669)
- median (p. 660)
- mode (p. 660)
- normal distribution (p. 692)
- outlier (p. 664)
- percentile (p. 663)
- probability distribution (p. 649)

- quartiles (p. 662)
- random sample (p. 677)
- range of a set of data (p. 669)
- sample (p. 677)
- sample proportion (p. 677)
- standard deviation (p. 669)
- standard normal curve (p. 693)
- z-score (p. 671)

Choose the correct term to complete each sentence.

1. A(n) __?__ is part of a population.

2. A(n) __?__ has a value substantially different from other data in a set.

3. A function that gives the probability of each event in a sample space is a(n) __?__.

4. A(n) __?__ involves repeated trials, each of which has two possible outcomes whose probabilities are constant throughout the trials.

5. Dispersion of data in a data set can be described by __?__.

Go Online
PHSchool.com

For: Vocabulary quiz
Web Code: agj-1251

Skills and Concepts

12-1 and 12-2 Objectives

▼ To make a probability distribution (p. 648)

▼ To use a probability distribution in conducting a simulation (p. 650)

▼ To find conditional probabilities (p. 654)

▼ To use formulas and tree diagrams (p. 655)

A **probability distribution** is a function that gives the probability of each event in a sample space. A **frequency table** lists outcomes and the number of times each occurs. A frequency table can be used to find **cumulative probability**, which is the probability of a range of events.

A **conditional probability** limits the sample space to a given event. The probability of event A, given event B, is written $P(A \mid B)$. You can find a conditional probability from a table, a tree diagram, or by the conditional probability formula.

$$P(A \mid B) = \frac{P(A \text{ and } B)}{P(B)}$$

6. Use the results in the table below for the Rock-Paper-Scissors game.
   a. Make a frequency table for the winner: Player 1, Player 2, or tie.
   b. Find P(Player 2 wins).

Rock-Paper-Scissors

Player 1	S	P	P	**R**	R	P	**P**	**P**	P	S	R	S	**P**	S	R
Player 2	P	R	**S**	S	**P**	**S**	R	R	P	P	R	S	R	P	**P**

R = Rock   P = Paper   S = Scissors   **Bold** = Winner

7. Two number cubes are rolled. Use a table to show the probability distribution for the product of the two numbers.

8. At a bank, the number of customers c who arrive at the teller counters each minute varies according to the distribution below. Simulate the number of customers over a ten-minute period.

Number of Customers Each Minute

c	0	1	2	3	4	5	6	7
$P(c)$	0.16	0.28	0.25	0.18	0.09	0.02	0.01	0.01

Use the frequency table below for Exercises 9 and 10.

Birthday Months of Respondents to a Survey

Month	J	F	M	A	M	J	J	A	S	O	N	D
Male	0	1	2	1	1	3	2	0	1	1	0	2
Female	0	1	0	1	0	2	1	3	1	0	4	1

9. Find P(birthday in August | female respondent).

10. Find P(male respondent | birthday in June).

Use these survey results for Exercises 11–13.

• Of all respondents, 60% have 1 sibling and 20% have 2 or more siblings.

• Of the respondents with 0 siblings, 90% have their own room.

• Of the respondents with 1 sibling, 20% do not have their own room.

• Of the respondents with 2 or more siblings, 50% have their own room.

11. Make a tree diagram that reflects the results of the survey.

12. Find P(own room | 0 siblings).   **13.** Find P(share room | 1 sibling).

12-3 Objectives

▼ To calculate measures of central tendency (p. 660)

▼ To draw and interpret box-and-whisker plots (p. 662)

You can use **measures of central tendency** to analyze data. The **mean** $\overline{x}$ equals the sum of the values divided by the number of values. The **median** is the middle value of a data set in numerical order. If the set has an even number of values, then the median is the mean of the middle two values. The **mode** is the most frequently occurring value. There can be more than one mode or no mode. A **bimodal** distribution has 2 modes. The second quartile is the median of the whole set. The first and third **quartiles** are, respectively, the medians of the values less than and greater than the median. A **box-and-whisker plot** displays data by using the quartiles to form a box and the minimum and maximum values to form whiskers. A **percentile** divides the range of a data set into two parts such that the part lying below the value contains a given percentage of the data. An **outlier** is a data value substantially different from the rest of the data.

Use the following set of values for Exercises 14–19.

13   12   15   18   14   16   18   12   13   14   14   17   15   8   17
16   12   16   14   15   13   13   17   15   14   18   16   12   12   13

14. Find the mean, median, and mode.   **15.** Make a box-and-whisker plot.

16. Find the 20th and 90th percentiles.   **17.** At what percentile is 15?

18. Identify the outlier.   **19.** Find the range without the outlier.

12-4 Objectives

▼ To find the standard deviation of a set of values (p. 668)

▼ To use standard deviation in real-world situations (p. 671)

You can use **measures of variation** to describe the spread of data. The **range of a set of data** is the difference between the maximum and minimum values. The **interquartile range** is the difference between the third and first quartiles. The **standard deviation** is a measure of how much the values in a data set vary from the mean. To find the standard deviation, (1) find the mean, (2) find the difference between each data value and the mean, (3) square each difference, (4) find the mean of the squares, and (5) take the square root of this mean. The **z-score** of a value is the number of standard deviations that value is from the mean.

Use the following set of values for Exercises 20–22.

$1.95 \quad $1.27 \quad $1.81 \quad $1.33 \quad $1.30 \quad $.99 \quad $1.63 \quad $1.49 \quad $1.39 \quad $1.25 \quad $1.50

20. Find the standard deviation.

21. Within how many standard deviations of the mean do all of the values fall?

22. Find the z-score of the value $1.85, to the nearest hundredth.

12-5 Objectives

▼ To find sample proportions (p. 677)

▼ To find the margin of error (p. 678)

A **sample** is part of a population. For a **random sample**, all members of the population are equally likely to be chosen for the sample. When an event occurs x times in a sample of size n, the **sample proportion** is the ratio $\frac{x}{n}$. When a random sample of size n is taken from a large population, the sample proportion has a **margin of error** of approximately $\pm \frac{1}{\sqrt{n}}$.

23. Of 50 people who rented clubs at a golf course, 38 were right-handed.
 a. Find the sample proportion as a percent.
 b. Find the margin of error.
 c. Find an interval likely to contain the true population proportion.

12-6 and 12-7 Objectives

▼ To find binomial probabilities (p. 685)

▼ To use binomial distributions (p. 687)

▼ To use a normal distribution (p. 692)

▼ To use the standard normal curve (p. 693)

A **binomial experiment** has repeated independent trials, each trial having two possible outcomes. In a binomial experiment with probability of success p and of failure q (so $p + q = 1$), the probability of x successes in n trials is $_{n}C_{x}p^{x}q^{n-x}$. This value is the **binomial probability**.

A **normal distribution** shows data that vary from the mean in a random manner. The pattern they form is a bell-shaped curve called a normal curve. The **standard normal curve** is a normal distribution centered on the y-axis. The mean is 0 and the standard deviation is 1. When a data set follows the normal curve, about 68% of the data fall within one standard deviation of the mean. About 95% of the data fall within two standard deviations of the mean.

24. A true-or-false quiz contains four questions. Design and describe a simulation you could use to find the probability of guessing three questions correctly.

25. Find the probability of 13 successes in 24 trials, given that the probability of success is 0.6 for each trial.

26. Use the binomial expansion of $(p + q)^n$ to write the binomial distribution for $n = 5$ and $p = 0.7$.

27. Sketch a curve for a normal distribution with mean 10 and standard deviation 4. Label the x-axis at one, two, and three standard deviations from the mean.

Chapter Test

Go Online
PHSchool.com
For: Chapter Test
Web Code: aga-1252

Graph the probability distribution for each sample space when two number cubes are rolled.

1. {both cubes the same number, each cube a different number}

2. {prime sum, composite sum}

 3. Writing Describe how a situation can have more than one sample space. Include an example.

Use the table below for Exercises 4–8.

How Many Current Music Groups Can You Name?

Age of Respondent	Number of Groups	
	0 – 4	5 or more
< 30	7	18
≥ 30	13	12

4. Make a frequency table for the ages of the respondents.

5. Make a frequency table for the number of groups named.

6. Find P(5 or more).

7. Find P(5 or more | age < 30).

8. Find P(age ≥ 30 | 0–4).

9. Find the mean, median, and mode for this set of values: 8, 9, 11, 12, 13, 15, 16, 18, 20.

10. Make a box-and-whisker plot for this set of values: 36, 36, 48, 65, 75, 82, 92, 101.

11. Find the 20th and 60th percentiles for this set of values: 36, 38, 42, 47, 51, 56, 62, 69, 70, 74.

12. Given the set of values below, at what percentiles are 78 and 81?
43 58 64 78 78 81 89 89 91 93

13. Identify the outlier of this set of values: 17, 15, 16, 15, 9, 18, 16.

14. Open-Ended Write a set of values that has a range of 10, a mean of 86, and a mode of 85.

15. Find the mean and the standard deviation for this set of values: 15, 17, 19, 20, 14, 23, 12.

16. A data set has a mean 30 and a standard deviation of 3. Find the z-score of the value 38.

Find the margin of error for each sample. Then find an interval likely to contain the true population proportion.

17. 15% of 457 teachers

18. 47% of 296 teens

19. 56% of 87 musicians

20. 23% of 100 bakers

A newspaper wants to take a poll about which candidate voters prefer for President. Identify any bias in each sampling method.

21. The newspaper interviews people at a political debate.

22. The newspaper publishes a number for people to call and express their opinion.

23. The newspaper calls people selected at random from the local telephone book.

Find the probability of x successes in n trials for the given probability of success p on each trial.

24. $x = 4, n = 10, p = 0.2$

25. $x = 3, n = 8, p = 0.6$

26. At a high school, 30% of the students buy class rings. You select five students at random. Find P(exactly two buy rings) and P(at least two buy rings).

27. A student guesses the answers to three questions on a true-or-false test. Design and describe a simulation to find the probability that the student guesses at least one of the questions correctly.

A set of data has a normal distribution with a mean of 29 and a standard deviation of 4. Find the percent of data within each interval.

28. from 25 to 33

29. from 21 to 25

30. greater than 29

31. less than 21

32. A data set is normally distributed with a mean of 37 and a standard deviation of 8.1. Sketch a normal curve for the distribution. Label the x-axis values at one, two, and three standard deviations from the mean.

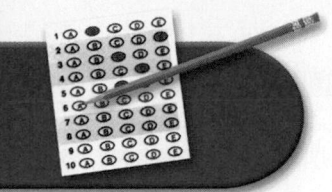

Standardized Test Prep

Multiple Choice

For Exercises 1–13, choose the correct letter.

1. Which polynomial has $(x - 1)$ as a factor?

Ⓐ $x^2 + 3x + 2$

Ⓑ $x^2 + 2x + 1$

Ⓒ $x^3 - x^2 - x + 1$

Ⓓ $x^3 - 3x - 2$

2. Which is the equation of an inverse variation for which $x = 5$ when $y = -28$?

Ⓕ $y = \frac{-x}{140}$ Ⓖ $y = \frac{-130}{x}$

Ⓗ $y = \frac{-x}{130}$ Ⓙ $y = \frac{-140}{x}$

3. Which parabola has focus $(3, 0)$ and directrix $x = -3$?

Ⓐ $y = \frac{1}{12}x^2$ Ⓑ $y = -\frac{1}{3}x^2$

Ⓑ $x = \frac{1}{12}y^2$ Ⓓ $x = \frac{1}{3}y^2$

4. Which is greatest for these data?

9   10   10   10   11   12   12   13   15

Ⓕ mean   Ⓖ median

Ⓗ range   Ⓙ mode

5. What are the quartiles of these data?

18   19   20   20   22   23   25   28   32

Ⓐ $Q_1 = 19.5, Q_2 = 22, Q_3 = 26.5$

Ⓑ $Q_1 = 20, Q_2 = 21, Q_3 = 26.5$

Ⓒ $Q_1 = 20, Q_2 = 22, Q_3 = 25$

Ⓓ $Q_1 = 19, Q_2 = 22.5, Q_3 = 28$

6. In which interval is the area above the x-axis and under the curve $y = 4x^2 + 1$ greatest?

Ⓕ $-5 \le x \le 1$ Ⓖ $1 \le x \le 3$

Ⓗ $1 \le x \le 4$ Ⓙ $2 \le x \le 5$

7. What are the foci of $\frac{x^2}{64} + \frac{y^2}{36} = 1$?

Ⓐ $(0, \pm10)$ Ⓑ $(\pm2\sqrt{7}, 0)$

Ⓒ $(\pm10, 0)$ Ⓓ $(0, \pm2\sqrt{7})$

8. Which graph has an asymptote at $x = 3$?

Ⓕ $y = \frac{1}{x + 3}$ Ⓖ $y = \frac{3}{x - 1}$

Ⓗ $y = \frac{x - 3}{x + 3}$ Ⓙ $y = \frac{3}{x - 3}$

9. Which function is the inverse of $f(x) = (x - 3)^2$?

Ⓐ $g(x) = \frac{x^2}{(3x - 1)^2}$ Ⓑ $g(x) = \frac{1}{(x - 3)^2}$

Ⓒ $g(x) = \sqrt{x} + 3$ Ⓓ $g(x) = \sqrt{x - 3}$

10. Which function has an asymptote at $x = -3$?

Ⓕ $y = \log_6 (x - 3) + 1$

Ⓖ $y = \log_6 (x + 3) + 1$

Ⓗ $y = \log_6 (x - 1) + 3$

Ⓙ $y = \log_6 (x - 1) - 3$

11. Solve $2 \log x - \log 4 = 2$.

Ⓐ 200   Ⓑ 20   Ⓒ 2   Ⓓ 0.5

12. You toss a number cube numbered 1 through 6. Find $P(\text{NOT a prime number})$.

Ⓕ $\frac{1}{6}$ Ⓖ $\frac{1}{3}$ Ⓗ $\frac{1}{2}$ Ⓙ $\frac{2}{3}$

13. Which equation represents an ellipse with a center at $(-1, 3)$ and a horizontal major axis?

Ⓐ $\frac{(x + 1)^2}{3^2} + \frac{(y - 3)^2}{12} = 1$

Ⓑ $\frac{(x - 1)^2}{3^2} + \frac{(y + 3)^2}{12} = 1$

Ⓒ $\frac{(x + 1)^2}{12} + \frac{(y - 3)^2}{3^2} = 1$

Ⓓ $\frac{(x - 1)^2}{12} + \frac{(y + 3)^2}{3^2} = 1$

Gridded Response

14. A stain on a page is 4 mm wide. You enlarged the image on a photocopier 6 times with 124% setting. What is the approximate width of the final image of the stain in millimeters?

15. Evaluate $\sum_{n=1}^{8} \frac{3n}{2}$.

16. Write the sum of the infinite geometric series as a fraction. $1 - 0.2 + 0.04 - \ldots$

Short Response

17. Solve the equation $\frac{x}{6} = \frac{x + 4}{9}$. Check your solution. Show your work.

18. State the property or properties used to justify the identity $9 \log 3 - 3 \log 9 = \log 27$.

Extended Response

19. Find the vertices, intercepts, asymptotes, and foci of the hyperbola $\frac{x^2}{16} - \frac{y^2}{9} = 1$.

20. Is the series $10{,}000 + 1000 + 100 + 10 + \ldots$ *arithmetic* or *geometric*? Find the sum of the first eight terms.

Activity Lab

Training Day

Applying Sequences The world is three-dimensional, but drawings are done on a two-dimensional surface. We know that railroad tracks are parallel, but to create a feeling of depth in a drawing, tracks are often drawn as though they meet. The point where they seem to meet is called a vanishing point. This technique is called perspective drawing.

Strong-Armed Laborer
To build the track of the Canadian Pacific railroad, a freight car loaded with crossties was hauled to the end of the trails. Workers carried the crossties farther down the roadbed to extend the rails.

Legendary Locomotive
During the Civil War, this engine was hijacked by Union soldiers who planned to blow up a bridge. Confederate troops pursued them, and after an 18-hour, 139-km (87-mile) chase, caught up with the engine and recaptured it.

Activity 1

Materials: paper and pencil, ruler

a. Draw a set of railroad tracks such that the lengths of the horizontal ties form a geometric sequence.

b. Write the first four terms of the sequence.

c. Write a recursive formula for the sequence.

d. Write an explicit formula for the sequence.

Spanning Three Generations
These three trains represent more than 25 years of development. The original "Bullet Train" (on the right) was built in 1964. Series 300 (on the left) was built in 1992. It has a top speed of 168 mi/h.

Activity 2

Find a small picture or drawing you want to enlarge. Follow the steps below to enlarge the drawing. Use the diagram below as a guide.

Step 1 Choose a point O to the right of the drawing.

Step 2 Choose and label some key points on the drawing as A, B, C, etc.

Step 3 Lightly draw $\overrightarrow{OA}$.

Step 4 To make a drawing with dimensions that are *three times* the size of the original picture, locate point A' on $\overrightarrow{OA}$ so that $OA' = 3 \cdot OA$.

Step 5 Repeat Steps 3 and 4 for the remaining points on the picture (each ray begins at point O). Use the new points to help you draw the figure with new dimensions. (In this example, the new drawing will have a scale factor of 3.)

Energy for Trains

Before the invention of the steam engine, heavy loads were transported along railroads using human or animal power. Steam locomotives have nearly disappeared in America. Locomotives are now diesel or electric.

Activity 3

a. Begin with a small, simple drawing (perhaps one of your own or a cartoon). Use the method from Activity 2 to create at least two size changes of the original drawing so that the scale factors form an arithmetic sequence. (The original drawing has a scale factor of 1.)

b. Write the first four terms of the arithmetic sequence of scale factors.

c. Write a recursive formula for the sequence.

d. Write an explicit formula for the sequence.

For: Information about trains
Web Code: age-1253

What You've Learned

- In Chapter 9, you learned to graph rational functions, some of which have graphs that are discontinuous in the coordinate plane.

- In Chapter 10, you learned to write and graph equations representing circles, ellipses, hyperbolas, and parabolas.

- In Chapters 11 and 12, you learned about patterns and probability.

 **Check Your Readiness**   **for Help** to the Lesson in green.

Analyzing Graphs of Rational Functions (Lesson 9-3)

Describe the vertical asymptotes and holes for each rational function.

1. $y = \dfrac{2}{x-3}$

2. $y = \dfrac{(x-5)(x-1)}{x-1}$

3. $y = \dfrac{x+2}{(2x+1)(x-4)}$

Simplifying Complex Fractions (Lesson 9-5)

Simplify each complex fraction.

4. $\dfrac{\frac{2}{a}}{\frac{1}{b}}$

5. $\dfrac{5+\frac{1}{2}}{2-\frac{1}{5}}$

6. $\dfrac{\frac{3}{c+d}}{2}$

7. $\dfrac{\frac{1}{4}}{\frac{4}{c}}$

8. $\dfrac{\frac{2}{3}}{\frac{6}{c+4}}$

9. $\dfrac{\frac{4}{x}}{\frac{2}{8}}$

10. $\dfrac{3-\frac{1}{2}}{\frac{7}{6}}$

11. $\dfrac{\frac{9}{m-n}}{\frac{3}{2m-2n}}$

Translating Conic Sections (Lesson 10-6)

Write an equation for each conic section. Then sketch the graph.

12. circle with center at $(1, -4)$ and radius 4

13. ellipse with center at $(2, 5)$, vertices at $(5, 5)$ and $(-1, 5)$, and co-vertices at $(2, 3)$ and $(2, 7)$

14. parabola with vertex at $(0, -3)$ and focus at $(0, 5)$

15. hyperbola with center at $(6, 1)$, one focus at $(6, 6)$, and one vertex at $(6, -2)$

Writing Formulas for Sequences (Lesson 11-1)

Find the next two terms in each sequence. Write a formula for the nth term. Identify each formula as *explicit* or *recursive*.

16. $16, 13, 10, 7, \ldots$

17. $-1, -8, -27, -64, -125, \ldots$

18. $9, 3, 1, \frac{1}{3}, \ldots$

Periodic Functions and Trigonometry

LESSONS

13-1 Exploring Periodic Data

13-2 Angles and the Unit Circle

13-3 Radian Measure

13-4 The Sine Function

13-5 The Cosine Function

13-6 The Tangent Function

13-7 Translating Sine and Cosine Functions

13-8 Reciprocal Trigonometric Functions

Key Vocabulary

- amplitude (p. 712)
- central angle (p. 726)
- cosecant (p. 763)
- cosine function (p. 743)
- cosine of θ (p. 720)
- cotangent (p. 763)
- coterminal angles (p. 719)
- cycle (p. 711)
- initial side (p. 718)
- intercepted arc (p. 726)
- period (p. 711)
- periodic function (p. 711)
- phase shift (p. 756)
- radian (p. 726)
- secant (p. 763)
- sine curve (p. 735)
- sine function (p. 734)
- sine of θ (p. 720)
- standard position (p. 718)
- tangent function (p. 749)
- tangent of θ (p. 749)
- terminal side (p. 718)
- unit circle (p. 720)

What You'll Learn Next

- In Chapter 13, you will learn how geometric measurement relates to trigonometry.

- You will learn to use radian measure.

- You will learn how to write and graph functions that describe periodic data.

Real-World Connection Applying what you learn, on page 729 you will solve a problem involving a satellite's orbit.

Exploring Periodic Data

What You'll Learn

- To identify cycles and periods of periodic functions
- To find the amplitude of periodic functions

... And Why

To make predictions about sound waves, as in Example 4

GO for Help Lesson 2-1

✓ Check Skills You'll Need

Determine whether each relation is a function.

1. $\{(2, 4), (1, 3), (-3, -1), (4, 6)\}$
2. $\{(2, 6), (-3, 1), (-2, 2)\}$
3. $\{(x, y)|\ x = 3\}$
4. $\{(x, y)|\ y = 8\}$
5. $\{(x, y)|\ x = y^2\}$
6. $\{(x, y)|\ x^2 + y^2 = 36\}$
7. $\{(a, b)|\ a = b^3\}$
8. $\{(w, z)|\ w = z - 36\}$

🔊 **New Vocabulary** • periodic function • cycle • period • amplitude

---

1 Identifying Periodic Functions

Activity: Periodic Cycles

Use the diagram below. Suppose you and a friend are the last two people seated on a Ferris wheel. Once the ride begins, the wheel moves at a constant speed. It takes 36 seconds to complete one revolution.

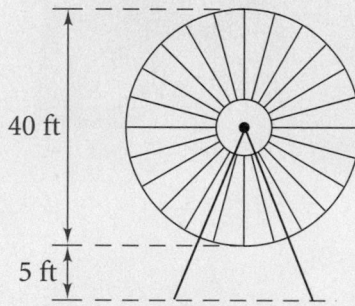

1. **a.** At 0 seconds, when the ride starts, how high above the ground are you?
   b. At what height are you at 9 seconds? At 18 seconds? At 27 seconds?
   c. At what height are you at 126 seconds? How many revolutions have you made?
   d. Predict where you will be at 3 minutes.

2. Sketch a graph showing the relationship between your height above the ground and the time since the ride began. Use $0 \le t \le 144$ for the domain, where $t = 0$ is the time at which the ride starts.

3. **Critical Thinking** How far (in feet) have you traveled after one revolution of the wheel? How far have you traveled at 144 seconds?

A **periodic function** repeats a pattern of *y*-values (outputs) at regular intervals. One complete pattern is a **cycle.** A cycle may begin at any point on the graph of the function. The **period** of a function is the horizontal length of one cycle.

1 EXAMPLE Identifying Cycles and Periods

Analyze the periodic function below. Identify one cycle in two different ways. Then determine the period of the function.

Begin at any point on the graph. Trace one complete pattern.

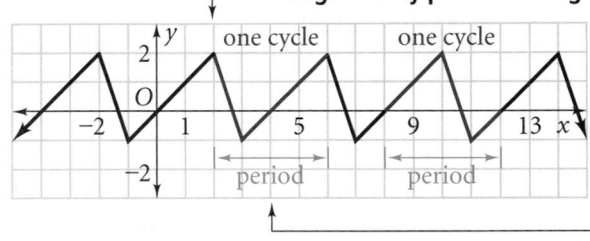

The beginning and ending *x*-values of each cycle determine the period of the function.

● Each cycle is 4 units long. The period of the function is 4.

✓ Quick Check **1** For each function, identify one cycle in two different ways. Then determine the period of the function.

a.
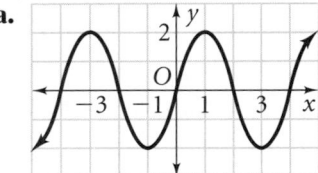

b.
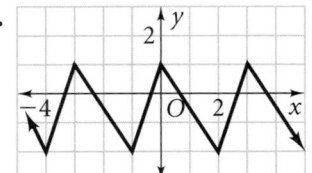

You can determine whether a function is periodic by analyzing its graph.

2 EXAMPLE Identifying Periodic Functions

Determine whether each function *is* or *is not* periodic. If it is, find the period.

a.
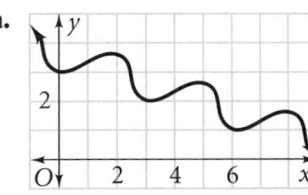

Although the graph shows similar curves, the *y*-values from one section do not repeat in other sections. The function *is not* periodic.

b.
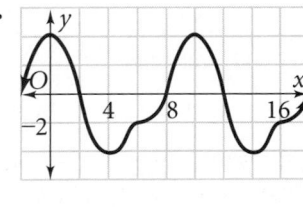

The pattern of *y*-values in one section repeats exactly in other sections. The function *is* periodic.

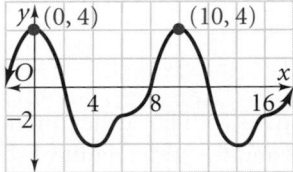

Find points at the beginning and end of one cycle. Subtract the *x*-values of the points: $10 - 0 = 10$. The pattern in the graph repeats every 10 units, so the period is 10.

✓ Quick Check ❷ Determine whether each function *is* or *is not* periodic. If it is, find the period.

a.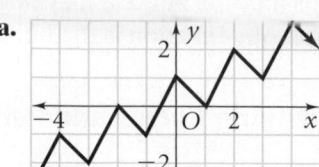

b.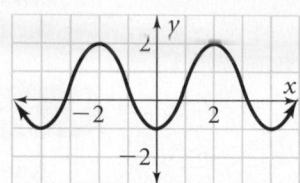

2 Finding the Amplitude of a Periodic Function

The amplitude of a periodic function measures the amount of variation in the function values.

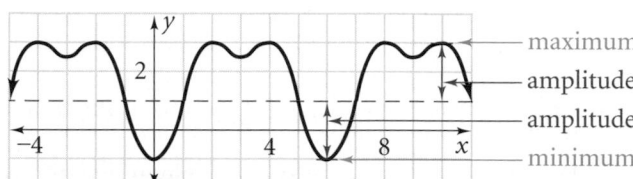

🔑 Key Concepts

Definition	Amplitude of a Periodic Function

The **amplitude** of a periodic function is half the difference between the maximum and minimum values of the function.

3 EXAMPLE Finding Amplitude of a Periodic Function

Find the amplitude of the periodic function at the right.

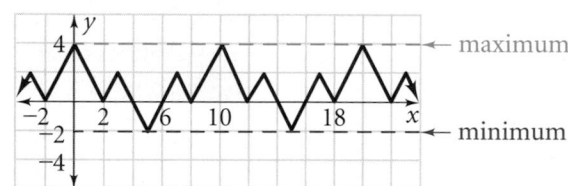

amplitude $= \frac{1}{2}$(maximum value $-$ minimum value)   **Use the definition of amplitude.**

$\qquad = \frac{1}{2}[4 - (-2)]$ **Substitute.**

$\qquad = \frac{1}{2}(6) = 3$ **Subtract within parentheses and simplify.**

● The amplitude of the function is 3.

✓ Quick Check ❸ Find the amplitude of each function.

a.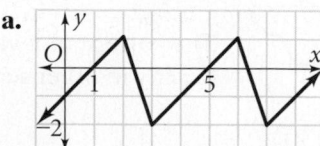

b.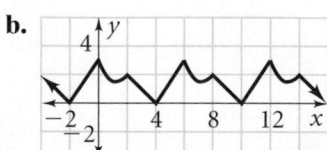

You can model some data with periodic functions. The rotation of a Ferris wheel, the beating of a heart, and the movement of sound waves are all examples of real-world events that generate periodic data.

4 EXAMPLE **Real-World** **Connection**

Sound Waves Sound is produced by periodic changes in air pressure called sound waves. The oscilloscope at the right shows the graph of a pure tone from a tuning fork. Find the period and the amplitude of the sound wave.

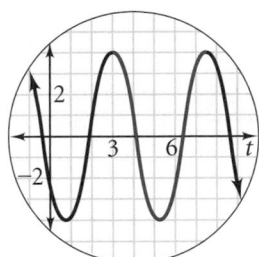

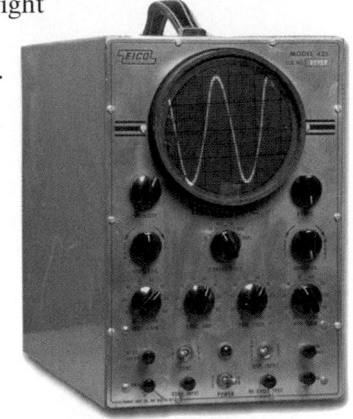

1 unit on the *t*-axis = 0.001 s

Real-World **Connection**

A microphone converts sound waves into an electrical signal, which can be shown as a graph on an oscilloscope.

One cycle of the sound wave occurs from 0.003 s to 0.0075 s. The maximum value of the function is 4, and the minimum value is -4.

period $= 0.0075 - 0.003$ **Use the definitions.** amplitude $= \frac{1}{2}[4 - (-4)]$

$\qquad = 0.0045$ **Simplify.** $\qquad = \frac{1}{2}(8) = 4$

The period of the sound wave is 0.0045 s. The amplitude is 4.

✓ **Quick Check** ④ Sketch the graph of a sound wave with a period of 0.004 s and an amplitude of 2.

EXERCISES

For more exercises, see *Extra Skill and Word Problem Practice.*

Practice and Problem Solving

Practice by Example

Example 1
(page 711)

Identify one cycle in two different ways. Then determine the period of the function.

1.

2.

3.

Example 2
(page 711)

Determine whether each function *is* or *is not* periodic. If it is, find the period.

4.
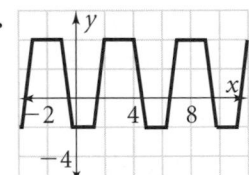

5.
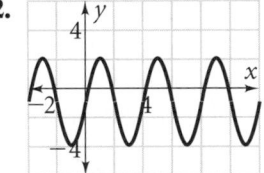

6.
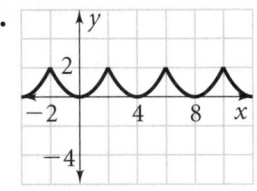

7.
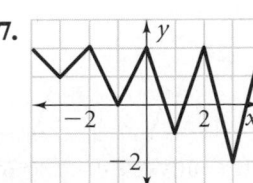

8.
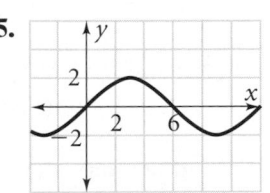
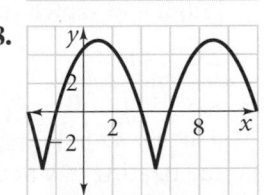

9.
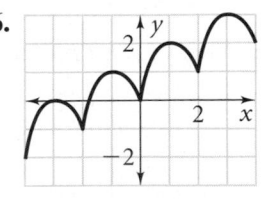
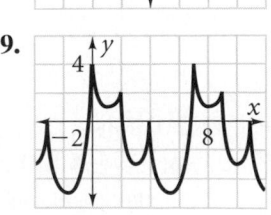

Examples 3 and 4
(pages 712 and 713)

Find the amplitude of each periodic function.

10.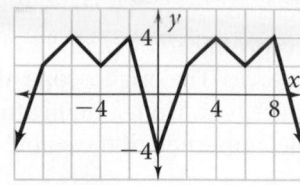

11.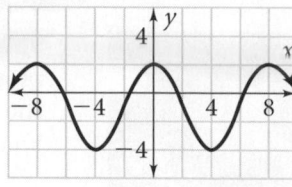

12.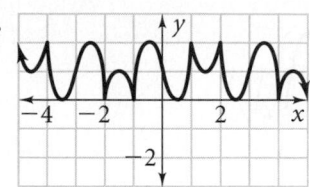

13.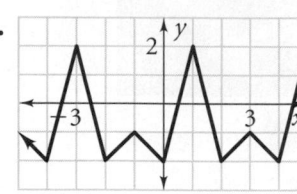

B Apply Your Skills

Sketch the graph of a sound wave with the given period and amplitude.

14. period 0.02, amplitude 4

15. period 0.005, amplitude 9

16. Complete each statement with x or y.
  a. You use ■-values to compute the amplitude of a function.
  b. You use ■-values to compute the period of a function.

Writing **Could you use a periodic function to represent each situation described below? Explain.**

17. the average monthly temperature in your community, recorded every month for three years

18. the population in your community, recorded every year for the last 50 years

19. the number of cars per hour that pass through an intersection near where you live, recorded for two consecutive work days

Health **Use the graph below for Exercises 20 and 21.**

20. A person's pulse rate is the number of times his or her heart beats in one minute. Each cycle in the graph represents one heartbeat. Find the pulse rate.

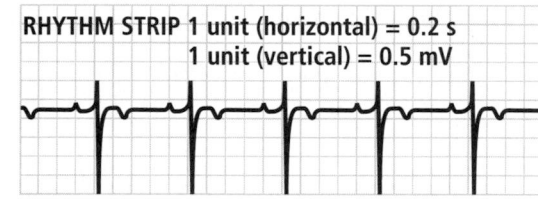

21. An electrocardiogram (EKG or ECG) measures the electrical activity of a person's heart in millivolts over time.
  a. What is the period of the EKG shown above?
  b. What is the amplitude of the EKG?

Real-World Connection

The carotid artery of the neck is a commonly used pulse point.

22. Open-Ended Sketch a graph of a periodic function that has a period of 3 and an amplitude of 2.

Find the maximum, minimum, and period of each periodic function. Then copy the graph and sketch two more cycles.

23.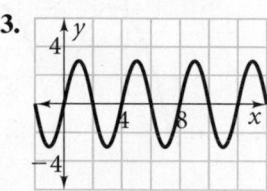

24.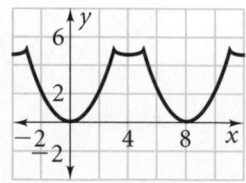

25.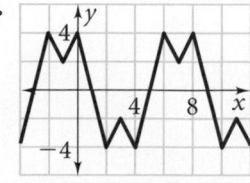

GO Online
Homework Video Tutor
Visit: PHSchool.com
Web Code: age-1301

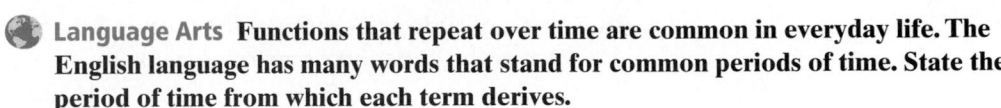

Language Arts Functions that repeat over time are common in everyday life. The English language has many words that stand for common periods of time. State the period of time from which each term derives.

26. annual **27.** biweekly **28.** quarterly **29.** hourly **30.** circadian

 **Challenge**

31. Suppose f is a periodic function. The period of f is 5 and $f(1) = 2$. Find $f(6)$, $f(11)$, and $f(-4)$.

32. Suppose g is a periodic function. The period of g is 24, $g(3) = 67$, and $g(8) = 70$. Find each function value.
  a. $g(27)$ **b.** $g(80)$ **c.** $g(-16)$ **d.** $g(51)$

33. Motion You are sitting on a pier watching the waves when you notice a bottle in the water. The bottle bobs so that it is between 2.5 ft and 4.5 ft below the pier. You know you can reach 3 ft below the pier. Suppose the bottle reaches its highest point every 5 s.
  a. Sketch a graph of the bottle's distance below the pier for 15 s. Assume that at $t = 0$, the bottle is closest to the pier.
  b. Find the period and the amplitude of the function.
  c. Estimation Use your graph to estimate the length of time the bottle is within reach during each cycle.

34. Calendar A day—the time Earth takes to rotate from one noon to the next—is a basic measure of time. A solar year is about 365.2422 days. We try to keep our calendar in step with the solar year.
  a. If every calendar year has 365 days, by how many days would the calendar year and the solar year differ after 100 years?
  b. If every fourth year has an extra "leap" day added, by how many days would the two systems differ after 100 years?
  c. If every hundred years the "leap" day is omitted, by how many days would the two systems differ after 100 years?
  d. Critical Thinking Why is it important for the difference between the calendar year and the solar year to be zero?

Real-World 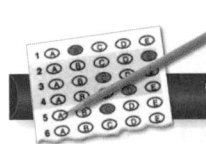 Connection

Coast Guard rescue jumpers time their pickups for the crests of the waves.

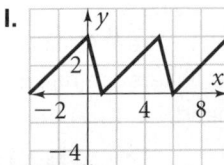 **Test Prep**

Multiple Choice

35. A periodic function goes through 5 complete cycles in 4 min. What is the period of the function?
  A. $\frac{1}{5}$ min   **B.** $\frac{1}{4}$ min   **C.** 48 s   **D.** 75 s

36. The period of a periodic function is 8 s. How many cycles does it go through in 30 s?
  F. $\frac{4}{15}$ cycle   **G.** 3.75 cycles   **H.** 22 cycles   **J.** 240 cycles

37. Which graph is NOT the graph of a periodic function?

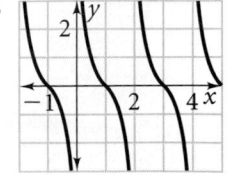

  A. I only   **B.** II only   **C.** III only   **D.** II and III

38. The amplitude of a periodic function is 2.5 and its minimum value is 0. What is the function's maximum value?

F. −2.5　　　　G. 0　　　　H. 2.5　　　　J. 5.0

Short Response

39. A periodic function completes *m* cycles in *n* seconds. What is the period of the function? Show your work.

Extended Response

40. A machine begins recording two periodic functions at the same time. The first has a period of 6 s. The second has a period of 7 s. After 20 s, the machine begins recording a third periodic function, with a period of 8 s. How many seconds after the machine begins recording the third function are all three functions at the beginning of their periods? Explain.

Mixed Review

Lesson 12-7

41. Sketch a normal curve for a distribution that has mean 57 and standard deviation 12. Label the *x*-axis values at one, two, and three standard deviations from the mean.

Lesson 11-1

Find the next two terms in each sequence. Write a formula for the *n*th term. Identify each formula as *explicit* or *recursive*.

42. 1, 3, 5, 7, 9, . . .　　　　**43.** 4, 6, 8, 10, 12, . . .　　　　**44.** 3, 6, 11, 18, 27, . . .

Lesson 10-6

Write an equation for each conic section. Then sketch the graph.

45. parabola with vertex $(-3, 2)$ and focus $(-3, 7)$

46. hyperbola with center $(5, -3)$, one focus at $(5, 0)$, and one vertex at $(5, -1)$

47. ellipse with center $(-2, 1)$, vertices at $(-6, 1)$ and $(2, 1)$, and co-vertices at $(-2, 3)$ and $(-2, -1)$

·········· **A Point in Time**

1500　　1600　　1700　　1800　　1900　　2000

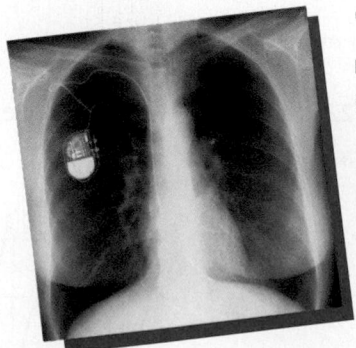

To human beings, the most important periodic function is the rhythm of the heart. About once per second, a nerve in the heart generates an electrical signal. This causes the heart to contract and force blood through the body.

In 1958, doctors placed the first pacemaker in a patient with a malfunctioning nerve. The creator of the device's control unit was Otis Boykin, an inventor from Dallas, Texas. He began his career testing automatic airplane controls. Today, more than a million pacemakers are helping people worldwide enjoy the normal rhythms of the human heart.

Go **Online**
PHSchool.com

For: Information about pacemakers
Web Code: age-2032

Special Right Triangles

In Geometry you learned about two special right triangles, the 45°-45°-90° triangle and the 30°-60°-90° triangle. The figures at the right summarize the relationships among the lengths of the sides of each triangle.

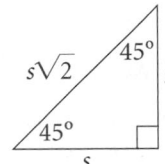
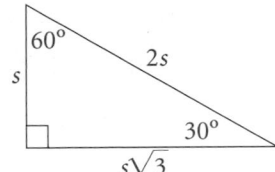

1 EXAMPLE Finding Side Lengths in a 45°-45°-90° Triangle

Find the missing side lengths in each figure.

a.

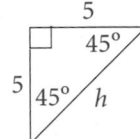

$$h = \sqrt{2} \cdot 5 \qquad \text{hypotenuse} = \sqrt{2} \cdot \text{leg}$$

$$h = 5\sqrt{2} \qquad \text{Simplify.}$$

b.

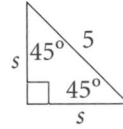

$$5 = \sqrt{2} \cdot s$$

$$s = \frac{5}{\sqrt{2}}$$

$$s = \frac{5\sqrt{2}}{2}$$

2 EXAMPLE Finding Side Lengths in a 30°-60°-90° Triangle

Find the missing side lengths in the triangle at the right.

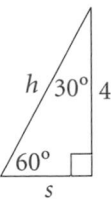

$$4 = \sqrt{3} \cdot s \qquad \text{longer leg} = \sqrt{3} \cdot \text{shorter leg}$$

$$s = \frac{4}{\sqrt{3}} = \frac{4\sqrt{3}}{3} \qquad \text{Divide and simplify.}$$

$$h = 2s \qquad \text{hypotenuse} = 2 \cdot \text{shorter leg}$$

$$= 2 \cdot \frac{4\sqrt{3}}{3} = \frac{8\sqrt{3}}{3} \qquad \text{Substitute } \frac{4\sqrt{3}}{3} \text{ for } s \text{ and simplify.}$$

EXERCISES

Use the given information to find the missing side length(s) in each 45°-45°-90° triangle. Rationalize any denominators.

1. hypotenuse 1 in.   **2.** leg 2 cm   **3.** hypotenuse $\sqrt{3}$ ft   **4.** leg $2\sqrt{5}$ m

Use the given information to find the missing side lengths in each 30°-60°-90° triangle. Rationalize any denominators.

5. shorter leg 3 in.   **6.** longer leg 1 cm   **7.** hypotenuse 1 ft

8. shorter leg $\sqrt{3}$ cm   **9.** hypotenuse $2\sqrt{2}$ ft   **10.** longer leg $2\sqrt{3}$ in.

11. hypotenuse $3\sqrt{2}$ m   **12.** longer leg $\sqrt{5}$ cm   **13.** shorter leg $\sqrt{13}$ mm

14. What is the ratio of the length to the width of a rectangle whose diagonals form a 90° angle? A 60° angle?

Angles and the Unit Circle

What You'll Learn

- To work with angles in standard position
- To find coordinates of points on the unit circle

. . . And Why

To use an ancient calendar, as in Example 3

✓ **Check Skills You'll Need**

GO **for Help** pages 54 and 876

For each measure, draw an angle with its vertex at the origin of the coordinate plane. Use the positive *x*-axis as one ray of the angle.

1. 90°   **2.** 45°   **3.** 30°

4. 150°   **5.** 135°   **6.** 120°

◄))) **New Vocabulary**
- standard position
- initial side
- terminal side
- coterminal angles
- unit circle
- cosine of θ
- sine of θ

---

1 Working With Angles in Standard Position

Vocabulary Tip

<u>Terminal</u> means "at an end" or "forming a boundary."

An angle is in **standard position** when the vertex is at the origin and one ray is on the positive *x*-axis. The ray on the *x*-axis is the **initial side** of the angle; the other ray is the **terminal side** of the angle.

Standard Position

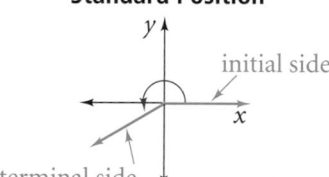

To measure an angle in standard position, find the amount of rotation from the initial side to the terminal side.

1 EXAMPLE **Measuring an Angle in Standard Position**

Find the measure of the angle at the right.

The angle measures 20° more than a straight angle of 180°.

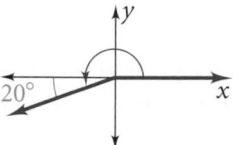

● Since $180 + 20 = 200$, the measure of the angle is 200°.

✓ **Quick Check** ❶ One full rotation contains 360 degrees. How many degrees are in one quarter of a rotation? In one half of a rotation? In three quarters of a rotation?

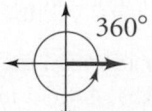 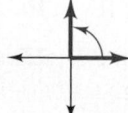  

The measure of an angle is positive when the rotation from the initial side to the terminal side is in the counterclockwise direction. The measure is negative when the rotation is clockwise.

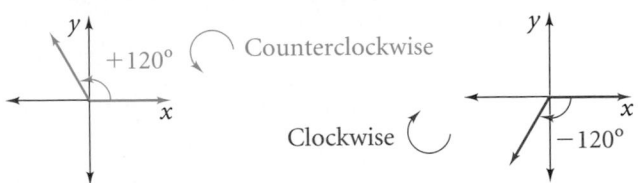

2 EXAMPLE Sketching an Angle in Standard Position

Sketch each angle in standard position.

a. 36° **b.** 315° **c.** −150°

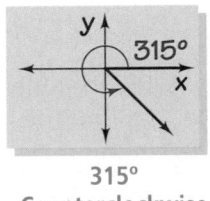 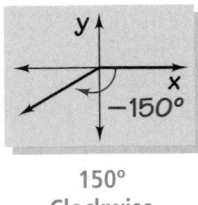

36°
Counterclockwise

315°
Counterclockwise

150°
Clockwise

✓ **Quick Check** ② Sketch each angle in standard position.
  a. 85° **b.** −320° **c.** 180°

Two angles in standard position are **coterminal angles** if they have the same terminal side.

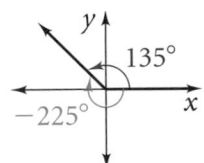

Angles that have measures 135° and −225° are coterminal.

3 EXAMPLE Real-World Connection

History The Aztec calendar stone has 20 divisions for the 20 days in each month of the Aztec year. The yellow angle marks the passage of 11 days. Find the measures of two coterminal angles that coincide with the angle. The terminal side of the angle is $\frac{11}{20}$ of a full rotation from the initial side.

$$\frac{11}{20} \cdot 360° = 198°$$

To find a coterminal angle, subtract one full rotation.

$$198° − 360° = −162°$$

Two coterminal angle measures for the angle in the photograph are 198° and −162°.

Real-World Connection

Archaeologists assembling a sample of Mesoamerican hieroglyphic text

✓ **Quick Check** ③ **a.** Find another angle coterminal with 198° by adding one full rotation.
  b. Reasoning Are angles with measures of 40° and 680° coterminal? Explain.
  c. Make a Conjecture Generalize how the measures of two coterminal angles are related.

Activity: Angles in a Circle

- Use a compass. Construct a circle with a radius of 1 in. on the coordinate plane. Place the center of the circle at the origin.

- Use a protractor. Draw an angle of 30°. Place one ray along the positive *x*-axis. Place the other ray in Quadrant I. Label the point where the second ray intersects the circle *P(x, y)*.

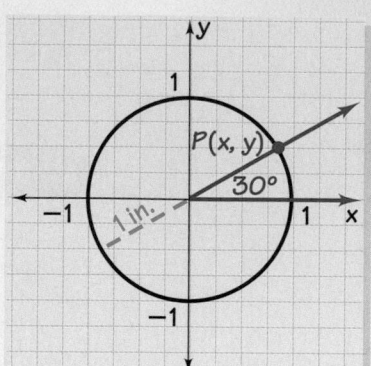

1. Identify the methods you could use to find the coordinates of *P*.

2. Choose one method and find the values of *x* and *y*. Express the coordinates in decimal form.

3. Use a calculator to find the values of cos 30° (read "cosine of 30 degrees") and sin 30° (read "sine of 30 degrees"). Compare these values to the values you found in Question 2.

4. **a.** Repeat the steps above using an angle of 45°. What are the coordinates of the new point *P*?
   b. Find cos 45° and sin 45° using your calculator. How do these values compare to those you found in part (a)?
   c. **Make a Conjecture** What is the relationship between the coordinates of a point *P* on the circle and the values of the sine and cosine of the angle containing *P*?

Vocabulary Tip

The Greek letter *θ* (pronounced THAY-tuh) is frequently used as a variable for angle measure.

The **unit circle** has a radius of 1 unit and its center at the origin of the coordinate plane. Points on the unit circle are related to periodic functions.

You can use the symbol *θ* for the measure of an angle in standard position.

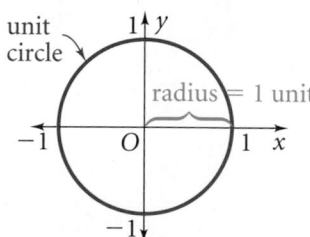

Key Concepts

Definition	Cosine and Sine of an Angle

Suppose an angle in standard position has measure *θ*. The **cosine of *θ*** (cos *θ*) is the *x*-coordinate of the point at which the terminal side of the angle intersects the unit circle. The **sine of *θ*** (sin *θ*) is the *y*-coordinate.

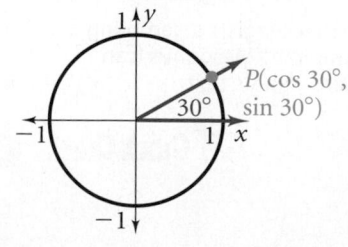

4 EXAMPLE Finding the Cosine and Sine of an Angle

Find the cosine and sine of 60°.

As the figure suggests, the x-coordinate of point A is $\frac{1}{2}$, so $\cos 60° = \frac{1}{2}$, or 0.5.

Use a 30°-60°-90° right triangle to find $\sin 60°$.

longer leg $= \sqrt{3} \cdot$ shorter leg

$= \sqrt{3} \cdot \frac{1}{2}$ **Substitute.**

$= \frac{\sqrt{3}}{2}$ **Multiply.**

≈ 0.87 **Simplify.**

The coordinates of the point at which the terminal side of a 60° angle intersects the unit circle are $(\frac{1}{2}, \frac{\sqrt{3}}{2})$, so $\cos 60° = 0.5$ and $\sin 60° = \frac{\sqrt{3}}{2} \approx 0.87$.

Problem Solving Hint

Quick Check ④ Draw each angle in a unit circle. Then find the cosine and sine of each angle.
 a. 45°   **b.** 30°   **c.** 120°

You can use right triangles to find the *exact* cosine and sine of an angle whose terminal side is not in Quadrant I.

5 EXAMPLE Finding Exact Values of Cosine and Sine

Find the exact values of $\cos(-120°)$ and $\sin(-120°)$.

Step 1 Sketch an angle of $-120°$ in standard position. Sketch a unit circle.

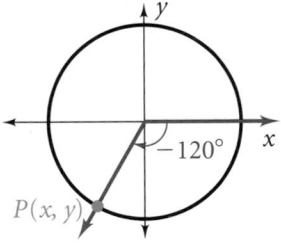

x-coordinate $= \cos(-120°)$
y-coordinate $= \sin(-120°)$

Step 2 Sketch a right triangle. Place the hypotenuse on the terminal side of the angle. Place one leg on the x-axis. (The other leg will be parallel to the y-axis.)

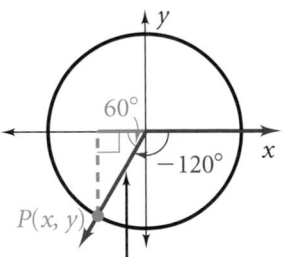

The triangle contains angles of 30°, 60°, and 90°.

Step 3 Find the length of each side of the triangle.

hypotenuse $= 1$ **The hypotenuse is a radius of the unit circle.**

shorter leg $= \frac{1}{2}$ **The shorter leg is half the hypotenuse.**

longer leg $= \frac{1}{2}\sqrt{3}$ **The longer leg is $\sqrt{3}$ times the short leg.**

$= \frac{\sqrt{3}}{2}$

Since the point lies in Quadrant III, both coordinates are negative. The shorter leg lies along the x-axis, so $\cos(-120°) = -\frac{1}{2}$, and $\sin(-120°) = -\frac{\sqrt{3}}{2}$.

 **Quick Check** ⑤ **a.** Use a calculator to find cos (−120°) and sin (−120°). How do these values compare to the exact values found in Example 5?

b. Find the exact values of cos 135° and sin 135°. Use properties of a 45°-45°-90° triangle. Use a calculator to find the decimal equivalents.

c. Find the exact values of cos 150° and sin 150°.

EXERCISES

For more exercises, see *Extra Skill and Word Problem Practice*.

Practice and Problem Solving

 Practice by Example

Find the measure of each angle in standard position.

Example 1
(page 718)

 **GO for Help**

1.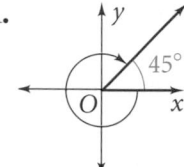

2.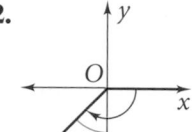

3.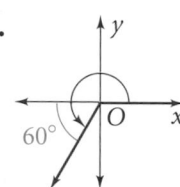

4.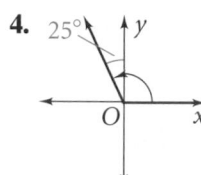

5.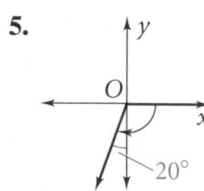

6.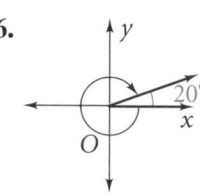

Example 2
(page 719)

Sketch each angle in standard position.

7. 40°   **8.** −130°   **9.** −270°   **10.** 120°   **11.** 95°

Example 3
(page 719)

Find the measure of an angle between 0° and 360° coterminal with each given angle.

12. 385°   **13.** 575°   **14.** −405°   **15.** −356°

16. 500°   **17.** −210°   **18.** 415°   **19.** −180°

20. Telephones Rotary telephones were widely used until the 1980s. Dialing a higher number (or 0) took longer because the dial moved through a larger central angle. Estimate the measures of two coterminal angles that coincide with the angle at the right.

Examples 4 and 5
(page 721)

Find the exact values of the cosine and sine of each angle. Then find the decimal values. Round your answers to the nearest hundredth.

21.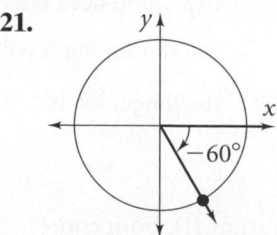

22.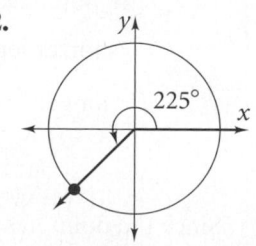

23.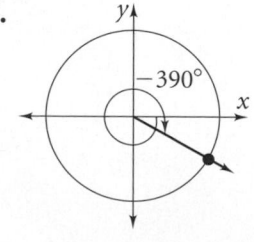

24. −240°   **25.** 390°   **26.** 315°   **27.** −30°   **28.** 135°

For each angle θ, find the values of cos θ and sin θ. Round your answers to the nearest hundredth.

29. $0°$ **30.** $32°$ **31.** $-45°$ **32.** $-210°$

33. $-95°$ **34.** $-10°$ **35.** $154°$ **36.** $90°$

Open-Ended Find a positive and a negative coterminal angle for the given angle.

37. $45°$ **38.** $-125°$ **39.** $-675°$ **40.** $400°$

41. $-85°$ **42.** $-425°$ **43.** $213°$ **44.** $-57°$

In which quadrant, or on which axis, does the terminal side of each angle lie?

45. $150°$ **46.** $210°$ **47.** $540°$ **48.** $-60°$ **49.** $0°$

50. a. Copy and complete the chart at the right.
    b. Suppose you know that cos θ is negative and sin θ is positive. In which quadrant does the terminal side of the angle lie?
    c. Writing Summarize how the quadrant in which the terminal side of an angle lies affects the sign of the sine and cosine of that angle.

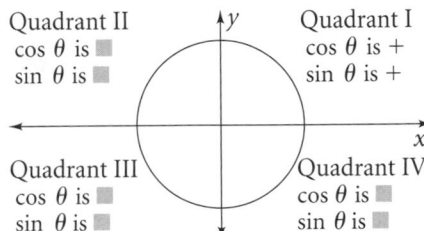

51. a. Use a calculator to find the value of each expression: cos 40°, cos 400°, and cos (−320°).
    b. Critical Thinking What do you notice about the values you found in part (a)? Explain.

52. Writing Explain how to find the sine and cosine of angles with measures of $0°, 90°, 180°, 270°,$ and $360°$ without using a calculator.

 **Challenge**

Sketch each angle in standard position. Use the unit circle and a right triangle to find exact values of the cosine and the sine of the angle.

53. $-300°$ **54.** $120°$ **55.** $225°$

56. $-780°$ **57.** $-405°$ **58.** $1020°$

59. Design Navajo sand paintings like the one at the right have many lines of symmetry. Suppose point A is on a unit circle. Find the coordinates of A.

60. Open-Ended Find the measures of four angles in standard position that have a sine of 0.5. (*Hint:* Use the unit circle and right triangles.)

61. Critical Thinking Suppose θ is an angle in standard position and $\cos \theta = -\frac{1}{2}$ and $\sin \theta = -\frac{\sqrt{3}}{2}$. Can the value of θ be 60°? Can it be −120°? Draw a diagram and justify your reasoning.

 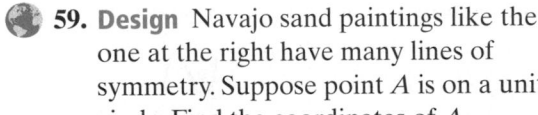

62. Navigation When navigators locate an object, they measure in a clockwise direction from due north. The measure of the angle is called the bearing. Suppose a lighthouse's bearing is 110° from a ship.

a. Sketch the diagram at the right on a coordinate plane. Place north along the positive y-axis.

b. Express the location of the lighthouse in terms of an angle in standard position.

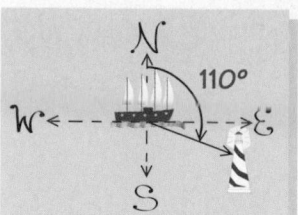

Test Prep

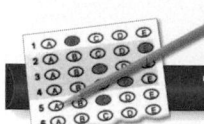

Multiple Choice

63. Which angle, in standard position, is NOT coterminal with the others?
A. −190°   **B.** −170°   **C.** 190°   **D.** 550°

64. An angle drawn in standard position has a terminal side that passes through the point ($\sqrt{2}$, −$\sqrt{2}$). What is one possible measure of the angle?
F. 45°   **G.** 225°   **H.** 315°   **J.** 330°

65. An angle of 120° is in standard position. What are the coordinates of the point at which the terminal side intersects the unit circle?
A. $\left(\frac{1}{2}, \frac{\sqrt{3}}{2}\right)$ **B.** $\left(-\frac{1}{2}, -\frac{\sqrt{3}}{2}\right)$ **C.** $\left(-\frac{\sqrt{3}}{2}, \frac{1}{2}\right)$ **D.** $\left(-\frac{1}{2}, \frac{\sqrt{3}}{2}\right)$

66. An angle of −225° is in standard position. Which points can lie on the terminal side of the angle?
I. $\left(\frac{\sqrt{2}}{2}, -\frac{\sqrt{2}}{2}\right)$ **II.** $\left(-\frac{\sqrt{2}}{2}, \frac{\sqrt{2}}{2}\right)$ **III.** $\left(-\frac{\sqrt{2}}{2}, -\frac{\sqrt{2}}{2}\right)$ **IV.** (−1, 1)
F. I and II   **G.** II and III   **H.** II and IV   **J.** I and III

Short Response

67. What is the exact value of cos (−210)°? Show your work.

Extended Response

68. Use an angle in standard position to find the exact value of $[\sin(-135°)]^2 + [\cos(-135°)]^2$. Show your work.

Mixed Review

Lesson 13-1

Determine whether each function *is* or *is not* periodic. If it is, find the period.

69. 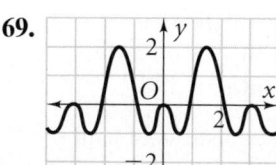   **70.** 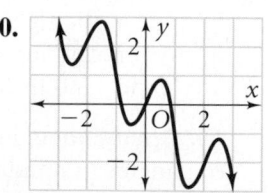   **71.**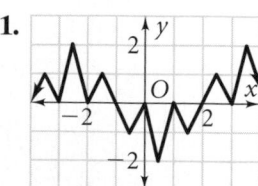

Lesson 12-1

Graph the probability distribution for each sample space.

72. {two coins heads, two coins tails, one coin heads and the other tails}

73. {the sum of two number cubes a prime number, the sum a composite number}

Lesson 10-5

Find the foci of each hyperbola. Draw the graph.

74. $\frac{y^2}{16} - \frac{x^2}{4} = 1$ **75.** $\frac{y^2}{25} - \frac{x^2}{100} = 1$ **76.** $\frac{x^2}{36} - \frac{y^2}{49} = 1$ **77.** $\frac{x^2}{81} - \frac{y^2}{64} = 1$

Measuring Radians

In the past, you have used degrees to measure angles. When angles are used in periodic functions, they are often measured in larger units called radians.

1. Measure the diameter of a cylinder and calculate its radius. On a piece of string, mark off a "number line" with each unit equal to the radius. Mark at least seven units.

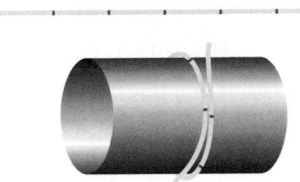

2. Wrap the string around the cylinder. How many radius units are needed to go around the cylinder one time?

3. Use the end of the cylinder to draw a circle on a sheet of paper. Keep the cylinder in place and wrap the string around it on the paper. Mark an arc of the circle equal to one radius unit of length.

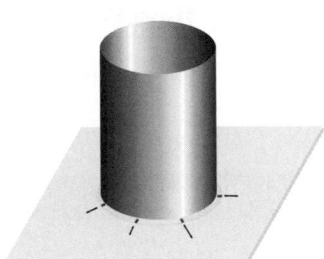

4. Remove the cylinder and string. Use paper folding to locate the center of the circle. (Fold the circle onto itself and crease the paper along a diameter. Repeat to get a second diameter.) Draw a central angle that intercepts one radius unit of arc.

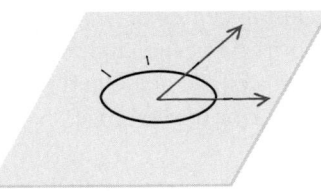

The measure of the angle you drew in Question 4 is 1 radian.

5. Use a protractor to measure the angle from Question 4 in degrees.

6. **Critical Thinking** The formula $C = 2\pi r$ relates the circumference of a circle C to its radius r. *Exactly* how many radians are in a 360° angle? Explain.

The diagram at the right shows that a rotation of 180° is equivalent to π radians.

7. Find the number of degrees in one radian by dividing 180 by π. How does your answer compare to the measurement you made in Question 5?

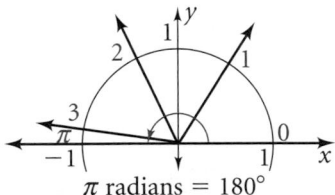

π radians = 180°

EXERCISES

Use the proportion $\frac{d°}{180°} = \frac{r \text{ radians}}{\pi \text{ radians}}$. Find the equivalent degree measure or radian measure.

1. 10° 2. 45° 3. 90° 4. 120° 5. 270°

6. 310° 7. 50° 8. 415° 9. 170° 10. 380°

11. $\frac{13\pi}{18}$ radians 12. $\frac{3\pi}{8}$ radians 13. $\frac{7\pi}{2}$ radians 14. $\frac{11\pi}{4}$ radians 15. $\frac{5\pi}{6}$ radians

Radian Measure

✓ **Check Skills You'll Need**

GO for Help page 898

Find the circumference of a circle with the given radius or diameter. Round your answer to the nearest tenth.

1. radius 4 in.
2. diameter 70 m
3. radius 8 mi
4. diameter 3.4 ft
5. radius 5 mm
6. diameter 6.3 cm

🔊 **New Vocabulary** • central angle • intercepted arc • radian

---

1 Using Radian Measure

A **central angle** of a circle is an angle with a vertex at the center of a circle. An **intercepted arc** is the portion of the circle with endpoints on the sides of the central angle and remaining points within the interior of the angle.

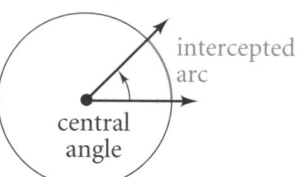

Vocabulary Tip

Radian is a shortened form of the phrase *radial angle*.

When a central angle intercepts an arc that has the same length as a radius of the circle, the measure of the angle is defined to be one **radian**. Like degrees, radians measure the amount of rotation from the initial side to the terminal side of an angle.

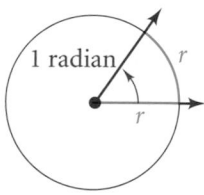

Because the circumference of a circle is $2\pi r$, there are 2π radians in any circle. Since 2π radians $= 360°$, and therefore π radians $= 180°$, you can use a proportion such as $\frac{d°}{180°} = \frac{r \text{ radians}}{\pi \text{ radians}}$ to convert between degrees and radians.

Real-World 🌐 Connection

Some pendulum rides travel through a complete revolution of 2π radians.

1 EXAMPLE Using a Proportion

a. Find the radian measure of an angle of 60°.

$\frac{60°}{180°} = \frac{r \text{ radians}}{\pi \text{ radians}}$ **Write a proportion.**

$60 \cdot \pi = 180 \cdot r$ **Write the cross-products.**

$r = \frac{60 \cdot \pi}{180}$ **Divide each side by 180.**

$= \frac{\pi}{3} \approx 1.05$ **Simplify.**

An angle of 60° measures about 1.05 radians.

b. Find the degree measure of $\frac{5\pi}{2}$ radians.

$$\frac{\frac{5\pi}{2}\text{ radians}}{\pi\text{ radians}} = \frac{d^\circ}{180^\circ}$$ **Write a proportion.**

$$\frac{\frac{5\pi}{2}}{\pi} = \frac{d}{180}$$

$$\frac{5\pi}{2} \cdot 180 = \pi \cdot d$$ **Write the cross-products.**

$$\frac{5\pi \cdot 180}{2 \cdot \pi} = d$$ **Divide each side by π.**

$$d = \frac{5\pi \cdot 180^{90}}{{}_{1}2 \cdot \pi}$$ **Simplify.**

$$= 450$$

An angle of $\frac{5\pi}{2}$ radians measures 450°.

✓ Quick Check ❶ Use a proportion for each conversion.

a. 85° to radians   **b.** 2.5 radians to degrees

The proportion $\frac{d^\circ}{180^\circ} = \frac{r\text{ radians}}{\pi\text{ radians}}$ leads to the following two convenient conversion factors.

🔑 Key Concepts

Summary	**Converting Between Radians and Degrees**

To convert degrees to radians, multiply by $\frac{\pi\text{ radians}}{180^\circ}$.

To convert radians to degrees, multiply by $\frac{180^\circ}{\pi\text{ radians}}$.

You can use the conversion factors and dimensional analysis to convert between angle measurement systems.

GO Online

Video Tutor Help
Visit: PHSchool.com
Web Code: age-0775

❷ **EXAMPLE** **Using Dimensional Analysis**

a. Find the degree measure of an angle of $-\frac{3\pi}{4}$ radians.

$$-\frac{3\pi}{4}\text{ radians} = -\frac{3\pi}{4}\text{ radians} \cdot \frac{180^\circ}{\pi\text{ radians}}$$ **Multiply by $\frac{180^\circ}{\pi\text{ radians}}$.**

$$= -\frac{3\pi}{{}_{1}4}\text{radians} \cdot \frac{{}^{45}180^\circ}{\pi\text{ radians}}$$ **Simplify.**

$$= -135^\circ$$

An angle of $-\frac{3\pi}{4}$ radians measures -135°.

b. Find the radian measure of an angle of 27°.

$$27^\circ = 27^\circ \cdot \frac{\pi}{180^\circ}\text{ radians}$$ **Multiply by $\frac{\pi\text{ radians}}{180^\circ}$.**

$$= {}^{3}27^\circ \cdot \frac{\pi}{{}_{20}180^\circ}\text{ radians}$$ **Simplify.**

$$= \frac{3\pi}{20}\text{ radians}$$

An angle of 27° measures $\frac{3\pi}{20}$ radians.

✓ Quick Check ❷ Use dimensional analysis to convert each degree measure from degrees to radians or from radians to degrees. (Express radian measures in terms of π.)

a. $\frac{\pi}{2}$ radians   **b.** 225° **c.** 2 radians   **d.** 150°

You can find the sine and cosine of angles in radian measure by first converting the radian measure to degrees and then using the unit circle.

3 EXAMPLE Finding Cosine and Sine of Radian Measures

Find the exact values of $\cos\left(\frac{\pi}{4} \text{ radians}\right)$ and $\sin\left(\frac{\pi}{4} \text{ radians}\right)$.

$\frac{\pi}{4}$ radians $\cdot \dfrac{180°}{\pi \text{ radians}} = 45°$ **Convert radians to degrees.**

Draw the angle. Complete a 45°-45°-90° triangle. Since the hypotenuse has length 1, both legs have length $\frac{\sqrt{2}}{2}$.

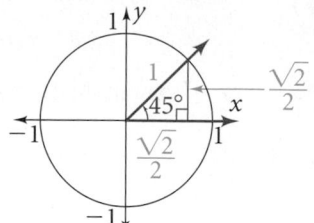

Thus, $\cos\left(\frac{\pi}{4} \text{ radians}\right) = \frac{\sqrt{2}}{2}$

and $\sin\left(\frac{\pi}{4} \text{ radians}\right) = \frac{\sqrt{2}}{2}$.

✓ Quick Check **3** **a.** Use a calculator to find $\cos\left(\frac{\pi}{4} \text{ radians}\right)$ and $\sin\left(\frac{\pi}{4} \text{ radians}\right)$. How do these values compare to the coordinates found in Example 3?

b. Explain how to use mental math to convert $\frac{\pi}{4}$ radians to degrees. (*Hint:* Begin with the relationship π radians $= 180°$.)

2 Finding the Length of an Arc

You can find the length of an intercepted arc by using the proportion
$$\frac{\text{arc length } s}{\text{circumference } 2\pi r} = \frac{\text{central angle measure } \theta \text{ radians}}{2\pi \text{ radians}}.$$
Simplifying this proportion results in the formula below.

 **Key Concepts**

Property	Length of an Intercepted Arc

For a circle of radius r and a central angle of measure θ (in radians), the length s of the intercepted arc is $s = r\theta$.

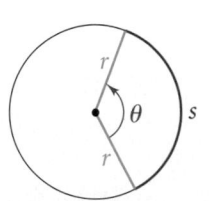

4 EXAMPLE Finding the Length of an Arc

Use the circle at the right. Find length s to the nearest tenth.

$s = r\theta$ **Use the formula.**

$= 3 \cdot \dfrac{5\pi}{6}$ **Substitute 3 for r and $\frac{5\pi}{6}$ for θ.**

$= \dfrac{5\pi}{2}$ **Simplify.**

≈ 7.9 **Use a calculator.**

The arc has a length of about 7.9 in.

✓ Quick Check **4** Find length b in Example 4. Round your answer to the nearest tenth.

5 **EXAMPLE** **Real-World Connection**

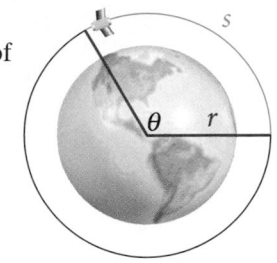

Weather Satellite A weather satellite in a circular orbit around Earth completes one orbit every 2 h. The radius of Earth is about 6400 km, and the satellite orbits 2600 km above Earth's surface. How far does the satellite travel in 1 h?

Since one complete revolution (orbit) takes 2 h, the satellite completes $\frac{1}{2}$ of a revolution in 1 h.

Step 1 Find the radius of the satellite's orbit.

$r = 6400 + 2600$ Add the radius of Earth and the distance from Earth's surface to the satellite.

$= 9000$ Simplify.

Step 2 Find the measure of the central angle the satellite travels through in 1 h.

$\theta = \frac{1}{2} \cdot 2\pi$ Multiply the fraction of the revolution by the number of radians in one complete revolution.

$= \pi$ Simplify.

Step 3 Find s for $\theta = \pi$.

$s = r\theta$ Use the formula.

$= 9000\pi$ Substitute 9000 for r and π for θ.

$\approx 28{,}274$ Simplify.

● The satellite travels about 28,000 km in 1 h.

 Quick Check **5** Find the length of the arc intercepted by each angle.
  a. $\angle AOB$
  b. $\angle COD$
  c. $\angle AOC$
  d. $\angle AOD$

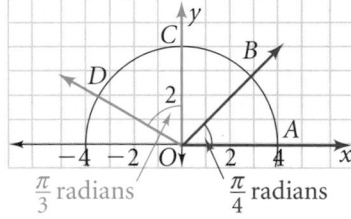

EXERCISES

For more exercises, see *Extra Skill and Word Problem Practice.*

Practice and Problem Solving

Write each measure in radians. Express the answer in terms of π and as a decimal rounded to the nearest hundredth.

  1. $-300°$

  2. $150°$

  3. $-90°$

  4. $-60°$

  5. $160°$

  6. $20°$

Write each measure in degrees. Round your answer to the nearest degree, if necessary.

  7. 3π radians

  8. $\frac{11\pi}{10}$ radians

  9. $-\frac{2\pi}{3}$ radians

  10. -3 radians

  11. 1.57 radians

  12. 4.71 radians

13. Copy and complete the diagram at the right. Fill in the missing measures in radians or degrees.

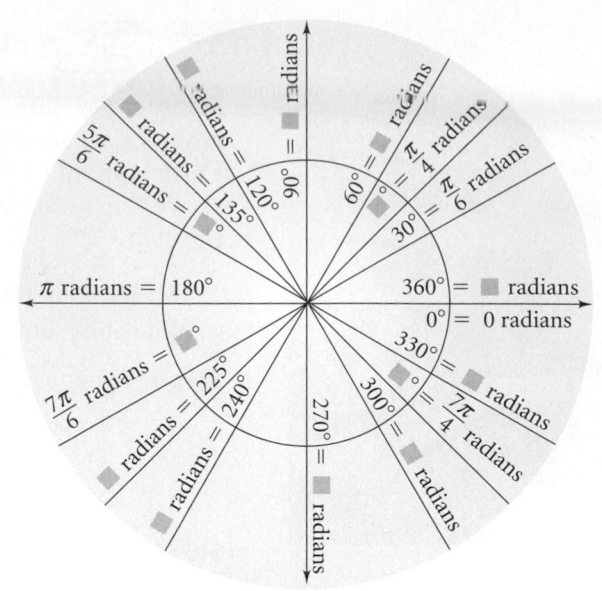

Example 3
(page 728)

The measure θ of an angle in standard position is given. Find the exact values of $\cos \theta$ and $\sin \theta$ for each angle measure.

14. $\frac{\pi}{6}$ radians

15. $\frac{\pi}{3}$ radians

16. $\frac{\pi}{2}$ radians

17. $\frac{2\pi}{3}$ radians

18. $\frac{5\pi}{6}$ radians

19. $-\frac{\pi}{2}$ radians

Example 4
(page 728)

Use each circle to find the length of the indicated arc. Round your answer to the nearest tenth.

20.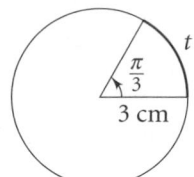

21.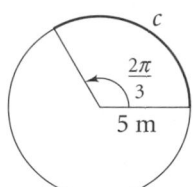

22.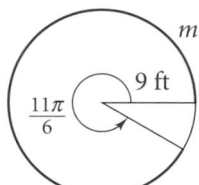

23.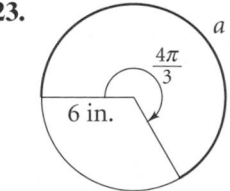

24.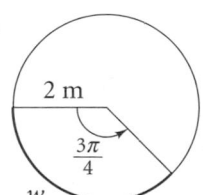

25.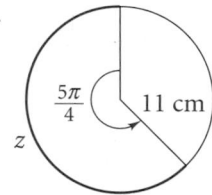

Example 5
(page 729)

Find the length of each arc.

26.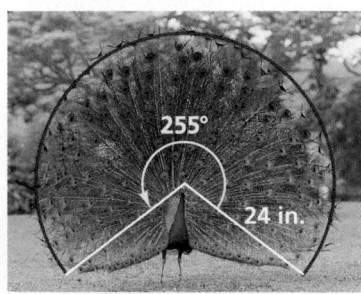

27.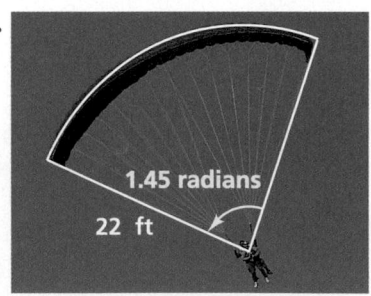

28. Space A geostationary satellite is positioned 35,800 km above Earth's surface. It takes 24 h to complete one orbit. The radius of Earth is about 6400 km.
  a. What distance does the satellite travel in 1 h?
  b. What distance does the satellite travel in 3 h?
  c. What distance does the satellite travel in 2.5 h?
  d. What distance does the satellite travel in 25 h?
  e. Critical Thinking After how many hours has the satellite traveled 200,000 km?

B Apply Your Skills **29. Automobile Design** Suppose a windshield wiper arm has a length of 22 in. and rotates through an angle of 110°. What distance does the tip of the wiper travel as it moves once across the windshield?

 30. Geography The 24 lines of longitude that approximate the 24 standard time zones are equally spaced around the equator.
  a. Suppose you use 24 central angles to divide a circle into 24 equal arcs. Express the measure of each angle in degrees and in radians.
  b. The radius of the equator is about 3960 mi. About how wide is each time zone at the equator?
  c. The radius of the Arctic Circle is about 1580 mi. About how wide is each time zone at the Arctic Circle?

In which quadrant, or on which axis, does the terminal side of each angle lie?

31. $\frac{4\pi}{3}$ radians   **32.** $-\frac{5\pi}{4}$ radians   **33.** $\frac{9\pi}{2}$ radians

34. $\frac{5\pi}{6}$ radians   **35.** $-\pi$ radians   **36.** $\frac{6\pi}{5}$ radians

Draw an angle in standard position with each given measure. Then find the values of the cosine and sine of the angle to the nearest hundredth.

37. $\frac{7\pi}{4}$ radians   **38.** $-\frac{2\pi}{3}$ radians   **39.** $\frac{5\pi}{2}$ radians

40. -2π radians   **41.** $\frac{7\pi}{6}$ radians   **42.** $-\frac{\pi}{5}$ radians

 43. a. Geometry Draw a unit circle on the coordinate plane. Then draw five angles in standard position measuring $\frac{\pi}{5}, \frac{4\pi}{5}, \frac{6\pi}{5}, \frac{9\pi}{5}$, and $\frac{3\pi}{10}$ radians.
  b. For each angle, complete a right triangle. Place the hypotenuse along the terminal side (from the origin to the unit circle). Place one leg along the *x*-axis. The other leg will be parallel to the *y*-axis.
  c. Critical Thinking Are the five triangles congruent? Justify your answer by using the values of sin θ and cos θ for each angle.

44. Open-Ended Draw an angle in standard position. Draw a circle with its center at the vertex of the angle. Find the measure of the angle in radians and degrees.

 45. Transportation Suppose the radius of a bicycle wheel is 13 in. (measured to the outside of the tire). Find the number of radians through which a point on the tire turns when the bicycle has moved forward a distance of 12 ft.

46. Error Analysis A student wanted to rewrite $\frac{9\pi}{4}$ radians in degrees. The screen shows her calculation. What error did the student make?

```
9*π/4*360/2*π
          3997.189782
```

Find the length of each arc. Also, assuming each angle to be in standard position, find the measures of two angles coterminal with the given angle.

47.

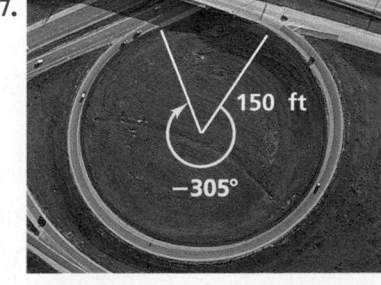

150 ft

−305°

48.

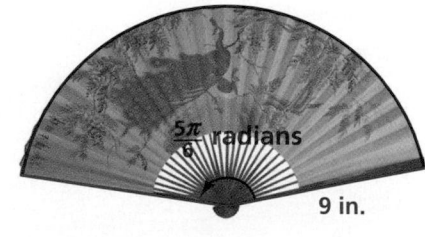

$\frac{5\pi}{6}$ radians

9 in.

GO **Online**
Homework Video Tutor
Visit: PHSchool.com
Web Code: age-1303

49. Writing Two angles are measured in radians. Explain how to tell whether the angles are coterminal without rewriting their measures in degrees.

50. Music A CD with diameter 12 cm spins in a CD player. Calculate how much farther a point on the outside edge of the CD travels in one revolution than a point 1 cm closer to the center of the CD.

51. Geography Assume that Earth is a sphere with radius 3960 miles. A town is at latitude 32° N. Find the distance in miles from the town to the North Pole. (*Hint:* Latitude is measured north and south from the equator.)

C Challenge

The given angle θ is in standard position. Find the radian measure of the angle that results after the given number of revolutions from the terminal side of θ.

52. $\theta = \frac{\pi}{2}$; 1 clockwise revolution

53. $\theta = \frac{\pi}{3}$; 2 clockwise revolutions

54. $\theta = -\frac{2\pi}{3}$; 1 counterclockwise revolution

55. $\theta = \frac{5\pi}{6}$; $2\frac{1}{2}$ counterclockwise revolutions

56. Reasoning Use the proportion $\dfrac{\text{measure of central angle}}{\text{measure of one complete rotation}} = \dfrac{\text{length of arc}}{\text{circumference}}$ to derive the formula $s = r\theta$. Use θ for the central angle measure and s for the arc length. Measure the rotation in radians.

57. a. Use the cartoon below. Use a calculator to evaluate the first three terms of Jason's expression to seven decimal places. Then evaluate the first four terms. Which is a better estimate of cos 60°?

FOX TROT by Bill Amend

b. Jason's expression will approximate the cosine of any angle if you know its radian measure. Write a general form of his expression by substituting x for $\frac{\pi}{3}$.

c. Use the general formula you wrote in part (b) to estimate $\cos\left(\frac{\pi}{10}\text{ radians}\right)$ to the nearest thousandth. What is the angle measure, in degrees?

Test Prep

Multiple Choice

58. Which pairs of measurements represent the same angle measures?

    I. 240°, $\frac{7\pi}{6}$ radians   **II.** 135°, $\frac{3\pi}{4}$ radians   **III.** 150°, $\frac{5\pi}{6}$ radians

    A. I and II only   **B.** I and III only   **C.** II and III only   **D.** I, II, and III

59. What is the exact value of $\cos\left(\frac{5\pi}{4}\text{ radians}\right)$?

    F. $-\frac{\sqrt{3}}{2}$ **G.** $-\frac{\sqrt{2}}{2}$ **H.** $-\frac{1}{2}$ **J.** $\frac{\sqrt{2}}{2}$

60. In a circle, an arc of length 8π cm is intercepted by a central angle of $\frac{2\pi}{3}$ radians. What is the radius of the circle?

    A. $\frac{3\pi}{16}$ cm   **B.** $\frac{16\pi}{3}$ cm   **C.** $\frac{16\pi^2}{3}$ cm   **D.** 12 cm

61. Two arcs have the same length. One arc is intercepted by an angle of $\frac{3\pi}{2}$ radians in a circle of radius 15 cm. If the radius of the other circle is 25 cm, what central angle intercepts the arc?

    F. $\frac{3\pi}{2}$ radians   **G.** $\frac{9\pi}{10}$ radians   **H.** $\frac{3\pi}{2}$ radians   **J.** $\frac{5\pi}{3}$ radians

Short Response   **62.** Describe the relationship between a central angle of one radian and the radius of the circle.

Mixed Review

Lesson 13-2   **Sketch each angle in standard position.**

    63. $15°$ **64.** $-75°$ **65.** $150°$ **66.** $-270°$ **67.** $-85°$

Lesson 12-4   **Find the mean and the standard deviation for each set of values.**

    68. 6 1 9 12 4 15 21 7 8 8

    69. 12 13 15 9 16 5 18 16 12 11 15

    70. 21 29 35 26 25 28 27 51 24 34

Lesson 10-3   **Write an equation of a circle with the given center and radius.**

    71. center $(0, 0)$, radius 8   **72.** center $(0, -5)$, radius 4

    73. center $(3, 7)$, radius 6.5   **74.** center $(-8, 4)$, radius 3

✓ Checkpoint Quiz 1   Lessons 13-1 through 13-3

Find the period and the amplitude of each periodic function.

1. 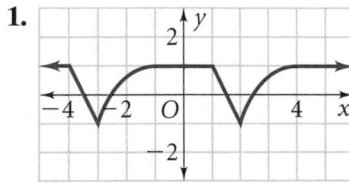   **2.**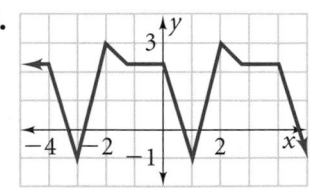

Find the exact values of sin θ and cos θ for an angle in standard position with each measure θ.

    3. $-45°$ **4.** $210°$ **5.** π radians   **6.** $\frac{\pi}{6}$ radians

Convert each angle measure into its equivalent in radians or degrees.

    7. $-180°$ **8.** $36°$ **9.** π radians   **10.** $\frac{4\pi}{3}$ radians

The Sine Function

What You'll Learn

- To identify properties of the sine function
- To graph sine curves

... And Why

To model light waves, as in Example 7

Use the graph. Find the value(s) of each of the following.

1. the period
2. the domain
3. the amplitude
4. the range

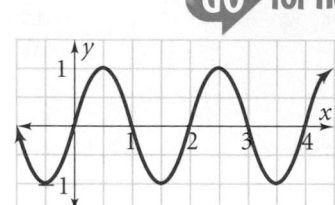

GO for Help Lesson 13-1

◀》 **New Vocabulary** • sine function • sine curve

---

1   Interpreting Sine Functions

Vocabulary Tip

Sine comes from the Latin word *sinus,* meaning "bay," a reference to the shape of the sine curve.

The **sine function,** $y = \sin \theta$, matches the measure θ of an angle in standard position with the y-coordinate of a point on the unit circle. This point is where the terminal side of the angle intersects the unit circle.

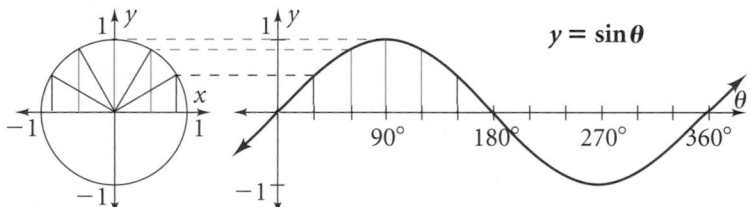

1 EXAMPLE   Interpreting the Sine Function in Degrees

Use the graph of the sine function.

a. What is the value of $y = \sin \theta$ for $\theta = 270°$?

The value of the function at $\theta = 270°$ is -1.

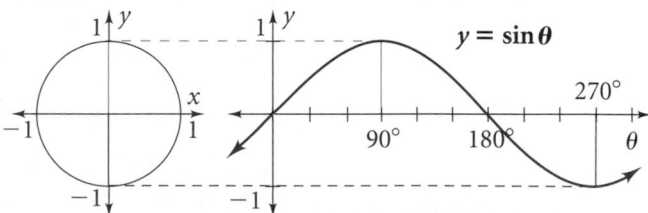

b. For what value of θ between 0° and 360° does the graph of $y = \sin \theta$ reach the maximum value of 1?

When $y = 1, \theta = 90°$.

✓ **Quick Check**   ❶ **a.** Extend the graph from Example 1 to include angle measures from 270° to 720°. Will the graph reach the maximum value of 1 again, and if so, where?

     b. Reasoning Is the sine function a periodic function? Explain.

As you have seen, an angle measure θ can be expressed in degrees or in radians. In this book, when no unit is mentioned you should use radians.

You can graph the sine function in radians. In the unit circle, you can show radian measures along the circle as lengths of arcs. In the graphs below, the points for 1, 2, and 3 radians are marked on the unit circle and on the θ-axis.

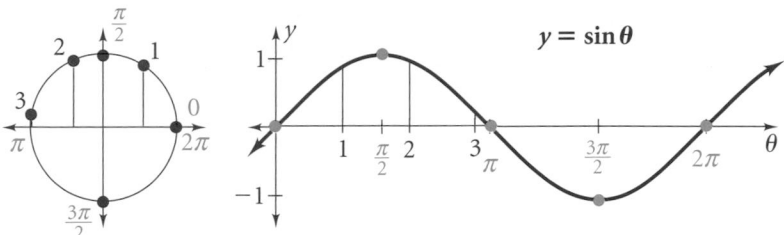

Real-World  **Connection**

If you mark a point on one of the blades of an eggbeater and plot the point's horizontal distance over time from the center of the eggbeater, the graph is a sine curve.

2 EXAMPLE **Estimating Sine Values in Radians**

Estimate each value from the graph. Check your estimate with a calculator.

a. sin 2

The sine function reaches its maximum value of 1 at $\frac{\pi}{2} \approx 1.57$. The value of the function at 2 is slightly less than 1, or about 0.9.

$\sin 2 \approx 0.9092974268$ **Use a calculator in radian mode.**

b. sin π

The sine function crosses the x-axis at π, so sin $\pi = 0$.

$\sin \pi = 0$ **Use a calculator in radian mode.**

✓ **Quick Check** **2** Use the graphs of sin θ from Examples 1 and 2.
a. Find the amplitude of the sine function.
b. Express the period of the sine function in degrees and in radians.
c. What are the domain and range of the sine function?

For: Sine Function Activity
Use: Interactive Textbook, 13-4

The graph of a sine function is called a **sine curve.** By varying the period, you get different sine curves.

3 EXAMPLE **Finding the Period of a Sine Curve**

Use the graph of $y = \sin 4\theta$ at the right.

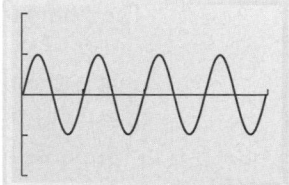

Xmin=0
Xmax=2π
Xscl=π/2
Ymin=−2
Ymax=2
Yscl=1

a. How many cycles occur in the graph at the right? How is the number of cycles related to the coefficient of θ in the equation?

The graph shows 4 cycles. The number of cycles is equal to the coefficient of θ.

Vocabulary Tip

The <u>period</u> of a function is the horizontal length of one cycle.

b. Find the period of $y = \sin 4\theta$.

$2\pi \div 4 = \frac{\pi}{2}$ **Divide the interval of the graph by the number of cycles.**

The period of $y = \sin 4\theta$ is $\frac{\pi}{2}$.

❸ Find the period of each sine curve below. For each graph, the θ-axis shows values from 0 to 2π.

a.

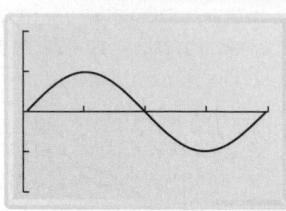

b.

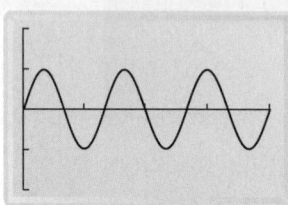

You can also vary the amplitude of a sine curve.

❹ **EXAMPLE** **Finding the Amplitude of a Sine Curve**

The graphing calculator screens at the right show several graphs of $y = a \sin \theta$. Each θ-axis shows values from 0 to 2π.

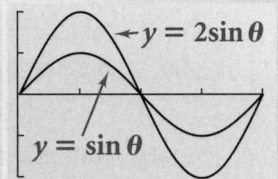

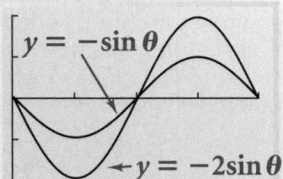

a. Find the amplitude of each sine curve. How does the value of a affect the amplitude?

The amplitude of $y = \sin \theta$ is 1, and the amplitude of $y = 2 \sin \theta$ is 2. The amplitude of $y = -\sin \theta$ is 1, and the amplitude of $y = -2 \sin \theta$ is 2. In each case, the amplitude of the curve is $|a|$.

b. How does a negative value of a affect the position of the curve?

When a is negative, the graph is a reflection in the x-axis.

✓ **Quick Check** ❹ Find the amplitude of each sine curve. Each interval on the y-axis represents one unit.

a.

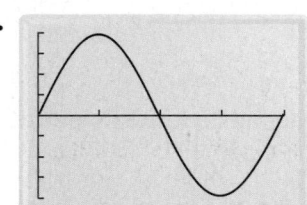

b.

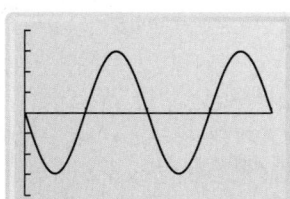

The summary box below lists the properties of sine functions.

 Key Concepts

Summary	Properties of Sine Functions

Suppose $y = a \sin b\theta$, with $a \neq 0, b > 0$, and θ in radians.

- $|a|$ is the amplitude of the function.

- b is the number of cycles in the interval from 0 to 2π.

- $\frac{2\pi}{b}$ is the period of the function.

You can use five points equally spaced through one cycle to sketch a sine curve. For $a > 0$, this five-point pattern is *zero–max–zero–min–zero*.

5 EXAMPLE Sketching a Graph

a. Sketch one cycle of a sine curve with amplitude 2 and period 4π.

Step 1 Choose scales for the y-axis and the θ-axis that are about equal ($\pi \approx 3$ units). On the θ-axis, mark one period (4π).

Step 2 Mark equal spaces through one cycle by dividing the period into fourths.

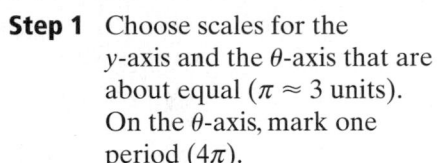
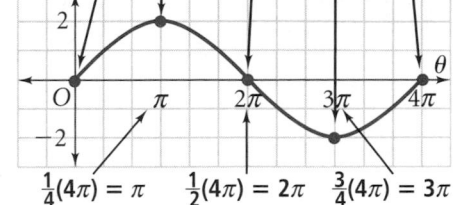

$$\tfrac{1}{4}(4\pi) = \pi \qquad \tfrac{1}{2}(4\pi) = 2\pi \qquad \tfrac{3}{4}(4\pi) = 3\pi$$

Step 3 Since the amplitude is 2, the maximum is 2 and the minimum is -2. Plot the five points and sketch the curve.

b. Use the form $y = a \sin b\theta$. Write an equation with $a > 0$ for the sine curve in part (a).

The amplitude is 2, and $a > 0$, so $a = 2$.
The period is 4π, and $4\pi = \frac{2\pi}{b}$, so $b = \frac{1}{2}$.
An equation for the function is $y = 2 \sin \frac{1}{2}\theta$.

✓ Quick Check **5 a.** Sketch one cycle of a sine curve with amplitude 3, period 4, and $a > 0$.
  b. Critical Thinking Predict the five-point pattern for graphing a sine curve when $a < 0$.
  c. Sketch one cycle of a sine curve with amplitude 2, period $\frac{2\pi}{3}$, and $a < 0$.

You can also graph sine functions from a given function rule.

6 EXAMPLE Graphing From a Function Rule

Sketch one cycle of $y = \frac{1}{2} \sin 2\theta$.

$|a| = \frac{1}{2}$, so the amplitude is $\frac{1}{2}$.

$b = 2$, so there are 2 cycles from 0 to 2π.

$\frac{2\pi}{b} = \frac{2\pi}{2} = \pi$, so the period is π.

Divide the period into fourths.

Using the values of the amplitude and period, plot the *zero–max–zero–min–zero* pattern.

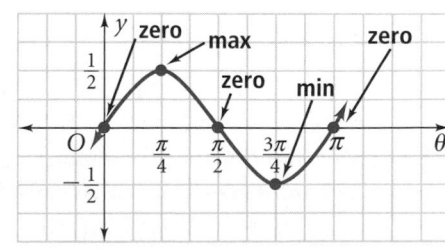

Sketch the curve.

✓ Quick Check **6** Sketch one cycle of the graph of each sine function.
  a. $y = 1.5 \sin 2\theta$ **b.** $y = 3 \sin \frac{\pi}{2}\theta$

You can use sine functions to model real-world situations.

7 **EXAMPLE** **Real-World** 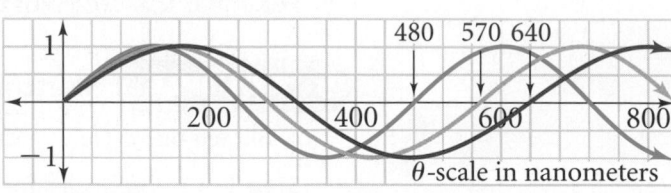 **Connection**

Multiple Choice The graph at the right models waves of red, blue, and yellow light. Which equation best models blue light?

θ-scale in nanometers

Ⓐ $y = \sin 240\pi\theta$ Ⓑ $y = \sin 480\pi\theta$ Ⓒ $y = \sin \frac{\pi}{480}\theta$ Ⓓ $y = \sin \frac{\pi}{240}\theta$

According to the graph, one blue cycle takes 480 nanometers to complete, so the period is 480.

To write an equation, first find b.

$\text{period} = \dfrac{2\pi}{b}$ **Use the relationship between the period and b.**

$480 = \dfrac{2\pi}{b}$ **Substitute.**

$b = \dfrac{2\pi}{480}$ **Multiply each side by $\frac{b}{480}$.**

An equation for blue light is $y = \sin \frac{2\pi}{480}\theta$ or $y = \sin \frac{\pi}{240}\theta$. The correct choice is D.

✓ **Quick Check** **7** Write equations for the sine curves that model the red and yellow light waves in Example 7.

EXERCISES

For more exercises, see *Extra Skill and Word Problem Practice.*

Practice and Problem Solving

A **Practice by Example**

Example 1
(page 734)

Use the graph at the right to find the value of $y = \sin \theta$ for each value of θ.

1. 30°   **2.** 45°   **3.** 120°

4. 180°   **5.** 240°   **6.** 300°

Example 2
(page 735)

Use the graph at the right to find the value of $y = \sin \theta$ for each value of θ.

7. $\frac{\pi}{2}$ radians   **8.** 3 radians

9. 4 radians   **10.** 5 radians

11. $\frac{3\pi}{2}$ radians   **12.** $\frac{7\pi}{4}$ radians

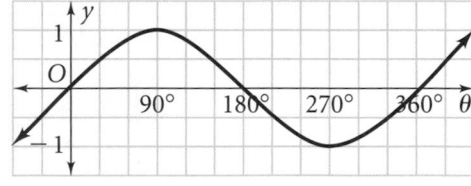

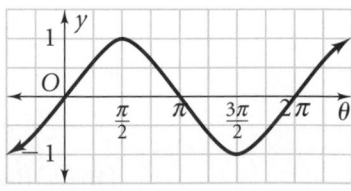

Examples 3 and 4
(pages 735 and 736)

How many cycles does each sine function have in the interval from 0 to 2π? Find the amplitude and period of each function.

13. 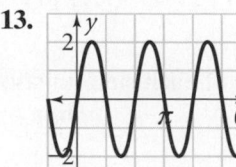   **14.** 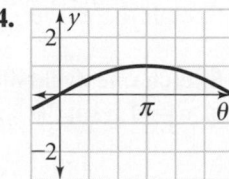   **15.**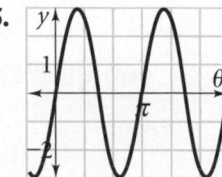

Example 5
(page 737)

Sketch one cycle of each sine curve. Assume $a > 0$. Write an equation for each graph.

16. amplitude 2, period $\frac{2\pi}{3}$

17. amplitude $\frac{1}{3}$, period π

18. amplitude 4, period 4π

19. amplitude 3, period 2π

20. amplitude 1, period 2

21. amplitude 1.5, period 3

Example 6
(page 737)

Sketch one cycle of the graph of each sine function.

22. $y = 2 \sin \theta$

23. $y = \sin 3\theta$

24. $y = -\sin \frac{\pi}{2}\theta$

25. $y = 2 \sin \pi\theta$

26. $y = 4 \sin \frac{1}{2}\theta$

27. $y = -4 \sin \frac{1}{2}\theta$

Example 7
(page 738)

Find the period of each sine curve. Then write an equation for each sine function.

28.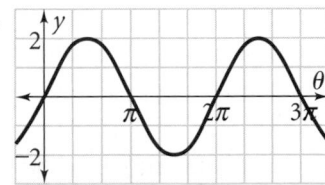

29.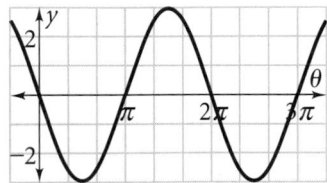

30.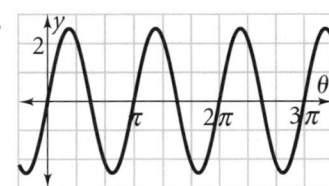

31.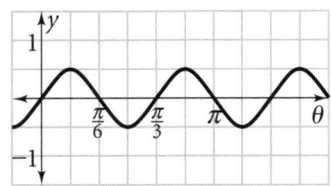

Test-Taking Tip

In a graph of a periodic function, a cycle easiest to see is often one that starts on an axis. Easiest of all is one that starts at the origin.

32.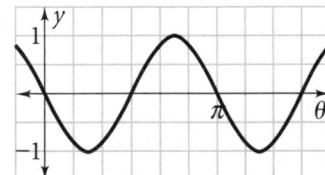

33.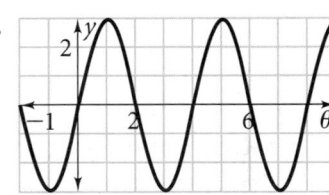

B **Apply Your Skills**

How many cycles does each sine function have in the interval from 0 to 2π? Find the amplitude and period of each function.

34. $y = \sin \theta$

35. $y = \sin 5\theta$

36. $y = \sin \pi\theta$

37. $y = 3 \sin \theta$

38. $y = -5 \sin \theta$

39. $y = -5 \sin 2\pi\theta$

40. a. Graph the functions $y = \sin \theta$, $y = 2 \sin \theta$, and $y = 3 \sin \theta$ on the same screen.
   b. Critical Thinking If a is positive, how does the graph of $y = a \sin \theta$ change as the value of a changes?

41. a. Graph the functions $y = 3 \sin \theta$ and $y = -3 \sin \theta$ on the same screen. How are the two graphs related?
   b. Graph the functions $y = \sin 3\theta$ and $y = \sin (-3\theta)$ on the same screen. How are the two graphs related?
   c. Critical Thinking How does the graph of $y = a \sin b\theta$ change when a is replaced with its opposite? How does the graph change when b is replaced with its opposite?

42. Use the formula period $= \frac{2\pi}{b}$ to find the period of each sine function.

   a. $y = 1.5 \sin 2\theta$

   b. $y = 3 \sin \frac{\pi}{2}\theta$

 43. Music The sound wave for the note A above middle C can be modeled by the function $y = 0.001 \sin 880\pi\theta$.
 a. What is the period of the function?
 b. What is the amplitude of the function?
 c. How many cycles of the graph are between 0 and 2π?

 44. Writing Suppose the independent variable θ is measured in degrees. Restate the properties of the sine function $y = a \sin b\theta$ on page 736 in terms of degrees. Which properties are affected by the conversion to degrees?

Find the period and amplitude of each sine function. Then sketch each function from 0 to 2π.

45. $y = -3.5 \sin 5\theta$ **46.** $y = \frac{5}{2} \sin 2\theta$ **47.** $y = -2 \sin 2\pi\theta$

48. $y = 0.4 \sin 3\theta$ **49.** $y = 0.5 \sin \frac{\pi}{3}\theta$ **50.** $y = -1.2 \sin \frac{5\pi}{6}\theta$

51. Open-Ended Write the equations of three sine functions with the same amplitude that have periods of 2, 3, and 4. Then sketch all three graphs on the same coordinate axes.

 52. Electricity One type of electric generator consists of a rotating magnetic field surrounded by stationary coils. The voltages produced by the generator can be modeled by sine curves. Suppose three coils are placed symmetrically around a magnetic field. The graph below shows the voltage produced in each coil.

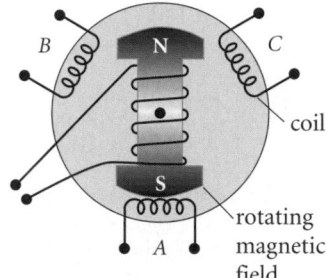

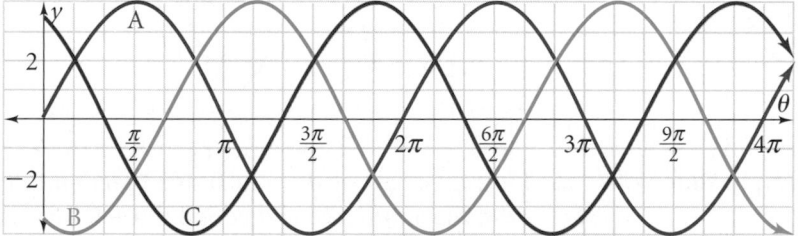

 a. Find the amplitude and period of each sine curve.
 b. Write an equation for the graph that models the voltage produced by coil A.
  c. Critical Thinking One of the graphs has the equation $y = 4 \sin\left(\theta - \frac{2\pi}{3}\right)$. Use your knowledge of translations in the coordinate plane to predict whether this is the equation for coil B or coil C. Check your prediction using a graphing calculator.

 Challenge **Sound** For sound waves, the period and the frequency of a pitch are reciprocals of each other: period $= \frac{\text{seconds}}{\text{cycle}}$ and frequency $= \frac{\text{cycles}}{\text{second}}$. Write an equation for each pitch. Let $\theta =$ time in seconds. Use $a = 1$.

53. the lowest pitch easily heard by humans: 30 cycles per second

54. the lowest pitch heard by elephants: 15 cycles per second

55. the highest pitch heard by bats: 120,000 cycles per second

Find the period and amplitude of each function. Sketch each function from 0 to 2π.

56. $y = \sin(\theta + 2)$ **57.** $y = \sin(\theta - 3)$ **58.** $y = \sin(2\theta + 4)$

Solar Year

March 21st
equal day and night

June 21st
longest day

Dec. 21st
shortest day

Sept. 22nd
equal day and night

Not drawn to scale

59. Astronomy Sunrise and sunset are defined as the times when someone at sea level sees the uppermost edge of the sun on the horizon. In Houston, Texas, at the spring equinox (March 21), there are 12 hours and 9 minutes of sunlight. Throughout the year, the variation from 12 hours 9 minutes of sunlight can be modeled by a sine function. The longest day (June 21) has 1 hour 55 minutes more sunlight than at the equinox. The shortest day (December 21) has 1 hour 55 minutes less sunlight.

a. Define the independent and dependent variables for a function that models the variation in hours of sunlight in Houston.

b. What are the amplitude and period of the function measured in days?

c. Write a function that relates the number of days away from the spring equinox to the variation in hours of sunlight in Houston.

d. Estimation Use your function from part (c). In Houston, about how much less sunlight does February 14 have than March 21?

e. Research Find the number of hours of sunlight in your area on June 21 and on December 21. Develop a sunlight model from your data. Use your model to predict the number of hours of sunlight you will have one week from now.

Test Prep

Multiple Choice

60. Which value is NOT the same as the other three values?

A. $\sin 100°$ **B.** $\sin 80°$ **C.** $\sin -80°$ **D.** $\sin -260°$

61. What is the amplitude of $y = 3 \sin 4\theta$?

F. $\frac{4}{3}$ **G.** 3   **H.** 4   **J.** 2π

62. Which answer choice describes $y = -\sin 2\theta$?

A. amplitude -1, period 4π **B.** amplitude 1, period π
C. amplitude 2, period $-\pi$ **D.** amplitude 2π, period 1

63. Which function has a period of 4π and an amplitude of 8?

F. $y = -8 \sin 8\theta$ **G.** $y = -8 \sin \frac{1}{2}\theta$ **H.** $y = 8 \sin 2\theta$ **J.** $y = 4 \sin 8\theta$

Short Response

64. Find the value of θ that is between $90°$ and $180°$ such that $\sin \theta = \sin 60°$. Show your work.

Extended Response

65. The period of a sine function is $30°$ and its amplitude is 1. Write the function in the form $y = a \sin b\theta$, where θ is in radians. Show your work.

Mixed Review

Lesson 13-3

Write each measure in radians. Express the answer in terms of π and as a decimal rounded to the nearest hundredth.

66. $-80°$ **67.** $150°$ **68.** $-240°$ **69.** $320°$ **70.** $-450°$

Lesson 12-2

71. A poll of teenagers in one town showed that 43% play a team sport. It also showed that 21% play varsity team sports. Find the probability that a teenager plays varsity sports, given that the teenager plays a team sport.

Lesson 11-1

Write an explicit formula for each sequence. Then find a_{15}.

72. $6, 5, 4, 3, \ldots$ **73.** $15, 18, 21, 24, \ldots$ **74.** $0.6, 1.4, 2.2, 3, \ldots$

You can use a graphing calculator to graph trigonometric functions in radians or degrees.

Go Online
PHSchool.com

For: Graphing calculator procedures
Web Code: age-2111

1 ACTIVITY Comparing Graphs in Radians and Degrees

Compare the graphs of $y = \cos x$ from $-360°$ to $360°$ and from -2π to 2π radians.

Step 1 Press MODE to change the mode to degrees. Adjust the window values. Graph the function.

Step 2 Change the mode to radians. Graph the function.

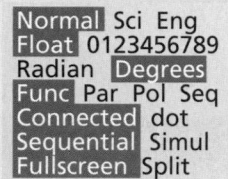

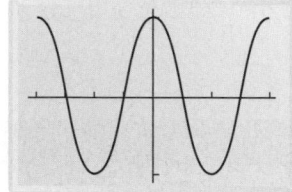

Xmin = −360   Ymin = −1.2
Xmax = 360   Ymax = 1.2
Xscl = 90   Yscl = 1

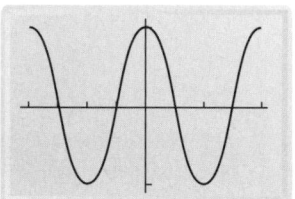

Xmin = −2π Ymin = −1.2
Xmax = 2π Ymax = 1.2
Xscl = π/2   Yscl = 1

The graphs appear to be identical, although in different windows. The function has a period of $360°$ or 2π radians.

● You can use the TRACE feature to evaluate trigonometric functions.

2 ACTIVITY Using the Trace Feature

Graph the function $y = \sin x$. Find $\sin 30°$ and $\sin 150°$.

Step 1 Change the mode to degrees. Adjust the window values.

Step 2 Graph the function. Use the TRACE key to find the y-values when $x = 30$ and $x = 150$.

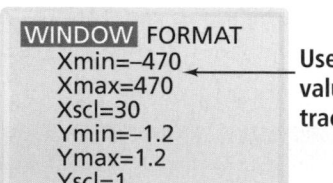

WINDOW FORMAT
Xmin=−470
Xmax=470
Xscl=30
Ymin=−1.2
Ymax=1.2
Yscl=1

Use these values to trace easily.

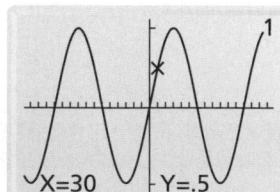

X=30   Y=.5

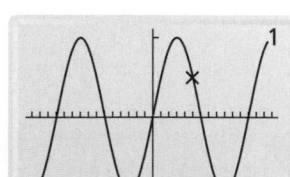

X=150   Y=.5

EXERCISES

Use appropriate window values to identify the period of each function in radians and in degrees. Then evaluate each function at 90°.

1. $y = \cos x$ **2.** $y = \sin x$ **3.** $y = \sin 3x$ **4.** $y = -3 \sin x$ **5.** $y = \cos (x + 30°)$

Writing **Graph the two functions in the same window. Compare the graphs. How are they similar? How are they different?**

6. $y = \sin x, y = \cos x$ **7.** $y = \sin x, y = \cos \left(x - \frac{\pi}{2}\right)$ **8.** $y = \sin x, y = \cos \left(x + \frac{\pi}{2}\right)$

The Cosine Function

✓ **Check Skills You'll Need**

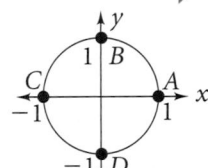

GO for Help Lesson 13-2

Find the *x*-coordinate of each point on the unit circle at the right.

1. *A*　　　　**2.** *B*

3. *C*　　　　**4.** *D*

🔊 **New Vocabulary** • cosine function

1　Graphing and Writing Cosine Functions

The **cosine function,** $y = \cos \theta$, matches the measure θ of an angle in standard position with the *x*-coordinate of a point on the unit circle. This point is where the terminal side of the angle intersects the unit circle.

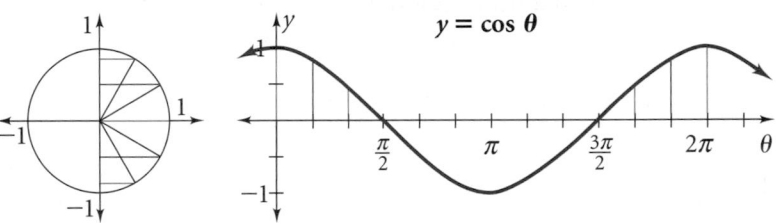

$y = \cos \theta$

1 EXAMPLE 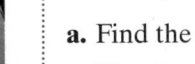 **Interpreting the Graph of Cos θ**

Use the graph shown above.

a. Find the domain, period, range, and amplitude of the cosine function.

The domain of the function is all real numbers.

The function goes from its maximum value of 1 and back again in an interval from 0 to 2π. The period is 2π.

The function has a maximum value of 1 and a minimum value of -1. The range is $-1 \le y \le 1$.

$$\text{amplitude} = \tfrac{1}{2}(\text{maximum} - \text{minimum})$$
$$= \tfrac{1}{2}[1 - (-1)]$$
$$= 1$$

b. Examine the cycle of the cosine function in the interval from 0 to 2π. Where in the cycle does the maximum value occur? Where does the minimum occur? Where do the zeros occur?

The maximum value occurs at 0 and 2π. The minimum value occurs at π. The zeros occur at $\frac{\pi}{2}$ and $\frac{3\pi}{2}$.

Real-World Connection

The distance over time between the center line of a metronome and a point on the metronome's swinging arm can be modeled with a cosine function.

✓ **Quick Check** ❶ Use the graphs below. How are the graphs of the sine and cosine functions alike? How are they different?

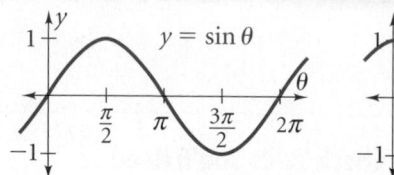

The cosine function has some of the same properties as the sine function.

 **Key Concepts**

Summary	**Properties of Cosine Functions**

Suppose $y = a \cos b\theta$, with $a \neq 0, b > 0$, and θ in radians.

- $|a|$ is the amplitude of the function.
- b is the number of cycles in the interval from 0 to 2π.
- $\frac{2\pi}{b}$ is the period of the function.

To graph a cosine function, locate five points equally spaced through one cycle. For $a > 0$, this five-point pattern is *max–zero–min–zero–max*.

❷ EXAMPLE **Sketching the Graph of a Cosine Function**

⬤nline active math

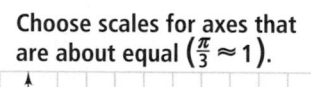

For: Cosine Function Activity
Use: Interactive Textbook, 13-5

Sketch the graph of $y = 1.5 \cos 2\theta$ in the interval from 0 to 2π.

$|a| = 1.5$, so the amplitude is 1.5.

$b = 2$, so the graph has two full cycles from 0 to 2π.

$\frac{2\pi}{b} = \pi$, so the period is π.

Divide the period into fourths. Plot five points for the first cycle. Use 1.5 for the maximum and -1.5 for the minimum. Repeat the pattern for the second cycle.

⬤ Sketch the curve.

Choose scales for axes that are about equal $\left(\frac{\pi}{3} \approx 1\right)$.

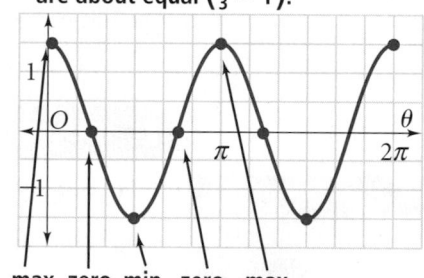

max zero min zero max

✓ **Quick Check** ❷ **a.** Graph the equations $y = \cos x$ and $y = -\cos x$ on the same coordinate plane. Compare the graphs.
b. Critical Thinking Write the five-point pattern to graph $y = a \cos b\theta$ when $a < 0$.
c. Sketch the cosine curve $y = -\frac{1}{2} \cos \pi\theta$ in the interval from 0 to 2π.

2 **Solving Trigonometric Equations**

Waves of water show periodic motion. Away from the shore, individual water molecules move up and down, returning to their initial position after a wave passes. Their height can be modeled with a cosine function.

3 **EXAMPLE** <u>Real-World</u> Connection

Wave Motion The figures at the right show the vertical motion of a particle in water as a wave moves by. Suppose 10-in. waves occur every 4 s. Write an equation that models the height of the particle as it moves from crest to crest.

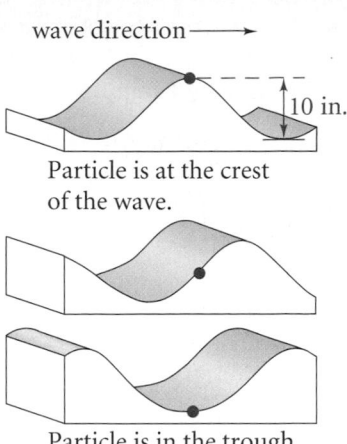

wave direction ——→

10 in.

Particle is at the crest of the wave.

The equation will have the form $y = a \cos b\theta$. Find values for a and b.

$a = \frac{10}{2}$ amplitude $= \frac{\text{maximum} - \text{minimum}}{2}$

$\quad = 5$ Simplify.

period $= \frac{2\pi}{b}$ Use the formula for the period.

$4 = \frac{2\pi}{b}$ The period is 4. Substitute.

$b = \frac{2\pi}{4}$ Multiply each side by $\frac{b}{4}$.

$\quad = \frac{\pi}{2}$ Simplify.

Particle is in the trough of the wave.

● An equation that models the height of the particle is $y = 5 \cos \frac{\pi}{2}\theta$.

✓ Quick Check **3** Write a cosine function for each description. Choose $a > 0$.
   a. amplitude 4, period 6π
   b. amplitude 2.5, period 8

You can solve an equation by graphing to find an exact location along a sine or cosine curve.

4 **EXAMPLE** Solving a Cosine Equation

Suppose you want to find the time t in seconds when the particle from Example 3 is exactly 3 in. above the average height represented by $y = 0$. Solve $5 \cos \frac{\pi}{2}t = 3$ in the interval from 0 to 8.

Step 1 Use two equations. Graph the equations $y = 3$ and $y = 5 \cos \frac{\pi}{2}t$ on the same screen.

Step 2 Use the **Intersect** feature to find the points at which the two graphs intersect.

The graph shows four solutions in the interval. They are $t \approx 0.6$, 3.4, 4.6, and 7.4.

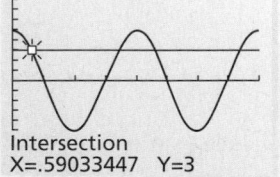

Xmin=0
Xmax=8
Xscl=1
Ymin=–8
Ymax=8
Yscl=1

Intersection
X=.59033447   Y=3

Graphing Calculator Hint

When you use the Intersect feature, move the cursor close to the desired point after the Guess? prompt appears.

● The particle is 3 in. above the average height at about 0.6, 3.4, 4.6, and 7.4 s.

✓ Quick Check **4** Find all solutions in the interval from 0 to 2π.
   a. $3 \cos 2t = -2$
   b. $-2 \cos \theta = 1.2$
   c. **Critical Thinking** In the interval from 0 to 2π, when is $-2 \cos \theta$ less than 1.2? Greater than 1.2?

EXERCISES

For more exercises, see *Extra Skill and Word Problem Practice*.

Practice and Problem Solving

Ⓐ Practice by Example

Example 1
(page 743)

GO for Help

Find the period and amplitude of each cosine function. At what values of x for $0 \le x \le 2\pi$ do the maximum value(s), minimum value(s), and zeros occur?

1.
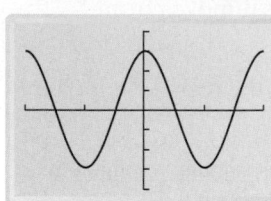
Xmin=−2π
Xmax=2π
Xscl=π
Ymin=−4
Ymax=4
Yscl=1

2.
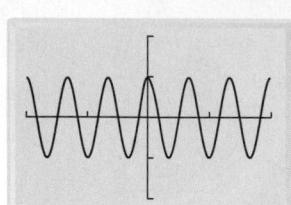
Xmin=−2π
Xmax=2π
Xscl=π
Ymin=−2
Ymax=2
Yscl=1

3.
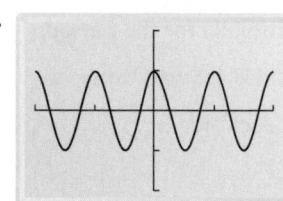
Xmin=−2π
Xmax=2π
Xscl=π
Ymin=−2
Ymax=2
Yscl=1

4.
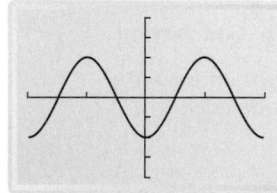
Xmin=−2π
Xmax=2π
Xscl=π
Ymin=−4
Ymax=4
Yscl=1

Example 2
(page 744)

Sketch the graph of each function in the interval from 0 to 2π.

5. $y = \cos 2\theta$ **6.** $y = -3 \cos \theta$ **7.** $y = -\cos 3t$ **8.** $y = \cos \frac{\pi}{2}\theta$ **9.** $y = -\cos \pi\theta$

Example 3
(page 745)

Write a cosine function for each description. Assume that $a > 0$.

10. amplitude 2, period π **11.** amplitude $\frac{\pi}{2}$, period 3   **12.** amplitude π, period 2

Write an equation of a cosine function for each graph.

13.
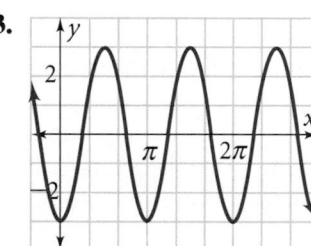

14.
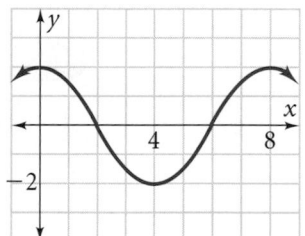

15. Wave Motion Suppose 8-in. waves pass every 3 s. Write an equation that models the height of a water molecule as it moves from crest to crest.

Example 4
(page 745)

Solve each equation in the interval from 0 to 2π. Round to the nearest hundredth.

16. $\cos 2t = \frac{1}{2}$ **17.** $20 \cos t = -8$ **18.** $-2 \cos \pi\theta = 0.3$

19. $3 \cos \frac{t}{3} = 2$ **20.** $\cos \frac{1}{4}\theta = 1$ **21.** $8 \cos \frac{\pi}{3}t = 5$

Ⓑ Apply Your Skills

Identify the period, range, and amplitude of each function.

22. $y = 3 \cos \theta$ **23.** $y = -\cos 2t$ **24.** $y = 2 \cos \frac{1}{2}t$ **25.** $y = \frac{1}{3} \cos \frac{\theta}{2}$

26. $y = 3 \cos \left(-\frac{\theta}{3}\right)$ **27.** $y = -\frac{1}{2} \cos 3\theta$ **28.** $y = 16 \cos \frac{3\pi}{2}t$ **29.** $y = 0.7 \cos \pi t$

Solve each equation in the interval from 0 to 2π. Round your answers to the nearest hundredth.

30. $\sin \theta = 0.6$ **31.** $-3 \sin 2\theta = 1.5$ **32.** $\sin \pi\theta = 1$

33. a. Solve $-2 \sin \theta = 1.2$ in the interval from 0 to 2π.
   b. Solve $-2 \sin \theta = 1.2$ in the interval $2\pi \le \theta \le 4\pi$. How are these solutions related to the solutions in part (a)?

34. a. Graph the equation $y = 5 \cos \frac{\pi}{2}\theta$ from Example 3.
   b. The independent variable θ represents time (in seconds). Find four times at which the particle is at the crest of a wave.
   c. For how many seconds during each cycle is the particle above the line $y = 0$? Below $y = 0$?

Real-World Connection

Commercial fishermen, including clam diggers, work in relation to the tides.

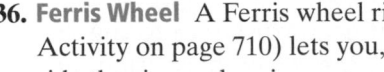
35. Tides The table at the right shows the times for high tide and low tide. The markings on the side of a local pier showed a high tide of 7 ft and a low tide of 4 ft on the previous day.

Tide Table	
High tide	4:03 A.M.
Low tide	10:14 A.M.
High tide	4:25 P.M.
Low tide	10:36 P.M.

   a. What is the average depth of water at the pier? What is the amplitude of the variation from the average depth?
   b. How long is one cycle of the tide?
   c. Write a cosine function that models the relationship between the depth of water and the time of day. Use $y = 0$ to represent the average depth of water. Use $t = 0$ to represent the time 4:03 A.M.
   d. Critical Thinking Suppose your boat needs at least 5 ft of water to approach or leave the pier. Between what times could you come and go?

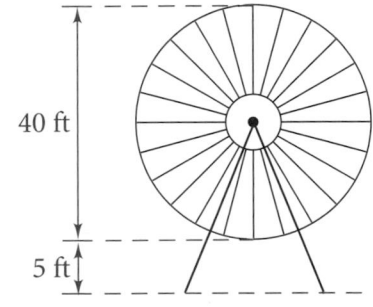

36. Ferris Wheel A Ferris wheel ride (see the Activity on page 710) lets you, in a sense, ride the sine and cosine waves.
   a. Recall the unit circle definitions of sine and cosine (pages 734, 743). Which function, sine or cosine, might serve as a better model for a Ferris wheel ride in the sense of riding a wave? Explain. (*Hint:* For a point on the unit circle, which function suggests vertical position?)
   b. Assume the Ferris wheel pictured turns counterclockwise. For a ride on the unit-circle sine wave, it would be ideal to begin your sine wave ride halfway up on the right side. On a Ferris wheel, however, you begin your ride at the bottom where you board your car. This means that your ride will be $\frac{\pi}{2}$ radians "out of phase" with $\sin x$. Graph $Y1 = \sin X$ and $Y2 = \sin\left(X - \frac{\pi}{2}\right)$ Explain the meaning of "out of phase."
   c. How does the amplitude of your sine wave ride compare with the amplitude of a unit-circle (1 ft radius) sine wave?
   d. How does the center of your Ferris wheel compare with the center of the unit circle?

GO Online
Homework Video Tutor
Visit: PHSchool.com
Web Code: age-1305

   e. Write a sine function that models your sine-wave Ferris wheel ride.
   f. Graph your function using screen dimensions $0 \le x \le 2\pi$ and $0 \le y \le 50$.
   g. How could you build the speed of the Ferris wheel into your model?
   h. How could you build the speed of the Ferris wheel into your graphical display? (*Hint:* Use parametric mode.)
   i. How can you relate the cosine function to a ride on the Ferris wheel?

C Challenge **37. a.** Graph $y = \cos \theta$ and $y = \cos\left(\theta - \frac{\pi}{2}\right)$ in the interval from 0 to 2π. What translation of the graph of $y = \cos \theta$ produces the graph of $y = \cos\left(\theta - \frac{\pi}{2}\right)$?
   b. Graph $y = \cos\left(\theta - \frac{\pi}{2}\right)$ and $y = \sin \theta$ in the interval from 0 to 2π. What do you notice?
   c. Critical Thinking Explain how you could rewrite a sine function as a cosine function.

38. Biology A helix is a three-dimensional spiral. The coiled strands of DNA and  the edges of twisted crepe paper are examples of helixes. In the diagram, the y-coordinate of each edge illustrates a cosine function. Write an equation for the y-coordinate of one edge.

39. Graph one cycle of $y = \cos \theta$, one cycle of $y = -\cos \theta$, and one cycle of $y = \cos (-\theta)$ on the same set of axes. Use the unit circle to explain any relationships you see among these graphs.

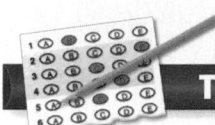

Test Prep

Multiple Choice

40. Which statement(s) is (are) true?

   I. $\cos \theta = \cos (-\theta)$ **II.** $\cos (\theta + 2\pi) = \cos \theta$ **III.** $\cos \pi = -\cos \pi$

   A. I and II only   **B.** II only   **C.** I and III only   **D.** I, II, and III

41. Which function has a period of 2π and an amplitude of 4?

   F. $f(x) = 2 \cos 4\theta$ **G.** $f(x) = 2 \cos \theta$

   H. $f(x) = 4 \cos 2\theta$ **J.** $f(x) = 4 \cos \theta$

42. Which equation corresponds to the graph shown at the right? The screen dimensions are $-4\pi \le x \le 4\pi$ and $-2 \le y \le 2$.

   A. $y = \frac{1}{2} \cos \frac{x}{4}$ **B.** $y = \frac{1}{2} \cos 4x$

   C. $y = 2 \cos \frac{x}{4}$ **D.** $y = 2 \cos 4x$

43. Which equation has the same graph as $y = -\cos t$?

   F. $y = \cos (-t)$ **G.** $y = \sin (t - \pi)$ **H.** $y = \cos (t - \pi)$ **J.** $y = -\sin t$

44. How many solutions does the equation $1 = -\sin 2t$ have for $0 \le t < 2\pi$?

   A. 1   **B.** 2   **C.** 3   **D.** 4

Short Response

45. Find the amplitude and period of $y = -0.2 \cos \frac{\pi}{3}\theta$.

46. Solve $75 \cos 4t = 12.5$ for t from 0 to 2π. Round your result(s) to the nearest hundredth.

47. For what value(s) of t in the interval from 0 to 2π is the value of $f(t) = 3 \cos 2t$ the least?

Mixed Review

Lesson 13-4

Sketch one cycle of each sine curve. Assume that $a > 0$. Then write an equation for each graph.

48. amplitude 1, period $\frac{\pi}{3}$ **49.** amplitude 2.5, period π **50.** amplitude 4, period 1

Lesson 12-5

Find the sample size that produces each margin of error.

51. $\pm 3\%$ **52.** $\pm 7\%$ **53.** $\pm 11\%$

Lesson 11-3

Write the explicit formula for each geometric sequence. List the first five terms.

54. $a_1 = 10, r = 3$ **55.** $a_1 = 12, r = -0.3$ **56.** $a_1 = 900, r = -\frac{1}{3}$

The Tangent Function

GO for Help Lesson 13-3

What You'll Learn

- To graph the tangent function

... And Why

To model the facade of a building, as in Example 3

Check Skills You'll Need

Use a calculator to find the sine and cosine of each value of θ. Then calculate the ratio $\frac{\sin \theta}{\cos \theta}$.

1. $\frac{\pi}{3}$ radians
2. 30 degrees
3. 90 degrees
4. $\frac{5\pi}{6}$ radians
5. $\frac{5\pi}{2}$ radians
6. 0 degrees

New Vocabulary
- tangent of θ
- tangent function

---

1   Graphing the Tangent Function

Vocabulary Tip

A line <u>tangent</u> to a circle intersects the circle at exactly one point.

The sine and cosine of an angle derive from the coordinates of a point on the unit circle. The tangent of an angle derives from the coordinates of a point on a line *tangent* to the unit circle.

For an angle θ in standard position, the **tangent of θ** is the y-coordinate of the point where the line containing the terminal side of the angle intersects the tangent line $x = 1$.

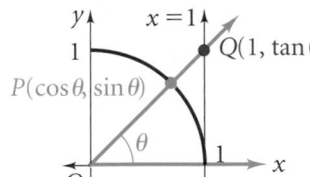

The line containing the terminal side of θ intersects the line $x = 1$ at Q.

The graph below shows one cycle of the **tangent function,** $y = \tan \theta$. Since the period is π, the asymptote that occurs at $\theta = \frac{\pi}{2}$ repeats every π units.

$y = \tan \theta$

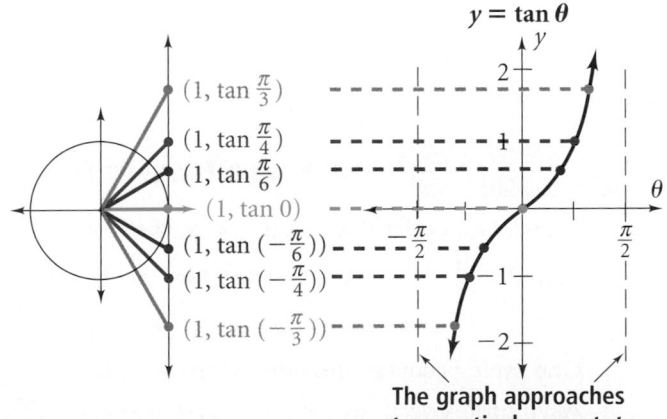

The graph approaches two vertical asymptotes.

You can estimate function values from the graph of the tangent function.

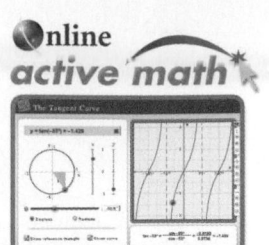

Online
active math

For: Tangent Function Activity
Use: Interactive Textbook, 13-6

1 **EXAMPLE** **Finding Tangent Values From a Graph**

Use the graph of $y = \tan \theta$ at the right to find each value.

a. $\tan \left(-\frac{\pi}{4}\right)$ $\tan \left(-\frac{\pi}{4}\right) = -1$
b. $\tan 0$ $\tan 0 = 0$
c. $\tan \frac{\pi}{4}$ $\tan \frac{\pi}{4} = 1$

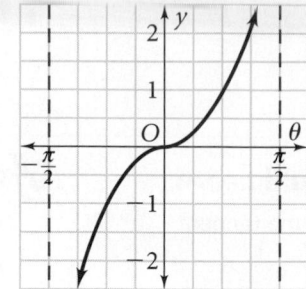

Quick Check **1** **a.** Use the graph in Example 1 to find $\tan \frac{\pi}{8}$ and $\tan \left(-\frac{\pi}{8}\right)$.

b. Critical Thinking Explain why the terminal side of an angle with measure $\frac{\pi}{2}$ *does not intersect* the tangent line.

The graph in Example 1 shows one cycle of the tangent function, $y = \tan \theta$. Since the period is π, the asymptote that occurs at $\theta = \frac{\pi}{2}$ is repeated every π units.

Key Concepts

Summary	**Properties of Tangent Functions**

Suppose $y = a \tan b\theta$, with $b > 0$ and θ in radians.

- $\frac{\pi}{b}$ is the period of the function.
- One cycle occurs in the interval from $-\frac{\pi}{2b}$ to $\frac{\pi}{2b}$.
- There are vertical asymptotes at each end of the cycle.

You can use asymptotes and three points to sketch one cycle of a tangent curve. As with sine and cosine, the five elements are equally spaced through one cycle. Use the pattern *asymptote–(−a)–zero–(a)–asymptote*. In the graph at the right, $a = b = 1$.

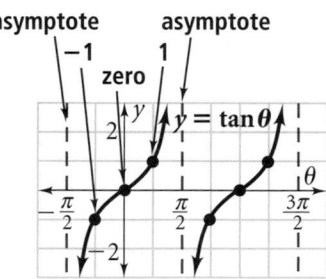

The next example shows how to use the period, asymptotes, and points to graph a tangent function.

2 **EXAMPLE** **Graphing a Tangent Function**

Sketch two cycles of the graph of $y = \tan \pi\theta$.

period $= \frac{\pi}{b}$ **Use the formula for the period.**

$= \frac{\pi}{\pi} = 1$ **Substitute π for b and simplify.**

One cycle occurs in the interval from $-\frac{1}{2}$ to $\frac{1}{2}$.

Asymptotes occur every 1 unit, at $\theta = -\frac{1}{2}, \frac{1}{2}$, and $\frac{3}{2}$.

Since $a = 1$, $\left(-\frac{1}{4}, -1\right)$ and $\left(\frac{1}{4}, 1\right)$ are on the graph.

Plot three points in each cycle. Sketch the curve.

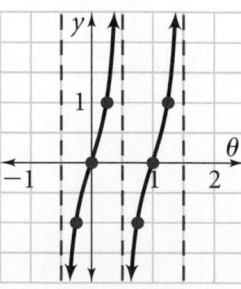

✅ **Quick Check** ❷ Sketch the graph of each tangent curve.

    a. $y = \tan 3\theta, 0 \le \theta \le \pi$ **b.** $y = \tan \frac{\pi}{2}\theta, 0 \le \theta < 3$

You can use the tangent function and a graphing calculator to solve problems involving angles.

❸ **EXAMPLE** **Real-World** 🌐 **Connection**

Design An architect is designing the front facade of a building to include a triangle, as shown in the figure. The base of the triangle is 200 ft wide. The function $y = 100 \tan \theta$ models the height of the triangle, where θ is the angle indicated. Graph the function in degree mode. What is the height of the triangle when $\theta = 16°$? What is the height when $\theta = 22°$?

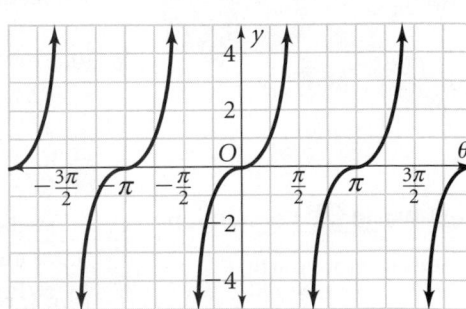

Not drawn to scale

Step 1 Graph the function.

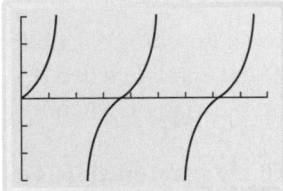

Xmin=0
Xmax=470
Xscl=50
Ymin=−300
Ymax=300
Yscl=90

Step 2 Use the TABLE feature.

X	Y₁
16	28.675
17	30.573
18	32.492
19	34.433
20	36.397
21	38.386
22	40.403
X=16	

When $\theta = 16°$, the height of the triangle is about 28.7 ft. When $\theta = 22°$, the height of the triangle is about 40.4 ft.

✅ **Quick Check** ❸ **a.** What is the height of the triangle when $\theta = 25°$?

    b. Reasoning The architect wants the triangle to be at least one story tall. The average height of a story is 14 ft. What must the measure of θ be for the height of the triangle to be at least 14 ft?

EXERCISES

For more exercises, see *Extra Skill and Word Problem Practice.*

Practice and Problem Solving

Ⓐ **Practice by Example**

Example 1
(page 750)

Use the graph of $y = \tan \theta$ to find each value. If the tangent is undefined at that point, write *undefined*.

1. $\tan (-\pi)$ **2.** $\tan \pi$

3. $\tan \frac{3\pi}{4}$ **4.** $\tan \frac{\pi}{2}$

5. $\tan \left(-\frac{7\pi}{4}\right)$ **6.** $\tan 2\pi$

7. $\tan \left(-\frac{3\pi}{4}\right)$ **8.** $\tan \frac{3\pi}{2}$

Example 2
(page 750)

Each graphing calculator screen shows the interval 0 to 2π. What is the period of each graph?

9.
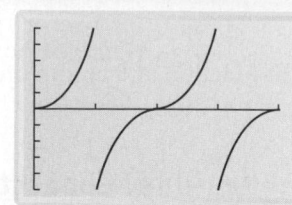

10.
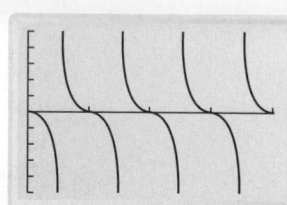

Identify the period and tell where two asymptotes occur for each function.

11. $y = \tan 5\theta$ 12. $y = \tan \frac{3\theta}{2}$ 13. $y = \tan 4\theta$ 14. $y = \tan \frac{2}{3\pi}\theta$

Sketch the graph of each tangent curve in the interval from 0 to 2π.

15. $y = \tan \theta$ 16. $y = \tan 2\theta$ 17. $y = \tan \frac{2\pi}{3}\theta$ 18. $y = \tan (-\theta)$

Example 3
(page 751)

Graph each function on the interval $0° < x < 470°$ and $-300 < y < 300$. Evaluate the function at $x = 45°, 90°,$ and $135°$.

19. $y = 50 \tan x$ 20. $y = -100 \tan x$ 21. $y = 125 \tan \left(\frac{1}{2}x\right)$

22. Suppose the architect in Example 3 reduces the length of the base of the triangle to 100 ft. The function that models the height of the triangle becomes $y = 50 \tan \theta$.
   a. Graph the function on a graphing calculator.
   b. What is the height of the triangle when $\theta = 16°$?
   c. What is the height of the triangle when $\theta = 22°$?

B   **Apply Your Skills**

Identify the period for each tangent function. Then graph each function in the interval from -2π to 2π.

23. $y = \tan \frac{\pi}{6}\theta$ 24. $y = \tan 2.5\theta$ 25. $y = \tan \left(-\frac{3}{2\pi}\theta\right)$

Solve each equation in the interval from 0 to 2π. Round your answers to the nearest hundredth.

26. $\tan \theta = 2$ 27. $\tan \theta = -2$ 28. $6 \tan 2\theta = 1$

29. a. Set your graphing calculator to Degree mode. Use window values $0 \le x \le 141$ and $-500 \le y \le 500$. Graph the functions $y = 100 \tan 2x$, $y = 200 \tan 2x$, and $y = 400 \tan 2x$ on the same set of axes. Sketch the graphs.
   b. Choose five values for x. Compare the y values. Explain how doubling the coefficient of the tangent function affects the output.
   c. Without graphing, make a prediction about the difference between the y-values of $y = 200 \tan x$ and $y = 600 \tan x$. Check your prediction on your graphing calculator.

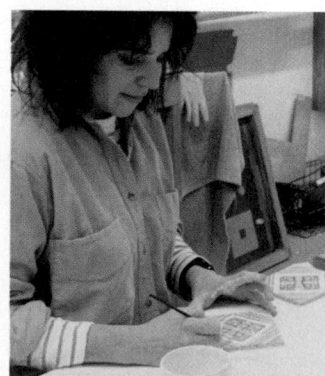

Real-World 🌐 **Connection**

Careers Ceramic artists work with a variety of geometric shapes.

30. **Ceramics** An artist is creating triangular ceramic tiles for a triangular patio. The patio will be an equilateral triangle with base 18 ft and height 15.6 ft.
   a. Find the area of the patio in square feet.
   b. The artist uses tiles that are isosceles triangles with base 6 in. The function $y = 3 \tan \theta$ models the height of the tiles, where θ is the measure of one of the base angles. Graph the function. Find the height of the tile when $\theta = 30°$ and when $\theta = 60°$.
   c. Find the area of one tile in square inches when $\theta = 30°$ and when $\theta = 60°$.
   d. Find the number of tiles the patio will require if $\theta = 30°$ and if $\theta = 60°$.

Homework Video Tutor

Visit: PHSchool.com
Web Code: age-1306

31. a. Open-Ended Write a tangent function.
   b. Graph the function on the interval -2π to 2π.
   c. Identify the period and the asymptotes of the function.

 32. Writing Explain how you can find the equations of the asymptotes of
$y = \tan b\theta$.

Use the function $y = 200 \tan x$ on the interval $0° \le x \le 141°$. Complete each ordered pair. Round your answers to the nearest whole number.

33. $(45°, \blacksquare)$ **34.** $(\blacksquare°, 0)$ **35.** $(\blacksquare°, -200)$ **36.** $(141°, \blacksquare)$ **37.** $(\blacksquare°, 550)$

Write an equation of a tangent function for each graph.

For a guide to solving
Exercise 38, see p. 755.

38.

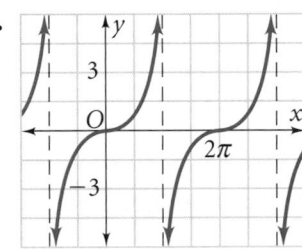

39.

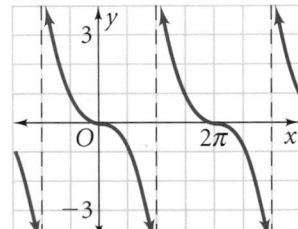

40.

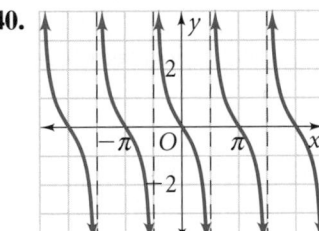

41.

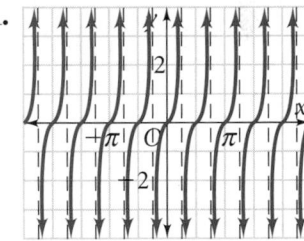

 42. Construction An architect is designing a hexagonal gazebo. The floor is a hexagon made up of six isosceles triangles. The function $y = 4 \tan \theta$ models the height of one triangle, where θ is the measure of one of the base angles and the base of the triangle is 8 ft long.
    a. Graph the function. Find the height of one triangle when $\theta = 60°$.
   b. Find the area of one triangle in square feet when $\theta = 60°$.
   c. Find the area in square feet covered by the gazebo when the triangles forming the hexagon are equilateral.

C Challenge **43. Geometry** The base of a square pyramid has side length 150 ft. The function $\ell = 75 \tan \theta$ models the slant height ℓ of the pyramid, where θ is the angle indicated in the figure.
   a. Graph the function $\ell = 75 \tan \theta$ as $Y_1 = 75 \tan X$ on a graphing calculator. Sketch the graph.
   b. Find the slant height of the pyramid when $\theta = 60°$.
   c. Find the surface area of the pyramid. (*Hint:* Don't forget to include the base of the pyramid.)

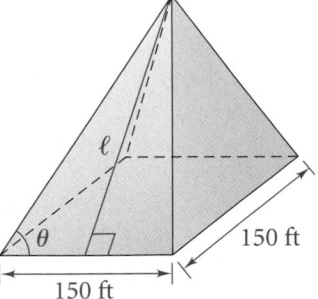

44. a. Graph $y = \tan x$, $y = a \tan x$ (with $a > 0$), and $y = a \tan x$ (with $a < 0$) on the same coordinate plane.
   b. Critical Thinking Recall the pattern of five elements for graphing a tangent function: *asymptote*−(−1)−*zero*−(1)−*asymptote*. How does the value of *a* affect this pattern?

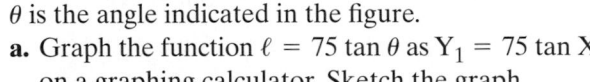

45. Geometry Use the drawing at the right and similar triangles. Justify the statement that $\tan \theta = \frac{\sin \theta}{\cos \theta}$.

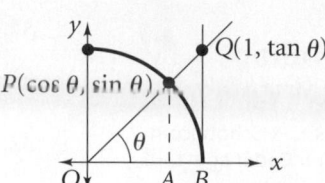

46. How many solutions does the equation $x = \tan x$ have for $0 \le x < 2\pi$? Explain.

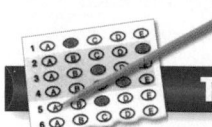

Test Prep

Multiple Choice

47. Which value is NOT defined?

A. $\tan 0$ **B.** $\tan \pi$ **C.** $\tan \frac{3\pi}{2}$ **D.** $\frac{1}{\tan \frac{\pi}{4}}$

48. What is the exact value of $\tan \frac{7\pi}{6}$?

F. $-\sqrt{3}$ **G.** $-\frac{\sqrt{3}}{3}$ **H.** $\frac{\sqrt{3}}{3}$ **J.** $\sqrt{3}$

49. Which pair of values are NOT equal?

A. $\tan \frac{\pi}{4}$, $-\tan \frac{3\pi}{4}$ **B.** $\tan \frac{\pi}{4}$, $\tan \frac{5\pi}{4}$

C. $\tan \theta$, $-\tan (-\theta)$ **D.** $\tan \theta$, $\tan (\pi - \theta)$

50. Which equation does NOT represent a vertical asymptote of the graph of $y = \tan \theta$?

F. $\theta = -\frac{\pi}{2}$ **G.** $\theta = 0$ **H.** $\theta = \frac{\pi}{2}$ **J.** $\theta = \frac{3\pi}{2}$

51. Which function has a period of 4π?

A. $y = \tan 4\theta$ **B.** $y = \tan 2\theta$ **C.** $y = \tan \frac{1}{2}\theta$ **D.** $y = \tan \frac{1}{4}\theta$

Short Response

52. Explain why there is no discussion of the amplitude of the tangent function in the lesson.

Extended Response

53. Compare the period of $y = \tan \theta$ with the period of $y = \sin \theta$. Use a graph of the two functions to support your statements.

Mixed Review

GO for Help

Lesson 13-5

Solve each equation in the interval from 0 to 2π. Round your answer to the nearest hundredth.

54. $\cos t = \frac{1}{4}$ **55.** $10 \cos t = -2$ **56.** $-2 \cos \theta = 0.7$

57. $3 \cos \frac{t}{5} = 1$ **58.** $\cos \frac{3}{4}\theta = -0.6$ **59.** $5 \cos \pi t = 0.9$

Lesson 12-3

Find the mean, median, and mode for each set of values.

60. 9   6   8   1   3   4   5   2   6   8   4   9   12   3   4   10   7   6

61. 45   42   39   35   41   45   49   42   43   48   32   51   42

62. 7.1   8.5   7.0   7.6   8.5   8.1   7.9   8.2   7.3   9.1   8.7   7.9

Lesson 11-2

Find the 27th term of each sequence.

63. $5, 8, 11, \ldots$ **64.** $59, 48, 37, \ldots$ **65.** $1, 3.5, 6, 8.5, \ldots$

66. $2.1, 1.7, 1.3, \ldots$ **67.** $-11, -5, 1, \ldots$ **68.** $6, -7, -20, \ldots$

Understanding Math Problems Read the problem below. Let the explanation guide you through reading a graph. Check your understanding with the exercises at the bottom of the page.

Write an equation of a tangent function for the graph.

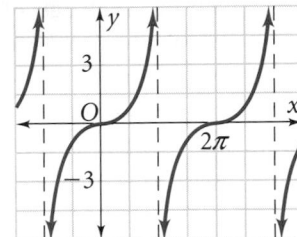

A graph shows data points of a function on a coordinate grid. When you read a graph, you identify information from the graph to help you solve the problem. As you look at a graph, ask yourself the following questions.

What relationship is shown in the graph?

The problem states that the graph shows a tangent function.

What information can I obtain from the graph?

Scale The scale on the y-axis shows that two grid lines represent 3 units. The scale on the x-axis shows that four grid lines represent 2π units, which means two grid lines represent π units. Redraw the graph and add labels to the x-axis.

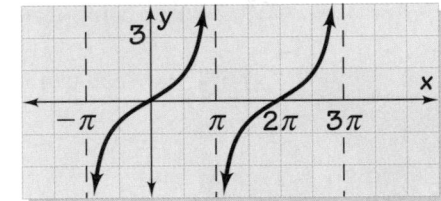

Asymptotes A tangent function has vertical asymptotes. Now that you've added labels, you can see that asymptotes occur at x-values of $-\pi, \pi$, and 3π.

Period The period is the horizontal distance between asymptotes.

$$\text{period} = \text{distance between asymptotes} = \pi - (-\pi) = 2\pi$$

Now you can use the information you've obtained from the graph to write an equation for the tangent function shown. The standard form for the equation of a tangent function is $y = \tan bx$. Since you know the period, you can find b.

$\text{period} = \frac{\pi}{b}$, so $b = \frac{\pi}{\text{period}} = \frac{\pi}{2\pi} = \frac{1}{2}$

Since $\left(-\frac{\pi}{2}, -1\right)$ is on the graph, $a = 1$.

An equation for the tangent function is $y = \tan \frac{1}{2}x$.

EXERCISES

For each graph below (a) identify the asymptotes; (b) identify the period; (c) write an equation for the function, and (d) find the zeros of the function.

1.

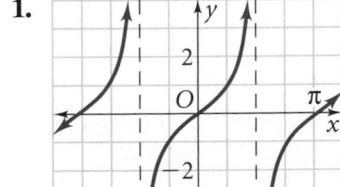

2.

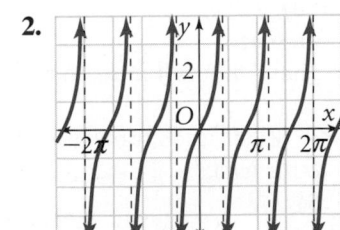

3.

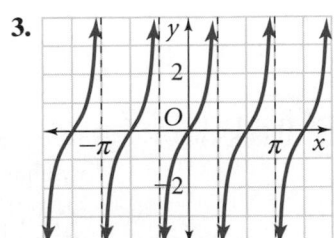

Translating Sine and Cosine Functions

What You'll Learn

- To graph translations of trigonometric functions
- To write equations of translations

. . . And Why

To analyze temperature data, as in Example 6

Graph each pair of equations on the same coordinate plane. Identify each translation as *horizontal*, *vertical*, or *diagonal*.

1. $y = 2x, y = 2x + 5$ **2.** $g(x) = |x|, f(x) = |x + 3|$

3. $y = -x, y = -x - 1$ **4.** $g(x) = |x|, h(x) = |x| - 4$

5. $y = -|x|, y = -|x - 2| + 1$ **6.** $y = x^2, y = (x + 3)^2 - 2$

🔊 **New Vocabulary**   • phase shift

---

1   Graphing Translations of Trigonometric Functions

Real-World 🌐 Connection

A modem (modulator-demodulator) uses phase shifts to convert data between digital signals, which use binary digits, and analog signals, which use waves.

You can translate periodic functions horizontally and vertically using the methods you have used for other functions.

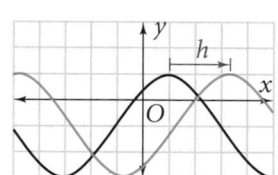 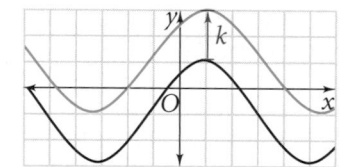

$g(x)$: horizontal translation of $f(x)$ $h(x)$: vertical translation of $f(x)$
$g(x) = f(x - h)$ $h(x) = f(x) + k$

Each horizontal translation of certain periodic functions is a **phase shift.**

When $g(x) = f(x - h)$, the value of h is the amount of the shift left or right. If $h > 0$, the shift is to the right. If $h < 0$, the shift is to the left.

1   EXAMPLE   Identifying Phase Shifts

What is the value of h in each translation? Describe each phase shift (use a phrase such as *3 units to the left*).

a. $g(x) = f(x - 2)$

     $h = 2$; the phase shift is 2 units to the right.

b. $y = \cos(x + 4)$
    $= \cos(x - (-4))$
   $h = -4$; the phase shift is 4 units to the left.

✓ **Quick Check** ❶ What is the value of h in each translation? Describe each phase shift (use a phrase such as *3 units to the left*).
     a. $g(t) = f(t - 5)$
     b. $y = \sin(x + 3)$

You can analyze a translation to determine how it relates to the parent function.

Video Tutor Help
Visit: PHSchool.com
Web Code: age-0775

2 EXAMPLE Graphing Translations

Use the graph of the parent function $y = \sin x$ at the left. Sketch each translation of the graph in the interval $0 \le x \le 2\pi$.

a. $y = \sin x + 3$

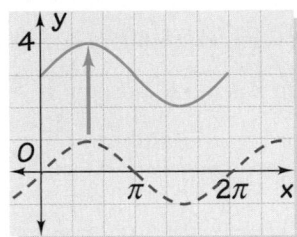

Translate the graph of $y = \sin x$ 3 units up.

b. $y = \sin \left(x - \frac{\pi}{2} \right)$

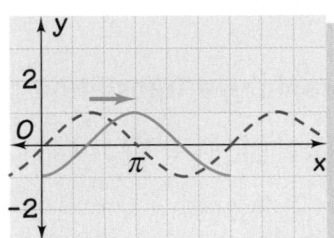

Translate the graph of $y = \sin x$ $\frac{\pi}{2}$ units to the right.

✓ **Quick Check** **2** Use the graph of $y = \sin x$ from Example 2. Sketch each translation of the graph in the interval $0 \le x \le 2\pi$. Which translation is a phase shift?
a. $y = \sin x - 2$ **b.** $y = \sin (x - 2)$

You can translate both vertically and horizontally to produce combined translations.

3 EXAMPLE Graphing a Combined Translation

Use the graph of the parent function $y = \sin x$ in Example 2. Sketch the translation $y = \sin (x + \pi) - 2$ in the interval $0 \le x \le 2\pi$.

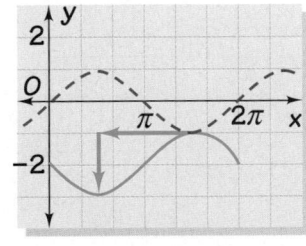

Translate the parent function π units to the left and 2 units down.

✓ **Quick Check** **3** The graph at the right shows $y = \cos x$.
Use it to graph each combined translation.
a. $y = \cos (x - 2) + 5$
b. $y = \cos (x + 1) + 3$

The translations graphed in Examples 2 and 3 belong to the families of the sine and cosine functions.

Key Concepts

Summary	Families of Sine and Cosine Functions

Parent Function
$y = \sin x$
$y = \cos x$

Transformed Function
$y = a \sin b(x - h) + k$
$y = a \cos b(x - h) + k$

- $|a|$ = amplitude (vertical stretch or shrink)
- $\frac{2\pi}{b}$ = period (when x is in radians and $b > 0$)
- h = phase shift, or horizontal shift
- k = vertical shift

You can use a simpler member of the sine or cosine families to help you graph a more complicated member.

4 EXAMPLE Graphing a Translation of $y = \sin 2x$

Sketch the graph of $y = \sin 2\left(x - \frac{\pi}{3}\right) - \frac{3}{2}$ in the interval from 0 to 2π.

Since $a = 1$ and $b = 2$, the graph is a translation of $y = \sin 2x$.

Step 1 Sketch one cycle of $y = \sin 2x$. Use five points in the pattern $zero-max-zero-min-zero$.

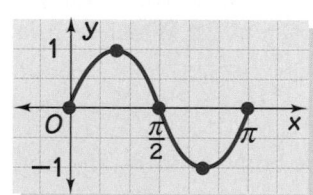

Step 2 Since $h = \frac{\pi}{3}$ and $k = -\frac{3}{2}$, translate the graph $\frac{\pi}{3}$ units to the right and $\frac{3}{2}$ units down. Extend the periodic pattern from 0 to 2π. Sketch the graph.

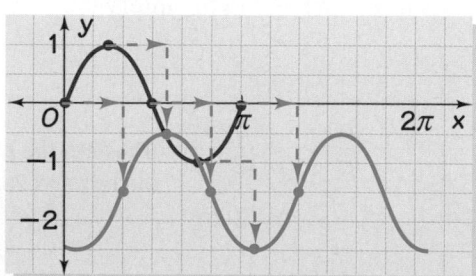

• The blue curve above is the graph of $y = \sin 2\left(x - \frac{\pi}{3}\right) - \frac{3}{2}$.

✓ Quick Check ④ Sketch each graph in the interval from 0 to 2π.
    a. $y = -3 \sin 2\left(x - \frac{\pi}{3}\right) - \frac{3}{2}$
    b. $y = 2 \cos \frac{\pi}{2}(x + 1) - 3$

You can write an equation to describe a translation.

5 EXAMPLE Writing a Translation

Write an equation for each translation.

a. $y = \sin x$, π units down

π units down means $k = -\pi$.

An equation is $y = \sin x - \pi$.

b. $y = -\cos x$, 2 units to the left

2 units to the left means $h = -2$.

An equation is $y = -\cos(x - (-2))$.

✓ Quick Check **5** Write an equation for each translation.

a. $y = \cos x$, $\frac{\pi}{2}$ units up

b. $y = 2 \sin x$, $\frac{\pi}{4}$ units to the right

6 EXAMPLE Real-World 🌐 Connection

Temperature Cycles The table at the left gives the typical high temperature in New Orleans, Louisiana, on several days of the year (January 1 = 1, February 1 = 32, and so on). Plot the data in the table. Write a cosine model for the data.

Day of Year	Temperature (°F)
16	62
47	65
75	71
106	79
136	85
167	90
197	91
228	90
259	87
289	79
320	70
350	64

Plot the data.

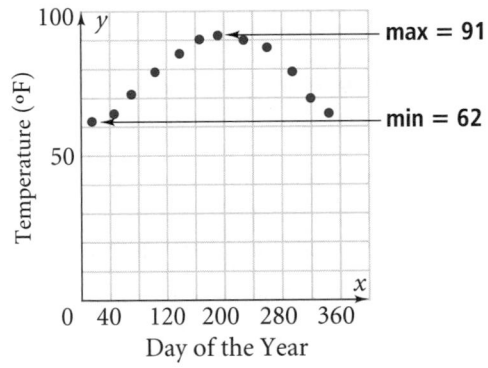

Use the form $y = a \cos b(x - h) + k$. Find values $a, b, h,$ and k.

amplitude $= \frac{1}{2}(\text{max} - \text{min})$

$= \frac{1}{2}(91 - 62)$

$= 14.5$

period $= \frac{2\pi}{b}$

$365 = \frac{2\pi}{b}$ **One complete cycle takes 365 days.**

$b = \frac{2\pi}{365}$

So (choosing $a > 0$), $a = 14.5$.

To find the values h and k, compare $y = 14.5 \cos \frac{2\pi}{365} x$ with the plot of the data.

phase shift: $h = 197 - 0$

$= 197$

vertical shift: $k = 91 - 14.5$

$= 76.5$

A model for the data is

$y = 14.5 \cos \frac{2\pi}{365}(x - 197) + 76.5$.

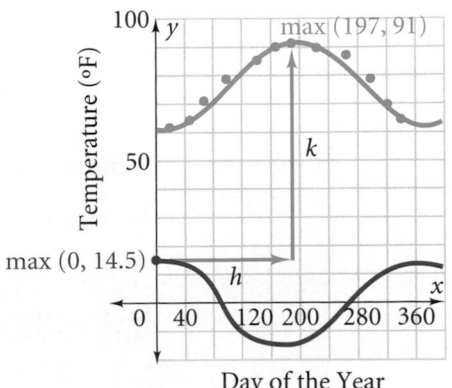

✓ **Quick Check** ⑥ **a. Estimation** Use the model from Example 6. Estimate the high temperature in New Orleans on September 1 (day 244).

b. Graphing Calculator Graph the model on your calculator. Use it to estimate the first day of the year that the high temperature is likely to reach 75°F.

EXERCISES

For more exercises, see *Extra Skill and Word Problem Practice.*

Practice and Problem Solving

 Practice by Example

Example 1
(page 756)

GO for Help

What is the value of *h* in each translation? Describe each phase shift (use a phrase like *3 units to the left*).

1. $g(x) = f(x + 1)$ **2.** $g(t) = f(t + 2)$

3. $h(z) = g(z - 1.6)$ **4.** $h(x) = f(x - 3)$

5. $y = \sin(x + \pi)$ **6.** $y = \cos\left(x - \frac{5\pi}{7}\right)$

Example 2
(page 757)

Use the function *f(x)* at the right. Graph each translation.

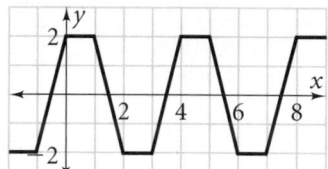

7. $f(x) + 1$ **8.** $f(x) - 3$

9. $f(x + 2)$ **10.** $f(x - 1)$

Graph each translation of $y = \cos x$ in the interval from 0 to 2π.

11. $y = \cos(x + 3)$ **12.** $y = \cos x + 3$ **13.** $y = \cos x - 4$

14. $y = \cos(x - 4)$ **15.** $y = \cos x + \pi$ **16.** $y = \cos(x - \pi)$

Example 3
(page 757)

Describe any phase shift and vertical shift in the graph.

17. $y = 3 \sin x + 1$ **18.** $y = 4 \cos(x + 1) - 2$

19. $y = \sin\left(x + \frac{\pi}{2}\right) + 2$ **20.** $y = \cos(x - 3) + 2$

Graph each function in the interval from 0 to 2π.

21. $y = 2 \sin\left(x + \frac{\pi}{4}\right) - 1$ **22.** $y = \sin\left(x + \frac{\pi}{3}\right) + 1$

23. $y = \cos(x - \pi) - 3$ **24.** $y = 2 \sin\left(x - \frac{\pi}{6}\right) + 2$

Example 4
(page 758)

Graph each function in the interval from 0 to 2π.

25. $y = 3 \sin \frac{1}{2} x$ **26.** $y = \cos 2\left(x + \frac{\pi}{2}\right) - 2$

27. $y = \frac{1}{2} \sin 2x - 1$ **28.** $y = \sin 3\left(x + \frac{\pi}{3}\right)$

29. $y = \sin 2(x + 3) - 2$ **30.** $y = 3 \sin \frac{\pi}{2}(x - 2)$

Example 5
(page 759)

Write an equation for each translation.

31. $y = \sin x, \pi$ units to the left   **32.** $y = \cos x, \frac{\pi}{2}$ units down

33. $y = \sin x, 3$ units up   **34.** $y = \cos x, 1.5$ units to the right

35. $y = \cos x, \frac{3}{2\pi}$ units to the left   **36.** $y = \sin x, 3\pi$ units down

Example 6
(page 759)

37. Temperature The table below shows water temperatures at a buoy in the Gulf of Mexico on several days of the year.

Water Temperatures in the Gulf of Mexico

Day of the Year	16	47	75	106	136	167	197	228	259	289	320	350
Temperature (°F)	71	69	70	73	77	82	85	86	84	82	78	74

SOURCE: *The USA Today Weather Almanac*

a. Plot the data.   **b.** Write a cosine model for the data.

Ⓑ Apply Your Skills

Write an equation for each translation.

38. $y = \sin x$, 2 units to the right and 4 units down

39. $y = \cos x$, 3 units to the left and π units up

40. $y = \sin x, \frac{\pi}{2}$ units to the right and 3.5 units up

Write a cosine function for each graph. Then write a sine function for each graph.

41.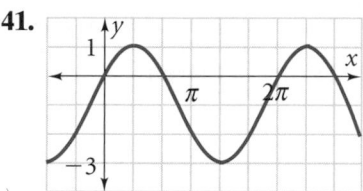

42.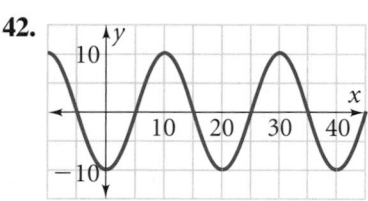

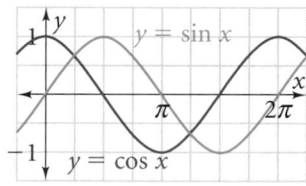

43. The graphs of $y = \sin x$ and $y = \cos x$ are shown at the left.
   a. What phase shift will translate the cosine graph onto the sine graph? Write your answer as an equation in the form $\sin x = \cos (x - h)$.
   b. What phase shift will translate the sine graph onto the cosine graph? Write your answer as an equation in the form $\cos x = \sin (x - h)$.

44. a. Critical Thinking Use a sine function to model the normal daily high temperature in New Orleans. Use the data given in Example 6 on page 759.
   b. Writing How do the sine and cosine models differ?
   c. Estimation Use your sine model to estimate the high temperature in New Orleans on December 1 (day 334).
   d. Graph your model. Use it to estimate the first day of the year that the high temperature is likely to reach 70°F.

45. a. Open-Ended Draw a periodic function. Find its amplitude and period. Then sketch a translation of your function 3 units down and 4 units to the left.
   b. Critical Thinking Suppose your original function is $f(x)$. Describe your translation using the form $g(x) = f(x - h) + k$.

GO ●nline
Homework Video Tutor
Visit: PHSchool.com
Web Code: age-1307

46. a. Write $y = 3 \sin (2x - 4) + 1$ in the form $y = a \sin b(x - h) + k$. (*Hint:* Factor where possible.)
   b. Find the amplitude and period. Describe any translations.

Ⓒ Challenge

Use a graphing calculator to graph each function in the interval from 0 to 2π. Then sketch each graph.

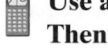

Graphing Calculator Hint
Change window values between exercises to see each graph clearly.

47. $y = \sin x + x$ **48.** $y = \sin x + 2x$

49. $y = \sin x - 0.5x$ **50.** $y = \cos x - x$

51. $y = \cos x - 2x$ **52.** $y = \cos x + x$

53. $y = \sin (x + \cos x)$ **54.** $y = \sin (x + 2 \cos x)$

Multiple Choice

55. Which function is a phase shift of $y = \sin \theta$ by 5 units to the left?

    A. $y = 5 \sin \theta$ **B.** $y = \sin \theta + 5$ **C.** $y = \sin(\theta + 5)$ **D.** $y = \sin 5\theta$

56. Which function is a translation of $y = \cos \theta$ by 5 units down?

    F. $y = -5 \cos \theta$ **G.** $y = \cos \theta - 5$

    H. $y = \cos(\theta - 5)$ **J.** $y = \cos(-5\theta)$

57. Which function is a translation of $y = \sin \theta$ that is $\frac{\pi}{3}$ units up and $\frac{\pi}{2}$ units to the left?

    A. $y = \sin\left(\theta + \frac{\pi}{3}\right) + \frac{\pi}{2}$ **B.** $y = \sin\left(\theta + \frac{\pi}{2}\right) + \frac{\pi}{3}$

    C. $y = \sin\left(\theta - \frac{\pi}{2}\right) + \frac{\pi}{3}$ **D.** $y = \sin\left(\theta - \frac{\pi}{3}\right) - \frac{\pi}{2}$

Short Response

58. Find values of a and b such that the function $y = \sin \theta$ can be expressed as $y = a \cos(\theta + b)$.

59. Write a function that is a transformation of $y = \sin \theta$ so that its amplitude is 4 and its minimum value is 1. Show your work.

Extended Response

60. Find all the values of θ between $-\pi$ and 2π for which $\sin \theta = 3 \sin \theta$. Show your work.

Mixed Review

Lesson 13-6

Identify the period of each function. Then tell where two asymptotes occur for each function.

61. $y = \tan 6\theta$ **62.** $y = \tan \frac{\theta}{4}$ **63.** $y = \tan 1.5\theta$ **64.** $y = \tan \frac{\theta}{6}$

Lesson 12-6

For the given probability of success p on each trial, find the probability of x successes in n trials.

65. $x = 4, n = 5, p = 0.2$ **66.** $x = 3, n = 5, p = 0.6$

67. $x = 4, n = 8, p = 0.7$ **68.** $x = 7, n = 8, p = 0.7$

Lesson 11-5

Evaluate the finite series for the specified number of terms.

69. $2 + 4 + 8 + \ldots; n = 5$ **70.** $3 + 12 + 48 + \ldots; n = 7$

71. $-1 - 6 - 36 + \ldots; n = 8$ **72.** $120 - 30 + 7.5 - \ldots; n = 5$

✓ Checkpoint Quiz 2   **Lessons 13-4 through 13-7**

Graph each function in the interval from -2π to 2π.

1. $y = \sin 4x$ **2.** $y = 3 \cos x$ **3.** $y = -2 \sin \pi x$

4. $y = 2 \cos \frac{\pi}{2}x$ **5.** $y = \tan 2x$ **6.** $y = -\tan x$

7. $y = \cos(x - 2)$ **8.** $y = \sin x + 4$ **9.** $y = 3 \tan \frac{\pi}{4}x$

10. Sketch the graph of $y = \sin 3x$ after a translation of 2 units to the right and π units down.

Reciprocal Trigonometric Functions

What You'll Learn

- To evaluate reciprocal trigonometric functions
- To graph reciprocal trigonometric functions

. . . And Why

To find indirect measurements, as in Example 6

✓ Check Skills You'll Need

GO for Help Lesson 7-8 and page 879

Find the reciprocal of each fraction.

1. $\frac{9}{13}$ **2.** $\frac{-5}{8}$ **3.** $\frac{1}{2\pi}$ **4.** $\frac{4m}{15}$ **5.** $\frac{14}{-t}$

Graph each pair of relations on the same coordinate plane.

6. $y = x,\ y = -x$ **7.** $y = x^2,\ y = \pm\sqrt{x}$

8. $y = |2x|,\ y = -|2x|$ **9.** $y = -6x^2,\ y = \pm\frac{\sqrt{6x}}{6}$

◀)) New Vocabulary
- cosecant
- secant
- cotangent

---

1   Evaluating Reciprocal Trigonometric Functions

In earlier lessons in this chapter, you studied three trigonometric functions—sine, cosine, and tangent. Three other functions—cosecant, secant, and cotangent—are related to reciprocals of the three you have used.

 Key Concepts

Definition	**Cosecant, Secant, and Cotangent Functions**

The cosecant (csc), secant (sec), and cotangent (cot) functions are defined using reciprocals. Their domains do not include the real numbers θ that make a denominator zero.

$$\csc\theta = \frac{1}{\sin\theta} \qquad \sec\theta = \frac{1}{\cos\theta} \qquad \cot\theta = \frac{1}{\tan\theta}$$

You can evaluate reciprocal trigonometric functions by using the definitions.

Graphing Calculator Hint

Caution! The keys for $\sin^{-1}$, $\cos^{-1}$, and $\tan^{-1}$ do not give reciprocals. They represent inverse trigonometric functions, which you will study in Chapter 14.

1 EXAMPLE   Using Reciprocals

a. Find $\csc 60°$.

Use a calculator in degree mode.

> 1/sin (60)
>   1.154700538

Use the definition.
$$\csc 60° = \frac{1}{\sin 60°}$$

b. Suppose $\cos\theta = \frac{5}{13}$. Find $\sec\theta$.

$\sec\theta = \frac{1}{\cos\theta}$ **Use the definition.**

$= \frac{1}{\frac{5}{13}}$ **Substitute.**

$= \frac{13}{5}$ **Simplify.**

✓ **Quick Check**   **1 a.** Suppose $\sin\theta = \frac{15}{8}$. Find $\csc\theta$.   **b.** Find $\cot 55°$ to the nearest hundredth.

You can use what you know about the unit circle to find exact values for reciprocal trigonometric functions.

2 **EXAMPLE** **Finding Exact Values**

Multiple Choice Which expression represents the exact value of csc 60°?

(A) $\dfrac{\sqrt{3}}{3}$ (B) $\dfrac{\sqrt{3}}{2}$ (C) $\dfrac{2\sqrt{3}}{3}$ (D) $\sqrt{3}$

Use the unit circle to find the exact value of sin 60°. Then write the reciprocal.

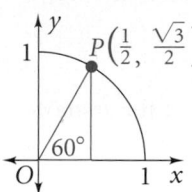

The y-coordinate of point P is $\dfrac{\sqrt{3}}{2}$.

$\csc 60° = \dfrac{1}{\sin 60°}$ **Use the definition.**

$= \dfrac{1}{\frac{\sqrt{3}}{2}}$ **Substitute.**

$= \dfrac{2}{\sqrt{3}}$ **Simplify.**

$= \dfrac{2\sqrt{3}}{3}$ **Rationalize the denominator.**

● The correct choice is C.

Quick Check ❷ Find each exact value.

a. sec 60°   **b.** cot 45°   **c.** csc 30°

You can also evaluate the reciprocal functions in radians.

3 **EXAMPLE** **Using Radians**

Evaluate each expression. Use your calculator's radian mode. Round to the nearest thousandth.

a. $\cot \dfrac{\pi}{3}$ **b.** sec (−1)

$\cot \dfrac{\pi}{3} = \dfrac{1}{\tan \frac{\pi}{3}}$ $\sec(-1) = \dfrac{1}{\cos(-1)}$

```
1/tan (π/3)
            .5773502692
```

```
1/cos (–1)
            1.850815718
```

● $\cot \dfrac{\pi}{3} \approx 0.577$ $\sec(-1) \approx 1.851$

Quick Check ❸ Use a calculator to evaluate each expression. Each angle is given in radians. Round to the nearest thousandth.

a. csc (−1.5)   **b.** sec 2   **c.** cot π

The graphs of reciprocal trigonometric functions have asymptotes where their denominators are zero.

4 **EXAMPLE** **Sketching a Graph**

Sketch the graphs of $y = \sin x$ and $y = \csc x$ in the interval from 0 to 2π.

Step 1 Make a table of values.

x	0	$\frac{\pi}{6}$	$\frac{\pi}{3}$	$\frac{\pi}{2}$	$\frac{2\pi}{3}$	$\frac{5\pi}{6}$	π	$\frac{7\pi}{6}$	$\frac{4\pi}{3}$	$\frac{3\pi}{2}$	$\frac{5\pi}{3}$	$\frac{11\pi}{6}$	2π
$\sin x$	0	0.5	0.9	1	0.9	0.5	0	-0.5	-0.9	-1	-0.9	-0.5	0
$\csc x$	■	2	1.2	1	1.2	2	■	-2	-1.2	-1	-1.2	-2	■

Step 2 Plot the points and sketch the graphs.

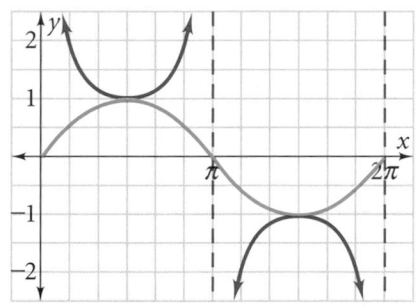

$y = \csc x$ will have a vertical asymptote wherever its denominator ($\sin x$) is 0.

✓ Quick Check **4** Graph $y = \tan x$ and $y = \cot x$ in the interval from 0 to 2π.

You can use a graphing calculator to graph trigonometric functions quickly.

5 **EXAMPLE** **Using Technology to Graph Reciprocals**

Graph $y = \sec x$. Find the value of $\sec 20°$.

Step 1 Use degree mode.
Graph $y = \frac{1}{\cos x}$.

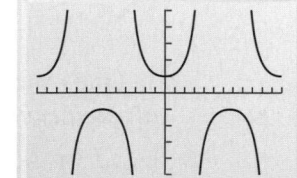

Xmin=−360
Xmax=360
Xscl=30
Ymin=−5
Ymax=5
Yscl=1

Step 2 Use the TABLE feature.

X	Y1	
20	1.0642	
21	1.0711	
22	1.0785	
23	1.0864	
24	1.0946	
25	1.1034	
26	1.1126	

X=20

● $\sec 20° \approx 1.0642$

✓ Quick Check **5** Use the graph of the reciprocal trigonometric function to find $\csc 45°$.

You can use a reciprocal trigonometric function to solve a real-world problem.

6 EXAMPLE Real-World 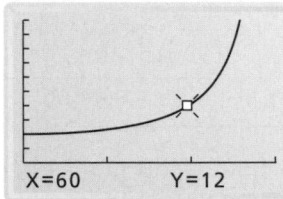 Connection

Indirect Measurement A handler of a parade balloon holds a line of length y. The length is modeled by the function $y = d \sec \theta$, where d is the distance from the handler of the balloon to the point on the ground just below the balloon, and θ is the angle formed by the line and the ground. Graph the function for $d = 6$. Find the length of line needed to form an angle of 60°.

$y = 6 \sec \theta = 6\left(\dfrac{1}{\cos \theta}\right) = \dfrac{6}{\cos \theta}$ **Use the definition of secant. Simplify.**

Graph the function. Use the **value** feature.

Xmin=0
Xmax=90
Xscl=30
Ymin=0
Ymax=30
Yscl=3

X=60   Y=12

● To form an angle of 60°, the line must be 12 ft long.

✓ **Quick Check** ❻ How long must the line be to form an angle of 30°? Of 45°? Of 85°?

EXERCISES

For more exercises, see *Extra Skill and Word Problem Practice.*

Practice and Problem Solving

A Practice by Example

Example 1
(page 763)

GO for Help

Evaluate each expression. Give your answer as a decimal rounded to the nearest hundredth.

1. csc 100°   **2.** csc 80°   **3.** cot $(-55°)$ **4.** sec 200°

Evaluate each expression. Write your answer in exact form.

5. Suppose $\tan \theta = \frac{20}{15}$. Find $\cot \theta$.   **6.** Suppose $\sin \theta = \frac{13}{18}$. Find $\csc \theta$.

7. Suppose $\cos \theta = -\frac{21}{35}$. Find $\sec \theta$.   **8.** Suppose $\tan \theta = -\frac{4}{3}$. Find $\cot \theta$.

Example 2
(page 764)

Find the exact value of each expression. If the expression is undefined, write *undefined*.

9. sec 45°   **10.** cot 60°   **11.** cot 90°   **12.** sec 180°

13. csc 0°   **14.** csc 60°   **15.** cot 0°   **16.** cot 30°

17. sec 90°   **18.** csc 30°   **19.** sec 60°   **20.** csc 45°

Example 3
(page 764)

Evaluate each expression to the nearest hundredth. Each angle is given in radians.

21. cot 3   **22.** sec π **23.** csc $\frac{\pi}{2}$ **24.** sec $(-\pi)$

25. sec 2.5   **26.** csc (-3.2) **27.** cot $\frac{\pi}{6}$ **28.** csc (-4.5)

Example 4
(page 765)

Graph each function in the interval from 0 to 2π.

29. $y = \sec 2\theta$ **30.** $y = \cot \theta$ **31.** $y = \csc 2\theta - 1$ **32.** $y = \csc 2\theta$

Example 5
(page 765)

Use the graph of the appropriate reciprocal trigonometric function to find each value. Round to four decimal places.

33. sec 30°   **34.** sec 80°   **35.** sec 110°   **36.** csc 30°

37. csc 70°   **38.** csc 130°   **39.** cot 30°   **40.** cot 60°

Example 6
(page 766)

41. Indirect Measurement A communications tower has wires anchoring it to the ground. Each wire is attached to the tower at a height 20 ft above the ground. The length y of the wire is modeled with the function $y = 20 \csc \theta$, where θ is the measure of the angle formed by the wire and the ground.
  a. Graph the function.
  b. Find the length of wire needed to form an angle of 45°.
  c. Find the length of wire needed to form an angle of 60°.
  d. Find the length of wire needed to form an angle of 75°.

Ⓑ Apply Your Skills

Evaluate each expression. Write your answer in exact form. If appropriate, also state it as a decimal rounded to the nearest hundredth. If the expression is undefined, write *undefined*.

42. $\cot(-45°)$ **43.** $\sec(-30°)$

44. $\csc(-90°)$ **45.** $\sec(-180°)$

Graph each function in the interval from 0 to 2π.

46. $y = \csc\theta - \frac{\pi}{2}$ **47.** $y = \sec\frac{1}{4}\theta$

48. $y = -\sec\pi\theta$ **49.** $y = \cot\frac{\theta}{3}$

Match each function with its graph.

50. $y = \frac{1}{\sin x}$ **51.** $y = \frac{1}{\cos x}$

52. $y = -\frac{1}{\sin x}$ **53.** $y = \frac{1}{\tan x}$

A.
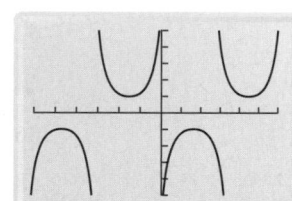

B.
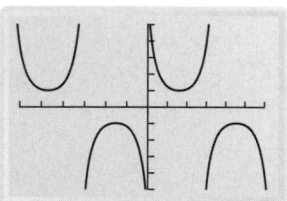

C.
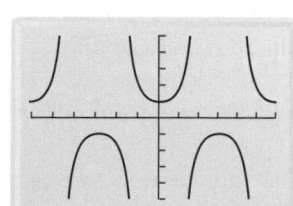

D.
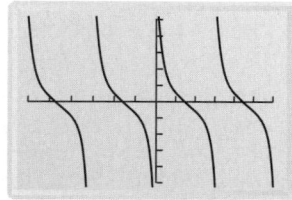

54. a. What are the domain, range, and period of $y = \csc x$?
  b. What is the relative minimum in the interval $0 \le x \le \pi$?
  c. What is the relative maximum in the interval $\pi \le x \le 2\pi$?

55. Reasoning Use the relationship $\csc x = \frac{1}{\sin x}$ to explain why each statement is true.
  a. When the graph of $y = \sin x$ is positive, so is the graph of $y = \csc x$.
  b. When the graph of $y = \sin x$ is near a y-value of -1, so is the graph of $y = \csc x$.

56. csc 180°   **57.** sec 90°   **58.** cot 0°

59. Indirect Measurement The function $y = 60 \sec \theta$ models the length y of a fire ladder as a function of the measure of the angle θ formed by the ladder and the horizontal when the hinge of the ladder is 60 ft from the building.
  a. Graph the function.
  b. In the photo, $\theta = 20°$. How far is the ladder extended?
  c. How far is the ladder extended when it forms an angle of 30°?
  d. Suppose the ladder is extended to its full length of 80 ft. What angle does it form with the horizontal? How far up a building can the ladder reach when fully extended? (*Hint:* Use the information in the photo.)

60. a. Graph $y = \tan x$ and $y = \cot x$ on the same axes.
   b. State the domain, the range, and the asymptotes of each function.
  c. Writing Compare the two graphs. How are they alike? How are they different?
  d. Geometry The graph of the cotangent function can be reflected about a line to graph the tangent function. Name at least two lines that have this property.

Graph each function in the interval from 0 to 2π. Describe any phase shift and vertical shift in the graph.

61. $y = \sec 2\theta + 3$ **62.** $y = \sec 2\left(\theta + \frac{\pi}{2}\right)$

63. $y = \csc 2\theta - 1$ **64.** $y = \csc 2\left(\theta - \frac{\pi}{2}\right)$

65. $y = -2 \sec (x - 4)$ **66.** $f(x) = 3 \csc (x + 2) - 1$

67. $y = \cot 2(x + \pi) + 3$ **68.** $g(x) = 2 \sec \left(3\left(x - \frac{\pi}{6}\right)\right) - 2$

69. a. Graph $y = -\cos x$ and $y = -\sec x$ on the same axes.
  b. State the domain, the range, and the period of each function.
  c. For which values of x does $-\cos x = -\sec x$? Justify your answer.
  d. Writing Compare the two graphs. How are they alike? How are they different?
  e. Reasoning Is the value of $-\sec x$ positive when $-\cos x$ is positive and negative when $-\cos x$ is negative? Justify your answer.

70. a. Critical Thinking Which expression gives the correct value of csc 60°?
  I. $\sin ((60^{-1})°)$ **II.** $(\sin 60°)^{-1}$ **III.** $(\cos 60°)^{-1}$
  b. Which expression in part (a) represents $\sin \left(\frac{1}{60}\right)°$?

 **Challenge**

71. Reasoning Each branch of $y = \sec x$ and $y = \csc x$ is a curve. Explain why these curves cannot be parabolas. (*Hint:* Do parabolas have asymptotes?)

72. Reasoning Consider the relationship between the graphs of $y = \cos x$ and $y = \cos 3x$. Use the relationship to explain the distance between successive branches of the graphs of $y = \sec x$ and $y = \sec 3x$.

73. a. Graph $y = \cot x$, $y = \cot 2x$, $y = \cot(-2x)$, and $y = \cot \frac{1}{2}x$ on the same axes.

   b. Make a Conjecture Describe how the graph of $y = \cot bx$ changes as the value of b changes.

74. a. Graph $y = \sec x$, $y = 2 \sec x$, $y = -3 \sec x$, and $y = \frac{1}{2} \sec x$ on the same axes.

   b. Make a Conjecture Describe how the graph of $y = b \sec x$ changes as the value of b changes.

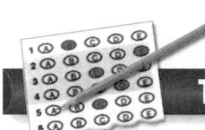

Test Prep

Gridded Response

For Exercises 75–78, suppose $\cos \theta = \frac{3}{5}$ and $\sin \theta > 0$. Enter each answer as a fraction.

75. What is $\tan \theta$? **76.** What is $\sec \theta$?

77. What is $\cot \theta$? **78.** What is $\csc \theta$?

For Exercises 79–82, suppose $\tan \theta = \frac{4}{3}$, $\sin \theta > 0$, and $-\frac{\pi}{2} \leq \theta < \frac{\pi}{2}$. Enter each answer as a decimal.

79. What is $\cot \theta + \cos \theta$? **80.** What is $(\sin \theta)(\cot \theta)$?

81. What is $\sec \theta \div \tan \theta$?

82. What is $\sin \theta + \cos \theta + \cot \theta + \csc \theta$?

Mixed Review

Lesson 13-7

Find the amplitude and period of each function. Describe any phase shift and vertical shift in the graph.

83. $y = 2 \sin x - 5$ **84.** $y = -\cos(x + 4) - 7$

85. $y = -3 \sin \left(x + \frac{\pi}{6}\right) + 4$ **86.** $y = 5 \cos \pi(x - 1.5) - 8$

Lesson 12-7

Sketch a normal curve for each distribution. Label the x-axis values at one, two, and three standard deviations from the mean.

87. mean = 25, standard deviation = 5

88. mean = 25, standard deviation = 10

Lesson 11-6

Write and evaluate a sum to approximate the area under each curve for the domain $-1 \leq x \leq 2$.
a. Use inscribed rectangles 1 unit wide.
b. Use circumscribed rectangles 1 unit wide.

89. $f(x) = 3x^2$ **90.** $y = x^2 + 4$

91. $g(x) = -x^2 + 4$ **92.** $g(x) = -x^2 + 8$

Using Mental Math

You can solve many problems quickly when you know the sine and cosine of special angles and the pattern of the y-values of the periodic function.

θ	0° or 0 radians	30° or $\frac{\pi}{6}$ radians	45° or $\frac{\pi}{4}$ radians	60° or $\frac{\pi}{3}$ radians	90° or $\frac{\pi}{2}$ radians
$\sin\theta$	0	$\frac{1}{2}$	$\frac{\sqrt{2}}{2}$	$\frac{\sqrt{3}}{2}$	1
$\cos\theta$	1	$\frac{\sqrt{3}}{2}$	$\frac{\sqrt{2}}{2}$	$\frac{1}{2}$	0

1 EXAMPLE

Find each exact value.

a. $\sin 150°$

The terminal side of the angle lies in Quadrant II and forms an angle of 30° with the x-axis.

$\sin 150° = \sin 30° = \frac{1}{2}$

b. $\cos\left(-\frac{\pi}{4}\right)$

The terminal side of the angle lies in Quadrant IV and forms an angle of $\frac{\pi}{4}$ radians with the x-axis.

$\cos\left(-\frac{\pi}{4}\right) = \cos\frac{\pi}{4} = \frac{\sqrt{2}}{2}$

2 EXAMPLE

Solve each equation in the interval from 0° to 360°. Give exact answers.

a. $\sin\theta = -\frac{\sqrt{2}}{2}$

The sine is negative, so the terminal side of the angle must lie in Quadrant III or IV. It forms an angle of 45° with the x-axis.

$\theta = 180° + 45° = 225°$

$\theta = 360° - 45° = 315°$

The solutions are 225° and 315°.

b. $\cos\left(\frac{\theta}{2}\right) = 0$

The cosine is 0, so the terminal side of the angle must lie on the y-axis. The angle must be 90° or 270°.

If $\frac{\theta}{2} = 90°$, then $\theta = 180°$.

If $\frac{\theta}{2} = 270°$, then $\theta = 540°$.

Since 540° > 360°, the only solution is 180°.

EXERCISES

Each angle extends outside Quadrant I. Find the exact value of each expression.

1. $\cos 150°$ **2.** $\sin -120°$ **3.** $\sin\left(\frac{5\pi}{6}\right)$ **4.** $\cos\left(\frac{2\pi}{3}\right)$

5. $\sin\left(-\frac{4\pi}{3}\right)$ **6.** $\cos\left(-\frac{5\pi}{4}\right)$ **7.** $\tan\left(\frac{2\pi}{3}\right)$ **8.** $\tan(-150°)$

Solve each equation in the interval from 0° to 360°. Give exact answers.

9. $\cos\theta = \frac{1}{2}$ **10.** $\sin\theta = \frac{\sqrt{2}}{2}$ **11.** $\sin\theta = 1$ **12.** $\cos\left(\frac{\theta}{4}\right) = \frac{1}{2}$

Chapter Review

Vocabulary Review

amplitude (p. 712)
central angle (p. 726)
cosecant (p. 763)
cosine function (p. 743)
cosine of θ (p. 720)
cotangent (p. 763)
coterminal angles (p. 719)
cycle (p. 711)

initial side (p. 718)
intercepted arc (p. 726)
period (p. 711)
periodic function (p. 711)
phase shift (p. 756)
radian (p. 726)
secant (p. 763)
sine curve (p. 735)

sine function (p. 734)
sine of θ (p. 720)
standard position (p. 718)
tangent function (p. 749)
tangent of θ (p. 749)
terminal side (p. 718)
unit circle (p. 720)

Go Online
PHSchool.com
For: Vocabulary quiz
Web Code: agj-1351

Choose the correct term to complete each sentence.

1. The   ?   of a function is the length of one cycle.

2. Centered at the origin of the coordinate plane, the   ?   has a radius of 1 unit.

3. The asymptote of the   ?   occurs at $\theta = \frac{\pi}{2}$ and repeats every π units.

4. A horizontal translation of a periodic function is a(n)   ?   .

5. The   ?   is the reciprocal of the cosine function.

Skills and Concepts

13-1 Objectives

▼ To identify cycles and periods of periodic functions (p. 710)

▼ To find the amplitude of periodic functions (p. 712)

A **periodic function** repeats a pattern of *y*-values at regular intervals. One complete pattern is called a **cycle.** A cycle may begin at any point on the graph. The **period** of a function is the length of one cycle. The **amplitude** of a periodic function is half the difference between its maximum and minimum values.

6. Determine whether the function at the right *is* or *is not* periodic. If it is, identify one cycle in two different ways. Then determine the period and amplitude.

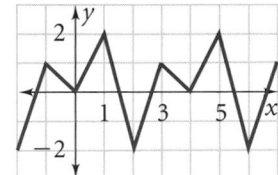

7. Sketch the graph of a wave with a period of 0.5 and an amplitude of 3.

13-2 Objectives

▼ To work with angles in standard position (p. 718)

▼ To find coordinates of points on the unit circle (p. 720)

An angle is in **standard position** if the vertex is at the origin and one ray, the **initial side**, is on the positive *x*-axis. The other ray is the **terminal side** of the angle. Two angles in standard position are **coterminal** if they have the same terminal side.

The **unit circle** has a radius of 1 unit and its center at the origin. The **cosine of θ** (cos θ) is the *x*-coordinate of the point where the terminal side of the angle intersects the unit circle. The **sine of θ** (sin θ) is the *y*-coordinate.

8. Find the measure of the angle in standard position at the right.

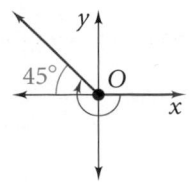

9. Sketch a −30° angle in standard position.

10. Find the measure of an angle between 0° and 360° coterminal with a −120° angle.

11. Find the exact coordinates of the point at which the terminal side of a 315° angle intersects the unit circle. Then find the decimal equivalents. Round your answers to the nearest hundredth.

13-3 Objectives

▼ To use radian measure for angles (p. 726)

▼ To find the length of an arc of a circle (p. 728)

A **central angle** of a circle is an angle whose vertex is at the center of a circle. An **intercepted arc** is the portion of the circle whose endpoints are on the sides of the angle and whose remaining points lie in the interior of the angle. A **radian** is the measure of a central angle that intercepts an arc equal in length to a radius of the circle.

To convert degrees to radians, multiply by $\frac{\pi \text{ radians}}{180°}$. To convert radians to degrees, multiply by $\frac{180°}{\pi \text{ radians}}$. When the measure of an angle θ is in radians and r is the radius, the length s of the intercepted arc is $s = r\theta$.

The measure θ of an angle in standard position is given.
a. Write each degree measure in radians and each radian measure in degrees rounded to the nearest degree.
b. Find the exact values of cos θ and sin θ for each angle measure.

12. 60°   **13.** −45°   **14.** 180°

15. 2π radians   **16.** $\frac{5\pi}{6}$ radians   **17.** $-\frac{3\pi}{4}$ radians

18. Use the circle to find the length of the indicated arc. Round your answer to the nearest tenth.

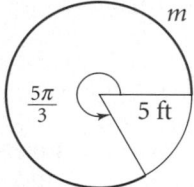

13-4 and 13-5 Objectives

▼ To identify properties of the sine function (p. 734)

▼ To graph sine curves (p. 737)

▼ To graph and write cosine functions (p. 743)

▼ To solve trigonometric equations (p. 744)

The **sine function** $y = \sin \theta$ matches the measure θ of an angle in standard position with the y-coordinate of a point on the unit circle. This point is where the terminal side of the angle intersects the unit circle. The graph of a sine function is called a **sine curve.**

The **cosine function** $y = \cos \theta$ matches the measure θ of an angle in standard position with the x-coordinate of a point on the unit circle. This point is where the terminal side of the angle intersects the unit circle.

For the sine function $y = a \sin b\theta$ and the cosine function $y = a \cos b\theta$, the amplitude equals $|a|$, there are b cycles from 0 to 2π, and the period is $\frac{2\pi}{b}$.

Sketch the graph of each function in the interval from 0 to 2π.

19. $y = 3 \sin \theta$ **20.** $y = 2 \cos \left(\frac{\pi}{2}\right)t$ **21.** $y = -\cos 2\theta$

22. For the graph at the right, how many cycles does the sine function have in the interval from 0 to 2π? Find the amplitude and period of the function. Then write an equation for the sine function.

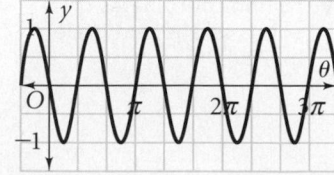

Write an equation of the function for each description or graph.

23. sine function, $a > 0$, amplitude 4, period 0.5π

24. cosine function, $a > 0$, amplitude 3, period π

25.

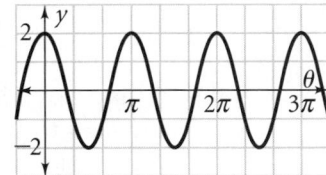

Solve each equation in the interval from 0 to 2π. Round to the nearest hundredth.

26. $\sin\theta = -0.7$ **27.** $\sin\left(\frac{\pi}{2}\right)\theta = 0.25$ **28.** $3\cos 4\theta = -2$

13-6 Objectives

▼ To graph the tangent function (p. 749)

The **tangent** of an angle θ in standard position is the y-coordinate of the point where the terminal side of the angle intersects the tangent line $x = 1$. A **tangent function** in the form $y = a\tan b\theta$ has a period of $\frac{\pi}{b}$.

Graph each function in the interval from 0 to 2π. Then evaluate the function at $t = \frac{\pi}{4}$ and $t = \frac{\pi}{2}$. If the tangent is undefined at that point, write _undefined_.

29. $y = \tan\left(\frac{1}{2}\right)t$ **30.** $y = \tan 3t$ **31.** $y = 2\tan t$

13-7 Objectives

▼ To graph translations of trigonometric functions (p. 756)

▼ To write equations of translations (p. 759)

Each horizontal translation of certain periodic functions is a **phase shift.** When $g(x) = f(x - h) + k$, the value of h is the amount of the horizontal shift and the value of k is the amount of the vertical shift.

Graph each function in the interval from 0 to 2π.

32. $y = \cos\left(x + \frac{\pi}{2}\right)$ **33.** $y = 2\sin x - 4$ **34.** $y = \sin(x - \pi) + 3$

Write an equation for each translation.

35. $y = \sin x, \frac{\pi}{4}$ units to the right   **36.** $y = \cos x, 2$ units down

---

13-8 Objectives

▼ To evaluate reciprocal trigonometric functions (p. 763)

▼ To graph reciprocal trigonometric functions (p. 765)

The **cosecant** (csc), **secant** (sec), and **cotangent** (cot) functions are defined using reciprocals. Their domains do not include the real numbers θ that make a denominator zero.

$$\csc\theta = \frac{1}{\sin\theta} \qquad\qquad \sec\theta = \frac{1}{\cos\theta} \qquad\qquad \cot\theta = \frac{1}{\tan\theta}$$

Evaluate each expression. Write your answer in exact form.

37. $\sec(-45°)$ **38.** $\cot 120°$ **39.** $\csc 150°$

Graph each function in the interval from 0 to 2π.

40. $y = 2\csc\theta$ **41.** $y = \sec\theta - 1$ **42.** $y = \cot\left(\frac{1}{4}\right)\theta$

Chapter 13

Chapter Test

Go Online
PHSchool.com
For: Chapter Test
Web Code: aga-1352

Determine whether each function *is* or *is not* periodic. If it is periodic, find the period and amplitude.

1.

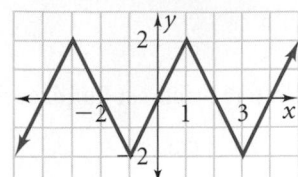

2.

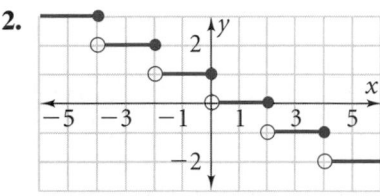

Find the measure of an angle between 0° and 360° coterminal with the given angle.

3. −32°   **4.** −229°   **5.** 375°

Write each measure in radians. Express the answer in terms of π and also as a decimal rounded to the nearest hundredth.

6. −225°   **7.** 120°   **8.** 600°

Write each measure in degrees. If necessary, round your answer to the nearest degree.

9. $\frac{5\pi}{6}$ **10.** −2.5π   **11.** 0.8

How many cycles does each sine function have in the interval from 0 to 2π? Find the amplitude and period of each function.

12.

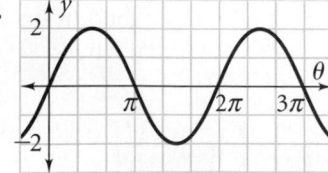

13.

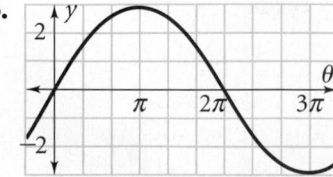

14. Open-Ended Sketch a function with period 7.

15. Writing Explain how to convert an angle measure in radians to an angle measure in degrees. Include an example.

16. Physics On each swing, a pendulum 18 inches long travels through an angle of $\frac{3\pi}{4}$ radians. How far does the tip of the pendulum travel in one swing? Round your answer to the nearest inch.

Find the amplitude and period of each function. Then sketch one cycle of the graph of each function.

17. $y = 4 \sin (2x)$ **18.** $y = 2 \sin (4x)$

Solve each equation in the interval from 0 to 2π. Give an exact answer and an answer rounded to the nearest hundredth.

19. $\cos t = \frac{1}{2}$ **20.** $2 \sin t = \sqrt{3}$

21. $3 \tan 2t = \sqrt{3}$ **22.** $\cos \frac{t\pi}{4} = 1$

Graph each function in the interval from 0 to 2π.

23. $y = 2 \cos x$ **24.** $y = -\cos \frac{\theta}{\pi}$

25. $y = 4 \sin x - 2$ **26.** $y = \cos (x + \pi)$

27. $y = \tan \frac{\theta}{3}$ **28.** $y = \tan \frac{\pi}{3}\theta$

Write an equation for each translation.

29. $y = \sin x$, 1 unit down

30. $y = \cos x$, 7.5 units to the right

31. $y = \sin x$, 3 units to the left, 1.5 units down

32. $y = \cos x$, $\frac{\pi}{2}$ units to the right, 8 units up

Evaluate each expression. Write your answer in exact form. If the expression is undefined, write *undefined*.

33. $\sin 30°$ **34.** $\cos 60°$

35. $\sin (-330°)$ **36.** $\csc (-330°)$

37. $\sec 270°$ **38.** $\tan 60°$

39. $\cos 45°$ **40.** $\cot (-60°)$

Graph each function in the interval from 0 to 2π.

41. $y = \cot \theta$ **42.** $y = \sec \theta + 1$

43. $y = \csc \frac{\theta}{2}$ **44.** $y = \csc (\theta + 1)$

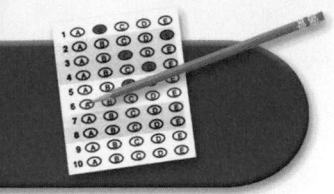
Standardized Test Prep

Reading Comprehension Read the passage below. Then answer the questions on the basis of what is *stated* or *implied* in the passage.

The Birthday Problem Suppose you are in a room of 25 people. How likely is it that at least two of the people celebrate their birthdays on the same day of the year? What about in a room of 100 people? Assume that no birthday occurs on February 29.

To answer such questions, first ask a related question: For any group of people, what is the probability that *no two* in the group have the same birthday? For a group of four people, using 365 as the number of days in a year, the probability is $\frac{365}{365} \cdot \frac{364}{365} \cdot \frac{363}{365} \cdot \frac{362}{365}$, or about 0.984. (For each person after the first, the number of days available for a "different birthday" decreases by 1.) Then it is easy to calculate the probability that at least two of the four have the same birthday: about $1 - 0.984$, or 0.016.

So you can calculate the probability that at least two of 25 people share a birthday by using the following expression.

$$1 - \frac{365}{365} \cdot \frac{364}{365} \cdot \frac{363}{365} \cdot \frac{362}{365} \cdot \ldots \cdot \frac{343}{365} \cdot \frac{342}{365} \cdot \frac{341}{365}$$

---

1. Which expression gives the probability that no two of three people have the same birthday?

- (A) $\frac{364}{365} \cdot \frac{363}{365} \cdot \frac{362}{365}$
- (B) $\frac{365}{365} \cdot \frac{364}{365} \cdot \frac{363}{365}$
- (C) $1 - \frac{364}{365} \cdot \frac{363}{365} \cdot \frac{362}{365}$
- (D) $1 - \frac{365}{365} \cdot \frac{364}{365} \cdot \frac{363}{365}$

2. Which expression gives the probability that at least two of three people have the same birthday?

- (F) $\frac{364}{365} \cdot \frac{363}{365} \cdot \frac{362}{365}$
- (G) $\frac{365}{365} \cdot \frac{364}{365} \cdot \frac{363}{365}$
- (H) $1 - \frac{364}{365} \cdot \frac{363}{365} \cdot \frac{362}{365}$
- (J) $1 - \frac{365}{365} \cdot \frac{364}{365} \cdot \frac{363}{365}$

3. Here is a different question: You meet 25 strangers, one at a time. With each meeting, what is the probability that a person has the same birthday as you?

- (A) $\frac{340}{365}$
- (B) $\frac{25}{365}$
- (C) $\frac{1}{25}$
- (D) $\frac{1}{365}$

4. In a group of 366, what is the probability that at least two people have the same birthday?

- (F) $\frac{1}{366}$
- (G) $1 - \frac{365}{366}$
- (H) 1
- (J) $\frac{366}{365}$

5. The reading passage contains the expression
$$1 - \frac{365}{365} \cdot \frac{364}{365} \cdot \frac{363}{365} \cdot \frac{362}{365} \cdot \ldots \cdot \frac{343}{365} \cdot \frac{342}{365} \cdot \frac{341}{365}.$$
What is another way to write that expression?

- (A) $1 - \frac{365 \cdot 364 \cdot 363 \ldots \cdot 341}{365!}$
- (B) $1 - \frac{365!}{341! \cdot 365^{25}}$
- (C) $1 - \frac{365!}{340! \cdot 365^{25}}$
- (D) $\frac{1 - 365!}{340! \cdot 365^{25}}$

6. In a group of five people, what is the probability that no two have the same birthday? What is the probability that at least two people in the group have the same birthday?

7. In a group of 15 people, what is the probability that no two have the same birthday? What is the probability that at least two people in the group have the same birthday?

8. Suppose you want a group for which the probability that at least two people have the same birthday is at least 50%. How many people do you need?

What You've Learned

- In Chapter 5, you learned to solve quadratic equations by finding square roots.

- In Chapter 7, you learned to find the inverse of a function.

- In Chapter 8, you learned about exponential and logarithmic functions, which are inverse functions. You learned to solve exponential and logarithmic equations by using inverse functions.

- In Chapter 13, you learned to use the sine, cosine, and tangent functions.

 **Check Your Readiness**

 for Help to the Lesson in green.

Solving Quadratic Equations (Lesson 5-5)

Solve each equation.

1. $4x^2 = 25$

2. $x^2 - 23 = 0$

3. $3x^2 = 80$

4. $8x^2 - 44 = 0$

5. $0.5x^2 = 15$

6. $6x^2 - 13 = 11$

Finding the Inverse of a Function (Lesson 7-7)

For each function f, find f^{-1} and the domain and range of f and f^{-1}. Determine whether f^{-1} is a function.

7. $f(x) = 5x + 2$

8. $f(x) = \sqrt{x + 3}$

9. $f(x) = \sqrt{3x - 4}$

10. $f(x) = \frac{5}{x}$

11. $f(x) = \frac{10}{x - 1}$

12. $f(x) = \frac{10}{x} - 1$

Solving Exponential and Logarithmic Equations (Lesson 8-5)

Solve each equation.

13. $4^x = \frac{1}{8}$

14. $\log 5x + 1 = -1$

15. $7^{3x} = 500$

16. $\log 3x + \log x = 9$

17. $\log(4x + 3) - \log x = 5$

18. $3^x = 243$

Evaluating Trigonometric Functions (Lessons 13-2 and 13-6)

For each value of θ, find the values of $\cos \theta$, $\sin \theta$, and $\tan \theta$. Round your answers to the nearest hundredth.

19. $48°$

20. $-105°$

21. $16°$

22. $\frac{5\pi}{6}$

Trigonometric Identities and Equations

Chapter 14

LESSONS

14-1 Trigonometric Identities

14-2 Solving Trigonometric Equations Using Inverses

14-3 Right Triangles and Trigonometric Ratios

14-4 Area and the Law of Sines

14-5 The Law of Cosines

14-6 Angle Identities

14-7 Double-Angle and Half-Angle Identities

◀)) **Key Vocabulary**

- Law of Cosines (p. 808)
- Law of Sines (p. 801)
- trigonometric identity (p. 778)
- trigonometric ratios for a right triangle (p. 792)

What You'll Learn Next

- In Chapter 14, you will learn to verify trigonometric identities.

- You will learn to solve trigonometric equations.

- By using trigonometric ratios, you will solve real-world problems involving right triangles.

Activity Lab Applying what you learn, on pages 834–835 you will do activities involving angles and balance.

777

Trigonometric Identities

GO for Help Lessons 1-1, 1-2, and 9-4

What You'll Learn

- To verify trigonometric identities

... And Why

To use trigonometric identities in simplifying expressions

✓ **Check Skills You'll Need**

Determine whether each equation is true for all real numbers x. Explain your reasoning.

1. $2x + 3x = 5x$

2. $-(4x - 10) = 10 - 4x$

3. $\frac{4x^2}{x} = 4x$

4. $\frac{x^2 + 1}{x - 1} = x + 1$

🔊 **New Vocabulary** • trigonometric identity

---

1 Verifying Trigonometric Identities

Technology Activity: Trigonometric Identities

1. Use a graphing calculator to graph $y_1 = \tan x$ and $y_2 = \frac{\sin x}{\cos x}$. If your calculator has the "animate" graph style, use it for y_2.

2. Graph $y_1 = (\cos x)^2 + (\sin x)^2$ and $y_2 = 1$.

3. **Make a Conjecture** In each Question 1 and 2, make a conjecture about the relationship between y_1 and y_2.

Real-World 🌎 **Connection**

Astronomers use trigonometry to determine the angles that locate an object in the celestial coordinate system. This system is similar to the system of latitude and longitude used on Earth.

A trigonometric equation such as $\csc \theta = \frac{1}{\sin \theta}$ is true for all values of θ except those for which $\sin \theta = 0$. A **trigonometric identity** is a trigonometric equation that is true for all values except those for which the expressions on either side of the equal sign are undefined. The three equations $\csc \theta = \frac{1}{\sin \theta}$, $\sec \theta = \frac{1}{\cos \theta}$, and $\tan \theta = \frac{1}{\cot \theta}$ are known as the reciprocal identities.

You can derive some other identities from the unit circle definitions of sine, cosine, and tangent. In the diagram below, $\cos \theta$, $\sin \theta$, and $\tan \theta$ are the coordinates of points P and Q. You can use the slope of $\overleftrightarrow{PQ}$ to show that $\tan \theta = \frac{\sin \theta}{\cos \theta}$.

slope $\overleftrightarrow{PQ} = \frac{\sin \theta - 0}{\cos \theta - 0}$ slope $= \frac{y_2 - y_1}{x_2 - x_1}$

$= \frac{\sin \theta}{\cos \theta}$

slope $\overleftrightarrow{PQ} = \frac{\tan \theta - 0}{1 - 0}$ slope $= \frac{y_2 - y_1}{x_2 - x_1}$

$= \tan \theta$

So, $\tan \theta = \frac{\sin \theta}{\cos \theta}$.   **Transitive Property of Equality**

$P(\cos \theta, \sin \theta)$ $x = 1$ $Q(1, \tan \theta)$

Using the reciprocal identity $\cot \theta = \frac{1}{\tan \theta}$ and the Tangent Identity $\tan \theta = \frac{\sin \theta}{\cos \theta}$, you can derive the Cotangent Identity $\cot \theta = \frac{\cos \theta}{\sin \theta}$.

$$\cot \theta = \frac{1}{\tan \theta} \qquad \textbf{Reciprocal identity}$$

$$= \frac{1}{\frac{\sin \theta}{\cos \theta}} \qquad \textbf{Substitute using the Tangent Identity.}$$

$$= \frac{\cos \theta}{\sin \theta} \qquad \textbf{Divide.}$$

Vocabulary Tip

The expression $\cos^2 \theta$ is equivalent to $(\cos \theta)^2$. The meaning of the phrase "cosine theta squared," when spoken, is not clear.

You can derive another identity from the definitions of $\cos \theta$ and $\sin \theta$. The ordered pair $(\cos \theta, \sin \theta)$ is a point on the unit circle, and for any point (x, y) on the unit circle, $x^2 + y^2 = 1$. So $\cos^2 \theta + \sin^2 \theta = 1$. This is one of the three Pythagorean identities.

To verify an identity, you should transform one side of the equation until it is the same as the other side. This eliminates the possibility of introducing errors that can be caused by squaring both sides of an equation or multiplying both sides of an equation by an expression that equals 0. These are the errors that can introduce extraneous roots when solving equations.

It is sometimes helpful to write all the functions in terms of sine and cosine.

For: Trig. Identity Activity
Use: Interactive Textbook, 14-1

1 EXAMPLE **Verifying Identities**

Verify the Pythagorean identity $1 + \tan^2 \theta = \sec^2 \theta$.

$$1 + \tan^2 \theta = 1 + \left(\frac{\sin \theta}{\cos \theta}\right)^2 \qquad \textbf{Tangent Identity}$$

$$= 1 + \frac{\sin^2 \theta}{\cos^2 \theta} \qquad \textbf{Simplify.}$$

$$= \frac{\cos^2 \theta}{\cos^2 \theta} + \frac{\sin^2 \theta}{\cos^2 \theta} \qquad \textbf{Write the fractions with common denominators.}$$

$$= \frac{\cos^2 \theta + \sin^2 \theta}{\cos^2 \theta} \qquad \textbf{Add.}$$

$$= \frac{1}{\cos^2 \theta} \qquad \textbf{Pythagorean identity}$$

$$= \sec^2 \theta \qquad \textbf{Reciprocal identity}$$

The left side of the equation has been transformed into the right side. Therefore the equation is an identity.

 **1** Verify the third Pythagorean identity, $1 + \cot^2 \theta = \csc^2 \theta$.

Key Concepts

Properties	**Trigonometric Identities**	
Reciprocal identities		
$\csc \theta = \frac{1}{\sin \theta}$	$\sec \theta = \frac{1}{\cos \theta}$	$\cot \theta = \frac{1}{\tan \theta}$
Tangent and cotangent identities		
$\tan \theta = \frac{\sin \theta}{\cos \theta}$	$\cot \theta = \frac{\cos \theta}{\sin \theta}$	
Pythagorean identities		
$\cos^2 \theta + \sin^2 \theta = 1$	$1 + \tan^2 \theta = \sec^2 \theta$	$1 + \cot^2 \theta = \csc^2 \theta$

There are many trigonometric identities in addition to the identities named in the summary above.

2 EXAMPLE Verifying Identities

Vocabulary Tip

The word <u>identity</u> is used in several ways.

additive identity: 0

multiplicative identity: 1

trigonometric identity: an equation true for all valid replacements of the variables

Verify the identity $\tan^2 \theta - \sin^2 \theta = \tan^2 \theta \sin^2 \theta$.

$$\tan^2 \theta - \sin^2 \theta = \left(\frac{\sin \theta}{\cos \theta}\right)^2 - \sin^2 \theta \qquad \text{Tangent Identity}$$

$$= \frac{\sin^2 \theta}{\cos^2 \theta} - \sin^2 \theta \qquad \text{Simplify.}$$

$$= \frac{\sin^2 \theta}{\cos^2 \theta} - \frac{\sin^2 \theta \cos^2 \theta}{\cos^2 \theta} \qquad \text{Write fractions with common denominators.}$$

$$= \frac{\sin^2 \theta - \sin^2 \theta \cos^2 \theta}{\cos^2 \theta} \qquad \text{Subtract.}$$

$$= \frac{\sin^2 \theta (1 - \cos^2 \theta)}{\cos^2 \theta} \qquad \text{Factor.}$$

$$= \frac{\sin^2 \theta (\sin^2 \theta)}{\cos^2 \theta} \qquad \text{Pythagorean identity}$$

$$= \frac{\sin^2 \theta}{\cos^2 \theta} \sin^2 \theta \qquad \text{Rewrite the fraction.}$$

$$= \tan^2 \theta \sin^2 \theta \qquad \text{Tangent Identity}$$

 **Quick Check** **2** Verify the identity $\sec^2 \theta - \sec^2 \theta \cos^2 \theta = \tan^2 \theta$.

You can use the trigonometric identities to simplify trigonometric expressions. Again, it is often helpful to write all the functions in terms of sines and cosines.

3 EXAMPLE Simplifying Expressions

Simplify the trigonometric expression $\csc \theta \tan \theta$.

$$\csc \theta \tan \theta = \frac{1}{\sin \theta} \cdot \tan \theta \qquad \text{Reciprocal Identity}$$

$$= \frac{1}{\sin \theta} \cdot \frac{\sin \theta}{\cos \theta} \qquad \text{Tangent Identity}$$

$$= \frac{\sin \theta}{\sin \theta \cos \theta} \qquad \text{Multiply.}$$

$$= \frac{1}{\cos \theta} \qquad \text{Simplify.}$$

$$= \sec \theta \qquad \text{Reciprocal identity}$$

So $\csc \theta \tan \theta = \sec \theta$.

 **Quick Check** **3** Simplify the trigonometric expression $\sec \theta \cot \theta$.

EXERCISES

For more exercises, see *Extra Skill and Word Problem Practice*.

Practice and Problem Solving

A Practice by Example

Examples 1 and 2
(pages 779 and 780)

GO for Help

Verify each identity.

1. $\cos \theta \cot \theta = \frac{1}{\sin \theta} - \sin \theta$

2. $\sin \theta \cot \theta = \cos \theta$

3. $\cos \theta \tan \theta = \sin \theta$

4. $\sin \theta \sec \theta = \tan \theta$

5. $\cos \theta \sec \theta = 1$

6. $\tan \theta \cot \theta = 1$

7. $\sin \theta \csc \theta = 1$

8. $\cot \theta = \frac{\csc \theta}{\sec \theta}$

Example 3
(page 780)

Simplify each trigonometric expression.

9. $\tan \theta \cot \theta$

10. $1 - \cos^2 \theta$

11. $\sec^2 \theta - 1$

12. $1 - \csc^2 \theta$

13. $\sec \theta \cot \theta$

14. $\cos \theta \tan \theta$

15. $\sin \theta \cot \theta$

16. $\sin \theta \csc \theta$

17. $\sec \theta \cos \theta \sin \theta$

18. $\sin \theta \sec \theta \cot \theta$

19. $\sec^2 \theta - \tan^2 \theta$

20. $\dfrac{\sin \theta}{\cos \theta \tan \theta}$

 Apply Your Skills

Simplify each trigonometric expression.

21. $\cos \theta + \sin \theta \tan \theta$

22. $\csc \theta \cos \theta \tan \theta$

23. $\tan \theta (\cot \theta + \tan \theta)$

24. $\sin^2 \theta + \cos^2 \theta + \tan^2 \theta$

> **Problem Solving Hint**
> To help remember the sec and csc reciprocal identities, notice that the initial letters of the functions in each identity are different.

25. $\cos^2 \theta \sec \theta \csc \theta$

26. $\sin \theta (1 + \cot^2 \theta)$

27. $\cot \theta \tan \theta - \sec^2 \theta$

28. $\sin^2 \theta \csc \theta \sec \theta$

29. $\cos \theta (1 + \tan^2 \theta)$

30. $\dfrac{\tan \theta}{\sec \theta - \cos \theta}$

31. $\sec \theta \cos \theta - \cos^2 \theta$

32. $\sin \theta \csc \theta - \cos^2 \theta$

33. $\csc \theta - \cos \theta \cot \theta$

34. $\cos \theta + \sin \theta \tan \theta$

35. $\sec \theta (1 + \cot^2 \theta)$

36. $\csc^2 \theta (1 - \cos^2 \theta)$

37. $\dfrac{\cos \theta \csc \theta}{\cot \theta}$

38. $\dfrac{\sin^2 \theta \csc \theta \sec \theta}{\tan \theta}$

Express the first trigonometric function in terms of the second.

39. $\sin \theta, \cos \theta$

40. $\tan \theta, \cos \theta$

41. $\cot \theta, \sin \theta$

42. $\csc \theta, \cot \theta$

43. $\cot \theta, \csc \theta$

44. $\sec \theta, \tan \theta$

Verify each identity.

Online
Homework Video Tutor
Visit: PHSchool.com
Web Code: age-1401

45. $\sin^2 \theta \tan^2 \theta = \tan^2 \theta - \sin^2 \theta$

46. $\sec \theta - \sin \theta \tan \theta = \cos \theta$

47. $\sin \theta \cos \theta (\tan \theta + \cot \theta) = 1$

48. $\dfrac{1 - \sin \theta}{\cos \theta} = \dfrac{\cos \theta}{1 + \sin \theta}$

49. $\dfrac{\sec \theta}{\cot \theta + \tan \theta} = \sin \theta$

50. $(\cot \theta + 1)^2 = \csc^2 \theta + 2 \cot \theta$

51. Express $\cos \theta \csc \theta \cot \theta$ in terms of $\sin \theta$.

52. Express $\dfrac{\cos \theta}{\sec \theta + \tan \theta}$ in terms of $\sin \theta$.

53. Open-Ended Create a trigonometric identity. (*Hint:* Start with a simple trigonometric expression and work backward.)

54. Writing Describe the similarities and differences in solving an equation and in verifying an identity.

 **Challenge**

Verify each identity.

55. $1 + \sec \theta = \dfrac{1 + \cos \theta}{\cos \theta}$

56. $\dfrac{1 + \tan \theta}{\tan \theta} = \cot \theta + 1$

57. $\dfrac{\cot \theta \sin \theta}{\sec \theta} + \dfrac{\tan \theta \cos \theta}{\csc \theta} = 1$

58. $\sin^2 \theta \tan^2 \theta + \cos^2 \theta \tan^2 \theta = \sec^2 \theta - 1$

Simplify each trigonometric expression.

59. $\dfrac{\cot^2 \theta - \csc^2 \theta}{\tan^2 \theta - \sec^2 \theta}$

60. $(1 - \sin \theta)(1 + \sin \theta) \csc^2 \theta + 1$

61. Physics When a ray of light passes from one medium into a second, the angle of incidence θ_1 and the angle of refraction θ_2 are related by Snell's law: $n_1 \sin \theta_1 = n_2 \sin \theta_2$, where n_1 is the index of refraction of the first medium and n_2 is the index of refraction of the second medium. How are θ_1 and θ_2 related if $n_2 > n_1$? If $n_2 < n_1$? If $n_2 = n_1$?

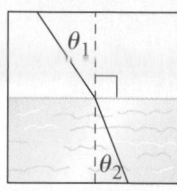

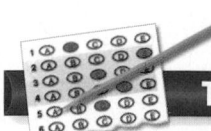

Test Prep

Multiple Choice

62. Which expression is NOT equal to the other three expressions?

A. $\dfrac{2}{\tan \theta}$ **B.** $\dfrac{\cot \theta}{\frac{1}{2}}$ **C.** $\dfrac{\sin \theta}{\frac{1}{2}\cos \theta}$ **D.** $\dfrac{2\cos \theta}{\sin \theta}$

63. Which equation is NOT true?

F. $\cos^2 \theta = 1 - \sin^2 \theta$ **G.** $\cot^2 \theta = \csc^2 \theta - 1$

H. $\sin^2 \theta = \cos^2 \theta - 1$ **J.** $\tan^2 \theta = \sec^2 \theta - 1$

64. Which expressions are equivalent?

   I. $(\sin \theta)(\csc \theta - \sin \theta)$ **II.** $\sin^2 \theta - 1$ **III.** $\cos^2 \theta$

A. I and II only   **B.** II and III only

C. I and III only   **D.** I, II, and III

65. How can you express $\csc^2 \theta - 2 \cot^2 \theta$ in terms of $\sin \theta$ and $\cos \theta$?

F. $\dfrac{1 - 2\cos^2 \theta}{\sin^2 \theta}$ **G.** $\dfrac{1 - 2\sin^2 \theta}{\sin^2 \theta}$

H. $\sin^2 \theta - 2 \cos^2 \theta$ **J.** $\dfrac{1}{\sin^2 \theta} - \dfrac{2}{\tan^2 \theta}$

66. Which expression is equivalent to $\dfrac{\tan \theta}{\cos \theta - \sec \theta}$?

A. $\csc \theta$ **B.** $\sec \theta$ **C.** $-\csc \theta$ **D.** $\tan^2 \theta$

Short Response

67. Show that $(\sec \theta + 1)(\sec \theta - 1) = \tan^2 \theta$ is an identity.

68. Show that $\dfrac{\cos x}{1 - \sin^2 x} = \sec x$ is an identity.

Mixed Review

Lesson 13-8

Graph each function in the interval from 0 to 2π.

69. $y = \csc (-\theta)$ **70.** $y = -\cot \theta$ **71.** $y = -\sec 0.5\theta$

72. $y = -\sec (0.5\theta + 2)$ **73.** $y = \cot \dfrac{\theta}{5}$ **74.** $y = \pi \sec \theta$

Lesson 13-2

Find the measure of an angle between 0° and 360° that is coterminal with the given angle.

75. 395°   **76.** 405°   **77.** −225°   **78.** −149°

79. 627°   **80.** −281°   **81.** 493°   **82.** −609°

Lesson 12-3

Make a box-and-whisker plot for each set of values.

83. 300   345   333   295   302   321

84. 32   48   87   43   62   15   49   51   47   36   50   109   64

Solving Trigonometric Equations Using Inverses

What You'll Learn

- To evaluate inverses of trigonometric functions
- To solve trigonometric equations

... And Why

To solve problems involving springs, as in Example 7

✓ **Check Skills You'll Need**

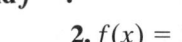 **for Help** Lessons 7-7, 13-2, and 13-6

For each function f, find f^{-1}.

1. $f(x) = x + 1$ **2.** $f(x) = 2x - 3$ **3.** $f(x) = x^2 + 4$

Find each value.

4. $\sin 30°$ **5.** $\cos \frac{\pi}{4}$ **6.** $\cos 135°$

7. $\tan(-\pi)$ **8.** $\tan 315°$ **9.** $\sin\left(-\frac{7\pi}{3}\right)$

1 Inverses of Trigonometric Functions

The cosine function $y = \cos \theta$ is periodic, so a horizontal line, such as the x-axis, can intersect the graph of $y = \cos \theta$ in infinitely many points. Therefore a vertical line can intersect the graph of the inverse of $y = \cos \theta$ in infinitely many points. The inverse of $y = \cos \theta$ is a relation that is not a function.

You can use a graph of an inverse function to find the measures of angles that have a given value of the function.

1 EXAMPLE Using a Graph to Find Angles With a Given Cosine

Use the graph of the inverse of $y = \cos \theta$ at the right.

a. Find the radian measures of the angles whose cosine is -1.

The line $x = -1$ intersects the graph at $(-1, \pi)$ and $(-1, -\pi)$. So the measures of two angles whose cosine is -1 are π and $-\pi$.

Other points of intersection are $(-1, \pm3\pi)$, $(-1, \pm5\pi)$, and so on. The measures of all the angles whose cosine is -1 can be written as $\pi + 2\pi n$, where n is any integer.

b. Find the radian measures of the angles θ whose cosine is 2.

The line $x = 2$ does not intersect the graph. 2 is not in the domain of the inverse of $y = \cos \theta$. There is no angle whose cosine is 2.

Inverse of $y = \cos \theta$

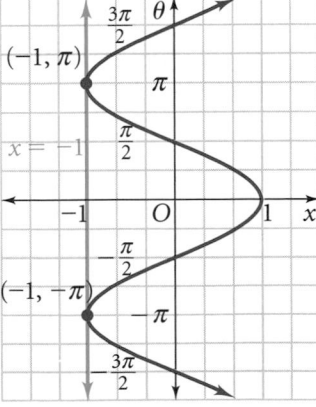

✓ **Quick Check** ❶ What are the radian measures of the angles whose cosine is 1.1? Whose cosine is 0? Whose cosine is -1.1?

You can use a unit circle to find angle measures for given sine or cosine values.

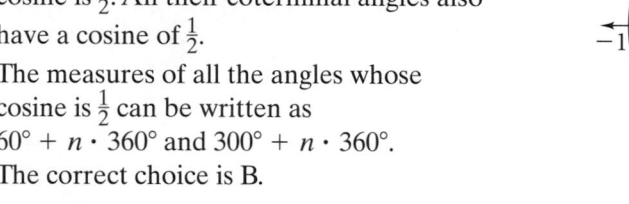

2 **EXAMPLE** Using a Unit Circle

Multiple Choice Find the degree measures of the angles whose cosine is $\frac{1}{2}$.

Ⓐ $30° + n \cdot 360°$ and $330° + n \cdot 360°$ Ⓑ $60° + n \cdot 360°$ and $300° + n \cdot 360°$

Ⓒ $30° + n \cdot 360°$ and $210° + n \cdot 360°$ Ⓓ $60° + n \cdot 360°$ and $120° + n \cdot 360°$

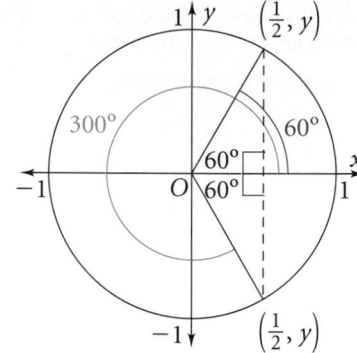

Draw a unit circle and mark the points on the circle that have x-coordinates of $\frac{1}{2}$. These points and the origin form 30°-60°-90° triangles. 60° and 300° are the measures of two angles whose cosine is $\frac{1}{2}$. All their coterminal angles also have a cosine of $\frac{1}{2}$.

The measures of all the angles whose cosine is $\frac{1}{2}$ can be written as $60° + n \cdot 360°$ and $300° + n \cdot 360°$.

The correct choice is B.

✓ **Quick Check** **2** Use a unit circle. Find the degree measures of all angles with the given cosine.

a. $-\frac{1}{2}$ **b.** $-\frac{\sqrt{3}}{2}$ **c.** $\frac{\sqrt{2}}{2}$

Vocabulary Tip

The expression $\cos^{-1} x$ represents the <u>inverse</u> <u>cosine</u> <u>function</u>. It is *not* the reciprocal of the cosine function, $\frac{1}{\cos x}$.

The domain of the cosine function can be restricted to $0 \le \theta \le \pi$ so that its inverse is a function. The inverse function is written $\theta = \cos^{-1} x$ and is read as "θ is the angle whose cosine is x."

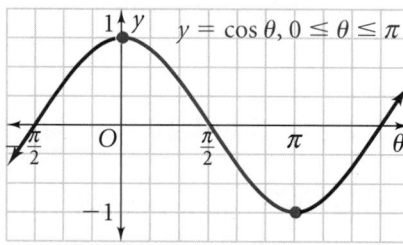 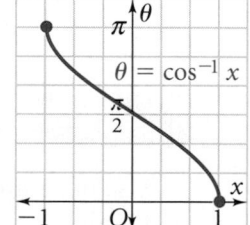

The domains are similarly restricted for $y = \sin \theta \left(-\frac{\pi}{2} \le \theta \le \frac{\pi}{2} \right)$ and $y = \tan \theta \left(-\frac{\pi}{2} < \theta < \frac{\pi}{2} \right)$ to obtain the inverse functions $\theta = \sin^{-1} x$ and $\theta = \tan^{-1} x$.

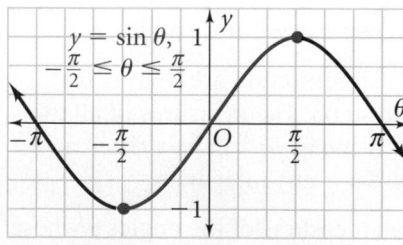 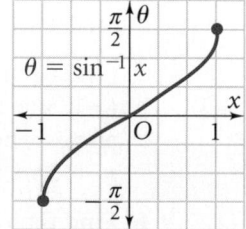

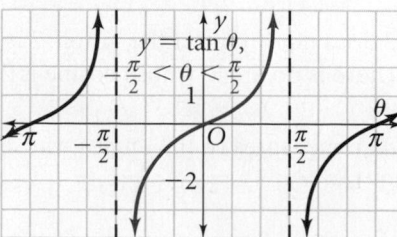 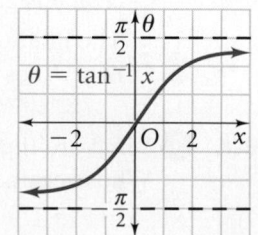

3 EXAMPLE Using a Calculator to Find the Inverse of Sine

Use a calculator and an inverse function to find the radian measures of all the angles whose sine is -0.9.

$\sin^{-1}(-0.9) \approx -1.12$ **Use a calculator.**

This angle is in Quadrant IV. The sine function is also negative in Quadrant III, as shown in the figure at the right. So $\pi + 1.12 \approx 4.26$ is another solution.

The radian measures of all the angles whose sine is -0.9 can be written as

$-1.12 + 2\pi n$ and $4.26 + 2\pi n$.

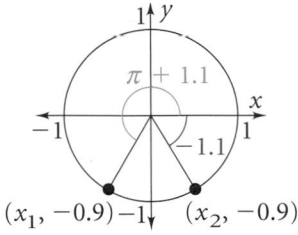

✓ Quick Check ❸ Find the radian measures of the angles.
a. angles whose sine is 0.44   b. angles whose sine is -0.73

4 EXAMPLE Using a Calculator to Find the Inverse of Tangent

Use a calculator and an inverse function to find the measure in radians of all the angles whose tangent is -0.84.

$\tan^{-1}(-0.84) \approx -0.70$ **Use a calculator.**

The tangent function is also negative in Quadrant II, as shown in the figure at the right. So $\pi - 0.70 \approx 2.44$ is another solution.

The radian measures of all the angles whose tangent is -0.84 can be written as

$-0.70 + 2\pi n$ and $2.44 + 2\pi n$.

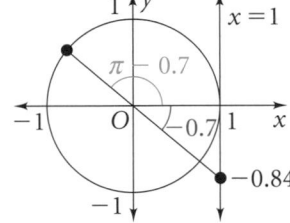

✓ Quick Check ❹ Find the radian measures of the angles.
a. angles whose tangent is 0.44   b. angles whose tangent is -0.73

2 Solving Trigonometric Equations

In contrast to trigonometric identities, most trigonometric equations are true for only certain values of the variable.

5 EXAMPLE Solving Trigonometric Equations

Solve $4\cos\theta - 1 = \cos\theta$ for $0 \le \theta < 2\pi$.

$4\cos\theta - 1 = \cos\theta$

$\quad\quad 3\cos\theta = 1$ **Add $1 - \cos\theta$ to each side.**

$\quad\quad\quad \cos\theta = \frac{1}{3}$ **Divide each side by 3.**

$\quad\quad \cos^{-1}\frac{1}{3} \approx 1.23$ **Use the inverse function to find one value of θ.**

The cosine function is also positive in Quadrant IV. So another value of θ is $2\pi - 1.23 \approx 5.05$. The two solutions between 0 and 2π are approximately 1.23 and 5.05.

**Quick Check** ⑤ Solve $3 \sin \theta + 1 = \sin \theta$ for $0 \le \theta < 2\pi$.

Sometimes you can solve trigonometric equations by factoring.

⑥ **EXAMPLE** **Solving by Factoring**

Solve $2 \cos \theta \sin \theta + \sin \theta = 0$ for $0 \le \theta < 2\pi$.

$2 \cos \theta \sin \theta + \sin \theta = 0$

$\quad \sin \theta (2 \cos \theta + 1) = 0$ **Factor.**

$\sin \theta = 0 \quad$ or $\quad 2 \cos \theta + 1 = 0$ **Zero-Product Property**

$\sin \theta = 0 \qquad\qquad\qquad \cos \theta = -\frac{1}{2}$ **Solve for cos θ.**

$\quad \theta = 0 \text{ and } \pi \qquad\qquad \theta = \frac{2\pi}{3} \text{ and } \frac{4\pi}{3}$ **Use the unit circle.**

The four values of θ are $0, \pi, \frac{2\pi}{3},$ and $\frac{4\pi}{3}$.

Quick Check ⑥ Solve $\sin \theta \cos \theta - \cos \theta = 0$ for $0 \le \theta < 2\pi$.

You can use trigonometric equations to solve problems involving repetitive events.

⑦ **EXAMPLE** **Real-World** 🌐 **Connection**

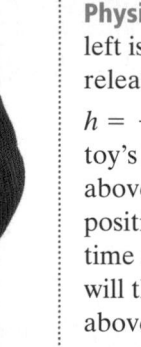

Real-World 🌐 **Connection**

The motion of an oscillating spring is called simple harmonic motion.

Physics The spring at the left is stretched and released. The equation $h = -4 \cos \frac{2\pi}{3}t$ models the toy's height h in inches above or below the rest position as a function of time t in seconds. When will the toy first be 2 in. above the rest position?

$$h = -4 \cos \tfrac{2\pi}{3}t$$

$2 = -4 \cos \tfrac{2\pi}{3}t$ **Substitute 2 for h.**

$-\tfrac{2}{4} = \cos \tfrac{2\pi}{3}t$ **Divide each side by -4.**

$-\tfrac{1}{2} = \cos \tfrac{2\pi}{3}t$ **Simplify.**

$\cos^{-1}\left(-\tfrac{1}{2}\right) = \tfrac{2\pi}{3}t$ **Use the inverse of the cosine to solve for t.**

$\tfrac{2\pi}{3} = \tfrac{2\pi}{3}t$ **Evaluate the inverse. Use the unit circle.**

$1 = t$ **Multiply each side by $\tfrac{3}{2\pi}$.**

The toy is 2 in. above the rest position at 1 s.

Quick Check ⑦ **a.** When will the toy in Example 7 first be 2 in. below the rest position? When will the toy next be 4 in. below the rest position?
b. You found that the toy in Example 7 is 2 in. above the rest position after 1 s. Will it ever be at that same position again? Explain.
c. How could you use a graphing calculator to solve Example 7?

EXERCISES

For more exercises, see *Extra Skill and Word Problem Practice*.

Practice and Problem Solving

 **Practice by Example**

Example 1
(page 783)

Use the graph of the inverse of $y = \sin \theta$ at the right.

1. Find the measures of the angles whose sine is -1.

2. Find the measures of the angles whose sine is 0.

3. Find the measures of the angles whose sine is 1.

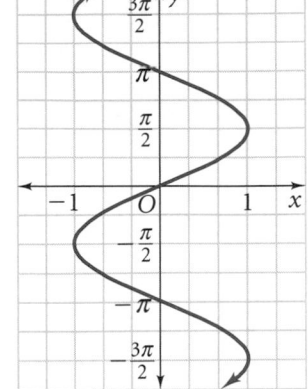

Example 2
(page 784)

Use a unit circle and 30°-60°-90° triangles to find the degree measures of the angles.

4. angles whose sine is $\frac{1}{2}$

5. angles whose tangent is $\frac{\sqrt{3}}{3}$

6. angles whose sine is $-\frac{1}{2}$

7. angles whose tangent is $-\sqrt{3}$

Examples 3 and 4
(page 785)

Use a calculator and inverse functions to find the radian measures of the angles.

8. angles whose tangent is 1

9. angles whose sine is 0.37

10. angles whose sine is (-0.78)

11. angles whose tangent is (-3)

12. angles whose cosine is (-0.89)

13. angles whose sine is (-1.1)

14. angles whose tangent is 5

15. angles whose cosine is 0.58

Example 5
(page 785)

Solve each equation for $0 \le \theta < 2\pi$.

16. $2 \sin \theta = 1$

17. $2 \cos \theta - \sqrt{3} = 0$

18. $4 \tan \theta = 3 + \tan \theta$

19. $2 \sin \theta - \sqrt{2} = 0$

20. $3 \cos \theta = 2$

21. $3 \tan \theta - 1 = \tan \theta$

22. $\sqrt{2} \cos \theta - \sqrt{2} = 0$

23. $3 \tan \theta + 5 = 0$

24. $2 \sin \theta = 3$

25. $2 \sin \theta = -\sqrt{3}$

Example 6
(page 786)

26. $(\cos \theta)(\cos \theta + 1) = 0$

27. $(\sin \theta - 1)(\sin \theta + 1) = 0$

28. $\tan^2 \theta + \tan \theta = 0$

29. $2 \sin^2 \theta - 1 = 0$

30. $\tan \theta = \tan^2 \theta$

31. $\sin^2 \theta + 3 \sin \theta = 0$

32. $\sin \theta = -\sin \theta \cos \theta$

33. $2 \sin^2 \theta - 3 \sin \theta = 2$

Example 7
(page 786)

34. **Physics** Two students set up a spring experiment similar to the one in Example 7. In their experiment, a weight was released 4 cm below the rest position. It rose to 4 cm above the rest position and returned to 4 cm below the rest position once every 4 seconds. The equation $h = -4 \cos\left(\frac{\pi}{2}t\right)$ models the height above and below the rest position at t seconds.
   a. Solve the equation for t.
   b. Find the times at which the weight is first at a height of 1 cm, 2 cm, and 3 cm above the rest position.
   c. Find the times at which the weight is at a height of 1 cm, 2 cm, and 3 cm below the rest position for the second time.

Each diagram shows one solution to the equation below it. Find the complete solution of each equation.

35.

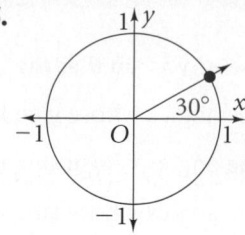

$5 \sin \theta = 1 + 3 \sin \theta$

36.

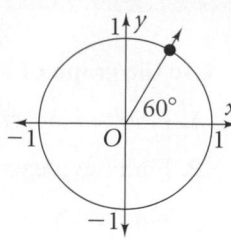

$6 \cos \theta - 5 = -2$

37.

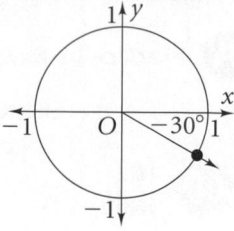

$4 \sin \theta + 3 = 1$

Solve each equation for $0 \le \theta < 2\pi$.

38. $\sec \theta = 2$

39. $\csc \theta = -1$

40. $\cot \theta = 10$

41. $\csc \theta = 3$

42. $\cot \theta = -10$

43. $\sec \theta = 1$

 44. Electricity The function $I = 40 \sin 60\pi t$ models the current I in amps that the electric generator shown at the left is producing after t seconds. When is the first time that the current will reach 20 amps? -20 amps?

45. Critical Thinking The graphing calculator screen below shows a portion of the graphs of $y = \sin \theta$ and $y = 0.5$.

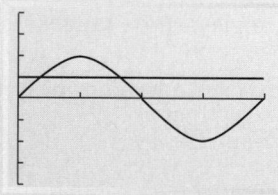

Xmin=0
Xmax=360
Xscl=90
Ymin=-2
Ymax=2
Yscl=0.5

a. Write the complete solution of $\sin \theta \ge 0.5$.
b. Write the complete solution of $\sin \theta \le 0.5$.
c. Writing Explain how you can solve inequalities involving trigonometric functions.

Find the complete solution in radians of each equation.

46. $2 \sin^2 \theta + \cos \theta - 1 = 0$

47. $\sin^2 \theta - 1 = \cos^2 \theta$

48. $2 \sin \theta + 1 = \csc \theta$

49. $3 \tan^2 \theta - 1 = \sec^2 \theta$

50. $\sin \theta \cos \theta = \frac{1}{2} \cos \theta$

51. $\tan \theta \sin \theta = 3 \sin \theta$

52. $2 \cos^2 \theta + \sin \theta = 1$

53. $\sin \theta \cot^2 \theta - 3 \sin \theta = 0$

54. $4 \sin^2 \theta + 1 = 4 \sin \theta$

55. $\tan \theta \cot \theta - \tan \theta + 2 \cot \theta = 0$

56. Error Analysis A student solved an equation as shown below. What error did the student make?

$$\theta = \cos^{-1} 0.5$$
$$= \frac{1}{\cos 0.5}$$
$$\approx \frac{1}{0.88}$$
$$\approx 1.14$$

GO Online
Homework Video Tutor
Visit: PHSchool.com
Web Code: age-1402

57. Error Analysis A student solved the equation $\sin^2 \theta = \frac{1}{2} \sin \theta$, $0 \le \theta < 2\pi$, as shown below. What error did the student make?

$$\sin^2 \theta = \frac{1}{2} \sin \theta$$

$$\sin \theta = \frac{1}{2}$$

$$\theta = \frac{\pi}{6} \text{ and } \frac{5\pi}{6}$$

Find the x-intercepts of the graph of each function.

58. $y = 2 \cos \theta + 1$

59. $y = 2 \sin^2 \theta - 1$

60. $y = \cos^2 \theta - 1$

61. $y = \tan^2 \theta - 1$

62. $y = 2 \sin^4 \theta - \sin^2 \theta$

63. $y = 2 \cos^2 \theta - 3 \cos \theta - 2$

64. Writing Describe the similarities and differences in solving the equations $4x + 1 = 3$ and $4 \sin \theta + 1 = 3$.

65. Find the complete solution of $\sin^2 \theta + 2 \sin \theta + 1 = 0$. (*Hint:* How would you solve $x^2 + 2x + 1 = 0$?)

66. a. Open-Ended Write three trigonometric equations whose complete solution is $\pi + 2\pi n$.
    b. Describe how you found the equations in part (a).

C Challenge

Solve each trigonometric equation for θ in terms of y.

Sample $y = 2 \sin 3\theta + 4$

$$\sin 3\theta = \frac{y - 4}{2}$$

$$3\theta = \sin^{-1}\left(\frac{y - 4}{2}\right)$$

$$\theta = \frac{1}{3} \sin^{-1}\left(\frac{y - 4}{2}\right)$$

67. $y = 2 \sin \theta$

68. $y = \cos 2\theta$

69. $y = 3 \sin (\theta + 2)$

70. $y = -4 \cos 2\pi\theta$

71. $y = \cos \theta + 1$

72. $y = 2 \cos \pi\theta + 1$

73. Parks A segment of a circle is the region formed by an arc of a circle and the line segment joining the endpoints of the arc. (The measure of the arc must be between 0 and 2π.) The expression below gives the area K in square feet of a segment in terms of the radius of the circle r in feet and the radian measure θ of the arc.

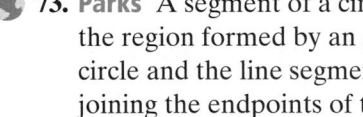

50 ft

$$K = \frac{r^2}{2}(\theta - \sin \theta)$$

    a. Suppose a circular park has a radius of 50 ft. Write an equation for the area of any segment of the park using $r = 50$.
    b. Use trial and error to approximate the measure of θ that makes the area of the segment 1500 ft^2.

74. Tides One day the tides at a point in Maine could be modeled by $h = 5 \cos \frac{2\pi}{13}t$, where h is the height of the tide in feet above the mean water level and t is the number of hours past midnight.

   a. At what times that day will the tide be 3 ft above the mean water level?

   b. At what times that day will the tide be *at least* 3 ft above the mean water level?

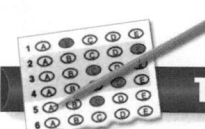

Test Prep

Multiple Choice

75. Which of the following is NOT equal to 60°?

   A. $\sin^{-1} \frac{\sqrt{3}}{2}$ **B.** $\cos^{-1} \frac{1}{2}$ **C.** $\tan^{-1} \sqrt{3}$ **D.** $\tan^{-1} \frac{\sqrt{3}}{3}$

76. In which quadrants are the solutions to $\tan \theta + 1 = 0$?

   F. Quadrants I and II   **G.** Quadrants II and III

   H. Quadrants II and IV   **J.** Quadrants III and IV

77. Which of these angles have a sine of about -0.6?

   I. 143.1°   **II.** 216.9°   **III.** 323.1°

   A. I and II only   **B.** I and III only

   C. II and III only   **D.** I, II, and III

78. What are the solutions of $2 \sin \theta - \sqrt{3} = 0$ for $0 \le \theta < 2\pi$?

   F. $\frac{\pi}{6}$ and $\frac{5\pi}{6}$ **G.** $\frac{\pi}{3}$ and $\frac{2\pi}{3}$

   H. $\frac{2\pi}{3}$ and $\frac{4\pi}{3}$ **J.** $\frac{4\pi}{3}$ and $\frac{5\pi}{3}$

79. Suppose $a > 0$. Under what conditions for a and b will $a \sin \theta = b$ have exactly two solutions in the interval $0 \le \theta < 2\pi$?

   A. $a = b$ **B.** $b > a$

   C. $a = -b$ **D.** $a > b > -a$

Short Response

80. Solve $2 \cos \theta = \sqrt{2}$ for $0 \le \theta < 2\pi$.

Extended Response

81. Solve $2 \sin^2 \theta = -\sin \theta$ for $0 \le \theta < 2\pi$. Show your work.

Mixed Review

Lesson 14-1

Simplify each expression.

82. $\cos^2 \theta \sec \theta \csc \theta$ **83.** $\sin \theta \sec \theta \tan \theta$

84. $\csc^2 \theta \, (1 - \cos^2 \theta)$ **85.** $\frac{\cos \theta \csc \theta}{\cot \theta}$

86. $\frac{\sec \theta}{\cot \theta + \tan \theta}$ **87.** $\frac{\sin \theta + \tan \theta}{1 + \cos \theta}$

Lesson 13-5

Write a cosine function for each description.

88. amplitude 4, period 8   **89.** amplitude 3, period 2π

90. amplitude 3π, period 1   **91.** amplitude $\frac{\pi}{4}$, period 3π

Lesson 12-2 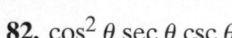 **92. Transportation** Ninety-eight percent of a railroad's trains depart on schedule. Eighty-nine percent of its trains depart and arrive on schedule. Find the probability that a train that departs on time also arrives on time.

Activity Lab

Lissajous Figures

FOR USE WITH LESSON 14-2

A clock pendulum swings in only one plane. Its oscillating path projected on a sheet of paper below it would be a segment. A pendulum supported by a string can move so that its path is a circle, ellipse, or other complicated curve. These curves are called Lissajous (lee suh zhoo) figures.

Lissajous figures can be described by parametric equations of this form.

$$x = a_1 \sin b_1(t - h_1)$$
$$y = a_2 \sin b_2(t - h_2)$$

x represents the oscillating motion in one direction and y represents the oscillating motion in the perpendicular direction. t is time, $|a_1|$ and $|a_2|$ are amplitudes of the oscillations, $\frac{b_1}{2\pi}$ and $\frac{b_2}{2\pi}$ are cycles per second, and h_1 and h_2 are phase shifts.

The parametric equations can be graphed with a graphing calculator. See page 124.

ACTIVITY

Set the calculator to radian and parametric mode. Set the window values as shown.

```
WINDOW
  Tmin=0
  Tmax=7
  Tstep=.05
  Xmin=-3
  Xmax=3
  Xscl=1
↓ Ymin=-2
```

```
WINDOW
↑ Tstep=.05
  Xmin=-3
  Xmax=3
  Xscl=1
  Ymin=-2
  Ymax=2
  Yscl=1
```

Graph each pair of parametric equations.

a. $x = 3 \sin 2(t - \pi)$

$y = 2 \sin 4(t - \pi)$

b. $x = 3 \sin 2\left(t - \frac{\pi}{3}\right)$

$y = 2 \sin 4(t - \pi)$

c. $x = 3 \sin 2(t - 1)$

$y = 2 \sin 3(t - 1)$

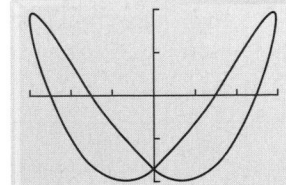 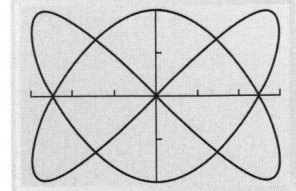

EXERCISES

Use your calculator to graph each pair of parametric equations. Sketch each graph.

1. $x = 2.1 \sin (t - 1)$

$y = 1.8 \sin (t - 2)$

2. $x = 3 \sin 2\left(t - \frac{3}{2}\right)$

$y = 2 \sin 3\left(t - \frac{2}{3}\right)$

3. $x = 3 \sin 3(t - 1)$

$y = 2 \sin 2(t - 1)$

4. Open-Ended Graph other Lissajous figures by changing the numbers in the equations. Sketch the interesting graphs and record their equations.

14-3

Right Triangles and Trigonometric Ratios

What You'll Learn

- To find lengths of sides in a right triangle
- To find measures of angles in a right triangle

. . . And Why

To design bridges, as in Example 3

✓ **Check Skills You'll Need**

△*ABC* is similar to △*RST*. Complete the following proportions.

1. $\frac{a}{b} = \frac{r}{\blacksquare}$

2. $\frac{a}{c} = \frac{\blacksquare}{t}$

3. $\frac{t}{r} = \frac{c}{\blacksquare}$

4. $\frac{c}{b} = \frac{\blacksquare}{s}$

GO **for Help** Skills Handbook page 872

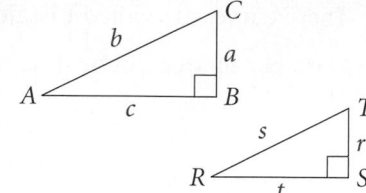

🔊 **New Vocabulary** • trigonometric ratios for a right triangle

---

1 Finding the Lengths of Sides in a Right Triangle

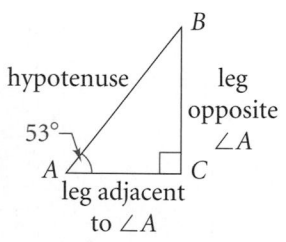

Activity: Right Triangle Ratios

Draw three right triangles, each one having an acute angle of 53°. Make the hypotenuse of the first triangle 10 cm long, and make the other two hypotenuses differ by at least 5 cm. Label the triangles 1, 2, and 3.

1. In each triangle, measure the lengths of the hypotenuse, the leg opposite the 53° angle, and the leg adjacent to the 53° angle. Copy the table below and record your measurements. Then calculate the three ratios for each triangle.

Triangle	Hyp. (cm)	Leg opp. ∠A (cm)	Leg adj. to ∠A (cm)	$\frac{opp.}{hyp.}$	$\frac{adj.}{hyp.}$	$\frac{opp.}{adj.}$
1	10	8.0	6.0	0.80	0.60	1.33
2	■	■	■	■	■	■
3	■	■	■	■	■	■

2. Reasoning What patterns do you see in the last three columns of the table? Check your results with others.

3. Make a Conjecture What is true about these ratios for all right triangles that have an acute angle of 53°?

The **trigonometric ratios for a right triangle** are the six different ratios of the sides of a right triangle. These ratios do not depend on the size of the right triangle. They depend only on the measures of the acute angles in the triangle.

792 Chapter 14 Trigonometric Identities and Equations

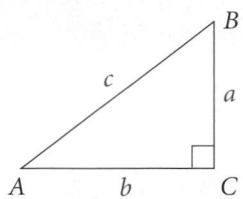

Vocabulary Tip

A <u>mnemonic device</u> is an arrangement or a process that helps you remember something. To remember trigonometric relationships, some students use the acronym "SOHCAHTOA" as a mnemonic device.

Sine:
Opposite over
Hypotenuse

Cosine:
Adjacent over
Hypotenuse

Tangent:
Opposite over
Adjacent

In a right triangle that has an acute $\angle A$, the ratios are defined as follows.

$$\sin A = \frac{\text{length of leg opposite } \angle A}{\text{length of hypotenuse}} = \frac{a}{c}$$

$$\cos A = \frac{\text{length of leg adjacent to } \angle A}{\text{length of hypotenuse}} = \frac{b}{c}$$

$$\tan A = \frac{\text{length of leg opposite } \angle A}{\text{length of leg adjacent to } \angle A} = \frac{a}{b}$$

$$\csc A = \frac{1}{\sin A} = \frac{\text{length of hypotenuse}}{\text{length of leg opposite } \angle A} = \frac{c}{a}$$

$$\sec A = \frac{1}{\cos A} = \frac{\text{length of hypotenuse}}{\text{length of leg adjacent to } \angle A} = \frac{c}{b}$$

$$\cot A = \frac{1}{\tan A} = \frac{\text{length of leg adjacent to } \angle A}{\text{length of leg opposite } \angle A} = \frac{b}{a}$$

1 EXAMPLE Real-World Connection

In the pyramid of Khafre, $AC \approx 108$ m and $m\angle A \approx 53°$.

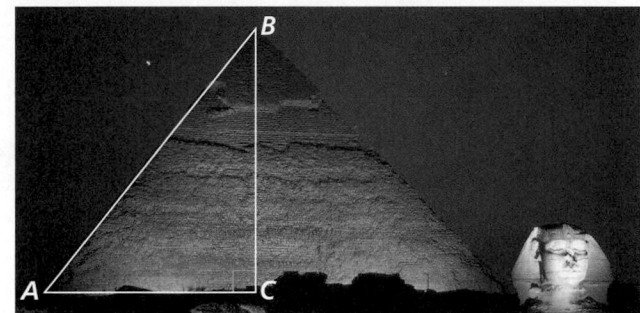

Egyptology Given that $\sin 53° \approx 0.80$, $\cos 53° \approx 0.60$, and $\tan 53° \approx 1.33$, find the height BC of the pyramid.

$$\tan A = \frac{BC}{AC} \qquad \textbf{definition of tan}$$

$$1.33 \approx \frac{BC}{108} \qquad \textbf{Substitute.}$$

$$BC \approx 108\,(1.33) \approx 144$$

● The height of the pyramid of Khafre is about 144 m.

✓ Quick Check ❶ Find the length of a lateral edge of the pyramid.

For acute angles, the unit circle definition of sine is equivalent to the definition of sine for right triangles.

sin θ using the unit circle

$\sin \theta = y\text{-coordinate of } P$

$\quad\; = PQ$

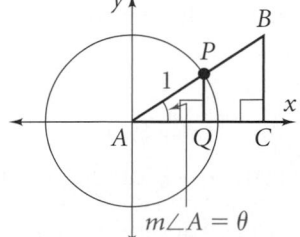

sin A using a right triangle

$$\sin A = \frac{\text{length of leg opposite } \angle A}{\text{length of hypotenuse}}$$

$$= \frac{BC}{AB}$$

Since $\triangle APQ$ and $\triangle ABC$ are similar triangles, $\frac{PQ}{PA} = \frac{BC}{AB}$.

So $\sin \theta = PQ = \frac{PQ}{1} = \frac{PQ}{PA} = \frac{BC}{AB} = \sin A$.

You can use a similar argument for each of the other five ratios. In each case, the definition based on a right triangle is equivalent to the corresponding unit circle definition for an acute angle.

2 EXAMPLE **Using a Right Triangle to Find Ratios**

In $\triangle ABC$, $\angle C$ is a right angle and $\sin A = \frac{5}{13}$. Find $\cos A$, $\cot A$, and $\sin B$ in fraction and in decimal form.

Step 1 Draw a diagram.

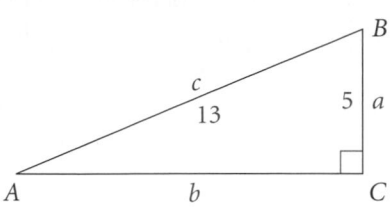

Step 2 Use the Pythagorean Theorem to find b.

$$c^2 = a^2 + b^2$$
$$13^2 = 5^2 + b^2$$
$$169 = 25 + b^2$$
$$144 = b^2$$
$$12 = b$$

Step 3 Calculate the ratios.

$$\cos A = \frac{\text{length of leg adjacent to } \angle A}{\text{length of hypotenuse}} = \frac{b}{c} = \frac{12}{13} \approx 0.9231$$

$$\cot A = \frac{\text{length of leg adjacent to } \angle A}{\text{length of leg opposite } \angle A} = \frac{b}{a} = \frac{12}{5} = 2.4$$

$$\sin B = \frac{\text{length of leg opposite } \angle B}{\text{length of hypotenuse}} = \frac{b}{c} = \frac{12}{13} \approx 0.9231$$

✓ Quick Check ❷ In $\triangle DEF$, $\angle D$ is a right angle and $\tan E = \frac{3}{4}$. Draw a diagram and find $\sin E$ and $\sec F$ in fraction and in decimal form.

If you are given the measures of an acute angle and a side of a right triangle, you can find the length of another side of the triangle.

3 EXAMPLE **Real-World 🌐 Connection**

Planning Park planners would like to build a bridge across a creek. Surveyors have determined that from 5 ft above the ground the angle of elevation to the top of an 8-ft pole on the opposite side of the creek is 5°. Find the length of the bridge to the nearest foot.

In the right triangle, the length of the leg opposite the 5° angle is 8 − 5, or 3 ft. You need to find the length of the leg adjacent to the 5° angle. Use the tangent ratio.

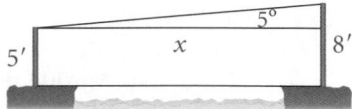

$$\tan 5° = \frac{3}{x}$$

$$x = \frac{3}{\tan 5°} \quad \textbf{Solve for } x.$$

$$\approx 34.29 \quad \textbf{Use a calculator in degree mode.}$$

The bridge will be about 34 ft long.

✓ Quick Check ❸ **a. Critical Thinking** What are the advantages and disadvantages of using cot 5° instead of tan 5° in solving Example 3?

b. Find the length of the bridge in Example 3 by using the 85° angle in the right triangle instead of the 5° angle.

To find the measure of an acute angle in a right triangle, you can use the inverses of the trigonometric functions.

4 **EXAMPLE**   **Finding Angle Measures**

In $\triangle DEF$, $\angle F$ is a right angle, $f = 13$, and $e = 5$. Find $m\angle D$ to the nearest tenth of a degree.

Step 1 Draw a diagram.

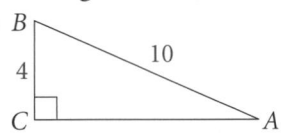

13 ← **Side f is opposite $\angle F$.**

5 ← **Side e is opposite $\angle E$.**

Step 2 Use a cosine ratio.

$$\cos D = \frac{5}{13}$$
$$m\angle D = \cos^{-1}\frac{5}{13}$$
$$\approx 67.38° \qquad \textbf{Use a calculator.}$$

● To the nearest tenth of a degree, $m\angle D$ is 67.4°.

 **Quick Check**   **4** Use a trigonometric ratio to find $m\angle A$ in each triangle.

a.

10

4

b.

5

9

5 **EXAMPLE**   **Real-World** **Connection**

Construction A wheelchair ramp must be constructed so the slope is not more than 1 in. of rise for every 1 ft of run. What is the maximum angle that the ramp can make with the ground, to the nearest tenth of a degree?

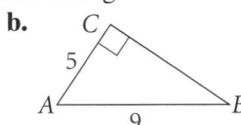

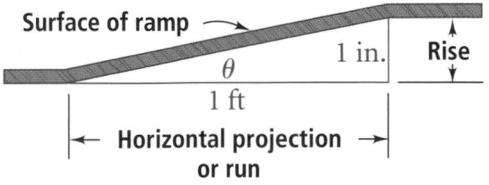

Surface of ramp

θ 1 in.   **Rise**

1 ft

← **Horizontal projection or run** →

Not drawn to scale

Let θ = the measure of the angle the ramp makes with the ground.

You know the length of the leg opposite the angle you need to find. You know the length of the leg adjacent to the angle you need to find. So, use the tangent ratio.

$$\tan \theta = \frac{1}{12} \qquad \textbf{Rewrite 1 ft as 12 in.}$$
$$\theta = \tan^{-1}\frac{1}{12} \qquad \textbf{Use the inverse of the tangent function.}$$
$$\theta \approx 4.8 \qquad \textbf{Use a calculator.}$$

● The angle between the ramp and the ground will be about 4.8°.

Real-World **Connection**

Federal regulations define allowable slopes for handicap-accessible facilities.

 **Quick Check**   **5** In $\triangle DEF$, $\angle F$ is a right angle, $d = 7$, and $f = 10$. Draw a diagram and find the remaining side length and angle degree measures. Round to the nearest tenth.

EXERCISES

For more exercises, see *Extra Skill and Word Problem Practice*.

Practice and Problem Solving

A Practice by Example

Example 1
(page 793)

 for Help

1. Ballooning From a hot-air balloon 3000 ft above the ground, you see a clearing whose angle of depression is 20°. Given that sin 20° ≈ 0.34, cos 20° ≈ 0.94, and tan 20° ≈ 0.36, find each distance to the nearest foot.

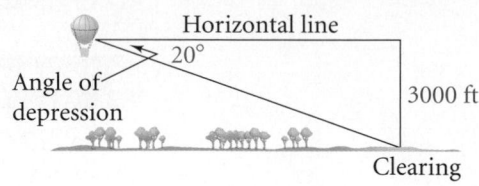

   a. your horizontal distance from the clearing
   b. your direct distance from the clearing

Example 2
(page 794)

2. In △ABC, find each value as a fraction and as a decimal. Round to the nearest hundredth.

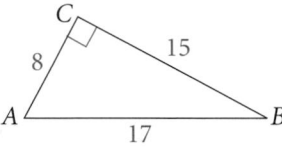

a. sin A	**b.** sec A
c. cot A	**d.** csc B
e. sec B	**f.** tan B

3. In △GHI, ∠H is a right angle, GH = 40, and cos G = $\frac{40}{41}$. Draw a diagram and find each value in fraction and in decimal form.

   a. sin G   **b.** sin I   **c.** cot G
   d. csc G   **e.** cos I   **f.** sec H

4. In △PQR, ∠R is a right angle and cot P = $\frac{5}{12}$. Draw a diagram. Find the values of the other five trigonometric functions of ∠P in fraction and in decimal form.

Example 3
(page 794)

Find each length *x*. Round to the nearest tenth.

5.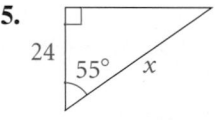

6.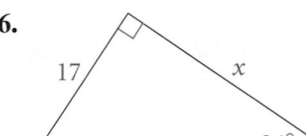

7.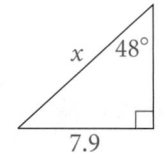

8. Indirect Measurement In 1915, the tallest flagpole in the world was in San Francisco.

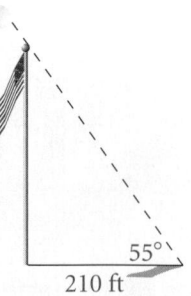

   a. When the angle of elevation of the sun was 55°, the length of the shadow cast by this flagpole was 210 ft. Find the height of the flagpole to the nearest foot.
   b. What was the length of the shadow when the angle of elevation of the sun was 34°?
   c. What do you need to assume about the flagpole and the shadow to solve these problems? Explain why.

Examples 4 and 5
(page 795)

Find each angle measure to the nearest tenth of a degree.

   9. $\cos^{-1} \frac{\sqrt{2}}{2}$ **10.** $\tan^{-1} 0.3333$ **11.** $\sin^{-1} \frac{3}{4}$

   12. $\tan^{-1} \sqrt{3}$ **13.** $\sin^{-1} 0.335$ **14.** $\cos^{-1} 0.992$

   15. $\tan^{-1} 3.552$ **16.** $\sin^{-1} 0.052$ **17.** $\cos^{-1} \frac{3}{8}$

In △ABC, ∠C is a right angle. Find the remaining sides and angles. Round your answers to the nearest tenth.

18. $b = 5, c = 10$ **19.** $a = 5, b = 6$ **20.** $b = 12, c = 15$

21. $a = 8.1, b = 6.2$ **22.** $b = 4.3, c = 9.1$ **23.** $a = 17, c = 22$

24. Rocketry An observer on the ground at point A watches a rocket ascend. The observer is 1200 ft from the launch point B. As the rocket rises, the distance d from the observer to the rocket increases.
   a. Write a model for $m\angle A$.
   b. Find $m\angle A$ if $d = 1500$ ft. Round your answer to the nearest degree.
   c. Find $m\angle A$ if $d = 2000$ ft. Round your answer to the nearest degree.

B Apply Your Skills

Sketch a right triangle with θ as the measure of one acute angle. Find the other five trigonometric ratios of θ.

25. $\sin \theta = \frac{3}{8}$ **26.** $\cos \theta = \frac{7}{20}$ **27.** $\cos \theta = \frac{1}{5}$

28. $\tan \theta = \frac{24}{7}$ **29.** $\csc \theta = \frac{21}{12}$ **30.** $\sec \theta = \frac{16}{9}$

31. $\cot \theta = \frac{5}{4}$ **32.** $\sin \theta = 0.35$ **33.** $\csc \theta = 5.2$

34. a. Engineering A radio tower has supporting cables attached to it at points 100 ft above the ground. Write a model for the length d of each supporting cable as a function of the angle θ that it makes with the ground.
   b. Find d when $\theta = 60°$ and when $\theta = 50°$.

In △ABC, ∠C is a right angle. Two measures are given. Find the remaining sides and angles. Round your answers to the nearest tenth.

35. $b = 8, c = 17$ **36.** $a = 7, b = 10$

37. $m\angle A = 52°, c = 10$ **38.** $m\angle A = 34.2°, b = 5.7$

39. $m\angle B = 17.2°, b = 8.3$ **40.** $m\angle B = 8.3°, c = 20$

41. A 150-ft pole casts a shadow 210 ft long. Find the measure of the angle of elevation of the sun.

42. Indirect Measurement A transit is 330 ft from the base of a building. The angles of elevation of the top and bottom of a flagpole situated on top of the building are 55° and 53°. Find the height of the flagpole.

43. Geometry An altitude inside a triangle forms angles of 36° and 42° with two of the sides. The altitude is 5 m long. Find the area of the triangle.

44. Construction When a crane's boom is at an angle of 70°, the top is 128 ft high. (See the diagram at the right.) How long is the boom? How far is the crane's cab from the bottom of the free-fall path of something dropped from the top of the boom?

45. a. In Example 4, use the Pythagorean Theorem to find EF.
   b. Use a trigonometric ratio to find EF.

46. Open-Ended If $\sin \theta = \frac{1}{2}$, describe a method you could use to find all the angles between 0° and 360° that satisfy this equation.

47. Reasoning Show that $\cos A$ defined as a ratio equals $\cos \theta$ using the unit circle.

GO for Help

For a guide to solving Exercise 42, see p. 800.

48. Baseball The bases on a baseball diamond form a square 90 ft on a side. The pitcher's plate is 60 ft 6 in. from the back corner of home plate.

a. About how far is the pitcher's plate from second base?

b. A line drive is 10 ft high when it passes over the third baseman, who is 100 ft from home plate. At what angle did the ball leave the bat? (Assume the ball is 4 ft above the ground when it is hit.)

 Challenge

Use the definitions of trigonometric ratios in right △ABC to verify each identity.

49. $\sec A = \dfrac{1}{\cos A}$ **50.** $\tan A = \dfrac{\sin A}{\cos A}$ **51.** $\cos^2 A + \sin^2 A = 1$

52. a. In △DEF below, h is the length of an altitude. Find h to the nearest tenth.
     b. For DF = 10.8, find the area of △DEF to the nearest tenth.
     c. Find the area of △RST to the nearest tenth.

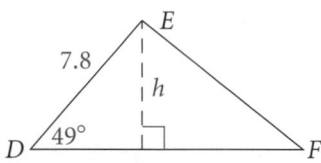

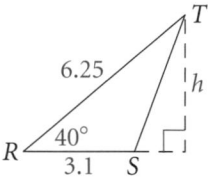

Vocabulary Tip

A regular polygon has congruent sides and congruent angles.

 53. Geometry A regular pentagon is inscribed in a circle of radius 10 cm.
     a. Find the measure of ∠C.
     b. Find the length of the diagonal PS.
     (*Hint:* First find RS.)

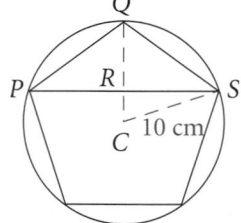

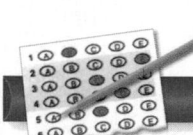 **Test Prep**

Multiple Choice

54. A ladder rests against a vertical building, as shown at the right. The ladder is 14 ft long and forms an angle of 76.5° with the ground. Which statement is NOT true?

   A. The bottom of the ladder is 13.6 ft from the base of the building.

   B. The bottom of the ladder is 3.3 ft from the base of the building.

   C. The top of the ladder is 13.6 ft from the ground.

   D. The ladder forms an angle of 13.5° with the building.

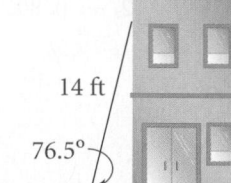

55. The sides of a rectangle are 25 cm and 8 cm. What is the measure of the angle formed by the short side and a diagonal of the rectangle?

   F. 17.7°   **G.** 18.7°   **H.** 71.3°   **J.** 72.3°

56. The figure at the right is a rectangle. What is the value of x?

A. 31.0   B. 36.9
C. 53.1   D. 59.0

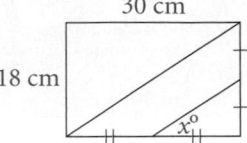
30 cm
18 cm
$x°$

57. In $\triangle XYZ$, $\angle Z$ is a right angle and $\tan X = \frac{8}{15}$. What is $\sin Y$?

F. $\frac{8}{17}$ G. $\frac{15}{17}$ H. $\frac{17}{15}$ J. $\frac{15}{8}$

58. In the right triangle at the right, $\cos y° = \frac{5}{13}$. If $x + 2z = 7.1$, what is the value of z?

A. 67.3   B. 22.6
C. −7.76   D. −30.1

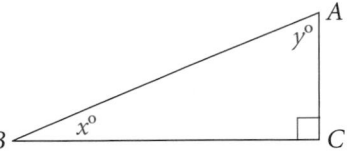
A
$y°$
B $x°$
C

Short Response

59. Find the measures of the acute angles of a right triangle, to the nearest tenth, if the legs are 135 cm and 95 cm.

Mixed Review

Lesson 14-2

Find the complete solution of each equation. Express your answer in degrees.

60. $\sec^2 \theta + \sec \theta = 0$ **61.** $2 \cos^2 \theta + 1 = 0$

62. $\cot \theta = \cot^2 \theta$ **63.** $\sin^2 \theta + 5 \sin \theta = 0$

Lesson 13-7

Graph each function in the interval from 0 to 2π.

64. $y = \sin (x - \pi) + 4$ **65.** $y = 3 \sin 2\left(x + \frac{\pi}{2}\right) - 5$

66. $y = \cos (x + \pi) - 3$ **67.** $y = -2 \cos \left(x - \frac{\pi}{3}\right) - 4$

Lesson 12-6

Use the binomial expansion of $(p + q)^n$ to calculate and graph each binomial distribution.

68. $n = 8, p = 0.2$ **69.** $n = 8, p = 0.4$ **70.** $n = 8, p = 0.8$

✓ Checkpoint Quiz 1   Lessons 14-1 through 14-3

Simplify each trigonometric expression.

1. $\sec \theta \cot \theta$ **2.** $\sec^2 \theta - 1$ **3.** $-1 - \cot^2 \theta$

Find the value of each expression to the nearest thousandth.

4. $\cos^{-1}\left(-\frac{\pi}{5}\right)$ **5.** $\sin^{-1} \frac{\pi}{10}$ **6.** $\tan^{-1} 4.35$

In $\triangle ABC$, $\angle C$ is a right angle. Find the remaining sides and angles. Round your answers to the nearest tenth.

7. $b = 14, c = 16$ **8.** $a = 7.9, b = 6.2$ **9.** $b = 29, c = 35$

10. Open-Ended Draw a right triangle. Measure the lengths of two sides, and then find the remaining sides and angles without measuring.

Understanding Word Problems Read the problem below. Then follow along with what Christiana thinks and writes. Check your understanding by solving the exercises at the bottom of the page.

Indirect Measurement A transit is 330 ft from the base of a building. The angles of elevation of the top and bottom of a flagpole situated on top of the building are 55° and 53°. Find the height of the flagpole.

What Christiana Thinks

A diagram will help me solve the problem.

I need the building, the flagpole on top, and two angles on the ground. One goes to the top of the pole and the other to the bottom. I'll use x and y for heights.

Aha! The height of the flagpole is $x - y$!

x is opposite the 55° angle.

330 is adjacent to the 55° angle.

I can use the tangent ratio to find x.

y is opposite the 53° angle and 330 is still the adjacent side. I can use tangent again to find y.

The height of the flagpole is $x - y$.

What Christiana Writes

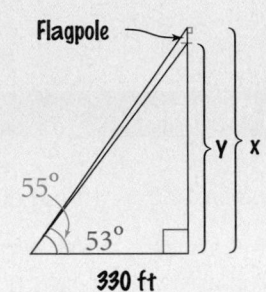

Flagpole

55°
53°
330 ft

$$\frac{x}{330} = \tan 55°$$
$$x = 330 \tan 55°$$
$$x \approx 471.3$$

$$\frac{y}{330} = \tan 53°$$
$$y = 330 \tan 53°$$
$$y \approx 437.9$$

$$\text{Height} = x - y$$
$$\approx 471.3 - 437.9$$
$$= 33.4$$

The height of the flagpole is 33.4 ft.

EXERCISES

1. A monument has a cylindrical base and a tall spire. You are standing 50 ft from the center of the base. The top and the bottom of the spire have elevation angles of 62° and 42°, respectively. How tall is the spire to the nearest foot?

2. You are standing 250 ft from the town water tower. The top and the bottom of the tank at the top of the tower have angles of elevation of 22° and 15° respectively. What is the height of the water tank to the nearest foot?

14-4

Area and the Law of Sines

What You'll Learn

- To find the area of any triangle and to use the Law of Sines

. . . And Why

To measure heights, as in Example 4

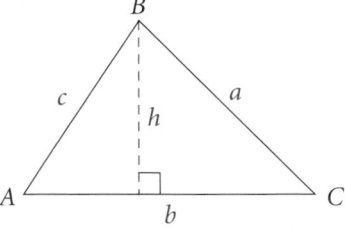

✓ Check Skills You'll Need

GO for Help Lesson 13-4

Simplify each expression.

1. $\dfrac{\sin 30°}{6}$ 2. $\dfrac{\sin 45°}{4}$ 3. $\dfrac{\sin 60°}{10}$

4. $\dfrac{\sin 30°}{12}$ 5. $\dfrac{\sin 45°}{8}$ 6. $\dfrac{\sin 60°}{9}$

Find the area of a triangle with the given base b and height h.

7. $b = 3$ cm, $h = 4$ cm   8. $b = 6$ in., $h = 15$ in.

9. $b = 5.2$ mm, $h = 12.6$ mm   10. $b = 6.17$ ft, $h = 3.25$ ft

◀) New Vocabulary ● **Law of Sines**

---

1 **Area and the Law of Sines**

Vocabulary Tip

An <u>oblique</u> <u>triangle</u> is a triangle that does not contain a right angle.

The formula for the area K of a triangle is $K = \frac{1}{2}bh$.

In any oblique $\triangle ABC$ with side lengths $a, b,$ and $c, h = c \sin A$. Therefore $K = \frac{1}{2}bh = \frac{1}{2}bc \sin A$. Similarly, $K = \frac{1}{2}ac \sin B$ and $K = \frac{1}{2}ab \sin C$.

1 EXAMPLE **Finding the Area of a Triangle**

Find the area of the triangle at the right.

In the triangle, $b = 5, c = 10,$ and $m\angle A = 31°$.

$K = \frac{1}{2}bc \sin A = \frac{1}{2}(5)(10) \sin 31°$

≈ 12.9

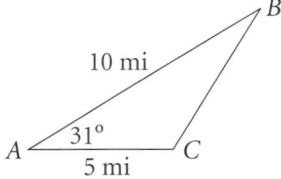

● The area is about 12.9 mi².

✓ Quick Check **1** A triangle has sides of lengths 12 in. and 15 in., and the measure of the angle between them is 24°. Find the area of the triangle.

Combining the three equations for the area of $\triangle ABC$ yields a useful formula.

$\frac{1}{2}bc \sin A = \frac{1}{2}ac \sin B = \frac{1}{2}ab \sin C$ **Transitive Property of Equality**

$\dfrac{\sin A}{a} = \dfrac{\sin B}{b} = \dfrac{\sin C}{c}$ **Divide by $\frac{1}{2}abc$.**

This relationship of the lengths of the sides of any triangle to the sines of the angles opposite them is known as the **Law of Sines.**

Theorem	Law of Sines

In $\triangle ABC$, let a, b, and c represent the lengths of the sides opposite $\angle A$, $\angle B$, and $\angle C$, respectively.

Then $\dfrac{\sin A}{a} = \dfrac{\sin B}{b} = \dfrac{\sin C}{c}$.

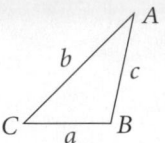

Vocabulary Tip

In math, <u>law</u> refers to a general property. The Law of Sines could have been named the Property of Sines.

You can use the Law of Sines to find missing measures of any triangle when you know the measures of

- two angles and any side, or
- two sides and the angle opposite one of them.

In Example 2, you are given the measures of two angles and a side.

2 EXAMPLE **Finding a Side of a Triangle**

In $\triangle PQR$, $m\angle R = 39°$, $m\angle Q = 32°$, and $PQ = 40$ cm. Find RQ.

Step 1 Draw and label a diagram.

Step 2 Find the measure of the angle opposite $\overline{RQ}$.

$m\angle P = 180° - 39° - 32° = 109°$

Step 3 Find RQ.

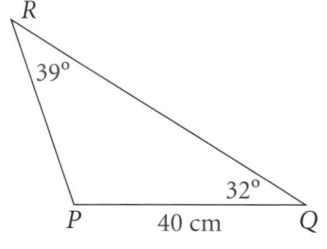

$\dfrac{\sin 109°}{RQ} = \dfrac{\sin 39°}{40}$ **Law of Sines**

$RQ = \dfrac{40 \sin 109°}{\sin 39°}$ **Solve for RQ.**

$RQ \approx 60.1$ cm **Use a calculator.**

 **②** In $\triangle KLM$, $m\angle K = 120°$, $m\angle M = 50°$, and $ML = 35$ yd. Find KL.

In Example 3, you are given the measures of two sides and an angle opposite one of the sides.

3 EXAMPLE **Finding an Angle of a Triangle**

In $\triangle RST$, $t = 7$, $r = 9$, and $m\angle R = 110°$. Find $m\angle S$.

Step 1 Draw and label a diagram.

Step 2 Find the measure of the angle opposite t.

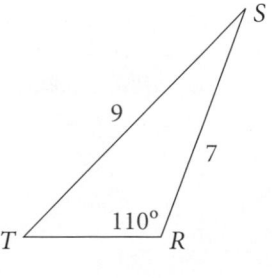

$\dfrac{\sin T}{7} = \dfrac{\sin 110°}{9}$ **Law of Sines.**

$\sin T = \dfrac{7 \sin 110°}{9}$ **Solve for sin T.**

$m\angle T = \sin^{-1}\left(\dfrac{7 \sin 110°}{9}\right)$ **Solve for $m\angle T$.**

$m\angle T \approx 47°$ **Use a calculator.**

Step 3 Find the measure of $\angle S$.

$m\angle S \approx 180° - 110° - 47° = 23°$

 **③** In $\triangle PQR$, $m\angle R = 97.5°$, $r = 80$, and $p = 75$. Find $m\angle P$.

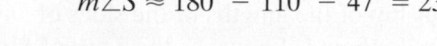

Surveyors can use the Law of Sines to measure the height of a mountain indirectly.

 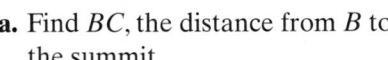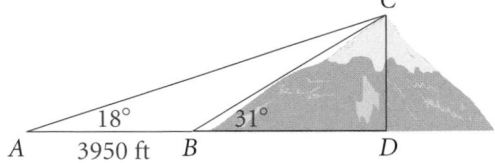
Surveying A surveyor locates points A and B at the same elevation and 3950 ft apart. At A, the angle of elevation to the summit of the mountain is 18°. At B, the angle of elevation is 31°.

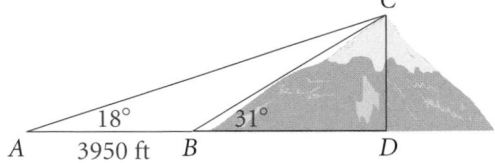

a. Find BC, the distance from B to the summit.

First find $m\angle ABC$ and $m\angle ACB$.

$m\angle ABC = 180° - 31° = 149°$
$m\angle ACB = 180° - 18° - 149° = 13°$

Now use the Law of Sines in $\triangle ABC$. Write a proportion that includes the side you know, AB, and the side you want, BC.

$\dfrac{\sin A}{BC} = \dfrac{\sin C}{AB}$ **Law of Sines**

$\dfrac{\sin 18°}{BC} = \dfrac{\sin 13°}{3950}$ **Substitute.**

$BC = \dfrac{3950 \sin 18°}{\sin 13°}$ **Solve for BC.**

$BC \approx 5426$ **Simplify.**

The distance from B to the summit is about 5426 ft.

b. Find CD, the height of the mountain.

In right $\triangle BCD$, you know BC and $m\angle B$. Use the sine ratio.

$\sin 31° \approx \dfrac{CD}{5426}$ **Definition of Sine**

$CD \approx 5426 \sin 31°$ **Solve for CD.**

$CD \approx 2795$ **Use a calculator.**

The summit is about 2795 ft higher than points A and B.

Quick Check **4** In $\triangle MNP$, $m\angle M = 35°$, $m\angle N = 120°$, and $MN = 48$. Find the length of the altitude of $\triangle MNP$ from vertex P.

The modern transit measures distances with a laser beam and stores data electronically.

EXERCISES

For more exercises, see *Extra Skill and Word Problem Practice.*

Practice and Problem Solving

 Practice by Example

Example 1
(page 801)

Find the area of each triangle. Round your answer to the nearest tenth.

1.

8 cm

51°

6 cm

2.

10 in.

15°

7 in.

3.

15 m

97°

11 m

4. A triangle has sides of lengths 10 cm and 16 cm, and the measure of the angle between them is 130°. Find the area of the triangle.

Example 2
(page 802)

Use the Law of Sines. Find the measure *x* to the nearest tenth.

5.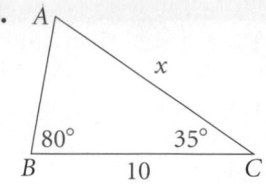

6.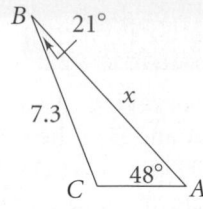

7.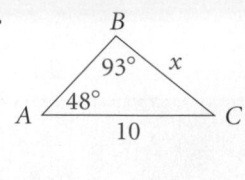

8. In $\triangle RST, m\angle R = 78°, m\angle T = 39°$, and $TS = 19$ in. Find RS.

9. In $\triangle JKL, m\angle L = 64°, j = 18$ m, and $m\angle K = 36°$. Find k.

10. In $\triangle RNP, m\angle N = 58°, n = 20$ in., and $m\angle R = 42°$. Find r.

Example 3
(page 802)

Use the Law of Sines. Find the measure *x* to the nearest tenth.

11.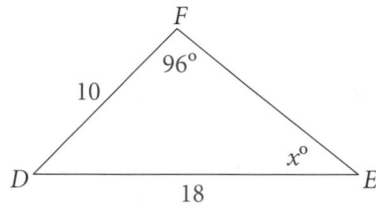

12.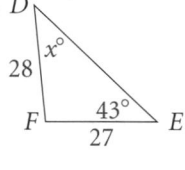

13. In $\triangle DEF, m\angle F = 43°, d = 16$ mm, and $f = 24$ mm. Find $m\angle D$.

14. In $\triangle ABC, m\angle A = 52°, c = 10$ ft, and $a = 15$ ft. Find $m\angle C$.

15. In $\triangle XYZ, m\angle Z = 33°, z = 35$ cm, and $x = 31$ cm. Find $m\angle X$.

Example 4
(page 803)

16. Surveying The distance from point *A* to the top of the hill is 2760 ft. The angle of elevation from *A* to the base of the tower is 28° and the angle of elevation from *A* to the top of the tower is 32°.

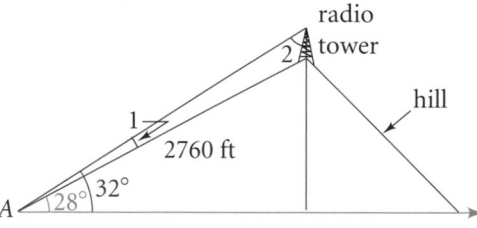

a. Find the measures of ∠1 and ∠2.
b. Find to the nearest foot the height of the tower above the top of the hill.

B **Apply Your Skills**

Find the remaining sides and angles in each triangle. Round your answers to the nearest tenth.

17.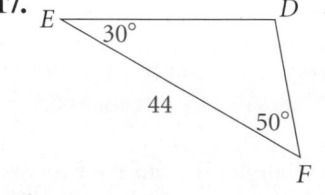

18.

19.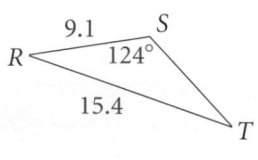

20.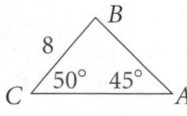

21.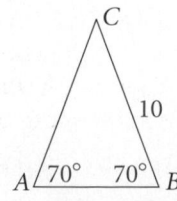

22.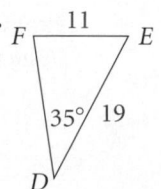

23. In $\triangle DEF, m\angle D = 54°, m\angle E = 54°$, and $d = 20$ in.

24. In $\triangle DEF, m\angle D = 54°, e = 8$ m, and $d = 10$ m.

804 Chapter 14 Trigonometric Identities and Equations

GO **O**nline
Homework Video Tutor
Visit: PHSchool.com
Web Code: age-1404

25. Critical Thinking In $\triangle ABC$, $a = 10$ and $b = 15$.
  a. Does the triangle have a greater area when $m\angle C = 1°$ or when $m\angle C = 50°$?
  b. Does the triangle have a greater area when $m\angle C = 50°$ or when $m\angle C = 179°$?
  c. For what measure of $\angle C$ does $\triangle ABC$ have the greatest area? Explain.

26. a. Open-Ended Sketch a triangle. Specify three of its measures so that you can use the Law of Sines to find the remaining measures.
  b. Solve for the remaining measures of the triangle.

 27. Forestry A forest ranger in an observation tower sights a fire 39° east of north. A ranger in a tower 10 miles due east of the first tower sights the fire at 42° west of north. How far is the fire from each tower?

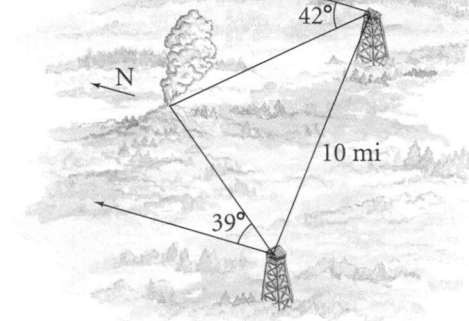

28. Geometry One of the congruent sides of an isosceles triangle is 10 cm long. One of the congruent angles has a measure of 54°. Find the perimeter of the triangle. Round your answer to the nearest centimeter.

29. Geometry The sides of a triangle are 15 in., 17 in., and 16 in. long. The smallest angle has a measure of 54°. Find the measure of the largest angle. Round your answer to the nearest degree.

Find the area of $\triangle ABC$. Round your answer to the nearest tenth.

30. $m\angle C = 68°$, $b = 12.9$, $c = 15.2$ **31.** $m\angle A = 52°$, $a = 9.71$, $c = 9.33$

32. $m\angle A = 23°$, $m\angle C = 39°$, $b = 14.6$ **33.** $m\angle B = 87°$, $a = 10.1$, $c = 9.8$

34. $m\angle A = 96°$, $m\angle C = 18°$, $a = 43.4$ **35.** $m\angle C = 33°$, $a = 1.2$, $b = 0.9$

36. $m\angle B = 40°$, $m\angle C = 80°$, $c = 5.5$ **37.** $m\angle A = 20°$, $b = 1$, $c = 5$

In $\triangle ABC$, $m\angle A = 40°$ and $m\angle B = 30°$. Find each value to the nearest tenth.

38. Find AC for $BC = 10.5$ m.   **39.** Find BC for $AC = 21.8$ ft.

40. Find AC for $AB = 81.2$ yd.   **41.** Find BC for $AB = 5.9$ cm.

 42. Measurement A vacant lot is in the shape of an isosceles triangle. It is between two streets that intersect at an 85.9° angle. Each of the sides of the lot that face these streets is 150 ft long. Find the length of the third side, to the nearest foot.

 **Challenge**   **43. Sailing** Buoys are located in the sea at points A, B, and C. $\angle ACB$ is a right angle. $AC = 3.0$ mi, $BC = 4.0$ mi, and $AB = 5.0$ mi. A ship is located at point D on $\overline{AB}$ so that $m\angle ACD = 30°$. How far is the ship from the buoy at point C? Round your answer to the nearest tenth of a mile.

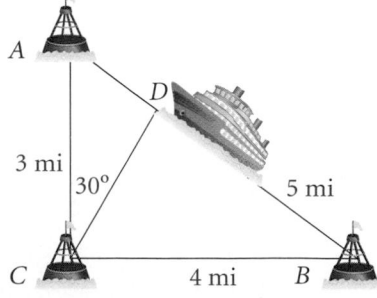

44. Writing Suppose you know the measures of all three angles of a triangle. Can you use the Law of Sines to find the lengths of the sides? Explain.

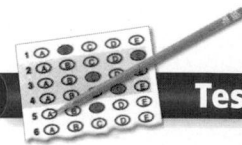

B

10

6   6

30°

A   C   D

45. **a.** In the diagram at the left, $m\angle A = 30°$, $AB = 10$, and $BC = BD = 6$. Use the Law of Sines to find $m\angle D$.
   b. Find $m\angle ABD$ and $m\angle ABC$.
   c. Reasoning Notice that two sides and a nonincluded angle of $\triangle ABC$ are congruent to the corresponding parts of $\triangle ABD$, but the triangles are not congruent. Must $\triangle EFG$ be congruent to $\triangle ABD$ if $EF = 10$, $FG = 6$, and $\angle E \cong \angle A$? Explain.

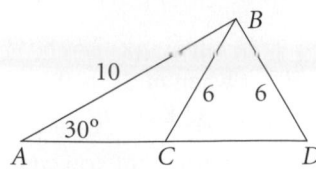

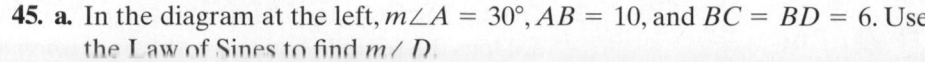

Multiple Choice

46. In $\triangle GDL$, $m\angle D = 57°$, $DL = 10.1$, and $GL = 9.4$. What is the best estimate for $m\angle G$?
   A. 64°   **B.** 51°   **C.** 39°   **D.** 26°

47. For which set of given information can you compute the area of a triangle?
   F. Given: the length of one side and the measure of the angle opposite it
   G. Given: the length of one side and the measure of an angle adjacent to it
   H. Given: the lengths of two sides and the measure of a nonincluded angle
   J. Given: the lengths of two sides and the measure of the included angle

48. A surveyor picks two points 250 m apart in front of a tall building. The angle of elevation from one point is 37°. The angle of elevation from the other point is 13°. What is the best estimate for the height of the building?
   A. 150 m   **B.** 138 m   **C.** 83 m   **D.** 56 m

Short Response

49. Two sides of a scalene triangle are 9 m and 14 m. The area of the triangle is 31.5 m². Find the measure of one of the angles of the triangle to the nearest tenth of a degree. Show your work.

Use the diagram for Exercises 50 and 51.

50. Let $m\angle N = 30°$. Find the measures of the other two angles to the nearest degree.

51. Let $m\angle M = 45°$. Find the area of the triangle to the nearest tenth of a square centimeter. Show your work.

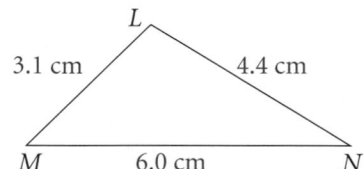

L

3.1 cm   4.4 cm

M   6.0 cm   N

Mixed Review

Lesson 14-3   **Find each angle measure to the nearest tenth of a degree.**

52. $\cos^{-1} \frac{3}{5}$ 53. $\tan^{-1} 0.4569$ 54. $\sin^{-1} \frac{5}{8}$ 55. $\tan^{-1} \sqrt{2}$

In $\triangle ABC$, $\angle B$ is a right angle. Find the remaining sides and angles. Round your answers to the nearest tenth.

56. $b = 5, c = 4$ 57. $a = 3, c = 3$ 58. $a = 10, b = 15$

59. $a = 1.6, c = 8.1$ 60. $a = 4.1, b = 9.4$ 61. $b = 100, c = 45$

Lesson 13-4   **Sketch one cycle of the graph of each sine function.**

62. $y = 4 \sin \theta$ 63. $y = 4 \sin \pi\theta$ 64. $y = \sin 4\theta$

Lesson 12-4   65. A set of values has a mean of 36 and a standard deviation of 5. Find the z-score of the value 43.

The Ambiguous Case

The triangles at the right have one pair of congruent angles and two pairs of congruent sides. But the triangles are not congruent. Notice that each of the congruent angles is opposite one of the congruent sides.

When you know the measures of two sides of a triangle and one of the opposite angles, there may be two triangles with those measurements. You can use the Law of Sines to find the other measures for both triangles.

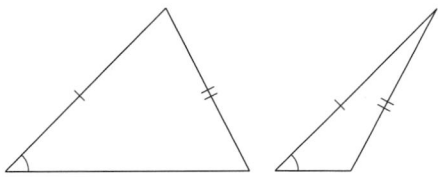

EXAMPLE

In each $\triangle ABC$ at the right, $m\angle A = 35°$, $a = 11$, and $b = 15$. Find $m\angle B$.

$\dfrac{\sin A}{a} = \dfrac{\sin B}{b}$ **Law of Sines**

$\dfrac{\sin 35°}{11} = \dfrac{\sin B}{15}$ **Substitute.**

$\sin B = \dfrac{15 \sin 35°}{11}$ **Solve for sin B.**

$m\angle B \approx \sin^{-1}\left(\dfrac{15 \sin 35°}{11}\right)$ **Find one value of m∠B.**

$m\angle B \approx 51°$ **Use a calculator.**

The sine function is also positive in Quadrant II. So another value of $m\angle B$ is about $180° - 51° = 129°$.

Because there are two possible angle measures for $\angle B$, there are two triangles that satisfy the given conditions. In one triangle the angle measures are about 35°, 51°, and 94°. In the other, the angle measures are about 35°, 129°, and 16°.

EXERCISES

In each $\triangle ABC$, find the measures for $\angle B$ and $\angle C$ that satisfy the given conditions. Draw diagrams to help you decide whether two triangles are possible. Remember that a triangle can have only one obtuse angle.

1. $m\angle A = 62°$, $a = 30$, and $b = 32$

2. $m\angle A = 16°$, $a = 12$, and $b = 37.5$

3. $m\angle A = 48°$, $a = 93$, and $b = 125$

4. $m\angle A = 112°$, $a = 16.5$, and $b = 5.4$

5. $m\angle A = 23.6°$, $a = 9.8$, and $b = 17$

6. $m\angle A = 155°$, $a = 12.5$, and $b = 8.4$

7. Multiple Choice You can construct a triangle with compass and straightedge when given three parts of the triangle (except for three angles). Which of the following given sets could result in the ambiguous case?
   Ⓐ Given: three sides
   Ⓑ Given: two sides and an included angle
   Ⓒ Given: two sides and a nonincluded angle
   Ⓓ Given: two angles and a nonincluded side

The Law of Cosines

What You'll Learn

• To use the Law of Cosines in finding the measures of sides and angles of a triangle

... And Why

To find the length of a sailing course, as in Example 1

✓ **Check Skills You'll Need**

Use the Law of Sines.

1. In $\triangle ABC$, $m\angle C = 33°$, $a = 17$, and $c = 21$. Find $m\angle A$.

2. In $\triangle RST$, $m\angle R = 59°$, $m\angle S = 45°$, and $r = 16$. Find t.

3. In $\triangle DEF$, $m\angle D = 55°$, $d = 18$, and $e = 21$. Find $m\angle F$.

GO ▶ **for Help** Lesson 14-4

◀)) **New Vocabulary** • Law of Cosines

---

1 The Law of Cosines

Since you can't use the Law of Sines to find the missing measures in the triangles at the right, another formula is needed.

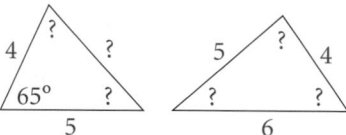

In this oblique $\triangle ABC$ with altitude h, let $AD = x$.

Then $DB = c - x$.

In $\triangle ADC$,
$b^2 = x^2 + h^2$ and
$\cos A = \frac{x}{b}$ or $x = b \cos A$.

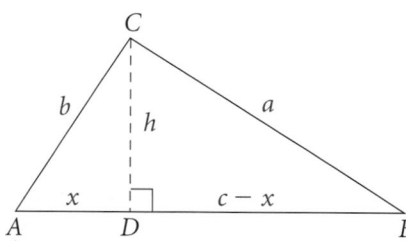

In $\triangle CBD$,

$a^2 = (c - x)^2 + h^2$	**Pythagorean Theorem**
$= c^2 - 2cx + x^2 + h^2$	**Square the binomial.**
$= c^2 - 2cx + b^2$	**Substitute b^2 for $x^2 + h^2$.**
$= c^2 - 2cb \cos A + b^2$	**Substitute $b \cos A$ for x.**
$= b^2 + c^2 - 2bc \cos A$	**Commutative Property of Addition**

The last equation relates the length of a side of any triangle to the measure of the opposite angle. It applies to any of the three sides and is called the **Law of Cosines.**

 Key Concepts

Theorem	**Law of Cosines**

In $\triangle ABC$, let a, b, and c represent the lengths of the sides opposite $\angle A$, $\angle B$, and $\angle C$, respectively.

$$a^2 = b^2 + c^2 - 2bc \cos A$$

$$b^2 = a^2 + c^2 - 2ac \cos B$$

$$c^2 = a^2 + b^2 - 2ab \cos C$$

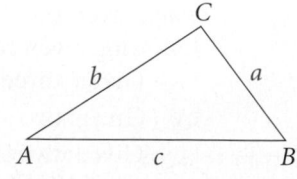

You can use the Law of Cosines to find missing measures in any triangle when you know the measures of

- two sides and the angle between them, or
- all three sides.

In this example, you are given the measures of two sides and the included angle.

1 EXAMPLE **Real-World 🌐 Connection**

Multiple Choice A racing committee wants to lay out a triangular course with a 40° angle between two sides of 3.5 mi and 2.5 mi. What will be the length of the third side?

Ⓐ 2.0 mi   Ⓑ 2.3 mi   Ⓒ 9.8 mi   Ⓓ 30.2 mi

Choose the form of the Law of Cosines that has a^2 on one side.

$a^2 = b^2 + c^2 - 2bc \cos A$

$a^2 = 2.5^2 + 3.5^2 - 2(2.5)(3.5) \cos 40°$ **Substitute.**

$\quad \approx 5.094$ **Use a calculator.**

$a \approx 2.3$ **Use a calculator.**

The third side of the triangular course will be about 2.3 mi long.

● The correct choice is B.

✓ **Quick Check** ❶ The lengths of two sides of a triangle are 8 and 10, and the measure of the angle between them is 40°. Find the length of the third side.

In this example, you are given the measures of three sides.

2 EXAMPLE **Finding an Angle Measure**

Find the measure of $\angle C$ in the triangle below. Round your answer to the nearest tenth of a degree.

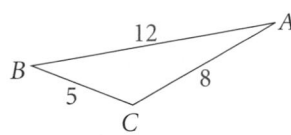

Choose the form of the Law of Cosines that contains $\angle C$.

$\quad c^2 = a^2 + b^2 - 2ab \cos C$

$\quad 12^2 = 5^2 + 8^2 - 2(5)(8) \cos C$ **Substitute.**

$\quad 144 = 25 + 64 - 80 \cos C$ **Simplify.**

$\quad 55 = -80 \cos C$ **Combine like terms.**

$\quad -\frac{55}{80} = \cos C$ **Solve for cos C.**

$\cos^{-1}\left(-\frac{55}{80}\right) = m\angle C$ **Solve for m∠C.**

$\quad m\angle C \approx 133.4°$ **Use a calculator.**

✓ **Quick Check** ❷ The lengths of the sides of a triangle are 10, 14, and 15. Find the measure of the angle opposite the longest side.

Sometimes you need to use the Law of Cosines followed by the Law of Cosines again or by the Law of Sines.

3 EXAMPLE Finding an Angle Measure

In $\triangle ABC$, $b = 6.2$, $c = 7.8$, and $m\angle A = 45°$. Find $m\angle B$.

Step 1 Draw a diagram.

Step 2 Find a. Since you cannot find $m\angle B$ directly, use the Law of Cosines to find a.

$a^2 = b^2 + c^2 - 2bc \cos A$

$a^2 = 6.2^2 + 7.8^2 - 2(6.2)(7.8) \cos 45°$ **Substitute.**

≈ 30.89 **Simplify.**

$a \approx \sqrt{30.89}$ **Solve for a.**

$a \approx 5.56$ **Find the principal square root.**

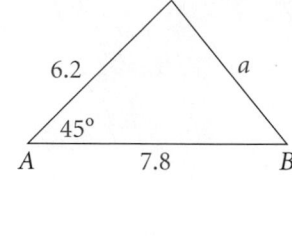

Problem Solving Hint

To help remember the formulas for the Law of Cosines, notice that the first and last letters are the same and the last one is capitalized.

Step 3 Now you can use the Law of Sines or the Law of Cosines to find $m\angle B$.

$\dfrac{\sin B}{6.2} \approx \dfrac{\sin 45°}{5.56}$ **Law of Sines**

$\sin B \approx \dfrac{6.2 \sin 45°}{5.56}$ **Solve for sin B.**

$m\angle B \approx \sin^{-1}\left(\dfrac{6.2 \sin 45°}{5.56}\right)$ **Solve for $m\angle B$. ($\angle B$ is not obtuse because $b < c$.)**

$\approx 52°$ **Use a calculator.**

✔**Quick Check** ❸ In $\triangle RST$, $s = 41$, $t = 53$, and $m\angle R = 126°$. Find $m\angle T$.

EXERCISES

For more exercises, see *Extra Skill and Word Problem Practice.*

Practice and Problem Solving

Ⓐ **Practice by Example**

Example 1
(page 809)

GO for Help

Use the Law of Cosines. Find the length of x to the nearest tenth.

1.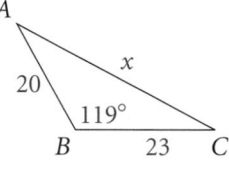

2.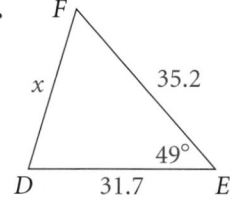

3.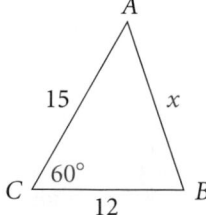

4. In $\triangle DEF$, $m\angle E = 54°$, $d = 14$ ft, and $f = 20$ ft. Find e.

5. In $\triangle RST$, $m\angle T = 32°$, $r = 10$ cm, and $s = 17$ cm. Find t.

6. In $\triangle ABC$, $m\angle B = 52°$, $a = 15$ in., and $c = 10$ in. Find b.

Example 2
(page 809)

Use the Law of Cosines. Find the measure of x to the nearest tenth of a degree.

7.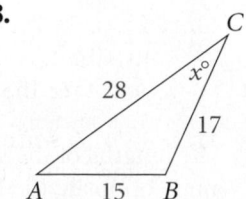

8.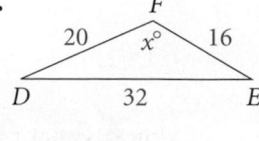

9.

10. In $\triangle DEF$, $d = 15$ in., $e = 18$ in., and $f = 10$ in. Find $m\angle F$.

11. In $\triangle ABC$, $a = 20$ m, $b = 14$ m, and $c = 16$ m. Find $m\angle A$.

12. In $\triangle DEF$, $d = 12$ ft, $e = 10$ ft, and $f = 9$ ft. Find $m\angle F$.

Example 3
(page 810)

Use the Law of Cosines and the Law of Sines. Find x to the nearest tenth.

13.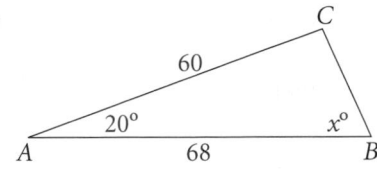

14.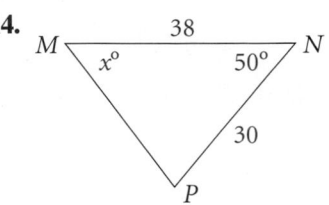

15. In $\triangle ABC$, $b = 4$ in., $c = 6$ in., and $m\angle A = 69°$. Find $m\angle C$.

16. In $\triangle RST$, $r = 17$ cm, $s = 12$ cm, and $m\angle T = 13°$. Find $m\angle S$.

17. In $\triangle DEF$, $d = 20$ ft, $e = 25$ ft, and $m\angle F = 98°$. Find $m\angle D$.

B **Apply Your Skills**

For each triangle, write the correct form of the Law of Cosines or the Law of Sines to solve for the measure in red. Use only the information given in blue.

18.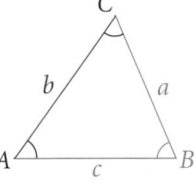

19.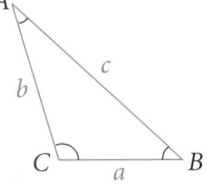

20.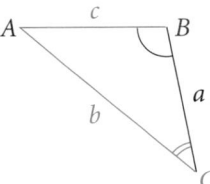

21.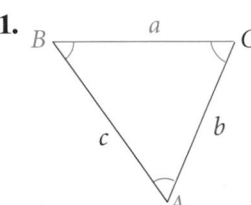

22.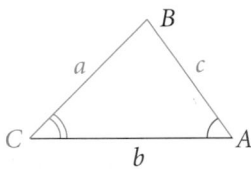

23.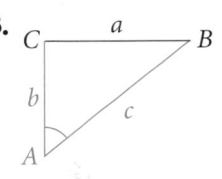

Find the remaining sides and angles in each triangle. Round your answers to the nearest tenth.

24.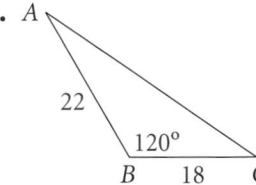

25.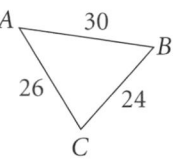

26.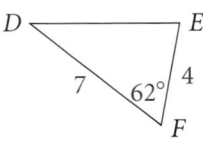

27.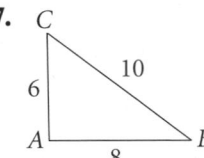

28.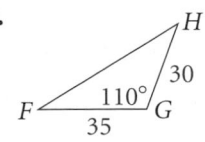

29.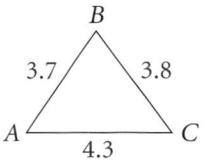

30. a. Open-Ended Sketch a triangle. Specify three of its measures so that you can use the Law of Cosines to find the remaining measures.
  b. Solve for the remaining measures of the triangle.

31. Sports A softball diamond is a square that is 65 ft on a side. The pitcher's mound is 46 ft from home plate. How far is the pitcher from third base?

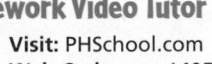

GO **Online**
Homework Video Tutor
Visit: PHSchool.com
Web Code: age-1405

Real-World Connection

Careers Pilots need navigation skills that include plotting a course on an aeronautical chart and computing flight time, headings, and fuel requirements.

 32. Writing Given the measures of three angles of a triangle, explain how to find the ratio of the lengths of two sides of the triangle.

 33. Geometry The lengths of the sides of a triangle are 7.6 cm, 8.2 cm, and 5.2 cm. Find the measure of the largest angle.

34. Navigation A pilot is flying from city A to city B, which is 85 mi due north. After flying 20 mi, the pilot must change course and fly 10° east of north to avoid a cloudbank.
   a. If the pilot remains on this course for 20 mi, how far will the plane be from city B?
   b. How many degrees will the pilot have to turn to the left to fly directly to city B? How many degrees from due north is this course?

In △ABC, m∠A = 53° and c = 7 cm. Find each value to the nearest tenth.

35. Find $m\angle B$ for $b = 6.2$ cm.   **36.** Find a for $b = 13.7$ cm.

37. Find a for $b = 11$ cm.   **38.** Find $m\angle C$ for $b = 15.2$ cm.

39. Find $m\angle B$ for $b = 37$ cm.   **40.** Find a for $b = 16$ cm.

In △RST, t = 7 ft and s = 13 ft. Find each value to the nearest tenth.

41. Find $m\angle T$ for $r = 11$ ft.   **42.** Find $m\angle T$ for $r = 6.97$ ft.

43. Find $m\angle S$ for $r = 14$ ft.   **44.** Find r for $m\angle R = 35°$.

45. Find $m\angle S$ for $m\angle R = 87°$.   **46.** Find $m\angle R$ for $m\angle S = 70°$.

 47. Geometry The lengths of the adjacent sides of a parallelogram are 54 cm and 78 cm. The larger angle measures 110°. What is the length of the longer diagonal? Round your answer to the nearest centimeter.

 48. Geometry The lengths of the adjacent sides of a parallelogram are 21 cm and 14 cm. The smaller angle measures 58°. What is the length of the shorter diagonal? Round your answer to the nearest centimeter.

49. Critical Thinking Does the Law of Cosines apply to a right triangle? That is, does $c^2 = a^2 + b^2 - 2ab \cos C$ remain true when $\angle C$ is a right angle? Justify your answer.

⊙ Challenge **50. Physics** A pendulum 36 in. long swings 30° from the vertical. How high above the lowest position is the pendulum at the end of its swing? Round your answer to the nearest tenth of an inch.

51. a. Find the length of the altitude to $\overline{PQ}$ in the triangle below.
   b. Find the area of $\triangle PQR$.

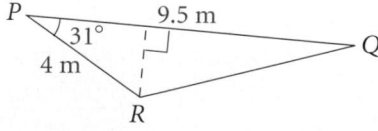

52. Find x in $\triangle ABC$.

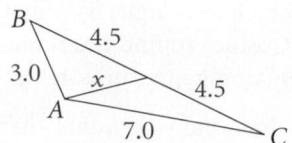

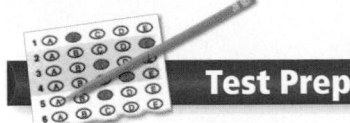
Gridded Response

Use the diagram below for Questions 53–58. Angle measures are in degrees.

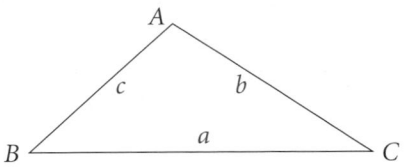

53. Let $a = 23.2$, $b = 18.5$, and $m\angle C = 42°$. Find c to the nearest tenth.

54. Use the information in Question 53 to find $m\angle A$ to the nearest tenth.

55. Suppose $a = 45.25$, $b = 39.75$, and $c = 20.65$. Find $m\angle B$ to the nearest tenth.

56. Use the information in Question 55 to find $m\angle C$ to the nearest tenth.

57. Suppose $b = 11.0$, $c = 11.7$, and $m\angle A = 22°$. Find the length of the altitude from A to the nearest tenth.

58. Use the information in Question 57 to find the area of $\triangle ABC$ to the nearest tenth of a square unit.

Mixed Review

Lesson 14-4

59. In $\triangle RST$, $m\angle R = 37°$, $m\angle T = 59°$, and $TS = 12$ in. Find RS.

60. In $\triangle JKL$, $m\angle L = 71°$, $j = 11$ m, and $m\angle K = 46°$. Find k.

61. In $\triangle MNP$, $m\angle N = 42°$, $n = 21$ in., and $m\angle M = 57°$. Find m.

62. In $\triangle DEF$, $m\angle F = 91°$, $d = 17$ mm, and $f = 21$ mm. Find $m\angle D$.

Lesson 13-6

Identify the period and tell where two asymptotes occur for each function.

63. $y = \tan 0.5\theta$ **64.** $y = \tan \frac{3\pi\theta}{2}$ **65.** $y = \tan(-3\theta)$ **66.** $y = \tan \frac{2\pi}{5}\theta$

Lesson 12-1

67. Use a table and a graph to show the probability distribution for the sum of two octahedral number cubes. $\{2, 3, 4, 5, 6, 7, 8, 9, 10, 11, 12, 13, 14, 15, 16\}$

Algebra at Work

·······················Acoustical Physicist

Acoustical physicists study sound to design concert halls, theaters, and auditoriums. They consider building materials, the shape of the hall, and the placement of people and equipment. Acoustical physicists ensure that sound is distributed evenly so that all of the people in the theater or auditorium hear equally well.

For: Information about acoustical physicists
Web Code: agb-2031

Angle Identities

GO for Help Lesson 14-1

What You'll Learn

- To verify and use angle identities
- To verify and use sum and difference identities

. . . And Why

To simplify trigonometric expressions and find values of trigonometric functions

✓ Check Skills You'll Need

Complete the three reciprocal identities.

1. $\csc \theta = \dfrac{1}{\blacksquare}$ **2.** $\sec \theta = \dfrac{1}{\blacksquare}$ **3.** $\cot \theta = \dfrac{1}{\blacksquare}$

Complete the three Pythagorean identities.

4. $\cos^2 \theta + \sin^2 \theta = \blacksquare$ **5.** $1 + \tan^2 \theta = \blacksquare$ **6.** $1 + \cot^2 \theta = \blacksquare$

---

1 Angle Identities

Real-World Connection

Over 2000 years ago, the Greek astronomer Hipparchus needed a table of trigonometric ratios to calculate the positions of the stars. He had to compute the table himself and he used angle identities to make the computations easier.

In the figure at the right, angles θ and $-\theta$ have the same amount of rotation, but the rotations are in opposite directions.

Point Q is a reflection of P in the x-axis. The x-coordinates of P and Q are the same and their y-coordinates are opposites. So $\cos(-\theta) = \cos \theta$ and $\sin(-\theta) = -\sin \theta$.

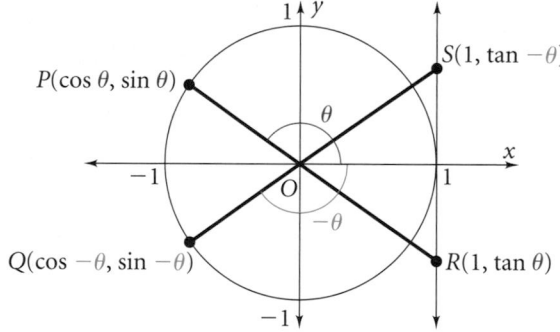

Similarly, R is the reflection of S in the x-axis. So $\tan(-\theta) = -\tan \theta$.

In the figure at the right, θ is a counterclockwise rotation from the positive x-axis and $\frac{\pi}{2} - \theta$ is the same amount of rotation clockwise from the positive y-axis.

Point Q is a reflection of P in the line $y = x$. If (x, y) are the coordinates of P, then (y, x) are the coordinates of Q. So $\cos\left(\frac{\pi}{2} - \theta\right) = \sin \theta$ and $\sin\left(\frac{\pi}{2} - \theta\right) = \cos \theta$.

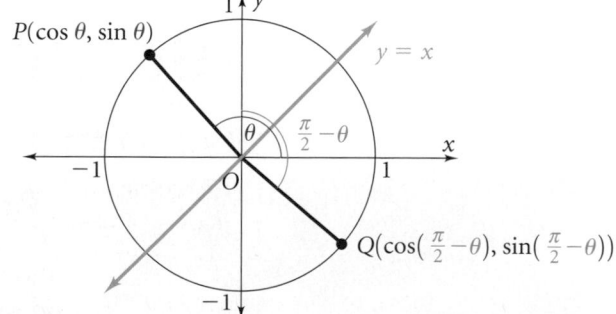

Then, by the Tangent Identity, $\tan\left(\dfrac{\pi}{2} - \theta\right) = \dfrac{\sin\left(\frac{\pi}{2} - \theta\right)}{\cos\left(\frac{\pi}{2} - \theta\right)} = \dfrac{\cos \theta}{\sin \theta} = \cot \theta$.

Key Concepts

Vocabulary Tip

The word <u>cofunction</u> is derived from complementary angle *function*.

Properties	**Angle Identities**

Negative angle identities

$$\sin{(-\theta)} = -\sin{\theta} \qquad \cos{(-\theta)} = \cos{\theta} \qquad \tan{(-\theta)} = -\tan{\theta}$$

Cofunction identities

$$\sin{\left(\frac{\pi}{2} - \theta\right)} = \cos{\theta} \qquad \cos{\left(\frac{\pi}{2} - \theta\right)} = \sin{\theta} \qquad \tan{\left(\frac{\pi}{2} - \theta\right)} = \cot{\theta}$$

---

1 EXAMPLE **Verifying Angle Identities**

Verify the identity $\sin{\left(\theta - \frac{\pi}{2}\right)} = -\cos{\theta}$.

$$\sin{\left(\theta - \tfrac{\pi}{2}\right)} = \sin{\left(-\left(\tfrac{\pi}{2} - \theta\right)\right)} \qquad -(a - b) = b - a$$

$$= -\sin{\left(\tfrac{\pi}{2} - \theta\right)} \qquad \sin{(-\theta)} = -\sin{\theta}$$

$$= -\cos{\theta} \qquad \sin{\left(\tfrac{\pi}{2} - \theta\right)} = \cos{\theta}$$

✓ **Quick Check** ❶ Verify the identity $\cos{\left(\theta - \frac{\pi}{2}\right)} = \sin{\theta}$.

You can use angle identities to solve trigonometric equations.

2 EXAMPLE **Solving Trigonometric Equations**

Solve $\sin{\theta} = \sin{\left(\frac{\pi}{2} - \theta\right)}$ for $0 \le \theta < 2\pi$.

$$\sin{\theta} = \sin{\left(\tfrac{\pi}{2} - \theta\right)}$$

$\sin{\theta} = \cos{\theta}$	cofunction identity
$\frac{\sin{\theta}}{\cos{\theta}} = 1$	Divide by $\cos{\theta}$.
$\tan{\theta} = 1$	Tangent Identity
$\theta = \tan^{-1}{1}$	Solve for one value of θ.

$$\theta = \frac{\pi}{4}$$

Another solution is $\frac{\pi}{4} + \pi$, or $\frac{5\pi}{4}$.

✓ **Quick Check** ❷ Solve $\sin{\left(\frac{\pi}{2} - \theta\right)} = \sec{\theta}$ for $0 \le \theta < 2\pi$.

3 EXAMPLE **Cofunction Identities in a Right Triangle**

The cofunction identities were derived using the unit circle. So they apply to an angle θ of any size. Use the definitions of the trigonometric ratios for a right triangle to derive a cofunction identity for $\sin{(90° - A)}$.

In a right triangle, the acute angles are complementary. So $A + B = 90°$ and $B = 90° - A$, where A and B are the measures of the acute angles.

$$\sin{(90° - A)} = \sin{B} \qquad \textbf{A and B are complementary angles.}$$

$$= \frac{b}{a} \qquad \textbf{definition of sine in a right triangle}$$

$$= \cos{A} \qquad \textbf{definition of cosine in a right triangle}$$

Quick Check ③ Derive a cofunction identity for sec $(90° - A)$.

2   Sum and Difference Identities

In the cofunction identities, any angle θ is subtracted from $\frac{\pi}{2}$. There are also identities for subtracting any two angles.

It is convenient to start with an identity for finding the cosine of the difference of two angles.

In the figure below, angles A, B, and $A - B$ are shown. Use the distance formula to find the square of the distance between P and Q.

$$(PQ)^2 = (x_1 - x_2)^2 + (y_1 - y_2)^2$$
$$= (\cos A - \cos B)^2 + (\sin A - \sin B)^2$$
$$= \cos^2 A - 2 \cos A \cos B + \cos^2 B + \sin^2 A - 2 \sin A \sin B + \sin^2 B$$
$$= 2 - 2 \cos A \cos B - 2 \sin A \sin B \quad \textbf{Use the Pythagorean identity}$$
$$\textbf{sin}^2\ \boldsymbol{\theta} + \textbf{cos}^2\ \boldsymbol{\theta} = \textbf{1.}$$

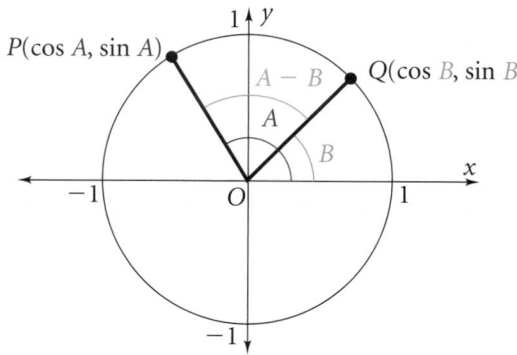

Now use the Law of Cosines to find $(PQ)^2$ in $\triangle POQ$.
$$(PQ)^2 = (PO)^2 + (QO)^2 - 2(PO)(QO) \cos (A - B)$$
$$= 1^2 + 1^2 - 2(1)(1) \cos (A - B)$$
$$= 2 - 2 \cos (A - B)$$

The Transitive Property for Equality tells you that the two expressions for $(PQ)^2$ are equal.

$$2 - 2 \cos (A - B) = 2 - 2 \cos A \cos B - 2 \sin A \sin B$$
$$-2 \cos (A - B) = -2 \cos A \cos B - 2 \sin A \sin B \quad \textbf{Subtract 2 from each side.}$$
$$\cos (A - B) = \cos A \cos B + \sin A \sin B \quad \textbf{Divide each side by } -\textbf{2.}$$

You can also derive an identity for $\sin (A - B)$. Then you can use the Tangent Identity to derive an identity for $\tan (A - B)$.

 Key Concepts

Properties	Angle Difference Identities
$\sin (A - B) = \sin A \cos B - \cos A \sin B$	
$\cos (A - B) = \cos A \cos B + \sin A \sin B$	
$\tan (A - B) = \frac{\tan A - \tan B}{1 + \tan A \tan B}$	

816   Chapter 14 Trigonometric Identities and Equations

4 EXAMPLE Using Angle Difference Identities

Find the exact value of cos 15°.

You know exact values for 30°, 60°, and 45°. Use the fact that 15° = 60° − 45°.

$\cos (A - B) = \cos A \cos B + \sin A \sin B$ **Cosine Angle Difference Identity**

$\cos (60° - 45°) = \cos 60° \cos 45° + \sin 60° \sin 45°$ **Substitute 60° for A and 45° for B.**

$= \frac{1}{2}\left(\frac{\sqrt{2}}{2}\right) + \frac{\sqrt{3}}{2}\left(\frac{\sqrt{2}}{2}\right)$ **Replace with exact values.**

$= \frac{\sqrt{2}}{4} + \frac{\sqrt{6}}{4}$ **Simplify.**

$= \frac{\sqrt{2} + \sqrt{6}}{4}$

So cos 15° = $\frac{\sqrt{2} + \sqrt{6}}{4}$.

 **Quick Check** ④ Find the exact value of sin 15°.

You can use the Negative Angle Identities and the Sine Angle Difference Identity to derive an identity for sin $(A + B)$.

$\sin (A + B) = \sin (A - (-B))$ **Rewrite as subtraction.**

$= \sin A \cos (-B) - \cos A \sin (-B)$ **Sine Angle Difference Identity**

$= \sin A \cos B - \cos A (-\sin B)$ **negative angle identities**

$= \sin A \cos B + \cos A \sin B$ **Simplify.**

You can similarly derive an identity for cos $(A + B)$. You can use the Tangent Identity to derive tan $(A + B)$.

Key Concepts

Properties	Angle Sum Identities
$\sin (A + B) = \sin A \cos B + \cos A \sin B$	
$\cos (A + B) = \cos A \cos B - \sin A \sin B$	
$\tan (A + B) = \frac{\tan A + \tan B}{1 - \tan A \tan B}$	

5 EXAMPLE Using Angle Sum Identities

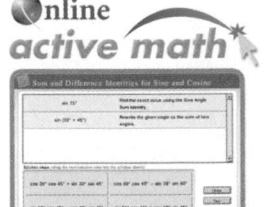

For: Identities Activity
Use: Interactive Textbook, 14-6

Find the exact value of sin 105°.

Use the fact that 105° = 60° + 45°.

$\sin (A + B) = \sin A \cos B + \cos A \sin B$ **Sine Angle Sum Identity**

$\sin (60° + 45°) = \sin 60° \cos 45° + \cos 60° \sin 45°$ **Substitute 60° for A and 45° for B.**

$= \frac{\sqrt{3}}{2}\left(\frac{\sqrt{2}}{2}\right) + \frac{1}{2}\left(\frac{\sqrt{2}}{2}\right)$ **Replace with exact values.**

$= \frac{\sqrt{6}}{4} + \frac{\sqrt{2}}{4}$ **Simplify.**

$= \frac{\sqrt{6} + \sqrt{2}}{4}$

So, sin 105° = $\frac{\sqrt{6} + \sqrt{2}}{4}$.

 **Quick Check** ⑤ Find the exact value of tan 105°.

EXERCISES

For more exercises, see *Extra Skill and Word Problem Practice.*

Practice and Problem Solving

A Practice by Example

Example 1
(page 815)

Verify each identity.

1. $\csc\left(\theta - \frac{\pi}{2}\right) = -\sec\theta$ 2. $\sec\left(\theta - \frac{\pi}{2}\right) = \csc\theta$

3. $\cot\left(\frac{\pi}{2} - \theta\right) = \tan\theta$ 4. $\csc\left(\frac{\pi}{2} - \theta\right) = \sec\theta$

5. $\tan\left(\theta - \frac{\pi}{2}\right) = -\cot\theta$ 6. $\sec\left(\frac{\pi}{2} - \theta\right) = \csc\theta$

Example 2
(page 815)

Solve each trigonometric equation for $0 \le \theta < 2\pi$.

7. $\cos\left(\frac{\pi}{2} - \theta\right) = \csc\theta$ 8. $\sin\left(\frac{\pi}{2} - \theta\right) = -\cos(-\theta)$

9. $\tan\left(\frac{\pi}{2} - \theta\right) + \tan(-\theta) = 0$ 10. $\sin^2\theta + \cos^2\theta = \sin\theta$

11. $\tan^2\theta - \sec^2\theta = \cos(-\theta)$ 12. $2\sin\left(\frac{\pi}{2} - \theta\right) = \sin(-\theta)$

13. $\tan\left(\frac{\pi}{2} - \theta\right) = \cos(-\theta)$ 14. $1 + \cot^2\theta = \csc\theta$

Example 3
(page 815)

Use the definitions of the trigonometric ratios for a right triangle to derive each cofunction identity.

15. a cofunction identity for $\csc(90° - A)$

16. a cofunction identity for $\cot(90° - A)$

Examples 4 and 5
(page 817)

Mental Math Find the value of each trigonometric expression.

17. $\cos 50° \cos 40° - \sin 50° \sin 40°$

18. $\sin 80° \cos 35° - \cos 80° \sin 35°$

19. $\sin 100° \cos 170° + \cos 100° \sin 170°$

20. $\cos 183° \cos 93° + \sin 183° \sin 93°$

Find each exact value. Use a sum or difference identity.

21. $\cos 105°$ 22. $\tan 105°$ 23. $\tan 15°$ 24. $\sin 75°$

25. $\cos 75°$ 26. $\tan 75°$ 27. $\cos 135°$ 28. $\tan 135°$

29. $\sin(-15°)$ 30. $\cos(-15°)$ 31. $\tan(-15°)$ 32. $\sin 225°$

33. $\cos 240°$ 34. $\sin 390°$ 35. $\cos(-300°)$ 36. $\tan 390°$

B Apply Your Skills

Verify each identity.

37. $\sin(A - B) = \sin A \cos B - \cos A \sin B$

38. $\tan(A - B) = \frac{\tan A - \tan B}{1 + \tan A \tan B}$

39. $\cos(A + B) = \cos A \cos B - \sin A \sin B$

40. $\tan(A + B) = \frac{\tan A + \tan B}{1 - \tan A \tan B}$

41. $\sin\left(x + \frac{\pi}{3}\right) + \sin\left(x - \frac{\pi}{3}\right) = \sin x$

42. $\sin\left(\frac{3\pi}{2} - x\right) = -\cos x$

GO Online
Homework Video Tutor
Visit: PHSchool.com
Web Code: age-1406

43. **Reasoning** Show that the equation $\sin(A + B) = \sin A + \sin B$ is *not* an identity by finding a counterexample, values for A and B for which the equation is false.

Rewrite each expression as a trigonometric function of a single angle measure.

44. $\sin 2\theta \cos \theta + \cos 2\theta \sin \theta$

45. $\sin 3\theta \cos 2\theta + \cos 3\theta \sin 2\theta$

46. $\cos 3\theta \cos 4\theta - \sin 3\theta \sin 4\theta$

47. $\cos 2\theta \cos 3\theta - \sin 2\theta \sin 3\theta$

48. $\dfrac{\tan 5\theta + \tan 6\theta}{1 - \tan 5\theta \tan 6\theta}$

49. $\dfrac{\tan 3\theta - \tan \theta}{1 + \tan 3\theta \tan \theta}$

 50. a. Graph $y = \sin 2x$ and $y = 2 \sin x$ on the same axes.
   b. Does $\sin 2x = 2 \sin x$ for all values of x? Is $\sin 2x = 2 \sin x$ an identity? Explain.
   c. Does $\sin 2x = 2 \sin x$ for any values of x? If so, what are they?
   d. Open-Ended Find an equation of the form $a \sin b = c \sin d$ whose solutions are $2\pi n$.

51. Gears The diagram at the right shows a gear whose radius is 10 cm. Point A represents a $60°$ counterclockwise rotation of point $P(10, 0)$. Point B represents a θ-degree rotation of point A. The coordinates of B are $(10 \cos (\theta + 60°), 10 \sin (\theta + 60°))$. Write these coordinates in terms of $\cos \theta$ and $\sin \theta$.

52. a. Critical Thinking A function is even if $f(-x) = f(x)$. A function is odd if $f(-x) = -f(x)$. Which trigonometric functions are even? Which are odd?
   b. Writing Are all functions either even or odd? Explain your answer. Give a counterexample if possible.

 **Challenge**

Use the sum and difference formulas to verify each identity.

53. $\cos (\pi - \theta) = -\cos \theta$

54. $\sin (\pi - \theta) = \sin \theta$

55. $\sin (\pi + \theta) = -\sin \theta$

56. $\cos (\pi + \theta) = -\cos \theta$

57. Reasoning For any parallelogram, prove that the sum of the squares of the lengths of the diagonals equals twice the sum of the squares of the lengths of two adjacent sides.

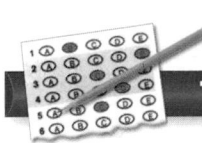 **Test Prep**

Multiple Choice

58. Which expressions are equivalent?
   I. $\cos \theta$ **II.** $\cos (-\theta)$ **III.** $\dfrac{\sin (-\theta)}{\tan (-\theta)}$

   A. I and II only   **B.** II and III only   **C.** I and III only   **D.** I, II, and III

59. Which expressions are equivalent?
   I. $-\tan \left(\frac{\pi}{2} - \theta\right)$ **II.** $\tan \left(\theta - \frac{\pi}{2}\right)$ **III.** $\tan \left(-\left(\frac{\pi}{2} - \theta\right)\right)$
   F. I and II only   **G.** II and III only   **H.** I and III only   **J.** I, II, and III

60. Which expression is equal to $\cos 50°$?
   A. $\sin 20° \cos 30° + \cos 20° \sin 30°$ **B.** $\sin 20° \cos 30° - \cos 20° \sin 30°$
   C. $\cos 20° \cos 30° + \sin 20° \sin 30°$ **D.** $\cos 20° \cos 30° - \sin 20° \sin 30°$

61. Which expression is NOT equivalent to $\cos \theta$?
   F. $-\sin (\theta - 90°)$ **G.** $-\cos (-\theta)$ **H.** $\sin (\theta + 90°)$ **J.** $-\cos (\theta + 180°)$

62. Which expression is an exact value for sin 15° ?

A. $\frac{\sqrt{2}}{2} \cdot \frac{\sqrt{3}}{2} + \frac{\sqrt{2}}{2} \cdot \frac{1}{2}$

B. $\frac{\sqrt{2}}{2} \cdot \frac{\sqrt{3}}{2} - \frac{\sqrt{2}}{2} \cdot \frac{1}{2}$

C. $\frac{\sqrt{2}}{2} \cdot \frac{1}{2} + \frac{\sqrt{2}}{2} \cdot \frac{\sqrt{3}}{2}$

D. $\frac{\sqrt{2}}{2} \cdot \frac{1}{2} - \frac{\sqrt{2}}{2} \cdot \frac{\sqrt{3}}{2}$

Short Response

63. Find an exact value for sin 165°. Show your work.

64. Use the fact that $\frac{\pi}{6} = \frac{\pi}{2} - \frac{\pi}{3}$ to find an exact value for $\cos \frac{\pi}{6}$. Show your work.

Mixed Review

Lesson 14-5

65. In $\triangle RST$, $m\angle S = 24°$, $r = 10$ ft, and $t = 18$ ft. Find s.

66. In $\triangle XYZ$, $m\angle Z = 51°$, $x = 13$ cm, and $y = 17$ cm. Find z.

67. In $\triangle DEF$, $m\angle F = 68°$, $d = 16$ mm, and $e = 21$ mm. Find f.

68. In $\triangle ABC$, $m\angle A = 87°$, $b = 22$ m, and $c = 19$ m. Find a.

Lesson 13-3

Write each measure in radians. Express the answer in terms of π and as a decimal rounded to the nearest hundredth.

69. 80°

70. −50°

71. −15°

72. 70°

73. 190°

74. 200°

Lesson 12-7

A set of data with a mean of 39 and a standard deviation of 6.2 is normally distributed. Find each value, given its distance from the mean.

75. +1 standard deviation

76. −2 standard deviations

77. +3 standard deviations

78. −1 standard deviation

✓ Checkpoint Quiz 2   Lessons 14-4 through 14-6

Find the area of $\triangle ABC$.

1. $m\angle A = 37°$, $b = 10$ cm, and $c = 12$ cm.

2. $m\angle B = 18°$, $a = 20$ ft, and $c = 25$ ft.

3. $m\angle B = 104°$, $a = 8$ m, and $c = 9$ m.

4. $m\angle C = 96°$, $a = 26$ in., and $b = 31$ in.

Find the remaining sides and angles in each triangle. Round your answers to the nearest tenth.

5. In $\triangle ABC$, $m\angle A = 27°$, $b = 17$ ft, and $c = 18$ ft.

6. In $\triangle DEF$, $d = 32$ mm, $e = 30$ mm, and $f = 35$ mm.

Simplify each trigonometric expression.

7. $\cos 60° \cos 20° - \sin 60° \sin 20°$

8. $\sin 90° \cos 27° - \cos 90° \sin 27°$

9. $\sin 150° \cos 290° + \cos 150° \sin 290°$

10. $\cos 233° \cos 154° + \sin 233° \sin 154°$

Double-Angle and Half-Angle Identities

What You'll Learn

- To verify and use double-angle identities
- To verify and use half-angle identities

... And Why

To find exact values of trigonometric functions

✓ **Check Skills You'll Need**   **GO for Help** Lesson 14-6

Complete the following angle identities.

1. $\cos (A - B) = $ ▧   **2.** $\cos (A + B) = $ ▧

3. $\tan (A - B) = $ ▧   **4.** $\sin (A - B) = $ ▧

5. $\sin (A + B) = $ ▧   **6.** $\tan (A + B) = $ ▧

---

1 Double-Angle Identities

You can use the angle sum identities to derive the double-angle identities.

Let $\theta = A = B$.

$\cos (A + B) = \cos A \cos B - \sin A \sin B$ **Cosine Angle Sum Identity**

$\cos (\theta + \theta) = \cos \theta \cos \theta - \sin \theta \sin \theta$ **Substitute θ for A and B.**

$\cos 2\theta = \cos^2 \theta - \sin^2 \theta$ **Simplify.**

You can use the Pythagorean identity $\sin^2 \theta + \cos^2 \theta = 1$ in the form $\sin^2 \theta = 1 - \cos^2 \theta$ to derive another identity for $\cos 2\theta$.

$\cos 2\theta = \cos^2 \theta - \sin^2 \theta$

$= \cos^2 \theta - (1 - \cos^2 \theta)$ **Substitute $1 - \cos^2 \theta$ for $\sin^2 \theta$.**

$= \cos^2 \theta - 1 + \cos^2 \theta$ **Remove parentheses.**

$= 2 \cos^2 \theta - 1$ **Simplify.**

You can use the Pythagorean theorem in the form $\cos^2 \theta = 1 - \sin^2 \theta$ to derive a third identity for $\cos 2\theta$.

$\cos 2\theta = \cos^2 \theta - \sin^2 \theta$

$= (1 - \sin^2 \theta) - \sin^2 \theta$ **Substitute $1 - \sin^2 \theta$ for $\cos^2 \theta$.**

$= 1 - 2 \sin^2 \theta$ **Simplify.**

You can use the other angle sum identities to derive double-angle identities for the sine and tangent.

 **Key Concepts**

Properties	**Double-Angle Identities**
$\cos 2\theta = \cos^2 \theta - \sin^2 \theta$	$\sin 2\theta = 2 \sin \theta \cos \theta$
$\cos 2\theta = 2 \cos^2 \theta - 1$	$\tan 2\theta = \dfrac{2 \tan \theta}{1 - \tan^2 \theta}$
$\cos 2\theta = 1 - 2 \sin^2 \theta$	

Using a Double-Angle Identity

Use a double-angle identity to find the exact value of $\cos 120°$.

$$\cos 120° = \cos (2 \cdot 60°) \qquad \text{Rewrite 120 as } (2 \cdot 60).$$
$$= \cos^2 60° - \sin^2 60° \qquad \text{Use a cosine double-angle identity.}$$
$$= \left(\tfrac{1}{2}\right)^2 - \left(\tfrac{\sqrt{3}}{2}\right)^2 \qquad \text{Replace with exact values.}$$
$$= -\tfrac{1}{2} \qquad \text{Simplify.}$$

✓ **Quick Check** ❶ Use a double-angle identity to find the exact value of $\sin 120°$.

You can use the double-angle identities to verify other identities.

2 EXAMPLE **Verifying an Identity**

Verify the identity $\cos 2\theta = \dfrac{1 - \tan^2 \theta}{1 + \tan^2 \theta}$.

$$\frac{1 - \tan^2 \theta}{1 + \tan^2 \theta} = \frac{1 - \tan^2 \theta}{\sec^2 \theta} \qquad \text{Pythagorean identity}$$

$$= \frac{1}{\sec^2 \theta} - \frac{\tan^2 \theta}{\sec^2 \theta} \qquad \text{Write as two fractions.}$$

$$= \frac{1}{\frac{1}{\cos^2 \theta}} - \frac{\frac{\sin^2 \theta}{\cos^2 \theta}}{\frac{1}{\cos^2 \theta}} \qquad \text{Express in terms of } \sin \theta \text{ and } \cos \theta.$$

$$= \cos^2 \theta - \sin^2 \theta \qquad \text{Simplify.}$$

$$= \cos 2\theta \qquad \text{double-angle identity}$$

✓ **Quick Check** ❷ Verify the identity $2 \cos 2\theta = 4 \cos^2 \theta - 2$.

2 Half-Angle Identities

You can use double-angle identities to derive half-angle identities.
Let $\theta = \frac{A}{2}$.

$$\cos 2\theta = 2 \cos^2 \theta - 1 \qquad \text{cosine double-angle identity}$$

$$\cos 2\left(\tfrac{A}{2}\right) = 2 \cos^2 \tfrac{A}{2} - 1 \qquad \text{Substitute } \tfrac{A}{2} \text{ for } \theta.$$

$$\frac{\cos A + 1}{2} = \cos^2 \tfrac{A}{2} \qquad \text{Solve for } \cos^2 \tfrac{A}{2}.$$

$$\pm\sqrt{\frac{\cos A + 1}{2}} = \cos \tfrac{A}{2} \qquad \text{Take the square root of each side.}$$

Similarly, $\sin \frac{A}{2} = \pm\sqrt{\dfrac{1 - \cos A}{2}}$ and $\tan \frac{A}{2} = \pm\sqrt{\dfrac{1 - \cos A}{1 + \cos A}}$.

🔑 **Key Concepts**

Properties	Half-Angle Identities

$$\sin \frac{A}{2} = \pm\sqrt{\frac{1 - \cos A}{2}} \qquad \cos \frac{A}{2} = \pm\sqrt{\frac{1 + \cos A}{2}} \qquad \tan \frac{A}{2} = \pm\sqrt{\frac{1 - \cos A}{1 + \cos A}}$$

Choose the positive or negative sign for each function depending on the quadrant in which $\frac{A}{2}$ lies.

3 EXAMPLE Using Half-Angle Identities

Use the half-angle identities to find each exact value.

a. $\sin 15°$

$$\sin 15° = \sin\left(\frac{30}{2}\right)° \qquad \text{Rewrite } 15° \text{ as } \frac{30°}{2}.$$

$$= \sqrt{\frac{1 - \cos 30°}{2}} \qquad \text{Use the principal square root, since } \sin 15° \text{ is positive.}$$

$$= \sqrt{\frac{1 - \frac{\sqrt{3}}{2}}{2}} \qquad \text{Substitute the exact value for } \cos 30°.$$

$$= \sqrt{\frac{2 - \sqrt{3}}{4}} \qquad \text{Simplify.}$$

$$= \frac{\sqrt{2 - \sqrt{3}}}{2} \qquad \text{Simplify.}$$

b. $\cos 150°$

$$\cos 150° = \cos\left(\frac{300}{2}\right)° \qquad \text{Rewrite } 150 \text{ as } \frac{300}{2}.$$

$$= -\sqrt{\frac{1 + \cos 300°}{2}} \qquad \text{Use the negative square root, since } \cos 150° \text{ is negative.}$$

$$= -\sqrt{\frac{1 + \left(\frac{1}{2}\right)}{2}} \qquad \text{Replace with an exact value.}$$

$$= -\sqrt{\frac{3}{4}} \qquad \text{Simplify.}$$

$$= -\frac{\sqrt{3}}{2} \qquad \text{Simplify.}$$

> **Problem Solving Hint**
> The quadrant of the terminal side of an angle determines the sign of the function.
>
> | Function | Positive in Quadrants |
> |----------|-----------------------|
> | sin | I, II |
> | cos | I, IV |
> | tan | I, III |

✓ **Quick Check** ❸ Use the half-angle identities to find the exact value of each expression.
a. $\sin 150°$ **b.** $\tan 150°$

4 EXAMPLE Using Half-Angle Identities

Given $\sin \theta = -\frac{24}{25}$ and $180° < \theta < 270°$, find $\sin \frac{\theta}{2}$.

First find $\cos \theta$.

$$\cos^2 \theta + \sin^2 \theta = 1 \qquad \text{Pythagorean identity}$$

$$\cos^2 \theta + \left(-\frac{24}{25}\right)^2 = 1 \qquad \text{Substitute.}$$

$$\cos^2 \theta = \frac{49}{25^2} \qquad \text{Solve for } \cos^2 \theta.$$

$$\cos \theta = -\frac{7}{25} \qquad \text{Choose the negative square root since } \theta \text{ is in Quadrant III.}$$

Now find $\sin \frac{\theta}{2}$.

Since $180° < \theta < 270°$, $90° < \frac{\theta}{2} < 135°$ and $\frac{\theta}{2}$ is in Quadrant II.

$$\sin \frac{\theta}{2} = \pm \sqrt{\frac{1 - \cos \theta}{2}} \qquad \text{half-angle identity}$$

$$= \sqrt{\frac{1 - \left(-\frac{7}{25}\right)}{2}} \qquad \text{Substitute. Choose the positive square root since } \frac{\theta}{2} \text{ is in Quadrant II.}$$

$$= \frac{4}{5} \qquad \text{Simplify.}$$

✓ **Quick Check** ❹ Use the information in Example 4 to find the exact values of $\cos \frac{\theta}{2}$ and $\tan \frac{\theta}{2}$.

EXERCISES

For more exercises, see *Extra Skill and Word Problem Practice.*

Practice and Problem Solving

A Practice by Example

Example 1
(page 822)

Example 2
(page 822)

Example 3
(page 823)

Example 4
(page 823)

Use a double-angle identity to find the exact value of each expression.

1. sin 240°   **2.** cos 120°   **3.** tan 120°   **4.** sin 90°

5. cos 240°   **6.** tan 240°   **7.** cos 600°   **8.** sin 600°

Use an angle sum identity to verify each identity.

9. $\sin 2\theta = 2 \sin \theta \cos \theta$ **10.** $\tan 2\theta = \dfrac{2 \tan \theta}{1 - \tan^2 \theta}$

Use a half-angle identity to find the exact value of each expression.

11. cos 15°   **12.** tan 15°   **13.** sin 15°   **14.** sin 22.5°

15. cos 22.5°   **16.** tan 22.5°   **17.** cos 90°   **18.** sin 7.5°

Given $\cos \theta = -\frac{4}{5}$ and $90° < \theta < 180°$, find the exact value of each expression.

19. $\sin \frac{\theta}{2}$ **20.** $\cos \frac{\theta}{2}$ **21.** $\tan \frac{\theta}{2}$ **22.** $\cot \frac{\theta}{2}$

Given $\cos \theta = -\frac{15}{17}$ and $180° < \theta < 270°$, find the exact value of each expression.

23. $\sin \frac{\theta}{2}$ **24.** $\cos \frac{\theta}{2}$ **25.** $\tan \frac{\theta}{2}$ **26.** $\sec \frac{\theta}{2}$

B Apply Your Skills

$\triangle RST$ has a right angle at $\angle T$. Use identities to show that each equation is true.

27. $\sin 2R = \dfrac{2rs}{t^2}$ **28.** $\cos 2R = \dfrac{s^2 - r^2}{t^2}$

29. $\sin 2S = \sin 2R$ **30.** $\sin^2 \frac{S}{2} = \dfrac{t - r}{2t}$

31. $\tan \frac{R}{2} = \dfrac{r}{t + s}$ **32.** $\tan^2 \frac{S}{2} = \dfrac{t - r}{t + r}$

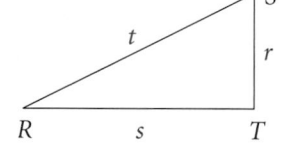

33. Critical Thinking If $\sin 2A = \sin 2B$, must $A = B$? Explain.

Given $\cos \theta = \frac{3}{5}$ and $270° < \theta < 360°$, find the exact value of each expression.

34. $\sin 2\theta$ **35.** $\cos 2\theta$ **36.** $\tan 2\theta$ **37.** $\csc 2\theta$

38. $\sin \frac{\theta}{2}$ **39.** $\cos \frac{\theta}{2}$ **40.** $\tan \frac{\theta}{2}$ **41.** $\cot \frac{\theta}{2}$

Use identities to write each equation in terms of the single angle θ. Then solve the equation for $0 \le \theta < 2\pi$.

42. $4 \sin 2\theta - 3 \cos \theta = 0$ **43.** $2 \sin 2\theta - 3 \sin \theta = 0$

44. $\sin 2\theta \sin \theta = \cos \theta$ **45.** $\cos 2\theta = -2 \cos^2 \theta$

Simplify each expression.

46. $2 \cos^2 \theta - \cos 2\theta$ **47.** $\sin^2 \frac{\theta}{2} - \cos^2 \frac{\theta}{2}$ **48.** $\dfrac{\cos 2\theta}{\sin \theta + \cos \theta}$

49. Open-Ended Choose an angle measure A.
 a. Find sin A and cos A.
 b. Use an identity to find sin $2A$.
 c. Use an identity to find cos $\frac{A}{2}$.

Homework Video Tutor

Visit: PHSchool.com
Web Code: age-1407

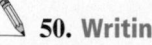
50. Writing Is $\frac{\tan \theta}{4} = \tan \frac{\theta}{4}$ an identity? Explain.

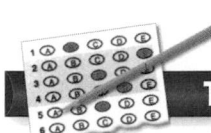

C **Challenge**

Use double-angle identities to write each expression, using trigonometric functions of θ instead of 4θ.

51. $\sin 4\theta$ **52.** $\cos 4\theta$ **53.** $\tan 4\theta$

Use half-angle identities to write each expression, using trigonometric functions of θ instead of $\frac{\theta}{4}$.

54. $\sin \frac{\theta}{4}$ **55.** $\cos \frac{\theta}{4}$ **56.** $\tan \frac{\theta}{4}$

57. Use the Tangent Half-Angle Identity and a Pythagorean identity to prove each identity.

     a. $\tan \frac{A}{2} = \dfrac{\sin A}{1 + \cos A}$ **b.** $\tan \frac{A}{2} = \dfrac{1 - \cos A}{\sin A}$

Test Prep

Multiple Choice

58. If θ is in Quadrant I and $\tan \theta = \frac{5}{12}$, what is the value of $\frac{\tan 4\theta}{5}$ to the nearest hundredth?

     A. 18.10   **B.** 0.33   **C.** 0.32   **D.** -23.90

59. If θ is in Quadrant I and $\sin \theta = \frac{3}{5}$, what is an exact value of $\sin 2\theta$?

     F. $\frac{9}{25}$ **G.** $\frac{24}{25}$ **H.** $\frac{6}{5}$ **J.** 73.7

Short Response

60. Use a half-angle identity to find an exact value of $\sin 67.5°$.

Extended Response

61. In the diagram at the right, line ℓ_1 forms an angle of θ with the positive x-axis and crosses the line $x = 1$ at $(1, 0.5)$. Line ℓ_2 forms an angle of 2θ with the positive x-axis. Find the coordinates of the point where ℓ_2 intersects $x = 1$. Show your work.

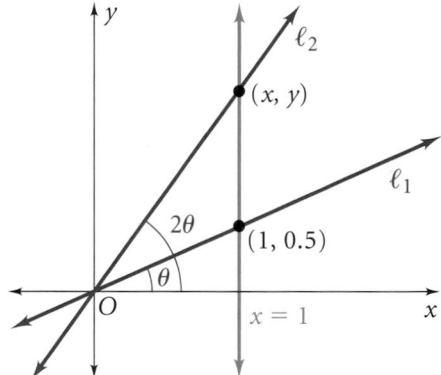

Mixed Review

for Help

Lesson 14-6

Lesson 13-1

Find each exact value. Use a sum or difference identity.

62. $\cos 405°$ **63.** $\sin (-300°)$ **64.** $\tan (-300°)$

Find the period and amplitude of each periodic function.

65. **66.**

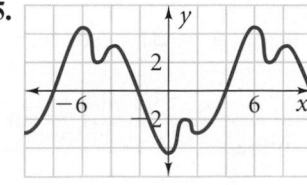

Open-ended questions ask you to create an example that satisfies certain given conditions. You may need to use your example to answer follow-up questions. As with extended-response questions, you should show all your work since you can receive partial credit.

EXAMPLE

For angles A and B, $A \neq B$ and $\sin A = \sin B$.
a. Find three pairs of values for A and B.
b. Write and prove a relation for A and B.

Here is a scoring rubric for a 4-point response.

[4] **a.** three pairs that satisfy the conditions
    b. $A + B = n\pi$, where n is an odd integer, or $A - B = 2n\pi$, or any other correct relation with a specific value of n; proves the relation.

[3] **a.** three pairs that satisfy the conditions
    b. $A + B = n\pi$, where n is an odd integer, or $A - B = 2n\pi$, or any other correct relation with a specific value of n; does not prove the relation.

[2] **a.** three pairs that satisfy the conditions
    b. no answer or incorrect answer

[1] **a.** one or two pairs that satisfy the conditions
    b. no answer or incorrect answer

The following response is worth 2 points.

a. $A = 0, B = \pi$
   $A = 0, B = 2\pi$
   $A = \frac{\pi}{6}, B = \frac{5\pi}{6}$
b. Let $A + B = 2\pi$. Then $A = 2\pi - B$.
  $\sin(2\pi - B) = \sin(2\pi)\cos(B) - \cos(2\pi)\sin(B)$
                $= 0 - (-1)\sin(B)$
                $= \sin(B)$

EXERCISES

1. Explain why the response above received only 2 points.

2. Write a 4-point response for the Example.

Find three sets of values for A and B, where $A \neq B$, that make each equation true. Write and prove a relation for A and B.

3. $\cos A = \cos B$ **4.** $\tan A = \tan B$

5. Find three sets of values for A and B such that $\sin(A + B) = \sin A + \sin B$. Write and prove a relation for A and B.

6. Find three pairs of values for A and B such that $\cos^2 A - \sin^2 A = \sin B$. Write and prove the relation for A and B.

Chapter Review

Vocabulary Review

Law of Cosines (p. 808)
Law of Sines (p. 801)

trigonometric identity (p. 778)

trigonometric ratios for a right triangle (p. 792)

Go Online
PHSchool.com
For: Vocabulary quiz
Web Code: agj-1451

Choose the correct vocabulary term to complete each sentence.

1. You can find missing measures of any triangle by using the ? if you know the measures of two angles and a side.

2. The six ratios of the lengths of the sides of a right triangle are known as the ? .

3. If you know the measures of two sides and the angle between them, you can use the ? to find missing parts of any triangle.

4. A trigonometric equation that is true for all values except those for which the expressions on either side of the equal sign are undefined is a ? .

5. The ? can be used to find missing measures of any triangle when you know two sides and the angle opposite one of them.

Skills and Concepts

14-1 Objectives

▼ To verify trigonometric identities (p. 778)

A **trigonometric identity** is a trigonometric equation that is true for all values except those for which the expressions on either side of the equal sign are undefined.

Reciprocal Identities

$$\csc \theta = \frac{1}{\sin \theta}$$

$$\sec \theta = \frac{1}{\cos \theta}$$

$$\cot \theta = \frac{1}{\tan \theta}$$

Tangent and Cotangent Identities

$$\tan \theta = \frac{\sin \theta}{\cos \theta}$$

$$\cot \theta = \frac{\cos \theta}{\sin \theta}$$

Pythagorean Identities

$$\cos^2 \theta + \sin^2 \theta = 1$$

$$1 + \tan^2 \theta = \sec^2 \theta$$

$$1 + \cot^2 \theta = \csc^2 \theta$$

Verify each identity.

6. $\sin \theta \tan \theta = \frac{1}{\cos \theta} - \cos \theta$

7. $\cos^2 \theta \cot^2 \theta = \cot^2 \theta - \cos^2 \theta$

Simplify each trigonometric expression.

8. $1 - \sin^2 \theta$

9. $\frac{\cos \theta}{\sin \theta \cot \theta}$

10. $\csc^2 \theta - \cot^2 \theta$

14-2 Objectives

▼ To evaluate inverses of trigonometric functions (p. 783)

▼ To solve trigonometric equations (p. 785)

The function $\cos^{-1} x$ is the inverse of $\cos \theta$ with the restricted domain $0 \le \theta \le \pi$. The function $\sin^{-1} x$ has domain $-\frac{\pi}{2} \le \theta \le \frac{\pi}{2}$, and $\tan^{-1} x$ has domain $-\frac{\pi}{2} < \theta < \frac{\pi}{2}$.

Use a unit circle and 30°-60°-90° triangles to find the value in degrees of each expression.

11. $\sin^{-1}\left(-\frac{\sqrt{3}}{2}\right)$

12. $\tan^{-1} \sqrt{3}$

13. $\tan^{-1}\left(-\frac{\sqrt{3}}{3}\right)$

14. $\cos^{-1} \frac{\sqrt{3}}{2}$

Use a calculator to find the value in radians of each expression.

15. $\sin^{-1} 0.33$ **16.** $\tan^{-1}(-2)$ **17.** $\cos^{-1}(-0.64)$ **18.** $\cos^{-1} 0.98$

Solve each equation for $0 \le \theta < 2\pi$.

19. $2 \cos \theta = 1$ **20.** $\sqrt{3} \tan \theta = 1$ **21.** $\sin \theta = \sin^2 \theta$

14-3 Objectives

▼ To find lengths of sides in a right triangle (p. 792)

▼ To find measures of angles in a right triangle (p. 795)

The six different ratios of the sides of a right triangle are known as the **trigonometric ratios for a right triangle**. These ratios depend on the size of the acute angles in the right triangle.

In a right triangle ABC that has an acute $\angle A$ and right $\angle C$, the ratios are defined as follows.

$$\sin A = \frac{\text{length of leg opposite } \angle A}{\text{length of hypotenuse}} = \frac{a}{c} \qquad \csc A = \frac{\text{length of hypotenuse}}{\text{length of leg opposite } \angle A} = \frac{c}{a}$$

$$\cos A = \frac{\text{length of leg adjacent to } \angle A}{\text{length of hypotenuse}} = \frac{b}{c} \qquad \sec A = \frac{\text{length of hypotenuse}}{\text{length of leg adjacent to } \angle A} = \frac{c}{b}$$

$$\tan A = \frac{\text{length of leg opposite } \angle A}{\text{length of leg adjacent to } \angle A} = \frac{a}{b} \qquad \cot A = \frac{\text{length of leg adjacent to } \angle A}{\text{length of leg opposite } \angle A} = \frac{b}{a}$$

In $\triangle ABC$, $\angle B$ is a right angle, $AB = 30$, and $\sec A = \frac{5}{3}$. Find each value in fraction and in decimal form.

22. $\cos A$ **23.** $\sin A$ **24.** $\tan C$

In $\triangle GHI$, $\angle H$ is a right angle. Find the remaining sides and angles. Round your answers to the nearest tenth.

25. $g = 3, i = 9$ **26.** $g = 12, h = 20$ **27.** $h = 55, i = 40$

14-4 Objectives

▼ To find the area of any triangle and to use the Law of Sines (p. 801)

You can find missing measures of any triangle if you know the measures of two angles and any side or if you know the measures of two sides and the angle opposite one of them by using the **Law of Sines.**

The Law of Sines states that for $\triangle ABC$, if a, b, and c represent the lengths of the sides opposite $\angle A$, $\angle B$, and $\angle C$, respectively, then $\frac{\sin A}{a} = \frac{\sin B}{b} = \frac{\sin C}{c}$.

Find the area of each triangle. Round your answers to the nearest hundredth.

28.

40°   7.3 m

5.6 m

29.

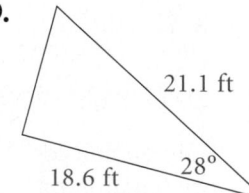

21.1 ft

18.6 ft   28°

30.

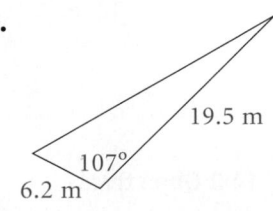

19.5 m

107°

6.2 m

31. In $\triangle LMN$, $m\angle L = 67°$, $m\angle N = 24°$, and $MN = 16$ in. Find LM to the nearest tenth.

32. In $\triangle XYZ$, $m\angle Z = 34°$, $x = 61$ cm, and $z = 42$ cm. Find $m\angle X$ to the nearest tenth.

You can find missing parts of any triangle when you know the measures of two sides and the angle between them, or all three sides, by using the **Law of Cosines**. For $\triangle ABC$, the following are true.

$$a^2 = b^2 + c^2 - 2bc \cos A \qquad b^2 = a^2 + c^2 - 2ac \cos B \qquad c^2 = a^2 + b^2 - 2ab \cos C$$

33. In $\triangle ABC$, $m\angle B = 45°$, $a = 24$ ft, and $c = 30$ ft. Find b to the nearest tenth.

34. In $\triangle DEF$, $d = 25$ in., $e = 28$ in., and $f = 20$ in. Find $m\angle F$ to the nearest tenth.

35. In $\triangle GHI$, $h = 8$, $i = 12$, and $m\angle G = 96°$. Find $m\angle I$ to the nearest tenth.

Angle identities are used to solve trigonometric equations.

Negative angle identities

$$\sin(-\theta) = -\sin\theta \qquad \cos(-\theta) = \cos\theta \qquad \tan(-\theta) = -\tan\theta$$

Cofunction identities

$$\sin\left(\frac{\pi}{2} - \theta\right) = \cos\theta \qquad \cos\left(\frac{\pi}{2} - \theta\right) = \sin\theta \qquad \tan\left(\frac{\pi}{2} - \theta\right) = \cot\theta$$

Angle difference identities

$$\sin(A - B) = \sin A \cos B - \cos A \sin B \qquad \tan(A - B) = \frac{\tan A - \tan B}{1 + \tan A \tan B}$$
$$\cos(A - B) = \cos A \cos B + \sin A \sin B$$

Angle sum identities

$$\sin(A + B) = \sin A \cos B + \cos A \sin B \qquad \tan(A + B) = \frac{\tan A + \tan B}{1 - \tan A \tan B}$$
$$\cos(A + B) = \cos A \cos B - \sin A \sin B$$

Verify each identity.

36. $\cos\left(\theta + \frac{\pi}{2}\right) = -\sin\theta$

37. $\sin^2\left(\theta - \frac{\pi}{2}\right) = \cos^2\theta$

Solve each trigonometric equation for $0 \le \theta < 2\pi$.

38. $\tan\left(\frac{\pi}{2} - \theta\right) = \cos\theta$

39. $1 + \tan^2\theta = \cos\theta$

You can use double-angle and half-angle identities to find exact values of trigonometric expressions. In the half-angle identities, choose the positive or negative sign for each function depending on the quadrant in which $\frac{A}{2}$ lies.

Double-angle identities

$$\cos 2\theta = \cos^2\theta - \sin^2\theta \qquad \sin 2\theta = 2\sin\theta\cos\theta \qquad \tan 2\theta = \frac{2\tan\theta}{1 - \tan^2\theta}$$
$$\cos 2\theta = 2\cos^2\theta - 1 \qquad \cos 2\theta = 1 - 2\sin^2\theta$$

Half-angle identities

$$\sin\frac{A}{2} = \pm\sqrt{\frac{1 - \cos A}{2}} \qquad \cos\frac{A}{2} = \pm\sqrt{\frac{1 + \cos A}{2}} \qquad \tan\frac{A}{2} = \pm\sqrt{\frac{1 - \cos A}{1 + \cos A}}$$

Use a double-angle identity to find the exact value of each expression.

40. $\sin 120°$
41. $\cos 90°$
42. $\tan 300°$

Use a half-angle identity to find the exact value of each expression.

43. $\cos 180°$
44. $\tan 60°$
45. $\sin 120°$

Chapter

14

Chapter Test

Go Online
PHSchool.com

For: Chapter Test
Web Code: aga-1452

Simplify each trigonometric expression.

1. $\sin \theta + \cos \theta \cot \theta$

2. $\sec \theta \sin \theta \cot \theta$

3. $\cot \theta (\tan \theta + \cot \theta)$

Verify each identity.

4. $\csc \theta \cos \theta \tan \theta = 1$ **5.** $\csc^2 \theta - \cot^2 \theta = 1$

6. $\sec \theta \cot \theta = \csc \theta$ **7.** $\sec^2 \theta - 1 = \tan^2 \theta$

Use a unit circle and 30°-60°-90° triangles to find the values of θ in degrees for each expression.

8. $\sin \theta = \frac{\sqrt{3}}{2}$ **9.** $\cos \theta = \frac{\sqrt{3}}{2}$

10. $\cos \theta = -1$ **11.** $\tan \theta = \sqrt{3}$

Solve each equation for $0 \le \theta < 2\pi$.

12. $4 \sin \theta + 2\sqrt{3} = 0$ **13.** $2 \cos \theta = 1$

14. $\sqrt{2} \sin \theta - 1 = 0$

In $\triangle ABC$, find each value as a fraction and as a decimal. Round to the nearest hundredth.

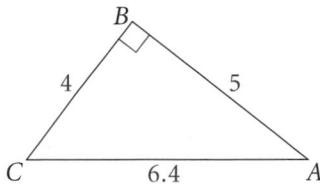

15. $\sin A$ **16.** $\sec A$ **17.** $\cot A$

18. $\csc C$ **19.** $\sec C$ **20.** $\tan C$

In $\triangle DEF$, $\angle F$ is a right angle. Find the remaining sides and angles. Round your answers to the nearest tenth.

21. $e = 6, f = 10$ **22.** $d = 10, e = 12$

23. $e = 21, f = 51$ **24.** $d = 5.5, e = 2.6$

25. Find the area of the triangle.

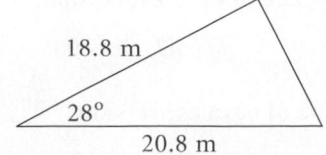

26. In $\triangle ABC$, $m\angle A = 45°$, $m\angle C = 23°$, and $BC = 25$ in. Find AB to the nearest tenth.

27. In $\triangle DEF$, $m\angle F = 56°$, $m\angle E = 34°$, and $DF = 10$ ft. Find EF to the nearest tenth.

28. In $\triangle GHI$, $m\angle I = 45°$, $g = 32$ cm, and $i = 52$ cm. Find $m\angle G$ to the nearest tenth.

29. In $\triangle JKL$, $m\angle J = 29°$, $l = 35$ m, and $j = 56$ m. Find $m\angle L$ to the nearest tenth.

 30. Writing Suppose you know the lengths of all three sides of a triangle. Can you use the Law of Sines to find the measures of the angles? Explain.

31. In $\triangle MNO$, $m\angle N = 45°$, $m = 20$ cm, and $o = 41$ cm. Find n to the nearest tenth.

32. In $\triangle PQR$, $p = 51$ ft, $q = 81$ ft, and $r = 61$ ft. Find $m\angle R$ to the nearest tenth.

33. In $\triangle STU$, $m\angle S = 96°$, $t = 8$ in., and $u = 10$ in. Find $m\angle U$ to the nearest tenth.

Verify each identity.

34. $-\sin \left(\theta - \frac{\pi}{2} \right) = \cos \theta$

35. $\csc \left(\theta + \frac{\pi}{2} \right) = \sec \theta$

36. $\csc \left(\theta - \frac{\pi}{2} \right) = -\sec \theta$

37. $\cos \left(-\theta - \frac{\pi}{2} \right) = \sin (-\theta)$

Solve each trigonometric equation for $0 \le \theta < 2\pi$.

38. $\sin \left(\frac{\pi}{2} - \theta \right) = \sec \theta$ **39.** $\cos \left(\frac{\pi}{2} - \theta \right) = \csc \theta$

40. $\cot \left(\frac{\pi}{2} - \theta \right) = \sin \theta$

Use a double-angle identity to find the exact value of each expression.

41. $\sin 60°$ **42.** $\cos 60°$ **43.** $\tan 60°$

Use a half-angle identity to find the exact value of each expression.

44. $\tan 30°$ **45.** $\sin 90°$ **46.** $\cos 180°$

47. Open-Ended Choose an angle measure A. Find $\sin A$ and $\cos A$. Then use the identities to find $\cos 2A$ and $\sin \frac{A}{2}$.

Standardized Test Prep

Go Online
PHSchool.com
For: End-of-course test
Web Code: aga-1454

Multiple Choice

For Exercises 1–32, choose the correct letter.

1. Which conic section is an ellipse?
Ⓐ $(x - 1)^2 + (y - 2)^2 = 4$
Ⓑ $(x + 4)^2 - (y - 3)^2 = 25$
Ⓒ $\frac{x^2}{36} + \frac{y^2}{81} = 100$
Ⓓ $\frac{x^2}{9} - \frac{y^2}{49} = 121$

2. How many solutions does the system
$\begin{cases} y = \frac{1}{2}x^3 - 1 \\ y = -x^2 + 4 \end{cases}$ have?
Ⓕ 0   Ⓖ 1   Ⓗ 2   Ⓙ 3

3. In which sequence is a_{25} the greatest?
Ⓐ $a_n = 2a_{n-1} + 7, a_1 = 5$
Ⓑ $a_n = 3n - 10$
Ⓒ $a_n = a_{n-1} + 18, a_1 = -7$
Ⓓ $a_n = n^2 - 200$

4. What is the inverse of the function $f(x) = x^3 + 4$?
Ⓕ $f^{-1}(x) = \frac{1}{3}x - 4$
Ⓖ $f^{-1}(x) = \sqrt[3]{x} - 4$
Ⓗ $f^{-1}(x) = \sqrt[3]{x - 4}$
Ⓙ $f^{-1}(x) = \sqrt[4]{x - 3}$

5. Which function shifts $y = |x + 1| - 3$ right 4 units and down 7 units?
Ⓐ $y = |x - 6| + 1$
Ⓑ $y = |x - 3| + 4$
Ⓒ $y = |x + 5| - 10$
Ⓓ $y = |x - 3| - 10$

6. Which is a direct variation that includes the point (10, 1)?
I. $y = 10x$ **II.** $y = 0.1x$
III. $xy = 10$ **IV.** $y = 0.5x - 4$
Ⓕ II only   Ⓖ I and III only
Ⓗ II, III, and IV   Ⓙ I only

7. Which of the following expressions is equivalent to $3 \log x + 2 \log y - \log x$?
I. $2 \log xy$ **II.** $\log x^2 + \log y^2$
III. $2 \log x + 2 \log y$ **IV.** $4 \log x - y$
Ⓐ I and II only   Ⓑ II and III only
Ⓒ III and IV only   Ⓓ I, II, and III only

8. Which graph represents a tangent function?

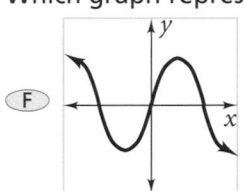
Ⓕ

Ⓖ
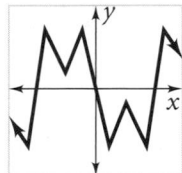

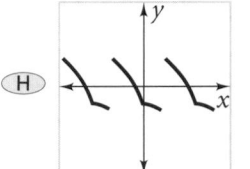
Ⓗ

Ⓙ
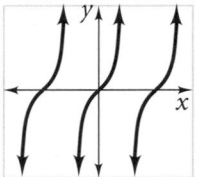

9. What is the solution of the matrix equation
$\begin{bmatrix} 10 & 9 & -5 \\ 3 & 12 & 7 \end{bmatrix} - X = \begin{bmatrix} 4 & -8 & 5 \\ 15 & -3 & 0 \end{bmatrix}$?
Ⓐ $\begin{bmatrix} 6 & 17 & -10 \\ -12 & 15 & 7 \end{bmatrix}$
Ⓑ $\begin{bmatrix} 14 & 1 & 0 \\ 18 & 9 & 7 \end{bmatrix}$
Ⓒ $\begin{bmatrix} 15 & 1 & -1 \\ 3 & 9 & 22 \end{bmatrix}$
Ⓓ $\begin{bmatrix} -6 & -17 & 10 \\ 12 & -15 & -7 \end{bmatrix}$

10. What is the distance of $4 - 5i$ from the origin?
Ⓕ 9 units
Ⓖ $\sqrt{41}$ units
Ⓗ 3 units
Ⓙ 1 unit

11. Which of the following is a simplification of $\frac{x^2 y^3 z}{4x} \div \frac{3xy^4 z^2}{2z}$?
Ⓐ $\frac{3x^3 y^7 z^3}{8xz}$
Ⓑ $\frac{3x^2 y^7 z^2}{8}$
Ⓒ $\frac{2x^2 y^3 z^2}{12x^2 y^4 z^2}$
Ⓓ $\frac{1}{6y}$

12. Which point is a solution of the following system?

$$\begin{cases} y \le 3x - 2 \\ y < 2x \\ x \ge -1 \\ y \ge -4 \end{cases}$$

- Ⓕ (0, 7)
- Ⓖ (−4, 1)
- Ⓗ (3, 1)
- Ⓙ (−1, −5)

13. The Law of Sines CANNOT be used as the first step in solving which of these triangles?

Ⓐ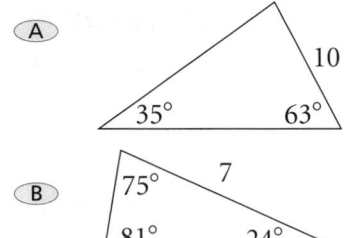

Ⓑ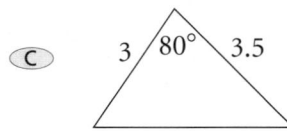

Ⓒ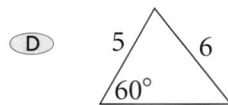

Ⓓ

14. What is the amplitude of $y = -4 \sin \frac{1}{2}x$?
- Ⓕ 4π
- Ⓖ 4
- Ⓗ $\frac{1}{2}$
- Ⓙ −4

15. What is $\frac{5\pi}{6}$ radians in degrees?
- Ⓐ 300°
- Ⓑ 150°
- Ⓒ 170°
- Ⓓ 80°

16. For $f(x) = x^2 - 1$ and $g(x) = |2x + 3|$, which has the greatest value?
- Ⓕ $f(g(3))$
- Ⓖ $g(f(2))$
- Ⓗ $g(f(-1))$
- Ⓙ $f(g(10))$

17. Which is the graph of an exponential function?

Ⓐ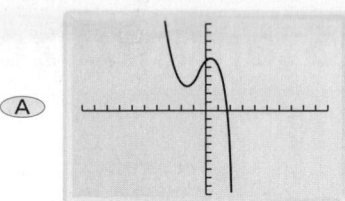

Ⓑ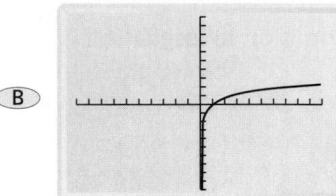

Ⓒ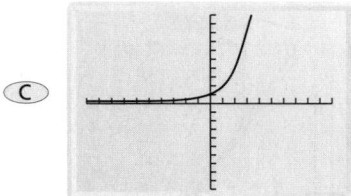

Ⓓ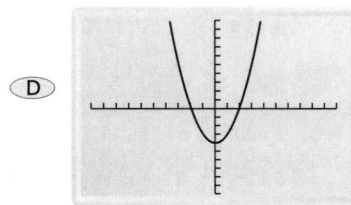

18. Which of the following expressions is equivalent to $3 \log x - 2 \log 2x$?
- Ⓕ $-\log x$
- Ⓖ $\log (-x)$
- Ⓗ $\log \frac{x}{2}$
- Ⓙ $\log \frac{x}{4}$

19. In $\triangle ABC$, $m\angle A = 36°$, $b = 12$, and $c = 25$. What is the length of a rounded to the nearest hundredth?
- Ⓐ 15.94
- Ⓑ 253.95
- Ⓒ 283.59
- Ⓓ 16.84

20. Which sequence has a common difference of 3?
- I. $a_n = a_{n-1} - 3$, $a_1 = 2$
- II. $a_n = 3$
- III. $a_n = a_{n-1} + 3$, $a_1 = -7$
- IV. $a_n = n^2 + 3$

- Ⓕ I only
- Ⓖ III only
- Ⓗ I and III
- Ⓙ II and IV

21. Which is greatest for the following data?

3, 4, 5, 5, 5, 5, 6, 7, 8, 9

- Ⓐ mean
- Ⓑ mode
- Ⓒ median
- Ⓓ range

22. Which of the following equations represents an ellipse?
- Ⓕ $3y^2 - x - 6y + 5 = 0$
- Ⓖ $x^2 + y^2 - 4x - 6y + 4 = 0$
- Ⓗ $4x^2 + y^2 - 16x - 6y + 9 = 0$
- Ⓙ $4x^2 - y^2 - 16x + 6y - 9 = 0$

23. Which curve has a period of 3?
- Ⓐ $y = 3 \sin 3\theta$
- Ⓑ $y = \cos \frac{\pi}{3} \theta$
- Ⓒ $y = \tan \frac{\pi}{3} \theta$
- Ⓓ $y = \frac{1}{3} \cos \theta$

24. Solve $10 - |4x + 1| < 7$.
- Ⓕ $x > \frac{1}{2}$
- Ⓖ $x < -1$ or $x > \frac{1}{2}$
- Ⓗ $x < -\frac{1}{2}$ or $x > 1$
- Ⓙ $-1 < x < \frac{1}{2}$

25. What are the roots of $\frac{x}{x - 18} = \frac{3x}{x^2 - 36}$?
   - **I.** 0   **II.** -3 **III.** 6
- Ⓐ I only
- Ⓑ I and II
- Ⓒ II and III
- Ⓓ I, II, and III

26. Let p and q vary inversely. If $p = -4$ when $q = 0.5$, what is q when p is 1?
- Ⓕ 2
- Ⓖ -2
- Ⓗ $\frac{1}{8}$
- Ⓙ $-\frac{1}{8}$

27. Find all the zeros of $f(x) = x(x - 3)^4$.
   - **I.** -3 **II.** 0   **III.** 3
- Ⓐ I and II
- Ⓑ I and III
- Ⓒ II and III
- Ⓓ III only

28. What is the degree of the polynomial $2x^5 + 3x - 1$?
- Ⓕ 2
- Ⓖ 3
- Ⓗ 4
- Ⓙ 5

29. What are the vertical asymptotes for the graph of $y = \frac{(x + 1)(x - 2)}{x^2 + x - 6}$?
   - **I.** $x = -1$ **II.** $x = 2$ **III.** $x = -3$
- Ⓐ I and III
- Ⓑ II only
- Ⓒ III only
- Ⓓ II and III

30. Which is equal to $\cos 120°$?
- Ⓕ $\cos 240°$
- Ⓖ $\cos 60°$
- Ⓗ $\cos 330°$
- Ⓙ $\cos 150°$

31. Which number completes the square for $x^2 - 3x$?
- Ⓐ 9
- Ⓑ $-\frac{3}{2}$
- Ⓒ $-\frac{9}{2}$
- Ⓓ $\frac{9}{4}$

32. There are 15 marbles in a bag: 2 are red, 8 are green, and 5 are blue. A marble is chosen at random and not replaced. A second marble is chosen at random. To the nearest whole percent, what is the probability that NEITHER marble is green?
- Ⓕ 19%
- Ⓖ 20%
- Ⓗ 89%
- Ⓙ 90%

Gridded Response

33. Express $\frac{5\pi}{9}$ radians in degrees.

34. A pendulum is 18 in. long. It swings through an angle of $\frac{3\pi}{4}$ radians. How far does the tip of the pendulum travel in one swing? Round your answer to the nearest inch.

35. Find a_{33} in the product $\begin{bmatrix} 2 & 1 \\ -6 & 5 \\ -1 & 3 \end{bmatrix} \cdot \begin{bmatrix} 8 & -2 & 0.5 \\ 4 & -7 & 10 \end{bmatrix}$.

Short Response

36. In $\triangle ABC$, $m\angle A = 56°$, $a = 8$, and $c = 6$. Show how to find $m\angle C$. Round to the nearest tenth.

37. Graph the function $y = \sin \left(x + \frac{\pi}{2} \right)$.

38. Divide $2x^4 + 4x^3 + 5x^2 + 9x - 2$ by $x + 2$. Show your work.

39. Write an equation of a rational function with asymptotes $y = 4$ and $x = -2$. Explain your work.

40. Simplify $(5 + 2i)(-3 + i)$. Show your work.

41. You put $600 into an account earning 5% annual interest, compounded continuously. How much will you have after 18 months? Show your work.

42. You roll three number cubes. Can the three events {rolling three of the same number, rolling exactly two of the same number, rolling all different numbers} be used to form a probability distribution? Explain.

43. You roll three number cubes. Find P(all three show the same number).

44. Find the inverse of the matrix $\begin{bmatrix} 6 & -2 \\ 11 & 3 \end{bmatrix}$.

Extended Response

45. In $\triangle ABC$, $m\angle A = 65°$, $b = 23$, and $c = 19$. Show how to find a. Round to the nearest hundredth.

46. Suppose you receive $350 for your birthday. You can put the money into an account earning 4.5% annual interest compounded continuously, or into an account earning 5% annual interest compounded monthly. Write and solve the equations that show how much you would have in each account after one year and after five years.

Activity Lab

A Question of Balance

Applying Trigonometry Why is it so difficult to walk on a balance beam? It is difficult because you must keep your body's center of gravity over a narrow base of support to maintain your balance. You can use this idea to calculate the maximum angle any object (or person) can tip without falling over.

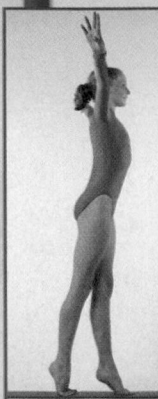

The Balance Beam

The balance beam, used only in women's gymnastics, is 5 m long but only 10 cm wide. A beam exercise lasts between 70 and 90 s. Each movement on the balance beam flows freely into the next, with the gymnast pausing only to hold the balance positions.

Activity 1

Materials: four pieces of 2×4 wood (16 in., 12 in., 8 in., 4 in. long), pencil, protractor

a. Use the diagram to write an equation relating θ to w and the length ℓ of the 2×4.

b. Tip a 16-in.-long piece of 2×4 on the edge of its narrow face. Use a protractor to measure the maximum angle the piece of 2×4 can tip without falling over. Use the equation from part (a) as a check.

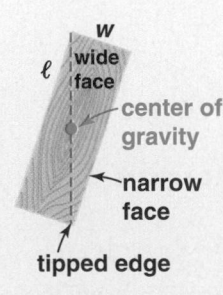

w
wide face
center of gravity
narrow face
tipped edge
ℓ

c. Repeat part (b) for pieces of 2×4 that measure 4 in., 8 in., and 12 in.

d. Reasoning Suppose you tip the 2×4 on the edge of its wide face instead of its narrow face. Write a new equation relating θ to ℓ and to n, the width of the narrow face. Use your new equation to calculate the value of θ for each of the 2×4 pieces from parts (b) and (c).

Balancing on a surfboard

To balance on a surfboard requires constant shifting of position due to the motion of the board on the water.

Balance in Ballet

To dance *en pointe* (on the tips of their toes), ballerinas rely on specially reinforced shoes.

Go Online
PHSchool.com
For: Information about balance
Web Code: age-1453

Balancing Act

The gymnast on the left below is holding a balance. The gymnast in the middle is in a precarious position, with his center of mass tipping over his foot. The gymnast on the right is tipping over, because his center of mass is no longer over his foot.

Activity 2

a. **Writing** Describe a method to measure the angle at which a piece of wood tips. (*Hints:* The diagram shows only one of the many places where you can measure θ. Also, large protractors are more accurate than small ones.)

b. Measure the angle at which each of the four pieces tips over on the edge of its narrow face.

c. Measure the angle at which each of the four pieces tips over on the edge of its wide face.

d. Compare your results from parts (b) and (c) with the angle measures you obtained in Activity 1.

● **Lesson 1-1** Replace each ■ with the symbol <, >, or = to make the sentence true.

1. -5 ■ -8

2. 7 ■ 7

3. 0.1 ■ 0.01

4. 12 ■ $\sqrt{12}$

5. $\frac{3}{8}$ ■ 0.375

6. $\frac{1}{5}$ ■ $\frac{1}{4}$

7. $\frac{1}{3}$ ■ 0.333

8. $\sqrt{6}$ ■ 3

● **Lesson 1-1** Find the opposite and the reciprocal of each number.

9. 102

10. -3.7

11. $2\frac{3}{4}$

12. -0.04

13. $\sqrt{2}$

14. $\pi - 4$

15. $-\frac{8}{5}$

16. 1.5

17. $\frac{6}{7}$

18. $\frac{3\pi}{2}$

19. 0.0001

20. $5\sqrt{7}$

● **Lesson 1-2** Evaluate each expression for the given values of the variables.

21. $6c + 5d - 4c - 3d + 3c - 6d; c = 4$ and $d = -2$

22. $10a + 3b - 5a + 4b + 1a + 5b; a = -3$ and $b = 5$

23. $3m + 9n + 6m - 7n - 4m + 2n; m = 6$ and $n = -4$

● **Lesson 1-3** Solve each equation. Check your answers.

24. $5 - w = 2w - 1$

25. $-2s = 3s - 10$

26. $2(x + 3) + 2(x + 4) = 24$

27. $8z + 12 = 5z - 21$

28. $7b - 6(11 - 2b) = 10$

29. $10k - 7 = 2(13 - 5k)$

● **Lesson 1-4** Solve each inequality. Graph the solution.

30. $3x - 8 \geq 1$

31. $7t + 4 \leq 3t$

32. $3v \leq 5v + 18$

33. $4a < 2a - 7$

34. $7 - x \geq 24$

35. $2(y - 3) + 7 < 21$

● **Lesson 1-4** Solve each compound inequality. Graph the solution.

36. $4r > -12$ and $2r < 10$

37. $5z \geq -10$ and $3z < 3$

38. $7x \geq 21$ and $8x \leq 56$

39. $3x < -6$ or $7x > 56$

40. $9b > 27$ and $4b \leq 44$

41. $5p \geq 10$ or $-2p < 10$

● **Lesson 1-5** Solve each equation. Check your answers.

42. $|4m + 2| = 10$

43. $|9 - 4z| = 53$

44. $|5x| = 30$

45. $|3x - 6| - 7 = 14$

46. $3|2d - 1| = 21$

47. $|2v + 3| - 6 = 14$

● **Lesson 1-5** Solve each inequality. Graph the solution.

48. $|3 - k| < 7$

49. $|2t + 7| \geq 4$

50. $|x - 2| < 6$

51. $2|w + 6| \leq 10$

52. $|3y - 5| + 6 > 15$

53. $3|2z + 5| + 2 \leq 8$

● **Lesson 1-6** Suppose you select a number at random from the sample space $\{1, 2, 3, 4, 5, 6, 7, 8, 9\}$. Find each theoretical probability.

54. P(a number that is a multiple of 5)

55. P(a number that is an integer)

56. P(a number that is a factor of twelve)

57. P(a number that is less than or equal to 4)

58. P(a number that is greater than 6)

59. P(a number that is a composite number)

● **Lessons 1-1, 1-2, and 1-3**

60. You can use the equation $T = 0.6(205 - \frac{a}{2} - r) + r$ to determine the target heart rate, T, for a cardiovascular workout for an athletic male a years old. His rest heart rate is r heartbeats per minute. What is the rest heart rate of an athletic 18-year-old male whose target heart rate is 144 heartbeats per minute?

61. A desktop computer now sells for 15% less than it did last year. The current price is $425. What was the price of the computer last year?

62. Mrs. Chavez invested $6000. She invested the money in two accounts—one with a 4% simple interest and the other with a 6% simple interest. At the end of the year, the total amount she earned in interest was $320. How much did Mrs. Chavez invest in each account?

63. A plane travels from New York City to San Francisco with an average speed of 550 mi/h. Another plane leaves from the same airport a half-hour later and travels the same route with an average speed of 625 mi/h. How many hours later will the second plane pass the first?

64. Mehmed and Colin run around a 450-meter track in opposite directions. They start at the same point and at the same time. Mehmed's speed is 2.0 m/s. Colin's speed is 2.5 m/s. How far will Colin have run when they meet again?

65. Angela is considering two job offers. Job A would pay a salary of $2500 plus a 4% commission on her total sales per month. Job B would pay $2200 plus an 8% commission on all sales over $2000 per month. What is the least amount Angela would have to sell each month for Job B to pay more than Job A?

66. Amando has $625 in his savings account. He wants to take a vacation that he estimates will cost $1300. If possible, he would like to have extra money to buy souvenirs for friends. Amando works 40 hours per week, earns $15 per hour, and saves 6% of each week's earnings. How many whole weeks must he work before he earns enough money to take the vacation?

67. A homeowner needs to rent some cleaning equipment. Company A will rent the machine he needs for $28 plus $4 per hour. Company B will charge $22 plus $4.75 per hour. For what range of hours will Company B charge less than Company A?

● **Lessons 1-4 and 1-5**

68. A metal part for a machine is now 5.85 inches long. The specifications call for it to be 5.72 inches long, with a tolerance of ±0.02 inch. By how much can a machinist decrease the length of the part?

● **Lesson 1-6**

69. In a group of 38 students, 15 take chemistry, 28 take Spanish, and 8 take both chemistry and Spanish. One student is selected at random from the group. What is the probability that the student takes neither chemistry nor Spanish?

70. A bag contains marbles of three different colors. You draw a marble, record its color, then put it back in the bag. The table shows the results of the 150 trials. What is the experimental probability of drawing a red marble?

Color	Frequency
Red	45
Blue	58
Yellow	47

71. Charles is one of a group of five students who have volunteered to work at the ticket table for a school band concert. If two students are selected at random to work at the ticket table, what is the probability that Charles will be one of the two?

72. Within a 10-by-10 grid of squares, two overlapping 6-by-6 squares are drawn. The area of overlap is 9 square units. If a dart hits the 10-by-10 square at a random point, what is the probability that it lands in one or both of the 6-by-6 squares?

Chapter 2

Extra Practice: Skills and Word Problems

● **Lesson 2-1** Determine whether each relation is a function. Justify your answer.

1. $\{(0,1),(1,0),(2,1),(3,1),(4,2)\}$

2. $\{(7,4),(4,9),(-3,1),(1,7),(2,8)\}$

3. $\{(1,4),(3,2),(5,2),(1,-8),(6,7)\}$

4. $\{(-5,1),(0,-3),(-2,1),(10,11),(7,1)\}$

5. $\{(9,3),(6,2),(3,2),(3,1),(6,-2)\}$

6. $\{(4,9),(5,3),(-2,0),(5,4),(8,1)\}$

● **Lesson 2-2** Graph each equation.

7. $y = x - 7$ **8.** $4x - y = 8$ **9.** $y = -x + 4$ **10.** $2x + 5y = 10$

11. $y = -4x + 3$ **12.** $-6x - 2y = 7$ **13.** $-2y = x - 2$ **14.** $3x - 8y = 9$

● **Lesson 2-2** Write in standard form the equation of each line.

15. slope $= 3; (-1, 4)$ **16.** slope $= -1; (0, 7)$ **17.** slope $= \frac{3}{4}; (2, 8)$

18. slope $= -\frac{2}{5}; (3, -9)$ **19.** slope $= \frac{8}{3}; (-2, 0)$ **20.** slope $= -5; (-3, -12)$

● **Lesson 2-2** Write in point-slope form the equation of the line through each pair of points.

21. $(0, 2)$ and $(-1, 3)$ **22.** $(1, 2)$ and $(-2, -4)$ **23.** $(11, 4)$ and $(3, 0)$

24. $(-4, -5)$ and $(-1, -8)$ **25.** $(-5, 6)$ and $(3, -10)$ **26.** $(12, 10)$ and $(0, 0)$

● **Lesson 2-2** Find the slope, y-intercept, and x-intercept of each line.

27. $y = 2x - 5$ **28.** $y = -x + 1$ **29.** $y = 4$ **30.** $y = 5x + 10$

31. $y = \frac{1}{3}x - 15$ **32.** $x = -7$ **33.** $y = -6x$ **34.** $y = -\frac{2}{5}x + 20$

● **Lesson 2-2** Write each equation in standard form.

35. $y = 3x + 9$ **36.** $4x = 6y - 9$ **37.** $2y = 8x - 7$ **38.** $y = -x + 1$

39. $0.3x + 1.2y = 2.4$ **40.** $y = \frac{2}{3}x + 15$ **41.** $x = 8 - y$ **42.** $\frac{1}{2}x - \frac{3}{4}y = 1$

● **Lesson 2-3** Write an equation of a direct variation that passes through each point.

43. $(3, 7)$ **44.** $(5, -8)$ **45.** $(-4, -10)$ **46.** $(-2, 9)$

47. $(-6, 6)$ **48.** $(6, -3)$ **49.** $(12, 8)$ **50.** $(-15, -1)$

● **Lesson 2-5** Graph each equation by writing two linear equations.

51. $y = |x - 2|$ **52.** $y = \left|x + \frac{1}{2}\right|$ **53.** $y = |4x + 3|$ **54.** $y = |4x - 3|$

55. $y = -|x + 4|$ **56.** $y = 2|x - 3|$ **57.** $y = |x + 4| - 2$ **58.** $y = \frac{4}{3}|2x - 1|$

● **Lesson 2-7** Graph each inequality.

59. $y < -x + 5$ **60.** $0.1x + 0.6y \geq 2$ **61.** $y \leq 3x - 1$ **62.** $x + 3y > 12$

63. $y \geq 5x - 3$ **64.** $6x + 2y \geq 7$ **65.** $y + 1 > \frac{1}{3}x + 2$ **66.** $5x - 4y \leq -3$

● **Lesson 2-1**

67. A garden has the shape of an isosceles triangle. The base of the triangle is 42 ft long, with an altitude of h ft. Write an equation that describes the area A of the garden as a function of h. What is the area of the garden for $h = 38$ ft?

68. To avoid air turbulence, a plane climbs from an altitude of 20,700 feet to a higher altitude at the rate of 325 feet per minute. Write a function that describes the altitude, y, of the plane x minutes after it begins its climb. Then find the altitude of the plane for $x = 5$.

● **Lesson 2-2**

69. The blueprint for a toy, shown at the right, identifies two perpendicular rods, each 5 in. long. Suppose each square in the coordinate grid measures 1 in.^{2} and the origin is O. Rods I and II are connected at point $A(4, 3)$.
a. Write an equation in slope-intercept form for the line containing Rod I.
b. Write an equation in point-slope form for the line containing Rod II.

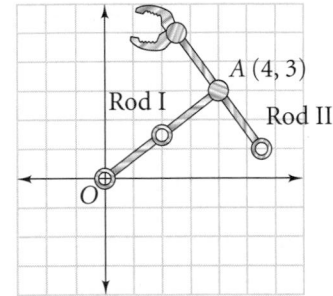

● **Lesson 2-3**

70. When a pump is turned on, it pumps water at a rate of 12 gal/min. What information do you need to know to decide if the volume of water in the tank varies directly with the time the pump is on? Explain.

71. Williamsville has streets that form a square grid. Adams Street forms the x-axis and Calvin Avenue forms the y-axis. A bank is located at $(100, 0)$, a bus stop at $(300, 0)$, and a post office at $(300, 200)$. Suppose a car departs somewhere on Adams Street, as shown at the right.
a. The minimum distance the car has to drive to get to the bank is an absolute value function $f(x)$, where x is the x-coordinate of the location of the car. Write an equation and draw the graph for $f(x)$.
b. Let $g(x)$ be the absolute value function that describes the minimum distance the car has to drive to get to the bus stop. Write an equation and draw the graph for this function.
c. Let $h(x)$ be the function that describes the minimum distance the car has to drive to get to the post office. Write an equation and draw the graph for this function.
d. Describe how the graphs in parts (a)–(c) are related.

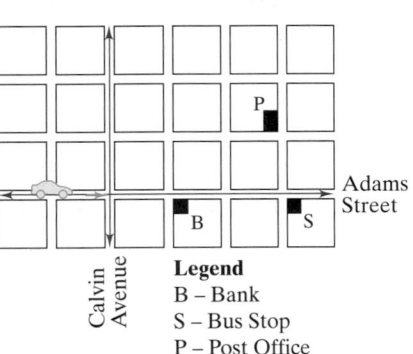

Legend
B – Bank
S – Bus Stop
P – Post Office

● **Lessons 2-4, 2-5, and 2-6**

72. The table shows the winning times in the men's Olympic 100-meter freestyle swimming event for the years 1960–2004. Use a graphing calculator.
a. Make a scatter plot of the data.
b. Find a line of best fit for the data. Round the coefficients to the nearest hundredth.
c. Use the equation for the line of best fit to predict the winning time for the event in the year 2012.

73. A truck rental company purchased a used truck for $18,000. It plans to rent the truck for $75 per day. Write an equation that describes how the profit, y, on the truck is related to the number of days, x, the truck earns rental income. Explain what the intercepts and slope of the graph of this function represent.

Years Since 1960	Winning Time
0	55.20
4	53.40
8	52.20
12	51.22
16	49.99
20	50.40
24	49.80
28	48.63
32	49.02
36	48.74
40	48.30
44	48.17

● **Lesson 2-7**

74. Andrea is going to buy x lbs of pasta salad and y lbs of chicken salad for a party. The pasta salad costs $4 per pound and the chicken salad costs $6 per pound. Andrea has at most $28 to spend. Write and graph an inequality that describes the relationship between x and y.

Chapter 3

Extra Practice: Skills and Word Problems

● **Lesson 3-1** Solve each system by graphing.

1. $\begin{cases} y = 2x + 1 \\ y = 4x - 5 \end{cases}$

2. $\begin{cases} x + y = 2 \\ y = 2x - 1 \end{cases}$

3. $\begin{cases} y = x + 4 \\ y = -2x + 3 \end{cases}$

4. $\begin{cases} 3x - 4y = 13 \\ 2x + y = 5 \end{cases}$

5. $\begin{cases} 2x = y - 7 \\ 4x - 2y = 14 \end{cases}$

6. $\begin{cases} x = 8 \\ x - y = 2 \end{cases}$

● **Lesson 3-2** Solve each system of equations.

7. $\begin{cases} x + y = 5 \\ x - y = -3 \end{cases}$

8. $\begin{cases} y = 3x - 1 \\ 2x + y = 14 \end{cases}$

9. $\begin{cases} 3x + 2y = 12 \\ x + y = 3 \end{cases}$

10. $\begin{cases} x - 4y = 16 \\ x + 2y = 4 \end{cases}$

11. $\begin{cases} y = 2x + 5 \\ y = 4 - x \end{cases}$

12. $\begin{cases} y = 5x - 1 \\ y = 14 \end{cases}$

● **Lesson 3-3** Solve each system of inequalities by graphing.

13. $\begin{cases} y \geq x - 3 \\ y \leq 3x + 7 \end{cases}$

14. $\begin{cases} 3x + 4y > 8 \\ y < 5x \end{cases}$

15. $\begin{cases} -x - 2y \geq -5 \\ y < 3 \end{cases}$

● **Lesson 3-4** Find the values of x and y that maximize or minimize the objective function.

16. $\begin{cases} x \leq 4 \\ y \leq 3 \\ x \geq 0 \\ y \geq 0 \end{cases}$

maximum for
$P = 2x + y$

17. $\begin{cases} x + y \leq 5 \\ y \geq x \\ x \geq 0 \end{cases}$

minimum for
$C = x + y$

18. $\begin{cases} 1 \leq x \leq 6 \\ 2 \leq y \leq 4 \\ x + y \geq 4 \end{cases}$

maximum for
$P = 3x + 2y$

19. A lunch stand makes $.75 in profit on each chef's salad and $1.20 in profit on each Caesar salad. On a typical weekday, it sells between 40 and 60 chef's salads and between 35 and 50 Caesar salads. The total number sold has never exceeded 100 salads. How many of each type of salad should be prepared to maximize profit?

● **Lesson 3-5** Graph each point in coordinate space.

20. $(0, 3, 0)$

21. $(4, 0, -2)$

22. $(0, 0, 5)$

23. $(1, 1, 0)$

24. $(0, 4, 2)$

25. $(-1, 2, 2)$

26. $(3, 0, 1)$

27. $(6, 1, 3)$

28. $(3, -1, 4)$

● **Lesson 3-5** Sketch the graph of each equation.

29. $x - y + z = 4$

30. $2x - y - z = 6$

31. $-x + y + 3z = 9$

32. $x + y + z = 5$

33. $-5x + 2y + 2z = 10$

34. $x - y + 3z = 3$

● **Lesson 3-6** Solve each system of equations.

35. $\begin{cases} x + y + z = 6 \\ x = 2y \\ z = x + 1 \end{cases}$

36. $\begin{cases} x - 2y + z = 8 \\ y - z = 4 \\ z = 3 \end{cases}$

37. $\begin{cases} 3x + y - z = 15 \\ x - y + 3z = -19 \\ 2x + 2y + z = 4 \end{cases}$

38. Carla has $2.40 in nickels and dimes. Deron has $5.50 in dimes and quarters. Deron has as many dimes as Carla has nickels and as many quarters as Carla has dimes. How many of each kind of coin does Carla have?

39. A kayaker can paddle 12 mi in 2 h moving with the river current. Paddling at the same pace, the trip back against the current takes 4 h. Assume that the river current is constant. Find what the kayaker's speed would be in still water.

40. Mrs. Mitchell put a total of $10,000 into two accounts. One account earns 6% simple annual interest. The other account earns 6.5% simple interest. After 1 year, the two accounts earned $632.50 interest. Find how much money was invested in each account.

41. Mr. Chandra bought 2 lbs of cheddar cheese and 3 lbs of chicken loaf. He paid $26.35. Mrs. Hsing paid $18.35 for 1.5 lbs of cheese and 2 lbs of chicken loaf. What was the price per pound of each item?

● Lesson 3-3

42. Leyla wants to buy fish, chicken, or some of each for weekend meals. The fish costs $4 per pound and the chicken costs $3 per pound. She will spend at least $11 but no more than $15.
a. Write a system of inequalities to model the situation.
b. Graph the system to show the possible amounts Layla could buy.

43. A furniture company makes desks and chairs. A carpenter can make a chair in 5 h and a desk in 8 h. Finishers take 2.5 h to paint a chair and 2 h to paint a desk. The carpentry department has enough people to work up to 400 h per week, and the finishing department can put in 120 h per week.
a. Write a system of inequalities to model the situation.
b. Graph the system to show the possible numbers of desks and chairs the company can produce in a week.

● Lesson 3-4

44. There are 20 true/false and 20 multiple choice questions on a test. A correct answer to a true/false question earns 10 points. A correct answer to a multiple choice question earns 12 points. The test makers determined that it takes, on average, 3 minutes to answer a true/false question and 4 minutes to answer a multiple choice question. Students have 1 hour to answer at most 18 questions of their choice. How many of each kind of question should a student answer correctly to get the greatest possible score?

45. A caterer must make at least 50 gal of potato soup and at least 120 gal of tomato soup. One chef can make 5 gal of potato soup and 6 gal of tomato soup in 1 h. Another chef can make 4 gal of potato soup and 12 gal of tomato soup in 1 h. The first chef earns $20/h. The second chef earns $22/h. How many hours should the company ask each chef to work to minimize the cost?

● Lessons 3-5 and 3-6

46. Three pumps can transfer 4150 gal of water per day when working at the same time. Pumps A and B together can transfer 3200 gal per day. Pumps A and C together can transfer 2900 gal per day. How many gallons can each pump transfer working alone?

47. For the school play, the Chavez family bought 2 student tickets, 1 adult ticket, and 2 senior tickets for $43. The Martinez family bought 3 student tickets and 2 adult tickets for $48. The Lynn family bought 4 student tickets, 2 adult tickets, and 1 senior ticket for $62. What was the price of each kind of ticket?

● **Lesson 4-1** State the dimensions of each matrix. Identify the indicated element.

1. $\begin{bmatrix} 3 & 1 & -5 \\ 6 & 9 & 10 \end{bmatrix}; a_{21}$

2. $\begin{bmatrix} 0.5 & 6.1 \\ -9.2 & 4.7 \end{bmatrix}; a_{11}$

3. $\begin{bmatrix} 56 & -83 & 12 \\ 101 & -71 & 49 \end{bmatrix}; a_{12}$

4. $\begin{bmatrix} 5 & 8 \\ -2 & 3 \\ 3 & 4 \end{bmatrix}; a_{21}$

5. $\begin{bmatrix} \frac{1}{4} & \frac{3}{8} \end{bmatrix}; a_{12}$

6. $\begin{bmatrix} 17 & -23 & 79 \\ 47 & 61 & 5 \end{bmatrix}; a_{22}$

● **Lesson 4-2** Find each sum or difference.

7. $\begin{bmatrix} -8 & 3 \\ 19 & -45 \end{bmatrix} + \begin{bmatrix} 12 & 64 \\ -7 & 63 \end{bmatrix}$

8. $\begin{bmatrix} 3.6 & -9.8 \\ 4.0 & -1.7 \end{bmatrix} - \begin{bmatrix} 0.8 & 3.4 \\ -6.1 & 7.9 \end{bmatrix}$

9. $\begin{bmatrix} 4 & 6 & -3 \\ 8 & -9 & -1 \end{bmatrix} - \begin{bmatrix} 10 & 7 & -3 \\ -9 & 2 & 7 \end{bmatrix}$

10. $\begin{bmatrix} -308 & 651 \\ 912 & -347 \end{bmatrix} + \begin{bmatrix} 105 & 318 \\ -762 & -438 \end{bmatrix}$

● **Lesson 4-3** Solve each matrix equation.

11. $\begin{bmatrix} 25 & -60 \\ 42 & 91 \end{bmatrix} + X = \begin{bmatrix} -37 & 61 \\ 85 & 37 \end{bmatrix}$

12. $\begin{bmatrix} -8 & 3 & 1 \\ -9 & 6 & 7 \end{bmatrix} - X = \begin{bmatrix} 5 & 8 & 3 \\ 4 & 2 & 6 \end{bmatrix}$

13. $X + \begin{bmatrix} 6 & 2 & 9 \\ 1 & 5 & 10 \end{bmatrix} = \begin{bmatrix} 11 & -5 & 16 \\ 3 & 6 & 8 \end{bmatrix}$

14. $X - \begin{bmatrix} 2.3 & 6.5 \\ 9.4 & -8.2 \end{bmatrix} = \begin{bmatrix} -4.7 & 3.6 \\ 9.4 & -5.8 \end{bmatrix}$

● **Lesson 4-3** For exercises 15–26, use matrices A, B, C, and D shown below. Perform the indicated operations if they are defined. If an operation is not defined, label it *undefined*.

$$A = \begin{bmatrix} 8 & 1 \\ -2 & 5 \end{bmatrix} \qquad B = \begin{bmatrix} -3 & 1 & 0 \\ -2 & -1 & 5 \end{bmatrix} \qquad C = \begin{bmatrix} 9 & 4 \\ 5 & 1 \\ 2 & 0 \end{bmatrix} \qquad D = \begin{bmatrix} 1 & 7 & 3 \\ 8 & 10 & -2 \end{bmatrix}$$

15. AB

16. BD

17. $2A$

18. CD

19. DA

20. $-3B$

21. $0.2A$

22. BA

23. $5C$

24. CB

25. $\frac{1}{2}D$

26. BC

● **Lesson 4-4** Use $\triangle ABC$ with coordinates $A(1, 5)$, $B(2, -1)$, and $C(4, 3)$. Write the coordinates of each image in matrix form.

27. a dilation 5 times the size

28. a translation 3 units left and 1 unit up

29. a translation 2 units right and 7 units down

30. a dilation one third the size

● **Lesson 4-5** Solve each matrix equation. If an equation cannot be solved, explain why.

31. $\begin{bmatrix} 2 & 1 \\ -1 & 7 \end{bmatrix} X = \begin{bmatrix} 8 & 1 \\ -12 & 41 \end{bmatrix}$

32. $\begin{bmatrix} -1 & 0 \\ 6 & 3 \end{bmatrix} X = \begin{bmatrix} -9 \\ -3 \end{bmatrix}$

33. $\begin{bmatrix} -3 & 5 \\ 1 & 8 \end{bmatrix} X = \begin{bmatrix} 29 \\ 58 \end{bmatrix}$

● **Lesson 4-7** Solve each system of equations. Check your answers.

34. $\begin{cases} x - y = 3 \\ x + y = 5 \end{cases}$

35. $\begin{cases} x - 2y = 7 \\ x + 3y = 12 \end{cases}$

36. $\begin{cases} 2x + 5y = 10 \\ x + y = 2 \end{cases}$

● **Lessons 4-1, 4-2, and 4-3**

37. A frozen yogurt supplier uses two machines to make chocolate and vanilla frozen yogurt. Both machines can be used in the morning and afternoon. Matrix A show the maximum hourly output of each machine. Matrix B shows how long the machines are used for production of each flavor.

Matrix A: **Output (gal/h)**

	Chocolate	Vanilla
Machine 1	4	5
Machine 2	7	8

Matrix B: **Time (h)**

	A.M.	P.M.
Chocolate	2	3
Vanilla	1	2

a. Compute the product AB of these matrices.
b. Describe what this product represents.

38. A distributor has orders for desk lamps and floor lamps from two motels. Matrix A shows the number of lamps each motel will purchase. Matrix B shows the cost of each type of lamp.

Matrix A:

	Desk	Floor
Motel 1	20	7
Motel 2	25	6

Matrix B:

	Cost
Desk	85
Floor	130

a. Compute the product AB of these matrices.
b. Describe what this product represents.

● **Lesson 4-4**

39. The matrix $\begin{bmatrix} \frac{\sqrt{3}}{2} & -\frac{1}{2} \\ \frac{1}{2} & \frac{\sqrt{3}}{2} \end{bmatrix}$ represents a 30° counterclockwise rotation. The preimage is $\triangle ABC$ with the vertices $A(1, 1)$, $B(1, 2)$, and $C(5, 4)$. Write a matrix for the vertices of the image.

● **Lessons 4-5 and 4-6**

40. County economists calculated that, in an average year, 9% of employed people lose their jobs and 86% of the unemployed find new jobs. The remaining people remain employed or unemployed, depending on their previous status. On January 1, the county has an unemployment rate of 7%. Calculate the expected unemployment rate for the next two years to the nearest tenth of a percent.

● **Lessons 4-7 and 4-8**

41. Margery got a total of 249 points on three tests. The combined scores on the first two tests were 95 more than the score on the third test. The score on the second test was 6 points more than the score on the first test. Write and solve a matrix equation to find the score on each test.

42. Leona's Diner offers 8-piece, 12-piece, and 16-piece family chicken meals. The table at the right lists the costs of three different orders. What is the price of each kind of meal?

8-piece meals	12-piece meals	16-piece meals	Total Cost
2	3	1	$96
4	5	0	$133
2	4	2	$134

43. At a diner, two hot dogs and one hamburger cost $10, while three hot dogs and two hamburgers cost $17.25. Write and solve a matrix equation to find the cost of a hot dog and a hamburger.

● **Lesson 5-1** Determine whether each function is *linear* or *quadratic*. Identify the quadratic, linear, and constant terms.

1. $y = 3x + 4$

2. $y = x^2 + 1$

3. $3x + 2y = 1$

4. $y = (x + 1)(x - 1)$

5. $y = 3 - x^2$

6. $y = 5x(x + 2)$

● **Lessons 5-2 and 5-3** Graph each function.

7. $y = 3x^2$

8. $y = (x + 3)^2 + 1$

9. $y = 2x^2 + 4$

10. $y = \frac{1}{2}(x - 3)^2$

11. $y = x^2 - 9$

12. $y = 2(x + 1)^2 - 5$

13. $y = (x + 1)^2 - 3$

14. $y = (x - 2)^2$

● **Lesson 5-4** Factor each expression.

15. $x^2 + 3x - 54$

16. $x^2 + 10x + 24$

17. $x^2 - 36$

18. $x^2 - 9x - 36$

19. $x^2 - 15x + 56$

20. $25x^2 + 70x + 49$

21. $7x^2 - 20x - 3$

22. $5x^2 + 23x - 10$

23. $\frac{1}{4}x^2 - 4$

24. $x^2 - 6x - 16$

25. $4x^2 + 12x + 40$

26. $4x^2 - 6x + 9$

● **Lesson 5-5** Solve each equation by factoring, by taking square roots, or by graphing. When necessary, round your answer to the nearest hundredth.

27. $x^2 + 4x - 1 = 0$

28. $4x^2 - 100 = 0$

29. $x^2 = -2x + 1$

30. $x^2 - 9 = 0$

31. $2x^2 + 4x = 70$

32. $x^2 - 30 = 10$

33. $x^2 + 4x = 0$

34. $x^2 + 3x + 2 = 0$

● **Lesson 5-6** Simplify each expression.

35. $(3 - i) + (5 - 2i)$

36. $(4 + 2i)(1 - i)$

37. $(4 + 2i) - (3 + 5i)$

38. $(8 - 3i)(6 + 9i)$

39. $(2 + 5i) - (-6 + i)$

40. $(-2 - 3i)(7 - i)$

● **Lesson 5-6** Solve each equation. Check your answers.

41. $x^2 + 16 = 0$

42. $4x^2 = -1$

43. $x^2 = -10$

44. $4x^2 + 48 = 0$

45. $-2x^2 = 5$

46. $x^2 + 3 = 0$

● **Lesson 5-6** Find the first three output values of each fractal-generating function. Use $z = 0$ as the first input value.

47. $f(z) = z^2 - i$

48. $f(z) = z^2 + 2 + i$

● **Lessons 5-7 and 5-8** Solve each equation by completing the square or using the Quadratic Formula.

49. $x^2 + 5x + 8 = 4$

50. $8x^2 + 64 = 0$

51. $2x^2 - 5x + 1 = 0$

52. $3x^2 = x - 9$

53. $x^2 + 10 = 4x - 2$

54. $x^2 - 7x = 0$

55. $x^2 + 4x + 4 = 0$

56. $x^2 - 7 = 0$

57. $x^2 + 8x - 17 = 0$

● **Lesson 5-8** Evaluate the discriminant of each equation. Tell how many solutions each equation has and whether the solutions are real or imaginary.

58. $x^2 + 4x = 17$

59. $2x^2 + x = -1$

60. $x^2 - 4x + 5 = 0$

61. $2x^2 + 5x = 0$

62. $x^2 - 19 = 1$

63. $3x^2 = 8x - 4$

64. $-2x^2 + 1 = 7x$

65. $4x^2 + 4x = -1$

● **Lesson 5-1**

66. The table shows the relation between the speed of a car and its stopping distance.

Speed (mi/h)	35	45	50	60
Stopping Distance (ft)	96	140	165	221

   a. Use a quadratic function to model the data.
   b. Predict the stopping distance for a car traveling at 65 mi/h.

● **Lessons 5-2 and 5-3**

67. Martin has 120 feet of fencing to enclose two rectangular play areas for children. He plans to enclose a rectangular area and then divide it into two equal sections, as shown in the figure.
   a. Find the dimensions of the largest total area Martin can enclose.
   b. Find the area of each of the small play areas.

68. Marnie throws a softball straight up into the air. The ball leaves her hand when it is exactly 5 ft from the ground. The height h of the ball, in feet, can be written as a function of time t, in seconds, as $h = -16t^2 + 40t + 5$.
   a. What is the maximum height the ball reaches?
   b. Marnie catches the ball 5 ft from the ground. How long was the ball in the air?

● **Lessons 5-4 and 5-5**

69. Hal's sister is 5 years older than Hal. The product of their ages is 456. How old are Hal and his sister?

70. A toy rocket is fired upward from the ground. The relation between its height h, in feet, and the time t from launch, in seconds, can be described by the equation $h = -16t^2 + 64t$. How long does the rocket stay more than 48 feet above the ground?

71. The expression $P(x) = 2500x - 2x^2$ describes the profit of a company that customizes bulldozers when it customizes x bulldozers in a month.
   a. How many bulldozers per month must the company customize to make the maximum possible profit? What is the maximum profit?
   b. Describe a reasonable domain and range for the function $P(x)$.
   c. For what number of bulldozers per month is the profit at least $750,000?

72. Flor is designing a kite with two perpendicular crosspieces that are 26 inches and 24 inches long, as shown in the figure. How long should $\overline{AK}$ be so that $\overline{AB} \perp \overline{BC}$ and $\overline{AD} \perp \overline{DC}$?

73. The lengths of the sides of a right triangle are x, $x + 4$, and $x + 8$ inches. What is the value of x? What is the length of the hypotenuse of the triangle?

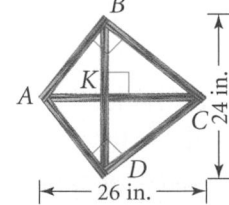

● **Lessons 5-6, 5-7, and 5-8**

74. The height y of a parabolic arch is given by $y = -\frac{1}{16}x^2 + 40$, where x is the horizontal distance from the center of the base of the arch. All distances are in feet.
   a. What is the highest point on the arch?
   b. How wide is the arch at the base to the nearest tenth of a foot?

75. An archer's arrow follows a parabolic path. The path of the arrow can be described by the equation $y = -0.005x^2 + 2x + 5$.
   a. Describe the meaning of the y-intercept of the graph of the equation.
   b. What is the horizontal distance the arrow travels before it hits the ground? Round your answer to the nearest foot.

● **Lesson 6-1** Write each polynomial in standard form. Then classify it by degree and by number of terms.

1. $a^2 + 4a - 5a^2 - a$

2. $3x - \frac{1}{3} - 5x$

3. $3n^2 + n^3 - n - 3 - 3n^3$

4. $15 - y^2 - 10y - 8 + 8y$

5. $6c^2 - 4c + 7 - 8c^2$

6. $3x^2 - 5x - x^2 + x + 4x$

● **Lesson 6-2** Write a polynomial function in standard form with the given zeros.

7. $x = 3, 2, -1$

8. $x = 1, 1, 2$

9. $x = -2, -1, 1$

10. $x = 1, 2, 6$

11. $x = -3, -1, 5$

12. $x = 0, 0, 2, 3$

13. $x = -2, 1, 2, 2$

14. $x = 2, 4, 5, 7$

● **Lesson 6-3** Divide.

15. $\left(x^3 - 3x^2 + 2\right) \div (x - 1)$

16. $\left(x^3 - x^2 - 6x\right) \div (x - 3)$

17. $\left(2x^3 + 10x^2 + 8x\right) \div (x + 4)$

18. $\left(x^4 + x^2 - 6\right) \div \left(x^2 + 3\right)$

19. $\left(x^2 - 4x + 2\right) \div (x - 2)$

20. $\left(x^3 + 11x + 12\right) \div (x + 3)$

● **Lesson 6-4** Solve each equation.

21. $t^3 - 3t^2 - 10t = 0$

22. $4m^3 + m^2 - m + 5 = 0$

23. $t^3 - 6t^2 + 12t - 8 = 0$

24. $2c^3 - 7c^2 - 4c = 0$

25. $w^4 - 13w^2 + 36 = 0$

26. $x^3 + 2x^2 - 13x + 10 = 0$

● **Lesson 6-5** Find the roots of each polynomial equation.

27. $x^3 + 2x^2 + 3x + 6 = 0$

28. $x^3 - 3x^2 + 4x - 12 = 0$

29. $3x^4 + 11x^3 + 14x^2 + 7x + 1 = 0$

30. $3x^4 - x^3 - 22x^2 + 24x = 0$

31. $45x^3 + 93x^2 - 12 = 0$

32. $8x^4 - 66x^3 + 175x^2 - 132x - 45 = 0$

● **Lesson 6-7** Evaluate each expression.

33. $6!$

34. $3!4!$

35. $\frac{7!}{4!}$

36. $\frac{6!2!}{8!}$

37. $_8P_5$

38. $_4C_1$

39. $_6C_2$

40. $_6P_2$

41. $_7C_3$

42. $_7P_3$

43. $2\left(_7C_5\right)$

44. $\frac{_7C_5}{_5C_2}$

● **Lesson 6-7** Indicate whether each situation involves a combination or a permutation. Then answer the question.

45. How many different orders can you choose to read six of the nine books on your summer reading list?

46. How many ways are there to choose five shirts out of seven to take to camp?

47. How many ways can you choose two out of four kinds of flowers for a bouquet?

● **Lesson 6-8** Use the Binomial Theorem to expand each binomial.

48. $(x - 1)^3$

49. $(3x + 2)^4$

50. $(4x + 10)^3$

51. $(2x + 5y)^4$

52. $\left(x^2 + 2\right)^4$

53. $(x + 2y)^7$

54. $(5x - y)^5$

55. $\left(x - 4y^3\right)^4$

56. Tonya wants to make a metal tray by cutting four identical square corner pieces from a rectangular metal sheet. Then she will bend the sides up to make an open tray.

   a. Let the length of each side of the removed squares be x in. Express the volume of the box as a polynomial function of x.

   b. Find the dimensions of a tray that would have a 384-in.^{3} capacity.

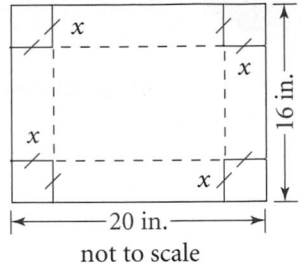

20 in.
not to scale

57. The product of three consecutive integers is 210. Use N to represent the middle integer.

   a. Write the product as a polynomial function of $P(N)$.

   b. Find the three integers.

58. To determine safe dosage of a medication, researchers measure the concentration of the medication in a patient's bloodstream. Let the function that models the concentration in parts per million at x hours after the medication is administered be $C(x) = -\frac{2}{3}x^4 + 8x^3 - \frac{130}{3}x^2 + 116x$.

   a. How many hours does it take for the medication to be completely eliminated from a patient's bloodstream?

   b. How many hours is the concentration above 80 parts per million?

59. A block of cheese is a cube whose side is x in. long. You cut off a 1-inch thick piece from the right side. Then you cut off a 3-inch thick piece from the top, as shown at the right. The volume of the remaining block is 2002 in.^{3}. What are the dimensions of the original block of cheese?

60. You can construct triangles by connecting three vertices of a convex polygon with n sides. The number of all possible such triangles can be represented as $f(n) = \frac{n^3 - 3n^2 + 2n}{6}$. Find the value of n such that you can construct 84 such triangles from the polygon.

61. You must answer exactly 12 out of 15 questions on a test. How many different ways can you select the questions to answer?

62. A lab assigns a three-digit identification to each subject in an experiment. No two subjects have the same identification. No digit can be repeated in an identification. What is the greatest number of subjects that can be used in the experiment?

63. To mark its eighth anniversary, Pizzeria Otto has a special coupon that offers the same price on a pizza with any combination of the 8 original toppings. Each pizza must have at least one topping. How many different kinds of pizza can be ordered with the coupon?

64. Ten friends want to take photographs of each other with exactly four of them in each picture. They want exactly one photograph with each combination. How many photographs do they need to take?

65. A total of 23 students will be coming to the end-of-the-year picnic. In how many ways can the teacher select 6 students for the clean-up crew?

66. City streets form a square grid. Each street runs one-way, either north or east. You want to take a taxi from a post office to a bank that is five blocks east and seven blocks north. How many different routes can the taxi take from the post office to the bank?

Extra Skills and Word Problems

Chapter 7

Extra Practice: Skills and Word Problems

● **Lesson 7-1** Simplify each radical expression. Use absolute value symbols as needed.

1. $\sqrt{36x^4}$ **2.** $\sqrt{c^{80}d^{50}}$ **3.** $\sqrt[4]{81x^{12}}$ **4.** $\sqrt[3]{-64}$

5. $\sqrt[5]{-32k^5}$ **6.** $\sqrt[4]{\frac{1}{16}w^{12}}$ **7.** $\sqrt[4]{m^{18}n^8}$ **8.** $\sqrt[3]{27y^{15}}$

● **Lesson 7-2** Multiply or divide and simplify. Assume that all variables are positive.

9. $\sqrt{3x^4} \cdot \sqrt{24x^3}$ **10.** $\sqrt[3]{4} \cdot \sqrt[3]{18}$ **11.** $\sqrt{5a^3} \cdot \sqrt{20a}$

12. $\frac{\sqrt{80}}{\sqrt{5}}$ **13.** $\frac{\sqrt{18x^5y}}{\sqrt{2x}}$ **14.** $\frac{\sqrt[3]{640w^3z^8}}{\sqrt[3]{5wz^4}}$

● **Lesson 7-3** Simplify.

15. $2\sqrt{7} + 3\sqrt{7}$ **16.** $\sqrt{32} + \sqrt{8}$ **17.** $\sqrt{7x} + \sqrt{28x}$

18. $3\sqrt{18} + 2\sqrt{72}$ **19.** $\sqrt{27} + \sqrt{48}$ **20.** $8\sqrt{45} - 3\sqrt{80}$

● **Lesson 7-4** Write each expression in simplest form. Assume that all variables are positive.

21. $\left(x^{-\frac{4}{3}}y^{\frac{3}{5}}\right)^{15}$ **22.** $\left(x^{\frac{1}{4}}y^{-\frac{3}{8}}\right)^{16}$ **23.** $\left(8x^{15}y^{-9}\right)^{-\frac{1}{3}}$ **24.** $\left(-27x^{-9}y^6\right)^{\frac{1}{3}}$

25. $\left(-32x^{-10}y^{15}\right)^{\frac{1}{5}}$ **26.** $\left(32x^{20}y^{-10}\right)^{-\frac{1}{5}}$ **27.** $\left(\frac{81y^{16}}{16x^{12}}\right)^{\frac{1}{4}}$ **28.** $\left(\frac{16x^{14}}{81y^{18}}\right)^{\frac{1}{2}}$

● **Lesson 7-5** Solve. Check for extraneous solutions.

29. $\sqrt{13x - 10} = 3x$ **30.** $\sqrt{x + 20} = x$

31. $(4x - 12)^{\frac{1}{2}} + 3 = x$ **32.** $(7x)^{\frac{1}{3}} = (5x + 2)^{\frac{1}{3}}$

33. $\sqrt{x - 2} - \sqrt{2x + 3} = -2$ **34.** $\sqrt{10x} - 2\sqrt{5x - 25} = 0$

● **Lesson 7-6** Let $f(x) = x^2$ and $g(x) = 3x + 1$. Evaluate each expression.

35. $(f \circ g)(0)$ **36.** $(f \circ g)(2)$ **37.** $(f \circ g)(-3)$

38. $(f \circ g)(5)$ **39.** $(g \circ f)(0)$ **40.** $(g \circ f)(1)$

41. $(g \circ f)(-1)$ **42.** $(f \circ f)(3)$ **43.** $(g \circ g)(4)$

● **Lesson 7-7** For each function f, find f^{-1} and the domain and range of f and f^{-1}. Determine whether f^{-1} is a function.

44. $f(x) = 6x + 1$ **45.** $f(x) = \sqrt{x + 4}$ **46.** $f(x) = \sqrt{x - 3}$

47. $f(x) = \sqrt{-5x + 2}$ **48.** $f(x) = 3x^2 + 1$ **49.** $f(x) = 2 - x^2$

● **Lesson 7-8** Graph each function.

50. $y = \sqrt{x}$ **51.** $y = \sqrt{x} - 1$ **52.** $y = \sqrt{x} + 3$

53. $y = \sqrt{x + 3}$ **54.** $y = 4\sqrt{x}$ **55.** $y = \frac{3}{4}\sqrt{x}$

56. $y = 2\sqrt{x - 5} + 2$ **57.** $y = \sqrt[3]{x} + 1$ **58.** $y = \sqrt[3]{x - 2} - 3$

Lessons 7-1, 7-2, and 7-3

59. The time T it takes a pendulum to make a full swing in each direction and return to its original position is called the period of the pendulum. The equation $T = 2\pi\sqrt{\frac{\ell}{32}}$ relates the length of the pendulum ℓ, in feet, to its period T, in seconds. How long is a pendulum if its period is 3 seconds? Round the answer to the nearest tenth.

60. You can use the expression $D = 1.2\sqrt{h}$ to approximate the visibility range D, in miles, from a height of h feet above ground.
a. Estimate the visibility from a height of 900 feet.
b. How far above ground is an observer whose visibility range is 84 miles?

61. You can approximate the speed of a falling object as $v = 8\sqrt{d}$, where v is the speed in feet per second and d is the distance, in feet, the object has fallen. Express d in terms of v.

Lessons 7-4, 7-5, and 7-6

62. Halina works in a department store. Three times per year she is allowed to combine her employee discount with special sale prices. Let x be the retail price of a blouse.
a. Halina's employee discount is 20%. Write a function $E(x)$ that represents the cost of the blouse after the discount.
b. Due to a manufacturer's incentive, the blouse is marked down 25%. Write a function $M(x)$ that represents the sale price.
c. The sales tax on clothing is 6%. Write a function $T(x)$ that describes the cost of a clothing item with sales tax included.
d. Halina found a blouse to which the discounts apply. Use the function composition $f = T \circ E \circ M$ to write the function $f(x)$ that represents the price Halina will pay for the blouse.

63. You invest p dollars in an account that earns a simple interest of 6%. The function that represents the account balance at the end of the year is $f(p) = 1.06p$.
a. Suppose that at the end of the year you deposit $500 in the account. Write a new function $g(p)$ that shows the balance that will earn interest in the second year.
b. At the end of every year you add $500 to the account. The interest rate remains 6%. Write a composition of functions f and g to find the account balance at the end of the third year, before adding the $500. Find that balance for an initial investment of $1000.

Lessons 7-7 and 7-8

64. You can use the function $f(x) = 331.4 + 0.6x$ to approximate the speed of sound in dry air, where x is the temperature in degrees Celsius.
a. Write an algebraic expression for the inverse function $f^{-1}(x)$.
b. Evaluate $f^{-1}(x)$ for $x = 350$. Round the result to the nearest whole number. Explain what your result represents.

65. Nisha built a model rocket. The initial speed of the rocket is 64 ft/s. The equation $h(t) = -16t^2 + 64t$ describes the relationship between the height of the rocket h, in feet, as a function of time t, in seconds.
a. Write an equation for h^{-1}. (*Hint*: Use $t(h) = \ldots$.) Is this relation a function? Explain what this relation represents.
b. Write a function that can be used to find how long it takes the object to reach a given height h as it moves upward.

Extra Practice: Skills and Word Problems

● **Lesson 8-1** Write an exponential equation $y = ab^x$ whose graph passes through the given points.

1. $(1, 10), (2, 25)$

2. $\left(2, 10\frac{2}{3}\right), (-1, 4.5)$

3. $(2, 6), (4, 54)$

4. $(-2, 0.05), (2, 12.8)$

5. $(2, 128), (-1, 16)$

6. $(-1, 12.25), (1, 4)$

● **Lesson 8-1** Without graphing, determine whether each equation represents exponential growth or exponential decay.

7. $y = 10^x$

8. $y = 327(0.05)^x$

9. $y = 1.023(0.98)^x$

10. $y = 0.5(1.67)^x$

11. $y = 1.14^x$

12. $y = 8(1.3)^x$

13. $y = 2\left(\frac{9}{10}\right)^x$

14. $y = 4.1(0.72)^x$

15. $y = 9.2(2.3)^x$

● **Lessons 8-1 and 8-2** Graph each equation.

16. $y = 3^x$

17. $y = 2(4)^x$

18. $y = 2^{-x}$

19. $y = \left(\frac{1}{4}\right)^x$

20. $y = 2^{3x}$

21. $y = 9^{-2x}$

22. $y = -0.1^x$

23. $y = -\left(\frac{1}{2}\right)^x$

● **Lesson 8-3** Write each equation in logarithmic form.

24. $100 = 10^2$

25. $9^3 = 729$

26. $64 = 4^3$

27. $\left(\frac{1}{2}\right)^4 = \frac{1}{16}$

28. $49^{\frac{1}{2}} = 7$

29. $\left(\frac{1}{3}\right)^{-3} = 27$

30. $625^{\frac{1}{4}} = 5$

31. $2^{-5} = \frac{1}{32}$

32. $6^2 = 36$

● **Lesson 8-3** Graph each logarithmic function.

33. $y = 2 \log x$

34. $y = \log_8 x$

35. $y = \log_4 (x + 1)$

36. $y = 3 + \log x$

37. $y = -1 + \log_2 x$

38. $y = \log (x - 2)$

39. $y = \log (x + 2)$

40. $y = \log (x - 5)$

● **Lesson 8-4** Write each expression as a single logarithm.

41. $\log 8 + \log 3$

42. $4(\log_2 x + \log_2 3)$

43. $3 \log x + 4 \log x$

44. $\log 4 + \log 2 - \log 5$

45. $\log r - \log t + 2 \log s$

46. $2 \log x - 4 \log y$

● **Lesson 8-4** Expand each logarithm.

47. $\log_b 2x^2y^3$

48. $\log_b 3m^3p^2$

49. $\log_b (4mn)^5$

50. $\log_b \frac{x^2}{2y}$

51. $\log_b \frac{(xy)^4}{2}$

52. $\log_b \sqrt[5]{x^3}$

● **Lessons 8-5 and 8-6** Solve each equation.

53. $\sqrt[3]{y^2} = 4$

54. $2 - 4^x = -62$

55. $\log x + \log 2 = 5$

56. $\log_3 (x + 1) = 4$

57. $e^x = 5$

58. $e^{\frac{x}{4}} = 5$

59. $\ln x - \ln 4 = 7$

60. $\log 4x = -1$

61. $\log 4 - \log x = -2$

62. $\ln 2 + \ln x = 4$

63. $4 + 5^x = 29$

64. $e^{3x} = 20$

Lessons 8-1 and 8-2

65. Mr. Andersen put $1000 into an account that earns 4.5% annual interest. The interest is compounded annually and there are no withdrawals. How much money will be in the account at the end of 30 years?

66. A manufacturer bought a new rolling press for $48,000. It has depreciated in value at an annual rate of 15%. What is its value 5 years after purchase? Round to the nearest hundred dollars.

67. You place $900 in an investment account that earns 6% interest compounded continuously. Find the balance after 5 years.

68. Bram invested $10,000 in an account that earns simple 5% interest annually.
  a. How much interest does the account earn in the first 10 years? Round to the nearest dollar.
  b. How much more would the account earn in interest in the first 10 years if the interest compounded continuously? Round to the nearest dollar.

69. Radium-226 has a half-life of 1660 years. How many years does it take a radium sample to decay to 55% of the original amount? Round your answer to the nearest year.

70. The population of Blinsk was 26,150 in 2000. In 2005, the population was 28,700. Find the growth function $P(x)$ that models the population.

Lessons 8-3 and 8-4

71. You can use the equation $N = k \log A$ to estimate the number of species N that live in a region of area A. The parameter k is determined by the conditions in the region. In a rain forest, 2700 species live in 500 km^2. How many species would remain if half of the forest area were destroyed by logging and farming?

72. The work done in joules (J) by a gas expanding from volume V_1 to volume V_2 is modeled by the equation $W = nRT \ln V_2 - nRT \ln V_1$, where n is the quantity of gas in moles (mol), T is the temperature in kelvin (K), and $R = 8.314 \frac{\text{J}}{\text{mol} \cdot \text{K}}$.
  a. Write the equation in terms of the ratio of the two volumes.
  b. Find the work done by 1 mol of gas at 300 K as it doubles its volume.

Lessons 8-5 and 8-6

73. The function $T(t) = T_r + (T_i - T_r)e^{kt}$ models Newton's Law of Cooling. It allows you to predict the temperature $T(t)$ of an object t minutes after it is placed in a constant-temperature cooling environment, such as a refrigerator. T_i is the initial temperature of the object, and T_r is the temperature inside the refrigerator. The number k is a constant for the particular object in question.
  a. A canned fruit drink takes 5 minutes to cool from 75°F to 68°F after it is placed in a refrigerator that keeps a constant temperature of 38°F. Find the value of the constant k for the fruit drink. Round to the nearest thousandth.
  b. What will be the temperature of the fruit drink after it has been in the refrigerator for 30 minutes?
  c. How long will the fruit drink have to stay in the refrigerator to have a temperature of 40°F?
  d. Will the fruit drink ever have a temperature of exactly 38°F? Explain.

74. The adult population of a city is 1,150,000. A consultant to a law firm uses the function $P(t) = 1,150,000(1 - e^{-0.03t})$ to estimate the number of people $P(t)$ who have heard about a major crime t days after the crime was first reported. About how many days does it take for 60% of the population to have been exposed to news of the crime?

● **Lesson 9-1** Suppose that x and y vary inversely. Write a function that models each inverse variation.

1. $x = 3$ when $y = 2$ **2.** $x = 4$ when $y = -1$ **3.** $x = 5$ when $y = 8$

4. $x = -6$ when $y = -2$ **5.** $x = -8$ when $y = 3$ **6.** $x = 10$ when $y = 15$

● **Lesson 9-2** Sketch the asymptotes and the graph of each equation.

7. $y = \dfrac{x+1}{x-2}$ **8.** $y = \dfrac{x-3}{(x+1)^2}$ **9.** $y = \dfrac{3x}{2x+1}$ **10.** $y = \dfrac{8-x}{x}$

11. $y = \dfrac{x-4}{x^2}$ **12.** $y = \dfrac{2x+1}{2x-1}$ **13.** $y = \dfrac{x}{x+3}$ **14.** $y = \dfrac{x+2}{x-4}$

● **Lesson 9-3** Find any points of discontinuity for each rational function.

15. $y = \dfrac{3x^2 + 2x}{x}$ **16.** $y = \dfrac{x^2 - 16}{x^2 + 4}$ **17.** $y = \dfrac{(x+2)(x-1)}{(x+2)^2(x-1)}$ **18.** $y = \dfrac{4}{x-6}$

19. $y = \dfrac{9x}{3x^3 - 6x}$ **20.** $y = \dfrac{x^2 + 7x + 12}{x+4}$ **21.** $y = \dfrac{x-7}{x-7}$ **22.** $y = \dfrac{x^2 - 3x + 2}{x-1}$

● **Lesson 9-4** Simplify each rational expression. What are the restrictions on the variables?

23. $\dfrac{x^2 + 9x + 18}{x+6}$ **24.** $\dfrac{x^2 + 3x + 2}{x-1} \cdot \dfrac{1-x}{x+2}$

25. $\dfrac{x^2 - 2x - 8}{x+3} \div \dfrac{x-4}{x+3}$ **26.** $\dfrac{2x^2 + 5x - 3}{x^2 - 4x} \cdot \dfrac{2x^3 - 8x^2}{x^2 + 6x + 9}$

27. $\dfrac{3x+1}{x^2 - 6x - 6} \div \dfrac{6x^2 + 11x + 3}{x^2 + 4x + 4}$ **28.** $\dfrac{3x^4 - x^3 - 2x^2}{6x^2 - 2x - 4}$

● **Lesson 9-5** Add or subtract. Simplify where possible.

29. $\dfrac{6x+1}{x+2} + \dfrac{2x-5}{2x+4}$ **30.** $\dfrac{8}{x^2 - 25} + \dfrac{9}{x-5}$

31. $\dfrac{x-3}{x^2 + 3x} + \dfrac{7}{x+3}$ **32.** $\dfrac{3x}{x^2 + 5x + 6} - \dfrac{2x}{x^2 + 8x + 16}$

33. $\dfrac{2}{x^2 - 1} - 3$ **34.** $\dfrac{2x}{x-5} - \dfrac{x}{x+7}$

● **Lesson 9-6** Solve each equation. Check your answers.

35. $\dfrac{x}{4} = \dfrac{x+1}{3}$ **36.** $\dfrac{2}{x^2 - 1} = \dfrac{4}{x+1}$

37. $\dfrac{3x}{5} + \dfrac{4}{x} = \dfrac{4x+1}{5}$ **38.** $\dfrac{3x}{x-2} = 4 + \dfrac{x}{5}$

39. $x + \dfrac{x}{4} - \dfrac{x}{5} = 21$ **40.** $\dfrac{3}{x+4} + \dfrac{5}{4} = \dfrac{18}{x+4}$

● **Lesson 9-7** Classify each pair of events as dependent or independent.

41. A main dish is selected at random; a type of salad is selected at random.

42. A department is selected at random; a class in that department is selected at random.

43. A volleyball team is selected at random from the league; one of the remaining teams is selected at random.

● **Lessons 9-1 and 9-2**

44. Sound intensity is inversely proportional to the square of the distance from the source—the farther from the source you are, the less intense the sound. Suppose the sound intensity is 30 watts per square meter (W/m^2) at 8 meters. What is the sound intensity at 4 meters?

45. The maximum load a cylindrical column can support varies directly as the fourth power of the diameter and inversely as the square of the height. A column that is 2 ft in diameter and 10 ft high can support up to 6 tons. If a column is 1 ft in diameter and 12 ft high, what is the maximum load it can support?

46. The force required to keep a car from skidding in a turn varies jointly with the mass of the car m, the square of its speed v, and the curvature k of the turn. The curvature is the reciprocal of the radius of the turn, $k = \frac{1}{r}$. Suppose it takes 2800 lb of force to keep an 1800-lb car from skidding at 45 mi/h on a curve with radius 425 ft. What force is needed to keep the car from skidding at 50 mi/h on a curve with a radius of 440 ft?

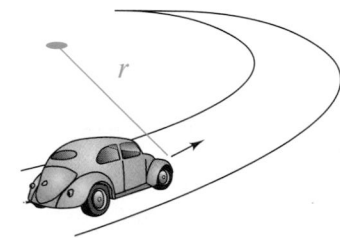

● **Lessons 9-3 and 9-4**

47. In her first 16 basketball games, Kimberlyn made 65.8% of her free throws. In the next game, she made 7 of 9 free throws. Let x be the number of free throws Kimberlyn tried in the first 16 games. Write a rational function that represents the percent of free throws made after 17 games.

48. The monthly cost $C(p)$ of removing p percent of pollutants from waste byproduct in manufacturing can be modeled by the function $C(p) = \frac{1500p}{100 - p}$. A manufacturer decides to spend $28,500 per month for removal of pollutants. What percent of the pollutant can the manufacturer expect to remove from the waste?

● **Lessons 9-5 and 9-6**

49. Michael rows downstream on a river. He then returns to the starting point. Michael traveled a total distance of 16 mi in 6.25 h. Michael's average rowing speed in still water is 4 mi/h. Assume the speed of the river current is constant. What is the speed of the river current?

50. It would take an apprentice house painter 1.5 h longer than his supervisor to paint an apartment. If they work together, they can complete the job in 4 h. About how long would it take the apprentice to complete the job working alone? Round your answer to the nearest tenth of an hour.

51. A master roofer can cover a garage in 1 h less than her new assistant. If they work together, they can complete the job in 7.75 h. How long would it take the assistant to complete the job working alone?

● **Lesson 9-7**

52. A game-show spinner has 26 equal sections labeled with the letters of the alphabet. What is the probability that on two consecutive spins you get your first and last initials, in that order?

53. The diagram at the right shows student membership in the math and science clubs. A student is selected at random. What is the probability that the student is a member of the math club *or* the science club?

54. You roll two number cubes. What is the probability that at least one of the numbers is prime *or* even?

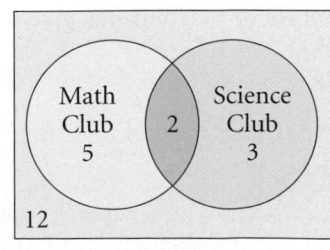

● **Lesson 10-1** Graph each equation. Identify the conic section and describe the graph and its lines of symmetry. Then find the domain and range.

1. $x^2 + y^2 = 4$

2. $x^2 - 16y^2 = 64$

3. $4x^2 + 9y^2 = 36$

4. $8x^2 - 16y^2 = 32$

5. $9x^2 + 9y^2 - 36 = 0$

6. $25x^2 + 4y^2 = 100$

● **Lesson 10-2** Write an equation of a parabola with its vertex at the origin.

7. focus at $(0, 3)$

8. directrix at $x = 4$

9. focus at $(0, -2)$

10. directrix at $y = \frac{1}{2}$

11. focus at $(0, 1)$

12. directrix at $x = 2$

13. directrix at $y = 3$

14. focus at $(0, -5)$

15. focus at $\left(\frac{3}{2}, 0\right)$

● **Lesson 10-2** Identify the focus and the directrix of the graph of each equation. Then sketch the graph.

16. $y = 4x^2$

17. $x = \frac{1}{16}y^2$

18. $-y = 10x^2$

19. $y^2 - 8x = 0$

20. $x^2 = 6y$

21. $y^2 = 20x$

22. $x^2 + 4y = 0$

23. $x^2 = -2y$

● **Lesson 10-3** Write an equation of a circle with the given center and radius.

24. center $(0, 0)$; radius 8

25. center $(-4, -6)$; radius 2

26. center $(-5, 1)$; radius 3

27. center $(1, 4)$; radius 5

28. center $(3, -2)$; radius 3.5

29. center $(0, -3)$; radius 1

● **Lesson 10-3** For each equation, find the center and radius of the circle.

30. $(x + 1)^2 + (y - 3)^2 = 4$

31. $(x + 6)^2 + (y + 9)^2 = 144$

32. $(x - 2)^2 + (y + 4)^2 = 16$

33. $(x + 8)^2 + (y - 1)^2 = 100$

34. $(x - 3)^2 + (y + 10)^2 = 25$

35. $(x - 7)^2 + (y - 2)^2 = 81$

● **Lesson 10-4** Find the foci for each equation of an ellipse. Then graph the ellipse.

36. $\frac{x^2}{9} + \frac{y^2}{25} = 1$

37. $\frac{x^2}{36} + \frac{y^2}{4} = 1$

38. $\frac{x^2}{100} + \frac{y^2}{121} = 1$

39. $\frac{x^2}{81} + \frac{y^2}{64} = 1$

40. $\frac{x^2}{49} + \frac{y^2}{144} = 1$

41. $\frac{x^2}{4} + y^2 = 1$

● **Lesson 10-5** Graph each equation.

42. $4x^2 - 25y^2 = 100$

43. $81x^2 - 16y^2 = 1296$

44. $y^2 - 4x^2 = 36$

45. $12x^2 - 3y^2 = 432$

46. $9x^2 - 121y^2 = 1089$

47. $x^2 - 64y^2 = 64$

● **Lesson 10-6** Identify the conic section represented by each equation. If it is a parabola, give the vertex. If it is a circle, give the center and radius. If it is an ellipse or a hyperbola, give the center and foci. Sketch the graph.

48. $(x + 1)^2 + (y - 2)^2 = 7$

49. $\frac{x^2}{89} + \frac{y^2}{62} = 1$

50. $\frac{x^2}{73} - \frac{y^2}{19} = 1$

51. $x + y^2 - 3y + 4 = 0$

52. $x^2 + y^2 + 16x - 6y = 11$

53. $3x^2 - 6x + y - 10 = 0$

● **Lessons 10-1 and 10-2**

54. The main mirror in the Hubble space telescope is parabolic. Its cross section is shown at the right. The focus of the parabola is 57.6 m from the vertex. Use this information and the diagram to find the equation of the parabola.

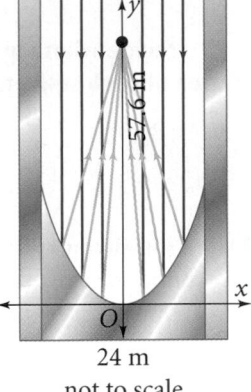

57.6 m

24 m

not to scale

55. Sports TV Group is designing a long-distance microphone for use at

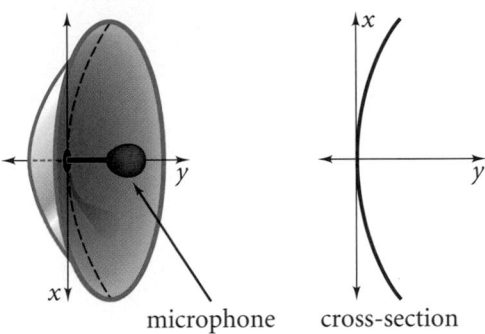

microphone   cross-section

football games. The microphone consists of a parabolic reflector and a sensor that is located at its focus. The equation for a cross section of the reflector is $y = \frac{1}{32}x^2$. All distances are measured in inches. What is the distance between the sensor and the vertex of the reflector?

● **Lessons 10-3 and 10-4**

56. A carpenter wants to cut a template for an elliptical window. He has a 10-ft by 3-ft rectangular piece of plywood. The carpenter plans to use a string to draw the top half of the ellipse, using a nail at each focus. The nails are along the bottom edge, 1 ft from each end.
  a. What length of string should the carpenter use to sketch the curve?
  b. If the x-axis is the bottom edge of the board, and $(0, 0)$ is the midpoint of that edge, what are the coordinates of the nails?
  c. Find the equation of the ellipse.

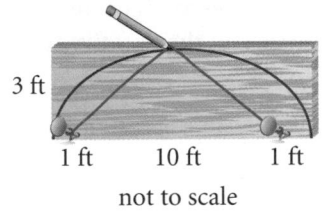

3 ft

1 ft   10 ft   1 ft

not to scale

57. A tanker truck carrying hazardous chemicals overturned on a highway, possibly spilling some of its cargo. Everyone within a 1.5-mile radius of the spill must be evacuated. The map that safety workers are using shows the spill site at coordinates $(4.5, 7)$. Each unit of measurement is 1 mi. Write an equation that describes the boundary of the evacuation region.

● **Lessons 10-5 and 10-6**

58. Some long-range navigation systems use hyperbolas to determine a ship's position. Suppose the system imposes coordinates so that the location of a ship is in the first quadrant. A ship is located at the intersection of the hyperbolas with equations $9x^2 - 4y^2 = 36$ and $16y^2 - x^2 = 25$. Find the coordinates of the ship to the nearest hundredth of a unit.

59. An engineer determines that the shape of a mirror surface in a motion sensor can be described by the equation $9x^2 - 25y^2 - 12x + 20y = 26$. Identify the conic section that represents the shape of the mirror.

60. One of the oldest known quadratic equations dates from the early Babylonian Empire about 1700 BC. An ancient mathematician posed this question:
  An area consists of two squares whose sum is 1000. The sides of one square are 10 less than $\frac{2}{3}$ of the sides of the other square. Find the sides of the squares.
  You can model the situation with a system: $x^2 + y^2 = 1000$; $y = \frac{2}{3}x - 10$.
  a. What conic section does the first equation represent?
  b. Use a graphing calculator to solve the system.
  c. Ancient Babylonians did not have graphing calculators. Use substitution to rewrite the system as a quadratic equation. Find the roots of the equation.
  d. In each of parts (b) and (c), you find two solutions. Explain why only one of them is reasonable for the situation.

Chapter 11 Extra Practice: Skills and Word Problems

- **Lesson 11-1** Decide whether each formula is *explicit* or *recursive*. Then find the first five terms of each sequence.

1. $a_n = 3n + 2$ **2.** $a_1 = 4; a_n = a_{n-1} + 7$ **3.** $a_n = 5n(n + 2)$

4. $a_1 = 2; a_n = a_{n-1} - 3$ **5.** $a_n = 6n^2 - 1$ **6.** $a_n = 6 - 2n$

- **Lesson 11-1** Find the next three terms in each sequence. Write an explicit and a recursive formula for each sequence.

7. $3, 5, 7, \ldots$ **8.** $19, 15, 11, \ldots$ **9.** $-12, -10.5, -9, \ldots$

10. $0.2, 0.5, 0.8, \ldots$ **11.** $-23, -36, -49, \ldots$ **12.** $25, 37.5, 50, \ldots$

- **Lesson 11-2** Find the arithmetic mean a_n of the given terms.

13. $a_{n-1} = 10, a_{n+1} = 20$ **14.** $a_{n-1} = 7, a_{n+1} = 19$ **15.** $a_{n-1} = -2, a_{n+1} = -7$

- **Lesson 11-3** Write the explicit formula for each geometric sequence. Then generate the first five terms.

16. $a_1 = 6, r = 2$ **17.** $a_1 = -27, r = \frac{1}{3}$ **18.** $a_1 = 1900, r = 0.1$

19. $a_1 = -5, r = 3$ **20.** $a_1 = 1, r = 4$ **21.** $a_1 = 500, r = 0.2$

- **Lesson 11-4** Use summation notation to write each arithmetic series for the specified number of terms. Then evaluate each series.

22. $21, 19, 17, 15, \ldots; 8$ terms   **23.** $4, 7, 10, 13, 16, 19, \ldots; 10$ terms

24. $-35, -28, -21, -14, \ldots; 7$ terms   **25.** $97, 96, 95, 94, 93, \ldots; 20$ terms

- **Lesson 11-4** For each sum, find the number of terms, the first term, and the last term. Then evaluate the sum.

26. $\displaystyle\sum_{n=1}^{5} (2n + 3)$ **27.** $\displaystyle\sum_{n=2}^{7} (4 - n)$ **28.** $\displaystyle\sum_{n=1}^{5} (n + 1)$ **29.** $\displaystyle\sum_{n=3}^{10} (3n - 5)$

- **Lesson 11-5** Find the sum of each infinite geometric series.

30. $4 + 2 + 1 + \frac{1}{2} + \ldots$ **31.** $3 - 1 + \frac{1}{3} - \frac{1}{9} + \ldots$ **32.** $2.2 - 0.22 + 0.022 - \ldots$

33. $0.9 + 0.09 + 0.009 + \ldots$ **34.** $5 - \frac{5}{2} + \frac{5}{4} - \frac{5}{8} + \ldots$ **35.** $1 + 0.1 + 0.01 + \ldots$

- **Lesson 11-5** Determine whether each series is *arithmetic* or *geometric*. Then find the sum to the given term.

36. $3 + 6 + 9 + 12 + 15 + \ldots; 10$th term   **37.** $3 + 6 + 12 + 24 + 48 + \ldots; 10$th term

38. $-1000 + 500 - 250 + 125 - \ldots; 7$th term   **39.** $87 + 72 + 57 + 42 + \ldots; 20$th term

- **Lesson 11-6** Write and evaluate sums to approximate the area under each curve for the domain $0 \le x \le 2$. First use inscribed rectangles 1 unit wide. Then use circumscribed rectangles 1 unit wide.

40. $f(x) = 2x^2$ **41.** $y = x^3$ **42.** $g(x) = 2x + 3$ **43.** $h(x) = |x + 3|$

● **Lesson 11-1**

44. A contractor must pay a penalty if work on a project is not completed on time. The penalty on the first day is $300. The penalty increases to $500 on the second day, to $700 on the third day, and so on.
a. Write an explicit formula that describes the sequence.
b. The contractor accumulated a penalty of $4500. How many days after the due date was the project completed?

45. Table tennis rules regulate the specific properties for the table, the ball, the net, and the paddles. According to the rules, a ball dropped from 30 cm above the table surface must bounce back to the height of 23 cm. This ratio of the drop height to the bounce height remains the same for any two consecutive bounces.
a. Write the first five terms of a sequence that describes the bounce heights after an initial drop of 30 cm. Round your answers to the nearest tenth.
b. Write an explicit formula that describes the sequence.

● **Lessons 11-2 and 11-4**

46. a. Find the common difference for the arithmetic sequence that has 17 as its twelfth term and 71 as its sixth term.
b. Write the explicit formula for the sequence.

47. The orchestra section of a theater has 25 seats in the front row, 27 seats in the second row, 29 seats in the third row, and so on. The pattern continues until the twelfth row. After that, every row has the same number of seats as row 12.
a. How many seats are there in row 12?
b. The orchestra section has 19 rows. How many seats are in the orchestra section?

● **Lessons 11-3 and 11-5**

48. A fruit fly receives genetic material from two parents. Each parent also receives genetic material from 2 parents. So each fruit fly receives genes from 4 grandparents, 8 great-grandparents, and so on. How many ancestors does a fruit fly have going back 15 generations?

49. Suppose a dropped ball bounces back to $\frac{4}{5}$ of its original height. A ball falls from a height of 5 feet and keeps bouncing until someone picks it up. Estimate the total vertical distance the ball travels if no one picks it up.

50. A new company hires an executive. The company is not expected to make a profit right away, so the executive agrees to an alternative payment scheme. The first month, he receives $.01. Each successive month his salary doubles, until his annual salary exceeds $200,000. Then this salary remains as the maximum level.
a. What is the total salary the executive receives in the first year?
b. After how many months will the company start paying the executive the maximum salary under the contract?
c. According to the contract, what is the maximum *annual* salary?

● **Lesson 11-6**

51. The city park is being renovated. In the renovated part shown at the right, there are two flower beds and a grass lawn between them. The equations of the flower bed boundaries are $y = \pm\frac{1}{2}\sqrt{16 + x^2}$. The units in the coordinate system are meters. Round all answers to the nearest hundredth.
a. Use 5 inscribed rectangles to estimate the area of each flower bed.
b. Use 5 circumscribed rectangles to estimate the same area.
c. Use the mean of your estimates in parts (a) and (b) to estimate the area of the lawn.

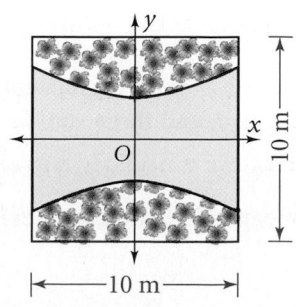

Extra Practice: Skills and Word Problems

● **Lesson 12-1** Graph the probability distribution for each sample space.

1. {the product of two number cubes an even number, the product an odd number}

2. {the sum of two number cubes a prime number, the sum a composite number}

● **Lesson 12-2** Use the data in the table to find each probability.

3. P(counselor a junior)

4. P(counselor female)

5. P(counselor a senior and male)

6. P(counselor a junior | counselor female)

7. P(counselor male | counselor a senior)

Characteristics of Camp Counselors

Grade Level	Male	Female
Junior	18	21
Senior	25	16

● **Lesson 12-3** Find the mean, median, and mode for each set of values.

8. 3 2 6 4 5 3 4 2 7 5 3

9. 16 62 24 13 21 35 24 17 20

10. 125 135 126 138 137 135 121

11. 6.1 9.5 3.8 4.6 6.1 2.3 3.7 2.1

● **Lesson 12-4** Find the mean, range, interquartile range, and standard deviation for each set of data.

12. 6 8 5 2 7 3 5 6 7

13. 25 29 21 19 30 26 28

14. 12 9 10 11 13 9 20

15. 100 98 101 100 102 97 100

● **Lesson 12-5** Find the margin of error for the sample proportion, given each sample size n.

16. $n = 90$

17. $n = 300$

18. $n = 125$

19. $n = 900$

20. $n = 1000$

21. $n = 5000$

● **Lesson 12-6** Find the probability of x successes in n trials for the given probability of success p on each trial.

22. $x = 2, n = 6, p = 0.7$

23. $x = 3, n = 8, p = \frac{2}{5}$

24. $x = 9, n = 10, p = 0.3$

25. $x = 7, n = 9, p = \frac{1}{5}$

26. $x = 4, n = 12, p = 0.8$

27. $x = 8, n = 11, p = 0.9$

● **Lesson 12-6** Use the binomial expansion of $(p + q)^n$ to calculate and graph each binomial distribution.

28. $n = 5, p = 0.2$

29. $n = 6, p = 0.4$

30. $n = 5, p = 0.7$

31. $n = 4, p = 0.2$

32. $n = 5, p = 0.4$

33. $n = 6, p = 0.8$

● **Lesson 12-7** Sketch a normal curve for each distribution. Label the x-axis values at one, two, and three standard deviations from the mean.

34. mean $= 30$, standard deviation $= 4$

35. mean $= 45$, standard deviation $= 11$

36. mean $= 10$, standard deviation $= 2$

37. mean $= 60$, standard deviation $= 12$

Lesson 12-1

38. Suppose you have a spinner with five congruent sections numbered 1 through 5 and another with seven congruent sections numbered 1 through 7. Make a table and a graph to show the probability distribution for the sum obtained by spinning both spinners at the same time.

Lesson 12-2

39. The probability that Luis wins the election for class president is $\frac{3}{5}$. The probability that Mac wins the election for class treasurer is $\frac{2}{3}$. The probability that both will win the office they are running for is $\frac{1}{2}$. What is the probability that Luis wins given that Mac wins?

40. You toss two number cubes. The sum of the numbers is greater than 5. What is the probability that you tossed the same number on each cube?

Lesson 12-3

41. All the scores on an Advanced Algebra final exam are shown below.

59 62 63 63 72 74 74 78 79 81
83 84 84 84 89 90 92 94 96 98

a. Find the mean, median, and mode for the data.
b. What percentile is the student who scored 89?
c. Draw a box-and-whisker plot for the data.
d. Identify any outliers in the data. Explain your choice.

Lesson 12-4

42. The table shows 12 monthly averages of daily high temperatures in °F for San Antonio, Texas.

49.3 53.5 61.7 69.3 75.5 82.2 85.0 84.9 79.3 70.2 60.4 52.2

a. Find the mean and the standard deviation of the data. Round to the nearest tenth.
b. The high temperature on April 1 was 50°F. What is the z-score for that day?

Lesson 12-5

43. In a survey of 380 art students 32% reported that their favorite color is red.
a. Find the margin of error for the sample.
b. Find an interval that is likely to contain the true population proportion.

Lesson 12-6

44. Jean is visiting her grandparents in Houston for five days. She wants to arrange a lunch with friends. If she picks a day at random, there is a 20% chance that all of her friends will be available to meet for lunch. What is the probability that all her friends are available to meet for lunch on three different days?

Lesson 12-7

45. The mean score on a quiz is 82 out of 100 possible points and the standard deviation is 4. Estimate the percent of scores that were 90 or higher.

46. A psychology professor gives a 100-item true/false test in a large college class. The mean score is 75.2 and the standard deviation is 8.1. The scores follow a normal distribution. What is the minimum score that is in the 99th percentile?

Extra Practice: Skills and Word Problems

● **Lesson 13-1** **Find the period and amplitude of each periodic function.**

1.
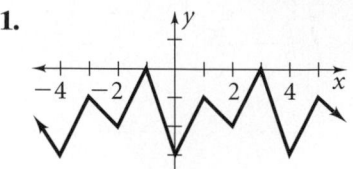

2.
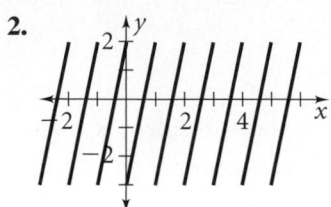

3.
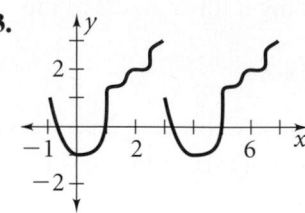

● **Lesson 13-2** **Sketch each angle in standard position.**

4. 15°

5. −230°

6. 400°

7. −145°

8. 280°

9. −750°

● **Lesson 13-3** **Write each measure in radians. Express the answer in terms of π and as a decimal rounded to the nearest hundredth.**

10. 100°

11. 270°

12. −45°

13. −550°

14. 425°

15. 10°

● **Lesson 13-3** **Write each measure in degrees. When necessary, round your answer to the nearest degree.**

16. 5π radians

17. −2 radians

18. $\frac{5\pi}{6}$ radians

19. -3π radians

20. $-\frac{13\pi}{10}$ radians

21. 9 radians

● **Lessons 13-4, 13-5, and 13-6** **Identify the amplitude or asymptotes, and the period for each function.**

22. $y = 4 \sin 3x$

23. $y = \cos 4x$

24. $y = \frac{1}{3} \tan \pi x$

25. $y = 2 \cos \frac{x}{4}$

26. $y = 3 \tan x$

27. $y = \frac{1}{9} \sin 5x$

● **Lessons 13-4, 13-5, and 13-6** **Sketch the graph of each function in the interval from 0 to 2π.**

28. $y = 2 \cos x$

29. $y = 3 \sin 2x$

30. $y = \tan \frac{x}{2}$

31. $y = -\sin 3x$

32. $y = -2 \tan \pi x$

33. $y = \cos 4x$

● **Lesson 13-7** **Graph each function in the interval from 0 to 2π.**

34. $y = -3 \cos (x + \pi) + 3$

35. $y = 2 \sin \left(2x - \frac{\pi}{3}\right) - 2$

36. $y = -\sin \left(x - \frac{\pi}{4}\right) + 1$

37. $y = 3 \cos \left(3x + \frac{\pi}{2}\right) - 1$

● **Lesson 13-8** **Evaluate each expression in radians.**

38. $\cot 1$

39. $\sec 4$

40. $\csc (-0.8)$

41. $\sec (-\pi)$

42. $\cot \frac{3\pi}{2}$

43. $\csc \frac{\pi}{4}$

44. $\sec 1.1$

45. $\cot 2$

46. $\csc 2.5$

Lesson 13-1

47. The graph at the right shows the temperature changes of a heating coil. Use the graph to find the amplitude and the period.

48. Describe four real-world situations that involve periodic changes. Explain how to find the amplitude and the period in each case.

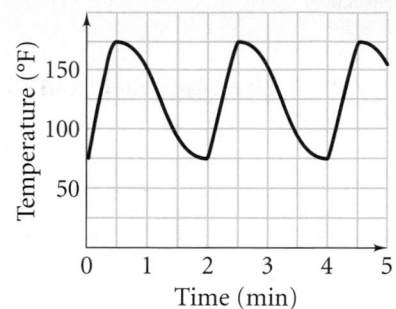

Lessons 13-2 and 13-3

49. Name two different times when the hands of a clock show each angle.
   a. $\frac{\pi}{3}$ radians
   b. $\frac{4\pi}{3}$ radians

50. a How much time passes as the minute hand of a clock sweeps $\frac{\pi}{4}$ radians?
   b. How much time passes as the hour hand sweeps $\frac{\pi}{4}$ radians?
   c. The hour hand of a clock is 3 in. long. What distance does the tip of the hour hand travel in 3.5 h? Round to the nearest tenth of an inch.

Lessons 13-4, 13-5, and 13-7

51. The graph at the right models the number of hours of daylight at a latitude of 40°N for a one-year period. The y-intercept is about 9.3 and the maximum is about 14.7. Each whole number on the x-axis corresponds to the beginning of a month (0 for January, 1 for February, and so on). Write an equation for the curve.

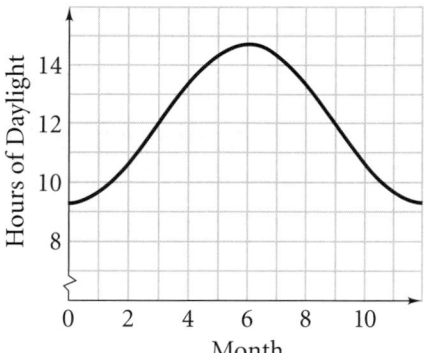

52. Earthquakes under the ocean can sometimes cause a dangerous wave called a tsunami. You can model the motion of a tsunami with the function $f(x) = a \cos bx$. Write an equation that models a tsunami that travels at 120 ft/s, has a period of 20 s, and has an amplitude of 60 ft.

53. The graph at the right approximates the number of hours of sleep that Kent gets each day in an average week. He usually gets at least 6.5 hours but no more than 8.5 hours of sleep on any given day. Write an equation that describes the graph.

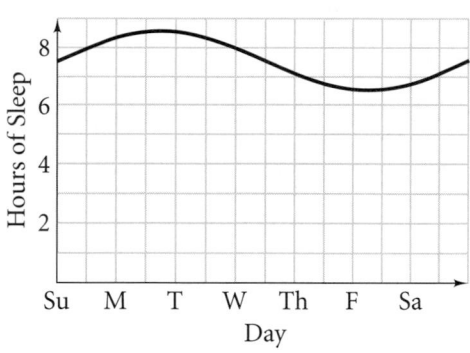

Lesson 13-6

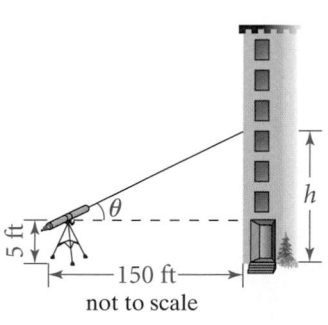

not to scale

54. Owen is using a telescope to measure a tall building down the street. Through the telescope, Owen can see the point on the building that is h ft above ground. The relationship between the position of the telescope and the height can be modeled by $h = 150 \tan \theta + 5$. Owen changed the angle θ from 70° to 75°. How much higher is the point on the building that he can see now?

Lesson 13-8

55. Gillian is building a model bridge. The bridge has a support tower in the middle that rises 30 cm above the bridge surface. The model has support cables attached at the top of the tower, going down to the bridge surface. The length of a support cable can be modeled as $y = 30 \csc x$, where x is the angle the cable forms with the bridge surface.
   a. Explain the meaning of the number 30 in the equation.
   b. The model is 160 cm long and the tower is in the middle. What is a reasonable range for the function? Explain.
   c. What is the angle at which a 60-cm cable is attached to the bridge?

● **Lesson 14-2** Use a unit circle and 30°-60°-90° triangles to find the degree measures of the angles.

1. angles whose sine is $\frac{\sqrt{3}}{2}$

2. angles whose cosine is $-\frac{1}{2}$

3. angles whose tangent is $\sqrt{3}$

● **Lesson 14-2** Use a calculator to find the value in radians of each expression.

4. $\tan^{-1}(-1.6)$

5. $\sin^{-1}(-2.8)$

6. $\sin^{-1} 1.2$

7. $\tan^{-1} 3.8$

8. $\cos^{-1} 0.5$

9. $\sin^{-1}(-2.1)$

10. $\tan^{-1} 1.3$

11. $\cos^{-1}(-1)$

● **Lesson 14-2** Solve each equation for $0 \le \theta \le 2\pi$.

12. $4\cos\theta = 3$

13. $\sqrt{3}\sin\theta + \sqrt{3} = 0$

14. $2\tan\theta + 3 = \tan\theta$

15. $(\tan\theta)\left(\tan\theta + \frac{1}{2}\right) = 0$

16. $\cos^2\theta - \frac{1}{3}\cos\theta = 0$

17. $\sin\theta\cos\theta + \sin\theta = 0$

● **Lesson 14-3** In $\triangle ABC$, $\angle C$ is a right angle. Find the remaining sides and angles. Round your answer to the nearest tenth.

18. $m\angle A = 29°, b = 8$

19. $a = 7, c = 9$

20. $m\angle B = 52°, b = 10$

21. $a = 2, b = 4$

22. $m\angle A = 37°, c = 12$

23. $b = 5, c = 8$

● **Lesson 14-3** In $\triangle RST$, $\angle S$ is a right angle, $RS = 24$, and $\cos R = \frac{12}{13}$. Draw a diagram and find each value in fraction and decimal form.

24. $\sin R$

25. $\sin T$

26. $\cos T$

27. $\cot R$

● **Lessons 14-4 and 14-5** Use the Law of Sines or the Law of Cosines. Find the measure x to the nearest tenth.

28.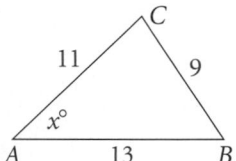

29.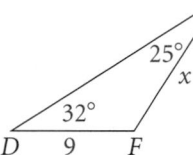

30.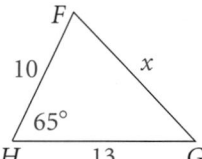

31.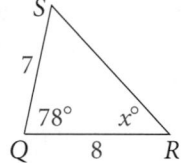

● **Lesson 14-6** Find each exact value. Use a sum or difference identity.

32. $\cos 15°$

33. $\sin 15°$

34. $\tan 315°$

35. $\cos 390°$

36. $\sin 105°$

37. $\tan 225°$

● **Lesson 14-7** Use a double-angle identity to find the exact value of each expression.

38. $\sin 120°$

39. $\cos 720°$

40. $\tan 480°$

41. $\cos 180°$

42. $\sin 180°$

43. $\cos 480°$

● **Lesson 14-7** Use a half-angle identity to find the exact value of each expression.

44. $\sin 90°$

45. $\cos 75°$

46. $\tan 75°$

47. $\sin 67.5°$

48. $\tan 67.5°$

49. $\cos 7.5°$

● **Lessons 14-1, 14-2, and 14-3**

50. A surveillance plane is flying at an altitude of 13 mi. The diagram shows how the visibility from the plane is defined by a circular arc limited by the tangent lines to the surface of Earth. Assume the radius of Earth to be 3950 mi. Use the diagram to find the visibility range (arc length).

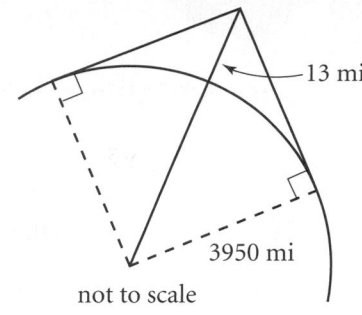

13 mi

3950 mi

not to scale

51. Two buildings on level ground are 200 feet apart. From the top edge of the shorter building, the angle of elevation to the top of the taller building is 24°, and the angle of depression to the bottom of the taller building is 35°. How tall is each building? Round to the nearest foot.

52. The function $y = 3 \cos \frac{\pi}{6} x + 9$ models the depth of water, in feet, at a pier in a 24-hour period starting at 6 A.M.
  a. Use a graphing calculator to sketch the function.
  b. Find the amplitude and the period of the function.
  c. Explain what the number 9 in the equation of the function represents.
  d. Find the first two times when the water level is 8 ft.

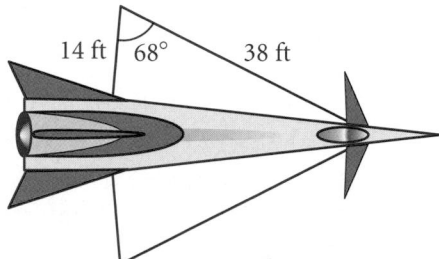

14 ft 68°   38 ft

53. The diagram shows an experimental aircraft with sweptback triangular wings. What is the area of each wing? Round to the nearest tenth of a square foot.

● **Lessons 14-4 and 14-5**

54. A landscaping company received a rough sketch of a triangular property from the property owner. The sketch, shown at the right, is not to scale. The owner is asking for a price quote to sod the land. Sod costs $2 per square foot. Can the landscaper estimate the cost of the job using the information provided? If so, find the estimate. If not, explain what information is missing.

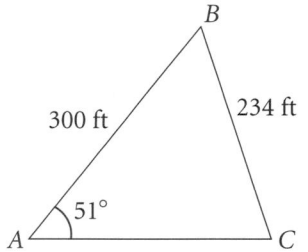

B

300 ft   234 ft

51°

A   C

55. Two spotters are observing a hot-air balloon. The spotters are 1.2 mi apart and the balloon is between them. One spotter reports an angle of elevation of 68°, and the other spotter reports an angle of elevation of 84°. What is the altitude of the balloon? Round to the nearest hundredth of a mile.

56. The Cairo tessellation is a tiling pattern that is used for many streets in Cairo, Egypt. The tiling uses identical pentagonal tiles. Each side has five congruent sides but it is not a regular pentagon. You can construct the Cairo tile as shown in the figure. Start with $\overline{AB}$. Find the midpoint M of the segment. Construct lines ME and MC at 45° to $\overline{AB}$. Use AB as a radius to mark off points E and C. Then use the same radius to mark point D. Find the measure of $\angle EAB$ to the nearest tenth of a degree.

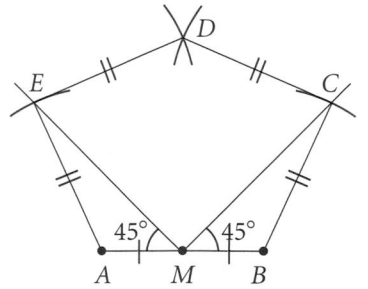

D

E   C

45°   45°

A   M   B

57. An entrepreneur wants to develop a property. The map of the property is a quadrilateral with vertices at points $(5, 5), (6, 9), (11, 10)$, and $(11, 5)$. Find the angle measures at each vertex to the nearest tenth of a degree.

● **Lessons 14-6 and 14-7**

58. Lines ℓ_1 and ℓ_2 pass through the origin and Quadrants I and III. Line ℓ_1 is the bisector of the angle formed by the x-axis and line ℓ_2. Lines ℓ_2 and $x = a$ intersect at (a, b). Lines ℓ_1 and $x = a$ intersect at (a, c). Express c as a function of a and b.

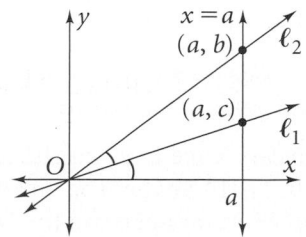

y

$x = a$

(a, b) ℓ_2

(a, c) ℓ_1

O x

a

Skills Handbook

Problem Solving Strategies

You may find these strategies helpful when solving word problems.

STRATEGY	WHEN TO USE IT
Draw a Diagram	The problem describes a picture or diagram.
Try, Check, Revise	Solving the problem directly is too complicated.
Look for a Pattern	The problem describes a relationship.
Make a Table	The problem has data that need to be organized.
Solve a Simpler Problem	The problem is complex or has numbers that are too cumbersome to use at first.
Use Logical Reasoning	You need to reach a conclusion using given information.
Work Backward	You need to find the number that led to the result in the problem.

Problem Solving: Draw a Diagram

EXAMPLE

Two students leave school at the same time and travel in opposite directions along the same road. One walks at a rate of 3 mi/h. The other bikes at a rate of 8.5 mi/h. How far apart are the students after two hours?

Draw a Diagram: walking 3 mi/h • 2h   biking 8.5 mi/h • 2h

```
          |←———|←—|       •       |—————→|————————————————→|
           6    3      School     8.5                     17
```

After two hours, the students will be 6 + 17, or 23 mi apart.

EXERCISES

1. A bug starts at point $P(0, 0)$. Each time it moves, it crawls one half the distance traveled in the previous move. It travels east, north, west, south, east, north, and so on, in order. Its first move is east 16 units. Where is the bug after six moves?

2. Draw a graph to check this statement: The graph of $y = 2(x - 3) + 1$ is the graph of $y = 2x + 1$ shifted to the right 3 units.

3. Suppose you have four metal rods with lengths 2 in., 5 in., 7 in., and 9 in. How could you use all four rods to measure a length of 1 in.?

4. Two cars leave Los Angeles at the same time and follow the same route toward the Grand Canyon. The first car averages 55 mi/h. The second car averages 65 mi/h. How far apart are the two cars after five hours?

Problem Solving: Try, Check, Revise

When you are not sure how to start solving a problem, try an answer and then test it. In the process of testing, you may see a way to revise your trial answer to get closer to the actual answer.

Skills Handbook

EXAMPLE

The automatic leg-counter at the Brazinski farm counted 114 legs as the pigs and ducks swarmed through the gate at feeding time. A total of 40 animals passed through the gate. How many pigs and how many ducks passed through the gate?

Try   20 pigs   **Test** $20 \cdot 4 =$ 80 legs
           20 ducks $20 \cdot 2 =$ $+40$ legs
                                                120 legs

Revise your guess. You need fewer pigs to bring the total number of legs down.

Try   18 pigs   **Test** $18 \cdot 4 =$ 72 legs
           22 ducks $22 \cdot 2 =$ $+44$ legs
                                                116 legs

The number is still too high.

Try   17 pigs   **Test** $17 \cdot 4 =$ 68 legs
           23 ducks $23 \cdot 2 =$ $+46$ legs
                                                114 legs

● Seventeen pigs and 23 ducks passed through the gate.

EXERCISES

1. Suppose the automatic leg-counter at the Brazinski farm counted 126 legs, but there were still a total of 40 animals. How many pigs and how many ducks passed through the gate?

2. Suppose the automatic leg-counter at the Brazinski farm counted 114 legs, but a total of 32 animals passed through the gate. How many pigs and how many ducks passed through the gate?

3. Marika biked a total of 110 mi during three days of training for a bicycle race. On the second day of her training session, she biked 15 mi more than on the first day but 5 mi less than on the third day. How many miles did she bike on the third day?

4. Use each of the integers from 1 to 9 once to fill the circles so that the sums along the spokes are equal. (Each spoke contains three numbers.)

5. Use each of the integers 2, 4, 6, 8, 12, 14, 16, 18, and 20 to fill the circles so that the sums along the spokes are equal.

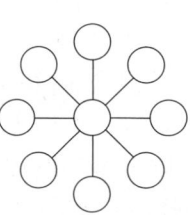

6. Find a and b such that $x^2 - x - 72 = (x + a)(x + b)$.

7. Approximate $\sqrt{385}$ to the nearest tenth.

8. Mr. Hoerner spent $45.50 last month to see 11 movies. If video rentals cost $3, movie matinees cost $4.50, and evening movies cost $7, how many of each type of movie did he see?

Problem Solving: Look for a Pattern and Make a Table

Some problems describe relationships that involve regular sequences of numbers or other things. To solve the problem you need to be able to recognize and describe the *pattern* that shows the relationship among the numbers or things. One way to organize the information is to *make a table*.

EXAMPLE

After scrounging around in the couch cushions, your father tells you he has found $2.40 in equal numbers of quarters, dimes, and nickels. He says you can have the money if you can tell him how many of each coin he has.

Make a table to help find a pattern.

Number of Nickels	1	2	3	4	5	6
Number of Dimes	1	2	3	4	5	6
Number of Quarters	1	2	3	4	5	6
Total Value	$.40	$.80	$1.20	$1.60	$2.00	$2.40

● Your father has six of each type of coin.

EXERCISES

1. Your father tells you that he has found $3.10 in equal numbers of quarters, nickels, and pennies. How many of each coin does he have?

2. **a.** A college radio station sponsors a contest once a week. One resident from a dormitory calls in and tries to answer ten questions correctly. Each correct answer earns the dorm $50, but each incorrect answer reduces the winnings by $25. Last week's contestant earned $350. How many answers were correct?

   b. The contest rules were changed so that each incorrect answer reduces the winnings by $50. A contestant earned $100. How many answers were correct?

3. **a.** Make tables to show the perimeters and areas of rectangles whose lengths are 1, 2, 3, 4, 5, 6, and 7 units and whose widths are 1, 2, 3, 4, 5, 6, and 7 units.
   b. Use the tables to find out whether there is a rectangle whose area and perimeter are numerically the same.

4. Lisa's school uniform is any combination of a white or light blue shirt, a dark blue skirt or a dark blue pair of slacks, and a plaid blazer. How many different outfits can she make?

5. How many different ways are there to make $.50 in change without using pennies?

6. How many different ways are there to make $.75 in change without using pennies?

7. How many ways can you roll two standard number cubes and get a sum of 7?

8. Suppose you have five 32¢ stamps and three 20¢ stamps. How many different amounts of postage could you make?

Problem Solving: Solve a Simpler Problem

By solving one or more simpler problems, you can often find a pattern that will help solve a more complicated problem.

> ## EXAMPLE

One thousand snap-together cubes make up a large cube measuring 10 units along each edge. The large cube is painted red and then taken apart. How many of the snap-together cubes are painted red on two sides?

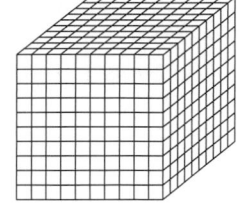

Begin with one snap-together cube, and then add cubes to make a larger cube. Find out whether there is a pattern.

Length of edge	1	2	3	4	5	. . .
Number of snap-together cubes	1	8	27	64	125	. . .
Number of cubes with two sides painted	0	0	12	24	36	. . .
Pattern			$12 \cdot 1$	$12 \cdot 2$	$12 \cdot 3$	. . .

The pattern is that there are $12 \cdot (n - 2)$ snap-together cubes painted red on two sides.

$12 \cdot (10 - 2) = 12 \cdot 8$ **Substitute 10 for n.**
$ = 96$

● There are 96 cubes that are painted red on two sides.

EXERCISES

1. Six different cuts are made through the center of a pizza. How many slices are formed?

2. a. Find each sum at the right.
   b. Describe a relationship between the number of addends and the sum of each addition in part (a).
   c. Evaluate $1 + 3 + 5 + \ldots + 997 + 999$.

$1 + 3 = \blacksquare$
$1 + 3 + 5 = \blacksquare$
$1 + 3 + 5 + 7 = \blacksquare$
$1 + 3 + 5 + 7 + 9 = \blacksquare$

3. Find the total number of squares of all sizes on a standard checkerboard, a board with eight units on a side.

4. Suppose your heart beats 68 times per minute.
   a. How many times had your heart beaten by your 15th birthday?
   b. If you live to be 87 years old, how many times will your heart have beaten?

5. a. The Steuben County Regional Soccer League has ten teams. During a season, each team plays every other team twice, once at home and once away. How many games are played in one season?
   b. Suppose there are s teams in the league. How many games are played in one season?

6. First, Second, Third, and Fourth Streets run east and west. They intersect A, B, and C Boulevards, which run north and south. How many different one-way paths are there from the intersection of First Street and A Boulevard to the intersection of Fourth Street and C Boulevard?

Problem Solving: Use Logical Reasoning

Some problems can be solved without using numbers. They can be solved by *logical reasoning,* given some information.

EXAMPLE

Four pigs (Julie, Snowball, Ladybug, and Tina) and their owners (Juan, Suzanne, LaShawn, and Trevor) went home happy after winning prizes at the county fair. None of the pigs have the same first initial as their owners. Juan's pig is not Tina. LaShawn's pig got her name because she was born during a blizzard. Match the owners with their pigs.

Make a table to organize what you know.

	Julie	Snowball	Ladybug	Tina
Juan	✗	✗		✗
Suzanne		✗		
LaShawn	✗	✔	✗	✗
Trevor		✗		✗

Juan's pig is not Tina, so put an ✗ in that box.

LaShawn's pig must be Snowball.

Since the pigs and their owners have different first initials, put an ✗ in each box along the main diagonal.

Use *logical reasoning* to complete the table.

	Julie	Snowball	Ladybug	Tina
Juan	✗	✗	✔	✗
Suzanne	✗	✗	✗	✔
LaShawn	✗	✔	✗	✗
Trevor	✔	✗	✗	✗

Juan must own Ladybug.

The only pig left for Suzanne is Tina.

The only possible pig for Trevor is Julie.

Juan owns Ladybug, Suzanne owns Tina, LaShawn owns Snowball, and Trevor owns Julie.

EXERCISES

1. The junior class is selling mugs with the school logo as part of a school-wide fundraising campaign. The top four salespeople in the class are Pat, Andy, Leon, and Shana. Pat sold more mugs than Andy but fewer than Leon. Shana also sold more than Andy, but she sold fewer than Pat. Andy sold the fewest mugs. Who sold the most mugs in the junior class?

2. Gregor has the same number of brothers as sisters. His sister Delores has twice as many brothers as sisters. How many children are in Gregor and Delores' family?

3. Ray has the same number of male classmates as female classmates. His classmate Rita has three fourths as many female classmates as male classmates. How many students are in the class?

4. Which expression(s) will be positive for all positive integers n?
   A. $2^n - n$ B. $n - 2^n$ C. $(n + 1) - 2^n$ D. $2^n - (n - 1)$ E. $2^n + n$

5. Four people, Luis, Marisa, Neil, and Ophelia, were on a bus. The florist sat next to Marisa. Luis and the surgeon are married to each other. The caterer, the editor, and Neil don't know each other. The surgeon was sitting behind Ophelia. Luis doesn't make salmon. Which person does which work?

Problem Solving: Work Backward

To solve some problems you need to start with the end result and work backward to the beginning.

> ### EXAMPLE
>
> A ball bounced four times, reaching one half its previous height with each bounce. After the fourth bounce, the ball reached a height of 2 ft. How high was the ball when it was dropped?
>
> Each bounce reaches one half the previous height. So multiply by two to find the previous height. Work backward.
>
> | Bounce | 4 | 3 | 2 | 1 |
> |--------|------|------|------|-------|
> | Height | 2 ft | 4 ft | 8 ft | 16 ft |
>
> After the first bounce, the ball reached a height of 16 ft, so it must have been dropped from a height of 2(16) or 32 ft.

EXERCISES

1. A ball bounced four times, reaching three fourths of its previous height with each bounce. After the fourth bounce, the ball reached a height of 27 cm. How high was the ball when it was dropped?

2. On Friday, Kamiko deposited $475 in her account. On Sunday, she withdrew $150. On Tuesday she deposited $25 and withdrew $50. On Wednesday she wrote a check for $127.50. She now has $627.45 in her account. How much was in Kamiko's account before she made Friday's deposit?

3. The diagram at the right shows the final resting place of a ball on a billiard table. Suppose the ball bounced off the cushions of the table four times. Show where the ball was when it was originally set in motion. (*Hint:* The ball makes equal angles with the side when it rebounds.)

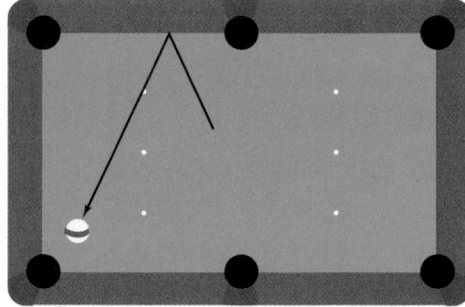

4. Suppose you start with a number. You multiply the number by 3, add 7, divide by $\frac{1}{2}$, subtract 5, and then divide by 12. The result is 5. What number did you start with?

5. Suppose you start with a number. You subtract 10, multiply by 3, add 5, multiply by $\frac{1}{4}$, and divide by $\frac{1}{3}$. The final result is 33. What number did you start with?

6. Derwood decided to sell a box of pencils. On Monday he sold half the pencils. On Tuesday he sold another 40 pencils. On Wednesday he sold half the pencils that were left. On Thursday he sold the remaining 25 pencils. How many pencils were in the box originally?

7. Tian rented a car to drive from his town to Chicago. The rental company charges $53 per day plus $.27 per mile. When Tian dropped the car off in Chicago three days later, his bill from the rental company was $453.57, which included 5% sales tax. How far from Chicago does Tian live?

Percents and Percent Applications

Percent means "per hundred." Find fraction, decimal, and percent equivalents by replacing one symbol for *hundredths* with another.

1 EXAMPLE Write each number as a percent.

a. $0.082 = 8.2\%$

b. $1.20 = 120\%$

Move the decimal point two places to the right and write a percent sign.

c. $\frac{3}{5} = \frac{60}{100} = 60\%$

Write the fraction as hundredths. Then replace hundredths with a percent sign.

d. $1\frac{1}{6} = \frac{7}{6}$
$= 1.166\overline{6}$
$= 116.\overline{6}\%$

First, use $7 \div 6$ to write $1\frac{1}{6}$ as a decimal.

2 EXAMPLE Write each percent as a decimal.

a. $50\% = 0.50 = 0.5$

b. $\frac{1}{2}\% = 0.5\% = 00.5\% = 0.005$

Move the decimal point two places to the left and drop the percent sign.

To model a percent problem with an equation, express each percent as a decimal. There are three basic kinds of percent problems.

3 EXAMPLE Use an equation to solve each percent problem.

a. What is 30% of 12?

$n = 0.3 \times 12$
$n = 3.6$

b. 18 is 0.3% of what?

$18 = 0.003 \times n$
$\frac{18}{0.003} = \frac{0.003n}{0.003}$
$6000 = n$

c. What percent of 60 is 9?

$n \times 60 = 9$
$60n = 9$
$n = \frac{9}{60} = 0.15 = 15\%$

EXERCISES

Write each number as a percent.

1. 0.46   **2.** 0.3   **3.** 0.294   **4.** 1.03   **5.** 0.007   **6.** 1.506

7. $\frac{1}{4}$ **8.** $\frac{3}{8}$ **9.** $\frac{2}{3}$ **10.** $\frac{4}{9}$ **11.** $1\frac{3}{20}$ **12.** $\frac{1}{200}$

Write each percent as a decimal.

13. 40%   **14.** 8%   **15.** 150%   **16.** 0.7%   **17.** 103.5%   **18.** 3.3%

Use an equation to solve each percent problem.

19. What is 25% of 50?   **20.** What percent of 58 is 37?   **21.** 120% of what is 90?

22. 8 is what percent of 40?   **23.** 15 is 75% of what?   **24.** 80% of 58 is what?

25. In Louisiana the state sales tax is 4%. If you buy a $15,000 car in Louisiana, how much tax will you pay?

26. The Mississippi River drains about 1,247,300 mi², which is 13.3% of the land area of North America. Estimate the total area of North America.

Operations With Fractions

To add or subtract fractions, use a common denominator. The common denominator is the least common multiple of the denominators.

1 EXAMPLE Simplify $\frac{2}{3} + \frac{3}{5}$.

$\frac{2}{3} + \frac{3}{5} = \frac{10}{15} + \frac{9}{15}$ **For 3 and 5, the least common multiple is 15.**

                  Write $\frac{2}{3}$ and $\frac{3}{5}$ as equivalent fractions with denominators of 15.

     $= \frac{19}{15}$ or $1\frac{4}{15}$ **Add the numerators.**

2 EXAMPLE Simplify $5\frac{1}{4} - 3\frac{2}{3}$.

$5\frac{1}{4} - 3\frac{2}{3} = 5\frac{3}{12} - 3\frac{8}{12}$ **Write equivalent fractions.**

         $= 4\frac{15}{12} - 3\frac{8}{12}$ **Write $5\frac{1}{4}$ as $4\frac{15}{12}$ so you can subtract the fractions.**

         $= 1\frac{7}{12}$ **Subtract the fractions. Then subtract the whole numbers.**

To multiply fractions, multiply the numerators and multiply the denominators. You can simplify by using a greatest common factor.

3 EXAMPLE Simplify $\frac{3}{4} \cdot \frac{8}{11}$.

Method 1 $\frac{3}{4} \cdot \frac{8}{11} = \frac{24}{44} = \frac{24 \div 4}{44 \div 4} = \frac{6}{11}$ **Method 2** $\frac{3}{{}_{1}4} \cdot \frac{8^{2}}{11} = \frac{6}{11}$

Divide 24 and 44 by 4, their greatest common factor.   **Divide 4 and 8 by 4, their greatest common factor.**

To divide fractions, use a reciprocal to change the problem to multiplication.

4 EXAMPLE Simplify $3\frac{1}{5} \div 1\frac{1}{2}$.

$3\frac{1}{5} \div 1\frac{1}{2} = \frac{16}{5} \div \frac{3}{2}$ **Write mixed numbers as improper fractions.**

         $= \frac{16}{5} \cdot \frac{2}{3}$ **Multiply by the reciprocal of the divisor.**

         $= \frac{32}{15}$ or $2\frac{2}{15}$ **Simplify.**

EXERCISES

Perform the indicated operation.

1. $\frac{3}{5} + \frac{4}{5}$ 2. $\frac{1}{2} + \frac{2}{3}$ 3. $4\frac{1}{2} + 2\frac{1}{3}$ 4. $6\frac{4}{5} + 1\frac{1}{9}$

5. $5\frac{3}{4} + 4\frac{2}{5}$ 6. $\frac{4}{5} - \frac{1}{5}$ 7. $\frac{2}{3} - \frac{3}{7}$ 8. $5\frac{1}{2} - 3\frac{2}{5}$

9. $8\frac{2}{5} - 1\frac{1}{10}$ 10. $7\frac{3}{4} - 4\frac{4}{5}$ 11. $\frac{3}{4} \cdot \frac{1}{2}$ 12. $\frac{9}{2} \cdot \frac{6}{7}$

13. $3\frac{4}{5} \cdot 10$ 14. $2\frac{1}{2} \cdot 3\frac{1}{5}$ 15. $6\frac{3}{4} \cdot 5\frac{2}{3}$ 16. $\frac{1}{2} \div \frac{1}{3}$

17. $\frac{6}{5} \div \frac{3}{5}$ 18. $8\frac{1}{2} \div 4\frac{1}{4}$ 19. $5\frac{5}{6} \div 2\frac{1}{3}$ 20. $3\frac{1}{6} \div 1\frac{3}{4}$

21. $7\frac{1}{2} + 3\frac{3}{4}$ 22. $3\frac{2}{3} \div \frac{1}{2}$ 23. $\frac{8}{9} - \frac{2}{3}$ 24. $7\frac{2}{7} \div 2\frac{3}{7}$

25. $\frac{7}{8} \cdot 5\frac{1}{2}$ 26. $2\frac{3}{4} \cdot \frac{5}{8}$ 27. $8 - 5\frac{5}{6}$ 28. $14\frac{1}{4} - 5\frac{2}{3}$

29. $4\frac{2}{3} + 1\frac{6}{11}$ 30. $5\frac{1}{4} \cdot 8$ 31. $3\frac{1}{2} \div 6$ 32. $8 \div 3\frac{5}{6}$

Ratios and Proportions

A *ratio* is a comparison of two quantities by division. You can write *equal ratios* by multiplying or dividing each quantity by the same nonzero number.

Ways to Write a Ratio

$a : b$ a to b $\frac{a}{b}$ $(b \neq 0)$

① EXAMPLE   Write $3\frac{1}{3} : \frac{1}{2}$ as a ratio in simplest form.

$$3\frac{1}{3} : \frac{1}{2} \longrightarrow \frac{3\frac{1}{3}}{\frac{1}{2}} = \frac{20}{3} \text{ or } 20 : 3$$

$\times 6$ (top and bottom)

In simplest form, both terms should be integers. Multiply by the common denominator, 6.

A rate is a ratio that compares different types of quantities. In simplest form for a rate, the second quantity is one unit.

② EXAMPLE   Write 247 mi in 5.2 h as a rate in simplest form.

$$\frac{247 \text{ mi}}{5.2 \text{ h}} = \frac{47.5 \text{ mi}}{1 \text{ h}} \text{ or } 47.5 \text{ mi/h}$$

$\div 5.2$ (top and bottom)

Divide by 5.2 to make the second quantity one unit.

A proportion is a statement that two ratios are equal. You can find a missing term in a proportion by using the cross products.

Cross Products of a Proportion

$$\frac{a}{b} = \frac{c}{d} \longrightarrow ad = bc$$

③ EXAMPLE   Write a proportion. Then solve.

The Copy Center charges $2.52 for 63 copies. At that rate, how much will the Copy Center charge for 140 copies?

cost $\longrightarrow$ $\frac{2.52}{63} = \frac{c}{140}$ $\longleftarrow$ copies   **Write each ratio as cost : copies.**

$2.52 \cdot 140 = 63c$ **Use cross products.**

$c = \frac{2.52 \cdot 140}{63}$ **Solve for c.**

$= 5.6$ or 5.60

EXERCISES

Write each ratio or rate in simplest form.

1. 15 to 20

2. 85 : 34

3. 38 g in 4 oz

4. 375 mi in 4.3 h

5. $\frac{84}{30}$

Solve each proportion.

6. $\frac{a}{5} = \frac{12}{15}$

7. $\frac{21}{12} = \frac{14}{x}$

8. $8 : 15 = n : 25$

9. $2.4 : c = 4 : 3$

10. $\frac{17}{8} = \frac{n}{20}$

11. $\frac{13}{n} = \frac{20}{3}$

12. $5 : 7 = y : 5$

13. $\frac{0.4}{3.5} = \frac{5.2}{x}$

14. $\frac{4}{x} = \frac{7}{6}$

15. $4 : n = n : 9$

16. A canary's heart beats 130 times in 12 s. Use a proportion to find how many times its heart beats in 50 s.

17. According to the label, there are 65 calories in 4 fl oz of pineapple juice. How many calories are in 14 oz of the juice?

Simplifying Expressions With Integers

To add two numbers with the same sign, *add* their absolute values. The sum has the same sign as the numbers. To add two numbers with different signs, find the *difference* between their absolute values. The sum has the same sign as the number with the greater absolute value.

1 EXAMPLE Add.

a. $-8 + (-5) = -13$ **b.** $-8 + 5 = -3$ **c.** $8 + (-5) = 3$

To subtract a number, add its opposite.

2 EXAMPLE Subtract.

a. $4 - 7 = 4 + (-7)$ **b.** $-4 - (-7) = -4 + 7$ **c.** $-4 - 7 = -4 + (-7)$
         $= -3$ $= 3$ $= -11$

The product or quotient of two numbers with the same sign is positive. The product or quotient of two numbers with different signs is negative.

3 EXAMPLE Multiply or divide.

a. $(-3)(-5) = 15$ **b.** $-35 \div 7 = -5$ **c.** $24 \div (-6) = -4$

4 EXAMPLE Simplify $2^2 - 3(4 - 6) - 12$.

Use the order of operations shown at the right.

$2^2 - 3(4 - 6) - 12 = 2^2 - 3(-2) - 12$
$ = 4 - 3(-2) - 12$
$ = 4 - (-6) - 12$
$ = 4 + 6 - 12$
$ = 10 - 12 = -2$

Order of Operations

1. Perform any operation(s) inside grouping symbols.
2. Simplify any terms with exponents.
3. Multiply and divide in order from left to right.
4. Add and subtract in order from left to right.

EXERCISES

Simplify each expression.

1. $-4 + 5$ **2.** $12 - 12$ **3.** $-15 + (-23)$ **4.** $4 - 17$ **5.** $-5 - 12$

6. $17 + (-18)$ **7.** $3 - (-5)$ **8.** $-8 - (-12)$ **9.** $-19 + 5$ **10.** $-8 + (-8)$

11. $(-7)(-4)$ **12.** $-120 \div 30$ **13.** $(-3)(4)$ **14.** $75 \div (-3)$ **15.** $(-6)(15)$

16. $(18)(-4)$ **17.** $-84 \div (-7)$ **18.** $(-13)(-3)$ **19.** $(-225) \div (-15)$ **20.** $-16 \div 8$

21. $-2(1 + 5) + (-3)(2)$ **22.** $-4(-2 - 5) + 3(1 - 4)$ **23.** $20 - (3)(12) + 4^2$

24. $\frac{-15}{-5} - \frac{36}{-12} + \frac{-12}{-4}$ **25.** $5^2 - 6(5 - 9)$ **26.** $4\left[(12)(3) - \frac{12}{3}\right]$

27. $(-3 + 2^3)\left(4 + \frac{-42}{7}\right)$ **28.** $(3 - 10)^2 + 3(-10)$ **29.** $(7 + 7)(7 - 7) - \frac{7}{-7}$

30. $5 - (-4)(-3) + 3^2$ **31.** $\left(\frac{-15}{5}\right)^2 + (7 - 4)^2$ **32.** $[4(-3)]^2 + 4(-3)^2$

Evaluating Formulas and Solving Literal Equations

To evaluate a formula, first substitute the known values for the variables. Then perform the indicated operations.

1 EXAMPLE Find the volume of a cone that has a radius of 5 in. and a height of 10 in. Use the formula $V = \frac{1}{3}\pi r^2 h$.

$V = \frac{1}{3}\pi r^2 h$

$\approx \frac{1}{3}(3.14)(5)^2(10)$ **Replace π with 3.14, r with 5, and h with 10.**

≈ 262 in.^{3} **Round your answer.**

Sometimes you do not know values for the variables in a formula, so you cannot substitute. To solve a formula or a literal equation for one of the variables in it, use properties of equality.

2 EXAMPLE Solve $P = 2(\ell + w)$ for w.

$P = 2(\ell + w)$

$\frac{P}{2} = \ell + w$ **Divide each side by 2.**

$\frac{P}{2} - \ell = w$ **Subtract ℓ from each side.**

Thus, $w = \frac{P}{2} - \ell$.

EXERCISES

Evaluate each formula. Give decimal answers to the nearest tenth.

1. $P = 2(\ell + w); \ell = 3.2, w = 4$

2. $c = 0.5q + 0.5n; q = 3, n = 5$

3. $d = rt; r = 35, t = 2.4$

4. $y = 3.5x + 2; x = 1.5$

5. $y = (x + 2)(x - 2); x = 5$

6. $A = s^2; s = 10.5$

7. $a = \sqrt{c^2 - b^2}; c = 5.5, b = 3$

8. $d = 0.5gt^2; g = -32, t = 4.5$

9. $y = 2x^2 - 3x + 1; x = 6$

10. $A = \frac{1}{2}(b_1 + b_2)h; b_1 = 13, b_2 = 9, h = 8$

11. $V = \pi r^2 h; r = 4.3, h = 9.1$

12. $A = \frac{1}{2}bh; b = 13.7, h = 8.5$

Solve each equation for the given variable.

13. $P = 2(\ell + w); \ell$

14. $d = rt; r$

15. $2a + b = c; b$

16. $I = Prt; P$

17. $\frac{1}{2}x = y; x$

18. $2(x + a) = c; a$

19. $m + n + p = q; m$

20. $\frac{c + d}{2} = a; c$

21. $mnp = q; m$

22. $y = mx + b; m$

23. $2r + 3s = 1; r$

24. $3a = 2b; b$

25. $A = \frac{1}{2}bh; b$

26. $V = \ell wh; h$

27. $c^2 = a^2 + b^2; b$

28. $m = \frac{a + b + c}{3}; b$

29. The formula $V = \frac{1}{2}\ell(A_1 + A_2)$ relates the volume V of a log to its length ℓ and the areas of the ends A_1 and A_2. Solve the formula for ℓ and find the length of a log that has a volume of 23 ft^3 and end areas of 0.32 ft^2 and 1.58 ft^2.

30. The formula $A = \frac{1}{2}h(b_1 + b_2)$ relates the area A of a trapezoid to its height h and the lengths of its bases b_1 and b_2. Solve the formula for b_1 and find the length of a base of a trapezoid that has an area of 43 cm^2, a height of 10 cm, and one base of 5.2 cm.

Area and Volume

The *area* of a plane figure is the number of square units contained in the figure. The *volume* of a space figure is the number of cubic units contained in the figure. Formulas for area and volume are listed on page 898.

1 EXAMPLE Find the area of each figure.

a.

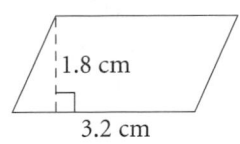

$A = bh$

$\quad = 3.2 \cdot 1.8$

$\quad = 5.76 \approx 5.8 \text{ cm}^2$

b.

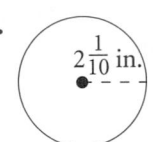

$A = \pi r^2$

$\quad \approx \frac{22}{7} \cdot \left(\frac{21}{10}\right)^2$

$\quad = \frac{693}{50} = 13\frac{43}{50} \text{ in.}^2$

c.

19 mm

8.5 mm

23 mm

$A = \frac{1}{2}(b_1 + b_2)h$

$\quad = \frac{1}{2}(19 + 23) \cdot 8.5$

$\quad = 178.5 \text{ mm}^2$

2 EXAMPLE Find the volume of each figure.

a.

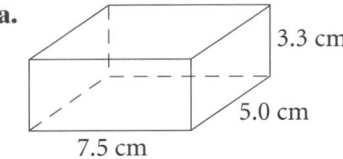

$V = \ell wh$

$\quad = 7.5 \cdot 5.0 \cdot 3.3$

$\quad = 123.75 \approx 124.8 \text{ cm}^3$

b.

24 ft

37 ft

37 ft

$V = \frac{1}{3}Bh$

$\quad = \frac{1}{3}(37^2) \cdot 24$

$\quad = 10{,}952 \text{ ft}^3$

c.

$V = \frac{4}{3}\pi r^3$

$\quad \approx \frac{4}{3} \cdot 3.14 \cdot 2.7^3$

$\quad = 82.40616 \approx 82.4 \text{ m}^3$

EXERCISES

Find the area of each figure.

1.

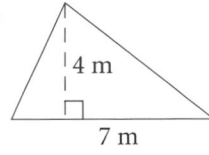

2.

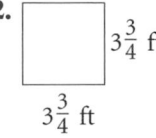

3.

9 cm

5 cm   4 cm

6 cm

4.

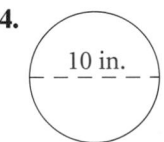

Find the volume of each figure.

5.

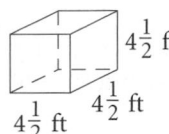

6.

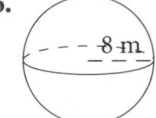

7.

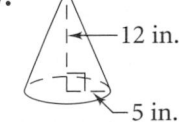

8.

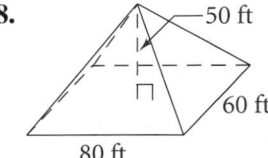

9. Find the area of a triangle with a base of 17 in. and a height of 13 in.

10. Find the volume of a rectangular box 64 cm long, 48 cm wide, and 58 cm high.

11. Find the surface area of the cube in Exercise 5.

12. Find the surface area of the rectangular solid in Example 2a.

The Coordinate Plane, Slope, and Midpoint

The *coordinate plane* is formed when two number lines intersect at right angles. The ordered pair $(-2, 4)$ identifies the location of a point on the plane. From the origin, move 2 units to the left and 4 units up.

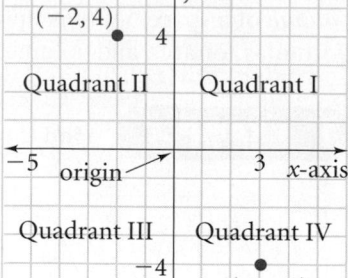

1 EXAMPLE In which quadrant would you find each point?

a. $(3, -4)$ Move 3 units right and 4 units down. The point is in Quadrant IV.
b. $(-2, -5)$ Move 2 units left and 5 units down. The point is in Quadrant III.

To find the slope of a line on the coordinate plane, choose two points on the line and use the slope formula.

2 EXAMPLE Find the slope of each line.

a.

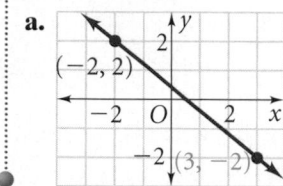

$$m = \frac{y_2 - y_1}{x_2 - x_1}$$

$$= \frac{2 - (-2)}{-2 - 3}$$

$$= \frac{4}{-5} \text{ or } -\frac{4}{5}$$

b.

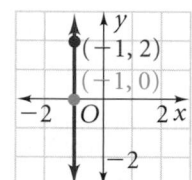

$$m = \frac{y_2 - y_1}{x_2 - x_1}$$

$$= \frac{2 - 0}{-1 - (-1)} = \frac{2}{0}$$

Since you cannot divide by zero, this line has an undefined slope.

Each coordinate of the midpoint of a segment is the mean of the corresponding coordinates of its endpoints. If (x_m, y_m) is the midpoint of the segment joining (x_1, y_1) and (x_2, y_2), then $x_m = \frac{x_1 + x_2}{2}$ and $y_m = \frac{y_1 + y_2}{2}$.

3 EXAMPLE Find the coordinates of the midpoint of the segment with endpoints $(-2, 5)$ and $(6, -3)$.

$\frac{-2 + 6}{2} = 2$ and $\frac{5 + (-3)}{2} = 1$, so the midpoint is $(2, 1)$.

EXERCISES

In which quadrant would you find each point?

1. $(3, 2)$ **2.** $(-4, 3)$ **3.** $(2, -3)$ **4.** $(4, -2)$ **5.** $(-4, -5)$ **6.** $(-1, -3)$

Graph each point on a coordinate plane.

7. $(4, 0)$ **8.** $(-3, 5)$ **9.** $(4, -3)$ **10.** $(-5, -2)$ **11.** $(0, -2)$ **12.** $(-4, 5)$

Find the slope of each line.

13.

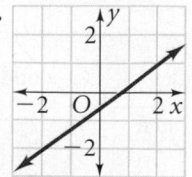

14.

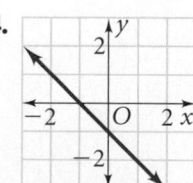

15.

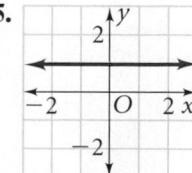

16. the line containing $(-3, 4)$ and $(2, -6)$

17. the line containing $(25, 40)$ and $(100, 55)$

Find the midpoint of the segment with the given endpoints.

18. $(-4, 4), (2, -5)$ **19.** $(3, 3), (7, -6)$ **20.** $(-1, -8), (0, -3)$ **21.** $(3, 4), (2, -6)$

Solving Linear Equations and Inequalities

To solve a linear equation having one variable, use inverse operations and properties of equality to get the variable alone on one side of the equal sign.

1 EXAMPLE Solve each equation.

a.
$$3x - 11 = -5$$
$$3x - 11 + 11 = -5 + 11 \quad \textbf{Add 11 to each side.}$$
$$3x = 6$$
$$\frac{3x}{3} = \frac{6}{3} \qquad\qquad \textbf{Divide each side by 3.}$$
$$x = 2$$

b.
$$\frac{2}{3}x + 1 = -5$$
$$\frac{2}{3}x + 1 - 1 = -5 - 1 \quad \textbf{Subtract 1 from each side.}$$
$$\frac{2}{3}x = -6$$
$$\frac{3}{2} \cdot \frac{2}{3}x = \frac{3}{2} \cdot (-6) \quad \textbf{Multiply each side by } \frac{3}{2}.$$
$$x = -9$$

Sometimes you can use the Distributive Property to simplify an equation.

2 EXAMPLE Solve each equation.

a.
$$2(x + 8) - 5 = 7$$
$$2x + 16 - 5 = 7 \qquad \textbf{Distribute to remove}$$
$$2x = -4 \qquad\qquad \textbf{parentheses.}$$
$$x = -2$$

b.
$$2x + 9 = 6x$$
$$2x - 2x + 9 = 6x - 2x \quad \textbf{Subtract 2x from}$$
$$9 = 4x \qquad\qquad \textbf{each side.}$$
$$\frac{9}{4} = x \text{ (or } x = 2.25)$$

In solving an inequality, you must reverse the order of the inequality when you multiply or divide each side by a negative number.

3 EXAMPLE Solve and graph each inequality.

a.
$$\frac{x}{3} - 2 > -4$$
$$\frac{x}{3} - 2 + 2 > -4 + 2$$
$$\frac{x}{3} > -2$$
$$3 \cdot \frac{x}{3} > 3(-2)$$
$$x > -6$$

b.
$$2x \geq 5x - 9$$
$$2x - 5x \geq 5x - 5x - 9 \quad \textbf{Divide each side}$$
$$-3x \geq -9 \qquad\qquad \textbf{by } -3 \textbf{ and}$$
$$\frac{-3x}{-3} \leq \frac{-9}{-3} \qquad\qquad \textbf{reverse the order}$$
$$x \leq 3 \qquad\qquad\quad \textbf{of the inequality.}$$

EXERCISES

Solve each equation.

1. $x + 4 = 3$

2. $3c - 7 = -13$

3. $8y - 3 + y = 51$

4. $6a = -48$

5. $\frac{1}{2}(s - 6) = 17$

6. $\frac{d}{3} = -8$

7. $\frac{4}{9}h = \frac{2}{3}$

8. $\frac{2}{3}r + 9 = 75$

9. $4(t + 5) = -36$

10. $7g - 3g + 2 = 6$

11. $3(x - 4) = 2x + 1$

12. $q + 4.5 = 3q - 2.7$

Solve and graph each inequality.

13. $9 + x \leq 15$

14. $-g < 5$

15. $7y + 2 \geq -12$

16. $9h > -18$

17. $\frac{s}{5} \geq 7$

18. $4 - a \leq 9$

19. $-\frac{c}{4} < 7$

20. $-\frac{3v}{5} > -\frac{9}{10}$

21. $t - 5.3 < -3.3$

22. $4y - 9y > -55$

23. $-5w > 2w - 21$

24. $\frac{3c}{7} \leq -\frac{2}{3}$

Absolute Value Equations and Inequalities

To solve an absolute value equation, get the absolute value by itself on one side of the equation. Then use the definition of absolute value to write two equations.

1 EXAMPLE Solve $|x| + 3 = 11$.

$|x| + 3 = 11$ **Subtract 3 from each side.**
$|x| = 8$ **The value of x is either 8 or -8.**
● $x = 8$ or $x = -8$

2 EXAMPLE Solve $|p - 20| = 4$.

$|p - 20| = 4$ **The value of the expression $p - 20$ is 4 or -4.**
$p - 20 = 4$ or $p - 20 = -4$ **Write two equations.**
● $p = 24$ or $p = 16$ **Solve for p.**

To solve an absolute value inequality, write two inequalities. Join the inequalities with *and* when $|x| < c$. Join them with *or* when $|x| > c$.

3 EXAMPLE Solve $|x - 3| < 5$. Graph the solution.

$|x - 3| < 5$
$x - 3 < 5$ and $x - 3 > -5$ **Write two inequalities joined by *and*.**
$x < 8$ and $x > -2$ **The solutions are all numbers less than 8 *and* greater than -2.**

●
```
←+—⊕—+—+—+—+—+—⊕—+→
  -2   0   2   4   6   8
```

4 EXAMPLE Solve $|x + 2| \geq 4$. Graph the solution.

$|x + 2| \geq 4$
$x + 2 \geq 4$ or $x + 2 \leq -4$ **Write two inequalities joined by *or*.**
$x \geq 2$ or $x \leq -6$ **The solutions are all numbers less than or equal to -6 *or* greater than or equal to 2.**

●
```
←●—+—+—+—+—+—●—+—+→
 -6  -4  -2   0   2   4
```

EXERCISES

Solve each equation.

1. $|y| = 8$ **2.** $|a| + 4 = 7$ **3.** $|c + 4| = 9$ **4.** $3|r| = 18$

5. $|5x| = 35$ **6.** $-7|p| + 4 = -17$ **7.** $|w - 8| = 7$ **8.** $|3t - 2| = 8$

9. $\frac{|v|}{4} = 5$ **10.** $\left|h + \frac{1}{2}\right| = 5\frac{1}{2}$ **11.** $|n - 7| = 0$ **12.** $8|z + 3| = 24$

Solve each inequality. Graph the solution.

13. $|x - 6| \leq 9$ **14.** $|a + 3| > 7$ **15.** $|r| \geq 7$ **16.** $|3y| > 39$

17. $|5p| \leq 12$ **18.** $4|k| + 3 \leq 5$ **19.** $|7x + 4| < 10$ **20.** $7|w - 5| \geq 21$

Graphing Two-Variable Equations and Inequalities

An equation in the form $Ax + By = C$ represents a line. To graph the line, first find the x-intercept and the y-intercept.

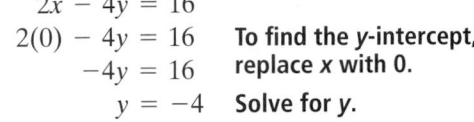 **EXAMPLE** Graph $2x - 4y = 16$.

$$2x - 4y = 16$$
$$2x - 4(0) = 16$$ **To find the x-intercept,**
$$2x = 16$$ **replace y with 0.**
$$x = 8$$ **Solve for x.**

The x-intercept is $(8, 0)$.

$$2x - 4y = 16$$
$$2(0) - 4y = 16$$ **To find the y-intercept,**
$$-4y = 16$$ **replace x with 0.**
$$y = -4$$ **Solve for y.**

The y-intercept is $(0, -4)$.

Plot the points $(8, 0)$ and $(0, -4)$. Then draw a line through the points.

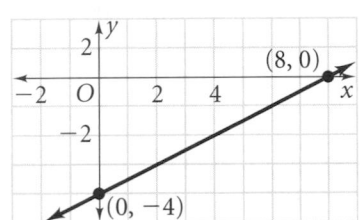

The equation $x = -3$ does not have a y-intercept. In this case, use *any* two points that lie on the line. For example, use $(-3, 1)$ and $(-3, 3)$.

A linear inequality describes a region of the coordinate plane that has a boundary line. Draw a dashed line when the inequality uses $<$ or $>$. Draw a solid line when the inequality uses $\le$ or $\ge$.

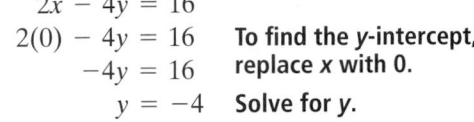 **EXAMPLE** Graph $2x + y > 5$.

First, graph the boundary line $2x + y = 5$. Use the x-intercept $(2.5, 0)$ and the y-intercept $(0, 5)$. Since the inequality uses $>$, draw a dashed line.

Next, test a point. Use $(0, 0)$.
$$2x + y > 5$$
$$2(0) + 0 > 5$$
$$0 > 5 \quad \textbf{False}$$

The inequality is *false* for $(0, 0)$.
Shade the region that does *not* contain $(0, 0)$.

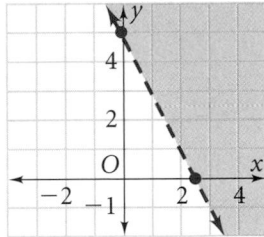

EXERCISES

Graph each equation or inequality.

1. $x + y = 6$
2. $2x + y = -4$
3. $x = 6$
4. $y = -3$
5. $3x - 2y = 12$
6. $x - 3y = -6$
7. $x - y = -3$
8. $y = x - 4$
9. $3x + 5y = 30$
10. $y = -4x + 5$
11. $2x - 5y = 20$
12. $4x + 7y = -21$
13. $y \ge -2$
14. $x + 2y < 8$
15. $4x - 4y > 8$
16. $x + 3y \le 12$
17. $x - 5 < 0$
18. $7x - 4y > 12$
19. $y - 3x \le 6$
20. $5x + 4y \ge 0$
21. $x + 5y \ge -8$
22. $y = \frac{2}{3}x + 2$
23. $\frac{2}{5}x - \frac{1}{2}y > 10$
24. $3y - x \le 0$

Operations With Exponents

An exponent indicates how many times a number is used as a factor.

1 EXAMPLE Write using exponents.

a. $3 \cdot 3 \cdot 3 \cdot 3 \cdot 3 = 3^5$

    ↑
   five factors of 3

b. $a \cdot a \cdot b \cdot b \cdot b \cdot b = a^2b^4$

    ↑   ↑
two factors of *a*; four factors of *b*

$2^n =$	$10^n =$
$2^2 = 4$	$10^2 = 100$
$2^1 = 2$	$10^1 = 10$
$2^0 = 1$	$10^0 = 1$
$2^{-1} = \frac{1}{2}$	$10^{-1} = \frac{1}{10}$
$2^{-2} = \frac{1}{4}$	$10^{-2} = \frac{1}{100}$

The patterns shown at the right indicate that $a^0 = 1$ and that $a^{-n} = \frac{1}{a^n}$.

2 EXAMPLE Write each expression so that all exponents are positive.

a. $a^{-2}b^3 = \frac{1}{a^2} \cdot b^3 = \frac{b^3}{a^2}$

b. $x^3y^0z^{-1} = x^3 \cdot 1 \cdot \frac{1}{z} = \frac{x^3}{z}$

You can simplify expressions that contain powers with the same base.

3 EXAMPLE Simplify each expression.

a. $b^5 \cdot b^3 = b^{5+3}$ **Add exponents to multiply powers with the same base.**

     $= b^8$

b. $\frac{x^5}{x^7} = x^{5-7}$ **Subtract exponents to divide powers with the same base.**

     $= x^{-2} = \frac{1}{x^2}$

You can simplify expressions that contain parentheses and exponents.

4 EXAMPLE Simplify each expression.

a. $\left(\frac{ab}{n}\right)^3 = \frac{a^3b^3}{n^3}$ **Raise each factor in the parentheses to the third power.**

b. $\left(c^2\right)^4 = c^{2 \cdot 4} = c^8$ **Multiply exponents to raise a power to a power.**

EXERCISES

Write each expression using exponents.

1. $x \cdot x \cdot x$

2. $x \cdot x \cdot x \cdot y \cdot y$

3. $a \cdot a \cdot a \cdot a \cdot b$

4. $\frac{a \cdot a \cdot a \cdot a}{b \cdot b}$

Write each expression so that all exponents are positive.

5. c^{-4}

6. $m^{-2}n^0$

7. $x^5y^{-7}z^{-3}$

8. $ab^{-1}c^2$

Simplify each expression. Use positive exponents.

9. d^2d^6

10. n^4n

11. $r^3 \cdot r^2 \cdot s^7 \cdot s$

12. $x^5y^2 \cdot xy^2z^6$

13. $\frac{a^5}{a^2}$

14. $\frac{c^7}{c}$

15. $\frac{n^3}{n^6}$

16. $\frac{a^5b^3}{ab^8}$

17. $(rt)^3$

18. $(3x)^2$

19. $\left(\frac{a}{b}\right)^4$

20. $\left(\frac{xz}{y}\right)^6$

21. $\left(c^3\right)^4$

22. $\left(\frac{x^2}{y^5}\right)^3$

23. $(u^4v^2)^3$

24. $\left(p^5\right)^{-2}$

25. $\frac{(2a^4)(3a^2)}{6a^3}$

26. $\left(x^{-2}\right)^3$

27. $(4a^2b)^3(ab)^2$

28. $\left(mg^3\right)^{-1}$

29. $g^{-3}g^{-1}$

30. $\frac{x^2y^3z^{-1}}{x^5yz^3}$

31. $\frac{(3a^3)^2}{18a}$

32. $\frac{c^3d^7}{c^{-3}d^{-1}}$

Factoring and Operations With Polynomials

When the terms of a polynomial are in descending order by degree and all like terms have been combined, the polynomial is in standard form.

① EXAMPLE   Perform each operation. Write in standard form.

a. $(3y^2 - 4y + 5) + (y^2 + 9y) = (3y^2 + y^2) + (-4y + 9y) + 5$ To add, group like terms.

$$= 4y^2 + 5y + 5$$ Write in standard form.

b. $8a^2(3a^2 - 5a - 2) = 8a^2(3a^2) + 8a^2(-5a) + 8a^2(-2)$ To multiply, distribute $8a^2$.

$$= 24a^4 - 40a^3 - 16a^2$$

c. $(n + 4)(n - 3) = n(n) + n(-3) + 4(n) + 4(-3)$ Distribute n and 4.

$$= n^2 - 3n + 4n - 12$$

$$= n^2 + n - 12$$

To factor a polynomial, first find the greatest common factor (GCF) of the terms. Then use the distributive property to factor out the GCF.

② EXAMPLE   Factor $6x^3 - 12x^2 + 18x$.

$6x^3 = 6 \cdot x \cdot x \cdot x;\ -12x^2 = 6 \cdot (-2) \cdot x \cdot x;\ 18x = 6 \cdot 3 \cdot x$ List the factors of each term. The GCF is $6x$.

$6x^3 - 12x^2 + 18x = 6x(x^2) + 6x(-2x) + 6x(3)$ Use the distributive property to factor out $6x$.

$$= 6x(x^2 - 2x + 3)$$

When a polynomial is the product of two binomials, you can work backward to find the factors.

$$x^2 + bx + c = (x + \blacksquare)(x + \blacksquare)$$

The *sum* of the numbers you use here must equal b.
The *product* of the numbers you use here must equal c.

③ EXAMPLE   Factor $x^2 - 13x + 36$.

Choose numbers that are factors of 36. Look for a pair with the sum -13. The numbers -4 and -9 have a product of 36 and a sum of -13. The factors are $(x - 4)$ and $(x - 9)$. So, $x^2 - 13x + 36 = (x - 4)(x - 9)$.

Factors	Sum
$-6 \cdot (-6)$	-12
$-4 \cdot (-9)$	-13

EXERCISES

Perform the indicated operations. Write each answer in standard form.

1. $(x^2 + 3x - 1) + (7x - 4)$ **2.** $(5y^2 + 7y) - (3y^2 + 9y - 8)$ **3.** $4x^2(3x^2 - 5x + 9)$

4. $-5d(13d^2 - 7d + 8)$ **5.** $(x - 5)(x + 3)$ **6.** $(n - 7)(n - 2)$

Factor each polynomial.

7. $a^2 - 8a + 12$ **8.** $b^3 + 6b^2$ **9.** $n^2 - 2n - 8$ **10.** $x^2 + 5x + 4$

11. $3m^2 - 9$ **12.** $y^2 + 5y - 24$ **13.** $s^3 + 6s^2 + 11s$ **14.** $2x^3 + 4x^2 - 8x$

15. $y^2 - 10y + 25$ **16.** $3r^2 - 48$ **17.** $2x^2 + 5x - 12$ **18.** $4w^2 - 9$

Scientific Notation and Significant Digits

In *scientific notation*, a number has the form $a \times 10^n$, where n is an integer and $1 \le a < 10$.

1 EXAMPLE Write 5.59×10^6 in standard form.

$5.59 \times 10^6 = 5\,590\,000$ **A positive exponent indicates a value greater than 1. Move the decimal point six places to the right.**

$= 5{,}590{,}000$

2 EXAMPLE Write 0.0000318 in scientific notation.

$0.0000318 = 3.18 \times 10^{-5}$ **Move the decimal point to create a number between 1 and 10 (five places to the right). Since the original number is less than 1, use a negative exponent.**

When a measurement is in scientific notation, all the digits of the number between 1 and 10 are *significant digits*. When you multiply or divide measurements, your answer should have as many significant digits as the least number of significant digits in any of the numbers involved.

3 EXAMPLE Multiply $(6.71 \times 10^8 \text{ mi/h})$ and $(3.8 \times 10^4 \text{ h})$.

$$(6.71 \times 10^8 \text{ mi/h})(3.8 \times 10^4 \text{ h}) = (6.71 \cdot 3.8)(10^8 \cdot 10^4)$$ **Rearrange factors.**

$$= 25.498 \times 10^{12}$$ **Add exponents when multiplying powers of 10.**

$$= 2.5498 \times 10^{13}$$ **Write in scientific notation.**

$$\approx 2.5 \times 10^{13} \text{ mi}$$ **Round to two significant digits.**

three significant digits   two significant digits

4 EXAMPLE Simplify $\dfrac{6.332 \times 10^5}{1.6 \times 10^{-2}}$.

$$\frac{6.332 \times 10^5}{1.6 \times 10^{-2}} = \frac{6.332}{1.6} \times 10^{5-(-2)}$$ **Subtract exponents when dividing powers of 10.**

$$= 3.9575 \times 10^7$$ **Simplify.**

$$\approx 4.0 \times 10^7$$ **Round to two significant digits.**

EXERCISES

Change each number to scientific notation or to standard form.

1. 1,340,000   **2.** 6.88×10^{-2} **3.** 0.000775   **4.** 0.0072   **5.** 1.113×10^5

6. 8.0×10^{-4} **7.** 1895   **8.** 2.3×10^3 **9.** 123,400   **10.** 7.985×10^4

Write each product or quotient in scientific notation. Round to the appropriate number of significant digits.

11. $(1.6 \times 10^2)(4.0 \times 10^3)$ **12.** $(2.5 \times 10^{-3})(1.2 \times 10^4)$ **13.** $(4.237 \times 10^4)(2.01 \times 10^{-2})$

14. $\dfrac{7.0 \times 10^5}{2.89 \times 10^3}$ **15.** $\dfrac{1.4 \times 10^4}{8.0 \times 10^2}$ **16.** $\dfrac{6.48 \times 10^6}{3.2 \times 10^5}$

17. $(1.78 \times 10^{-7})(5.03 \times 10^{-5})$ **18.** $(7.2 \times 10^{11})(5 \times 10^6)$ **19.** $(8.90 \times 10^8) \div (2.36 \times 10^{-2})$

20. $(3.95 \times 10^4) \div (6.8 \times 10^8)$ **21.** $(4.9 \times 10^{-8}) \div (2.7 \times 10^{-2})$ **22.** $(3.972 \times 10^{-5})(4.7 \times 10^{-4})$

Operations With Radicals

To simplify a radical, remove all perfect square factors from the radicand.

1 EXAMPLE Simplify $\sqrt{75}$.

$\sqrt{75} = \sqrt{25 \cdot 3} = \sqrt{25} \cdot \sqrt{3} = 5\sqrt{3}$ **Use the property $\sqrt{ab} = \sqrt{a} \cdot \sqrt{b}$.**

2 EXAMPLE Simplify $\sqrt{18} - \sqrt{50} + \sqrt{27}$.

$$\sqrt{18} - \sqrt{50} + \sqrt{27} = \sqrt{9 \cdot 2} - \sqrt{25 \cdot 2} + \sqrt{9 \cdot 3}$$ **Simplify each radical.**

$$= 3\sqrt{2} - 5\sqrt{2} + 3\sqrt{3}$$ **Use the distributive property**

$$= (3 - 5)\sqrt{2} + 3\sqrt{3}$$ **to combine like terms.**

$$= -2\sqrt{2} + 3\sqrt{3}$$

To remove a radical from the denominator of a fraction, you *rationalize* the denominator. Make the denominator rational by multiplying by a form of 1.

3 EXAMPLE Simplify each expression.

a. $\dfrac{5}{\sqrt{3}} = \dfrac{5}{\sqrt{3}} \cdot \dfrac{\sqrt{3}}{\sqrt{3}}$ **Multiply the fraction by $\dfrac{\sqrt{3}}{\sqrt{3}}$ to make the denominator a rational number.**

$\qquad = \dfrac{5\sqrt{3}}{\sqrt{9}} = \dfrac{5\sqrt{3}}{3}$

b. $\dfrac{2}{\sqrt{3}} \cdot \sqrt{\dfrac{5}{6}} = \dfrac{2}{\sqrt{3}} \cdot \dfrac{\sqrt{5}}{\sqrt{6}}$ **Use the property $\sqrt{\dfrac{a}{b}} = \dfrac{\sqrt{a}}{\sqrt{b}}$.**

$\qquad = \dfrac{2\sqrt{5}}{\sqrt{18}}$ **Multiply radicals.**

$\qquad = \dfrac{2\sqrt{5}\sqrt{2}}{\sqrt{18}\sqrt{2}}$ **Multiply by $\dfrac{\sqrt{2}}{\sqrt{2}}$ to make the denominator a rational number.**

$\qquad = \dfrac{2\sqrt{10}}{\sqrt{36}}$

$\qquad = \dfrac{2\sqrt{10}}{6} = \dfrac{\sqrt{10}}{3}$

EXERCISES

Simplify each radical expression.

1. $\sqrt{36}$ 2. $\sqrt{72}$ 3. $\sqrt{18}$ 4. $\sqrt{108}$ 5. $\sqrt{54}$

6. $\sqrt{60}$ 7. $\sqrt{300}$ 8. $\sqrt{\dfrac{1}{2}}$ 9. $\dfrac{2}{\sqrt{3}}$ 10. $\dfrac{3}{\sqrt{5}}$

11. $\dfrac{\sqrt{2}}{\sqrt{5}}$ 12. $\dfrac{\sqrt{3}}{\sqrt{8}}$ 13. $\dfrac{1}{\sqrt{2}} \cdot \dfrac{\sqrt{3}}{\sqrt{2}}$ 14. $\sqrt{\dfrac{2}{3}} \cdot \sqrt{\dfrac{5}{6}}$ 15. $\dfrac{\sqrt{2}}{3} \cdot \sqrt{\dfrac{8}{5}}$

16. $\sqrt{\dfrac{2}{7}} \cdot \sqrt{\dfrac{8}{7}}$ 17. $\dfrac{2}{\sqrt{2}} \cdot \sqrt{\dfrac{5}{3}}$ 18. $\sqrt{2} + \sqrt{2}$

19. $3\sqrt{5} + 2\sqrt{5}$ 20. $7\sqrt{7} - \sqrt{7}$ 21. $4\sqrt{3} - 3\sqrt{3}$

22. $\sqrt{18} + \sqrt{98}$ 23. $\sqrt{8} - \sqrt{50}$ 24. $\sqrt{6} + \sqrt{24}$

25. $\sqrt{40} + \sqrt{90}$ 26. $\sqrt{27} + \sqrt{75} - \sqrt{12}$ 27. $\sqrt{45} + \sqrt{20} + \sqrt{5}$

28. $\sqrt{3} - \sqrt{75} + \sqrt{18}$ 29. $\sqrt{98} + \sqrt{50} - \sqrt{5}$ 30. $\sqrt{5} + \sqrt{3} - \sqrt{180}$

The Pythagorean Theorem and the Distance Formula

In a right triangle, the sum of the squares of the lengths of the legs is equal to the square of the length of the hypotenuse. Use this relationship, known as the Pythagorean Theorem, to find the length of a side of a right triangle.

The Pythagorean Theorem

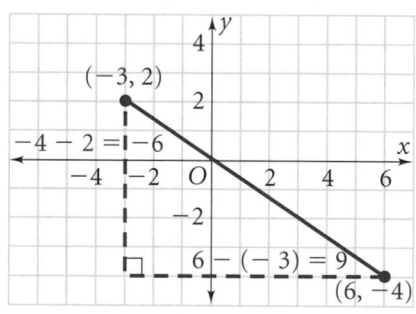

$$a^2 + b^2 = c^2$$

1 EXAMPLE Find m in the triangle below, to the nearest tenth.

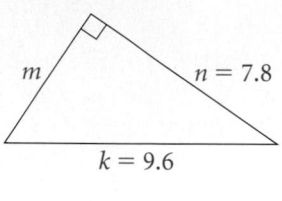

$$m^2 + n^2 = k^2$$
$$m^2 + 7.8^2 = 9.6^2$$
$$m^2 = 9.6^2 - 7.8^2$$
$$m^2 = 31.32$$
$$m = \sqrt{31.32}$$
$$\approx 5.6$$

Thus, m is about 5.6 units.

To find the distance between two points on the coordinate plane, use the distance formula.

The distance d between any two points (x_1, y_1) and (x_2, y_2) is
$$d = \sqrt{(x_2 - x_1)^2 + (y_2 - y_1)^2}.$$

2 EXAMPLE Find the distance between $(-3, 2)$ and $(6, -4)$.

$$d = \sqrt{(6 - (-3))^2 + (-4 - 2)^2}$$
$$= \sqrt{9^2 + (-6)^2}$$
$$= \sqrt{81 + 36}$$
$$= \sqrt{117}$$
$$\approx 10.8$$

Thus, d is about 10.8 units.

EXERCISES

In each problem, a and b are the lengths of the legs of a right triangle and c is the length of the hypotenuse. Find each missing length.

1. c if $a = 6$ and $b = 8$

2. a if $b = 12$ and $c = 13$

3. b if $a = 8$ and $c = 17$

4. c if $a = 10$ and $b = 3$

5. a if $b = 7$ and $c = 25$

6. b if $a = 24$ and $c = 40$

7. a if $b = 100$ and $c = 114$

8. b if $a = 12.0$ and $c = 30.1$

9. c if $a = 8.3$ and $b = 3.3$

Find the distance between each pair of points, to the nearest tenth.

10. $(0, 0), (4, -3)$

11. $(-5, -5), (1, 3)$

12. $(-1, 0), (4, 12)$

13. $(0, 15), (17, 0)$

14. $(-4, 2), (4, -2)$

15. $(-8, -8), (8, 8)$

16. $(-1, 1), (1, -1)$

17. $(-2, 9), (0, 0)$

18. $(-5, 3), (4, 3)$

19. $(-2, 1), (3, 4)$

20. $(3, -2), (3, 5)$

21. $(5, 4), (-3, 1)$

Bar and Circle Graphs

Sometimes you can draw different graphs to represent the same data, depending on the information you want to share. A *bar graph* is useful for comparing amounts; a *circle graph* is useful for comparing percents.

 **EXAMPLE**   Display the 1998 data on immigration to the United States in a bar graph and a circle graph.

Immigration to the United States, 1998

Place of Origin	Immigrants (1000's)
Africa	40.7
Asia	219.7
Europe	90.8
North America	253.0
South America	45.4

SOURCE: U.S. Immigration and Naturalization Service.
Go to **www.PHSchool.com** for a data update.
Web Code: agg-9041

To make a bar graph, place the categories along the bottom axis. Decide on a scale for the side axis. An appropriate scale would be 0–300, marked in intervals of 50. For each data item, draw a bar whose height is equal to the data value.

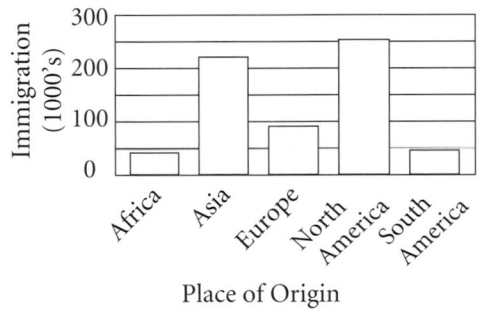

To make a circle graph, first find the *percent* of the data in each category. Then express each percent as a decimal and multiply by 360° to find the size of each *central angle*.

$$\text{Africa} \longrightarrow \frac{40.7}{649.6} \approx 0.06 \text{ or } 6\%$$

$$0.06 \times 360° \approx 22°$$

Draw a circle and use a protractor to draw each central angle.

Immigration to the United States, 1998

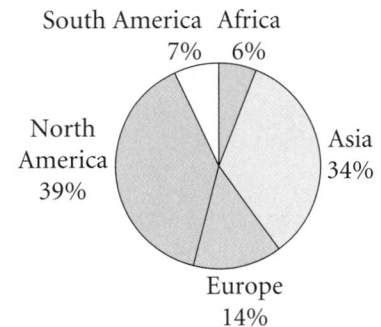

EXERCISES

Display the data from each table in a bar graph and a circle graph.

1.

NASA Space Shuttle Expenses, 2000

Operation	Millions of Dollars
Orbiter, integration	698.8
Propulsion	1,053.1
Mission, launch operations	738.8
Flight operations	244.6
Ground operations	510.3

SOURCE: U.S. National Aeronautics and Space Administration.
Go to **www.PHSchool.com** for a data update.
Web Code: agg-9041

2.

Cable TV Revenue, 1999

	Millions of Dollars
Advertising, programs	20,068
Basic service	26,890
Pay-per-view, premium services	6,324
Installation	765
Other	5,727

SOURCE: U.S. Census Bureau. Go to **www.PHSchool.com** for a data update.
Web Code: agg-9041

Descriptive Statistics and Histograms

For numerical data, you can find the *mean*, the *median*, and the *mode*.

Mean   The sum of the data values in a data set divided by the number of data values

Median   The middle value of a data set that has been arranged in increasing or decreasing order. If the data set has an even number of values, the median is the mean of the middle two values.

Mode   The most frequently occurring value in a data set

① EXAMPLE   Find the mean, median, and mode for the following data set.

$$5 \quad 7 \quad 6 \quad 3 \quad 1 \quad 7 \quad 9 \quad 5 \quad 10 \quad 7$$

Mean $\dfrac{5 + 7 + 6 + 3 + 1 + 7 + 9 + 5 + 10 + 7}{10} = 6$

Median $5, 7, 6, 3, 1, 7, 9, 5, 10, 7$ **Rearrange the numbers from least to greatest.**

            $1, 3, 5, 5, 6, 7, 7, 7, 9, 10$ **The median is the mean of the two middle numbers, 6 and 7.**

            The median is $\dfrac{6 + 7}{2} = 6.5$.

Mode   The most frequently occurring data value is 7.

The frequency of a data value is the number of times it occurs in a data set.
A *histogram* is a bar graph that shows the frequency of each data value.

② EXAMPLE   Use the survey results to make a histogram for the cost of a movie ticket at various theaters.

Survey of Movie Ticket Prices
$5 $6 $5 $7 $6 $7 $6 $8 $6

Movie Ticket Prices

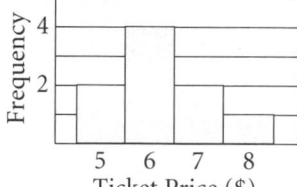

EXERCISES

Find the mean, the median, and the mode of each data set.

1. −3   4   5   5   −2   7   1   8   9

2. 0   0   1   1   2   3   3   5   3   8   7

3. 2.4   2.4   2.3   2.3   2.4   12.0

4. 1   1   1   1   2   2   2   3   3   4

5. 1.2   1.3   1.4   1.5   1.6   1.7   1.8

6. −4   −3   −2   −1   0   1   2   3   4

Make a histogram for each data set.

7. 7   4   8   6   6   8   7   7   5   7

8. 73   75   76   75   74   75   76   74   76   75

Operations With Rational Expressions

A *rational expression* is an expression that can be written in the form $\frac{\text{polynomial}}{\text{polynomial}}$, where the denominator is not zero. A rational expression is in simplest form if the numerator and denominator have no common factors except 1.

1 EXAMPLE Write the expression $\frac{4x + 8}{x + 2}$ in simplest form.

$\frac{4x + 8}{x + 2} = \frac{4(x + 2)}{x + 2}$ **Factor the numerator.**

$= 4$ **Divide out the common factor $x + 2$.**

To add or subtract two rational expressions, use a common denominator.

2 EXAMPLE Simplify $\frac{x}{2y} + \frac{x}{3y}$.

$\frac{x}{2y} + \frac{x}{3y} = \frac{x}{2y} \cdot \frac{3}{3} + \frac{x}{3y} \cdot \frac{2}{2}$ **The common denominator of $3y$ and $2y$ is $6y$.**

$= \frac{3x}{6y} + \frac{2x}{6y}$

$= \frac{5x}{6y}$ **Add the numerators. Place the sum over the common denominator.**

To multiply rational expressions, first find and divide out any common factors in the numerators and the denominators. Then multiply the remaining numerators and denominators. To divide rational expressions, first use a reciprocal to change the problem to multiplication.

3 EXAMPLE Simplify $\frac{40x^2}{21} \div \frac{5x}{14}$.

$\frac{40x^2}{21} \div \frac{5x}{14} = \frac{40x^2}{21} \cdot \frac{14}{5x}$ **Change dividing by $\frac{5x}{14}$ to multiplying by the reciprocal, $\frac{14}{5x}$.**

$= \frac{{}^{8}\cancel{40x}^{\,21}}{3\cancel{21}} \times \frac{\cancel{14}^{\,2}}{{}_{1}\cancel{5x}}$ **Divide out the common factors 5, x, and 7.**

$= \frac{16x}{3}$ **Multiply the numerators ($8x \cdot 2$). Multiply the denominators ($3 \cdot 1$).**

EXERCISES

Write each expression in simplest form.

1. $\frac{4a^2b}{12ab^3}$
2. $\frac{5n + 15}{n + 3}$
3. $\frac{x - 7}{2x - 14}$
4. $\frac{28c^2(d - 3)}{35c(d - 3)}$

Perform the indicated operation.

5. $\frac{3x}{2} + \frac{5x}{2}$
6. $\frac{3x}{8} + \frac{5x}{8}$
7. $\frac{5}{h} - \frac{3}{h}$
8. $\frac{6}{11p} - \frac{9}{11p}$

9. $\frac{3x}{5} - \frac{x}{2}$
10. $\frac{13}{2x} - \frac{13}{3x}$
11. $\frac{7x}{5} + \frac{5x}{7}$
12. $\frac{5a}{b} + \frac{3a}{5b}$

13. $\frac{7x}{8} \cdot \frac{32x}{35}$
14. $\frac{3x^2}{2} \cdot \frac{6}{x}$
15. $\frac{8x^2}{5} \cdot \frac{10}{x^3}$
16. $\frac{7x}{8} \cdot \frac{64}{14x}$

17. $\frac{16}{3x} \div \frac{5}{3x}$
18. $\frac{4x}{5} \div \frac{16}{15x}$
19. $\frac{x^3}{8} \div \frac{x^2}{16}$
20. $\frac{3}{n^2} \div 9n^4$

Tables

Table 1 Measures

United States Customary	Metric

Length

12 inches (in.) = 1 foot (ft)	10 millimeters (mm) = 1 centimeter (cm)
36 in. = 1 yard (yd)	100 cm = 1 meter (m)
3 ft = 1 yd	1000 mm = 1 meter
5280 ft = 1 mile (mi)	1000 m = 1 kilometer (km)
1760 yd = 1 mi	

Area

144 square inches (in.^2) = 1 square foot (ft^2)	100 square millimeters (mm^2) = 1 square centimeter (cm^2)
9 ft^2 = 1 square yard (yd^2)	10,000 cm^2 = 1 square meter (m^2)
43,560 ft^2 = 1 acre (a)	10,000 m^2 = 1 hectare (ha)
4840 yd^2 = 1 acre	

Volume

1728 cubic inches (in.^3) = 1 cubic foot (ft^3)	1000 cubic millimeters (mm^3) = 1 cubic centimeter (cm^3)
27 ft^3 = 1 cubic yard (yd^3)	1,000,000 cm^3 = 1 cubic meter (m^3)

Liquid Capacity

8 fluid ounces (fl oz) = 1 cup (c)	1000 milliliters (mL) = 1 liter (L)
2 c = 1 pint (pt)	1000 L = 1 kiloliter (kL)
2 pt = 1 quart (qt)	
4 qt = 1 gallon (gal)	

Mass

16 ounces (oz) = 1 pound (lb)	1000 milligrams (mg) = 1 gram (g)
2000 lb = 1 ton (t)	1000 g = 1 kilogram (kg)
	1000 kg = 1 metric ton

Temperature

32°F = freezing point of water	0°C = freezing point of water
98.6°F = normal body temperature	37°C = normal body temperature
212°F = boiling point of water	100°C = boiling point of water

Time	
60 seconds (s) = 1 minute (min)	365 days = 1 year (yr)
60 minutes = 1 hour (h)	52 weeks (approx.) = 1 year
24 hours = 1 day (d)	12 months = 1 year
7 days = 1 week (wk)	10 years = 1 decade
4 weeks (approx.) = 1 month (mo)	100 years = 1 century

Table 2 Math Symbols

$0.\overline{3}$	$0.333\ldots$	p. 5
$\ldots$	and so on	p. 5
π	pi, an irrational number, approximately equal to 3.14	p. 5
$\approx$	is approximately equal to	p. 6
$\cdot$	multiplication sign, times ($\times$)	p. 7
( )	parentheses for grouping	p. 7
[ ]	brackets for grouping	p. 7
$\frac{1}{a}$	reciprocal of a, $a \neq 0$	p. 7
$\lvert a \rvert$	absolute value of a	p. 8
$\neq$	is not equal to	p. 12
$=$	equals	p. 18
$\overset{?}{=}$	Is the statement true?	p. 18
$a : b$	ratio of a to b	p. 20
$^\circ$	degree(s)	p. 22
%	percent	p. 22
$>$	is greater than	p. 26
$\leq$	is less than or equal to	p. 26
$\geq$	is greater than or equal to	p. 26
$<$	is less than	p. 26
AB	length of segment AB; distance between points A and B	p. 30
$\triangle ABC$	triangle ABC	p. 30
$P(\text{event})$	probability of the event	p. 40
(x, y)	ordered pair	p. 54
{ }	set braces	p. 55
$f(x)$	f of x; the function value at x	p. 58
$\{x \mid x > 0\}$	the set of all x, such that x is greater than zero	p. 62
x_1, x_2, etc.	specific values of the variable x	p. 64
y_1, y_2, etc.	specific values of the variable y	p. 64
b	y-intercept of a linear function	p. 65
m	slope of a linear function	p. 65
$[x]$	greatest integer	p. 71
$\pm$	plus or minus	p. 94
$\begin{bmatrix} 1 & 2 \\ 3 & 4 \end{bmatrix}$	matrix	p. 168
a_{mn}	element in the mth row and nth column of matrix A	p. 169
A'	A prime	p. 192
A^{-1}	inverse of matrix A	p. 199
$\begin{vmatrix} a & b \\ c & d \end{vmatrix}$	determinant of a matrix	p. 200
$\det A$	determinant of matrix A	p. 200
$\sqrt{x}$	nonnegative square root of x	p. 266
i	the imaginary number $\sqrt{-1}$	p. 274
$n!$	n factorial	p. 345
$_nC_r$	combinations of n things taken r at a time	p. 346
$_nP_r$	permutations of n things taken r at a time	p. 346
a^n	nth power of a	p. 368
a^{-n}	$\frac{1}{a^n}$, $a \neq 0$	p. 368
$\sqrt[n]{a}$	the principal nth root of a	p. 370
$(g \circ f)(x)$	$g(f(x))$	p. 399
$*$	multiply (in a spreadsheet formula)	p. 402
$\wedge$	raised to a power (in a spreadsheet formula)	p. 402
$f^{-1}(x)$	the inverse of function f	p. 408
e	the number $2.71828\ldots$	p. 441
$\log_b x$	logarithm of x, base b	p. 447
$\ln x$	$\log_e x$	p. 470
$\sum\limits_{n=1}^{5}$	summation	p. 621
∞	infinity	p. 627
$P(A \mid B)$	probability of event A, given event B	p. 655
$\bar{x}$	mean of data values of x	p. 660
σ	sigma	p. 669
θ	theta, measure of an angle	p. 720
$\cos \theta$	cosine of θ	p. 720
$\sin \theta$	sine of θ	p. 720
$\tan \theta$	tangent of θ	p. 749
$\csc \theta$	cosecant of θ	p. 763
$\cot \theta$	cotangent of θ	p. 763
$\sec \theta$	secant of θ	p. 763
$\cos^{-1} x$	the angle whose cosine is x	p. 784
$\sin^{-1} x$	the angle whose sine is x	p. 784
$\tan^{-1} x$	the angle whose tangent is x	p. 784
$\angle A$	angle A	p. 792
$m\angle A$	measure of angle A	p. 793

Tables

Table 3 Squares and Square Roots

Number n	Square n^2	Positive Square Root $\sqrt{n}$	Number n	Square n^2	Positive Square Root $\sqrt{n}$	Number n	Square n^2	Positive Square Root $\sqrt{n}$
1	1	1.000	51	2601	7.141	101	10,201	10.050
2	4	1.414	52	2704	7.211	102	10,404	10.100
3	9	1.732	53	2809	7.280	103	10,609	10.149
4	16	2.000	54	2916	7.348	104	10,816	10.198
5	25	2.236	55	3025	7.416	105	11,025	10.247
6	36	2.449	56	3136	7.483	106	11,236	10.296
7	49	2.646	57	3249	7.550	107	11,449	10.344
8	64	2.828	58	3364	7.616	108	11,664	10.392
9	81	3.000	59	3481	7.681	109	11,881	10.440
10	100	3.162	60	3600	7.746	110	12,100	10.488
11	121	3.317	61	3721	7.810	111	12,321	10.536
12	144	3.464	62	3844	7.874	112	12,544	10.583
13	169	3.606	63	3969	7.937	113	12,769	10.630
14	196	3.742	64	4096	8.000	114	12,996	10.677
15	225	3.873	65	4225	8.062	115	13,225	10.724
16	256	4.000	66	4356	8.124	116	13,456	10.770
17	289	4.123	67	4489	8.185	117	13,689	10.817
18	324	4.243	68	4624	8.246	118	13,924	10.863
19	361	4.359	69	4761	8.307	119	14,161	10.909
20	400	4.472	70	4900	8.367	120	14,400	10.954
21	441	4.583	71	5041	8.426	121	14,641	11.000
22	484	4.690	72	5184	8.485	122	14,884	11.045
23	529	4.796	73	5329	8.544	123	15,129	11.091
24	576	4.899	74	5476	8.602	124	15,376	11.136
25	625	5.000	75	5625	8.660	125	15,625	11.180
26	676	5.099	76	5776	8.718	126	15,876	11.225
27	729	5.196	77	5929	8.775	127	16,129	11.269
28	784	5.292	78	6084	8.832	128	16,384	11.314
29	841	5.385	79	6241	8.888	129	16,641	11.358
30	900	5.477	80	6400	8.944	130	16,900	11.402
31	961	5.568	81	6561	9.000	131	17,161	11.446
32	1024	5.657	82	6724	9.055	132	17,424	11.489
33	1089	5.745	83	6889	9.110	133	17,689	11.533
34	1156	5.831	84	7056	9.165	134	17,956	11.576
35	1225	5.916	85	7225	9.220	135	18,225	11.619
36	1296	6.000	86	7396	9.274	136	18,496	11.662
37	1369	6.083	87	7569	9.327	137	18,769	11.705
38	1444	6.164	88	7744	9.381	138	19,044	11.747
39	1521	6.245	89	7921	9.434	139	19,321	11.790
40	1600	6.325	90	8100	9.487	140	19,600	11.832
41	1681	6.403	91	8281	9.539	141	19,881	11.874
42	1764	6.481	92	8464	9.592	142	20,164	11.916
43	1849	6.557	93	8649	9.644	143	20,449	11.958
44	1936	6.633	94	8836	9.695	144	20,736	12.000
45	2025	6.708	95	9025	9.747	145	21,025	12.042
46	2116	6.782	96	9216	9.798	146	21,316	12.083
47	2209	6.856	97	9409	9.849	147	21,609	12.124
48	2304	6.928	98	9604	9.899	148	21,904	12.166
49	2401	7.000	99	9801	9.950	149	22,201	12.207
50	2500	7.071	100	10,000	10.000	150	22,500	12.247

Table 4 Trigonometric Ratios

Angle	Sine	Cosine	Tangent
1°	0.0175	0.9998	0.0175
2°	0.0349	0.9994	0.0349
3°	0.0523	0.9986	0.0524
4°	0.0698	0.9976	0.0699
5°	0.0872	0.9962	0.0875
6°	0.1045	0.9945	0.1051
7°	0.1219	0.9925	0.1228
8°	0.1392	0.9903	0.1405
9°	0.1564	0.9877	0.1584
10°	0.1736	0.9848	0.1763
11°	0.1908	0.9816	0.1944
12°	0.2079	0.9781	0.2126
13°	0.2250	0.9744	0.2309
14°	0.2419	0.9703	0.2493
15°	0.2588	0.9659	0.2679
16°	0.2756	0.9613	0.2867
17°	0.2924	0.9563	0.3057
18°	0.3090	0.9511	0.3249
19°	0.3256	0.9455	0.3443
20°	0.3420	0.9397	0.3640
21°	0.3584	0.9336	0.3839
22°	0.3746	0.9272	0.4040
23°	0.3907	0.9205	0.4245
24°	0.4067	0.9135	0.4452
25°	0.4226	0.9063	0.4663
26°	0.4384	0.8988	0.4877
27°	0.4540	0.8910	0.5095
28°	0.4695	0.8829	0.5317
29°	0.4848	0.8746	0.5543
30°	0.5000	0.8660	0.5774
31°	0.5150	0.8572	0.6009
32°	0.5299	0.8480	0.6249
33°	0.5446	0.8387	0.6494
34°	0.5592	0.8290	0.6745
35°	0.5736	0.8192	0.7002
36°	0.5878	0.8090	0.7265
37°	0.6018	0.7986	0.7536
38°	0.6157	0.7880	0.7813
39°	0.6293	0.7771	0.8098
40°	0.6428	0.7660	0.8391
41°	0.6561	0.7547	0.8693
42°	0.6691	0.7431	0.9004
43°	0.6820	0.7314	0.9325
44°	0.6947	0.7193	0.9657
45°	0.7071	0.7071	1.0000
46°	0.7193	0.6947	1.0355
47°	0.7314	0.6820	1.0724
48°	0.7431	0.6691	1.1106
49°	0.7547	0.6561	1.1504
50°	0.7660	0.6428	1.1918
51°	0.7771	0.6293	1.2349
52°	0.7880	0.6157	1.2799
53°	0.7986	0.6018	1.3270
54°	0.8090	0.5878	1.3764
55°	0.8192	0.5736	1.4281
56°	0.8290	0.5592	1.4826
57°	0.8387	0.5446	1.5399
58°	0.8480	0.5299	1.6003
59°	0.8572	0.5150	1.6643
60°	0.8660	0.5000	1.7321
61°	0.8746	0.4848	1.8040
62°	0.8829	0.4695	1.8807
63°	0.8910	0.4540	1.9626
64°	0.8988	0.4384	2.0503
65°	0.9063	0.4226	2.1445
66°	0.9135	0.4067	2.2460
67°	0.9205	0.3907	2.3559
68°	0.9272	0.3746	2.4751
69°	0.9336	0.3584	2.6051
70°	0.9397	0.3420	2.7475
71°	0.9455	0.3256	2.9042
72°	0.9511	0.3090	3.0777
73°	0.9563	0.2924	3.2709
74°	0.9613	0.2756	3.4874
75°	0.9659	0.2588	3.7321
76°	0.9703	0.2419	4.0108
77°	0.9744	0.2250	4.3315
78°	0.9781	0.2079	4.7046
79°	0.9816	0.1908	5.1446
80°	0.9848	0.1736	5.6713
81°	0.9877	0.1564	6.3138
82°	0.9903	0.1392	7.1154
83°	0.9925	0.1219	8.1443
84°	0.9945	0.1045	9.5144
85°	0.9962	0.0872	11.4301
86°	0.9976	0.0698	14.3007
87°	0.9986	0.0523	19.0811
88°	0.9994	0.0349	28.6363
89°	0.9998	0.0175	57.2900
90°	1.0000	0.0000	

Tables

Table 5 Random Numbers

71133	15379	62220	83119	33872	80881	54263	35427
50631	71600	00133	22447	76212	94621	91026	89499
92641	47157	49324	27674	04501	30142	49180	17909
06747	85629	84240	41917	84067	44264	40953	20516
10967	26366	60323	55523	09686	47962	59778	99479
08945	67385	60015	91676	72694	49757	86540	32359
22437	77933	00815	21862	25049	30840	01760	60655
78658	17681	63881	99741	74067	35810	11989	68048
23006	64650	50777	06226	64703	73487	34815	35296
67218	66215	14219	61908	18165	17261	45017	29303
03020	75784	91506	02237	88056	15027	04040	96770
94965	75820	50994	31050	67304	16730	29373	96700
07845	69584	70548	52973	72302	97594	92241	15204
42665	29990	57260	75846	01152	30141	35982	96088
04003	36893	51639	65625	28426	90634	32979	05449
32959	06776	72420	55622	81422	67587	93193	67479
29041	35939	80920	31801	38638	87905	37617	53135
63364	20495	50868	54130	32625	30799	94255	03514
27838	19139	82031	46143	93922	32001	05378	42457
94248	29387	32682	86235	35805	66529	00886	25875
40156	92636	95648	79767	16307	71133	15714	44142
44293	19195	30569	41277	01417	34656	80207	33362
71878	31767	40056	52582	30766	70264	86253	07179
24757	57502	51033	16551	66731	87844	41420	10084
55529	68560	50069	50652	76104	42086	48720	96632
39724	50318	91370	68016	06222	26806	86726	52832
80950	27135	14110	92292	17049	60257	01638	04460
21694	79570	74409	95087	75424	57042	27349	16229
06930	85441	37191	75134	12845	67868	51500	97761
18740	35448	56096	37910	35485	19640	07689	31027
40657	14875	70695	92569	40703	69318	95070	01541
52249	56515	59058	34509	35791	22150	56558	75286
86570	07303	40560	57856	22009	67712	19435	90250
62962	66253	93288	01838	68388	55481	00336	19271
78066	09117	62350	58972	80778	46458	83677	16125
89106	30219	30068	54030	49295	48985	01624	72881
88310	18172	89450	04987	02781	37935	76222	93595
20942	90911	57643	34009	20728	88785	81212	08214
93926	66687	58252	18674	18501	22362	37319	33201
88294	55814	67443	77285	36229	26886	66782	89931
29751	08485	49910	83844	56013	26596	20875	34568
11169	15529	33241	83594	01727	86595	65723	82322
06062	54400	80649	70749	50395	48993	77447	24862
87445	17139	43278	55031	79971	18515	61850	49101
39283	22821	44330	82225	53534	77235	42973	60190

Properties and Formulas

Order of Operations
1. Perform any operation(s) inside grouping symbols.
2. Simplify any terms with exponents.
3. Multiply and divide in order from left to right.
4. Add and subtract in order from left to right.

Properties of Exponents
For any nonzero number a and any integers m and n:

$a^0 = 1, a \neq 0$ $\qquad$ $a^m \cdot a^n = a^{m+n}$

$\dfrac{a^m}{a^n} = a^{m-n}$ $\qquad$ $(a^m)^n = a^{mn}$

$a^{-n} = \dfrac{1}{a^n}$ $\qquad$ $a^{\frac{1}{n}} = \sqrt[n]{a}$

$(ab)^n = a^n b^n$ $\qquad$ $\left(\dfrac{a}{b}\right)^n = \dfrac{a^n}{b^n}$

Properties of Square Roots
For any numbers $a \geq 0$ and $b \geq 0$,
$\sqrt{ab} = \sqrt{a} \cdot \sqrt{b}$.
For any numbers $a \geq 0$ and $b > 0$,
$\sqrt{\dfrac{a}{b}} = \dfrac{\sqrt{a}}{\sqrt{b}}$.

The Pythagorean Theorem
In a right triangle, the sum of the squares of the lengths of the legs is equal to the square of the length of the hypotenuse.
$a^2 + b^2 = c^2$

The Converse of the Pythagorean Theorem
If a triangle has sides of lengths a, b, and c, and $a^2 + b^2 = c^2$, then the triangle is a right triangle with hypotenuse of length c.

The Distance Formula
The distance d between any two points (x_1, y_1) and (x_2, y_2) is $d = \sqrt{(x_2 - x_1)^2 + (y_2 - y_1)^2}$.

The Midpoint Formula
The midpoint M of a line segment with endpoints $A(x_1, y_1)$ and $B(x_2, y_2)$ is $\left(\dfrac{x_1 + x_2}{2}, \dfrac{y_1 + y_2}{2}\right)$.

Parent Function and Function Families
If a, k and h are positive numbers and $f(x)$ is a parent function, then
$f(x) + k$ shifts $f(x)$ up k units;
$f(x) - k$ shifts $f(x)$ down k units;
$f(x + h)$ shifts $f(x)$ left h units;
$f(x - h)$ shifts $f(x)$ right h units.
$af(x)$ stretches $f(x)$ vertically if $a > 1$
$af(x)$ shrinks $f(x)$ vertically if $0 < a < 1$
$-f(x)$ reflects $f(x)$ across the x-axis

Multiplication Counting Principle
If there are m ways to make a first selection and n ways to make a second selection, there are $m \times n$ ways to make the two selections.

Number of Permutations
The number of permutations of n items of a set arranged r items at a time is
$_nP_r = \dfrac{n!}{(n-r)!}$ for $1 \leq r \leq n$.

CHAPTER 1

The Identity Properties
For every real number a:
$a + 0 = a$ $\quad$ and $\quad$ $0 + a = a$
$a \cdot 1 = a$ $\quad$ and $\quad$ $1 \cdot a = a$

Closure
For all real numbers a and b, $a + b$ and $a \cdot b$ are real numbers.

The Commutative Properties
For all real numbers a and b:
$a + b = b + a$ and $a \cdot b = b \cdot a$

The Inverse Properties
For every real number a:
$a + (-a) = 0$ and $a \cdot \dfrac{1}{a} = 1$ $(a \neq 0)$

The Associative Properties
For all real numbers a, b, and c:
$(a + b) + c = a + (b + c)$
$(a \cdot b) \cdot c = a \cdot (b \cdot c)$

The Distributive Property
For all real numbers a, b, and c:
$a(b + c) = ab + ac$

Properties of Equality
Let a, b, and c represent real numbers.

Reflexive: $a = a$

Symmetric: If $a = b$, then $b = a$.

Transitive: If $a = b$ and $b = c$, then $a = c$.

Addition: If $a = b$, then $a + c = b + c$.

Subtraction: If $a = b$, then $a - c = b - c$.

Multiplication: If $a = b$, then $ac = bc$.

Division: If $a = b$ and $c \neq 0$, then $\dfrac{a}{c} = \dfrac{b}{c}$.

Substitution: If $a = b$, then b may be substituted for a in any expression to obtain an equivalent expression.

Properties of Inequality

Let a, b, and c represent real numbers.

Transitive: If $a \leq b$ and $b \leq c$, then $a \leq c$.

Addition: If $a \leq b$, then $a + c \leq b + c$.

Subtraction: If $a \leq b$, then $a - c \leq b - c$.

Multiplication:
If $a \leq b$ and $c > 0$, then $ac \leq bc$.
If $a \leq b$ and $c < 0$, then $ac \geq bc$.

Division:
If $a \leq b$ and $c > 0$, then $\frac{a}{c} \leq \frac{b}{c}$.
If $a \leq b$ and $c < 0$, then $\frac{a}{c} \geq \frac{b}{c}$.

CHAPTER 2

Slope Formula

$$\text{slope} = \frac{\text{vertical change (rise)}}{\text{horizontal change (run)}} = \frac{y_2 - y_1}{x_2 - x_1},$$
where $x_2 - x_1 \neq 0$.

Point-Slope Equation of a Line

The line through point (x_1, y_1) with slope m has the equation $y - y_1 = m(x - x_1)$.

CHAPTER 3

Vertex Principle of Linear Programming

If there is a maximum or a minimum value of the linear objective function, it occurs at one or more vertices of the feasible region.

CHAPTER 4

Matrix Addition

Let A, B, and C represent $m \times n$ matrices.

Closure: $A + B$ is an $m \times n$ matrix.

Commutative: $A + B = B + A$

Associative: $(A + B) + C = A + (B + C)$

Additive Identity: There exists a unique $m \times n$ matrix O such that $O + A = A + O = A$.

Additive Inverse: For each A, there exists a unique opposite $-A$ such that $A + (-A) = O$.

Matrix Subtraction

If two matrices A and B have the same dimensions, then $A - B = A + (-B)$.

Scalar Multiplication

Let A, B, and O represent $m \times n$ matrices, and let c and d represent scalars.

Closure: cA is an $m \times n$ matrix.

Associative: $(cd)A = c(dA)$

Distributive:
$c(A + B) = cA + cB$
$(c + d)A = cA + dA$

Multiplicative Identity: $1 \cdot A = A$

Zero: $0A = O$ and $cO = O$

Matrix Multiplication

Let A, B, and C represent $n \times n$ matrices.

Closure: AB is an $n \times n$ matrix.

Associative: $(AB)C = A(BC)$

Distributive:
$A(B + C) = AB + AC$
$(B + C)A = BA + CA$

Zero: $OA = AO = O$, where O has the same dimensions as A.

CHAPTER 5

Graph of a Quadratic Function in Standard Form

The graph of $y = ax^2 + bx + c$ is a parabola when $a \neq 0$.
When $a > 0$, the parabola opens up. When $a < 0$, the parabola opens down.
The axis of symmetry is the line $x = -\frac{b}{2a}$.

The x-coordinate of the vertex is $-\frac{b}{2a}$.

The y-coordinate of the vertex is the value of

y when $x = -\frac{b}{2a}$, or $y = f\left(-\frac{b}{2a}\right)$.

The y-intercept is $(0, c)$.

Graph of a Quadratic Function in Vertex Form

The graph of $y = a(x - h)^2 + k$ is the graph of $y = ax^2$ translated h units horizontally and k units vertically.
When h is positive the graph shifts right; when h is negative the graph shifts left.
When k is positive the graph shifts up; when k is negative the graph shifts down.
The vertex is (h, k), and the axis of symmetry is the line $x = h$.
When $a > 0$, the parabola opens up. When $a < 0$, the parabola opens down.

Factoring Perfect Square Trinomials
$a^2 + 2ab + b^2 = (a + b)^2$
$a^2 - 2ab + b^2 = (a - b)^2$

Factoring a Difference of Two Squares
$a^2 - b^2 = (a + b)(a - b)$

Zero-Product Property
If $ab = 0$, then $a = 0$ or $b = 0$.
Example: If $(x + 3)(x - 7) = 0$, then $(x + 3) = 0$
or $(x - 7) = 0$.

Square Root of a Negative Real Number
For any positive real number a, $\sqrt{-a} = i\sqrt{a}$.
Example: $\sqrt{-4} = i\sqrt{4} = i \cdot 2 = 2i$
Note that $(\sqrt{-4})^2 = (i\sqrt{4})^2 = i^2\sqrt{4}^2 = -1 \cdot 4 = -4$ (not 4).

Quadratic Formula
The roots of $ax^2 + bx + c = 0$ are
$x = \dfrac{-b \pm \sqrt{b^2 - 4ac}}{2a}$.

The Discriminant
The standard form of a quadratic equation is
$ax^2 + bx + c = 0$. The discriminant is the value of
the expression $b^2 - 4ac$.
$b^2 - 4ac > 0 \Rightarrow$ two real solutions
$b^2 - 4ac = 0 \Rightarrow$ one real solution
$b^2 - 4ac < 0 \Rightarrow$ two complex solutions

CHAPTER 6

Factor Theorem
The expression $x - a$ is a linear factor of a polynomial
if and only if the value a is a zero of the related
polynomial function.

Remainder Theorem
If a polynomial $P(x)$ of degree $n \geq 1$ is divided by
$(x - a)$, where a is a constant, then the remainder
is $P(a)$.

Sum and Difference of Cubes
$a^3 + b^3 = (a + b)(a^2 - ab + b^2)$
$a^3 - b^3 = (a - b)(a^2 + ab + b^2)$

Rational Root Theorem
If $\dfrac{p}{q}$ is in simplest form and is a rational root of
the polynomial equation
$a_nx^n + a_{n-1}x^{n-1} + \ldots + a_1x + a_0 = 0$ with
integer coefficients, then p must be a factor of a_0
and q must be a factor of a_n.

Irrational Root Theorem
Let a and b be rational numbers and let $\sqrt{b}$ be an
irrational number. If $a + \sqrt{b}$ is a root of a polynomial
equation with rational coefficients, then the conjugate
$a - \sqrt{b}$ also is a root.

Imaginary Root Theorem
If the imaginary number $a + bi$ is a root of a
polynomial equation with real coefficients, then the
conjugate $a - bi$ also is a root.

Fundamental Theorem of Algebra
If $P(x)$ is a polynomial of degree $n \geq 1$ with
complex coefficients, then $P(x) = 0$ has at least
one complex root.

Corollary
Including imaginary roots and multiple roots, an nth
degree polynomial equation has exactly n roots; the
related polynomial function has exactly n zeros.

Binomial Theorem
For every positive integer n,
$(a + b)^n = {}_nC_0a^n + {}_nC_1a^{n-1}b + {}_nC_2a^{n-2}b^2 + \ldots + {}_nC_{n-1}ab^{n-1} + {}_nC_nb^n$.

Chapter 7

nth Root of a^n
For any negative real number a, $\sqrt[n]{a^n} = |a|$ when n
is even.

Multiplying Radical Expressions
If $\sqrt[n]{a}$ and $\sqrt[n]{b}$ are real numbers, then
$\sqrt[n]{a} \cdot \sqrt[n]{b} = \sqrt[n]{ab}$.

Dividing Radical Expressions
If $\sqrt[n]{a}$ and $\sqrt[n]{b}$ are real numbers and $b \neq 0$, then
$\dfrac{\sqrt[n]{a}}{\sqrt[n]{b}} = \sqrt[n]{\dfrac{a}{b}}$.

Chapter 8

Properties of Logarithms
For any positive numbers, M, N, and $b, b \neq 1$:
$\log_b MN = \log_b M + \log_b N$
$\log_b \dfrac{M}{N} = \log_b M - \log_b N$
$\log_b M^x = x \log_b M$

Change of Base Formula
For any positive numbers, M, b, and c, with
$b \neq 1$ and $c \neq 1$, $\log_b M = \dfrac{\log_c M}{\log_c b}$.

Chapter 9

Probability of *A* and *B*
If *A* and *B* are independent events, then
$P(A \text{ and } B) = P(A) \cdot P(B)$.

Probability of *A* or *B*
If *A* and *B* are mutually exclusive events, then
$P(A \text{ or } B) = P(A) + P(B)$.
If *A* and *B* are not mutually exclusive events, then
$P(A \text{ or } B) = P(A) + P(B) - P(A \text{ and } B)$.

Chapter 10

Conic Section	Form of Equation
Parabola	vertex (h, k) $y = a(x - h)^2 + k$ $x = a(y - k)^2 + h$
Circle	center (h, k) $(x - h)^2 + (y - k)^2 = r^2$
Ellipse	center (h, k) $\dfrac{(x - h)^2}{a^2} + \dfrac{(y - k)^2}{b^2} = 1$ $\dfrac{(x - h)^2}{b^2} + \dfrac{(y - k)^2}{a^2} = 1$
Hyperbola	center (h, k) $\dfrac{(x - h)^2}{a^2} - \dfrac{(y - k)^2}{b^2} = 1$ $\dfrac{(y - k)^2}{a^2} - \dfrac{(x - h)^2}{b^2} = 1$

Chapter 11

Arithmetic Sequence Formulas
Recursive: $a_1 =$ a given value; $a_n = a_{n-1} + d$
Explicit: $a_n = a_1 + (n - 1)d$
In these formulas, a_n is the *n*th term, a_1 is the first term, *n* is the number of the term, and *d* is the common difference.

Geometric Sequence Formulas
Recursive: $a_1 =$ a given value; $a_n = a_{n-1} \cdot r$
Explicit: $a_n = a_1 \cdot r^{n-1}$
In these formulas, a_n is the *n*th term, a_1 is the first term, *n* is the number of the term, and *r* is the common ratio.

Sum of a Finite Arithmetic Series
The sum S_n of a finite arithmetic series
$a_1 + a_2 + a_3 + \ldots + a_n$ is $S_n = \frac{n}{2}(a_1 + a_n)$, where a_1 is the first term, a_n is the *n*th term, and *n* is the number of terms.

Sum of a Finite Geometric Series
The sum S_n of a finite geometric series
$a_1 + a_2 + a_3 + \ldots + a_n$ is $S_n = \frac{a_1(1 - r^n)}{1 - r}$, where a_1 is the first term, *r* is the common ratio, and *n* is the number of terms.

Sum of an Infinite Geometric Series
An infinite geometric series with $|r| < 1$ converges to the sum *S* given by the following formula:
$S = \dfrac{a_1}{1 - r}$

Chapter 12

Conditional Probability Formula
For any two events *A* and *B* from a sample space with $P(A) \neq 0$,
$P(B \mid A) = \dfrac{P(A \text{ and } B)}{P(A)}$

Margin of Error Formula
When a random sample of size *n* is taken from a large population, the sample proportion has a margin of error of approximately $\pm \frac{1}{\sqrt{n}}$.

Binomial Probability
For repeated independent trials, each with a probability of success *p* and a probability of failure *q* (with $p + q = 1$), the probability of *x* successes in *n* trials is ${}_nC_x p^x q^{n-x}$.

Chapter 13

Converting Between Radians and Degrees
To convert degrees to radians, multiply by $\frac{\pi \text{ radians}}{180°}$.
To convert radians to degrees, multiply by $\frac{180°}{\pi \text{ radians}}$.

Length of an Intercepted Arc
For a circle of radius *r* and a central angle of measure θ (in radians), the length *s* of the intercepted arc is $s = r\theta$.

Properties of Sine Functions
Suppose $y = a \sin b\theta$, with $a \neq 0, b > 0$, and θ in radians.
$|a|$ is the amplitude of the function.
b is the number of cycles in the interval from 0 to 2π.
$\frac{2\pi}{b}$ is the period of the function.

Properties of Cosine Functions

Suppose $y = a \cos b\theta$, with $a \neq 0, b > 0$, and θ in radians.

$|a|$ is the amplitude of the function.

b is the number of cycles in the interval from 0 to 2π.

$\frac{2\pi}{b}$ is the period of the function.

Properties of Tangent Functions

Suppose $y = a \tan b\theta$, with $b > 0$ and θ in radians.

$\frac{\pi}{b}$ is the period of the function.

One cycle occurs in the interval from $-\frac{\pi}{2b}$ to $\frac{\pi}{2b}$.

There are vertical asymptotes at each end of the cycle.

Translations of Sine and Cosine Functions

$y = a \sin b(x - h) + k$ and $y = a \cos b(x - h) + k$ represent translations of $y = a \sin bx$ and $y = a \cos bx$.

- $|a|$ = amplitude
- $\frac{2\pi}{b}$ = period (when x is in radians and $b > 0$)
- h = phase shift, or horizontal shift
- k = vertical shift

Cosecant, Secant, and Cotangent Functions

The cosecant (csc), secant (sec), and cotangent (cot) functions are defined using reciprocals. Their domains include all real numbers θ except those that make a denominator zero.

$$\csc \theta = \frac{1}{\sin \theta} \qquad \sec \theta = \frac{1}{\cos \theta} \qquad \cot \theta = \frac{1}{\tan \theta}$$

Chapter 14

Trigonometric Identities

Reciprocal Identities:

$$\csc \theta = \frac{1}{\sin \theta} \qquad \sec \theta = \frac{1}{\cos \theta} \qquad \cot \theta = \frac{1}{\tan \theta}$$

Tangent and Cotangent Identities:

$$\tan \theta = \frac{\sin \theta}{\cos \theta} \qquad \cot \theta = \frac{\cos \theta}{\sin \theta}$$

Pythagorean Identities:

$$\cos^2 \theta + \sin^2 \theta = 1$$
$$1 + \tan^2 \theta = \sec^2 \theta$$
$$1 + \cot^2 \theta = \csc^2 \theta$$

Trigonometric Ratios for a Right Triangle

In $\triangle ABC$ with $\angle C$ a right angle:

$$\sin A = \frac{\text{length of leg opposite } \angle A}{\text{length of hypotenuse}} = \frac{a}{c}$$

$$\cos A = \frac{\text{length of leg adjacent to } \angle A}{\text{length of hypotenuse}} = \frac{b}{c}$$

$$\tan A = \frac{\text{length of leg opposite } \angle A}{\text{length of leg adjacent to } \angle A} = \frac{a}{b}$$

$$\csc A = \frac{\text{length of hypotenuse}}{\text{length of leg opposite } \angle A} = \frac{c}{a}$$

$$\sec A = \frac{\text{length of hypotenuse}}{\text{length of leg adjacent to } \angle A} = \frac{c}{b}$$

$$\cot A = \frac{\text{length of leg adjacent to } \angle A}{\text{length of leg opposite } \angle A} = \frac{b}{a}$$

Law of Sines

In $\triangle ABC$, let $a, b,$ and c represent the lengths of the sides opposite $\angle A, \angle B,$ and $\angle C$, respectively.

Then $\frac{\sin A}{a} = \frac{\sin B}{b} = \frac{\sin C}{c}$.

You can use the Law of Sines to find missing measures of any triangle when you know the measures of two angles and any side, or two sides and the angle opposite one of them.

Law of Cosines

In $\triangle ABC$, let $a, b,$ and c represent the lengths of the sides opposite $\angle A, \angle B,$ and $\angle C$, respectively.

$$a^2 = b^2 + c^2 - 2bc \cos A$$
$$b^2 = a^2 + c^2 - 2ac \cos B$$
$$c^2 = a^2 + b^2 - 2ab \cos C$$

You can use the Law of Cosines to find missing parts of any triangle when you know the measures of two sides and the angle between them, or all three sides.

Angle Identities

Negative Angle Identities:

$$\sin (-\theta) = -\sin \theta$$
$$\cos (-\theta) = \cos \theta$$
$$\tan (-\theta) = -\tan \theta$$

Cofunction Identities:

$$\sin \left(\frac{\pi}{2} - \theta \right) = \cos \theta$$
$$\cos \left(\frac{\pi}{2} - \theta \right) = \sin \theta$$
$$\tan \left(\frac{\pi}{2} - \theta \right) = \cot \theta$$

Angle Difference Identities

$$\sin (A - B) = \sin A \cos B - \cos A \sin B$$
$$\cos (A - B) = \cos A \cos B + \sin A \sin B$$
$$\tan (A - B) = \frac{\tan A - \tan B}{1 + \tan A \tan B}$$

Angle Sum Identities

$$\sin (A + B) = \sin A \cos B + \cos A \sin B$$
$$\cos (A + B) = \cos A \cos B - \sin A \sin B$$
$$\tan (A + B) = \frac{\tan A + \tan B}{1 - \tan A \tan B}$$

Double Angle Identities

$$\sin 2\theta = 2 \sin \theta \cos \theta$$
$$\cos 2\theta = \cos^2 \theta - \sin^2 \theta$$
$$\cos 2\theta = 2 \cos^2 \theta - 1$$
$$\cos 2\theta = 1 - 2 \sin^2 \theta$$
$$\tan 2\theta = \frac{2 \tan \theta}{1 - \tan^2 \theta}$$

Formulas from Geometry

You will use a number of geometric formulas as you work through your algebra book. Here are some perimeter, area, and volume formulas.

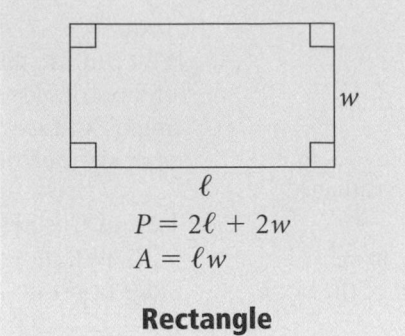

$$P = 2\ell + 2w$$
$$A = \ell w$$

Rectangle

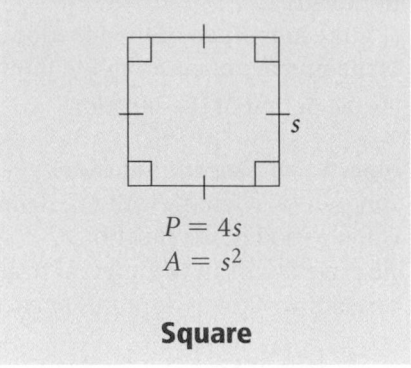

$$P = 4s$$
$$A = s^2$$

Square

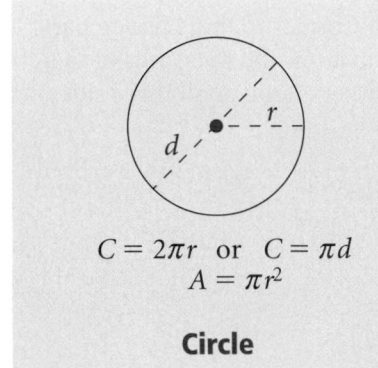

$$C = 2\pi r \quad \text{or} \quad C = \pi d$$
$$A = \pi r^2$$

Circle

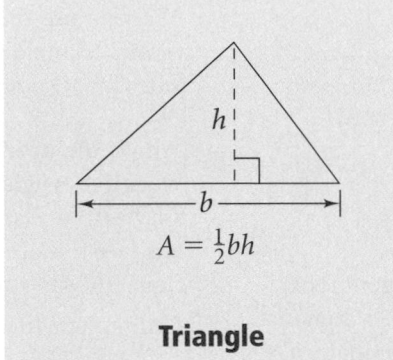

$$A = \tfrac{1}{2}bh$$

Triangle

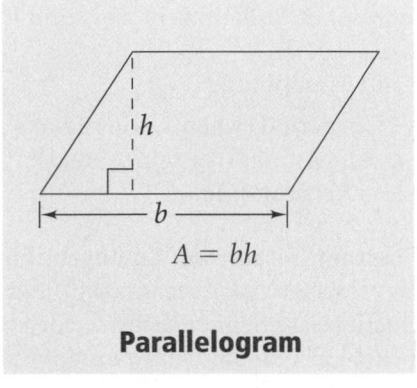

$$A = bh$$

Parallelogram

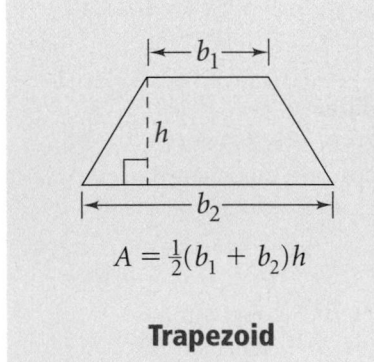

$$A = \tfrac{1}{2}(b_1 + b_2)h$$

Trapezoid

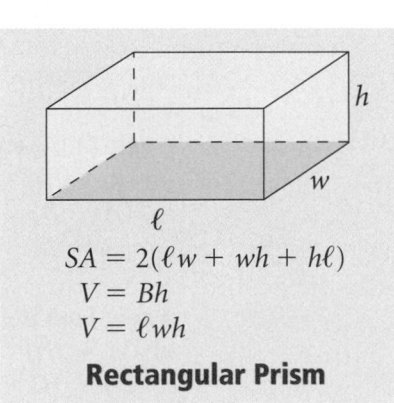

$$SA = 2(\ell w + wh + h\ell)$$
$$V = Bh$$
$$V = \ell wh$$

Rectangular Prism

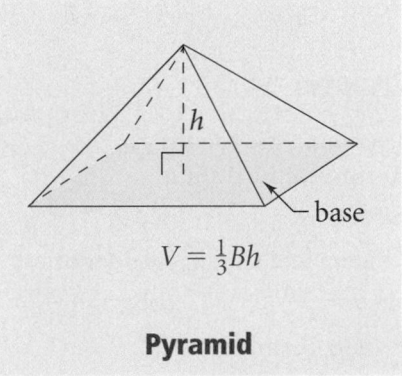

$$V = \tfrac{1}{3}Bh$$

Pyramid

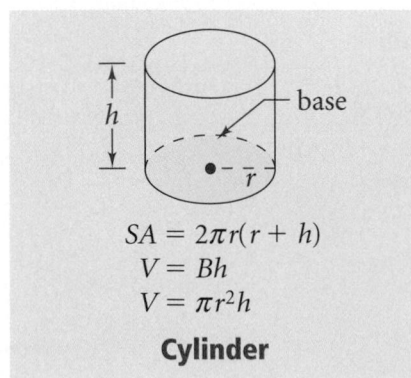

$$SA = 2\pi r(r + h)$$
$$V = Bh$$
$$V = \pi r^2 h$$

Cylinder

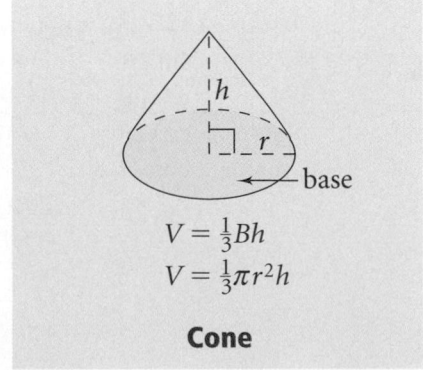

$$V = \tfrac{1}{3}Bh$$
$$V = \tfrac{1}{3}\pi r^2 h$$

Cone

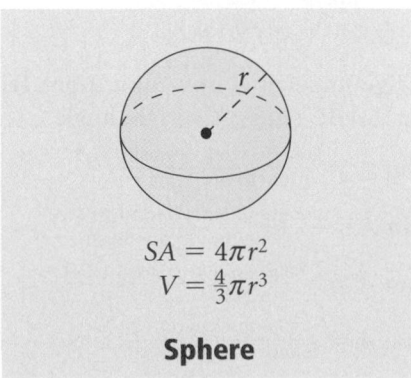

$$SA = 4\pi r^2$$
$$V = \tfrac{4}{3}\pi r^3$$

Sphere

English/Spanish Illustrated Glossary

 A

EXAMPLES

Absolute value function (p. 88)   A function of the form $f(x) = |mx + b| + c$, where $m \neq 0$, is an absolute value function.

$f(x) = |3x - 2| + 3$
$f(x) = |2x|$

Función de valor absoluto (p. 88)   Una función de la forma $f(x) = |mx + b| + c$, donde $m \neq 0$, es una función de valor absoluto.

Absolute value of a complex number (p. 275)   The absolute value of a complex number is its distance from the origin on the complex number plane. In general, $|a + bi| = \sqrt{a^2 + b^2}$.

$|3 - 4i| = \sqrt{3^2 + (-4)^2} = 5$

Valor absoluto de un número complejo (p. 275)   El valor absoluto de un número complejo es la distancia a la que está del origen en el plano de números complejo. Generalmente, $|a + bi| = \sqrt{a^2 + b^2}$.

Absolute value of a real number (pp. 8, 33)   The absolute value of a real number is its distance from zero on the number line.

If $x \geq 0$, then $|x| = x$. If $x < 0$, then $|x| = -x$.

$|3| = 3$
$|-4| = 4$

Valor absoluto de un número real (pp. 8, 33)   El valor absoluto de un número real es la distancia a la que el número se encuentra de cero en la recta numérica.

Si $x \geq 0$, entonces $|x| = x$. Si $x < 0$, entonces $|x| = -x$.

Additive inverse (p. 7)   The opposite or additive inverse of any number a is $-a$. The sum of opposites is 0.

$3 + (-3) = 0$
$5.2 + (-5.2) = 0$

Inverso aditivo (p. 7)   El opuesto o inverso aditivo de cualquier número a es $-a$. La suma de los opuestos es 0.

Algebraic expression (p. 12)   An expression that contains one or more variables is called an algebraic expression or a variable expression.

$2x + 3$
$z - y$

Expresión algebraica (p. 12)   Una expresión que contiene una o más variables es llamada expresión algebraica o expresión variable.

Amplitude of a periodic function (p. 712)   The amplitude of a periodic function is half the difference between the maximum and minimum values of the function.

The maximum and minimum values of $y = 4 \sin x$ are 4 and -4, respectively.
amplitude $= \dfrac{4 - (-4)}{2} = 4$

Amplitud de una función periódica (p. 712)   La amplitud de una función periódica es la mitad de la diferencia entre los valores máximo y mínimo de la función.

Arithmetic mean (p. 607)   The arithmetic mean of any two numbers is their sum divided by two.

Media aritmética (p. 607)   La media aritmética de dos números cualesquiera es la suma de los números dividida por dos.

The arithmetic mean of 12 and 15 is $\frac{12 + 15}{2} = 13.5$.

Arithmetic sequence (p. 606)   In an arithmetic sequence, the difference between consecutive terms is constant. The constant is called the common difference.

Progresión aritmética (p. 606)   En una progresión aritmética la diferencia entre términos consecutivos es un número constante. El número constante se llama la diferencia común.

The arithmetic sequence $1, 5, 9, 13, \ldots$ has a common difference of 4.

Arithmetic series (p. 620)   An arithmetic series is a series whose terms form an arithmetic sequence.

Serie aritmética (p. 620)   Una serie aritmética es una serie cuyos términos forman una progresión aritmética.

$1 + 5 + 9 + 13 + 17 + 21$ is an arithmetic series with six terms.

Asymptote (p. 433)   An asymptote is a line that a graph approaches as x or y increases in absolute value.

Asíntota (p. 433)   Una asíntota es una recta a la cual se acerca una gráfica a medida que x o y aumentan de valor absoluto.

The function $y = \frac{x + 2}{x - 2}$ has $x = 2$ as a vertical asymptote and $y = 1$ as a horizontal asymptote.

Augmented matrix (p. 222)   An augmented matrix contains the coefficients and constants from a system of equations.

Matriz aumentada (p. 222)   Una matriz aumentada contiene los coeficientes y constantes de un sistema de ecuaciones.

linear system   augmented matrix

$\begin{cases} x + 4 = 6 \\ -2x + 5y = 7 \end{cases}$ $\left[\begin{array}{cc|c} 1 & 4 & 6 \\ -2 & 5 & 7 \end{array}\right]$

Axis of symmetry (p. 239)   The axis of symmetry is the line that divides a figure into two parts that are mirror images.

Eje de simetría (p. 239)   El eje de simetria es la recta que divide una figura en dos partes que son imágenes una de la otra.

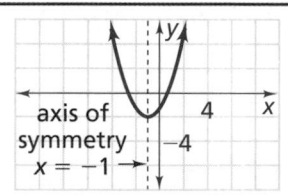

$y = x^2 + 2x - 1$

▼ **B**

Bimodal (p. 660)   A bimodal data set has two modes.

Bimodal (p. 660)   Un conjunto bimodal de datos tiene dos modas.

$\{1, 2, 3, 3, 4, 5, 6, 6\}$

mode $= 3$ and 6

Binomial experiment (p. 685) A binomial experiment is one in which the situation involves repeated trials. Each trial has two possible outcomes (success or failure), and the probability of success is constant throughout the trials.

Experimento binomial (p. 685) Un experimento binomial es un experimento que requiere varios ensayos. Cada ensayo tiene dos resultados posibles (éxito o fracaso), y la probabilidad de éxito es constante durante todos los ensayos.

Binomial probability (p. 687) In a binomial experiment with probability of success p and probability of failure q, the probability of x successes in n trials is given by $_nC_x\, p^x q^{n-x}$.

Probabilidad binomial (p. 687) En un experimento binomial con una probabilidad de éxito p y una probabilidad de fracaso q, la probabilidad de x éxitos en n ensayos se expresa con $_nC_x\, p^x q^{n-x}$.

Suppose you roll a standard number cube and that you call rolling a 1 a success. Then $p = \frac{1}{6}$ and $q = \frac{5}{6}$. The probability of rolling nine 1's in twenty rolls is $_{20}C_9\left(\frac{1}{6}\right)^9\left(\frac{5}{6}\right)^{11} \approx 0.0022$.

Binomial Theorem (p. 354) For every positive integer n,
$(a + b)^n = {_nC_0}a^n + {_nC_1}a^{n-1}b^1 + \ldots + {_nC_{n-1}}a^1b^{n-1} + {_nC_n}b^n$. The numbers $_nC_0, {_nC_1}, \ldots, {_nC_n}$ are often called binomial coefficients.

Teorema binomial (p. 354) Para todo número entero positivo n,
$(a + b)^n = {_nC_0}a^n + {_nC_1}a^{n-1}b^1 + \ldots + {_nC_{n-1}}a^1b^{n-1} + {_nC_n}b^n$. Los números $_nC_0, {_nC_1}, \ldots, {_nC_n}$ a menudo se llaman coeficientes del binomio.

$$(2x - 3)^3 = {_3C_0}(2x)^3 + {_3C_1}(2x)^2(-3)^1$$
$$+ {_3C_2}(2x)^1(-3)^2 + {_3C_3}(-3)^3$$
$$= 8x^3 - 36x^2 + 54x - 27$$

Box-and-whisker plot (p. 662) A box-and-whisker plot is a method of displaying data that uses quartiles to form the center box and the maximum and minimum values to form the whiskers.

Gráfica de cajas (p. 662) Una gráfica de cajas es un método para mostrar datos que utiliza cuartiles para formar una casilla central y los valores máximos y mínimos para formar los conectores.

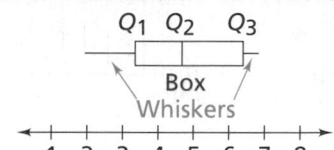
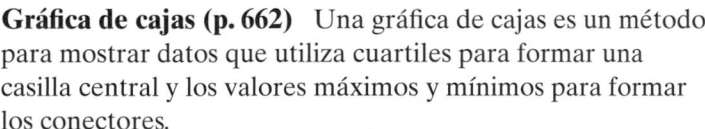

Branch (p. 495) Each piece of a discontinuous graph is called a branch.

Rama (p. 495) Cada segmento de una gráfica discontinua se llama rama.

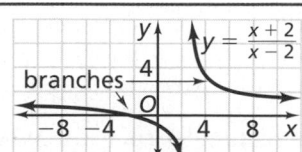

Center of a circle (p. 561) The center of a circle is the point that is the same distance from every point on the circle.

Centro de un círculo (p. 561) El centro de un círculo es el punto que está situado a la misma distancia de cada punto del círculo.

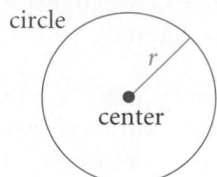

Center of rotation (p. 194) The center of rotation is the fixed point of a rotation transformation.

Centro de rotación (p. 194) El centro de rotación es el punto fijo de una transformación por rotación.

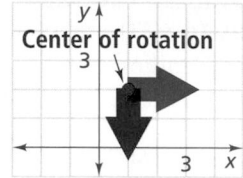

Central angle (p. 726) A central angle of a circle is an angle whose vertex is at the center of a circle.

Ángulo central (p. 726) El ángulo central de un círculo es un ángulo cuyo vértice está situado en el centro del círculo.

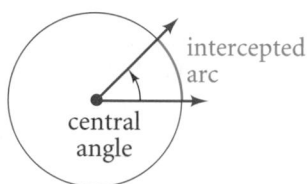

Change of Base Formula (p. 462) $\log_b M = \frac{\log_c M}{\log_c b}$, where $M, b,$ and c are positive numbers, and $b \neq 1$ and $c \neq 1$.

$$\log_3 8 = \frac{\log 8}{\log 3} \approx 1.8928$$

Fórmula de cambio de base (p. 462) $\log_b M = \frac{\log_c M}{\log_c b}$, donde M, b y c son números positivos y $b \neq 1$ y $c \neq 1$.

Circle (p. 561) A circle is the set of all points in a plane at a distance r from a given point. The standard form of the equation of a circle with center (h, k) and radius r is $(x - h)^2 + (y - k)^2 = r^2$.

Círculo (p. 561) Un círculo es el conjunto de todos los puntos situados en un plano a una distancia r de un punto dado. La forma normal de la ecuación del círculo cuyo centro es (h, k) y cuyo radio es r es $(x - h)^2 + (y - k)^2 = r^2$.

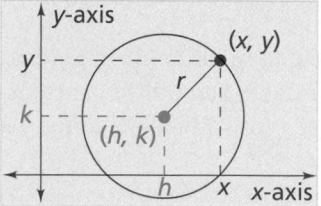

Circumscribed rectangles (p. 636) When approximating the area under a curve, circumscribed rectangles are partially above the curve. Their combined area generally is greater than the area under the curve.

Rectángulos circunscritos (p. 636) Al aproximar el área que queda dentro de una curva, los rectángulos circunscritos quedan parcialmente por fuera de la curva. Generalmente, su área total es mayor que el área dentro de la curva.

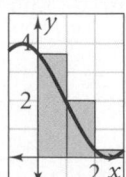

Coefficient (p. 13)   The numerical factor in a term is the coefficient.

Coeficiente (p. 13)   El factor numérico de un término es el coeficiente.

The coefficient of $-3k$ is -3.

Coefficient matrix (p. 214)   When representing a system of equations with a matrix equation, the matrix containing the coefficients of the system is the coefficient matrix.

Matriz de coeficientes (p. 214)   Al representar un sistema de ecuaciones con una ecuación de matriz, la matriz que contiene los coeficientes del sistema es la matriz de coeficientes.

$$\begin{cases} x + 2y = 5 \\ 3x + 5y = 14 \end{cases}$$

coefficient matrix $\begin{bmatrix} 1 & 2 \\ 3 & 5 \end{bmatrix}$

Combination (p. 346)   Any unordered selection of r objects from a set of n objects is a combination. The number of combinations of n objects taken r at a time is $_nC_r = \frac{n!}{r!(n-r)!}$ for $0 \le r \le n$.

Combinación (p. 346)   Cualquier selección no ordenada de r objetos tomados de un conjunto de n objetos es una combinación. El número de combinaciones de n objetos, cuando se toman r objetos cada vez, es $_nC_r = \frac{n!}{r!(n-r)!}$ para $0 \le r \le n$.

The number of combinations of seven items taken four at a time is

$$_7C_4 = \frac{7!}{4!(7-4)!} = 35.$$

There are 35 ways to choose four items from seven items without regard to order.

Combined variation (p. 490)   When one quantity varies with respect to two or more other quantities, the relation is a combined variation.

Variación combinada (p. 490)   Cuando una cantidad varía con respecto a otras dos o más cantidades, la relación es una variación combinada.

$y = kx^2\sqrt{z}$

$z = \frac{kx}{y}$

Common difference (p. 606)   A common difference is the difference between consecutive terms of an arithmetic sequence.

Diferencia común (p. 606)   La diferencia común es la diferencia entre los términos consecutivos de una progresión aritmética.

The arithmetic sequence $1, 5, 9, 13, \ldots$ has a common difference of 4.

Common logarithm (p. 447)   A common logarithm is a logarithm that uses base 10. You can write the common logarithm $\log_{10} y$ as $\log y$.

Logaritmo común (p. 447)   El logaritmo común es un logaritmo de base 10. El logaritmo común $\log_{10} y$ se expresa como $\log y$.

$\log 1 = 0$

$\log 10 = 1$

$\log 50 = 1.698970004 \ldots$

Common ratio (p. 612)   A common ratio is the ratio of consecutive terms of a geometric sequence.

Razón común (p. 612)   Una razón común es el número que resulta al dividir términos consecutivos en una progresión geométrica.

The geometric sequence $2.5, 5, 10, 20, \ldots$ has a common ratio of 2.

Completing the square (p. 282)   Completing the square is the process of finding the constant term of a perfect square trinomial.

Completar el cuadrado (p. 282)   Completar el cuadrado es el proceso de hallar el término constante de un trinomio cuadrado perfecto.

$x^2 - 12x + \blacksquare$

$x^2 - 12x + \left(\frac{-12}{2}\right)^2$

$x^2 - 12x + 36$

Complex conjugates (p. 338) Number pairs of the form $a + bi$ and $a - bi$ are complex conjugates.

The complex numbers $2 - 3i$ and $2 + 3i$ are complex conjugates.

Conjugados complejos (p. 338) Los pares de números de la forma $a + bi$ y $a - bi$ son conjugados complejos.

Complex fraction (p. 516) A complex fraction is a fraction that has a fraction in its numerator or denominator or in both its numerator and denominator.

$\dfrac{\frac{2}{1}}{5}$

$\dfrac{\frac{2}{7}}{\frac{3}{2}}$

Fracción compleja (p. 516) Una fracción compleja es una fracción que contiene otra fracción en el numerador o en el denominador, o en ambos.

Complex number plane (p. 275) You can use the complex number plane to represent a complex number geometrically. Locate the real part of the number on the horizontal axis and the imaginary part on the vertical axis.

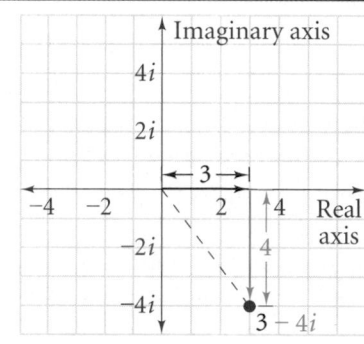

Plano de números complejos (p. 275) Plano que sirve para representar geométricamente los números complejos. Se localiza la parte real del número en el eje horizontal y la parte imaginaria en el eje vertical.

Complex numbers (p. 275) Imaginary numbers and real numbers together make up the set of complex numbers. A complex number can be written in the form $a + bi$, where a and b are real numbers, including 0, and i is $\sqrt{-1}$.

$6 + i$

$7, 2i$

Números complejos (p. 275) Los números imaginarios y los números reales componen el conjunto de números complejos. Un número complejo es cualquier expresión de la forma $a + bi$, donde a y b son números reales, incluido 0, e i es $\sqrt{-1}$.

Composite function (p. 399) A composite function is a combination of two functions such that the output from the first function becomes the input for the second function.

$$f(x) = 2x + 1 \quad g(x) = x^2 - 1$$
$$(g \circ f)(5) = g(f(5)) = g(2(5) + 1)$$
$$= g(11)$$
$$= 11^2 - 1 = 120$$
$$(f \circ g)(5) = f(g(5)) = f((5)^2 - 1)$$
$$= f(24)$$
$$= 2(24) + 1 = 49$$

Función compuesta (p. 399) Una función compuesta es la combinación de dos funciones. La cantidad de salida de la primera función es la cantidad de entrada de la segunda función.

Compound inequality (p. 28) A compound inequality is a pair of inequalities joined by *and* or *or*.

$-1 < x$ and $x \leq 3$

$x < -1$ or $x \geq 3$

Desigualdad compuesta (p. 28) Una desigualdad compuesta se forma con dos desigualdades enlazadas por medio de una *y* o una *o*.

Conditional probability (p. 654) A conditional probability contains a condition that may limit the sample space for an event. The notation $P(B \mid A)$ is read "the probability of event B, given event A." For any two events A and B in the sample space,

$$P(B \mid A) = \frac{P(A \text{ and } B)}{P(A)}.$$

Probabilidad condicional (p. 654) Una probabilidad condicional contiene una condición que puede limitar el espacio muestral de un suceso. La notación $P(B \mid A)$ se lee "la probabilidad del suceso B, dado el suceso A". Para dos sucesos cualesquiera A y B en el espacio muestral,

$$P(B \mid A) = \frac{P(A \text{ y } B)}{P(A)}.$$

Suppose that 83% of an airline's flights depart on schedule. Suppose also that 75% of its flights depart and arrive on schedule.

$P(\text{arrives on time} \mid \text{departs on time})$

$= \dfrac{P(\text{departs and arrives on time})}{P(\text{departs on time})}$

$= \dfrac{0.75}{0.83}$

≈ 0.9

Conic section (p. 547) A conic section is a curve formed by the intersection of a plane and a double cone.

Sección cónica (p. 547) Una sección cónica es una curva que se forma por la intersección de un plano con un cono doble.

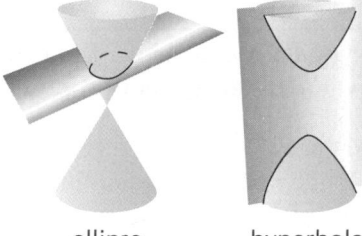

ellipse   hyperbola

Conjugates (p. 337) Number pairs of the form $a + \sqrt{b}$ and $a - \sqrt{b}$ are conjugates.

Conjugados (p. 337) Los pares de números con la forma $a + \sqrt{b}$ y $a - \sqrt{b}$ son conjugados.

$5 + \sqrt{3}$ and $5 - \sqrt{3}$ are conjugates.

Constant matrix (p. 214) When representing a system of equations with a matrix equation, the matrix containing the constants of the system is the constant matrix.

Matriz de constantes (p. 214) Al representar un sistema de ecuaciones con una ecuación matricial, la matriz que contiene las constantes del sistema es la matriz de constantes.

$\begin{cases} x + 2y = 5 \\ 3x + 5y = 14 \end{cases}$

constant matrix $\begin{bmatrix} 5 \\ 14 \end{bmatrix}$

Constant of variation (pp. 72, 488, 490) The constant of variation is the value of k in the direct variation $y = kx$ or the value of k in the indirect variation $xy = k$. A joint variation also has a constant of variation.

Constante de variación (pp. 72, 488, 490) La constante de variación es el valor de k en una variación directa $y = kx$, o el valor de k en la variación indirecta $xy = k$. Una variación conjunta también tiene una constante de variación.

In $y = 3.5x$, the constant of variation k is 3.5. In $xy = 5$, the constant of variation k is 5.

Constraints (p. 139) Constraints are restrictions on the variables of the objective function in a linear programming problem. *See* **Linear programming.**

Restricciones (p. 139) Las restricciones son limitaciones a las variables de una función objetiva en un problema de programación lineal. *Ver* **Linear programming.**

Continuously compounded interest formula (p. 444) The formula for continuously compounded interest is $A = Pe^{rt}$.

Fórmula de interés compuesto continuo (p. 444) La fórmula para el interés compuesto continuo es $A = Pe^{rt}$.

Suppose that $P = \$1200$, $r = 0.05$, and $t = 3$. Then

$$A = 1200e^{0.05 \cdot 3}$$
$$= 1200(2.718\ldots)^{0.15}$$
$$\approx 1394.20$$

Converge (p. 627) An infinite geometric series converges when $|r| < 1$, where r is the common ratio of the related sequence.

Convergir (p. 627) Una serie geométrica infinita converge cuando $|r| < 1$, donde r es la razón común de la progresión.

$1 + \frac{1}{2} + \frac{1}{4} + \frac{1}{8} + \cdots$ converges.

Coordinate space (p. 146) Coordinate space is a three-dimensional space where each point is described uniquely using an ordered triple of numbers.

Espacio de coordenadas (p. 146) Un espacio de coordenadas es un espacio tridimensional en el cual cada punto es definido de manera única por una tripleta ordenada de números.

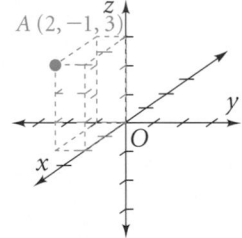

Cosecant function (p. 763) The cosecant (csc) function is the reciprocal of the sine function. For all real numbers θ except those that make $\sin \theta = 0$, $\csc \theta = \frac{1}{\sin \theta}$.

Función cosecante (p. 763) La función cosecante (csc) se define como el recíproco de la función seno. Para todos los números reales θ, excepto aquéllos para los que $\sin \theta = 0$, $\csc \theta = \frac{1}{\sin \theta}$.

If $\sin \theta = \frac{5}{13}$, then $\csc \theta = \frac{13}{5}$.

Cosine function (p. 743) The cosine function, $y = \cos \theta$, matches the measure θ of an angle in standard position with the x-coordinate of a point on the unit circle. This point is where the terminal side of the angle intersects the unit circle.

Función coseno (p. 743) La función coseno, $y = \cos \theta$, equivale a la medida θ de un ángulo en posición normal con la coordenada x de un punto en el círculo unitario. Este punto es el punto de intersección entre el lado terminal del ángulo y el círculo unitario.

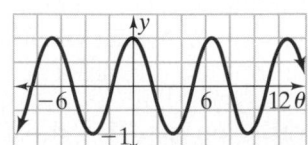

Cosine of θ (p. 720)   The cosine of an angle measure θ (cos θ) is the x-coordinate of the point at which the terminal side of the angle intersects the unit circle.

Coseno de θ (p. 720)   El coseno de un ángulo que mide θ (cos θ) es la coordenada x del punto de intersección del lado terminal del ángulo y el círculo unitario.

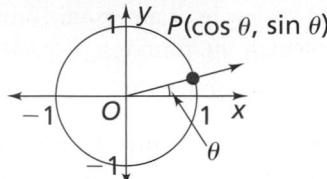

Cotangent function (p. 763)   The cotangent (cot) function is the reciprocal of the tangent function. For all real numbers θ except those that make tan θ = 0, $\cot \theta = \frac{1}{\tan \theta}$.

Función cotangente (p. 763)   La función cotangente (cot) es el recíproco de la función tangente. Para todos los números reales θ, excepto aquéllos para los que tan θ = 0, $\cot \theta = \frac{1}{\tan \theta}$.

If $\tan \theta = \frac{5}{12}$, then $\cot \theta = \frac{12}{5}$.

Coterminal angles (p. 719)   Two angles in standard position are coterminal if they have the same terminal side.

Ángulos coterminales (p. 719)   Dos ángulos que están en posición normal son coterminales si tienen el mismo lado terminal.

Angles that have measures 135° and −225° are coterminal.

Co-vertices (of an ellipse) (p. 568)   The endpoints of the minor axis of an ellipse are the co-vertices of the ellipse.

Covértices (de una elipse) (p. 568)   Los puntos de intersección entre una elipse y los ejes menores son los covértices de la elipse.

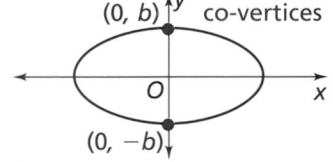

Cramer's Rule (p. 221)   Cramer's Rule is a method of solving a system of linear equations using determinants. D is the determinant of the system's coefficient matrix. Form the determinants D_x and D_y by replacing the corresponding column of the coefficient matrix with the terms of the constant matrix.

Regla de Cramer (p. 221)   La regla de Cramer es un método para resolver por medio de determinantes un sistema de ecuaciones lineales. D es el determinante de la matriz de coeficientes del sistema. Se forman los determinantes D_x y D_y reemplazando la columna correspondiente de la matriz de coeficientes con los términos de la matriz constante.

$$\begin{cases} x + 2y = 6 \\ -x + y = -6 \end{cases}$$

$$D = \begin{vmatrix} 1 & 2 \\ -1 & 1 \end{vmatrix} = 3$$

$$D_x = \begin{vmatrix} 6 & 2 \\ -6 & 1 \end{vmatrix} = 18$$

$$D_y = \begin{vmatrix} 1 & 6 \\ -1 & -6 \end{vmatrix} = 0$$

$$x = \frac{D_x}{D} = 6 \qquad y = \frac{D_y}{D} = 0$$

Cumulative probability (p. 648)   Probability over a continuous range of events is cumulative probability.

Probabilidad acumulativa (p. 648)   La probabilidad que existe a lo largo de una serie continua de sucesos es la probabilidad acumulativa.

Cycle (p. 711) A cycle of a periodic function is an interval of x-values over which the function provides one complete pattern of y-values.

Ciclo (p. 711) El ciclo de una función periódica es un intervalo de valores de x de los cuales la función produce un patrón completo de valores de y.

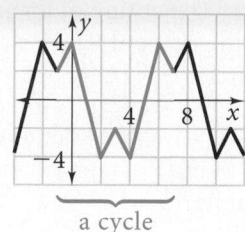

a cycle

Decay factor (p. 433) In an exponential function of the form $y = ab^x$, b is the decay factor if $0 < b < 1$.

Factor de decremento (p. 433) En una función exponencial de la forma $y = ab^x$, b es el factor de decremento si, $0 < b < 1$.

In the equation $y = 0.5^x$, 0.5 is the decay factor.

Degree of a polynomial (p. 307) The degree of a polynomial is the largest degree of any term of the polynomial.

Grado de un polinomio (p. 307) El grado de un polinomio es el grado mayor de cualquier término del polinomio.

$P(x) = x^6 + 2x^3 - 3$

degree 6

Degree of a term (p. 307) The exponent of the variable in a term determines the degree of the term.

Grado de un término (p. 307) El exponente de la variable de un término determina el grado del término.

$x^2 \leftarrow$ degree 2

$3y^3 \leftarrow$ degree 3

$-4a^{12} \leftarrow$ degree 12

Dependent events (p. 531) Two events are dependent if the occurrence of one event affects the probability of the second event.

Sucesos dependientes (p. 531) Cuando el resultado de un suceso influye en la probabilidad de que ocurra el segundo suceso, los dos sucesos son dependientes.

You have a bag with red and blue marbles. You draw one marble at random and then another without replacing the first. The colors drawn are dependent events. A red marble on the first draw changes the probability for each color on the second draw.

Dependent system (p. 120) A system of equations that does not have a unique solution is a dependent system.

Sistema dependiente (p. 120) Un sistema de ecuaciones es dependiente cuando no tiene una solución única.

$\begin{cases} y = 2x + 3 \\ -4x + 2y = 6 \end{cases}$ represents two equations for the same line, so it has many solutions. It is a dependent system.

Dependent variable (p. 62) If a function is defined by an equation using the variables x and y, where y represents output values, then y is the dependent variable.

Variable dependiente (p. 62) Si una función es definida por una ecuación que usa las variables x e y, donde y representa valores de salida, entonces y es la variable dependiente.

$y = 2x + 1$

y is the dependent variable.

Determinant (p. 200)   The determinant of a square matrix is a real number that can be computed from its elements according to a specific formula.

The determinant of $\begin{bmatrix} 3 & -2 \\ 5 & 6 \end{bmatrix}$ is $3(6) - 5(-2) = 28$.

Determinante (p. 200)   El determinante de una matriz cuadrada es un número real que se puede calcular a partir de sus elementos por medio de una fórmula específica.

Difference of cubes (p. 328)   A difference of cubes is an expression of the form $a^3 - b^3$. It can be factored as $(a - b)(a^2 + ab + b^2)$.

$x^3 - 27 = (x - 3)(x^2 + 3x + 9)$

Diferencia de dos cubos (p. 328)   La diferencia de dos cubos es una expresión de la forma $a^3 - b^3$. Se puede factorizar como $(a - b)(a^2 + ab + b^2)$.

Difference of two squares (p. 263)   A difference of two squares is an expression of the form $a^2 - b^2$. It can be factored as $(a + b)(a - b)$.

$25a^2 - 4 = (5a + 2)(5a - 2)$
$m^6 - 1 = (m^3 + 1)(m^3 - 1)$

Diferencia de dos cuadrados (p. 263)   La diferencia de dos cuadrados es una expresión de la forma $a^2 - b^2$. Se puede factorizar como $(a + b)(a - b)$.

Dilation (p. 192)   A dilation is a transformation that can change the size of a figure. When the center of the dilation is the origin, you can use scalar multiplication to find the coordinates of the vertices of an image.

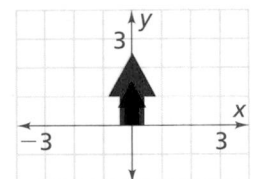

Dilatación (p. 192)   Una dilatación es una transformación que puede cambiar el tamaño de una figura. Cuando el centro de dilatación está en el origen, se hallan las coordenadas de los vértices de la imagen por medio de la multiplicación de escalar.

Direct variation (p. 72)   A linear function defined by an equation of the form $y = kx$, where $k \neq 0$, represents direct variation.

$y = 3.5x, y = 7x, y = -\frac{1}{2}x$

Variación directa (p. 72)   Una función lineal definida por una ecuación de la forma $y = kx$, donde $k \neq 0$, representa una variación directa.

Directrix (p. 555)   The directrix of a parabola is the fixed line used to define a parabola. Each point of the parabola is the same distance from the focus and the directrix.

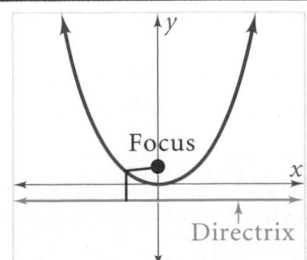

Directriz (p. 555)   La directriz de una parábola es la recta fija con que se define una parábola. Cada punto de la parábola está a la misma distancia del foco y de la directriz.

Discriminant (p. 291) The discriminant of the quadratic trinomial $ax^2 + bx + c$ is $b^2 - 4ac$. The discriminant determines the number of real roots that the quadratic equation $ax^2 + bx + c = 0$ has. If $b^2 - 4ac < 0$, the equation has no real roots; if $b^2 - 4ac = 0$, the equation has one real root; if $b^2 - 4ac > 0$, the equation has two real roots.

$3x^2 - 6x + 1$

$\text{discriminant} = (-6)^2 - 4(3)(1)$

$= 36 - 12 = 24$

The equation has two real roots.

Discriminante (p. 291) El discriminante del trinomio cuadrático $ax^2 + bx + c$ es $b^2 - 4ac$. El discriminante determina la cantidad de raíces reales que tiene la ecuación $ax^2 + bx + c = 0$. Si $b^2 - 4ac < 0$, la ecuación no tiene raíces reales; si $b^2 - 4ac = 0$, la ecuación tiene una raíz real; si $b^2 - 4ac > 0$, la ecuación tiene dos raíces reales.

Diverge (p. 627) An infinite geometric series diverges when $|r| \geq 1$, where r is the common ratio of the related sequence.

$1 + 2 + 4 + 8 + \cdots$ diverges.

Divergir (p. 627) Una serie geométrica infinita diverge cuando $|r| \geq 1$, donde r es la razón común de la progresión relacionada.

Domain (p. 56) The domain of a relation is the set of all inputs, or x-coordinates, of the ordered pairs.

In the relation $\{(0, 1), (0, 2), (0, 3), (0, 4), (1, 3), (1, 4), (2, 1)\}$, the domain is $\{0, 1, 2\}$. In the function $f(x) = x^2 - 10$, the domain is all real numbers.

Dominio (p. 56) El dominio de una relación es el conjunto de todos los valores de entrada, o coordenadas x, de los pares ordenados.

Ellipse (p. 568) An ellipse is the set of points P in a plane such that the sum of the distances from P to two fixed points F_1 and F_2 is a given constant k. The standard form of the equation of an ellipse with its center at the origin is $\frac{x^2}{a^2} + \frac{y^2}{b^2} = 1$ if the major axis is horizontal and $\frac{x^2}{b^2} + \frac{y^2}{a^2} = 1$ if the major axis is vertical, where $a > b$.

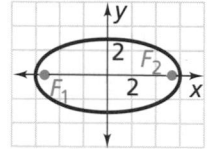

$\frac{x^2}{36} + \frac{y^2}{9} = 1$

$F_1 = \left(-3\sqrt{3}, 0\right), F_2 = \left(3\sqrt{3}, 0\right)$

Elipse (p. 568) Una elipse es el conjunto de puntos P situados en un plano tal que la suma de las distancias entre P y dos puntos fijos F_1 y F_2 es una constante dada k. La forma normal de la ecuación de una elipse con su centro en el origen es $\frac{x^2}{a^2} + \frac{y^2}{b^2} = 1$ si el eje mayor es horizontal y $\frac{x^2}{b^2} + \frac{y^2}{a^2} = 1$ si el eje mayor es vertical, donde $a > b$.

Equal matrices (p. 177) Equal matrices are matrices with the same dimensions and equal corresponding elements.

Matrices A and B are equal.

Matrices equivalentes (p. 177) Dos matrices son equivalentes si y sólo si tienen las mismas dimensiones y sus elementos correspondientes son iguales.

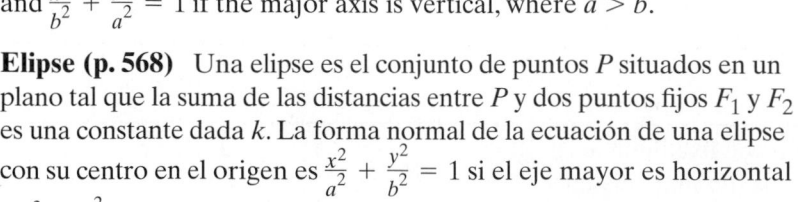

Equivalent systems (p. 127)   Linear systems that have the same solution(s) are equivalent systems.

Sistemas equivalentes (p. 127)   Sistemas lineales que tienen la misma solución o soluciones son sistemas equivalentes.

Evaluate (p. 12)   To evaluate an expression, substitute numbers for the variables in the expression and then simplify the expression following the order of operations.

Evaluar (p. 12)   Para evaluar una expresión, se sustituyen las variables de la expresión por números y luego se simplifica la expresión siguiendo el orden de las operaciones.

When $x = 2$ and $y = -1$, $2x + 3y$ evaluates to 1.

Expand (p. 353)   You expand a binomial raised to a power by multiplying and then writing the resulting polynomial in standard form.

Desarrollar (p. 353)   Para desarrollar un binomio elevado a una potencia, se multiplica y luego se escribe el polinomio resultante en forma normal.

$$(x + 4)^3$$
$$= (x + 4)(x + 4)^2$$
$$= (x + 4)(x^2 + 8x + 16)$$
$$= x^3 + 8x^2 + 16x + 4x^2 + 32x + 64$$
$$= x^3 + 12x^2 + 48x + 64$$

Experimental probability (p. 40)   The experimental probability of an event is the ratio

$$\frac{\text{number of times the event occurs}}{\text{number of trials}}.$$

Probabilidad experimental (p. 40)   La probabilidad experimental de un suceso es la razón

$$\frac{\text{número de veces que el suceso ocurre}}{\text{número de ensayos}}.$$

Suppose a basketball player has scored 19 times in 28 attempts at a basket. The experimental probability of the player's scoring is $P(\text{score}) = \frac{19}{28} \approx 0.68$, or 68%.

Explicit formula (p. 602)   An explicit formula expresses the nth term of a sequence in terms of n.

Fórmula explícita (p. 602)   Una fórmula explícita expresa el n-ésimo término de una progresión en función de n.

Let $a_n = 2n + 5$ for positive integers n. If $n = 7$, then $a_7 = 2(7) + 5 = 19$.

Exponential equation (p. 461)   An equation of the form $b^{cx} = a$, where the exponent includes a variable, is called an exponential equation. You can solve an exponential equation by taking the logarithm of each side of the equation.

Ecuación exponencial (p. 461)   Una ecuación de la forma $b^{cx} = a$, donde el exponente incluye una variable, se llama ecuación exponencial. Dicha ecuación se resuelve hallando el logaritmo de cada lado de la ecuación.

$$5^{2x} = 270$$
$$\log 5^{2x} = \log 270$$
$$2x \log 5 = \log 270$$
$$2x = \frac{\log 270}{\log 5}$$
$$2x \approx 3.4785$$
$$x \approx 1.7392$$

English/Spanish Glossary

Exponential function (pp. 430, 441) The general form of an exponential function is $y = ab^x$, where x is a real number, $a \neq 0$, $b > 0$, and $b \neq 1$. When $b > 1$, the function models exponential growth with growth factor b. When $0 < b < 1$, the function models exponential decay with decay factor b.

Función exponencial (pp. 430, 441) La forma general de una función exponencial es $y = ab^x$, donde x es un número real, $a \neq 0$, $b > 0$ y $b \neq 1$. Cuando $b > 1$, la función representa un incremento exponencial con factor de incremento b. Cuando $0 < b < 1$, la función representa el decremento exponencial con factor de decremento b.

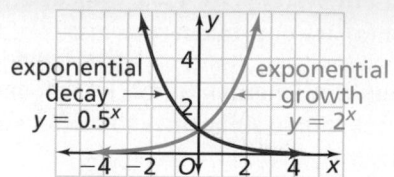

Extraneous solution (p. 34) An extraneous solution is a solution of an equation derived from an original equation but it is not a solution of the original equation.

Solución extraña (p. 34) Una solución extraña es una solución de una ecuación derivada de una ecuación dada, pero que no satisface la ecuación dada.

$$\sqrt{x - 3} = x - 5$$
$$x - 3 = x^2 - 10x + 25$$
$$0 = x^2 - 11x + 28$$
$$0 = (x - 4)(x - 7)$$
$$x = 4 \text{ or } 7$$

The number 7 is a solution, but 4 is not, since $\sqrt{4 - 3} \neq 4 - 5$.

Factor Theorem (p. 315) The expression $x - a$ is a linear factor of a polynomial if and only if the value a is a zero of the related polynomial function.

Teorema de factores (p. 315) La expresión $x - a$ es un factor lineal de un polinomio si y sólo si el valor a es un cero de la función del polinomio relacionada.

The value 2 makes the polynomial $x^2 + 2x - 8$ equal to zero. So, $x - 2$ is a factor of $x^2 + 2x - 8$.

Factoring (p. 259) Factoring is rewriting an expression as the product of its factors.

Descomposición factorial (p. 259) Descomponer en factores es convertir una expresión en el producto de sus factores.

expanded form   factored form
$x^2 + x - 56$ $(x + 8)(x - 7)$

Feasible region (p. 140) In a linear programming problem, the feasible region contains all the values that satisfy the constraints on the objective function.

Región factible (p. 140) En un problema de programación lineal, la región factible contiene todos los valores que satisfacen las restricciones de la función objetiva.

EXAMPLES

Focus (plural: foci) (pp. 555, 568, 575) The focus of a conic section is a point used to define a conic section.

A parabola is the set of all points that are the same distance from the parabola's focus and its directrix. An ellipse is the set of all points P such that the sum of the distances from each point P to the two foci of the ellipse is a constant. A hyperbola is the set of all points P such that the difference of the distances from each point P to the two foci of the hyperbola is a constant.

Foco (pp. 555, 568, 575) El foco de una sección cónica es el punto con el que se define una sección cónica.

Una parábola es el conjunto de todos los puntos que están a la misma distancia del foco y la directriz de la parábola. Una elipse es el conjunto de todos los puntos P tal que la suma de las distancias de cada punto P a los dos focos de la elipse es una constante. Una hipérbola es el conjunto de todos los puntos P tal que la diferencia de las distancias de cada punto P a los dos focos de la hipérbola es una constante.

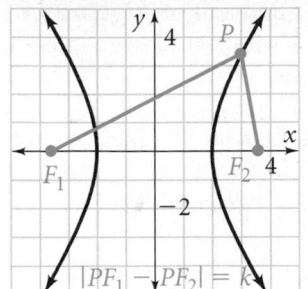

F_1 and F_2 are foci.

Frequency table (p. 648) A frequency table is a list of the outcomes in a sample space and the number of times each outcome occurs.

Tabla de frecuencias (p. 648) Una tabla de frecuencias es una lista de los resultados de un espacio muestral y el número de veces que cada resultado ocurre.

Roll	Freq.
1	5
2	9
3	7
4	8
5	8
6	3

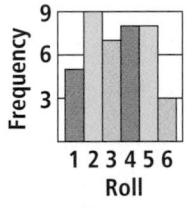

Suppose that you roll a standard number cube 40 times and that each number occurs as often as shown in the table. The table is a frequency table and the diagram to its right is a frequency diagram, or histogram.

Function (p. 57) A function is a relation in which each element of the domain is paired with exactly one element of the range.

Función (p. 57) Una función es una relación que asigna exactamente un valor del dominio a cada valor del rango.

The relation $y = 3x^3 - 2x + 3$ is a function. $f(x) = 3x^3 - 2x + 3$ is the same relation written in function notation.

Function notation (p. 58) If f is the name of a function, the function notation $f(x)$ also indicates the function name, but also represents a range value for the domain value x. You read the function notation $f(x)$ as "f of x" or "a function of x." Note that $f(x)$ does *not* mean "f times x."

Notación de una función (p. 58) Si f es el nombre de una función, la notación de la función $f(x)$ indica el nombre de la función, pero también representa un rango de valores para el dominio de valores de x. La notación de una función $f(x)$ se lee "f de x" o "función de x". Hay que recordar que $f(x)$ no significa "f multiplicado por x".

When the value of x is 3, $f(3)$, read "f of 3," represents the value of the function at 3.

English/Spanish Glossary

Fundamental Theorem of Algebra (p. 341) If $P(x)$ is a polynomial of degree $n \geq 1$ with complex coefficients, then $P(x) = 0$ has at least one complex root.

$P(x) = 3x^3 - 2x + 3$ is of degree 3, so $P(x) = 0$ has at least one complex root.

Teorema fundamental de álgebra (p. 341) Si $P(x)$ es un polinomio de grado $n \geq 1$ con coeficientes complejos, entonces $P(x) = 0$ tiene por lo menos una raíz compleja.

G

Geometric mean (p. 614) The geometric mean of any two positive numbers is the positive square root of the product of the two numbers.

The geometric mean of 12 and 18 is $\sqrt{12 \cdot 18} \approx 14.6969$.

Media geométrica (p. 614) La media geométrica de dos números positivos es la raíz cuadrada positiva del producto de los dos números.

Geometric sequence (p. 612) In a geometric sequence, the ratio of consecutive terms is constant. The constant is called the common ratio.

The geometric sequence 2.5, 5, 10, 20, 40, . . . has a common ratio of 2.

Progresión geométrica (p. 612) En una progresión geométrica, la razón de términos consecutivos es un valor constante. La constante se llama razón común.

Geometric series (p. 626) A geometric series is the sum of the terms in a geometric sequence.

One geometric series with five terms is $2.5 + 5 + 10 + 20 + 40$.

Serie geométrica (p. 626) Una serie geométrica es la suma de términos en una progresión geométrica.

Greatest common factor (GCF) of an expression (p. 259) The greatest common factor (GCF) of an expression is the common factor of each term of the expression that has the greatest coefficient and the greatest exponent.

The GCF of $4x^2 + 20x - 12$ is 4.

Máximo factor común de una expresión (p. 259) El máximo común factor de una expresión es el factor común de cada término de la expresión que tiene el mayor coeficiente y el mayor exponente.

Growth factor (p. 430) In an exponential function of the form $y = ab^x$, b is the growth factor if $b > 1$.

In the exponential equation $y = 2^x$, 2 is the growth factor.

Factor de incremento (p. 430) En una función exponencial de la forma $y = ab^x$, b es el factor de incremento si $b > 1$.

H

Hyperbola (p. 575) A hyperbola is a set of points P in a plane such that the difference between the distances from P to the foci F_1 and F_2 is a given constant k. $|PF_1 - PF_2| = k$

The standard form of an equation of a hyperbola centered at $(0, 0)$ is $\frac{x^2}{a^2} - \frac{y^2}{b^2} = 1$ if the transverse axis is horizontal and $\frac{y^2}{a^2} - \frac{x^2}{b^2} = 1$ if the transverse axis is vertical.

Hipérbola (p. 575) Una hipérbola es un conjunto de puntos P en un plano tal que la diferencia entre las distancias de P a los focos F_1 y F_2 es una constante k dada. $|PF_1 - PF_2| = k$

La forma normal de la ecuación de una hipérbola centrada en $(0, 0)$ es $\frac{x^2}{a^2} - \frac{y^2}{b^2} = 1$, si el eje transversal es horizontal, y $\frac{y^2}{a^2} - \frac{x^2}{b^2} = 1$, si el eje transversal es vertical.

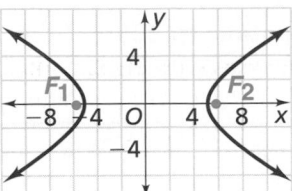

$$\frac{x^2}{5^2} - \frac{y^2}{3^2} = 1$$

I

i **(p. 274)** The imaginary number i is the principal square root of -1.　　$i = \sqrt{-1}$ and $i^2 = -1$.

i **(p. 274)** El número imaginario i es la raíz cuadrada principal de -1.

Image (p. 192) An image is a figure obtained by a transformation of a preimage.

Imagen (p. 192) Una imagen es la figura que resulta después de que la preimagen sufre una transformación.

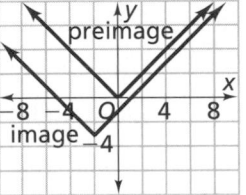

Imaginary number (p. 274) An imaginary number is any number of the form $a + bi$, where $b \neq 0$ and $i = \sqrt{-1}$. A number of the form bi is a pure imaginary number.

$2 + 3i$

$7i$

i

Número imaginario (p. 274) Un número imaginario es todo número de la forma $a + bi$, donde $b \neq 0$ e $i = \sqrt{-1}$. Un número de la forma bi es un número imaginario puro.

Imaginary Root Theorem (p. 338) If the imaginary number $a + bi$ is a root of a polynomial equation with real coefficients, then the conjugate $a - bi$ also is a root.

$2 + 3i$ is a root of $x^2 - 4x + 13 = 0$, so $2 - 3i$ is also a root.

Teorema de la raíz imaginaria (p. 338) Si el número imaginario $a + bi$ es la raíz de la ecuación de un polinomio con coeficientes reales, entonces el conjugado $a - bi$ también es una raíz.

English/Spanish Glossary

Inconsistent system (p. 120) A system of equations that has no solution is an inconsistent system.

Sistema incompatible (p. 120) Un sistema incompatible es un sistema de ecuaciones para el cual no hay solución.

$\begin{cases} y = 2x + 3 \\ -2x + y = 1 \end{cases}$ is a system of parallel lines, so it has no solution. It is an inconsistent system.

Independent events (p. 531) When the outcome of one event does not affect the probability of a second event, the two events are independent.

Sucesos independientes (p. 531) Cuando el resultado de un suceso no altera la probabilidad de otro, los dos sucesos son independientes.

The results of two rolls of a number cube are independent. Getting a 5 on the first roll does not change the probability of getting a 5 on the second roll.

Independent system (p. 120) A system of linear equations that has a unique solution is an independent system.

Sistema independiente (p. 120) Un sistema de ecuaciones lineales que tenga una sola solución es un sistema independiente.

$\begin{cases} x + 2y = -7 \\ 2x - 3y = 0 \end{cases}$ has the unique solution $(-3, -2)$. It is an independent system.

Independent variable (p. 62) If a function is defined by an equation using the variables x and y, where x represents input values, then x is the independent variable.

Variable independiente (p. 62) Si una función es definida por una ecuación con las variables x e y, donde x representa los valores de entrada, entonces x es la variable independiente.

$y = 2x + 1$

x is the independent variable.

Index (p. 370) With a radical sign, the index indicates the degree of the root.

Índice (p. 370) Con un signo de radical, el índice indica el grado de la raíz.

index 2   index 3   index 4

$\sqrt{16}$ $\sqrt[3]{16}$ $\sqrt[4]{16}$

Initial side of an angle (p. 718) When an angle is in standard position, the initial side of the angle is given to be on the positive x-axis. The other ray is the terminal side of the angle.

Lado inicial de un ángulo (p. 718) Cuando un ángulo está en posición normal, el lado inicial del ángulo se ubica en el eje positivo de las x. El otro rayo, o semirrecta, forma el lado terminal del ángulo.

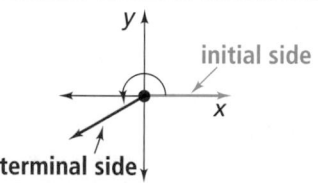

Inscribed rectangles (p. 635) When approximating the area under a curve, inscribed rectangles are completely under the curve. Their combined area generally is less than the area under the curve.

Rectángulos inscritos (p. 635) Cuando se aproxima el área situada dentro de una curva, los rectángulos inscritos quedan completamente contenidos en la curva. Generalmente, su área total es menor que el área dentro de la curva.

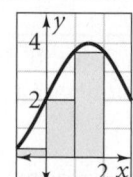

Intercepted arc (p. 726)   An intercepted arc is the portion of a circle whose endpoints are on the sides of a central angle of the circle and whose remaining points lie in the interior of the angle.

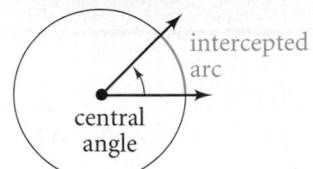

Arco interceptado (p. 726)   Un arco interceptado es la porción de un círculo cuyos extremos quedan sobre los lados de un ángulo central del círculo y cuyos puntos restantes quedan en el interior del ángulo.

Interquartile range (p. 669)   The interquartile range of a set of data is the difference between the third and first quartiles.

The first and third quartiles of the data set $\{2, 3, 4, 5, 5, 6, 7, 7\}$ are 3.5 and 6.5. The interquartile range is $6.5 - 3.5 = 3$.

Intervalo intercuartil (p. 669)   El rango intercuartil de un conjunto de datos es la diferencia entre el tercero y el primer cuartiles.

Inverse functions (p. 409)   If function f pairs a value b with a then its inverse, denoted f^{-1}, pairs the value a with b. If f^{-1} is also a function, then f and f^{-1} are inverse functions.

If $f(x) = x + 3$, then $f^{-1}(x) = x - 3$.

Funciones inversas (p. 409)   Si la función f empareja un valor b con a, entonces su inversa, cuya notación es f^{-1}, empareja el valor a con b. Si f^{-1} también es una función, entonces f y f^{-1} son funciones inversas.

Inverse relation (p. 407)   If a relation pairs element a of its domain with element b of its range, the inverse relation "undoes" the relation and pairs b with a. If (a, b) is an ordered pair of a relation, then (b, a) is an ordered pair of its inverse.

Relación inversa (p. 407)   Si una relación empareja el elemento a de su dominio con el elemento b de su rango, la relación inversa "deshace" la relación y empareja b con a. Si (a, b) es un par ordenado de una relación, entonces (b, a) es un par ordenado de su inversa.

Inverse variation (p. 488)   A relation represented by an equation of the form $y = \frac{k}{x}$ or $xy = k$, where $k \neq 0$, is an inverse variation with the constant of variation k.

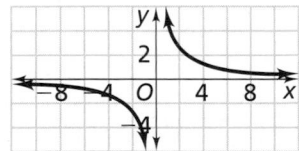

Variación inversa (p. 488)   Una relación representada por la fórmula $y = \frac{k}{x}$ o $xy = k$, donde $k \neq 0$, es una variación inversa con la constante de variación k.

$xy = 5$, or $y = \frac{5}{x}$

Irrational Root Theorem (p. 337)   Let a and b be rational numbers and let $\sqrt{b}$ be an irrational number. If $a + \sqrt{b}$ is a root of a polynomial equation with rational coefficients, then the conjugate $a - \sqrt{b}$ also is a root.

$2 + \sqrt{3}$ is a root of $x^2 - 4x + 1 = 0$, so $2 - \sqrt{3}$ is also a root.

Teorema de la raíz irracional (p. 337)   Sean a y b números racionales y sea $\sqrt{b}$ un número irracional. Si $a + \sqrt{b}$ es una raíz de una ecuación de un polinomio con coeficientes racionales, entonces el conjugado $a - \sqrt{b}$ también es una raíz.

English/Spanish Glossary

Joint variation (p. 490) If one variable varies directly with respect to each of two or more other variables, the relation is a joint variation.

$z = 8xy$
$T = kPV$

Variación conjunta (p. 490) Si una variable varía directamente con respecto a cada una de dos o más variables, la relación es una variación conjunta.

L

Law of Cosines (p. 808) In $\triangle ABC$, let a, b, and c represent the lengths of the sides opposite $\angle A$, $\angle B$, and $\angle C$, respectively. Then

$a^2 = b^2 + c^2 - 2bc \cos A,$

$b^2 = a^2 + c^2 - 2ac \cos B,$ and

$c^2 = a^2 + b^2 - 2ab \cos C$

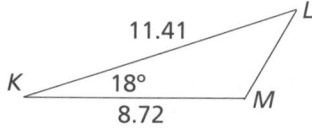

$LM^2 = 11.41^2 + 8.72^2 -$
$2(11.41)(8.72) \cos 18°$

$LM^2 \approx 16.9754$

$LM \approx 4.12$

Ley de cosenos (p. 808) En $\triangle ABC$, sean a, b y c las longitudes de los lados opuestos a $\angle A$, $\angle B$ y $\angle C$, respectivamente. Entonces

$a^2 = b^2 + c^2 - 2bc \cos A,$

$b^2 = a^2 + c^2 - 2ac \cos B$ y

$c^2 = a^2 + b^2 - 2ab \cos C$

Law of Sines (p. 801) In $\triangle ABC$, let a, b, and c represent the lengths of the sides opposite $\angle A$, $\angle B$, and $\angle C$, respectively. Then

$\dfrac{\sin A}{a} = \dfrac{\sin B}{b} = \dfrac{\sin C}{c}.$

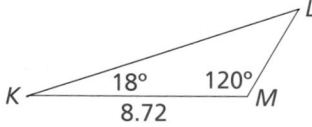

$m\angle L = 180 - (120 + 18) = 42°$

$\dfrac{KL}{\sin 120°} = \dfrac{8.72}{\sin 42°}$

$KL = \dfrac{8.72 \sin 120°}{\sin 42°}$

$KL \approx 11.26$

Ley de senos (p. 801) En $\triangle ABC$, sean a, b y c las longitudes de los lados opuestos a $\angle A$, $\angle B$ y $\angle C$, respectivamente. Entonces

$\dfrac{\text{sen } A}{a} = \dfrac{\text{sen } B}{b} = \dfrac{\text{sen } C}{c}.$

Like radicals (p. 380) Like radicals are radical expressions that have the same index and the same radicand.

$4\sqrt[3]{7}$ and $\sqrt[3]{7}$ are like radicals.

Radicales semejantes (p. 380) Los radicales semejantes son expresiones radicales que tienen el mismo índice y el mismo radicando.

Limits (p. 621) Limits in summation notation are the least and greatest integer values of the index n.

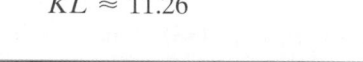

Límites (p. 621) Los límites en notación de sumatoria son el menor y el mayor valor del índice n en números enteros.

Linear equation (p. 62)   A linear equation in two variables is an equation that can be written in the form $ax + by = c$. *See also* **Standard form of a linear equation.**

Ecuación lineal (p. 62)   Una ecuación lineal de dos variables es una ecuación que se puede escribir de la forma $ax + by = c$. *Ver también* **Standard form of a linear equation.**

$y = 2x + 1$ can be written as $-2x + y = 1$.

Linear function (p. 62)   A function whose graph is a line is a linear function. You can represent a linear function with a linear equation.

Función lineal (p. 62)   Una función cuya gráfica es una recta es una función lineal. La función lineal se representa con una ecuación lineal.

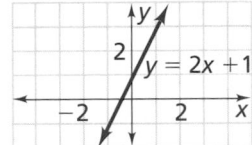

Linear inequality (p. 101)   A linear inequality is an inequality in two variables whose graph is a region of the coordinate plane that is bounded by a line. Each point in the region is a solution of the inequality. A sign of $\leq$ or $\geq$ indicates a solid boundary line. A sign of $<$ or $>$ indicates a dashed boundary line.

Desigualdad lineal (p. 101)   Una desigualdad lineal es una desigualdad de dos variables cuya gráfica es una región del plano de coordenadas delimitado por una recta. Cada punto de la región es una solución de la desigualdad. El signo $\leq$ o $\geq$ denota que hay una recta de delimitación continua. El signo $<$ o $>$ denota que la recta de delimitación es punteada.

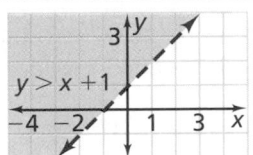

$y > x + 1$

Linear programming (p. 139)   Linear programming is a technique that identifies the minimum or maximum value of some quantity. This quantity is modeled with an objective function. Limits on the variables in the objective function are constraints, written as linear inequalities.

Programación lineal (p. 139)   La programación lineal es un método que permite identificar las condiciones que elevan al máximo o reducen al mínimo una cantidad. Se hace un modelo de esta cantidad con una función objetiva. Los límites de las variables en la función objetiva son restricciones, expresadas como desigualdades lineales.

Restrictions: $x \geq 0$, $y \geq 0$, $x + y \leq 7$, and $y \leq -2x + 8$

Objective function: $B = 2x + 4y$

Graph the restrictions to find the coordinates of each vertex.

Evaluate $B = 2x + 4y$ at each vertex.

The minimum value of B occurs when $x = 0$ and $y = 0$. The maximum value of B occurs when $x = 0$ and $y = 7$.

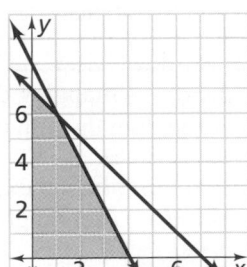

Linear system (p. 118) A linear system is a set of two or more linear equations that use the same variables.

Sistema lineal (p. 118) Un sistema lineal es un conjunto de dos o más ecuaciones lineales con las mismas variables.

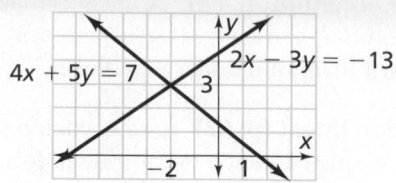

Logarithm (p. 447) A logarithm to the base b of a positive number y is defined as follows:
If $y = b^x$, then $\log_b y = x$.

$\log_2 8 = 3$

$\log_{10} 100 = 2$

$\log_5 5^7 = 7$

Logaritmo (p. 447) El logaritmo de base b de un número positivo y se define así:
Si $y = b^x$, entonces $\log_b y = x$.

Logarithmic equation (p. 463) An equation that includes a logarithmic expression is called a logarithmic equation.

$\log_3 x = 4$

Ecuación logarítmica (p. 463) Una ecuación que incluye una expresión logarítmica se llama ecuación logarítmica.

Logarithmic function (p. 448) A logarithmic function is the inverse of an exponential function.

Función logarítmica (p. 448) Una función logarítmica es la inversa de una función exponencial.

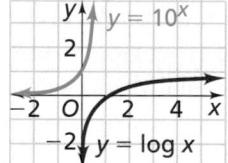

Major axis of an ellipse (p. 568) The major axis of an ellipse is the segment that contains the foci and has its endpoints on the ellipse. These endpoints are vertices of the ellipse.

Eje mayor de una elipse (p. 568) El eje mayor de una elipse es el segmento que contiene los focos y tiene los puntos extremos de la elipse. Los extremos son los vértices de la elipse.

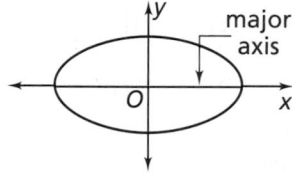

Mapping diagram (p. 56) A mapping diagram describes a relation by linking elements of the domain with elements of the range.

Mapa (p. 56) Un mapa describe una relación al unir los elementos del dominio con los elementos del rango.

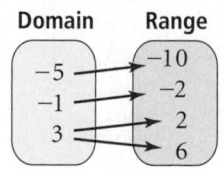

Margin of error (p. 679) A sample proportion should be reported with an estimate of error, called the margin of error. When a random sample of size n is taken from a large population, the sample proportion has a margin of error of about $\pm\frac{1}{\sqrt{n}}$.

Margen de error (p. 679) Una proporción muestral debe incluir una estimación del error, que se llama margen de error. Cuando se hace una muestra aleatoria de tamaño n de una población grande, la proporción muestral tiene un margen de error de aproximadamente $\pm\frac{1}{\sqrt{n}}$.

A set of 500 items is taken from a population for sampling. The margin of error for a sample proportion is about $\pm\frac{1}{\sqrt{500}} \approx \pm 0.045$.

Matrix (p. 168) A matrix is a rectangular array of numbers written within brackets. A matrix with m horizontal rows and n vertical columns is an $m \times n$ matrix.

Matriz (p. 168) Una matriz es un conjunto de números encerrados en corchetes y dispuestos en forma de rectángulo. Una matriz que contenga m filas y n columnas es una matriz $m \times n$.

$$A = \begin{bmatrix} 1 & -2 & 0 & 10 \\ 9 & 7 & -3 & 8 \\ 2 & -10 & 1 & -6 \end{bmatrix}$$

The number 2 is the element in the third row and first column. A is a 3×4 matrix.

Matrix addition (p. 174) You add two matrices with the same dimensions by adding their corresponding elements.

Suma matricial (p. 174) Para sumar dos matrices que tengan las mismas dimensiones se suman sus elementos correspondientes.

$$\begin{bmatrix} 2 & -3 \\ 0 & 4 \end{bmatrix} + \begin{bmatrix} -1 & 0 \\ 5 & -6 \end{bmatrix}$$
$$= \begin{bmatrix} 2 + (-1) & -3 + 0 \\ 0 + 5 & 4 + (-6) \end{bmatrix}$$
$$= \begin{bmatrix} 1 & -3 \\ 5 & -2 \end{bmatrix}$$

Matrix element (p. 169) Every item listed in a matrix is an element of the matrix. An element is identified by its position in the matrix.

Elemento matricial (p. 169) Cada cifra de una matriz es un elemento de la matriz. El elemento se identifica según la posición que ocupa en la matriz.

$$A = \begin{bmatrix} 1 & -2 & 0 & 10 \\ 9 & 7 & -3 & 8 \\ 2 & -10 & 1 & -6 \end{bmatrix}$$

Element a_{21} is 9, the element in the second row and first column.

Matrix equation (p. 176) A matrix equation is an equation in which the variable is a matrix.

Ecuación matricial (p. 176) Una ecuación matricial es una ecuación en que la variable es una matriz.

Solve $X + \begin{bmatrix} 3 & -2 \\ 5 & 1 \end{bmatrix} = \begin{bmatrix} 4 & 0 \\ 0 & 3 \end{bmatrix}$.

$$X + \begin{bmatrix} 3 & -2 \\ 5 & 1 \end{bmatrix} = \begin{bmatrix} 4 & 0 \\ 0 & 3 \end{bmatrix}$$

$$X = \begin{bmatrix} 4 & 0 \\ 0 & 3 \end{bmatrix} - \begin{bmatrix} 3 & -2 \\ 5 & 1 \end{bmatrix} = \begin{bmatrix} 1 & 2 \\ -5 & 2 \end{bmatrix}$$

Matrix multiplication (p. 184) To find element c_{ij} of the product matrix AB, multiply each element in the ith row of A by the corresponding element in the jth column of B, and then add. If A is an $m \times n$ matrix and B is an $n \times p$ matrix, then the product matrix AB is an $m \times p$ matrix.

Multiplicación matricial (p. 184) Para encontrar el elemento c_{ij} del producto de la matriz AB, se multiplica cada elemento de la fila i de A por el elemento respectivo de la columna j de B y luego se suman. Si A es una matriz $m \times n$ y B es una matriz $n \times p$, entonces el producto de la matriz AB es una matriz $m \times p$.

$$\begin{bmatrix} 1 & 1 \\ 2 & 3 \\ 0 & 2 \end{bmatrix} \begin{bmatrix} 4 & 2 \\ 5 & 6 \end{bmatrix}$$

$$= \begin{bmatrix} (1)(4) + (1)(5) & (1)(2) + (1)(6) \\ (2)(4) + (3)(5) & (2)(2) + (3)(6) \\ (0)(4) + (2)(5) & (0)(2) + (2)(6) \end{bmatrix}$$

$$= \begin{bmatrix} 9 & 8 \\ 23 & 22 \\ 10 & 12 \end{bmatrix}$$

Mean (p. 660) The sum of the data values divided by the number of data values is the mean. *See also* **Arithmetic mean.**

Media (p. 660) La suma de los valores de datos dividida por el número de valores de datos sumados es la media. *Ver también* **Arithmetic mean.**

$\{1, 2, 3, 3, 6, 6\}$

$$\text{mean} = \frac{1 + 2 + 3 + 3 + 6 + 6}{6}$$
$$= \frac{21}{6} = 3.5$$

Measures of central tendency (p. 660) The mean, the median, and the mode are single, central values that help describe a set of data. They are called measures of central tendency.

Medidas de tendencia central (p. 660) La media, la mediana y la moda son los valores centrales únicos que permiten describir un conjunto de datos. Se llaman medidas de tendencia central.

$\{1, 2, 3, 3, 4, 5, 6, 6\}$

mean = 3.75

median = 3.5

modes = 3 and 6

Measures of variation (p. 669) Measures of variation, such as the range, the interquartile range, and the standard deviation, describe how the data in a data set are spread out.

Medidas de dispersión (p. 669) Las medidas de dispersión, tal como el rango, el intervalo intercuartil y la desviación típica, describen cómo se dispersan los datos en un conjunto de datos.

Median (p. 660) The median is the middle value in a data set. If the data set contains an even number of values, the median is the mean of the two middle values.

Mediana (p. 660) La mediana es el valor situado en el medio en un conjunto de datos. Si el conjunto de datos contiene un número par de valores, la mediana es la media de los dos valores del medio.

$\{1, 2, 3, 3, 4, 5, 6, 6\}$

$$\text{median} = \frac{3 + 4}{2} = \frac{7}{2} = 3.5$$

Minor axis of an ellipse (p. 568) The minor axis of an ellipse is the segment perpendicular to the major axis at its midpoint. The endpoints of the minor axis are on the ellipse and are the co-vertices of the ellipse.

Eje menor de una elipse (p. 568) El eje menor de una elipse es el segmento perpendicular al eje mayor en su punto medio. Los extremos del eje menor están en la elipse y son los covértices de la elipse.

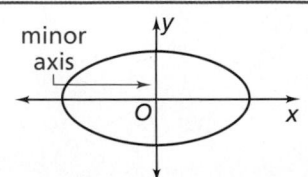

Mode (p. 660) The mode is the most frequently occurring value (or values) in a set of data.

$\{1, 2, 3, 3, 4, 5, 6, 6\}$
The modes are 3 and 6.

Moda (p. 660) La moda es el valor o valores que ocurren con mayor frecuencia en un conjunto de datos.

Monomial (p. 307) A monomial is either a real number, a variable, or a product of real numbers and variables with whole number exponents.

$1, x, 2z, 4ab^2$

Monomio (p. 307) Un monomio es un número real, una variable o un producto de números reales y variables cuyos exponentes son números enteros.

Multiple zero (p. 316) If a linear factor is repeated in the complete factored form of a polynomial, the zero related to that factor is a multiple zero.

The zeros of the function $P(x) = 2x(x - 3)^2(x + 1)$ are $0, 3$, and -1. Since $(x - 3)$ occurs twice as a factor, the zero 3 is a multiple zero.

Cero múltiplo (p. 316) Si un factor lineal se repite en la forma factorizada completa de un polinomio, el cero relacionado con ese factor es un cero múltiplo.

Multiplicative identity matrix (p. 199) For an $n \times n$ square matrix, the multiplicative identity matrix is an $n \times n$ square matrix I, or $I_{n \times n}$, with 1's along the main diagonal and 0's elsewhere.

$$I_{2 \times 2} = \begin{bmatrix} 1 & 0 \\ 0 & 1 \end{bmatrix}$$

$$I_{3 \times 3} = \begin{bmatrix} 1 & 0 & 0 \\ 0 & 1 & 0 \\ 0 & 0 & 1 \end{bmatrix}$$

Matriz de identidad multiplicativa (p. 199) Para una matriz cuadrada $n \times n$, la matriz de identidad multiplicativa es la matriz cuadrada I de $n \times n$, o $I_{n \times n}$, con unos por la diagonal principal y ceros en los demás lugares.

Multiplicative inverse (p. 7) The multiplicative inverse, or reciprocal, of any nonzero number a is $\frac{1}{a}$. The product of reciprocals is 1.

$5 \times \frac{1}{5} = 1$

Inverso multiplicativo (p. 7) El inverso multiplicativo, o recíproco, de todo número racional distinto de cero a es $\frac{1}{a}$. El producto de números recíprocos es 1.

Multiplicative inverse of a matrix (p. 199) If A and X are $n \times n$ matrices, and $AX = XA = I$, then X is the multiplicative inverse of A, written A^{-1}.

$$A = \begin{bmatrix} 2 & 1 \\ 4 & 0 \end{bmatrix}$$

$$X = \begin{bmatrix} 0 & \frac{1}{4} \\ 1 & -\frac{1}{2} \end{bmatrix}$$

Inverso multiplicativo de una matriz (p. 199) Si A y X son matrices $n \times n$, y $AX = XA = I$, entonces X es el inverso multiplicativo de A, expresado como A^{-1}.

$$AX = \begin{bmatrix} 1 & 0 \\ 0 & 1 \end{bmatrix} = I, \text{ so } X = A^{-1}$$

English/Spanish Glossary

Multiplicity (p. 316) The multiplicity of a zero of a polynomial function is the number of times the related linear factor is repeated in the factored form of the polynomial.

Multiplicidad (p. 316) La multiplicidad de un cero de una función polinomial es el número de veces que el factor lineal relacionado se repite en la forma factorizada del polinomio.

The zeros of the function $P(x) = 2x(x - 3)^2(x + 1)$ are $0, 3$, and -1. Since $(x - 3)$ occurs twice as a factor, the zero 3 has multiplicity 2.

Mutually exclusive events (p. 533) When two events cannot happen at the same time, the events are mutually exclusive. If A and B are mutually exclusive events, then $P(A \text{ or } B) = P(A) + P(B)$.

Sucesos mutuamente excluyentes (p. 533) Cuando dos sucesos no pueden ocurrir al mismo tiempo, son mutuamente excluyentes. Si A y B son sucesos mutuamente excluyentes, entonces $P(A \text{ o } B) = P(A) + P(B)$.

Rolling an even number E and rolling a multiple of five M on a standard number cube are mutually exclusive events.

$$P(E \text{ or } M) = P(E) + P(M)$$
$$= \frac{3}{6} + \frac{1}{6}$$
$$= \frac{4}{6}, \text{ or } \frac{2}{3}$$

---

n factorial (p. 345) For any positive integer n, n factorial (or $n!$) is $n(n - 1) \times \ldots \times 3 \times 2 \times 1. 0! = 1$.

n factorial (p. 345) Para cualquier número entero positivo n, n factorial (o $n!$) es $n(n - 1) \times \ldots \times 3 \times 2 \times 1. 0! = 1$.

$4! = 4 \times 3 \times 2 \times 1 = 24$

---

nth root (p. 369) For any real numbers a and b, and any positive integer n, if $a^n = b$, then a is an nth root of b.

raíz n-ésima (p. 369) Para todos los números reales a y b, y todo número entero positivo n, si $a^n = b$, entonces a es la n-ésima raíz de b.

$\sqrt[5]{32} = 2$ because $2^5 = 32$.

$\sqrt[4]{81} = 3$ because $3^4 = 81$.

Natural logarithmic function (p. 470) The function $y = \log_e x$ is the natural logarithmic function. It is the inverse of $y = e^x$. It is commonly written as $y = \ln x$.

Función logarítmica natural (p. 470) La función $y = \log_e x$ es la función logarítmica natural. Es la inversa de $y = e^x$. Generalmente se expresa como $y = \ln x$.

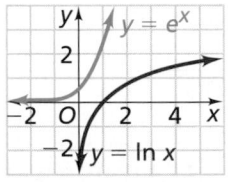

$\ln e^3 = 3$

$\ln 10 \approx 2.3026$

$\ln 36 \approx 3.5835$

Normal distribution (p. 692) A normal distribution shows data that vary randomly from the mean in the pattern of a bell-shaped curve.

Distribución normal (p. 692) Una distribución normal muestra, con una curva en forma de campana, datos que varían alcatoriamento respecto de la media.

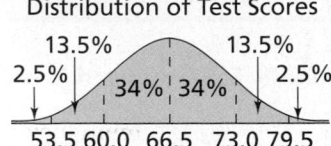

Distribution of Test Scores

13.5% 13.5%
2.5% 34% 34% 2.5%
53.5 60.0 66.5 73.0 79.5

In a class of 200 students, the scores on a test were normally distributed. The mean score was 66.5 and the standard deviation was 6.5. The number of students who scored greater than 73 was about 13.5% + 2.5% of those who took the test.

16% of 200 = 32

About 32 students scored 73 or higher on the test.

Objective function (p. 139) In a linear programming model, the objective function is a model of the quantity that you want to make as large or as small as possible. *See* **Linear programming**.

Función objetiva (p. 139) En un modelo de programación lineal, la función objetiva es un modelo de la cantidad que se quiere aumentar o disminuir cuanto sea posible. *Ver* **Linear programming**.

Opposite (p. 7) The opposite or additive inverse of any number a is $-a$. The sum of opposites is 0.

Opuesto (p. 7) El opuesto o inverso aditivo de todo número a es $-a$. La suma de dos opuestos es 0.

$3 + (-3) = 0$

$5.2 + (-5.2) = 0$

Ordered triples (p. 146) Ordered triples of the form (x, y, z) represent the location of a point in coordinate space.

Tripletas ordenadas (p. 146) Las tripletas ordenadas de la forma (x, y, z) representan la ubicación de un punto en el espacio de coordenadas.

$(2, 4, 5)$
$(0, 1, 2)$
$(0, 0, 0)$

Outlier (p. 664) An outlier is a data value that is substantially different from the other values in a data set.

Valor extremo (p. 664) Un valor extremo es un valor que difiere sustancialmente de los demás valores de un conjunto de datos.

The outlier in the data set $\{56, 64, 73, 59, 98, 65, 59\}$ is 98.

Parabola (pp. 239, 555)   A parabola is the graph of a quadratic function. It is the set of all points P in a plane that are the same distance from a fixed point F, the focus, as they are from a line d, the directrix.

Parábola (pp. 239, 555)   La parábola es la gráfica de una función cuadrática. Es el conjunto de todos los puntos P situados en un plano a la misma distancia de un punto fijo F, o foco, y de la recta d, o directriz.

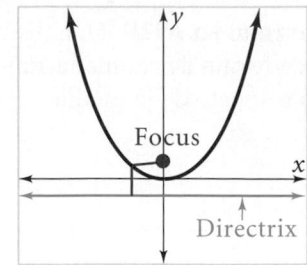

Parameter (p. 97)   A parameter is a symbol, usually a letter, that represents a constant. In a function rule, a parameter helps describe a transformation of a function.

In $f(x) = a(x - h)^2 + k$, a, h, and k are parameters. x is the independent variable.

Parámetro (p. 97)   Un parámetro es un símbolo, generalmente una letra, que representa una constante. En la regla de una función, el parámetro sirve para describir la transformación de la función.

Parent function (p. 93)   A family of functions is a group of functions with common characteristics. A parent function is the simplest function with these characteristics.

$y = x$ is the parent function for the functions of the form $y = x + k$.

Función elemental (p. 93)   Una familia de funciones es un grupo de funciones con características comunes. La función elemental es la función más simple que reúne esas características.

Pascal's Triangle (p. 353)   Pascal's Triangle is a triangular array of numbers whose nth row contains the coefficients of the terms of the binomial expansion of $(a + b)^{n-1}$.

Triángulo de Pascal (p. 353)   El triángulo de Pascal es una matriz triangular de números cuya fila n-ésima contiene los coeficientes de los términos del desarrollo del binomio $(a + b)^{n-1}$.

Pascal's Triangle
```
            1
          1   1
        1   2   1
      1   3   3   1
    1   4   6   4   1
  1   5  10  10   5   1
```

Percentile (p. 663)   A percentile is a number from 0 to 100 that you can associate with a value in a data set to indicate the percent of the data that are less than or equal to it. If x is the 63rd percentile, then 63% of the data are less than or equal to x.

Percentil (p. 663)   El percentil es un número del 0 al 100 que se puede asociar con un valor de un conjunto de datos para indicar el porcentaje de los datos que son menores que o iguales a él. Si x es el 63° percentil, entonces 63% de los datos son menores que o iguales a x.

Perfect square trinomial (p. 262)   A perfect square trinomial is the product you obtain when you square a binomial.

Trinomio cuadrado perfecto (p. 262)   Un trinomio cuadrado perfecto se obtiene al elevar al cuadrado un binomio.

perfect square   binomial
   trinomial   square
$$16x^2 - 24x + 9 = (4x - 3)^2$$

Period of a function (p. 711) The period of a periodic function is the horizontal length of one cycle.

Período de una función (p. 711) El período de una función periódica es el intervalo horizontal de un ciclo.

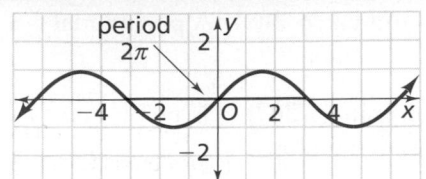

The periodic function $y = \sin x$ has period 2π.

Periodic function (p. 711) A periodic function repeats a pattern of y-values at regular intervals.

Función periódica (p. 711) Una función periódica repite un patrón de valores y a intervalos regulares.

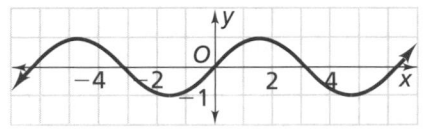

$y = \sin x$

Permutation (p. 345) A permutation is an arrangement of items in a particular order. The number of permutations of n objects taken r at a time is $_nP_r = \frac{n!}{(n-r)!}$ for $1 \le r \le n$.

Permutación (p. 345) Una permutación es la disposición de objetos en un orden determinado. El número de permutaciones de n objetos seleccionados r veces es $_nP_r = \frac{n!}{(n-r)!}$ para $1 \le r \le n$.

$$_8P_5 = \frac{8!}{(8-5)!}$$
$$= \frac{8 \cdot 7 \cdot 6 \cdot 5 \cdot 4 \cdot 3!}{3!}$$
$$= 8 \times 7 \times 6 \times 5 \times 4$$
$$= 6720$$

Phase shift (p. 756) A horizontal translation of a periodic function is a phase shift.

Cambio de fase (p. 756) Una traslación horizontal de una función periódica es un cambio de fase.

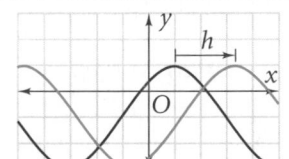

$g(x)$: horizontal translation of $f(x)$
$g(x) = f(x - h)$

Point of discontinuity (p. 501) A point of discontinuity is the x-coordinate of a point where the graph of a function breaks into branches. A rational function has a point of discontinuity at $x = a$ if a is a number for which the denominator of the function is zero.

Punto de discontinuidad (p. 501) Un punto de discontinuidad es la coordenada x de un punto donde la gráfica de una función se divide en ramas. Una función racional tiene un punto de discontinuidad en $x = a$, si a es un número para el cual el denominador de la función es cero.

$f(x) = \frac{2}{x-2}$ has a point of discontinuity at $x = 2$.

Point-slope form (p. 65) The point-slope form of an equation of a line is $y - y_1 = m(x - x_1)$, where m is the slope of the line and (x_1, y_1) is a point on the line.

Forma punto-pendiente (p. 65) La forma punto-pendiente de una ecuación lineal es $y - y_1 = m(x - x_1)$, donde m es la pendiente de la recta y (x_1, y_1) es un punto de la recta.

$y - 3 = 2(x - 1)$
$y + 4 = 5(x - 2)$
$y - 2 = 3(x + 2)$

Polynomial (p. 307)   A polynomial is a monomial or the sum of monomials.

$$3x^3 + 4x^2 - 2x + 5$$
$$8x$$
$$x^2 + 4x + 2$$

Polinomio (p. 307)   Un polinomio es un monomio o la suma de dos o más monomios.

Polynomial function (p. 307) $P(x) = a_n x^n + a_{n-1} x^{n-1} + \ldots + a_1 x + a_0$ is a polynomial function when n is a nonnegative integer and the coefficients $a_n, \ldots, a_0$ are real numbers.

Función polinomial (p. 307) $P(x) = a_n x^n + a_{n-1} x^{n-1} + \ldots + a_1 x + a_0$ es una función polinomial, donde n es un entero no negativo y los coeficientes $a_n, \ldots, a_0$ son números reales.

Preimage (p. 192)   The preimage is the original figure before a transformation.

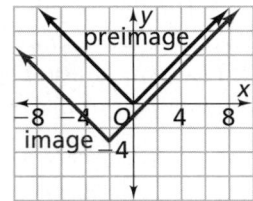

Preimagen (p. 192)   La preimagen es la figura original antes de sufrir una transformación.

Principal root (p. 370)   When a number has two real roots, the positive root is called the principal root. A radical sign indicates the principal root. The principal root of a negative number a is $i\sqrt{|a|}$.

The number 25 has two square roots, 5 and -5. The principal square root, 5, is indicated by the symbols $\sqrt{25}$ or $25^{\frac{1}{2}}$.

Raíz principal (p. 370)   Cuando un número tiene dos raíces reales, la raíz positiva es la raíz principal. El signo del radical indica la raíz principal. La raíz principal de un número negativo a es $i\sqrt{|a|}$.

Probability distribution (p. 649)   A probability distribution is a function that tells the probability of each outcome in a sample space.

Distribución de probabilidades (p. 649)   Una distribución de probabilidades es una función que señala la probabilidad de que cada resultado ocurra en un espacio muestral.

Roll	Fr.	Prob.
1	5	0.125
2	9	0.225
3	7	0.175
4	8	0.2
5	8	0.2
6	3	0.075

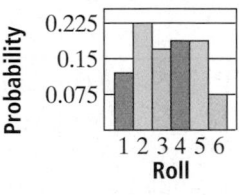

The table and graph both show the experimental probability distribution for the outcomes of 40 rolls of a standard number cube.

Quadratic equation (p. 267)   A quadratic equation is one that can be written in the standard form $ax^2 + bx + c = 0$, where $a \neq 0$.

$$2x^2 + 3x + 1 = 0$$

Ecuación cuadrática (p. 267)   Una ecuación cuadrática es una ecuación que se puede expresar en forma normal como $ax^2 + bx + c = 0$, donde $a \neq 0$.

Quadratic Formula (p. 289) A quadratic equation written in standard form $ax^2 + bx + c = 0$, can be solved using the Quadratic Formula.

$$x = \frac{-b \pm \sqrt{b^2 - 4ac}}{2a}$$

If $-x^2 + 3x + 2 = 0$, then

$$x = \frac{-3 \pm \sqrt{(3)^2 - 4(-1)(2)}}{2(-1)}$$

$$= \frac{-3 \pm \sqrt{17}}{-2}$$

Fórmula cuadrática (p. 289) Toda ecuación cuadrática $ax^2 + bx + c = 0$ escrita en forma normal se puede resolver por medio de la fórmula cuadrática.

$$x = \frac{-b \pm \sqrt{b^2 - 4ac}}{2a}$$

Quadratic function (p. 238) A quadratic function is a function that can be written in the standard form $f(x) = ax^2 + bx + c$, where $a \neq 0$. Its graph is a parabola.

Función cuadrática (p. 238) Una función cuadrática se puede expresar con la forma normal $f(x) = ax^2 + bx + c$, donde $a \neq 0$. Su gráfica es una parábola.

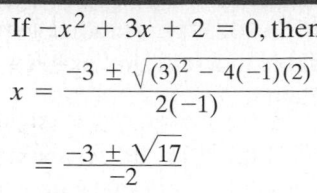

$y = x^2 + 2x - 2$

Quartiles (p. 662) Quartiles are values that separate a finite data set into four equal parts. The second quartile (Q_2) is the median of the data. The first and third quartiles (Q_1 and Q_3) are the medians of the lower half and upper half of the data, respectively.

Cuartiles (p. 662) Los cuartiles son valores que separan un conjunto finito de datos en cuatro partes iguales. El segundo cuartil (Q_2) es la mediana de los datos. Los cuartiles primero y tercero (Q_1 y Q_3) son las medianas de la mitad superior e inferior de los datos, respectivamente.

$\{2, 3, 4, 5, 5, 6, 7, 7\}$

$Q_1 = 3.5$

Q_2 (median) $= 5$

$Q_3 = 6.5$

R

Radian (p. 726) One radian is the measure of a central angle of a circle that intercepts an arc equal in length to a radius of the circle. You can use a proportion to convert an angle measure between different units.

$$\frac{\text{degree measure}}{180} = \frac{\text{radian measure}}{\pi}$$

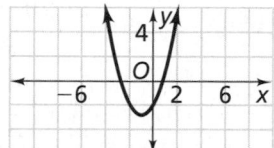

Thus, $60° = \frac{\pi}{3}$ radians.

Radián (p. 726) Un radián es la medida del ángulo central de un círculo que corta un arco de la misma longitud que el radio del círculo. Se puede usar una proporción para convertir la medida de un ángulo de una unidad de medida a la otra.

$$\frac{\text{medida en grados}}{180} = \frac{\text{medida de radián}}{\pi}$$

Radical equation (p. 391) A radical equation is an equation that has a variable in a radicand or has a variable with a rational exponent.

$(\sqrt{x})^3 + 1 = 65$

$x^{\frac{3}{2}} + 1 = 65$

Ecuación radical (p. 391) La ecuación radical es una ecuación que contiene una variable en el radicando o una variable con un exponente racional.

Radical function (p. 415) A radical function is a function that can be written in the form $f(x) = a\sqrt[n]{x - h} + k$, where $a \neq 0$. For even values of n, the domain of a radical function is the real numbers $x \geq h$. *See also* **Square root function.**

$f(x) = \sqrt{x - 2}$

Función radical (p. 415) Una función radical es una función que puede expresarse como $f(x) = a\sqrt[n]{x - h} + k$, donde $a \neq 0$. Para n par, el dominio de la función radical son los números reales tales que $x \geq h$. *Ver también* **Square root function.**

Radicand (p. 370) The number under a radical sign is the radicand.

The radicand in $3\sqrt[4]{7}$ is 7.

Radicando (p. 370) La expresión que aparece debajo del signo radical es el radicando.

Radius (p. 561) The radius r of a circle is the distance between the center of the circle and any point on the circumference.

Radio (p. 561) El radio r de un círculo es la distancia entre el centro del círculo y cualquier punto de la circunferencia.

Random sample (p. 677) In a random sample, each member of the population is as likely to be chosen for the sample as every other member.

Let the set of all females between the ages of 19 and 34 be the population. A random selection of 900 females between those ages would be a sample of the population.

Muestra aleatoria (p. 677) En una muestra aleatoria es igualmente probable que cada miembro de la población sea escogido para la muestra.

Range (p. 56) The range of a relation is the set of all outputs or y-coordinates of the ordered pairs.

In the relation $\{(0, 1), (0, 2), (0, 3), (0, 4), (1, 3), (1, 4), (2, 1)\}$, the range is $\{1, 2, 3, 4\}$. In the function $f(x) = |x - 3|$, the range is the set of real numbers greater than or equal to 0.

Rango (p. 56) El rango de una relación es el conjunto de todas las salidas posibles, o coordenadas y, de los pares ordenados.

Range of a set of data (p. 669) The range of a set of data is the difference between the greatest and least values.

The range of the set $\{3.2, 4.1, 2.2, 3.4, 3.8, 4.0, 4.2, 2.8\}$ is $4.2 - 2.2 = 2$.

Rango de un conjunto de datos (p. 669) El rango de un conjunto de datos es la diferencia entre el valor máximo y el valor mínimo de los datos.

Rational exponent (p. 385)   If the nth root of a is a real number and m is an integer, then $a^{\frac{1}{n}} = \sqrt[n]{a}$ and $a^{\frac{m}{n}} = \sqrt[n]{a^m} = \left(\sqrt[n]{a}\right)^m$. If m is negative, $a \neq 0$.

$4^{\frac{1}{3}} = \sqrt[3]{4}$

$5^{\frac{3}{2}} = \sqrt{5^3} = \left(\sqrt{5}\right)^3$

Exponente racional (p. 385)   Si la raíz n-ésima de a es un número real y m es un número entero, entonces $a^{\frac{1}{n}} = \sqrt[n]{a}$ y $a^{\frac{m}{n}} = \sqrt[n]{a^m} = \left(\sqrt[n]{a}\right)^m$. Si m es negativo, $a \neq 0$.

Rational function (p. 501)   A rational function $f(x)$ can be written as $f(x) = \dfrac{P(x)}{Q(x)}$, where $P(x)$ and $Q(x)$ are polynomial functions. The domain of a rational function is all real numbers except those for which $Q(x) = 0$.

Función racional (p. 501)   Una función racional $f(x)$ se puede expresar como $f(x) = \dfrac{P(x)}{Q(x)}$, donde $P(x)$ y $Q(x)$ son funciones de polinomios. El dominio de una función racional son todos los números reales excepto aquéllos para los cuales $Q(x) = 0$.

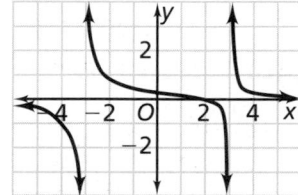

The function $y = \dfrac{x-2}{x^2-9}$ is a rational function with three branches separated by asymptotes $x = -3$ and $x = 3$.

Rational Root Theorem (p. 335)   If $\frac{p}{q}$ is in simplest form and is a rational root of the polynomial equation $a_n x^n + a_{n-1} x^{n-1} + \ldots + a_1 x + a_0 = 0$ with integer coefficients, then p must be a factor of a_0 and q must be a factor of a_n.

Teorema de la raíz racional (p. 335)   Si $\frac{p}{q}$ está en su forma más simple y es la raíz racional de la ecuación del polinomio $a_n x^n + a_{n-1} x^{n-1} + \ldots + a_1 x + a_0 = 0$ con números enteros como coeficientes, entonces p debe ser factor de a_0 y q debe ser factor de a_n.

The polynomial equation $10x^3 + 6x^2 - 11x - 2 = 0$ has leading coefficient 10 (with factors $\pm 1, \pm 2, \pm 5, \pm 10$) and constant term -2 (with factors ± 1 and ± 2). Its only possible rational roots are $\pm 1, \pm 2, \pm \frac{1}{2}, \pm \frac{1}{5}, \pm \frac{2}{5}, \pm \frac{1}{10}$.

Rationalize the denominator (p. 376)   To rationalize the denominator of an expression, rewrite it so there are no radicals in any denominator and no denominators in any radical.

$\dfrac{1}{\sqrt{2}} = \dfrac{1}{\sqrt{2}} \times \dfrac{\sqrt{2}}{\sqrt{2}} = \dfrac{\sqrt{2}}{2}$

Racionalizar el denominador (p. 376)   Para racionalizar el denominador de una expresión, ésta se escribe de modo que no haya radicales en ningún denominador y no haya denominadores en ningún radical.

Reciprocal (p. 7)   The reciprocal or multiplicative inverse of any nonzero number a is $\frac{1}{a}$. The product of reciprocals is 1.

$5 \times \frac{1}{5} = 1$

Recíproco (p. 7)   El valor recíproco, o inverso multiplicativo, de un número a cuyo valor no es cero es $\frac{1}{a}$. El producto de un número y su valor recíproco es 1.

English/Spanish Glossary

Reciprocal function (p. 495)   A reciprocal function is a function that can be written in the form $f(x) = \frac{a}{x - h} + k$, where $a \neq 0$. The domain of a reciprocal function is all real numbers except $x = h$.

$$f(x) = \frac{1}{2x + 5}$$
$$p(v) = \frac{3}{v} + 5$$

Función recíproca (p. 495)   Una función recíproca es una función que puede expresarse como $f(x) = \frac{a}{x - h} + k$, donde $a \neq 0$. El dominio de una función recíproca son todos los números reales excepto aquéllos para los que se cumple que $x = h$.

Recursive formula (p. 602)   A recursive formula defines the terms in a sequence by relating each term to the ones before it.

Let $a_n = 2.5a_{n-1} + 3a_{n-2}$.
If $a_5 = 3$ and $a_4 = 7.5$, then
$a_6 = 2.5(3) + 3(7.5) = 30$.

Fórmula recursiva (p. 602)   Una fórmula recursiva define cada término de una progresión en función del término o términos precedentes.

Reflection (p. 193)   A reflection, or flip, is a transformation that maps a point in the plane to its mirror image, using a specific line as the mirror.

Reflexión (p. 193)   Una reflexión es una transformación en la que se voltea una figura sobre una línea específica, que actúa a manera espejo.

preimage   image

Relation (p. 55)   A relation is a set of pairs of input and output values.

$\{(0, 1), (0, 2), (0, 3), (0, 4), (1, 3)\}$

Relación (p. 55)   Una relación es cualquier conjunto de pares ordenados de valores de entrada y valores de salida.

Relative maximum (minimum) (p. 315)   The y-value of a point on the graph of a function that is higher (lower) than the nearby points of the graph is a relative maximum (minimum).

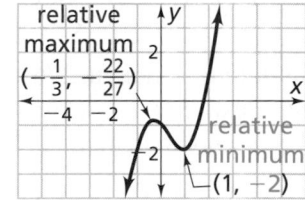

Máximo (mínimo) relativo (p. 315)   El valor y de un punto en la gráfica de una función que es mayor (menor) que los de los puntos cercanos es un máximo (mínimo) relativo.

Remainder Theorem (p. 323)   If a polynomial $P(x)$ of degree $n \geq 1$ is divided by $(x - a)$, where a is a constant, then the remainder is $P(a)$.

If $P(x) = x^3 - 4x^2 + x + 6$ is divided by $x - 3$, then the remainder is $P(3) = 3^3 - 4(3)^2 + 3 + 6 = 0$ (which means that $x - 3$ is a factor of $P(x)$).

Teorema del residuo (p. 323)   Si un polinomio $P(x)$ de grado $n \geq 1$ se divide por $(x - a)$, donde a es una constante, el residuo es $P(a)$.

Root (p. 268)   A root of a function is the input value for which the value of the function is zero. A root of an equation is a value that makes the equation true. *See also* **Zero of a function.**

-2 and 3 are roots of the function $f(x) = (x + 2)(x - 3)$ and the equation $(x + 2)(x - 3) = 0$.

Raíz (p. 268)   La raíz de una función es el valor de entrada para el cual el valor de la función es cero. La raíz de una ecuación es un valor que hace verdadera la ecuación. *Ver también* **Zero of a function.**

Rotation (p. 194) A rotation is a transformation that turns a figure about a fixed point called the center of rotation.

Rotación (p. 194) Rotación es una transformación que hace girar una figura alrededor de un punto fijo llamado centro de rotación.

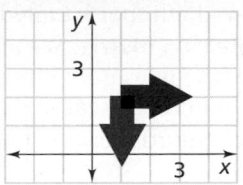

Row operations (p. 223) To solve a system of equations using an augmented matrix, you can use one or more of the following row operations:

• Switch any two rows.

• Multiply a row by a constant.

• Add one row to another.

• Combine one or more of these steps.

Operaciones de filas (p. 223) Para resolver un sistema de ecuaciones por medio de una matriz aumentada, se puede usar una o más de las siguientes operaciones de filas.

• Intercambiar dos filas.

• Multiplicar una fila por una constante.

• Sumar una fila a otra.

• Combinar uno o más de estos pasos.

Sample (p. 677) A sample is information gathered from only part of a population.

Muestra (p. 677) Una muestra contiene información reunida solamente de una parte de una población.

Let the set of all males between the ages of 19 and 34 be the population. A random selection of 900 males between those ages would be a sample of the population.

Sample proportion (p. 677) If an event occurs x times in a sample of size n, the sample proportion is $\frac{x}{n}$.

Proporción muestral (p. 677) Si un suceso ocurre x veces en un espacio muestral de tamaño n, la proporción de la muestra es $\frac{x}{n}$.

For a random selection of 900 males, 350 preferred red shirts to green shirts. The sample proportion would be $\frac{350}{900} = \frac{7}{18}$.

Sample space (p. 41) The set of all possible outcomes of an experiment is called the sample space.

Espacio muestral (p. 41) El espacio muestral es el conjunto de todos los resultados posibles de un suceso.

When you roll a number cube, the sample space is $\{1, 2, 3, 4, 5, 6\}$.

EXAMPLES

Scalar (p. 182) A real number is called a scalar for certain special uses, such as multiplying a matrix. *See also* **Scalar multiplication.**

Escalar (p. 182) Un número real se llama escalar en ciertos casos especiales, como en la multiplicación de una matriz. *Ver también* **Scalar multiplication.**

$$2.5\begin{bmatrix} 1 & 0 \\ -2 & 3 \end{bmatrix} = \begin{bmatrix} 2.5(1) & 2.5(0) \\ 2.5(-2) & 2.5(3) \end{bmatrix}$$
$$= \begin{bmatrix} 2.5 & 0 \\ -5 & 7.5 \end{bmatrix}$$

Scalar multiplication (p. 182) Scalar multiplication is an operation that multiplies a matrix A by a scalar c. To find the resulting matrix cA, multiply each element of A by c.

Multiplicación escalar (p. 182) La multiplicación escalar es la que multiplica una matriz A por un número escalar c. Para hallar la matriz cA resultante, multiplica cada elemento de A por c.

$$2.5\begin{bmatrix} 1 & 0 \\ -2 & 3 \end{bmatrix} = \begin{bmatrix} 2.5(1) & 2.5(0) \\ 2.5(-2) & 2.5(3) \end{bmatrix}$$
$$= \begin{bmatrix} 2.5 & 0 \\ -5 & 7.5 \end{bmatrix}$$

Scatter plot (p. 80) A scatter plot is a graph that relates two different sets of data by plotting the data as ordered pairs. You can use a scatter plot to determine a relationship between the data sets.

Diagrama de puntos (p. 80) Un diagrama de puntos es una gráfica que relaciona dos conjuntos de datos presentando los datos como pares ordenados. El diagrama de puntos sirve para definir la relación entre conjuntos de datos.

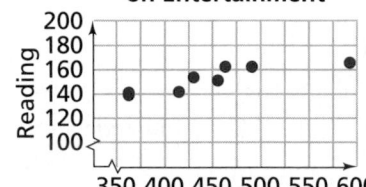

Dollars Spent Per Capita on Entertainment

SOURCE: U.S. Bureau of Labor Statistics.
Go to **www.PHSchool.com** for a data update.

Secant (p. 763) The secant (sec) function is the reciprocal of the cosine function. For all real numbers θ except those that make $\cos \theta = 0$, $\sec \theta = \frac{1}{\cos \theta}$.

Secante (p. 763) La función secante (sec) es el recíproco de la función coseno. Para todos los números reales θ, excepto aquéllos para los que $\cos \theta = 0$, $\sec \theta = \frac{1}{\cos \theta}$.

If $\cos \theta = \frac{5}{13}$, then $\sec \theta = \frac{13}{5}$.

Sequence (p. 600) A sequence is an ordered list of numbers.

Progresión (p. 600) Una progresión es una sucesión de números.

$1, 4, 7, 10, \ldots$

Series (p. 619) A series is the sum of the terms of a sequence. The series is finite (infinite) if the corresponding sequence has finitely (infinitely) many terms..

Serie (p. 619) Una serie es la suma de los términos de una progresión. La serie es finita (infinita) si la progresión correspondiente tiene una cantidad finita (infinita) de términos.

The series $3 + 6 + 9 + 12 + 15$ corresponds to the sequence 3, 6, 9, 12, 15. The sum of the series is 45.

Shrink (p. 96)   A vertical shrink of a function f by the factor a, $0 < a < 1$, is a transformation of f that multiplies all y-values by a.

Reducción (p. 96)   La reducción vertical de una función f por el factor a, donde $0 < a < 1$, es una transformación de f que multiplica todos los valores de y por a.

$g(x) = \frac{1}{2}x^2$ is a vertical shrink of $f(x) = x^2$

Simplest form of a rational expression (p. 509)   A rational expression is in simplest form when its numerator and denominator are polynomials that have no common divisors.

Forma simplificada de una expresión racional (p. 509)   Una expresión racional no se puede simplificar más cuando su numerador y su denominador son polinomios que ya no contienen factores comunes.

$$\frac{x^2 - 7x + 12}{x^2 - 9} = \frac{(x-4)(x-3)}{(x+3)(x-3)}$$
$$= \frac{x-4}{x+3}, \text{ where } x \neq -3$$

Simulation (p. 40)   When actual trials are difficult to conduct, you can find experimental probability by using a simulation, which is a model of one or more events.

Simulación (p. 40)   Cuando es difícil realizar los ensayos de un experimento, se puede determinar la probabilidad experimental por medio de una simulación, o modelo de uno o más sucesos del experimento.

Suppose a weather forecaster predicts a 50% chance of rain for the next three days. You can use three coins landing heads up to simulate three days in a row of rain.

Sine curve (p. 735)   A sine curve is the graph of a sine function.

Sinusoide (p. 735)   Sinusoide es la gráfica de la función seno.

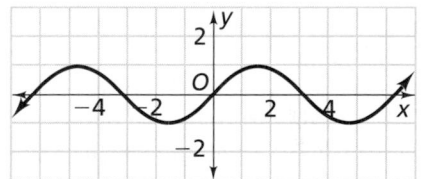

Sine function (p. 734)   The sine function, $y = \sin \theta$, matches the measure θ of an angle in standard position with the y-coordinate of a point on the unit circle. This point is where the terminal side of the angle intersects the unit circle.

Función seno (p. 734)   La función seno, $y = \text{sen } \theta$, equivale a la medida θ de un ángulo en posición normal con la coordenada y de un punto dado en el círculo unitario. Este punto es la intersección del lado terminal y el círculo unitario.

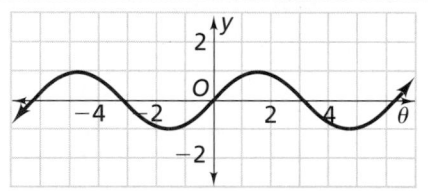

Sine of θ (p. 720)   The sine of an angle measure θ ($\sin \theta$) is the y-coordinate of the point at which the terminal side of the angle intersects the unit circle.

Seno de θ (p. 720)   El seno de un ángulo que mide θ ($\text{sen } \theta$) es la coordenada y del punto de intersección entre el lado terminal del ángulo y el círculo unitario.

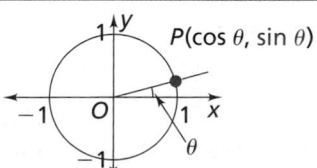

English/Spanish Glossary

Slope of a line (p. 64) The slope of a non-vertical line is the ratio of the vertical change to a corresponding horizontal change. The slope of a vertical line is undefined.

$$\text{slope} = \frac{\text{vertical change}}{\text{horizontal change}} = \frac{y_2 - y_1}{x_2 - x_1}, \text{where } x_2 - x_1 \neq 0$$

Pendiente de una recta (p. 64) La pendiente de una recta no vertical es la razón del cambio vertical y el cambio horizontal. La pendiente de una recta vertical no está definida.

$$\text{pendiente} = \frac{\text{cambio vertical}}{\text{cambio horizontal}} = \frac{y_2 - y_1}{x_2 - x_1}, \text{donde } x_2 - x_1 \neq 0$$

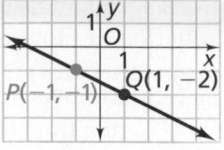

The slope of the line through points $(-1, -1)$ and $(1, -2)$ is
$$\frac{-2 - (-1)}{1 - (-1)} = \frac{-1}{2} = -\frac{1}{2}.$$

Slope-intercept form (p. 65) The slope-intercept form of an equation of a line is $y = mx + b$, where m is the slope and b is the y-intercept.

Forma pendiente-intercepto (p. 65) La forma pendiente-intercepto de una ecuación lineal es $y = mx + b$, donde m es la pendiente y b es el intercepto en y.

$y = 8x + 2$

$y = -x + 1$

$y = -\frac{1}{2}x - 14$

Solution of an equation (p. 18) A solution of an equation is a number that makes the equation true.

Solución de una ecuación (p. 18) Una solución de una ecuación es cualquier número que haga verdadera la ecuación.

The solution of $2x - 7 = -12$ is $x = -2.5$.

Square matrix (p. 199) A square matrix is a matrix with the same number of columns as rows.

Matriz cuadrada (p. 199) Una matriz cuadrada es la que tiene la misma cantidad de columnas y filas.

Matrix A is a square matrix.

$$A = \begin{bmatrix} 1 & 2 & 0 \\ -1 & 0 & -2 \\ 1 & 2 & 3 \end{bmatrix}$$

Square root equation (p. 391) A square root equation is a radical equation in which the radical has index 2.

Ecuación de raíz cuadrada (p. 391) Una ecuación de raíz cuadrada es una ecuación radical en la cual el radical tiene índice 2.

$\sqrt{x} = 4$

Square root function (p. 415) A square root function is a function that can be written in the form $f(x) = a\sqrt{x - h} + k$, where $a \neq 0$. The domain of a square root function is all real numbers $x \geq h$.

Función de raíz cuadrada (p. 415) Una función de raíz cuadrada es una función que puede ser expresada como $f(x) = a\sqrt{x - h} + k$, donde $a \neq 0$. El dominio de una función de raíz cuadrada son todos los números reales tales que $x \geq h$.

$f(x) = 2\sqrt{x - 3} + 4$

Standard deviation (p. 669)   Standard deviation is a measure of how much the values in a data set vary, or deviate, from the mean, $\overline{x}$. To find the standard deviation, follow five steps:

- Find the mean of the data set.
- Find the difference between each data value and the mean.
- Square each difference.
- Find the mean of the squares.
- Take the square root of the mean of the squares. This is the standard deviation.

$\{0, 2, 3, 4, 6, 7, 8, 9, 10, 11\}$

$\overline{x} = 6$

standard deviation $= \sqrt{12} \approx 3.46$

Desviación típica (p. 669)   La desviación típica denota cuánto los valores de un conjunto de datos varían, o se desvían, de la media, $\overline{x}$. Para hallar la desviación típica, se siguen cinco pasos:

- Se halla la media del conjunto de datos.
- Se calcula la diferencia entre cada valor de datos y la media.
- Se eleva al cuadrado cada diferencia.
- Se halla la media de los cuadrados.
- Se calcula la raíz cuadrada de la media de los cuadrados. Ésa es la desviación típica.

Standard form of a linear equation (p. 63)   The standard form of a linear equation is $Ax + By = C$, where A, B, and C are real numbers, and A and B are not both zero.

In standard form, the equation $y = \frac{4}{3}x - 1$ is $4x + (-3)y = 3$.

Forma normal de una ecuación lineal (p. 63)   La forma normal de una ecuación lineal es $Ax + By = C$, donde A, B, y C son números reales, y A y B son valores distintos de cero.

Standard form of an equation of a circle (p. 561)   *See* **Circle.**

$(x - 3)^2 + (y - 4)^2 = 4$

Forma normal de la ecuación de un círculo (p. 561)   *Ver* **Circle.**

Standard form of an equation of an ellipse (p. 568)   *See* **Ellipse.**

$\dfrac{x^2}{5^2} + \dfrac{y^2}{3^2} = 1$

Forma normal de la ecuación de una elipse (p. 568)   *Ver* **Ellipse.**

Standard form of an equation of a hyperbola (p. 575)   *See* **Hyperbola.**

$\dfrac{x^2}{5^2} - \dfrac{y^2}{3^2} = 1$

Forma normal de la ecuación de una hipérbola (p. 575)   *Ver* **Hyperbola.**

Standard form of a polynomial (p. 307)   The standard form of a polynomial has the terms in descending order by degree. A one-variable polynomial in standard form has no two terms with the same degree, since all like terms have been combined.

$2x^3 - 5x^2 - 2x + 5$

Forma normal de un polinomio (p. 307)   Un polinomio está en forma normal cuando sus términos están en orden descendente por grados. Un polinomio de una variable en forma normal no tiene dos términos del mismo grado puesto que todos los términos han sido combinados.

English/Spanish Glossary

Standard form of a quadratic equation (p. 267) *See* **Quadratic equation.**

$2x^2 + 5x + 2 = 0$

Forma normal de una ecuación cuadrática (p. 267) *Ver* **Quadratic equation.**

Standard form of a quadratic function (p. 238) The standard form of a quadratic function is $f(x) = ax^2 + bx + c$, where $a \neq 0$.

$f(x) = 2x^2 + 5x + 2$

Forma normal de una función cuadrática (p. 238) La forma normal de una función cuadrática es $f(x) = ax^2 + bx + c$, donde $a \neq 0$.

Standard normal curve (p. 693) The standard normal curve is a normal distribution centered on the y-axis. The mean of the standard normal curve is 0. The standard deviation is 1.

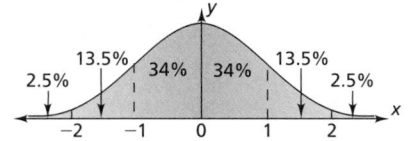

Curva normal en posición normal (p. 693) La curva normal es la distribución normal centrada en el eje y. La media de la curva normal es 0. La desviación normal es 1.

Standard position of an angle (p. 716) An angle is in standard position when the vertex is at the origin of a coordinate system and one ray is on the positive x-axis.

$x^3 + 27 = (x + 3)(x^2 - 3x + 9)$

Posición normal de un ángulo (p. 716) Un ángulo está en posición normal cuando su vértice está en el origen de un sistema de coordenadas y uno de sus lados está sobre el eje x positivo.

Stretch (p. 96) A vertical stretch of a function f by the factor a, $a > 1$, is a transformation of f that multiplies all y-values by a.

$g(x) = 2x^2$ is a vertical stretch of $f(x) = x^2$.

Ampliación (p. 96) Una ampliación vertical de una función f por el factor a, donde $a > 1$, es una transformación de f que multiplica todos los valores de y por a.

Sum of cubes (p. 328) The sum of cubes is an expression of the form $a^3 + b^3$. It can be factored as $(a + b)(a^2 - ab + b^2)$.

$x^3 + 27 = (x + 3)(x^2 - 3x + 9)$

Suma de dos cubos (p. 328) La suma de dos cubos es una expresión de la forma $a^3 + b^3$. Se puede factorizar como $(a + b)(a^2 - ab + b^2)$.

Synthetic division (p. 321) Synthetic division is a method of dividing polynomials in which you omit all variables and exponents and perform the division on the list of coefficients. You also reverse the sign of the divisor so that you can add throughout the process, rather than subtract.

$$
\begin{array}{r|rrrrr}
-3 & 2 & 5 & 0 & -2 & -8 \\
   &   & -6 & 3 & -9 & 33 \\
\hline
   & 2 & -1 & 3 & -11 & 25
\end{array}
$$

Divide $2x^4 + 5x^3 - 2x - 8$ by $x + 3$.
$2x^4 + 5x^3 - 2x - 8$ divided by $x + 3$ gives $2x^3 - x^2 + 3x - 11$ as quotient and 25 as remainder.

División sintética (p. 321) La división sintética es un método de dividir polinomios según el cual se omiten todas las variables y los exponentes y se hace la división con la lista de coeficientes. También se puede invertir el signo del divisor para sumar en vez de restar durante el proceso.

System of equations (p. 118) A system of equations is a set of two or more equations using the same variables.

$$\begin{cases} 2x - 3y = -13 \\ 4x + 5y = 7 \end{cases}$$

Sistema de ecuaciones (p. 118) Un sistema de ecuaciones es un conjunto de dos o más ecuaciones que contienen las mismas variables.

Tangent function (p. 749) The tangent function, $y = \tan \theta$, matches the measure θ of an angle in standard position with the y-coordinate of the point at which the line containing the terminal side of a central angle of the unit circle intersects the tangent line $x = 1$.

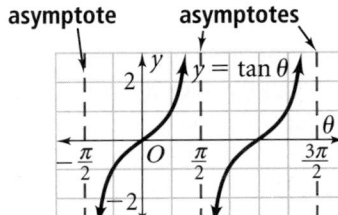

Función tangente (p. 749) La función tangente, $y = \tan \theta$, equivale a la medida θ de un ángulo en posición normal, con la coordenada y del punto donde la recta que contiene el lado terminal de un ángulo central del círculo unitario corta la tangente $x = 1$.

Tangent of θ (p. 749) The tangent of an angle measure θ ($\tan \theta$) is the y-coordinate of the point at which the line containing the terminal side of the angle intersects the tangent line $x = 1$.

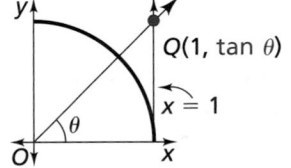

Tangente de θ (p. 749) La tangente de un ángulo que mide θ ($\tan \theta$) es la ordenada y del punto donde la recta que contiene el lado terminal del ángulo corta la tangente $x = 1$.

Term of a sequence (p. 600) Each number in a sequence is a term.

$1, 4, 7, 10, \ldots$
The second term is 4.

Término de una progresión (p. 600) Cada número de una progresión es un término.

Term of an expression (p. 13) A term is a number, a variable, or the product of a number and one or more variables.

The expression $4x^2 - 3y + 7.3$ has 3 terms.

Término de una expresión (p. 13) Un término es un número, una variable o el producto de un número y una o más variables.

Terminal side of an angle (p. 718) See *Initial side of an angle*.

Lado terminal de un ángulo (p. 718) *Ver Initial side of an angle*.

Theoretical probability (p. 41) If a sample space has n equally likely outcomes, and an event A occurs in m of these outcomes, then the theoretical probability of event A is $P(A) = \frac{m}{n}$.

Use the set $\{1, 4, 9, 16, 25, 36, 49, 64, 81, 100\}$. The probability that a number selected at random is greater than 50 is $P(A) = \frac{3}{10} = 0.3$.

Probabilidad teórica (p. 41) Si un espacio muestral tiene n resultados con la misma probabilidad de ocurrir, y ocurre un suceso A en m de estos resultados, entonces la probabilidad teórica del suceso A es $P(A) = \frac{m}{n}$.

Tolerance (p. 36) The difference between a desired measurement and its maximum and minimum allowable values is the tolerance. The tolerance equals one half of the difference between the maximum and minimum values.

A manufacturing specification calls for a dimension d of 10 cm with a tolerance of 0.1 cm. The allowable difference between d and 10 is less than or equal to 0.1.

Tolerancia (p. 36) La diferencia entre una medida deseada y sus valores máximo y mínimo permitidos es la tolerancia. La tolerancia equivale a la mitad de la diferencia entre los valores máximo y mínimo.

Trace (p. 148) If a plane in a three-dimensional xyz-coordinate system intersects the xy-, yz-, or xz-plane in a line, then that line is a trace of the given plane.

Trazo (p. 148) Si un plano en un sistema tridimensional de coordenadas xyz interseca el plano xy, yz o xz en una recta, entonces esa recta es una traza del plano dado.

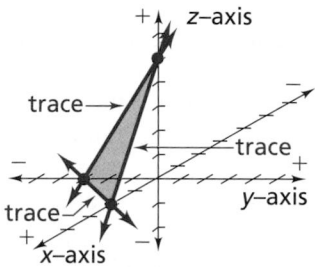

Transformation (p. 192) A transformation of a function $y = af(x - h) + k$ is a change made to the value of at least one of the parameters a, h, and k.

$g(x) = 2(x - 3)^2$ is a transformation of $f(x) = x^2$.

Transformación (p. 192) Una transformación de una función $y = af(x - h) + k$ es un cambio en el valor de uno de los parámetros a, h y k.

Translation (p. 191) A translation is a transformation that slides a graph or figure horizontally, vertically, or both without changing the size or shape of the graph or figure.

Traslación (p. 191) Una traslación es el proceso de deslizar una gráfica o figura horizontalmente, verticalmente, o en ambos sentidos, pero sin cambiar ni el tamaño ni la forma de la gráfica o figura.

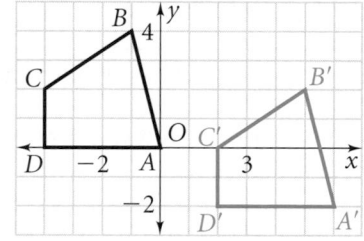

Transverse axis of a hyperbola (p. 575) The transverse axis of a hyperbola is the segment that lies on the line containing the foci and has endpoints on the hyperbola. The endpoints are the vertices of the hyperbola.

Eje transversal de una hipérbola (p. 575) El eje transversal de una hipérbola es el segmento que pasa por la recta donde se encuentran los focos y que tiene los extremos sobre la hipérbola. Los extremos son los vértices de la hipérbola.

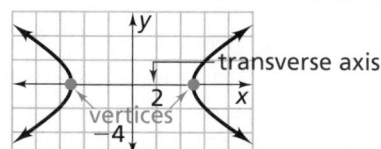

Trend line (p. 80) A trend line is a line that approximates the relationship between the data sets of a scatter plot. You can use a trend line to make predictions.

Línea de tendencia (p. 80) La línea de tendencia es una línea que aproxima la relación entre los conjuntos de datos en un diagrama de puntos. La línea de tendencia permite hacer predicciones.

Used Car Prices

Trigonometric identity (p. 778) A trigonometric identity is a trigonometric equation that is true for all values except those for which an expression on either side of the equal sign is undefined.

$$\tan \theta = \frac{\sin \theta}{\cos \theta}$$

Identidad trigonométrica (p. 778) Una identidad trigonométrica es una ecuación trigonométrica que satisface todos los valores excepto aquéllos para los cuales las expresiones a cada lado del signo igual no están definidas.

Trigonometric ratios for a right triangle (p. 792) The trigonometric ratios for a right triangle are the six different ratios of the sides of a right triangle. These ratios do not depend on the size of the right triangle. They depend only on the measures of the acute angles in the triangle. In a right triangle that has an acute $\angle A$, the ratios are defined as follows.

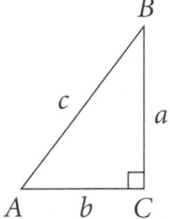

$$\sin A = \frac{a}{c}$$
$$\csc A = \frac{1}{\sin A} = \frac{c}{a}$$

$$\cos A = \frac{b}{c}$$
$$\sec A = \frac{1}{\cos A} = \frac{c}{b}$$

$$\tan A = \frac{a}{b}$$
$$\cot A = \frac{1}{\tan A} = \frac{b}{a}$$

Razones trigonométricas para un triángulo rectángulo (p. 792)
Las razones trigonométricas de un triángulo rectángulo son las seis razones de los lados de dicho triángulo. Esas razones no dependen del tamaño del triángulo rectángulo. Dependen sólo de la magnitud de los ángulos agudos del triángulo. En un triángulo rectángulo que tenga un ángulo agudo $\angle A$, las razones se definen así.

$$\operatorname{sen} A = \frac{a}{c}$$
$$\csc A = \frac{1}{\operatorname{sen} A} = \frac{c}{a}$$

$$\cos A = \frac{b}{c}$$
$$\sec A = \frac{1}{\cos A} = \frac{c}{b}$$

$$\tan A = \frac{a}{b}$$
$$\cot A = \frac{1}{\tan A} = \frac{b}{a}$$

English/Spanish Glossary

Unit circle (p. 720) The unit circle has a radius of 1 unit and its center is at the origin of the coordinate plane.

Círculo unitario (p. 720) El círculo unitario tiene un radio de 1 unidad y el centro está situado en el origen del plano de coordenadas.

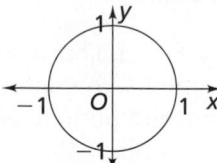

Variable (p. 12) A variable is a symbol, usually a letter, that represents one or more numbers.

Variable (p. 12) Una variable es un símbolo, generalmente una letra, que representa uno o más valores.

x, a, k

Variable expression (p. 12) An expression that contains one or more variables is an algebraic expression, or a variable expression.

Expresión variable (p. 12) Una expresión que contenga una o más variables es una expresión algebraica o expresión variable.

$2x + 3, z - y$

Variable matrix (p. 214) When representing a system of equations with a matrix equation, the matrix containing the variables of the system is the variable matrix.

Matriz variable (p. 214) Al representar un sistema de ecuaciones con una ecuación de matricial, la matriz que contenga las variables del sistema es la matriz variable.

$$\begin{cases} x + 2y = 5 \\ 3x + 5y = 14 \end{cases}$$

variable matrix $\begin{bmatrix} x \\ y \end{bmatrix}$

Vertex form of a quadratic function (p. 252) The vertex form of a quadratic function is $f(x) = a(x - h)^2 + k$, where (h, k) are the coordinates of the vertex of the function.

Forma del vértice de una función cuadrática (p. 252) La forma del vértice de una función cuadrática es $f(x) = a(x - h)^2 + k$, donde (h, k) son las coordenadas del vértice de la función.

$f(x) = x^2 + 2x - 1 = (x + 1)^2 - 2$
The vertex is $(-1, -2)$.

Vertex of a function (p. 88) A vertex of a function is a point where the function reaches a maximum or a minimum value.

Vértice de una función (p. 88) El vértice de una función es el punto donde la función alcanza un valor máximo o mínimo.

Vertex of a parabola (p. 239) The vertex of a parabola is the point where the function for the parabola reaches a maximum or a minimum value. The parabola intersects its axis of symmetry at the vertex.

Vértice de una parábola (p. 239) El vértice de una parábola es el punto donde la función de la parábola alcanza un valor máximo o mínimo. La parábola y su eje de simetría se intersecan en el vértice.

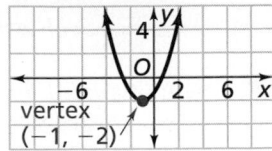

The vertex of the quadratic function $y = x^2 + 2x - 1$ is $(-1, -2)$.

Vertical-line test (p. 57) You can use the vertical-line test to determine whether a relation has at least one element of the domain paired with more than one element of the range. If a vertical line passes through two or more points on the graph, then the relation is *not* a function.

Prueba de la recta vertical (p. 57) La prueba de la recta vertical permite determinar si en una relación hay por lo menos un elemento del dominio al que corresponde más de un elemento del rango. Si una recta vertical del sistema de coordenadas pasa por dos o más puntos de la gráfica, quiere decir que la relación *no es* una función.

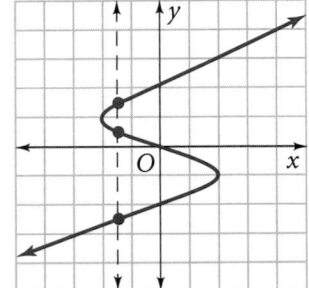

Vertices of a hyperbola (p. 575) The endpoints of the transverse axis of a hyperbola are the vertices of the hyperbola.

Vértices de una hipérbola (p. 575) Los dos puntos de intersección de la hipérbola y su eje mayor son los vértices de la hipérbola.

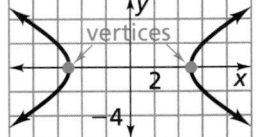

Vertices of an ellipse (p. 568) The endpoints of the major axis of an ellipse are the vertices of the ellipse.

Vértices de una elipse (p. 568) Los dos puntos de intersección de la elipse y su eje mayor son los vértices de la elipse.

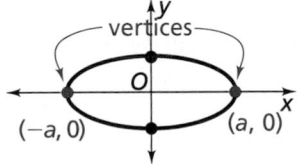

x- **and** *y*-**intercepts (p. 63)** The point at which a line crosses the *x*-axis (or the *x*-coordinate of that point) is an *x*-intercept. The point at which a line crosses the *y*-axis (or the *y*-coordinate of that point) is a *y*-intercept.

Intercepto en *x* **e intercepto en** *y* **(p. 63)** El punto donde una recta corta el eje *x* (o la coordenada *x* de ese punto) es el intercepto en *x*. El punto donde una recta cruza el eje *y* (o la coordenada *y* de ese punto) es el intercepto en *y*.

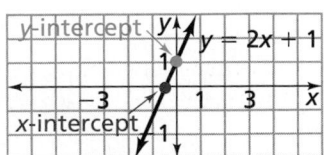

The *x*-intercept of $y = 2x + 1$ is $\left(-\frac{1}{2}, 0\right)$ or $-\frac{1}{2}$.
The *y*-intercept of $y = 2x + 1$ is $(0, 1)$ or 1.

Zero matrix (p. 175) The zero matrix O, or $O_{m \times n}$, is the $m \times n$ matrix whose elements are all zeros. It is the additive identity matrix for the set of all $m \times n$ matrices.

$$\begin{bmatrix} 1 & 4 \\ 2 & -3 \end{bmatrix} + O = \begin{bmatrix} 1 & 4 \\ 2 & -3 \end{bmatrix}$$

Matriz cero (p. 175) La matriz cero, O, o $O_{m \times n}$, es la matriz $m \times n$ cuyos elementos son todos ceros. Es la matriz de identidad aditiva para el conjunto de todas las matrices $m \times n$.

Zero of a function (p. 268) A zero of a function is any value of the variable for which the function is 0. On the graph of a function, each x-intercept represents a zero.

Cero de una función (p. 268) Un cero de una función es cualquier valor de la variable para el cual la función es 0. En la gráfica de una función, cada intercepto en x representa un cero.

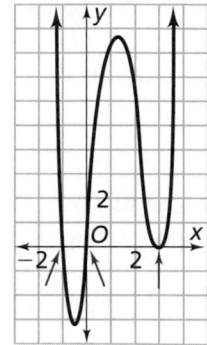

The zeros of the function $P(x) = 2x(x - 3)^2(x + 1)$ are 0, 3, and -1.

Zero-Product Property (p. 267) If the product of two or more factors is zero, then one of the factors must be zero.

$(x - 3)(2x - 5) = 0$

$x - 3 = 0$ or $2x - 5 = 0$

Propiedad del cero del producto (p. 267) Si el producto de dos o más factores es cero, entonces uno de los factores debe ser cero.

z-score (p. 671) The z-score of a value is the number of standard deviations that the value is from the mean.

$\{0, 2, 3, 4, 6, 7, 8, 9, 10, 11\}$

$\overline{x} = 6$

Puntaje z (p. 671) El puntaje z de un valor es el número de desviaciones normales que tiene ese valor de la media.

standard deviation $= \sqrt{12} \approx 3.46$

For 8, z-score $= \dfrac{8 - 6}{\sqrt{12}} \approx 0.58$.

Answers to Instant Check System™

Chapter 1

Check Your Readiness   p. 2

1. 0 **2.** −2 **3.** −2.09 **4.** 8.05 **5.** −$\frac{3}{4}$ **6.** $\frac{11}{12}$ **7.** $10\frac{7}{10}$
8. $3\frac{1}{2}$ **9.** −42 **10.** 72 **11.** 9 **12.** −9.8 **13.** −$3\frac{1}{3}$
14. −$5\frac{1}{2}$ **15.** −$4\frac{2}{3}$ **16.** −$\frac{3}{4}$ **17.** −21 **18.** 7.35
19. −$\frac{1}{6}$ **20.** −$\frac{3}{5}$ **21.** −20 **22.** 8 **23.** 0.97 **24.** −5
25. 55 **26.** 3

Lesson 1-1   pp. 4–8

Check Skills You'll Need 1. 7.2 **2.** 4 **3.** −13.5 **4.** 6.8
5. −5 **6.** −1

Quick Check 1. rational numbers; rational numbers
2.

$$-2\frac{1}{4} \quad -\sqrt{2} \qquad 0.\overline{3}$$

3. $-\sqrt{0.08} > -\sqrt{0.1}, -\sqrt{0.1} < -\sqrt{0.08}$
4a. $-400, \frac{1}{400}$ **b.** $-4\frac{1}{5}, \frac{5}{21}$ **c.** $0.002, -500$
d. $\frac{4}{9}, -\frac{9}{4} \left(\text{or} -2\frac{1}{4}\right)$ **5a.** Identity Prop. of Add.
b. Assoc. Prop. of Add. **6a.** 10, 1.5, 3 **b.** for
values of x such that $x \le 0$

Lesson 1-2   pp. 12–15

Check Skills You'll Need 1. 16 **2.** 6 **3.** $\frac{8}{3}$ **4.** 195 **5.** 21
6. −1

Quick Check 1a. $\frac{7}{2}$ **b.** 26 **c.** 4 **2a.** −16
b. −3 **c.** −69 **3a.** about 45%; about 43%
b. Answers may vary. Sample: Changing patterns
in minority populations might lead to more voter
turnout. Less stable international conditions
might arouse voter concerns. **4a.** $-3x^2 + 6x$
b. $-4r - 4s$ **5a.** $10x$ **b.** $10c + 2d$

Lesson 1-3   pp. 18–21, 24

Check Skills You'll Need 1. $-4x + 3$ **2.** $7x + 3y - 1$
3. $8g + 2h$ **4.** $\frac{x}{3}$ **5.** $2y$ **6.** $-3c + 1$

Quick Check 1a. −11 **b.** 2 **2a.** 35 **b.** 3
3. $b_1 = \frac{2A}{h} - b_2$ **4a.** $x = \frac{15}{a + b}, a \ne -b$
b. $x = \frac{a(d - b)}{2}, a \ne 0$ **5.** 8 cm wide; 16 cm long
6. 36 cm; 39 cm; 45 cm **7.** about 86.4 seconds,
or 1 minute 26.4 seconds

Checkpoint Quiz 1 1. $-1, 0.3, \frac{2}{3}, 7$ **2.** Comm. Prop. of

Add., Assoc. Prop. of Add., Dist. Prop. **3.** $a + 2b$
4. $a^2 + a - 7$ **5.** 5 **6.** $\frac{3}{2}$, or $1\frac{1}{2}$ **7.** 2 **8.** $r = \frac{A - p}{pt}$,
$p \ne 0, t \ne 0$ **9.** $x = \frac{4b}{7a}, a \ne 0$ **10.** width = 76 yd,
length = 236 yd

Lesson 1-4   pp. 26–29

Check Skills You'll Need 1. true **2.** false **3.** false
4. false **5.** true **6.** true **7.** −6 **8.** 15

Quick Check
1a. $x < 11$
5 6 7 8 9 10 11 12 13
b. $n \le -2$
−6−5−4−3−2−1 0 1 2
2a. All real numbers are solutions.
−4−3−2−1 0 1 2 3 4 **b.** no solutions
c. values of a less than or equal to 0; values of
a greater than 0 **3.** at least $55,000
4.
2 3 4 5 6 7 8 9 10 z
5. $x < 4$ or $x > 5$
−1 0 1 2 3 4 5 6 7
6. by at least 0.03 in., but by no more than 0.43 in.

Lesson 1–5   pp. 33–36, 38

Check Skills You'll Need 1. 14 **2.** 16 **3.** 2.3 **4.** $x > 3$
5. $a \ge 4$ **6.** $t < 9$

Quick Check 1. $\frac{5}{3}, -3$ **2.** $-\frac{13}{3}, 5$ **3a.** 1 **b.** no
solutions **c.** Answers may vary; any positive real
number. **4.** $x < -2$ or $x > 5$
−3−2−1 0 1 2 3 4 5 6 7
5. $-8\frac{4}{5} < z < 7\frac{3}{5}$
−12−10−8−6−4−2 0 2 4 6 8 10
6. $|C - 28.125| \le 0.375$

Checkpoint Quiz 2
1. $x \le 5$
−2−1 0 1 2 3 4 5 6 7
2. $x < 5\frac{4}{7}$
−2−1 0 1 2 3 4 5 6 7
3. $z > -1$
−4−3−2−1 0 1 2 3 4 5
4. $w > 1$ or $w < -3$
−6−5−4−3−2−1 0 1 2 3 4
5. $-15 \le x \le 7$
−16−14−12−10−8−6−4−2 0 2 4 6 8

6. $x < -2$ or $x > 2$
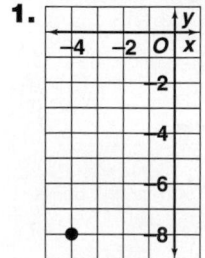
-4 -3 -2 -1 0 1 2 3 4

7. $-\frac{5}{2}, \frac{11}{2}$ **8.** $\frac{1}{6}$ **9.** $13 < 3n + 3 < 16, n = 4$
10. $PR - RQ < PQ < PR + RQ; 4 < PQ < 26$

Lesson 1-6   pp. 39–42

Check Skills You'll Need   **1.** 37.5%   **2.** $183\frac{1}{3}$%   **3.** 0.43%
4. 0.25%   **5.** 104%   **6.** 300%

Quick Check   **1.** $\frac{29}{40}$, or 0.725, or 72.5%   **2.** $\frac{3}{50}$, or
6%   **3.** $\frac{1}{2}$, or 50%   **4.** $\frac{1}{4}$, or 25%   **5a.** $\frac{1}{16}$, or 6.25%
b. $\frac{5}{16}$, or 31.25%

Chapter 2

Check Your Readiness   p. 52

1.
-2 0 2 4 6

2.
-4 -2 0 2

3.
-2 0 2 4 6   **4.** $6s$ **5.** $4a + b$

6. $xy - y + x$ **7.** $1.5g$ **8.** 0 **9.** $3b - 2c - 2$
10. $6f - 5d$ **11.** $3h + 3g$ **12.** $-2z + 5$
13. $2g - 4dg - 12d$ **14.** $8v - 6$ **15.** $7t - 3st - 5s$
16. $-2 < x < 8$
-2 0 2 4 6 8

17. $a \le 0$
-4 -2 0 2

18. $x > -1$
-2 0 2 4

19. $x < -4$ or $x > \frac{10}{3}$
-6 -4 -2 0 2 4 6

20. $-\frac{1}{2} \le d \le \frac{25}{4}$
-2 0 2 4 6 8

21. $-24 \le f \le 18$
-30 -20 -10 0 10 20 30   **22.** $\frac{15}{64}$ **23.** $\frac{1}{32}$

24. $\frac{11}{32}$ **25.** $\frac{13}{16}$ **26.** $\frac{27}{32}$ **27.** $\frac{13}{16}$

Lesson 2-1   pp. 55–61

Check Skills You'll Need

1.   **2.** 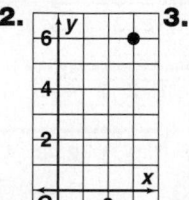   **3.**

---

4. 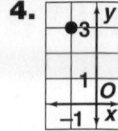   **5.**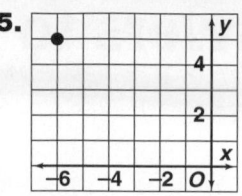

6. 1, 2, 4, 7   **7.** 5, 3, −1, −7   **8.** 3, 1, 9, 51
9. 4, 3, 1, 2

Quick Check

1a. 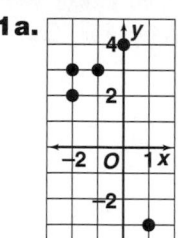   **b.**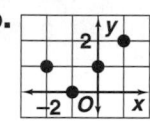

2a. domain {−3, 0, 2, 4}, range {2, 1, 4, −3}
b. domain {−3, −1, 1}, range {−4, −2, 1, 3}
3a. domain range   **b.** domain range   **4a.** function

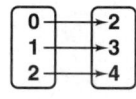   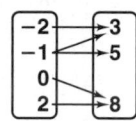

b. not a function   **5a.** not a function   **b.** function
c. not a function   **6a.** −14, −5, 10   **b.** $-\frac{13}{4}, -1, \frac{11}{4}$
c. $\frac{6}{5}, \frac{3}{5}, -\frac{2}{5}$

Lesson 2-2   pp. 62–70

Check Skills You'll Need   **1.** $\frac{17}{3}, 7, \frac{23}{3}, \frac{29}{3}$ **2.** $-\frac{16}{5}, -2, -\frac{7}{5}, \frac{2}{5}$
3. −5, 1, 4, 13   **4.** $-9, -8, -\frac{15}{2}, -6$

Quick Check

1a. 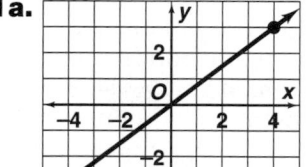   **b.**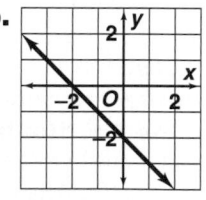

c. 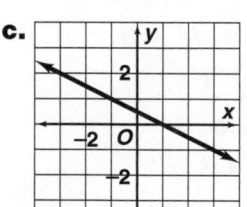   **2a.**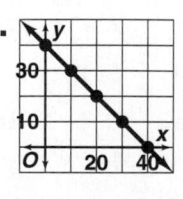

$y = 40 - x$, x-intercept (40, 0), y-intercept (0, 40).
When there are 0 children, the train holds 40 adults.
When there are 0 adults, the train holds 40
children. **b.** Answers may vary. Sample: Each
seat holds one person, whether adult or child.

3a. $\frac{2}{3}$ **b.** $-\frac{6}{7}$ **4a.** $2x - y = 10$ **b.** $\frac{5}{6}x - y = -\frac{11}{6}$
5a. $y - 0 = -\frac{1}{4}(x - 5)$ **b.** $y + 1 = -\frac{9}{4}(x + 2)$
c. $y - 1 = \frac{4}{9}(x - 5)$ **6a.** $-\frac{3}{2}$ **b.** $-\frac{4}{3}$ **c.** $-\frac{A}{B}$, $B \neq 0$,
undefined, $B = 0$
7a. $y = -\frac{1}{5}x + \frac{14}{5}$

b. $y = \frac{2}{3}x - \frac{1}{3}$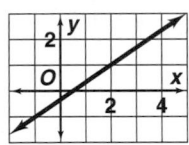

c. $x = 5$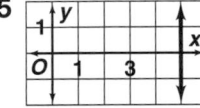

Check Skills You'll Need 1. $y = \frac{x}{4}$ **2.** $y = \frac{5}{12}x$ **3.** $y = 20$
4. $y = 30x$ **5.** $y = 7$ **6.** true **7.** true **8.** false
9. true

Quick Check 1a. yes; $k = \frac{1}{3}$, $y = \frac{1}{3}x$ **b.** no
c. no **2a.** yes; $k = 0.5$ **b.** no **c.** yes; $k = \frac{5}{2}$ **d.** no
3a. π **b.** 33.4 cm **4a.** 8 **b.** 28 **c.** −0.6 **d.** 0.2

Checkpoint Quiz 1 1. (9, 0), (0, −3) **2.** $\left(-\frac{5}{7}, 0\right)$, (0, 5)

3. (0, 0), (0,0) **4.** $\left(-\frac{5}{2}, 0\right)$, (0, 10) **5.** $y = 2x - 9$

6. $y = 4x - 2$ **7.** $y = -\frac{3}{5}x - 2$ **8.** $y = -\frac{2}{3}x + 2$
9a. $y = 7x$ **b.**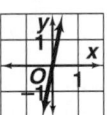

Both intercepts are 0 when no one has bought
any tickets. **c.** Answers may vary. Sample: No; the
number of people must be a whole number. **10.** A

Check Skills You'll Need 1. 3.6, −1.7 **2.** 1.5, −3.5
3. −1, $\frac{1}{10}$ **4.** −6, −2, $-\frac{4}{3}$ **5.** 6, $\frac{11}{2}$, 3

Quick Check 1a. $h = -20t + 1350$; the slope is
negative. **b.**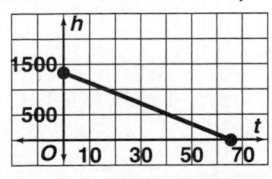

The h-intercept (0, 1350) represents the starting
height at time 0. **2a.** The candle is burning down
at the rate of $\frac{1}{4}$ inch per hour. **b.** the original

height of the candle **c.** $y = -2x + 9$ **3a.** $3\frac{1}{2}$ in.
b. $6\frac{1}{4}$ in. **c.** after 25 hours
4a.

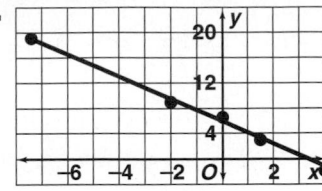

A linear model is reasonable; models may vary.
Sample: $y = -1.92x + 6$

b.

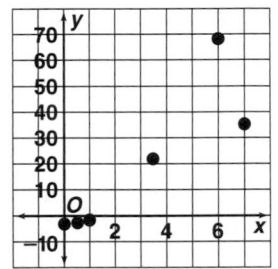

not reasonable

Check Skills You'll Need

1.   **2.**   **3.**

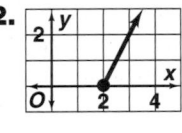 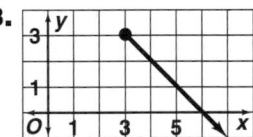

Quick Check

1a.   **b.**

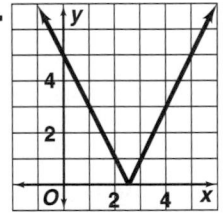 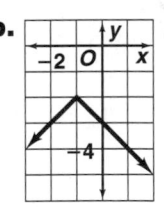

2a.

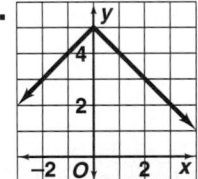

b.

3a.   **b.**

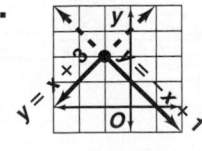

4a. The graph would stretch vertically by a factor of 3. **b.**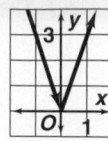

Lesson 2-6 pp. 93–97, 100

Check Skills You'll Need

1. 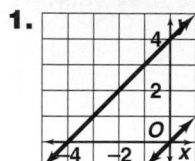 **2.**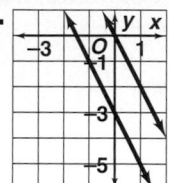

3. 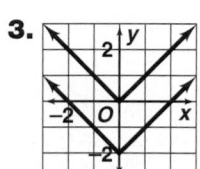 **4.**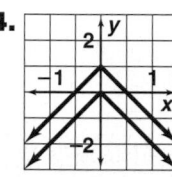

5. 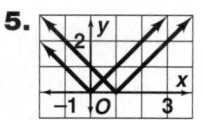 **6.**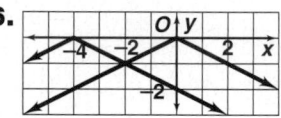

Quick Check 1a. $y = x + 1$ is $y = x$ shifted 1 unit up.

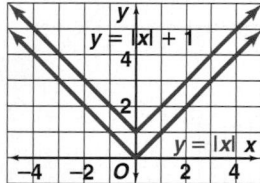

b. $y = |x| - \frac{1}{2}$; $y = |x| + 3.5$.

2a. $y = \left|x + \frac{3}{2}\right|$

b. The graph is translated 1 unit to the right.

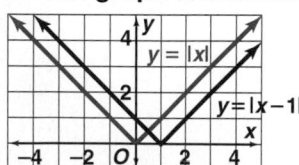

3. Answers may vary. Sample: 4.5 units right and 3 units up

4a. The graph is a vertical shrink by a factor of $\frac{1}{3}$.

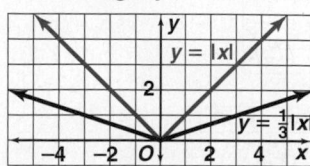

b. $y = 3|x|$

5. $y = -5|x|$

Checkpoint Quiz 2

1. 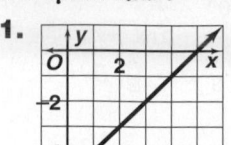 **2.** 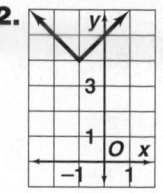 **3.**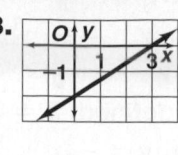

4. 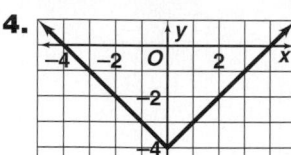 **5.**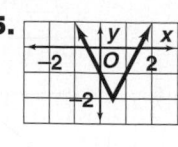

6. 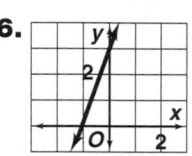 **7.** $y = x - 4$ **8.** $y = |x + 5| - 3$

9a. 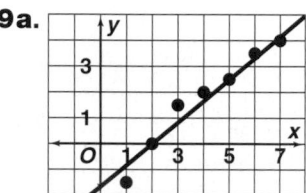 **b.** about 7 **10.** D

Lesson 2-7 pp. 101–104

Check Skills You'll Need 1. $p \leq 1.25$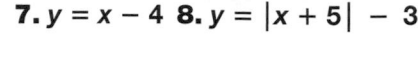

2. $t > 13$

3. $t \leq -3$

4. $c = \pm 4.5$

5. $b = 2, 8$

6. $h \leq -3.5$ or $h \geq 3.5$

Quick Check

1a. 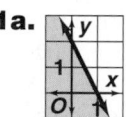 **b.** 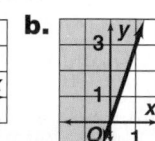 **c.**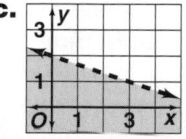

2a. at least 3; Answers may vary. Sample: (2, 5), (1, 6), (0, 7) **b.** $7x + 5y \geq 35$, $x > 0$, $y > 0$

3a. 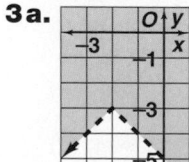 **b.**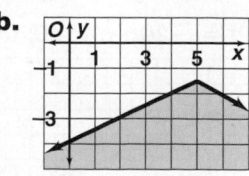

4a. $y \leq |x + 4| - 3$ **b.** $y \geq 2x + 5$

Chapter 3

Check Your Readiness p. 116

1. $7x - 1$ **2.** $5 - p$ **3.** $-6z + 10$ **4.** $r - 4$

5. $a \leq \frac{3}{2}$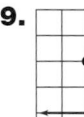

6. $b > 2$

7. $c < -12$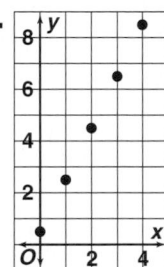

8. $d \leq -1$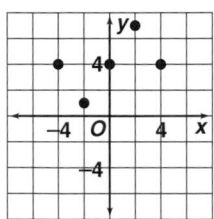

9. 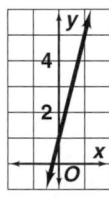 **10.**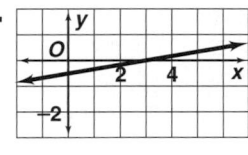

11. 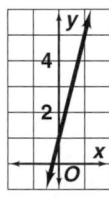 **12.**

13. 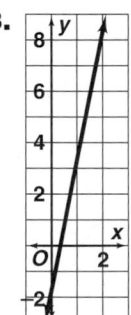 **14.**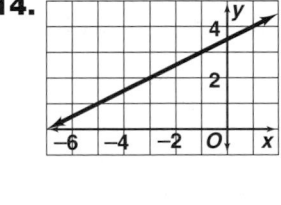

15. $y = 6x$ 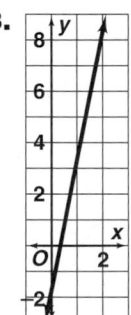 **16.**

17. 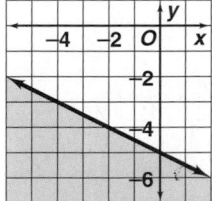 **18.**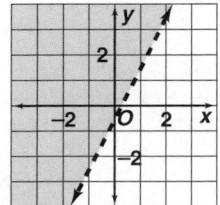

19.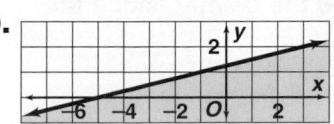

Lesson 3-1 pp. 118–120

Check Skills You'll Need

1. 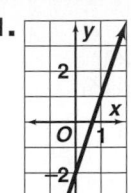 **2.**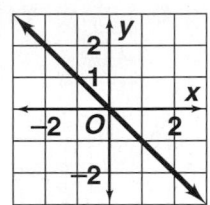

3.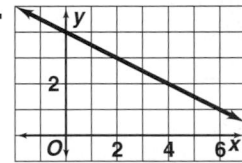

4, 5, 6.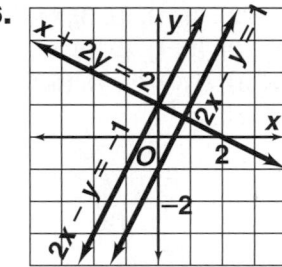

Quick Check

1. (1, 3)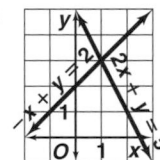

2a. 2008 — men: 43.46 s, women: 47.31 s, 2024 — men: 43.07 s, women: 45.89 s **b.** It would mean that eventually the 400-m run would be run in zero seconds, and this could not happen.
3a. inconsistent **b.** dependent **c.** independent

Lesson 3-2 pp. 125–127

Check Skills You'll Need 1. -4 **2.** x **3.** $-5x$ **4.** $-8y$ **5.** 1
6. -2 **7.** $-\frac{1}{4}$

Quick Check 1.a. $(-6, -6)$ **b.** $(2, 6)$

2. $\begin{cases} c = 15.49x \\ c = 6 + 13.99x \end{cases}$ The number of CDs is 4.

3a. $(4, -1)$ **b.** $(-2, 1)$ **4.** Answers may vary. Sample: Multiply (1) by -5. Multiply (2) by 3. Add equations together, solving for y. Substitute the value of y into either original equation and solve for x. **5a.** infinite number of solutions $\{(x, y)| -3x + 5y = 7\}$ **b.** no solution

Lesson 3-3
pp. 133–135, 138

Check Skills You'll Need 1. $x > \frac{33}{5}$ 2. $y \leq -14$ 3. $x > -\frac{7}{5}$

4.  5. 6.  7.

8. 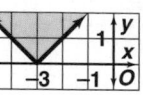 9.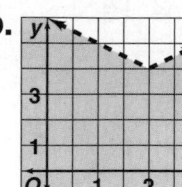

Quick Check

1a. (0, 1), (1, 2), (2, 3), (3, 4), (4, 5), (5, 6), (6, 7)

1b. (1, 0), (2, 1), (2, 0), (3, 2), (3, 1), (3, 0), (4, 3), (4, 2), (4, 1), (4, 0), (5, 3), (5, 2), (5, 1), (5, 0), (6, 3), (6, 2), (6, 1), (6, 0), (7, 2), (7,1), (7,0), (8, 1), (8, 0), (9, 1), (9, 0), (10, 0)

2a. 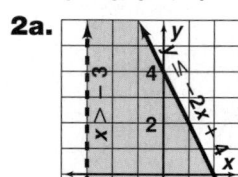 **b.**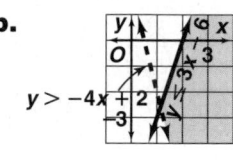

3. $\begin{cases} 550 \leq m \leq 800 \\ v \leq 800 \\ v + m \geq 1100 \end{cases}$

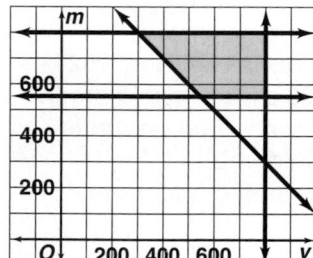

4a. 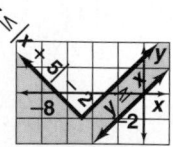 **b.**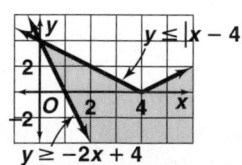

Checkpoint Quiz 1 1. (4, −3) 2. (7, 0) 3. (2, −4) 4. (1, 3)

5. $\begin{cases} 2n + 3m = 158 \\ 2n + 5m = 181 \end{cases}$ $61.75 cost per night, $11.50 cost per meal **6.** approximately 4.8 years

7a. $\begin{cases} h \geq 18 \\ s \geq 12 \\ s + h \leq 35 \end{cases}$ **b.**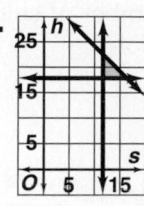

8. 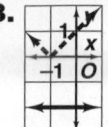 9. 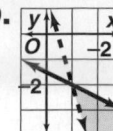 10.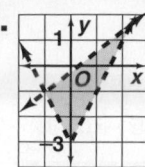

Lesson 3-4
pp. 139–141

Check Skills You'll Need 1. (2, −3) 2. (1, 2) 3. (1, 1)

4. 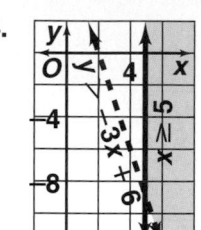 5. 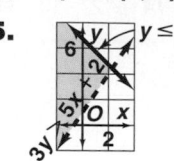 $y \leq -x + 7$

6. 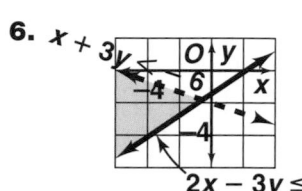 $2x - 3y \leq 4$

Quick Check 1. $P = 2(0) + 3(0) = 0$, $P = 2(2) + 3(0) = 4$, $P = 2(4) + 3(3) = 17$, $P = 2(0) + 3(7) = 21$
When $x = 0$ and $y = 7$, P is maximized at 21.
When $x = 0$ and $y = 0$, P is minimized at 0.
2. Order 25 cases of mixed nuts and no cases of roasted peanuts.

Lesson 3-5
pp. 146–148, 151

Check Skills You'll Need 1. x: −3, y: 6 2. x: 18, y: 4
3. x: −8, y: 3 4. x: 10, y: −8

5.  6. 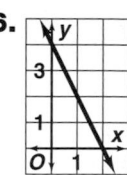 7. 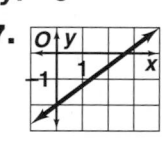 8.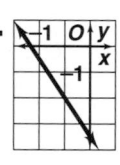

Quick Check

1a. 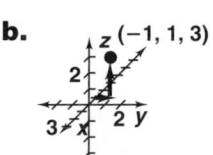 (0, −4, −2) **b.** (−1, 1, 3)

c. (3, −5, 2) 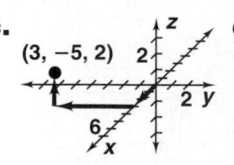 **d.** (3, 3, −3)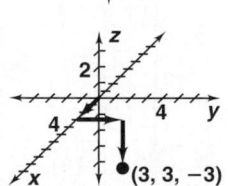

2a. (0, 5, 0) **b.** outside the helmet, since the helmet is curved

3a.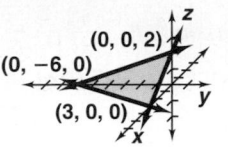

b.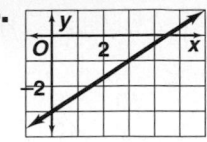

c.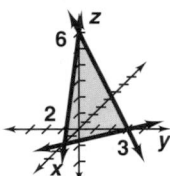

Checkpoint Quiz 2 1. C = 25 for (5, 5) **2.** 300 acres corn and 100 acres soybeans

3. 3x + 2y + z = 6

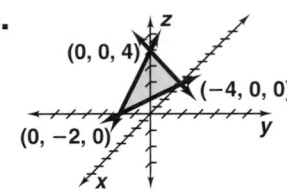

4. 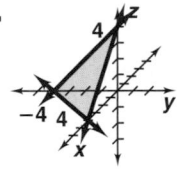 **5.**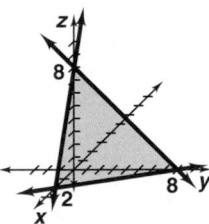

Lesson 3-6　　　　　pp. 152–156

Check Skills You'll Need 1. (3, −5) **2.** no solution

3. (1, −4) **4.** 1 **5.** 1 **6.** $\frac{1}{2}$ **7.** yes **8.** yes

Quick Check 1a. (1, 2, −1) **b.** (3, 3, 1) **c.** No; you wouldn't need to use any of the original equations twice. **2.** (2, −1, 1) **3a.** (4, 1, 5) **b.** (2, 0, −6) **4.** $1400 growth, $1100 income, and $700 money market

Chapter 4

Check Your Readiness　　　　　p. 166

1. 6 **2.** $\frac{1}{3}$ **3.** $-\frac{3}{8}$ **4.** $\frac{7}{12}$ **5.** $\frac{10}{3}$ **6.** −9 **7.** $-\frac{17}{4}$

8. all real numbers **9.** $t > -\frac{11}{4}$ **10.** $s < 2$

11. 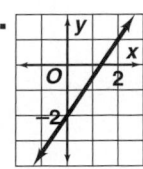 **12.** 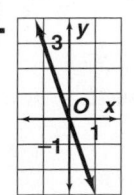 **13.**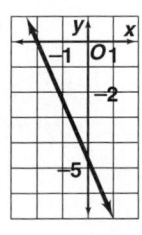

14. 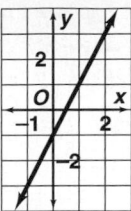 **15.**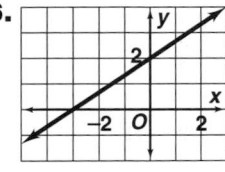

16. 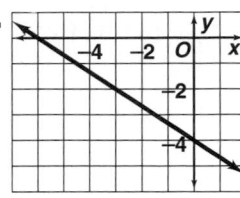 **17.**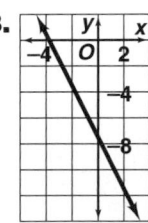

18. **19.** $\left(\frac{1}{2}, -4\right)$ **20.** $\left(-\frac{2}{3}, -\frac{2}{3}\right)$ **21.** $\left(\frac{3}{4}, \frac{11}{4}\right)$
22. (7, 9, −6) **23.** (0, 0, 8)
24. (7, 5, 0)

Lesson 4-1　　　　　pp. 168–170

Check Skills You'll Need 1. 3.116 million units; 4.115 million units **2.** 0.829 million units **3.** 3.126 million units **4.** The export percent increase of 8.3% was larger than the 48.9% increase for the imports.

Quick Check 1a. 2 × 3 **b.** 1 × 3 **c.** 3 × 2
2a. 15 **b.** 17 **c.** 10.4 **d.** 24

3a.

	China	Russia	United States
Production	42	46	71
Consumption	43	28	98

b. Add a new column for each additional country.
c. A c × d matrix has c rows and d columns, while a d × c matrix has d rows and c columns.

4a.
$$\begin{bmatrix} 9.725 & 9.700 & 9.587 & 9.137 & 9.837 & 9.837 \\ 9.650 & 8.537 & 9.712 & 9.412 & 9.775 & 9.725 \\ 9.512 & 9.650 & 9.725 & 9.700 & 9.712 & 9.475 \end{bmatrix}$$
b. 9.837; Paul Hamm's score on the parallel bars

Lesson 4-2　　　　　pp. 174–177

Check Skills You'll Need 1. $\begin{bmatrix} 14 & 4 \\ 2 & -1 \end{bmatrix}$ **2.** $\begin{bmatrix} 3 & 1 \\ -3 & -2 \end{bmatrix}$

3. $\begin{bmatrix} 1 & -3 \\ -2 & -2 \end{bmatrix}$ **4.** $\begin{bmatrix} 4 & 13 \\ -2 & 12 \end{bmatrix}$ **5.** $\begin{bmatrix} 4 & -6 \\ 8 & -3 \end{bmatrix}$

6. $\begin{bmatrix} 6 & -2 \\ 1 & 7 \end{bmatrix}$

Quick Check **1a.** $\begin{bmatrix} 4 & 7 & -3 \\ -6 & 1 & 19 \end{bmatrix}$

b. $\begin{bmatrix} -15 & 25 \\ -1 & 1 \\ -2 & 15 \end{bmatrix}$ **2a.** $\begin{bmatrix} 0 & 0 \\ 0 & 0 \end{bmatrix}$ **b.** $\begin{bmatrix} -1 & 10 & -5 \\ 0 & 2 & -3 \end{bmatrix}$

3a. $\begin{bmatrix} 10 & -12 & 7 \\ -8 & -4 & -2 \end{bmatrix}$ **b.** $\begin{bmatrix} 0 & 4 \\ -3 & 14 \end{bmatrix}$ **4.** $\begin{bmatrix} 11 & 7 \\ -6 & -1 \end{bmatrix}$

5a. no **b.** yes **6a.** $x = 30, y = 2$
b. $x = -3, y = 7$

Lesson 4-3 pp. 182–186, 189

Check Skills You'll Need **1.** $\begin{bmatrix} 9 & 15 \\ 6 & 24 \end{bmatrix}$ **2.** $\begin{bmatrix} -20 \\ 35 \end{bmatrix}$

3. $\begin{bmatrix} -4 & 12 & 16 \\ 0 & -8 & -20 \end{bmatrix}$

Quick Check **1.** $\begin{bmatrix} -45 & 36 & -30 & 0 \\ -60 & 30 & -21 & 0 \end{bmatrix}$

2a. $\begin{bmatrix} 7 & -12 & 58 \\ -9 & 24 & -10 \end{bmatrix}$ **b.** $\begin{bmatrix} 20 & 3 & 29 \\ -5 & 52 & 17 \end{bmatrix}$

3a. $\begin{bmatrix} 1 & 6 \\ 2 & 0 \end{bmatrix}$ **b.** $\begin{bmatrix} -1 & 0 & -3 \\ 7 & 5 & -2 \end{bmatrix}$

4a. $\begin{bmatrix} 12 & -12 \\ -5 & 0 \end{bmatrix}$ **b.** No; explanations may vary.
Sample: For the matrices in part (a),

$$AB = \begin{bmatrix} 12 & -12 \\ -5 & 0 \end{bmatrix}.$$

However, $BA = \begin{bmatrix} 3 & -3 \\ -29 & 9 \end{bmatrix}$, so $AB \neq BA$.

5a. [105] **b.** Product does not exist. **6a.** *RS* is defined, but *SR* is undefined.

b. $RS = \begin{bmatrix} 28 & 10 & -6 & -16 \\ 32 & 20 & -9 & -32 \end{bmatrix}$

Checkpoint Quiz 1 **1.** 3×2; 1 **2.** 2×3; -2 **3.** 3×3; 5

4. $\begin{bmatrix} -2 & 4 \\ 6 & 16 \end{bmatrix}$ **5.** $\begin{bmatrix} 1 & 5 \\ -4 & -7 \end{bmatrix}$ **6.** $\begin{bmatrix} 4.5 & 6 \\ 27 & -18 \end{bmatrix}$

7. $\begin{bmatrix} 42 & 46 \\ 3 & 1 \end{bmatrix}$ **8.** $\begin{bmatrix} 50 & 117 \\ 278 & 495 \end{bmatrix}$

9. Make sure that the number of columns in the first matrix is the same as the number of rows in the second matrix.

10. Answers may vary. Sample: $2X +$
$\begin{bmatrix} 1 & 2 & 2 & 4 \\ 0 & 3 & 0 & 5 \end{bmatrix} = \begin{bmatrix} 25 & 16 & -4 & 20 \\ 18 & 3 & -22 & 7 \end{bmatrix}$

Lesson 4-4 pp. 191–195

Check Skills You'll Need

1.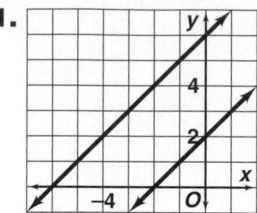
$y = x + 6$

2.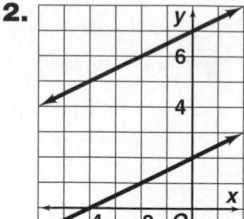
$f(x) = \frac{1}{2}x + 7$

3.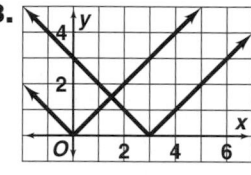
$g(x) = |x - 3|$

4.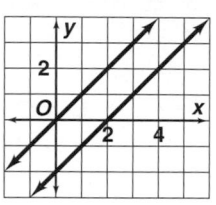
$y = x - 2$

5.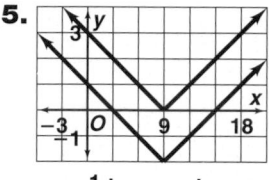
$y = \frac{1}{3}|x - 3| - 2$

6.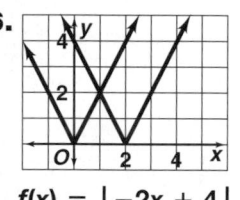
$f(x) = |-2x + 4|$

Quick Check **1a.** Subtract 6 from each x-coordinate and add 2 to each y-coordinate.

b. $\begin{bmatrix} -3 & -3 & -3 & -3 & -3 \\ 2 & 2 & 2 & 2 & 2 \end{bmatrix}$

c. $(-3, -3), (-4, 1), (-8, 2), (-2, 5), (1, 2)$

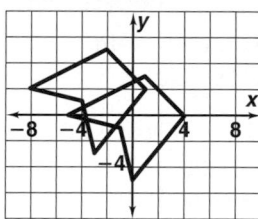

2a. $(-20, 0), (32, -4), (16, 20)$

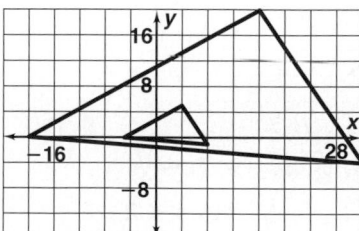

b. (−1, 0), (1.6, −0.2), (0.8, 1)

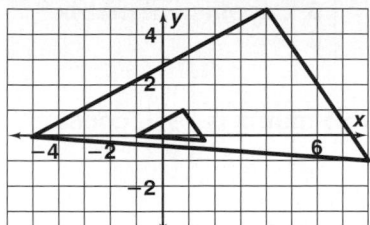

c. (7.5, 0), (−12, 1.5), (−6, −7.5)

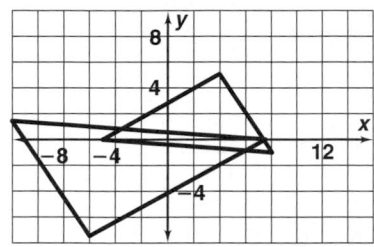

3a. $\begin{bmatrix} 3 & 4 & -1 \\ 0 & 4 & 1 \end{bmatrix}$

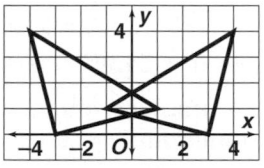

b. $\begin{bmatrix} -3 & -4 & 1 \\ 0 & -4 & -1 \end{bmatrix}$

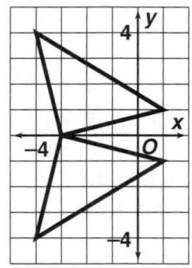

c. $\begin{bmatrix} 0 & 4 & 1 \\ -3 & -4 & 1 \end{bmatrix}$

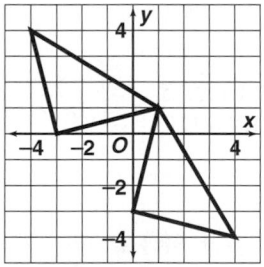

d. $\begin{bmatrix} 0 & -4 & -1 \\ 3 & 4 & -1 \end{bmatrix}$

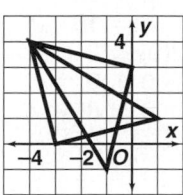

4a. $\begin{bmatrix} -1 & -1 & -4 & -3 \\ 1 & 3 & 6 & 1 \end{bmatrix}$

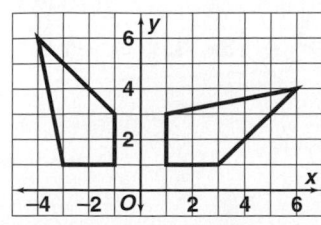

b. $\begin{bmatrix} -1 & -3 & -6 & -1 \\ -1 & -1 & -4 & -3 \end{bmatrix}$

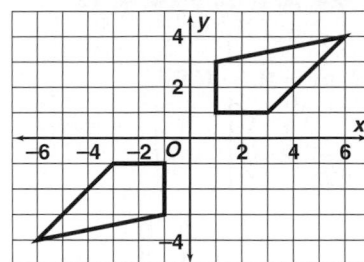

c. $\begin{bmatrix} 1 & 1 & 4 & 3 \\ -1 & -3 & -6 & -1 \end{bmatrix}$

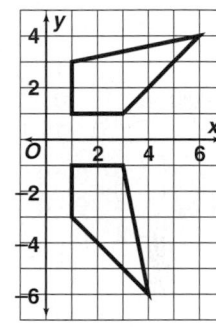

d. $\begin{bmatrix} 1 & 3 & 6 & 1 \\ 1 & 1 & 4 & 3 \end{bmatrix}$

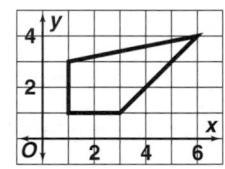

Lesson 4-5   pp. 199–203

Check Skills You'll Need 1a. 12 **b.** 12 **c.** 0 **2a.** −12
b. −12 **c.** 0 **3a.** 12 **b.** −12 **c.** 24 **4a.** −12 **b.** 12
c. −24

Quick Check 1a. $\begin{bmatrix} 2 & 1 \\ 2.5 & 1 \end{bmatrix}\begin{bmatrix} -2 & 2 \\ 5 & -4 \end{bmatrix} =$

$\begin{bmatrix} 2(-2) + 1(5) & 2(2) + 1(-4) \\ 2.5(-2) + 1(5) & 2.5(2) + 1(-4) \end{bmatrix} = \begin{bmatrix} 1 & 0 \\ 0 & 1 \end{bmatrix}$

b. $\begin{bmatrix} -2 & -5 \\ -3 & -8 \end{bmatrix}\begin{bmatrix} -8 & 5 \\ 3 & -2 \end{bmatrix} =$

$\begin{bmatrix} -2(-8) + (-5)(3) & -2(5) + (-5)(-2) \\ -3(-8) + (-8)(3) & -3(5) + (-8)(-2) \end{bmatrix}$

$= \begin{bmatrix} 1 & 0 \\ 0 & 1 \end{bmatrix}$ **2a.** 0 **b.** 10 **c.** −9

3a. yes; $\begin{bmatrix} 1.5 & -2 \\ -0.5 & 1 \end{bmatrix}$ **b.** yes; $\begin{bmatrix} -\frac{24}{11} & \frac{23}{33} \\ \frac{10}{11} & \frac{-5}{33} \end{bmatrix}$

4a. $\begin{bmatrix} 0 & -2 \\ 0 & 4 \end{bmatrix}$ **b.** $\begin{bmatrix} -2 \\ 1 \end{bmatrix}$

5a. 43.3%, 62.0%, 70.3%; 73.9% **b.** about
11,829 people **c.** about 102 people

Check Skills You'll Need **1.** -24 **2.** 0 **3.** -24 **4.** 12
5. 12 **6.** 0

Quick Check **1a.** 27 **b.** 22 **c.** 0 **2.** -1087

3a. The matrices $\begin{bmatrix} 0 & 0 & 1 \\ 0.2 & -0.2 & 0 \\ 0 & -1 & 1 \end{bmatrix}$ and

$\begin{bmatrix} 1 & 5 & -1 \\ 1 & 0 & -1 \\ 1 & 0 & 0 \end{bmatrix}$ have a product of $\begin{bmatrix} 1 & 0 & 0 \\ 0 & 1 & 0 \\ 0 & 0 & 1 \end{bmatrix}$, so

they are inverses.

b. The matrices $\begin{bmatrix} 0 & 1 & 0 \\ 1 & 0 & 1 \\ 0 & 1 & 0 \end{bmatrix}$ and $\begin{bmatrix} 3 & 4 & 1 \\ -2 & 0 & 2 \\ 1 & 5 & 3 \end{bmatrix}$ have

a product of $\begin{bmatrix} -2 & 0 & 2 \\ 4 & 9 & 4 \\ -2 & 0 & 2 \end{bmatrix}$, so they are not

inverses.

4a. The matrices $\begin{bmatrix} 0 & 0 & 2 \\ 1 & 3 & -2 \\ 1 & -2 & 1 \end{bmatrix}$ and

$\begin{bmatrix} 0.1 & 0.4 & 0.6 \\ 0.3 & 0.2 & -0.2 \\ 0.5 & 0 & 0 \end{bmatrix}$ have a product of $\begin{bmatrix} 1 & 0 & 0 \\ 0 & 1 & 0 \\ 0 & 0 & 1 \end{bmatrix}$,

so they are inverses.

b. $\begin{bmatrix} 9 \\ -5 \\ 0 \end{bmatrix}$ **5.** POETRY

Checkpoint Quiz 2 **1.** $A'(-2, 8)$, $B'(-8, 0)$, $C'(2, -2)$
2. $A'(-4, 7)$, $B'(-7, 3)$, $C'(-2, 2)$ **3.** $A'(4, 1)$, $B'(0, 4)$,
$C'(-1, -1)$ **4.** $A'(-4, 1)$, $B'(0, 4)$, $C'(1, -1)$

5. $\begin{bmatrix} 2 & 3 \\ -4 & -5 \end{bmatrix}$ **6.** $\begin{bmatrix} 5 \\ 2 \\ 6 \end{bmatrix}$ **7.** $\begin{bmatrix} -2 \\ 8 \end{bmatrix}$ **8.** -10 **9.** 18

10. -71

Check Skills You'll Need **1.** $(2, 4)$ **2.** $(0, 6, 3)$ **3.** $(3, -3, 9)$

Quick Check **1a.** $\begin{bmatrix} 3 & 2 \\ 0 & 1 \end{bmatrix}\begin{bmatrix} x \\ y \end{bmatrix} = \begin{bmatrix} 16 \\ 5 \end{bmatrix}$;

coefficient matrix is $\begin{bmatrix} 3 & 2 \\ 0 & 1 \end{bmatrix}$, variable matrix is $\begin{bmatrix} x \\ y \end{bmatrix}$,

constant matrix is $\begin{bmatrix} 16 \\ 5 \end{bmatrix}$.

b. $\begin{bmatrix} 1 & -1 & 1 \\ 1 & -2 & -1 \\ 2 & -1 & 2 \end{bmatrix}\begin{bmatrix} x \\ y \\ z \end{bmatrix} = \begin{bmatrix} 0 \\ 5 \\ 8 \end{bmatrix}$; coefficient matrix

is $\begin{bmatrix} 1 & -1 & 1 \\ 1 & -2 & -1 \\ 2 & -1 & 2 \end{bmatrix}$, variable matrix is $\begin{bmatrix} x \\ y \\ z \end{bmatrix}$, constant

matrix is $\begin{bmatrix} 0 \\ 5 \\ 8 \end{bmatrix}$. **2a.** $(-1, 4)$ **b.** $(-2, 8)$

3a. $2(4) + (-10) + 3(1) \overset{?}{=} 1$
$8 - 10 + 3 \overset{?}{=} 1$
$1 = 1$
$5(4) + (-10) - 2(1) \overset{?}{=} 8$
$20 - 10 - 2 \overset{?}{=} 8$
$8 = 8$
$4 - (-10) - 9(1) \overset{?}{=} 5$
$4 + 10 - 9 \overset{?}{=} 5$
$5 = 5$

b. $(1.25, 2.5, -1.75)$

4. one large bead = \$1.95, one small bead = \$.55

5a. yes **b.** The graphing calculator indicates that
there is a "singular matrix" error.

Check Skills You'll Need **1.** -3 **2.** 1 **3.** 11 **4.** -18 **5.** 15
6. -35

Quick Check **1.** $(1, 2)$ **2a.** In D, replace the
coefficients of z with the constants. **b.** $y = 1$,

$z = 1$ **3a.** $\begin{bmatrix} 1 & -5 & | & 15 \\ 3 & 3 & | & 3 \end{bmatrix}$ **b.** $\begin{bmatrix} 1 & 2 & 3 & | & -4 \\ 0 & 1 & -2 & | & 8 \\ 0 & 0 & 1 & | & -3 \end{bmatrix}$

4a. $\begin{cases} 5x + 7y = -3 \\ -8y = 6 \end{cases}$ **b.** $\begin{cases} -x + 3z = -4 \\ 7x + 2y - z = 0 \\ y + 2z = -3 \end{cases}$

5. $(-15, 5)$

6a. $3(4) - 2(1) + 4(0) \overset{?}{=} 10$
$12 - 2 + 0 \overset{?}{=} 10$
$10 = 10$ ✓
$4 + 4(1) - 2(0) \overset{?}{=} 8$
$4 + 4 - 0 \overset{?}{=} 8$
$8 = 8$ ✓

b. $(-1, 2, 3)$

Chapter 5

Check Your Readiness   p. 236

1. $4x^2 - 5x$ **2.** $\frac{11x^2}{30}$ **3.** $-7x^2 - 13x$ **4.** $\frac{2}{3}$ **5.** -1.8
6. 1

7. 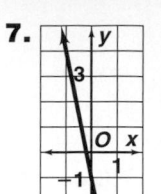 **8.** 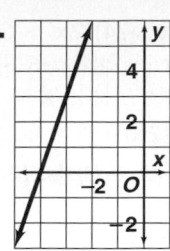 **9.**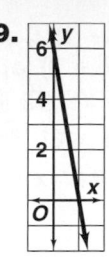

10. 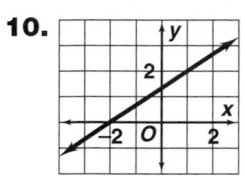 **11.**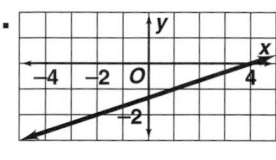

12. 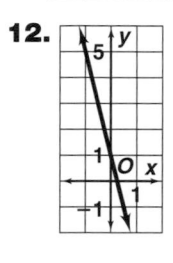 **13.**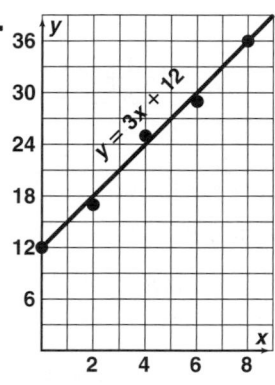

Sample: $y = 3x + 12$

14.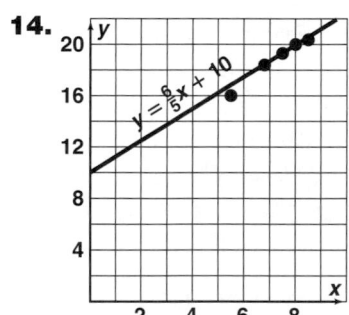

Sample: $y = \frac{6}{5}x + 10$

15. 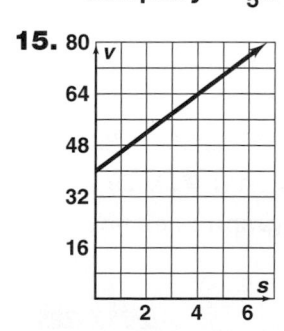 **16.** $y = |x|$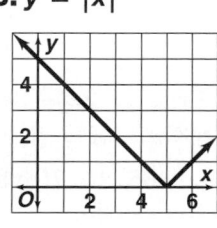

$v = 6s + 40$

Lesson 5-1 pp. 238–240

Check Skills You'll Need **1.** $-3, -1, 0, 1, 3$ **2.** $9, 1, 0, 1,$ 9 **3.** $3, 1, 0, -1, -3$ **4.** $-9, -1, 0, -1, -9$ **5.** $3, \frac{1}{3},$ $0, \frac{1}{3}, 3$ **6.** $-3, -\frac{1}{3}, 0, -\frac{1}{3}, -3$ **7.** $y = -\frac{3}{4}x + 2$ **8.** $y = 2x + 7$ **9.** $y = -\frac{1}{6}x + 3$

Quick Check **1a.** linear; none, $5x$, none
b. quadratic; $3x^2$, $-16x$, 5 **c.** quadratic; x^2, $3x$,
none **2a.** $(1, -1)$, $x = 1$; $P'(3, 3)$, $Q'(0, 0)$
b. $(-1, 2)$, $x = -1$; $P'(0, 1)$, $Q'(-3, -2)$
3. $y = -2x^2 + 3x - 1$ **4a.** 73 mm **b.** 39 mm
c. No; the tank is empty at 109 seconds.

Lesson 5-2 pp. 245–247

Check Skills You'll Need **1.** 3 **2.** -1 **3.** -4 **4.** $(0, 0)$
5. $\left(-\frac{3}{2}, 0\right)$ **6.** $\left(-\frac{7}{3}, 0\right)$

7. 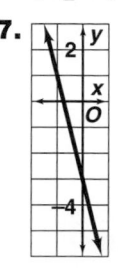 **8.** 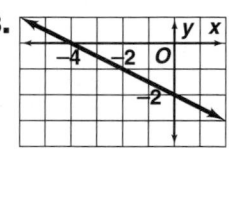 **9.**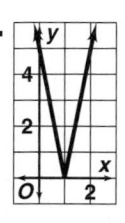

Quick Check

1a. 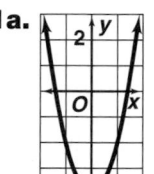 **b.** 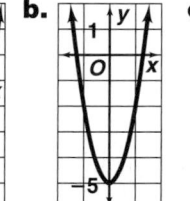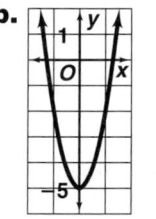 **c.** $(0, 0)$

2a. 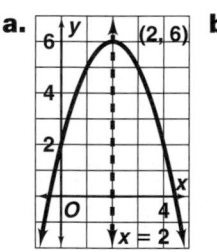 **b.**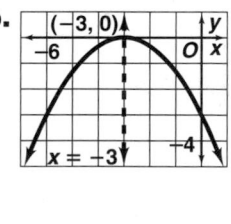

3a. 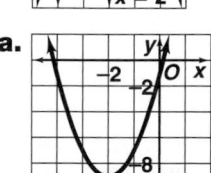 minimum: -9
b. none

4. \$10; \$500

Lesson 5-3 pp. 252–255, 258

Check Skills You'll Need
1. $y = x$ **2.** $y = |x|$

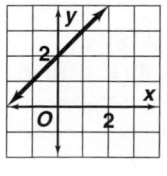 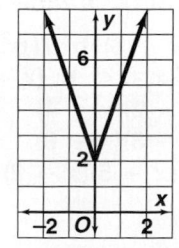

Answers to Instant Check System **955**

Instant Check System Answers

3. $y = |x|$

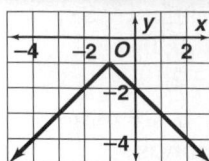

4. $y = x - 2$ **5.** $y = -|x + 1| - 1$

Quick Check

1a.

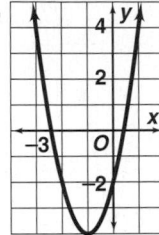

b. Check students' work.
2. $y = 2(x + 1)^2$ **3.** $y = 0.00015(x - 2000)^2$
4. $y = -3(x - 2)^2 + 17$

Checkpoint Quiz 1 **1.** $y = x^2 + 6x + 3$
2. $y = -2x^2 + 4x + 1$ **3.** $y = 5x^2 - 10x$

4. 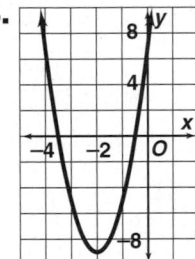 **5.**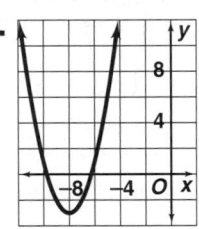

6.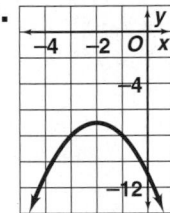

7. max.; 14 **8.** min.; 7 **9.** $y = -3(x + 1)^2 - 5$;
$(-1, -5)$; $x = -1$ **10.** Answers may vary.
Sample: $y = (x - 3)^2 + 2$; $x = 3$; $(0, 11)$, $(6, 11)$

Lesson 5-4   pp. 259–263

Check Skills You'll Need **1.** $x^2 + 5x - 1$
2. $6x^2 - 10x - 3$ **3.** $4x^2 - x - 10$ **4.** $-2x^2 + 10x$
5. $4x^2 - 28x + 49$ **6.** $16x^2 - 9$

Quick Check **1a.** $3(3x^2 + x - 6)$ **b.** $7(p^2 + 3)$ **c.**
$2w(2w + 1)$ **2a.** $(x + 2)(x + 4)$ **b.** $(x + 4)(x + 8)$ **c.**
$(x + 4)(x + 10)$ **3a.** $(x - 2)(x - 4)$
b. $(x - 3)(x - 4)$ **c.** $(x - 3)(x - 8)$
4a. $(x + 2)(x - 16)$ **b.** $(x + 5)(x - 2)$

---

c. $(x + 5)(x - 1)$ **5a.** $(x + 4)(2x + 3)$
b. $(x + 1)(4x + 3)$ **c.** $(x - 2)(2x - 3)$
6a. $(x - 1)(2x + 9)$ **b.** $(x - 6)(3x + 2)$
c. $(x + 2)(4x - 3)$ **7a.** $(2x + 3)^2$ **b.** $(8x - 1)^2$
c. $(5x + 9)^2$ **8a.** $(x - 8)(x + 8)$ **b.** $(2a + 7)(2a - 7)$

Lesson 5-5   pp. 267–269

Check Skills You'll Need **1.** $(x + 7)(x - 2)$ **2.** $4x(x - 3)$
3. $(3x - 4)(3x + 4)$

4. 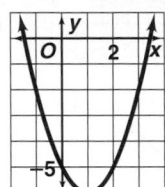 **5.**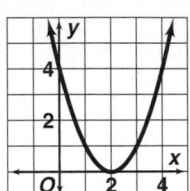

6.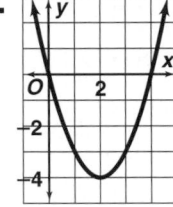

Quick Check **1a.** $-9, 2$ **b.** $-3, 1$ **c.** $0, \frac{1}{2}$
2a. $-\frac{5}{2}, \frac{5}{2}$ **b.** $-2\sqrt{2}, 2\sqrt{2}$ **c.** $-\frac{1}{2}, \frac{1}{2}$ **3a.** 5 s
b. $t = 5$ or $t = -5$, and use positive solution
because it describes time; check students' work.
4. 4.56 **5a.** $-1.24, 3.24$ **b.** $-0.81, 0.31$

Lesson 5-6   pp. 274–277, 280

Check Skills You'll Need **1.** 5 **2.** $2\sqrt{17}$ **3.** 13 **4.** $2\sqrt{34}$
5. $x\sqrt{2}$ **6.** $5x$

Quick Check **1a.** $i\sqrt{2}$ **b.** $2i\sqrt{3}$ **c.** $6i$ **d.** $\sqrt{a^2} = |a|$,
$(\sqrt{a})^2 = a$ **2.** $7 + 3i\sqrt{2}$ **3a.** $2\sqrt{13}$ **b.** $\sqrt{29}$
c. 4 **4a.** $5i$ **b.** $-4 + 3i$ **c.** $-a - bi$ **5a.** $6 - i$
b. $4 - 2i$ **c.** $4 - 3i$ **6a.** -84 **b.** $9 - 38i$
c. $43 - 24i$ **7a.** $\pm 4i$ **b.** $\pm i\sqrt{30}$ **c.** $\pm\frac{1}{2}i$ **8.** $-1 + i$,
$-1 - i$, $-1 + 3i$

Checkpoint Quiz 2 **1.** $(2x - 3)(x + 2)$ **2.** $5(x + 3)(x - 3)$
3. $(2x - 9)^2$ **4.** $-4, 1$ **5.** 1 **6.** $\pm 11i$ **7.** $\sqrt{29}$
8. $\sqrt{82}$ **9.** $\sqrt{65}$ **10.** No; the graph does not
intersect the x-axis.

Lesson 5-7   pp. 282–285

Check Skills You'll Need **1.** $x^2 - 6x + 9$ **2.** $4x^2 - 4x + 1$
3. $x^2 + 8x + 13$ **4.** ± 5 **5.** $\pm 4\sqrt{3}$ **6.** $\pm 2i$ **7.** $\pm\frac{3}{4}$
Quick Check **1.** $-2, 16$ **2.** $\frac{49}{4}$ **3a.** $-2 \pm 2\sqrt{2}$
b. $1 \pm \sqrt{2}$

4a. $x^2 - 8x + 36 = 0$; $(4 + 2i\sqrt{5})^2 - 8(4 + 2i\sqrt{5}) + 36 = 16 + 2(8i\sqrt{5}) + (2i\sqrt{5})^2 - 32 - 16i\sqrt{5} + 36 = (16 - 20 - 32 + 36) + (16i\sqrt{5} - 16i\sqrt{5}) = 0$; $(4 - 2i\sqrt{5})^2 - 8(4 - 2i\sqrt{5}) + 36 = 16 + 2(-8i\sqrt{5}) + (-2i\sqrt{5})^2 - 32 + 16i\sqrt{5} + 36 = 16 - 20 - 32 + 36 + (-16i\sqrt{5} + 16i\sqrt{5}) = 0$

b. The graph has no x-intercepts, so no real solutions. **c.** $-3 \pm 5i$ **5a.** $-2, \frac{3}{2}$ **b.** $\frac{3}{4} \pm \frac{i\sqrt{23}}{4}$
6a. $y = (x - 5)^2 - 27$ **b.** $y = \left(x + \frac{5}{2}\right)^2 - \frac{13}{4}$

7a. (280, 38,000) **b.** The coefficient of s^2 is negative, so the parabola opens downward.

Lesson 5-8 pp. 289–293

Check Skills You'll Need **1.** $y = -10x^2 + 8$ **2.** $y = x^2 + 4x + 3$ **3.** $y = -x^2 + 4x + 1$ **4.** $y = 8x^2 + 2x - 1$
5. 24 **6.** 84 **7.** -48 **8.** 89

Quick Check **1.** $-1, \frac{4}{3}$ **2a.** $-1 \pm \frac{i\sqrt{2}}{2}$

b.

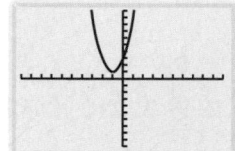

The graph does not intersect the x-axis.
3a. $\frac{1}{2}, \frac{3}{2}$ **b.** $-2 \pm 3\sqrt{5}$; $-8.71, 4.71$
4a. one real solution **b.** two imaginary solutions
5. Yes; the discriminant is positive.

Chapter 6

Check Your Readiness p. 304

1. $y = 2x^2 + 1$ **2.** $y = -\frac{1}{4}x^2 - 1$
3. $y = 3x^2 - 6x + 3$

4.

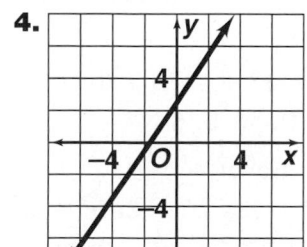

5.

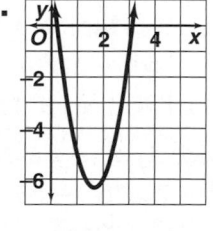

6.

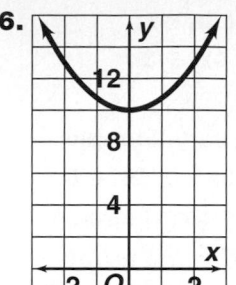

7. $x = -0.25, 1$
8. $x \approx -6.39, 4.39$
9. $x \approx -6.38, 0.38$
10. $x = -4, 9$

11. $x = 3, \frac{7}{2}$ **12.** $x = \frac{2 \pm \sqrt{13}}{3}$
13. 24; 2 real solutions **14.** 0; 1 real solution
15. 0; 1 real solution **16.** $\frac{50}{101}$

Lesson 6-1 pp. 306–309

Check Skills You'll Need **1.** x **2.** $3x^2y - 8xy^2$ **3.** $7x^2 - 3x$ **4.** 1 term **5.** 2 terms **6.** 3 terms

Quick Check **1a.** $-2x + 5$; linear binomial
b. $5x^3 + x^2 - 4x$; cubic trinomial **c.** $-2x^5 + 6$; quintic binomial **2.** Answers may vary. Sample: No; when $x = 25$ then, based on the cubic model, $y \approx 3.76$, but because of its turning points the cubic model is unreliable. **3.** 75.9 million troy oz

Lesson 6-2 pp. 313–316

Check Skills You'll Need **1.** $(x + 4)(x + 3)$ **2.** $(x + 10)(x - 2)$ **3.** $(x - 12)(x - 2)$ **4.** $x^2 + 4x$
5. $x^2 + 2x + 1$ **6.** $x^3 - 4x^2 - 3x + 18$

Quick Check **1.** $x^3 + 4x^2 + 5x + 2$
2. $3x(x - 4)(2x + 3)$ **3.** $V \approx 3014$ in.^{3}, depth 10.5 in., length 20.5 in., width 14 in. **4a.** 7, 5, 3

b.

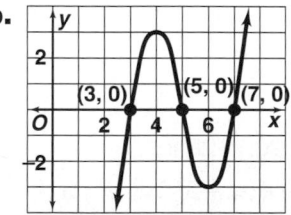

5a. $y = x^3 + 5x^2 + 2x - 8$ **b.** $y = x^3 + 6x^2 + 8x$
c. Answers may vary. Sample: The zero at 0 can be from $x = 0, x^2 = 0, x^3 = 0$, and so on. Each power will lead to a different answer. **6a.** -1, multiplicity of 3 **b.** 2, multiplicity of 2

Lesson 6-3 pp. 320–23, 326

Check Skills You'll Need **1.** $x^2 - x - 10$ **2.** $2x^2 - 5x - 3$
3. $x^2 + 3x - 9$ **4.** $3x^2 + 9x - 30$ **5.** $4x^3 - 2x^2 + 5x + 9$; 4, -2, 5, 9 **6.** $5x^3 - 9x^2 + 10$; 5, -9, 0, 10
7. $-x^2 + 2x + 7$; -1, 2, 7 **8.** $-3x^4 + x^3 - 7x^2$; -3, 1, -7, 0, 0

Quick Check 1. $x + 1$, R 5 **2a.** yes **b.** no
3. $x^2 + 3x - 2$, R -4 **4a.** $x^2 - 4x + 3$
b. $(x + 2)(x - 3)(x - 1)$ **5.** -69

Checkpoint Quiz 1 1. Answers may vary. Sample:
$y = (x + 1)^2(x + 2)(x + 3)$ **2.** $-3x^3 + 5x + 6$;
degree 3, 3 terms **3.** $x^4 - 3x^2 + \frac{5}{2}x$; degree 4,
3 terms **4.** $3x^2 + 9x - 12$; degree 2, 3 terms
5. 1, 2 (mult. 2) **6.** $-\frac{1}{2}$, 4 **7.** 0 (mult. 3),
3, -1 (mult. 2) **8.** $x^2 + 2x + 1$ **9.** $2x^2 - 3x + 1$
10. 479

Lesson 6-4   pp. 327–330

Check Skills You'll Need

1. (1, 4) 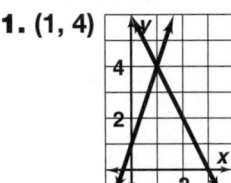 **2.** $\left(1, \frac{2}{3}\right)$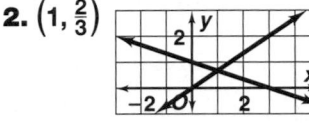

3. no points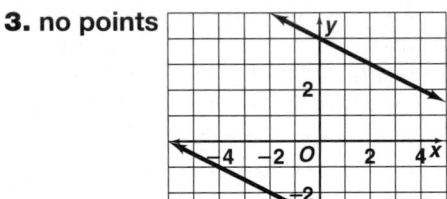

4. $(x - 5)(x + 3)$ **5.** $(x - 7)(x - 2)$ **6.** $(x + 5)(x + 1)$

Quick Check

1. $x = -1$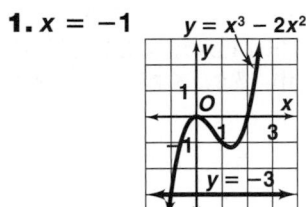

2. 22.7125 in., 25.7125 in., 20.7125 in.

3. $(2x - 1)(4x^2 + 2x + 1)$ **4a.** $-2, 1 \pm i\sqrt{3}$ **b.** $\frac{1}{3}$,
$\frac{-1 \pm i\sqrt{3}}{6}$ **5a.** $(x^2 + 6)(x^2 + 1)$ **b.** $(x^2 - 5)(x^2 + 2)$
6. $3i, -3i, i\sqrt{2}, -i\sqrt{2}$

Lesson 6-5   pp. 335–338

Check Skills You'll Need 1. $\pm1, \pm2, \pm3, \pm4, \pm6, \pm12$
2. $\pm1, \pm2, \pm3, \pm4, \pm6, \pm8, \pm12, \pm24$ **3.** $\pm1, \pm2$,
$\pm3, \pm4, \pm6, \pm9, \pm12, \pm18, \pm36$ **4.** $\pm1, \pm2, \pm3$,
$\pm4, \pm6, \pm8, \pm12, \pm16, \pm24, \pm48$
5. $x^3 - 5x^2 + 7x - 35$ **6.** $x^3 + 2x^2 - 3x - 6$

---

7. A rational number can be written as the
quotient of two integers $\frac{a}{b}$, where $b \neq 0$.
8. Irrational numbers cannot be written as
quotients of integers. **9.** An imaginary number is a
nonreal number of the form $a + bi$, where $b \neq 0$.

Quick Check 1. 4 **2a.** $\pm\sqrt{5}, 2$ **b.** $-1, \frac{1 \pm i\sqrt{2}}{3}$
3a. $2 + \sqrt{7}, -\sqrt{5}$ **b.** No; the Irrational Root
Theorem does not apply unless you know that all
of the coefficients of the polynomial are rational.
4a. $-3i, -2 - i$ **b.** 4 or greater
5a. $x^3 - 3x^2 + x + 5 = 0$ **b.** $x^4 + 5x^2 + 4 = 0$

Lesson 6-6   pp. 341–343

Check Skills You'll Need 1. 2 **2.** 3 **3.** 5 **4.** $\pm4i$
5. $1 \pm i\sqrt{2}$ **6.** $\frac{-5 \pm i\sqrt{7}}{4}$

Quick Check 1. 4 complex roots, number of real
roots: 0, 2, or 4, possible rational roots: $\pm1, \pm3$
2a. 2, $\pm2i$ **b.** You can verify the real zeros by
graphing the function. You can verify the complex
zeros by substituting the values into the function.

Lesson 6-7   pp. 345–347, 351

Check Skills You'll Need 1. 30, 240 **2.** $\frac{4}{5}$ **3.** 210 **4.** 42
5. 36 **6.** 60 **7.** 192

Quick Check 1. 720 **2.** 720 **3a.** 252 **b.** 28
c. 480,700 **4.** 77,520; 125,970 **5.** 638

Checkpoint Quiz 2 1. 1, 3, -2 **2.** $\frac{1}{3}, \frac{-1 \pm i\sqrt{3}}{6}$ **3.** ±3,
$\pm i\sqrt{5}$ **4.** $\frac{1}{2}, \frac{-1 \pm i\sqrt{3}}{2}$ **5.** $-2, 2, -\frac{4}{3}$ **6a.** $3 + 5i$,
$-\sqrt{2}$ **b.** Degree must be ≥ 4. **7.** 5; by the
corollary to the Fundamental Theorem of Algebra
8a. 744 **b.** 10 **9a.** 21 **b.** 35 **c.** 35 **d.** 21
10. 5040

Lesson 6-8   pp. 353–355

Check Skills You'll Need 1. $x^2 + 4x + 4$ **2.** $4x^2 + 12x +$
9 **3.** $x^3 - 9x^2 + 27x - 27$ **4.** $a^4 + 4a^3b + 6a^2b^2 +$
$4ab^3 + b^4$ **5.** 1 **6.** 5 **7.** 10 **8.** 10 **9.** 5

Quick Check 1. $a^8 + 8a^7b + 28a^6b^2 +$
$56a^5b^3 + 70a^4b^4 + 56a^3b^5 + 28a^2b^6 + 8ab^7 + b^8$
2. $x^4 - 8x^3 + 24x^2 - 32x + 16$ **3a.** $v^9 + 9v^8w +$
$36v^7w^2 + 84v^6w^3 + 126v^5w^4 + 126v^4w^5 +$
$84v^3w^6 + 36v^2w^7 + 9vw^8 + w^9$ **b.** $c^5 - 10c^4 +$
$40c^3 - 80c^2 + 80c - 32$ **4a.** about 0.387
b. about 0.349

Chapter 7

Check Your Readiness   p. 366

1. $3y^2 - 14y + 8$ **3.** $x^3 + 4x^2 - 15x - 18$ **5.** $8b^3$
7. $6a^6$ **9.** $-2, 7$ **11.** $-4, \frac{2}{3}$ **15.** domain $\{1, 2, 3, 4\}$,
range $\{2, 3, 4, 5\}$ **17.** domain $\{x \mid x \in R\}$,
range $\{y \mid y \in R\}$

19. 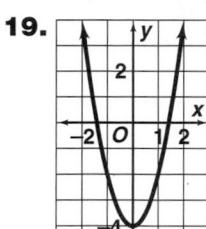 **21.**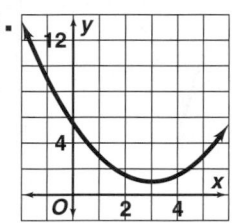

Lesson 7-1   pp. 369–371

Check Skills You'll Need **1.** 5^2 **2.** 0.3^2 **3.** $\left(\frac{2}{7}\right)^2$ **4.** $(x^5)^2$
5. $(x^2y)^2$ **6.** $(13x^3y^6)^2$

Quick Check **1a.** $0; -1; 2$ **b.** 0.01 and -0.01,
no real square root, $\frac{6}{11}$ and $-\frac{6}{11}$ **2a.** -3 **b.** 3 **c.** 7
3a. $2|x|y^2$ **b.** $-3c^2$ **c.** $x^2|y^3|$ **4a.** 2.29 in. **b.** 2.8 in.
c. 2.92 in.

Lesson 7-2   pp. 374–377

Check Skills You'll Need **1.** 6 **2.** 3 **3.** 3 **4.** x^2 **5.** ab
6. $5a^3b^4$

Quick Check **1a.** 6 **b.** -3 **c.** not possible
2. $5x^2\sqrt{2}$; $x\sqrt[3]{18x}$ **3.** $42x^3y\sqrt{3}$ **4a.** 3 **b.** $2x\sqrt{x}$
c. $4x^3\sqrt[4]{x^2}$ **5a.** $\frac{\sqrt{35}}{5}$ **b.** $\frac{x\sqrt{5y}}{5y}$ **c.** $\frac{\sqrt[3]{18x^2}}{3x}$ **6.** $t = \frac{\sqrt{da}}{a}$

Lesson 7-3   pp. 380–382, 384

Check Skills You'll Need **1.** $15x^2 + 2x - 8$
2. $-24x^2 + 71x - 35$ **3.** $x^2 - 16$ **4.** $16x^2 - 25$
5. $x^2 + 10x + 25$ **6.** $4x^2 - 36x + 81$

Quick Check **1a.** $5\sqrt{7}$ **b.** cannot combine
c. $9\sqrt{xy}$ **2.** $60\sqrt{2}$ in. or about 84.9 in. **3.** $2\sqrt{2}$
4. $5 - 2\sqrt{6}$ **5.** 3 **6.** $39 + 10\sqrt{15}$

Checkpoint Quiz 1 **1.** $|b|c^2$ **2.** xy^2 **3.** $-a$ **4.** $-y^2$
5. $8\sqrt{3} + 24$ **6.** $12x^3y\sqrt{35}$ **7.** $12\sqrt[3]{3} - 9\sqrt[3]{2}$
8. $\frac{4\sqrt{10x}}{45x}$ **9.** -7 **10.** $\frac{20\sqrt{7} - 25}{87}$

Lesson 7-4   pp. 385–388

Check Skills You'll Need **1.** $\frac{1}{16}$ **2.** $\frac{1}{9x^2}$ **3.** $\frac{1}{125x^6y^3}$ **4.** $\frac{1}{2}$
5. $\frac{16b^{12}}{a^8}$ **6.** $\frac{b^2}{16a^6}$

Quick Check 1a. 2 b. 2 c. 4 2a.

Quick Check **1a.** 2 **b.** 2 **c.** 4 **2a.** $\frac{1}{\sqrt[8]{y^3}}$, $\sqrt[5]{z^2}$
b. $x^{\frac{2}{3}}$, $y^{\frac{3}{2}}$ **c.** If m is negative, $a^{\frac{m}{n}} = \frac{1}{(\sqrt[n]{a})^m}$, and if
$a = 0$, then the denominator of the fraction would
be zero. Since this cannot happen, $a \neq 0$.
3. about 0.270 revolutions per second, or about
16 revolutions per minute **4a.** $\frac{1}{125}$ **b.** 8 **c.** 16
5. $\frac{1}{2x^5}$

Lesson 7-5   pp. 391–394

Check Skills You'll Need **1.** $-3, 2$ **2.** $-2, 7$ **3.** $1, -\frac{3}{2}$
4. $-\frac{1}{3}, 2$ **5.** $-\frac{5}{2}, \frac{1}{2}$ **6.** $-\frac{2}{3}, \frac{3}{2}$

Quick Check **1.** 7 **2.** 6 **3.** about 25.1 watts; it is
4 times the power of a 10-cm cell. **4.** 10 **5.** 5

Lesson 7-6   pp. 398–400, 404

Check Skills You'll Need **1.** D: $\{0, 2, 4\}$, R: $\{-5, -3, -1\}$
2. D: $\{-1, 0, 1\}$, R: 0 **3.** D: all real numbers, R: all
real numbers **4.** D: all real numbers, R: all real
numbers ≥ 0 **5.** 10 **6.** 28

Quick Check **1.** $(f + g)(x) = 5x^2 + x + 1$, domain: all
real numbers; $(f - g)(x) = 5x^2 - 9x - 1$, domain:
all real numbers **2.** $(f \cdot g)(x) = 12x^3 + 8x^2 - 17x +$
5, domain: all real numbers; $\left(\frac{f}{g}\right)(x) = 3x + 5$,
domain: all real numbers except $\frac{1}{2}$
3a. $(f \circ g)(x) = x^2 - 2$, $(f \circ g)(-5) = 23$ **b.** No; the
order in which operations are performed changes
between $(f \circ g)$ and $(g \circ f)$, which changes what
each composition equals. **4a.** Let $f(x) = 0.9x$ and
$g(x) = 0.75x$. Then $(g \circ f)(x) = g(0.9x) = 0.75(0.9x)$.
b. $(f \circ g)(x) = f(0.75x) = 0.9(0.75)x$. **c.** It makes no
difference.

Checkpoint Quiz 2 **1.** $81x^4$ **2.** $\frac{1}{4y^2}$ **3.** 5 **4.** $5, -\frac{29}{5}$
5. $-\frac{2}{3}, -1$ **6.** -2 **7.** $\frac{15}{4}$ **8.** 0 **9.** $\frac{7}{2}$ **10.** 43

Lesson 7-7   pp. 406–409

Check Skills You'll Need

1. 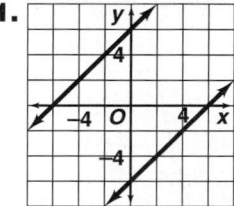 **2.**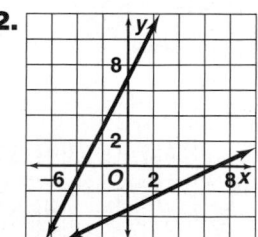

3. 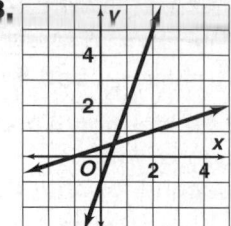 **4.**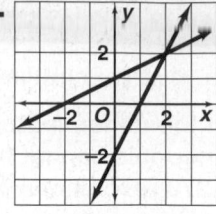

5. 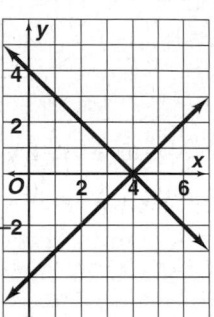 **6.**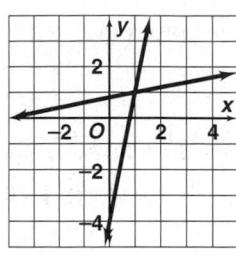

Quick Check 1a. The line $y = x$ is the perpendicular bisector of each segment connecting a point in s to the corresponding point in the inverse of s. The graph of the inverse of s is a reflection in the line $y = x$ of the graph of s. **b.** yes; no **2a.** Yes; no; for every x-value except 3 in the domain of the inverse there are two y-values. **b.** $y = \frac{1}{3}x + \frac{10}{3}$; it is a function because for each value of x there is only one y-value.

3.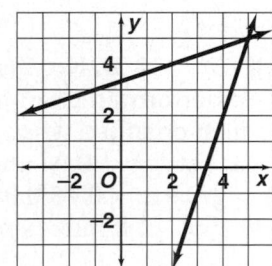

4a. D: all real numbers, R: all real numbers
b. $f^{-1}(x) = \frac{-x + 10}{3}$ **c.** D: all real numbers, R: all real numbers **d.** 3 **e.** 2 **5.** $v = 8\sqrt{d}$; ≈44 ft/s **6.** 777, −5802

Lesson 7-8   **pp. 414–417**

Check Skills You'll Need

1. 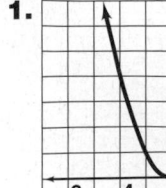 **2.**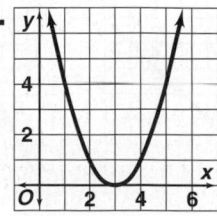

---

3. 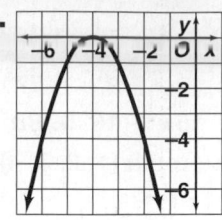 **4.**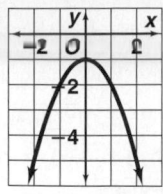

5. 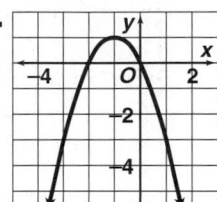 **6.**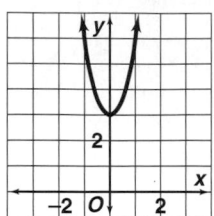

Quick Check

1. 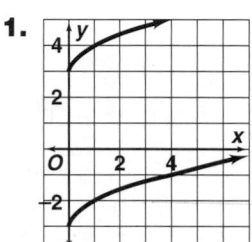 **2.**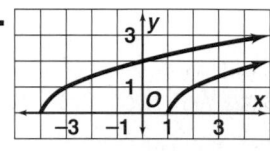

3.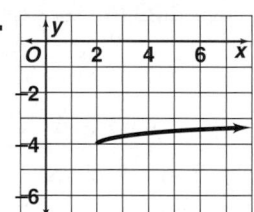

4.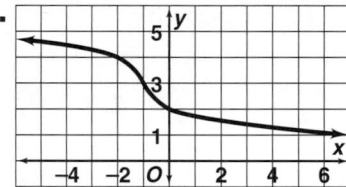

5. about 60 m; it is about $\frac{1}{4}$ the height.
6. $y = 2\sqrt[3]{x - 3} + 3$; the graph is the graph of $y = 2\sqrt[3]{x}$ translated 3 units right and 3 units up.

Chapter 8

Check Your Readiness   **p. 428**

1. 0.1, 1, 10, 100, 1000 **2.** $\frac{4}{9}, \frac{2}{3}, 1, \frac{3}{2}, \frac{9}{4}$
3. 12, 0, 0, 0, 12

4a. $n = 3d$ 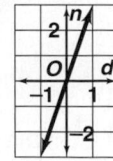 **b.** 84 acorns **c.** The function would be $n = 9 + 3d$, and the graph would shift 9 units upward.

5. $y = x^2 - 4x$ **6.** $y = 3x^2 - 2x + 7$

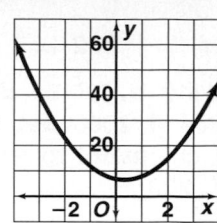 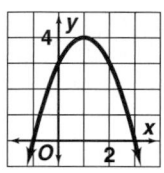

7. $y = -x^2$ **8.** $y = 3x^2$

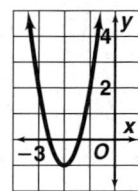

9.

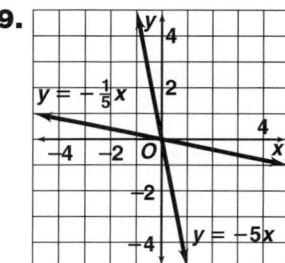

10.

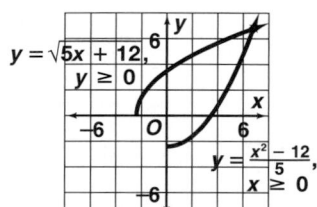

11.

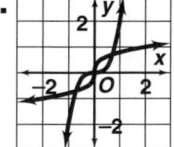

Lesson 8-1   pp. 430–434

Check Skills You'll Need **1.** 8 **2.** 16 **3.** 2 **4.** 9 **5.** 1 **6.** $\frac{1}{4}$

Quick Check

1a. 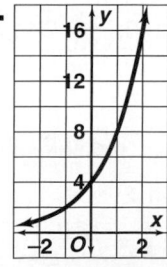 **b.**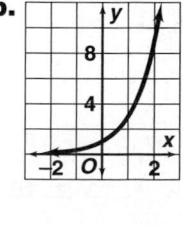

2a. about 338 million **b.** The growth factor may
change. **c.** $y = 281(1.014)^x$; about 346 million
3. $y = 0.25(4)^x$

4a. exponential decay **b.** exponential growth
c. exponential decay

5a. $y = 0$ 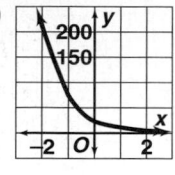 **b.** $y = 0$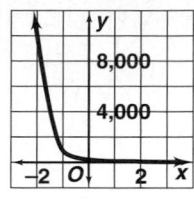

6. about $3900

Lesson 8-2   pp. 439–442, 445

Check Skills You'll Need **1.** $y = |x + 2| + 1$
2. $y = -|x| - 2$ **3.** $y = (x - 1)^2 - 2$
4. $y = -(x + 1)^2 + 3$ **5.** $y = \frac{1}{x^5}$ **6.** $y = x$
7. $y = x^5$ **8.** $33

Quick Check

1a. 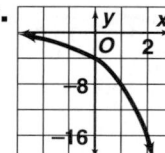 **b.**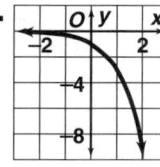

2a. 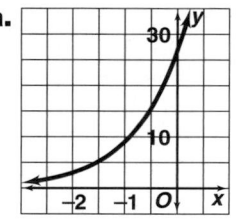 **b.**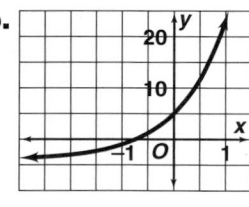

c.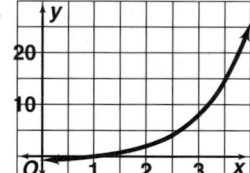

3. $y = 90\left(\frac{1}{2}\right)^{\frac{2}{35}x}$; about 71 mg **4a.** 54.5982
b. 0.0498 **c.** 1.6487 **5.** $1479.00

Checkpoint Quiz 1 **1.** exponential growth; 45%
increase **2.** exponential decay; 1% decrease
3. exponential growth; 70% increase
4. exponential decay; 20% decrease

5. 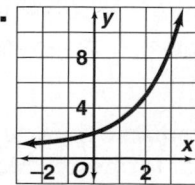 **6.**

7. 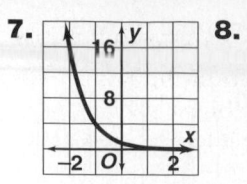 **8.**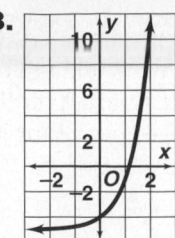

9. Answers may vary. Sample: The population of Smallville was 1200 in 1990. It was growing at a rate of 1% per year. Find the population in 2010.
10. $y = 100\left(\frac{1}{2}\right)^{\frac{1}{30}x}$; about 9.9 mg

---

Lesson 8-3   pp. 446–449

Check Skills You'll Need 1. 2 **2.** 16 **3.** 3 **4.** 2

5. 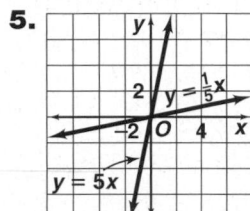 **6.**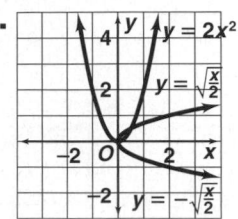

7. 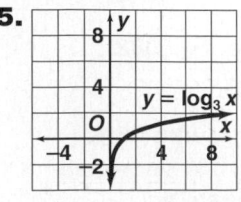 **8.**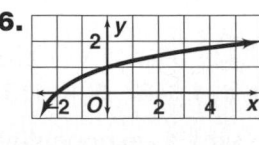

Quick Check 1. The earthquake in California released about 1265 times as much energy as the earthquake in Alabama. 2a. $\log_3 729 = 6$
b. $3 = \log_{\frac{1}{2}}\left(\frac{1}{8}\right)$ **c.** $0 = \log_{10} 1$ **3a.** $-\frac{5}{6}$ **b.** $\frac{3}{2}$ **c.** 2
4. 3.2×10^{-9}

5. 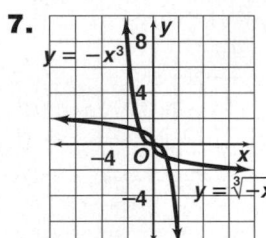 **6.**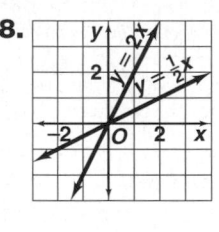

Lesson 8-4   pp. 454–456

Check Skills You'll Need 1. 5 **2.** −1 **3.** $\frac{2}{3}$ **4.** 24 **5.** 2187
6. $\frac{1}{27}$ **7.** 36

Quick Check 1a. Product Property b. Power Property, Quotient Property 2a. $\log 2$ **b.** No; they do not have the same base. **3a.** $\log_2 7 + \log_2 b$
b. $2 \log y - 2 \log 3$ **c.** $3 \log_7 a + 4 \log_7 b$
4. about 6 decibels

Lesson 8-5   pp. 461–464, 468

Check Skills You'll Need 1. 1 **2.** 2 **3.** $\frac{4}{3}$ **4.** $\frac{1}{25}$

Quick Check 1a. 1.2619 **b.** 0.8496 **c.** 0.2009
2. 0.4634 **3.** 0.4634 **4.** 2068 **5a.** 3.7227, $\log_8 2301$
b. Sample: Use a calculator to raise 2 to the 2.465 power. **6.** 3.45 **7.** 200

Checkpoint Quiz 2

1. 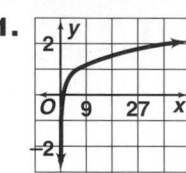 **2.**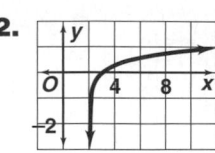

3. $3 \log s - 5 \log r$ **4.** $2 \log_6 3 + 2 \log_6 x + 2 \log_6 y$
5. $\log_6 4 + \frac{1}{2} \log_6 x$ **6.** 3 **7.** 20 **8.** 1000
9. $\log 2 \approx 0.3010$, $\log_3 2 \approx 0.6309$, $\log_2 3 \approx$
1.5850, $2^3 = 8$, $3^2 = 9$ **10.** Rewrite $\log_2 10$
as $\frac{\log 10}{\log 2}$ and evaluate it to get ≈ 3.322. Then set
$3.322 = \log_3 x$. Rewrite to get $3.322 = \frac{\log x}{\log 3}$ and
solve. Convert $\log x = 1.585$ to $10^{1.585} = x$ or
$x \approx 38.46$. So $\log_2 10 \approx \log_3 38.46$.

Lesson 8-6   pp. 470–472

Check Skills You'll Need 1. 148.413 **2.** 40.171 **3.** 0.135
4. 0.368 **5.** 11.417 **6.** 81 **7.** $\frac{1}{2}$ **8.** 65,536

Quick Check 1a. $\ln 8$ **b.** $\ln x^3 y$ **c.** $\ln \sqrt[4]{3x}$
2a. ≈ 5.4 km/s; no **b.** One could increase its mass ratio or its exhaust velocity. **3a.** 1.105
b. 439,605,247.8 **c.** 488,262.4 **4a.** 2.401 **b.** 1.605
5. 6.5%

Chapter 9

Check Your Readiness   p. 486

1. $\frac{7}{27}$ **2.** $\frac{1}{3}$ **3.** $\frac{5}{9}$ **4.** $\frac{22}{27}$ **5.** $\frac{22}{27}$ **6.** $\frac{12}{27}$ **7.** $\frac{4}{3}$; −4 **8.** $-\frac{2}{3}$; 2
9. $-\frac{10}{3}$; 10 **10.** $-\frac{16}{7}$; $\frac{48}{7}$ **11.** $(x + 3)(x - 2)$
12. $(4x + 5)(x + 3)$ **13.** $(3x - 5)(3x + 5)$
14. $(x - 6)^2$ **15.** $(3x + 4)(x + 2)$ **16.** $(x - 3)(x - 2)$
17. 1, −8 **18.** −6, −8 **19.** 4, 2 **20.** 0, $-\frac{2}{3}$ **21.** 8, $\frac{1}{2}$
22. 15, −2

Lesson 9-1   pp. 488–490

Check Skills You'll Need 1. 10 **2.** 15 **3.** 1.2

Quick Check 1. $y = \frac{0.42}{x}$ **2a.** inverse; $y = \frac{0.72}{x}$
b. neither **c.** direct; $y = 15x$
3a. about 5,000,000 min, or about 10 yr
b. about 27 beats per min

4. *A* varies jointly with the height and the sum of the bases. **5.** $V = \frac{\sqrt{2}}{6}e^3$

Lesson 9-2   pp. 495–498

Check Skills You'll Need   **1.** 2 units up   **2.** 2 units left **3.** 3 units down   **4.** 3 units right   **5.** 4 units left and 5 units down   **6.** 10 units right and 7 units up

Quick Check

1.

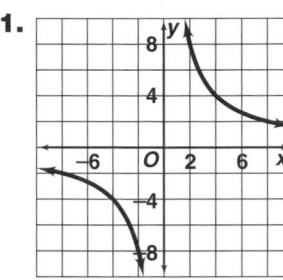

2. The graph of $y = \frac{2}{x}$ is a stretch of $y = \frac{1}{x}$ by the factor 2. The graph of $y = -\frac{2}{x}$ is the reflection of $y = \frac{2}{x}$ in the x-axis. The graph of $y = \frac{0.5}{x}$ is a shrink of $y = \frac{1}{x}$ by the factor 0.5. The graph of $y = -\frac{0.5}{x}$ is the reflection of $y = \frac{0.5}{x}$ in the x-axis.

3a. 2.28 ft, 1.81 ft, 1.52 ft   **b.** As the pipe becomes very short, the pitch becomes very high (great frequency). As the pipe becomes very long, the pitch becomes low (frequency near 0).

4. $x = -7$ and $y = -3$

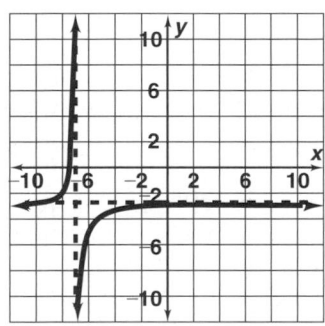

5a. $y = -\frac{1}{x + 4} + 5$ **b.**

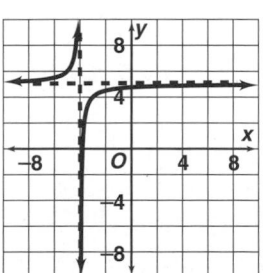

Lesson 9-3   pp. 501–505, 508

Check Skills You'll Need   **1.** $(x + 3)(x + 2)$ **2.** $(x - 4)(x - 2)$ **3.** $(x - 3)(x - 9)$ **4.** $(2x - 7)(x + 4)$ **5.** $(2x - 5)(x - 3)$ **6.** $(2x - 3)(x - 8)$ **7.** $3, -4$ **8.** $-4, 7$ **9.** $3, 6$

Quick Check   **1a.** $-4, 4$ **b.** none   **c.** $-4, 2$ **2a.** Since 1 and -3 are the zeroes of the denominator and neither is a zero of the numerator, $x = 1$ and $x = -3$ are vertical asymptotes.   **b.** The graph of this function is the

same as the graph of $y = \frac{1}{x + 3}$, except that it has a hole at $x = 2$. The vertical asymptote is $x = -3$. **c.** The graph of this function is the same as the graph of $y = x - 1$, except that it has a hole at $x = -1$.   **3a.** $y = -2$ **b.** $y = 2$

4.

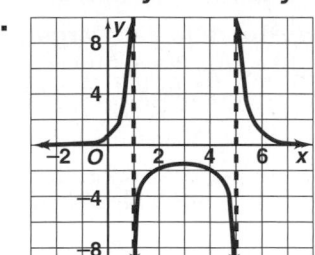

5a. Answers may vary. Sample: Graph $y = 8$ and use the Intersection feature to find that the graphs intersect at $x = 16,103.2$. So the number of discs produced must be greater than 16,103. **b.** $x = 100$; $y = 0.25$ **c.** Answers may vary. Sample: The vertical asymptote means that if you produce 100 or fewer discs you won't sell any, since the first 100 are samples. The horizontal asymptote means that the average cost will never go below $.25, since that is how much each disc costs to produce.

Checkpoint Quiz 1   **1.** $z = 5xy$ **2.** $z = \frac{20x}{y}$ **3.** $z = \frac{180}{xy}$ **4.** Answers may vary. Sample: Both have vertical asymptote $x = 0$ and horizontal asymptote $y = 0$. $y = \frac{4}{x}$ is closer to the axes.   **5.** Answers may vary. Sample: $y_2 = \frac{1}{x} + 5$ is a vertical translation of $y_1 = \frac{1}{x}$ up 5 units.   **6.** Answers may vary. Sample: $y_2 = \frac{1}{x - 1} + 2$ has vertical asymptote of $x = 1$ and horizontal asymptote $y = 2$. $y_2 = \frac{1}{x + 1} - 2$ has vertical asymptote $x = -1$ and horizontal symptote $y = -2$.

7.

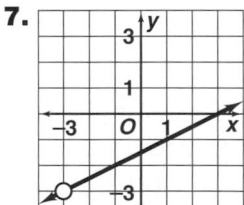

8.

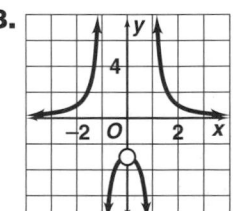

9.

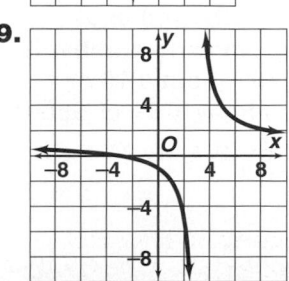

10.

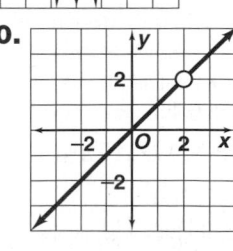

Lesson 9-4   pp. 509–511

Check Skills You'll Need   **1.** $(2x - 1)(x - 1)$ **2.** $(2x + 3)(2x - 3)$ **3.** $(5x + 1)(x + 1)$

4. $10(x + 1)(x - 1)$ **5.** $\frac{5}{16}$ **6.** $\frac{1}{3}$ **7.** $\frac{1}{3}$ **8.** $\frac{6}{35}$ **9.** $\frac{5}{32}$
10. $\frac{3}{2}$ **11.** $\frac{3}{4}$ **12.** $\frac{2}{3}$

Quick Check 1a. $-\frac{3}{x}$; $x \neq 0, y \neq 0$
b. $\frac{-3(x + 2)}{(x - 2)(x - 4)}$; $x \neq 2$ or 4 **c.** $\frac{2x + 1}{x - 3}$; $x \neq 2$ or 3
2a. $\frac{2r}{5}$ **b.** As m gets larger, the ratio gets larger.
3. $\frac{a - 2}{a(a - 1)}$; $a \neq 0, 1, -1,$ or -2 **4.** $\frac{3(a + 5)(a - 3)}{(a + 1)(a + 4)}$;
$a \neq -1, -4,$ or 4

Lesson 9-5 pp. 514–517, 520

Check Skills You'll Need 1. 21 **2.** 30 **3.** 187 **4.** 210
5. $\frac{17}{38}$ **6.** $\frac{19}{75}$ **7.** $\frac{11}{72}$ **8.** $\frac{137}{180}$

Quick Check 1. 4 cm **2a.** $6(x - 5)(x + 5)(x + 2)$
b. $10(x + 2)(x - 2)(x + 1)$ **3.** $\frac{3x^2 - 18x + 4}{4(x - 6)(x + 2)}$
4a. $\frac{-3x^2 - 21x - 4}{6(x + 5)(x + 7)}$ **b.** $\frac{-x^2 + 5x + 2}{3(x - 1)(x - 2)(x + 2)}$ **5a.** $\frac{1}{xy}$
b. $\frac{6y}{2y - 1}$ **c.** $\frac{x^3 - 4x^2 + x + 2}{2x^2 + 4x}$

Checkpoint Quiz 2 1. $\frac{3(x - 8)}{25(x - 4)}$ **2.** $\frac{2}{3}$ **3.** 2 **4.** $\frac{y(y - 5)}{2(y + 4)}$
5. $\frac{4(6y^2 + x^2)}{9x^3y^3}$ **6.** $\frac{41}{15(y + 5)}$ **7.** $\frac{5xy - 12}{2y(y + 2)}$
8. $\frac{3x^3 - x^2 - 11x}{x^2 - 2}$ **9.** $\frac{2x}{y}$ **10.** $\frac{y(3x + 1)}{x(4y + 5)}$

Lesson 9-6 pp. 522–524

Check Skills You'll Need 1. $15t^2$ **2.** 8 **3.** $3h^3$
4. $(y + 2)(y - 1)$ **5.** $z(2z + 1)$ **6.** $(k + 2)(k - 2)$

Quick Check 1a. no solution **b.** $-3, 2$ **2.** $2, -2$ **3.** 10
mi/h downhill, 6 mi/h uphill **4a.** Maria: 6.75 h,
Paco: 13.5 h **b.** Adrian: 4.5 h, Phillip: 9 h

Lesson 9-7 pp. 531–534

Check Skills You'll Need 1. $\frac{7}{36}$ **2.** $\frac{25}{36}$ **3.** $\frac{1}{2}$ **4.** 72

Quick Check 1. Independent; the number of marbles
is the same after the marble is replaced.
2a. $\frac{1}{25}$ or 4%; $\frac{1}{40}$ or 2.5% **b.** $\frac{1}{1000}$ or 0.1% **3a.** Not
mutually exclusive since 2 is both even and
prime. **b.** Mutually exclusive since no number is
both even and less than 2. **4a.** about 0.26 or
about 26% **b.** about 0.47 or about 47% **c.** about
0.79 or about 79% **5a.** $\frac{5}{9}$ **b.** $\frac{2}{3}$

Chapter 10

Check Your Readiness p. 544

1. quadratic; $-x^2, 6x, 1$ **2.** linear; none, $-12x$,
-18 **3.** linear; none, $x, -\frac{13}{2}$ **4.** quadratic; $-8x^2$,
$28x$, none **5.** quadratic; $-2x^2, -3x, 6$ **6.** linear;
none, $-x, -10$

7. 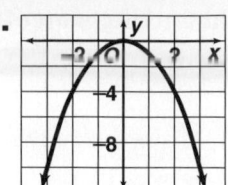 **8.**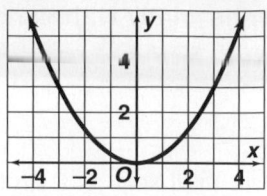

9. 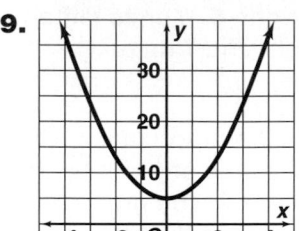 **10.**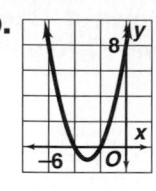

11. 16 **12.** $\frac{25}{4}$ **13.** 49

14. $y = (x + 3)^2 - 2$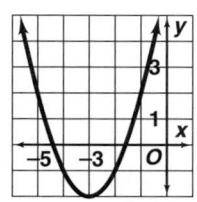

15. $y = 2(x - 1)^2 + 8$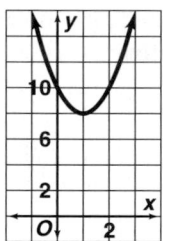

16. $y = -3\left(x - \frac{1}{6}\right)^2 + \frac{1}{12}$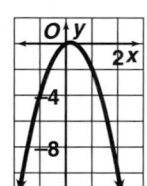

17. $\frac{1}{2}, i\sqrt{5}, -i\sqrt{5}$ **18.** $\frac{1}{2}, 1$ **19.**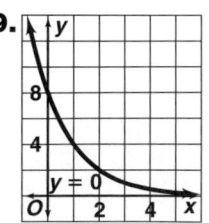

20. 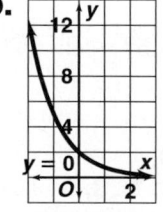 **21.**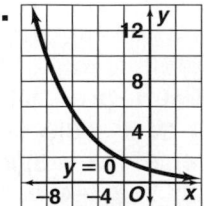

Lesson 10-1 pp. 547–550

Check Skills You'll Need 1. −2, 6 **2.** −3, −1.5 **3.** −4, 3
4. ±2, −4 **5.** 3, 9 **6.** ±0.5, 1

Quick Check

1a.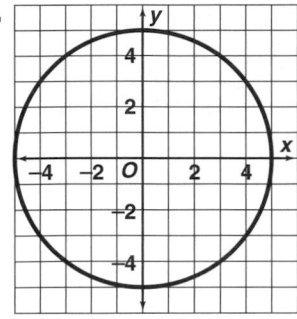

The graphs are the same.

b. Rewrite $x^2 + y^2 = 25$ as $y^2 = 25 - x^2$. Then take the square root of both sides, which gives you $y = \pm\sqrt{25 - x^2}$. **c.** When $x = 6$, $25 - x^2 = -11$. $\sqrt{-11}$ is not a real number.

2a. 4 units; 3 units; an ellipse is oblong instead of round. It has 2 axes of symmetry rather than infinitely many. **b.** (1, −2.9), (−1, 2.9), (−1, −2.9)

c.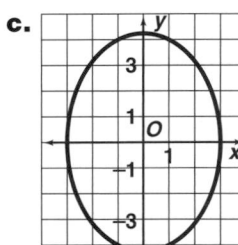

It is an ellipse with center (0, 0). The x-intercepts are 3 and −3 and the y-intercepts are $3\sqrt{2}$ and $-3\sqrt{2}$.

3a. No; there are vertical lines that intersect the graph in more than one point. **b.** Answers may vary. Sample: Solving $x^2 - y^2 = 9$ for y gives $y = \pm\sqrt{x^2 - 9}$. For $-3 < x < 3$, the value of $x^2 - 9$ is negative and $\sqrt{x^2 - 9}$ is not a real number. **c.** $y = x$ and $y = -x$; asymptotes

4. center: (0, 0); no x-intercepts, y-intercepts: −4, 4; domain: all real numbers, range: all y such that $y \geq 4$ or $y \leq -4$ **5a.** Answers may vary. Sample: All equations have an x^2-term, a y^2-term, and no other terms on the left side. There is a positive constant term and nothing else on the right side. **b.** Answers may vary. Sample: The related domains and ranges are all different. The absolute values of the coefficients of x^2 and y^2 are equal for $x^2 - y^2 = 1$, but the signs of the coefficients are different. The absolute values of the coefficients of x^2 and y^2 are equal for $x^2 + y^2 = 16$, and the signs are the same. The absolute values of the coefficients of x^2 and y^2 are different for $9x^2 + 25y^2 = 225$, but the signs are the same.

Lesson 10-2 pp. 555–558

Check Skills You'll Need 1. 8 **2.** 4 **3.** 3 **4.** $\frac{1}{8}$ **5.** $2\sqrt{2}$
6. $\sqrt{65}$ **7.** $\sqrt{73}$

Quick Check 1. $x = \frac{1}{8}y^2$ **2.** $x = \frac{1}{2}y^2$
3. $y = \frac{1}{33}x^2$ **4.** (0, 3), $y = -3$
5. (−3, −1), (−3, −1.75),
$y = -\frac{1}{4}$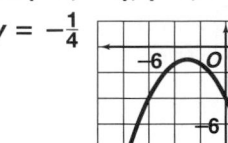

Lesson 10-3 pp. 561–564, 566

Check Skills You'll Need 1. 4 **2.** 7 **3.** $2\sqrt{5}$ **4.** $4\sqrt{3}$
5. $6\sqrt{2}$ **6.** 1 **7.** 4 **8.** 9

Quick Check 1. $(x - 5)^2 + (y + 2)^2 = 64$
2a. $(x + 5)^2 + (y + 3)^2 = 1$
b. $(x - 2)^2 + (y - 3)^2 = 9$
3. $x^2 + (y + 4)^2 = 1$ **4.** (−8, −3), 11
5.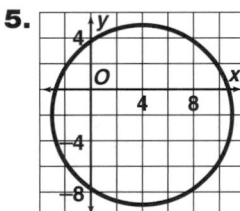

Checkpoint Quiz 1 1. (0, 0), $\left(0, \frac{1}{12}\right)$, $y = -\frac{1}{12}$;
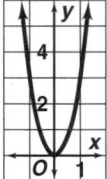

2. (0, −2), $\left(\frac{1}{16}, -2\right)$, $x = -\frac{1}{16}$;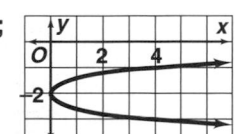

3. (3, −1), $\left(3, -\frac{3}{4}\right)$, $y = -\frac{5}{4}$;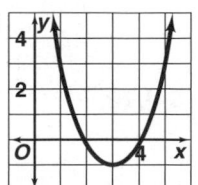

4. $(x + 6)^2 + (y - 3)^2 = 64$ **5.** 4 units left and 6 units up

Lesson 10-4   pp. 560–570

Check Skills You'll Need 1. ±4 **2.** ±4√3 **3.** ±6 **4.** 34
5. −16 **6.** 7

Quick Check 1. $\frac{x^2}{9} + \frac{y^2}{36} = 1$ **2.** $\frac{x^2}{36} + \frac{y^2}{225} = 1$

3. $(2\sqrt{2}, 0), (-2\sqrt{2}, 0)$;

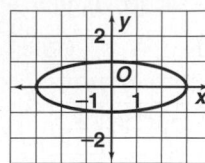

4. $\frac{x^2}{64} + \frac{y^2}{81} = 1$

Lesson 10-5   pp. 574–577, 580

Check Skills You'll Need 1. $y = -\frac{5}{2}x$ **2.** $y = \frac{1}{3}x$
3. $y = \pm 2\sqrt{x^2 - 4}$ **4.** $y = \pm\frac{3}{5}\sqrt{x^2 + 25}$
5. $y = \pm\frac{3}{2}\sqrt{x^2 - 36}$

Quick Check 1.

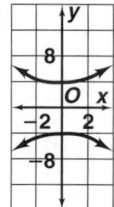

2. $(\sqrt{34}, 0), (-\sqrt{34}, 0)$;

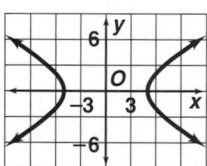

3. $\dfrac{x^2}{4.770 \times 10^{12}} - \dfrac{y^2}{3.668 \times 10^{12}} = 1$

Checkpoint Quiz 2 1. $\frac{x^2}{25} + \frac{y^2}{16} = 1$ **2.** $\frac{x^2}{25} + \frac{y^2}{29} = 1$
3. $\frac{x^2}{100} + \frac{y^2}{149} = 1$ **4.** $(\sqrt{65}, 0), (-\sqrt{65}, 0)$

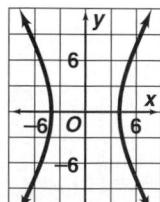

5. $(0, 2\sqrt{34}), (0, -2\sqrt{34})$

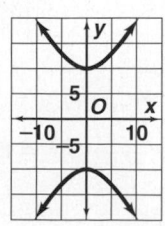

6. $(\sqrt{85}, 0), (-\sqrt{85}, 0)$

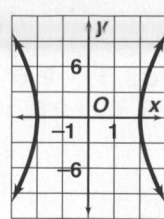

7. $(0, \sqrt{89}), (0, -\sqrt{89})$

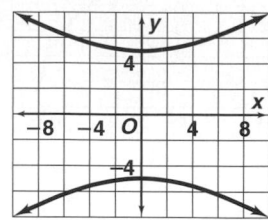

8. $\frac{x^2}{121} - \frac{y^2}{104} = 1$ **9.** $\frac{x^2}{16} - \frac{y^2}{9} = 1$
10. $\frac{y^2}{64} - \frac{x^2}{12.25} = 1$

Lesson 10-6   pp. 582–585

Check Skills You'll Need 1. $y = x^2$; 4 units up **2.** $y = x^2$;
3 units right and 2 units down **3.** $y = x^2$; 1 unit up
4. $y = x^2$; 5 units left, 6 units up
5. $y = (x - 3)^2 - 8$ **6.** $y = (x + 5)^2 - 32$
7. $y = 2(x + 2)^2 - 3$ **8.** $y = 4\left(x - \frac{3}{2}\right)^2 - 6$

Quick Check 1. $\dfrac{(x - 1)^2}{25} + \dfrac{(y + 4)^2}{4} = 1$

2. $\dfrac{(y - 3)^2}{16} - \dfrac{(x - 2)^2}{33} = 1$ **3.** $\dfrac{(x - 100)^2}{784} - \dfrac{y^2}{9216} = 1$

4. circle with center (6, −2) and radius 4√3;

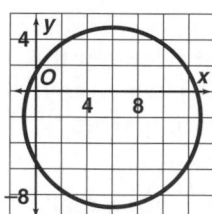

Chapter 11

Check Your Readiness   pp. 598

1. 9, 11, 13, 15 **2.** 1, 6, 11, 16 **3.** 0.9, 1.1, 1.3, 1.5
4. −2, −7, −12, −17 **5.** $3\frac{1}{3}, 7\frac{1}{3}, 11\frac{1}{3}, 15\frac{1}{3}$
6. −12, −15, −18, −21 **7.**

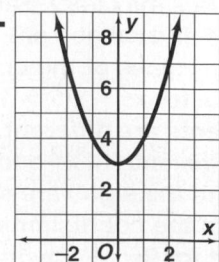

8. 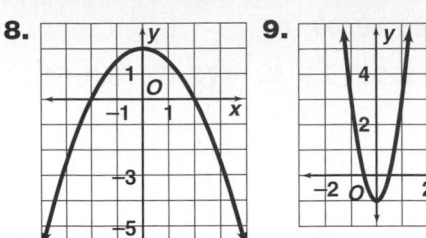 **9.**

10. **11.** **12.**
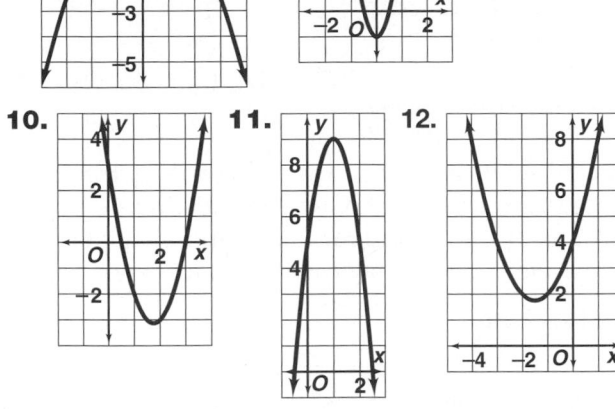

13. 4 **14.** −4 **15.** 0.4 **16.** 50 **17.** $5x^2$
18. $-0.3y^4$ **19.** $|x^3y^5|$ **20.** $11y^{12}$ **21.** $\frac{4}{3}$ **22.** $\frac{3}{4}$
23. $\frac{5}{3}$ **24.** $\frac{5}{18}$

Lesson 11-1   pp. 600–602

Check Skills You'll Need **1.** 13, 15; add 2. **2.** −14, −16; subtract 2. **3.** 3125, 15,625; multiply by 5. **4.** 20, 15; subtract 5. **5.** 8, 4; divide by 2. **6.** 20, 23; add 3. **7.** 128, 256; multiply by 2. **8.** −19, −23; subtract 4.

Quick Check **1a.** Add 7; 55, 62, 69. **b.** Divide by 3; 3, 1, $\frac{1}{3}$. **2a.** 3.2 ft **b.** 10th bounce **3.** 22, 30
4a. 1, 4, 9, 16, 25, 36; 400 **b.** $a_n = n^2$ **c.** No; a_1 is not given.

Lesson 11-2   pp. 606–607

Check Skills You'll Need **1.** Subtract 2. **2.** Add 17.
3. Add $\frac{3}{7}$. **4.** Subtract $\frac{1}{4}$.

Quick Check **1a.** no **b.** yes; −3 **2a.** The first term in the sequence, 1100, was the amount of money with *no* participants, so there is one more term than the number of participants. **b.** 149
3a. 40.5 **b.** $\dfrac{a_6 + a_7}{2}$

Lesson 11-3   pp. 612–614, 617

Check Skills You'll Need **1.** 16 **2.** 21 **3.** 1000 **4.** $\frac{100}{3}$

Quick Check **1a.** 5, 15, 45, 135, 405, 1215, 3645, 10,935, 32,805, 98,415; the tenth term is the ninth term times 3. **b.** Geometric; the common ratio is −4. **c.** Arithmetic; the common difference is +12.
2a. 4,261,625,379 **b.** −34 **3a.** 40 or −40 **b.** 7.5 or −7.5 **c.** 378 or −378

Checkpoint Quiz 1 **1.** arithmetic; 15 **2.** geometric; 3 **3.** arithmetic; −3 **4.** geometric; 0.5 **5.** geometric; −0.5 **6.** arithmetic; −2 **7.** 6.25 **8.** 82 **9.** 1 **10.** To find the arithmetic mean, add the terms and divide by 2. To find the geometric mean, multiply the terms and find the square root of the product.

Lesson 11-4   pp. 619–621

Check Skills You'll Need **1.** 25 **2.** −42 **3.** $a_n = 2 + 2n$
4. $a_n = -2 + 3n$ **5.** $a_n = -11 - 6n$
6. $a_n = 19 - 9n$

Quick Check **1a.** 0.3 + 0.6 + 0.9 + 1.2 + 1.5 + 1.8 + 2.1 + 2.4 + 2.7 + 3.0; 16.5
b. 100 + 125 + 150 + 175 + 200 + 225; 975
2a. 31 **b.** 252 **3a.** $\displaystyle\sum_{n=1}^{6} n$ **b.** $\displaystyle\sum_{n=1}^{9} (5n - 2)$
4a. 10, −2, 7; 25 **b.** 4, $\frac{3}{2}$, 3; 9 **c.** 4, 4, 25; 54

Lesson 11-5   pp. 626–628, 631

Check Skills You'll Need **1.** $193\frac{3}{4}$ **2.** 120 **3.** −22 **4.** −75
5. $\frac{12}{5}$ **6.** $\frac{4}{3}$ **7.** $\frac{2}{3}$ **8.** $\frac{99}{16}$

Quick Check **1a.** $a_1 = -45, r = -3, n = 5$;
−2745 **b.** $a_1 = \frac{1}{3}, r = \frac{1}{3}, n = 4; \frac{40}{81}$ **2a.** To find the amount 20% larger than a given amount, multiply by 1.2, which is equivalent to 120%. **b.** The common ratio becomes 1.25. **c.** Yes; they will have $1407.35. **3a.** converges **b.** diverges
4. a. 2 **b.** 2

Checkpoint Quiz 2 **1.** arithmetic; 900 **2.** geometric; 29,524 **3.** geometric; −7.9375 **4.** arithmetic; 1200 **5.** geometric; 239.0625 **6.** arithmetic; 6150 **7.** $\frac{15}{14}$
8. 4 **9.** Answers may vary. Sample: $\frac{1}{2} + \frac{1}{4} + \frac{1}{8}$
10. No; the common difference causes arithmetic series to diverge.

Lesson 11-6   pp. 635–637

Check Skills You'll Need **1.** 4 ft^2 **2.** 2.75 m^2 **3.** 0.62 cm^2
4. $34\frac{7}{16}$ in.^{2}

Quick Check **1a.** 1545; it is much larger.
b. 1370; the mean is most accurate; it is between the other measures known to be smaller and larger than the actual value.

2a.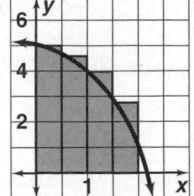

b. The left side values give the height of the circumscribed rectangles. **c.** 0.5(5) + 0.5(4.75) + 0.5(4) + 0.5(2.75) = 8.25 units²; it is greater than Example 2. **3a.** $4\frac{1}{3}$ **b.** $8\frac{2}{3}$ **c.** $5\frac{1}{4}$

Chapter 12

1. 120 **2.** 720 **3.** 144 **4.** 1 **5.** 6 **6.** 35 **7.** $a^5 + 5a^4b + 10a^3b^2 + 10a^2b^3 + 5ab^4 + b^5$ **8.** $j^3 + 9j^2k + 27jk^2 + 27k^3$ **9.** $m^2 + 1.4m + 0.49$
10. $0.000064 + 0.00192t + 0.024t^2 + 0.16t^3 + 0.6t^4 + 1.2t^5 + t^6$ **11.** ±0.1 **12.** ±0.071
13. ±0.063 **14.** ±0.051 **15.** ±0.048 **16.** ±0.036
17. 0.08 **18.** 0.125 **19.** 0.085 **20.** 0.865 **21.** 0.06

Lesson 12-1   pp. 648–651

Check Skills You'll Need 1. yes **2.** no **3.** no **4.** $\frac{1}{18}$
5. $\frac{1}{4}$ **6.** 1

Quick Check

1.

Type	Number
Acute	13
Right	7
Obtuse	5
Total	25

2. 0.857

3. Answers may vary. Sample:

Rolling One Number Cube

Numbers	1	2	3	4	5	6
Frequency	1	1	1	1	1	1
Probability	$\frac{1}{6}$	$\frac{1}{6}$	$\frac{1}{6}$	$\frac{1}{6}$	$\frac{1}{6}$	$\frac{1}{6}$

4a. The Plant Color Distribution would be most useful for avoiding white plants because it shows the total probability of growing green plants, which is the desired outcome.

b.

Genotype			
Event	GG	Gw	ww
Frequency	1	2	1
Probability	$\frac{1}{4}$	$\frac{1}{2}$	$\frac{1}{4}$

Plant Color		
Event	Green	White
Frequency	3	1
Probability	$\frac{3}{4}$	$\frac{1}{4}$

Lesson 12-2   pp. 654–656

Check Skills You'll Need 1. $\frac{1}{16}$ **2.** $\frac{1}{16}$ **3.** $\frac{3}{16}$ **4.** $\frac{9}{16}$
5. $\frac{7}{16}$ **6.** $\frac{9}{16}$

Quick Check 1. $\frac{7}{14}$ or $\frac{1}{2}$ **2.** about 0.021 or 2.1% **3.** 0.9
4. 0.33

Lesson 12-3   pp. 660–664, 667

Check Skills You'll Need
1. 0.2 0.3 0.6 0.7 0.8 0.9 1.2; 0.7 **2.** 11 15 17 18 21 21 23; 18 **3.** 2.6 3.9 7.8 9.1 10.4 11.7 15.6; 9.1

4. 76 80 82 84 86 86 89; 84

Quick Check 1. ≈ 3.6, 3.7, 2.8 **2.** ≈ 73.42; 73.5; 61, 70, 77, 83, 85

3.
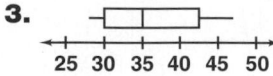

4.
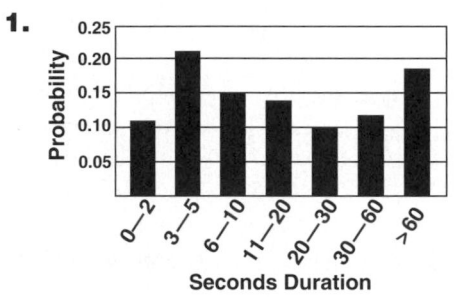 $Q_1 = 84$, $Q_2 = 85$, $Q_3 = 86$

5a. 21 **b.** 65 **c.** 71 **6a.** Yes; it is unlikely that the water temperature of a lake would change by 25°F. **b.** No; 98 would represent the busiest night of the week and it may relate to a weekly event.

Checkpoint Quiz 1

1.

2. 0.385 **3.** No; when $x = 1$, $P(x) = -\frac{1}{2}$, and probability is never negative. **4.** $\frac{12}{57}$ **5.** $\frac{5}{8}$ **6.** $\frac{23}{43}$
7. $\frac{45}{68}$ **8.** 5.69, 5, 4 **9.** 3.82, 2.85, no mode

Lesson 12-4   pp. 668–672

Check Skills You'll Need 1. 4.9 **2.** 2.5 **3.** 10.5 **4.** 9 **5.** 7
6. 8.03

Quick Check 1a. range: 14, interquartile range: 6
b. Yes; answers may vary.

1	2	3	4	5	6	7	8	9	10
1	1	1	1	1	10	10	10	10	10

c. Yes; sample:

1	2	3	4	5	6	7	8	9	10
3	3	3	5	5	6	6	8	8	8

2. 80, ≈ 18.7 **3.** 8, about 4.0 **4a.** 1 **b.** No; three standard deviations from the mean is 46.3, which is less than 48. **5.** 100

Lesson 12-5   pp. 677–680

Check Skills You'll Need 1. $\frac{1}{2}$ **2.** $-\frac{1}{3}$ **3.** $\frac{1}{6}$ **4.** $-\frac{1}{11}$ **5.** $\frac{\sqrt{2}}{10}$
6. $-\frac{1}{9}$

Quick Check 1. 52% **2a.** Yes; the sample is biased because it overrepresents students who live in a warm climate. **b.** Answers may vary. Sample: Every 10 years, the United States conducts a census of the population to find exactly how many people live in the country.

3. B; a larger sample has less variation, which corresponds to a smaller standard deviation.
4a. 100 **b.** 625 **c.** 2500 **5.** 71%, ±9%, 62% to 80%

Lesson 12-6   pp. 685–688, 691

Check Skills You'll Need 1. 6 **2.** 1 **3.** 10 **4.** $x^3 + 6x^2 + 12x + 8$ **5.** $w^4 - 4w^3y + 6w^2y^2 - 4wy^3 + y^4$
6. $m^3 + 3m^2n + 3mn^2 + n^3$ **7.** $t^4 + 12t^3s + 54t^2s^2 + 108ts^3 + 81s^4$ **8.** $a^5 + 10a^4b + 40a^3b^2 + 80a^2b^3 + 80ab^4 + 32b^5$ **9.** $p^6 + 6p^5q + 15p^4q^2 + 20p^3q^3 + 15p^2q^4 + 6pq^5 + q^6$

Quick Check 2a. P (one prize) $= 3(0.4)^1(0.6)^2 = 0.432$; P(no prize) $= 1(0.6)^3 = 0.216$ **b.** 1
3a. 0.2637 **b.** 0.2335 **4.** 0.9933

Checkpoint Quiz 2 1. $33.8\overline{3}$, 20, 6.20 **2.** 11, 5, 1.63
3. 2.375, 4, 1.41 **4.** 228 **5a.** This survey may be biased because it overrepresents people who shop for CDs online and entirely misses those who do not have internet access. **b.** Answers may vary. Sample: Survey a random selection of students in homerooms for each grade level.
6a. $0.3441 \approx 34.4\%$ **b.** ±3.8% **c.** 30.6% to 38.2%
7. 25 **8.** 0.343 **9.** 0.4096 **10.** 0.0768

Lesson 12-7   pp. 692–694

Check Skills You'll Need 1. 8, 10, 14, 16 **2.** 14.7, 15.7, 17.7, 18.7 **3.** 4, 5.5, 8.5, 10 **4.** 18.6, 20.3, 23.7, 25.4 **5.** 15.7, 16.6, 18.4, 19.3 **6.** 30.7, 31.9, 34.3, 35.5

Quick Check 1a. 71% **b.** 88%

2.

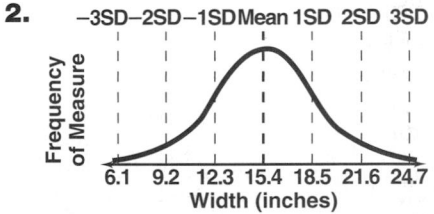

3a. 68 responses **b.** 13 or 14 responses
4a. 47 or 48 students **b.** 76 is about 1 SD above the mean. About 13.5% + 2.5% should receive grades above 76. 16% of 140 is about 22.

Chapter 13

Check Your Readiness   p. 708

1. vertical asymptote $x = 3$ **2.** hole at $x = 1$
3. vertical asymptotes $x = -\frac{1}{2}$ and $x = 4$ **4.** $\frac{2b}{a}$
5. $\frac{55}{18}$ **6.** $\frac{3}{2(c + d)}$ **7.** $\frac{c}{16}$ **8.** $\frac{c + 4}{9}$ **9.** $\frac{16}{x}$ **10.** $\frac{15}{7}$ **11.** 6
12. $(x - 1)^2 + (y + 4)^2 = 16$;

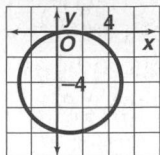

13. $\frac{(x - 2)^2}{9} + \frac{(y - 5)^2}{4} = 1$;

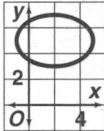

14. $y = \frac{1}{32}x^2 - 3$;

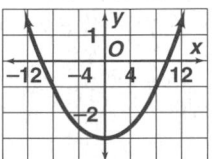

15. $\frac{(y - 1)^2}{9} - \frac{(x - 6)^2}{16} = 1$;

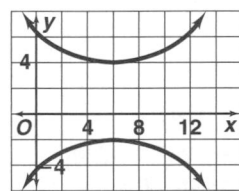

16. 4, 1; $a_n = 19 - 3n$, explicit; $a_1 = 16$, $a_n = a_{n-1} - 3$, recursive **17.** $-216, -343$; $a_n = -n^3$, explicit **18.** $\frac{1}{9}, \frac{1}{27}$; $a_n = 9\left(\frac{1}{3}\right)^{n-1}$, explicit; $a_1 = 9$, $a_n = \frac{1}{3} \cdot a_{n-1}$, recursive

Lesson 13-1   pp. 710–713

Check Skills You'll Need 1. yes **2.** yes **3.** no **4.** yes
5. no **6.** no **7.** yes **8.** yes

Quick Check 1a. from −3 to 1 or 0 to 4; 4
b. from −4 to −1 or 0 to 3; 3 **2a.** not periodic
b. periodic; 4 **3a.** 1.5 **b.** 1.5

4.

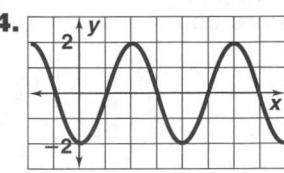

1 unit on the x-axis is 0.001 s.

Lesson 13-2   pp. 718–722

Check Skills You'll Need

1. 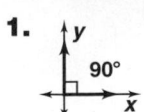   **2.** 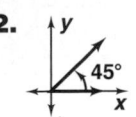   **3.**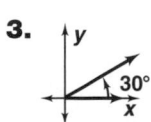

4. 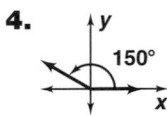   **5.** 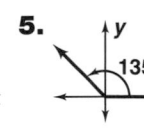   **6.**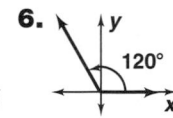

Quick Check 1. 90°; 180°; 270°

2a. 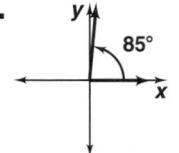 **b.**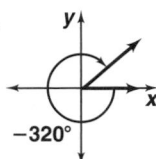

c.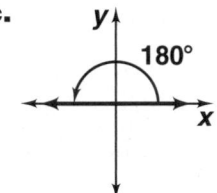

3a. 558° **b.** No; 40° is coterminal with 400° and 760°. **c.** Answers may vary. Sample: The difference between measures of two coterminal angles is a multiple of 360°.

4a. 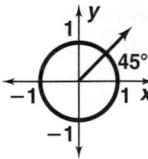 **b.**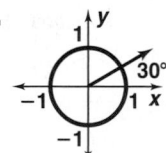

$\frac{\sqrt{2}}{2} \approx 0.707, \frac{\sqrt{2}}{2} \approx 0.707$ $\frac{\sqrt{3}}{2} \approx 0.87, 0.5$

c.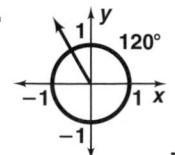

$-0.5, \frac{\sqrt{3}}{2} \approx 0.87$

5a. −0.5, −0.87; the values are equal and are the rounded decimal values of $-\frac{1}{2}$ and $-\frac{\sqrt{3}}{2}$.

b. $-\frac{\sqrt{2}}{2}, \frac{\sqrt{2}}{2}$; ≈−0.707, ≈0.707 **c.** $-\frac{\sqrt{3}}{2}, \frac{1}{2}$

Lesson 13-3   pp. 726–729, 733

Check Skills You'll Need 1. 25.1 in. **2.** 219.9 m
3. 50.3 mi **4.** 10.7 ft **5.** 31.4 mm **6.** 19.8 cm

Quick Check 1a. ≈1.48 radians **b.** ≈143.24°
2a. 90° **b.** $\frac{5\pi}{4}$ radians **c.** ≈114.59° **d.** $\frac{5\pi}{6}$ radians

3a. 0.71, 0.71; these values are the rounded decimal equivalent of $\frac{\sqrt{2}}{2}$. **b.** π radians = 180°, so $\frac{\pi}{4}$ radians becomes $\frac{180°}{4}$, which is 45°. **4.** 6.3 in.
5a. ≈3.14 units **b.** ≈4.19 units **c.** ≈6.28 units
d. ≈10.47 units

Checkpoint Quiz 1 1. 5, 1 **2.** 4, 2 **3.** $-\frac{\sqrt{2}}{2}, \frac{\sqrt{2}}{2}$
4. $-\frac{1}{2}, -\frac{\sqrt{3}}{2}$ **5.** 0, −1 **6.** $\frac{1}{2}, \frac{\sqrt{3}}{2}$ **7.** −π radians
8. $\frac{\pi}{5}$ radians **9.** 180° **10.** 240°

Lesson 13-4   pp. 734–738

Check Skills You'll Need 1. 2 **2.** all real numbers **3.** 1
4. all real numbers between −1 and 1, inclusive

Quick Check 1a. yes; at 450° **b.** Yes; the y-values repeat at regular intervals. **2a.** 1 **b.** 360°, 2π radians **c.** domain: all real numbers, range: all real numbers between −1 and 1, inclusive **3a.** 2π
b. $\frac{2\pi}{3}$ **4a.** 4 **b.** 3

5a. 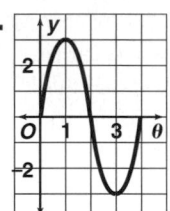   **b.** zero-min-zero-max-zero

c.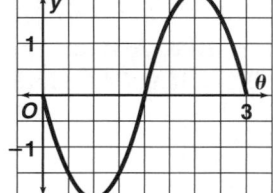

6a. 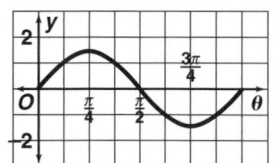 **b.**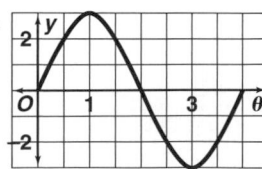

7. $y = \sin \frac{\pi}{320}\theta, y = \sin \frac{\pi}{285}\theta$

Lesson 13-5   pp. 743–745

Check Skills You'll Need 1. 1 **2.** 0 **3.** −1 **4.** 0

Quick Check 1. They are the same curve translated $\frac{\pi}{2}$ units horizontally.

2a.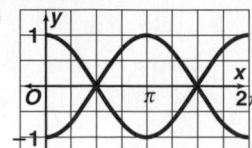

They are reflections of each other over the x-axis.

b. min-zero-max-zero-min

c.

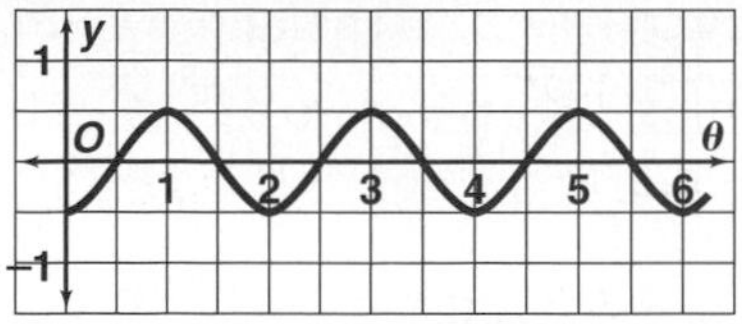

3a. $y = 4 \cos \frac{1}{3}\theta$ **b.** $y = 2.5 \cos \frac{\pi}{4}\theta$ **4a.** 1.2, 2.0, 4.3, 5.1 **b.** 2.2, 4.1 **c.** $0 \leq \theta < 2.2$ and $4.1 < \theta \leq 2\pi$; $2.2 < \theta < 4.1$

Lesson 13-6 pp. 749–751

Check Skills You'll Need **1.** ≈0.87, 0.5; ≈1.73 **2.** 0.5, ≈0.87; ≈0.58 **3.** 1, 0; undefined **4.** 0.5, ≈−0.87; ≈−0.58 **5.** 1, 0; undefined **6.** 0, 1; 0

Quick Check **1a.** 0.4, −0.4 **b.** The terminal side of $\frac{\pi}{2}$ lies on the line $x = 0$, which cannot intersect $x = 1$.

2a.

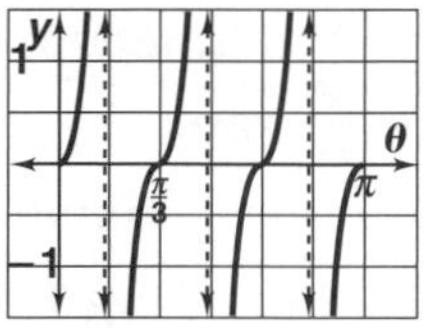

b.

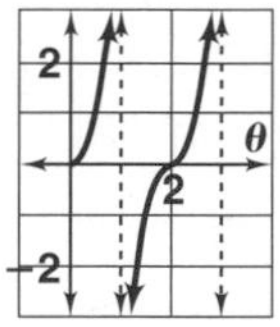

3a. 46.6 ft **b.** 8°

Lesson 13-7 pp. 756–760, 762

Check Skills You'll Need

1.

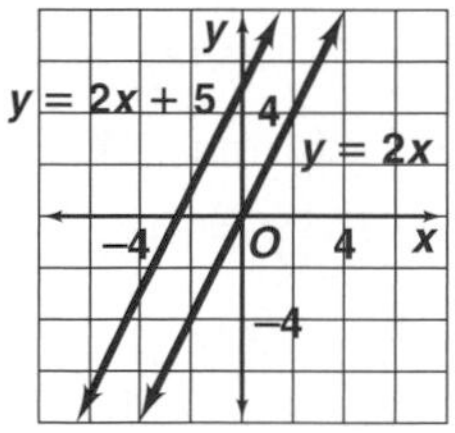

vertical

2.

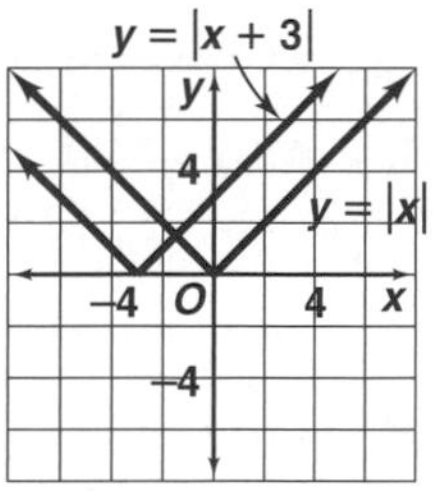

horizontal

3.

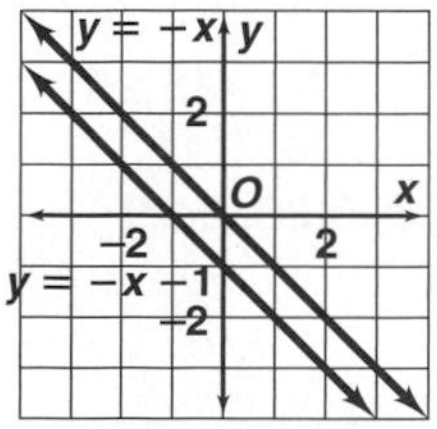

vertical

4.

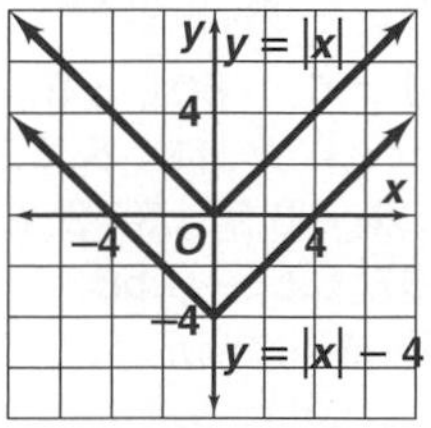

vertical

5.

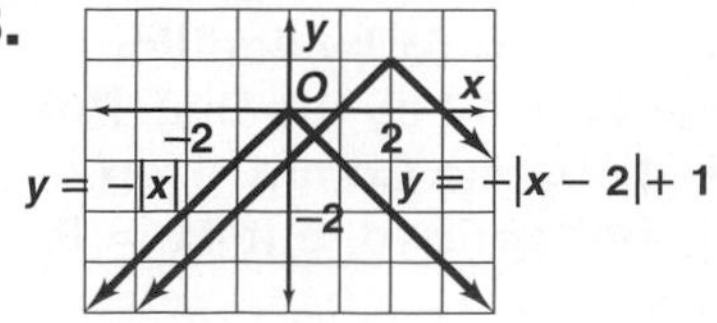

diagonal

6.

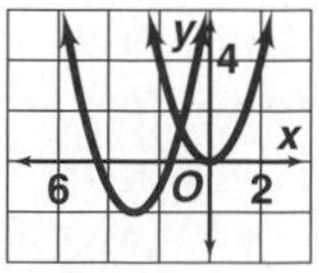

diagonal

Quick Check **1a.** 5; 5 units to the right **b.** −3; 3 units to the left

2a.

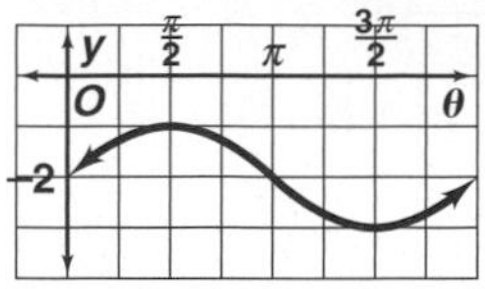

b.

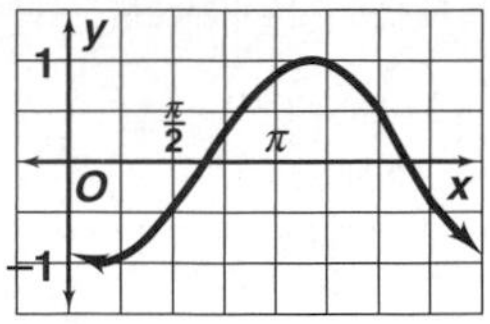

(b) is a phase shift.

3a.

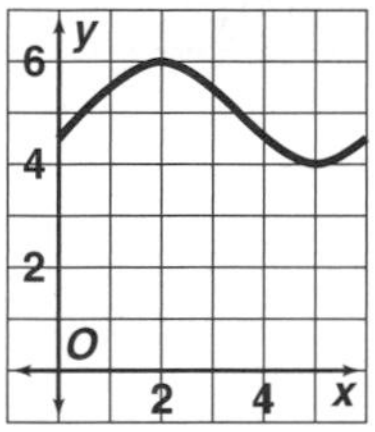

b.

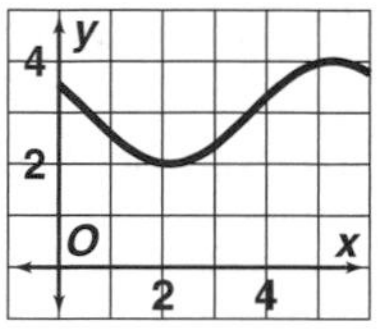

4a.

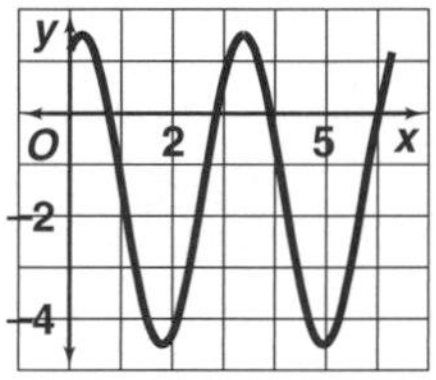

b.

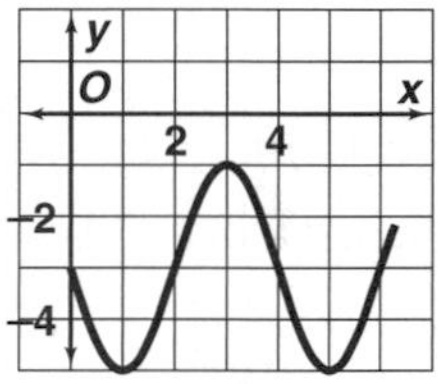

5a. $y = \cos x + \frac{\pi}{2}$ **b.** $y = 2 \sin\left(x - \frac{\pi}{4}\right)$
6a. 86.5° **b.** day 100

Checkpoint Quiz 2

1.

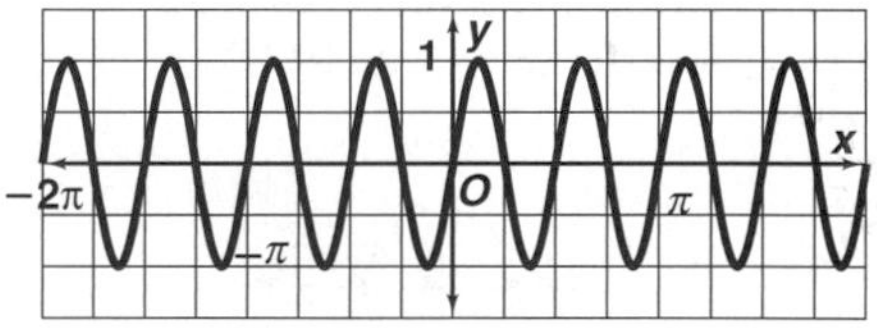

2.

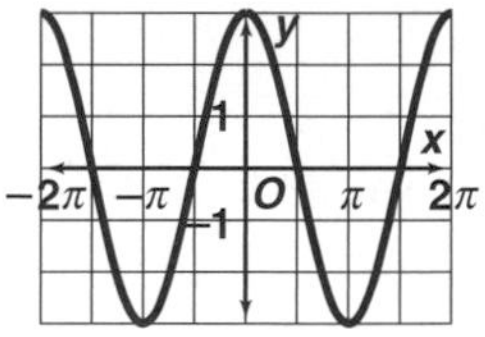

3.

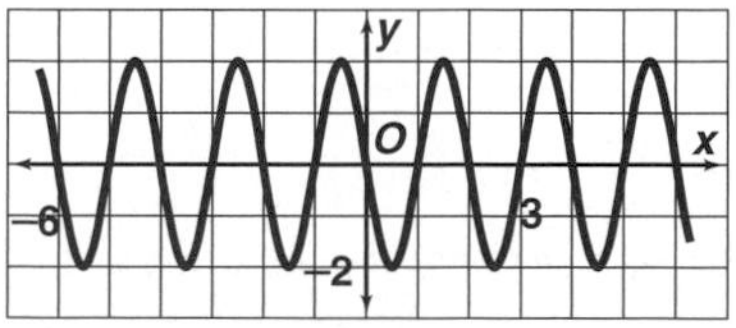

4.

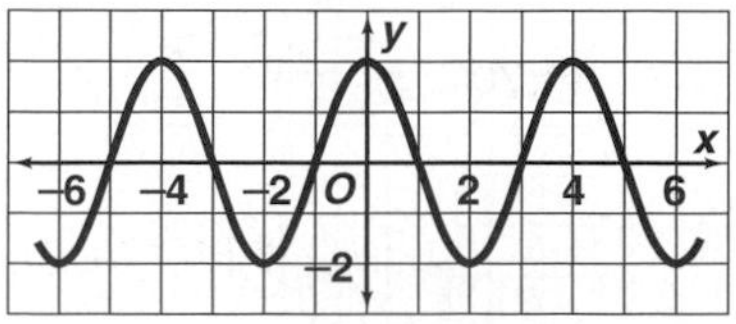

5.

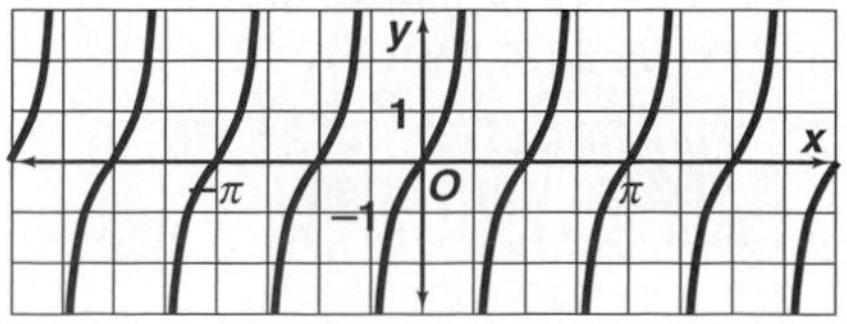

6.

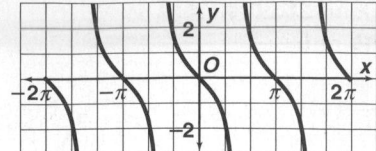

7.

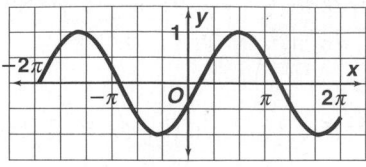

8.

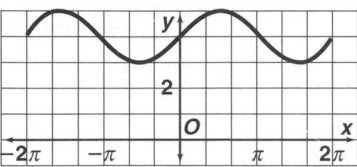

9.

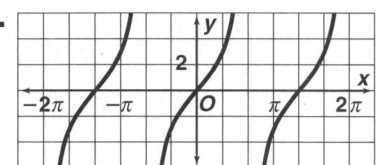

10.

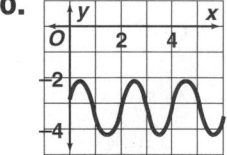

Lesson 13-8   pp. 763–766

Check Skills You'll Need 1. $\frac{13}{9}$ **2.** $-\frac{8}{5}$ **3.** 2π
4. $\frac{15}{4m}$ **5.** $-\frac{t}{14}$

6.

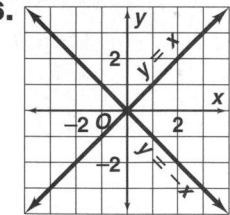

7.

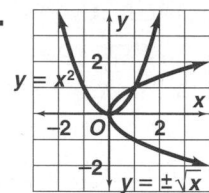

8.

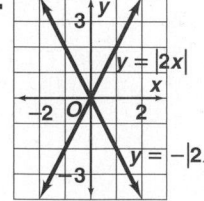

9.

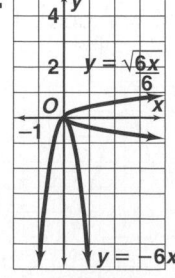

Quick Check 1a. $\frac{8}{15}$ **b.** ≈ 0.70 **2a.** 2 **b.** 1 **c.** 2
3a. -1.003 **b.** -2.403 **c.** undefined

4.

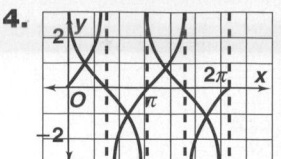

5. ≈ 1.4142 **6.** 6.9 ft; 8.5 ft; 68.8 ft

Chapter 14

Check Your Readiness   p. 776

1. $\pm\frac{5}{2}$ **2.** $\pm\sqrt{23}$ **3.** $\pm\frac{4\sqrt{15}}{3}$ **4.** $\pm\frac{\sqrt{22}}{2}$ **5.** $\pm\sqrt{30}$
6. ± 2 **7.** Domain of f is $\{x \mid x \in R\}$, range of f is
$\{y \mid y \in R\}$; $f^{-1}(x) = \frac{x-2}{5}$, domain of f^{-1} is
$\{x \mid x \in R\}$, range of f^{-1} is $\{y \mid y \in R\}$. f^{-1} is a
function. **8.** Domain of f is $\{x \mid x \in R, x \geq -3\}$,
$x \geq 0$ range of f is $\{y \mid y \in R, y \geq 0\}$; $f^{-1}(x) =$
$x^2 - 3$, domain of f^{-1} is $\{x \mid x \in R, x \geq 0\}$, range
of f^{-1} is $\{y \mid y \in R, y \geq -3\}$. f^{-1} is a function.
9. Domain of f is $\{x \mid x \in R, x \geq \frac{4}{3}\}$, range of f is
$\{y \mid y \in R, y \geq 0\}$; $f^{-1}(x) = \frac{x^2 + 4}{3}$ $x \geq 0$, domain of
f is $\{x \mid x \in R, x \geq 0\}$, range of f^{-1} is $\{y \mid y \in R,$
$y \geq \frac{4}{3}\}$. f^{-1} is a function. **10.** Domain of f is
$\{x \mid x \in R, x \neq 0\}$, range of f is $\{y \mid y \in R, y \neq 0\}$;
$f^{-1}(x) = \frac{5}{x}$, domain of f^{-1} is $\{x \mid x \in R, x \neq 0\}$,
range of f^{-1} is $\{y \mid y \in R, y \neq 0\}$. f^{-1} is a function.
11. Domain of f is $\{x \mid x \in R, x \neq 1\}$, range of f is
$\{y \mid y \in R, y \neq 0\}$; $f^{-1}(x) = \frac{10}{x} + 1$, domain of f^{-1} is
$\{x \mid x \in R, x \neq 0\}$, range of f^{-1} is $\{y \mid y \in R, y \neq 1\}$.
f^{-1} is a function. **12.** Domain of f is $\{x \mid x \in R,$
$x \neq 0\}$, range of f is $\{y \mid y \in R, y \neq -1\}$; $f^{-1}(x) =$
$\frac{10}{x+1}$, domain of f^{-1} is $\{x \mid x \in R, x \neq -1\}$, range of
f^{-1} is $\{y \mid y \in R, y \neq 0\}$. f^{-1} is a function.

13. -1.5 **14.** 0.002 **15.** ≈ 1.065 **16.** $\approx 18{,}257$
17. $\approx 3 \times 10^{-5}$ **18.** 5 **19.** 0.67, 0.74, 1.11
20. $-0.26, -0.97, 3.73$ **21.** 0.96, 0.28, 0.29
22. $-0.87, 0.5, -0.58$

Lesson 14-1   pp. 778–780

Check Skills You'll Need 1. Yes; $2x + 3x = (2 + 3)x$ by
the Dist. Prop. and $(2 + 3)x = 5x$ by addition.
2. Yes; $-(4x - 10) = -4x + 10$ by the Dist. Prop.,
and $-4x + 10 = 10 - 4x$ by the Comm. Prop.
3. No; for $x = 0$, $\frac{4x^2}{x}$ is not defined, but $4x = 0$.

4. No; for $x = 1$, $\frac{x^2 + 1}{x - 1}$ is not defined, but
$x + 1 = 2$.

Quick Check 1. $1 + \cot^2 \theta = 1 + \left(\frac{\cos \theta}{\sin \theta}\right)^2 =$
$1 + \frac{\cos^2 \theta}{\sin^2 \theta} = 1 + \frac{1 - \sin^2 \theta}{\sin^2 \theta} = 1 + \frac{1}{\sin^2 \theta} - \frac{\sin^2 \theta}{\sin^2 \theta} =$
$1 + \csc^2 \theta - 1 = \csc^2 \theta$ **2.** $\sec^2 \theta -$
$\sec^2 \theta \cos^2 \theta = \left(\frac{1}{\cos \theta}\right)^2 - \left(\frac{1}{\cos \theta}\right)^2 \cos^2 \theta =$
$\frac{1}{\cos^2 \theta} - \frac{1}{\cos^2 \theta} \cdot \cos^2 \theta = \frac{1}{\cos^2 \theta} - \frac{\cos^2 \theta}{\cos^2 \theta} =$
$\frac{1 - \cos^2 \theta}{\cos^2 \theta} = \frac{\sin^2 \theta}{\cos^2 \theta} = \tan^2 \theta$ **3.** $\csc \theta$

Lesson 14-2   pp. 783–786

Check Skills You'll Need 1. $f^{-1}(x) = x - 1$
2. $f^{-1}(x) = \frac{x + 3}{2}$ **3.** $f^{-1}(x) = \pm\sqrt{x - 4}$
4. 0.5 **5.** $\frac{\sqrt{2}}{2}$ **6.** $-\frac{\sqrt{2}}{2}$ **7.** 0 **8.** -1 **9.** $-\frac{\sqrt{3}}{2}$

Quick Check 1. none, $\frac{\pi}{2} + \pi n$, none
2a. $120° + n \cdot 360°$ and $240° + n \cdot 360°$
b. $150° + n \cdot 360°$ and $210° + n \cdot 360°$
c. $45° + n \cdot 360°$ and $315° + n \cdot 360°$
3a. $0.46 + 2\pi n$ and $2.69 + 2\pi n$
b. $-0.82 + 2\pi n$ and $3.96 + 2\pi n$ **4a.** $0.41 + 2\pi n$
and $3.56 + 2\pi n$ **b.** $-0.63 + 2\pi n$ and $2.51 + 2\pi n$
5. $\frac{11\pi}{6}$ and $\frac{7\pi}{6}$ **6.** $\frac{\pi}{2}$ and $\frac{3\pi}{2}$ **7a.** $\frac{1}{2}$ s; 3 s **b.** At 2 s;
the toy will reach a maximum at 4 in. and then
come back down, again hitting 2 in. at 2 s.
c. Let $y_1 = -4 \cos \frac{2\pi}{3} t$ and let $y_2 = 2$. Graph.
Trace and calculate the intersection.

Lesson 14-3   pp. 792–795, 799

Check Skills You'll Need 1. s **2.** r **3.** a **4.** t

Quick Check 1. 180 m

2.

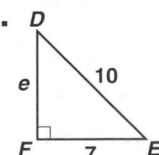

$\frac{3}{5} = 0.6, \frac{5}{3} \approx 1.67$

3a. Answers may vary. Sample: An advantage is
that simplification of the equation is easier. A
disadvantage is that you have to press an extra
button on the calculator to get the cotangent
function. **b.** ≈ 34.29 ft **4a.** 23.58° **b.** 56.25°

5.

$e \approx 7.14$; $m\angle E \approx 45.6°$, $m\angle D \approx 44.4°$

Checkpoint Quiz 1 1. $\csc \theta$ **2.** $\tan^2 \theta$ **3.** $-\csc^2 \theta$
4. 2.25 **5.** 0.320 **6.** 1.345 **7.** $a \approx 7.7$,
$m\angle A \approx 29.0°$, $m\angle B \approx 61.0°$ **8.** $c \approx 10.0$,

$m\angle A \approx 51.9°$, $m\angle B \approx 38.1°$ **9.** $a \approx 19.6$,
$m\angle A \approx 34.0°$, $m\angle B \approx 56.0°$

Lesson 14-4   pp. 801–803

Check Skills You'll Need 1. $\frac{1}{12}$ **2.** $\frac{\sqrt{2}}{8}$ **3.** $\frac{\sqrt{3}}{20}$ **4.** $\frac{1}{24}$ **5.** $\frac{\sqrt{2}}{16}$
6. $\frac{\sqrt{3}}{18}$ **7.** 6 cm^2 **8.** 45 in.^{2} **9.** 32.8 mm^2
10. 10.03 ft^2

Quick Check 1. 36.6 in.^{2} **2.** 31.0 yd **3.** 68.4° **4.** 56.4

Lesson 14-5   pp. 808–810

Check Skills You'll Need 1. 26.2° **2.** 18.1 **3.** 52.1° or
17.9°

Quick Check 1. 6.4 **2.** 75.3° **3.** 30.7°

Lesson 14-6   pp. 814–817, 820

Check Skills You'll Need 1. $\sin \theta$ **2.** $\cos \theta$ **3.** $\tan \theta$ **4.** 1
5. $\sec^2 \theta$ **6.** $\csc^2 \theta$

Quick Check 1. $\cos\left(\theta - \frac{\pi}{2}\right) =$
$\cos\left(-\left(\frac{\pi}{2} - \theta\right)\right) = \cos\left(\frac{\pi}{2} - \theta\right) = \sin \theta$
2. $0, \pi$ **3.** $\sec(90° - A) = \csc A$
4. $\frac{\sqrt{6} - \sqrt{2}}{4}$ **5.** $-2 - \sqrt{3}$

Checkpoint Quiz 2 1. 36.1 cm^2 **2.** 77.3 ft^2 **3.** 34.9 m^2
4. 400.8 in^2 **5.** $a = 8.2$ ft, $m\angle B = 69.7°$, $m\angle C =$
83.3° **6.** $m\angle D = 58.4°$, $m\angle E = 53.0°$, $m\angle F =$
68.7° **7.** $\cos 80°$ **8.** $\sin 63°$ **9.** $\sin 80°$

Lesson 14-7   pp. 821–823

Check Skills You'll Need 1. $\cos A \cos B + \sin A \sin B$
2. $\cos A \cos B - \sin A \sin B$ **3.** $\frac{\tan A - \tan B}{1 + \tan A \tan B}$
4. $\sin A \cos B - \cos A \sin B$ **5.** $\sin A \cos B +$
$\cos A \sin B$ **6.** $\frac{\tan A + \tan B}{1 - \tan A \tan B}$

Quick Check 1. $\frac{\sqrt{3}}{2}$ **2.** $2 \cos 2\theta =$
$2(2 \cos^2 \theta - 1) = 4 \cos^2 \theta - 2$ **3a.** $\frac{1}{2}$ **b.** $-\frac{\sqrt{3}}{3}$
4. $-\frac{3}{5}, -\frac{4}{3}$

Selected Answers

Chapter 1

EXERCISES 1. natural numbers, whole numbers, integers, rational numbers, real numbers
3. irrational numbers, real numbers **9.** whole numbers, rational numbers **11.** irrational numbers, rational numbers

13.

$$-6\ -5\ -4\ -3\ -2\ -1\ 0\ 1$$

15.

$$-1\ 0\ 1\ 2\ 3\ 4$$

17. > **19.** > **25.** $-\frac{1}{4} > -\frac{1}{3}$, $-\frac{1}{3} < -\frac{1}{4}$ **27.** $-2.\overline{3} < 2.\overline{1}$, $2.\overline{1} > -2.\overline{3}$ **35.** $-3\frac{3}{5}, \frac{5}{18}$

37. $1\frac{7}{2}, -\frac{2}{7}$ **43.** Comm. Prop. of Add. **45.** Comm. Prop. of Mult. **49.** 0.06 **51.** 1.6 **57.** $-3\frac{1}{2}$ **59.** $\frac{1}{2}$

61. -5 **65.** natural numbers, whole numbers, integers, rational numbers, real numbers
67. irrational numbers, real numbers **71.** >
73. < **79.** Answers may vary. Sample: 4 is a whole number, but $\frac{1}{4}$ is not a whole number.
81. 0 is a whole number, and since $-0 = 0$, the opposite of 0 is a whole number.

EXERCISES 1. -30 **3.** 368 **9.** 1 ft **11.** 64 ft
13. 0.013 mm **15.** 0.4 mm **17.** $1210
19. $1464.10 **21.** $4a$ **23.** $-9a + b$ **37.** $4a$ **39.** 17
41. 66 **47.** $-\frac{3}{4}a^2 + 2b^2$ **49.** $\frac{7y^2}{12} + \frac{2y}{15}$ **55.** C **57.** G
63. Assoc. Prop. of Add., Comm. Prop. of Add., Assoc. Prop. of Add., Identity Prop. of Mult., Dist. Prop. of Add., Simplify. **75.** $-4.3, -|3.4|, |-3.4|, |-4.3|$, **77.** $-\sqrt{\frac{1}{8}}, -\sqrt{\frac{1}{10}}, \sqrt{\frac{1}{16}}, \sqrt{\frac{1}{4}}$ **79.** > **81.** <

EXERCISES 1. 23 **3.** $\frac{17}{2}$ **9.** 8 **11.** 2 **17.** $h = \frac{2A}{b}$
19. $w = \frac{V}{lh}$ **23.** $x = \frac{c}{a+b}, a \neq -b$
25. $x = a(c - b)$ or $ac - ab, a \neq 0$ **29.** 4 h
31. width = 4.5 cm, length = 7.5 cm **37.** 3
39. $\frac{3}{2}$ **43.** $r_2 = \frac{Rr_1}{r_1 - R}$ **45.** $v = \frac{h + 5t^2}{t}$ **51.** ≈ 4.03 m
55. $x = ab - b^2 - a, b \neq 0$ **57.** $x = \frac{b+d}{c-a}, a \neq c$

EXERCISES 1. $x \leq -\frac{1}{2}$

$$-3\ -2\ -1\ 0\ 1\ 2\ 3\ 4\ 5$$

3. $a > 11$ **15.** The longest side is less than 21 cm.
17. 40 students **19.** $-4 \leq x \leq 2$

$$-7\ -6\ -5\ -4\ -3\ -2\ -1\ 0\ 1\ 2\ 3\ 4$$

21. $-5 < x \leq 6$ **23.** All real numbers are solutions.

$$-4\ -3\ -2\ -1\ 0\ 1\ 2\ 3\ 4$$

25. $x \leq -3$ or $x \geq 9$ **27.** between $4\frac{1}{2}$ and $5\frac{1}{2}$ days
29. $z \geq 6$ **31.** $x \geq -48$ **39.** Dist. Prop.; arithmetic; Sub. Prop. of Inequality; Mult. Prop. of Inequality **41.** $-1 < x < 8$ **43.** no solutions

EXERCISES 1. $-6, 6$ **3.** $-6, 12$ **11.** $\frac{2}{3}$ **13.** $-4, 8$
17. $x \leq -3$ or $x \geq 13$

$$-6\ -4\ -2\ 0\ 2\ 4\ 6\ 8\ 10\ 12\ 14\ 16\ 18$$

19. all real numbers **23.** $-2\frac{2}{3} < y < 3\frac{1}{3}$

$$-5\ -4\ -3\ -2\ -1\ 0\ 1\ 2\ 3\ 4\ 5\ 6$$

25. no solution **29.** $|k - 50.5| \leq 0.5$
31. $|b - 52.5| \leq 2.5$ **35.** $-\frac{3}{2}, -1$ **37.** $-\frac{1}{3}$
45. $x \leq -8$ or $x \geq 5$ **47.** $t < -\frac{3}{2}$ or $t > 2$
55. C **59.** $|x - 9.55| \leq 0.02, 9.53 \leq x \leq 9.57$

EXERCISES 1. $\frac{161}{340}$ or about 47%; $\frac{179}{340}$ or about 53% **7.** $\frac{1}{2}$, or 50% **9.** $\frac{4}{5}$, or 80% **11.** $\frac{19}{125}$, or 15.2%
13. $\frac{14}{25}$, or 56% **15.** {Gg, Gg, gg, gg}; $\frac{1}{2}$, or 50%
17. $\frac{1}{16}$, or 6.25% **19.** $\frac{1}{4}$, or 25% **21a.** 1 **b.** 0
25. $\frac{52}{147}$, or 35.4% **27.** $\frac{31}{147}$, or 21.1% **29.** $\frac{1}{2}$ **31.** 0
35. $\frac{4}{9}$ **37.** $\frac{4}{9}$ **39.** $\approx 6.4\%$

1. additive inverse **2.** sample space **3.** solution of an equation **4.** compound inequality
5. reciprocal **6.** experimental probability
7. theoretical probability **8.** extraneous solution
9. simulation **10.** absolute value **11.** real numbers, irrational numbers **12.** real numbers, rational numbers, integers **13.** real numbers, rational numbers, integers, whole numbers, natural numbers **14.** real numbers, irrational numbers **15.** real numbers, rational numbers
16. > **17.** > **18.** > **19.** <

20. 3.4; $-\frac{1}{3.4}$

$$-6\ -4\ -2\ 0\ 2\ 4\ 6$$

21. $-4 - \pi$; $\frac{1}{4 + \pi}$

$$-8\ -6\ -4\ -2\ 0\ 2\ 4\ 6\ 8$$

22. $-1\frac{7}{8}; \frac{8}{15}$

$$-3\ -2\ -1\ 0\ 1\ 2\ 3$$

23. $-\sqrt{12};\ \dfrac{1}{\sqrt{12}}$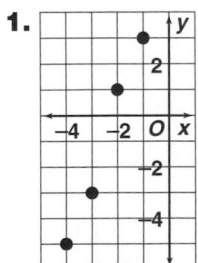
−4 −2 0 2 4

24–28. Answers may vary. Samples:
24. $(x + 3)(1) = x + 3$ **25.** $(2x + 7) + 3y = 2x + (7 + 3y)$ **26.** $3(2x − 4) = 6x − 12$ **27.** $(5x)(3y) = (3y)(5x)$ **28.** $10z + 0 = 10z$ **29.** 4 **30.** 19 **31.** $5b$
32. 11 **33.** 10 **34.** 5 **35.** 4 **36.** −8 **37.** $\dfrac{b − a^2}{a}$, $a \neq 0, b \neq 0$ **38.** 10 cm, 6 cm **39.** 525 mi/h
40. 70°, 110°
41. $z \leq \dfrac{2}{5}$
0 1 2 3

42. $x > 2$
−2 −1 0 1 2 3

43. $y > 4.5$
0 1 2 3 4 5 6

44. $−1 \leq x \leq 1$
−3 −2 −1 0 1 2 3

45. $x \leq \dfrac{3}{2}$ or $x > 6$
0 1 2 3 4 5 6 7

46. $y \geq \dfrac{5}{3}$
−2 −1 0 1 2 3

47. $\$155{,}850 \leq A \leq \$415{,}850$ **48.** 1 **49.** $\dfrac{1}{5}$, 9
50. no solutions
51. $−\dfrac{1}{3} \leq x \leq \dfrac{5}{3}$
−2 −1 0 1 2 3

52. $y < 0$ or $y > 18$
−4 0 4 8 12 16 20

53. $x < −4$ or $x > 6$
−6 −4 −2 0 2 4 6 8

54. $|x − 43.6| \leq 0.1$ **55.** $\dfrac{1}{2}$ **56.** $\dfrac{5}{8}$ **57.** $\dfrac{1}{2}$ **58.** $\dfrac{3}{8}$
59. $\dfrac{5}{8}$ **60.** about 9%

CHAPTER 2

Lesson 2-1   pp. 59–61

EXERCISES

1. 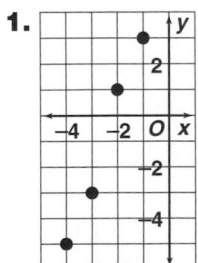   **3.**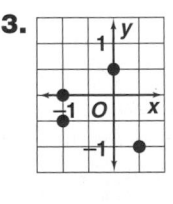

5. (−2, −2), (−1, 1), (1, 1), (1, 0), (3, 3), (3, −2); domain {−2, −1, 1, 3}, range {−2, 0, 1, 3}
7. (−2, 0), (−1, 2), (0, 3), (1, 2), (2, 0); domain = {−2, −1, 0, 1, 2}, range = {0, 2, 3} **9.** domain range
13. function **15.** function

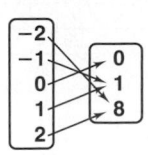

---

17. not a function **19.** function **23.** 13, 7, −3.5, −14 **25.** −2, −4, −7.5, −11
33.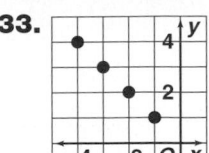

domain {−4, −3, −2, −1}, range {1, 2, 3, 4}
35. domain $\left\{ −\dfrac{3}{2}, \dfrac{1}{2}, \dfrac{3}{2}, \dfrac{5}{2} \right\}$, range $\left\{ −\dfrac{1}{2}, \dfrac{1}{2} \right\}$
37. domain {−2, −1, 0, 9}, range {2, 5, 7}, not a function **39.** domain {−3.2 ≤ x ≤ 3.2}, range {−1 ≤ y ≤ 1}, not a function **41.** B **43.** yes
45. no

Lesson 2-2   pp. 67–70

EXERCISES

1. 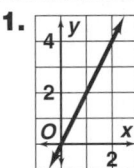   **9a.**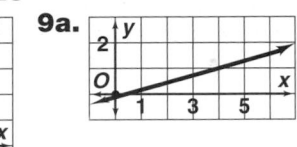

$y = 0.23x$, domain {$x \mid x \in$ R and $x \geq 0$}, range {$y \mid y \in$ R and $y \geq 0$} **b.** x-intercept (0, 0), y-intercept (0, 0); when no miles have been driven, there is no cost. **c.** 0.23 represents a cost of $.23 per mile driven. **11.** −1 **13.** 3 **21.** $\dfrac{5}{6}x − y = \dfrac{19}{3}$
23. $y = −2$ **27.** $y − 0 = \dfrac{5}{4}(x − 1)$
29. $y + 1 = −\dfrac{4}{3}(x − 0)$ **33.** $\dfrac{3}{2}$ **35.** $−\dfrac{A}{B}$
39. $y = \dfrac{5}{2}x + \dfrac{13}{2}$ 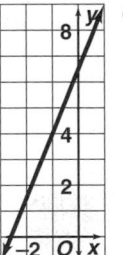 **41.** $x = 1$

43. 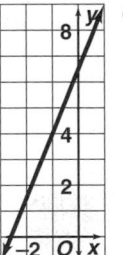   **51.** $\dfrac{1}{3}$ **53.** $−\dfrac{1}{4}$

55. −1; (0, 1000), (1000, 0) **57.** 54; (0, −1), $\left(\dfrac{1}{54}, 0 \right)$
63. $−\dfrac{5}{13}$ **65.** $−\dfrac{7}{10}$ **67.** $y = 3x + 2$ **69.** B
71. $y = −1$ **73.** $y = \dfrac{5}{6}x + \dfrac{10}{3}$

75. $3x − 2y = 2$ **77.** $3x + 12y = −4$

Extension

1. 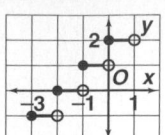 **3.**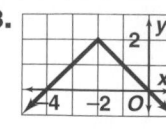

5. $f(x) = \begin{cases} -3x - 10, & \text{if } x \le -2 \\ \frac{1}{2}x - 3, & \text{if } -2 < x < 2 \\ 2x - 6, & \text{if } x \ge 2 \end{cases}$

Lesson 2-3

EXERCISES 1. yes; 2, $y = 2x$ **3.** no **9.** yes;
12 **11.** yes; −2 **17.** $\frac{2}{7}$; $-\frac{10}{7}$ **19.** −1; 5 **25.** 4 **27.** $\frac{5}{3}$
29. no **31.** yes; $k = 1.3$, $y = 1.3x$ **33.** $y = 2x$
35. $y = -\frac{9}{2}x$ **41.** 9 **43.** 90
47. Yes; $y = -\frac{5}{6}x$ contains the point $\left(15, -12\frac{1}{2}\right)$.

Lesson 2-4

EXERCISES
1. $d = 62.5h + 15$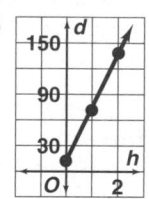

3. $h = 8x + 60$ **5.** $y = 0.5x + 0.75$; 3.25 lb
7. $y = 1.75x + 1.75$; $8.40
9.
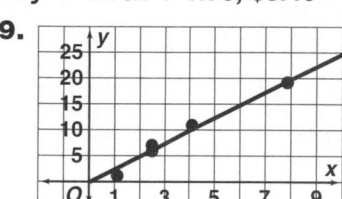

Linear model is reasonable; models may vary.
Sample: $y = 2.6x - 0.6$ **11.** not reasonable
13a.
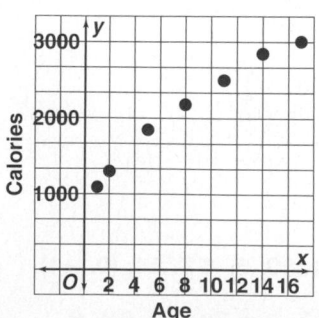

Answers may vary. Sample: $y = 110x + 1170$
b. 2930 Cal **c.** Answers may vary. Sample: No;
adults need fewer Calories, not more.
15. $y = -4x + 10$ **17.** $y = -7.5x - 2.5$ **23.** 104.5
25. 13

Lesson 2-5

EXERCISES
1.

x	0	−1	1	−2	2
y	0	4	4	8	8

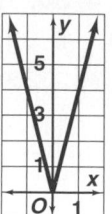

11.
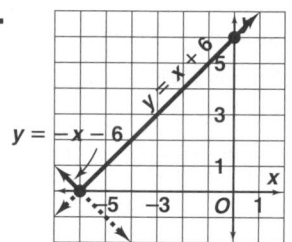

19. 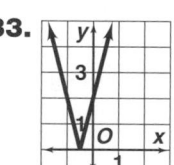 **29.** B **31.** A

33.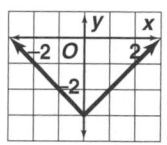

51. A

Lesson 2-6

EXERCISES 1. 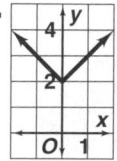 **3.**

5. $y = |x| - \frac{2}{3}$ **7.** $y = |x| + 2$
9. Translate $y = |x|$ left 5 units;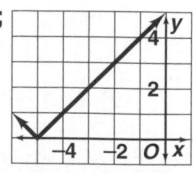

11. Translate $y = |x|$ left 2 units;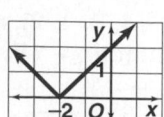

13. $y = |x - 3|$

17. 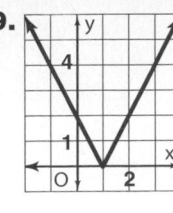 **19.**

23. $y = 2|x|$ **25.** $y = \frac{2}{3}|x|$

29. vertical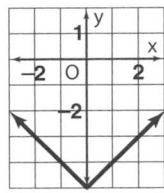

31. horizontal 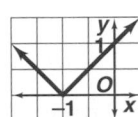 **35.** $y = |x - 2| - 2$

37. $y = -\frac{1}{2}|x + 2| + 4$ **43.** $y = -|x| - 3$

45. $y = 2|x| + 11$ **47.** $y = -|x - p| + q$

Lesson 2-7   pp. 104–106

EXERCISES

1. 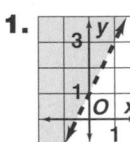 **11.** 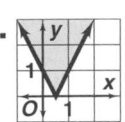 **21.** $5x + 3y \le 9$

23.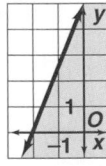

Chapter Review   pp. 109–111

1. dependent **2.** relations **3.** sometimes
4. point-slope **5.** sometimes **6.** not a function;
domain: {1, 3, 5, 8}, range: {0, 1, 2, 3, 8}
7. function; domain: {−10, −6, 5, 6, 10}, range:
{2, 3, 4, 7} **8.** not a function;
domain: $\left\{ -2, -\frac{3}{2}, -1, \frac{1}{2}, 1, 2, 3 \right\}$,
range: $\left\{ -\frac{7}{2}, -\frac{1}{2}, 0, \frac{1}{2}, \frac{3}{2}, 2, \frac{5}{2} \right\}$
9. function; domain: {−4, −2, −1, 1, 3},
range: {−1, 2, 4} **10.** function;
domain: $\left\{ -2, -1, \frac{1}{2}, 3 \right\}$, range: {2} **11.** 6, 4.5, 1
12. $-3\frac{3}{4}, -3\frac{3}{16}, -1\frac{7}{8}$ **13.** $2\frac{5}{6}, 2\frac{5}{24}, \frac{3}{4}$ **14.** $3x + y = 12$
15. $2x - y = 1$ **16.** $2, \left(\frac{3}{4}, 0 \right), \left(0, -\frac{3}{2} \right)$

17. $\frac{M}{N}; \left(\frac{P}{M}, 0 \right), \left(0, -\frac{P}{N} \right)$ **18.** −1; (5, 0), (0, 5)

19a. $y = -\frac{1}{2}x + 7$
b. $y = 2x - 13$
c.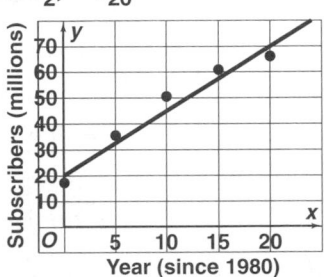

20. no **21.** no **22.** yes; 1; $y = x$ **23.** −4; 1.2
24. $\frac{10}{3}$; −1 **25.** $\frac{7}{2}$; $-1\frac{1}{20}$
26a and b.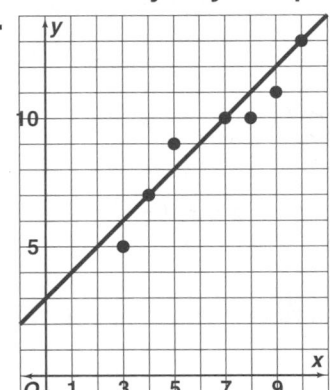

Answers may vary. Sample: $y = 2.5x + 21.5$
c. Answers may vary. Sample: about 96.5 million
27.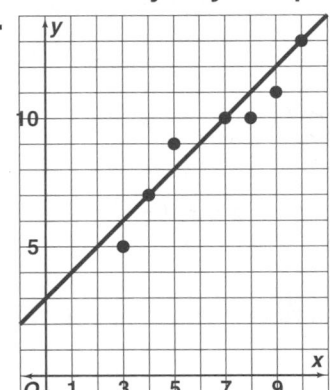

Answers may vary. Sample: reasonable;
$y = x + 3$; 18
28.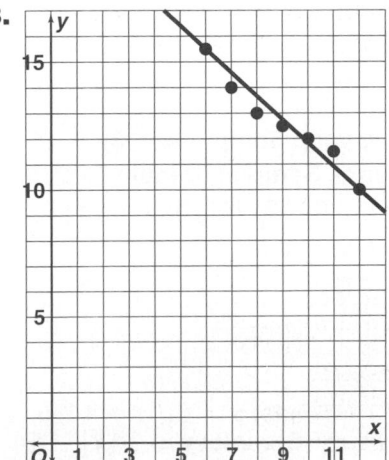

Answers may vary. Sample: reasonable;
$y = -0.8 + 19.9$; 7.9

29.
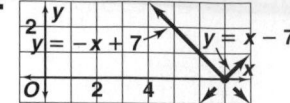

30.
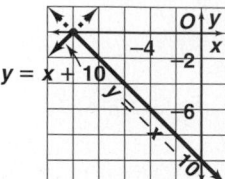

31.
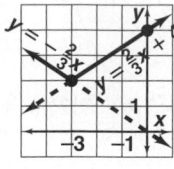

32. $y = |x - 2| + 4$ **33.** $y = |x + 3|$
34. $y = |x - 5| + 2$ **35.** $y = |x - 4| + 1$

36.
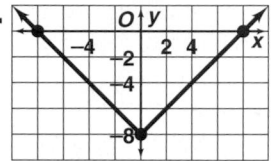

37.
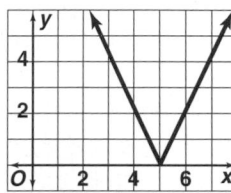

38.
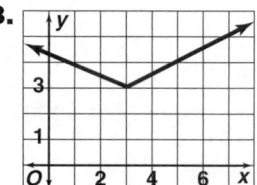

39.
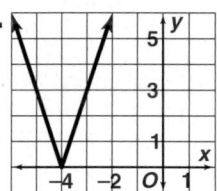

40.
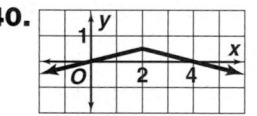

41.
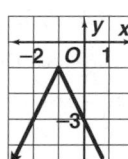

42.
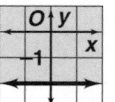

43.
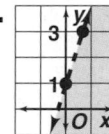

44.
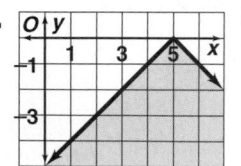

45.
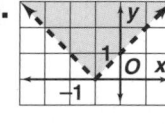

46a. Answers may vary. Sample: $x + 3y \leq 15$
b. Answers may vary. Sample: domain {1, 2, 3, 4, 5, 6, 7, 8, 9, 10, 11, 12, 13, 14, 15}, range {1, 2, 3, 4, 5}

c.
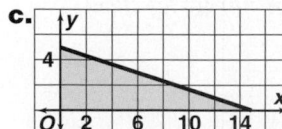

47. Answers may vary. Sample: $y \leq -|x| - 1$

Chapter 3

EXERCISES
1. (3, 1)
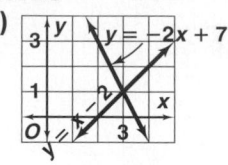

3. (−2, 4)
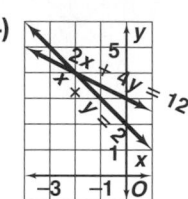

11. $\begin{cases} y = 0.22x + 67.5 \\ y = 0.15x + 75.507 \end{cases}$; about 2085

13. dependent **15.** inconsistent
25. infinitely many solutions

$3 = 4y + x$
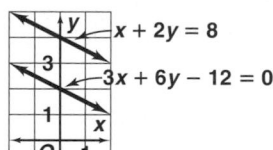

27. no solution

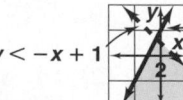

39. dependent **41.** inconsistent

EXERCISES 1. (0.5, 2.5) **3.** (20, 4)

13a. $\begin{cases} d = 0.50m \\ d = 15 \end{cases}$ **b.** 30 miles

15a. $\begin{cases} p = 28 \\ p = 8 + 0.35d \end{cases}$ **b.** 58 **19.** (2, 4)
21. (2, −2) **31.** {(a, d) | −3a + d = −1} **33.** no solution **45.** (m, n) = (4, −3) **47.** (t, v) = (50, 750)
57. Substitution; the first equation is solved for y.
59. Substitution; the second equation is solved for y.

EXERCISES 1. (0, 4), (0, 5), (0, 6), (0, 7), (0, 8)
5. no **7.**

$y < -x + 1$ $y \leq 2x + 2$

9.

$y \leq 3$ $y \leq \frac{1}{2}x + 1$

17. $\begin{cases} a + c \geq 40 \\ c \leq 30 \end{cases}$

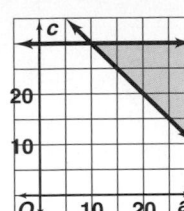

19. 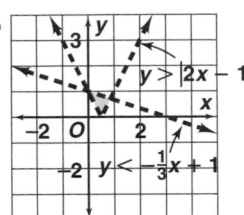 **21.**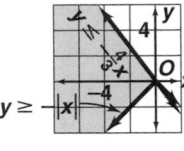

31. A, B **33.** A, B

43. 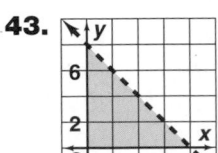 **45.**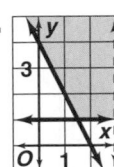

Lesson 3-4 pp. 142–144

EXERCISES 1. When $x = 4$ and $y = 2$, P is maximized at 16. **3.** When $x = 6$ and $y = 8$, C is minimized at 36.

5. 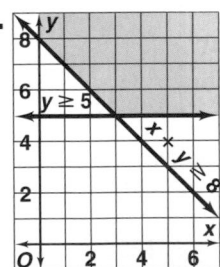 vertices: (3, 5), (0, 8); minimized at (0, 8)

11. 70 spruce; 0 maple **13.** A

15. 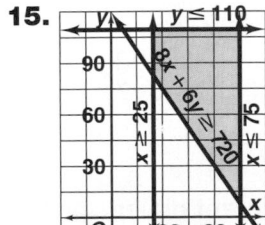 vertices: (75, 20), (75, 110), $\left(25, 86\frac{2}{3}\right)$, (25, 110); minimized when $C = 633\frac{1}{3}$ at $\left(25, 86\frac{2}{3}\right)$

Lesson 3-5 pp. 149–151

EXERCISES 1. 1 unit back, 5 units right
3. 2 units forward, 5 units up

5.

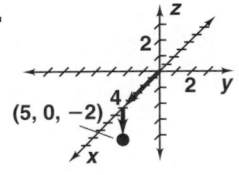

13. (0, 0, 0) **15.** (0, 40, 0)

19. 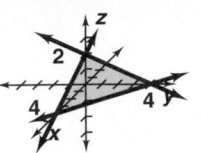 **27.**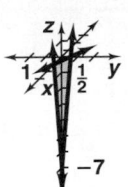

37. Mt. Kilimanjaro **39.** Vildivia Seamount

Lesson 3-6 pp. 157–159

EXERCISES 1. (4, 2, −3) **3.** (2, 1, −5)
11. $(a, b, c) = (2, 3, -2)$ **13.** (5, 2, 2)
19. $220,000 was placed in short-term notes. $440,000 was placed in government bonds. $340,000 was placed in utility bonds.
21. 50 nickels, 10 dimes, and 15 quarters
23. one solution **25.** (8, 1, 3) **27.** $\left(\frac{1}{2}, 2, -3\right)$
39. 75 apples; 25 pears

Chapter Review pp. 161–163

1. A **2.** D **3.** B **4.** E **5.** C **6.** (−2, −3) **7.** (2, 4)
8. no solution **9.** (−2, 0) **10.** (3, 6) **11.** no solution **12.** consistent and dependent
13. consistent and independent **14.** inconsistent
15. 20 checks **16.** (10, −4) **17.** (0, 4) **18.** (1, 9)
19. (3, 7) **20.** no solution **21.** $\left(\frac{7}{24}, \frac{1}{24}\right)$
22. 1 serving of roast beef and 2 servings of mashed potatoes

23. 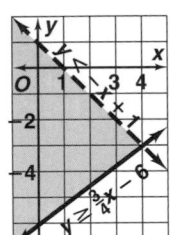 **24.**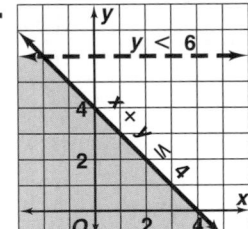

25.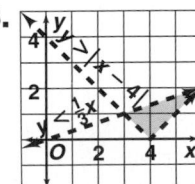

26. Let r = number of gallons of regular coffee, and d = number of gallons of decaffeinated coffee.
$r + d \geq 10$
$\frac{1}{3}r \geq d$

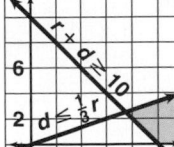

27.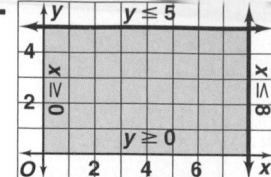

vertices: (0, 0), (8, 0), (8, 5), (0, 5)
$C = 0$ at (0, 0)

28.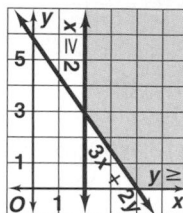

vertices: (4, 0) (2, 3)
$C = 11$ at (2, 3)

29.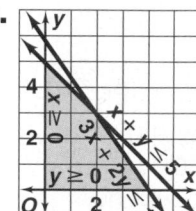

vertices: (0, 0), (4, 0), (2, 3), (0, 5)
$P = 25$ at (0, 5)

30. 50 of each type

31. 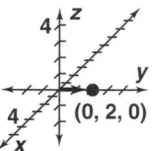 **32.**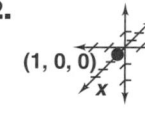

33. 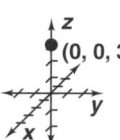 **34.**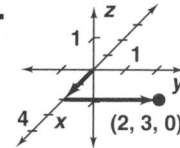

35.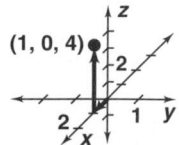

36. (3, 3, 1) **37.** (0, −2, 2) **38.** (−2, 2, −1)
39. (0, 0, 3)
40. 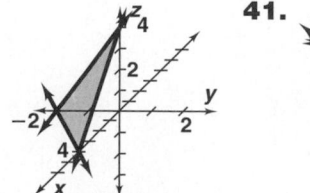 **41.**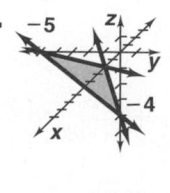

42.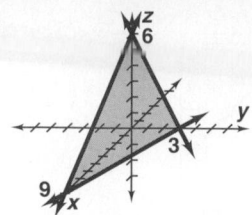

43. (2, 5, 3) **44.** no solution **45.** (6, 0, −2)

Chapter 4

Lesson 4-1   pp. 170–173

1. 3×3 **3.** 1×2 **7.** −3 **9.** $\frac{1}{2}$
13.

	Week 1	Week 2	Week 3	Week 4
Novels	175	154	201	180
Biogr.	100	93	110	92
Sci-Fi.	93	81	114	100
Nonfiction	100	104	103	110

15.

	1998	1999	2000	2001	2002	2003
CDs	847.0	933.9	942.5	881.9	803.3	745.9
DVDs	0.5	2.5	3.3	7.9	10.7	17.5

3.3, which represents 3.3 million DVDs shipped in 2000

17. 2×6, 6×2 **21.** 2×3; 1 **23.** 1×3; 12

Lesson 4-2   pp. 178–180

EXERCISES

1a.

Anita Allen		Mary Beth Lagorashvili	
Shoot	952	Shoot	760
Fence	720	Fence	832
Swim	1108	Swim	1252
Ride	1172	Ride	1144
Run	1044	Run	1064

b. 4996; 5052

3. $\begin{bmatrix} 1 & 3 \\ 4 & 0 \end{bmatrix}$ **5.** $\begin{bmatrix} 0 & 0 \\ 0 & 0 \end{bmatrix}$ **11.** $\begin{bmatrix} -9 & -2 & 12 \\ -15 & 11 & -7 \end{bmatrix}$

13. $\begin{bmatrix} -4 & -1 \\ -1 & -2 \end{bmatrix}$

15. No; the matrices have different dimensions.
17. $x = 2$, $t = \frac{3}{5}$ **19.** $B + D$ cannot be added because they do not have the same dimensions.

21. $\begin{bmatrix} -6 & -3 \\ -4 & -2 \\ -2 & 5 \end{bmatrix}$ **23.** B **25.** $\begin{bmatrix} 9 & 62 \\ 125 & -11 \end{bmatrix}$

29. $a = 2$, $b = \frac{9}{4}$, $c = -1$, $d = 0$, $f = \frac{1}{2}$, $g = -4$
31. $c = \frac{5}{2}$, $d = \frac{2}{5}$, $f = 7$, $g = 5$, $h = -1$

Lesson 4-3 pp. 186–189

1. $\begin{bmatrix} 9 & 12 \\ 18 & -6 \\ 3 & 0 \end{bmatrix}$ **3.** $\begin{bmatrix} -3 & -6 \\ 9 & -3 \end{bmatrix}$ **9.** $\begin{bmatrix} 8 & -2.5 \\ -1.5 & -1 \end{bmatrix}$

11. $\begin{bmatrix} 5 & -12 \\ 9 & -6 \end{bmatrix}$ **13.** $\begin{bmatrix} -8 & 0 \\ 0 & -8 \end{bmatrix}$

19a.

	Lilies	Carnations	Daisies
Arrangement 1	3	0	0
Arrangement 2	3	4	0
Arrangement 3	0	3	4

b.

	Cost
Lilies	2.15
Carnations	0.90
Daisies	1.30

c.

	Cost
Arrangement 1	6.45
Arrangement 2	10.05
Arrangement 3	7.90

21. defined **23.** undefined

31. $\begin{bmatrix} -9 & 7 & 4 \\ 8 & 2 & -3 \end{bmatrix}$ **33.** $\begin{bmatrix} 1 & 0 & -1 \\ 0 & 1 & -1 \end{bmatrix}$

35. B **37.** 4×4;

$\begin{bmatrix} a & 0 & b & 0 \\ a-2e & 0 & b & -2f \\ 2e & 0 & 0 & 2f \\ -a+e & 0 & -b & f \end{bmatrix}$

39. $\begin{bmatrix} 9 & -6 \\ 15 & -3 \\ -6 & -12 \end{bmatrix}$ **41.** $\begin{bmatrix} 17 & -24 \\ -33 & -7 \\ 69 & -18 \end{bmatrix}$

Lesson 4-4 pp. 195–198

EXERCISES 1. $\begin{bmatrix} -2 & -2 & 2 & 2 \\ 2 & 6 & 6 & 2 \end{bmatrix}$

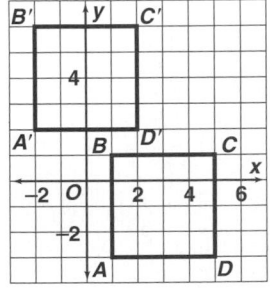

5.

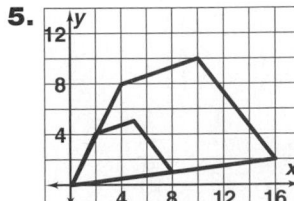

11.

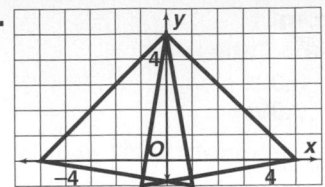

13. $\begin{bmatrix} 3 & -3 & -3 & 3 \\ -3 & -6 & -3 & -6 \end{bmatrix}$ **15.** $\begin{bmatrix} 3 & 2 & 2 & 3 & 5 \\ 1 & 2 & 3 & 4 & 2.5 \end{bmatrix}$

17.

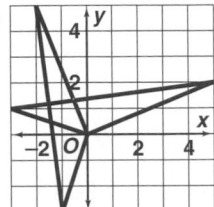

21. $\begin{bmatrix} 0 & 4 & 8 & 6 \\ 0 & 4 & 4 & 2 \end{bmatrix}$ **23.** $\begin{bmatrix} -4 & 0 & 0 & -3 & -4 \\ 1 & 2 & 4 & 6 & 2 \end{bmatrix}$

27. $\begin{bmatrix} -12 & 4 & -4 \\ 4 & 8 & 16 \end{bmatrix}$ **29.** $\begin{bmatrix} -1.5 & 0.5 & -0.5 \\ 0.5 & 1 & 2 \end{bmatrix}$

35. A **39.** $f: \begin{bmatrix} 1 & 2 & 4 & 5 & 2 \\ 2 & 1 & 2 & 5 & 4 \end{bmatrix}$, $g: \begin{bmatrix} 2 & 4 & 8 & 10 & 4 \\ 4 & 2 & 4 & 10 & 8 \end{bmatrix}$;

dilation **41.** $f: \begin{bmatrix} -2 & 1 & -5 \\ 0 & 3 & 3 \end{bmatrix}$, $g: \begin{bmatrix} 2 & 5 & -1 \\ -2 & 1 & 1 \end{bmatrix}$;

1 translation **43.**

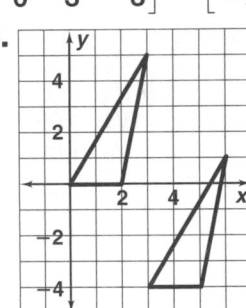

Lesson 4-5 pp. 203–205

EXERCISES 1. $\begin{bmatrix} 3 & 2 \\ 4 & 3 \end{bmatrix}\begin{bmatrix} 3 & -2 \\ -4 & 3 \end{bmatrix} =$

$\begin{bmatrix} 3(3)+2(-4) & 3(-2)+2(3) \\ 4(3)+3(-4) & 4(-2)+3(3) \end{bmatrix} = \begin{bmatrix} 1 & 0 \\ 0 & 1 \end{bmatrix}$

3. $\begin{bmatrix} \frac{1}{5} & -\frac{1}{10} \\ 0 & \frac{1}{4} \end{bmatrix}\begin{bmatrix} 5 & 2 \\ 0 & 4 \end{bmatrix} =$

$\begin{bmatrix} \frac{1}{5}(5)+(-\frac{1}{10})(0) & \frac{1}{5}(2)+(-\frac{1}{10})(4) \\ 0(5)+\frac{1}{4}(0) & 0(2)+\frac{1}{4}(4) \end{bmatrix} = \begin{bmatrix} 1 & 0 \\ 0 & 1 \end{bmatrix}$

5. 0 **7.** $-\frac{11}{40}$ **15.** yes; $\begin{bmatrix} -1 & 3 \\ 1 & -2 \end{bmatrix}$ **17.** yes; $\begin{bmatrix} 0 & \frac{1}{2} \\ \frac{1}{3} & -\frac{1}{6} \end{bmatrix}$

23. No solutions; the determinant of $\begin{bmatrix} 0 & -4 \\ 0 & -1 \end{bmatrix}$ is 0.

25. a.

To \ From	No Cable	Cable
No Cable	0.98	0.005
Cable	0.02	0.995

b. about 20,100 people **c.** about 19,897 people
27. −120 **29.** 2 **31.** yes **33.** No; answers may vary.

Sample: The product is $\begin{bmatrix} 0 & 1 \\ 1 & 0 \end{bmatrix}$. **35.** yes; $\begin{bmatrix} -5 & 7 \\ 3 & -4 \end{bmatrix}$

37. yes; $\begin{bmatrix} 0.5 & 0 \\ 0 & 0.5 \end{bmatrix}$

Lesson 4-6   pp. 209–211

EXERCISES 1. 20 **3.** −14 **5.** 6 **7.** −7314.14

9. no **11.** $\begin{bmatrix} 5 \\ 8 \\ 2 \end{bmatrix}$ **13.** PORTRAIT **17.** −3 **19.** 1

21. $\begin{bmatrix} 0.4 & 0.4 & 0.2 \\ -0.6 & -0.6 & 0.2 \\ -0.2 & 0.8 & 0.4 \end{bmatrix}$ **23.** no inverse

Extension   p. 213

1.

	N_1	N_2	N_3	N_4
N_1	0	1	0	1
N_2	1	0	1	1
N_3	0	1	0	1
N_4	1	1	1	0

3.

	V_1	V_2	V_3	V_4	V_5
V_1	0	1	0	0	0
V_2	1	0	1	0	0
V_3	0	1	0	1	1
V_4	0	0	1	0	1
V_5	0	0	1	1	0

5.

	A	B	C	D
A	0	1	0	0
B	0	0	0	0
C	0	1	1	1
D	1	1	0	1

7. 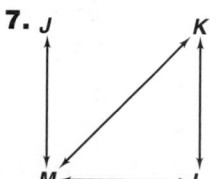 **9.**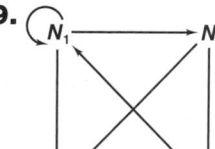

Lesson 4-7   pp. 217–219

EXERCISES 1. $\begin{bmatrix} 1 & 1 \\ 1 & -2 \end{bmatrix}\begin{bmatrix} x \\ y \end{bmatrix} = \begin{bmatrix} 5 \\ -4 \end{bmatrix}$; coefficient

matrix is $\begin{bmatrix} 1 & 1 \\ 1 & -2 \end{bmatrix}$, variable matrix is $\begin{bmatrix} x \\ y \end{bmatrix}$, constant

matrix is $\begin{bmatrix} 5 \\ -4 \end{bmatrix}$. **3.** $\begin{bmatrix} 3 & 5 \\ 1 & 1 \end{bmatrix}\begin{bmatrix} a \\ b \end{bmatrix} = \begin{bmatrix} 0 \\ 2 \end{bmatrix}$; coefficient

matrix is $\begin{bmatrix} 3 & 5 \\ 1 & 1 \end{bmatrix}$, variable matrix is $\begin{bmatrix} a \\ b \end{bmatrix}$, constant

matrix is $\begin{bmatrix} 0 \\ 2 \end{bmatrix}$. **7.** (2, 1) **9.** $\left(\frac{1}{2}, 20\right)$ **17.** yes **19.** yes

23. $\begin{bmatrix} 6 \\ 2 \end{bmatrix}$ **25.** $\begin{bmatrix} 16 \\ -22 \end{bmatrix}$ **27.** (2, 4) **29.** (4, 1, 3)

Lesson 4-8   pp. 224–227

EXERCISES 1. (2, 0) **3.** (3, 1)

7. $\begin{bmatrix} 3 & -7 & 3 & | & -3 \\ 1 & 1 & 2 & | & -3 \\ 2 & -3 & 5 & | & -8 \end{bmatrix}$ **9.** $\begin{cases} 5x + y = -3 \\ -2x + 2y = 4 \end{cases}$

11. $\begin{cases} 2x + y + z = 1 \\ x + y + z = 2 \\ x - y + z = -2 \end{cases}$ **13.** (−2, −6)

15. (6.25, −6.25) **19.** (3, 1, 1) **21.** no unique solution **25.** (−3, 5) **27.** (4, 8) **29.** (1, 1, −1) **31.** (4, 0, 1) **33.** C **35.** (2, 0, 3) **37.** no unique solution **39.** almonds: $2/lb, pecans: $4/lb, pistachios: $6/lb

Chapter Review   pp. 229–231

1. matrix **2.** transformations **3.** determinants **4.** equal matrices **5.** zero matrix **6.** matrix equation **7.** square matrix **8.** preimage **9.** scalar product **10.** identity matrix **11.** 2×3; −7 **12.** 3×2; −5 **13.** 3×3; 78 **14.** 226 **15.** 50

16. about 9% **17.** [1 −8 12] **18.** $\begin{bmatrix} t - 1 \\ 3 \end{bmatrix}$

19. $\begin{bmatrix} -3 & 10 \\ -3 & 3 \end{bmatrix}$ **20.** $\begin{bmatrix} 2 & 8 & 13 \\ 33 & 0 & -7 \end{bmatrix}$

21. $x = -2, w = 8, r = 4, t = -1$

22. $t = -4, y = \frac{11}{2}, r = 4, w = 5$

23. $\begin{bmatrix} 18 & 3 & 0 & 24 \\ -12 & 9 & 21 & 33 \end{bmatrix}$ **24.** $\begin{bmatrix} -9 & 7 \\ -8 & -8 \end{bmatrix}$

25. undefined **26.** $\begin{bmatrix} -6 & 10 & 21 & 41 \\ -28 & 10 & 28 & 28 \end{bmatrix}$

27. $\begin{bmatrix} -14 & -2 \\ 43 & -7 \end{bmatrix}$ **28.** $\begin{bmatrix} 4 & -1 & 2 \\ -1 & -2 & 3 \end{bmatrix}$

29. $\begin{bmatrix} 0 & -5 & -2 \\ 5 & 4 & 9 \end{bmatrix}$ **30.** $\begin{bmatrix} -3 & 2 & -1 \\ 1 & 0 & 5 \end{bmatrix}$

31. $\begin{bmatrix} 1 & 0 & 5 \\ 3 & -2 & 1 \end{bmatrix}$ **32.** $\begin{bmatrix} 1 & 0 & 5 \\ -3 & 2 & -1 \end{bmatrix}$

33. $\begin{bmatrix} 1.5 & -1 & 0.5 \\ 0.5 & 0 & 2.5 \end{bmatrix}$ **34.** $\begin{bmatrix} 6 & -4 & 2 \\ 2 & 0 & 10 \end{bmatrix}$

35. $\begin{bmatrix} -1 & 0 & -5 \\ 3 & -2 & 1 \end{bmatrix}$ **36.** 24; $\begin{bmatrix} \frac{1}{6} & -\frac{1}{24} \\ 0 & \frac{1}{4} \end{bmatrix}$

37. 0; does not exist **38.** 42; $\begin{bmatrix} \frac{5}{42} & -\frac{1}{42} \\ -\frac{4}{21} & \frac{5}{21} \end{bmatrix}$

$$\textbf{39. } 6;\begin{bmatrix} \frac{1}{3} & -\frac{2}{3} & 0 \\ -\frac{1}{6} & \frac{1}{3} & -\frac{1}{2} \\ \frac{1}{3} & \frac{1}{3} & 0 \end{bmatrix} \quad \textbf{40. } \begin{bmatrix} 1 & 2 \\ -1 & 0 \end{bmatrix} \quad \textbf{41. } \begin{bmatrix} -4 \\ -7 \end{bmatrix}$$

42. $\begin{bmatrix} 2 \\ 2 \end{bmatrix}$ **43.** $\begin{bmatrix} 2 & 1 \\ 3 & 2 \end{bmatrix}$ **44.** no unique solution

45. no unique solution **46.** 3 small canoes, 2 large canoes **47.** $(4, -7)$ **48.** $(6, 0, -2)$

Chapter 5

Lesson 5-1   pp. 241–243

EXERCISES 1. linear; none, x, 4 **3.** quadratic;

$3x^2$, $-6x$, none **11.** $(-1, 0)$, $x = -1$ **13.** $P'(6, 9)$,

$Q'(2, 1)$ **17.** $y = x^2 - 5x + 2$ **19.** $y = x^2 + 2x$

21a. $y = -16x^2 + 33x + 46$, where x is the

number of seconds after release and y is the

height in ft. **b.** 28.5 ft

23. $y = 4x^2$ **25.** no **27.** $\left(-\frac{1}{2}, -\frac{1}{2}\right)$, $x = -\frac{1}{2}$

29. $\left(\frac{1}{2}, 0\right)$, $x = \frac{1}{2}$

Lesson 5-2   pp. 248–251

EXERCISES

1. 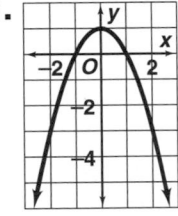 **3.** 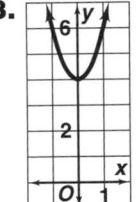 **11.**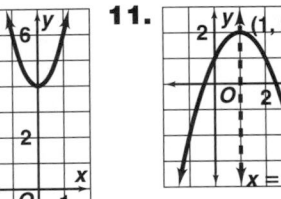

13. 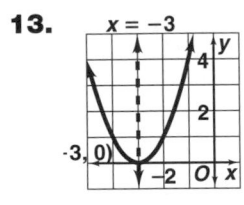 **23.**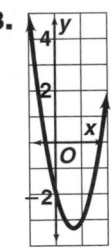

min, $-\frac{10}{3}$

25.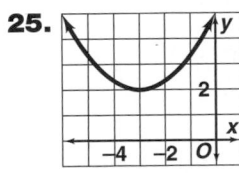

min, 2

29. 2 s; 64 ft

31. 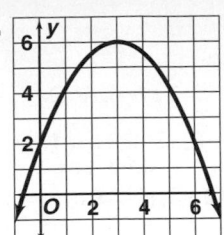 **33.**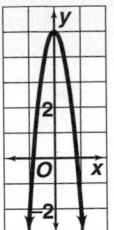

37. B **39.** A **45.** -3 **47.** 2 **49.** $y = -4x^2 - 3$

51. $y = 10x^2 - 1$ **55.** B **57.** $y = x^2 + 1$; up

59. $y = -\frac{1}{2}x^2 + 1$; down

Lesson 5-3   pp. 255–258

EXERCISES

1. 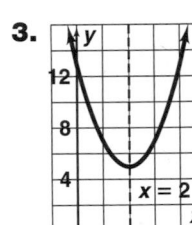 **3.**

13. $y = \frac{1}{4}x^2$ **15.** $y = -(x - 2)^2$ **17.** $y = (x - 2)^2$

19. $y = 6(x + 3)^2 - 2$ **21.** $(-20, 0)$, -600

23. $(-5.5, 0)$, 726 **27.** $y = (x - 2)^2 + 2$

29. $y = 6x^2 - 10$

37.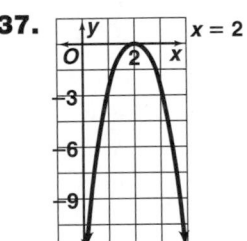

43. $y = -7(x - 1)^2 + 2$ **45.** $y = -\frac{1}{2}(x + 3)^2 + 6$

51. $y = 25x^2 + 60x + 27$ **53.** $y = 2x^2 + 22x$

59. yes **61.** no; $y = -3\left(x + \frac{1}{3}\right)^2 + \frac{4}{3}$ **69.** $a = 3$,

$k = -1$ **71.** $a = \frac{1}{5}$, $k = 1$

Lesson 5-4   pp. 263–265

EXERCISES 1. 3; $3(a^2 + 3)$ **3.** x; $x(x - 2)$

7. $(x + 1)(x + 2)$ **9.** $(x + 2)(x + 5)$

31. $(x + 4)(3x - 5)$ **33.** $(x - 2)(7x + 6)$

47. $5x - 1$ by $5x - 1$ **51.** $9(x + 2)(x - 2)$

53. $3(2y + 5)(2y - 5)$ **67.** $(x - 70)$ ft

Selected Answers

Lesson 5-5 pp. 270–272

EXERCISES **1.** $-4, -2$ **3.** $-1, \frac{3}{2}$ **7.** $-4, 4$ **9.** $-4, 4$ **13.** $0, 4$ **15.** $-\frac{7}{2}, \frac{7}{2}$ **21.** $-1.32, 8.32$ **23.** $-1.67,$ -1.5 **25.** $-0.94, 2.34$ **33.** B **37.** $3, 8$ **39.** $-\frac{1}{2}, 3$

Lesson 5-6 pp. 278–280

EXERCISES **1.** $2i$ **3.** $i\sqrt{15}$ **11.** $2 + i\sqrt{3}$ **13.** $6 - 2i\sqrt{7}$ **19.** 2 **21.** $2\sqrt{2}$ **25.** $-5 + 3i$ **27.** $3 + 2i$ **29.** $6 + 3i$ **31.** $7 + 4i$ **41.** $\pm 5i$ **43.** $\pm\frac{8i\sqrt{3}}{3}$ **47.** $-i, -1 - i, i$ **49.** $1 - i, 1 - 3i,$ $-7 - 7i$ **51.** $\pm 7i$ **55.** B **57.** $288i$ **59.** $10 - 4i$

Lesson 5-7 pp. 285–287

EXERCISES **1.** $-4, -2$ **3.** $-1, 3$ **7.** 81 **9.** 144 **13.** $-4, 7$ **15.** $-3 \pm 4i\sqrt{2}$ **29.** $y = -(x - 2)^2 + 3$ **31.** $y = (x + 2)^2 - 3$ **35.** $y = \frac{1}{2}(x - 5)^2 - \frac{1}{2};$ $\left(5, -\frac{1}{2}\right)$ **37a.** $(60, 5000)$ **b.** positive rational numbers less than 130; whole numbers up to 5000 **c.** \$60; \$5000 **41.** $-20, 20$ **43.** $-16, 16$ **51.** $-12 \pm 3\sqrt{17}$ **53.** $\frac{1}{4} \pm \frac{\sqrt{57}}{12}$

Lesson 5-8 pp. 293–295

EXERCISES **1.** $1, 3$ **3.** $-\frac{7}{2}, 1$ **23.** $\frac{5}{3} \pm \frac{\sqrt{10}}{3}$; $0.61,$ 2.72 **25.** $-\frac{1}{6}, 1$ **31.** -4; two, imaginary **33.** 0; one, real **41.** $1, 10$ **43.** $-\frac{3}{2}, \frac{1}{2}$ **53a.** $w(18 - w) = 36$ **b.** 2.29 in. by 15.71 in. **57.** two **59.** none **67a.** $x^2 = 100\pi$ **b.** 17.72 cm

Chapter Review pp. 299–301

1. perfect square trinomial **2.** quadratic formula **3.** vertex form of a quadratic function **4.** zero of a function **5.** discriminant **6.** quadratic; $-2x^2, 5x, 3$ **7.** quadratic; $-x^2, x, 3$ **8.** linear; none, $-4x, 3$ **9.** $(0, -1), x = 0, (2, 3)$ and $(-1, 0)$ **10.** $(-2, 1), x = -2, (-2, 1)$ and $(-4, 0)$ **11.** $(1, -4), x = 1, (3, -1)$ and $\left(2, -3\frac{1}{4}\right)$ **12a.** $y = 614x^2 - 342x + 4962,$ where $x = 0$ corresponds to 1995 and y is in thousands. **b.** around 1999 **c.** $y = -25.5x^2 +$ $917.8x + 4776.7$ **d.** around 2007 **e.** $\approx 13,000,000$

13.

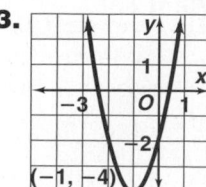

vertex $(-1, -4)$, y-intercept: -2; $x = -1$

14.

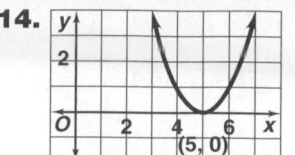

vertex $(5, 0)$, y-intercept: 25; $x = 5$

15.

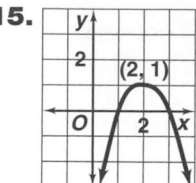

vertex $(2, 1)$, y-intercept: -3; $x = 2$

16.

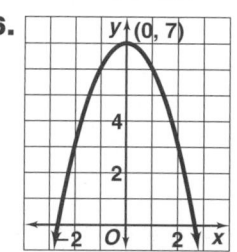

vertex $(0, 7)$, y-intercept: 7; $x = 0$

17. $y = \left(x + \frac{1}{2}\right)^2 - 12\frac{1}{4}$; minimum: $-12\frac{1}{4}$ **18.** $y = -(x - 1)^2 + 3$; maximum: 3 **19.** $y = 2(x + 2)^2 - 11$; minimum: -11 **20.** $y = -0.5(x - 0)^2 + 5$; maximum: 5 **21.** $y = -\frac{1}{2}(x - 1)^2 + 2$; maximum: 2 **22.** $y = \frac{4}{9}(x - 3)^2 - 1$; minimum: -1 **23.** $y = \frac{1}{2}(x - 0)^2 - 2$; minimum: -2 **24.** $0, 7$ **25.** $-4, 2$ **26.** $-6, 0$ **27.** $2 - 2\sqrt{2}, 2 + 2\sqrt{2}$ **28.** $-1, 4$ **29.** $-0.85, 5.85$ or $\frac{5 \pm 3\sqrt{5}}{2}$ **30.** $\frac{2}{3}, 4$ **31.** $-1, 4$ **32.** -4 **33.** 3 **34.** $\frac{3}{2}$ **35.** $-3, 3$ **36.** $-\frac{1}{3}, \frac{5}{2}$ **37.** $-\frac{3}{2}, -\frac{1}{2}$ **38.** $-2.61, 1.28$ or $\frac{-2 \pm \sqrt{34}}{3}$ **39.** $5i$ **40.** $-1 + i\sqrt{2}$ **41.** $-4 - i$ **42.** $3i\sqrt{3}$ **43.** $4 + 8i\sqrt{2}$ **44.** $\sqrt{10}$ **45.** $\sqrt{13}$ **46.** 4 **47.** $-4 + 6i$ **48.** $51 + 21i$ **49.** $8 + 6i$ **50.** $2 + 16i$ **51.** $-2 + i$; **52.** $4 - 3i$;

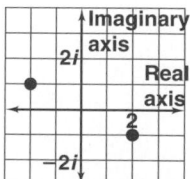

53. $7 + 4i$; **54.** $2i$;

55. $-i\sqrt{2}, i\sqrt{2}$ **56.** $-i\sqrt{5}, i\sqrt{5}$ **57.** $-2i, 2i$
58. $\frac{-i\sqrt{6}}{3}, \frac{i\sqrt{6}}{3}$ **59.** $-i, -1-i, i$ **60.** $i, 1+i, -i$
61. $-1, \frac{1}{3}$ **62.** $-\frac{3}{2} + \frac{i\sqrt{91}}{2}, -\frac{3}{2} - \frac{i\sqrt{91}}{2}$
63. $1 + i\sqrt{3}, 1 - i\sqrt{3}$ **64.** $\frac{1}{2} + \frac{3i\sqrt{3}}{2}, \frac{1}{2} - \frac{3i\sqrt{3}}{2}$
65. $-\frac{3}{4} + \frac{\sqrt{73}}{4}, -\frac{3}{4} - \frac{\sqrt{73}}{4}$ **66.** $-\frac{3}{4}, 1$
67. $y = \left(x + \frac{3}{2}\right)^2 - \frac{13}{4}; \left(-\frac{3}{2}, -\frac{13}{4}\right)$
68. $y = 2\left(x - \frac{1}{4}\right)^2 - \frac{9}{8}; \left(\frac{1}{4}, -\frac{9}{8}\right)$
69. $y = \left(x + \frac{1}{2}\right)^2 + \frac{7}{4}; \left(-\frac{1}{2}, -\frac{7}{4}\right)$ **70.** 2 real solutions; $3 + \sqrt{7}, 3 - \sqrt{7}$ **71.** 2 imaginary solutions; $\frac{7}{4} + \frac{i\sqrt{31}}{4}, \frac{7}{4} - \frac{i\sqrt{31}}{4}$ **72.** 2 real solutions; $3 + \sqrt{5}, 3 - \sqrt{5}$

Chapter 6

Lesson 6-1   pp. 309–311

EXERCISES 1. $10x + 5$; linear binomial
3. $2m^2 + 7m - 3$; quadratic trinomial **13.** $y = x^3 + 1$ **15.** $y = 1.5x^3 + x^2 - 2x + 1$ **19.** $y = x^3 - 10x^2$; 2023 **21.** $y = -0.03948x^3 + 2.069x^2 - 17.93x + 106.9$; 206 **25.** $x^3 + 4x$; cubic binomial **27.** 7; constant monomial **33.** $-c^2 + 16$; binomial **35.** $16x^2 - x - 5$; trinomial **47.** $30x^3 - 10x^2$; binomial **49.** $b^3 - 6b^2 + 9b$; trinomial

Extension   p. 312

1. $(\nearrow, \nearrow)$ **3.** $(\nearrow, \searrow)$ **5.** $(\searrow, \nearrow)$ **7.** $(\nearrow, \searrow)$ **9.** $(\searrow, \searrow)$

Lesson 6-2   pp. 317–319

EXERCISES 1. $x^2 + x - 6$ **3.** $x^3 - 7x^2 + 15x - 9$
7. $x(x - 6)(x + 6)$ **9.** $5x(2x^2 - 2x + 3)$
13. about 24.2, -1.4; 0, -5, 1 **15a.** $h = x$, $\ell = 16 - 2x$, $w = 12 - 2x$
b. $V = x(16 - 2x)(12 - 2x)$
c.
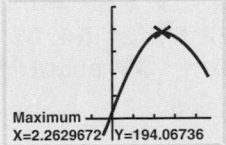
194 in.^{3}, 2.26 in.

17. 2, -9
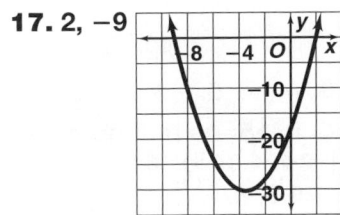

21. $y = x^3 - 18x^2 + 107x - 210$
23. $y = x^3 + 9x^2 + 15x - 25$ **29.** -3 (mult. 3)
31. $-1, 0, \frac{1}{2}$ **37.** 2 x^3 blocks, 15 x^2 blocks, 31 x blocks, 12 unit blocks **39.** $V = 12x^3 - 27x$
41. $y = -2x^3 + 9x^2 - x - 12$
43. $y = 3x(x - 8)(x - 1)$ **45.** $y = x^2(x + 4)(x - 1)$
47. about 10.5, -7.1; $\frac{3}{2}$, 4, 6 **49.** about -2.98, -6.17; 1.5 **51.** Answers may vary. Sample: $y = x^3 - 3x^2 - 10x$ **53.** $y = x^4 - 4x^3 - 7x^2 + 22x + 24$ **55.** 0 (mult. 2), -1 (mult. 2)

Lesson 6-3   pp. 324–326

EXERCISES 1. $x - 8$ **3.** $x^2 + 4x + 3$, R 5 **9.** no
11. yes **13.** $x^2 + 4x + 3$ **15.** $x^2 - 11x + 37$, R -128 **23.** $y = (x + 1)(x + 3)(x - 2)$ **25.** $\ell = x + 3$ and $h = x$ **27.** 0 **29.** 12 **37.** $x^2 + 4x + 5$
39. $x^4 - x^3 + x^2 - x + 1$ **43.** yes **45.** no
49. yes **51.** no **53.** $x^3 - 2x^2 - 2x + 4$, R -35
55. $x^3 - 4x^2 + x$

Lesson 6-4   pp. 330–332

EXERCISES 1. $-2, 1, 5$ **3.** 0, 1
13. $(x - 10)(x^2 + 10x + 100)$ **15.** 3, $\frac{-3 \pm 3i\sqrt{3}}{2}$
17. 5, $\frac{-5 \pm 5i\sqrt{3}}{2}$ **21.** $(x^2 - 7)(x - 1)(x + 1)$
23. $(x^2 - 3)(x - 2)(x + 2)$ **27.** $\pm 3, \pm 1$ **29.** $\pm 4, \pm 2i$
33. $-1, 3.24, -1.24$ **35.** $-2, -3, 1, 2$ **41.** D
43. $\frac{4}{3}, \frac{-2 \pm 2i\sqrt{3}}{3}$ **45.** $\pm 5, \pm i\sqrt{2}$
61. $V = x^2(4x - 2)$, 4 in. by 4 in. by 16 in.
63. $-\frac{5}{2}, 1; y = (2x + 5)(x - 1)$
65. $-1, 2, 2; y = (x + 1)(x - 2)^2$

Lesson 6-5   pp. 339–340

EXERCISES 1. $\pm 1, \pm 2$; 1 **3.** $\pm 1, \pm 2, \pm 4$; -1 **7.** 2, $\pm i\sqrt{5}$ **9.** $-3, 1, \frac{7}{2}$ **13.** $-\sqrt{5}, \sqrt{13}$ **15.** $1 + \sqrt{10}$, $2 - \sqrt{2}$ **19.** $x^3 - x^2 + 9x - 9 = 0$ **21.** $x^3 - 2x^2 + 16x - 32 = 0$ **25.** $\pm\frac{1}{12}, \pm\frac{1}{6}, \pm\frac{1}{4}, \pm\frac{1}{2}, \pm\frac{1}{3}, \pm\frac{2}{3}, \pm\frac{3}{4}, \pm 1, \pm\frac{3}{2}, \pm 2, \pm 3, \pm 6; \frac{1}{2}, \frac{3}{2}, \frac{2}{3}$ **27.** $\pm\frac{7}{3}, \pm\frac{1}{6}, \pm\frac{1}{2}, \pm\frac{1}{3}, \pm\frac{7}{6}, \pm 1, \pm\frac{3}{2}, \pm 3, \pm\frac{7}{2}, \pm 7, \pm\frac{21}{2}, \pm 21; \frac{1}{3}, -\frac{7}{2}, 1, 3$
29. $x^4 - 6x^3 + 14x^2 - 24x + 40 = 0$ **31.** $x^4 - 6x^3 + 2x^2 + 30x - 35 = 0$ **33.** Sometimes true; since -2 is a factor of 8, -2 is a possible root of the equation. **35.** Sometimes true; since $\sqrt{5}$ and $-\sqrt{5}$ are conjugates, they can be roots of a

polynomial equation with integer coefficients
37. D

Lesson 6-6   pp. 343–344

EXERCISES 1. 3 complex roots; number of real roots: 1 or 3; possible rational roots: ±1 **3.** 4 complex roots; number of real roots: 0, 2, or 4; possible rational roots: 0 **9.** −1, $\frac{1 \pm i\sqrt{7}}{4}$ **11.** 4, $\frac{1 \pm i\sqrt{3}}{2}$ **17.** 4 complex roots; number of real roots: 0, 2, or 4; possible rational roots: ±$\frac{1}{2}$, ±1, ±2, ±$\frac{13}{2}$, ±13, ±26 **19.** 3 complex roots; number of real roots: 1 or 3; possible rational roots: ±$\frac{1}{3}$, ±$\frac{2}{3}$, ±1, ±$\frac{4}{3}$, ±2, ±3, ±4, ±6, ±12 **21.** 4, ±3i **23.** −6, $\frac{-1 \pm i}{2}$

Lesson 6-7   pp 348–351

EXERCISES 1. 120 **3.** 6,227,020,800 **9a.** 24 **b.** 120 **11.** 56 **13.** 1680 **19.** 4, 151, 347, 200 **21.** 15 **23.** 1 **29.** 4368 **31.** 2600 **33.** true because of the Comm. Prop. of Add. **35.** False; answers may vary. Sample: (3 + 2)! = 120 and 3! + 2! = 8 **39.** C **43.** 84 **45.** 5 **47.** permutation **49.** combination **51.** 210 **53.** 5 **55a.** 56 **b.** 56 **57.** 3024 **59.** 24

Lesson 6-8   pp. 355–357

EXERCISES 1. $a^3 + 3a^2b + 3ab^2 + b^3$ **3.** $a^4 + 4a^3b + 6a^2b^2 + 4ab^3 + b^4$ **13.** $x^4 + 4x^3y + 6x^2y^2 + 4xy^3 + y^4$ **15.** $s^2 - 2st + t^2$ **21a.** about 25% **b.** about 21% **c.** about 12% **23.** $x^7 + 7x^6y + 21x^5y^2 + 35x^4y^3 + 35x^3y^4 + 21x^2y^5 + 7xy^6 + y^7$ **25.** $81x^4 - 108x^3y + 54x^2y^2 - 12xy^3 + y^4$ **43a.** about 31% **b.** about 16% **c.** about 16% **45.** $_8C_4x^4y^4$ **47.** 7, $7r^6s$ **49.** $80x^2$ **51.** $264x^{10}$ **59a.** $(s + 0.5)^3$ **b.** $s^3 + 1.5s^2 + 0.75s + 0.125$ **61.** 13, d^{12}, $12d^{11}e$ **63.** 6, $32a^5$, $80a^4b$

Chapter Review   pp. 359–361

1. degree **2.** standard form of a polynomial **3.** multiplicity **4.** complex conjugates **5.** combinations **6.** $3p^3 - 2p$; cubic binomial **7.** $-5x^9 + 3$; degree 9 binomial **8.** $-x^5 - x^3 + x$; quintic trinomial **9.** $4x^3 + 2x^2 + 2x$; cubic trinomial **10.** $x^7 + x^4 - x^2 + x + 5$; degree 7, 5 terms **11.** s; linear monomial **12.** cubic: $y = 62.2685x^3 - 303.194x^2 + 481.8148x - 248.522$; quartic: $y = 984.375x^4 - 6631.481x^3 + 16,498.68x^2 - 17,954.685x + 7208.88$;

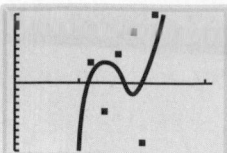 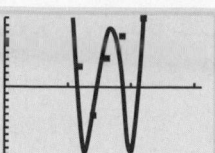

The quartic model better fits the data.
13. $f(x) = x(x - 4)(x + 3)$; −3, 0, 4; rel. max. ≈ 12.60, rel. min. ≈ −20.75 **14.** $g(x) =$ $(2 - x)(2 + x)$; −2, 2; rel. max. = 4 **15.** $y = x^3(x + 2)^4$; 0 (mult. 3), −2 (mult. 4); rel. max. = 0, rel. min. ≈ −1.07 **16.** $f(x) = x^4 + 3x^3 - 4x^2 - 12x$ **17.** $f(x) = x^3 - 4x^2 + 5x - 2$ **18.** $f(x) = x^4 + 2x^3 - 3x^2$ **19.** $f(x) = x^3 + 6x^2 + 12x + 8$ **20.** $x^2 + 5x + 8$, R 12; check students' work. **21.** $x^3 - x^2 + x - 2$, R 4; check students' work. **22.** $(x + 1)(x - 3)(x - 1)$ **23.** $(x - 3)^2(x + 2)$ **24.** 93 **25.** −30 **26.** 77 **27.** −9 **28.** −1, 1.38, 3.62 **29.** −1.78 **30.** 0 **31.** −1.52 **32.** −1.63 **33.** no real solution **34.** $(x - 2)(x^2 + 2x + 4)$; 2, −1 ± $i\sqrt{3}$ **35.** $t^4(2t - 1)(2t + 1)$; 0, $\frac{1}{2}$, $-\frac{1}{2}$ **36.** $(2x + 1)(4x^2 - 2x + 1)$; $-\frac{1}{2}$, $\frac{1 \pm i\sqrt{3}}{4}$ **37.** $x(x - 4)(x - 1)$; 0, 1, 4 **38.** $x(x^2 - 2x - 5)$; 0, 1 ± $\sqrt{6}$ **39.** $(x + 2)^2(x^2 - 2x + 4)^2$; −2, 1 ± $i\sqrt{3}$ **40.** 3 complex roots; number of real roots: 3 or 1; possible rational roots: ±1, ±2, ±3, ±6; roots 1, 2, 3 **41.** 4 complex roots; number of real roots: 4, 2, or 0; possible rational roots: ±1, ±2, ±4, ±8, ±$\frac{1}{2}$, ±$\frac{1}{5}$, ±$\frac{2}{5}$, ±$\frac{4}{5}$, ±$\frac{8}{5}$, ±$\frac{1}{10}$; roots: −1, −$\frac{1}{2}$, $\frac{4}{5}$, 2 **42.** 4 complex roots; number of real roots: 4, 2, or 0; possible rational roots: ±1, ±7; roots: ±1.26, ±2.10 **43.** 4 complex roots; number of real roots: 4, 2, or 0; possible rational roots: ±1, ±2, ±4; roots: −1, −2 **44.** 3 complex roots; number of real roots: 3 or 1; possible rational roots: ±1, ±5; roots: −1, 2 ± i **45.** 4 complex roots; number of real roots: 4, 2, or 0; possible rational roots: ±1, ±2, ±3, ±6, ±9, ±18; roots: ±3, 1 ± i **46.** $x^3 - 2x^2 + x - 2 = 0$ **47.** $x^4 - 16x^3 + 91x^2 - 216x + 182 = 0$ **48.** $x^4 - 10x^3 + 39x^2 - 70x + 50 = 0$ **49.** $x^5 - 6x^4 + 11x^3 - 24x^2 + 28x = 0$ **50.** $x^4 - 8x^3 + 23x^2 - 42x + 30 = 0$ **51.** $x^4 - 12x^2 + 35 = 0$ **52.** 72 **53.** 24 **54.** 35 **55.** 30 **56.** 2 **57.** 120 **58.** $4320x^3y^3$ **59.** about 27%

Chapter 7

Lesson 7-1   pp. 372–373

EXERCISES 1. 15, −15 **3.** none **5.** −4 **7.** −$\frac{1}{2}$ **9.** 2, −2 **11.** 0.3, −0.3 **13.** 6 **15.** no real-number root **21.** 4|x| **23.** $x^4|y^9|$ **29.** 1.34 in. **31.** 0.48 cm **33.** 10, −10 **35.** 0.5, −0.5 **37.** $\sqrt[3]{-64}$, $\sqrt[6]{64}$, $-\sqrt[3]{-64}$, $\sqrt{64}$ **39.** 0.5 **41.** 0.2 **59.** Some; they are equal for $x ≥ 0$. **61.** Some; they are equal for $x ≥ 0$.

Lesson 7-2 — pp. 377–379

EXERCISES 1. 16 **3.** -9 **9.** $2x\sqrt{5x}$ **11.** $5x^2\sqrt{2x}$
17. $2\sqrt[3]{12}$ **19.** $7x^3y^4\sqrt{6y}$ **23.** 10 **25.** $2x^2y^2\sqrt{2}$
27. $\frac{\sqrt{2x}}{2}$ **29.** $\frac{\sqrt[3]{4x}}{2}$ **35.** $r = \frac{\sqrt{Gm_1m_2F}}{F}$ **37.** $10\sqrt{2}$
39. $3x^6y^5\sqrt{2y}$ **55.** 212 mi/h greater

Lesson 7-3 — pp. 382–384

EXERCISES 1. $6\sqrt{6}$ **3.** cannot combine
7. $33\sqrt{2}$ **9.** $7\sqrt{2}$ **13.** $8 + 4\sqrt{5}$ **15.** $63 - 38\sqrt{2}$
19. 14 **21.** -40 **23.** $-2 + 2\sqrt{3}$ **25.** $13 + 7\sqrt{3}$
27. $13\sqrt{2}$ **29.** $48\sqrt{2x}$

Lesson 7-4 — pp. 388–390

EXERCISES 1. 6 **3.** 7 **11.** $\sqrt[5]{x}$ **13.** $\sqrt[5]{y^2}$ or $(\sqrt[5]{y})^2$
19. $7^{\frac{1}{2}}x^{\frac{3}{2}}$ **21.** $(7x)^{\frac{3}{2}}$ **27.** ≈ 15.1 m **29.** ≈ 1.6 m
31. 16 **33.** 64 **39.** $\frac{1}{x^4}$ **41.** $\frac{5}{x^{\frac{2}{3}}}$ **51.** -3
53. 729 **63.** A **65.** $x^{\frac{1}{2}}$ **67.** $x^{\frac{1}{2}}$

Lesson 7-5 — pp. 394–396

EXERCISES 1. 16 **3.** 22 **7.** $3, -13$ **9.** 18 **13.** 30.6 ft
15. 3 **17.** $-3, -4$ **21.** 3 **23.** 1 **35.** 4 **37.** 23

Lesson 7-6 — pp. 400–404

EXERCISES 1. $x^2 + 3x + 5$ **3.** $-x^2 + 3x + 5$
13. $2x^2 + 2x - 4$; domain: all real numbers
15. $2x^2 - 2$; domain: all real numbers
21. $x^2 + 5$; 14, 9 **23.** 104 **25.** 16 **31.** 1 **33.** -3
43a. $f(x) = 0.9x$ **b.** $g(x) = x - 2000$ **c.** \$14,200
d. \$14,400 **45.** $x^2 - x + 7$ **47.** $x^2 - 5x - 3$
51. $-3x^2 + 2x + 16$, domain: all real numbers
53. $3x^3 + 8x^2 - 4x + 16$, domain: all real numbers
59. -4 **61.** 2 **63.** $3x^2, 9x^2$ **65.** $12x^2 + 2, 6x^2 + 4$
71a. $P(x) = 5295x - 1000$ **b.** \$158,750
73. $(f + g)(x) = f(x) + g(x)$ Def. of Function Add.
    $= 3x - 2 + (x^2 + 1)$ Substitution
    $= x^2 + 3x - 2 + 1$ Comm. Prop.
    $= x^2 + 3x - 1$ arithmetic
75. $(f \circ g)(x) = f(g(x))$ def. of comp. functions
    $= f(x^2 + 1)$ substitution
    $= 3(x^2 + 1) - 2$ substitution
    $= 3x^2 + 3 - 2$ Dist. Prop.
    $= 3x^2 + 1$ arithmetic

Lesson 7-7 — pp. 410–412

EXERCISES

1.

x	0	1	0	2
y	1	2	3	4

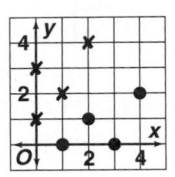

5. $y = \frac{1}{3}x - \frac{1}{3}$; yes **7.** $y = -\frac{1}{3}x + \frac{4}{3}$; yes

15.

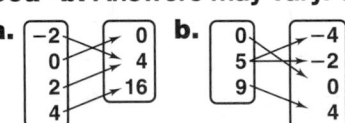

23. $f^{-1}(x) = \frac{x - 4}{3}$, and the domain and range
for both f and f^{-1} are all real numbers; f^{-1} is a
function. **25.** $f^{-1}(x) = x^2 - 7$, $x \geq 0$, domain f:
$\{x|x \geq -7\}$, range f: $\{y|y \geq 0\}$, domain f^{-1}: $\{x|x \geq 0\}$, and range f^{-1}: $\{y|y \geq -7\}$; f^{-1} is a
function. **29a.** $F = \frac{5}{9}(C - 32)$; yes **b.** $-3.89°F$
31. 10 **33.** 0.2 **35.** $f^{-1}(x) = \pm\sqrt{\frac{2x + 8}{3}}$; no
37. $f^{-1}(x) = \frac{x^2 - 6x + 10}{2}$, $x \geq 3$; yes **47.** $f^{-1}(x) = x^2$,
$x \leq 0$, domain of f: $\{x|x \leq 0\}$, range of f: $\{y|y \leq 0\}$,
domain of f^{-1}: $\{x|x \leq 0\}$, range of f^{-1}: $\{y|y \geq 0\}$,
and f^{-1} is a function.
49. $f^{-1}(x) = 3 - x^2$, $x \geq 0$, domain of f: $\{x|x \leq 3\}$,
range of f: $\{y|y \geq 0\}$, domain of f^{-1}: $\{x|x \geq 0\}$,
range of f^{-1}: $\{y|y \leq 3\}$, and f^{-1} is a function.
59a–b. Answers may vary. Sample:

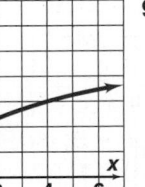

61. $n = s\sqrt{2}$; $3\sqrt{2}$ in. $\approx$ 4.2 in.

Lesson 7-8 — pp. 417–419

EXERCISES

1.

9.

19.

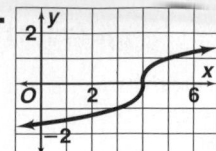

25. 147 **27.** −8.11 **31.** $y = 3\sqrt{x - 1}$; the graph is the graph of $y = 3\sqrt{x}$ translated 1 unit to the right. **33.** $y = -14\sqrt{x + 1}$; the graph is the graph of $y = -14\sqrt{x}$ translated 1 unit to the left.

Chapter Review pp. 423–425

1. radicand **2.** index **3.** rationalize the denominator **4.** are not **5.** rational exponents **6.** composite function **7.** rational exponents **8.** inverse functions **9.** a radical equation **10.** principal root **11.** 12 **12.** −0.4 **13.** 7 **14.** 0.5 **15.** −3 **16.** $7|xy^5|$ **17.** $-4y^3$ **18.** $(a - 1)^2$ **19.** $3x^3$ **20.** $(y + 3)^2$ **21.** $4x^4y^2\sqrt{2xy}$ **22.** 20 **23.** $6\sqrt[3]{2}$ **24.** $10x^2y\sqrt[3]{12y^2}$ **25.** $7x^2\sqrt{2}$ **26.** $15x^3y^2\sqrt{x}$ **27.** $6xy\sqrt[4]{2y}$ **28.** 4 **29.** $2y\sqrt[3]{y}$ **30.** $5x$ **31.** $6xy\sqrt{3x}$ **32.** $3a^2b\sqrt[3]{b}$ **33.** $\frac{2\sqrt{3}}{3}$ **34.** $\frac{x\sqrt{6x}}{4}$ **35.** $\frac{\sqrt[3]{5x^2}}{x^2}$ **36.** $\frac{a^3\sqrt{ab}}{4b}$ **37.** $\frac{y\sqrt[3]{150x}}{10x^2}$ **38.** $6\sqrt{3}$ **39.** $7 - 3\sqrt{3}$ **40.** 43 **41.** $2\sqrt{2x}$ **42.** $\frac{42 - 12\sqrt{3}}{37}$ **43.** $-\frac{\sqrt{2} + \sqrt{10}}{4}$ **44.** $\sqrt[5]{3}$ **45.** $\sqrt[3]{x^2}$ **46.** $\sqrt[4]{\frac{1}{8}}$ **47.** $\sqrt[5]{3}$ **48.** $\sqrt[4]{\frac{1}{p^9}}$ **49.** 81 **50.** 216 **51.** x **52.** $x^{\frac{5}{6}}$ **53.** $\frac{y^4}{x^6}$ **54.** −42 **55.** 2 **56.** 121 **57.** $x^2 - x + 7$ **58.** $-x^2 + 5x + 3$ **59.** $2x^3 - x^2 - 11x + 10$ **60.** $x^2 - 5x - 3$ **61.** $\frac{x^2 - 3x + 2}{2x + 5}, x \neq -\frac{5}{2}$ **62.** 1 **63.** 25 **64.** 9 **65.** 1 **66.** $c^2 - 6c + 9$ **67.** $y = \frac{1}{6}x - \frac{1}{3}$; yes **68.** $y = \left(\frac{x - 1}{2}\right)^{\frac{1}{3}}$; yes **69.** $y = \pm\sqrt[4]{x} + 2$; no **70.** $y = x^2 - 2, x \geq 0$; yes **71.** 5 **72.** −5 **73.** 6 **74.** t

75.

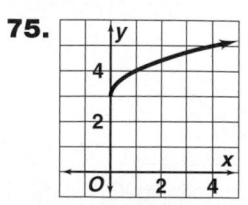

76.

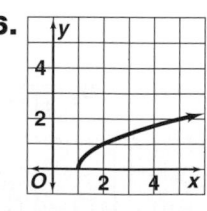

77.

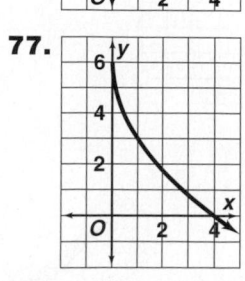

78.

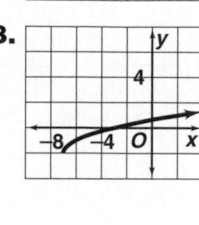

Chapter 8

EXERCISES

1.

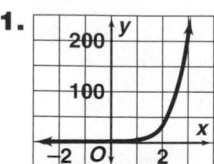

9a. 1.0126 **b.** $y = 6.08(1.0126)^x$, where $x = 0$ corresponds to 2000 **11.** $y = 2.5(7)^x$ **13.** $y = 5(0.6)^x$ **17.** exponential decay **19.** exponential decay

25.

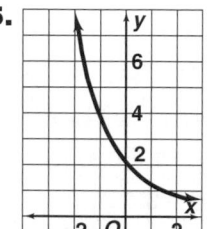

$y = 0$ is the horizontal asymptote.

33. $y = 12,000(0.9)^x$; 6377 **35a.** $y = 6500(0.857)^x$ **b.** $4091.25 **37.** 30% increase **39.** 70% decrease **43a.** about 5.6% **b.** about 0.0017% **47.** 6 **49.** 0.45

EXERCISES 1. Asymptote is $y = 0$.

9.

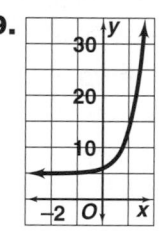

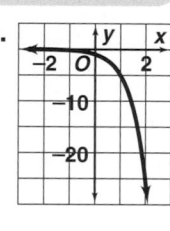

15. $y = 50\left(\frac{1}{2}\right)^{\frac{1}{14.3}x}$; 0.85 mg **17.** $y = 24\left(\frac{1}{2}\right)^{\frac{1}{5730}x}$; 0.64 mg **19.** 403.4288 **21.** 1 **25.** $448.30 **27.** 0 **33.** $y = -3^x$; $y = -3^{x-8} + 2$ **35.** $y = -3\left(\frac{1}{3}\right)^x$; $y = -3\left(\frac{1}{3}\right)^{x+5} - 1$ **37.** 8.7 yr **41.** $399.97 **43.** exponential growth **45.** exponential growth

---

EXERCISES 1. The earthquake in Missouri released about 1.97 times more energy. **3.** The earthquake in Missouri released about 8,759,310 times more energy. **7.** $3 = \log 1000$ **9.** $\log \frac{1}{10} = -1$ **15.** $\frac{1}{2}$ **17.** $\frac{3}{2}$ **27.** 6.3×10^{-3} **29.** 7.9×10^{-4}

35.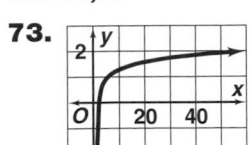

41. 0.6990; 0 **43.** −1.0969; −2 **53.** $128 = 2^7$
55. $16,807 = 7^5$ **65.** $y = 0.5^x$ **67.** $y = 2^{x-1}$

73. 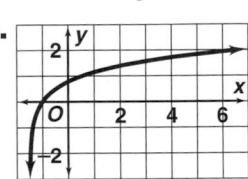 **75.**

77. domain $\{x \mid x > 0\}$, range: all reals
79. domain $\{x \mid x > 0\}$, range: all reals

Lesson 8-4   pp. 457–459

EXERCISES 1. Product Property **3.** Power
Property **11.** $\log 14$ **13.** $\log 972$ **19.** $3 \log x +$
$5 \log y$ **21.** $\log_4 5 + \frac{1}{2} \log_4 x$ **31.** 9 dB **33.** −2
35. 6 **45.** 1.4772 **47.** 2.097 **57.** 0.00001 **59.** False;
$\frac{1}{2} \log_3 3 = \log_3 3^{\frac{1}{2}}$, not $\log_3 \frac{3}{2}$.
61. False; the two logs have different bases.
73. $\log_3 \sqrt[4]{2x}$ **75.** $\log \frac{27}{2}$ **79.** $3 \log 2 + \frac{3}{2} \log x -$
$3 \log 5$ **81.** $\log 2 + \frac{1}{2} \log 4 + \frac{1}{2} \log r - \log s$

Lesson 8-5   pp. 464–468

EXERCISES 1. 1.5850 **3.** 2.7320 **13.** 0.5690
15. 4.7027 **17.** 6 **19.** 0.64 **25.** $\log 14$ **27.** $\log 972$
33. 0.05 **35.** 33 **43.** $100,000 \sqrt{5} \approx 223,606.8$
45. $\frac{1}{4}$ **51.** $2 = 10\left(\frac{1}{2}\right)^{\frac{x}{1.17}}$, about 2.7 min. **53.** −1
55. $\frac{1}{2}$ **61a.** Let x equal the number of years after
2000. Florida growth factor = 1.0213,
$y = 15,982,378 \cdot (1.0213)^x$; New York growth
factor = 1.0054, $y = 18,976,457 \cdot (1.0054)^x$ **b.** 2011
69. $\frac{\log 8}{\log 3}$ **71.** $\frac{\log 3.3}{\log 9}$ **77a.** top up: 10^{-5} W/m²,
top down: $10^{-2.5}$ W/m² **b.** 99.67% **79.** 2.9315
81. 0.6225

Lesson 8-6   pp. 472–475

EXERCISES 1. $\ln 125$ **3.** $\ln 4$ **11.** 24.13
13. 25 seconds **15.** 0.135 **17.** 1488.979
23. 2.890 **25.** 2.401 **29.** 6 years **31.** 1 **33.** 10
39. 301 **41.** sometimes **43.** always
45. about 19.8 hours **47.** 3.6 **49.** 9.4 **55.** 542.31
57. 0.0794

Chapter Review   pp. 479–481

1. growth factor **2.** common logarithm
3. asymptote **4.** logarithm **5.** exponential
equation **6.** exponential growth; 400%

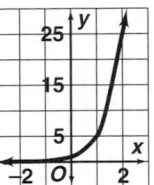

7. exponential growth; 300%

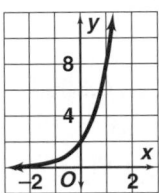

8. exponential growth; 280%

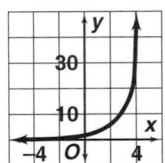

9. exponential decay; −75%

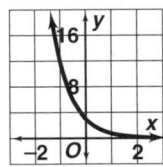

10. $y = \frac{25}{7}\left(\frac{7}{5}\right)^x$ **11.** $y = 0.0015(10)^x$
12. $y = 2.25\left(\frac{1}{3}\right)^x$ **13.** $y = \left(\frac{1}{3}\right)^x$
14. $y = 12,500(0.91)^x$; $7800 **15.** $y = 50(1.03)^x$; $58
16. $y = 1500(0.2)^x$; 2.4 **17.** $y = 2(1.4)^x$; 7.6832
18. $y = 3^x$ reflected over the x-axis and translated
up 1 unit

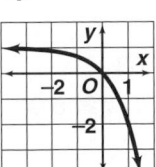

19. $y = 8^x$ translated down 1 unit

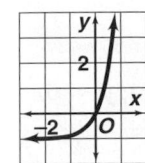

20. $y = 2(2)^x$ translated left 1 unit and up 3 units

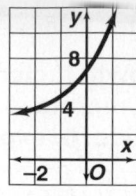

21. $y = 2\left(\frac{1}{3}\right)^x$ reflected over the x-axis and translated 2 units

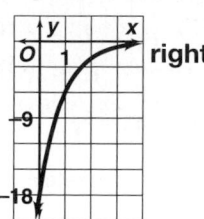 right

22. $1100.76 **23.** $291.91 **24.** $645.23
25. 2.7183 **26.** 0.3679 **27.** 148.4132 **28.** 0.6065
29. $y = 3\left(\frac{1}{2}\right)^{\frac{x}{1620}}$; $\approx$2.937 mg **30.** 2.0×10^{-6}
31. 7 **32.** $2 = \log_6 36$ **33.** $-3 = \log_2 0.125$
34. $3 = \log_3 27$ **35.** $-3 = \log 0.001$ **36.** 6
37. -2 **38.** -5 **39.** 0
40.
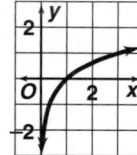
41.
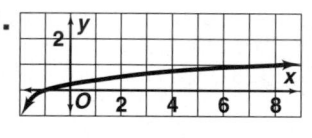

42.
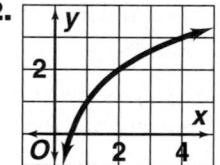
43.
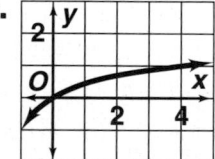

44. $\log 24$ **45.** $\log_2 \frac{5}{3}$ **46.** $\log_3 7x^4$ **47.** $\log \frac{z}{y}$
48. $2\log_4 x + 3\log_4 y$; Product and Power Properties **49.** $\log 4 + 4\log s + \log t$; Product and Power Properties **50.** $\log_3 2 - \log_3 x$; Quotient Property **51.** $2\log(x + 3)$; Power Property **52.** 1.76 dB **53.** 2.38 **54.** 3.26 **55.** 4.65 **56.** 1.37 **57.** 1 **58.** $\approx$0.66 **59.** $\approx$0.67 **60.** $\approx$3.06 **61.** $\frac{10}{3}$ **62.** 8 **63.** 50 **64.** 7,625,597,484,987 **65.** $\log_5 91.68$ **66.** about 18.2 h **67.** 0.83 **68.** 2.26 **69.** 4.31 **70.** 0.00018 **71.** 3.77 **72.** 6.03 **73.** 3.4%

Chapter 9

Lesson 9-1 pp. 491–493

EXERCISES **1.** $y = \frac{11}{x}$ **3.** $y = \frac{1}{x}$ **7.** direct; $y = 5x$
9. direct; $y = 2x$ **13.** $y = \frac{100}{x}$; 10 **15.** $y = -\frac{5}{3x}$; $-\frac{1}{6}$
17. A varies jointly with b and h. **19.** V varies jointly with B and h. **25.** $z = 10xy$; 360
27. $z = \frac{4}{xy}$; $\frac{1}{9}$ **29.** 18 **31.** $\frac{1}{4}$ **35.** 7200 rpm **37.** $18\frac{2}{3}$

39. 2 **40.** 2.625 **15.** 8 **49.** 32 **51.** $\frac{40}{3}$ **53.** 32
55. quartered; divided by 16

Lesson 9-2 pp. 498–500
EXERCISES
1.
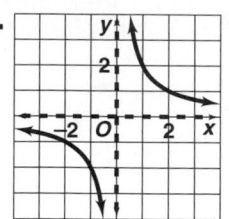

5.
The graph is in Quadrant II and Quadrant IV. The graph is a reflection of the graph of $y = \frac{3}{x}$.

7.
The graph is in Quadrant II and Quadrant IV. The graph is a reflection of the graph of $y = \frac{5}{x}$.

11. 7.67 ft **13.** 1.84 ft
15.
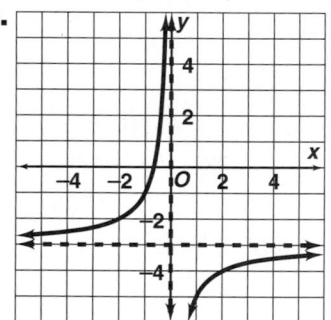

23. $y = \frac{2}{x + 2} + 3$ **27.** $y = \frac{0.5}{x}$ **29.** $y = -\frac{8.3}{x}$
33.
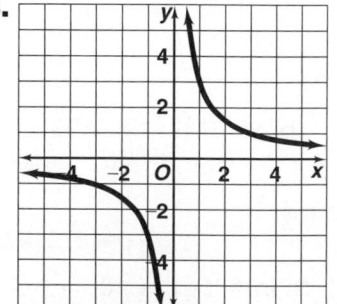

41.
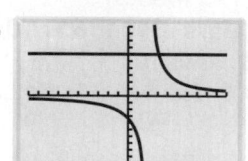 (3, 6)

990 Selected Answers

Lesson 9-3   pp. 505–508

EXERCISES **1.** $x = 0, x = 2$ **3.** $x = 1, x = -1$
11. hole at $x = -5$ **13.** vertical asymptote
at $x = -1$, hole at $x = 2$ **19.** $y = 0$ **21.** $y = 1$

25.   **31a.** $y = \dfrac{0.19x + 210{,}000}{x - 500}$

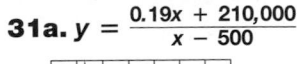

b. \$46.88; \$14.68 **c.** more than 21,916 discs **d.** $x =$
500, $y = 0.19$ **33.** vertical asymptote at $x = -2$

35.

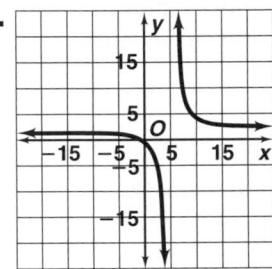

43a. $y = \dfrac{20{,}000x + 200{,}000}{x + 1}$

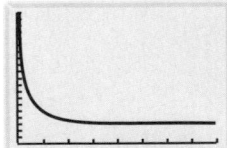

```
WINDOW FORMAT
Xmin=0
Xmax=40
Xscl=4
Ymin=0
Ymax=200000
Yscl=10000
```

b. \$65,000; \$25,806.45

Lesson 9-4   pp. 511–513

EXERCISES **1.** $\frac{1}{2x - 1}$; $x \neq 0$ or $\frac{1}{2}$ **3.** $b + 1$; $b \neq 1$
7. $\frac{7}{15x^2}$; $x \neq 0, y \neq 0$ **9.** $\frac{4}{3}$; $y \neq \frac{1}{2}$ or 3 **13.** $\frac{2}{3x^2y^2}$;
$x \neq 0, y \neq 0$ **15.** $\frac{5(x + y)}{3}$; $x \neq y$ **19.** $\frac{(x - 8)}{(x - 10)}$;
$x \neq -3$ or 10 **21.** $\frac{y(y + 3)}{12(y + 4)}$; $x \neq 0, y \neq -4$ or 3
27. $\frac{a + 3}{(a - 3)(a - 3)}$; $a \neq -4, -3,$ or 3 **29.** $\frac{4}{x}$; $x \neq 0$,
$-5, 4,$ or 1 **33.** $\frac{(x - 1)^3}{(x + 4)}$, $x \neq -4, 0, 1$ **35.** $\frac{18x^5}{y^2}$, $y \neq 0$
37a. 1.2 m/s² **b.** 2.68 m/s²

Lesson 9-5   pp. 517–520

EXERCISES **1.** $\frac{120}{59} \approx 2.03$ in. **5.** $(x - 1)(x + 1)$
$(x + 1)$ **7.** $18(2x - 7)(x + 3)$ **11.** $\frac{2(d - 2)}{2d + 1}$
13. $\frac{7x^2 + 20x - 18}{(x - 3)(x + 3)(x + 4)}$ **17.** $\frac{-3(2y + 1)}{2y - 1}$

19. $\frac{x^2 - 24}{3x(x + 3)}$ **23.** $\frac{15}{28}$ **25.** $\frac{b}{9}$ **31.** $\frac{3x - 8}{4x^2}$
33. $\frac{2x^3 - x^2 + 1}{x^2(x + 1)(x - 1)}$ **45.** $\frac{2x - 5y}{2(3x + 2y)}$ **47.** x

Lesson 9-6   pp. 524–527

EXERCISES **1.** 5 **3.** 10 **11.** 10 **13.** 2
23. passenger train: 112 mi/h, freight train:
92 mi/h **25.** $1\frac{5}{7}$ h **27.** $E = mc^2$ **29.** $c = \sqrt{a^2 - b^2}$
39. 3 **41.** no solution

Lesson 9-7   pp. 534–537

EXERCISES **1.** independent **3.** dependent **5.** $\frac{1}{6}$
7. 0.54 **11.** Mutually exclusive since if the
numbers are equal, then the sum is even.
13. 47% **15.** $\frac{14}{15}$ **17.** $\frac{26}{35}$ **19.** $\frac{1}{2}$ **21.** $\frac{5}{6}$ **27.** $\frac{7}{12}$
29. $\frac{31}{56}$ **31.** 13% **33.** 98% **37.** $\frac{4}{15}$ **39.** $\frac{1}{15}$ **41.** $\frac{1}{11}$
43. $\frac{7}{15}$ **45a.** $\frac{1}{4}$ **b.** $\frac{1}{64}$

Chapter Review   pp. 539–541

1. mutually exclusive **2.** simplest form
3. independent events **4.** branch **5.** point of
discontinuity **6.** $y = \frac{150}{x}$; 30 **7.** $y = \frac{60}{x}$; 12
8. $y = \frac{180}{x}$; 36 **9.** $y = \frac{72}{x}$ **10.** not possible
11. $y = 6x$ **12.** $z = \frac{7}{4}xy$; 56 **13.** $z = \frac{4x}{y}$; 2
14. $z = \frac{x^3}{y}$; 8 **15.** R varies jointly with k, m and
the square of n. **16.** W varies inversely with the
square of d. **17.** P varies directly with x and
inversely with the product of z and the square of y.

18.

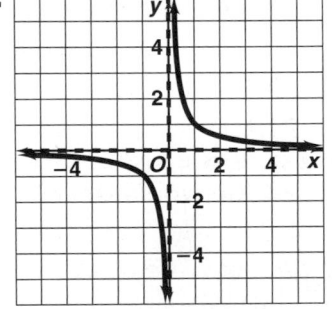

19.

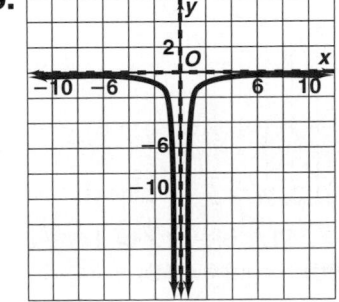

20.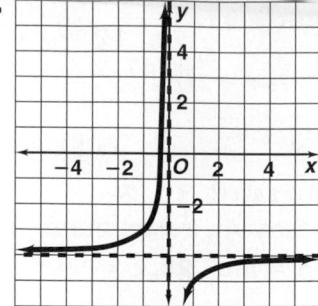

21.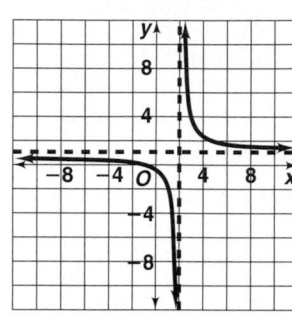

22. $y = \frac{4}{x} + 3$ **23.** $y = \frac{4}{x - 2} + 2$ **24.** $y = \frac{4}{x + 3} - 4$

25. 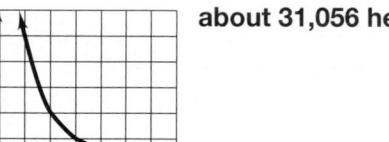 about 31,056 headsets

26. -7 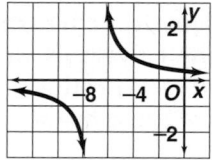 vertical asymptote $x = -7$, horizontal asymptote $y = 0$

27. $-2, 1$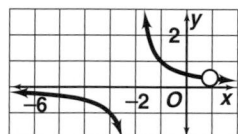

vertical asymptote $x = -2$, horizontal asymptote $y = 0$, hole at $x = 1$

28. $1, -1$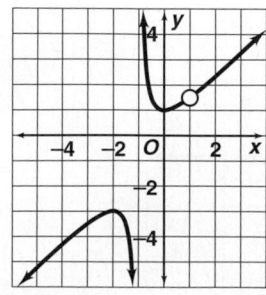

vertical asymptote $x = -1$, hole at $x = 1$

29. no points of discontinuity

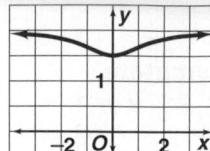

horizontal asymptote $y = 2$

30. $\frac{(x - 1)(x + 1)}{x + 3}$; $x \neq -4, -3$, or 6

31. $\frac{(2x - 1)(x + 1)}{x + 4}$; $x \neq -4, -1$, or 0 **32.** $\frac{r}{3}$

33. 12 cm **34.** $\frac{3(3x - 4)}{(x - 2)(x + 2)}$

35. $\frac{-x^2 + 3x + 2}{x(x + 1)(x - 1)(x + 3)}$ **36.** $\frac{8}{15}$ **37.** $\frac{1}{4(x + y)}$

38. -1 **39.** no solution **40.** $-12, 9$ **41.** 7.5 h, 15 h **42.** dependent **43.** independent
44. not mutually exclusive **45.** not mutually exclusive **46.** $\frac{1}{3}$ **47.** $\frac{2}{3}$ **48.** $\frac{5}{6}$

Chapter 10

Lesson 10-1 pp. 550–553

EXERCISES

1.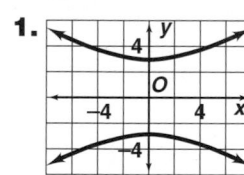

Hyperbola: center (0, 0), y-intercepts at $\pm\frac{5\sqrt{3}}{3}$, no x-intercepts, the lines of symmetry are the x- and y-axes; domain: all real numbers, range:
$y \geq \frac{5\sqrt{3}}{3}$ or $y \leq -\frac{5\sqrt{3}}{3}$. **17.** center (0, 0), x-intercepts at ± 3, y-intercepts at ± 2; domain: $-3 \leq x \leq 3$, range: $-2 \leq y \leq 2$ **19.** center (0, 0), x-intercepts at ± 3, no y-intercepts; domain: $x \leq -3$ or $x \geq 3$, range: all real numbers
23. 19 **25.** 18

29.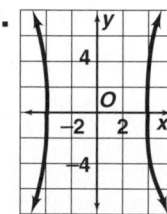

Hyperbola: center (0, 0), x-intercepts ± 4, the lines of symmetry are the x- and y-axes; domain: $x \leq -4$ or $x \geq 4$, range: all real numbers.

35.

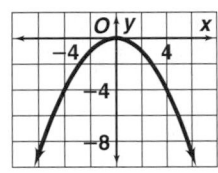

$x^2 + y^2 = 36$ **39.** D

41, 43. Answers may vary. Samples are given.
41. $(\sqrt{2}, 1)$ **43.** $(2, 0)$

Lesson 10-2   pp. 558–560

EXERCISES 1. $y = \frac{1}{8}x^2$ **3.** $x = -\frac{1}{12}y^2$ **7.** $x = \frac{1}{24}y^2$
9. $y = \frac{1}{28}x^2$ **13.** $y = \frac{1}{6}x^2$ **17.** $\left(0, \frac{1}{4}\right), y = -\frac{1}{4}$
19. $\left(-\frac{1}{2}, 0\right), x = -\frac{1}{2}$
25. $(0, 0), (0, -1), y = 1$

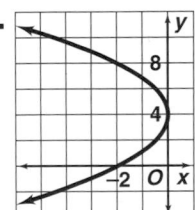

37. $y = \frac{1}{400}x^2$ **39.** $x = -\frac{1}{28}y^2$ **43.** $x = -\frac{1}{8}y^2$
45. $x = y^2$

47.

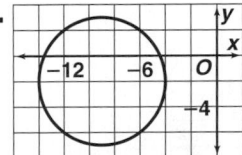

53. $x = -\frac{1}{2}(y - 1)^2 + 1$

Lesson 10-3   pp. 564–566

EXERCISES 1. $x^2 + y^2 = 100$ **3.** $(x - 2)^2 +$
$(y - 3)^2 = 20.25$ **9.** $x^2 + (y + 1)^2 = 9$
11. $(x - 2)^2 + (y + 4)^2 = 25$ **17.** $(x + 3)^2 +$
$(y - 4)^2 = 9$ **19.** $(1, 1), 1$ **21.** $(3, -1), 6$

27.

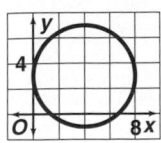

35. $x^2 + y^2 = 16$ **37.** $x^2 + y^2 = 25$ **45.** $(x + 6)^2 +$
$(y - 13)^2 = 49$ **47.** $(x + 2)^2 + (y - 7.5)^2 = 2.25$
55. $(0, 0), \sqrt{2}$ **57.** $(0, 0), \sqrt{14}$
65. circle; $(x - 4)^2 + (y - 3)^2 = 16$;

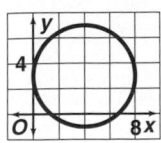

Lesson 10-4   pp. 571–573

EXERCISES 1. $\frac{x^2}{16} + \frac{y^2}{9} = 1$ **3.** $\frac{x^2}{9} + y^2 = 1$
9. $\frac{x^2}{2.25} + \frac{y^2}{0.25} = 1$ **11.** $\frac{x^2}{36} + \frac{y^2}{100} = 1$
19. $(0, 4), (0, -4)$

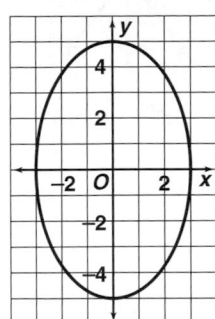

27. $\frac{x^2}{100} + \frac{y^2}{64} = 1$ **29.** $\frac{x^2}{89} + \frac{y^2}{64} = 1$ **33.** $(\sqrt{5}, 0),$
$(-\sqrt{5}, 0)$ **35.** $(0, 4\sqrt{2}), (0, -4\sqrt{2})$ **45.** $\frac{x^2}{16} + y^2 = 1$
47. $\frac{x^2}{4} + \frac{y^2}{16} = 1$ **51.** $\frac{x^2}{25} + \frac{y^2}{4} = 1$ **53.** $\frac{x^2}{702.25} +$
$\frac{y^2}{210.25} = 1$

Lesson 10-5   pp. 578–580

EXERCISES

1.

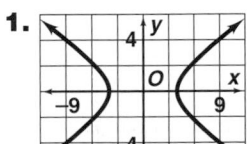

11. $(0, \sqrt{113}), (0, -\sqrt{113})$;

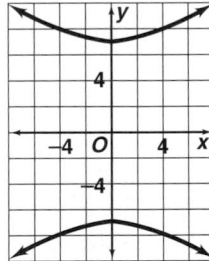

19. $\frac{x^2}{69,169} - \frac{y^2}{96,480} = 1$ **21.** $\frac{x^2}{192,432,384} -$
$\frac{y^2}{170,203,465} = 1$ **23.** $\frac{x^2}{9} - \frac{y^2}{16} = 1$ **25.** $y^2 - \frac{x^2}{3} = 1$
27.

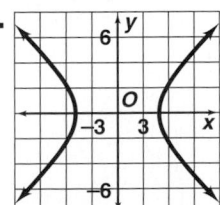

31. $\frac{y^2}{9} - x^2 = 1$

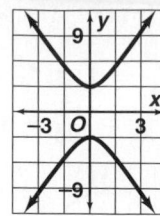

33. $y = \pm\frac{1}{2}\sqrt{2x^2 - 8}$; (2, 0), (−2, 0)

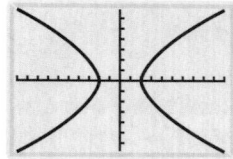

41. (±1, 0), $y = \pm\frac{1}{3}x$ **43.** (±5, 0), $y = \pm\frac{4}{5}x$

Lesson 10-6   pp. 585–588

EXERCISES

1. $\frac{(x + 2)^2}{9} + \frac{(y - 1)^2}{4} = 1$ **3.** $\frac{x^2}{36} + \frac{(y + 4)^2}{25} = 1$

5. $\frac{(x + 3)^2}{16} - \frac{(y + 3)^2}{9} = 1$ **7.** $\frac{(x + 1)^2}{9} - \frac{(y - 2)^2}{40} = 1$

11. $\frac{(x - 175)^2}{1936} - \frac{y^2}{28,689} = 1$

13. $(x + 6)^2 + y^2 = 81$;
circle, center (−6, 0),
radius 9

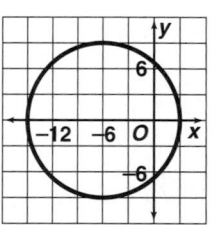

29. $(x + 6)^2 + (y - 9)^2 = 81$

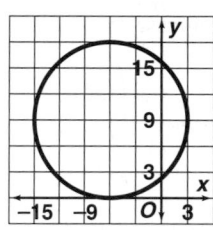

33. $\frac{(x - 1)^2}{9} + \frac{(y + 1)^2}{16} = 1$ **35.** $(x + 4)^2 +$
$(y + 4)^2 = 25$ **37.** $(x - 8)^2 + (y - 2)^2 = 4$

39. $y - 5 = 4(x - 3)^2$

49.

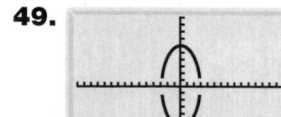   ellipse, $\frac{x^2}{9} + \frac{y^2}{36} = 1$

Chapter Review   pp. 591–593

1. directrix **2.** major axis **3.** standard form of an
equation of a circle **4.** radius **5.** transverse axis

6.

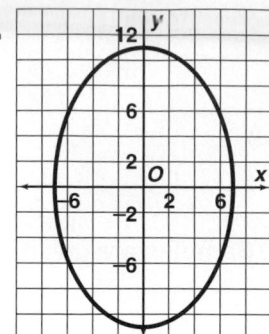

ellipse; x-axis and
y-axis;
domain: $-7 \le x \le 7$
range: $-11 \le y \le 11$

7.

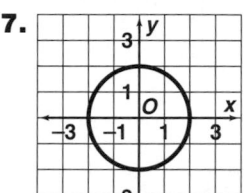

circle; every line through the
center; domain: $-2 \le x \le 2$
range: $-2 \le y \le 2$

8.

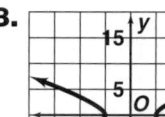

hyperbola; x-axis and y-axis;
domain: $x \le -5$ or $x \ge 5$
range: all real numbers

9.

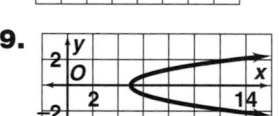

parabola; x-axis; domain: $x \ge 5$, range: all real
numbers **10.** center (0, 0); (±4, 0); domain: $x \ge 4$
or $x \le -4$, range: all real numbers **11.** center
(0, 0); (0, ±2), (±3, 0); domain: $-3 \le x \le 3$, range:
$-2 \le y \le 2$ **12.** $y = \frac{1}{8}x^2 + 1$ **13.** $x = -\frac{1}{12}y^2 + 1$
14. $x = \frac{1}{20}y^2$ **15.** $y = -\frac{1}{20}x^2$ **16.** $y = \frac{1}{24}x^2$
17. $y = \frac{1}{10}x^2$ **18.** $y = 3x^2$
19. $\left(0, \frac{1}{20}\right), y = -\frac{1}{20}$

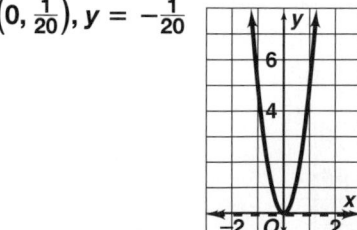

20. $\left(\frac{1}{8}, 0\right), x = -\frac{1}{8}$

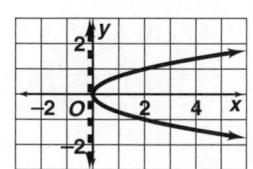

---

21. $(-2, 0)$, $x = 2$

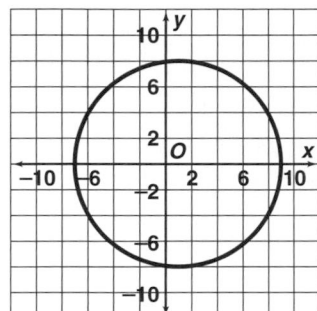

22. $x^2 + y^2 = 16$ **23.** $(x - 8)^2 + (y - 1)^2 = 25$

24. $(x + 3)^2 + (y - 2)^2 = 100$ **25.** $(x - 5)^2 + (y + 3)^2 = 64$ **26.** $(x - 3)^2 + (y - 1)^2 = 9$

27. $(x + 1)^2 + y^2 = 4$

28. center $(1, 0)$, radius 8

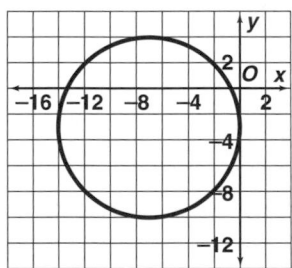

29. center $(-7, -3)$, radius 7

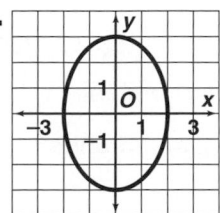

30. $\frac{x^2}{17} + \frac{y^2}{16} = 1$ **31.** $\frac{x^2}{25} + \frac{y^2}{29} = 1$ **32.** $\frac{x^2}{9} + \frac{y^2}{10} = 1$

33. $\frac{x^2}{40} + \frac{y^2}{36} = 1$ **34.** $\frac{x^2}{64} + \frac{y^2}{16} = 1$

35.

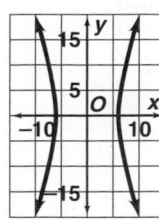

foci $(0, \pm\sqrt{5})$

36.

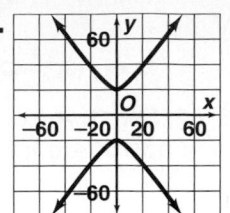

foci $(\pm 3\sqrt{29}, 0)$

37.

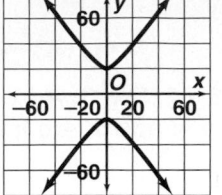

foci $(0, \pm\sqrt{569})$

38.

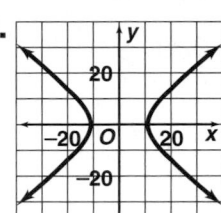

foci $(\pm\sqrt{202}, 0)$

39. $\dfrac{x^2}{1.148 \times 10^{10}} - \dfrac{y^2}{3.395 \times 10^{10}} = 1$

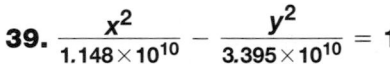

40. $\dfrac{(x - 3)^2}{4} + \dfrac{(y + 2)^2}{9} = 1$ **41.** $\dfrac{(x - 6)^2}{9} - \dfrac{(y - 3)^2}{16} = 1$

42. $\dfrac{(x - 77.5)^2}{1640.25} - \dfrac{y^2}{4366} = 1$

43. hyperbola; center $(0, -2)$, foci $(0, -2 \pm 2\sqrt{10})$

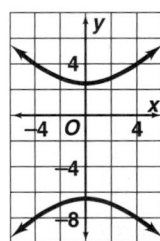

44. circle, center $\left(-\frac{3}{2}, 2\right)$, radius $\frac{\sqrt{61}}{2}$

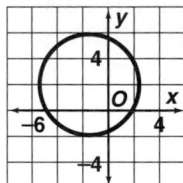

45. parabola; vertex $\left(-\frac{1}{2}, -\frac{169}{4}\right)$

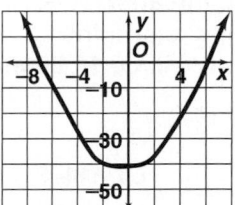

46. ellipse; center $(1, -2)$, foci $\left(\frac{3 \pm \sqrt{51}}{3}, -2\right)$

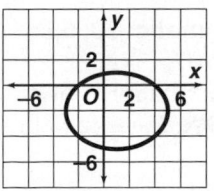

Chapter 11

Lesson 11-1   pp. 603–605

EXERCISES 1. Subtract 3; 65, 62, 59. **3.** Add one more to each term (add 3, add 4, add 5, etc.); 25, 33, 42.

11.

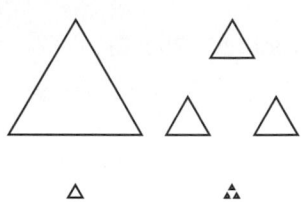

13. $a_n = a_{n-1} - 2, a_1 = 43$; 33 **15.** $a_n = a_{n-1} - 5, a_1 = 6$; −14 **19.** $a_n = \frac{1}{n+1}$; $\frac{1}{13}$ **21.** $a_n = 4n - 1$; 47 **25.** explicit; 0, 1, 3, 6, 10 **27.** recursive; −2, 6, −18, 54, −162 **33.** 20, 23; $a_n = 3n + 2$; explicit or $a_n = a_{n-1} + 3, a_1 = 5$; recursive **35.** 216, 343; $a_n = n^3$; explicit **45.** 26, 677; 458, 330; 2.1×10^{11} **47.** 25, 36, 49, 64 **51a.** 25 boxes **b.** 110 boxes **c.** 9 levels

Lesson 11-2   pp. 608–610

EXERCISES 1. no **3.** no **11.** 127 **13.** 12.5 **21.** −7.5 **23.** 13 **31.** 4 **33.** 13 **47.** 15 **49.** 22 **53.** $a_n = 0 + 6(n - 1), a_n = a_{n-1} + 6, a_1 = 0$ **55.** $a_n = -4 + 4(n - 1), a_n = a_{n-1} + 4, a_1 = -4$ **63.** −4, −10, −16 **65.** −8, −17, −26 **71a.** $20, $45, $75, $110, $150, $195, $245, $300, $360, $425, $495 **b.** $a_n = a_{n-1} + \$20 + \$5(n - 1), a_1 = \$20$ **c.** $495

Extension   p. 611

1a. fifth **b.** seventh **c.** sixth **d.** fourth **3a.** 1, 1, 2, 3, 5, 8, 13, 21, 34, 55 **b.** 143; 13; the answer is the seventh term. **c.** Check students' work; the answer is the seventh term. **d.** It will be 11 times the seventh term.

Lesson 11-3   pp. 614–617

EXERCISES 1. yes; 2; 16, 32 **3.** yes; −2; 16, −32 **13.** $a_n = 5 \cdot (-3)^{n-1}$; 5, −15, 45, −135, 405 **15.** $a_n = \frac{1}{2}\left(\frac{2}{3}\right)^{n-1}$; $\frac{1}{2}, \frac{1}{3}, \frac{2}{9}, \frac{4}{27}, \frac{8}{81}$ **23.** 1530 **25.** 1.5 **29.** arithmetic; 125, 150 **31.** arithmetic; 50, 55 **37.** 6561, 2187, 729, or −6561, 2187, −729 **39.** 10, 8, 6.4, or −10, 8, −6.4 **43.** 12,288 **45.** 201,326,592 **49.** 16 **51.** 10 **59.** 7

Lesson 11-4   pp. 622–624

EXERCISES 1. 21 + 18 + 15 + 12 + 9 + 6 + 3; 84 **3.** 100 + 99 + 98 + 97 + 96 + 95; 585 **7.** 32 **9.** 264 **13.** $\sum_{n=1}^{4} 2n$ **15.** $\sum_{n=1}^{7} (n + 4)$ **19.** 5, 1, 9; 25 **21.** 6, 4, −1; 9 **25.** sequence; infinite **27.** series; finite **33a.** 91 **b.** 83 **35.** 110 **37.** 5150

Lesson 11-5   pp. 628–631

EXERCISES 1. 255 **3.** 381 **9.** converges; has a sum **11.** converges; has a sum **19.** 1 **21.** $\frac{9}{2}$ **25.** arithmetic; 420 **27.** geometric; 96.47 **33.** 4 **35.** no sum **41.** $\frac{7}{8}$

Extension   p. 633

1. $1 + 3 + 5 + 7 + 9 + 11 \stackrel{?}{=} 6^2$, 36 = 36; $1 + 3 + 5 + 7 + 9 + 11 + 13 \stackrel{?}{=} 7^2$, 49 = 49; $1 + 3 + 5 + 7 + 9 + 11 + 13 + 15 \stackrel{?}{=} 8^2$, 64 = 64
3. For $n = 1$, $\frac{1}{1(1 + 1)} = \frac{1}{1 + 1}$

Assume
$$\frac{1}{1 \cdot 2} + \frac{1}{2 \cdot 3} + \frac{1}{3 \cdot 4} + \ldots + \frac{1}{k(k + 1)} = \frac{k}{k + 1}$$
Prove
$$\frac{1}{1 \cdot 2} + \frac{1}{2 \cdot 3} + \frac{1}{3 \cdot 4} + \ldots + \frac{1}{k(k + 1)} + \frac{1}{(k + 1)((k + 1) + 1)} = \frac{k + 1}{(k + 1) + 1}$$
Proof
$$\frac{1}{1 \cdot 2} + \frac{1}{2 \cdot 3} + \frac{1}{3 \cdot 4} + \ldots + \frac{1}{k(k + 1)} + \frac{1}{(k + 1)((k + 1) + 1)} = \frac{k}{k + 1} + \frac{1}{(k + 1)((k + 1) + 1)} =$$
$$\frac{k(k + 2)}{(k + 1)(k + 2)} + \frac{1}{(k + 1)((k + 1) + 1)} =$$
$$\frac{k(k + 2) + 1}{(k + 1)((k + 1) + 1)} = \frac{k^2 + 2k + 1}{(k + 1)((k + 1) + 1)} =$$
$$\frac{(k + 1)^2}{(k + 1)((k + 1) + 1)} = \frac{k + 1}{(k + 1) + 1}$$

Lesson 11-6   pp. 637–639

EXERCISES 1. total produced **3.** miles **7.** 110 units² **9.** $A = \sum_{n=1}^{2} 1f(a_n)$ **a.** 0.5 units² **b.** 2.5 units² **11.** $A = \sum_{n=1}^{2} 1f(a_n)$ **a.** 3 units² **b.** 7 units² **19.** 2.5 units² **21.** 3.3 units²

25. 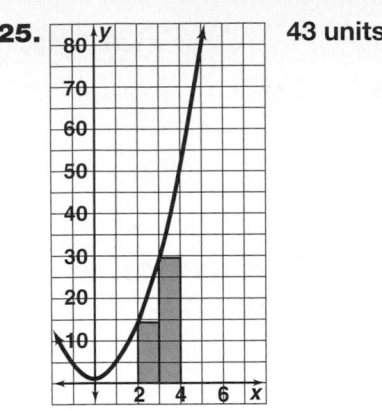 43 units^2

33. 7.5 units^2 **35.** 3.46 units^2

Chapter Review pp. 641–643

1. limits **2.** circumscribed rectangles
3. sequence **4.** converges **5.** common ratio
6. $a_n = a_{n-1} + 17, a_1 = 5; 73, 90, 107$
7. $a_n = -7a_{n-1}, a_1 = 1; 2401; -16,807; 117,649$
8. $a_n = a_{n-1} + 9, a_1 = -2; 34, 43, 52$
9. $a_n = 3n - 2; 34$ **10.** $a_n = 2^n; 4096$
11. $a_n = 6n^2 - 30; 834$ **12.** Answers may vary.
Sample: If the formula uses the previous term,
then it is recursive; otherwise it is explicit. **13.** no
14. yes; $d = 15; a_{32} = 468$ **15.** yes; $d = 3; a_{32} =$
100 **16.** 5 **17.** 101.5 **18.** −4.9 **19.** 5 **20.** −10.5,
−8, −5.5 **21.** 1.4, 0.8, 0.2 **22.** 11 **23.** 0.5 **24.** If
the terms of the sequence have a common
difference, then the sequence is arithmetic.
25. yes; $r = \frac{1}{2}, a_n = 1\left(\frac{1}{2}\right)^{n-1}, \frac{1}{16}, \frac{1}{32}$ **26.** no
27. yes; $r = 1.2, a_n = 3(1.2)^{n-1}, 6.2208, 7.46496$
28. 6 **29.** 20 **30.** 0.04 **31.** −10, −5, −2.5 **32.** $-\frac{1}{3}$,
$-\frac{2}{3}, -\frac{4}{3}$ **33.** $3\frac{1}{2}, 12\frac{1}{4}, 42\frac{7}{8}$ **34.** $\sum_{n=1}^{5} 13 - 3n; 20$
35. $\sum_{n=1}^{7} 45 + 5n; 455$ **36.** $\sum_{n=1}^{11} 4.6 + 1.4n; 143$
37. $\sum_{n=1}^{8} 23 - 2n; 112$ **38.** 3, −8, 26; 27 **39.** 9, 4, 8;
54 **40.** 11, $-\frac{10}{3}$, −10; $-\frac{220}{3}$ **41.** No; she will have
only 1150 available by the end of the fifth year.
42. $4\frac{121}{243}$ **43.** 31 **44.** 53.125 **45.** $14\frac{7}{18}$
46. converges; $S = 187.5$ **47.** diverges; no sum
48. diverges; no sum **49.** converges; $S = 2$
50. $A = \sum_{n=1}^{2} 1 \cdot f(a_n)$ **a.** 1 unit^2 **b.** 5 units^2
c. $\frac{8}{3}$ units^2 **51.** $A = \sum_{n=1}^{2} 1 \cdot f(a_n)$ **a.** 3 units^2

b. 11 units^2 **c.** 6 units^2 **52.** $A = \sum_{n=1}^{2} 1 \cdot f(a_n)$
a. 6 units^2 **b.** 14 units^2 **c.** $10.\overline{6}$ units^2

53. $A = \sum_{n=1}^{2} 1 \cdot f(a_n)$ **a.** 7 units^2
b. 9 units^2 **c.** 8 units^2

54. $A = \sum_{n=1}^{2} 1 \cdot f(a_n)$ **a.** 9 units^2 **b.** 17 units^2
c. 12 units^2 **55.** $A = \sum_{n=1}^{2} 1 \cdot f(a_n)$ **a.** 7 units^2
b. 11 units^2 **c.** $8\frac{2}{3}$ units^2

Chapter 12

Lesson 12-1 pp. 651–653

EXERCISES

1.

Object	Frequency
Rock	11
Paper	10
Scissors	15
Total	36

3. 0.11 **5.** 0.53

7. Number of Days Per Month

Days	28	29	30	31
Frequency	3	1	16	28
Probability	$\frac{3}{48}$	$\frac{1}{48}$	$\frac{16}{48}$	$\frac{28}{48}$

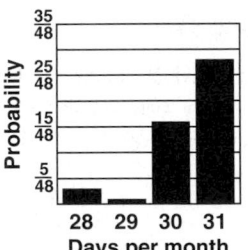

9. 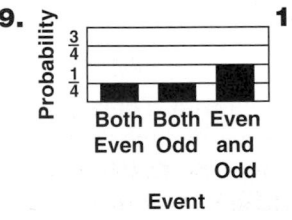 **13.**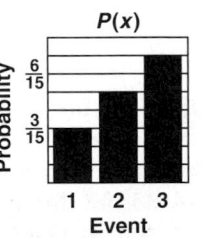

Lesson 12-2 pp. 656–658

EXERCISES 1. 0.9 **3.** $0.\overline{6}$ **5.** 0.405
7. 0.562 **9.** 45%

11. 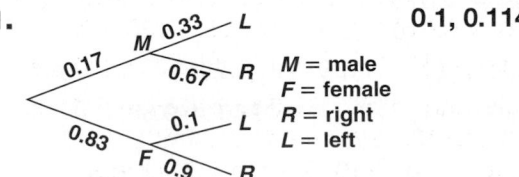 0.1, 0.114

M = male
F = female
R = right
L = left

19. $P(C)$ **21.** $P(R|W)$

Extension   p. 659

1. 0.9508 **3.** 0.9998 **5.** $\frac{2}{3}$ or about 67% **7.** 0.08
9. 0.84

Lesson 12-3   pp. 664–667

EXERCISES 1. 4.36, 3, 1 **3.** 600.3, 535.5, 499

5.
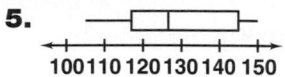
100 110 120 130 140 150

7.
66 70 74 78 82 86 90

9. 6, 18 **11.** 0 **15.** 381; this value raises the mean. **17.** 60th

Lesson 12-4   pp. 672–674

EXERCISES 1. 5, 2.5 **3.** 704, 461 **5.** 15.1, 3.5
7. 10,259.18; 68.67 **9.** 3 standard deviations
11. −1.4 **13.** 0 **15.** 14.6, 52.3; the bird speeds
are more spread out than the cat speeds.
17. 2001: ≈6707; 2002: ≈6738 **21a.** 53.8, 3.4
b. 7; 9; 10 **23.** ≈75.8; ≈8.7 **25.** ≈0.007; ≈0.08

Lesson 12-5   pp. 680–683

EXERCISES 1. 73% **3.** 92% **5.** very little bias
7. C; this sample has the smallest standard
deviation, which most likely indicates a larger
sample. **9.** ±7% **11.** ±3% **13.** 400 **15.** ±4%;
55% to 63% **17a.** 63% **b.** ±5% **c.** 58% to 68%
19a. 94% **b.** ±18% **c.** 76% to 100% **27.** 31%,
±13% **29.** 63%, ±5%

Lesson 12-6   pp. 688–691

EXERCISES 1. Each guess is a trial. There are 5
trials. Each correct answer is a success. The
probability of a success on a single trial is 0.5.
Check students' designs and simulations.
5. 25% **7.** 0% **9.** 0.1361 **11.** 0.0015
13. $P(0) = 0.0156$
$P(1) = 0.0938$
$P(2) = 0.2344$
$P(3) = 0.3125$
$P(4) = 0.2344$
$P(5) = 0.0938$
$P(6) = 0.0156$
15. 0.2824 **17.** 0.1109 **19.** 0.2051
25a. ${}_{40}C_3 \cdot \left(\frac{1}{7}\right)^3\left(\frac{6}{7}\right)^{37} = 0.0960 = 9.6\%$

Lesson 12-7   pp. 695–698

EXERCISES 1. 43% **3.** 43 men

5.
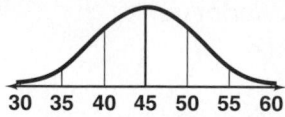
30 35 40 45 50 55 60

9. 79.1 **11.** 68% **15.** 32% **19.** 2.5% **21.** 100%
23. 50% **27a.** 209 **b.** 41 **c.** 127 – 250

Chapter Review   pp. 701–703

1. sample **2.** outlier **3.** probability distribution
4. binomial experiment **5.** measures of variation

6a.

Winner	Freq.
Player 1	8
Player 2	4
Ties	3
Total	15

b. P(Player 2 wins) $= \frac{4}{15}$

9. $\frac{3}{14}$ **10.** $\frac{3}{5}$ **11.**
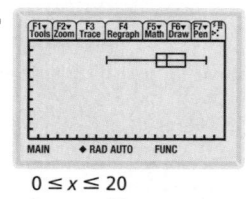

12. 0.9 **13.** 0.2 **14.** 14.4; 14; 12, 13, 14

15.
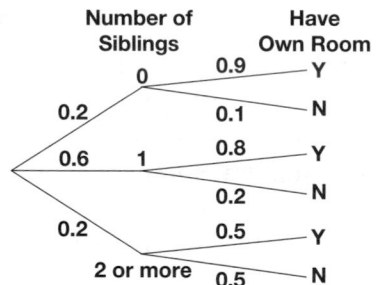
$0 \le x \le 20$
$0 \le y \le 10$

16. 20th percentile = 13, 90th percentile = 18
17. 53rd percentile **18.** 8 **19.** 6 **20.** 0.26 **21.** 2
22. ≈1.56 **23a.** 76% **b.** ±14% **c.** from 62% to
90% **24.** Answers may vary. Sample: Each guess
is a trial. There are 4 trials. Since there are 2
equally likely answers, the probability of success
is 0.5. Let 1 represent a correct response and 2
an incorrect response. Generate 4 random
numbers, either 1 or 2, 10 times. The probability
is one tenth the number of times there are exactly
three 1's. **25.** 0.137

27.
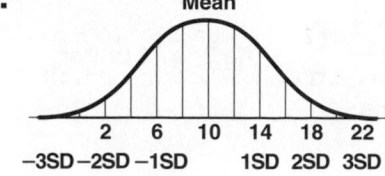
Mean
2   6   10   14   18   22
−3SD −2SD −1SD   1SD 2SD 3SD

Chapter 13

Lesson 13-1   pp. 713–716

EXERCISES 1. 5 **3.** 4 **5.** periodic; 12
7. not periodic **11.** 3 **13.** 2

15.

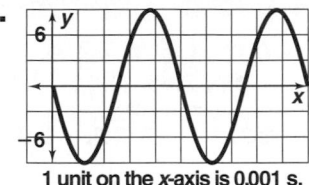

1 unit on the *x*-axis is 0.001 s.

17. Answers may vary. Sample: Yes; average
monthly temperatures for three years should be
cyclical due to the variation of the seasons.
19. Answers may vary. Sample: Yes; traffic that
passes through an intersection should be at the
same levels for the same times of day for two
consecutive work days. **21a.** 1 s **b.** 1.5 mV
23. 3, −3, 4;

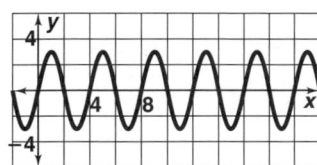

27. 2 weeks **29.** 1 hour

Lesson 13-2   pp. 722–724

EXERCISES 1. 45° **3.** 240°

7.

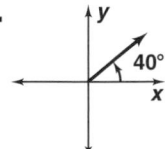

13. 215° **15.** 4° **21.** $\frac{1}{2}$, $\frac{\sqrt{3}}{2}$; 0.50, 0.87
23. $\frac{\sqrt{3}}{2}$, $-\frac{1}{2}$; 0.87, −0.50 **25.** $\frac{\sqrt{3}}{2}$, $\frac{1}{2}$; 0.87, 0.50
27. $\frac{\sqrt{3}}{2}$, $-\frac{1}{2}$; 0.87, −0.50 **29.** 1.00, 0.00
31. 0.71, −0.71 **37–39.** Answers may vary.
Samples: **37.** 405°, −315° **39.** 45°, −315° **45.** II
47. negative *x*-axis **51a.** 0.77, 0.77, 0.77
b. The cosines of the three angles are equal
because the angles are coterminal.

Lesson 13-3   pp. 729–733

EXERCISES 1. $-\frac{5\pi}{3}$, −5.24 **3.** $-\frac{\pi}{2}$, −1.57 **7.** 540°
9. −120° **15.** $\frac{1}{2}$, $\frac{\sqrt{3}}{2}$ **17.** $-\frac{1}{2}$, $\frac{\sqrt{3}}{2}$ **21.** 10.5 m
23. 25.1 in. **27.** ≈32 ft **29.** ≈42.2 in. **31.** III
33. positive *y*-axis

37.

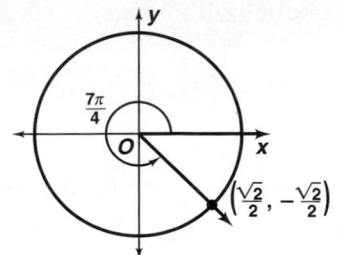

0.71, −0.71

45. ≈11 radians **47.** ≈798 ft; 55°, −665°
51. ≈4008.7 mi

Lesson 13-4   pp. 738–741

EXERCISES 1. $\frac{1}{2}$ **3.** ≈0.9 **7.** 1 **9.** ≈−0.8
13. 3; 2, $\frac{2\pi}{3}$ **15.** 2; 3, π

17.

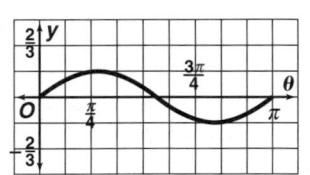

$y = \frac{1}{3}\sin 2\theta$

23.

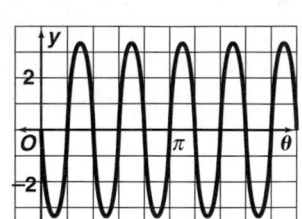

29. 2π; $y = -3\sin\theta$ **31.** $\frac{\pi}{3}$; $y = \frac{1}{2}\sin 6\theta$
35. 5; 1, $\frac{2\pi}{5}$ **37.** 1; 3, 2π
43a. $\frac{1}{440}$ **b.** 0.001 **c.** 880π
45. $\frac{2\pi}{5}$, 3.5

Lesson 13-5   pp. 746–748

EXERCISES 1. 2π, 3; max: 3, min: −3, zeros: $\frac{\pi}{2}$, $\frac{3\pi}{2}$
3. π, 1; max: 1, min: −1, zeros: $\frac{\pi}{4}$, $\frac{3\pi}{4}$, $\frac{5\pi}{4}$, $\frac{7\pi}{4}$

5.

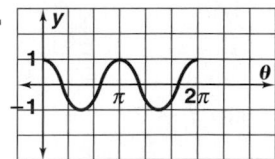

11. $y = \frac{\pi}{2}\cos\frac{2\pi}{3}\theta$ **13.** $y = -3\cos 2\theta$ **17.** 1.98,
4.30 **19.** 2.52 **23.** π, −1 ≤ y ≤ 1, 1
25. 4π, $-\frac{1}{3}$ ≤ y ≤ $\frac{1}{3}$, $\frac{1}{3}$ **31.** 1.83, 2.88, 4.97, 6.02
33a. 3.79, 5.64 **b.** 10.07, 11.92; these values are
the sums of the values from part (a) and 2π.

35a. 5.5 ft; 1.5 ft **b.** about 12 h 22 min
c. $y = 1.5 \cos \frac{2\pi t}{742}$
d. 12:17 A.M.–7:49 A.M., 12:39 P.M.–8:11 P.M.

Lesson 13-6   pp. 751–754

EXERCISES 1. 0 **3.** -1 **9.** π **11.** $\frac{\pi}{5}$, $\theta = -\frac{\pi}{10}, \frac{\pi}{10}$
13. $\frac{\pi}{4}$, $\theta = -\frac{\pi}{8}, \frac{\pi}{8}$ **15.**

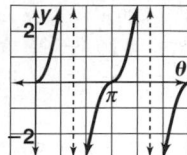

19.

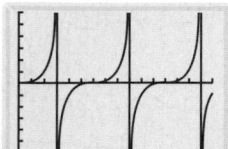

50, undefined, -50

23. 6

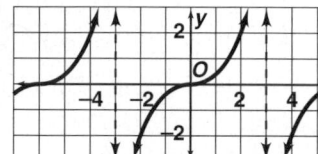

27. 2.03, 5.18 **33.** 200 **35.** 135 **39.** $y = -\tan\left(\frac{1}{2}x\right)$
41. $y = \tan(2x)$

Lesson 13-7   pp. 760–762

EXERCISES 1. -1; 1 unit to the left
3. 1.6; 1.6 units to the right

7.

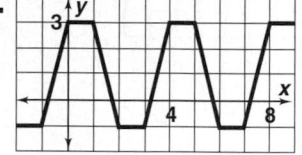

11.

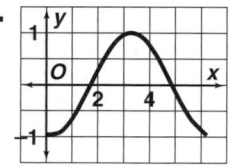

17. 3, 2π; 1 unit up **19.** 1, 2π; $\frac{\pi}{2}$ units left
and 2 units up

21.

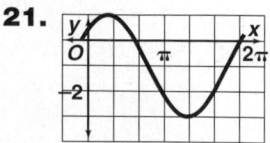

25.

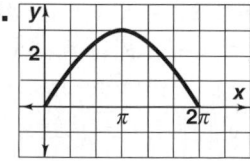

31. $y = \sin(x + \pi)$ **33.** $y = \sin x + 3$
37a.

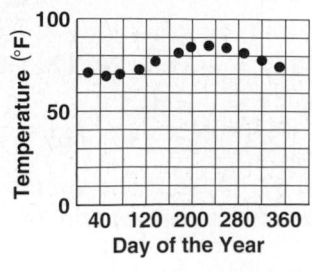

b. $y = 8.5 \cos \frac{2\pi}{365}(x - 228) + 77.5$
39. $y = \cos(x + 3) + \pi$ **41.** $y = 2\cos\left(x - \frac{\pi}{3}\right) - 1$;
$y = 2\sin\left(x + \frac{\pi}{6}\right) - 1$

Lesson 13-8   pp. 766–769

EXERCISES 1. 1.02 **3.** -0.70 **5.** $\frac{3}{4}$ **7.** $-\frac{5}{3}$ **9.** $\sqrt{2}$
11. 0 **21.** -7.02 **23.** 1

29.

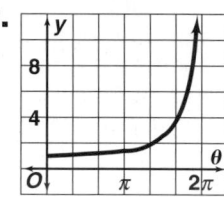

33. 1.1547 **35.** -2.9238

43. $\frac{2\sqrt{3}}{3}$; 1.15 **45.** -1

47.

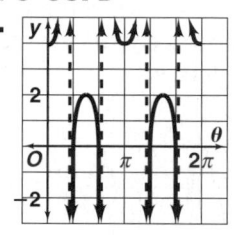

51. C **53.** D
61.

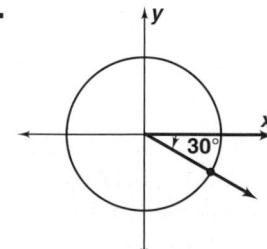

3 units up

Chapter Review   pp. 771–773

1. period **2.** unit circle **3.** tangent function
4. phase shift **5.** secant function **6.** periodic; 4, 2
7. Answers may vary. Sample:

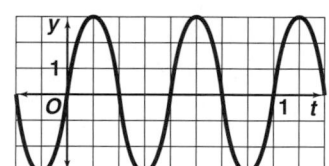

8. $-225°$

9.

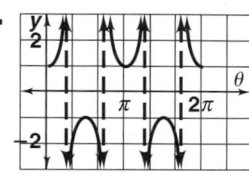

10. 240° **11.** $\left(\frac{\sqrt{2}}{2}, -\frac{\sqrt{2}}{2}\right)$; (0.71, -0.71) **12a.** $\frac{\pi}{3}$
b. $\frac{1}{2}$, $\frac{\sqrt{3}}{2}$ **13a.** $-\frac{\pi}{4}$ **b.** $\frac{\sqrt{2}}{2}$, $-\frac{\sqrt{2}}{2}$ **14a.** π **b.** -1, 0
15a. 360° **b.** 1, 0 **16a.** 150° **b.** $-\frac{\sqrt{3}}{2}$, $\frac{1}{2}$
17a. $-135°$ **b.** $-\frac{\sqrt{2}}{2}$, $-\frac{\sqrt{2}}{2}$ **18.** 26.2 ft

19.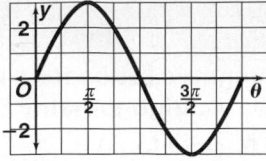

20.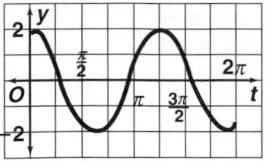

21.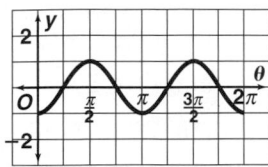

22. 3 cycles; 1, $\frac{2\pi}{3}$; $y = -\sin 3\theta$ **23.** $y = 4 \sin 4\theta$
24. $y = 3 \cos 2\theta$ **25.** $y = 2 \cos 2\theta$ **26.** 3.92, 5.51
27. 0.16, 1.84, 4.16, 5.84 **28.** 0.58, 1.00, 2.15, 2.57, 3.72, 4.14, 5.29, 5.71

29. 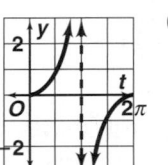 0.41, 1

30. 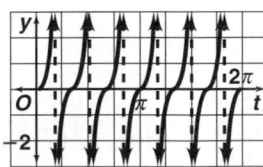 −1, undefined

31. 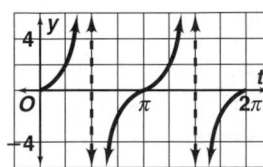 2, undefined

32.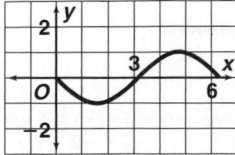

33.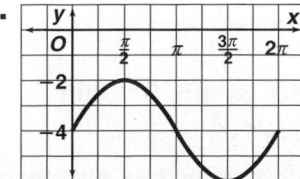

35. $y = \sin\left(x - \frac{\pi}{4}\right)$ **36.** $y = \cos x - 2$ **37.** $\sqrt{2}$
38. $-\frac{\sqrt{3}}{3}$ **39.** 2

40.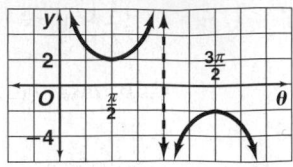

41.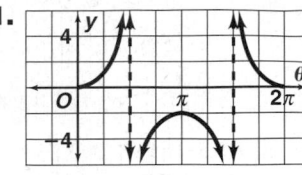

42.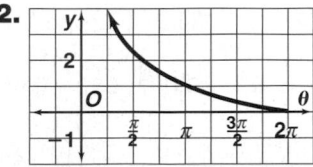

Chapter 14

Lesson 14-1 pp. 780–782

EXERCISES 1. $\cos \theta \cot \theta = \cos \theta \left(\frac{\cos \theta}{\sin \theta}\right) = \frac{1 - \sin^2 \theta}{\sin \theta} = \frac{1}{\sin \theta} - \sin \theta$ **3.** $\cos \theta \tan \theta = \cos \theta \left(\frac{\sin \theta}{\cos \theta}\right) = \sin \theta$ **9.** 1 **11.** $\tan^2 \theta$ **21.** $\sec \theta$
23. $\sec^2 \theta$ **39.** $\pm\sqrt{1 - \cos^2 \theta}$ **41.** $\frac{\pm\sqrt{1 - \sin^2 \theta}}{\sin \theta}$
45. $\sin^2 \theta \tan^2 \theta = \sin^2 \theta \left(\frac{\sin^2 \theta}{\cos^2 \theta}\right) = (1 - \cos^2 \theta)\left(\frac{\sin^2 \theta}{\cos^2 \theta}\right) = \frac{\sin^2 \theta - \sin^2 \theta \cos^2 \theta}{\cos^2 \theta} = \frac{\sin^2 \theta}{\cos^2 \theta} - \frac{\sin^2 \theta \cos^2 \theta}{\cos^2 \theta} = \tan^2 \theta - \sin^2 \theta$

Lesson 14-2 pp. 787–790

EXERCISES 1. $-\frac{\pi}{2} + 2\pi n$ **3.** $\frac{\pi}{2} + 2\pi n$ **5.** $30° + n \cdot 360°$ and $210° + n \cdot 360°$ or $30° + n \cdot 180°$
7. $120° + n \cdot 360°$ and $300° + n \cdot 360°$ or $120° + n \cdot 180°$ **9.** $0.38 + 2\pi n$ and $2.76 + 2\pi n$
17. $\frac{\pi}{6}, \frac{11\pi}{6}$ **19.** $\frac{\pi}{4}, \frac{3\pi}{4}$ **35.** $30° + n \cdot 360°$ and $150° + n \cdot 360°$ **37.** $210° + n \cdot 360°$ and $330° + n \cdot 360°$
39. $\frac{3\pi}{2}$ **41.** 0.34, 2.80 **47.** $\frac{\pi}{2} + 2\pi n, \frac{3\pi}{2} + 2\pi n$
49. $\frac{\pi}{4} + \frac{\pi}{2}n$ **59.** $0.79 + \pi n, 2.36 + \pi n$
61. $0.79 + \pi n, 2.36 + \pi n$ **65.** $\frac{3\pi}{2} + 2\pi n$

Lesson 14-3 pp. 796–799

EXERCISES 1a. ≈8333 ft **b.** ≈8824 ft
3a. $\frac{9}{41} \approx 0.22$ **b.** $\frac{40}{41} \approx 0.98$ **c.** $\frac{40}{9} \approx 4.44$ **d.** $\frac{41}{9} \approx 4.56$ **e.** $\frac{9}{41} \approx 0.22$ **f.** not defined **5.** 41.8 **7.** 10.6
9. 45.0° **11.** 48.6° **19.** $c \approx 7.8$, $\angle A = 39.8°$, $\angle B = 50.2°$ **21.** $c \approx 10.2$, $\angle A = 52.6°$, $\angle B = 37.4°$

25. $\cos \theta = \frac{\sqrt{55}}{8}$, $\tan \theta = \frac{3\sqrt{55}}{55}$, $\csc \theta = \frac{8}{3}$, $\sec \theta = \frac{8\sqrt{55}}{55}$, $\cot \theta = \frac{\sqrt{55}}{3}$

35. $a = 15$, $m\angle A \approx 61.9°$, $m\angle B \approx 28.1°$
37. $a \approx 7.9$, $b \approx 6.2$, $m\angle B = 38°$
41. 35.5° **43.** 20.3 m²

Lesson 14-4 · pp. 803–806

EXERCISES 1. 18.7 cm² **3.** 81.9 m² **5.** 10.9
7. 7.4 **11.** 33.5° **13.** 27.0° **15.** 28.8°
17. $m\angle D = 100°$, $e = 22.3$, $f = 34.2$ **19.** $m\angle T = 29.3°$, $m\angle R = 26.7°$, $r = 8.3$ **27.** 7.5 mi, 7.9 mi
29. 66° **31.** 44.5 **33.** 49.4 **39.** 28.0 ft **41.** 4.0 cm

Extension · p. 807

1. 70.4 and 47.6°, or 109.6° and 8.4° **3.** 87.3° and 44.7°, or 92.7° and 39.3° **5.** 44.0° and 112.4°, or 136.0° and 20.4°

Lesson 14-5 · pp. 810–813

EXERCISES 1. 37.1 **3.** 13.7 **7.** 47.3° **9.** 125.1°
13. 60.4° **15.** 71.7° **19.** $c^2 = a^2 + b^2 - 2ab \cos C$ **21.** $\frac{\sin A}{a} = \frac{\sin B}{b}$ **25.** $m\angle A = 50.1°$, $m\angle B = 56.3°$, $m\angle C = 73.6°$ **27.** $m\angle A = 90°$, $m\angle B = 36.9°$, $m\angle C = 53.1°$ **31.** 38.9 ft **33.** 77.2°
35. 57.1° **37.** 8.8 cm **41.** 32.6° **43.** 67.2°
47. 109 cm

Lesson 14-6 · pp. 818–820

EXERCISES 1. $\csc\left(\theta - \frac{\pi}{2}\right) = \csc\left(-\left(\frac{\pi}{2} - \theta\right)\right) = -\csc\left(\frac{\pi}{2} - \theta\right) = -\sec\theta$ **7.** $\frac{\pi}{2}, \frac{3\pi}{2}$ **9.** $\frac{\pi}{4}, \frac{3\pi}{4}, \frac{5\pi}{4}, \frac{7\pi}{4}$
15. $\sec A$ **17.** 0 **19.** −1
21. $\frac{\sqrt{2} - \sqrt{6}}{4}$ **23.** $2 - \sqrt{3}$
37. $\sin (A - B) = \sin (A + (-B)) = \sin A \cos (-B) + \cos A \sin (-B) = \sin A \cos B - \cos A \sin B$ **45.** $\sin 5\theta$ **47.** $\cos 5\theta$

Lesson 14-7 · pp. 824–825

EXERCISES 1. $-\frac{\sqrt{3}}{2}$ **3.** $-\sqrt{3}$ **9.** $\sin 2\theta = \sin (\theta + \theta) = \sin \theta \cos \theta + \cos \theta \cdot \sin \theta = 2 \sin \theta \cos \theta$ **11.** $\frac{\sqrt{2 + \sqrt{3}}}{2}$ **13.** $\frac{\sqrt{2 - \sqrt{3}}}{2}$ **19.** $\frac{3\sqrt{10}}{10}$
21. 3 **23.** $\frac{4\sqrt{17}}{17}$ **25.** −4 **27.** $\sin 2R = 2 \sin R \cos R = 2\frac{r}{t} \cdot \frac{s}{t} = \frac{2rs}{t^2}$ **29.** $\sin 2S = 2 \sin S \cos S = 2 \cdot \frac{s}{t} \cdot \frac{r}{t} = \frac{2sr}{t^2} = 2 \sin R \cos R = \sin 2R$ **35.** $-\frac{7}{25}$ **37.** $-\frac{25}{24}$ **43.** $\sin \theta (4 \cos \theta - 3) = 0$; $0, \pi, 0.723, 5.560$ **47.** $-\cos \theta$

Chapter Review · pp. 827–829

1. Law of Sines **2.** trigonometric ratios for a right triangle **3.** Law of Cosines **4.** trigonometric identity **5.** Law of Sines **6.** $\sin \theta \tan \theta = \frac{\sin^2 \theta}{\cos \theta} = \frac{1 - \cos^2 \theta}{\cos \theta} = \frac{1}{\cos \theta} - \frac{\cos^2 \theta}{\cos \theta} = \frac{1}{\cos \theta} - \cos \theta$
7. $\cos^2 \theta \cot^2 \theta = (1 - \sin^2 \theta) \cot^2 \theta = \cot^2 \theta - \sin^2 \theta \cot^2 \theta = \cot^2 \theta - \sin^2 \theta \cdot \frac{\cos^2 \theta}{\sin^2 \theta} = \cot^2 \theta - \cos^2 \theta$ **8.** $\cos^2 \theta$ **9.** 1 **10.** 1 **11.** −60°
12. 60° **13.** −30° **14.** 30° **15.** $0.34 + 2\pi n$, $2.80 + 2\pi n$ **16.** $-1.11 + 2\pi n$, $2.03 + 2\pi n$
17. $2.27 + 2\pi n$, $4.02 + 2\pi n$ **18.** $0.20 + 2\pi n$, $6.08 + 2\pi n$ **19.** $\frac{\pi}{3}, \frac{5\pi}{3}$ **20.** $\frac{\pi}{6}, \frac{7\pi}{6}$ **21.** $0, \frac{\pi}{2}, \pi$
22. $\frac{3}{5}$, 0.6 **23.** $\frac{4}{5}$, 0.8 **24.** $\frac{3}{4}$, 0.75 **25.** 9.5, 18.4°, 71.6° **26.** 16, 36.9°, 53.1° **27.** 37.7, 43.3°, 46.7°
28. 13.14 m² **29.** 92.12 ft² **30.** 57.81 m²
31. 7.1 in. **32.** 54.3° or 125.7° **33.** 21.4 ft **34.** 43.9° **35.** 52.2° **36.** $\cos\left(\theta + \frac{\pi}{2}\right) = \cos \theta \cdot \cos\left(\frac{\pi}{2}\right) - \sin \theta \cdot \sin\left(\frac{\pi}{2}\right) = \cos \theta \cdot 0 - \sin \theta \cdot 1 = -\sin \theta$
37. $\sin^2\left(\theta - \frac{\pi}{2}\right) = \sin^2\left(-\left(\frac{\pi}{2} - \theta\right)\right) = \left(-\sin\left(\frac{\pi}{2} - \theta\right)\right) \cdot \left(-\sin\left(\frac{\pi}{2} - \theta\right)\right) = (-\cos \theta)(-\cos \theta) = \cos^2 \theta$ **38.** $\frac{\pi}{2}$ and $\frac{3\pi}{2}$ **39.** 0
40. $\frac{\sqrt{3}}{2}$ **41.** 0 **42.** $-\sqrt{3}$ **43.** −1 **44.** $\sqrt{3}$ **45.** $\frac{\sqrt{3}}{2}$

Extra Practice

CHAPTER 1 1. > **3.** > **9.** $-102, \frac{1}{102}$ **11.** $-2\frac{3}{4}, \frac{4}{11}$
21. 28 **23.** 14 **25.** 2 **27.** −11
31. $t \leq -1$
33. $a < -\frac{7}{2}$
37. $-2 \leq z < 1$
39. $x < -2, x > 8$
43. −11, 15.5 **45.** −5, 9
49. $t \leq -5.5, t \geq -1.5$
51. $-11 \leq w \leq -1$
55. 1 **57.** $\frac{4}{9}$ **61.** $500 **63.** $3\frac{2}{3}$ **65.** $11,500
67. less than 8 h **69.** $\frac{3}{38}$ **71.** $\frac{2}{5}$

CHAPTER 2 1. Yes; each x-value has exactly one y-value. **3.** No; the x-value 1 has two y-values.
15. $3x - y = -7$ **17.** $3x - 4y = -26$
21. $y - 2 = -1(x - 0)$ **23.** $y - 0 = \frac{1}{2}(x - 3)$
27. 2, −5, 2.5 **29.** 0, 4, none **35.** $3x - y = -9$

37. $8x - 2y = 7$ **43.** $y = \frac{7}{3}x$ **45.** $y = 2.5x$

51. 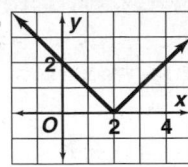 **59.**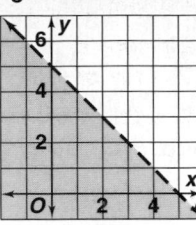

67. $A(h) = 21h$; 798 ft^2 **69.** $y = \frac{3}{4}x$

71. a. $f(x) = |x - 100|$ **b.** $g(x) = |x - 300|$
c. $h(x) = |x - 300| + 200$ **d.** They are translations of each other. **73.** $y = 75x - 18{,}000$; The intercept, $-18{,}000$, represents the initial investment; the slope, 75, is the rental income per day.

CHAPTER 3

1. 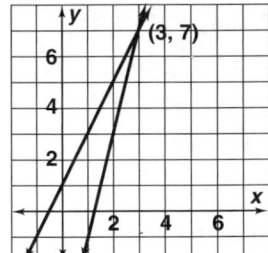 **7.** (1, 4) **9.** (6, −3)

13.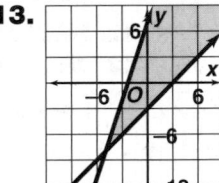

17. (0, 0) **19.** 50 chef's salads and 50 Caesar salads

29.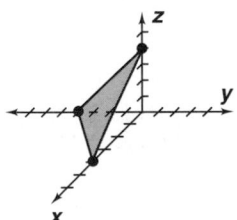

35. (2, 1, 3) **37.** (2, 3, −6) **39.** 4.5 mi/h **41.** $4.70 per lb of cheese, $5.65 per lb of chicken loaf

43. a.
$\begin{cases} 5x + 8y \le 400 \\ 2.5x + 2y \le 120 \\ x \ge 0 \\ y \ge 0 \end{cases}$

b.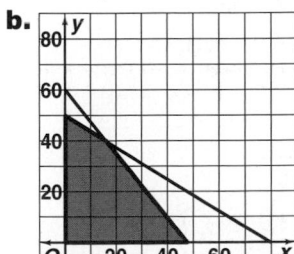

45. first chef: $3\frac{1}{3}$ h; second chef: $8\frac{1}{3}$ h
47. Student: $6; Adult: $15; Senior: $8

CHAPTER 4

1. 2×3; 6 **3.** 2×3; −83 **7.** $\begin{bmatrix} 4 & 67 \\ 12 & 18 \end{bmatrix}$

9. $\begin{bmatrix} -6 & -1 & 0 \\ 17 & -11 & -8 \end{bmatrix}$ **11.** $\begin{bmatrix} -62 & 121 \\ 43 & -54 \end{bmatrix}$

13. $\begin{bmatrix} 5 & -7 & 7 \\ 2 & 1 & -2 \end{bmatrix}$ **15.** $\begin{bmatrix} -26 & 7 & 5 \\ -4 & -7 & 25 \end{bmatrix}$

17. $\begin{bmatrix} 16 & 2 \\ -4 & 10 \end{bmatrix}$ **27.** $\begin{bmatrix} 5 & 10 & 20 \\ 25 & -5 & 15 \end{bmatrix}$

29. $\begin{bmatrix} 3 & 4 & 6 \\ -2 & -8 & -4 \end{bmatrix}$ **31.** $\begin{bmatrix} \frac{68}{15} & -\frac{34}{15} \\ -\frac{16}{15} & \frac{83}{15} \end{bmatrix}$ **33.** $\begin{bmatrix} 2 \\ 7 \end{bmatrix}$

35. (9, 1) **37. a.** Machine 1 $\begin{bmatrix} 13 & 22 \\ 22 & 37 \end{bmatrix}$
Machine 2

b. Machine 1 makes 13 gal of frozen yogurt in the A.M. and 22 gal in the P.M. Machine 2 makes 22 gal in the A.M. and 37 gal in the P.M.

39. $\begin{bmatrix} \frac{\sqrt{3}-1}{2} & \frac{\sqrt{3}-2}{2} & \frac{5\sqrt{3}-4}{2} \\ \frac{\sqrt{3}+1}{2} & \frac{2\sqrt{3}+1}{2} & \frac{4\sqrt{3}+5}{2} \end{bmatrix}$

41. $\begin{bmatrix} 1 & 1 & 1 \\ 1 & 1 & -1 \\ -1 & 1 & 0 \end{bmatrix} \begin{bmatrix} x \\ y \\ z \end{bmatrix} \begin{bmatrix} 249 \\ 95 \\ 6 \end{bmatrix}$; $x = 83$, $y = 89$, $z = 77$

43. $\begin{bmatrix} 2 & 1 \\ 3 & 2 \end{bmatrix} \begin{bmatrix} x \\ y \end{bmatrix} = \begin{bmatrix} 10 \\ 17.25 \end{bmatrix}$; $x = 2.75$, $y = 4.50$

45. orchestra: $25; balcony: $15

CHAPTER 5
1. linear; none, $3x$, 4

3. linear; none, $-\frac{3}{2}x$, $\frac{1}{2}$ **7.**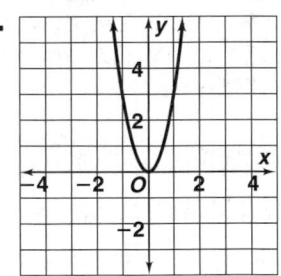

15. $(x + 9)(x - 6)$ **17.** $(x - 6)(x + 6)$
27. 0.24, −4.24 **29.** 0.41, −2.41 **35.** $8 - 3i$
37. $1 - 3i$ **41.** $\pm 4i$ **43.** $\pm i\sqrt{10}$ **47.** $-i$, $-1 - i$, i
49. −1, −4 **51.** $\frac{5}{4} \pm \frac{\sqrt{17}}{4}$ **59.** 108; 2, real
61. 25; 2, real **67. a.** 30 ft by 20 ft **b.** 300 ft^2
69. 19 years old; 24 years old
71. a. 625 bulldozers; $781,250
b. $x \ge 0$; $P(x) \le \$781{,}250$ **c.** $500 \le x \le 750$
73. 20 in **75. a.** The archer releases the arrow 5 ft about the ground. **b.** 402 ft

CHAPTER 6
1. $-4a^2 + 3a$; quadratic binomial
3. $-2n^3 + 3n^2 - n - 3$; cubic polynomial of 4 terms **7.** $y = x^3 - 4x^2 + x + 6$
9. $y = x^3 + 2x^2 - x - 2$ **15.** $x^2 - 2x - 2$
17. $2x^2 + 2x$ **21.** 0, −2, 5 **23.** 2 **27.** −2, $\pm i\sqrt{3}$
29. −1, $\frac{-5 \pm \sqrt{13}}{6}$ **33.** 720 **35.** 210

45. permutation; 60,480 orders **47.** combination;
6 ways **49.** $81x^4 + 216x^3 + 216x^2 + 96x + 16$
51. $16x^4 + 160x^3y + 600x^2y^2 + 1000xy^3 + 625y^4$
57. a. Answers may vary. Sample:
$P(N) = (N - 1)N(N + 1) = N^3 - N$ **b.** 5, 6, 7
59. 14 in. by 14 in. by 14 in. **61.** 455 ways
63. 255 kinds of pizza **65.** 100,947 ways

CHAPTER 7 1. $6x^2$ **3.** $3|x^3|$ **9.** $6x^3\sqrt{2x}$ **11.** $10a^2$

15. $5\sqrt{7}$ **17.** $3\sqrt{7x}$ **21.** $\frac{y^9}{x^{20}}$ **23.** $\frac{y^3}{2x^5}$ **29.** no solution

31. 3, 7 **35.** 1 **37.** 64 **45.** $f^{-1}(x) = x^2 - 4, x \geq 0$;
domain of f: $\{x \geq -4\}$, range of f: $\{y \geq 0\}$,
domain of f^{-1}: $\{x \geq 0\}$, range of f^{-1}: $\{y \geq -4\}$;
f^{-1} is a function.

51.

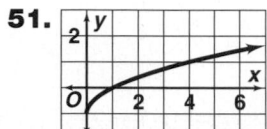

59. 7.3 ft **61. a.** 36 mi **b.** 4900 ft
63. a. $E(x) = 0.8x$ **b.** $M(x) = 0.75x$
c. $T(x) = 1.06x$ **d.** $f(x) = 0.636x$
65. a. $f^{-1} = \frac{x - 331.4}{0.6}$
b. 31°C; The speed of sound is 350 m/s at 31°C.

CHAPTER 8 1. $y = 4(2.5)^x$ **3.** $y = \frac{2}{3}(3)^x$
7. exponential growth **9.** exponential decay
17.

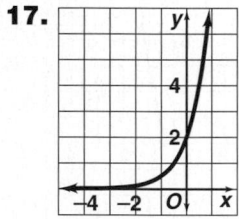

25. $\log_9 729 = 3$ **27.** $\log_{\frac{1}{2}} \frac{1}{16} = 4$ **41.** $\log 24$
43. $\log x^7$ **47.** $\log_b 2 + 2\log_b x + 3\log_b y$
49. $5(\log_b 4 + \log_b m + \log_b n)$ **53.** ± 8
55. 50,000 **65.** $3745.32 **67.** $1214.87
69. 1432 y **71.** 2399 species **73. a.** -0.042
b. 48.5°F **c.** 69.5 min **d.** no; 38°F is the horizontal
asymptote of the function.

CHAPTER 9 1. $y = \frac{6}{x}$ **3.** $y = \frac{40}{x}$
7.

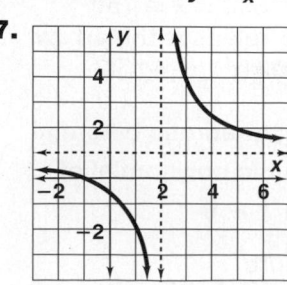

15. 0 **17.** $-2, 1$ **23.** $x + 3; x \neq -6$
25. $x + 2; x \neq -3, 4$ **29.** $\frac{14x - 3}{2(x + 2)}$ **31.** $\frac{8x - 3}{x(x + 3)}$
35. -4 **37.** $-5, 4$ **41.** independent **43.** dependent
45. about 0.26 tons **47.** $f(x) = \frac{0.658x + 7}{x + 9}$
49. 2.4 mi/h **51.** about 16 h **53.** $\left(\frac{1}{26}\right)^2$ **55.** $\frac{35}{36}$

CHAPTER 10 1.

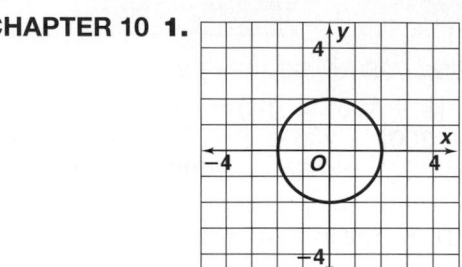

Circle; every line through (0, 0) is a line of
symmetry, radius 2; domain: $-2 \leq x \leq 2$,
range: $-2 \leq y \leq 2$. **7.** $y = \frac{1}{12}x^2$ **9.** $y = -\frac{1}{8}x^2$
17. (4, 0), $x = -4$;

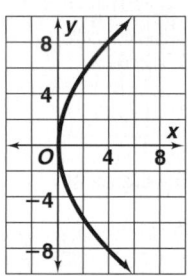

25. $(x + 4)^2 + (y + 6)^2 = 4$ **27.** $(x - 1)^2 +$
$(y - 4)^2 = 25$ **31.** $(-6, -9)$, 12 **33.** $(-8, 1)$, 10
37. $(\pm 4\sqrt{2}, 0)$

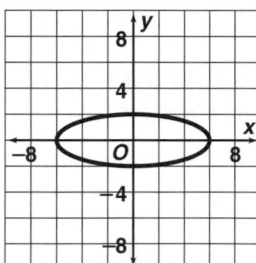

49. ellipse; center (0, 0), foci $(\pm 3\sqrt{3}, 0)$

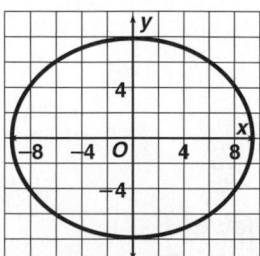

55. 8 in. **57.** $(x - 4.5)^2 + (y - 7)^2 = 1.5^2$
59. a. hyperbola **b.** $(-1.316, 0.4)$, $(2.648, 0.4)$

CHAPTER 11 1. explicit; 5, 8, 11, 14, 17
3. explicit; 15, 40, 75, 120, 175 **7.** 9, 11, 13;
$a_n = 2n + 1$; $a_1 = 3$, $a_n = a_{n-1} + 2$
9. -7.5, -6, -4.5; $a_n = -13.5 + 1.5n$;
$a_1 = -12$, $a_n = a_{n-1} + 1.5$ **13.** 15 **15.** -4.5
17. $a_n = -27\left(\frac{1}{3}\right)^{n-1}$; -27, -9, -3, -1, $-\frac{1}{3}$
19. $a_n = -5(3)^{n-1}$; -5, -15, -45, -135, -405
23. $\sum\limits_{n=1}^{10}(3n + 1)$; 175 **25.** $\sum\limits_{n=1}^{20}(-n + 98)$; 1750
27. 6, 2, -3; -3 **29.** 8, 4, 25; 116 **31.** $\frac{9}{4}$ **33.** 1
37. geometric; 3069 **39.** arithmetic; -1110
41. $0 + 1 = 1$; $1 + 8 = 9$ **43.** $3 + 4 = 7$; $4 + 5 = 9$
45. a. 23, 17.6, 13.5, 10.4, 7.9 **b.** $a_n = 30\left(\frac{23}{30}\right)^n$
47. a. 47 seats **b.** 761 seats **49.** 45 ft
51. a. 44.49 m² **b.** 53.86 m² **c.** 49.18 m²

CHAPTER 12 1.

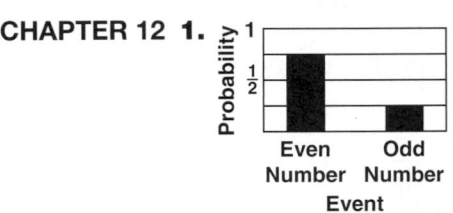

3. $\frac{39}{80}$ **5.** $\frac{25}{80}$ **9.** 25.8, 21, 24 **11.** 4.8, 4.2, 6.1
13. 25.429, 11, 8, 3.81 **15.** 99.71, 5, 3, 1.578
17. $\pm 6\%$ **19.** $\pm 3\%$ **23.** $0.2787 \approx 28\%$
25. $0.0003 \approx 0.03\%$
29. $P(k = 0) = 0.0467$
$\quad P(k = 1) = 0.1866$
$\quad P(k = 2) = 0.3110$
$\quad P(k = 3) = 0.2765$
$\quad P(k = 4) = 0.1382$
$\quad P(k = 5) = 0.0369$
$\quad P(k = 6) = 0.0041$

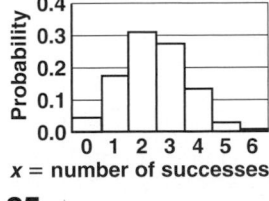

35.

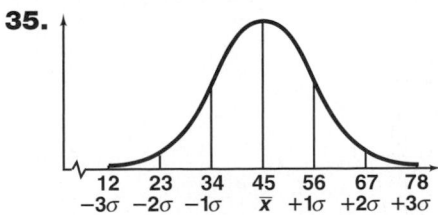

39. $\frac{1}{3}$ **41. a.** 79.95; 82; 84 **b.** 70th percentile
c.

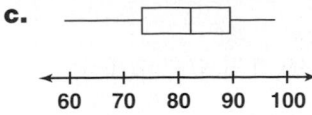

d. Answers may vary. Sample: None; all the scores are reasonably close to the other scores.
43. a. about 5% **b.** 102 to 141 students **45.** 2.5%

CHAPTER 13 1. 4, $1\frac{1}{2}$ **3.** 4, 2
11. $\frac{3\pi}{2}$, 4.71 **13.** $\frac{-55\pi}{18}$, -9.60 **17.** $-115°$
19. $-540°$ **23.** 1, $\frac{\pi}{2}$ **25.** 2, 8π

29. 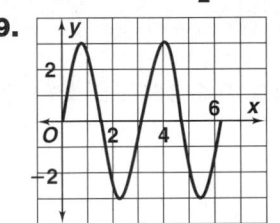 **35.**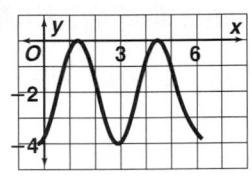

39. -1.5299 **41.** -1 **47.** 50°F; 2 min
49. a. 2:00; 10:00 **b.** 4:00, 8:00
51. $y = -3.15 \cos\left(\frac{\pi}{6}x\right) + 12.45$
53. $y = \sin\left(\frac{2\pi}{7}x\right) + 7.5$
55. a. Answers may vary. Sample: The height of the tower, 30 cm, is the scale factor that gives the length of the cable when multiplied by csc x.
b. Explanations may vary. Sample: 30 to about 85.5 cm; The length of the cable is at least 30 cm, and the longest cable must still be attached to the bridge. So the longest cable is at most $\sqrt{30^2 + \left(\frac{160}{2}\right)^2} \approx 85.44$ cm long.
c. $\frac{\pi}{6}$ radians or 30°

CHAPTER 14 1. $60° + n \cdot 360°$ and $120° + n \cdot 360°$ **3.** $60° + n \cdot 360°$ and $240° + n \cdot 360°$
5. no solution **7.** 1.313 **13.** $\frac{3\pi}{2}$
15. 0, π, 2.6779, 5.8195, 2π
19. $b = 5.7$, $\angle A = 51.1°$, $\angle B = 38.9°$
21. $c = 4.5$, $\angle A = 26.6°$, $\angle B = 63.4°$ **25.** $\frac{12}{13}$, 0.923
27. $\frac{12}{5}$, 2.4 **29.** 11.3 **31.** 46.3 **33.** $\frac{\sqrt{6} - \sqrt{2}}{4}$ **35.** $\frac{\sqrt{3}}{2}$
39. 1 **41.** -1 **45.** $\frac{\sqrt{6} - \sqrt{2}}{4}$ **47.** $\frac{\sqrt{2 + \sqrt{2}}}{2}$
51. 140 ft, 229 ft **53.** 352.3 ft² **55.** 2.36 mi
57. 76°, 1153°, 78.7°, 90°

Skills Handbook

p. 864 **1.** $\left(13, 6\frac{1}{2}\right)$ **3.**

p. 865 **1.** 23 pigs and 17 ducks **3.** 45 mi
p. 866 **1.** ten of each coin
p. 867 **1.** 12 slices **3.** 204
p. 868 **1.** Leon **3.** 15 students

p. 869 **1.** $85\frac{1}{3}$ cm

3.
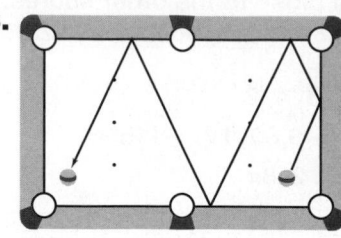

p. 870 **1.** 46% **3.** 29.4% **13.** 0.4 **15.** 1.5 **19.** 12.5 **21.** 75

p. 871 **1.** $1\frac{2}{5}$ **3.** $6\frac{5}{6}$

p. 872 **1.** 3 to 4 **3.** 9.5 g/oz **7.** 8 **9.** 1.8

p. 873 **1.** 1 **3.** −38

p. 874 **1.** 14.4 **3.** 84 **13.** $\ell = \frac{P}{2} - w$ **15.** $b = c - 2a$

p. 875 **1.** 14 m^2 **3.** 30 cm^2 **5.** 91.1 ft^3 **7.** 314.2 in.^{3} **9.** 110.5 in.^{2} **11.** 121.5 ft^2

p. 876 **1.** I **3.** IV **13.** $\frac{3}{4}$ **15.** 0 **19.** $\left(5, -\frac{3}{2}\right)$ **21.** $\left(\frac{5}{2}, -1\right)$

p. 877 **1.** −1 **3.** 6

13. $x \le 6$

15. $y \ge -2$
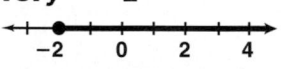

p. 878 **1.** 8, −8 **3.** 5, −13

13. $-3 \le x \le 15$

15. $r \le -7$ or $r \ge 7$

p. 879

1.
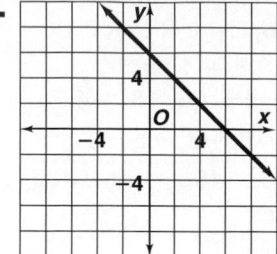

p. 880 **1.** x^3 **3.** a^4b **5.** $\frac{1}{c^4}$ **7.** $\frac{x^5}{y^7z^3}$ **9.** d^8 **11.** r^5s^8

p. 881 **1.** $x^2 + 10x - 5$ **3.** $12x^4 - 20x^3 + 36x^2$ **7.** $(a - 6)(a - 2)$ **9.** $(n - 4)(n + 2)$

p. 882 **1.** 1.34×10^6 **3.** 7.75×10^{-4} **11.** 6.4×10^5 **13.** $\approx 8.52 \times 10^2$

p. 883 **1.** 6 **3.** $3\sqrt{2}$

p. 884 **1.** 10 **3.** 15 **11.** 10 **13.** 22.7

p. 885

1.
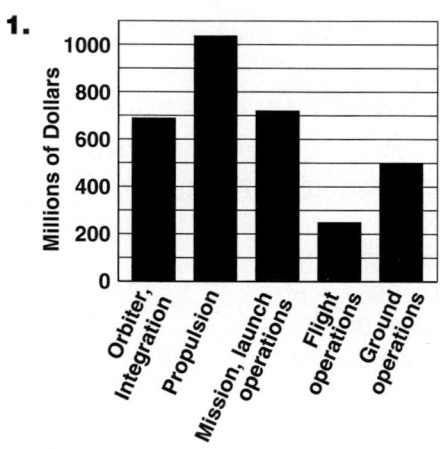

p. 886 **1.** 3.8, 5, 5 **3.** 4.0, 2.4, 2.4

p. 887 **1.** $\frac{a}{3b^2}$ **3.** $\frac{1}{2}$ **5.** $4x$ **7.** $\frac{2}{h}$

Index

A

Abscissa, 54

Absolute value, 33
of complex number, 275, 301
of real number, 8, 33

Absolute value equations, 33–34, 49, 878

Absolute value function, 88–90, 111

Absolute value inequalities, 35–36, 103–104

Absolute value symbols, 371

Absolute value systems of inequalities, 135

ACT preparation. *See* Test Prep

Active Math Online, 6, 28, 42, 57, 89, 95, 102, 118, 127, 135, 141, 175, 193, 247, 253, 269, 292, 316, 323, 371, 417, 434, 440, 448, 489, 497, 504, 558, 564, 570, 577, 606, 614, 636, 663, 688, 735, 744, 750, 758, 779, 817

Activity. *See also* Data analysis; Technology
Adding Fractions–Extended, 514
Analyzing Data Spread, 668
Analyzing Graphs, 118
Analyzing Hyperbolas, 574
Angles in a Circle, 720
Arithmetic Series, 619
Binomial Probability, 685
Checking for Extraneous Solutions, 394
Counting Zeros, 341
Estimating Square Roots, 4
Factoring, 259
Finding a Minimum Value, 139
Finding the Line of Best Fit, 86
Generating a Pattern, 600
Geometric Sequences, 612
Graphs of Polynomial Functions, 306
Hands-On, 39, 531
Inverses, 406
Linear Inequalities, 101
Periodic Cycles, 710
Point-Slope Form, 64
Properties of Logarithms, 454
Right Triangle Ratios, 792
Technology, 118, 306, 394, 582, 778
Tournament Play, 432
Translating a Geometric Figure, 191
Translating Conic Sections, 582
Trigonometric Identities, 778
Using Matrices, 184
Using the Line of Best Fit to Estimate, 87
Using the Line of Best Fit to Predict, 86
Vertex Form, 252

Activity Lab
Applying Conic Sections, 596–597
Applying Exponential Functions, 484–485

Applying Functions, 114–115
Applying Inequalities, 234–235
Applying Quadratic Functions, 364–365
Applying Sequences, 706–707
Applying Trigonometry, 834–835
Area Under a Curve, 699
As the Ball Flies, 364–365
Bridges, Beams, and Tension, 114–115
Building a Business, 234–235
Completing the Square, 281
Conic Sections, 546
Continuous Probability, 676
A Crowded House, 484–485
Evaluating Series, 634
Exponential and Logarithmic Inequalities, 476–477
Extraneous Solutions, 521
Fibonacci Sequence, 611
Finding a Line of Best Fit, 86–87
Fitting Exponential Curves to Data, 438
Geometry and Infinite Series, 625
Graphing calculator, 124, 145, 244, 296–297, 413, 420–421, 438, 469, 476–477, 494, 528–529, 554, 567, 589, 634, 699, 742, 791
Graphing Conic Sections, 554
Graphing Inverses, 413
Graphing Rational Functions, 494
Graphing Trigonometric Functions, 742
Hands-On, 281, 546, 725
Linear and Exponential Models, 469
Linear Programming, 145
Lissajous Figures, 791
Martian Math, 596–597
Measuring Radians, 725
Modeling Using Residuals, 244
Parametric Equations, 124
Pascal's Triangle, 352
Quadratic Inequalities, 296–297
A Question of Balance, 834–835
Radical Inequalities, 420–421
Rational Inequalities, 528–529
Solving Quadratic Systems, 589
Solving Systems Using Tables, 132
Spreadsheets, 25
Technology, 25, 86–87, 124, 145, 181, 244, 296–297, 413, 420–421, 438, 469, 476–477, 494, 528–529, 554, 567, 589, 634, 699, 742, 791
Training Day, 706–707
Using Parametric Equations, 567
Working with Matrices, 181
Writing Equations From Roots, 273
Writing Expressions From Tables, 11

Addition. *See also* Summation
of complex numbers, 276
of fractions, 514–515
of functions, 398
of matrices, 174–175, 181, 191–192, 230
of polynomials, 881

of radical expressions, 380–381
of rational expressions, 515

Addition property
of equality, 18
of inequality, 26

Additive identity matrix, 175

Additive inverse
of complex number, 276
of matrix, 175
opposites, 7, 47–48

Algebra at Work. *See also* Careers
acoustical physicist, 813
demographer, 412
economist, 537
landscape architect, 251
market researcher, 683
miniaturist, 77
quality control engineer, 326
radiologist, 151
wildlife biologist, 24

Algebra 1 Review
Coordinate Plane, 54
Properties of Exponents, 368
Square Roots and Radicals, 266

Algebra tiles, 260, 281

Algebraic expressions, 12–14, 48

Ambiguous Case (Law of Sines), 807

Amplitude
of cosine function, 744
defined, 712, 771
of periodic function, 712–713, 738–739, 771
of sine curve, 736

Amplitude modulation (AM) radio, 712

Analyzing data. *See* Data analysis

And (compound inequality), 28, 48–49

Angle(s)
central, 726, 772, 885
in a circle, 720
congruent, 807
cosine of, 720–722, 728, 771, 784, 827–828
coterminal, 719, 771
initial side of, 718, 771
measuring, 718–719, 725, 795, 809, 810
radian measure, 725, 726–729, 772
sine of, 720–722, 728, 771
in standard position, 718–719, 771
tangent of, 749, 773
terminal side of, 718, 771, 823
of triangle, 802
in unit circle, 720–722, 771

Angle difference identities, 816–817, 829

Angle identities, 814–817, 829

Angle sum identities, 816, 817, 829

Applications. *See* Algebra at Work; Careers; Point in Time; Real-World Connections

Arc, 645
finding length of, 728–729
intercepted, 726, 728, 772

Area
under curve, 635–637, 643, 699
formulas for, 801, 898
Law of Sines and, 801–802, 828
of triangle, 801–802

Arithmetic mean, 607, 641

Arithmetic sequences
defined, 606, 641
formulas for, 607
identifying and generating, 606–607, 642

Arithmetic series, 619–621, 642

Assessment. *See also* Instant Check System; Open-Ended; Test-Taking Strategies
Chapter Review, 47–49, 109–111, 161–163, 229–231, 299–301, 359–361, 423–425, 479–481, 539–541, 591–593, 641–643, 701–703, 771–773, 827–829
Chapter Test, 50, 112, 164, 232, 302, 362, 426, 482, 542, 594, 644, 704, 774, 830
Checkpoint Quiz, 24, 38, 77, 100, 138, 151, 189, 211, 258, 280, 326, 351, 384, 404, 445, 468, 508, 520, 566, 580, 617, 631, 667, 691, 733, 762, 799, 820
Cumulative Review, 113, 233, 363, 483, 595, 705, 831–833
Mixed Review, 10, 17, 24, 31, 38, 45, 61, 70, 77, 84, 92, 100, 106, 123, 130, 138, 144, 151, 159, 173, 180, 189, 198, 205, 211, 219, 227, 243, 251, 258, 265, 272, 280, 287, 295, 311, 319, 326, 332, 340, 344, 351, 357, 373, 379, 384, 390, 396, 404, 412, 419, 437, 445, 452, 459, 468, 475, 493, 500, 508, 513, 520, 527, 537, 553, 560, 566, 573, 580, 588, 605, 610, 617, 624, 631, 639, 653, 658, 667, 674, 683, 691, 698, 716, 724, 733, 741, 748, 754, 762, 769, 782, 790, 799, 806, 813, 820, 825
Quick Check, 6, 7, 8, 12, 13, 14, 19, 20, 21, 27, 28, 29, 33, 34, 35, 36, 40, 41, 42, 55, 56, 57, 58, 63, 64, 65, 66, 67, 72, 73, 74, 78, 79, 80, 89, 90, 94, 95, 96, 97, 102, 103, 104, 119, 120, 125, 126, 127, 134, 135, 140, 141, 147, 148, 153, 154, 155, 156, 168, 169, 170, 175, 176, 177, 182, 183, 184, 185, 186, 192, 193, 194, 195, 200, 201, 202, 203, 207, 208, 214, 215, 216, 217, 221, 222, 223, 224, 239, 240, 245, 246, 247, 253, 254, 255, 259, 260, 261, 262, 263, 267, 268, 269, 274, 275, 276, 277, 282, 283, 284, 285, 290, 291, 292, 307, 308, 309, 313, 314, 315, 316, 321, 322, 323, 327, 328, 329, 330, 336, 337, 338, 342, 343, 345, 346, 347, 354, 355, 370, 371, 374, 375, 376, 377, 380, 381, 382, 385, 386, 387, 388, 391, 392, 393, 398, 399, 400, 407, 408, 409, 415, 416, 417, 430, 431, 432, 433, 434, 439, 440, 441, 442, 446, 447, 448, 449, 455, 456, 461, 462, 463, 464, 470, 471, 472, 489, 490, 495, 496, 497, 498, 502, 503, 504, 505, 509, 510, 511, 515, 516, 517, 522, 523, 524, 532, 533, 534, 548, 549, 550, 555, 556, 557, 558, 562, 563, 564, 569, 570, 576, 577, 583, 584, 585, 601, 602, 606, 607, 613, 614, 620, 621, 627, 628, 636, 637, 648, 649, 650, 651, 654, 655, 656, 660, 661, 662, 663, 664, 669, 670, 671, 672, 677, 678, 679, 680, 686, 687, 688, 692, 693, 694, 711, 712, 713, 718, 719, 721, 722, 727, 728, 729, 734, 735, 736, 737, 738, 744, 745, 750, 751, 756, 757, 758, 759, 760, 763, 764, 765, 766, 779, 780, 783, 784, 785, 786, 793, 794, 795, 801, 802, 803, 809, 810, 815, 816, 817, 822, 823
Reading Comprehension, 51, 165, 303, 427, 543, 645, 775
Test Prep, 10, 17, 23, 31, 38, 45, 61, 70, 76, 84, 92, 99–100, 106, 113, 123, 130, 137, 144, 150, 159, 165, 173, 180, 189, 198, 205, 210, 219, 227, 233, 243, 251, 258, 265, 272, 280, 287, 295, 303, 311, 319, 325, 332, 340, 344, 350, 357, 363, 373, 379, 384, 390, 396, 403–404, 411–412, 419, 427, 437, 444–445, 452, 459, 467–468, 474–475, 483, 493, 500, 507–508, 513, 519–520, 527, 537, 543, 552–553, 560, 566, 573, 579–580, 588, 595, 605, 610, 616–617, 624, 630–631, 639, 645, 653, 658, 666–667, 674, 682–683, 690, 697–698, 705, 715–716, 724, 732–733, 741, 748, 754, 762, 769, 775, 782, 790, 798–799, 806, 813, 819–820, 825, 831–833

Associative property
of matrix addition, 175
of matrix multiplication, 186
of real numbers, 7
of scalar multiplication, 183

Asymptotes, 433, 503, 504, 540, 575, 750, 755

Augmented matrix, 222–224

Average. *See* Mean

Axis
of ellipse, 568, 592
of hyperbola, 575, 593
imaginary, 275
major, 568, 592
minor, 568, 592
real, 275
of symmetry, parabola, 239, 299, 555
transverse, 575, 593
x- and *y*-, 54, 146–148
z-, 146–148

B

Baca, Judith Francisca, 211

Balance, 834–835

Bar graph, 885

Base *e*, 441–442, 470–472, 481

Best fit, line or curve of, 86–87, 244, 308, 438

Bias, in sample, 677, 678

Bimodal data, 660, 702

Binomial(s), 260
expansion of, 353–354, 361
multiplying, 881

Binomial distribution, 687–688, 703

Binomial experiment, 685–686, 703

Binomial probability, 685–687, 703

Binomial radical expressions, 381–382

Binomial Theorem, 354–355, 361

Boundary line, 101, 111

Box-and-whisker plots, 662–664, 702

Branches
of hyperbola, 548, 575
of inverse variation graph, 495–496, 540

Break-even point, 130

C

CALC feature, of graphing calculator, 145, 505, 670, 699

Calculator. *See* Graphing calculator

Cannot Be Determined, as test answer, 590

Careers. *See also* Algebra at Work
agriculturist, 650
air traffic controller, 579
business owner, 403
carpenter, 318
ceramic artist, 752
consumer researcher, 349
craftsman, 403
custom tailor, 285
dispatcher, 671
financial planner, 627
graphic designer, 613
groomer, 122
hot-air balloonist, 78
mason, 526
microbiologist, 143
neonatal nurse, 692
park planner, 794
picture framer, 249
pilot, 812
psychologist, 444
radio broadcaster, 532
smoke jumper, 268
sound engineer, 740
stadium designer, 157
support personnel, 535
video game programmer, 505

Center
of circle, 561, 563–564, 592
of ellipse, 548, 549, 568
of hyperbola, 548, 575
of rotation, 194

Central angle, 726, 772, 885

Central tendency, measures of, 660–662, 702, 886

Challenge exercises. *See* Enrichment

Change of Base Formula, 462–463

Chapter Review. *See* Assessment

Chapter Test. *See* Assessment

Check Skills You'll Need. *See* Instant Check System

Check Your Readiness. *See* Instant Check System

Checkpoint Quiz. *See* Instant Check System

Circle, 561–564
angles in, 720

center of, 561, 563–564, 592
central angle of, 726, 772, 885
circumference of, 726
conic section, 547–548, 550, 561–564, 592
defined, 561, 592
equation of, 561–563, 583, 592
finding center and radius of, 563
graphing, 547–548, 564
intercepted arc, 726, 728, 772
moiré pattern, 550
radius of, 561, 563–564, 592
translations of, 562
unit, 720–722, 771, 784, 827–828

Circle graph, 885

Circumference, 726

Circumscribed rectangles, 635, 643

Closure property
of matrix addition, 175
of matrix multiplication, 186
of real numbers, 7
of scalar multiplication, 183

Coefficient, 13, 353, 354

Coefficient matrix, 214, 216, 231

Cofunction identities, 815–816, 829

Combinations, 346–347, 361

Combined translation, 95

Combined variation, 490, 539

Common difference, 606, 641

Common factors, 259–262

Common logarithm, 447, 480

Common ratio, 612, 642

Communication. *See* Critical Thinking;
Error Analysis; Justifying Steps;
Vocabulary Builder; Vocabulary
Tips; Writing

Commutative property
of matrix addition, 175
of real numbers, 7

Compass, 720

Completing the square, 281, 282–285, 293, 301

Complex conjugates, 338, 361

Complex fractions, 516–517, 540

Complex number(s)
absolute value of, 275, 301
adding, 276
additive inverse of, 276
complex conjugate, 338, 361
defined, 275, 301
fractals, 277, 279
identifying, 274–275
multiplying, 276
operations with, 276–277
simplifying imaginary numbers, 275
solutions to quadratic equations, 277, 283, 290

Complex number plane, 275, 301

Composite function, 399, 425

Composition
of functions, 399–400
of inverse functions, 409

Compound inequalities, 28–29, 36, 48

Compound interest, 441–442, 480

Computer. *See* Technology

Computer spreadsheets, 25, 257, 402, 630

Conditional probability
comparing, 659
defined, 654, 701
finding, 654–655, 701
formula for, 655
tree diagrams and, 656, 659

Conic sections, 596–597
circle, 547–548, 550, 561–564, 592
defined, 547, 591
ellipse, 548, 550
equations of, 582–584
families of, 583
graphing, 547–550, 554, 591
hyperbola, 548–549, 550
identifying, 549–550, 585
moiré pattern, 550
parabola, 547, 555–558
translations of, 582–585, 593
using paper cutouts, 546

Conjectures. *See* Make a Conjecture

Conjugates, 337, 361
complex, 338, 361
multiplying, 381–382, 424
radical, 381–382

Connections. *See* Algebra at Work;
Careers; Interdisciplinary
Connections; Point in Time; Real-
World Connections

Constant matrix, 214, 231

Constant of variation, 72, 110, 488, 490

Constant term, 238, 307

Constraints, 139, 162

Continuous function, 57

Continuous probability, 676

**Continuously compounded interest
formula,** 441–442, 480

Convergence, 627–628, 643

Coordinate geometry, 205, 218, 220, 319, 698. *See also* Conic sections;
Graph(s); Translations

Coordinate plane, 54, 876

Coordinate space, 146–148, 163

Corollary, 342

Cosecant function, 763, 773

Cosines, Law of, 808–810, 829

Cosine equation, 745

Cosine functions, 743–745, 772
defined, 743
families of, 758
finding inverse of, 785, 827–828
graphing and writing, 743–744
radian measures, 728
translating, 756–760
unit circles and, 720–722, 728, 771, 784, 827–828

Cosine of angle, 720–722, 728, 771

Cotangent function, 763, 773

Cotangent identity, 779, 827

Coterminal angles, 719, 771

Counting methods
combinations, 346–347, 361
permutations, 345–346, 361

Co-vertices of ellipse, 568, 592

Cramer's Rule, 221–222, 231

Critical Thinking, 8, 10, 13, 23, 27, 31, 34, 44, 69, 87, 90, 98, 99, 103, 119, 122, 137, 144, 150, 153, 169, 185, 191, 192, 198, 203, 204, 205, 222, 240, 243, 247, 257, 265, 271, 280, 281, 286, 294, 311, 318, 325, 332, 344, 350, 373, 378, 383, 386, 396, 399, 411, 413, 418, 422, 431, 437, 443, 451, 455, 458, 463, 465, 471, 474, 492, 494, 499, 505, 510, 512, 517, 518, 521, 526, 536, 548, 549, 554, 560, 566, 571, 586, 594, 596, 602, 604, 608, 609, 616, 618, 623, 630, 636, 638, 639, 644, 650, 653, 658, 666, 673, 674, 678, 681, 682, 697, 723, 725, 740, 747, 753, 761, 768, 788, 794, 805, 812, 819, 824

Cross products, 872

Cube root function, 416

Cubes
difference of, 328, 360
sum of, 328, 360

Cubic functions, 307, 328

CubicReg feature, of graphing calculator, 308

Cumulative probability, 648, 701

Cumulative Review. *See* Assessment

Curves
area under, 635–637, 643, 699
of best fit, 86–87, 244, 308, 438
fitting data to, 240, 244, 308, 438
Lissajous figures, 791
sine, 735–736
standard normal, 693–694, 703

Cycle
of cosine function, 744
defined, 711
identifying, 711
periodic, 710, 771
of sine function, 735–736
of tangent function, 749, 750

Cylinders, radius of, 725

D

Data analysis, 660–664. *See also*
Mathematical modeling
bar graph, 885
bimodal data, 660, 702
binomial distribution, 685–688, 703
binomial experiment, 685–686, 703
box-and-whisker plots, 662–664, 702
circle graph, 885
data spread, 668
exercises, 83, 98, 110, 144, 179, 203, 350, 506, 635
histogram, 886
interquartile range, 669, 703

margin of error, 679–680, 703
mean, 660, 702, 886
measures of central tendency, 660–662, 702, 886
measures of variation, 669, 703
median, 660, 702, 886
mode, 660, 702, 886
normal distribution, 692–694, 703
outlier, 664, 702
percentiles, 663, 702
probability distributions, 648–651, 701
quartile, 662, 702
random sample, 677, 703
range of, 669, 703
sample, 677–680, 703
sample proportion, 677, 678, 703
standard deviation, 668–672, 675, 703
standard normal curve, 693–694, 703
z-score, 671–672, 693–694

Data collection, 60, 436, 652, 674, 681, 689
Data interpretation, 228
Data modeling, 78–79, 240, 244, 308–309. *See also* Mathematical modeling
Data organizing
into matrices, 169–170
in tables, 453
Data spread, 668
Decay factor, 433, 479
Degrees
converting to and from radians, 727, 772
of polynomial, 307, 359
of term, 307, 359
Denominator
containing radical expressions, 266
least common, 523
rationalizing, 376–377, 382, 423, 883
Dependent events, 531–532, 541
Dependent system, 120, 161
Dependent variable, 62, 110
Detached coefficients, method of, 322
Determinant, 200, 206–207
Diagrams
drawing, 358
mapping, 56, 109
tree, 655–656, 659
Difference identities for angles, 816–817, 829
Difference of cubes, 328, 360
Difference of two squares, 263, 300
Digits, significant, 882
Dilation, 190, 192–193, 230
Dimensions of matrices, 168, 185, 229
Dimensional analysis, 490, 727–728
Direct variation, 72–74, 110, 489
Directed graph, 212–213
Directrix of parabola, 555, 557–558, 591
Discontinuity, 501–503, 540
Discrete function, 57
Discrete mathematics
Binomial Theorem, 354–355, 361
combinations, 346–347, 361

linear programming, 139–141, 145, 162
Multiplication Counting Principle, 345, 346
networks, 212–213
permutations, 345–346, 361
scatter plot, 80, 86, 110
sequence. *See* Sequences
tree diagram, 655–656, 659
Discriminant, 291–292, 293, 301
Disp feature, of graphing calculator, 567
DispGraph feature, of graphing calculator, 567
Distance formula, 561
Distribution
binomial, 687–688, 703
normal, 692–694, 703
probability, 648–651, 701
Distributive property
of matrix multiplication, 186
of real numbers, 7
of scalar multiplication, 183
simplifying algebraic expressions, 13
solving equations, 19
Divergence, 627, 643
Division
of binomial radical expressions, 382
of fractions, 871
of functions, 398, 399
of polynomials, 320–323, 360
of radical expressions, 375–377
of rational expressions, 511
synthetic, 321–323, 360
Division property
of equality, 18
of inequality, 26
simplifying algebraic expressions, 13–14
of square roots, 266
Domain
of functions, 398
of relations, 56, 109
Dorling Kindersley Activity Lab
Applying Conic Sections, 596–597
Applying Exponential Functions, 484–485
Applying Functions, 114–115
Applying Inequalities, 234–235
Applying Quadratic Functions, 364–365
Applying Sequences, 706–707
Applying Trigonometry, 834–835
Double-angle identities, 821–822, 829
Drawing
diagrams, 358
ellipses, 572
perspective, 706
DrawInv feature, of graphing calculator, 413

E

e
base of exponential function, 441–442, 470–472, 481
natural logarithmic function, 470–472, 481

Eccentricity, of ellipse, 571
Elimination
solving linear systems, 126, 127, 162
solving three-variable systems, 152–154
Ellipse
center of, 548, 549, 568
co-vertices of, 568, 592
defined, 568, 592
drawing, 572
eccentricity of, 571
equation of, 568–569, 583
focus of, 568, 570, 592
graphing, 548
major axis of, 568, 592
minor axis of, 568, 592
moiré pattern, 550
translations, 583, 593
vertices of, 568, 592
Ellipsis points, 619
End behavior, 312
Endpoints, 71
Enrichment. *See also* Extensions
Challenge exercises, 16, 23, 31, 37, 44, 60, 69, 76, 83, 91, 99, 105, 122, 130, 137, 143, 150, 158, 172, 180, 188, 204, 218, 226, 243, 250, 257, 265, 271, 279, 287, 295, 311, 319, 325, 332, 340, 344, 350, 357, 373, 378, 383, 389, 396, 403, 411, 418, 436, 444, 451, 459, 467, 474, 492, 499, 507, 512, 519, 527, 536, 560, 572, 579, 587, 604, 609, 615, 623, 630, 638, 653, 657, 666, 674, 682, 690, 697, 715, 740, 747, 753, 761, 768, 781, 789, 798, 805, 812, 819, 825
Equal matrices, 177, 230
Equality, properties of, 18
Equations. *See also* Function(s); Inequalities
absolute value, 33–34, 49, 878
of circle, 561–563, 583, 592
of conic sections, 582–584
cosine, 745
of ellipse, 568–569, 583
equivalent, 585
exponential. *See* Exponential equations
graphing, 62–64, 110, 118–120, 161, 879
of hyperbola, 575, 577, 583, 584
linear. *See* Linear equations
literal, solving, 874
logarithmic, 462–464, 470–472, 481
matrix. *See* Matrix equation
natural logarithmic, 471
of parabola, 253–254, 555–557, 558, 583
parametric, 124, 413, 567, 791
polynomial. *See* Polynomial equations
quadratic. *See* Quadratic equations
radical, 391–393, 425
rational, 522–524
solution to, 18, 48
solving by graphing, 119, 268, 269, 293, 327–328, 461, 589
solving by tables, 132, 269, 293, 462
square root, 391, 416, 425

systems of. *See* Systems of equations
in three variables, 148, 152–156, 163
transformations, 252–253, 469
translations, 759–760
translations of functions, 94, 111
trigonometric, 744–745, 785–786, 815
writing to solve problems, 20–21

Equilateral triangle, 601, 648

Equivalent compound inequality, 36

Equivalent equations, 585

Equivalent systems, 127, 154, 162

Error, margin of, 679–680, 703

Error Analysis, 17, 30, 76, 82, 150, 158,
171, 204, 250, 264, 294, 324, 332,
340, 378, 383, 389, 450, 457, 466,
512, 518, 528, 536, 565, 572, 608,
630, 665, 673, 731, 788, 789

Estimation
of area under a curve, 636
exercises that use, 9, 172, 242, 397, 760,
761
of square roots, 4
as test-taking strategy, 640
using line of best fit, 87

Evaluating
algebraic expressions, 12–13, 48
determinants, 206–207
formulas, 874
infinite geometric series, 627–628
logarithmic functions, 446–448
polynomial functions, 323
reciprocal trigonometric functions,
763–764
series, 627–628, 634

Expanding
binomials, 353–354, 361
logarithms, 455

Experimental probability, 39–40, 49, 649

Explicit formula, 602, 607, 613, 641

Exponents
in algebraic expression, 12
properties of, 368, 387
rational, 385–388, 393, 424

Exponential decay, 432–434, 440

Exponential equations
defined, 461, 481
solving, 472
solving by graphing, 461
solving by tables, 462
solving using logarithms, 461
writing from graphs, 432

Exponential functions, 484–485
analyzing, 433
base *e*, 441–442, 470–472, 481
decay factor, 433, 479
defined, 430, 479
depreciation, 434
exponential decay, 432–434, 440
exponential growth, 430–432, 479
family of, 439–441
fitting to data, 438
graphing, 430, 439–440
growth factor, 430, 479
parent, 439–441, 495–497

properties of, 439–442
transforming into linear functions, 469
writing, 432

Exponential growth, 430–432, 479

Exponential inequalities, 476–477

Exponential models, 469

ExpReg feature, of graphing calculator,
462

Expressions
algebraic, 12–14, 48
equivalent, 13
evaluating, 12–13, 48
logarithmic, 446–448, 454–455, 481
quadratic. *See* Quadratic expressions
radical. *See* Radical expressions
rational. *See* Rational expressions
simplifying, 12–14, 48
terms of, 13, 238, 307
trigonometric, 780
variable, 12
writing from tables, 11

Extended response exercises, 31, 38, 45,
61, 92, 100, 113, 123, 144, 160, 173,
189, 198, 233, 243, 265, 280, 287,
295, 319, 332, 340, 357, 363, 379,
384, 412, 419, 437, 459, 475, 483,
493, 500, 527, 595, 610, 617, 653,
667, 690, 705, 716, 724, 741, 754,
762, 790, 825, 833

Extension
The Ambiguous Case, 807
Comparing Conditional Probabilities,
659
End Behavior, 312
Mathematical Induction, 632–633
Networks, 212–213
Piecewise Functions, 71

Extra Practice, 836–863

Extraneous solution, 34, 48, 393, 394, 521

Extrapolate, 310

F

Factor(s)
common, 259
decay, 433, 479
defined, 259
greatest common factor (GCF), 259,
300
growth, 430, 479
linear, 313
of polynomial function, 315–316
prime, 313

Factor Theorem, 315, 360

Factor trees, 313

Factorial notation, 345, 361

Factoring
defined, 259
difference of cubes, 328, 360
difference of two squares, 263, 300
greatest common factor, 259, 300
perfect square trinomial, 262, 300
polynomials, 313–316, 320–323,
328–330, 360, 881
quadratic expressions, 259–262

quadratic trinomial, 260–262
solving polynomial equations by,
328–330
solving quadratic equations by, 267,
293, 300
solving trigonometric equations by,
786
sum of cubes, 328, 360

Family(ies)
of conic sections, 583
of exponential functions, 439–441
of functions, 93–97
of logarithmic functions, 449
of quadratic functions, 253
of radical functions, 415
of reciprocal functions, 495–498
of sine and cosine functions, 758

Feasible region, 140, 162

Fibonacci sequence, 611

Finite graph, 212–213

Finite sequences, 619

Finite series, 619–621, 626–627, 634, 642

Flip. *See* Reflections

Focus (foci)
of ellipse, 568, 570, 592
of hyperbola, 575, 576–577
of parabola, 555, 557–558, 591

FOIL, 238, 424

Formulas
for area, 801, 898
for arithmetic sequences, 607
for binomial probability, 687
Change of Base, 462–463
for conditional probability, 655
for continuously compounded
interest, 441, 480
for converting between radians and
degrees, 727
for distance, 561
evaluating, 874
explicit, 602, 607, 613, 641
generating mathematical patterns
with, 602
for geometric sequences, 613
for geometric series, 626
Law of Cosines, 808
Law of Sines, 802
for length of intercepted arc, 728
for margin of error, 679
Quadratic, 289–291, 293, 301
radical expressions in, 397
recursive, 602, 607, 613, 641
slope, 64, 876
solving for one variable, 19
spreadsheet, 25
for standard deviation, 669
for sum of arithmetic series, 620
for sum of geometric series, 628
for volume, 490

Fractal, 277, 279

Fractal geometry, 603

Fractions
adding, 514–515
complex, 516–517, 540
dividing, 871

multiplying, 871
subtracting, 871
Frequency table, 648–649, 701, 702
Function(s). *See also* Equations; Graph(s)
absolute value, 88–90, 111
adding, 398
amplitude of, 712–713, 736, 744, 771
applying, 114–115
composite, 399, 425
composition of, 399–400
continuous, 57
cosecant, 763, 773
cosine. *See* Cosine functions
cotangent, 763, 773
cube root, 416
cubic, 307, 328
defined, 57, 109
discrete, 57
dividing, 398, 399
domain of, 398
exponential. *See* Exponential functions
family of, 93–97
identifying, 57–58
inverse, 406–409, 413, 414–415, 425
linear, 62, 110, 238, 469
logarithmic, 446–449, 480
maximum and minimum values of, 139–140, 247, 315, 360
multiplying, 398, 399
natural logarithmic, 470–472, 481
objective, 139, 162
operations with, 398–399, 425
parent. *See* Parent function
period of, 735, 755, 771
periodic. *See* Periodic functions
piecewise, 71
polynomial. *See* Polynomial functions
quadratic. *See* Quadratic functions
radical, 414–417
range of, 398
rational, 494, 501–505, 540
reciprocal, 495–498
reciprocal trigonometric, 763–766
secant, 763, 773
sine. *See* Sine functions
square root, 415–416, 425
step, 71
subtracting, 398
tangent, 749–751, 773
translations. *See* Translations
trigonometric. *See* Trigonometric functions
truth, 421
vertical-line test, 57–58
zeros of. *See* Zeros of functions
Function notation, 58, 109
Function rules, 58, 737
Fundamental Theorem of Algebra, 341–343, 361

G

Gauss, Carl Friedrich, 341
GCF (greatest common factor), 259, 300
Geometric mean, 614, 642

Geometric probability, 42, 49
Geometric sequences, 612–614
defined, 612, 642
formulas for, 613
graph of, 614
identifying, 613
Geometric series
defined, 626, 643
finite, 626–627, 634
formula for, 626
infinite, 625, 627–628
Geometric transformations, 190, 191–195, 230
Geometry
coordinate, 205, 218, 220, 319, 698. *See also* Conic sections; Graph(s); Translations
exercises that use, 14, 15, 20, 22, 30, 32, 38, 42, 43, 48, 60, 62, 69, 73, 76, 83, 100, 128, 137, 150, 158, 159, 191, 192, 196, 197, 218, 227, 242, 264, 286, 295, 311, 317, 318, 324, 330, 331, 349, 356, 362, 372, 378, 402, 405, 410, 411, 426, 444, 490, 602, 604, 605, 610, 625, 731, 753, 754, 768, 797, 798, 805, 812
fractal, 603
infinite series and, 625, 627–628
Geometry Review
Formulas, 898
Geometric Transformations, 190
Radical Expressions in Formulas, 397
Special Right Triangles, 717
Golden ratio, 269, 291, 383
Golden rectangle, 269, 270, 291
Graph(s)
of absolute value function, 88–90, 111
of circle, 547–548, 564
of conic sections, 547–550, 554, 591
of cosine function, 743–744
of cube root function, 416
directed, 212–213
of ellipse, 548
end behavior of, 312
of exponential decay, 433
of exponential function, 430, 439–440
finite, 212–213
from function rule, 737
of geometric sequence, 614
of hyperbola, 548–549, 576
of inequalities, 26–28
of inverse, 413
of inverse relation, 408
of inverse variation, 495
of linear equation, 62–64, 110
of linear inequalities, 101–103, 111
of logarithmic function, 448–449
of parabola, 245–246, 253, 299, 557–558
of periodic function, 739
of piecewise function, 71
points on coordinate plane, 54
of polynomial equation, 327–328
of polynomial function, 306, 312
of quadratic equation, 268, 269, 293
of quadratic function, 239, 245–246, 299

of rational function, 494, 504–505
of real numbers, 6
of reciprocal functions, 495–496
of reciprocal trigonometric functions, 765–766
of relations, 55–56, 556
of sine function, 737–738
solving equations by, 119, 268, 269, 293, 327–328, 461, 589
solving exponential equations by, 461
solving linear systems by, 119, 589
solving polynomial equations by, 327–328
solving quadratic equations by, 268, 269, 293
solving square root equations by, 416
solving systems of equations by, 119, 589
of square root function, 416
of systems of inequalities, 134–135, 162
of systems of linear equations, 118–120, 161, 589
of tangent function, 749–751
of three-dimensional coordinate space, 146–148, 163
translating trigonometric functions, 756–758
translations, 93–97, 497–498
Graphing calculator
absolute value function, 89
Activity Lab, 86, 124, 145, 244, 296–297, 413, 420–421, 438, 469, 476–477, 494, 528–529, 554, 567, 634, 699, 742, 791
angles in circle, 720
angles of triangle, 802, 809, 810
area under a curve, 637, 699
CALC feature of, 145, 505, 670, 699
checking for extraneous solutions, 394
comparing models of data, 308–309
CubicReg feature of, 308
determinant of matrix, 207
Disp feature of, 567
DispGraph feature of, 567
DrawInv feature of, 413
evaluating finite series, 634
evaluating reciprocal trigonometric functions, 764
exercises that use, 90, 91, 98, 121, 122, 209, 210, 225, 226, 232, 241, 242, 243, 270, 288, 295, 304, 309, 310, 311, 317, 318, 319, 330, 331, 332, 350, 359, 417, 436, 437, 442, 444, 450, 464, 499, 565, 578, 579, 587, 588, 616, 629, 638, 639, 652, 653, 664, 673, 690, 722, 728, 740, 746, 752, 753, 760, 761, 766, 767, 768, 787, 806, 828
ExpReg feature of, 462
graphing conic sections, 554
graphing polynomial functions, 306
intersect feature of, 745
inverse of function, 413
inverse of sine, 785
inverse of tangent, 785
length of arc, 728
line of best fit, 86–87
linear and exponential models, 469

linear programming, 145
LinReg feature of, 86–87, 119, 244, 308
LIST feature of, 661
LOGIC menu of, 421
MATH feature of, 355, 651, 687
matrix equation, 215
matrix operations, 181
MODE feature of, 494, 742
parametric equation, 567
PRB menu of, 345, 347
PRGM feature of, 567
Prompt feature of, 567
QuadReg feature of, 240, 244, 299, 308
QuarticReg feature of, 308–309
Radian feature of, 567
radical inequalities, 420–421
random numbers, 40
rref feature of, 224
side of triangle, 802, 803, 809
STAT feature of, 244, 438, 469, 612, 670
STAT PLOT feature of, 612, 663
systems of inequalities, 135
systems of linear equations, 118, 215, 220
Table option of, 296
TBLSET feature of, 420
TEST menu of, 421
Tmax feature of, 567
Tmin feature of, 567
TRACE feature of, 87, 124, 441, 494, 567, 578, 663, 742
Tstep feature of, 567
value option of, 145
VARS feature of, 567
X1T feature of, 567
Y1T feature of, 567
zero option of, 145
ZOOM feature of, 86, 89, 413, 438, 562, 637
ZSquare feature of, 89
Graphing Calculator Hints, 42, 89, 184, 192, 208, 215, 327, 345, 347, 355, 371, 386, 441, 502, 562, 612, 637, 651, 745, 761, 763
Greatest common factor (GCF), 259, 300
Greatest integer function, 71
Gridded response examples, 46, 79, 126, 185, 285, 323, 380, 442, 515
Gridded response exercises, 23, 46, 75, 84, 113, 130, 205, 233, 258, 350, 363, 380, 396, 467–468, 473, 483, 537, 566, 595, 630–631, 674, 705, 769, 813, 833
Growth factor, 430, 479
Guided Problem Solving, 32, 107, 131, 220, 288, 333, 405, 453, 530, 581, 618, 675, 755, 800
Guo Shoujing, 617

H

Halayudha, 353
Half-angle identities, 822–823, 829
Hands-On Activity, 39, 531

Hands-On Activity Lab, 281, 546
Harmonic mean, 519
Hinges (quartiles), 662, 702
Hipparchus, 814
Histogram, 886
History and Math, 158, 232, 250, 587, 719. *See also* Point in Time
History of Math. *See* Point in Time
Homework Video Tutor, 9, 16, 22, 37, 44, 60, 68, 75, 82, 91, 98, 105, 122, 129, 136, 143, 149, 158, 171, 179, 187, 197, 204, 210, 218, 225, 242, 249, 257, 264, 270, 279, 286, 294, 310, 318, 325, 332, 339, 343, 349, 356, 373, 378, 383, 389, 395, 402, 411, 418, 436, 443, 450, 458, 466, 474, 492, 499, 506, 512, 518, 525, 535, 551, 559, 565, 572, 578, 586, 604, 608, 615, 623, 629, 638, 652, 657, 665, 673, 681, 689, 696, 714, 723, 731, 739, 747, 753, 761, 767, 781, 788, 797, 805, 811, 818, 824
Horizontal asymptotes, 504, 540
Horizontal line, 66
Horizontal translation, 94–95, 252, 415, 756–758, 773
Hyperbola, 550
analyzing, 574
axes of, 575, 593
branches of, 548, 575
center of, 548, 575
defined, 575, 593
equation of, 575, 577, 583, 584
focus of, 575, 576–577
graphing, 548–549, 576
moiré pattern, 550
translations, 584, 593
vertices of, 575, 593

I

***i,* imaginary number,** 274–275, 301
Identities, trigonometric. *See* Trigonometric identities
Identity matrix
additive, 175
multiplicative, 199, 231
Identity property, 7, 175, 183
Image, 192, 230
Imaginary axis, 275
Imaginary number(s), 274–275, 301. *See also* Complex number(s)
Imaginary Root Theorem, 338, 361
Inclusive events, 533
Inconsistent system, 120, 161
Independent events, 531–532, 541
Independent system, 120, 161
Independent variable, 62, 110
Index of radical, 370, 423
Indirect measurement, 766, 767, 768, 796, 797, 800
Induction, mathematical, 632–633

Inequalities
absolute value, 35–36, 103–104, 135
applying, 234–235
compound, 28–29, 36, 48
equivalent compound, 36
exponential, 476–477
graphs of, 26–28
linear. *See* Linear inequalities
logarithmic, 476–477
properties of, 26
quadratic, 296–297
radical, 420–421
rational, 528–529
simplified compound, 36
solutions of, 26–28
systems of, 133–135, 162
writing, 104
Infinite geometric series, 625, 627–628
Infinite sequences, 619
Infinite series, 619, 625, 627–628
Initial side of angle, 718, 771
Inscribed rectangles, 635, 643
Instant Check System
Check Skills You'll Need, 4, 12, 18, 26, 33, 39, 55, 62, 72, 78, 88, 93, 101, 118, 125, 133, 139, 146, 152, 168, 174, 182, 191, 199, 206, 214, 221, 238, 245, 252, 259, 267, 274, 282, 289, 306, 313, 320, 327, 335, 341, 345, 353, 369, 374, 380, 385, 391, 398, 406, 414, 430, 439, 446, 454, 461, 470, 488, 495, 501, 509, 514, 522, 531, 547, 555, 561, 568, 574, 582, 600, 606, 612, 619, 626, 635, 648, 654, 660, 668, 677, 685, 692, 710, 718, 726, 734, 743, 749, 756, 763, 778, 783, 792, 801, 808, 814, 821
Check Your Readiness, 2, 52, 116, 166, 236, 304, 366, 428, 486, 544, 598, 646, 708, 776
Checkpoint Quiz, 24, 38, 77, 100, 138, 151, 189, 211, 258, 280, 326, 351, 384, 404, 445, 468, 508, 520, 566, 580, 617, 631, 667, 691, 733, 762, 799, 820
Quick Check, 6, 7, 8, 12, 13, 14, 19, 20, 21, 27, 28, 29, 33, 34, 35, 36, 40, 41, 42, 55, 56, 57, 58, 63, 64, 65, 66, 67, 72, 73, 74, 78, 79, 80, 89, 90, 94, 95, 96, 102, 103, 104, 119, 120, 125, 126, 127, 134, 135, 140, 141, 147, 148, 153, 154, 155, 156, 168, 169, 170, 175, 176, 177, 182, 183, 184, 185, 186, 192, 193, 194, 195, 200, 201, 202, 203, 207, 208, 214, 215, 216, 217, 221, 222, 223, 224, 239, 240, 245, 246, 247, 253, 254, 255, 259, 260, 261, 262, 263, 267, 268, 269, 274, 275, 276, 277, 282, 283, 284, 285, 290, 291, 292, 307, 308, 309, 313, 314, 315, 316, 321, 322, 323, 327, 328, 329, 330, 336, 337, 338, 342, 343, 345, 346, 347, 354, 355, 370, 371, 374, 375, 376, 377, 380, 381, 382, 385, 386, 387, 388, 391, 392, 393, 398, 399, 400, 407, 408, 409, 415, 416, 417, 430, 431, 432, 433, 434, 439, 440, 441, 442, 446, 447, 448, 449, 455, 456, 461, 462, 463, 464, 470, 471, 472, 489, 490, 495, 496, 497, 498, 502, 503, 504, 505, 509, 510, 511, 515,

516, 517, 522, 523, 524, 532, 533, 534, 548, 549, 550, 555, 556, 557, 558, 562, 563, 564, 569, 570, 576, 577, 583, 584, 585, 601, 602, 606, 607, 613, 614, 620, 621, 627, 628, 636, 637, 648, 649, 650, 651, 654, 655, 656, 660, 661, 662, 663, 664, 669, 670, 671, 672, 677, 678, 679, 680, 686, 687, 688, 692, 693, 694, 711, 712, 713, 718, 719, 721, 722, 727, 728, 729, 734, 735, 736, 737, 738, 744, 745, 750, 751, 756, 757, 758, 759, 760, 763, 764, 765, 766, 779, 780, 783, 784, 785, 786, 793, 794, 795, 801, 802, 803, 809, 810, 815, 816, 817, 822, 823

Intercepted arc, 726, 728, 772

Interdisciplinary Connections
  archaeology, 389, 442, 451, 467
  architecture, 197, 287, 510, 622
  art, 4, 58, 269, 270, 291
  astronomy, 467, 573, 588, 741, 778, 814
  biology, 41, 444, 473, 481, 693, 695, 748
  botany, 442
  chemistry, 61, 445, 448, 450, 453, 467, 480
  civil engineering, 254
  ecology, 142
  economics, 123, 247, 401, 437
  electrical engineering, 15
  engineering, 15, 254, 797
  geography, 150, 731, 732
  geology, 665
  geometry, 14, 15, 20, 22, 30, 32, 38, 42, 43, 48, 60, 62, 69, 73, 76, 83, 100, 128, 137, 150, 158, 159, 191, 192, 196, 197, 218, 227, 242, 264, 286, 295, 311, 317, 318, 324, 330, 331, 349, 356, 362, 372, 378, 402, 405, 410, 411, 426, 444, 490, 602, 604, 605, 610, 625, 731, 753, 754, 768, 797, 798, 805, 812
  history, 158, 232, 250, 587, 719
  language arts, 715
  literature, 208, 209, 210, 347
  medicine, 440, 692
  meteorology, 37, 665
  microbiology, 143
  music, 139, 185, 467, 496, 519, 732, 740
  oceanography, 436, 661, 663
  physics, 15, 218, 241, 248, 249, 271, 295, 302, 377, 378, 383, 389, 396, 443, 474, 480, 482, 490, 492, 512, 519, 614, 630, 644, 774, 782, 786, 787, 812
  psychology, 136, 444
  science, 79
  seismology, 446, 449, 465, 696
  social science, 649
  social studies, 83
  sociology, 689
  statistics, 174, 535, 690
  weather, 130, 390, 652, 656, 657, 664, 688
  zoology, 436, 462, 466, 489

Interest, 25, 441–442, 472, 480

Internet Links. *See* Active Math Online; Homework Video Tutor; Lesson Quiz Online; Video Tutor Help Online; Vocabulary Quiz Online

Interpolate, 310

Interquartile range, 669, 703

Intersect feature, of graphing calculator, 745

Inverse
  additive, 7, 47–48, 175, 276
  finding, 7
  multiplicative, 7, 47–48, 408
  of trigonometric functions, 783–785, 827–828

Inverse function, 406–409, 413, 414–415, 425

Inverse matrix
  additive, 175
  of coefficient matrix, 215, 216, 231
  encoding and decoding messages, 208
  multiplicative, 175, 199, 200, 207, 231
  solving matrix equations, 201–203, 208, 214–217
  solving systems of equations, 214–217

Inverse properties of real numbers, 7

Inverse relations, 406–409, 425

Inverse trigonometric function, 783–785, 827–828

Inverse variations, 488–489, 495, 539, 540

Irrational numbers, 5

Irrational Root Theorem, 337, 361

Isosceles triangle, 648

J

Joint variation, 490
Justifying Steps, 16, 30, 50

K

Koch snowflake, 601

L

Law of Cosines, 808–810, 829
Law of Large Numbers, 678
Law of Sines, 801–803, 807, 828
Least common denominator, 523
Least common multiple, 515
Least squares method, 87
Left end behavior, 312
Lesson Quiz Online, 9, 17, 23, 31, 37, 45, 61, 69, 75, 83, 91, 99, 105, 123, 129, 137, 143, 149, 159, 173, 179, 189, 197, 205, 209, 219, 227, 243, 249, 257, 265, 271, 279, 287, 295, 311, 319, 325, 331, 339, 343, 351, 357, 373, 379, 383, 389, 395, 403, 411, 419, 437, 445, 451, 459, 467, 473, 493, 499, 507, 513, 519, 527, 535, 551, 559, 565, 573, 579, 587, 605, 609, 615, 623, 631, 639, 653, 657, 667, 673, 681, 691, 697, 715, 723, 733, 741, 747, 753, 761, 769, 781, 789, 799, 805, 811, 819, 825

Like radicals, 380, 424
Like terms, combining, 14

Limits, 621, 642

Line(s). *See also* Linear equations; Linear inequalities; Linear systems
  horizontal, 66
  parallel, 66
  perpendicular, 66, 67
  slope of, 64–66, 110
  vertical, 66, 110
  x-intercept, 63
  y-intercept, 63

Linear equations
  direct variation, 72–74, 110
  graphing, 62–64, 110
  modeling, 78–80, 110, 244, 308, 469
  piecewise function, 71
  point-slope form of, 64–65, 66, 110
  slope formula, 64, 876
  slope-intercept form of, 65–66, 110
  solving, 877
  standard form of, 63, 66, 110
  systems of. *See* Linear systems
  transforming exponential equations, 469

Linear factor, 313

Linear function, 62, 110, 469

Linear inequalities
  defined, 101, 111
  graphing, 101–103, 111
  solving, 877
  systems of, 133–135, 162

Linear programming, 139–141, 145, 162

Linear regression line, 86

Linear systems
  classifying, 120
  defined, 118, 161
  dependent, 120, 161
  equivalent, 127, 154, 162
  graphing, 118–120, 161, 589
  inconsistent, 120, 161
  independent, 120, 161
  of inequalities, 134–135, 162
  parametric equations, 124
  solving by elimination, 126, 127, 162
  solving by graphing, 119, 589
  solving by substitution, 125–126, 162
  solving using augmented matrices, 222–224
  solving using Cramer's Rule, 221–222, 231
  solving using matrix equations, 214–217
  solving using tables, 132, 133–134
  without a unique solution, 127

Linear term, 238

LinReg feature, of graphing calculator, 86–87, 119, 244, 308

Lissajous figures, 791

LIST feature, of graphing calculator, 661

Literal equation, solving, 874

Logarithm(s)
  Change of Base Formula, 462–463
  common, 447, 480
  defined, 447
  evaluating, 447–448

expanding, 455
expressions, 446–448, 454–455, 481
modeling sound, 456
natural, 470–472, 481
properties of, 454–456, 464
simplifying, 455

Logarithmic equations, 462–464, 470–472, 481

Logarithmic expressions, 446–448, 454–455, 481

Logarithmic functions, 446–449
defined, 448, 480
families of, 449
graphing, 448–449
natural, 470–472, 481
writing and evaluating, 446–448

Logarithmic inequalities, 476–477

LOGIC menu, of graphing calculator, 421

Logical operators, 421

Long division of polynomials, 320–321

M

Major axis, 568, 592

Make a Conjecture, 64, 150, 190, 205, 281, 306, 319, 419, 454, 574, 611, 625, 720, 769, 792

Manipulatives. *See also* Graphing calculator
algebra tiles, 260, 281
compass, 720
index cards, 39, 306
number cubes, 531, 541, 553, 652, 701
protractor, 720, 834, 835

Mapping diagram, 56, 109

Margin of error, 679–680, 703

Math at Work. *See* Algebra at Work; Careers

MATH feature, of graphing calculator, 355, 651, 687

Math in the Media, 188

Mathematical induction, 632–633

Mathematical modeling. *See also* Simulations
infinite series, 625
inverse variation, 488
linear equations, 78–80, 110, 244, 308, 469
polynomial functions, 308–309, 314
predictions, 79–80
quadratic functions, 240, 244, 308
trend line, 80, 110
using equations of circles, 563
using rational equations, 523–524
using residuals, 244
using sine functions, 738

Mathematical patterns, 600–602. *See also* Patterns

Matrices
adding, 174–175, 181, 191–192, 230
additive identity, 175
additive inverse, 175
augmented, 222–224
coefficient, 214, 216, 231

constant, 214, 231
Cramer's Rule, 221–222, 231
defined, 168, 176, 229
determinant of, 200, 206–207
dilation, 192–193
dimensions of, 168, 185, 229
directed graph, 212, 213
elements of, 169, 177, 229
equal, 177, 230
exercises that use, 271, 294
identifying, 168–169
multiplicative identity, 199, 231
multiplicative inverse, 199, 200, 207, 231
multiplying, 184–186, 230
organizing data into, 169–170
product, 183, 185, 186
reflection, 193–194
rotation, 194–195
row operations, 223, 231
scalar multiplication, 182–183, 230
square, 199, 231
subtracting, 176
transformations of geometric figures, 191–195, 230
translations, 191–192, 230
variable, 214, 231
writing vertices as, 192
zero, 175

Matrix equation
solving, 176–177, 230
solving using equal matrices, 177, 230
solving using inverse matrices, 201–203, 208, 214–216
solving using scalars, 183–184
used to solve systems of linear equations, 214–217

Maximum and minimum values of functions, 139–140
of quadratic functions, 247
relative, 315, 360

Mean
arithmetic, 607, 641
of data set, 660, 702, 886
defined, 660, 702
geometric, 614, 642
harmonic, 519

Measurement
of angles, 718–719, 725, 795, 809, 810
exercises that use, 59, 81, 318, 426, 805
indirect, 766, 767, 768, 796, 797, 800
in radians, 725, 726–729, 772

Measures of central tendency, 660–662, 702, 886

Measures of variation, 669, 703

Median, 660, 702, 886

Mental Math, 187, 273, 465, 473, 552, 770, 818

Method of detached coefficients, 322

Minimum value. *See* Maximum and minimum values of functions

Minor axis, 568, 592

Mixed Review, 10, 17, 24, 31, 38, 45, 61, 70, 77, 84, 92, 100, 106, 123, 130, 138, 144, 151, 159, 173, 180, 189, 198, 205, 211, 219, 227, 243, 251, 258,

265, 272, 280, 287, 295, 311, 319, 326, 332, 340, 344, 351, 357, 373, 379, 384, 390, 396, 404, 412, 419, 437, 445, 452, 459, 468, 475, 493, 500, 508, 513, 520, 527, 537, 553, 560, 566, 573, 580, 588, 605, 610, 617, 624, 631, 639, 653, 658, 667, 674, 683, 691, 698, 716, 724, 733, 741, 748, 754, 762, 769, 782, 790, 799, 806, 813, 820, 825

Mode, 660, 702

MODE feature, of graphing calculator, 494, 742

Models and modeling. *See* Mathematical modeling; Simulations

Modem, 756

Moiré pattern, 550

Monomial, 260

Multiple, least common, 515

Multiple choice examples, 14, 96, 104, 119, 140, 177, 222, 263, 292, 328, 347, 392, 409, 431, 472, 490, 534, 556, 585, 590, 601, 628, 654–655, 664, 738, 764, 784, 809

Multiple choice exercises, 9, 10, 17, 31, 37, 38, 43, 45, 61, 69, 70, 76, 83, 91, 92, 99–100, 105, 106, 113, 123, 129, 137, 143, 144, 149, 150, 159, 173, 179, 180, 187, 189, 196, 198, 209, 210, 219, 225, 227, 243, 249, 251, 257, 265, 270, 272, 279, 280, 287, 295, 311, 319, 325, 331, 332, 339, 340, 344, 348, 357, 363, 373, 379, 383, 384, 389, 390, 395, 403–404, 409, 411–412, 419, 422, 435, 437, 443, 444–445, 451, 452, 459, 465, 474–475, 478, 493, 499, 500, 507–508, 513, 519–520, 525, 527, 529, 535, 538, 551, 552–553, 559, 560, 565, 571, 573, 586, 588, 605, 610, 616, 624, 639, 653, 658, 666–667, 682–683, 690, 697, 705, 715–716, 724, 732–733, 741, 748, 754, 762, 782, 790, 798–799, 806, 807, 819–820, 825

Multiple events, probability of, 531–534

Multiple zero, 316, 360

Multiplication
of binomial radical expressions, 381
of binomials, 881
of complex numbers, 276
of conjugates, 381, 424
of fractions, 871
of functions, 398, 399
of matrices, 184–186, 230
of radical expressions, 374–375
of rational expressions, 510
scalar, 182–183, 230
simplifying algebraic expressions, 13
of square roots, 266

Multiplication Counting Principle, 345, 346

Multiplication property
of equality, 18
of inequality, 26

simplifying algebraic expressions, 13
of square roots, 266
Multiplicative identity matrix, 199, 231
Multiplicative identity property of scalar multiplication, 183
Multiplicative inverses
of matrices, 199, 200, 207, 231
reciprocals, 7, 47–48
Multiplicative Property of Zero
matrix multiplication, 186
real number multiplication, 13
scalar multiplication, 183
Multiplicity, 316, 360
Mutually exclusive events, 533

N

n **factorial,** 345, 361
Natural logarithm, 470–472, 481
Natural logarithmic equation, 471
Natural logarithmic function, 470–472, 481
Natural numbers, 5
Negative angle identities, 815, 829
Negative square root, 5
Networks, 212–213
New Vocabulary, 4, 12, 18, 26, 33, 39, 55, 62, 72, 78, 88, 93, 101, 118, 125, 139, 146, 168, 174, 182, 191, 199, 214, 221, 238, 252, 259, 267, 274, 282, 289, 306, 313, 320, 327, 335, 341, 345, 353, 369, 374, 380, 385, 391, 398, 406, 414, 430, 439, 446, 461, 470, 488, 495, 501, 509, 514, 531, 547, 555, 561, 568, 574, 600, 606, 612, 619, 626, 635, 648, 654, 660, 668, 677, 685, 692, 710, 718, 726, 734, 743, 749, 756, 763, 778, 792, 801, 808
Non-mutually exclusive events, 533
Normal curves, 693–694, 703
Normal distributions, 692–694, 703
Notation
factorial, 345, 361
function, 58, 109
scientific, 882
summation, 621, 642
*n*th **root,** 369, 370
Number(s)
complex. *See* Complex number(s)
imaginary, 274–275, 301
irrational, 5
natural, 5, 275
random, 40, 43, 651, 892
rational, 5, 275
real. *See* Real numbers
roots of. *See* Roots of numbers
simplifying, 274, 275, 387
whole, 5, 275
Number cubes, 531, 541, 553, 652, 701
Number line, 6
Number of combinations, 346
Number of permutations, 346

O

Objective function, 139, 162
Oblique triangle, 801
Odds, 652
Open-Ended, 9, 16, 23, 31, 37, 44, 48, 50, 69, 75, 82, 91, 98, 105, 107, 111, 112, 122, 129, 143, 158, 160, 164, 173, 180, 188, 189, 190, 191, 205, 209, 218, 225, 232, 242, 249, 257, 258, 264, 270, 271, 294, 302, 309, 318, 325, 331, 332, 340, 343, 349, 372, 378, 383, 389, 396, 402, 411, 418, 426, 427, 436, 443, 444, 445, 450, 457, 466, 474, 482, 492, 499, 512, 518, 526, 527, 536, 542, 552, 565, 567, 572, 587, 594, 604, 608, 611, 612, 615, 623, 629, 631, 638, 639, 667, 689, 697, 698, 704, 714, 723, 731, 740, 753, 761, 774, 781, 789, 791, 797, 799, 805, 811, 819, 824, 830
Open-ended questions, answering, 826
Operations
order of, 873
row, 223, 231
Opposites
additive inverse, 7, 47–48
additive inverse matrices, 175
simplifying algebraic expressions, 13
Or (compound inequality), 28, 48
Order of operations, 873
Ordered pairs, 54–56
Ordered triples, 146, 163
Ordering, real numbers, 6
Ordinate, 54
Origin, 54, 146
Oscilloscope, 713
Outlier, 664, 702

P

Parabolas, 555–558
axis of symmetry, 239, 299, 555
conic sections, 547, 555–558
defined, 239, 555
directrix, 555, 557–558, 591
equation of, 253–254, 555–557, 558, 583
focus of, 555, 557–558, 591
graphing, 245–246, 253, 557–558
maximums and minimums, 247
points on, 239
properties of, 246
transformations, 252–255
vertex of, 239, 299
Parabolic solar mirrors, 557
Parallel lines, 66
Parameters, 97
Parametric equations, 124, 413, 567, 791
Parent function, 93–95, 97, 111
exponential, 439–441, 495–497
quadratic, 253
reciprocal, 495–498
trigonometric, 758

Pascal, Blaise, 353
Pascal's Triangle, 352, 353–354, 361, 611
Paths, finite graphs, 212–213
Patterns. *See also* Sequences; Series
exercises that use, 252, 273
formulas to generate, 602
mathematical, 600–602
moiré, 550
Test-Taking Tip, 328
Percent, 870
Percentile, 663, 702
Perfect square trinomial, 262, 282, 300
Perimeter, 14
Period
of cosine function, 744
defined, 711, 771
of function, 735, 755, 771
of sine curve, 735–736
of tangent function, 750
Periodic cycles, 710
Periodic functions. *See also* Trigonometric functions
amplitude of, 712–713, 739, 771
defined, 712, 771
graph of, 739
identifying, 710–712
translations, 756–760, 773
Permutations, 345–346, 361
Perpendicular lines, 66, 67
Perspective drawing, 706
Phase shift, 756, 773
Piecewise function, 71
Plane
complex number, 275, 301
coordinate, 54, 876
sketching, 148
Point in Time
moon landing, 475
murals, 211
pacemakers, 716
sun's movements, 617
Titanic, 553
Point of discontinuity, 501–503, 540
Point-slope form, 64, 65, 66, 110
Polygons, regular, 798
Polynomial(s)
adding, 881
binomial expansion, 353–354, 361
classifying, 307
defined, 307, 359
degree of, 307, 359
dividing, 320–323, 360
equivalent statements about, 316
factored form of, 313–315
factoring, 313–316, 320–323, 328–330, 360, 881
long division of, 320–321
operations with, 881
standard form of, 307, 313
synthetic division, 321–323, 360
Polynomial equations
Fundamental Theorem of Algebra, 341–343, 361

Imaginary Root Theorem, 338, 361
Irrational Root Theorem, 337, 361
number of roots, 341–343
Rational Root Theorem, 335–337, 361
roots of. *See* Roots of polynomial equations
solving by factoring, 328–330
solving by graphing, 327–328
solving higher–degree, 330
writing equations from roots, 338, 361

Polynomial functions
defined, 307, 359
end behavior, 312
evaluating, 323
Factor Theorem, 315, 360
factors of, 315–316
graphing, 306, 312
modeling, 308–309, 314
multiple zeros, 316, 360
relative maximums or minimums, 315
zeros of, 315–316, 341–343

Population, 431, 434, 462, 465, 484–485, 534

Positive (principal) square root, 5, 266

Power Property of Logarithms, 454–455

PRB menu, of graphing calculator, 345, 347

Predictions, 79–80, 86

Preimage, 192, 230

PRGM feature, of graphing calculator, 567

Prime factor, 313

Principal root, 370, 423

Principal (positive) square root, 5, 266

Principles. *See also* Law; Theorems
Multiplication Counting Principle, 345, 346
Vertex Principle of Linear Programming, 140

Probability
area under curve and, 699
binomial, 685–687, 703
Binomial Theorem, 354–355, 361
conditional, 654–656, 659, 701
continuous, 676
cumulative, 648, 701
of dependent events, 531–532, 541
exercises, 151, 356
experimental, 39–40, 49, 649
geometric, 42, 49
of independent events, 531–532, 541
of multiple events, 531–534
of mutually exclusive events, 533
normal distribution, 692–694, 703
sample space, 41
standard normal curve, 693–694, 703
theoretical, 41–42, 49

Probability distribution, 648–651, 701

Problem Solving Hints, 12, 62, 69, 91, 134, 158, 216, 226, 444, 499, 516, 522, 555, 584, 685, 721, 781, 810, 823

Product matrix, 183, 185, 186

Product Property of Logarithms, 454–455

Programming, linear, 139–141, 145, 162

Prompt feature, of graphing calculator, 567

Proof, 23

Properties
absolute value inequalities, 35
addition, 18, 26
additive identity, 175
additive inverse, 175
angle difference identities, 816, 829
angle identities, 815
angle sum identities, 817, 829
associative, 7, 175, 183, 186
closure, 7, 175, 183, 186
cofunction identities, 815, 829
commutative, 7, 175
conditional probability, 655
cosine functions, 744
dimensions of product matrix, 185
distributive, 7, 13, 19, 183, 186
division, 13, 18, 26, 266
double–angle identities, 821
equality, 18
exponential functions, 439–442
exponents, 368, 387
factoring differences of squares, 263
half-angle identities, 822
horizontal asymptotes, 504
identity, 7, 175, 183
inequalities, 26
logarithms, 454–456, 464
matrix addition, 175
matrix multiplication, 186
matrix subtraction, 176
multiplication, 13, 18, 26, 266
multiplication of radical expressions, 374–375
multiplicative of zero, 13, 183, 186
negative angle identities, 815, 829
parabolas, 246
probability of independent events, 532
probability of mutually exclusive events, 533
quadratic functions, 246
rational exponents, 387
rational functions, 501–504
real numbers, 7–8, 274
reflexive, 18
scalar multiplication, 183
simplifying algebraic expressions, 13
sine functions, 736
square roots, 266
substitution, 18
subtraction, 13, 18, 26
symmetric, 18
tangent functions, 750
transitive, 18, 26
vertex principle of linear programming, 140
vertical asymptotes, 503
zero, multiplicative, 13, 183, 186
Zero Product, 267, 300, 315

Proportions
cross products, 872
direct variation problem, 74

sample, 677, 678, 703
using to find radian measure, 726–727

Protractor, 720, 834, 835

Pythagorean identities, 779, 816, 827

Pythagorean Theorem, 4, 275, 884

Q

Quadrants, 54

Quadratic, 282

Quadratic equations
complex solutions to, 277, 283, 290
discriminant of, 291–292, 293, 301
parabola, 555–557
perfect-square trinomial equation, 282–284, 300
solving by completing the square, 282–284, 293, 301
solving by factoring, 267, 293, 300
solving by finding square roots, 268, 293
solving by graphing, 268, 269, 293
solving by tables, 269, 293
solving using discriminant, 291–292, 293, 301
solving using Quadratic Formula, 289–291, 293, 301
standard form of, 267, 300
types of solutions, 293
writing from roots, 273
Zero Product Property, 267, 300, 315

Quadratic expressions
difference of squares, 263, 300
factoring, 259–262
factoring by using, 329
factoring trinomials, 260–262
perfect square trinomials, 262

Quadratic Formula, 289–291, 293, 301

Quadratic functions, 364–365
applying, 364–365
classifying, 238
defined, 238
family of, 253
graphs of, 239, 245–246, 299
maximums and minimums, 247
modeling with, 240, 244, 308
perfect square trinomials, 282
properties of, 246
rewriting by completing the square, 284–285
standard form of, 238, 246, 299
transformations, 252–255
vertex form of, 252–255, 284–285, 300
zeros of functions, 268, 300

Quadratic inequalities, 296–297

Quadratic systems, 589

Quadratic term, 238

Quadratic trinomials, 260–262

QuadReg feature, of graphing calculator, 240, 244, 299, 308

QuarticReg feature, of graphing calculator, 308–309

Quartile, 662, 702

Quick Check. *See* Instant Check System

Quotient Property of Logarithms, 454–455

R

Radian(s)
  comparing graphs in, 742
  converting to and from degrees, 727, 772
  defined, 726, 772
  evaluating reciprocal trigonometric functions, 764
  measuring in, 725, 726–729, 772

Radian feature, of graphing calculator, 567

Radical conjugates, 381–382

Radical equations, 391–393, 425

Radical expressions
  adding, 380–381
  binomial, 381–382
  conjugates, 381, 424
  converting to and from radical form, 386
  dividing, 375–377
  in formulas, 397
  index of, 370, 423
  like radicals, 380, 424
  multiplying, 374–375
  principal root, 370, 423
  radicand, 370, 423
  rational exponents and, 385–388, 424
  rationalizing denominator, 376–377, 382, 423, 883
  simplifying, 266, 371, 375, 381, 883
  square roots, 266
  subtracting, 380–381

Radical functions, 414–417

Radical inequalities, 420–421

Radical symbol, 266

Radicand, 370, 423

Radius
  of circle, 561, 563–564, 592
  of cylinder, 725

Random numbers, 40, 43, 651, 892

Random sample, 677–678, 703

Range
  of functions, 398
  interquartile, 669, 703
  of relations, 56, 109
  of set of data, 669, 703

Rate, 872

Ratio
  common, 612, 642
  golden, 269, 291, 383
  for right triangle, 792–794, 828
  trigonometric, 720–722, 828, 891
  using, 20

Rational equations, 522–524

Rational exponents, 385–388, 393, 424

Rational expressions
  adding, 515
  complex fractions, 516–517, 540
  dividing, 511

least common multiples, 515
  multiplying, 510
  operations with, 887
  simplest form of, 509, 540
  simplifying, 509–510, 540–541
  subtracting, 516

Rational functions. *See also* Inverse variations
  defined, 501
  graphing, 494, 504–505
  horizontal asymptotes, 504, 540
  point of discontinuity, 501–503, 540
  properties of, 501–504
  vertical asymptotes, 503, 540

Rational inequalities, 528–529

Rational numbers, 5, 275

Rational Root Theorem, 335–337, 361

Rationalizing denominators, 376–377, 382, 423, 883

Reading Comprehension. *See* Assessment

Real numbers, 5–8
  absolute value of, 8, 33
  graphing, 6
  ordering, 6
  properties of, 7–8, 274
  as solutions of inequalities, 27
  square root of, 274
  subsets of, 5

Real-World Connections. *See also* Algebra at Work; Careers; Point in Time
  acoustics, 466, 573
  advertising, 122, 351
  aerodynamics, 523, 569
  aeronautics, 21
  agriculture, 151, 264, 417, 696
  air pollution, 294
  air quality, 143
  air traffic control, 579
  automobiles, 80, 294, 409, 526, 731
  aviation, 77
  balance, 834–835
  banking, 122, 161, 615
  baseball, 798
  basketball, 36, 506
  boats, 346, 372
  break-even point, 130
  budgeting, 498
  business, 121, 180, 187, 188, 216, 225, 256, 294, 435, 505, 506, 535, 643
  calendar, 715
  carpentry, 318
  ceramics, 752
  circular dwellings, 561
  circus, 418
  classroom management, 133
  coins, 265
  college admissions, 135
  college enrollment, 533
  colors, 226
  commission, 70, 106
  communications, 202–203, 241, 436, 629
  computer use, 682

construction, 20, 30, 250, 458, 492, 658, 753, 795, 797
consumer issues, 349, 400
consumer spending, 691
cooking, 104, 143
cost analysis, 67
crafts, 620
cryptography, 208, 209
custom tailoring, 285
data collection, 60, 436, 652, 674, 681, 689
depreciation, 434
design, 95, 147, 157, 264, 512, 526, 550, 613, 723, 731, 751
discounts, 426
dog grooming, 122
earnings, 164, 674
education, 623, 694
Egyptology, 793
Eiffel Tower, 66
Einstein's formula, 377
elections, 13, 16, 129, 131, 347, 682
electricity, 9, 392, 740, 788
electronics, 418
energy, 169, 392, 670, 671, 673, 675
entertainment, 82, 102, 204, 603
environment, 75
estimation, 9, 172, 242, 397, 760, 761
exercise, 205
fabric design, 95
fees, 122, 126
Ferris wheel, 747
finance, 157, 604
financial planning, 627
firefighting, 268, 270
focal length of lens, 515
food preparation, 351
forestry, 805
fractals, 277, 279
fuel economy, 526
fund-raising, 67, 128, 136, 137, 607
games, 49, 505, 697
gardening, 271
gas mileage, 76, 499
gears, 819
genetics, 356, 650, 680, 689
global positioning system, 146
gold, 308
golden ratio, 269, 291, 383
golf, 616
government, 666
grades, 403
graphic arts, 193
gymnastics, 170
harmonic mean, 519
health, 493, 714
hockey, 292
hot-air ballooning, 78, 796
hydraulics, 240, 394
income, 673
indirect measurement, 766, 767, 768, 796, 797, 800
industrial design, 512
industry, 526, 535
interest, 442, 472
interior design, 264
Internet access, 129

investing, 15, 22, 156, 164, 443, 472, 473, 482, 560, 644
jobs, 172
landscape design, 526
light, 551, 738
machinery, 563
manufacturing, 90, 179, 248, 251, 264, 286, 699
market research, 650–651, 655
marketing, 653, 689
masonry, 526
matrices, 271, 294
measurement, 59, 81, 318, 426, 805
mechanics, 492
merchandising, 686
metalwork, 317
modeling, 560
money management, 156
motion, 715, 745, 746, 786
musical, 50
nature, 611
navigation, 584, 724, 812
noise control, 456, 458
nutrition, 81, 82, 153, 162, 218, 226
odds, 652
optics, 559
packaging, 249, 310, 371, 395
parabolas, 239
parade balloons, 766
parks, 789, 794
Pascal, Blaise, 353
pendulum, 726, 743
pet transportation, 328
physical fitness, 231
picture framing, 249
pipes, 263
planning, 794
population, 431, 434, 462, 465, 484–485, 534
postal rates, 242
prices, 182
product design, 147
production, 698
profit, 141, 163, 403
public opinion, 678
public works, 442
purchasing, 164
quality control, 29, 687, 689, 697
racing, 809
radio, 532
recreation, 6, 112
retail sales, 172
revenue, 28, 188, 248
road safety, 242, 409
rocketry, 797
safety, 242, 409, 653
sailing, 805
sales, 82, 164, 172, 226, 401
satellites, 378, 729
savings, 50, 330, 443, 474, 609
shopping, 126, 138, 217
simple harmonic motion, 786
solar energy, 392, 557
sound, 451, 456, 458, 466, 552, 713, 740
space, 386, 471, 473, 577, 730
sports, 22, 44, 60, 119, 157, 178, 286, 288, 300, 355, 669, 811
stadium design, 157

stamps, 242, 283, 341
surveying, 803, 804
surveys, 657, 680, 681, 683
technology, 173, 257, 402, 623, 630
telephones, 722
temperature, 759, 761
tests, 49, 174, 536, 695
tides, 747, 790
track and field, 84, 666, 696
transportation, 63, 78, 111, 112, 128, 172, 328, 526, 609, 652, 659, 731, 790
travel, 90, 213, 314
tsunamis, 559
unicycles, 247
vacuum bottle, 331
video game programming, 505
vital statistics, 309
volume, 322–323, 394
volunteerism, 524
wage policy, 507
water conservation, 73
water supply, 411
wave motion, 745, 746
weather satellite, 729
wildlife, 682
windmill, 195
windows, 94, 380
woodworking, 249, 525

Reasonableness
of domain/range, 460
of solution, 460

Reasoning, 9, 81, 115, 122, 179, 245, 288, 324, 325, 352, 389, 458, 507, 600, 627, 681, 732, 767, 768, 769, 792, 797, 806, 818, 819. *See also* Critical Thinking; Error Analysis; Justifying Steps; Make a Conjecture

Reciprocal, 7, 47–48

Reciprocal functions
defined, 495
family of, 495–498
graphing, 495–496
graphing translations of, 497–498

Reciprocal identities, 778, 779, 781, 827

Reciprocal trigonometric functions, 763–766

Rectangles
calculating area under curve, 635–636, 643
circumscribed, 635, 643
golden, 269, 270, 291
inscribed, 635, 643

Recursive formula, 602, 607, 613, 641

Reflections, 96, 97, 190, 193–194

Reflexive property of equality, 18

Regular polygon, 798

Relations
defined, 55, 109
domain and range, 56, 109
functions, 57–58
graphing, 55–56, 556
inverse, 406–409, 425
mapping diagrams, 56, 109

Relative maximums and minimums, 315, 360

Remainder Theorem, 323, 360

Residual, 244

Review. *See* Algebra 1 Review; Assessment; Extra Practice; Geometry Review; Mixed Review; Skills Handbook

Right end behavior, 312

Right triangles
cofunction identities in, 815, 829
side lengths of, 717, 792–794
special, 717
trigonometric ratios for, 792–794, 828

Roots of numbers
cube, 416
exponent form, 385–388
finding, 370
nth root, 369, 370
principal root, 370, 423
radical expressions, 371
square. *See* Square root(s)

Roots of polynomial equations
finding by factoring, 328–330, 360
finding by graphing, 327–328
Fundamental Theorem of Algebra, 341–343, 361
Imaginary Root Theorem, 338, 361
Irrational Root Theorem, 337, 361
Rational Root Theorem, 335–337, 361
solving higher-degree equations, 330
writing equations from roots, 338

Roots of quadratic equations, 273

Rotation, 190, 194–195, 230

Row operations, 223, 231

Rref feature, of graphing calculator, 224

Rubric-based exercises. *See* Extended response exercises; Short response exercises

S

Sample(s), 677–680, 703
bias in, 677, 678
margin of error in, 679–680, 703
random, 677–678, 703

Sample proportion, 677, 678, 703

Sample space, 41

SAT preparation. *See* Test Prep

Scalar, 182, 230

Scalar multiplication, 182–183, 230

Scalar products, 183, 230

Scalene triangle, 648

Scatter plots, 80, 86, 110

Scientific notation, 882

Secant function, 763, 773

Sequences
applying, 706–707
arithmetic, 606–607, 641, 642
defined, 600, 641
explicit formulas, 602, 607, 613, 641
Fibonacci, 611
finite, 619
generating, 601

Index

geometric, 612–614, 642
infinite, 619
recursive formulas, 602, 607, 613, 641
sum of. *See* Series
terms in, 600

Series
arithmetic, 619–621, 642
defined, 619, 642
evaluating, 627–628, 634
finding sum of, 621
finite, 619–621, 626–627, 634, 642
geometric, 626–628, 643
infinite, 619, 625, 627–628
writing in summation notation, 621

Short response exercises, 10, 17, 31, 38, 45, 61, 70, 76, 84, 92, 106, 108, 113, 123, 137, 144, 150, 159, 180, 189, 198, 210, 219, 233, 251, 265, 272, 287, 295, 311, 319, 325, 332, 340, 344, 357, 363, 373, 379, 384, 390, 404, 412, 419, 437, 445, 452, 459, 483, 493, 500, 508, 513, 520, 527, 553, 560, 573, 588, 595, 605, 610, 616, 624, 639, 658, 667, 690, 698, 705, 716, 724, 733, 741, 748, 754, 762, 782, 790, 799, 806, 820, 825, 833

Shrink. *See* Stretch and Shrink
Sides
of right triangles, 717, 792–794
of triangles, 802, 803, 809

Sigma
lower case, 669
upper case, 621, 627, 642

Sign(s)
negative, 557

Significant digits, 882
Simplest form
of rational expression, 509, 540
writing expressions in, 388

Simplified compound inequality, 36
Simplifying
complex fractions, 516–517, 540
expressions, 13–14, 48
expressions with rational exponents, 385–388
imaginary numbers, 275
logarithms, 455
natural logarithms, 470
numbers, 274, 275, 387
numbers with rational exponents, 387
radical expressions, 266, 371, 375, 381, 883
rational expressions, 509–510, 540–541
trigonometric expressions, 780

Simulations, 40, 650–651. *See also* Mathematical modeling
Sines, 720–722, 728, 771
Law of, 801–803, 828

Sine curve, 735–736
Sine functions, 734–738, 772
defined, 734
families of, 758
finding inverse of, 785, 827–828
graphing, 737–738

interpreting, 734–736
radian measures, 728
translating, 756–760
unit circles and, 720–722, 728, 771, 827–828

Skills Handbook, 864–887
Skills maintenance. *See* Mixed Review
Slope
defined, 64, 110
finding, 64
formula for, 64, 876
horizontal lines, 66
perpendicular lines, 66, 67
point-slope form, 64–65, 66, 110
slope-intercept form, 65–66, 110
vertical lines, 66, 110

Slope-intercept form, 65–66, 110
Solution
complex, 277, 290
to equation, 18, 48
extraneous, 34, 48, 393, 394, 521
to inequality, 26–29

Special right triangles, 717
Spreadsheets, 25, 257, 402, 630
Square(s)
completing, 281, 282–285, 293, 301
difference of, 263, 300
perfect square trinomial, 262, 282, 300
table of, 890

Square matrix, 199, 231
Square root(s)
division property of, 266
estimating, 4
multiplying, 266
negative, 5
of negative real number, 274
positive, 5, 266
principal root, 5, 266
radical expressions, 266
solving quadratic equations, 268, 293
table of, 890

Square root equations, 391, 416, 425
Square root functions, 415–416, 425
Standard deviation, 668–672
defined, 669, 703
finding, 668–671, 703
in problem solving, 675
using, 671–672

Standard form
of equation of circle, 561, 583, 592
of equation of ellipse, 568, 569, 583
of equation of hyperbola, 575, 577, 583, 584
of equation of parabola, 583
of linear equation, 63, 66, 110
of polynomial, 307, 313
of quadratic equation, 267, 300
of quadratic function, 238, 246, 299

Standard normal curve, 693–694, 703
Standard position of angle, 718–719, 771
Standardized Test Prep. *See* Test Prep
STAT feature, of graphing calculator, 244, 438, 469, 612, 670

STAT PLOT feature, of graphing calculator, 612, 663
Statistics, exercises, 174, 535, 690. *See also* Data analysis
Step function, 71
Stretch and Shrink, 96, 97, 253, 416
Subsets, of real numbers, 5
Substitution
solving linear systems, 125–126, 162
solving three-variable systems, 155–156, 163

Substitution property of equality, 18
Subtraction
of fractions, 871
of functions, 398
of matrices, 176
of radical expressions, 380–381
of rational expressions, 516

Subtraction property
of equality, 18
of inequality, 26
simplifying algebraic expressions, 13

Sum
of cubes, 328, 360
of infinite geometric series, 628

Sum identities for angles, 816, 817, 829
Summation. *See also* Addition
area under a curve, 635–637, 643
finite arithmetic series, 619–621, 642
finite geometric series, 626–627, 634
infinite geometric series, 625, 627–628

Summation notation, 621, 642
Symbols
absolute value, 371
radical, 266
sigma, 621, 627, 642, 669
summation, 621, 627, 642
tables of, 889
theta, 720

Symmetric property of equality, 18
Symmetry, 245
axis of, 239, 299, 555

Synthetic division, 321–323, 360
Systems of equations
classifying, 120
defined, 118, 161
dependent, 120, 161
equivalent, 127, 154, 162
graphing, 118–120, 161, 589
inconsistent, 120, 161
independent, 120, 161
linear. *See* Linear systems
linear programming, 139–141, 145, 162
quadratic, 589
solving algebraically, 125–127, 589
solving by elimination, 126, 127, 162
solving by graphing, 119, 589
solving by substitution, 125–126, 162
solving using augmented matrices, 222–224
solving using Cramer's Rule, 221–222, 231
solving using matrix equations, 214–217

solving using tables, 132, 133–134
solving without a unique solution, 127
three-variable, 152–156, 163

Systems of inequalities, 133–135, 162, 297

T

Table(s)
data organization and, 453
frequency, 648–649, 701, 702
of measures, 888
of random numbers, 892
reading data in, 453
solving exponential equations by, 462
solving quadratic equations by, 269, 293
solving systems using, 132, 133–134
of squares and square roots, 890
of symbols, 889
of trigonometric ratios, 891
using, 654
writing expressions from, 11

Table option, of graphing calculator, 296

Tangent function, 749–751, 773

Tangent identity, 779, 827

Tangent of angle, 749, 773

TBLSET feature, of graphing calculator, 420

Technology. *See also* Graphing calculator; Spreadsheets
Activity, 118, 306, 394, 582, 778
Activity Lab, 25, 86–87, 124, 145, 181, 244, 296–297, 413, 420–421, 438, 469, 476–477, 494, 528–529, 554, 567, 589, 634, 699, 742, 791
exercises, 173, 257, 402, 623, 630
modem, 756
oscilloscope, 713
parabolic solar mirrors, 557
transit, 803

Term(s), 13, 48
in algebraic expressions, 13
coefficient of, 13
combining like, 14
constant, 238, 307
defined, 600, 641
degree of, 307, 359
in polynomials, 307
in quadratic functions, 238
in sequences, 600

Terminal side of angle, 718, 771, 823

Tessellation, 191, 196

TEST menu, of graphing calculator, 421

Test Prep
Cumulative Review, 113, 233, 363, 483, 595, 705, 831–833
exercises, 10, 17, 23, 31, 38, 45, 61, 70, 76, 84, 92, 99–100, 106, 113, 123, 130, 137, 144, 150, 159, 173, 180, 189, 198, 205, 210, 219, 227, 233, 243, 251, 258, 265, 272, 280, 287, 295, 311, 319, 325, 332, 340, 344, 350, 357, 373, 379, 384, 390, 396, 403–404, 411–412, 419, 437, 444–445, 452, 459, 467–468, 474–475, 493, 500, 507–508, 513, 519–520, 527,

537, 552–553, 560, 566, 573, 579–580, 588, 595, 605, 610, 616–617, 624, 630–631, 639, 645, 653, 658, 666–667, 674, 682–683, 690, 697–698, 705, 715–716, 724, 732–733, 741, 748, 754, 762, 769, 775, 782, 790, 798–799, 806, 813, 819–820, 825, 831–833
Reading Comprehension, 51, 165, 303, 427, 543, 645, 775

Testing. *See* Assessment

Test-Taking Strategies
Answering Open-Ended Questions, 826
Answering the Question Asked, 700
Choosing *Cannot Be Determined*, 590
Drawing a Diagram, 358
Eliminating Answers, 538
Finding Multiple Correct Answers, 422
Interpreting Data, 228
Testing Multiple Choices, 478
Using Estimation, 640
Using Mental Math, 770
Using a Variable, 298
Writing Extended Responses, 160
Writing Gridded Responses, 46
Writing Short Responses, 108

Test-Taking Tips, 14, 29, 69, 79, 96, 104, 119, 126, 140, 177, 184, 222, 263, 284, 293, 323, 328, 381, 393, 408, 431, 442, 472, 490, 515, 535, 556, 557, 585, 601, 628, 654, 664, 739, 764, 784, 809

Theorems
Binomial Theorem, 354–355, 361
Factor Theorem, 315, 360
Fundamental Theorem of Algebra, 341–343, 361
Imaginary Root Theorem, 338, 361
Irrational Root Theorem, 337, 361
Law of Cosines, 808–810, 829
Law of Sines, 801–803, 828
Pythagorean Theorem, 4, 275, 884
Rational Root Theorem, 335–337, 361
Remainder Theorem, 323, 360

Theoretical probability, 41–42, 49

Theta, 720

Three-dimensional coordinate space, 146–148, 163

Three-variable system of equations, 152–156, 163

Tmax feature, of graphing calculator, 567

Tmin feature, of graphing calculator, 567

Tolerance, 36

Trace, 148

TRACE feature, of graphing calculator, 87, 124, 441, 494, 567, 578, 663, 742

Transformations
defined, 97
dilations, 190, 192–193, 230
geometric, 190, 191–195, 230
image, 192, 230
of parabolas, 252–255
preimage, 192, 230
of quadratic functions, 252–255

reflections, 96, 97, 190, 193–194
rotations, 190, 194–195, 230
translations. *See* Translations
using matrix operation, 191–195, 230

Transit, 803

Transitive property
of equality, 18
of inequality, 26

Translations
of circles, 562
combined, 95
of conic sections, 582–585, 593
of cosine functions, 756–760
defined, 93, 230, 582
of ellipses, 583, 593
equations of, 759–760
geometric, 190, 191
graphing, 93–97, 497–498
horizontal, 94–95, 253, 415, 756–758, 773
of hyperbolas, 584, 593
of inverse variations, 540
phase shifts, 756, 773
of reciprocal functions, 497–498
of sine functions, 756–760
of trigonometric functions, 756–760, 773
using matrix addition, 191–193, 230
vertical, 94, 95, 253, 415

Transverse axis, 575, 593

Tree diagram, 655–656, 659

Trend line, 80, 110

Triangles
ambiguous case, 807
area of, 801–803
equilateral, 601, 648
finding angle of, 802, 809, 810
45°-45°-90°, 717
isosceles, 648
Law of Cosines, 808–810, 829
Law of Sines, 801–803, 828
oblique, 801
Pascal's, 352, 353–354, 361, 611
Pythagorean Theorem, 4, 275, 884
right. *See* Right triangles
scalene, 648
sides of, 802, 803, 809
30°-60°-90°, 717

Trigonometric equations, 744–745, 785–786, 815

Trigonometric expressions, simplifying, 780

Trigonometric functions
cosecant, 763, 773
cosine. *See* Cosine functions
cotangent, 763, 773
graphing, 742, 756–758
inverses of, 783–786, 827–828
phase shift, 756, 773
reciprocal, 763–766
secant, 763, 773
sine, 720–722, 728, 734–738, 756–760, 772
tangent, 749–751, 773
translations, 756–760, 773

Trigonometric identities
angle, 814–816, 829
angle difference, 816–817, 829
angle sum, 816, 817, 829
cofunction, 815, 829
cotangent, 779, 827
defined, 778, 827
double-angle, 821–822, 829
half-angle, 822–823, 829
negative angle, 815, 829
properties of, 779
Pythagorean, 779, 816, 827
reciprocal, 778, 779, 781, 827
tangent, 779, 827
using to simplify expressions, 780
verifying, 778–780, 822

Trigonometric ratios, 720–722, 828, 891
for a right triangle, 792–794, 828

Trinomials, 260–262, 282, 300, 307

Truth function, 421

Tstep feature, of graphing calculator, 567

U

Unit circle
angles in, 720–722, 771
cosine of angle, 720–722, 728, 771, 784, 827–828
defined, 720, 771
sine of angle, 720–722, 728, 771, 827–828
tangent of angle, 749

V

Value option, of graphing calculator, 145

Vanishing point, 706

Variable(s), 12, 48
dependent, 62, 110
independent, 62, 110
using, 298

Variable expressions, 12

Variable matrix, 214, 231

Variance, 673

Variation
combined, 490, 539
constant of, 72, 110, 488, 490
direct, 72–74, 110, 489
inverse, 488–489, 495, 539, 540
joint, 490
measures of, 669, 703

VARS feature, of graphing calculator, 567

Vertex, 88, 253, 284
of absolute value function, 88, 111

co-vertices, 568, 592
of ellipse, 568, 592
finite graph, 212–213
of hyperbola, 575, 593
matrix representation of, 192
of parabola, 239, 299

Vertex form of quadratic function, 252–255, 284–285, 300

Vertex Principle of Linear Programming, 140

Vertical asymptotes, 502, 503, 540

Vertical line, 66, 110

Vertical-line test, 57–58

Vertical shrink, 96, 97, 253, 416

Vertical stretch, 96, 97, 253, 416

Vertical translation, 94, 95, 253, 415

Video Tutor Help Online, 18, 27, 58, 67, 73, 103, 120, 127, 174, 200, 274, 282, 290, 321, 381, 387, 447, 455, 511, 516, 523, 607, 613, 621, 727, 757, 794

Vocabulary Builder
Continuous and Discrete, 334
High-Use Academic Words, 85
Reasonable Context, 460
Variable and Parameter, 684

Vocabulary Quiz Online, 47, 109, 161, 229, 299, 359, 423, 479, 539, 591, 641, 701, 771, 827

Vocabulary Review, 47, 109, 161, 229, 299, 359, 423, 479, 539, 591, 641, 701, 771, 827

Vocabulary Tip, 5, 7, 8, 19, 34, 40, 57, 64, 72, 83, 88, 93, 101, 120, 123, 139, 140, 141, 148, 168, 176, 183, 191, 192, 196, 207, 222, 238, 245, 246, 252, 253, 259, 260, 269, 275, 282, 284, 307, 310, 314, 315, 316, 320, 322, 329, 335, 342, 369, 370, 385, 398, 399, 408, 433, 434, 443, 447, 449, 455, 470, 488, 490, 495, 496, 501, 533, 547, 550, 568, 571, 574, 575, 582, 606, 619, 621, 627, 648, 649, 660, 662, 669, 670, 677, 693, 712, 718, 720, 726, 734, 735, 736, 749, 779, 780, 784, 793, 798, 801, 802, 815

Volume, 322–323, 394, 490

W

Whole numbers, 5, 275

Writing, 10, 17, 23, 25, 30, 37, 44, 50, 60, 76, 77, 81, 83, 98, 105, 112, 122, 124,
129, 137, 143, 149, 158, 164, 171, 180, 184, 188, 189, 196, 204, 210, 213, 217, 226, 232, 242, 250, 257, 264, 271, 278, 286, 294, 302, 310, 318, 325, 332, 340, 344, 349, 350, 352, 356, 362, 368, 373, 378, 383, 389, 395, 402, 403, 411, 413, 418, 426, 437, 438, 443, 450, 458, 465, 468, 469, 474, 482, 492, 496, 499, 506, 512, 518, 526, 542, 551, 554, 559, 566, 567, 579, 586, 594, 604, 608, 615, 617, 623, 630, 634, 638, 644, 652, 657, 659, 665, 666, 667, 673, 674, 681, 689, 694, 695, 704, 714, 723, 732, 740, 742, 753, 761, 768, 774, 781, 788, 789, 805, 812, 819, 824

X

x-axis, 54, 146–148
x-coordinate, 54
x-intercept, 63, 148
X1T feature, of graphing calculator, 567

Y

y-axis, 54, 146–148
y-coordinate, 54
y-intercept, 63, 246
Y1T feature, of graphing calculator, 567

Z

z-axis, 146–148
Zero matrix, 175
Zero option, of graphing calculator, 145
Zero Product Property, 267, 300, 315
Zeros of functions, 268
multiplicity of, 316, 360
polynomial functions, 315–316, 341–343
quadratic functions, 268, 300
z-intercept, 148
ZOOM feature, of graphing calculator, 86, 89, 413, 438, 562, 637
z-score, 671–672, 693–694
ZSquare feature, of graphing calculator, 89

Acknowledgments

Staff Credits

The people who made up the High School Mathematics team—representing design services, editorial, editorial services, education technology, image services, marketing, market research, production services, publishing processes, and strategic markets—are listed below. Bold type denotes the core team members.

Leora Adler, **Scott Andrews,** Carolyn Artin, Stephanie Bradley, Amy D. Breaux, Peter Brooks, Judith D. Buice, Ronit Carter, Lisa J. Clark, Bob Cornell, Sheila DeFazio, Marian DeLollis, Kathleen Dempsey, Jo DiGiustini, Delphine Dupee, Emily Ellen, Janet Fauser, Debby Faust, Suzanne Feliciello, Frederick Fellows, Jonathan Fisher, Paula Foye, Paul Frisoli, **Patti Fromkin,** Paul Gagnon, Melissa Garcia, Jonathan Gorey, Jennifer Graham, **Ellen Granter,** Barbara Hardt, Daniel R. Hartjes, Richard Heater, Kerri Hoar, Jayne Holman, Karen Holtzman, Angela Husband, Kevin Jackson-Mead, Al Jacobson, Misty-Lynn Jenese, **Elizabeth Lehnertz,** Carolyn Lock, Diahanne Lucas, Catherine Maglio, **Cheryl Mahan,** Barry Maloney, Meredith Mascola, Ann McSweeney, Eve Melnechuk, Terri Mitchell, Sandy Morris, Cindy Noftle, Marsha Novak, Marie Opera, Jill Ort, **Michael Oster,** Steve Ouellette, Dorothy M. Preston, Rashid Ross, Donna Russo, Suzanne Schineller, Siri Schwartzman, Malti Sharma, Dennis Slattery, Emily Soltanoff, Deborah Sommer, Kathryn Smith, Lisa Smith-Ruvalcaba, Kara Stokes, Mark Tricca, Paula Vergith, Nate Walker, Diane Walsh, Merce Wilczek, **Joe Will,** Amy Winchester, Mary Jane Wolfe, Helen Young, Carol Zacny

Additional Credits: J. J. Andrews, Sarah Aubry, Jonathan Kier, Lucinda O'Neill, Sara Shelton, Ted Smykal, Michael Torocsik

Cover Design

Brainworx Studio

Cover Photos

Water drops, Martin Dohrn/Science Photo Library/Photo Researchers, Inc.
Spiral staircase, Bryan Reinhart/Masterfile Corporation

Technical Illustration

Argosy Illustration; Nesbitt Graphics, Inc.

Illustration

Argosy Illustration: 91
Kenneth Batelman: 75, 143, 179, 212, 240, 308, 350, 431, 507b, 663, 751
Dorling Kindersley Ltd./Richard Bonson: 484 br, 484 bl, 485b, 597 m
Dorling Kindersley Ltd.: 485 t
Jim DeLapine: 507
GeoSystems Global Corporation: 150
John Edwards Inc.: 79, 187 226 b, 473, 651, 674 tl
Dennis Harms: 174; 182, 352, 385, 649 b
Lois Leonard Stock: 190
Seymour Levy: 141 149
Ron Magnes: 202, 203, 204
Steve McEntee: 661

Jim Nuttle: 56
Brucie Rosch: 9, 156, 169, 188, 351, 370, 456, 652, 681 t, 761
Gary Torrisi: 208, 716, 805 t, 573, 603 b, 604 l
J/B Woolsey Associates: 171, 226 t, 317 mr, 318, 331, 348, 371, 553 br, 654, 665, 679, 696 b, 759
XNR Productions: 566

Photo Research

Sharon Donahue

Photography

Front Matter: Page viii, Bruno Perousse/Age Fotostock; **x,** Bob Daemmrich/Stock Boston; **xi,** Andrew Syred/Science Photo Library/Photo Researchers, Inc.; **xii,** SuperStock, Inc.; **xiii,** ©2000 by Consumers Union of the United States, Inc., Yonkers, New York 10703-1057, a nonprofit organization. Reprinted with permission from the march 2000 issue of Consumer Reports, for educational purposes only.; **xiv,** Getty Images, Inc.; **xix,** Raymond Gehman/Corbis; **xv,** NASA; **xvi,** Getty Images, Inc.; **xvii,** Getty Images, Inc.; **xviii,** Getty Images, Inc.; **xx,** Lawrence Migdale/Photo Researchers, Inc.; **xxi,** Chris Bensley/Stock Boston.

Chapter 1: Pages 2, 3, Chris Hondoros/Newsmakers/Getty Images, Inc.; **4,** Art Institute of Chicago, Illinois/Lauros-Giraudon, Paris/SuperStock, Inc.; **6,** Jeff Greenberg/PhotoEdit; 13, Charles Gupton/Stock Boston; **15,** Bob Daemmrich Photography, Inc.; **16,** Jonathan Nourock/Getty Images, Inc.; **20,** Bob Daemmrich/Stock Boston; **21,** SuperStock, Inc.; **22,** Bruno Perousse/Age Fotostock; **24,** Jeff Henry/Peter Arnold, Inc.; **28,** Bob Daemmrich/Stock Boston; **30,** Jon Riley; **36,** Time Pannell/Corbis; **37,** Northeast River Forecast Center/NOAA; **39 l,** Richard Haynes; **39 m, r,** Ken O'Donoghue; **41,** Ken O'Donoghue; **44,** Tim Davis/Allstock/PictureQuest.

Chapter 2: Pages 52, 53 Bridge design by Vebjorn Sand/Photo by Terje S. Johansen; **55,** Richard Megna/Fundamental Photographs; **56,** Jim Chatwin/Index Stock Imagery/PictureQuest; **58,** Dirk Weisheit/DDB Stock Photo; **61,** Bob Rowan/Corbis; **63,** Figaro Magazine/Getty Images, Inc.; **66 t,** Patrick Ingrand/ Getty Images, Inc.; **66 b,** Pearson Education, Inc.; **69,** Texas Instruments; **76,** Vanessa Vick/Photo Researchers, Inc.; **77 l,** Stacy Pick/Stock Boston; **77 r,** George A. Robinson/Getty Images, Inc.; **78,** AP Photo/Brietling Orbiter; **80,** Getty Images, Inc.; **82,** PhotoDisc, Inc./Getty Images, Inc.; **90,** Martin Rogers/Stock Boston/PictureQuest; **91,** Russ Lappa; **94,** Bill Aron/PhotoEdit; **95,** The British Museum; **97 both,** ©The Design Library, New York; **102 t,** Joe Sohm/Stock Boston; **102 b,** M. Grecco/Stock Boston; **114 t all,** ©John T. Fowler. All rights reserved.; **114-115,** Dorling Kindersley; **115 tl,** Bridge design by Vebjorn Sand/Photo by Terje S. Johansen; **115 tm,** Getty Images, Inc.; **115 tr,** L'Institute Bibliotheque, Paris.

Chapter 3: Pages 116, 117, Renee Lynn/Photo Researchers, Inc.; **119,** AP Photo/Thomas Kienzle; **121 l,** PhotoDisc, Inc./Getty Images, Inc.; **121 m,** Corbis; **121 r,** Getty Images, Inc.; **122,** David Young-Wolff/PhotoEdit; **126,** PhotoDisc, Inc./Getty Images, Inc.; **132,** Russ Lappa; **133,** Stock Boston; **135,** Bob Daemmrich/Stock Boston; **137,** Bob Daemmrich/Stock Boston; **141 both,** Mark Thayer; **143,** Bob Daemmrich Photography, Inc.; **146,** David Weintraub/Stock Boston; **147,** Mark Thayer; **149,** Zigy Kaluzny/Getty Images, Inc.; **151 l,** Jose L. Pelaze/Corbis; **151 r,** 1992 SIU Biomed Comm/Custom Medical Stock Photo; **153,**

Acknowledgments

Pearson Education; **157,** AP Photo/Paul Sakuma; **158,** Getty Images, Inc.

Chapter 4: Pages 166, 167, Michael Newman/PhotoEdit; **169,** Michael Newman/PhotoEdit; **170,** AP Photo/L.G. Patterson; **174,** Frank Siteman/Stock Boston; **179,** AP Photo/John Bazemore; **182,** Jeff Greenberg/Omni-Photo Communications, Inc.; **185 both,** Andrew Syred/Science Photo Library/Photo Researchers, Inc.; **188,** Atlantic Feature ©1996 by Mark Parisi; **193,** Russ Lappa; **193 inset,** William Taufic/Corbis; **195,** George Holton/Photo Researchers, Inc.; **197,** Jerry Clapsaddle; **202,** The New York Times; **209,** AP Photo/The Daily Times, Marc F. Henning; **210,** AP Photo/Lincoln Journal Star, Robert Becker; **211,** ©1976-2002 Photos courtesy of SPARC; **216,** Russ Lappa; **218,** David Simson/Stock Boston; **234 background,** Dag Sundberg/Getty Images, Inc.; **234 l,** Jeremy Horner/Corbis; **234 m, r,** Hershey Foods Corporation. Photos provided by JPL Productions; **235 tl,** Hershey Foods Corporation. Photos provided by JPL Productions; **235 tr,** Dorling Kindersley; **235 m all,** Hershey Foods Corporation. Photos provided by JPL Productions; **235 bl,** Dorling Kindersley; **235 br,** Greg Pease/Getty Images, Inc.

Chapter 5: Pages 236, 237, Pearson Education/Prentice Hall College Division; **239,** Jon Chomitz; **242 t,** Fish & Wildlife Service; **242 b,** AP Photo/St. Cloud Times, Paul Middlestaedt; **247,** Marty Katz/The Image Works; **249,** Michael Newman/PhotoEdit; **250,** James L. Stanfield/National Geographic Image Collection; **251,** Michael Epstein/PhotoEdit; **254,** SuperStock, Inc.; **256,** Finagle A Bagel; **263,** Doug Menuez/PhotoDisc, Inc./Getty Images, Inc.; **264,** Jeff Greenberg/Visuals Unlimited; **268,** Mike McMillan/Spotfire Images; **269,** Portrait of a Man, 1773-1775, 12" x 16 1/4", Museo De Zaragoza; **270,** Asian Art Museum of San Francisco, The Avery Brundage Collection, B60 M427; **277,** Prentice Hall; **278,** © Robotman reprinted by permission of Newspaper Enterprise Association, Inc.; **279,** Prentice Hall; **281,** Jon Chomitz; **283,** Courtesy of Craig Smorynski; **285,** Michael Newman/PhotoEdit; **286,** Prentice Hall; **287,** Petyer Pearson/Getty Images, Inc.; **288,** Prentice Hall; **291,** Getty Images, Inc.; **292,** Reuters New Media Inc./Corbis; **294,** AP/Wide World Photos.

Chapter 6: Pages 304, 305, AP Photo/Eric Risberg; **308,** National Geographic Society; **314,** Spencer Grant/Stock Boston; **317,** Greg Pease/Getty Images, Inc.; **318,** Bob Daemmrich/Stock Boston/PictureQuest; **322,** Museo Archeologico, Florence, Italy/Art Resource, New York; **326,** Corbis; **328,** Nik Kleinberg/Stock Boston; **331,** James A. Sugar/Corbis; **334,** Craig Smorynski; **341,** C. Marvin Lang; **346,** Getty Images, Inc.; **347,** PhotoEdit; **349 t,** ©2000 by Consumers Union of the United States, Inc. Yonkers, New York 10703-1057, a nonprofit organization. Reprinted with permission from the March 2000 issue of Consumer Reports, for educational purposes only.; **349 b,** Peanuts reprinted by permission of United Feature Syndicate, Inc.; **353,** Jean-Loup Charmet/Photo Researchers, Inc.; **355,** Andy Lyons/Allsport/Getty Images, Inc.; **356,** Getty Images, Inc.; **364 t,** Colorsport; **364 b both,** Dorling Kindersley; **364-365,** Glyn Kirk/Action Plus; **365 t,** Colorsport; **365 m,** Allsport/Getty Images, Inc.; **365 b,** Vincent Laforet/Allsport/Getty Images, Inc.

Chapter 7: Pages 366, 367, U.S. Space & Rocket Center; **372,** Getty Images, Inc.; **377,** Sidney Harris; **378,** PhotoDisc, Inc./Getty Images, Inc.; **383,** Judy Canty/Stock Boston; **386,** Jason Grow/Corbis; **389,** An Keren/Sovfoto/Eastfoto/PictureQuest; **392,** Jean-Claude LeJeune/Stock Boston; **395,** Russ Lappa; **400,** Robert Brenner/PhotoEdit; **401 l,** Amy C. Etra/PhotoEdit; **401 r,** Robert Fried/Stock Boston; **403,** Stone/Getty Images, Inc.; **409,** AP Photo/The Saginaw News, Bernie Eng; **411,** Tony Freeman/PhotoEdit; **412,** Bob Daemmrich/The Image Works; **418,** Ringling Bros. and Barnum & Bailey Combined Shows, Inc.

Chapter 8: Pages 428, 429, Richard Pasley/Stock Boston; **431,** Spencer Grant/PhotoEdit; **432,** AP Photo/University of Illinois, Mark Jones; **436,** AP Photo/Bob Care; **440,** Peter Berndt, MD/Custom Medical Stock Photo; **443,** Bill Aron/PhotoEdit; **444,** Laura Dwight/Omni-Photo Communications, Inc.; **446,** AP Photo/Lauren McFalls; **448,** L.S. Stepanowicz/Bruce Coleman, Inc.; **451,** James King-Holmes/Science Photo Library/Photo Researchers, Inc.; **456,** John Neubauer/PhotoEdit; **458,** Reuters NewMedia Inc./Corbis; **462,** Jeff Greenberg/PhotoEdit; **465,** Andrew Rafkind/Getty Images, Inc.; **466,** Catherine Karnow/Corbis; **467,** Andy Sacks/Getty Images, Inc.; **471,** NASA; **474,** David Young-Wolff/PhotoEdit; **475,** NASA; **475 inset,** NASA/Bruce Coleman, Inc.; **476,** The British Museum/HIP/The Image Works; **477,** ABPL/Daryl Balfour/Animals Animals; **484 l,** Photograph by Halliday Historic Photograph Co., circa 1905. Courtesy of Society for the Preservation of New England Antiquities; **484 r,** Peter Vanderwarker Photographs.

Chapter 9: Pages 486, 487, David Breashears /Arcturus Motion Pictures; **489,** Kevin Dodge/Masterfile; **492,** Bob Daemmrich/Stock Boston; **496,** Robert Freck/Getty Images, Inc.; **499,** Comstock Images; **505,** Dennis O'Clair/Getty Images, Inc.; **510,** Tom Dietrich/Getty Images, Inc.; **512,** 1992 Jeffrey Muir Hamilton/Stock Boston; **514 both,** Mark Thayer; **519,** Bob Daemmrich Photography, Inc.; **523,** Courtesy of Lightning Cycle Dynamics, Inc.; **526 t,** Reprinted with special permission of King Features Syndicate.; **526 b,** Morton Beebe/Corbis; **531 t,** Jon Chomitzl **531 b,** Jon Chomitz; **532,** Mark C. Burnett/Stock Boston; **534,** Prentice Hall; **535,** Pitney Bowes, Inc.; **537,** H. Dratch/The Image Works.

Chapter 10: Pages 544, 545, NASA; **547,** Jeff Smith; **548 both,** Jeff Smith; **551,** Richard Pasley/Stock Boston; **553,** Painting by Ken Marschall from Titanic: an Illustrated History ©1992, A Madison Press Book; **557,** Getty Images, Inc.; **559 t,** Prentice Hall; **559 b,** Woody Woodworth/SuperStock, Inc.; **561,** Molly & Georg Gerster/Comstock Images; **563,** Michael Rosenfeld/Getty Images, Inc.; **565,** Susan Van Etten/Stock Boston; **569,** NASA Langley Research Center; **572,** Ken O'Donoghue; **579,** Ed Young/Science Photo Library/Photo Researchers, Inc.; **587,** Collection of the Lowe Art Museum, University of Miami. Museum Purchase in memory of Shelia Natasha Simrod Friedman, #92.0094; **596,** Dorling Kindersley; **596-597,** NASA; **597,** NASA.

Chapter 11: Pages 598, 599, Doug Wechsler/Vireo; **600 t,** Bob Daemmrich/The Image Works; **600 m,** Laura Dwight/PhotoEdit; **600 b,** Will & Deni McIntyre/Photo Researchers, Inc.; **601,** Prentice Hall; **603,** AP/Wide World Photos; **604,** From Not Strictly By The Numbers ©Carolina Mathematics/Carolina Biological Supply Company; **606,** Arthur Tilley/Getty Images, Inc.; **607,** AP Photo/Michael Tweed; **609,** James Lamb/Getty Images, Inc.; **611 l,** Jane Grushow/Grant Heilman Photography, Inc.; **611 ml,** Ed Reschke/Peter Arnold, Inc.; **611 mr,** Joy Spurr/Bruce Coleman, Inc.; **611 r,** Ed Reschke/Peter Arnold, Inc.; **612,** Ken O'Donoghue; **613,** Cindy Charles/PhotoEdit; **614,** Paul Barton/Corbis; **616,** Corel Corp.; **617 both,** China Stock; **620 t,** Russ Lappa; **620 b,** Prentice Hall; **622,** The Image Works; **623,** Russ Lappa; **627,** Myrleen Ferguson/PhotoEdit; **628,** Scott Camazine/Photo Researchers, Inc.; **630,** Leonard Lessin/Peter Arnold, Inc.; **635,** Doug Wechsler/Vireo.

Chapter 12: Pages 646, 647, Getty Images, Inc.; **650,** P. Dumas/Eurelios/Science Photo Library/Photo Researchers, Inc.; **653,** Tony Freeman/PhotoEdit; **655,** Jose Carillo/PhotoEdit; **656,** AP Photo/Don Heupel; **666,** Corbis; **669,** AP Photo/Michael